Dictionary of Literary Biography

Documentary Series

Yearbooks

Concise Series

Concise Dictionary of American Literary Biography, 7 volumes (1988-1999): *The New Consciousness, 1941-1968; Colonization to the American Renaissance, 1640-1865; Realism, Naturalism, and Local Color, 1865-1917; The Twenties, 1917-1929; The Age of Maturity, 1929-1941; Broadening Views, 1968-1988; Supplement: Modern Writers, 1900-1998.*

Concise Dictionary of British Literary Biography, 8 volumes (1991-1992): *Writers of the Middle Ages and Renaissance Before 1660; Writers of the Restoration and Eighteenth Century, 1660-1789; Writers of the Romantic Period, 1789-1832; Victorian Writers, 1832-1890; Late-Victorian and Edwardian Writers, 1890-1914; Modern Writers, 1914-1945; Writers After World War II, 1945-1960; Contemporary Writers, 1960 to Present.*

Concise Dictionary of World Literary Biography, 10 volumes projected (1999-   ): *Ancient Greek and Roman Writers; German Writers; African, Caribbean, and Latin American Writers; South Slavic and Eastern European Writers.*

Russian Novelists in the Age of Tolstoy and Dostoevsky

Dictionary of Literary Biography® • Volume Two Hundred Thirty-Eight

Russian Novelists in the Age of Tolstoy and Dostoevsky

Edited by
J. Alexander Ogden
University of South Carolina
and
Judith E. Kalb
University of South Carolina

A Bruccoli Clark Layman Book
The Gale Group
Detroit • San Francisco • London • Boston • Woodbridge, Conn.

Printed in the United States of America

The paper used in this publication meets the minimum requirements
of American National Standard for Information Sciences–Permanence
Paper for Printed Library Materials, ANSI Z39.48-1984. ∞™

Library of Congress Cataloging-in-Publication Data

Russian novelists in the age of Tolstoy and Dostoevsky / edited by J. Alexander Ogden and
Judith E. Kalb.
    p. cm.–(Dictionary of literary biography: v. 238)
"A Bruccoli Clark Layman book."
Includes bibliographical references and index.
ISBN 0-7876-4655-5 (alk. paper)
1. Russian fiction–19th century–Bio-bibliography–Dictionaries. 2. Novelists, Russian–19th century–
Biography–Dictionaries. I. Ogden, J. Alexander. II. Kalb, Judith E. III. Series.

PG3098.3.R874 2001
891.73'3'03–dc21   00-053515
[B]   CIP

10 9 8 7 6 5 4 3 2 1

For our parents

Contents

Plan of the Series

. . . Almost the most prodigious asset of a country, and perhaps its most precious possession, is its native literary product—when that product is fine and noble and enduring.

Mark Twain*

The advisory board, the editors, and the publisher of the *Dictionary of Literary Biography* are joined in endorsing Mark Twain's declaration. The literature of a nation provides an inexhaustible resource of permanent worth. Our purpose is to make literature and its creators better understood and more accessible to students and the reading public, while satisfying the needs of teachers and researchers.

To meet these requirements, *literary biography* has been construed in terms of the author's achievement. The most important thing about a writer is his writing. Accordingly, the entries in *DLB* are career biographies, tracing the development of the author's canon and the evolution of his reputation.

The purpose of *DLB* is not only to provide reliable information in a usable format but also to place the figures in the larger perspective of literary history and to offer appraisals of their accomplishments by qualified scholars.

The publication plan for *DLB* resulted from two years of preparation. The project was proposed to Bruccoli Clark by Frederick G. Ruffner, president of the Gale Research Company, in November 1975. After specimen entries were prepared and typeset, an advisory board was formed to refine the entry format and develop the series rationale. In meetings held during 1976, the publisher, series editors, and advisory board approved the scheme for a comprehensive biographical dictionary of persons who contributed to literature. Editorial work on the first volume began in January 1977, and it was published in 1978. In order to make *DLB* more than a dictionary and to compile volumes that individually have claim to status as literary history, it was decided to organize volumes by topic, period, or

From an unpublished section of Mark Twain's autobiography, copyright by the Mark Twain Company

genre. Each of these freestanding volumes provides a biographical-bibliographical guide and overview for a particular area of literature. We are convinced that this organization—as opposed to a single alphabet method—constitutes a valuable innovation in the presentation of reference material. The volume plan necessarily requires many decisions for the placement and treatment of authors. Certain figures will be included in separate volumes, but with different entries emphasizing the aspect of his career appropriate to each volume. Ernest Hemingway, for example, is represented in *American Writers in Paris, 1920–1939* by an entry focusing on his expatriate apprenticeship; he is also in *American Novelists, 1910–1945* with an entry surveying his entire career, as well as in *American Short-Story Writers, 1910–1945, Second Series* with an entry concentrating on his short fiction. Each volume includes a cumulative index of the subject authors and articles.

Since 1981 the series has been further augmented by the *DLB Yearbooks*, which update published entries, add new entries to keep the *DLB* current with contemporary activity, and provide articles on literary history. There have also been nineteen *DLB Documentary Series* volumes which provide illustrations, facsimiles, and biographical and critical source materials for figures works, or groups judged to have particular interest for students. In 1999 the *Documentary Series* was incorporated into the *DLB* volume numbering system beginning with *DLB 210, Ernest Hemingway.*

We define literature as the *intellectual commerce of a nation:* not merely as belles lettres but as that ample and complex process by which ideas are generated, shaped, and transmitted. *DLB* entries are not limited to "creative writers" but extend to other figures who in their time and in their way influenced the mind of a people. Thus the series encompasses historians, journalists, publishers, book collectors, and screenwriters. By this means readers of *DLB* may be aided to perceive literature not as cult scripture in the keeping of intellectual high priests but firmly positioned at the center of a nation's life.

DLB includes the major writers appropriate to each volume and those standing in the ranks behind them. Scholarly and critical counsel has been sought in deciding which minor figures to include and how full their entries should be. Wherever possible, useful references are made to figures who do not warrant separate entries.

Each *DLB* volume has an expert volume editor responsible for planning the volume, selecting the figures for inclusion, and assigning the entries. Volume editors are also responsible for preparing, where appropriate, appendices surveying the major periodicals and literary and intellectual movements for their volumes, as well as lists of further readings. Work on the series as a whole is coordinated at the Bruccoli Clark Layman editorial center in Columbia, South Carolina, where the editorial staff is responsible for accuracy and utility of the published volumes.

One feature that distinguishes *DLB* is the illustration policy—its concern with the iconography of literature. Just as an author is influenced by his surroundings, so is the reader's understanding of the author enhanced by a knowledge of his environment. Therefore *DLB* volumes include not only drawings, paintings, and photographs of authors, often depicting them at various stages in their careers, but also illustrations of their families and places where they lived. Title pages are regularly reproduced in facsimile along with dust jackets for modern authors. The dust jackets are a special feature of *DLB* because they often document better than anything else the way in which an author's work was perceived in its own time. Specimens of the writers' manuscripts and letters are included when feasible.

Samuel Johnson rightly decreed that "The chief glory of every people arises from its authors." The purpose of the *Dictionary of Literary Biography* is to compile literary history in the surest way available to us—by accurate and comprehensive treatment of the lives and work of those who contributed to it.

The *DLB* Advisory Board

Introduction

The second half of the nineteenth century was an extraordinary time in Russian history and literature, and the two were closely linked. Radicals and revolutionaries demanded extreme changes in Russian government and society, and czars and their reactionary advisers responded for the most part with efforts to solidify imperial authority rather than diminish it. While the 1860s stand out as a period when a realistic czar was spurred to enact meaningful governmental and social reforms, often extremists on both sides managed to block the various middle paths sought by moderates, both liberal and conservative. This incendiary situation eventually culminated in the revolutions of 1905 and 1917, followed by the abolition of the monarchy and the onset of Soviet rule.

Russian writers played a fundamental role in the political events and discussions of this period. As the age of Realism in Russian literature dawned, literary critics urged social and political involvement from writers, who were thought to have a responsibility to portray, respond to, and, in so doing, influence the events around them. The novel proved invaluable in this process, for its characters and the relationships among them provided a variety of voices that could represent differing opinions and trends. Such literary characters as Ivan Aleksandrovich Goncharov's Oblomov (emblematic, according to the critic Nikolai Aleksandrovich Dobroliubov, of the slothful "superfluity" affecting Russia's upper classes) or Ivan Sergeevich Turgenev's Bazarov (a member of the "nihilist" generation of the 1860s) assumed real life in the discussions of the day. As writers proved adept at circumventing the censors to address dangerous issues through the smoke-screen of literature, the authority of the Russian writer grew in the eyes of the expanding reading public and eventually in some cases assumed near-religious proportions. By 1880, when the novelist Fyodor Dostoevsky spoke at a celebration in honor of the Russian poet Aleksandr Sergeevich Pushkin (1799–1837) held in Moscow, he was hailed as a prophet; and by the end of the century the novelist Leo Tolstoy had created his own version of Christianity and had been deemed dangerous by both church and state. In addition to having social relevance and influence, a significant number of novels of this period are works of artistic genius, ranging from Dostoevsky's haunting and powerful *Brat'ia Karamazovy* (The Brothers Karamazov, 1879–1880) to Tolstoy's masterpiece *Voina i mir* (War and Peace, 1865–1869). Indeed, the decades under discussion in this volume have become widely known as the age of the great Russian novel. This introduction seeks to place the Russian novel in context, first providing an overview of the history of the period and then surveying the development of the novel in Russia.

The tempestuous political events of the period had their roots in the preceding half-century. The nineteenth century had begun with the accession to the throne of Alexander I (reigned 1801–1825), welcomed originally as a saintly figure committed to improving the lot of his subjects after the reign of his father, the arbitrary Paul I (assassinated in 1801). Influenced in his upbringing by his remarkable grandmother Catherine II (the Great), Alexander I developed education in Russia by establishing several universities and schools, and he initially pondered abolishing serfdom, the system by which millions of Russians were the property of the owners of the estates where they lived and worked. Alexander I also relied upon his reform-minded adviser Mikhail Mikhailovich Speransky, eventually rejecting, however, Speransky's proposal of a constitution. The first half of Alexander's reign also encompassed Russia's triumphant victory in the war against Napoleon Bonaparte, later described in Tolstoy's *Voina i mir*. The liberal tendencies of Alexander's rule did not last: the second half of his reign was marked by his reliance on General Aleksei Andreevich Arakcheev, whose name became synonymous with cruelty, rigidity, and reaction. In fact, Arakcheev's influence was considered so important that the second portion of Alexander's reign came to be known as the "Arakcheevshchina."

Disappointment over the lack of reform under Alexander I was partially responsible for the revolt of the Decembrists, a group of liberal noblemen who, seeking a constitutional government and the end of serfdom, staged a rebellion shortly after Alexander's death in November of 1825. The new czar, Alexander's brother Nicholas I (reigned 1825–1855), punished the conspirators harshly, taking a personal interest in their executions or Siberian exiles, and under the shadow of the rebellion he proceeded to inaugurate a period of reaction in Russian history in an effort to "freeze" his country's development. Count Sergei Semenovich Uvarov, Minister of Education under Nicholas I, gave Nicholas's natural conservatism an ideological framework with the formula "Orthodoxy, Autocracy, and Nationality." Nicholas was firmly committed to the power of the throne, and he reacted with alarm and further reactionary measures to the revolutions that swept Europe in 1848, as well as to the Polish insurrection of 1830 against Russian rule. The historian Bernard Pares characterizes the period as one of "complete suffocation," and historian Nicholas V. Riasanovsky concurs, assessing the censorship policies of the time: "Censorship reached ridiculous proportions, with new agencies appearing, including 'a censorship over the censors.' The censors, to cite only a few instances of their activities, deleted 'forces of nature' from a textbook in physics, probed the hidden meaning of an ellipsis in an arithmetic book, changed 'were killed' to 'perished' in an account of Roman emperors . . . and worried about the possible concealment of secret codes in musical notations." This difficult situation worsened after Russia's defeat in the Crimean War (1853–1856), which pitted the Russians against the Turks, who were supported by the French and the British. A defining period in the war was the siege of Sevastopol', later described in the early stories of Tolstoy, who had served there while in the military. Many of the writers who became prominent in the second half of the century were born and came of age during the difficult years of Nicholas I's reign, among them Dostoevsky, who spent years in Siberian exile after his arrest in 1849 as a member of the Petrashevsky Circle, a group headed by Mikhail Vasil'evich Butashevich-Petrashevsky that met periodically to discuss utopian socialist ideas and social issues.

The advent of Alexander II (reigned 1855–1881) to the Russian throne was an occasion for rejoicing among liberal-minded Russians. Nicholas I's son, who had been tutored by the poet Vasilii Andreevich Zhukovsky and who later came to be known as the "Czar-Liberator" for freeing the serfs in 1861, recognized the troubled state of his country and the need to improve it. He embarked upon a series of reforms that eventually touched much of Russian society: the abolition of serfdom, the restructuring of regional political structures through the zemstvo system of locally governed units, the overhaul of the legal system (which has been seen as the most successful of the "Great Reforms"), changes in Russia's banking system, the liberalization of educational policy, and the restructuring of military service. With the emancipation of the serfs a few years before the freeing of the slaves in the United States, Alexander II fundamentally altered the nature of Russian society and sought to correct a leading cause of popular discontent. The emancipation heralded the decline of the gentry and the eventual creation of a middle class in Russia. Yet, in ways the freeing of the serfs did not go far enough. Many protested the terms under which the emancipation had occurred: the former serfs received minimal land and in some cases had to pay the landlords for it. Several uprisings on the part of the peasants themselves took place in subsequent years as the former serfs faced difficult conditions.

The peasants were not alone in their discontent. Another rebellion in Poland in 1863 failed, resulting in the imposition of strict Russification policies in Poland and along the Polish borders of Russia. Meanwhile, as Alexander II's reforms took effect, they paradoxically created a thirst for further reforms. Students in particular rallied to the cause of reform and, at times, revolution. In 1866 a student named Dmitrii Karakozov attempted to assassinate the czar. While the effort failed, it had lasting results: with some exceptions (the restructuring of the army, for instance, took place in 1874) the reforms of the preceding years came to a halt. Turning toward reaction, Alexander II appointed the conservative Count Dmitrii Andreevich Tolstoy as Minister of Education, and gradually restrictions on universities, the zemstvos, and the press took effect. The pendulum had shifted once more; and again, a revolutionary act had provoked reaction.

Turgenev's *Ottsy i deti* (Fathers and Sons) is the work perhaps most emblematic of the tensions between generations inherent in Russian society in the era of the Great Reforms. Written in 1862 but set in 1859, Turgenev's novel juxtaposes the "fathers'" generation of the 1840s with that of the "children," the so-called new men and new women of the 1860s. The older generation is portrayed as Romantic and idealistic, influenced by German philosophy, while the younger generation stands for positivism, utilitarianism, and Realism. Turgenev portrayed these young "radicals" or "nihilists" in the character of Bazarov, who would rather dissect frogs than enjoy art or music. The "men of the forties" had had their own political differences: it has become customary to divide them loosely into "Slavophiles," or those who rejected excessive Westernization and sought a return to native Russian traditions, and "Westernizers," who urged Russians to learn from and emulate Western development in the spirit of the Westernizing Czar Peter I (the Great, reigned 1682–1725). Yet, despite their differing visions of Russia and its future, the two groups had substantially more in common with each other than they had with the next generation. The Bazarovs of Russia sought to reject much of received wisdom, whether in philosophy, art, or social custom.

Their mantras were "critical realism" and science; in their iconoclastic zeal they failed to value the poetry of Pushkin or the concept of beauty. They were followers of the critics Nikolai Gavrilovich Chernyshevsky, Dobroliubov, and Dmitrii Ivanovich Pisarev, who rejected "art for art's sake" and called instead for a literature focused solely on meaningful discussions of Russia's current conditions and future path. Many of the radical thinkers were *raznochintsy* (members of different classes), which meant that they were the children of minor officials, priests, or other workers rather than scions of the nobility, as earlier generations of Russian writers had been. As Riasanovsky notes, the word *intelligentsia*, with its connotations of critical intellectualism, dates from this period.

In fact, political engagement has long been seen as a hallmark of modern Russian writing, and Russia's radical critics of the 1860s were not the first to call for "socially relevant" literature. The critic Vissarion Grigor'evich Belinsky (1811–1848), who has been called the father of Russian criticism, had already asserted in his articles of the 1840s the transformative power of Russian literature and the need for Russian writers to involve themselves in the pressing social issues of the day; for example, Belinsky read Pushkin's *Evgenii Onegin, roman v stikhakh* (Eugene Onegin, a Novel in Verse, 1825–1832) as an "encyclopedia of Russian life" and Nikolai Vasil'evich Gogol's short stories as scathing portraits of the ills of Russian society. Belinsky combined his political convictions with often astute artistic judgments, welcoming into the Russian literary arena such remarkable talents as Mikhail Iur'evich Lermontov, Gogol, and Dostoevsky. One of the reasons for Dostoevsky's arrest in 1849 was his reading at the Petrashevsky Circle of Belinsky's famous letter to Gogol, which took Gogol to task for a turn to conservatism in his last work; the letter was taboo in Nicholas I's Russia.

While Belinsky's own intellectual trajectory took him through the complexities of German metaphysics to a view of art as "an analysis of society," his radical successors might be seen as more narrow and limited in their intellectual approach. Dobroliubov, who may have been the inspiration for Turgenev's Bazarov, viewed literature through a rather confining prism that permitted so artistically rich a work as Goncharov's *Oblomov* (1859) to function primarily as a political text, one that revealed the sunken depths of Russian society through the slothfulness of its privileged title character. Ralph E. Matlaw notes that in Dobroliubov's famous article "Chto takoe oblomovshchina?" (What is Oblomovitis? 1859) "Oblomov is merely a repellent nonentity, a symbol of the disease produced by the institution of serfdom." Dobroliubov's article also pointed to an important phenomenon in Russian culture, which he saw epitomized in Oblomov: that of "the superfluous man," the Russian aristocrat who represents weakness, uselessness, and the inability to make decisions and act productively. Dobroliubov's fellow critic Pisarev identified himself with Bazarov and called unabashedly for useful shoes over useless Shakespeare. Chernyshevsky, like Dobroliubov the son of a priest and therefore also a *raznochinets*, created a literary and political storm with his reviews of contemporary literature and with his own novel *Chto delat'?* (What Is to Be Done? 1863), which inspired a generation of Russian youth to emulate the "new" men and women he portrayed. Chernyshevsky, who wrote his novel while awaiting Siberian exile, is known in particular for his review of Turgenev's story "Asia" (1858), with its love story dismissed by Chernyshevsky as follows: "Forget about them, those erotic questions! They are not for the reader of our time, who is busy with problems of administrative and judicial improvements, financial reforms, and the emancipation of the serfs."

The power of the critics was unquestionable. As novels and criticism appeared in the "thick journals" of the day, readers could partake of literature on the one hand and prescriptions for how to read it on the other. Ivan Afanas'evich Kushchevsky's little-known 1871 novel *Nikolai Negorev* portrays this process admirably, as he shows students in the period of the Great Reforms being carried away by literature and criticism; the students are inspired to the point of creating their own literary journal. Meanwhile, whether or not authors agreed with the critics' radical agenda, they made political and social questions fundamental elements of their work. Dostoevsky's *Besy* (The Devils, 1871–1872) dealt with the dangers that Dostoevsky, grown conservative following his exile, believed were inherent in the radical movement. Tolstoy's *Anna Karenina* (1875–1877) dealt with issues concerning the zemstvos in addition to its more famous story of adultery.

Anna Karenina also touched upon another important and controversial theme of the period: that of the "woman question." While Tolstoy judged Anna harshly for her adultery with Captain Vronsky, nonetheless his portrayal of the difficulties Anna faces through social ostracism and separation from her son provides insight into some aspects of women's lives in late-nineteenth-century Russia. Chernyshevsky's *Chto delat'?* presented a different vision of possibilities for Russian women. His heroine Vera Pavlovna arranges a marriage to escape a difficult family situation, lives separately from her husband, and starts a dressmaking shop to help poor women. Chernyshevsky's novel clearly struck a chord, as many young Russian women sought to break away from the strictures of Russian family life: at this time women needed their father's or husband's permission to work; divorces were hard to obtain; and it was difficult for women to pursue higher education. As Barbara Heldt notes, the confined nature of many women's lives and experiences meant that the literature produced by women was in ways different from that of male writers, who were able, for instance, to spend a night on the streets with the homeless, as did Tolstoy. Yet, women played an important role in the literary process, often using male or nongendered pseudonyms. Writers such as Avdot'ia Iakovlevna Panaeva (who wrote under the name of N. Stanitsky) and Evgeniia Tur (pseudonym of Elizaveta Sailhas de Tournemir) devoted particular attention in their works to the situation of women at this time; Panaeva and Tur also presided over literary salons, where writers could introduce new works or discuss current literary trends. Russian women increasingly went abroad to universities; when they encountered revolutionary ideas in Europe, the alarmed Russian government in 1873 summoned them back to newly opened educational institutions in Russia. This concession came too late, however, and women played a large role in the revolutionary movements of the 1870s and beyond.

By the 1870s the radical movement had come of age. Chief among the radicals' concerns were the peasants, who were struggling financially in the wake of the emancipation. This concern manifested itself in the new credo of Populism (*narodnichestvo*). Guilt-ridden over their own education and the privileges they had enjoyed, as they saw it, at the expense of the peasantry, many young Russian men and women turned to "the people"–in whom they posited a distinctive and important "Russianness" they themselves were lacking–in order both to teach and to learn. One phase of this commitment, called "Going to the People," reached its height from 1873 to 1874, when groups of young people went into the countryside, in some cases to become teachers and doctors, in other cases to preach revolution to the peasants. The latter process was for the most part a miserable failure, as bewildered peasants turned their would-be saviors over to the police, and arrests of the crusaders mounted. Interest in the peasantry manifested itself in the literary sphere as well. Novelists such as Nikolai Nikolaevich Zlatovratsky, Pavel Vladimirovich Zasodimsky, and Fedor Mikhailovich Reshetnikov depicted the difficulties of peasant life in their works. Perhaps most memorably, Tolstoy donned peasant garb, renounced his prior writings, and wrote stories specifically intended for a peasant audience.

As Pares writes, the radical movement of this period consisted essentially of two groups, both of which were opposed to the government and committed to the peasantry. The first group, influenced by the Populist thinkers and critics Petr Lavrovich Lavrov and Nikolai Konstantinovich Mikhailovsky, called for education and propaganda as the instruments of change. The second group, inspired by the anarchist Mikhail Aleksandrovich Bakunin, called for armed insurrection; an example of his ideals came in the Nechaev conspiracy, a plot against the government, which Dostoevsky later portrayed in *Besy*. When the "Going to the People" movement failed to motivate the peasantry to wholesale revolutionary fervor, the revolutionaries decided that if the peasants would not revolt, then the revolutionaries must do it for them. The result of this decision was a wave of terrorism directed by the "People's Will" organization, founded in 1879, against government officials and Czar Alexander II himself. The czar survived several assassination attempts, which included the destruction of the Imperial train and the dining room at the czar's palace.

The international front was no calmer, as Russia plunged into war with Turkey in 1877. At issue was the fate of the Balkans: in 1875 Herzegovina and Bosnia had rebelled against Turkish rule, and the Turks had put down a Bulgarian rebellion in 1876. A wave of Pan-Slavism swept many in Russian society, including Dostoevsky, who preached the Pan-Slavic cause in his *Dnevnik pisatelia* (Diary of a Writer, 1876–1881). Russian army officers volunteered to fight in the Serb army: Tolstoy's Vronsky in *Anna Karenina* is one such officer. The Russians were victorious in the war, which ended in 1878, but the advantageous treaty the Russians had negotiated with the Turks was changed substantially by Great Britain and Austria-Hungary. The government's acceptance of lesser terms invoked the wrath of conservatives who felt that the czar had betrayed his Slavic brethren, and the Russian public reacted to the settlement with a loss of confidence in their government.

Beset on several fronts, the government now realized that a change in policy was essential. The czar appointed General Mikhail Tarielovich Loris-Melikov to head a Supreme Executive Commission intended to combat terrorism and at the same time to further the reforms that had started at the beginning of Alexander II's reign. In so doing, the government hoped to keep the liberal members of the intelligentsia from joining forces irrevocably with the radical revolutionaries. This effort on the part of the government was interpreted by many Russian intellectuals, eager for any efforts from the government to correct the disastrous political situation, as a sign of a potential "thaw." As Marcus Levitt explains, the Pushkin Celebration of 1880, when a monument to the poet was dedicated, occurred at the time of this "thaw" and became associated with this effort at political rapprochement. Reminiscences of the event point to the surprise many Russians felt that a monument was being erected to a writer, rather than a political figure. In fact, the celebration represents a striking example of the complex relationship between literature and politics in Russia: the figure of Pushkin became representative of the political allegiances and agendas of different parties.

For in addition to signifying an improvement of relations between the intelligentsia and the autocracy, the Pushkin Celebration came to be viewed by various Russian intellectuals as an opportunity to achieve a reconciliation between the conservative and liberal branches of the intelligentsia, both of which claimed Pushkin as their inspiration. Thus, intellectuals ranging in political views from the moderate liberal Turgenev to the conservative Dostoevsky came together to laud Pushkin and set aside, at least briefly, their own political differences. While Turgenev hoped for further reforms in Russia and felt that these reforms could best be achieved under the aegis of the czar and his government, Dostoevsky, on the contrary, longed to see a strong czar heading a Russian Orthodox state. Both men, however, were alarmed by the waves of terrorism sweeping Russia, and both hoped to see Loris-Melikov's efforts succeed. As the two men were considered the respective heads of the liberal and conservative factions at the celebration, their speeches on Pushkin were eagerly anticipated as statements of their political positions. Turgenev, in fact, devoted the bulk of his speech to discussing Pushkin and the importance of art; his speech was considered disappointing. Dostoevsky's speech turned out to be the major sensation of the celebration. The speech, while ostensibly about Pushkin, was in fact dedicated to Dostoevsky's conservative and messianic political agenda. Moved to tears by Dostoevsky's oratory, members of the audience fainted; long-time enemies swore to love one another; and even Turgenev, who had been estranged from Dostoevsky for years, wept and embraced his adversary. In the aftermath of the celebration, however, the rapture caused by Dostoevsky's words faded, and the old antagonisms reasserted themselves. The celebration had not, as Dostoevsky had hoped, brought the liberals into the conservative fold, nor had it fulfilled Turgenev's hopes of combating revolutionary radicalism through its affirmation of the liberal ideals, expounded earlier by the "men of the forties," of beauty and culture.

Indeed, the celebration was noteworthy not only for its famous participants but also for its missing major figures. Tolstoy, uninterested in official festivities, had opted not to attend. More important, perhaps, the revolutionary radicals were not represented at the event. The radicals were alarmed by Loris-Melikov, who was winning the support of the liberals and who, they feared, would detract from revolutionary fervor. Loris-

Melikov had in fact embarked upon a course of reforms, and it seemed that Alexander II was ready to listen to his proposals. Before he could ponder them thoroughly, the "Czar-Liberator" was killed in March of 1881 by an assassin from the People's Will.

With the murder of Alexander II by the revolutionaries, a familiar pattern reasserted itself. Alexander II's replacement, his son Alexander III (reigned 1881–1894), was a staunch reactionary, who from the start of his reign made his conservative convictions clear. The new czar declared war on the revolutionaries, strengthened censorship, enhanced the position of the gentry, rendered the lives of the peasants more difficult, and increased government control over universities. Alexander III returned to a policy of "Orthodoxy, Autocracy, and Nationality," which proved difficult for the non-Russians and non-Orthodox in his realm. Jews suffered in particular, as pogroms, or murderous and vandalistic attacks on Jewish villages, were not only disregarded but even encouraged by some authorities. Quotas were set for Jewish students at the universities, and permitted places of residence for Jews were curtailed. Many Jews emigrated from Russia at this time. Again, literature portrayed and responded to prevailing social conditions. The writer Vsevolod Vladimirovich Krestovsky epitomized in his later works the anti-Semitism of the day, while various texts by Nikolai Semenovich Leskov present a more nuanced view of Jews in Russia and the conditions they faced.

Alexander III was succeeded by his son Nicholas II (reigned 1894–1917), Russia's last czar. A devoted family man but an unsuccessful ruler, Nicholas for the most part continued his father's repressive policies and eventually proved too weak to withstand the competing political pressures of his reign. A disastrous war with Japan from 1904 to 1905 opened the way to revolution in 1905, following which Nicholas grudgingly acceded to demands for a constitutional monarchy, though he attempted gradually to limit the freedoms the term entailed. By 1914 Russia was embroiled once again in war, this time in World War I, which became increasingly unpopular among the Russian people. In 1917 Nicholas II abdicated the Russian throne, and a provisional government was installed in his place. Later that year the revolutionary Bolsheviks, promising land to the people and an end to the war, staged a coup to take over the Russian government. In 1918 the Bolsheviks ordered Nicholas II and his family brutally assassinated in the basement of the house in Ekaterinburg where they had been exiled. The Bolsheviks and their successors ruled Russia for the next seven decades.

As the monarchy entered its final years, many of the stars of Russia's novelistic pantheon were dying. A new generation of Russian writers, the Symbolists, came into prominence at the turn of the twentieth century. The Symbolists decried the political thrust that had been assigned to literature, and they unabashedly sought meaning in other, mystical realms. While novels, some brilliant, continued to be written, and prose writers such as Maksim Gorky achieved renown, poetry in the early years of the twentieth century regained a status it had lost since the Golden Age, represented by Pushkin's verse, in the first decades of the nineteenth century. Poets such as Aleksandr Aleksandrovich Blok, Valerii Iakovlevich Briusov, and Andrei Bely became leading figures in Russian intellectual life, as did representatives of the Acmeist and Futurist movements in the years before the 1917 revolution. Russia's age of the great Realist novel had ended.

The Russian novel had arisen quickly in comparison to its Western European counterparts, but it did not appear fully formed out of nowhere. The appearance of the novel in Russia dates to the latter part of the eighteenth century. Fedor Aleksandrovich Emin's adventure tale *Nepostoiannaia fortuna, ili Pokhozhdenie Miramonda* (Inconstant Fortune, or The Adventures of Miramond, 1763) was the first original novel written in Russian, and over the next seven years Emin followed it with several other novels and translations, all intended to reach a broad audience. Mikhail Dmitrievich Chulkov's *Prigozhaia povarikha, ili Pokhozhdenie razvratnoi zhenshchiny* (The Comely Cook, or The Adventures of a Debauched Woman), another early novel, was more successful artistically than Emin's efforts had been. The first part of this work was published in 1770; the rest remained unpublished, probably for reasons of censorship, and has been lost. Often compared to Daniel Defoe's *Moll Flanders* (1722) and probably drawing on Pierre Marivaux's *La Vie de Marianne* (The Life of Marianne, 1731–1741), Chulkov's *Prigozhaia povarikha* is, as Harold B. Segel notes in his *The Literature of Eighteenth-Century Russia* (1967), "the best Russian eighteenth-century specimen of the European 'rogue novel' with a 'fallen woman' as its heroine."

The novel was not, however, generally considered to be one of the important genres of Russian literature in the late eighteenth or early nineteenth centuries; indeed, much of contemporary literary opinion held it in utter contempt. Poetry was exalted; occupying oneself with either writing or reading novels was seen as a useless and even dangerous waste of time. Aleksandr Petrovich Sumarokov gave dire warnings about the consequences of reading novels in his "O chtenii romanov" (On Reading Novels, 1759), and other attacks on the novel at this time came from Mikhail Matveevich Kheraskov. (The latter's own novels appeared only somewhat later.) Staunch defense of the novel came from a group of writers who were responsible for trans-

lating many Baroque and adventure novels from the French in the 1750s and 1760s. These writers, grouped around the first private Russian literary journal, felt that time spent on novels could be productive, as shown by the programmatic title of their journal: *Prazdnoe vremia, v pol'zu upotreblennoe* (Idle Time for Good Use, 1759–1760).

Kheraskov, once he started writing novels, produced works that drew on classical antiquity, mythology, and Masonic allegory. Another significant novelist of the late eighteenth century, Matvei Komarov, reworked folkloric, carnivalesque forms. As these examples suggest, the Russian novel arose from several disparate elements and sources, both native and foreign. This multifaceted character was true of the novel everywhere; Philip Stevick notes in *The Theory of the Novel* (1967) that "The novel . . . is a mixed genre. Its origins lie in a dozen different forms: essay, romance, history, the 'character,' biography, comic and sentimental drama, and so on. Traditionally, it is flexible and indeterminate in its form." In Russia, the balance of these various contributions was influenced by the fact that Russia did not have the advantage of a long development of secular literature of the sort seen in Western Europe from the Renaissance onward. The native precursors of the novel, such as *Povest' o Frole Skabeeve* (The Tale of Frol Skabeev), dating from the early seventeenth century, are as close to the medieval tradition and to folklore as they are to Western literature of the seventeenth and early eighteenth centuries. Later, when novelists as disparate as Dostoevsky, Tolstoy, and Chernyshevsky looked back for models in a premodern native written tradition, they often turned to medieval hagiography. The development from a late-medieval tradition to the undisputed flourishing of a modern literature took place in Russia over the course of little more than a century, and this hectic pace continued in the nineteenth century as well. As Belinsky noted, given how quickly Russia absorbed new forms and ways of thinking, different generations lived in what elsewhere would have seemed like different centuries.

While Russian sources were thus clearly important in the development of the Russian novel, Western novels had a decisive impact. In the course of the eighteenth century there were translations into Russian of many of the most important novels of the West. English contributions included Daniel Defoe's *Robinson Crusoe* and Henry Fielding's *Tom Jones* in the 1760s and 1770s, and works by Oliver Goldsmith, Samuel Richardson (*Pamela, Clarissa Harlowe,* and *Sir Charles Grandison*), and Laurence Sterne (*A Sentimental Journey*) in the 1780s and 1790s. Catherine the Great herself commissioned a translation of Jonathan Swift's *Gulliver's Travels*. Alain René Lesage's *Histoire de Gil Blas de Santillane* appeared in Russian in 1754–1755, Paul Scarron's *Roman comique* (Comic Novel) in 1763, and Jean Jacques Rousseau's *Julie ou la Nouvelle Héloïse* in 1769. Johann Wolfgang von Goethe's *Die Leiden des jungen Werthers* (The Sorrows of Young Werther) was translated in 1781.

Despite highbrow disapproval, novels had already gained great popular appeal by the late eighteenth century. Nikolai Mikhailovich Karamzin, in his "O knizhnoi torgovle" (On the Book Trade, 1802), noted that "An inquiring person would wish to know, perhaps, what kinds of book have the readiest sale among us? I inquired about this of many booksellers, and all without thinking answered: 'Novels!'" By the end of the eighteenth century, notes Victor Terras in his *History of Russian Literature* (1991), "most major foreign novels, and many second- and third-rate novels, had found their way to the Russian reader."

The popularity of the novel increased further in the first two decades of the nineteenth century, although it was still overshadowed by verse during this period, the "Golden Age" of Russian poetry. Vasilii Trofimovich Narezhny, later called Russia's first real novelist by Belinsky, achieved only modest success with his novels *Rossiiskii Zhil'blaz ili pokhozhdeniia kniazia Gavrily Simonovicha Chistiakova* (A Russian Gil Blas, or the Adventures of Prince Gavrila Simonovich Chistiakov, 1814) and *Aristion, ili Perevospitanie* (Aristion, or Reeducation, 1822). As with Chulkov's *Prigozhaia povarikha,* much of Narezhny's first novel was banned by censors; only the first three parts appeared in 1814, while the last three were not published until 1938.

Russian audiences increasingly sought out translated historical novels and in particular the works of Sir Walter Scott, whose books appeared in Russian throughout the 1820s. Soon Russian novelists took up his themes and style, and historical subjects dominated in the novels of the late 1820s and 1830s. Mikhail Nikolaevich Zagoskin's *Iurii Miloslavsky, ili Russkie v 1612 godu* (Iurii Miloslavsky, or the Russians in 1612, 1829) was praised by literary society and by popular audiences alike, going through several editions and translations into Western European languages. Zagoskin followed up with several other historical works, including *Roslavlev, ili Russkie v 1812 godu* (Roslavlev, or the Russians in 1812, 1830) and *Askol'dova mogila* (Askol'd's Grave, 1833). Another of the popular and influential Russian historical novelists of the early 1830s was Ivan Ivanovich Lazhechnikov, whose *Poslednii Novik, ili Zavoevanie Lifliandii v tsarstvovanie Petra Velikogo* (The Last Courtier, or the Conquest of Livonia During the Rule of Peter the Great, 1831–1833) was the first of a series of successful historical novels from this writer. Similarly successful and particularly innovative in his manipulation of genres and subjects was Aleksandr Fomich

Vel'tman; his novels in the 1830s include time travel, settings in the distant future and past, Sternean digressive narration, and incorporation of folklore and legend.

Several important novelists in the 1820s and 1830s were equally active on the practical side of the publishing business, including Osip Ivanovich Senkovsky, Nikolai Alekseevich Polevoi, and the notorious Faddei Venediktovich Bulgarin, whose name, in the words of Ronald LeBlanc, has become "synonymous in Russia with viciousness, opportunism, and avarice of the most amoral kind." Bulgarin was co-editor of several St. Petersburg periodicals, including *Severnyi arkhiv* (Northern Archive), *Syn otechestva* (Son of the Fatherland), and *Severnaia pchela* (The Northern Bee). His 1829 novel *Ivan Vyzhigin* (originally subtitled *Russkii Zhilblaz* [A Russian Gil Blas], alluding both to Lesage and Narezhny) was wildly popular with readers, including highly placed reactionaries right up to Czar Nicholas I himself. The novel quickly sold out its first two print runs and led to many sequels, imitations, and parodies by Bulgarin and several others. Some of these sound like bad modern movie sequels: one minor author's parodies included *The Death of Ivan Vyzhigin, Ivan Vyzhigin's Genealogy,* and *Ivan Vyzhigin's Godfather,* all published in 1831, with a similar number appearing the following year and devoted to Vyzhigin's various adventures and family members.

Polevoi and Senkovsky, in addition to writing novels, edited two of Russia's first encyclopedic journals and constantly agitated for a larger reading public. Polevoi, as publisher of *Moskovskii telegraf* (The Moscow Telegraph) from 1825 to 1834, either wrote or translated much of the contents of this liberal journal himself. Going against the reigning policies in this time of reaction, Polevoi benefited as a publisher from none of the official approval and privileges that Bulgarin received. *Moskovskii telegraf* was eventually closed after printing a negative review of a government-sponsored performance of Nestor Vasil'evich Kukol'nik's historical play *Ruka Vsevyshnego otechestvo spasla* (The Hand of the Almighty Saved the Fatherland, 1834). Senkovsky, an erudite orientalist, critic, writer, and publisher, edited *Biblioteka dlia chteniia* (Library for Reading) from 1834 to 1856, to which he contributed the novel *Ideal'naia krasavitsa* (An Ideal Beauty, 1841–1844) and other prose.

When looking in this period for the antecedents to the great Realist novels of later in the century, readers should not limit themselves to novels. As it had from its beginnings, the novel continued to draw on advances in other realms of writing, including short fiction, memoir literature, and journalism. Writers in these other genres made many crucial advances in the vivid observation of place, exploration of psychology and character, motivation of action, and other elements essential to the growth of the Realist novel. Among works that were particularly significant in the development of Russian prose fiction are Aleksandr Nikolaevich Radishchev's *Puteshestvie iz Peterburga v Moskvu* (Journey from Petersburg to Moscow, 1790), Karamzin's *Pis'ma russkogo puteshestvennika* (Letters of a Russian Traveler, 1791–1801), and later and most significantly, the prose works of Pushkin.

Pushkin's prose fiction was written during the last decade of his life (1827–1837) and focused in general on forms shorter than the full-fledged novel. His stories, particularly the five stories in *Povesti pokoinogo Ivana Petrovicha Belkina* (Tales of the Late Ivan Petrovich Belkin, 1831), are particularly noteworthy for the conciseness and precision characteristic of Pushkin's prose as a whole; they are much the opposite of the prolix writing typical of the novelistic tradition until that time. Pushkin's longest completed work of prose fiction, *Kapitanskaia dochka* (The Captain's Daughter, 1836), drew on his research into the Pugachev uprising under Catherine the Great and showed Pushkin's mastery of the form of the historical novel. The work is in fact closer to a *povest'* (tale, novella) than a novel in length, but Pushkin consistently referred to it as a novel in his letters and elsewhere.

Pushkin's greatest contribution to the evolution of the novel in Russia, however, was made not in prose but in poetry, in his *Evgenii Onegin*. This witty, brilliant work is self-consciously playful in its genre, narration, and use of language. Melding elements of the novel, comedy, epic, and satire, Pushkin at the same time creates a strict verse form that was distinctive enough to become known ever after as the "Onegin stanza." Pushkin, who places himself and various contemporary references into the text, also alludes in his description of his heroine Tat'iana to the popularity that foreign novels were enjoying in Russia: "Seeing herself as a creation– / Clarissa, Julie, or Delphine– / by writers of her admiration, / Tatyana, lonely heroine, / roamed the still forest like a ranger, / sought in her book, that text of danger, / and found her dreams, her secret fire, / the full fruit of her heart's desire" (translated by Charles Johnson). Thus Tat'iana is shaped by her reading, as are many of the characters in later nineteenth-century Russian fiction, including some of the best-known characters in the novels of Tolstoy, Dostoevsky, Turgenev, and Goncharov.

The status of *Evgenii Onegin* as a "novel in verse" may seem paradoxical. But it is worth noting that the three best novels of the early part of the century, and the only ones that exerted lasting influence and are still universally read, are all problematic in their "novel-ness": Pushkin's *Evgenii Onegin,* Lermontov's *Geroi nashego vremeni* (A Hero of Our Time, 1840), and Gogol's *Mertvye dushi* (Dead Souls, 1842). The elements of Lermontov's novel are largely self-contained stories loosely knit together, while Gogol called his work a *poema* (narrative poem), not a novel, and he never was able to find a satisfactory way to conclude it, leaving much undone after burning his attempts. William Mills Todd III, discussing these three works in his study *Fiction and Society in the Age of Pushkin* (1986), writes, "in very different ways *Eugene Onegin, A Hero of Our Time,* and *Dead Souls* stretch most familiar conceptions of the novel nearly to the breaking point, not only our conceptions, but those of their initial readers, a century and a half ago."

In moving from poetry to prose, Pushkin, Lermontov, and Gogol demonstrate individually a transformation that was taking place in Russian literature as a whole. Pushkin and Lermontov were the outstanding figures of the Golden Age of poetry; Gogol, on the contrary, marked the dawn of a new age of mature native prose. After the utter failure of his *Gants Kiukhel'garten* (Hanz Kuechelgarten, 1829), published when he was twenty, Gogol turned exclusively to prose. Starting at first with short stories, Gogol culminated his career in the struggle with *Mertvye dushi.*

Only in the half-century from the 1840s to the 1890s, roughly the period covered by this volume, did the Russian novel reach its maturity and attain international importance and even preeminence. Some reasons for the shift from the earlier period into this new era of the novel include a growing middle-class readership, new forms of publication to reach that readership, a rethinking of the role literature should play in the lives of its readers (leading in turn to new expectations and demands placed on literature), and an international environment in which the concerns of Realism occupied most writers all across Europe.

As Stevick notes, "It has been obvious to the most disparate of observers–from Samuel Johnson to Karl Marx to Lionel Trilling–that the novel is a middle-class genre. Such an observation has implications both extrinsic and intrinsic. It implies, extrinsically, that the novel emerged as a specific genre at least partly as a response to a new kind of audience. . . . Intrinsically, such an observation implies that the novel, almost by definition, must come to terms with the middle class." In Russia, the middle class as conventionally defined was still small in the 1840s; and any reader of the novels of the period will realize that by no means all of them are predominantly peopled by middle-class characters. But something significant had happened to the Russian reading public. Changes in Russian society meant that the numbers of people who needed to work and worried about feeding themselves and a family, yet still had enough time and education to enjoy reading, were growing significantly. As noted, children of minor officials and village clergy were increasingly less likely to be satisfied with the limited options open to their parents, leading to the newfound "mixed-class" force of the *raznochintsy*. Many young men and women progressed from a traditional education (whether at a village school, a gymnasium, or a seminary) to an active desire to participate in public life, making up for the deficiencies in their official education through assiduous reading and discussions with fellow students. Thus, as Jeffrey Brooks has shown in a 1985 study, the Russian reading public grew enormously in the second half of the nineteenth century.

Meanwhile, newly written, original works of literature were more available to a wider audience than ever before. Russian literary life earlier in the century had been dominated by salons and exclusive circles; in the Golden Age of poetry, few of those engaged in serious literature were concerned with "crass concerns" of making money or reaching a broad audience. Much of the poetry of the Romantic age was written "for the few," while the 1830s and 1840s were a time of rapidly expanding audiences and a demand for popular prose that could reach its audience efficiently and quickly. Monthly and weekly magazines proved to be the perfect vehicle.

Russian journalism was already well established, as seen in the efforts of figures such as Polevoi, Bulgarin, and Senkovsky, all of whom were advocates of a wider reading public. Polevoi, son of a Siberian merchant, had criticized the gentry and praised the merchant class, and, in the words of Mary Jo White, tirelessly used his journal "to cultivate a wider reading public, a broad middle-class audience, and so to democratize literature and learning." Bulgarin explicitly wrote for a "middle-class" audience, and the purpose of Senkovsky's *Biblioteka dlia chteniia* was to provide easy and enjoyable reading for a large and diverse audience. All three of these men, however, had faced a literary community that often looked down on their activities. As prose came to dominance, and as a more diverse cross-section of the population became active not just as readers but also as writers, Russian literary life became inseparably tied to the various periodicals that served as its means of dissemination. Nearly all of the writers in this volume were regular contributors to the journals of their day, and many also served as journal editors at some point in their careers.

During the 1840s and 1850s a new form of periodical emerged—the so-called thick journal, distinguished from the already established encyclopedic journals not so much by size or expanse of subject matter, since both were substantial and wide-ranging, but rather by a particular ideological bent. Among the most important of such journals were *Otechestvennye zapiski* (Notes of the Fatherland), *Sovremennik* (The Contemporary), and *Russkii vestnik* (The Russian Herald). Many of the large novels of nineteenth-century Russian writers appeared first or exclusively in these or other thick journals; in fact, it was not uncommon for a given journal to be serializing more than one long novel at the same time.

Increasingly, readers and writers placed new demands on literature, coming to it with conceptions of its role quite different from those held by their predecessors. Unlike the audiences of the Romantic era, when the predominant form of long fiction had been the historical novel, new audiences wanted literature that dealt with contemporary issues and society. At first, readers were fascinated with the mainly short works of the Natural School of the 1840s, which focused on the least fortunate and most pitiful urban dwellers; increasingly, though, they looked for forms that could capture the whole scope of society, and the long Realist novel perfectly satisfied this desire. "The novel," as E. M. Forster wrote, "is sogged with humanity."

Novels can be variously defined, but perhaps the best definitions have to do with the world that a given novelist creates for his readers. In the words of the twentieth-century writer Joseph Conrad, "every novelist must begin by creating for himself a world, great or little, in which he can honestly believe. This world cannot be made otherwise than in his own image: it is fated to remain individual and a little mysterious, and yet it must resemble something already familiar to the experience, the thoughts and the sensations of his readers." There is a tension inherent in this "resemblance" to something "familiar," and it can be felt particularly strongly in Russian novels of the second half of the nineteenth century and the spirited debates that raged around them. Some blamed a novel for not being "close enough to life" or for being out of step with pressing current issues; others might see a novel as being too "ethnographic," simply chronicling life in a particular environment and showing no evidence of attention to even basic issues of style and form. The "accursed questions" that agitated Russian society in this period were all addressed in literature, and even readers today who are distanced in both time and place from the events and debates described find themselves captured by the issues involved.

The extent to which the greatest novels of the period were intrinsically linked to the realities of nineteenth-century Russian society has sometimes made it difficult to discuss them on purely artistic grounds. Vladimir Nabokov, another novelist of the twentieth century and a passionate advocate for the autonomy of art, cautions readers that, "We should always remember that the work of art is invariably the creation of a new world, so that the first thing we should do is to study that new world as closely as possible, approaching it as something brand new, having no obvious connection with the worlds we already know." While this advice is useful for any appreciation of a novel on its own merits, certainly in the case of the Russian Realist novel close attention to the historical context of the work will also yield rich results.

Searching for a definition of what unites and defines the works classed together under the heading of Russian Realism, D. S. Mirsky sees the common trait as "a sympathetic attitude to human beings, without distinction (not only of class but) of intrinsic moral significance." No matter how elevated or debased the surroundings, no matter how noble or low the actions and motivations of characters, all of them are worthy of a reader's attention. While inheriting many of the features of earlier Russian literature, the novels of this period were also written with full awareness of contemporaneous literary developments in Western Europe; translations of Victor Hugo, Eugène Sue, Alexandre Dumas *père,* Jules Janin, and Honoré de Balzac all appeared in *Moskovskii telegraf,* and George Sand, Emile Zola, Charles Dickens, and Guy de Maupassant were all extremely influential. In fact, in Mirsky's phrase, "Gogol and George Sand were the father and mother of Russian realism and its accepted masters during the initial stages."

Unlike the defining characteristics of earlier periods, though, "realism is perhaps the first major literary development whose Russian version is not a more or less belated response to ideas generated in Western Europe," as Hugh McLean has noted. For the first time the rest of the world began to pay avid attention to Russian literature and soon came to acknowledge the preeminent place of the Russian novel in world fiction. In the introduction to his classic *Aspects of the Novel* (1927) Forster wrote, "An unpleasant and unpatriotic truth has here to be faced. No English novelist is as great as Tolstoy—that is to say has given so complete a picture of man's life, both on its domestic and heroic side. No English novelist has explored man's soul as deeply as Dostoevsky." As Yale professor William Lyon Phelps wrote in 1911, hoping to persuade "some American and English readers to substitute in their leisure hours first-class novels for fourth and fifth class" ones, "Russian fiction is like German music—the best in the world."

Some of the figures in the present volume are among the giants of world literature; others, however, are relatively unknown, and in several cases the articles appearing here are the most detailed treatment of these writers' lives and works available in English. Taken as a whole, the entries in this volume provide a detailed portrait of the styles, concerns, and historical involvement of the novel in Russia in the second half of the nineteenth century. The novelists represent an artistic range from master stylists, such as (in different ways) Turgenev and Leskov, to those who were more a part of popular culture and are important as a reflection of the flavor of the era rather than as artistic exemplars. Our hope is that, by giving attention to once popular but now forgotten novelists alongside their more well-known contemporaries, this volume will inspire further research into some of the still unexplored territories of Russian literary history. The criterion for inclusion in this volume (for those figures not covered in other volumes of the *Dictionary of Literary Biography* related to this period) has been the authorship of at least one significant novel; some writers represented are as well or better known for their works in other genres.

— J. Alexander Ogden and Judith E. Kalb

Note on Bibliography

The first bibliographic rubric in each entry is Works, which encompasses separately published books and pamphlets as well as works of substantial length (novels, novellas, dramas) that appeared only in periodical form. If a work was both serialized and published separately, we have tried when possible to provide bibliographic information on both publications, since publication in periodical form was often of primary importance for works that appeared in the period covered by this volume. The common genre of the *povest'* (tale, novella) provides a particular challenge, since *povesti* range in length from short stories to novels. Some appeared as separate publications; many appeared only in periodicals. In most cases we have included these works under the first rubric. Important shorter works published in periodical form are found under the Selected Periodical Publications rubric.

Contributors to the volume have provided the fullest bibliographical information available to them at the time of writing. Bibliographies have been checked when applicable against Kseniia Dmitrievna Muratova, ed., *Istoriia russkoi literatury XIX veka. Bibliograficheskii ukazatel'* (Leningrad: Akademiia Nauk SSSR, 1962), Avgusta Vladimirovna Mez'er, comp., *Russkaia slovesnost' s XI po XIX stoletiia vkliuchitel'no. Bibliograficheskii ukazatel' proizvedenii russkoi slovesnosti v sviazi s istoriei literatury i kritikoi. Knigi i zhurnalnye stati,* volume 2 (St. Petersburg: Tipografiia Altshulera, 1902), and P. A. Nikolaev, ed., *Russkie pisateli, 1800–1917: biograficheskii slovar',* 4 volumes to date (Moscow: Bol'shaia Rossiiskaia entsiklopediia, 1992–   ). Readers are referred to these publications for further bibliographic detail.

Note on Dates, Names, and Transliteration

All dates in this volume appear according to the calendar in use in Russia at the time, which in almost all cases (pre-1918) was the Julian calendar (Old Style). To convert to the Gregorian calendar (New Style), add twelve days for dates in the nineteenth century, thirteen days for pre-1918 dates in the twentieth century.

Russian names, titles, and quotations are transliterated according to the standard Library of Congress transliteration system (without diacritics, but preserving hard and soft signs), with the following exceptions. Surnames with the adjectival ending -yi or -ii are changed to -y. This exception will be seen most frequently in the ending -sky (rather than -skii). Czars are given anglicized names (Alexander, Nicholas), Gogol appears without his final soft sign, and Leo Tolstoy and Fyodor Dostoevsky appear in their commonly accepted forms. Moscow and St. Petersburg are given their English names. Books published in St. Petersburg during the twentieth century use the name for the city in place at time of publication (St. Petersburg, Petrograd, Leningrad, St. Petersburg).

In accord with standard scholarly practice, prerevolutionary Russian orthography has been modernized. Readers should note, however, that listings for nineteenth-century books and periodicals in library catalogues usually preserve the peculiarities of prerevolutionary spelling. Thus, for example, our modern spellings *Rassvet, Vestnik Evropy,* and *Moskovskie vedomosti* correspond to prerevolutionary *Razsviet, Viestnik Evropy,* and *Moskovskiia viedomosti.*

Acknowledgments

This book was produced by Bruccoli Clark Layman, Inc. Karen L. Rood is senior editor. Tracy Simmons Bitonti and Penelope M. Hope were the in-house editors. Assistance with bibliographical research and translation was provided by Olga Karabanova.

Production manager is Philip B. Dematteis.

Administrative support was provided by Ann M. Cheschi, Amber L. Coker, and Angi Pleasant.

Accounting supervisor is Ann-Marie Holland.

Copyediting supervisor is Phyllis A. Avant. The copyediting staff includes Brenda Carol Blanton, Allen E. Friend Jr., Melissa D. Hinton, William Tobias Mathes, Rebecca Mayo, Nancy E. Smith, and Elizabeth Jo Ann Sumner.

Editorial associates are Andrew Choate and Michael S. Martin.

Database manager is José A. Juarez.

Layout and graphics supervisor is Janet E. Hill. The graphics staff includes Karla Corley Brown and Zoe R. Cook.

Office manager is Kathy Lawler Merlette.

Photography supervisor is Paul Talbot. Photography editors are Charles Mims and Scott Nemzek.

Permissions editor is Jeff Miller.

Digital photographic copy work was performed by Joseph M. Bruccoli.

The SGML staff includes Frank Graham, Linda Dalton Mullinax, Jason Paddock, and Alex Snead.

Systems manager is Marie L. Parker.

Typesetting supervisor is Kathleen M. Flanagan. The typesetting staff includes Patricia Marie Flanagan, Mark J. McEwan, Pamela D. Norton, and Alison Smith. Freelance typesetters are Wanda Adams and Vicki Grivetti.

Walter W. Ross did library research. He was assisted by Steven Gross and the following librarians at the Thomas Cooper Library of the University of South Carolina: circulation department head Tucker Taylor; reference department head Virginia W. Weathers; Brette Barclay, Marilee Birchfield, Paul Cammarata, Gary Geer, Michael Macan, Tom Marcil, Rose Marshall, and Sharon Verba; interlibrary loan department head John Brunswick; and interlibrary loan staff Robert Arndt, Hayden Battle, Barry Bull, Jo Cottingham, Marna Hostetler, Marieum McClary, Erika Peake, and Nelson Rivera.

The editors would like to thank Matthew J. Bruccoli for his invitation to edit this volume and for his support. We are grateful to in-house editors Tracy Bitonti and Penny Hope, who once more rose with dedication, humor, and flexibility to the challenges presented by a Russian volume. Thanks are due as well to Christine Rydel, who provided willing and informed advice throughout this project. In the initial stages of the volume, consultations with Lazar Fleishman, Gregory Freidin, Monika Greenleaf, and William Mills Todd III were particularly helpful. We would like to acknowledge the scholarly generosity of Jehanne Gheith and Mary Zirin, who shared with us their expertise on Russian women writers. June Pachuta Farris assisted us greatly by answering queries on bibliographies for specific writers, such as Leo Tolstoy, and on general bibliographic issues. We are also grateful for the support of our colleagues at the University of South Carolina. Our families, as ever, provided inspiration.

Russian Novelists in the Age of Tolstoy and Dostoevsky

Dictionary of Literary Biography

Petr Dmitrievich Boborykin

(15 August 1836 – 12 August 1921)

John McNair
University of Queensland

WORKS: *Odnodvorets,* in *Biblioteka dlia chteniia,* 161 (September 1860): 1–70 (separate pagination);

Rebenok, in *Biblioteka dlia chteniia,* 163 (November 1861): 1–59 (separate pagination);

V put'-dorogu!, in *Biblioteka dlia chteniia,* nos. 1–5, 9, 12 (1862); nos. 5–8, 12 (1863); nos. 9–12 (1864); (St. Petersburg: Vnutrenniaia strazha i E. Arnol'd, 1864);

Zemskie sily, in *Biblioteka dlia chteniia,* nos. 1–8 (1865); (St. Petersburg: Imp. Akademiia nauk, 1865);

V chuzhom pole, in *Russkii vestnik,* nos. 10, 12 (1866); (St. Petersburg: A. M. Kotomin, 1872);

Zhertva vecherniaia, in *Vsemirnyi trud,* nos. 1, 2, 4, 5, 7 (1868); (St. Petersburg: M. Khan, 1868); revised and enlarged edition (St. Petersburg: N. A. Shigin, 1872);

Na sud, in *Vsemirnyi trud,* nos. 1–5 (1869); (St. Petersburg, 1869);

Solidnye dobrodeteli, in *Otechestvennye zapiski,* nos. 9–12 (1870); (St. Petersburg: E. P. Pechatkin, 1871);

Povesti i rasskazy (St. Petersburg: Morigerovsky, 1872);

Povesti (St. Petersburg: M. O. Vol'f, 1871?);

Teatral'noe iskusstvo (St. Petersburg: N. Nekliudov, 1872);

Del'tsy, in *Otechestvennye zapiski,* nos. 4–12 (1872); nos. 1–5 (1873); (St. Petersburg: V. Tushkov, 1874);

Polzhizni, in *Vestnik Evropy,* nos. 11–12 (1873); (St. Petersburg: Kekhribardzhi, 1874);

Doktor Tsybul'ka, in *Otechestvennye zapiski,* nos. 3–6 (1874); (Moscow: Salaev, 1875);

V usad'be i na poriadke, in *Vestnik Evropy,* no. 1 (1875); *Dolgo-li?,* in *Otechestvennye zapiski,* no. 10 (1875); *V usad'be i na poriadke. Dolgo-li? Povesti* (St. Petersburg: Kekhribardzhi, 1876);

Povesti (St. Petersburg: Kekhribardzhi, 1876);

Likhie bolesti, in *Otechestvennye zapiski,* 10 (1876): 293–380; 11 (1876): 5–86; (St. Petersburg, 1877);

Ne u del, in *Slovo,* 1 (1878): 1–67;

Sami po sebe, in *Slovo,* 9–10 (1878): 1–56; 11 (1878): 1–52; 12 (1878): 113–189;

3

Sytye: P'esa v 5-i aktakh, in *Slovo,* no. 11 (1879); (St. Petersburg: V. Demakov, 1879);

Iskusstvo chteniia (St. Petersburg: V. Demakov, 1882);

Kitai-gorod, in *Vestnik Evropy,* nos. 1–5 (1882); (St. Petersburg: M. O. Vol'f, 1883);

Teoriia teatral'nogo iskusstva (St. Petersburg: V. S. Kurochkin, 1882);

Doktor Moshkov. P'esa v 4-kh aktakh, in *Izvestiia Literatury,* no. 2 (1884); (St. Petersburg: A. E. Landau, 1885);

Sochineniia, 12 volumes (St. Petersburg: M. O. Vol'f, 1884–1886);

Za rabotu, in *Nov',* nos. 13–18 (1885);

Kleimo. Drama v 4-kh aktakh (Moscow: E. N. Rassokhina, 1886);

Narodnyi teatr (Moscow: Novosti, 1886);

Iz novykh, in *Vestnik Evropy,* nos. 1–6 (1887);

Na ushcherbe, in *Vestnik Evropy,* nos. 1–6 (1890);

Poumnel, in *Russkaia mysl',* nos. 10–12 (1890);

Povesti dlia vzroslykh (Moscow: V. I. Az, 1891);

S boiu, in *Artist,* 13 (1891): 28–57 (supplement);

Vasilii Terkin, in *Vestnik Evropy,* nos. 1–6 (1892); (Moscow: I. D. Sytin, 1895);

Trup. Povest', in *Severnyi vestnik,* no. 4 (1892); (Moscow: Posrednik, 1893);

Pered chem-to, in *Severnyi vestnik,* nos. 10, 11 (1892); (Stuttgart: Karl Malkomes, 1893);

Pereval, in *Vestnik Evropy,* nos. 1–6 (1894);

Khodok, in *Vestnik Evropy,* nos. 1–6 (1895);

Kniaginia, in *Vestnik Evropy,* 1 (1896): 34–99; 2 (1896): 497–559; 3 (1896): 45–94; 4 (1896): 521–604; 5 (1896): 28–65; 6 (1896): 565–609;

Po-drugomu, in *Vestnik Evropy,* 1 (1897): 119–188; 2 (1897): 567–640; 3 (1897): 5–75; 4 (1897): 459–534;

Sobranie romanov, povestei i rasskazov, 12 volumes (St. Petersburg: A. F. Marks, 1897);

Tiaga, in *Vestnik Evropy,* 1 (1898): 32–116; 2 (1898): 503–589; 3 (1898): 44–101; 4 (1898): 453–511; 5 (1898): 5–55;

Kuda idti?, in *Vestnik Evropy,* 1 (1899): 19–83; 2 (1899): 445–524; 3 (1899): 5–89; 4 (1899): 429–511;

Nakip'. Komediia v 4-kh aktakh (St. Petersburg, 1899); republished as *Povetrie* in *Teatr i iskusstvo,* supplement, no. 1 (1900);

Evropeiskii roman v XIX stoletii. Roman na zapade za dve treti veka (St. Petersburg: M. Stasiulevich, 1900);

Roman na zapade za dve treti veka (St. Petersburg, 1900);

Zhestokie, in *Russkaia mysl',* 1 (1901): 1–61; 2 (1901): 1–61; 3 (1901): 1–73; 4 (1901): 1–69; 5 (1901): 1–49; 6 (1901): 1–51;

Istinno-nauchnoe znanie. Otvet moim kritikam (Moscow: I. N. Kushnerev, 1901);

Vechnyi gorod (itogi perezhitogo) (Moscow: I. N. Kushnerev, 1903);

Uprazdniteli, in *Russkaia mysl',* 11 (1904): 1–80;

Za polveka. Moi vospominaniia, published in installments in *Russkaia mysl', Golos minuvshego, Minuvshie gody,* and *Russkaia starina* (1906–1913); edited, with an introduction and notes, by B. P. Koz'min (Moscow: Zemlia i fabrika, 1929);

Velikaia razrukha (Moscow: V. I. Sablin, 1908);

Ne pervye, ne poslednie. Rasskazy dlia detei srednego vozrasta (St. Petersburg & Moscow: M. O. Vol'f, 1908);

Stolitsy mira. Tridsat' let vospominanii (Moscow: Sfinks, 1911);

Obmirshchenie (Moscow: Sfinks, 1912);

Odna dusha. Rasskaz (Moscow: Universal'naia biblioteka, 1918).

Editions and Collections: *Kitai-gorod* (Krasnodar: Krasnodarskoe knizhn. izd-vo, 1957; Moscow: Goslitizdat, 1957);

Vospominaniia, 2 volumes, edited and annotated by E. Vilenskaia and L. Roitberg (Moscow: Khudozhestvennaia literatura, 1965);

Povesti i rasskazy, compiled, edited, and annotated by Sergei I. Chuprinin (Moscow: Sovetskaia Rossiia, 1984);

Sochineniia, 3 volumes, edited and annotated by Chuprinin (Moscow: Khudozhestvennaia literatura, 1993).

PLAY PRODUCTIONS: *Odnodvorets,* Moscow, Malyi Theatre, 1 December 1861;

Rebenok, Moscow, Malyi Theatre, 8 January 1862;

Nakip', St. Petersburg, Aleksandrinskii Theatre, 2 December 1899.

OTHER: I. Leman [Johann-Gottlieb Lehmann], *Khimiia. Polnoe karmannoe rukovodstvo k teoreticheskoi i prakticheskoi khimii,* 3 volumes, translated by Boborykin (St. Petersburg: M. O. Vol'f, 1860–1867);

"Sud'by russkogo romana," in *Pochin. Sbornik obshchestva liubitelei rossiiskoi slovesnosti na 1895 g.* (Moscow: Tipo-lit. Vysochaishe utverzhdennogo "Russkogo t-va pechatnogo i izdatel'skogo dela," 1895), pp. 182–209;

"Podgnivshie vekhi," in *V zashchitu intelligentsii. Sbornik statei* (Moscow: Zaria, 1909), pp. 129–138.

SELECTED PERIODICAL PUBLICATIONS: "Analiz i sistematika Tena," *Vsemirnyi trud,* 11 (1867): 247–293; 12 (1867): 1–34;

"Phénomènes du drame moderne," *Philosophie positive,* 2 (January–June 1868): 80–98;

"Nihilism in Russia," *Fortnightly Review,* 4, no. 20 (August 1868): 117–138;

"Del criticismo russo," *Rivista europea*, 2, fasc. 2 (1875): 218–225; fasc. 3 (1875): 462–470;

"Real'nyi roman vo Frantsii," *Otechestvennye zapiski*, 6, ii (1876): 329–357; 7, ii (1876): 38–92;

"Mysli o kritike literaturnogo tvorchestva," *Slovo*, 5, ii (1878): 59–71;

"Motivy i priemy russkoi belletristiki," *Slovo*, 6, ii (1878): 48–62;

"Krasota, zhizn' i tvorchestvo," *Voprosy filosofii i psikhologii*, 16 (1893): 71–108; 17 (1893): 30–62;

"Metody izucheniia romana," *Severnyi vestnik*, 11, i (1894): 8–24;

"English Influence in Russia," *Contemporary Review*, 68 (July 1895): 50–57;

"L'évolution du roman russe," *L'Humanité nouvelle*, 7 (1900): 410–424;

"Russkaia intelligentsiia," *Russkaia mysl'*, 12 (1904): 80–88.

Largely forgotten by modern readers, Petr Dmitrievich Boborykin is remembered by historians of Russian literature chiefly for the sheer volume of his output, which apart from some twenty-six novels, more than one hundred shorter works of prose fiction, and almost thirty plays, includes full-length histories of the European novel and the modern theater; two substantial volumes of reminiscences (as well as many uncollected memoirs); essays on philosophy, psychology, aesthetics, literary theory, stagecraft, and intellectual history; and a voluminous corpus of occasional journalism. To many of his contemporaries, such prodigious productivity seemed ironically disproportionate to Boborykin's modest share of literary talent, so that the verbs *boborykat'* (to write immoderately and tediously–attributed to Mikhail Evgrafovich Saltykov [pseudonym, Shchedrin]) and *oboborykinit'sia* (to become dazed from a surfeit of Boborykin–coined by Petr Nikitich Tkachev) gained some currency, and "Pierre Bobo" himself became a favorite target for satirists and parodists (most notably Fyodor Dostoevsky and Viktor Petrovich Burenin).

At the same time, however, some of his novels, stories, and plays had in their day considerable impact on the reading (and theatergoing) public, while during his lifetime literary scholars such as Semen Afanasievich Vengerov and Dmitrii Nikolaevich Ovsianiko-Kulikovsky argued persuasively for a serious recognition of his achievement. Fulfilled in his vocation as *bytopisatel'* (social chronicler), Boborykin took as his special theme the life of the Russian intelligentsia in the decades between Emancipation and Revolution, following its vicissitudes in volume after volume and even claiming to have invented the term itself. To this self-appointed task he brought a consuming interest in

ideas, the outlook of a "scientific" positivist, and a remarkable sense for the topical. In many ways more at home in Western Europe than in Russia, Boborykin aspired to the role of cultural intermediary, keeping his contemporaries abreast of the latest European ideas; he played a significant part, for example, in disseminating Emile Zola's literary theories even before the publication of *Le roman expérimental* (The Experimental Novel) in Russia in 1879. For this reason he was sometimes called "the Russian Zola" and is now usually included among the Russian epigones of naturalism, although (in the terms he himself habitually used) he remained as both practitioner and theoretician a staunch champion of the *trezvyi realizm* (sober realism) of the Russian novel.

Descended on his father's side from an old boyar family and on his mother's from the landowning gentry, Petr Dmitrievich Boborykin was born in Nizhnii Novgorod on 15 August 1836. Because his parents had already separated, he was brought up in the home of his paternal grandfather, Petr Bogdanovich Grigor'ev, a protégé of Emperor Paul who had retired from the service with the rank of general to his mansion in Nizhnii and his estate in the surrounding countryside. Neither Boborykin's grandparents nor his mother (increasingly prone to "nervous prostration") took much part in his early education beyond providing tutors in French and German and permitting access to Petr Bogdanovich's library and visits to the theaters of the town. The local classical gymnasium, which Petr began to attend in 1846, despite the repressive discipline generally associated with the reign of Nicholas I, provided a more liberal environment than his grandfather's house, and while there he developed his interest in contemporary Russian and European literature, even writing a few stories that won the praise of his contemporaries. His first visit to Moscow, early in 1853, not only brought the first real contact with his father but encouraged him in his passion for the theater.

Later that year Boborykin began his university studies in Kazan, enrolling in the special course in *kameralistika* (administrative studies). In November 1855, however, he transferred to the University of Derpt (Tartu, Estonia), attracted by its European traditions and its reputation in the exact sciences, which had become his chief interest; there, along with chemistry, anatomy, and physiology, he studied medicine, although with no thought of becoming a practitioner. By 1858 he had begun to consider a literary career, and by the time he left Derpt (without completing his degree) in December 1860, he had written three plays and had one of them (*Odnodvorets*, The Smallholder) appear in print that same year. His first published work, however, was the first volume of his translation of a textbook on chemistry by Johann-Gottlieb Lehmann.

Caricature of Boborykin under siege from angry readers and subscribers after his monthly journal, Biblioteka dlia chteniia *(Library for Reading), ceased publication in June 1865 (from* Iskra *[The Spark], 1865)*

Boborykin now moved to St. Petersburg, transferring to the university there (from which he graduated with a diploma in administrative studies in September 1861) and launching himself as a professional writer, although within a few weeks, following the death of his grandfather, he had become a substantial landowner with an assured annual income. By February 1862 his career had prospered to such an extent that two of his plays—*Odnodvorets* and *Rebenok* (The Infant, 1861)—had been successfully performed at the Malyi Theatre in Moscow (the first in 1861 and the second in January 1862), the first installment of his first novel, *V put'-dorogu!* (On the Road!, 1862–1864), had appeared in the St. Petersburg monthly *Biblioteka dlia chteniia* (Library for Reading), and he had made his debut as a regular feuilletonist in that same journal. A year later, in February 1863, following overtures from the publisher Viacheslav Petrovich Pechatkin, he became owner and editor of *Biblioteka dlia chteniia* and began his determined but foredoomed efforts to raise its declining fortunes.

V put'-dorogu!, which appeared—in sometimes irregular installments—between January 1862 and November 1864, spans most of Boborykin's tenure as editor and is the most directly autobiographical of his novels, a bildungsroman that follows the intellectual and moral development of his alter ego Boris Telepnev as a schoolboy in Nizhnii Novgorod and as a student at Kazan and Derpt. So rambling and diffuse that an anonymous reviewer in the satirical journal *Iskra* (The Spark) in January 1864 rechristened it *Poteriannyi put'* (The Lost Way), the novel finally brings its hero and his friends to the point at which their emergence into the world becomes emblematic of the predicament of the new generation seeking an outlet for its idealism and desire "to be of use" on the eve of the 1860s. Similar echoes of the age of the "great reforms" are found in *Zemskie sily* (Powers of the Land, 1865), an unfinished novel the serial publication of which was abruptly terminated with the collapse of *Biblioteka dlia chteniia,* and in all of the five plays that Boborykin published in the journal. They also resonate in the feuilletons and leading articles in which the editor urged his principles of open-minded social enquiry and disinterested altruism, free of prejudice and "tendency." In the increasingly politicized atmosphere of Russian intellectual life, these appeals to moderate liberalism only further alienated the radicals on whose support the fate of the "thick" journals so much depended. Despite Boborykin's initial success in attracting new contributors and readers to *Biblioteka dlia chteniia,* its financial position (the full details of which had probably been concealed from him at the time of purchase) failed to improve, and following the publication of *Nekuda* (Nowhere to Go) by M. Stebnitsky (Nikolai Semenovich Leskov) in 1864, began to deteriorate rapidly. Widely regarded as an attack on Russian radicalism, Leskov's novel provoked outrage, much of it directed at *Biblioteka dlia chteniia* and its unfortunate editor. Contributions were withdrawn and subscriptions canceled, and, all remedies having failed, the journal appeared for the last time in June 1865. By March of the following year, its debts were put at more than thirty thousand rubles, for which Boborykin accepted personal responsibility. Having sold the estates inherited from his grandfather, he paid off what he could and undertook to settle all outstanding claims in installments from his earnings.

The impact of this fiasco on Boborykin's literary career can hardly be overestimated. On one hand, the need to discharge his debts (finally settled only in 1886), as well as earn his living, accounts for his conspicuous industry and his immoderate productivity as a writer. On the other hand, the opprobrium attaching to him from the *Nekuda* episode was never wholly forgotten and was certainly a factor in his failure to win the critical recognition he believed to be his due. In the shorter term, however, the collapse of *Biblioteka dlia chteniia* had its positive aspect also, for it encouraged Boborykin in his resolve to travel to Europe.

Arriving in Paris in the autumn of 1865, he made the city his home for almost five years, returning there from shorter sojourns in London, Madrid, Vienna, Prague, and Berlin. He attended lectures at the Sorbonne, the Collège de France, and—even contemplating a career on the stage—the Conservatoire, and under the tutelage of the Russian Positivist Grigorii Nikolaevich Vyrubov worked his way systematically through the writings of the Positivist Auguste Comte, whose ideas had first attracted him as a student in Derpt. Some time later, in the lectures of Hippolyte Adolphe Taine at the École des Beaux-Arts, he heard expounded the principles of a "scientific" aesthetics consistent with Comte's "scientific-philosophic" doctrine. These principles were the main sources of the Weltanschauung that was thereafter to inform Boborykin's sustained attempt to record and evaluate the phenomena of contemporary life.

During these years in Paris he embarked on a new career as foreign correspondent, providing for *Sankt-Peterburgskie vedomosti* (St. Petersburg News) not only regular pieces on French politics but also occasional theater reviews and (in 1870) dispatches from the battlefields of the Franco-Prussian War. More substantial were his contributions to the monthly press, such as an essay on Taine for the St. Petersburg journal *Vsemirnyi trud* (Universal Labor) in 1867, in which he first joined issue with the "metaphysical" tradition of Russian "civic" criticism; a survey of modern drama for *La Philosophie positive* (published in Paris by Vyrubov and Emile Littré); and the article "Nihilism in Russia," which appeared in *The Fortnightly Review* in August 1868. Neither of the two plays he wrote in Paris had any success, but between 1866 and 1871 he produced four novels (as well as many novellas and short stories). The most significant of these is *Zhertva vecherniaia* (Victim of the Night, 1868), which had an immediate succès de scandale. Set in St. Petersburg high society, it is presented as the confession of a young widow seduced by the roué writer Dombrovich and rescued from a life of idle debauchery by the high-minded radical Labazin. His example of noble self-sacrifice, however, only convinces the heroine that moral regeneration is beyond her reach, and she commits suicide. The novel was generally seen as a pornographic roman à clef and was apparently saved from the censor only by the intervention of Alexander II. Finding little that was new in its exposé of a corrupt society and its exposition of the "woman question," Vengerov, in his *Kritiko-biograficheskii slovar'* (Critical-Biographical Dictionary, 1895) suggests it was rather *Solidnye dobrodeteli* (Solid Virtues, 1870) that in its unflattering picture of fashionable liberalism marked a new phase in Boborykin's attempt as a novelist "to reflect the age and capture the moment."

During his stay in Russia from late 1871 until early 1873 Boborykin devoted much of his time to the theater, though less as a dramatist (both of the plays he wrote during this period were rejected by the theatrical censor) than as an educator and theoretician. The lectures on "the art of the theater" he delivered in the spring of 1871 at the St. Petersburg Actors' Club were published the following year as *Teatral'noe iskusstvo* (1872) and provoked considerable interest. Taking a "scientific" approach to the depiction of "the truth of life" and "the defining characteristics of the age and the nation" on the stage, this treatise also offered some trenchant criticism of the shortcomings of the contemporary Russian theater, in particular its neglect of professional training for actors and other stage workers, its attachment to routine, and the inadequacies of its management. Boborykin pursued all these matters in lectures, articles, and pamphlets over the next decades.

In 1871, in the Actors' Club, Boborykin became acquainted with one of the actresses new to the Aleksandrinskii company that season, Sofiia Aleksandrovna Zborzhevskaia, née Kalmykova, who performed under the name Severtsova. A widow (or perhaps divorcée) some nine years his junior, she had first attracted his attention in Paris, where she had begun her stage career as Mlle. Delnord in the Vaudeville theater. They were married in November 1872, embarking a month afterward on the first of the many European journeys that they made during their long life together. The marriage was childless.

Although this period of residence abroad was prolonged by illness until the autumn of 1875, Boborykin's life now settled into a regular routine. Much of the year was spent in St. Petersburg (with frequent visits to Moscow), while the summer, autumn, and sometimes also the winter months were given over to travel—to the Baltic, Germany, France, Switzerland, or Italy; only the outbreak of hostilities in the Balkans in 1877, when Boborykin resumed his duties as special correspondent from the theater of war, disrupted the pattern. His creative writing occupied the months spent abroad, while his time in Russia was given over to broadening his acquaintance with Russian life and to his work as journalist, publicist, and lecturer. In the mid 1870s, for example, he wrote a weekly Sunday feuilleton for *Sankt-Peterburgskie vedomosti,* and from 1878 until the 1890s he became a regular contributor to the Moscow newspaper *Russkie vedomosti* (Russian News). He continued to write about the theater, provoking controversy in particular with his observations on the "cult" of Aleksandr Nikolaevich Ostrovsky, while in an essay on the realist novel in France, published in the June and July issues of *Otechestvennye zapiski* (Notes of the Fatherland) in 1876, he entered the debate then raging over "Zola-

П. Д. БОБОРЫКИНЪ.

ПОЛЖИЗНИ

РОМАНЪ ВЪ ДВУХЪ КНИГАХЪ.

С. ПЕТЕРБУРГЪ.
ИЗДАНІЕ А. Е. КЕХРИБАРДЖИ.
1874.

Title page for Polzhizni *(Half a Life), Boborykin's novel
about an agronomist's attempts to modernize
the rural economy*

ism," defending the experimental novel from the censure of Russian utilitarian criticism.

During the 1870s and 1880s Boborykin's novels (and to a lesser extent his novellas and short stories) appeared regularly year after year over two or three issues in one or another of the "thick" monthlies—*Otechestvennye zapiski, Vestnik Evropy* (The Herald of Europe), *Slovo* (The Word), and later *Russkaia mysl'* (Russian Thought)—and established him as one of the fixtures of Russian literary life. They are the products of the workmanlike approach to his craft he described in an interview published in the newspaper *Novosti i birzhevaia gazeta* (News and Stockmarket Gazette) on 7 January 1895:

> I take some phenomenon, some "area of life," and jot it down in a single phrase. For the most part it is this note that serves as the title of the future novel. . . . You will find any number of these jottings in my notebooks. . . . This is what the French call the *idée-mère.* . . . I do not use the

idea that has occurred to me at once, but sometimes leave it undeveloped for a year or two. . . . Then I set to work on a summary, and my attention is focused on the detailed working out of the basic idea, rather than of the plot. . . .

> After that I set down the *dramatis personae* as in a play; next to each of the characters you will find a detailed resumé (his or her past and present), and also their physical description.

The "areas of life" selected for examination range from the stockmarket boom of the early 1870s (*Del'tsy* [The Operators, 1872–1873]) through various phenomena of the next twenty years, such as attempts to modernize the rural economy (*Polzhizni* [Half a Life, 1873]), educational reforms (*Doktor Tsybul'ka* [Dr. Tsybul'ka, 1874]), the rise of Populism (*Likhie bolesti* [Grave Disorders, 1876]) and Pan-Slavism (*Sami po sebe* [All by Themselves, 1878]), the first stirrings of industrial capitalism (*Kitai-gorod* [Kitai-gorod–the traditional merchant quarter of Moscow–1882]) to the gradual awakening of social life after the decade of reaction that followed the assassination of the Czar-Liberator Alexander II in 1881 (*Za rabotu* [To Work!, 1885–1886] and *Iz novykh* [The New Men, 1887]). The *idée-mère* (generating idea) common to all these works is the effect of the changing social climate on the collective psychology of the intelligentsia as it seeks a *delo* (cause) in the national life, or, more particularly, the conflict between this altruistic impulse and the realities of Russian life: corruption, cynicism, inertia, and compromise. The "progressives" in *Del'tsy* flee from triumphant materialism to lick their wounds and "work on themselves" in Europe; the agronomist Grechukhin in *Polzhizni*, seduced from his efforts to improve the lot of the peasants by an affair with his employer's wife, seeks his moral renewal in America; Meshcherin in *Likhie bolesti* sees no escape from the surrounding "poverty of thought, lifelessness and, as it were, bureaucratic emptiness"; Nida in *Sami po sebe* and Nogaitseva in *Iz Novykh* feel condemned by their sex and their milieu to empty, useless lives; and the former radical Paltusov in *Kitai-gorod,* sensing in the merchant-businessmen of Moscow a vitality lacking in his own class, casts in his lot with them only to succumb to the temptations of ambition and avarice.

Plot in these novels, as the author himself suggests, is secondary to the development of the "main idea" and depends on more or less predictable variations on the familiar themes of love, lust, and the desire for money and power. *Fabula* (The narrative) resolves itself into a series of scenes and dialogues, reminding the reader that the novelist is also a dramatist; and indeed, from 1883, after an interval of more than ten years, Boborykin again began writing for the stage, producing a series of comedies and dramas—*Ne u del* (Out of Office, 1878), *Sytye* (Fat Cats, 1879), *Doktor Moshkov* (Dr. Moshkov, 1885), and *S boiu* (Pitched Battle, 1891)—exploring similar "areas of life" and themes. In characterization, too, the novelist's methods resemble those of the dramatist, as he seems to acknowledge in the 1895 interview: though the dramatis personae may proliferate as chapter succeeds chapter, they are (with perhaps a few exceptions) drawn from a comparatively narrow range of stock types, both positive (the idealists and the "Turgenevan" heroines) and negative (careerists, predatory males, manipulative matriarchs, and sensualists of both sexes). "Dossiers" are appended to provide (sometimes lengthy) personal histories, while further individualizing details are furnished by meticulous description of dress and appearance and careful reproduction of habits of speech and gesture. This attention to circumstantial detail, also seen in the treatment of setting and decor, is a feature of Boborykin's method noted with some asperity by Nikolai Konstantinovich Mikhailovsky in his "Literatura i zhizn'" (Literature and Life) column in *Russkoe bogatstvo* (Russian Riches) in April 1895:

> [He] piles on images and scenes, heaps them up like goods in the furniture department of the Trading Arcade, and with forensic exactitude he describes a chocolate-colored plaid, an "irregular nose" (I don't know what this irregular nose is, but it figures often in Mr. Boborykin's works), green velveteen upholstery, the "bold pattern" of a pair of trousers, and so on and so forth—and it all turns out to be "pure art."

To others among his contemporaries, Boborykin's methods were redolent less of "pure art" than of pure naturalism. The author himself rejected any direct comparison with Zola but conceded that his procedures were similar to those of Alphonse Daudet. Superficial resemblances apart, however, the circumstantial realism of Boborykin's chronicles of the intelligentsia bears as much relation to the clinical documentation of the experimental novel as their affirmation of the values of enlightenment and gradual progress does to its philosophical determinism and moral indifferentism.

The novelist's investigation of the phenomena of Russian life and the psyche of the thinking classes continued throughout the 1890s and beyond. *Na ushcherbe* (On the Wane, 1890), *Pereval* (The Pass, 1894), and *Khodok* (The Go-between, 1895) examine the responses of both male and female members of the intelligentsia to successive historical phases and ideological shifts: political reaction, famine and epidemic, Tolstoyism, recrudescent populism and Marxism. *Vasilii Terkin* (1892) introduces a new type, the self-made intellectual of peasant stock whose social idealism embraces concern for the welfare of the land itself. *Tiaga* (Drawing Force, 1898)—with its faint echoes of *L'Assomoir*

Boborykin, circa 1900 (portrait by Iosif Braz; from Rampa i zhizn' *[Footlights and Life], 1910)*

(1877) and *Germinal* (1885) perhaps the most "Zolaist" of Boborykin's novels—is concerned with both the dawning political awareness of the working class and the tragic legacy of popular drunkenness. *Kniaginia* (The Princess, 1896) returns to the "woman question," presenting a heroine who finds scope for social action through her liberalizing influence on her bureaucrat husband. *Po-drugomu* (Another Way, 1897), *Kuda idti?* (Whither Now?, 1899), and *Zhestokie* (The Cruel Ones, 1901) highlight various manifestations of fin-de-siècle decadence: Nietzscheanism, aestheticism, mysticism, apocalypticism, sexual (and homosexual) promiscuity; while *Obmirshchenie* (Profanation, 1904–1905) records the impact of secularism and progress on the traditional mores of the Old Believers. *Velikaia razrukha* (Wrack and Ruin, 1908) takes the chronicle as far as the revolutionary year of 1905; although, seen through the eyes of an "old idealist" of the 1840s whose Socialist Revolutionary granddaughter perishes on the barricades and whose Social Democrat grandson falls victim to Bolshevik-Menshevik rivalries, the triumph of *pugachevshchina* (Pugachev-like terror) seems a betrayal of the values he clings to.

The novella *Poumnel* (Older and Wiser, 1890), rather than any of these novels, heralded a change in Boborykin's literary fortunes. Its depiction of a populist-turned-bureaucrat determined to pursue his old ideals in his new career, and of his wife, who, first condemning his apostasy, encourages him in his attempt to "be of use," provoked (according to Mikhailovsky, writing again in *Russkoe bogatstvo* in April 1895) "lively interest and serious critical atten-

Boborykin on the fiftieth anniversary of his literary debut (caricature by Gosh for Novoe vremia *[New Times], 1910)*

tion." In January 1895 Vengerov published a balanced but sympathetic study of the writer under the heading "Otzyvchivyi pisatel'" (A Responsive Writer) in the monthly supplement of the newspaper *Nedelia* (The Week). In 1897 the St. Petersburg publisher A. F. Marks issued a twelve-volume collection of novels and stories written since the last omnibus edition of Boborykin's prose had appeared in the mid 1880s—effectively the second series of his collected works. In 1899 his play *Nakip'* (Froth on the Surface), first performed at the Aleksandrinskii Theatre in St. Petersburg on 2 December, was the talk of the season that included the premiere of Antonin Pavlovich Chekhov's *Diadia*

Vania (Uncle Vanya) at the Moscow Art Theatre. In 1900 the fortieth anniversary of Boborykin's literary debut was celebrated at banquets in Moscow and St. Petersburg; two years later he was elected an honorary member of the Imperial Academy of Sciences. In the following decade Dmitrii Ovsianiko-Kulikovsky devoted whole chapters to Boborykin in his *Istoriia russkoi literatury* (History of Russian Literature, 1908–1910) and his *Istoriia russkoi intelligentsii* (History of the Russian Intelligentsia, 1910), and in 1910 Boborykin's fiftieth jubilee was the occasion for further festivities. Despite this recognition, the theme of his own neglect at the hands of Russian literary criticism remains a dominant one in Boborykin's later correspondence.

The loss of sight in his right eye in 1888 had done little to diminish Boborykin's productivity. From the beginning of the new century he turned increasingly to the shorter narrative genres, and after *Velikaia razrukha* he published only novellas and short stories, among them several tales for children. After *Nakip'* he wrote only a few more plays but remained active as a "man of the theater" in the widest sense, particularly in the organization of actors' schools and workshops and as a lecturer on drama and stagecraft. Withdrawing from his regular journalistic commitments in the early 1890s, he began to publish occasional reminiscences of his own life and travels: *Za polveka* (Half a Century, published in installments between 1906 and 1913), *Stolitsy mira* (Capitals of the World, 1911), and memoirs of his encounters with literary and political celebrities in Russia and Europe; the latter were to become a staple of his literary output until his death. He also followed new interests as a lecturer on aesthetics, philosophy, and psychology, publishing articles in both specialist journals and the popular press. "Krasota, zhizn' i tvorchestvo" (Beauty, Life, and Creativity, 1893) brings these interests together, defending "pure art" as an autonomous sphere of mental activity while at the same time asserting the obligation of art to reflect the life of society.

Boborykin's most ambitious project during these years, however, was the history of the nineteenth-century European novel (conceived at the end of the 1880s under the influence of the literary-critical theories of Taine, Emile Hennequin, Ferdinand Brunetière, and others). The first volume, *Roman na zapade za dve treti veka* (The Novel in the West Over Two-thirds of a Century), appeared to a mixed reception in 1900; work on the second volume, *Sud'by russkogo romana* (The Fortunes of the Russian Novel), continued until 1912, although publication was delayed for a variety of reasons and finally abandoned following the outbreak of war in 1914. Boborykin's sometimes idiosyncratic account of the great tradition of "sober" and "objective" Russian realism, with its critique of "metaphysical" criticism, its rejection of Gogolian moral satire and Tolstoyan didacticism, and its praise for the lesser realists of the 1860s and 1870s, was never to reach its audience.

Boborykin's annual winter sojourn in Russia in 1912–1913 was his last. Immediately following the declaration of World War I in August 1914, he made plans to return to Russia from Italy but was forced to abandon them on the advice of his doctor. Thereafter, he and his wife moved to Switzerland, finally settling in Lugano. An involuntary exile, he craved contact with his compatriots, and in his seventy-ninth year again found work—as special correspondent for many Russian newspapers. Since his assets in Germany were frozen and his access to funds in Russia was limited, writing was also a necessity. Feeling increasingly isolated and depressed, he was at first cheered by the news from Russia in February 1917, although any optimism about a "new beginning" for his homeland soon gave way to dismay at the activities of the Bolsheviks. The October Revolution severed all communication with his correspondents in Russia and cut off his only source of income. While he continued to write, publishing memoirs and fiction in a variety of emigré organs, he could no longer earn a living. Through the Society of Russian Writers in Paris, Ivan Alekseevich Bunin was able to provide some financial assistance, but from 1920 Boborykin's health began to decline. On 4 June 1921 he suffered a stroke from which he never recovered; he died on 12 August 1921, and after his cremation, his ashes were deposited in a communal cinerarium—effectively a pauper's grave. Sofiia Aleksandrovna survived him by almost four years.

Boborykin had definite views about his place in Russian literature. Recognizing the genius of Ivan Sergeevich Turgenev, Dostoevsky, and Leo Tolstoy, Boborykin numbered himself among those conscientious *bytopisateli* (chroniclers of everyday life) whose contribution to the novel's expanding reflection of life he believed hardly less significant than theirs. To younger writers such as Chekhov, Maksim Gorky, and the neorealists of the early twentieth century he was condescending, frequently (if privately) expressing resentment that they so readily won credit for innovations in content and form that more properly belonged to himself.

Few have taken him at his own evaluation, and those contemporaries who were warmest in his praise seldom forbore to acknowledge also his failings as an artist: prolixity, diffuseness, superficiality, a general lack of "vivid originality," as Mikhailovsky put it in his *Literaturnye vospominaniia i sovremennaia smuta* (Literary Recollections and Our Contemporary Unrest, 1907). In their absorbing concern with contemporaneity, his works remain time bound, their message of gradualist melior-

ism of merely historical interest to later generations. Since his death only a handful of them have been republished—most of them for the first time in Sergei Chuprinin's three-volume selection in 1993. During the Soviet period, only one of his novels—*Kitai-gorod*—appeared in print, albeit in several editions, for while this novel in particular could be (and was) presented as an illustration of Marxist theories of Russian economic development, Boborykin, as an exponent of naturalism, remained excluded from the canon of critical (and therefore socialist) realism. Elaborating on this view, the standard literary histories relegated him to the ranks of the ideologically suspect, and only in recent years have scholars, both in Russia and outside it, examined the limits of Boborykin's naturalism and its relevance to his theory and practice as a novelist in any rigorous way.

Whatever the fate of Boborykin's literary reputation, however, there can be no doubt about his significance as a representative literator of his age. Few Russian writers have lived so fully in the literary movement of their times, and few of his contemporaries embodied so completely the aspirations and the values of the reading public itself—that *izbrannoe men'shinstvo* (select minority) he made the object of his special study.

Letters:

"Iz perepiski P. D. Boborykina," compiled and edited by A. M. Mudrov, *Izvestiia Azerbaidzhanskogo gosudarstvennogo universiteta*, 6 / 7 (1926): 137–150;

"P. D. Boborykin v perepiske s A. A. Izmailovym," compiled and edited by Mudrov, *Izvestiia Azerbaidzhanskogo gosudarstvennogo universiteta*, 8 / 10 (1927): 12–24.

Interview:

I. Em. "Kak rabotaiut nashi pisateli: P. D. Boborykin," *Novosti i Birzhevaia gazeta*, 7 (7 January 1895): 2.

Bibliographies:

S. A. Vengerov, *Kritiko-biograficheskii slovar' russkikh pisatelei i uchenykh*, volume 4, part 1 (St. Petersburg: M. Stasiulevich, 1895), pp. 191–192;

Vengerov, *Istochniki slovaria russkikh pisatelei*, volume 1 (St. Petersburg: Imp. Akad. Nauk, 1900), pp. 264–267.

References:

Kirsten Blanck, "Boborykin als Literaturtheoretiker," *Die Welt der Slaven*, 26, no. 2 (1981): 259–273;

Blanck, *P. D. Boborykin: Studien zur Theorie und Praxis des naturalistischen Romans in Russland* (Wiesbaden: Otto Harrassowitz, 1990);

V. E. Cheshikhin, *Sovremennoe obshchestvo v proizvedeniiakh Boborykina i Chekhova* (Odessa: Znanie, 1899);

Sergei I. Chuprinin, "Chekhov i Boborykin. (Nekotorye problemy naturalisticheskogo dvizheniia v russkoi literature kontsa XIX veka)," in *Chekhov i ego vremia* (Moscow: Nauka, 1977), pp. 138–158;

Chuprinin, "'Figuranty'–sreda–real'nost'. (K kharakteristike russkogo naturalizma)," *Voprosy literatury,* 7 (1979): 125–160;

Chuprinin, "Moskva i moskvichi v tvorchestve Petra Dmitrievicha Boborykina," in P. D. Boborykin, *Kitai-gorod: Roman v piati knigakh; Proezdom: Povest'* (Moscow: Moskovskii rabochii, 1985), pp. 5–18;

Chuprinin, "P. D. Boborykin–istorik russkoi literatury," *Izvestiia AN SSSR: Seriia literatury i iazyka,* 35, no. 3 (1976): 221–228;

Chuprinin, "Trudy i dni P. D. Boborykina," in P. D. Boborykin, *Sochineniia v trekh tomakh* (Moscow: Khudozhestvennaia literatura, 1993), volume 1, pp. 5–26;

L. A. Iezuitova, "O 'naturalisticheskom' romane v russkoi literature kontsa XIX–nachala XX vekov," in *Problemy poetiki russkogo realizma XIX veka* (Leningrad: izd-vo Leningradskogo gos. universiteta, 1984), pp. 228–264;

A. M. Linin, "K istorii burzhuaznogo stilia v russkoi literature," *Izvestiia Rostovskogo-na-Donu Pedagogicheskogo Instituta,* 6 (1935): 51–135;

John McNair, "Boborykin and his Chronicles of the Russian Intelligentsia," in *The Golden Age of Russian Literature and Thought,* edited by Derek Offord (Basingstoke: Macmillan, 1992; New York: St. Martin's Press, 1992), pp. 149–167;

McNair, "Death in Lugano: The Last Years of P. D. Boborykin," *Australian Slavonic and East European Journal,* 10, no. 2 (1996): 127–137;

McNair, "Nihilism, Positivism and Progress: Boborykin on the Russian Intelligentsia," in *Slavic Themes: Papers from Two Hemispheres,* edited by Boris Christa and others (Neuried: Hieronymus, 1988), pp. 203–223;

McNair, "Persecution by Parody: The Literary Trial(s) of Piotr Boborykin," *New Zealand Slavonic Journal* (1994): 113–126–Festschrift in honor of Patrick Waddington;

McNair, "P. D. Boborykin and his *History of the European Novel,*" *Irish Slavonic Studies,* 3 (1982): 14–38;

McNair, "P. D. Boborykin, Hippolyte Taine and the English Novel: A Russian Experiment in 'Scientific' Criticism," *Forum for Modern Language Studies,* 19, no. 4 (1983): 301–320;

McNair, "*The Reading Library* and the Reading Public: The Decline and Fall of *Biblioteka dlia chteniia,*" *Slavonic and East European Review,* 70, no. 2 (1992): 213–227;

McNair, "A Russian European: Boborykin in England," *Slavonic and East European Review,* 63, no. 4 (1985): 540–559;

Dmitrii Ovsianiko-Kulikovsky, *Istoriia russkoi intelligentsii: Itogi khudozhestvennoi literatury XIX v.* (Moscow: V. M. Sablin, 1910), pp. 317–338;

Ovsianiko-Kulikovsky, *Istoriia russkoi literatury v XIX veke,* volume 5 (Moscow: izd-vo t-va Mir, 1910), pp. 134–144, 528–529;

Ewa Slawecka, *Piotr Boborykin: Z dziejów naturalizmu w Rosji* (Kraków: Wydawnictwo Naukowe WSP, 1981);

V. Ia. Svetlov, "Letopisets nashego vremeni. Poslednie 25 let deiatel'nosti Boborykina,"*Ezhemesiachnoe literaturnoe prilozhenie k zhurnalu "Niva,"* 9 (1896): 79–114;

S. A. Vengerov, "Boborykin, Petr Dmitrievich, izvestnyi romanist," in his *Kritiko-biograficheskii slovar' russkikh pisatelei i uchenykh,* volume 4, part 1 (St. Petersburg: M. Stasiulevich, 1895), pp. 191–241;

Vengerov, "Otzyvchivyi pisatel'," *Knizhki "Nedeli,"* 1 (1895): 163–181;

Z. Vengerova, "P. D. Boborykin: k 40-letiiu ego lit. deiatel'nosti," *Obrazovanie,* 11 (1900): 34–42; 12 (1900): 18–27;

E. Vilenskaia and L. Roitberg, "P. D. Boborykin i ego vospominaniia," in P. D. Boborykin, *Vospominaniia v dvukh tomakh,* volume 1 (Moscow: Khudozhestvennaia literatura, 1965), pp. 5–36.

Papers:

A substantial archive comprising Petr Dmitrievich Boborykin's manuscripts, correspondence, and other materials is divided between the Russian State Archive of Literature and Art (RGALI) in Moscow and the Institute of Russian Literature (Pushkin House) of the Russian Academy of Sciences in St. Petersburg. A smaller but significant collection of items relating to the last years of Boborykin's life in the possession of his widow in Switzerland at the time of her death (see S. A. Boborykina, "Rukopisnoe nasledie P.D. Boborykina," *Poslednie novosti,* 1318, 12 August 1924: 2), and offered for purchase to the Soviet Academy of Sciences by her creditors after her death, has yet to be traced.

Nikolai Gavrilovich Chernyshevsky

(12 July 1828 – 17 October 1889)

Andrew M. Drozd
University of Alabama

WORKS: *Kriticheskie stat'i,* in *Sovremennik* (1854–1861); (St. Petersburg: Izd. M. N. Chernyshevskogo, 1893);

Estetika i poeziia, in *Sovremennik* (1854–1861); (St. Petersburg: Izd. M. N. Chernyshevskogo, 1893);

Esteticheskie otnosheniia iskusstva k deistvitel'nosti (St. Petersburg: Eduard Prats, 1855);

Ocherki Gogolevskogo perioda russkoi literatury, in *Sovremennik* (1855–1856); (St. Petersburg: Izd. M. N. Chernyshevskogo, Tip. V. A. Tikhanova, 1892);

Aleksandr Sergeevich Pushkin, ego zhizn' i sochineniia, anonymous (St. Petersburg, 1856);

Zametki o sovremennoi literature 1856–1862 gg., in *Sovremennik* (1856–1862); (St. Petersburg: Izd. M. N. Chernyshevskogo, 1894);

Lessing, ego vremia, ego zhizn' i deiatel'nost' (St. Petersburg: Tip. Glavnogo shtaba po voenno-uchebnym zavedeniiam, 1857);

Stat'i po krest'ianskomu voprosu, in *Sovremennik* (1857–1859); (St. Petersburg: Izd. M. N. Chernyshevskogo, 1905);

Russkii chelovek na Rendez-vous. Razmyshleniia po prochtenii povesti g. Turgeneva "Asia," in *Atenei,* no. 18 (1858); (Geneva: M. Elpidin, 1901);

Antropologicheskii printsip v filosofii, anonymous, in *Sovremennik,* nos. 4–5 (1860); (Geneva: H. Georg, 1875);

Chto delat'? [What Is to Be Done?], in *Sovremennik* (1863); (Geneva: M. Elpidin, 1867); first translated by Benjamin R. Tucker as *What's to Be Done? A Romance* (Boston: Tucker, 1886); revised and abridged by Ludmila B. Turkevich as *What Is to Be Done?* (New York: Vintage, 1961); expanded and with a new preface by Cathy Porter (London: Virago, 1982);

Sochineniia, 4 volumes (Geneva: M. Elpidin, 1867–1870);

Kaven'iak (Geneva: Tip. A. Trusova, 1874);

O zemle kak elemente bogatstva (Geneva: M. Elpidin, 1874);

O nekotorykh usloviiakh sposobstvuiushchikh umnozheniiu narodnogo kapitala (Geneva: M. Elpidin, 1874);

Nikolai Gavrilovich Chernyshevsky, 1853

Bor'ba partii vo Frantsii (Geneva: H. Georg, 1875);

Iul'skaia monarkhiia (Geneva, 1875);

Prolog. Roman iz nachala shestidesiatykh godov. Chast' I: Prolog Prologa, anonymous (London: Vpered, 1877);

Obshchina i gosudarstvo (Geneva: M. Elpidin, 1877);

Kritika filosofskikh predubezhdenii protiv obshchinnogo vladeniia (Geneva: M. Elpidin, 1877);

Ekonomicheskaia deiatel'nost' i zakonodatel'stvo (Geneva: M. Elpidin, 1877);

Pis'ma bez adresa (Geneva: M. Elpidin, 1890);

Nauchilis'-li? (Geneva: M. Elpidin, 1898);

Literaturnoe nasledie, 3 volumes, edited by N. A. Alekseev, M. N. Chernyshevsky, and S. N. Chernov (Moscow: Gosudarstvennoe izdatel'stvo, 1928–1930);

Povesti v povesti (Moscow: Izdatel'stvo Vsesoiuznogo obshchestva politikatorzhan i ssyl'no-poselentsev, 1930);

Dnevnik, 2 volumes, edited by Alekseev (Moscow: Izdatel'stvo Politkatorzhan, 1931–1932);

Iz avtobiografii, edited by V. A. Sushitsky (Saratov: Saratovskoe obl. izd-vo, 1937);

Neopublikovannye proizvedeniia, edited by Alekseev (Saratov: Saratovskoe oblastnoe gosudarstvennoe izdatel'stvo, 1939);

Masteritsa varit' kashu (Moscow: Isskustvo, 1953).

Editions and Collections: *Polnoe sobranie sochinenii N. G. Chernyshevskogo,* 10 volumes, edited by Mikhail Nikolaevich Chernyshevsky (St. Petersburg: Izdanie M. N. Chernyshevskogo, 1905–1906);

Izbrannye sochineniia v piati tomakh, 5 volumes (Moscow-Leningrad, 1928–1935);

Stat'i po estetike (Moscow: Gosudarstvennoe sotsial'no-ekonomicheskoe izdatel'stvo, 1938);

Estetika (Moscow-Leningrad: Iskusstvo, 1939);

Literaturno-kriticheskie stat'i, edited by N. F. Bel'chikov (Moscow: Khudozhestvennaia literatura, 1939);

Polnoe sobranie sochinenii, 16 volumes, edited by V. Ia. Kirpotin and others (Moscow: Khudozhestvennaia literatura, 1939–1953);

Izbrannye ekonomicheskie proizvedeniia, 3 volumes, edited by Ivan Dmitrievich Udal'tsov (Moscow: Gosudarstvennoe izdatel'stvo politicheskoi literatury, 1948–1949);

Izbrannye pedagogicheskie vyskazyvaniia, edited by N. N. Razumovsky (Moscow: Izdatel'stvo Akademii Pedagogicheskikh Nauk RSFSR, 1949);

O klassikakh russkoi literature, edited by N. V. Bogoslovsky (Moscow: Gosudarstvennoe izdatel'stvo detskoi literatury, 1949);

Izbrannye literaturno-kriticheskie stat'i, edited by A. V. Zapadov (Leningrad: Lenizdat, 1950);

Izbrannye sochineniia (Moscow: Gosudarstvennoe izdatel'stvo khudozhestvennoi literatury, 1950);

Ob iskusstve: stat'i, retsenzii, vyskazyvaniia, edited by Bogoslovsky (Moscow: Izdatel'stvo Akademii Khudozhestv SSSR, 1950);

Izbrannye filosofskie sochineniia, 3 volumes, edited by M. M. Grigor'ian (Moscow: Gospolitizdat, 1950–1951);

Estetika i literaturnaia kritika, edited by B. I. Bursov (Moscow-Leningrad: Gosudarstvennoe izdatel'stvo khudozhestvennoi literatury, 1951);

Izbrannye literaturno-kriticheskie stat'i, edited by Bogoslovsky (Moscow: Gosudarstvennoe izdatel'stvo detskoi literatury, 1953);

Izbrannye pedagogicheskie proizvedeniia, edited by V. Z. Smirnov (Moscow: Izdatel'stvo Akademii Pedagogicheskikh Nauk RSFSR, 1953);

Estetika, edited by G. A. Sokolov (Moscow: Gosudarstvennoe izdatel'stvo khudozhestvennoi literatury, 1958);

Sobranie sochinenii, 5 volumes, edited by Iu. S. Melent'eva (Moscow: Pravda, 1974);

Chto delat'? (Leningrad: Nauka, 1975)–includes the published text and the rough draft;

Izbrannye proizvedeniia v trekh tomakh, 3 volumes (Leningrad: Khudozhestvennaia literatura, 1978);

Pis'ma bez adresa, edited by A. S. Bushmin, F. F. Kuznetsov, A. F. Smirnov, N. N. Skatov, and G. M. Fridlender (Moscow: Sovremennik, 1979);

Literaturnaia kritika, 2 volumes (Moscow: Khudozhestvennaia literatura, 1981);

Ocherki Gogolevskogo perioda russkoi literatury, edited by A. A. Zhuk (Moscow: Khudozhestvennaia literatura, 1984);

Pis'ma bez adresa, edited by V. R. Shcherbina and I. V. Kondakov (Moscow: Sovetskaia Rossiia, 1986);

Sochineniia v dvukh tomakh, 2 volumes, edited by Igor' Konstantinovich Pantin (Moscow: Mysl', 1986–1987).

Editions in English: *A Vital Question; or What is to Be Done?* translated by Nathan Haskell Dole and S. S. Skidelsky (New York: Crowell, 1886); republished as *What Is To Be Done?* with an introduction by Kathryn Feuer (Ann Arbor, Mich.: Ardis, 1986);

Selected Philosophical Essays (Moscow: Foreign Languages Publishing House, 1953; Westport, Conn.: Hyperion Press, 1981);

"L. N. Tolstoy's *Childhood* and *Boyhood* and *Military Tales*" and "The Russian at the *Rendez-vous*," in *Belinsky, Chernyshevsky, and Dobrolyubov: Selected Criticism,* edited by Ralph E. Matlaw (New York: Dutton, 1962), pp. 93–129;

"The Aesthetic Relations of Art to Reality" and "The Anthropological Principle in Philosophy," in *Russian Philosophy,* volume 2, edited by James M. Edie, James P. Scanlan, and Mary-Barbara Zeldin (Chicago: Quadrangle Books, 1965), pp. 11–60;

What Is to Be Done? translated by Michael R. Katz (Ithaca, N.Y.: Cornell University Press, 1989);

Prologue. A Novel from the Beginning of the 1860s, translated by Katz (Evanston, Ill.: Northwestern University Press, 1995).

OTHER: Nikolai Aleksandrovich Dobroliubov, *Sochine-niia,* 4 volumes, edited by Chernyshevsky (St. Petersburg: Tip. Iosafata Ogrizko, 1862);

Materialy dlia biografii N. A. Dobroliubova, sobrannye v 1861–1862 godakh, compiled by Chernyshevsky (Moscow: Izd. K. T. Soldatenkova, 1890).

TRANSLATIONS: Thomas Babington Macaulay, *Rasskazy iz istorii Anglii,* 2 volumes, translated by Chernyshevsky and others (St. Petersburg: Tip. Glavnogo shtaba ego velichestva po voenno-uchebnym zavedeniiam, 1858);

Friedrich Christoph Schlosser, *Istoriia vosemnadtsatogo sto-letiia i deviatnadtsatogo do padeniia Frantsuzskoi imperii,* 8 volumes, translated by Chernyshevsky and others (St. Petersburg, 1858–1860);

John Stuart Mill, *Osnovaniia politicheskoi ekonomii s nekoto-rymi iz ikh primenenii k obshchestvennoi filosofii* (St. Petersburg: Karl Vul'f, 1860);

Schlosser, *Vsemirnaia istoriia,* 8 volumes, translated by Chernyshevsky and others (St. Petersburg: Izd. A. Serno-Solov'evicha, Tip. Iosafata Ogrizko, 1861–1863);

Schlosser, *Vsemirnaia istoriia,* volume 16 (St. Petersburg: Izd. M. O. Vol'fa, 1865);

William Lant Carpenter, *Energiia v prirode* (St. Petersburg: Izd. L. F. Panteleeva, 1885);

Georg Weber, *Vseobshchaia istoriia,* 11 volumes, translated by Chernyshevsky under the pseudonym Andreev (Moscow: Izd. K. T. Soldatenkova, 1885–1889);

Otto Schrader, *Sravnitel'noe iazykovedenie i pervobytnaia istoriia* (St. Petersburg: Tip. Ministerstva putei soobshcheniia, 1886);

Herbert Spencer, *Osnovnye nachala* (St. Petersburg: Izd. L. F. Panteleeva, 1897).

SELECTED PERIODICAL PUBLICATIONS:
"Detstvo i otrochestvo. Sochinenie grafa L. N. Tol-stogo. Spb. 1856. Voennye rasskazy grafa L. N. Tolstogo. Spb. 1856," *Sovremennik,* 60, no. 12 (1856);

"Proiskhozhdenie teorii blagotvornosti bor'by za zhizn'," as "An Old Transformist," *Russkaia mysl',* no. 9 (1888).

Nikolai Gavrilovich Chernyshevsky remains one of the most controversial figures in Russian literature and intellectual life. Chernyshevsky rose to prominence in the period after Russia's defeat in the Crimean War. During the "thaw" that followed decades of "freeze" under the conservative Nicholas I, intellectual life in Russia revived with great vigor. Chernyshevsky was already well educated and well placed to take advan-

Ol'ga Sokratovna Vasil'eva, whom Chernyshevsky married in 1853

tage of the new era of freedom in Russia. However, he was far too visible a public figure when this era ended.

From 1855 to 1862 Chernyshevsky was the lead-ing radical journalist in Russia, working for the "thick journal" *Sovremennik* (The Contemporary). During this time Chernyshevsky battled many of the ideas held by the older generation of intellectuals and forcefully her-alded the coming of a new generation, the so-called Russian nihilists. In contrast to the older generation of Russian intellectuals who were of aristocratic origin, Chernyshevsky was of more modest birth. As a result, he came to exemplify the *raznochintsy* (those born of the various nonaristocratic ranks) and its newly found place in Russian society. Chernyshevsky's battles with the older generation coincided with a split that took place in Russian society: the division of the progressive camp into liberals and radicals. As a result, Cherny-shevsky became anathema to Russian liberals (as well as conservatives and reactionaries), while he was the idol of the younger, radicalized generation of Russians. Chernyshevsky exercised enormous influence not only on his contemporaries but on generations to follow. His writings on aesthetics had great influence in the visual arts on the nineteenth-century Russian artists known as *Peredvizhniki* (The Wanderers) and their revolt from prevailing aesthetic norms. In the field of politics many Russian radicals and revolutionaries counted Chernyshevsky as a formative influence. Throughout the nineteenth century, anarchists, Russian Marxists, and Russian populists all looked to Chernyshevsky with special reverence. And Chernyshevsky was among the first leftists in Russia to challenge Charles Darwin's theories and set the stage for a more sober assessment of Darwin's legacy.

While the left in Russia was generally unanimous in praise of Chernyshevsky, the right and much of the center was far more hostile. For them Chernyshevsky was the source of all evil in Russian society and directly to blame for the injection of revolutionary poison into it. This split regarding Chernyshevsky continued into the twentieth century, with the Bolshevik regime that took power in 1917 proclaiming him to be one of its pantheon of gods, but with most observers in the West taking a generally negative view of Chernyshevsky's legacy, seeing in him a crude materialist/utilitarian and a hater of art and aesthetics. However, while his supporters generally praise Chernyshevsky for his role in the Russian revolutionary tradition and his detractors condemn him for the same, all agree that Chernyshevsky was a key figure in Russia in the middle of the nineteenth century.

Nikolai Gavrilovich Chernyshevsky was born the son of an Orthodox priest, Gavriil Ivanovich Chernyshevsky, on 12 July 1828 in the provincial town of Saratov on the lower Volga River. His mother, Evgeniia Egorovna (née Golubeva), was the daughter of an Orthodox priest, and Gavriil Ivanovich had married her as part of his appointment to replace her father at the Sergievskaia Church in Saratov. From all indications, Gavriil Ivanovich approached his priestly station mainly as a means of livelihood. While it does seem clear that the family was a believing one, there is little to indicate that it was overly zealous in its faith. And although he was given the traditional religious upbringing, including attendance at a seminary, young Chernyshevsky was exposed to liberal, secular influences at an early age.

Young Chernyshevsky was an avid reader and a polyglot. He had use of his father's library, which was excellent for a provincial one. Chernyshevsky became acquainted with many of the cultural issues that occupied the Russian press via the so-called "thick journals,"

acquiring his first exposure to critics Vissarion Grigor'evich Belinsky and Aleksandr Ivanovich Herzen. Through the library he also first encountered the influences of the West. The work of George Sand particularly impressed him. To supplement his avid reading, young Chernyshevsky developed a strong desire and an unusual ability for learning foreign languages. As a mere youth he had already acquired mastery of Latin, Greek, Hebrew, German, French, Polish, Tatar, and even some English. By the time Chernyshevsky approached adulthood, he was quite well read and far too cosmopolitan for the traditional vocation of a provincial priest. The final impetus away from that choice, however, was provided by a grievance of the elder Chernyshevsky, who had been passed over for a promotion. The family therefore decided to send the younger Chernyshevsky to St. Petersburg for a university education.

At St. Petersburg University (1846–1850) Chernyshevsky was exposed to many crucial influences and underwent a process of radicalization. He watched the revolutions of 1848 rise and fall throughout Europe. Moreover, acquaintances who were involved with the revolutionary Petrashevsky Circle, in particular Aleksandr Vladimirovich Khanykov, introduced him to Western authors such as Charles Fourier and Ludwig Feuerbach. Thus, he became acquainted with much of the radical literature being produced in Western Europe. Chernyshevsky was close to becoming a member of the Circle, but the group was arrested before he made the decision to join.

After graduating from the university in 1850, Chernyshevsky returned to Saratov on 12 March 1851 to take a position as a teacher of Russian literature at a local gymnasium. During his stay in Saratov, on 26 January 1853, Chernyshevsky met Ol'ga Sokratovna Vasil'eva, the daughter of a somewhat unconventional local doctor, and proposed marriage in short order. Chernyshevsky's parents overtly disapproved of his choice of a wife; Chernyshevsky, however, chose this moment to assert his independence and stood by his intended bride. His mother died shortly afterward and, in what seemed a scandalous and disrespectful act to many, Chernyshevsky refused to postpone the wedding, which took place on 29 April 1853. Moreover, he and his new wife left for St. Petersburg shortly thereafter, in May 1853.

Upon his return to St. Petersburg, Chernyshevsky had intentions of pursuing an academic career. During the winter of 1853–1854 he passed a series of examinations for his master's (*magisterskaia*) degree in literature. However, there ensued a twenty-month battle with his adviser, Aleksandr Vasil'evich Nikitenko, over his thesis, *Esteticheskie otnosheniia iskusstva k deistvitel'nosti*

(The Aesthetic Relations of Art to Reality, 1855), because of philosophical differences. In his thesis Chernyshevsky chose to do battle with the prevailing idealist aesthetics, taking a stance that greatly irritated his adviser. Nikitenko, with the aid of Avraam Sergeevich Norov, the Minister of Public Education, managed to hold up the defense of the thesis for many months. Contributing to Chernyshevsky's difficulties was the fact that the details of his case began to gain notoriety. When the public defense of the thesis finally took place in May 1855, it was something of a great cultural event, causing a furious reaction.

Chernyshevsky's thesis rather forcefully announced a new aesthetics and was celebrated by the Russian youth of the time as a most exciting event, while the older writers, especially Ivan Sergeevich Turgenev, condemned it. As Charles Moser has stated, "Chernyshevsky could scarcely have hoped to exert a more powerful influence on Russian society than he in fact did through this short work." In *Esteticheskie otnosheniia iskusstva k deistvitel'nosti* Chernyshevsky attacks idealist aesthetic theory. He does not specify Georg Wilhelm Friedrich Hegel, but rather an epigone, Friedrich Theodor Vischer, and his *Aesthetik oder Wissenschaft des Schönen* (Aesthetics or Science of the Beautiful, 1846–1857).

What particularly irked Chernyshevsky about idealist aesthetics was the philosophical assumption that everyday reality was imperfect, inferior to an unseen transcendental reality. Further, idealist aesthetics assumed that since art was in touch with this transcendental reality, a work of art must be perfect, superior to anything that exists in reality. While Chernyshevsky's rejection of this formulation is often interpreted as an attack on art, such is not the case. Chernyshevsky does not attack art itself, but simply what he regards as a faulty philosophical assumption. For Chernyshevsky, there is no transcendental reality and thus nothing for art or the artist to be in touch with. Rather, Chernyshevsky argues that art is a part or a subset of reality; it does not exist apart from reality and thus cannot be superior to it. Chernyshevsky then examines several key concepts (the sublime, the tragic) in the field of aesthetics and redefines them on a nonidealist basis. Likewise, Chernyshevsky goes on to note the damage done by the strictures of idealist aesthetics and its insistence that beauty is the sole subject of art. In particular, Chernyshevsky notes the distortions and monotony to which this idea has led. In direct contrast to idealist aesthetics Chernyshevsky argues that anything in reality, not just beauty, is fair game for art. On a more practical level Chernyshevsky condemns the monotonous nature of artistic production with its insistence on a love theme. Chernyshevsky posits that a work of art need not focus on love but on anything that is of interest to

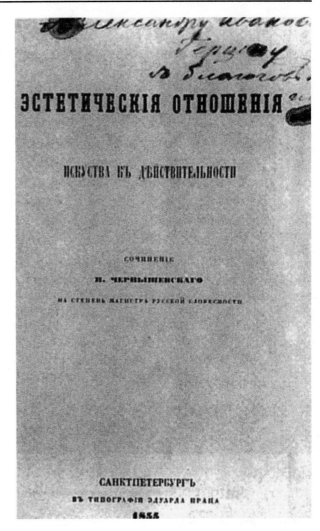

Title page for the copy of his master's thesis, Esteticheskie otnosheniia iskusstva k deistvitel'nosti *(The Aesthetic Relations of Art to Reality, 1855), that Chernyshevsky gave to Aleksandr Ivanovich Herzen (A. I. Herzen Museum, Moscow)*

the artist. Thus, far from condemning art or restricting it, Chernyshevsky seeks to expand its boundaries and free it from the strictures imposed by idealist aesthetics.

Although Chernyshevsky did manage to hold his defense and pass it, any further career in academia was clearly closed to him. Indeed, Norov managed to hold up the paperwork on Chernyshevsky's degree until the end of 1858. Thus, Chernyshevsky had to find another outlet for his intellectual energies and a means of a livelihood. He found both in the flourishing press of the "thick journals." Since his return to St. Petersburg in 1853 he had contributed to both Andrei Aleksandrovich Kraevsky's *Otechestvennye zapiski* (Notes of the Fatherland) and Nikolai Alekseevich Nekrasov's *Sovremennik.* But as the rivalry between Kraevsky and Nekrasov worsened, Kraevsky forced the issue, and Chernyshevsky made a choice in favor of *Sovremennik* in April 1855.

Nekrasov was impressed by Chernyshevsky's writing and was convinced that he had found a rising star. Chernyshevsky's capacity for sustained hard work and his ability to focus on the burning issues of the day made him invaluable to Nekrasov. However, Chernyshevsky's presence at *Sovremennik* irritated Nekrasov's colleagues, particularly Turgenev, Tolstoy, and Dmitrii Vasil'evich Grigorovich. These men disliked Chernyshevsky's aesthetics, and the publication of his thesis caused a considerable amount of tension. For the time being Nekrasov's colleagues managed to work with Chernyshevsky, although in their private meetings and correspondence they reveled in calling Chernyshevsky *pakhnushchii klopami* ("the one who smells of bedbugs") or *klopovoniaiushchii gospodin* ("the bedbug-stinking gentleman"). In a particularly revealing episode, Turgenev, Grigorovich, Vasilii Petrovich Botkin, and Aleksandr Vasil'evich Druzhinin gathered in 1855 for a house party at which they composed a comic skit belittling Chernyshevsky. This skit was reworked and published by Grigorovich in September 1855 in *Biblioteka dlia chteniia* as "Shkola gostepriimstva" (The School of Hospitality).

Despite the complaints from his colleagues at *Sovremennik,* Nekrasov began to entrust more responsibility to Chernyshevsky. In April 1856 Nekrasov's colleagues attempted to have Chernyshevsky replaced by Apollon Aleksandrovich Grigor'ev in the criticism section, but Nekrasov stuck by his younger colleague. Moreover, when he went abroad in August 1856, he entrusted the editorial responsibilities to Chernyshevsky, irritating the others further. Although Chernyshevsky's relationship with the other writers occasionally improved, one by one they abandoned *Sovremennik,* with Turgenev being the last to leave in 1860.

As the other writers left the journal, Chernyshevsky was handed even more responsibility and influence. Under his direction *Sovremennik* began to concentrate more on economic, social, and political questions in order to keep up with the shift in public interest. Members of the younger generation appeared to fill the void left at *Sovremennik* by Tolstoy's and Turgenev's departures. In particular, Chernyshevsky found a close colleague in Nikolai Aleksandrovich Dobroliubov, to whom he turned over the literary criticism section of the journal in 1857 so that he could concentrate more on political and economic questions. Accompanying this change was a monumental growth in popularity for *Sovremennik:* from 1854 to 1856 subscriptions averaged about 3,000, but by 1860 they had reached 6,500. This increase put *Sovremennik* far ahead of its competitors as the most widely read monthly in Russia.

During his relatively brief publishing career in St. Petersburg, Chernyshevsky produced several articles and reviews on a wide variety of topics (including philosophy, economics, politics, history, literature, and aesthetics), some of which are milestones of Russian culture. Many Western scholars see Chernyshevsky as a man who was primarily interested in radical politics and used other fields, such as literary criticism, as merely a "cover" for crusading radical journalism. However, about half of Chernyshevsky's output during these years deals with literary criticism and/or questions of aesthetics. As scholar Dennis Reinhartz states, "to believe that nearly fifty percent of Chernyshevsky's most significant work was nothing more than an aegis for the remainder is unrealistic to the point of being ridiculous." Indeed, not only did Chernyshevsky review many works of Russian literature and engage in serious discussions of aesthetic questions, but also he occasionally turned his attention to such problems as Russian versification, which, as René Wellek has stated, indicates "serious study of technical matters." A more balanced appraisal reveals Chernyshevsky as a man seriously, but not exclusively, interested in literature and aesthetics.

Any student of Chernyshevsky's journalistic work must also be cognizant of the fact that he wrote under conditions of censorship. While restrictions were relaxed after Russia's defeat in the Crimean War, the censorship was still in existence, and much remained taboo. Therefore Chernyshevsky, like many other Russian writers, had to resort to something known as "Aesopian language" in order to get certain ideas into print. For the modern reader in the English-language world, Russian journalism of the nineteenth century is frustrating, if not infuriating. For readers used to the more-or-less open expression of ideas, the Russian writers' long-winded, roundabout, tangential discussions can be quite tedious. However, it must be remembered that writers of the time were simply not free to say what they wanted to say. Although a clever writer could often make a mockery of the censorship, it was there nonetheless. In this regard, Chernyshevsky was an excellent embodiment of nineteenth-century Russian journalism. While technically following the restrictions of the censorship, Chernyshevsky published article after article in which he not only managed to get his radical ideas across but even taunted the censor.

Despite some personal difficulties with Tolstoy, Chernyshevsky created a masterpiece of literary criticism in 1856 with "Detstvo i otrochestvo. Sochinenie grafa L. N. Tolstogo. Spb. 1856. Voennye rasskazy grafa L. N. Tolstogo. Spb. 1856," his review in *Sovre-*

Alekseevskii ravelin, *the building in the Peter and Paul Fortress of St. Petersburg where Chernyshevsky was imprisoned from July 1862 until May 1864*

mennik of Tolstoy's early works: *Detstvo* (Childhood, 1852), *Otrochestvo* (Boyhood, 1854), and the Sevastopol sketches (1854–1856). Chernyshevsky was the first to draw attention to the distinguishing feature of Tolstoy's fiction: the concentration on the psychic process. Without the benefit of Tolstoy's later works or his personal documents, Chernyshevsky was able to discern that the secret of Tolstoy's success was his introspection. In this review Chernyshevsky made a significant contribution to the field of literary criticism by coining two terms: *vnutrennii monolog* (interior monologue) and *dialektika dushi* (the dialectic of the soul). In addition, the review is notable because Chernyshevsky defends the autonomy of the artist from outside pressures. In particular, he defends Tolstoy from the charge that he failed in *Detstvo* to introduce either a love story or social questions. Chernyshevsky felt Tolstoy should be praised for not disfiguring his works with material that is foreign to the idea of the work.

In 1855 and 1856 Chernyshevsky also produced a series of articles for *Sovremennik* titled *Ocherki Gogolevskogo perioda russkoi literatury* (Essays on the Gogolian Period of Russian Literature). While not quite the cultural milestone of the Tolstoy review, as Wellek has stated, these essays show that Chernyshevsky "had the makings of an intellectual historian." Chernyshevsky's essays performed an important function at the time: he provided the Russian reading public with a history of the preceding generation of writers and critics. In particular, Chernyshevsky presented a summary of the works of Russian critics Nikolai Alekseevich Polevoi, Osip Ivanovich Senkovsky, Stepan Petrovich Shevyrev, and Nikolai Ivanovich Nadezhdin. Moreover, taking advantage of the relaxation of the censorship following the accession of Alexander II, Chernyshevsky reacquainted the Russian public with the life and works of Belinsky, quoting extensively from Belinsky's writing. Although somewhat tiresome for modern readers, these quotations were a great service to the Russian reading public. At the time Belinsky's works had not yet been collected in book form and were simply unavailable to many readers.

Chernyshevsky ranks Belinsky much higher than his predecessors, arguing that Belinsky was the first genuine historian of Russian literature who had clear ideas about the nature of literary history. Chernyshevsky takes pains to show the logic and continuity in Belinsky's intellectual development. Chernyshevsky's essays did much to resurrect Belinsky's memory and assure him a permanent place in the canon of Russian literary criticism. Also, in these essays Chernyshevsky made his famous statements on the importance of both literature and literary critics in Russia, arguing that in Russia, literature is the entire intellectual life of the nation.

A little-known aspect of Chernyshevsky's legacy relevant to this period is his role in the establishment of the Aleksandr Pushkin cult in Russia. While Chernyshevsky's admiration for Nikolai Vasil'evich Gogol is well known, his admiration for Pushkin is often ignored or downplayed. Yet, during his best years Chernyshevsky devoted a significant amount of attention to the so-called father of Russian literature. In 1855 Chernyshevsky published in *Sovremennik* a review of Pavel Vasil'evich Annenkov's collection of Pushkin's works, *Sochineniia Pushkina* (The Works of Pushkin, 1855). In the review Chernyshevsky labels Pushkin the first truly great Russian poet and argues that he has earned the right to eternal glory in Russian literature. Chernyshevsky followed up this review with an anonymously published booklet titled *Aleksandr Sergeevich Pushkin, ego zhizn' i sochineniia* (Alexander Sergeevich Pushkin, His Life and Works, 1856). Chernyshevsky's stated goal in writing the booklet was to familiarize Russian youth with the great poet. Chernyshevsky speaks in reverent tones about Pushkin, claiming that no educated Russian can pronounce Pushkin's name without deep respect. With these works Chernyshevsky ensured that Pushkin would not be remembered only by the more conservative "art for art's sake" group of writers and critics, but would be canonized as well by the radical left. Chernyshevsky's endorsement of Pushkin, combined with Belinsky's assessment of the great poet, helped to pave the way for the universal acceptance of Pushkin as the unquestioned father of Russian literature.

In 1860 Chernyshevsky published an essay in *Sovremennik* titled *Antropologicheskii printsip v filosofii* (The Anthropological Principle in Philosophy), which became another milestone of Russian culture. Although its argument was by no means universally accepted, this work resonated among the more radical elements of Russian society and has long remained an emblem that concisely defines the "men of the sixties." Chernyshevsky's rejection of the dual nature of man clearly undermined many premises of the existing order in Russia. Supporters of that order were not slow to take notice, and this particular work convinced many in Russian society that Chernyshevsky was a "dangerous man."

Antropologicheskii printsip v filosofii is a good example of Chernyshevsky's use of Aesopian language. It is ostensibly a review of Petr Lavrovich Lavrov's *Ocherki voprosov prakticheskoi filosofii* (Essays on Problems of Practical Philosophy, 1860), but Chernyshevsky quickly abandons the discussion of the latter work and engages in his own exposition, some of which is seemingly pointless. But at the very end of the work, following more than eighty pages of discussion, Chernyshevsky includes a paragraph in which he boldly explains his anthropological principle. He openly attacks the concept of man as a creature with a dual nature—that is, an immortal soul and mortal, material body—and asserts that man has only one, nonsupernatural nature, grounded in this reality. The ploy obviously worked, for Chernyshevsky's essay was passed by the censor and published despite its radical nature. The authorities were alarmed enough to issue a reprimand to the particular censor who passed the essay, but by this time the article had already appeared in print and had its effect.

Chernyshevsky analyzes many of the key concepts of the idealist philosophical definition of man and debunks each of them. Chernyshevsky does state that there are two categories of phenomena with regard to man: those of a material order (a man eats, walks) and those of a moral order (a man thinks, feels, wishes). However, Chernyshevsky insists on man's unitary nature and attempts to redefine many key concepts (such as good and evil) on this basis. In particular, Chernyshevsky is concerned with disputing idealist philosophical claims regarding the motives for man's behavior. For Chernyshevsky, man is a subjective being that acts in his own interests. In his extended discussion Chernyshevsky clearly recognizes that the science of his time had not explained everything about man, particularly phenomena of the moral order. However, he argues that this fact does not constitute proof of the dual nature of man, and he confidently expresses the view that with time science will achieve a better understanding of man.

By this point Alexander II had announced his intention to liberate the serfs in Russia (an event that occurred in 1861), and Chernyshevsky began to devote increasing attention to this issue. In articles in *Sovremennik* he consistently argued for the most generous emancipation possible. When it became clear that the government intended to liberate the serfs on the best possible terms for the gentry, and that the Russian liberals were willing to abide by this plan, Chernyshevsky adopted an uncompromising stance. After the actual emancipation proclamation was made public and had been accepted by much of the Russian public, the czarist government became determined to deal with troublesome radicals such as Chernyshevsky, who was labeled "a dangerous man." As a result, on 7 July 1862 Chernyshevsky was arrested and imprisoned.

After arresting Chernyshevsky, however, the czarist government faced an annoying problem: the utter lack of evidence of any wrongdoing. The government had suspected Chernyshevsky of organizing the student disturbances in 1861 and 1862, but surveillance revealed nothing that could be used at a trial. Likewise, the initial charge on which Chernyshevsky was arrested–having illegal ties with the émigré writer Herzen–was so flimsy that it did not figure into his eventual trial. Yet, despite the lack of evidence, the government kept Chernyshevsky in prison without formal charges; proper legal procedure was hardly its main concern. Rather, it was determined to keep Chernyshevsky out of circulation.

With time, however, the lack of evidence began to be a source of embarrassment, and the government was in serious need of a case against Chernyshevsky. Therefore, it manufactured one, charging Chernyshevsky with participation in the writing and dispersing of the revolutionary proclamation "Barskim Krest'ianam ot ikh dobrozhelatelei poklon" (A Bow to the Landlords' Peasants from Their Well-Wishers) that had appeared in 1861. The case was greatly aided by the false testimony of one Vsevolod Dmitrievich Kostomarov, who conveniently provided some damning documents. Greatly aided by these false documents and other questionable evidence, the government was finally able to bring Chernyshevsky to court for trial. As Evgenii Lampert has described it, "The proceedings turned, in fact, into a cruel farce, and they stand as one of the greatest judicial crimes in Russian pre-revolutionary legal history." Chernyshevsky was formally sentenced in February 1864 to fourteen years of hard labor to be followed by permanent exile in Siberia. As a part of the ritual mercy shown by the czar, the sentence of hard labor was cut in half.

As a part of his punishment Chernyshevsky was put through the ceremony of a civil execution on 19 May 1864. At the public ceremony Chernyshevsky was forced to climb a scaffold wearing a sign around his neck with the words "state criminal" on it. After his sentence was read out, he was forced to kneel while a sword (albeit a weakened one) was broken over his head. He was never again a free man. Fearing a demon-

stration of support for the prisoner and perhaps possible retaliation for his treatment, the government quickly dispatched him from St. Petersburg to his term in Siberia. The government had good reason to remove him as fast as possible. The radical youth was in a most uncompromising mood because of the treatment Chernyshevsky had received. Moreover, even some of the strongest supporters of the regime were beginning to express grave doubts over Chernyshevsky's unjust treatment. But despite the loss of some face, the czarist regime had achieved what it wanted: Chernyshevsky was effectively silenced.

Chernyshevsky was sent to Siberia on 20 May 1864, leaving Ol'ga Sokratovna and his two sons, Mikhail and Aleksandr, behind in the care of his cousin, Aleksandr Nikolaevich Pypin. The rigors of the journey greatly weakened his health, and the harsh conditions of his term of hard labor furthered the decline. Furthermore, after this term was finished in 1871, Chernyshevsky was sent to the village of Viliuisk in the extreme north to serve out his exile. The government was determined to keep this dangerous man as isolated as possible. Accordingly, it settled him in a backwater where the inhabitants were non-Russian. This caution was misplaced, however, for Chernyshevsky was clearly a broken man. Although he maintained his defiant spirit to the end, his health, which had never been particularly good, was shattered forever.

Contributing to Chernyshevsky's harsh treatment was the fact that Czar Alexander II seemed to have had a personal hatred of him. Upon Alexander's order, Chernyshevsky was placed in the severe *Alekseevskii ravelin* in the Peter and Paul Fortress when he was arrested. In addition, the czar followed the details of Chernyshevsky's arrest, investigation, and trial with great interest. Moreover, in subsequent years Alexander II was adamant in refusing to commute Chernyshevsky's sentence. Despite the many entreaties of the writer's family, friends, and even some rather highly placed officials, throughout the remainder of Alexander's life Chernyshevsky was consistently kept in the harshest conditions possible.

While the various essays Chernyshevsky published in *Sovremennik* had a major impact on Russian society, his most important work in this regard is the novel *Chto delat'?* (What Is to Be Done? 1863), begun after Chernyshevsky had been in prison for six months. While some have celebrated the novel and others have disparaged it, all agree on its unquestioned role in Russian society of the nineteenth century. Generations of young Russians were radicalized by reading the novel, and well into the twentieth century many young Russians consciously patterned their own lives after the events and characters presented in *Chto delat'?*

Page from the manuscript for Chto delat'? *(What Is to Be Done? 1863), written while Chernyshevsky was imprisoned in the Peter and Paul Fortress (Central State Archives of Literature and Art, Moscow)*

In late 1862 Chernyshevsky asked the prison commandant, Aleksei Fedorovich Sorokin, for permission to write a novel. The request was granted, and Chernyshevsky began work on 14 December 1862. Realizing that if his trial and sentencing were to take place, he would probably be unable to publish his work, Chernyshevsky worked intensely on the manuscript. After completing the first two chapters of the novel, Chernyshevsky submitted them to the investigative commission in charge of his case in January 1863. These chapters were held by the commission for ten days and then sent to the chief of police on 26 January. The manuscript was then passed on to the journal *Sovremennik* and was promptly lost by Nekrasov in a cab. Nekrasov reported the loss to the police; an advertisement was placed; and the manuscript was returned in short order.

On 12 February 1863 Chernyshevsky sent chapter 3 to the commission, with continuations following on 26, 28, and 30 March. Chernyshevsky finished the novel on 4 April 1863 and sent the ending to the commission on 6 April. The entire novel was completed in a span of less than four months. While Chernyshevsky continued his work on the novel, the first chapters had already appeared in *Sovremennik*. The first two chapters, approved by the censor on 15 February and 4 March, appeared in the third issue on 19 March 1863. The third chapter, approved on 20 April, appeared in issue four on 28 April. The last chapters came out in the fifth issue on 30 May 1863, after having been passed by the censor on 27 April and 18 May. Thus appeared one of the most subversive works of all time, written while its author was incarcerated by the government authorities. Nekrasov's loss of the initial installment and the aid of the St. Petersburg police in its return have only added to the aura of mystery surrounding this novel. The circumstances are so improbable that some have even speculated that the czarist authorities conspired to let Chernyshevsky publish the novel in the hopes that he would embarrass himself by the effort.

Chto delat'? is a bildungsroman. The setting is St. Petersburg of the 1850s, and the novel is concerned with the genesis of the younger generation of Russians that later formed the men of the 1860s (or the "nihilists," as their detractors often labeled them). The novel traces protagonist Vera Pavlovna Rozal'skaia's upbringing under an oppressive mother and her liberation from her family by marriage to a medical student, Lopukhov. The arrangements of this marriage are unconventional, with each partner having a separate, inviolable room. Vera Pavlovna later falls in love with her husband's best friend, Kirsanov, and to resolve the crisis Lopukhov fakes his suicide and goes to America. The novel then traces Vera Pavlovna's second marriage to Kirsanov.

Toward the end of the novel Lopukhov returns under an alias, finds love, and remarries. At the end of the novel, the two couples have settled down together and are on the verge of taking some qualitative, but unstated, leap in their political development. In addition to adventures provided by the love intrigue, the novel has also attracted attention because of Vera Pavlovna's attempt to set up a cooperative made up of women who were formerly of questionable character but who share equally and enthusiastically in the direction of the venture. Likewise, Vera Pavlovna's fourth dream, which depicts a distant future that has come about because of cooperative ventures, seems to offer the reader a blueprint of a model society and a means to get there.

Traditionally *Chto delat'?* is studied more for its content than its form. In the Soviet Union, Lenin's unabashed admiration for Chernyshevsky's novel ensured its placement on the list of great books. It was seen as a forerunner of Soviet-sanctioned Socialist Realism and interpreted as a great contribution to the revolutionary movement. Soviet scholars especially stressed the character Rakhmetov, who plays almost no role in the plot but was seen as Chernyshevsky's model of a revolutionary superman. While declaring the novel a classic, Soviet scholarship was mostly concerned with the political ideas expressed in the novel and rarely analyzed the work as literature. In the West scholars have generally interpreted *Chto delat'?* as a weak, belated turn to literature by Chernyshevsky necessitated by the circumstances of his imprisonment. The novel is rarely treated as literature in Western criticism. Instead, it is regarded as a sociopolitical document important only for its further elaboration of Chernyshevsky's ideas and for its effect on Russian society. While Soviet scholarship routinely praised Chernyshevsky for his literary efforts and Western scholarship generally condemned him for the same, both shared the same basic assumption: *Chto delat'?* is not a novel like other novels, but merely a cover for the author to express his political views.

What the refusal to treat *Chto delat'?* as literature misses, however, is that it represents a rather bold attempt in formal terms by Chernyshevsky. The novel is hardly traditional or conventional in form. Chernyshevsky displays an amazing lack of concern with generic and stylistic purity, combining many different elements ranging from a parody of contemporary adventure novels to a modern hagiography. Chernyshevsky consciously subverts many of the techniques of literature up to his time by such tactics as making his work devoid of nature descriptions and introducing many characters at the end of the novel. While this experimentation and subversion of previous literary

The civil execution of Chernyshevsky conducted in Mytnaia Square, St. Petersburg, on 19 May 1864, just before he was sent to Siberia (from Liudmila Danilovna Mikitich, Saint-Petersburg, Petrograd: A City of Writers and Poets, *1991)*

norms might make the novel unwieldy, the novel is held together by the organizing pole of the main character, Vera Pavlovna, and by Chernyshevsky's ubiquitous narrator. *Chto delat'?* is a work that engages in an intense polemic with prevailing aesthetic norms and self-consciously discusses the manner in which it is written. Much of this polemic is achieved by means of an alternation of narrative and metanarrative, in which the purported author of the novel consistently digresses from the plot in order to address the reader regarding themes and techniques of literature.

The most infamous example of metanarrative in *Chto delat'?* comes in the deliberately misplaced "Foreword" to the novel, in which Chernyshevsky's narrator introduces himself to the reader, claiming to be the actual author of the work. He asserts that he has no literary talent and, moreover, that any merit to be found in the novel is owing to its truth. This passage forms the key to understanding or misunderstanding *Chto delat'?* If the novel is approached as a mere cover by Chernyshevsky for his political views, then this admission by the author to a lack of talent confirms that the

novel is not truly literature and need not be read as such. However, bearing in mind that Chernyshevsky had long been a master of Aesopian language, these statements by his narrator should be cause for suspicion. And if readers approach *Chto delat'?* as literature, then they must be careful not to identify the narrator with the author and not to trust the narrator. In short, a more literary interpretation of Chernyshevsky's foreword would see it as a device designed to provoke an unsophisticated reading of the novel, especially by the censor.

In writing *Chto delat'?* Chernyshevsky quite consciously operated within the tradition of Russian and Western literature. He was well read in Western literature, and echoes of, or responses to, such writers as Jean-Jacques Rousseau, Laurence Sterne, Charles Dickens, and William Makepeace Thackeray are clearly apparent. The best-known example is the influence of George Sand, whose *Jacques* (1834) has long been noted as an important predecessor in terms of plot for Chernyshevsky's novel. In *Jacques* a husband has to deal with the fact that his wife has fallen in love with another man. To resolve the situation, he kills himself in order to free his wife to marry her lover. While this situation is without question important for understanding Chernyshevsky's text, one must remember that *Chto delat'?* is not simply a response to Sand's *Jacques*, which had long been known in Russia and had provoked responses from Russian writers, including Herzen's *Kto vinovat?* (Who Is To Blame?, 1845–1846), Druzhinin's *Polinka Saks* (1847), and Mikhail Vasil'evich Avdeev's *Podvodnyi kamen'* (The Reef, 1860). Chernyshevsky's novel therefore represents one in a series of responses to *Jacques* and reacts not only to that novel but to previous Russian responses. These previous works had treated the love triangle as inherently catastrophic for all the participants. Chernyshevsky, however, presents his readers with a love triangle in which the participants not only do not experience catastrophe but go on to lead happy, fulfilling lives. Finally, while *Jacques* is an important precursor for *Chto delat'?*, too often this influence is stressed to the exclusion of Sand's other novels. But as Emily Klenin notes, *Chto delat'?* is a response not only to *Jacques* but to all of Sand's works.

Within the tradition of Russian literature, Chernyshevsky clearly draws to some degree on the three great predecessors: Pushkin, Gogol, and Mikhail Iur'evich Lermontov. Pushkin's *Evgenii Onegin* (published in full in 1833) is another important predecessor for *Chto delat'?*, especially its narrator and his digressions. Like Pushkin's narrator, Chernyshevsky's narrator claims to know the characters personally but does not function as a participant in the action. Also like Pushkin's narrator, Chernyshevsky's often digresses from the plot. Within these digressions the narrator addresses the stylized images of his readers, especially the "perspicacious" reader. While Pushkin's digressions are lyrical and Chernyshevsky's are "publicistic," the narrative digressions in Chernyshevsky's novel are clearly modeled on Pushkin's device.

Chernyshevsky also responds to Turgenev's *Ottsy i deti* (Fathers and Sons, 1862). Indeed, *Chto delat'?* is often treated as little more than a retort to Turgenev's novel. Many critics argue that Chernyshevsky was displeased by the image of the "nihilists" provided by Turgenev and attempted to battle this slander by his own, positive portrayal. However, close scrutiny fails to reveal any major polemic by Chernyshevsky. There are indeed superficial links: Chernyshevsky uses the name Kirsanov for one of his characters and, like Turgenev's Bazarov, the two main male characters in *Chto delat'?* are known for dissecting frogs. Clearly, Chernyshevsky gives a more positive portrayal of the so-called Russian nihilists than did Turgenev. But the setting of *Chto delat'?* is far different from that of *Ottsy i deti*, as is the plot development. To demonstrate that Chernyshevsky parodies or subverts any specific element in Turgenev's novel is a rather difficult task. The superficial references to *Ottsy i deti* (and to other works by Turgenev, such as "Pervaia liubov'" [First Love, 1860]) in *Chto delat'?* more likely represent a device by Chernyshevsky to mislead certain readers, particularly the censors.

While a point-by-point polemic with Turgenev is absent in *Chto delat'?,* the novel does include rather clear polemics with Fyodor Dostoevsky's *Diadiushkin son* (Uncle's Dream, 1859) and Tolstoy's *Semeinoe schast'e* (Family Happiness, 1859). In *Diadiushkin son* there is a matriarch, Mar'ia Aleksandrovna, who attempts to sell off her daughter in marriage. Dostoevsky's narrator playfully claims that he would like to write a eulogy for Mar'ia Aleksandrovna but is unable to do so. In a pointed response Chernyshevsky names his matriarch Mar'ia Aleksevna, and although his Mar'ia Aleksevna is a more vulgar, abusive character than Dostoevsky's matriarch, Chernyshevsky's narrator does provide an extended eulogy for her. Likewise, Chernyshevsky polemicizes with Tolstoy about the "woman question." Whereas Tolstoy had asserted in *Semeinoe schast'e* that a woman's happiness was to be found only in marriage and children, Chernyshevsky rejects such a thesis in his novel. Vera Pavlovna's story does not culminate with marriage; rather, marriage is only the beginning of her journey. Moreover, while the reader is briefly informed (so briefly that many have missed it) that Vera Pavlovna has a child, there are no odes to motherhood in *Chto delat'?* In a most pointed turn on Tolstoy's work, in which the characters resort to abstract terminology ("A" and "B") in order to discuss their feelings, Cherny-

shevsky's Lopukhov uses this same terminology when proposing a ménage à trois, something completely abhorrent to Tolstoy's militant moralism.

While Chernyshevsky is clearly influenced by previous Russian literature, *Chto delat'?* also represents a conscious break from that tradition in several respects. First, earlier Russian literature had consistently presented unworthy male characters to its readers. In some cases the male characters are outright scoundrels; in others they are simply weak and ineffectual. Typically in previous Russian literature, the male character's unworthiness is exemplified by his failure with regard to love. In contrast, female characters were often presented as the embodiments of great virtue, creatures so good that they bore the "burden of terrible perfection." Chernyshevsky rejects this dichotomy in *Chto delat'?* Far from being either scoundrels or weak cowards, the two main male characters, Lopukhov and Kirsanov, are worthy men. As a result, by the end of the novel both men have passed the test of love. Moreover, not only are Lopukhov and Kirsanov both worthy men but also in this contrast of men and women Vera Pavlovna, while positive, is no example of perfection. Thus, Chernyshevsky consciously reduced the gulf that separated male and female characters in Russian literature.

A corollary to this concern is the positive male hero. Russian literature before *Chto delat'?* is notoriously lacking such a character. The most positive hero that had appeared in Russian literature up to that point was Insarov in Turgenev's *Nakanune* (On the Eve, 1860)—who, however, was not a Russian but a Bulgarian by nationality. Through the depiction of Lopukhov and Kirsanov in *Chto delat'?* Chernyshevsky clearly responds to this deficiency. Many other writers rejected Chernyshevsky's answer to the question of the positive hero (or his supposed answer), but none could ignore it. Chernyshevsky squarely puts the question of the positive hero to the forefront in Russian literature and forces other writers to respond.

In terms of content, *Chto delat'?* is often interpreted as a "how-to" novel that preaches feminism, materialism, utilitarianism, utopian socialism, and revolutionary asceticism. Of these various "isms," feminism is the most appropriate, for there is little doubt that Chernyshevsky was concerned with the "woman question." The liberation of women is clearly a major theme of the novel. The other ideologies so often ascribed to the novel, however, are far more problematic. Critics generally assume that the characters are nothing more than Chernyshevsky's mouthpieces, and that is where the failure to appreciate that *Chto delat'?* is literature, not an ideological tract, has had its biggest impact. While Chernyshevsky's various characters do espouse certain ideologies, sometimes quite forcefully, a careful reading

The prison in the northern Siberian village of Viliuisk where Chernyshevsky was sent in 1871 (from Evgenii Lampert, Sons Against Fathers, *1965)*

of the novel reveals that not only are these ideologies not endorsed by Chernyshevsky's narrator, but quite often the narrator mocks them, as in the case of Lopukhov's and Kirsanov's materialism and utilitarianism. Moreover, a careful reading demonstrates that in many cases these ideologies prove to be unsatisfactory and are to be rejected. *Chto delat'?* is the story of Vera Pavlovna's personal development, not a how-to novel. Particularly revealing is that by the end of the novel, Pavlovna is abandoning her infamous cooperative venture for a medical career. Rather than being a ready-made answer to the question of what is to be done, Chernyshevsky's novel demonstrates what is not to be done. The question posed in the title is not explicitly answered.

The appearance of *Chto delat'?* sent a shock wave through Russian society. Despite a government ban on the novel and attempts to recall all issues of *Sovremennik* in which it appeared, *Chto delat'?* circulated widely among the Russian youth and became its Bible. Manuscript copies passed from hand to hand, and several émigré editions were published and smuggled into Russia. Unlike previous Russian literature, *Chto delat'?* managed to tap the psyche of the Russian youth and move them to action. Many young Russians in the 1860s called themselves followers of Chernyshevsky and professed to act in his name, even using the term "Chernyshevtsy" to refer to themselves. As one contemporary, the critic Aleksandr Mikhailovich Skabichevsky, has described it, the influence of *Chto delat'?* on the Russian youth was simply phenomenal:

> We read the novel almost like worshippers, with the kind of piety with which we read religious books, and without the slightest trace of a smile on our lips. The influence of the novel on our society was colossal. It played a great role in Russian life, especially among the leading members of the intelligentsia who were embarking on the road to socialism, bringing it down a bit from the world of drama to the problem of our social evils, sharpening its image as the goal which each of us had to fight for.

Not only Chernyshevsky's supporters but also his detractors were unanimous regarding the popularity of the novel. As Professor P. Tsitovich of Odessa University was pained to admit, every schoolgirl and student was "considered a dunce if she was not acquainted with the exploits of Vera Pavlovna." Mikhail Nikiforovich Katkov, the editor of *Russkii vestnik* (The Russian Herald), sounded a similar note when he said of the younger generation that they were treating *Chto delat'?* the way Muslims revere the Koran.

On the level of daily life, many young men and women consciously began to model their lives on the main characters of *Chto delat'?* Fictitious marriages, although a phenomenon that existed prior to the appearance of the novel, blossomed under its influence. These were conducted so that young women could escape an oppressive familial home and/or seek higher education. Likewise, many young couples consciously modeled their lifestyles on the novel, including the adoption of separate, inviolable rooms for each partner. *Chto delat'?* remained particularly powerful for Russian women: even major figures of the early twentieth century, such as activists Aleksandra Mikhailovna Kollontai and Inessa Armand, continued to look upon the novel as a model of behavior.

Following the actions of Vera Pavlovna, many young Russians began to set up cooperative/communal ventures. Again, such phenomena had appeared before Chernyshevsky wrote his novel; but after *Chto delat'?* communal ventures began to spring forth everywhere. Reportedly, young people would sit around a table with a copy of the novel in front of them and plan a cooperative venture. Perhaps the most famous of these communes, the Znamenskii Commune founded by Vasilii Sleptsov, was inspired directly by *Chto delat'?* Most of these ventures were not particularly successful, while others were utter failures. However, the image continued to influence generations.

Other young Russians took up direct revolutionary activity after reading the novel. The most flamboyant was Nikolai Ishutin, who consciously modeled his behavior on the character Rakhmetov. Ishutin is said to have recognized only three great men in history: Jesus Christ, St. Paul, and Chernyshevsky. In a gesture that undoubtedly imitates Rakhmetov, Ishutin obtained a job on a Volga River steamboat, using it as a base for his radical activities. A more significant group comprised the young Russians who attempted to assassinate Czar Alexander II in 1866. These people, often referred to as the Karakozovites, had all read the novel and claimed that they had turned to terrorism under its influence. Indeed, they even chose 4 April 1866 as the date for their attempt so as to coincide with what many thought was an implicit call to revolution in *Chto delat'?* Chernyshevsky so moved the younger generation in Russia that many even hatched plots to rescue him from Siberia.

Not just immediate contemporaries but several generations of Russians counted the reading of *Chto delat'?* as a key moment in their radicalization. Both Chernyshevsky and his novel were widely revered on the Left in Russia by adherents of all trends (Populist,

anarchist, and Marxist). With the Bolshevik victory in 1917 *Chto delat'?* assumed the status of a great book in the Soviet Union. The novel became required reading in Soviet schools, but paradoxically this official recognition resulted in a loss of feeling for the book. Admiration for the novel quickly acquired a ritualistic character rather than an expression of sincere conviction. Since the fall of the Soviet Union both Chernyshevsky and his novel have fallen into disrepute.

After completing *Chto delat'?* Chernyshevsky turned to a new literary project, a novel titled *Povesti v povesti* (Tales Within a Tale, 1930), while still in prison. Chernyshevsky worked on the novel from 21 July 1863 to 1 January 1864, but it was not published in his lifetime and thus had no significance for his contemporaries. Despite this fact, however, *Povesti v povesti* is important for two reasons. First, in the various forewords he wrote for the novel, Chernyshevsky clearly plays the same game he had played in *Chto delat'?*, attempting to provoke his readers into an unsophisticated reading. While this provocation in *Chto delat'?* has often been missed by observers, there can be little doubt in the passages from *Povesti v povesti* that Chernyshevsky attempts to lure certain readers into approaching his work in an unsophisticated manner. With these facts in mind, certain passages in *Chto delat'?*, which was completed only months before, cannot be interpreted in the naive manner in which they have traditionally been perceived.

In addition, in one particularly important variant to the foreword (dated 10 October 1863), Chernyshevsky outlines something that he calls the "objective" novel. In this foreword Chernyshevsky discusses his plan to write a novel in which the author's attitudes are not at all evident. Chernyshevsky argues that not a single such work exists in Russian literature; all previous literature is clearly "subjective." As a model Chernyshevsky cites William Shakespeare, whose characters speak while the author himself is silent. The creation of an "objective" novel, Chernyshevsky argues, is a difficult but important task. The concept of the "objective" novel developed by Chernyshevsky was later cited by Mikhail Bakhtin in his 1963 study *Problemy poetiki Dostoevskogo* (Problems of Dostoevsky's Poetics). For Bakhtin, in this foreword Chernyshevsky came quite close to the concept of the polyphonic novel, which demonstrates that such a concept was "in the air" when Dostoevsky wrote his novels.

Although the conditions of his servitude in Siberia were harsh, Chernyshevsky did not abandon his literary efforts. From 1867 to 1870, while serving in the Aleksandrovskii silver smelting plant near Irkutsk, Chernyshevsky worked on the novel *Prolog* (Prologue, 1877). Well aware that he had no hope for publication

Chernyshevsky in 1888

asking him to do what he could to get it published. Pypin also attempted to prevent the appearance of this novel; however, Chernyshevsky managed to send out a second copy, which made its way to London. Pypin, who had learned of this copy, attempted to persuade the émigrés in London not to publish the work. Eventually a compromise was reached, and the first part of the novel was published anonymously.

Prolog consists of two parts. The first, titled *Prolog prologa* (Prologue to the Prologue) is the story of protagonist Aleksei Ivanych Volgin in the year 1857, shortly after the Russian government has announced its intention to emancipate the serfs. The novel is autobiographical, with Volgin standing for Chernyshevsky and each of the characters rather easily traced to an historical figure. The second part, titled *Iz dnevnika Levitskogo* (Levitsky's Diary) is a fragment that was abandoned by Chernyshevsky but included in the 1906 text. *Iz dnevnika Levitskogo* consists of entries in the journal of one Vladimir Alekseich Levitsky, who is based on Chernyshevsky's younger radical colleague Dobroliubov.

Although Franco Venturi has characterized *Prolog* as Chernyshevsky's "finest work" and Anatoly Lunacharsky wrote that he "read this book with genuine delight" and was unable to tear himself away from it, from a formal point of view *Prolog* has less to offer the reader than *Chto delat'?* The bold experimentation Chernyshevsky had demonstrated in his previous effort is not apparent in this novel. Rather, *Prolog* is quite conventional in its form. *Prolog prologa* consists of a traditional third-person narration with several quoted conversations. The metanarrative and mixing of formal styles that appears in *Chto delat'?* is absent. Likewise, the second part, *Iz dnevnika Levitskogo,* is also traditional in its form, consisting of a series of first-person diary entries. While the bold experimentation demonstrated in *Chto delat'?* and *Povesti v povesti* seemed to promise much, *Prolog* is clearly not a step forward in terms of formal composition.

While lacking in formal experimentation, *Prolog* does have much to offer the modern reader. In terms of content, readers interested in the late 1850s in Russia will find it rather intriguing to read the synopsis of a participant more than a decade after the events. Moreover, since he was writing with little expectation of publication in Russia, Chernyshevsky wrote quite openly, with little regard for censorship. Thus, the political discussions in the novel are much more straightforward than the articles he legally published in *Sovremennik*. Among the topics of discussion are the coming emancipation of the serfs and evaluations of plans to liberate them, the proper role of a radical/revolutionary, and the "woman question." In addition, the novel has much

within Russia, he wrote with less fear of the censorship. Rather, Chernyshevsky intended *Prolog* to be published abroad, either in French or English translation. However, the novel remained unpublished until 1877, when only the first half of the novel was published in the original Russian in London, without the author's name. In 1883 this edition was reprinted in the émigré journal *Znamia* (Banner). The entire text of the novel was not published until 1906, when Chernyshevsky's son, Mikhail Nikolaevich Chernyshevsky, took advantage of the liberalization following the 1905 revolution to bring out his father's works.

Prolog was intended as the middle part of a trilogy. The first part of the trilogy, "Starina" (Olden Times), was written and sent to Chernyshevsky's cousin, Aleksandr Nikolaevich Pypin, who later destroyed the manuscript, fearing its overt political content. The third part of the trilogy, "Rasskazy iz belogo zala" (Tales from the White Hall), was never written. Chernyshevsky also sent the manuscript for *Prolog* to Pypin,

to offer the reader in terms of humor. Chernyshevsky was not devoid of a sense of humor, and his depictions, especially that of Count Chaplin, can be quite amusing. Finally, again not fearing the censorship, Chernyshevsky dealt more openly with the relationship between the sexes, and as Michael R. Katz has stated, *Prolog* "is without doubt the most erotic of nineteenth-century Russian novels."

Although *Chto delat'?* and *Prolog* are the only works to achieve much notice among scholars, Chernyshevsky did try his hand many times at literature. He made several attempts at creative writing while a student, although none of these were published in his lifetime. After his arrest, Chernyshevsky devoted a significant portion of his efforts to fiction. Much of the material was destroyed for various reasons, and all that remains are summaries provided in letters or accounts of contemporaries. The material that is still extant is barely known among scholars and little studied. Despite the obscurity in which these works languish, they are considerable in number. From Chernyshevsky's student days, the fragments "Teoriia i praktika" (Theory and Practice) and "Poniman'e" (Understanding) are still extant. From the time of his incarceration in the Peter and Paul Fortress, the novella *Alfer'ev*, the unfinished novel *Povesti v povesti,* and the cycle "Melkie rasskazy" (Petty Stories) have survived. And from the years of Chernyshevsky's exile, in addition to *Prolog*, there are such works as the novellas *Istoriia odnoi devushki* (One Girl's Story), and *Vechera u kniagini Starobel'skoi* (Evenings with Princess Starobel'skaia); the plays *Drama bez razviazki* (A Drama with no Denouement), *Velikodushnyi muzh* (The Magnanimous Husband), and *Masteritsa varit' kashu* (The Master Workwoman Cooks Kasha, 1906); the historical tale "Potomok Barbarussy" (Barbarossa's Descendant); and the unfinished novel *Otbleski siianiia* (Radiant Reflections). While mostly unstudied, these works do offer some surprises for Western scholars. For example, the Soviets considered "Znamenie na krovle" (A Sign on the Roof) a prediction of the destruction of the world via the atomic bomb. Thus, it was not included in the thirteenth volume of his *Polnoe sobranie sochinenii* (Complete Collected Works, 1939–1953) where it belonged but appeared only later in the sixteenth, supplemental volume.

After the death of Alexander II, Chernyshevsky was finally allowed to move to a southern location because of health considerations in August 1883. The long years in the harsh northern Siberian climate had already broken him. However, the government still chose a location that was out of the way, settling upon Astrakhan. Chernyshevsky was allowed to rejoin his family, although by this time his children were adults

with lives of their own. From all indications, his years in Astrakhan were lonely and frustrating. In particular, he was reduced to doing translations of Western authors in order to make ends meet. Because the government still refused to allow anything with his name on it to appear in print, he had to accept whatever means of earning a living he could.

In 1888, one year before his death, Chernyshevsky made his last significant contribution to the Russian intellectual scene. This effort was not fiction but an essay devoted to a discussion of Charles Darwin and his theory of natural selection. Up to this time in Russian society Darwin's theories had been received with great admiration by most educated Russians. The main criticism came from religious conservatives, but Chernyshevsky had long been dissatisfied with Darwin. In 1888 he decided to speak out and published "Proiskhozhdenie teorii blagotvornosti bor'by za zhizn'" (The Origin of the Theory of the Beneficence of the Struggle for Existence) in *Russkaia mysl'* (Russian Thought) under the name "An Old Transformist." In this essay Chernyshevsky traces the development of Darwin's career and notes how Darwin consistently failed to deliver the promised elaboration of his theories. Regarding natural selection, Chernyshevsky argues that Darwin takes his theory not so much from facts evidenced in biology, but from Thomas Malthus and his *Essay on the Principle of Population* (1798). Chernyshevsky rebukes Darwin for taking the struggle for existence and elevating it to positive principle.

Although the essay was not published under his name, many in Russia knew who the actual author was, mostly through word-of-mouth. Chernyshevsky's critique produced an immediate response in Russian society. By this time Chernyshevsky was a sainted figure among Russian progressives, and the critique of Darwin by such a preeminent figure caused everyone to take notice. Even an old adversary, Tolstoy, labeled Chernyshevsky's analysis "beautiful." The stage was now set for a more sober assessment of Darwin in Russian society.

As Chernyshevsky's health progressively worsened, and it was clear that his time was near, the government finally allowed him to go back to Saratov in June 1889. There he lived the last four months of his life, dying on 17 October 1889.

Although he has fallen into disrepute in Russia since the collapse of the Soviet Union, Chernyshevsky's place in Russian history and culture cannot be ignored. However much his detractors might wish to exorcise his name from the books, Chernyshevsky was too integral a part of nineteenth-century Russian society. And if he is acknowledged but only in a demonic or distorted form, then the question arises of how a man who was so untalented, stupid, or evil could be so influential. A more balanced assessment, not influenced by the ideological considerations of the Cold War, would evaluate Chernyshevsky on his own merits and not simply dismiss him because Lenin liked him. Well into the twentieth century, Chernyshevsky's legacy appears in unexpected ways. For example, the Russian critic of rock and roll music, Artemii Troitsky, titled his 31 January 1991 article published in *Literaturnaia gazeta* (Literary Gazette) "Russkii rok na rendez-vous," which, consciously or unconsciously, clearly recalls the title of one of Chernyshevsky's famous essays, *Russkii chelovek na rendez-vous,* published in *Atenei* (1858). If one ever hopes to achieve a realistic understanding of Russian culture, Chernyshevsky must be included in the picture.

Letters:

Chernyshevsky v Sibiri: Perepiska s rodnymi, 3 volumes, edited by E. A. Liatsky (St. Petersburg: Ogni, 1912–1913);

Perepiska Chernyshevskogo s Nekrasovym, Dobroliubovym i A. S. Zelenym. 1855–1862 (Moscow: Moskovskii rabochii, 1925).

Bibliographies:

M. N. Chernyshevsky, *O Chernyshevskom. Bibliografiia. 1854–1910.* second edition (St. Petersburg, 1911);

V. A. Sushitsky, *Saratovskii universitet i N. G. Chernyshevsky, 1909–1934 gg.* (1934);

M. M. Klevensky, E. N. Kusheva, and O. P. Markova, *Russkaia podpol'naia i zarubezhnaia pechat'. Bibliograficheskii ukazatel'. 1. Donarodovol'cheskii period. 1831–1879. Vypusk I. Knigi, broshiury, listovki.* (Moscow, 1935), pp. 135–138;

L. M. Dobrovol'sky, "Bibliografiia," in *N. G. Chernyshevsky. 1889–1939. Sbornik statei i materialov* (Leningrad: Goslitizdat, 1940), pp. 204–205;

N. N. Gribanovsky, *N. G. Chernyshevsky v viliuiskoi ssylke (Bibliograficheskii ukazatel')* (Iakutsk: Gosizdat IaASSR, 1947);

N. M. Chernyshevskaia, "Bibliografiia pisem N. G. Chernyshevskogo" in *Uchenye zapiski* (Saratovskii gosudarstvennyi universitet) 19 (1948): 142–195;

E. I. Ryskin, in his "N. G. Chernyshevsky," *Osnovnye izdaniia sochinenii russkikh pisatelei. XIX vek.* (Moscow: Goskul'tprosvetizdat, 1948), pp. 162–166;

Ryskin, in his "Nikolai Gavrilovich Chernyshevsky," *Bibliograficheskie ukazateli russkoi literatury XIX veka* (Moscow: Vsesoiuznaia knizhnaia palata, 1949), pp. 155–159;

F. Maisky, "Bibliograficheskii ukazatel' o zhizni i deiatel'nosti N. G. Chernyshevskogo" in his *N. G.*

Chernyshevsky v Zabaikal'e (1864–1871 gg.) (Chita, 1950), pp. 119–136;

M. M. Grigor'ian, ed., *Nikolai Gavrilovich Chernyshevsky; rekomendatel'nyi ukazatel' literatury* (Moscow, 1953);

M. K. Gotovskaia and others, comp., *Nikolai Gavrilovich Chernyshevsky: Kratkii rekomendatel'nyi ukazatel' literatury* (Moscow, 1953);

V. V. Sel'chuk, *Velikie russkie revoliutsionnye demokraty: Belinsky, Gertsen, Chernyshevsky, Dobroliubov; kratkii obzor literatury* (Moscow: Gosudarstvennaia Biblioteka SSSR, 1954);

B. P. Koz'min, *Chernyshevsky, Nikolai Gavrilovich* (1955);

P. A. Suponitskaia and A. Ia. Il'ina, *N. G. Chernyshevsky: ukazatel' literatury, 1960–1970* (Saratov: Izdatel'stvo Saratovskogo universiteta, 1976);

Suponitskaia, *N. G. Chernyshevsky: ukazatel' literatury, 1971–1981* (Saratov: Izdatel'stvo Saratovskogo universiteta, 1985).

Biographies:

Iurii M. Steklov, *N. G. Chernyshevsky, ego zhizn' i deiatel'nost' (1828–1889),* second edition (Moscow: Gosudarstvennoe izdatel'stvo, 1928);

A. P. Skaftymov, *Zhizn' i deiatel'nost' N. G. Chernyshevskogo,* second edition (Saratov: OGIZ, 1947);

N. M. Chernyshevskaia, *Letopis' zhizni i deiatel'nosti N. G. Chernyshevskogo* (Moscow: Gosudarstvennoe izdatel'stvo, 1953);

B. Riurikov, *N. G. Chernyshevsky. Kritiko-biograficheskii ocherk* (Moscow: Gosudarstvennoe izdatel'stvo khudozhestvennoi literatury, 1961);

William F. Woehrlin, *Chernyshevskii. The Man and the Journalist* (Cambridge, Mass.: Harvard University Press, 1971);

N. Naumova, *Nikolai Gavrilovich Chernyshevsky,* second edition (Leningrad: Prosveshchenie, 1974);

A. A. Demchenko, *N. G. Chernyshevsky. Nauchnaia biografiia,* 4 volumes (Saratov: Izdatel'stvo Saratovskogo universiteta, 1978–1994);

Anatolii Lanshchikov, *N. G. Chernyshevsky,* second edition (Moscow: Sovremennik, 1987).

References:

Julia Alissandratos, "Hagiographical Commonplaces and Medieval Prototypes in N. G. Chernyshevsky's *What is to be Done?*," *St. Vladimir's Theological Quarterly,* 26, no. 2 (1982): 103–117;

Mikhail Bakhtin, *Problems of Dostoevsky's Poetics,* edited and translated by Caryl Emerson (Minneapolis: University of Minnesota Press, 1984), pp. 65–69;

N. L. Brodsky and N. P. Sidorov, *Kommentarii k romanu N. G. Chernyshevskogo "Chto delat'?"* (Moscow: Mir, 1933);

Richard L. Brown, "Chernyshevskii, Dostoevskii, and the Peredvizhniki: Towards a Russian Realist Aesthetic?" dissertation, Ohio University, 1980;

Frederick C. Copleston, S.J., *Philosophy in Russia From Herzen to Lenin and Berdyaev.* (Notre Dame, Ind.: University of Notre Dame Press, 1986), pp. 100–111;

Andrew M. Drozd, *Chernyshevskii's What Is to Be Done?: A Reevaluation* (Evanston, Ill.: Northwestern University Press, 2001);

V. E. Evgen'ev-Maksimov, *Sovremennik pri Chernyshevskom i Dobroliubove* (Leningrad: Goslitizdat, 1936);

Joseph Frank, "N. G. Chernyshevsky: A Russian Utopia," *Southern Review,* new series, 3, no. 1 (1967): 68–84;

Richard Freeborn, *The Russian Revolutionary Novel. Turgenev to Pasternak* (Cambridge: Cambridge University Press, 1982), pp. 21–28;

Henry Gifford, *The Hero of His Time. A Theme in Russian Literature* (London: Edward Arnold, 1950), pp. 177–198;

Mamikon Meerovich Grigoruian, *N. G. Chernyshevsky's World Outlook* (Moscow: Foreign Languages Publishing House, 1954);

U. A. Gural'nik, *Nasledie N. G. Chernyshevskogo-pisatelia i sovetskoe literaturovedenie* (Moscow: Nauka, 1980);

Richard Hare, *Pioneers of Russian Social Thought* (London: Oxford University Press, 1951), pp. 171–211;

Michael R. Katz, "English Translations of *What is to Be Done?,*" *Slavic Review,* 46 (Spring 1987): 125–131;

Katz, "Vera Pavlovna's Dreams in Chernyshevskii's *What is to be Done?,*" in *Issues in Russian Literature Before 1917,* edited by J. Douglas Clayton (Columbus, Ohio: Slavica, 1989), pp. 150–161;

Emily Klenin, "On the Ideological Sources of *Čto delat'?*: Sand, Družinin, Leroux," *Zeitschrift für slavische Philologie,* 51, no. 2 (1991): 367–405;

Evgenii Lampert, *Sons Against Fathers* (Oxford: Clarendon Press, 1965), pp. 94–223;

K. N. Lomunov, ed., *"Chto delat'?" N. G. Chernyshevskogo. Istoriko-funktsional'noe issledovanie* (Moscow: Nauka, 1990);

N. O. Lossky, *History of Russian Philosophy* (New York: International Universities Press, 1951), pp. 47–70;

A. V. Lunacharsky, *Stat'i o Chernyshevskom,* edited by E. M. Mel'nikova (Moscow: Goslitizdat, 1958);

Thomas Garrigue Masaryk, *The Spirit of Russia,* volume 2 (London: Allen & Unwin, 1919), pp. 2–53;

Rufus Mathewson, *The Positive Hero in Russian Literature* (New York: Columbia University Press, 1958), pp. 80–107;

Marcia Morris, *Saints and Revolutionaries* (Albany: State University of New York Press, 1993), pp. 136–147;

Gary Saul Morson, *The Boundaries of Genre: Dostoevsky's Diary of a Writer and the Traditions of Literary Utopia* (Austin: University of Texas Press, 1981), pp. 99–104;

Charles A. Moser, *Esthetics as Nightmare. Russian Literary Theory, 1855–1870* (Princeton: Princeton University Press, 1989), pp. 138–149;

N. Naumova, *Roman N. G. Chernyshevskogo "Chto delat'?"* (Leningrad: Khudozhestvennaia literatura, 1972);

Derek Offord, "Dostoyevsky and Chernyshevsky," *Slavonic and East European Review,* 57 (October 1979): 509–530;

T. I. Ornatskaia, "Roman N. G. Chernyshevskogo *Chto delat'?* (K istorii teksta)," *Russkaia literatura,* no. 3 (1977): 115–127;

Irina Paperno, *Chernyshevskii and the Age of Realism. A Study in the Semiotics of Behavior* (Stanford, Cal.: Stanford University Press, 1988);

N. G. O. Pereira, *The Thought and Teachings of N. G. Černyševskij* (The Hague & Paris: Mouton, 1975);

M. T. Pinaev, *N. G. Chernyshevsky. Khudozhestvennoe tvorchestvo (Posobie dlia studentov)* (Moscow: Prosveshchenie, 1984);

G. V. Plekhanov, *N. G. Chernyshevsky* (St. Petersburg: Shipovnik, 1910);

Alexis E. Pogorelskin, "Pypin and Chernyshevsky: the *Prolog* Affair Reconsidered," *Oxford Slavonic Papers,* new series, 14 (1981): 107–120;

E. I. Pokusaev, *N. G. Chernyshevsky,* fifth edition (Moscow: Prosveshchenie, 1976);

Pokusaev, ed., *N. G. Chernyshevsky. Stat'i, issledovaniia i materialy,* 10 volumes (Saratov: Izdatel'stvo Saratovskogo universiteta, 1958–1987);

Francis B. Randall, *N. G. Chernyshevskii* (New York: Twayne, 1967);

P. Reifman, *N. G. Chernyshevsky* (Tartu: Tartuskii gosudarstvennyi universitet, 1973);

Dennis Reinhartz, "N. G. Chernyshevsky on Aesthetics and Art: The Role of the Artist in a Revolution," dissertation, New York University, 1971;

James Allen Rogers, "Russian Opposition to Darwinism in the Nineteenth Century," *Isis,* 65, no. 229 (December 1974): 487–505;

Rogers, "The Russian Populists' Response to Darwin," *Slavic Review,* 22, no. 3 (September 1963): 456–468;

Iu. K. Rudenko, *Chernyshevsky-romanist i literaturnye traditsii* (Leningrad: Izdatel'stvo Leningradskogo universiteta, 1989);

Rudenko, *Roman N. G. Chernyshevskogo "Chto delat'?" Esteticheskoe svoeobrazie i khudozhestvennyi metod* (Leningrad: Izdatel'stvo Leningradskogo universiteta, 1979);

A. P. Skaftymov, *Nravstvennye iskaniia russkikh pisatelei. Stat'i i issledovaniia o russkikh klassikakh* (Moscow: Khudozhestvennaia literatura, 1972), pp. 219–338;

V. G. Smolitsky, *Iz ravelina. O sud'be romana N. G. Chernyshevskogo "Chto delat'?",* second edition (Moscow: Kniga, 1977);

Richard Stites, *The Women's Liberation Movement in Russia. Feminism, Nihilism, and Bolshevism* (Princeton: Princeton University Press, 1978), pp. 89–99;

Gleb Struve, "*Monologue Intérieur:* The Origins of the Formula and the First Statement of its Possibilities," *PMLA,* 69 (December 1954): 1101–1111;

G. E. Tamarchenko, *Chernyshevsky-romanist* (Leningrad: Khudozhestvennaia literatura, 1976);

Tamarchenko, *Romany N. G. Chernyshevskogo* (Saratov: Saratovskoe knizhnoe izdatel'stvo, 1954);

Victor Terras, *Belinskij and Russian Literary Criticism. The Heritage of Organic Aesthetics* (Madison: University of Wisconsin Press, 1974), pp. 234–245;

Daniel P. Todes, *Darwin without Malthus* (New York: Oxford University Press, 1989), pp. 37–38;

P. Tsitovich, *Chto delali v romane "Chto delat'?"* fourth edition (Odessa: G. Ul'rikh, 1879);

Adam Ulam, *The Bolsheviks* (New York: Macmillan, 1965), pp. 54–70;

Franco Venturi, *Roots of Revolution* (New York: Knopf, 1960), pp. 129–186;

N. A. Verderevskaia, *Roman N. G. Chernyshevskogo «Chto delat'?» Posobie dlia uchashchikhsia* (Moscow: Prosveshchenie, 1982);

Verderevskaia, *Stanovlenie tipa raznochintsa v russkoi realisticheskoi literature 40-60kh godov XIX veka* (Kazan': Kazan'skii gosudarstvennyi pedagogicheskii institut, 1975), pp. 106–134;

G. Verkhovsky, *O romane N. G. Chernyshevskogo "Chto delat'?"* (Iaroslavl': Iaroslavskoe knizhnoe izdatel'stvo, 1959);

Alexander Vucinich, *Darwin in Russian Thought* (Berkeley: University of California Press, 1988), pp. 146–150;

Andrzej Walicki, *A History of Russian Thought From the Enlightenment to Marxism* (Stanford, Cal.: Stanford University Press, 1979), pp. 183–221;

René Wellek, *A History of Modern Criticism: 1750–1950. The Later Nineteenth Century* (New Haven: Yale University Press, 1965), pp. 238–245;

Wellek, "Social and Aesthetic Values in Russian Nineteenth-Century Literary Criticism (Belinskii, Chernyshevskii, Dobroliubov, Pisarev)," in *Continuity and Change in Russian and Soviet Thought,* edited by Ernest J. Simmons (Cambridge, Mass.: Harvard University Press, 1955), pp. 388–391;

Nicholas G. Žekulin, "Forerunner of Socialist Realism: The Novel 'What to do?' by N. G. Chernyshevsky," *Slavonic and East European Review,* 41 (1963): 467–483;

V. V. Zenkovsky, *A History of Russian Philosophy,* volume 1 (New York: Columbia University Press, 1953), pp. 320–343;

Margaret Ziolkowski, *Hagiography and Modern Russian Literature* (Princeton: Princeton University Press, 1988), pp. 191–195.

Papers:

Nikolai Gavrilovich Chernyshevsky's papers are housed at the Russian State Archive of Literature and Art, Moscow.

Grigorii Petrovich Danilevsky
(A. Skavronsky)
(14 April 1829 – 6 December 1890)

Ekaterina Rogatchevskaia
University of Glasgow

WORKS: *Eskisy o Finliandii* (St. Petersburg, 1848);

Pis'ma iz stepnoi derevni, in *Biblioteka dlia chteniia,* no. 12 (1850);

Krymskie stikhotvoreniia, in *Biblioteka dlia chteniia,* no. 105 (1851);

Pir u poeta Katulla, in *Panteon russkoi stseny,* no. 10 (1852);

Stepnye skazki (St. Petersburg: Tip. I. Fishona, 1852);

Slobozhane. Malorossiiskie rasskazy (St. Petersburg: Tip. I. Fishona, 1854);

Osnov'ianenko, in *Otechestvennye zapiski* (1855); (St. Petersburg: V Tip. Koroleva, 1856);

Iziumskie vechernitsy (St. Petersburg, 1856);

Ukrainskie skazki, in *Russkii vestnik,* nos. 1–2 (1858); eighth edition (St. Petersburg: Deshevaia biblioteka A. S. Suvorina, 1888);

Selo Sorokopanovka, as A. Skavronsky, in *Sovremennik,* no. 2 (1859);

Iz Ukrainy. Skazki i povesti (St. Petersburg: Tip. O. Strugovshchikova, 1860);

Volia. Dva romana iz byta beglykh (St. Petersburg, 1864)—comprises *Beglye v Novorossii,* first published in *Vremia,* nos. 1–2 (1862); and *Beglye vorotilis',* first published in *Vremia,* nos. 1–3 (1863);

Ukrainskaia starina: Materialy dlia istorii ukrainskoi literatury i narodnogo obrazovaniia (Khar'kov: Izdanie Zalenskogo i Liubarskogo, 1866);

Novye mesta. Roman, in *Russkii vestnik,* nos. 1–2 (1867); (St. Petersburg: Tip. V. V. Komarova, 1890);

Novye sochineniia, 2 volumes (St. Petersburg, 1868);

Deviatyi val (Khristova nevesta). Roman, in *Vestnik Evropy,* nos. 1–3 (1874); (St. Petersburg, 1874);

Potemkin na Dunae (1790), in *Vestnik Evropy,* no. 2 (1878); (St. Petersburg: Tip. M. M. Stasiulevicha, 1878);

Mirovich. Istoricheskii roman; Potemkin na Dunae. Poslednie zaporozhtsy (St. Petersburg: A. S. Suvorin, 1880)—*Mirovich* first published in *Vestnik Evropy,* nos. 6–8 (1879);

Na Indiiu pri Petre I; Potemkin na Dunae; istoricheskie romany (St. Petersburg: A. S. Suvorin, 1885)—*Na Indiiu pri*

Grigorii Petrovich Danilevsky (A. Skavronsky)

Petre I first published in *Vestnik Evropy,* no. 12 (1880);

Kniazhna Tarakanova. Istoricheskii roman; Umanskaia reznia (Poslednie zaporozhtsy). Istoricheskaia povest' (St. Petersburg: A. S. Suvorin, 1886)—*Kniazhna Tarakanova* first published in *Vestnik Evropy,* no. 5 (1883); translated by Ida de Mouchanoff as *The Princess*

Tarakanova. A Dark Chapter of Russian History (London: Swan Sonnenschein, 1891; New York: Macmillan, 1891);

Vosem'sot dvadtsat' piatyi god, in *Istoricheskii vestnik,* no. 7 (1883);

Ozero-slobodka. Skazka (Poltava: Tip. Gub. pravleniia, 1885);

Sozhzhennaia Moskva, in *Russkaia mysl',* 1–2 (1886); (St. Petersburg: A. S. Suvorin, 1887); translated by A. S. Rappoport as *Moscow in Flames* (London: Stanley Paul, 1917; New York: Brentano's, 1917);

Znakomstvo s Gogolem, in *Istoricheskii vestnik,* no. 12 (1886);

Semeinaia starina (St. Petersburg: A. S. Suvorin, 1887);

Pervaia iskra. Otryvok iz istoricheskogo romana, in *Russkaia mysl',* no. 1 (1888);

Chernyi god (Pugachevshchina). Istoricheskii roman, in *Russkaia mysl',* no. 12 (1888) and nos. 1–3 (1889);

Istoricheskie rasskazy: Tsar' Aleksei s sokolom; Vecher v tereme tsaria Alekseia; Ekaterina Velikaia na Dnepre (St. Petersburg: A. S. Suvorin, 1889);

Tsarevich Aleksei. Istoricheskaia povest', in *Russkaia mysl',* nos. 1–2 (1892);

Ne vytantsovalos'. Povest' (St. Petersburg: Tip. V. V. Komarova, 1893);

Ioann Antonovich: 1740–1764, compiled by I. V. Novikov (Moscow: Armada, 1994).

Editions and Collections: *Sochineniia (1847–1890),* seventh edition, 9 volumes (St. Petersburg: Tipografiia M. M. Stasiulevicha, 1892–1893);

Polnoe sobranie sochinenii, eighth and ninth editions, 24 volumes (St. Petersburg: A. F. Marks, 1901, 1902);

Beglye v Novorossii. Volia. (Beglye vorotilis') (Moscow: Goslitizdat, 1956);

Mirovich. Kniazhna Tarakanova. Sozhzhennaia Moskva (Moscow: Izvestiia, 1961);

Mirovich. Sozhzhennaia Moskva (Moscow: Pravda, 1981);

Beglye v Novorossii. Volia. Kniazhna Tarakanova (Moscow: Pravda, 1983);

Sozhzhennaia Moskva. Kniazhna Tarakanova (Voronezh: Izdatel'stvo Voronezhskogo universiteta, 1985);

Potemkin na Dunae (Moscow: Detskaia literatura, 1992);

Istoricheskie romany, edited by N. G. Il'inskaia (Moscow: Russkaia kniga, 1993);

Potemkin (Moscow: Armada, 1994);

Sobranie sochinenii, 10 volumes (Moscow: "TERRA," 1995).

PLAY PRODUCTION: *Pir u poeta Katulla,* St. Petersburg, Aleksandrinskii Theatre, November 1852.

OTHER: "Chumaki," in *Russkie ocherki,* compiled by B. O. Kosteliants and P. A. Sidorov, volume 1 (Moscow: Goslitizdat, 1956).

TRANSLATIONS: *Richard III,* in *Biblioteka dlia chteniia,* no. 3 (1850);

Cymbeline, in *Biblioteka dlia chteniia,* no. 8 (1851).

To say that Grigorii Petrovich Danilevsky has been forgotten over the years is an exaggeration; his moderate liberal views meant that his work was not forbidden during the Soviet period, and the attractive topics he favored encouraged his continuing appeal after his death. Deeply devoted to literary work, Danilevsky wrote in a variety of genres, from poetry to stories to translations of Shakespearean tragedies. Nevertheless, in the history of Russian literature as well as the memory of Russian readers, Danilevsky is known primarily for three of his many historical novels: *Mirovich* (1879), *Kniazhna Tarakanova* (1883; translated as *The Princess Tarakanova. A Dark Chapter of Russian History,* 1891) and *Sozhzhennaia Moskva* (1886; translated as *Moscow in Flames,* 1917).

Grigorii Petrovich Danilevsky was born on 14 April 1829 in the village of Danilovka, in the Iziumskii area (Uezd) of Khar'kov province. Descended from wealthy Ukrainian gentry, Danilevsky was proud of his ancestors and interested in his family history, which he evoked in the series of stories *Semeinaia starina* (Family History, 1871–1873). The founder of the family line was a Cossack named Danilo, famous because of Peter the Great's visit to his house en route to the Battle of Poltava in 1709. Danilevsky's great-grandmother had served as maid of honor to Catherine the Great. Danilevsky's parents kept for the most part to their estate, where Danilevsky spent his early years. His father, Petr Ivanovich, died in 1839 at the age of thirty-seven, when the boy was only ten years old. Danilevsky's mother, née Ekaterina Grigor'evna Kupchinova, married again, this time to Mikhail Mikhailovich Ivanchin-Pisarev. In later letters to his mother, Danilevsky attested to Ivanchin-Pisarev's kindness toward him, writing that he was grateful. Danilevsky was extremely close to his mother, a good musician and a well-educated woman interested in both Russian and French literature. She was the first person to exert a strong influence on the future writer, as she communicated her interest in the arts to her sons (Danilevsky's half brother was a promising artist, but died young). Danilevsky later recalled his mother's "cordial and genteel sociability" (*radushnaia svetskaia obshchitel'nost'*) and her "refined, exceptional mind."

From 1841 to 1846 Danilevsky studied at the Moscow University Gentry Pension, where such famous Russian authors as Vasilii Andreevich Zhukovsky, Aleksandr Sergeevich Griboedov, and Mikhail Iur'evich Lermontov had also received their educations. There Danilevsky began his early attempts at writing verse. Danilevsky continued his education at St. Petersburg University, where, despite his strong interest in literature, he chose for practical reasons to study law. Nonetheless, in his second year at the university Danilevsky was awarded a silver medal for an essay on Aleksandr Sergeevich Pushkin and Ivan Andreevich Krylov, in which he compared the two writers' creative methods. Danilevsky thoroughly enjoyed his studies, proclaiming in a 15 February 1847 letter to his mother, "If only I could be a student my whole life!" He took advantage of life in St. Petersburg and began associations with various journals. As he later recalled in an 1889 letter to his friend Nikolai Ivanovich Poliansky (the husband of Ivanchin-Pisarev's niece), "I had started writing earlier, and in 1846 my first piece, the poem 'Vesna' [Spring, later published under the title "Slavianskaia Vesna" (The Slavic Spring)], was published as an anonymous work in [Nestor Vasil'evich] Kukol'nik's *Illiustratsiia* [The Illustration]. At that time I had just enrolled at St. Petersburg University." As for Danilevsky's poems written in the Moscow period, they were published later. In 1901 at least two of them, "Privet Rodine" (Regards to Motherland, 1845) and "Raskaianie razboinika" (The Brigand's Repentance, 1844), were included in his collected works.

On 22 April 1849 Danilevsky was arrested for his alleged involvement in the revolutionary Petrashevsky Circle, a group of young intellectuals and literary people who met in the 1840s to discuss social and philosophical problems. Although the police found some forbidden literature in Danilevsky's apartment, he did not end up facing trial and was released on 10 July from the Peter and Paul Fortress for lack of evidence. Thereafter, Danilevsky always demonstrated moderate liberal views and in his later writings sought at times to deny completely any previous revolutionary activity. Danilevsky graduated from the university in 1850 and the same year was given a position as clerical assistant in the Ministry of Education; until 1857 he served on various commissions in the same ministry.

Danilevsky's first substantial work was his cycle of poems *Krymskie stikhotvoreniia* (Crimean Poems), which appeared in *Biblioteka dlia chteniia* (Library for Reading) in 1851; the critic Ivan Ivanovich Panaev noted Lermontov's influence on the cycle. This initial period of Danilevsky's literary activity

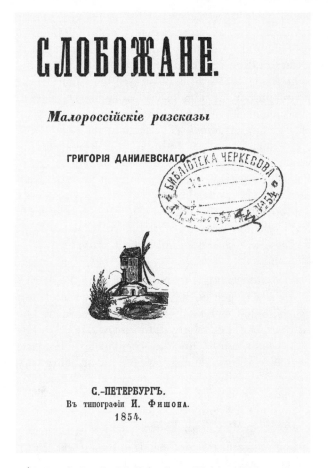

Title page for Danilevsky's Slobozhane. Malorossiiskie rasskazy *(The People from the Sloboda Region: Little Russian Tales), a popular collection of short stories influenced by Nikolai Vasil'evich Gogol (The Kilgour Collection of Russian Literature, Houghton Library, Harvard University)*

was marked as well by his interest in translations. Starting from the 1840s and continuing for more than a decade, Danilevsky translated such authors as Voltaire, Novalis, Heinrich Heine, Adam Mickiewicz, and George Gordon, Lord Byron, as well as two tragedies by William Shakespeare, *Cymbeline* (1849, published in 1851) and *Richard III* (1850). In an 1889 letter to Poliansky, Danilevsky confessed with a good deal of pride:

P. A. Pletnev [at that time the president of St. Petersburg University] suggested to me while I was still a student that I should translate this piece [*Cymbeline*], as it was Pushkin's favorite. Pushkin had always been surprised as to why *Romeo and Juliet* was so popular in Russian theaters when this tragedy was completely unknown.

Danilevsky's Shakespearean translations were not, however, a success. Because of their complicated style and the attitude of censors they were not staged, and they received negative reviews. These reviews, however, appeared in the most influential contemporary Russian journals, *Otechestvennye zapiski* (Notes of the Fatherland) and *Sovremennik* (The Contemporary), which in itself pleased the vanity of the young author. Despite his critical failure Danilevsky experimented with drama once again in his 1852 play *Pir u poeta Katulla* (The Feast at the Poet Catullus') which he called "episodes from Roman life, in verse." The play was staged that November in St. Petersburg with the famous actor Vasilii Andreevich Karatygin in the leading role. Although Danilevsky was not close to theatrical circles, he always admired Karatygin, and he wrote a brief poem—"Pamiati V. A. Karatygina" (In Memory of V. A. Karatygin, 1853)—after the actor's death.

Apart from poems and translations Danilevsky also was engaged during this period in writing short essays, notes, and satires in various newspapers and journals in St. Petersburg and Moscow. He was a regular contributor to the newspaper *Vedomosti Sankt-Peterburgskoi gorodskoi politsii* (St. Petersburg City Police Record), where he published "Vypiski iz putevogo al'boma. Eskizy Finliandii" (Extracts from a Travel Diary: Finnish Sketches); a separate edition was published as *Eskizy Finliandii* in 1848.

In spite of the fact that Danilevsky was a prolific and rather successful journalist, his connections in the artistic circles of the capital were superficial: he had no close friends or protectors. One unkind critic mentioned in a private letter that the cause of Danilevsky's loneliness at that time was his desperate wish to be famous. Danilevsky's meetings with poet Iakov Petrovich Polonsky, however, with whom he maintained a long friendship, date to 1850. A year later Danilevsky met Nikolai Vasil'evich Gogol, whom he had long admired and who greatly influenced his work of this period. Danilevsky dedicated an article in the newspaper *Moskovskie vedomosti* (Moscow News) to Gogol, as well as one essay in his cycle *Pis'ma iz stepnoi derevni* (Letters from a Steppe Village, 1850), in which he expressed his admiration for Gogol's writing and offered the reader his own understanding of Gogol's images. In the summer of 1852 Danilevsky visited Gogol's place of birth, as described in his essay "Khutorok bliz Dikan'ki" (A Small Farm Near Dikan'ka) in *Moskovskie vedomosti* (14 October 1852). And in 1854 Danilevsky published a book of short stories, *Slobozhane. Malorossiiskie rasskazy* (The People from the Sloboda Region: Little Russian Tales), which was influenced by Gogol. The book met with popular success, though it was criticized in various periodicals. Danilevsky later wrote about his encoun-

ters with Gogol in *Znakomstvo s Gogolem* (Acquaintance with Gogol, 1886).

As a staff member of the Ministry of Education, Danilevsky took part in a scholarly expedition organized by the ministry to the provinces of Kursk, Khar'kov, and Poltava in the summer of 1854. Danilevsky's task was to examine various archives, primarily monasterial, and to present a list of the most valuable historical documents held there. One result was his article "Chastnye i obshchestvennye sobraniia starinnykh aktov i istoricheskikh dokumentov v Khar'kovskoi gubernii" (Private and Public Collections of Old Deeds and Historical Documents in Khar'kov Province, 1856) published in *Zhurnal Ministerstva narodnogo prosveshcheniia*. In 1855 the author traveled to the provinces of Poltava and Ekaterinoslav to collect historical material on Peter the Great's epoch; a year later his article "Poltavskaia starina v otnoshenii ko vremeni Petra Velikogo" (Old Documents from the Poltava Province Relating to Peter the Great's Time) was also published in *Zhurnal Ministerstva narodnogo prosveshcheniia*. In 1856 Danilevsky was one of a group of writers and scholars invited by Grand Prince Konstantin Nikolaevich to take part in a trip to study the Azov Sea region as well as Russian and Ukrainian settlements on the Don and Dnieper Rivers.

Danilevsky's other works of this period involve his interest, like that of Gogol, in his native Ukraine. He translated Ukrainian folktales into Russian in his *Stepnye skazki* (The Steppe Tales, 1852), *Ukrainskie skazki* (Ukrainian Tales, 1858), and *Iz Ukrainy. Skazki i povesti* (From Ukraine: Tales and Stories, 1860). He also wrote biographies of famous Ukrainian thinkers such as the writer Grigorii Fedorovich Kvitko-Osnov'ianenko and the philosopher Grigorii Savvich Skovoroda. His works on these figures later became part of his collection *Ukrainskaia starina* (Early Days of the Ukraine, 1866), which was awarded the Uvarov prize in 1868 by the Academy of Sciences.

In 1857 a new phase in Danilevsky's life began when he left St. Petersburg for Ukraine, where he remained for the next twelve years with only occasional visits to the capital. He also married Iuliia Zamiatina, the daughter of a local landowner. Despite being far from the capital city, Danilevsky was not removed from politics. He was elected a deputy to the Khar'kov Committee on Peasant Affairs and later became a member of the School Council and obtained other civil posts. In addition, he liberated several of his serfs (the government-mandated emancipation did not come until 1861). Many of his literary works of this period are also related to contemporary politics, particularly the question of the peasantry.

In 1859 Danilevsky published his novella *Selo Sorokopanovka* (The Village of Sorokopanovka) in *Sovremennik*. The radical editorial board of *Sovremennik* did not share Danilevsky's more moderate aesthetic views or political principles, and Danilevsky had realized before submitting his work that it would be difficult for him to publish in this leading journal. He later claimed in a letter that Aleksandr Ivanovich Herzen had suggested that he submit the work under a pseudonym, and Danilevsky successfully did just that, using the name A. Skavronsky. When Danilevsky's cunning was uncovered by the editorial board at *Sovremennik*, several of its members were shocked and even furious. Mikhail Evgrafovich Saltykov-Shchedrin in particular lashed out at Danilevsky in evaluations of his work and compared Skavronsky-Danilevsky to the twin characters Bobchinsky and Dobchinsky in Gogol's *Revizor* (The Government Inspector, 1836). Nonetheless, *Sovremennik* editor Nikolai Alekseevich Nekrasov viewed Danilevsky's work more positively, and Danilevsky planned to publish a new novel, *Beglye v Novorossii* (Fugitives in Novorossiia, 1862), in this journal. The combined negative votes of editorial board members Nikolai Gavrilovich Chernyshevsky and Saltykov-Shchedrin rendered this impossible, however; *Beglye v Novorossii* and its sequel, *Beglye vorotilis'* (The Fugitives Return, 1863), which were grouped together under the title *Volia* (Freedom, 1864), appeared in the journal *Vremia* (Time), edited by Fyodor Dostoevsky and his brother Mikhail. These novels, too, appeared under the pseudonym "Skavronsky."

The novels are devoted to a discussion of the plight of the peasantry before the emancipation of the serfs: Danilevsky compares the serfs to American slaves and their masters to slaveowners. As scholar T. V. Romanova notes, Danilevsky hid the harshness of his message in a tale of adventures and chance episodes; Saltykov-Shchedrin responded by claiming in a review that Danilevsky's novels "took place in an imaginary state and obviously not in Novorossiia." Nonetheless, the novels were the first ones written in the immediate wake of the emancipation, and they made Danilevsky "quite famous," as Fyodor Dostoevsky wrote in his review of *Beglye v Novorossii*. The novels aroused particular interest in Ukraine and the Novorossiisk region, where several complimentary reviews appeared in local journals. The mixed reactions point to a further phenomenon in the writer's professional life: Danilevsky had a tendency during these years to publish his works in journals that spanned a broad ideological spectrum. Some of the liberal journals were taken aback when Danilevsky published his novels in the journal of the more conservative Dostoevsky brothers and at the same time strove to publish other work with them.

In 1869 a third phase of Danilevsky's career began when the writer returned to St. Petersburg and commenced work at the Ministry of Internal Affairs as a clerk on various commissions. Literary activities continued as well, and in 1870 Danilevsky became an assistant editor of the newspaper *Pravitel'stvennyi vestnik* (The Government Herald). He served as the chief editor starting in 1881. In this newspaper Danilevsky published two appreciative articles on Leo Tolstoy. Foreshadowing his own later interest in historical novels, Danilevsky devoted particular attention to those critics who had found Tolstoy's treatment of the Napoleonic War in *Voina i mir* (War and Peace, 1863–1869) less than accurate historically. Danilevsky lauded Tolstoy's treatment and visited Tolstoy at Iasnaia Poliana in 1885. He re-created his own version of the Napoleonic War in his novel *Sozhzhennaia Moskva*.

Danilevsky's next two novels were still dedicated to contemporary Russian subjects, however. The novel *Novye mesta* (New Places, 1867) discusses the provincial gentry harshly; this novel also met with criticism from Saltykov-Shchedrin in *Sovremennik*. The novel *Deviatyi val (Khristova nevesta)* (The Ninth Wave [Bride of Christ]), which Danilevsky wrote over a period of several years, was originally supposed to be published in *Otechestvennye zapiski* but was eventually published in *Vestnik Evropy* (The Herald of Europe) in 1874. The novel negatively portrayed clergymen and monasteries.

Danilevsky changed his focus in subsequent novels, turning chiefly to historical novels, tales, and short stories, which he published in various periodicals. Before the late 1860s he had published such works occasionally, such as his short stories "Ekaterina Velikaia na Dnepre" (Catherine the Great on the Dnieper, 1858), "Tsar' Aleksei s sokolom" (Czar Alexei with a Falcon, 1856), and "Vecher v tereme tsaria Alekseia" (An Evening in Czar Alexei's Chamber, 1856). Now, however, using his position in the Ministry of Internal Affairs to gain access to private and official historical documents in secret archives, he devoted himself to gathering data for a novel on eighteenth-century Russian history. His novel *Mirovich* was written in 1875, though its publication was partially blocked by the censorship, as the topic was forbidden; it was eventually published, though with significant cuts, in *Vestnik Evropy* in 1879. The novel tells the tale of Vasilii Mirovich, who in 1764 attempted to free former Czar Ivan VI, who had been proclaimed czar at the age of one and had been nominally on the throne four hundred and four days. Ivan had been

ПОТЕМКИНЪ НА ДУНАѢ

1790-й годъ.

ИСТОРИЧЕСКАЯ ПОВѢСТЬ.

Г. П. Данилевскаго.

С.-ПЕТЕРБУРГЪ.
Типографія М. Стасюлевича, Вас. Остр., 2 л., 7.
1878

Title page for Potemkin na Dunae (1790) *(Potemkin on the Danube [1790]), Danilevsky's novel about Prince Grigorii Aleksandrovich Potemkin*

imprisoned in 1741, after Empress Elizabeth had gained power in a coup, and he had been kept in prison by Elizabeth's successor, Catherine II. During the attempt at freeing him, the former czar was killed; Catherine then had Mirovich executed for his rebellion. Danilevsky drew both on the materials he had gathered and on his own family lore in his treatment of Mirovich's story. In his acknowledgments to the novel Danilevsky wrote:

> my great-grandfather on my father's side was Mirovich's compatriot and fellow. His wife, my great-grandmother, was a lady in waiting to Catherine the Great when the latter was only Peter III's spouse. My great-grandmother saved her husband through her connections after a search was conducted at his place following the Shlusselburg catastrophe. She remembered everything very well and sometimes talked with family members about Mirovich and why he had tried to save Prince Ivan Antonovich. Her daughter-in-law, the mother of my father, was of the Roslavlevs family, who

along with the Orlovs played a significant role in Catherine the Great's accession to the throne. A woman possessed of a splendid mind, good breeding and a remarkable memory, my grandmother had good relations with her mother-in-law, never parted from her, and died in her old age, when I was nine. Many of her stories I wrote following my uncle, her eldest son, who also passed on to me an interesting eighteenth-century family document.

In his novel Danilevsky tried to analyze Mirovich's motives and characterized him without sympathy, but with some understanding. Mirovich was descended from wealthy and famous Ukrainian gentry, but his ancestors had been punished by Peter the Great and had lost almost all their property, leaving Mirovich poor and miserable. He was moved in his attempt both by vanity and a desire to become famous and rich. Although Danilevsky was quite concerned about historical veracity and even criticized his predecessors in approaches to this topic for their unrealistic and unhistorical descriptions (among them the English writer James Grant, who had written the novel *The Secret Dispatch* in 1869), he did not measure up to his own specifications at all times. The story of the young girl Poliksena Pchelkina, who forces Mirovich to act for the salvation of the former czar, seems highly unnatural. There are other elements to the novel that are historically implausible or impossible, including conversations between Mirovich and the famous Russian scientist and poet Mikhail Vasil'evich Lomonosov in his own house, Mirovich's meetings with Peter III's aide Gudovich, and scenes of Lomonosov's acquaintance with specific young poets and authors, including Denis Ivanovich Fonvizin, Gavriil Romanovich Derzhavin, and Nikolai Ivanovich Novikov. In addition, the thoughts of Danilevsky's characters, the reasons for their actions, and their views often seem too simple for people involved in high-level political affairs and experienced in court intrigues. It is possible that this simplification was the result of Danilevsky's choice to focus on individuals and their lives rather than on the historical events surrounding them.

Danilevsky followed *Mirovich* with a series of additional novels: *Potemkin na Dunae (1790)* (Potemkin on the Danube [1790], 1878), which described the last days and death of Catherine II's favorite, Prince Grigorii Aleksandrovich Potemkin; *Umanskaia reznia* (Uman Slaughter, 1878), which dealt with the confrontation of Poland and Russia and the subsequent subjection of Poland; and *Na Indiiu pri Petre I* (To India in Peter I's Time, 1880), which included the story of the unsuccessful military action undertaken by Prince Berkovich from 1717 to 1721. In 1883

Danilevsky's second major historical novel devoted to eighteenth-century Russian history, *Kniazhna Tarakanova,* was published. Danilevsky told the story of Tarakanova, a pretender who claimed to be the daughter of the unmarried Empress Elizabeth. According to legends, Tarakanova was a smart adventuress well acquainted with members of European society and conversant in several languages. She was arrested by Aleksei Orlov and then imprisoned in the Peter and Paul Fortress, where she died of consumption. Danilevsky chose to present Tarakanova from a psychological point of view, suggesting his own understanding of her intentions and purposes and painting her as a stronger and more impressive figure than had generally been supposed. Both *Mirovich* and *Kniazhna Tarakanova* were popular with Russian readers, although critics were less generous, blaming the author for a poor description of the age or the absence of a central idea. Others, however, praised Danilevsky for a realistic and accurate historical presentation.

The most popular and at the same time probably the weakest of Danilevsky's historical novels, as many critics have agreed, was *Sozhzhennaia Moskva,* which dealt with Russia's war with Napoleon in 1812. Danilevsky appeared to have more difficulty depicting his own century than the preceding one; perhaps this difficulty explains why he had stopped working on the novel *Vosem'sot dvadtsat' piatyi god* (The Year 1825, chapters of which were published in 1883) several years before writing *Sozhzhennaia Moskva.* Critics commonly recognized that Danilevsky's novel was not only influenced by Tolstoy's *Voina i mir* but was also heavily dependent on the memoirs of Vasilii Perovsky (the illegitimate son of the Minister of Public Education Aleksei Kirillovich Razumovsky). Although Perovsky had never married, in the novel Danilevsky described a romantic love story between Perovsky, whose name Danilevsky did not change, and a character named Avrora Kramalina. Danilevsky's contemporaries easily recognized in Avrora the war hero and popular author Nadezhda Andreevna Durova. Danilevsky depicted other historical figures in his novel as well, such as the artist Vasilii Tropinin and the *prikazshchik* (steward) Maksim Sokolov, but he combined them with additional characters who were simply based on types. This method proved to be counterproductive, as readers were tempted to compare real people they had known to Danilevsky's characters and then were left dissatisfied with their comparisons; this disappointment in turn led to a lack of interest in and appreciation of the novel.

In Danilevsky's last major historical novel, *Chernyi god* (The Black Year, 1888–1889), lauded by the literary historian Semen Afanas'evich Vengerov as Danilevsky's most successful work, the author dealt with the peasant uprising led by the Don Cossack Emelian Pugachev in 1773. Buoyed by the numbers who joined his revolt, Pugachev declared himself Czar Peter III, not dead as commonly thought but miraculously free after having survived his wife Catherine II's coup to take over his throne; the rebel leader was then executed by Catherine II in 1774. Danilevsky tried to present this historical episode as a tragedy witnessed by common people (among them the Duganovs, whose family history took center stage in his tale).

None of Danilevsky's historical novels can be described as a masterpiece. His interest in psychology and the common people's behavior, combined with his historical knowledge, was not always supported by commensurate literary skills and methods. At the same time it should be noted that in his investigation of historical situations that had attracted Russian authors before (for example, Pushkin's *Kapitanskaia dochka* [The Captain's Daughter, 1835], which also treated the Pugachev rebellion, or Tolstoy's *Voina i mir,* or Mikhail Nikolaevich Zagoskin's *Roslavlev, ili Russkie v 1812* [Roslavlev, or the Russians in 1812, 1831], dedicated to the 1812 war with Napoleon), Danilevsky remained original and sometimes even unpredictable.

In addition to historical novels, Danilevsky also wrote short, macabre stories, and he combined nine of them in his "Russian Dekameron." The story "Zhizn' cherez sto let" (Life One Hundred Years From Now) is the most interesting. Danilevsky presented his vision of the future, which in the story is witnessed by the Russian student Poroshin. According to the story, Western Europe would be conquered by China in 1930. Europe would be called at this point "The United States of Europe," and it would become a Chinese colony, as would America. Meanwhile, the Chinese emperor would obtain the title of "Bogdykhan of Europe." Russian loyalty to China would be rewarded with permission to establish a separate Greek-Slavonic republic on the Balkans. Furthermore, the Russians would drive the British out of India and call Calcutta their third capital (joining St. Petersburg and Moscow). France would keep its political peculiarities, but would be ruled by Jews. Another noteworthy story is "Progulka domovogo" (The Walk of the House Spirit). In this fantasy Danilevsky presented the mysterious adventures of a gentleman who travels to the city cemetery in the same cab every night for an entire month. In the short story "Mertvets-ubiitsa" (The Murderer-Corpse) Danilevsky combined a frightening plot with historical characters (Catherine the Great and Stepan Ivanovich Sheshkovsky).

At the beginning of the 1890s Danilevsky started to work on a big novel about the tragic fate of Prince Aleksei, Peter the Great's son, killed after disagreeing with his father's plans to modernize Russia. The novel remained unfinished upon Danilevsky's death from kidney disease in 1890. The first part of it appeared in *Russkaia mysl'* (Russian Thought) in 1892. Danilevsky, who is buried in his native Ukraine, played a significant role in the popularization of Russian and Ukrainian history among common readers.

Letters:

M. G. Danilevsky, *Danilevsky po lichnym ego pis'mam i literaturnoi perepiske* (Khar'kov, 1893);

N. Barsukov, *Zhizn' i trudy M. P. Pogodina,* volume 11 (St. Petersburg, 1897), pp. 75, 76, 408, 409, 414, 433; volume 12 (St. Petersburg, 1898), pp. 195, 210, 219, 221, 235; volume 14 (St. Petersburg, 1910), p. 359;

M. M. Stasiulevich i ego sovremenniki v ikh perepiske, volume 5 (St. Petersburg, 1913), pp. 306–324;

Iu. G. Oksman, *I. S. Turgenev,* volume 1 (Odessa: Vseukrainskoe gosudarstvennoe izdatel'stvo, 1921), pp. 111–112;

K. P. Pobedonostsev i ego korrespondenty, volume 1, part 1 (Moscow-Petrograd: Gosudarstvennoe izdatel'stvo, 1923), pp. 350–352;

N. N. Apostolov, *Lev Tolstoy i ego sputniki* (Moscow: Gosizdat, 1928), pp. 217–218;

Neizdannye pis'ma k A. N. Ostrovskomu (Moscow-Leningrad: Academia, 1932), pp. 92–96;

Pis'ma k A. V. Druzhininu (Moscow: Gosizdat, 1948), pp. 109–117.

Bibliographies:

Grigorii Petrovich Danilevsky, "Perevody sochinenii G. P. Danilevskogo," in his *Polnoe sobranie sochinenii,* volume 10 (St. Petersburg: A. F. Marks, 1902), pp. 132–136;

"Khronologicheskii ukazatel' k sochineniiam G. P. Danilevskogo," in Danilevsky's *Polnoe sobranie sochinenii,* volume 9 (St. Petersburg: A. F. Marks, 1902), pp. 163–165;

"Arkhiv G. P. Danilevskogo," *Otchet Imperatorskoi Publichnoi biblioteki za 1908 god* (Petrograd, 1915), pp. 59–82;

I. V. Vladislavlev, *Russkie pisateli. Opyt bibliograficheskogo posobiia po russkoi literature XIX–XX stoletii,* fourth

edition (Moscow-Leningrad: Gosudarstvennoe izdatel'stvo, 1924), p. 46f.

Biographies:

"G. P. Danilevsky. Nekrolog," *Pravitel'stvennyi vestnik,* no. 268 (8 December 1890);

B-rne, "Vospominaniia o Danilevskom," *Donskaia pchela,* no. 46 (16 June 1891);

A. O., "Iz literaturnykh vospominanii," *Novoe vremia,* no. 8720 (8 June 1900);

S. A. Vengerov, "G. P. Danilevsky," *Istochniki slovaria russkikh pisatelei,* volume 2 (St. Petersburg: Tipografiia Imperatorskoi Akademii nauk, 1900–1917), pp. 190–193;

S. S. Trubachev, "G. P. Danilevsky (Biograficheskii ocherk)," in Danilevsky's *Polnoe sobranie sochinenii,* volume 1 (St. Petersburg: A. F. Marks, 1902), pp. i–lxxxiii;

D. I. Bagalei, *Materialy dlia biografii iuzhno-russkikh nauchno-literaturnykh deiatelei XIX veka,* book 1 (Kiev, 1903);

R. I. Sementkovsky, "Sredi otoshedshikh. (Iz moikh vospominanii)," *Istoricheskii vestnik,* nos. 7–8 (1917), pp. 103–106;

T. V. Romanova, "Danilevsky, Grigorii Petrovich," in *Russkie pisateli. Biobibliograficheskii slovar',* volume 1 (Moscow: Prosveshchenie, 1990), pp. 244–249;

E. V. Sviiasov, "Danilevsky, Grigorii Petrovich," in *Russkie pisatelei 1800–1917. Biograficheskii slovar',* volume 2 (Moscow: Nauchnoe izdatel'stvo "Bol'shaia Rossiliskaia entsiklopediia," 1992), pp. 80–82.

References:

V. Bibikov, "G. P. Danilevsky," *Den',* no. 9 (11 December 1890);

V. Enisherlov, "Pis'ma avtora *Sozhzhennoi Moskvy,*" in his *Vremen proslezhivaia sviaz'* (Moscow: Sovremennik, 1985), pp. 24–32;

V. A. Gromov, "Nekrasov i istoriia publikatsii romana G. P. Danilevskogo *Deviatyi val* (1873)," *Nekrasovskii sbornik,* volume 9 (Leningrad: Nauka, 1988), pp. 148–154;

N. Ilinskaia, "G. P. Danilevsky i ego romany iz istorii XVIII veka," in Danilevsky's *Istoricheskie romany* (Moscow: Russkaia kniga, 1993), pp. 5–18;

L. Kh. Kimova, *G. P. Danilevsky–istoricheskii romanist* (Moscow: Avtoreferat dissertatsii na soiskanie uchenoi stepeni kandidata filologicheskikh nauk, 1981);

Kimova, "Nravstvennoe i istoricheskoe v romane Danilevskogo *Kniazhna Tarakanova,*" *Filologicheskie nauki,* no. 1 (1981);

S. S. Levin, "Sovremennye literaturnye deiateli, volume 1: G. P. Danilevsky," *Istoricheskii vestnik,* 40 (1890): 154–170;

L. Mirkut, "G. Danilewski i F. Dostojewski," *Przegląd rusystyczny,* nos. 3/4 (1986);

Mirkut, "G. Danilewski. Sylwetka i kontakty literackie pisarza," *Slavia orientalis,* nos. 3/4 (1985);

Mirkut, "Twórczość G. Danilewskiego. Stan i perspektywy badań," *Slavia orientalis,* no. 3 (1981);

Mikhail Evgrafovich Saltykov-Shchedrin, "Literaturnaia podpis' A. Skavronskogo," in his *Sobranie sochinenii,* volume 5 (Moscow: Khudozhestvennaia literatura, 1966), pp. 334–336;

Saltykov-Shchedrin, "Novye sochineniia G. P. Danilevskogo," in his *Polnoe sobranie sochinenii,* volume 9 (Moscow: Khudozhestvennaia literatura, 1970), pp. 257–261;

Saltykov-Shchedrin, "Volia. Dva romana iz zhizni beglykh A. Skavronskogo," in his *Polnoe sobranie sochinenii,* volume 5 (Moscow: Khudozhestvennaia literatura, 1966), pp. 408–416;

M. Serebriansky, *Sovetskii istoricheskii roman* (Moscow: Gosudarstvennoe izdatel'stvo khudozhestvennoi literatury, 1936), pp. 40–41;

E. V. Sviiasov, "Danilevsky v literaturnoi polemike nachala 1860-kh gg.," *Russkaia literatura,* 4 (1981): 170–180;

Sviiasov, "Do istorii napisannia pratsi Danilevskogo *Osnov'ianenko*," *Radians'ke literaturoznavstvo,* no. 12 (1980);

Sviiasov, *G. P. Danilevsky v literaturno-obshchestvennom protsesse kontsa 1840-kh nachala 1860-kh gg.* (Leningrad: Avtoreferat dissertatsii na soiskanie uchenoi stepeni kandidata filologicheskikh nauk, 1982);

E. S. Vilenskaia, "G. P. Danilevsky i ego roman iz zhizni beglykh," in Danilevsky's *Beglye v Novorossii. Volia* (Moscow: Gosudarstvennoe izdatel'stvo khudozhestvennoi literatury, 1956), pp. 3–18.

Papers:

Letters from and to Grigorii Petrovich Danilevsky and other unpublished materials are in the Manuscript Division of the Russian National Library (St. Petersburg), in the Russian State Archive of Literature and Arts (Moscow), in the Special Collection of the Institute of Russian Literature (St. Petersburg), in the Russian State Navy Archive (St. Petersburg), and in the Russian State Historical Archive (St. Petersburg).

Fyodor Dostoevsky

(30 October 1821 – 28 January 1881)

Harriet Murav
University of California at Davis

WORKS: *Bednye liudi. Roman,* in *Peterburgskii sbornik* (St. Petersburg: N. Nekrasov, 1846), pp. 1–166; (St. Petersburg: E. Prats, 1847); translated as *Poor Folk* (New York: Harper, 1887);

Dvoinik: Prikliucheniia gospodina Goliadkina, in *Otechestvennye zapiski,* 2 (1846); revised as *Dvoinik: Peterburgskaia poema* (St. Petersburg: F. Stellovsky, 1866); translated by George Bird as *The Double: A Poem of St. Petersburg* (London: Harwell, 1956; Bloomington: Indiana University Press, 1958);

Netochka Nezvanova. Istoriia odnoi zhenshchiny, in *Otechestvennye zapiski,* 1, 2, 5 (1849); translated by Constance Garnett as *Nyetochka Nyezvanov,* in *The Friend of the Family or Stepanichkovo and Its Inhabitants and Another Story* (London: Heinemann, 1920);

Diadiushkin son. Iz mordasovskikh letopisei, in *Russkoe slovo,* 3 (1859): 27–172; translated by Whishaw as "Uncle's Dream" in *Uncle's Dream and The Permanent Husband* (London: Vizetelly, 1888);

Selo Stepanchikovo i ego obitateli. Iz zapisok neizvestnogo [The Village of Stepanchikovo and Its Inhabitants], in *Otechestvennye zapiski,* 11 (1859): 65–206; 12 (1859): 343–410; translated by Whishaw as *The Friend of the Family,* in *The Friend of the Family and The Gambler* (London: Vizetelly, 1887);

Sochineniia, 2 volumes, edited by N. A. Osnovsky (Moscow, 1860);

Zapiski iz mertvogo doma [Notes from the House of the Dead], chapter 1 in *Russkii mir,* 6, 7 (1860); chapters 1–4 in *Russkii mir,* 1 (1861); published in full in *Vremia,* 4, 9–11 (1861); 1–3, 5, 12 (1862); (St. Petersburg: Tipografiia Ogrizko, 1862); first translated by H. Sutherland Edwards as *Prison Life in Siberia* (London: J. & R. Maxwell, 1887?);

Unizhennye i oskorblennye. Iz zapisok neudavshegosia literatora [The Insulted and the Injured], in *Vremia,* 1–7 (1861); first translated by Frederick Whishaw as *Injury and Insult,* second edition (London: Vizetelly, 1887);

Zimnie zametki o letnikh vpechatleniiakh, in *Vremia,* 2 (1863): 289–318; 3 (1863); (St. Petersburg: F. Stellovsky,

Fyodor Dostoevsky in the early 1860s

1866); translated by Richard Lee Renfield, with a foreword by Saul Bellow, as *Winter Notes on Summer Impressions* (New York: Criterion, 1955);

Zapiski iz podpol'ia [Notes from Underground], in *Epokha,* 1, 2 (1864); translated by C. Hogarth as *Letters from the Underworld,* in *Letters from the Underworld and Other Tales* (London: Dent, 1913);

Polnoe sobranie sochinenii, volumes 1–4, edited by Dostoevsky (St. Petersburg: F. Stellovsky, 1865–1870);

Igrok, first published as volume 3 of *Polnoe sobranie sochinenii* (1866); translated by Whishaw as *The*

Gambler, in *The Friend of the Family and The Gambler* (London: Vizetelly, 1887);

Prestuplenie i nakazanie, in *Russkii vestnik,* 1, 2, 4, 6–8, 11–12 (1866); (St. Petersburg: A. F. Bazunov, E. Prats, and Ia. Veidenshtraukh, 1867); translated as *Crime and Punishment* (London: Vizetelly / New York: Crowell, 1886);

Idiot, in *Russkii vestnik,* 1, 2, 4–12 (1868); (St. Petersburg: Tipografiia K. Zamyslovskogo, 1874); translated by Whishaw as *The Idiot* (London: Vizetelly, 1887);

Vechnyi muzh [The Eternal Husband], in *Zaria,* 1, 2 (1870); (St. Petersburg: A. F. Bazunov, 1871); first translated by Whishaw as *The Permanent Husband,* in *Uncle's Dream and The Permanent Husband* (London: Vizetelly, 1888);

Besy [The Devils], in *Russkii vestnik,* 1, 2, 4, 7, 9–11 (1871); 11–12 (1872); (St. Petersburg: Tipografiia K. Zamyslovskogo, 1873); first translated by Garnett as *The Possessed* (New York: Macmillan, 1913);

Podrostok [The Adolescent], in *Otechestvennye zapiski,* 1, 2, 4, 5, 9, 11, 12 (1875); (St. Petersburg: Tipografiia A. Transhelia, 1876); first translated by Garnett as *A Raw Youth* (London: Heinemann, 1916);

Brat'ia Karamazovy, in *Russkii vestnik,* 1, 2, 4–6, 8–11 (1879); 1, 4, 7–11 (1880); (St. Petersburg: Tipografiia brat'ev Panteleevykh, 1881); translated by Garnett as *The Brothers Karamazov* (London: Heinemann, 1912).

Editions and Collections: *Polnoe sobranie sochinenii,* 14 volumes (St. Petersburg: A. G. Dostoevskaia, 1882–1883);

Polnoe sobranie khudozhestvennykh proizvedenii, 13 volumes, edited by B. Tomashevsky and K. Khalabaev (Leningrad: GIZ, 1926–1930);

Polnoe sobranie sochinenii v tridtsati tomakh, edited by V. G. Bazanov, G. M. Fridlender, and others (Leningrad: Nauka, 1972–1991);

Polnoe sobranie sochinenii F. M. Dostoevskogo: Kanonicheskie teksty, edited by V. N. Zakharov (Petrozavodsk: Izdatel'stvo Petrozavodskogo universiteta, 1995–);

Besy. Roman v trekh chastiakh, edited by Liudmila Saraskina (Moscow: Soglasie, 1996).

Editions in English: *Crime and Punishment,* translated by Constance Garnett (New York: Macmillan, 1913);

The Idiot, translated by Garnett (London: Heinemann, 1913); revised and edited with an introduction by Avrahm Yarmolinsky (New York: Limited Editions Club, 1956);

A Gentle Creature and Other Stories, translated with an introduction by David Magarshack (London: J. Lehmann, 1950);

The Devils, translated by David Magarshack (Harmondsworth, U.K.: Penguin, 1953);

The Idiot, translated and with an introduction by Magarshack (Harmondsworth, U.K.: Penguin, 1954);

Memoirs from the House of the Dead, translated by Jessie Coulson (London: Oxford University Press, 1956);

The Brothers Karamazov, 2 volumes, translated by Magarshack (Harmondsworth, U.K.: Penguin, 1958);

Notes from Underground and The Grand Inquisitor, selected, translated, and with an introduction by Ralph E. Matlaw (New York: Dutton, 1960);

Notes from Underground, White Nights, The Dream of a Ridiculous Man, and Selections from The House of the Dead, translated by Andrew R. MacAndrew (New York: New American Library, 1961);

The Gambler, Bobok, A Nasty Story, translated by Coulson (Harmondsworth, U.K.: Penguin, 1966);

The Notebooks for Crime and Punishment, edited and translated by Edward Wasiolek (Chicago & London: University of Chicago Press, 1967);

The Notebooks for The Idiot, translated by Katharine Strelsky, edited by Wasiolek (Chicago & London: University of Chicago Press, 1967);

The Notebooks for The Possessed, translated by Victor Terras, edited by Wasiolek (Chicago & London: University of Chicago Press, 1968);

The Notebooks for The Brothers Karamazov, edited and translated by Wasiolek (Chicago & London: University of Chicago Press, 1971);

The Gambler, with Polina Suslova's Diary, translated by Terras, edited by Wasiolek (Chicago: University of Chicago Press, 1972);

The Brothers Karamazov, translated by Garnett, revised by Matlaw (New York: Norton, 1976);

The Adolescent, translated by MacAndrew (New York: Norton, 1981);

The Double: Two Versions, translated by Evelyn Harden (Ann Arbor, Mich.: Ardis, 1985);

Winter Notes on Summer Impressions, translated by David Patterson (Evanston, Ill.: Northwestern University Press, 1988);

Crime and Punishment, translated by Coulson, edited by George Gibian, second edition (New York: Norton, 1989);

Notes from Underground, translated and edited by Michael R. Katz (New York: Norton, 1989);

Crime and Punishment, translated by David McDuff (Harmondsworth, U.K.: Viking, 1991);

The Brothers Karamazov, translated by Richard Pevear and Larissa Volokhonsky, with an introduction by Malcolm V. Jones (New York: Knopf, 1992);

Devils, translated by Katz (Oxford: Oxford University Press, 1992);

Crime and Punishment, translated by Pevear and Volokhonsky, with an introduction by W. J. Leatherbarrow (New York: Knopf, 1993);

Notes from Underground, translated by Pevear and Volokhonsky (New York: Knopf, 1993);

An Accidental Family, translated by Richard Freeborn (Oxford: Oxford University Press, 1994);

Demons, translated and annotated by Pevear and Volokhonsky (New York: Knopf, 1994);

A Writer's Diary, 2 volumes, translated and annotated by Kenneth Lantz (Evanston, Ill.: Northwestern University Press, 1994);

The Eternal Husband and Other Stories, translated and annotated by Pevear and Volokhonsky (New York: Bantam, 1997).

OTHER: Honoré de Balzac, *Eugénie Grandet,* translated by Dostoevsky, *Panteon,* 6, 7 (1844);

"Polzunkov," in *Illiustrirovannyi al'manakh* (St. Petersburg: I. Panaev and N. Nekrasov, 1848), pp. 502–516;

Vremia, edited by Dostoevsky (1861–April 1863);

Epokha, edited by Dostoevsky (1864–1865);

"Dnevnik pisatelia," column in *Grazhdanin* (1873);

Dnevnik pisatelia, one-man journal by Dostoevsky (1876–1877, 1880, 1881); translated and annotated by Boris Brasol as *The Diary of a Writer,* 2 volumes (New York: Scribners, 1949; London: Cassell, 1951).

SELECTED PERIODICAL PUBLICATIONS:
"Gospodin Prokharchin. Rasskaz," *Otechestvennye zapiski,* 10 (1846): 151–178;

"Khoziaika. Povest'," *Otechestvennye zapiski,* 10 (1847): 396–424; 11 (1847): 381–414;

"Slaboe serdtse. Povest'," *Otechestvennye zapiski,* 2 (1848): 412–446;

"Chuzhaia zhena i muzh pod krovat'iu. Proisshestvie neobyknovennoe," *Otechestvennye zapiski,* 1 (1848): 50–58; 11 (1848): 158–175;

"Chestnyi vor (Iz zapisok neizvestnogo)," first published as "Rasskazy byvalogo cheloveka," in *Otechestvennye zapiski,* 4 (1848): 286–306;

"Elka i svad'ba (Iz zapisok neizvestnogo)," *Otechestvennye zapiski* (1848): 44–49;

"Belye nochi: Sentimental'nyi roman (Iz vospominanii mechtatelia)," *Otechestvennye zapiski,* 12 (1848): 357–400;

"Malen'kii geroi. Iz neizvestnykh memuarov," *Otechestvennye zapiski,* 8 (1857): 359–398;

"Skvernyi anekdot," *Vremia,* 11 (1862): 299–352;

"Krokodil," *Epokha,* 2 (1865): 1–40;

"Bobok," *Grazhdanin* (1873);

"Mal'chik u Khrista na elke," *Dnevnik pisatelia* (January 1876);

"Muzhik Marei," *Dnevnik pisatelia* (February 1876);

"Krotkaia: Fantasticheskii rasskaz," *Dnevnik pisatelia* (November 1876);

"Son smeshnogo cheloveka: Fantasticheskii rasskaz," *Dnevnik pisatelia* (April 1877);

Pushkin. Ocherk, in *Dnevnik pisatelia* (1880).

Among European writers of the nineteenth century Fyodor Dostoevsky is the preeminent novelist of modernity. He explored the far-ranging moral, religious, psychological, social, political, and artistic ramifications of the breakdown of traditional structures of authority and belief. He chronicled the rise and fall of the modern secular individual and traced the totalitarian potential of the new ideologies of his time, including socialism. He examined, as no one had previously, the potential for violence and the abuse of power in all forms of human interaction. His engagement with the ongoing issues of his time, his highly dramatic and melodramatic plots, his never-ending search for a more adequate form of religious expression, and his experimentation with narrative structure, character, and authorial voice give his fiction its unusual qualities.

Fyodor Mikhailovich Dostoevsky was born on 30 October 1821 in the Moscow Mariinskii Hospital, where his father, Mikhail Andreevich Dostoevsky, was a staff doctor. The second of seven children, he was closest to his older brother, Mikhail. Dostoevsky later wrote with warmth about his mother, Mariia Fedorovna, but wrote nearly nothing about his father and is reported to have said that his childhood was difficult and joyless. The correspondence between his parents, written in the effulgent, sentimental style of the time, reveals little. The Mariinskii Hospital served the indigent, and inasmuch as the Dostoevsky family was quartered on its premises, the young boy gained impressions of urban poverty that he later was able to use in his fiction and journalism. Walks in the hospital gardens and readings from the Bible, the *Lives of the Saints,* and Nikolai Mikhailovich Karamzin's *Istoriia gosudarstva Rossiiskogo* (History of the Russian State, 1818–1829) were the main family activities of Dostoevsky's early childhood.

In 1828 Mikhail Andreevich Dostoevsky was granted a nobleman's rank, and shortly thereafter the family purchased an estate at Darovoe. Little is known about this period except for the fragmentary accounts the author himself provided in his journal *Dnevnik pisatelia* (Diary of a Writer, 1876–1877, 1880, 1881). Most of this material also served Dostoevsky's ideological projects of the 1870s—including, for example, his argument about the necessary link between the educated

The novelist's parents, Mariia Fedorovna Dostoevskaia and Mikhail Andreevich Dostoevsky, in 1823 (portraits by Popov; from Peter Sekirin,
The Dostoevsky Archive, *1997)*

classes and the peasantry. In Dostoevsky's 1876 autobiographical fragment, "Muzhik Marei" (The Peasant Marei), the author describes himself as a child playing in the woods on his father's estate. He recounts how he was terrified by the cry "a wolf is coming" and was tenderly comforted by a peasant named Marei. Scholars have commented on the Mariological, feminine, and maternal motifs introduced in the portrait of the peasant. In *Dnevnik pisatelia* Dostoevsky also describes how in 1832 a large portion of the family estate went up in flames. His nanny offered the family her own money for rebuilding. According to Dostoevsky, the simple Russian woman, like the simple peasant Marei, exemplified the virtues of the Russian people as a whole.

In 1837 Dostoevsky's mother died, and in the same year Dostoevsky's father enrolled him in the Military Engineering Academy in St. Petersburg. Dostoevsky's formal education before this time was limited to a boarding school in Moscow. An episode from his journey to St. Petersburg made an overwhelming impression on Dostoevsky. He witnessed a system for making horses go faster. A courier beat the coachman on the back of his neck with his fist, and with every blow the coachman whipped the horses. Dostoevsky used this

scene later in *Zapiski iz podpol'ia* (Notes from Underground, 1864) and indirectly in *Prestuplenie i nakazanie* (Crime and Punishment, 1866) in Raskol'nikov's dream of the peasant who beats his mare. He also referred to this scene in *Dnevnik pisatelia* as an "emblem" of human brutality. Not every representation of the uneducated classes was positive.

In addition to engineering, the training at the Military Engineering Academy focused on parade and drill. Dostoevsky was not a brilliant student. According to a story that may be apocryphal, Dostoevsky's version of a graduation project—a plan for the best fortress—had no entrance or exit, causing Czar Nicholas I to remark that the future author was a "fool." While still in school, Dostoevsky developed an intense friendship with another student at the academy, Ivan Shidlovsky. Dostoevsky's letters to his father from the Military Engineering Academy are mostly requests for money, but to his older brother, Mikhail, he wrote about his love for literature, especially the works of Friedrich Schiller and Homer. Dostoevsky compared Homer to Christ, arguing that in the *Iliad* Homer's vision with regard to the ancient world was similar to Christ's with regard to the new world. At the end of his life, in *Dnevnik pisatelia, Brat'ia Karamazovy* (The Brothers Karamazov, 1879–1880), and his speech on Aleksandr Sergeevich Pushkin, Dostoevsky returned to the idea of universal organization and harmony, carving out a special role both for himself and for Russia in achieving these ends.

In 1839 Dostoevsky's father died in mysterious circumstances, giving rise to a set of conflicting versions of his death. According to one account, Mikhail Andreevich was killed by his own peasants in revenge for his harsh treatment of them. The other, more likely version is that he died of a stroke. The death or absence of the father is a significant theme in Dostoevsky's work from his early fiction to his last novel. Ivan Karamazov's line "Who does not desire the death of his father?" has added fuel to psychoanalytic interpretations of Dostoevsky's epilepsy, which Freud famously diagnosed as "hystero-epilepsy," a form of neurosis. However, according to this theory, Dostoevsky felt so guilty about his own desire for his father's death that he had to inflict on himself a form of punishment, which took the form of epileptic attacks. According to the account left by Dr. Stepan Dmitrievich Ianovsky, who treated Dostoevsky in the first part of his life, Dostoevsky did not experience severe attacks of epilepsy in the late 1830s, when his father died, but in the late 1840s.

Upon completing his training and receiving his officer's rank, Dostoevsky served for one year in the draftsman's section of the engineering department in St. Petersburg before retiring in 1844 in order, as he said, to devote himself to literature. In the same year his anonymous translation of Honoré de Balzac's *Eugénie Grandet* appeared in print.

In 1844 Dostoevsky had begun work on his first work of fiction, *Bednye liudi* (Poor Folk, 1846). He was at that time sharing an apartment with the writer Dmitrii Vasil'evich Grigorovich. Dostoevsky later wrote to Mikhail that he had revised and refined the work and that he was pleased with its overall structure. It was published in 1846 to great critical acclaim. Grigorovich presented the manuscript to the writer and critic Nikolai Alekseevich Nekrasov, who spent all night reading it and the next morning told the critic Vissarion Grigor'evich Belinsky that a new Gogol had appeared. Belinsky said that Dostoevsky had produced the first "social novel" in Russia and had made the truth accessible even to the most unthinking reader. Dostoevsky later wrote a parody of his own critical reception in *Unizhennye i oskorblennye* (The Insulted and the Injured, 1861).

In *Bednye liudi,* an epistolary novel, Makar Devushkin, a timid and gentle clerk (his name suggests girlishness), cannot save Varvara from what he thinks

is an unwanted marriage. According to critic Mikhail Bakhtin, the artistic highlight of the work, in distinction from Nikolai Vasil'evich Gogol's Petersburg stories, is that the portrait of the hero's consciousness of his inner self is drawn by showing the "hero's orientation toward another's word." According to Makar, the poor person is always eavesdropping to find out whether he is the object of another's speech. In a letter written to his brother after the publication of the novel, Dostoevsky complained that the public "was used to seeing the author's face in his characters and could not conceive that Devushkin and not Dostoevsky was speaking." This problem was not limited to *Bednye liudi.* Dostoevsky's readers continued to identify the author with the ideological positions taken by his characters, and sometimes with their criminal acts.

Near the end of *Bednye liudi,* Makar Devushkin remarks to himself that "everything has doubled" within him. Dostoevsky's next work, *Dvoinik* (The Double), later subtitled *Peterburgskaia poema* (A Petersburg Poem), was also published in 1846 but was not well received at the time. Belinsky wrote that insanity belonged in the lunatic asylum and not in literature. *Dvoinik* told the bizarre story of another Gogolian little clerk, Iakov Petrovich Goliadkin. The name, like so many names in Dostoevsky, is significant. The root suggests "nakedness." At several points in the novella he feels himself being stared at, blushes, and attempts to hide. Goliadkin repeatedly insists that he is his "own person" and wears masks only at masquerades but encounters his double in the form of Goliadkin Junior, an insolent and more daring version of himself. Goliadkin Junior insinuates himself into the hero's good graces, discovers his weaknesses, including his social ambition and resentment, and finally usurps his position entirely.

One of the important aspects of the Petersburg theme explored by Dostoevsky in this and other works is the overwhelming presence of the official bureaucracy and its negative effects on the individual. When he is discovered at a party without an invitation, Goliadkin's protest to his superiors that "this is my private life" suggests the opposite, the complete absence of a personal life or even an identity of his own. In *Zapiski iz podpol'ia* the hero remarks that he could not become anything, neither good nor bad, not "even an insect." The multiple dimensions of this general malaise of the nineteenth century is one of Dostoevsky's chief concerns. Later he wrote about the loss of a traditional religious framework and separation from people as two of the underlying causes for the dissolution of the personality, but in this earlier period he, like other authors of the time, emphasized the deleterious effect of the imperial city itself.

The mock execution of Dostoevsky and the other members of the radical Petrashevsky circle, 22 December 1849 (from V. S. Nechaeva, ed., Fedor
Mikhailovich Dostoevsky v portretakh, illiustratsiiakh, dokumentakh, *1972)*

Dmitrii Chizhevsky, in an article first published in 1928, was among the first critics to expound on the significance of the double as a philosophical problem in Dostoevsky's works, including *Besy* (The Devils, 1871–1872), *Podrostok* (The Adolescent, 1875), and *Brat'ia Karamazovy*. According to Chizhevsky, Dostoevsky's fiction, beginning with *Dvoinik,* revealed the instability of individual existence, not as a psychological or social problem, but as an ontological problem. The Russian Enlightenment focused single-mindedly on the efficacy of reason as a tool to remake reality. Chizhevsky writes that Dostoevsky's Goliadkin is hollowed out under the pressure of the rational principle embodied in the rule of Czar Nicholas I. Chizhevsky saw a link between the instability of Goliadkin's personality and a similar lack of fixed definition in Stavrogin and Ivan Karamazov. Deprived of any other opportunity for the expression of unique selfhood, these heroes use the only means available to them, which, according to Chizhevsky, was their sense of shame.

In "Khoziaika" (The Landlady), published in 1847, Dostoevsky attempts to unite the Petersburg theme with motifs from folklore and romantic litera-

ture. Most critics, from Dostoevsky's time to the present, have seen little merit in this work, which borrows its fundamental plot from E. T. A. Hoffman. Ordynov, a student of the natural sciences, falls under the spell of the mysterious Katerina and the equally mysterious Murin, an old man who is her lover and may also be her father. The near-incestuous relationship between a father figure and his daughter or adopted daughter becomes an arena in which to investigate the abuse of power. The heroine of "Khoziaika" confesses that her "disgrace and shame" are dear to her, "the same as joy and happiness." Dostoevsky significantly expands this personality trait (the derivation of pleasure from shame) in other works—for example, in the hero of *Zapiski iz podpol'ia,* in Nastas'ia Filippovna of *Idiot* (The Idiot, 1868), and in Fedor Pavlovich Karamazov.

In the years 1848–1849 Dostoevsky continued work on his Petersburg theme, combining social criticism with the development of the hero as "dreamer." The first-person narrator of "Belye nochi" (White Nights, 1848) reflects on the charming but sickly and deceptive beauty of St. Petersburg. He describes himself as a "dreamer" who has cut himself off from "real life" for the sake of his own inventions. He has no desires because he is "the artist of his own life." During his lonely walks, the hero meets Nasten'ka, whose isolated life is similar to his, except that she has already formed a romantic attachment to a young man. The budding love between the narrator and Nasten'ka forms the basis for the story, which ends with the hero's pathetic words to the effect that his "minute of bliss" with Nasten'ka is enough for his whole life. As Victor Terras has shown, the hero of *Zapiski iz podpol'ia* is an older, embittered version of the narrator of "Belye nochi." "Slaboe serdtse" (A Weak Heart, 1848) is another St. Petersburg tale of a "dreamer" with strong echoes of Pushkin's "Mednyi vsadnik" (Bronze Horseman, 1833). It tells the story of a young clerk, Vasia Shumkov, who is engaged to be married but ends up losing his sanity over work that he has not finished on time. The shock of his superior's leniency actually causes the breakdown. At the end of the story, Vasia's friend Arkadii has a vision of St. Petersburg as a fantastic dream that will fade into the fog of the evening.

Netochka Nezvanova (1849) is a first-person narrative of a young girl, a female "dreamer." Its three parts are only loosely strung together: first, Netochka's miserable childhood with her stepfather and mother; then the time she spends as the ward of a prince; and finally, her early adolescence in the home of the prince's grown daughter. Netochka's stepfather, the half-mad and drunken musician Efimov, convinces the child that her mother is responsible for his failure as an artist. When the mother dies, Netochka's fantasy of living happily ever after with her stepfather comes to no avail. Efimov dies, and the next phase of Netochka's life begins. Settled in the prince's household, Netochka receives an education in the style of Jean-Jacques Rousseau and falls in love with the prince's youngest daughter, Katia, one of Dostoevsky's many proud, beautiful, and willful Katerinas. When their passion for each other is discovered, Netochka is sent to live with the prince's stepdaughter, Aleksandra Mikhailovna, and her husband Petr Aleksandrovich. In their home, as in her earliest childhood, a mystery dominates the relations between the husband and his timid wife. Netochka's talent as a singer is discovered and she begins professional training. As in other works from this period, the turning point in Netochka's development and awareness comes with her secret discovery of a library. She discovers in the library "a threshold to a new life." In this novel, as in other works from the early period, Dostoevsky explores nonnormative sexual relationships, which include the quasi-incestuous relationship between Efimov and Netochka and the homoerotic relationship between Netochka and Katia. Terras and Joe Andrew discuss this aspect of the early work in their criticism.

Dostoevsky never finished *Netochka Nezvanova*. In April of 1849 he was arrested for his political activity, which included participation in the Petrashevsky reading and discussion circle. Mikhail Butashevich-Petrashevsky, a well-known St. Petersburg figure, worked in the Ministry of Foreign Affairs and had a large collection of banned books. He was the author of *Karmannyi slovar' inostrannykh slov* (Pocket Dictionary of Foreign Words, 1845–1846), a radical political tract in the form of a dictionary. Members of the circle talked about such issues as socialism, freedom of the press, changes in the judicial system, and the emancipation of the serfs. Dostoevsky had taken part in a more radical group, the Pal'm-Durov circle, which had planned to acquire a printing press and distribute leaflets against the government. Aleksandr Pal'm and Sergei Durov were both writers; Pal'm's patriotic literary works were part of the reason his sentence was reduced. Dostoevsky also was involved in another faction, centered on Nikolai Aleksandrovich Speshnev, who believed in the need for rebellion. Dostoevsky had, in the presence of a government informer, read aloud Belinsky's letter to Gogol, which criticized the church and other Russian institutions, including the government. Dostoevsky later compared his political beliefs to an illness. He wrote that he had been "infected" by a "disease" in which he was convinced that the foundations of society—the family, religion, and the right to property—were immoral. Dostoevsky and his older and younger brothers were arrested, although Andrei and Mikhail were released for lack of evidence. Lengthy isolation in the St. Peter and Paul Fortress during the investigation and secret trial did not prevent Dostoevsky from continuing his creative life: he completed the story "Malen'kii geroi" (A Little Hero) while in prison. It was published nearly a decade later in 1857.

A court appointed by Czar Nicholas I in November of 1849 condemned Dostoevsky and other members of the Petrashevsky circle to death. In early December the death sentence was commuted, and in Dostoevsky's case the punishment was reduced first to eight years and then to four years of hard labor, to be followed by service in the army with a restoration of civil rights. On 22 December 1849 Dostoevsky and his fellow-prisoners were told, however, that they would be executed by firing squad. The ceremonial breaking of the swords was carried out; the prisoners were divided into groups of three, and the first group was tied to stakes. At the last moment, the execution was stopped, and the prisoners were informed of their real sentences. According to Joseph Frank, mock execu-

The stockade around the Omsk prison camp, where Dostoevsky spent the years 1850–1854 at hard labor

tions were the norm when death sentences were commuted by the czar, but usually prisoners were informed in advance that the execution would be nothing more than a ceremony. What made this one unusual was that the prisoners did not know that their lives were to be spared. Czar Nicholas I wanted to make a great impression on the Petrashevsky circle.

He succeeded. The anticipation of death and the sudden reprieve left two prisoners in a state of insanity. Life imitated Dostoevsky's art: Vasia Shumkov, the hero of "Slaboe serdtse," goes mad from "gratitude," according to one of the other characters in the story. In a letter written afterward to his brother, Dostoevsky described himself as having undergone a spiritual beheading: "The head that created, lived the higher life of art . . . that head has already been cut from my shoulders." In subsequent works Dostoevsky wrote about the horror of certain death. In *Idiot,* for example, Prince Myshkin describes how the prisoner greedily takes in his last impressions as he is being driven to the execution and counts the seconds as the guillotine blade falls. In the same letter Dostoevsky wrote with great vividness about his fear that the images he had created, if not permitted to take form in writing, would poison his bloodstream. Bakhtin and other critics have described the living and embodied quality of the Dostoevskian hero's "idea." The idea is not an abstraction but a force compelling the hero to act in a particular way. Something of that quality is evident in the language of Dostoevsky's letter of 1849.

Dostoevsky served four years in a hard labor stockade in Omsk, followed by six years of army service in Semipalatinsk. He wrote two novellas in Siberia, neither of which has received much critical acclaim. *Selo Stepanchikovo i ego obitateli* (The Village of Stepanchikovo and Its Inhabitants, 1859) is notable for its portrait of the petty domestic tyrant Foma Fomich Opiskin, a former lackey, buffoon, and sponger, and first in the long list of extraordinary fools in Dostoevsky's works. Dostoevsky comments that perhaps the enormous ambition of such figures is nothing more than a distortion of their feeling of self-worth, which had been crushed early on. Foma Fomich had been a "literary man" but had not been recognized. Several critics have seen a parody of Gogol in Opiskin. Dostoevsky's letters show that he was worried about having been cut off from everything that was new in Russia, so perhaps he was thinking of himself as well.

In February of 1857 Dostoevsky married Mariia Dmitrievna Isaeva. Her husband, an alcoholic, had recently died, leaving her with a young son and without income. Traces of the Isaevas can be seen in Dostoevsky's portrait of the Marmeladovs in *Prestuplenie i nakazanie*. Dostoevsky had a rival for Isaeva's affections, Nikolai Vergunov, and according to rumor, Isaeva had an affair with Vergunov even after she and Dostoevsky were married. The marriage was, by all accounts, not congenial. One of the problems had to do with Dostoevsky's epilepsy. In prison his attacks had lessened (the story that he first began to experience severe epilepsy

Mariia Dmitrievna Isaeva, whom Dostoevsky married in 1857

after a flogging he received in the stockade is a myth). The severity of his attacks increased after his release. During his honeymoon Dostoevsky suffered an epileptic seizure that shocked his wife. He later wrote that if he had known he had real epilepsy, he never would have married. Mariia Dmitrievna was also ill with tuberculosis.

Dostoevsky used his illness as grounds to petition the czar for a swifter return to St. Petersburg. Alexander II had ascended the throne in 1855, and the usual expectations about amnesty were heightened by his reputation for gentleness. As part of this effort to secure his freedom, Dostoevsky also wrote a few jingoistic odes in relation to the Crimean War, which were never published. Baron Aleksandr Egorovich Vrangel, the public prosecutor in Semipalatinsk with important family connections in St. Petersburg, made repeated efforts to help Dostoevsky. Nonetheless, the restoration of Dostoevsky's rights, the freedom to retire from army service, permission to publish, and permission to return to the capital progressed slowly. Even after Dostoevsky came back to European Russia, his final departure for St. Petersburg was delayed for a few more months, which he spent in Tver. He was allowed to return to St. Peters-

burg in December of 1859, under the watch of the secret police.

All the experiences that flowed from Dostoevsky's arrest—his imprisonment in St. Petersburg, the mock execution, life in the stockade in Omsk, and army service afterward in Semipalatinsk—had a profound impact on his writing. He wrote about his time in Siberia explicitly in letters to his brother and other correspondents, and in *Zapiski iz mertvogo doma* (Notes from the House of the Dead, 1861). Dostoevsky later drew upon his Siberian experiences in the creation of characters for his novels, including both criminals and saintly sufferers. In entries written for *Dnevnik pisatelia* in the 1870s, Dostoevsky also used his experiences in the stockade to reflect on questions of the national mission and character of Russia and to promote his own public image. In his essay "Odna iz sovremennykh fal'shei" (One of the Contemporary Falsehoods, 1873) written for his regular column in *Grazhdanin* (The Citizen), Dostoevsky aptly noted that "to tell the story of the rebirth of my convictions would be very difficult," suggesting presumably that his immediate contact with the people led to a resurgence of his religious and national-patriotic beliefs. He wrote that neither he nor the other members of the Petrashevsky circle felt regret for what they had done, that nothing "broke" them. The only circumstance that changed their views was their "contact with the people, solidarity with them in their common misfortune." Yet, Dostoevsky's letter to his brother Mikhail in 1854, written immediately upon release from the Omsk fortress, emphasizes the "hatred" the ordinary convicts—Dostoevsky calls them "150 enemies"—demonstrated toward noblemen such as Dostoevsky. From the 1860s to the 1870s Dostoevsky reworked and transformed his writings about his experience in prison and in Siberia, shifting the tenor of his remarks.

An often-quoted 1854 letter to Natal'ia D. Fonvizina offers a self-portrait of Dostoevsky's religious faith at the time. He wrote that he was and would always remain "a child of the century, a child of disbelief and doubt." If Dostoevsky may be credited with having some insight into his own state of mind, his letter suggests that the "rebirth" he later alluded to was an ongoing process. In the letter he added that in his best moments he had created his own credo, the belief that there was nothing more beautiful, profound, or perfect than Christ, and that even if Christ were shown to be outside the truth, he would "prefer to remain with Christ than with the truth." Dostoevsky emphasizes Christ's role as an ideal or model, downplaying more traditional aspects of Christology. Dostoevsky's religious beliefs did not remain static but evolved significantly over the course of his writing career. One factor remained constant throughout—his belief in the moral power of art. Aesthetics play a central role in the structure of his belief. In *Idiot* Prince Myshkin says that "beauty will save the world." In *Besy* Tikhon complains that Stavrogin's confession is "ugly." Robert Louis Jackson's explication of "form and formlessness" in *Brat'ia Karamazovy* demonstrates the connection Dostoevsky made between the moral and the aesthetic sense. Dostoevsky's 1880 address on the occasion of the Pushkin jubilee places the great Russian poet at the center of a messianic vision, once again revealing the link between spiritual renewal and art.

Zapiski iz mertvogo doma, Dostoevsky's thinly fictionalized account of his experience in the Omsk fortress, takes the form of loosely strung together impressions, vignettes, and scenes from prison life, beginning with first impressions and ending with release from the "house of the dead." The narrator is the nobleman Gorianchikov, imprisoned for the murder of his wife. Dostoevsky later wrote that some readers believed he had committed Gorianchikov's crime. One of the most powerful scenes concerns the prisoners' bathhouse. The filth and steam, the "roaring" of the prisoners, on whose heat-reddened bodies the scars of endured floggings stand out, and the sound of their chains make Gorianchikov think that he has entered hell. The portrait gallery includes the sadistic stockade commander, who enjoyed limitless power over the prisoners; the criminal Gazin, "a human-sized spider"; the mild Dagestan Tartar, Alei, "one of the best encounters I have ever had"; and the nobleman Il'insky, surprisingly nonchalant, who was imprisoned for the murder of his father but turned out not to have committed the crime. Dostoevsky later used Il'insky as a prototype for Dmitrii Karamazov in *Brat'ia Karamazovy.* Reflections on prison and society appear throughout *Zapiski iz mertvogo doma.* The narrator remarks on the incommensurability between crimes and punishments and the debilitating effect that corporal punishment has on the development of civil society. He also remarks on the morally uplifting qualities of the prisoners' theater—a living proof of what Schiller called the "aesthetic education of mankind."

A noticeable detachment and almost ethnographic stance in relation to the world of the stockade characterize the tone of the narration. Readers never come close to the narrator or author except to discover that one of the unanticipated hardships of prison life, aside from the leg irons prisoners wore, was the constant forced company of the other convicts. Gorianchikov discloses at the end that he finally understands he will never be accepted into this world, because he is a nobleman. Dostoevsky reestablished himself as a literary figure of importance with *Zapiski iz mertvogo doma.* Nikolai Gavrilovich Chernyshevsky took an active

interest in republishing excerpts from *Zapiski iz mertvogo doma;* Leo Tolstoy and Ivan Sergeevich Turgenev praised it; and Dostoevsky was often asked to give public readings from it. It is one of the first in a long line of Russian and Soviet prison memoirs.

Unizhennye i oskorblennye is a Dickensian novella about "careers, connections, money, and marriage." The work includes elements of *Netochka Nezvanova* and Dostoevsky's later work *Podrostok.* It is narrated in the first person by a young man, Ivan Petrovich, a budding writer who is fatally ill. Dostoevsky uses the figure of Ivan Petrovich to connect his pre-Siberian and post-Siberian selves: the young man has won acclaim for his work about a little clerk. The allusion is to Dostoevsky's own *Bednye liudi.* The two plotlines in *Unizhennye i oskorblennye* feature conflicts between fathers and daughters. In the first plot, Natasha Ikhmenev is in love with Alesha, the son of her father's enemy, Prince Valkovsky. Earlier, Prince Valkovsky had accused Natasha and her parents of attempting to entrap Alesha in a marriage. Valkovsky is now engaged in litigation against Natasha's father, his former steward.

Natasha leaves her father's house in order to become Alesha's mistress. Alesha is a naive, gullible figure—a proto-Prince Myshkin in some respects—who cannot decide between two women and who persists in believing in his father's goodness, despite the senior Valkovsky's machinations against him. The father plans to have Alesha marry a rich heiress, Katia, and to declare the young couple legally incapable of managing their own money. Together with his new bride, Katia's stepmother, he plans to assume control of the young people's income. Prince Valkovsky's violence against his offspring is not only limited to his son, Alesha, but also manifests itself in his relation to his other child, his daughter, Nelly, whom he refuses to acknowledge. For the most part, the novel was not well received by the critics. The Russian writer Evgeniia Tur found it lacking in artistic merit. In contrast, the critic Nikolai Aleksandrovich Dobroliubov, writing in 1861, emphasized that social and political conditions created the "insulted and the injured" personalities of this work and of *Dvoinik* as well. Dobroliubov argued that the sense of injured pride signaled a potential for healthy social change.

In addition to works of fiction, Dostoevsky's other literary projects of the time were the journals *Vremia* (Time) and *Epokha* (Epoch), which he edited together with his brother Mikhail. The journals included most significantly Dostoevsky's own work and articles by the writers Nikolai Nikolaevich Strakhov and Apollon Aleksandrovich Grigor'ev. *Unizhennye i oskorblennye* was serialized in *Vremia.* In this period of his early journalism (as in the later writings of the

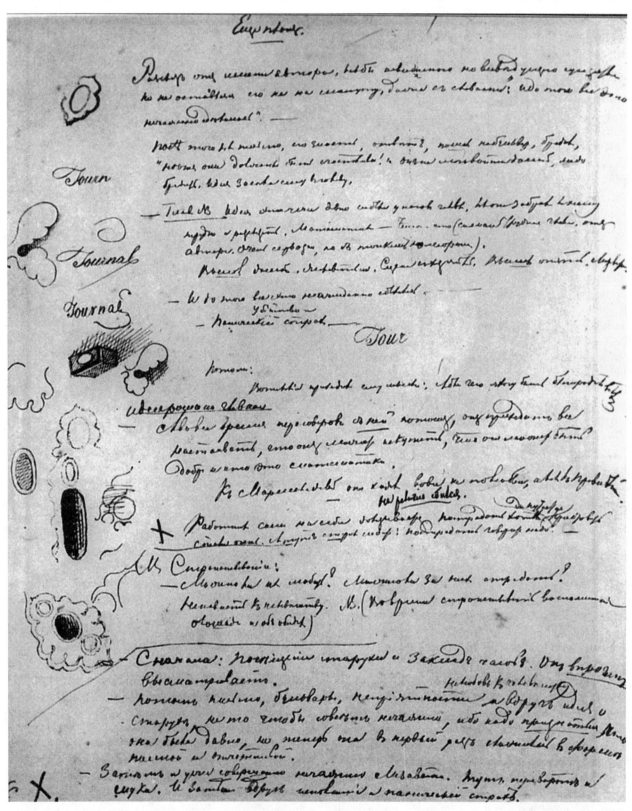

Notes for Prestuplenie i nakazanie *(Crime and Punishment), first published in* Russkii vestnik *(The Russian Herald) in 1866 (Manuscript Department, Russian State Library, Moscow)*

1870s) Dostoevsky promulgated a doctrine known as *pochvennichestvo*. The term, based on the word for soil or earth, suggests "rootedness." Dostoevsky advocated the necessity of a union between the Russian people and those responsible for enlightening them. An example of this doctrine appears in his *Dnevnik pisatelia* for 1876, in the essay "Neobkhodimyi kontrakt s narodom" (The Necessary Contract with the People). Dostoevsky's most important nonfiction work published in *Vremia* was based on his trip to Europe in 1862, which he undertook in part to consult specialists for his epilepsy. *Zimnie zametki o letnikh vpechatleniiakh* (Winter Notes on Summer Impressions, 1863) gives Dostoevsky a chance to reflect further on the relation between individuals and their native countries and on the separation between the Russian educated classes, whose sights were set on Europe, and the ordinary Russian people. Some of his comments reflect the genre of the travelogue, such as his characterizations of the highly efficient way the French collect data about visitors to their country. The work as a whole is more philosophical than journalistic, with a particular focus on the relations between the individual and society and the grounds for those relations. Dostoevsky writes about the difficulty of achieving brotherhood in Western society, in which the main emphasis is on the individual. He comes to the seemingly paradoxical conclusion that the highest form of individualism is voluntary self-sacrifice.

In *Zimnie zametki o letnikh vpechatleniiakh* Dostoevsky develops the ideological kernel of *Zapiski iz podpol'ia*. He writes that if people are offered food and work and asked in return only the slightest diminution of their personal freedom, the offer will be refused in favor of the opportunity to exercise one's own will without any restriction: "freedom is better." The 1864 work elaborates on this point. The "Crystal Palace"–the underground writer's shorthand for the rationally organized utopias of socialism–will not succeed, because people value their own individual irrational desires, their suffering, and their freedom more than anything else. The nameless "antihero" has no identity other than his argumentative and endlessly self-canceling writing. He is, to use the language of his text, not born from the bosom of nature but from a chemical process. The pathologically self-conscious, alienated, and isolated writer is ultimately dehumanized and without an identity. He could not become anything, he says, "neither evil, nor good, nor a scoundrel, nor honest, nor a hero, nor an insect." He is the antithesis of the "rootedness" Dostoevsky had written about in this period. The underground writer's sole occupation is deriving pleasure from his sense of humiliation. He compares himself to a mouse, which is always insulted but incapable of taking revenge, thus building around itself a "stink-

ing mess" of doubt. He is proof that happiness and pleasure are not necessarily the product of the rational calculation of one's own advantage.

Zapiski iz podpol'ia is divided into two parts: "Podpol'e" (Underground) and "Po povodu mokrogo snega" (Apropos of the Wet Snow). In the first part, the narrator introduces himself and his philosophy, and in the second he narrates an episode from his younger years. There are several kinds of memories, he notes: some which one does not reveal to everyone, some which one reveals not even to friends, and some which one keeps secret even from oneself. "Po povodu mokrogo snega" belongs to this last category. The underground "antihero" discloses a shameful act and his despair at his bookishness and failure to enter "living life." Dostoevsky complained in a letter that the censors had eliminated the sections of the work in which the necessity of faith was introduced.

Zapiski iz podpol'ia occupies an important place in the history of modern thought beyond the polemics of Dostoevsky's own time and place. The work both looks back to the eighteenth century and looks forward to the twentieth century and beyond. The Russian émigré philosopher Lev Shestov argues that it is not in the work of Immanuel Kant but in Dostoevsky's *Zapiski iz podpol'ia* that the true "Critique of Pure Reason" can be found. (Dostoevsky had himself expressed interest in Kant's "Critique" upon his release from prison a decade earlier.) Dostoevsky rejects the mechanistic model of human behavior found in Denis Diderot's *Le neveu de Rameau* (Rameau's Nephew, 1761) and also rejects the prescription for the rational organization of human happiness found in Chernyshevsky's *Chto delat'?* (What Is to Be Done?, 1863). His portrait of narcissism and other forms of neurosis in *Zapiski iz podpol'ia* anticipates the development of psychoanalytic models in the twentieth century. In his philosophical rejection both of traditional values and of his critique of Enlightenment faith in human progress and reason, the underground writer refuses the comfort of any system of belief whatsoever, thus anticipating existentialism. The work radically questions the possibility of human fellowship or community. But it also suggests a somewhat less pessimistic view. Bakhtin claims that the underground writer's deliberate self-distortion is a way of asserting his freedom to define himself. There is something positive in his self-torment. Shestov noted that such extreme self-reproach was characteristic of the confessions of the saints. Both Bakhtin and Shestov hint at the possibility of moral renewal in the underground writer.

The tormented philosophy of the underground writer is the wellspring of Dostoevsky's great ideological heroes, from Raskol'nikov to Ivan Karamazov, who test the limits of rationalism and reject the notion that

Anna Grigor'evna Dostoevskaia, the novelist's second wife, 1871

history shows evidence of rational progress. The representation of the modern antihero sets a new departure for European literature. *Zapiski iz podpol'ia* serves as a source for works by Albert Camus, André Gide, Jean-Paul Sartre, and Hermann Hesse, and was important to the American writers Saul Bellow and Isaac Rosenfeld. In Russian literature, the influence of *Zapiski iz podpol'ia* can be traced in such writers as Leonid Nikolaevich Andreev, Fedor Kuz'mich Sologub, Vsevolod Mikhailovich Garshin, and Mikhail Petrovich Artsybashev in the early part of the twentieth century, and in the period following the revolution, in such writers as Iurii Karlovich Olesha.

In 1863 Dostoevsky made a second trip to Europe, this time to pursue his love affair with Apollinariia Prokof'evna Suslova, a writer whose life fit the literary model of the emancipated woman of the times. Mariia Dmitrievna, Dostoevsky's wife, died in 1864, the same year that he lost his brother Mikhail. Dostoevsky later proposed marriage to another woman

writer, Anna Vasil'evna Korvin-Krukhovskaia. He was unhappy with Suslova and unsuccessful with Krukhovskaia. An indirect hint of the relationship with Suslova can be seen in *Zapiski iz podpol'ia*. The hero says that his servant, Apollon, is his "executioner." Suslova served as the prototype for Polina in *Igrok* (The Gambler, 1866), the novel that Dostoevsky completed in breathtaking speed by dictating it in twenty-six days to the stenographer Anna Grigor'evna Snitkina, who became his second wife on 15 February 1867. The time pressure was the result of Dostoevsky's debts and those he had assumed when his brother died.

Igrok tells the story of a Russian family living abroad in a city called Ruletenburg. The family includes a widowed general; his stepdaughter Polina; his young children; their tutor, Aleksei Ivanovich; and various hangers-on—including the disreputable Frenchman de Grieux, to whom the general owes money, and the equally disreputable Mademoiselle Blanche, whom the general would like to marry but cannot because he has no money. The characters await the death of the general's mother, "la baboulinka." Instead of dying, however, she appears in Ruletenburg—fierce, eccentric, and apparently determined to gamble away everyone's inheritance. The spinning roulette wheel dominates the lives of the characters. The young hero, the tutor Aleksei Ivanovich, like the "antihero" of *Zapiski iz podpol'ia,* has lost his connection to reality, to his own interests, and to broader social interests, as one of the other characters remarks. He has even rejected his own memories. Gambling takes on a metaphysical dimension for him as a way of testing himself and his fate.

Dostoevsky uses a similar concept of the hero's test of himself as the basis for *Prestuplenie i nakazanie*. He attempted to sell the idea of the work to the editor of the *Russkii vestnik* (The Russian Herald), Mikhail Nikiforovich Katkov, by describing it as a "psychological account of a crime." The hero, Rodion Romanovich Raskol'nikov, a poor student, falls prey to "certain strange half-baked ideas" and decides to extricate himself from his position "all at once." He robs and murders an old pawnbroker, who is "not good for anything." In the completed version of the novel, Raskol'nikov attempts to justify his crime on the grounds that he wants to help his poor mother and his sister, Dunia. His sister has agreed to an unwanted marriage to the businessman Luzhin in order to keep Raskol'nikov at the university.

Dostoevsky emphasizes in the letter to Katkov that the "entire psychological process of the crime unfolds" only afterward. He explains how "unanswered questions arise before the murderer, unsuspected and unexpected feelings torment his soul." The murderer, according to Dostoevsky, is ultimately forced to confess because his own feelings demand it. Dostoevsky insisted to Katkov that his idea was "not eccentric" and had an immediate connection to contemporaneous events—he pointed to newspaper accounts of crimes committed by educated, "developed" individuals. What Dostoevsky referred to as the "half-baked ideas" of the time enter the ideological debates that the characters carry on in the novel. Utilitarianism plays a central role. Luzhin asserts that "science says: 'love yourself above all, because everything in the world is based on personal interest.'" Raskol'nikov argues that the crimes the other characters have been discussing, including his own crime, the murder of the pawnbroker and her sister, occurred in accordance with Luzhin's theory. Raskol'nikov thus directly reveals one crucial dimension of the ideological center of the novel and its chief rhetorical device, the undermining of an idea by carrying it to an absurd extreme. Dostoevsky embodies the economic model of rational self-interest in a character who is cut off from all of humanity.

Dostoevsky had experimented with this narrative kernel—the hero and his idea—in *Zapiski iz podpol'ia,* but he significantly expands on it in *Prestuplenie i nakazanie.* Originally, Raskol'nikov's story was to have taken the form of a first-person confession, like *Zapiski iz podpol'ia,* but Dostoevsky settled instead on an omniscient narrator, greatly enhancing the dramatic impact of the narrative. The "psychological account of the crime" unfolds in the series of meetings Raskol'nikov has with Porfirii Petrovich, the examining magistrate; Sonia Marmeladova, a saintly prostitute; and Svidrigailov, a villainous and depraved character. Dostoevsky creates in Porfirii Petrovich an extraordinarily skilled detective, who tells his chief suspect that he knows how to ensnare a criminal psychologically. Porfirii Petrovich has a sociological perspective on the crime; he tells Raskol'nikov that the crime is "a gloomy contemporary case, a case of our time, when the human heart has darkened; when the phrase is cited that 'blood refreshes.'" Svidrigailov, according to Konstantin Mochulsky, is Raskol'nikov's "double." His is the path of renunciation of the moral law. Dostoevsky repeats in Svidrigailov a negative feature he had used earlier in "Elka i svad'ba" (A Christmas Tree and a Wedding, 1848)—namely, a pathological attraction for young girls. Svidrigailov has absolutely no hope of redemption: his vision of eternity is a small bathhouse, with spiders in the corners.

The dramatic pattern of Raskol'nikov's meetings with the other characters reveals that his motivation and his potential for good and evil cannot be reduced to the economic calculus that he himself points to in discussion with his adversary Luzhin. In Balzac's *Le Père Goriot* (1835) Rastignac proposes that an individual may commit a crime in order to help humanity. For Raskol'nikov the noble ideal is insincere, one of his many masks. He murders not for the sake of an idea, but for his own sake, in order to test himself. Is he merely ordinary, or is he extraordinary, a Napoleonic figure who can transgress the boundaries of morality to achieve his goal? Raskol'nikov's three meetings with Sonia Marmeladova are particularly important in this regard. The confrontations with Sonia are three failed attempts at self-definition, three self-disclosures that do not add up to one coherent whole. As in *Zapiski iz podpol'ia,* the artistic representation of the fragmentation of the self, which Bakhtin calls the hero's "unfinalizability" and Philip Rahv calls "the principle of uncertainty or indeterminacy," is the main feature of Dostoevsky's experimentation with the construction of character.

The modern story of the dissolution of a personality is only one side of the novel, however. Through Sonia, whose face conveys "insatiable compassion," and her father, the drunkard Marmeladov, the perspective of the novel opens beyond the social reality of St. Petersburg in the 1860s and the ideological debates and new problems of the time. Sonia's father, a civil servant fallen on hard times, has close links to the downtrodden characters of Dostoevsky's early fiction. Raskol'nikov meets him in the opening part of the novel and learns from him that Sonia has taken up prostitution in order to help her family. Like Makar Devushkin in *Bednye liudi,* who declares passionately that the rich and the poor are brothers, Marmeladov, too, has a vision of reconciliation, but his introduces an eschatological dimension to the novel. He tells Raskol'nikov that at the Last Judgment, Jesus will forgive even the drunkards. The religious and folkloric themes Dostoevsky introduces through Marmeladov receive fuller development in Raskol'nikov's relationship with Sonia. In general, Dostoevsky's entire construction of the "folk" and folk culture shifts significantly toward a positive evaluation in the mature fiction in comparison to earlier treatments, such as Ordynov in "Khoziaika." In *Prestuplenie i nakazanie* Sonia reads Raskol'nikov the New Testament story of the resurrection of Lazarus, which has important implications for Raskol'nikov's own story. The funeral feast for Marmeladov, with its carnivalesque suspension of judgment and its mock trial, sustains the alternative narrative line, interrupting the detective story and the psychological account of Raskol'nikov's unraveling. Dostoevsky returned to a similarly double perspective in his last novel, *Brat'ia Karamazovy,* in which a murder, its detection, and the problems of resurrection and theodicy receive equal attention.

Upon publication in 1866, *Prestuplenie i nakazanie* was immediately praised for the depth of its psychological analysis. In contrast, the radical critic Dmitrii Ivanovich Pisarev emphasized the depth of Dostoevsky's social-economic analysis, arguing that Raskol'nikov was driven by the "struggle for existence." Turgenev and Anatolii Fedorovich Koni, a leading jurist, both praised the work. Some radical critics charged that Dostoevsky had misrepresented the younger generation and its ideas. The symbolist poet Viacheslav Ivanovich Ivanov read *Prestuplenie i nakazanie* in a mythic-religious framework, comparing this and Dostoevsky's other works to ancient tragedy. According to Ivanov, Raskol'nikov's guilt is the guilt of all humanity toward Mother Earth. In Ivanov's view, Raskol'nikov acts in the role of the scapegoat, the substitute sacrificial victim. Gide, whose own writing was influenced by *Prestuplenie i nakazanie,* argues that while Raskol'nikov fails in his attempt to be more than ordinary, Friedrich Nietzsche took his idea of the superman from *Prestuplenie i nakazanie.* Nietzsche likely formulated his idea before he encountered Dostoevsky in French translation. However, *Prestuplenie i nakazanie* is one of the works on the basis of which Nietzsche said that Dostoevsky was "the only psychologist from whom he had anything to learn." The Russian philosopher Nikolai Aleksandrovich Berdiaev saw in Raskol'nikov's crime the crisis of modern, rational humanism with its self-glorification of the individual. Thomas Mann called this work the greatest crime novel of all time.

One of most productive sources of Dostoevsky criticism in general and *Prestuplenie i nakazanie* in particular has been psychoanalysis and other forms of scientific psychology. R. D. Laing and Karen Horney are among the many professional psychologists who use Raskol'nikov and other Dostoevskian heroes as examples of psychological phenomena. Alfred Bem, a Russian émigré scholar, wrote a series of sophisticated literary studies published in the 1930s that traced the structure of the id and guilt in *Prestuplenie i nakazanie* and in Dostoevsky's early fiction in general. In addition to this type of interpretation, recent criticism of the novel has focused on such questions as Raskol'nikov's literary predecessors—Pushkin's Hermann from *Pikovaia dama* (The Queen of Spades, 1834) is an example—narrative structure and the function of time, and the significance of religious imagery and language in the work. In *Problems of Dostoevsky's Poetics,* Bakhtin emphasizes the importance of Raskol'nikov's consciousness; everything in the novel is "projected against him and dialogically reflected in him." Bakhtin also discusses the significance of the threshold and public square in this work as particularly important forms of boundary space where carnivalization takes place.

The publication of *Prestuplenie i nakazanie* did not relieve the financial difficulties Dostoevsky faced. Pursuit by his creditors led him to return again to Europe. Dostoevsky and Anna Grigor'evna spent the years 1867–1871 abroad, where he wrote *Idiot* and most of *Besy.* In 1867 he gambled, begged his editor for money, pawned his wife's jewelry and clothing, and started writing his next novel. The Dostoevskys had their first child, a girl whom they named Sonia, in early 1868, but she died three months later. Another daughter, Liubov', was born in Dresden in 1869. Dostoevsky's feelings about his life in Europe may be deduced from a line at the end of *Idiot:* "All of your Europe is only a fantasy, and all of us abroad are only a fantasy."

Idiot was his portrait of a "wholly good man," Prince Myshkin, to whom he referred in his notebooks as "Prince Christ." *Idiot* offers a counterpoint to *Prestuplenie i nakazanie,* not only because of the opposed qualities of the heroes, Myshkin and Raskol'nikov, but also because of the narrative qualities of the two works. The earlier novel is generally praised for its tight narrative construction, unlike the later work, in which the action starts, stops, and meanders. However, the notebooks for the novel reveal extensive work on the development of the prince's character, who in earlier versions of the novel is "pathologically proud."

The novel begins with the meeting of Prince Myshkin and Parfen Rogozhin on a train arriving in St. Petersburg. The prince has been in Switzerland, where he received treatment for a mysterious nervous illness; he is on his way to see his distant relatives, the Epanchins. Gania Ivolgin, General Epanchin's secretary, an utterly ordinary young man, is in love with Aglaia Epanchina, but he is being offered money to marry off Nastas'ia Filippovna, the femme fatale of the novel. As a young girl, Nastas'ia Filippovna was seduced by her guardian, Afanasii Totsky. As a grown woman, she attempts to take revenge on her victimizer by socially shaming him. By the conclusion of his first day, the prince has become closely involved in the lives of the Epanchins and the less reputable Ivolgins. He has inherited a fortune and has become Rogozhin's rival for the hand of Nastas'ia Filippovna. In the second part of the novel, Rogozhin attempts to murder the prince. The action switches to Pavlovsk, where Dostoevsky introduces such characters as Lebedev, who interprets the development of railways in Russia as a fulfillment of the Apocalypse of John. The third part is occupied for the most part with Ippolit Terent'ev's lengthy "Necessary Confession," which anticipates Ivan Karamazov's "Rebellion." In the fourth and final part, Prince Myshkin is engaged to Aglaia Epanchina. The novel concludes with a stunningly written reunion of Rogozhin and Prince Myshkin.

This novel, like *Brat'ia Karamazovy,* includes debates about faith and its destruction. In answer to Rogozhin's question as to whether he believes in God, Prince Myshkin offers several parables. A peasant over-

Notes for Besy *(The Devils), first published in* Russkii vestnik *in 1871–1872 (Manuscript Department, Russian State Library, Moscow)*

come with desire for his friend's silver watch slits his friend's throat while asking Christ for forgiveness. A mother sees her baby smile at her for the first time and crosses herself, explaining to the prince that God's joy at seeing a sinner pray is the same as her delight in her baby. The prince is struck by the simple Russian woman's ability to grasp a profound Christian truth. Dostoevsky introduces a national motif by having Prince Myshkin suggest that Russia will play a special role in the future resurrection of humanity–a belief that he expanded later in his journalism. At an evening party given in his honor, the prince tells the aristocratic guests that they will be servants in the future and urges them to find happiness in simple joys, in nature, and in children. The prince's ecstatic discourse culminates in an epileptic fit.

The detailed description of Prince Myshkin's epileptic attacks has drawn the attention of Dostoevsky's biographers and critics, some of whom attribute Myshkin's feelings to Dostoevsky himself. The novel presents multiple perspectives on the disorder and its meaning both for the sufferer and for those around him. Dostoevsky's first wife was apparently horrified by his epilepsy, but Anna Grigor'evna took Dostoevsky's illness more in stride, although she despaired at her own sense of helplessness–there was little she could do, she reports, but loosen the sick man's collar. She writes that Dostoevsky himself was afraid of dying during his epileptic attacks. In *Idiot* Prince Myshkin experiences the warning sign of an attack as a moment of intense but also "serene, harmonious joy." The prince feels united with all of existence and says later that he understands what is meant by the suspension of time. However, Myshkin himself questions the meaning of his experience by asking "what if all these moments and flashes of a higher self-awareness were nothing other than disease?" The inner experience and its interpretation contrast sharply with the impression the attack makes on those who witness it. The distortion of the facial features, convulsions in the entire body, an awful cry–all create an impression of intolerable horror in passersby.

In one of his works of art criticism, Dostoevsky had written that sacred art must convey not only the concrete historical reality of the figures described in the Gospels, but also the transcendent meaning of these figures. In providing conflicting perspectives on Myshkin's epileptic attacks and their meaning both for Myshkin and for those around him, Dostoevsky meets his own criterion for sacred art. The physical expression of a diseased body may be a part of a transcendent religious experience for the sufferer. The question about the artistic representation of transcendence is important to *Idiot*, which includes a treatise in miniature on the topic. In his "Confession" Ippolit Terent'ev, dying of tuberculosis, describes a picture by Hans Holbein the Younger of Christ just taken down from the cross. "Here there is only nature," says Ippolit. He asks how Jesus' disciples, upon seeing the "corpse," could believe that it could be resurrected and be a source of resurrection for others. This painting could lead its viewers to lose faith, as Prince Myshkin points out. Ippolit says that the painting makes him imagine nature as "an enormous, implacable deaf beast" and then corrects himself, saying that a more truthful image would be "an enormous machine of the latest manufacture" that destroyed a "great and invaluable Being." The problem of resurrection, both literal and figurative, which occupies Dostoevsky throughout the writing of the mature fiction paradoxically receives its bleakest treatment in this novel about a "wholly beautiful man."

Just as the characters in *Idiot* experience doubts about faith, similar doubts have occurred to readers of *Idiot* in both the nineteenth and the twentieth centuries–not about faith, but about Dostoevsky's capacities as an artist to create a transcendent and realistic hero who suffers from epilepsy. Konstantin Mochulsky and Michael Holquist both find sanctity and salvation to be topics unsuitable for novels. The contingent linear temporal structure of ongoing social reality does not mesh easily with the eternal vertical structure of sacred time. Dostoevsky anticipated the problem by having the narrator remark in the notebooks to *Idiot* that his view of "reality" was unique but that he also could agree with those who said he was a "bad artist." Some critics argue that the apparent artistic failures of the work encourage the reader's active interpretation. Dostoevsky's "Prince Christ" is an astute judge of character, capable of profound analyses of both others and himself. He tells the boxer Keller that he, too, has "double thoughts." But he cannot choose between two women, Aglaia Epanchina and Nastas'ia Filippovna. Murray Krieger and Caryl Emerson, among others, argue that even though Myshkin can discern the other characters' better natures, he cannot prevent, and on the contrary, may even hasten, their and his own disastrous fates. Other readings of the novel examine its narrative voices in terms of Bakhtin's concept of polyphony (Robin Feuer Miller, for example) and offer an analysis of its narrative structure in light of the structure of the unconscious (Elizabeth Dalton). Diana Burgin and Olga Matich have written about sexuality and the subversion of gender roles in *Idiot*, focusing on Prince Myshkin and Nastas'ia Filippovna.

Vechnyi muzh (The Eternal Husband, 1870) is a reworking of the 1848 farce "Chuzhaia zhena i muzh pod krovat'iu" (Another Man's Wife and a Husband Under the Bed). The story examines the peculiar bond between the male victim and male perpetrators of adultery. Pavel Pavlovich Trusotsky, the so-called eternal husband, comes to St. Petersburg to find his late wife's lovers, including Aleksei Ivanovich Vel'chaninov. In the opening, Vel'chaninov notices that Trusotsky is following him, but it occurs to him that perhaps he himself is tailing Trusotsky. As the plot unfolds, Trusotsky uses the child of his wife and Vel'chaninov as a way of punishing his wife's lover. Like the hero of *Zapiski iz podpol'ia,* to which this work directly alludes, Trusotsky cultivates his anger and resentment, seeking opportunities for fresh humiliation and jealousy. As in so many other works of Dostoevsky, the story examines how the "insulted and injured" may become aggressors themselves. The relationship between the two men is paramount to the action of the story. Trusotsky insists on accompanying Vel'chaninov to his new fiancée's home. Trusotsky both nurses Vel'chaninov during an attack of illness and nearly kills him, leading Vel'chaninov to call Trusotsky a "Quasimodo" who fell in love with his wife's lover. The ending of the story recapitulates the fundamental plot. The two protagonists confront each other once again over the same object—a beautiful young woman. The theme of adultery, centrally important to the nineteenth-century European novel in general, receives a particular twist in Dostoevsky's story—namely, the emphasis on the male victim's need for suffering and his relationship with the aggressor. Dostoevsky's story may have been influenced in part by Gustave Flaubert's *Madame Bovary* (1857), which he read. In the critical literature, Gide and René Girard in particular have found *Vechnyi muzh* to be one of Dostoevsky's masterpieces. For Girard it embodies the logic of "triangular desire," the mediation of a subject's desire for an object through a third party.

In the late 1860s, after completing work on *Idiot* and *Vechnyi muzh,* which he wrote rapidly and without his usual agony, Dostoevsky returned to a project he had begun previously, titled in his notebooks "Zhitie velikogo greshnika" (The Life of a Great Sinner). Elements of this sketch appear in *Besy* in the characters of Tikhon and Stavrogin and in *Podrostok.* Living in Europe, Dostoevsky followed events at home with intense interest, especially the notorious Nechaev affair of 1869. A student group, "The People's Justice," led by Sergei Gennadievich Nechaev, murdered one of their own members. Whether Nechaev ordered the murder as a means of cementing the group by a bond of blood was not established. Dostoevsky saw in the crime a confirmation of his own earlier novelistic projections in *Prestuplenie i nakazanie* about the pernicious influence of radical thought on the shaky moral groundwork of the younger generation of Russians. He described his wish to write a "novel-pamphlet" in which he would express his ideas without restraint, even if it

meant that he would gain the reputation of a retrograde. His novel, which evolved into something far greater than a mere political pamphlet, directly attacked the revolutionary ideology formulated by Nechaev and Mikhail Aleksandrovich Bakunin in their *Katekhizis revoliutsionera* (Catechism of a Revolutionary, 1869).

In *Idiot* Dostoevsky inserts the story of Prince Myshkin's otherworldly rapture into the fabric of St. Petersburg society of the 1860s. The prince's message of joy goes largely unheard, and everyday life continues in its accustomed tracks. The vision of *Besy* is far darker: the continuity of everyday life comes under question. In the world of *Besy,* Russian reality is dominated by crime, scandal, suicide, moral depravity, self-delusion, and insanity. The Nechaev episode is one of many disasters depicted in this apocalyptic novel.

At the center of the novel is Nikolai Stavrogin, who fascinates and destroys nearly everyone who comes into contact with him. He tempts the other characters by serving as the screen on which they paint their own fantasies. His beautiful face is nothing more than a mask; in the words of his half-mad and prophetic wife, Mar'ia Lebiadkina, he is "a bad actor." Theatricality and imposture of various kinds function in *Besy* as a metaphor for the loss of order and authority, both political and moral. Stavrogin conceals his marriage and welcomes the attentions of a young aristocratic lady, Liza, who spends a night with him. Dasha Shatov plays the role of confidante and nurse to Stavrogin. Her brother Ivan Shatov, a former serf of Stavrogin's mother, has learned his fervent Slavophilism from Stavrogin. Shatov proclaims his belief in the Russian people and the Russian God, but when pressed by Stavrogin, admits that he himself does not yet believe in God. Stavrogin tells him: "You reduce God to a simple attribute of nationality." The Symbolist writer Dmitrii Sergeevich Merezhkovsky leveled this charge against Dostoevsky as well.

At the same time that Stavrogin tutored Shatov in Slavophilism, he imbued the engineer Aleksei Kirillov with an insane nihilism. In this novel, unlike *Idiot,* epilepsy comes without ecstatic aura: Kirillov also experiences an epileptic cessation of time, but in contrast to Prince Myshkin, his message is far from joyful. Kirillov believes that suicide will liberate humanity from the fear of death and the afterworld, and a new creature will be born, a man-god. Even this bleak vision of human freedom is compromised, as Kirillov becomes enmeshed in the political machinations of Petr Verkhovensky, the Nechaev figure.

Verkhovensky receives the epithet of a "clever serpent." His tongue is "unusually long and narrow," and his speech is rapid and insinuating. Petr is literally and figuratively the offspring of a "man of the forties." His

The novelist's children Liubov' (born 1869) and Fedor (born 1871) in the 1870s

father, Stepan Trofimovich Verkhovensky, is a mixture of such figures as Aleksandr Ivanovich Herzen, Nikolai Platonovich Ogarev, and Timofei Nikolaevich Granovsky. These writers were grounded in a philosophy of idealism and a literature of romanticism, sharply opposed by the "men of the sixties," politically radical writers such as Chernyshevsky and Dobroliubov, for whom, to use the language of the novel, "boots are more important than Pushkin." Dostoevsky lays the blame for the nihilism of the 1860s on the liberalism of the 1840s. Stepan Trofimovich Verkhovensky is not only Petr's father but also served as tutor and father figure to Nikolai Stavrogin.

Petr Verkhovensky infiltrates the highest levels of authority in the town, pitting the foolish and weak governor Von Lembke against his foolish and even more gullible wife, who feels herself to have been specially chosen for the role as guiding light before the younger generation. At the same time, Petr Verkhovensky convinces the local radicals that he is connected to revolutionary cells all over Russia. The local circle includes

the theoretician Shigalev, who dismisses all previous socialists, from Plato to Charles Fourier, as dreamers. Shigalev explains his philosophy by stating that having started from the premise of "unlimited freedom," he concludes with the premise of "unlimited despotism." While Shigalev theorizes, Verkhovensky schemes and acts. He plans to foment rebellion and make Stavrogin agree to play the role of Ivan Czarevich, the pretender to the throne. Stavrogin has generated considerable critical controversy, adding to the mythology surrounding Dostoevsky himself. One of the controversies has to do with the sources for Stavrogin. Nikolai Speshnev, whom Dostoevsky knew from his time with the Petrashevsky circle, is certainly a key prototype. Dostoevsky is said to have referred to Speshnev as his "Mephistopheles." Another controversy arises out of the censorship and self-censorship of the ninth chapter of the second part of the novel. Immediately following Petr Verkhovensky's proposal that Stavrogin seek the throne, the would-be czar visits the monk Tikhon and confesses to him. *Russkii vestnik,* in which the novel first appeared in serial form during 1871–1872, refused the chapter, and in the subsequent publication of the novel in 1873 Dostoevsky did not include it. The Soviet Academy of Sciences edition of Dostoevsky's complete works similarly omitted the chapter. In 1996 Liudmila Saraskina published a new edition of *Besy,* which restores the suppressed chapter to its rightful place.

In the chapter, Tikhon reads Stavrogin's written account of what seems to be his rape of a young girl and her subsequent suicide. Leonid P. Grossman has described Dostoevsky's extraordinary artistry in Stavrogin's confession. According to Grossman, Dostoevsky produced a highly convincing representation of an ugly crime in an ugly, official style, breaking the norms of literary decorum. Bakhtin, in contrast, emphasizes the underlying dynamic of Dostoevsky's dialogic art in Stavrogin's confession. Stavrogin desperately needs another's ear but refuses the forgiveness that he seeks. Forgiveness from the confessor presupposes an understanding of the confessing speaker and possible domination over him. According to Bakhtin, Dostoevsky draws attention to the flow of power inherent in the speech situation of confession.

The confession was apparently so convincing that speculation as to Dostoevsky's own possible involvement in a similar crime arose in his lifetime. Nikolai Strakhov, a critic and one of Dostoevsky's first biographers, perpetrated the rumor that Dostoevsky had sexually assaulted a young girl. The origin of the rumor may be related to an incident Dostoevsky reported from the time of his childhood. While serving at the Mariinskii Hospital, Dostoevsky's father attended a girl who had been raped and died from her injuries. Dostoevsky subsequently said that he considered this crime the most terrible of all and that he used it to "punish" his hero Stavrogin in *Besy.*

The various scandals depicted within the world of *Besy* pursued not only its author but also those whom he portrayed in the novel. For example, Dostoevsky took the opportunity in a different part of his work to lampoon Turgenev, with whom he had previously quarreled. Dostoevsky owed Turgenev money and disagreed with him about the contribution of Russia to civilization. In *Besy* Turgenev appears as the "great writer" Karmazinov. He nervously demands to know from Petr Verkhovensky when the revolution will begin, and yet he entrusts Verkhovensky with his manuscript. Karmazinov declares his contempt for Russia and love of Europe. At the disastrous fête for the poor governesses, Karmazinov reads his work "Merci," a pastiche of Turgenev's writing. In fact *Besy* as a whole engaged seriously with the problems raised in Turgenev's *Ottsy i deti* (Fathers and Sons, 1862). Stepan Trofimovich Verkhovensky explicitly compares his own son to Baz-

arov. The chief difference between the two works is that in Dostoevsky's novel the intergenerational conflict seems incapable of resolution.

Besy was received critically by contemporary readers, as those in favor of the student movements of the time accused Dostoevsky of slandering an entire generation as insane fanatics. The radical critic Nikolai Konstantinovich Mikhailovsky (who, upon Dostoevsky's death, characterized him as having a "cruel talent") gave sarcastic praise to Dostoevsky's "brilliant psychiatric talent" in the novel; in so doing he implied that Dostoevsky's own psychological state was somehow peculiar and extreme. Dostoevsky planned to publish a direct response to his critics: notes for this piece begin by raising the question of "who is healthy and who is insane." Further, in a column he published in 1873, Dostoevsky asserted that he himself was an "old Nechaevite," in the sense that he had been a member of the Petrashevsky circle. In fact, to read *Besy* solely in the context of other antinihilist novels of its time and as nothing more than the political pamphlet its author said it would be reduces the complexity of its artistry and oversimplifies the conflicting ideologies of its author. *Besy* was not Dostoevsky's last word on such questions as the meaningfulness of history.

For many twentieth-century critics, *Besy* signals the end of the nineteenth-century realist tradition. As Edward Said remarks in *Beginnings: Intention and Method* (1975), text, time, and understanding fall out of sync in *Besy.* Normal genealogy is suspended; the family is shattered; and the events of the novel seem to overtake the control of their creator. The narrative structure of the novel contributes to this sense of disorder. The narrator also plays a role as a character in the novel, a fact that leads to inconsistencies in his narrative report. He emphasizes the gaps in his knowledge and his lack of skill as a narrator. In *Dostoevsky and the Novel* (1977), Holquist argues that the division of Stavrogin's persona among all the other characters—for example, Shatov and Kirillov—signals the disruption of the coherent individual self upon which the realist novel usually depends. Instead of the story of the formation of a personality and the development of character, *Besy* is a revelation of the disintegration of personality. Dostoevsky's incomplete narrative account, his destruction of the image of the family, and his deliberate deformation of the integral personality signal a break with the history of the nineteenth-century realist novel, the best examples of which in Russia are the work of Turgenev and Tolstoy. *Besy* provides a transition to new literary forms of the twentieth century. However modernist Dostoevsky's depiction of total breakdown may seem in terms of its narrative structure, it may not in fact signal the acceptance of a modernist sensibility. The novel also

An 1880 photograph of the house in Staraia Russa that Dostoevsky rented not long after his return to Russia in 1871 and eventually bought

points the other way to reveal an anachronistic, pre-modern historical and religious sensibility in which a "time of troubles" heralds the restoration of a divinely willed order. One might thus draw a parallel between *Besy* and Andrei Donat'evich Siniavsky's autobiographical novel *Spokoinoi nochi* (Goodnight, 1984). The technique of fantastic realism and the supernatural and demonic motifs that dominate that novel are greatly beholden to *Besy*. J. M. Coetzee's 1994 novel *The Master of Petersburg* is loosely based on *Besy* and on episodes from Dostoevsky's life.

Dostoevsky, his wife, and their young daughter Liubov' returned from Europe to St. Petersburg in the summer of 1871. The writing of *Besy* was completed there. Shortly after their arrival, Anna Grigor'evna gave birth to a son, Fedor. The family rented a house in Staraia Russa, which they eventually were able to buy. The next year Dostoevsky became editor of a right-wing journal, *Grazhdanin* (The Citizen), owned by Prince Vladimir Petrovich Meshchersky. Dostoevsky soon came to view his editorial responsibilities as a heavy burden that took away too much time from his

creative life. In 1873 he spent two days in jail for printing the words of the czar without prior permission. Dostoevsky's own column in the journal was titled "Dnevnik pisatelia." In it he published autobiographical and biographical sketches (including portraits of Belinsky and Herzen), literary and social criticism, and short fiction of his own. In a piece called "Sreda" (The Environment) he argued as he had done so many times before against the theory that socioeconomic conditions are responsible for crime. "Vlas" is an extended commentary on the Nekrasov poem of the same title, in which Dostoevsky notes two conflicting tendencies in the Russian people—an urge to "leap into the abyss" and the opposite pull toward salvation. He concludes that the most essential feature of all is the need for suffering. Among the works of fiction published in *Grazhdanin* is the extraordinary "Bobok," a dialogue of voices issuing from the still-living consciousnesses of rotting corpses in a graveyard. The corpses agree to play a game of confessions, similar to Ferdyshenko's parlor game in *Idiot,* and they proclaim their eagerness to lose their sense of shame and "bare themselves" before one another. The publication of *Besy* and the association with Meshchersky, and through him, Konstantin Petrovich Pobedonostsev, the future head of the Synod, led to vociferous criticism of Dostoevsky in the liberal press.

Dostoevsky resigned from his editorial post in 1874, citing poor health. In notebooks from February of the same year he mentions a "novel about children, exclusively about children, and about a child-hero." Children had appeared both in the prehistory of *Idiot,* in the circle of children Prince Myshkin gathers around himself, and in his relations with the youths Ippolit and Kolia Ivolgin. A new focus on children and groups of children emerges as a distinct layer of Dostoevsky's late writings, in the novel *Podrostok* (also translated as *A Raw Youth*), in his 1876 and 1877 *Dnevnik pisatelia* (then published as an independent journal), and in his last novel, *Brat'ia Karamazovy.* In the notebooks, Dostoevsky describes plans for a novel along the lines of Turgenev's *Ottsy i deti.* The central theme of all this work is what Dostoevsky identified as the absence of a guiding principle and the loss of unity in all segments of Russian society—from the educated upper classes to the peasantry. This "decomposition" or "breakdown" could be found not only between social groups but also within members of the same group and within the Russian family. Dostoevsky remarked that children were at odds with their parents.

The problem of decomposition and disorder had also been central to *Besy.* In that work, however, Dostoevsky had emphasized the faults of the "sons" and their utter rejection of the "fathers." Like the earlier work, *Podrostok* reproduces events from Russian political life, specifically the political trial of the circle of Aleksandr Vasil'evich Dolgushin, charged with circulating proclamations to stir up rebellion. Dolgushin, tried in 1874, becomes "Dergachev" in the novel. The members of this political group are on the whole represented in a more positive light than the members of the political circle in *Besy,* with the possible exception of Kraft, who commits suicide because he believes Russia is a second-class country. Unlike in *Besy,* in *Podrostok* the "sons" yearn for renewal and turn toward the "fathers" for guidance. The young hero's search for a guiding principle and his need for a father overlap.

Podrostok is the diary of one year in the life of Arkadii Makarovich Dolgoruky, the illegitimate son of Andrei Petrovich Versilov, a member of the nobility, and Sof'ia Andreevna, married to one of Versilov's serfs, Makar Dolgoruky. The "Dolgoruky" name, which belonged to a noble family of great eminence in Russian history, was considerably tarnished in the 1870s. Russian readers of the time would have been alerted to the significance of the name and its ramifica-

tions for the exploration in the novel of the problems of the Russian nobility. When asked in school whether he is a "Prince Dolgoruky," Arkadii answers by saying that he is just "plain Dolgoruky." Dostoevsky in this way draws attention to the fallen nobility. Arkadii grew up neglected by Versilov but "fell in love" with him nonetheless; he was mocked and beaten at school because of his illegitimacy and was the particular victim of the bully Lambert, whom he meets again in the course of the novel as a blackmailer. As a way of overcoming his loneliness and social disgrace Arkadii decides to devote himself entirely to his "idea." Like Raskol'nikov he seeks "freedom and power"—not by means of murder, but by becoming a Rothschild. Dostoevsky had used a similar feature in the character of Gania Ivolgin in *Idiot.* Arkadii stints himself on food and clothing and gives up his education in order to accumulate money, but he is distracted from his single-minded pursuit by a good deed he performs and by his involvement with a dissolute young prince, from whom he takes money.

The entangled plot of the novel, as in works from the 1840s and *Idiot,* again concerns money, careers, and marriages. Versilov is involved in a court case against the family of Prince Sokolsky, including Prince Sokolsky's son, and the Prince's daughter, Katerina Nikolaevna Akhmakova. Arkadii comes into possession of a letter Katerina Akhmakova has written seeking legal help to have her father declared mentally incompetent. She fears that if her father discovers the letter, she will lose all chances for her inheritance, which depends on the outcome of the Sokolsky-Versilov court case. Arkadii has the opportunity to use the letter as a weapon against both Versilov and Katerina, with whom both Versilov and Arkadii are in love. As the novel progresses, Arkadii comes to a better understanding of both his legal father, Makar, who became a religious pilgrim, and his natural father, Versilov. Eventually Arkadii renounces his "idea."

Dostoevsky created the image of Versilov out of a composite of real and literary figures of the 1830s and 1840s, including Aleksandr Sergeevich Griboedov's character Chatsky from *Gore ot uma* (Woe from Wit, finished between 1823 and 1824); Petr Iakovlevich Chaadaev (1794–1856), declared insane by Czar Nicholas I for his criticisms of Russia; and in particular, the foremost liberal thinker of the nineteenth century, Aleksandr Ivanovich Herzen (1812–1870). Well-educated and with an air of superiority, Versilov has spent several fortunes. He defines the nobility as the aggregate of the best people—those who preserve knowledge, enlightenment, and the highest ideals. He left Russia for Europe, but says that he did so in service to Russia, which lives not for itself but for an idea. Europeans no longer value

Dostoevsky in 1880 (photograph by M. Panov)

their own history and culture, but Versilov, a self-declared "Russian European," loves Europe more than any European national can. The love for Europe and Russia, like Versilov's love for the two women, Sof'ia and Katerina Akhmakova, does not resolve itself, and Versilov experiences firsthand the "decomposition" that dominates the novel as a whole. He has an episode of "doubling," and splits Sof'ia's icon in two.

Dostoevsky uses the epilogue to reflect on the literary status of the novel and his relation to other writers of the time, particularly Tolstoy. Responding to Arkadii's "notes," his former tutor comments on the nature of Russian life in general, observing that only in the family and in the hereditary nobility can some measure of order or structure be found in Russia, and that this structure could be the basis for a Russian literary aesthetic. What has happened recently, he says, is that the fathers are eroding the Russian family and its traditions to the point at which an author seeking to present beauty and finished aesthetic forms in the Russian family would be forced to write an historical novel. The beautiful forms found in other novels belong to Russian history, not to the Russian present. Dostoevsky alludes

to Tolstoy's *Voina i mir* (War and Peace, 1863–1869), which had been serialized in the same journal and at the same time as *Prestuplenie i nakazanie.* Arkadii belongs to an "accidental family," a family that has merged with the general chaos and disorder of the times, and the incomplete nature of his diary–*Podrostok*–speaks for its link to the nature of ongoing social reality. Dostoevsky defends the seemingly random and incomplete qualities of his own narrative art and indirectly names himself as a poet of modernity.

In 1875 Dostoevsky announced that he would publish a separate one-man monthly journal, *Dnevnik pisatelia,* which would resemble a newspaper in format, but would constitute "something whole, a book, written by one pen." It was to be a diary "in the literal sense of the word," including an account of his impressions and experiences, but it would also include fiction, and for the most part, it would be about "real events." The major thematic layers of *Dnevnik pisatelia* are politics, both domestic and foreign, literature, and court cases, which, as several critics have noted, form the "creative laboratory" for *Brat'ia Karamazovy.* The journal ran from 1876 to 1877, with one issue published in 1880 and one in 1881. The critical literature typically insists on a separation between Dostoevsky the artist and Dostoevsky the journalist. According to this view, his genius was in the artistic depiction of the competing voices and consciousnesses of his characters in dramatic conflict with one another. His journalism, in contrast, falls flat because of the more limited opportunities for dramatic interaction. *Dnevnik pisatelia* has been attacked for its jingoistic and anti-Semitic politics, especially evident, for example, in his discussions of the Slavic cause in the Balkans and in the chapter of the March 1877 issue titled "Evreiskii vopros" (The Jewish Question). Dostoevsky attempts to resolve the "dissolution" he had described in *Podrostok* by resorting to the messianic idea of Russia as the sole Christ-bearing nation. *Dnevnik pisatelia* also includes important short fiction, including "Krotkaia: Fantasticheskii rasskaz" (A Meek One: A Fantastic Tale, 1876) and "Son smeshnogo cheloveka: Fantasticheskii rasskaz" (The Dream of a Ridiculous Man: A Fantastic Tale, 1877), both of which received extensive and favorable critical treatment. *Dnevnik pisatelia* reveals the manner in which Dostoevsky transformed items he found in the newspaper into works of art. For example, a real-life suicide on which he comments in an earlier issue of *Dnevnik pisatelia* becomes the central plot element of "Krotkaia." *Dnevnik pisatelia,* with its combination of newspaper events, sociological observation, politics, personal confession, and political commentary may be seen as a Dostoevsky novel without the veneer of a plot, an attempt to move beyond the conventions of the realist novel in an even more extreme fashion than his own previous works had done. Its hero is Dostoevsky himself, now able to communicate directly with the reading audience. *Dnevnik pisatelia* made Dostoevsky a well-known public figure with many correspondents, to whom he referred as his "collaborators."

In 1878 Dostoevsky informed readers of his *Dnevnik pisatelia* that he was suspending publication because of illness. The real reason was to work on his next novel. In the same year Dostoevsky and Anna Grigor'evna lost their three-year-old son Aleksei from what Dostoevsky believed was epilepsy. He had in this period developed a friendship with the philosopher Vladimir Sergeevich Solov'ev, with whom he visited the Optyna Pustin monastery after his son's death. Dostoevsky wrote in a letter that he and Solov'ev believed in a "real, literal, personal resurrection." This belief was the central theme of his last work, the sum total of all his writing, often compared to Dante's and Balzac's works in scope and stature. *Brat'ia Karamazovy,* serialized in *Russkii vestnik* in 1879–1880, uses a murder as the fulcrum of its plot. The motivation for the murder is not the trial of an ideology as in *Prestuplenie i nakazanie* or the furthering of revolutionary politics as in *Besy,* but the rivalry between a father, Fedor Pavlovich Karamazov, and his sons. The murder, its detection, and the trial of the defendant occupy what the narrator calls the external side of the novel. Fedor Pavlovich is a dissolute landowner, tavern-keeper, and buffoon. Dostoevsky wrote in a letter that "we are all nihilists; we are all Fedor Pavlovichs." Fedor Pavlovich's nihilism is not that of Turgenev's Bazarov, who rejects authority and old-fashioned principles, but a more thoroughgoing rejection of all ideals and beliefs. He "besmirches everything he touches," as one of the characters puts it. With his first wife he had a son, Dmitrii, whom he all but abandoned and who now returns to his father as a grown man, seeking to claim the inheritance that he mistakenly believes his fathers owes him. Dmitrii, who is fond of quoting Schiller, calls himself a noxious Karamazov insect. He proclaims his love for God even as he performs morally reprehensible acts. Dmitrii embodies the "breadth" of character that Dostoevsky, in "Vlas," had described as typically Russian: as Dmitrii himself says, he strives for the ideal of the Madonna but ends up with the "ideal of Sodom." Dmitrii and Fedor Pavlovich compete for the affections of Grushenka, a femme fatale who started out as one of the insulted and injured. At the same time, Dmitrii is engaged to Katerina Ivanovna, a society woman, whose love for him is intermixed with tyrannical impulses.

Fedor Pavlovich's second marriage produced two sons, Ivan and Alesha. Ivan grew up painfully aware of his dependence on the charity of others. A brilliant student, he makes a name for himself in his journalism and criticism, and inexplicably he comes to the provinces to live with his father. Alesha, the third son, has set his heart on becoming a monk and lives in the cell of the elder Zosima, his spiritual father. Remarkably healthy and rosy-cheeked, free of the disease and hesitancy of Prince Myshkin, Alesha believes in the holiness of his elder. Zosima, like Tikhon in *Besy,* is based in part on the figure of Tikhon of Zadonsk. Another son, Smerdiakov, was born after Fedor Pavlovich allegedly raped the holy fool of the town, Stinking Lizaveta. Smerdiakov hates Russia, loves death, rejects literary art, and strives to imitate Ivan and even anticipates his wishes. Fedor Pavlovich loves beauty, after his own fashion, but Smerdiakov does not. Dostoevsky develops the device of the "double" with extraordinary skill in his last work. Smerdiakov has the uncanny ability to be present even when he is not.

At the philosophical core of the novel is the fifth of its twelve books, "Pro and Contra," including Ivan's "Rebellion." This segment and *Zapiski iz podpol'ia* are probably the best known of all of Dostoevsky's writings. Ivan asks how the suffering of children can be part of God's plan for the redemption of the world. The court cases on which Dostoevsky had commented in his *Dnevnik pisatelia,* most of which concerned child abuse, such as the notorious Kronenberg case, became the central evidence in Ivan's indictment of God's world and ongoing historical reality. Ivan "returns his entrance ticket" because the price of universal harmony—the suffering of the innocent—is too high. Dostoevsky wrote in a letter to Konstantin Pobedonostsev that Ivan's arguments are the essence of the idea of destruction and anarchism of the time. Ivan was Dostoevsky's distillation of socialism. As in his earlier works—especially *Zapiski iz podpol'ia, Besy,* and *Podrostok*—for Dostoevsky the chief flaw of socialism was that it offered humanity "bread" and other forms of material well-being in exchange for individual choice and indeed, individuality. In *Brat'ia Karamazovy* Dostoevsky presents his vision of socialism in the form of a "legend" that Ivan narrates to Alesha. It is set during the time of the Spanish Inquisition, in Seville. Christ reappears, and the Grand Inquisitor arrests him and then explains how the Inquisition has been "correcting" his work. Ivan's Grand Inquisitor views humanity as a herd, incapable of God's freedom and enslaved by "miracle, mystery, and authority." The weak and childlike human beings to whom the Grand Inquisitor ministers need to be fed, to be rewarded and punished, and above all, to have a common object of worship. The lofty example of Jesus is only for the few; the many, in contrast, depend on the constant and all-pervasive discipline of the Inquisitor. Dostoevsky was so effective in

Dostoevsky's study in his last St. Petersburg apartment

mounting the arguments of the Grand Inquisitor that several critics–including Vasilii Vasil'evich Rozanov, the Russian religious philosopher, and English novelist and critic D. H. Lawrence–believed that the author shared the Inquisitor's beliefs.

In Shigalev's system in *Besy,* the leveling of individual talent and accomplishment was to be accomplished by brute force, but in Ivan's "Legend," a more subtle calculus, based on human need, leads to the same end of total despotism. In both these works, Dostoevsky is said to have predicted the terror of Stalinism and other forms of totalitarianism in the twentieth century. Dostoevsky, who prided himself on the "realism" of his works and insisted that he predicted real events, might have derived some grim satisfaction from these acknowledgments of his prescience.

Dostoevsky wrote that the refutation of Ivan's arguments comes "indirectly" in book 6, which immediately follows Ivan's conversation with Alesha. "A Russian Monk" includes Alesha's transcription of the life and sayings of the elder Zosima in a highly stylized form. In the notebooks to the novel, Zosima says that the meaning of historical reality–"the essence of things"–cannot be grasped on earth. The ideal of

Christ is not an impossibility for human beings, because Christ's image was a human one, and it is found among the Russian people. Dostoevsky has Zosima express the idea that the possibility of "paradise on earth" is within the grasp of human beings, as long as they orient themselves toward the image of Christ and take on the responsibility of active love and brotherhood: "each is responsible for all." Dostoevsky notes in a letter that he shares Zosima's "thoughts" but not the form or the language in which they were expressed. He also wrote that the refutation of Ivan comes in the novel as a whole. The possibility of meaning in historical reality is hinted at in the carefully rendered allusions of the novel to the Bible, and in its time frame, in which images from the past offer guidance and hope in the present. The subplots involving children are important in this regard. Dmitrii's impulse toward redemption centers on the image of a child. Alesha befriends the young Kolia Krasotkin, a budding Ivan, and nurtures relationships between the schoolchildren and the dying Iliusha Snegirov, whose father Dmitrii has insulted.

During its serial publication *Brat'ia Karamazovy* was reviewed extensively in the Russian press. Konstantin Nikolaevich Leont'ev protested the overly "rosy" Christianity of the elder Zosima, arguing that it distorted the principles of Russian Orthodoxy. In 1894 Rozanov published a study of Dostoevsky's works as a whole, focusing in particular on *Brat'ia Karamazovy*. Although Rozanov reserved special praise for Ivan's "Rebellion" and the "Legend of the Grand Inquisitor," he also saw great profundity in Zosima's belief that God had taken "seeds from the other world" and placed them on earth. The perhaps overly simplistic question as to whether Dostoevsky sided with Ivan or Zosima has concerned critics. Albert Camus's *L'Homme révolté* (The Rebel, 1951) argued that Ivan's rebellion, based on reason alone, leads to insanity. Other critics, notably Jackson, see in Ivan's suffering a form of imitation of Christ and thus an unwitting refutation of his rejection of Christ. Robert L. Belknap has also shown how Dostoevsky refutes Ivan's claims by a series of ad hominem arguments. Sven Linner and Jostein Børtnes examine the religious dimensions of the novel, and Valentina Evgen'eva Vetlovskaia has shown the significance of the "Life of Aleksei the Man of God" for the character of Alesha.

One of the open critical questions about *Brat'ia Karamazovy* has to do with the fate of Alesha and the possibility of a second installment of the novel. There is some evidence, in the narrator's reference to two novels, the main one being the second, and in the memoirs of the publisher A. S. Suvorin and others, who write that Dostoevsky planned to write a second volume in which Alesha would become a revolutionary and commit a political crime. Violent attacks against the authorities were on the increase in the late 1870s. One of the best-known incidents took place in 1878, when Vera Zasulich shot at the Governor-General of St. Petersburg. Viktor Shklovsky's *Za i protiv: Zametki o Dostoevskom* (For and Against: Remarks on Dostoevsky, 1957) supports Suvorin on this point. Igor' Volgin's *Poslednii god Dostoevskogo* (Dostoevsky's Last Year, 1986) explores the possibility in detail, arguing that Dostoevsky's closeness to court circles did not mean he had become an unabashed apologist for the czar and autocracy. Not all critics accept that Dostoevsky planned to write a second installment.

In June of 1880, Dostoevsky delivered a speech at the memorial ceremonies honoring the national poet of Russia, Pushkin. According to Dostoevsky, Pushkin had embodied the uniquely Russian characteristic of universal receptivity and humanism. Pushkin demonstrated the Russian genius for uniting what was best in all the European nations. Dostoevsky used an idea that he had previously put in the mouth of Versilov in *Podrostok*, that for the true Russian, the fate of Europe was as precious as the fate of Russia. The Slavophile Ivan Sergeevich Aksakov, according to Dostoevsky,

Dostoevsky's grave at the Aleksandr Nevsky Lavra cemetery in St. Petersburg (photograph by Judith E. Kalb)

characterized the speech as an "historical event." Turgenev, from whom Dostoevsky had been estranged for many years, embraced him with open arms. Dostoevsky had resolved the subject of their earlier quarrel by answering the question of what contribution Russia had made to Western civilization. Dostoevsky wrote to his wife that the hall was in "hysterics" when he spoke of the unity of humankind, and that people called him a "prophet" and swore to each other to "be better." The Pushkin address was published in the single issue of Dostoevsky's *Dnevnik pisatelia* for 1880. The epilogue of *Brat'ia Karamazovy*, including Alesha's speech at the stone, was written in the afterglow of the Pushkin speech. Alesha calls upon the schoolchildren to remember themselves united in harmony around their dead friend, Iliusha. Alesha transforms the funeral into a memorial not only to the dead but also to the living, gathered around Iliusha's stone, and, like Dostoevsky in the Pushkin speech, takes the opportunity to "utter the ultimate word of great, universal harmony."

Dostoevsky died on 28 January 1881 of complications from emphysema. The crowd at his funeral was estimated at fifty thousand people. The mood at the event was characterized by eyewitnesses as having the solemn yet joyful spirit of a national holiday. After Dostoevsky died, Vladimir Solov'ev praised him in the same terms that Dostoevsky had used to praise Pushkin—as the prophet of Russia.

The study of Dostoevsky, both inside and outside Russia, has been shaped in important ways by his status in that country. In 1972 the massive thirty-volume edition of the complete works of Dostoevsky was undertaken by the Russian Academy of Sciences in St. Petersburg (Leningrad). This edition, with its extensive explanatory notes, bibliographical references, publication histories, draft editions, and variant versions, has been the crucial resource for generations of Dostoevsky scholars all over the world. Since the collapse of the Soviet Union, aspects of Dostoevsky's work that were neglected have come to the foreground. These aspects include a closer examination of his politics, both his critique of socialism and his rapprochement with czarist circles, and the study of religious themes and motifs in his works, long the provenance of Vetlovskaia, among others. Scholars are taking advantage of a greater variety of critical approaches, including feminism, ethnic studies, and the work of Jacques Derrida, Jacques Lacan, and Emmanuel Levinas. At the same time, a new tendency has emerged, which emphasizes Dostoevsky's Christianity above all else. In 1995 a new Russian edition of his complete works was begun under the supervision of V. N. Zakharov, which uses the orthography of the nineteenth-century original. Saraskina's 1996 edition of *Besy* includes an anthology of criticism not widely available to Russian readers previously. The publication of hard-to-find memoirs and new studies based on archival documents continues. An important source book that exemplifies this type of work is the three-volume chronicle of Dostoevsky's life based on his letters and other documents, edited by N. F. Budanova and G. M. Fridlender (1993–1995). In both Russia and the West, the work of Bakhtin has been established as a cornerstone of Dostoevsky criticism.

Letters:

F. M. Dostoevsky, *Pis'ma v chetyrekh tomakh,* 4 volumes, edited with commentary by A. S. Dolinin (Moscow: Gosudarstvennoe izdatel'stvo khudozhestvennoi literatury, 1928);

Selected Letters of Fyodor Dostoevsky, edited by Joseph Frank and David I. Goldstein, translated by Andrew R. MacAndrew (New Brunswick & London: Rutgers University Press, 1987);

David Lowe, ed. and trans., *Complete Letters,* 5 volumes— volume 1 co-edited and co-translated with Ronald Meyer (Ann Arbor, Mich.: Ardis, 1988).

Bibliographies:

Anna Grigor'evna Dostoevskaia, *Bibliograficheskii ukazatel' sochinenii i proizvedenii iskusstva, otnosiashchikhsia k zhizni i deiatel'nosti F. M. Dostoevskogo, sobrannykh v "Muzei pamiati F. M. Dostoevskogo" v Moskovskom istoricheskom muzee im. Imperatora Aleksandra III, 1846–1903* (St. Petersburg: Pantaleev, 1906);

V. V. Akopdzhanova, S. V. Belov, and others, *F. M. Dostoevsky: Bibliografiia proizvedenii F. M. Dostoevskogo i literatury o nem, 1917–1965* (Moscow: Izdatel'stvo Kniga, 1968);

S. V. Belov, ed., *Dostoevsky i teatr, 1846–1877: Bibliograficheskii ukazatel'* (Leningrad: LGITMiK, 1980);

Garth M. Terry, "Dostoevsky Studies in Great Britain: A Bibliographical Survey," in Malcolm V. Jones and Terry, eds., *New Essays on Dostoevsky* (Cambridge: Cambridge University Press, 1983), pp. 215–244;

W. J. Leatherbarrow, *Fedor Dostoevsky: A Reference Guide* (Boston, Mass.: G. K. Hall, 1990).

Biographies:

Orest F. Miller and Nikolai Strakhov, *Biografiia, pis'ma, i zametki iz zapisnoi knizhki F. M. Dostoevskogo* (St. Petersburg: A. S. Suvorin, 1883);

Apollinariia Prokof'evna Suslova, *Gody blizosti s Dostoevskim: Dnevnik, povest', pis'ma,* edited by A. S. Dolinin (Moscow: Izdatel'stvo Sabashnikovykh, 1928); English translation in Fyodor Dostoevsky, *The Gambler with Polina Suslova's Diary,* translated by Victor Terras, edited by Edward Wasiolek (Chicago: University of Chicago Press, 1972);

Andrei Mikhailovich Dostoevsky, *Vospominaniia* (Leningrad: Izdatel'stvo pisatelei v Leningrade, 1930);

E. H. Carr, *Dostoevsky (1821–1881): A New Biography* (London: Allen & Unwin, 1931);

Leonid P. Grossman, *Zhizn' i trudy Dostoevskogo: Biografiia v datakh i v dokumentakh* (Moscow-Leningrad: Academia, 1935);

N. F. Bel'chikov, *Dostoevsky v protsesse petrashevtsev* (Moscow-Leningrad: AN SSSR, 1936);

Konstantin Mochulsky, *Dostoevsky: His Life and Work,* translated, with an introduction by Michael A. Minihan (Princeton: Princeton University Press, 1947);

Avrahm Yarmolinsky, *Dostoevsky: His Life and Art,* second edition, revised and enlarged (New York: Criterion Books, 1957);

David Magarshack, *Dostoevsky* (London: Secker & Warburg, 1962);

Grossman, *F. M. Dostoevsky: Zhizn' zamechatel'nykh liudei,* second edition (Moscow: Molodaia gvardiia, 1965);

Pierre Pascal, *Dostoïevski: L'homme et l'oeuvre* (Lausanne: L'Age d'homme, 1970);

V. S. Nechaeva, ed., *F. M. Dostoevsky v portretakh, illiustratsiiakh, dokumentakh* (Moscow: Prosveshchenie, 1972);

Joseph Frank, *Dostoevsky: The Seeds of Revolt, 1821–1849* (Princeton: Princeton University Press, 1976);

Frank, *Dostoevsky: The Years of Ordeal, 1850–1859* (Princeton: Princeton University Press, 1983);

Frank, *Dostoevsky: The Stir of Liberation, 1860–1865* (Princeton: Princeton University Press, 1986);

Anna Grigor'evna Dostoevskaia, *Vospominaniia* (Moscow: Izdatel'stvo "Pravda," 1987);

Geir Kjetsaa, *Fyodor Dostoyevsky: A Writer's Life* (London: Macmillan, 1988);

N. F. Budanova and G. M. Fridlender, eds., *Letopis' zhizni i tvorchestva F. M. Dostoevskogo v trekh tomakh,* 3 volumes (St. Petersburg: Gumanitarnoe agentstvo "Akademicheskii proekt," 1993–1995);

Nina Pelikan Straus, *Dostoevsky and the Woman Question: Rereadings at the End of the Century* (New York: St. Martin's Press, 1994);

Frank, *Dostoevsky: The Miraculous Years, 1865–1871* (Princeton: Princeton University Press, 1995).

References:

Joe Andrew, *Narrative and Desire in Russian Literature, 1822–1849: The Feminine and the Masculine* (New York: St. Martin's Press, 1993);

Dominique Arban, *Les années d'apprentissage de Fiodor Dostoïevski* (Paris: Payot, 1967);

Mikhail Bakhtin, *Problems of Dostoevsky's Poetics,* edited and translated by Caryl Emerson (Minneapolis: University of Minnesota Press, 1984);

Robert L. Belknap, *The Structure of The Brothers Karamazov* (The Hague: Mouton, 1967);

Jostein Børtnes, *Visions of Glory: Studies of Early Russian Hagiography,* translated by Børtnes and Paul L. Nielson (Oslo: Solum Fortag, 1988);

Diana Burgin, "Prince Myshkin, the True Lover and 'Impossible Bridegroom': A Problem in Dostoevskian Narrative," *SEEJ,* 27 (1983): 158–175;

Robert L. Busch, *Humor in the Major Novels of F. M. Dostoevsky* (Columbus, Ohio: Slavica, 1987);

Jacques Catteau, *Dostoevsky and the Process of Literary Creation,* translated by Audrey Littlewood (Cambridge: Cambridge University Press, 1989);

Dmitrii Chizhevsky, "K probleme dvoinika (iz knigi o formalizme v etike)," in *O Dostoevskom: Sbornik statei,* volume 1, edited by A. L. Bem (Prague, 1928), pp. 9–38; English translation in *Dostoevsky: A Collection of Critical Essays,* edited by Rene Wellek (Englewood Cliffs, N.J.: Prentice-Hall, 1962);

Elizabeth Dalton, *Unconscious Structure in "The Idiot": A Study in Literature and Psychoanalysis* (Princeton: Princeton University Press, 1979);

Donald Fanger, *Dostoevsky and Romantic Realism: A Study of Dostoevsky in Relation to Balzac, Dickens, and Gogol,* Northwestern University Press Studies in Russian Literature and Theory (Evanston, Ill.: Northwestern University Press, 1998);

André Gide, *Dostoevsky* (New York: New Directions, 1961);

René Girard, *Deceit, Desire, and the Novel: Self and Other in Literary Structure,* translated by Yvonne Freccero (Baltimore: Johns Hopkins University Press, 1965);

David Goldstein, *Dostoevsky and the Jews,* University of Texas Press Slavic Series, no. 3 (Austin & London: University of Texas Press, 1981);

Michael Holquist, *Dostoevsky and the Novel* (Evanston, Ill.: Northwestern University Press, 1977);

Vyacheslav Ivanov, *Freedom and the Tragic Life: A Study in Dostoevsky,* translated by Norman Cameron (New York: Farrar, Straus & Cudahy, 1960);

Robert Louis Jackson, *The Art of Dostoevsky: Deliriums and Nocturnes* (Princeton: Princeton University Press, 1981);

Jackson, *Dialogues with Dostoevsky: The Overwhelming Questions* (Stanford, Cal.: Stanford University Press, 1993);

Jackson, *Dostoevsky's Quest for Form—A Study of His Philosophy of Art* (New Haven: Yale University Press, 1966);

Jackson, *Dostoevsky's Underground Man in Russian Literature,* Slavistic Printings and Reprintings, no. 15 (The Hague: Mouton, 1958);

Sven Linner, *Starets Zosima in "The Brothers Karamazov": A Study in the Mimesis of Virtue,* Stockholm Studies in Russian Literature, 4 (Stockholm: Almqvist and Wiksell, 1975);

Olga Matich, "The Idiot: A Feminist Reading," in *Dostoevsky and the Human Condition after a Century,* Contributions to the Study of World Literature, 16, edited by Alexei Ugrinsky, Frank Lambasa, and Valiia Ozolins (New York: Greenwood Press, 1986);

Robin Feuer Miller, *Dostoevsky and The Idiot: Author, Narrator, and Reader* (Cambridge, Mass.: Harvard University Press, 1981);

Gary Saul Morson, *The Boundaries of Genre: Dostoevsky's Diary of a Writer and the Traditions of Literary Utopia* (Austin: University of Texas Press, 1981);

Harriet Murav, *Holy Foolishness: Dostoevsky's Novels and the Poetics of Cultural Critique* (Stanford, Cal.: Stanford University Press, 1992);

Nina Perlina, *Varieties of Poetic Utterance: Quotation in The Brothers Karamazov* (Lanham, Md.: University Presses of America, 1985);

James Rice, *Dostoevsky and the Healing Art: An Essay in Literary and Medical History* (Ann Arbor, Mich.: Ardis, 1985);

Gary Rosenshield, *Crime and Punishment: The Techniques of the Omniscient Narrator* (Lisse: Peter de Ridder, 1978);

L. M. Rozenblium, *Tvorcheskie dnevniki Dostoevskogo* (Moscow: Nauka, 1981);

Liudmila Saraskina, *Fedor Dostoevsky: Odolenie demonov* (Moscow: Soglasie, 1996);

Vladimir Seduro, *Dostoevski's Image in Russia Today* (Belmont, Mass.: Nordland, 1975);

Victor Terras, *Reading Dostoevsky* (Madison: University of Wisconsin Press, 1998);

Terras, *The Young Dostoevsky, 1846–1849: A Critical Study,* Slavistic Printings and Reprintings, no. 69 (The Hague: Mouton, 1969);

Valentina Evgen'evna Vetlovskaia, "Alyosha Karamazov and the Hagiographic Hero," in *Dostoevsky: New Perspectives,* edited by Robert Louis Jackson (Englewood Cliffs, N.J.: Prentice Hall, 1984), pp. 206–226;

Igor' Volgin, *Poslednii god Dostoevskogo: Istoricheskie zapiski* (Moscow: Sovetskii pisatel', 1986);

René Wellek, ed., *Dostoevsky: A Collection of Critical Essays* (Englewood Cliffs, N.J.: Prentice Hall, 1962);

V. N. Zakharov, ed., *Novye aspekty v izuchenii Dostoevskogo: Sbornik nauchnykh trudov* (Petrozavodsk: Izdatel'stvo Petrozavodskogo universiteta, 1994).

Papers:

Manuscripts, letters, and papers of Fyodor Dostoevsky are located in Moscow in the Manuscript Division of the Russian State Library, the Russian State Archive of Literature and Art (RGALI, formerly TsGALI), and the State Historical Museum, and in St. Petersburg at the Institute of Russian Literature (IRLI, Pushkin House).

Aleksandr Vasil'evich Druzhinin

(8 October 1824 – 19 January 1864)

L. K. Mansour
United States Military Academy

WORKS: *Polin'ka Saks,* in *Sovremennik,* no. 12 (1847), I: 155–228;

Rasskaz Alekseia Dmitricha, in *Sovremennik,* no. 2 (1848), II: 209–304;

Lola Montes, in *Illiustrirovannyi Al'manakh* (1848), II: 1–27—withdrawn from distribution;

Doktor i patsient. Sobranie pisem, dnevnikov i rasskazov. Freilein Vil'gel'mina, in *Sovremennik,* no. 6 (1848), I: 103–158;

Zhiuli, roman v dvukh chastiakh, in *Sovremennik,* no. 1 (1849), I: 5–164;

Sharlotta Sh–ts, istinnoe proisshestvie, in *Sovremennik,* no. 12 (1849), I: 287–312;

Ne vsiakomu slukhu ver'. Komediia dlia domashnego spektakelia, in *Sovremennik,* no. 11 (1850), I: 61–98;

Petergofskii fontan, in *Biblioteka dlia chteniia,* no. 12 (1850), I: 53–112;

Pevitsa, in *Sovremennik,* no. 12 (1851), I: 131–170;

Istoriia odnoi kartiny, in *Sovremennik,* no. 11 (1851), I: 5–28;

Mademoiselle Jeannette, in *Biblioteka dlia chteniia,* no. 12 (1852), I: 167–206;

Dve vstrechi, in *Biblioteka dlia chteniia,* no. 12 (1854), I: 127–154;

Pashen'ka. Provintsial'nyi rasskaz, in *Otechestvennye zapiski,* no. 1 (1854): 5–62;

Dramy iz obydennoi, preimushchestvenno stolichnoi zhizni, part 1, *Razdum'e artista,* in *Sovremennik,* 43, no. 2 (1854), special section: 17–20; part 2, *Opasnye sosedi,* in *Sovremennik,* 44, no. 3 (1854), special section: 38–41;

Derevenskii rasskaz, in *Biblioteka dlia chteniia,* no. 3 (1855), I: 52–94;

Russkii cherkes, in *Biblioteka dlia chteniia,* no. 11 (1855), I: 93–141;

Legenda o kislykh vodakh, in *Sovremennik,* nos. 3–4 (1855), I: 11–85, 241–314;

Iz putevykh rasskazov dorozhnogo cheloveka, in *Biblioteka dlia chteniia,* no. 9 (1856): 41–60; no. 10 (1856): 1–32;

Obruchennye, in *Biblioteka dlia chteniia,* no. 10 (1857), I: 297–346; no. 11 (1857), I: 3–53; no. 12 (1857), I: 73–124;

Aleksandr Vasil'evich Druzhinin

Peterburgskaia idilliia. Povest' v fel'etonnom rode, in *Biblioteka dlia chteniia,* no. 4 (1857): 267–298; no. 5 (1857): 42–75;

Zakat solntsa. Rasskaz beznadezhnogo kholostiaka, in *Vek,* no. 1 (1861): 27–32;

Proshloe leto v derevne, in *Russkii vestnik,* no. 2 (1862), I: 664–702; no. 3 (1862), I: 380–416; nos. 5–6 (1862), I: 42–76, 509–551; nos. 7–8 (1862), I: 67–114, 610–658; no. 9 (1862), I: 197–238.

Editions and Collections: *Sobranie sochinenii A. V. Druzhinina v vos'mi tomakh,* 8 volumes, edited by N. V.

Gerbel' (St. Petersburg: Tipografiia Imperatorskoi Akademii Nauk, 1865–1867);

Polin'ka Saks (Moscow: Goslitizdat, 1955);

Literaturnaia kritika (Moscow: Sovetskaia Rossiia, 1983);

Povesti. Dnevnik (Moscow: Nauka, 1986);

Prekrasnoe i vechnoe (Moscow: Sovremennik, 1988);

Polin'ka Saks. Dnevnik (Moscow: Pravda, 1989).

Edition in English: *Polinka Saks; and, The Story of Aleksei Dmitrich,* translated by Michael R. Katz (Evanston, Ill.: Northwestern University Press, 1992).

PLAY PRODUCTION: *Ne vsiakomu slukhu ver'. Komediia dlia domashnego spektakelia,* Aleksandrinskii Theatre, 1855.

OTHER: "Dramaticheskii fel'eton o fel'etone i fel'etonistakh," in *Russkii fel'eton,* edited by A. V. Zapadavov and E. P. Prokhorov (Moscow: Gosudarstvennoe izdatel'stvo politicheskoi literatury, 1958).

TRANSLATIONS: William Shakespeare, *Korol' Lir,* in *Sovremennik,* no. 12 (1856), I: 169–342; (St. Petersburg, 1857);

Shakespeare, *Koriolan',* in *Biblioteka dlia chteniia,* no. 12, (1858), special section: 1–151;

Shakespeare, *Korol' Richard Tretii,* in *Sovremennik,* no. 5, (1862), special section: 1–170;

Shakespeare, *Korol' Dzhon,* in *Sobranie sochinenii A. V. Druzhinina,* 3 (1865).

SELECTED PERIODICAL PUBLICATIONS:

"Pis'ma inogorodnogo podpischika o russkoi zhurnalistike," in *Sovremennik* (1849–1851, 1854, 1856); *Biblioteka dlia chteniia* (1852–1853, 1856);

Santimental'noe puteshestvie Ivana Chernoknizhnika po peterburgskim dacham, as Ivan Chernoknizhnikov, in *Sovremennik,* no. 7 (1850), VI: 54–74; no. 8 (1850), VI: 177–257; no. 12 (1850), VI: 193–197;

"Pis'ma inogorodnogo podpischika ob angliiskoi literature i zhurnalistike," in *Sovremennik* (1852–1853, 1856); *Biblioteka dlia chteniia* (1856);

"Zametki peterburgskogo turista," in *Sankt-Peterburgskie vedomosti,* nos. 8, 14, 20, 26, 29, 41, 47, 53, 59, 65, 73, 79, 90, 101, 120, 228, 234, 240, 246, 252, 259, 263, 270, 274, 280 (1855); nos. 3, 8, 14, 20, 31, 43, 53, 65, 77, 87, 97 (1856);

"Zametki i uveselitel'nye ocherki peterburgskogo turista," in *Biblioteka dlia chteniia,* no. 11 (1856), VII: 75–92; no. 12 (1856), VII: 179–193; no. 1 (1857), VII: 78– 92; no. 2 (1857), VII: 143–163; no. 10 (1857), VII: 155–168;

"Zametki peterburgskogo turista," in *Vek,* nos. 38–39 (1860);

"Novye zametki peterburgskogo turista," in *Vek,* nos. 1, 3, 5, 7, 9, 11, 13, 15, 17, 24, 42 (1861);

"Uveselitel'no-filosofskie ocherki peterburgskogo turista," in *Severnaia pchela,* nos. 291, 305, 340 (1862); nos. 5, 19 (1863).

Aleksandr Vasil'evich Druzhinin, famous in his time as the author of the enormously popular sentimental tale *Polin'ka Saks* (1847), was also an influential literary critic and polemicist, a widely read essayist and humorist, an unrivaled popularizer and translator of English literature and, for a time, Leo Tolstoy's closest adviser. Druzhinin is best known today as chief defender of "pure art" in a struggle that began in the mid 1850s with radical literary critics. Though ostensibly about aesthetics, this battle, coming just at the end of thirty years of oppressive rule by Czar Nicholas I, was in effect the opening act in the protracted social struggle that culminated in the October Revolution of 1917.

Druzhinin was born into a somewhat atypical family for Russia in the first half of the nineteenth century. His father, Vasilii F. Druzhinin, was an official in the postal treasury. He rose from obscurity through the so-called table of ranks, a civil service merit system instituted by Peter the Great a hundred years previously, to the rank of State Councilor, equal to that of general in the Russian army. This rank secured the privilege of heritable nobility. In 1820 the family took up residence at a sizable estate (about 6,200 acres) not far from St. Petersburg. There was a family legend, propagated until well into the twentieth century, that the father had received it as a reward for saving a chest of government money as Moscow burned around the invading French in 1812. It was, in fact, money from his wife, Mariia Pavlovna Shiriaeva, that bought the property, whereupon it was renamed "Mariinskoe" in her honor. Whatever he himself believed, Druzhinin respected his father greatly while remaining tenderly attached to his mother, with whom he often shared living arrangements to the end of his thirty-nine years. Mariinskoe later became Druzhinin's summer retreat from the yearly cholera epidemics in St. Petersburg and a workshop where he entertained the literary elite of Russia and produced many of his articles, translations, and stories.

Judging from Druzhinin's early writing, which he admitted was heavily autobiographical, his parents' marriage was not a happy one. The mother's infidelities were the subject of gossip among the servants, and the family financial situation slowly deteriorated as the rural economy of Russia, dependent on serf labor, proved less and less viable. As a result, Aleksandr, a hypersensitive child born some eight years after two older brothers, seems early on to have formed a sensitivity to the complications of family life that bordered on aversion. Nevertheless, he received a fair education at the hand of domestic tutors and could speak five languages—including English, French, Italian, and German—by age sixteen. A precocious reader, he had from his earliest years free rein of his father's large personal library. Voltaire and other eighteenth-century philosophers were his early favorites, but he also read German poets, especially Friedrich Schiller and Johann Wolfgang von Goethe; English eighteenth-century novelists; and Latin and Greek classics, most likely in French translation.

In 1840 Druzhinin's parents determined he should follow his father into civil service, and they enrolled him in the Corps of Pages, a boarding school for boys from noble families, where he studied for four miserable years. At the Corps of Pages a source of constant embarrassment and shame for him was that his father had earned his patents of nobility, rather than being born to them. Boys born to families with ancient lineage took every opportunity to remind lower-born bench mates of their inferior status. To compound the misery, Druzhinin's father's death the year following his son's entry into the corps led for a time to the family's impoverishment and temporary loss of their estate. From the experiences he describes in stories set in thinly disguised replicas of the corps, Druzhinin apparently developed an abiding disdain for aristocratic "ninnies" and resolved that he would at all costs learn to beat them at their own game. He emerged from the corps affecting all the manners of an elegantly dressed, perfectly polished English gentleman—a style perennially favored by young blades in Russia since the end of the Napoleonic Wars. More importantly for his work as a writer, he began searching during this time, primarily in the arts and literature, for a way to mimic the absolute imperturbability and equanimity of an English gentleman in all his dealings with the world.

Graduates of the corps were eligible for a range of prestigious military and government posts; consequently, though he had no real interest in military service, Druzhinin decided to join his older brothers in the Finland Guards Regiment. His military colleagues quickly discerned in him a love for reading coupled with a glaring unsuitability to military duties and made him regimental librarian, in which capacity he began three years of intense study of European literature. Judging by the references in *Polin'ka Saks,* which he published toward the end of his military service, he was reading everything from the plays of William Shakespeare and tales by François Rabelais to novels by George Sand and tracts by Pierre-Joseph Proudhon and other radical writers. While many of the young Russian writers who later became famous in the Golden Age of Russian prose were studying German speculative philosophy in courses at the state universities in St. Petersburg and Moscow or in the famous "philosophical circles" that formed separately from official classes, Druzhinin immersed himself in authors who were heavily influenced by British empiricist philosophy with its emphasis on sensation and feeling. As a result, though he soon made fast friends and lifelong colleagues among the university crowd, his political and aesthetic views developed along paths more down-to-earth than those of his contemporaries.

In late winter of 1847, his last year in the Finland Guards, Druzhinin published in the widely read thick journal *Sovremennik* (The Contemporary) his first major work, an epistolary novel titled *Polin'ka Saks.* It was a huge success. Vissarion Grigor'evich Belinsky, chief critic at the journal and the arbiter of literary merit for most of reading Russia, greeted its publication warmly, finding Polin'ka's psychological portrait particularly deep. Female readers from across the empire seemed especially to appreciate the freedom the author had given his young heroine, Polin'ka, to find her own way in life. Far from being a feminist, even for his own time (for example, he believed women incapable of writing poetry), Druzhinin was keen to show the pernicious effects of the "finishing" undergone by young women in the "noble ladies' institutes" and young women's pensions of patriarchal Russia.

Polin'ka's husband, the other major figure in the novel, is a worldly-wise and industrious government official named Konstantin Saks, a composite of all the honest government workers Druzhinin, as a boy, had observed gathered around his father's table. A veteran of war in the Caucasus, Saks is plainspoken and rational, chaste and fair, though not without a certain tendency toward impatience. He takes on the exasperating task of instructing the thoughtful yet naive young Polin'ka in the higher life of the mind. Druzhinin's villain, Prince Galitsky, is a feckless and cynical former lover who reappears just as Saks is leaving for the provinces on business. The story line is borrowed quite consciously from *Jacques* (1834), a novel by Sand. At one point Saks even gives Polin'ka Sand's early novels to read, but as a sign of Polin'ka's limited life experience, she soon grows tired of them and throws them aside. In this way Druzhinin signals that Sand's story is necessary not so much to supply conceits for a clever tale as to reveal the complexity of his characters' psychology.

The reckless and destructive behavior of the upper class of Russia receives special criticism in the novel. The prince's sister, a bored and depraved aristocratic tart, toys with Polin'ka's emotions, fanning the embers of her superficial attraction to the prince into a

Vasilii Petrovich Botkin, Ivan Sergeevich Turgenev, and Druzhinin in 1855 (drawing by Dmitrii Vasil'evich Grigorovich, from Russkie pisateli, 1800–1917: Biograficheskii slovar', *volume 2, 1992)*

consuming flame that ravages her honest devotion to Saks and ruins her family. The prince has been spoiled by the privileges of class to the point that he can slyly comment on his "greatness and power" as he lies at Polin'ka's feet, sobbing about his love for her.

The central problem of the story, however, is Polin'ka's need to transcend the infantile stage of development in which a pseudoeducation has left her. Just as her decency and innocence remain unaltered from childhood, so, too, do her judgment, reason, and taste—a condition that leads inexorably to unfortunate consequences. When Prince Galitsky first reappears, Polin'ka feels only a generous pity for him, and her decency transforms Galitsky's lust to possess her into something approaching sincere love. By this time in his life, though, Druzhinin had adopted Voltaire's skepticism about the power of naive goodness. In time, the prince persuades Polin'ka to respond in kind to his transformed affection, and their affair is found out. According to societal and literary norms of the day, the betrayed husband has no choice but to demand satisfaction for lost honor. But true to his liberal ideals of personal freedom, Druzhinin gives all the main figures the ability to rise above such limitations. Though suffering great torment, Saks determines to step aside and allow

the lovers to choose for themselves how to live. Polin'ka's emotions and insight begin to mature, and her growing up leads to a renewed and deeper love for Saks. Even the prince, whose scheming, lust, and vanity are the emblems of the stock aristocratic rape-artist in Romantic tales, shows new facets of his personality, adding solicitude for Polin'ka's safety once they are found out and admiration for Saks's self-effacement and compassion for his new wife when she falls ill. Still, neither of the two young lovers quite survives being given the responsibility to live as the heart dictates. Polin'ka dies of consumption; the prince is left to wander Europe alone; and Saks retires from the service to a life in the provinces.

Polin'ka Saks influenced an entire generation of Russians. When Tolstoy in 1891 replied to a request to provide a recommended reading list, among a handful of other titles he remembered *Polin'ka Saks* as a novel that had made a "very great" impression on him at age twenty. At the time of its publication he would have been the same age as the prince and intimately acquainted with the life such people led. Tormented by his own imitation of that life, he probably recognized in the social and family issues raised in the story the same questions he was posing to himself in diary entries, letters, and notes, and which appeared in all his novels starting with *Semeinoe schast'e* (Family Happiness, 1859).

Druzhinin published his second major work of fiction, *Rasskaz Alekseia Dmitricha* (Aleksei Dmitrich's Story), in 1848, also in *Sovremennik*. At first glance the story is merely another account of a sensitive boy's coming of age. But this novella is also a closely observed comparison of radically different ways of child-rearing and a meditation on the tragedy that is family life among the middling *dvorianstvo* (service nobility) of Russia. In the course of five "evenings" Aleksei tells the story of his upbringing in a house filled with bickering and petty scandal. Sent to a boarding school, he becomes fast friends with Kostia, a free-spirited boy whose desultory upbringing in the Russian countryside has followed, quite accidentally, the principles Jean-Jacques Rousseau prescribed in his *Emile* (1762). Druzhinin uses this fictional setting to evaluate the relative merits of a family life purged of the flaws he had come to know only too well in his own upbringing. Judging from Aleksei's abortive love affair with Verinka, Kostia's equally independent sister, which fails largely as a result of her own family entanglements, Druzhinin held out little hope for any solution to this question. In his own life, though his journals often refer to his strong attraction to women and theirs to him, he never once seriously contemplated marriage.

Druzhinin's subsequent stories and novellas tended more and more toward Dostoevskian themes as he examined the psychology of his characters, finding ever deeper conflict between the rational mind and the will. His novella *Lola Montes* was ready for publication in March of 1848 but was abruptly withdrawn and published only after his death. The censor objected to the "anti-family" tendency evinced in the heroine Lola's moderately sadistic dreams of vengeance on the older man to whom her parents had married her. In the next two years Druzhinin published half a dozen other short stories and novellas with equally dark themes. The most successful, *Petergofskii fontan* (Peterhof Fountain), was based on a story of infidelity, incest, and suicide that he had heard among his acquaintances. Heavily censored, it was barely recognizable to the author himself when it was printed in December of 1850.

With the relative success of his early literary works, Druzhinin became a regular contributor to *Sovremennik*. His intense though short-lived friendship with Belinsky, the leading critic of the journal, his knowledge of foreign literatures, and his unabashed love for Russian writing placed him in direct line to become chief literary critic when Belinsky died of consumption in early 1848. Druzhinin's new position was complicated immediately by the reaction of the Russian government to anti-monarchist uprisings throughout

Europe in the same year, known as the "Springtime of the Nations." In Hungary the revolts were suppressed at the point of Russian bayonets, and Czar Nicholas I, determined to quarantine the democratic contagion, initially closed many "westernizing" journals in St. Petersburg and Moscow, suspecting them of "seditious thinking." *Sovremennik* was chief among them. The czar strengthened the censorship bureau and forbade the publication of work that touched on sensitive topics, specifically disallowing references to government bureaucracy, the church, or the sanctity of family life, which were precisely Druzhinin's topics.

In this fear-filled atmosphere, with the best Russian writers silenced, the young critic turned his readers' attention abroad. But he felt that simply to report on works by foreign writers was not enough. Instead, Druzhinin attempted to fill the gaps in cultural understanding that gave Russian readers difficulty in understanding fully what they read. He wrote a series called *Galereia zamechatel'nykh pisatelei* (Gallery of Great Writers, 1851) and later added other critical biographies spiked with lengthy translated passages to introduce the figures from English literature worthy of attention in pre-emancipation Russia. Among them were the satirical playwright Richard Sheridan, the critic Samuel Johnson, the satirist William Makepeace Thackeray, the historical novelist Walter Scott, the proto-realist poet George Crabbe, the American novelist James Fenimore Cooper, and the essayist Ralph Waldo Emerson. In all his essays Druzhinin promoted the values of clear expression, craftsmanship, and "the absence of phrases," by which he meant sincerity. For example, Crabbe, whose story "Peter Grimes" (1810) was made into an opera one hundred thirty-five years later, was praised by Druzhinin for the affectionate though unflinching realism with which he depicted life in the English countryside.

In these same years Druzhinin began a series of feuilletons for *Sovremennik* initially titled *Pis'ma inogorodnogo podpischika* (Letters from an Out-of-town Subscriber, 1849–1856). The feuilleton, a mixed genre imported from French journalism in the 1840s, refined features of the cultural events review, the essay, the humorous sketch, and the gossip column. The main function of this series, as Druzhinin saw it, was to educate public taste in a pleasurable way. At first he reviewed Russian journals, but as the censorship bureau made presenting these critiques increasingly complicated, he turned to reviewing Western European periodicals, particularly British journals, such as the *Edinburgh Review* and *Blackwood's Magazine,* often commenting on the Russian scene under the cover of stories about literary conflicts abroad. In his reports on foreign journals, he tended to side with critics such as Théophile Gautier in France, who eschewed woolly philosophical speculation for impressionistic descriptions of the feelings elicited by an opera, play, or novel; or Francis, Lord Jeffrey, the leading British cultural critic, who believed that pleasure encountered in a work of art arose directly from personal associations stimulated in the observer's memory.

With the death of Czar Nicholas I in 1855, however, serious literary and social questions could again be addressed in public. Druzhinin immediately became embroiled in a controversy over the utility of art with radical materialist critics led by Nikolai Gavrilovich Chernyshevsky, a priest's son turned radical publicist, who had just joined *Sovremennik*. The radicals demanded that all artistic effort be turned toward solving the social problems of Russia. For them, literature was a surrogate for real life, a kind of teaching aid needed to instruct those who had not learned logic or did not know how to read a textbook. Druzhinin countered, in a series of critical articles, that good writers approached subjects with no conscious intent to teach anything. Instead, they sought to show what did or was likely to happen in life, without conforming their vision to the beliefs of any movement or school, much less any political party. Druzhinin encapsulated his ideas in the phrase *chistoe i svobodnoe tvorchestvo* (pure and autonomous creativity). Precisely at that time Pavel Vasil'evich Annenkov, a friend and collaborator at *Sovremennik,* was publishing materials for a biography and authoritative edition of works by the poet Aleksandr Sergeevich Pushkin. In a lengthy review of this project published in March 1855 under the title "A. S. Pushkin: Poslednee izdanie ego sochinenii" (A. S. Pushkin and the Recent Publication of his Works), Druzhinin seized on Pushkin as the Russian exemplar of a "pure artist." Druzhinin wrote that Pushkin's nature comprised a harmony of all the necessary characteristics of a true poet: passion, a fine memory, and abiding curiosity, tempered by northern "phlegmatism" that curbed excessive idealism and dispelled illusions about the world. Pushkin himself had often claimed for himself the freedom Druzhinin touted: "Poet, crave not the public's love" read the first line of one oft-quoted poem from 1835. All great art was true to life, Druzhinin wrote, confident that any reader of good faith and sufficient life experience would know what that was. For him there could be no diverging from the truth, no false coloration, neither darker nor lighter than things appeared in life. He roundly criticized writers of the "Natural School," ostensibly imitators of Nikolai Gogol's satires on venal bureaucrats, provincial boors, and urban would-be social climbers, who had developed among Russian readers a taste for socially engaged literature. In a programmatic article in the journal *Biblioteka dlia chteniia* (Library for Reading) titled "Kritika gogolevskogo perioda russkoi literatury i nashi k nei otnosheniia" (Our Criticism of the Gogol

Period of Russian Literature, 1856), Druzhinin countered that the grotesque characters and plots of the "School," so often praised by Belinsky and other proponents of socially engaged literature, did not exist anywhere in reality, and therefore, were mere "fantasies," the daydreams of scribblers whose first and only purpose in writing was to teach some political lesson.

Despite a long history of vilification by radical critics and Soviet-era commentators, Druzhinin's "Pushkinian School" was only distantly related to the "art-for-art's-sake" movement promoted by more extreme aesthetes in the West. He agreed with his radical opponents that literature in Russia played an important role in that it was the only forum for public debate on social issues. But anything worth teaching, Druzhinin wrote, would automatically be conveyed by a dispassionate portrayal of things as they were, with all the dynamic contradictions of their beauties and faults.

In November 1855, in the midst of this fight, the arrival of young Leo Tolstoy had a galvanizing effect on the "liberals" of *Sovremennik*. Druzhinin and his colleagues—such as Nikolai Alekseevich Nekrasov (the chief editor for the journal and a renowned poet), Ivan Sergeevich Turgenev (one of Russia's greatest story writers), and Vasilii Petrovich Botkin (well known for his articles and essays on European culture)—saw in Tolstoy's realistic prose a potent antidote to the excesses of the Natural School. But among these exquisitely educated sophisticates, Tolstoy, fresh from battle in the Crimea and the Caucasus, seemed determined from the start to play the "provincial gentleman." Affecting a touchy sense of self-worth, he scandalized the urbane crowd at *Sovremennik* with his categorical, if largely uninformed, disdain for the opera, Shakespeare's plays, and Homer. Druzhinin, too, was at first shocked, then amused, and finally intrigued by the young writer's diatribes. A careful observer of character, Druzhinin could see that precisely because educated Russians venerated Western cultural goods, Tolstoy felt duty-bound to denigrate them. Druzhinin admired and openly envied Tolstoy's independence of judgment and lust for life, giving the young artillery officer a dashing Caucasian nickname, "bashibuzuk" (head-breaker), a term he had likely heard among the veterans back at the Finland Guards. Leafing through Tolstoy's diary from the period makes plain that trips to gypsy camps outside the capital, gaming tables of aristocratic salons, and brothels in the poorer quarters took up quite as much time as arguments about literature. Despite signs of incipient tuberculosis as early as 1850, Druzhinin was well-known in his circle as a reveler and was often the one who showed Tolstoy around the darker corners of the capital. In his own journal from the period, Druzhinin jokingly referred to these excursions as *chernoknizhie*

Contributors to Sovremennik *(The Contemporary) in March 1856: (seated) Ivan Aleksandrovich Goncharov, Ivan Sergeevich Turgenev, Druzhinin,
and Aleksandr Nikolaevich Ostrovsky; (standing) Leo Tolstoy and Dmitrii Vasil'evich Grigorovich*

(black arts) and included them in the slightly fictionalized reports from the demimonde and other St. Petersburg haunts, variously signed "Ivan Chernoknizhnikov"
or "Petersburg Tourist," pseudonyms he had first used in
Sovremennik in 1850. Druzhinin infused these feuilletons with an Epicurean worldview according to
which equanimity was to be found, even in the
worst of times, in poetry, light humor, and the company of friends and "congenial" women. Already
before Tolstoy's arrival, stories by Druzhinin of
"Ivan" and other *Sovremennik* contributors under
mildly humorous pseudonyms were entertaining
readers at *Sankt-Peterburgskie vedomosti* (St. Petersburg
News), a local St. Petersburg paper. Tolstoy appears
under the name "Khaldeev" (roughly translated as
"Mr. Magician").

Druzhinin came to exercise a strong influence on
Tolstoy, who was attracted to Druzhinin's direct way of
addressing issues and evident erudition, a fact that has
been disputed by only the most obstinate of radical and
Soviet commentators. Druzhinin and Tolstoy's collaboration was particularly intense in 1856 when the two
men were meeting almost daily, sometimes twice in the
same day, as Druzhinin advised Tolstoy in detail concerning works in progress. For example, upon reading
Tolstoy's autobiographical story "Iunost'" (Youth,
1857), Druzhinin cautioned Tolstoy against an overreli-
ance on subtle physical traits in characterizing a psychology. "At times," he chided Tolstoy in one letter, "it
seems you are ready to claim that the shape of some
character's thighs somehow indicates clearly his desire
to travel to India."

He framed a public response to Tolstoy's work in
three articles published in 1856 in *Biblioteka dlia chteniia:*
"'Metel', 'Dva gusara'. Povesti grafa L. N. Tolstogo"
("The Snowstorm," "Two Hussars." Tales by Count
L. N. Tolstoy), "'Ocherki iz krest'ianskogo byta' A. F.
Pisemskogo" (Sketches from Peasant Life by A. F.

Pisemsky), and "'Voennye rasskazy' grafa L. N. Tolstogo" (War Stories by Count L. N. Tolstoy), in which he heaped special praise on Tolstoy's widely admired *Sevastopol'skie rasskazy* (Sevastopol Stories, 1855–1856). Druzhinin found Tolstoy's account of the quiet fortitude of Russian soldiery far superior to any writing in English journals on the same campaign. Tolstoy, he wrote, was able to depict each participant on the battlefield as an individual, without recourse to the "types" so common in less capable writing. Busy at the same time translating *King Lear* (1605), the first of his long-lived translations from Shakespeare, Druzhinin told friends that he was working daily to turn the obstinate young author toward a reexamination of the classics he claimed to despise, in particular Shakespeare. He sensed in Tolstoy a comparable talent for drawing distinct, "three-dimensional" characters. In print he praised Tolstoy above all, though, for eschewing the kind of voyeuristic "daguerreotype" writing common to war reporting that makes the battlefield just another exotic place readers may visit for a moment. He found that Tolstoy, far from alienating the readers from the events described, allowed them to feel what soldiers felt during a bombardment or while advancing under fire. Druzhinin claimed Tolstoy's talent was a "rare confluence of powerful analysis and refined poetry," combined with closely observed life experiences. He wrote that Tolstoy succeeded in depicting the soldier's life at Sevastopol, or the landowner's dealings with his peasants, because he himself had taken part in events similar to those narrated. Druzhinin strongly urged Tolstoy to develop the last theme, because little of worth had been written about country life from the point of view of the gentry, though they were central to the social reality of Russia. The seeds of this advice apparently fell on fertile soil, if the "Levin" chapters in *Anna Karenina* (1873–1877), written twenty years later, are any indication.

Later, in May 1858, Druzhinin advised Tolstoy against a plan conceived with his close friend, the poet of refined personal verses Afanasii Afanas'evich Fet, to publish a literary journal that would promote "eternal values" in art. While supporting the idea in principle, Druzhinin knew well the obstacles confronting such a project. Beginning in April 1856 he had taken over general editorial responsibility for the moribund journal *Biblioteka dlia chteniia,* with the intent of employing it to woo the public away from the radicals. But in the years leading up to emancipation of the serfs in 1861, radicalism among literate Russians was on the rise. In such an atmosphere Druzhinin's signature evenhandedness, his distaste for personal attacks, and a preference for gradualist politics were not calculated to win subscriptions for his journal. Amply forewarned, Tolstoy abandoned his own publishing plans. Yet, in 1859, still intent on converting public taste to writing that "speaks to all readers of all time," he addressed the *Obshchestvo liubitelei rossiiskoi slovesnosti* (Society of Lovers of Russian Literature), repeating Druzhinin's warning that politically involved literature was inherently ephemeral. When in October 1859 Tolstoy decided to "quit literature for good," Druzhinin, attempting to dissuade him, wrote, "You are one of four or five writers all Russia looks to for a way forward" in both literature and social questions. But literary celebrity in St. Petersburg had not brought Tolstoy the kind of emotional warmth or inner peace he apparently craved. He complained especially bitterly about Druzhinin's coldness, and later commentators have noted similarities between Druzhinin's forced humor and aloofness and Tolstoy's subsequent depiction of Speransky in *Voina i mir* (War and Peace, 1863–1869) and later, of Anna Karenina's stiff and dessicated bureaucrat husband.

Druzhinin's light sarcasm and gentlemanly moderation won him enemies on both the left and the right. Fyodor Dostoevsky never quite forgave Druzhinin for his flippant, though substantially accurate, review of Dostoevsky's early stories "Belye nochi" (White Nights, 1848) and *Netochka Nezvanova* (as yet incomplete in 1849). Druzhinin wrote that however unclear the world was to the main characters themselves, Dostoevsky as author had an obligation to make their image clear, giving the reader more concrete details. Dostoevsky responded with nasty caricatures of Druzhinin over the next ten years, particularly in the story *Selo Stepanchikovo i ego obitateli* (The Village of Stepanchikovo and its Inhabitants, 1859). He seems, nevertheless, to have taken Druzhinin's criticisms to heart when rearranging earlier works for republication. Druzhinin did not live to see Dostoevsky's best work, which began to appear only in the mid 1860s.

After 1860 Druzhinin's health faltered, forcing him to give up editorship of *Biblioteka dlia chteniia.* Yet, he continued to write—publishing dozens of articles, translations, and feuilletons—mostly having to do with foreign literature and politics. Druzhinin's biographers note that while in 1848 reactionary censorship forced Druzhinin to stop writing about Russian literature and take up European writing, twelve years later radical public opinion forced him to do the same. For a time he did take on joint editorial duties at *Vek* (The Age), a journal designed to educate and inform members of the fledgling Russian middle class. At the same time he reviewed British literary happenings and wrote on the American Civil War for *Russkii vestnik* (Russian Herald), *Sankt-Peterburgskie vedomosti* (St. Petersburg News), and other papers.

In this same period Druzhinin brought to fruition his plans for an *Obshchestvo dlia posobiia nuzhdaiushchimsia literatoram i uchenym* (Literary Fund for Destitute Writers and Scholars). He had first published a design for the fund in November of 1857, moved by the success of a similar institution in Great Britain. In a coup of personal diplomacy perhaps only he could have brought off, Druzhinin reconciled all competing literary "parties" just long enough to found this organization, which thrived under various names into the 1990s. Similarly, Druzhinin's funeral in the winter of 1864 following his death from tuberculosis on 19 January was occasion for a reconciliation between Turgenev and Ivan Aleksandrovich Goncharov, both contributors to *Sovremennik* and friends of Druzhinin who had been feuding for years. Though in the last years he had been estranged from Druzhinin, Nekrasov also appeared at the funeral to eulogize him.

For decades after his death, Druzhinin remained in disrepute among the left-leaning and later among Soviet commentators. His views were systematically simplified, his legacy reduced to the "salon sensibility" said to characterize his feuilletons. At the same time, his more serious articles went unprinted until the 1970s. Now that his writing can be examined with more objectivity, Druzhinin's work is enjoying something of a revival in Russian studies. He is recognized for having written with an evenhandedness and erudition rare for his time that make his best work still worth reading.

Letters:

Pis'ma k A. V. Druzhininu (1850–1863), edited by P. S. Popov (Moscow: Gosudarstvennyi Literaturnyi Muzei, 1948).

Biography:

Anmartin-Mihal Brojde, *A. V. Druzhinin: Zhizn' i tvorchestvo* (Copenhagen: Rosenkilde & Bagger, 1986)—includes an overview in English, pp. 494–504.

References:

N. Belchikov, "P. V. Annenkov, A. V. Druzhinin i S. S. Dudishkin," *Ocherki po istorii russkoi kritiki,* edited by A. Lunacharsky (Moscow: Gosudarstvennoe Izdatel'stvo, 1929), pp. 263–304;

Anmartin-Mihal Brojde, "Better Late Than Never," *Soviet Studies in Literature,* 11, no. 4 (Fall 1975): 3–19;

Brojde, "Druzhinin's View of American Life and Literature," *Canadian-American Slavic Studies,* 10, no. 3 (Fall 1976): 382–399;

Brojde, "Perceptions of Shakespeare by A. V. Druzhinin," in *We and They* (Copenhagen: Rosenkilde & Bagger, 1984), pp. 63–71;

Brojde, "A. V. Druzhinin: Zhizn' i tvorchestvo" (Copenhagen: Rosenkilde & Bagger, 1986);

Kornei Chukovsky, "Tolstoi i Druzhinin v 60-kh godax," *Liudi i knigi 60-kh godov* (Moscow: Gosizdat, 1934);

Boris F. Egorov, *Bor'ba esteticheskikh idei v Rossii serediny XIX veka* (Leningrad: Iskusstvo, 1982), pp. 48–136;

Boris Eikhenbaum, "Nasledie Belinskogo i L'va Tolstogo," *Voprosy literatury,* 4 (June 1961): 124–148;

George Genereux, "Alexander Druzhinin's Writings on English Literature," dissertation, University of California, Los Angeles, 1968;

Genereux, "The Crisis in Russian Literary Criticism: 1856–the Decisive Year," *Russian Literary Triquarterly,* 17 (1982): 117–140;

Charles A. Moser, *Esthetics as Nightmare: Russian Literary Theory 1855–70* (Princeton: Princeton University Press, 1989);

Derek Offord, *Portraits of Early Russian Liberals: A Study of the Thought of T. N. Granovsky, V. P. Botkin, P. V. Annenkov, A. V. Druzhinin and K. D. Kaverin* (Cambridge: Cambridge University Press, 1985);

Helen Szyrman Shulak, "Aleksandr Druzhinin and His Place in Russian Criticism," dissertation, University of California, Berkeley, 1967.

Papers:

Most of Aleksandr Vasil'evich Druzhinin's letters, drafts for published and unpublished works, and personal notes are held by the Russian State Archive for Literature and the Arts (RGALI, formerly TsGALI) in Moscow, Russian Federation. Some materials can be found at the Tolstoy Museum in Moscow and in the Russian National Library in St. Petersburg.

Ekaterina Oskarovna Dubrovina

(29 May 1846 – 10 January 1913)

Judith E. Kalb
University of South Carolina

WORKS: *Sfinks, Delo,* nos. 10–12 (1877); (St. Petersburg, 1877);

Peterburgskaia l'vitsa. Povest' iz velikosvetskoi zhizni (St. Petersburg: Tip. A. Transhelia, 1878);

Nemizida. Original'nyi roman (1880);

Ocherki i rasskazy (St. Petersburg: V. V. Komarov, 1884);

V tumane zhizni (St. Petersburg: V. V. Komarov, 1884);

Zakoronelyi (St. Petersburg: V. V. Komarov, 1884);

Zhenskaia mest' (St. Petersburg, 1884);

Mertvetsy-mstiteli. Roman-khronika (St. Petersburg, 1888);

Chertova kuklia. Istoricheskaia povest' (St. Petersburg, 1889);

Dve povesti: I. Pod kashtanami. II. Sovremennaia Tsirtseia (St. Petersburg, 1889);

Rukhnuvshii velikan (St. Petersburg, 1889);

Opal'nyi. Istoricheskii roman v 2-kh ch. (St. Petersburg, 1890);

Ot plakhi k pochesti. Istoricheskii roman iz epokhi zavoevanii Sibiri (St. Petersburg, 1890);

Chem zhit'? in *Russkoe bogatstvo,* no. 10 (1890); (St. Petersburg: A. A. Kaspari, 1910);

Cherez dvadtsat' let (St. Petersburg, 1891);

Zasluzhennaia kara. Istoricheskii roman vremen Arakcheeva (St. Petersburg: Rodina, 1891);

Iz t'my vekov. Istoricheskii roman (St. Petersburg, 1892);

Sila dolga (St. Petersburg, 1892);

Beskrovnaia mest'. Istoricheskii roman (St. Petersburg, 1894);

Zhertva trekh chestoliubii. Istoricheskii roman (St. Petersburg: A. A. Kaspari, 1897);

Na Petrovskom zavode. Vospominaniia E. O. Dubrovinoi (St. Petersburg: Izdatel', 1898);

Bez viny–rasplata (Moscow: Univ. tip., 1899);

Opomnilas' (St. Petersburg: V. V. Komarov, 1899);

Pobeda liubvi (Moscow: Univ. tip., 1899);

Pod natiskom strasti (St. Petersburg: A. A. Kaspari, 1899);

Chudnaia (St. Petersburg: A. A. Kaspari, 1900);

Babushkiny vnusheniia (St. Petersburg: A. A. Kaspari, 1901);

Pod gnetom zastoia (St. Petersburg: A. A. Kaspari, 1902);

Pod shum zimnei v'iugi. Rasskazy (Moscow, 1902);

Romany, povesti, i rasskazy (St. Petersburg, 1902);

Ekaterina Oskarovna Dubrovina

Otzhivaiushchie tipy. Rasskazy. I. Iz mraka k svetu. II. Tikhie vody (St. Petersburg: A. A. Kaspari, 1903);

Liubov' (St. Petersburg: A. A. Kaspari, 1904);

U Tarasovoi gory. Rasskaz (St. Petersburg: A. A. Kaspari, 1904);

Sobranie sochinenii, 11 volumes (St. Petersburg, 1910–1911);

Gipnoz–popustitel'. Roman iz Tiflisskoi ugolovnoi khroniki (Tiflis: Rossinchukova, 1911);

Pristroilas'. Rasskaz; Deti gor. Rasskaz; Gadanie. Rasskaz (St. Petersburg: A. A. Kaspari, 1911);

V tenetakh liubvi (St. Petersburg: A. A. Kaspari, 1913).

SELECTED PERIODICAL PUBLICATION:
"Pamiati M. L. Mikhailova," in *Beseda,* no. 12 (1905); republished in *Vospominaniia,* by N. V. Shelgunov, L. P. Shelgunova, and M. L. Mikhailov, volume 2 (Moscow, 1967).

One of the first female professional writers in Russia, Ekaterina Oskarovna Dubrovina is significant both for the extent of her creative output and for the popularity she enjoyed with the reading public during the last decades of the nineteenth century. An incomplete listing of her works in 1900 showed that Dubrovina already had produced more than forty novels as well as equivalent numbers of novellas and short stories. Published in a variety of journals and newspapers, her tales feature characters ranging from coldhearted, shallow society maidens to oppressed and poverty-stricken women "of the people." In addition to treating contemporary themes, particularly those involving women, Dubrovina also wrote historical novels; among her chosen topics were Ivan the Terrible's Russia and the reign of Czar Alexander I.

Dubrovina was born Ekaterina Oskarovna Deikhman on 29 May 1846 in Irkutsk, Siberia, and grew up on the eastern side of Lake Baikal at the Petrovsk ironworks factory managed by her father, Oskar Aleksandrovich Deikhman. According to Dubrovina's memoir *Na Petrovskom zavode* (At the Petrovsk Factory, 1898), Oskar Deikhman was "an attractive blond, with a kind, open face of the purely Germanic type." Well liked by his employees and valued by friends as "a man of broad intellect, magnificent heart, and a rare goodness of spirit," Deikhman devoted himself to the Petrovsk factory to such an extent that it became the central ironworks factory of Eastern Siberia. He later directed a similar factory in Nerchinsk. Dubrovina's paternal grandmother, Ekaterina Pavlovna Mevius, was a proud descendant of Martin Luther and raised her children as Lutherans. She objected to her son Oskar's marriage to a poverty-stricken noblewoman, but Dubrovina's mother, Aleksandra Petrovna, was a devoted spouse and parent, possessed of "beauty, a mind, and a loving heart," as her daughter later wrote. According to Dubrovina's portrayal in *Na Petrovskom zavode,* Aleksandra Petrovna maintained a warm and hospitable home. Frequent guests at the Deikhmans' included Ivan Ivanovich Gorbachevsky, a nobleman who had taken part in the Decembrist uprising of 1825 and had as a result been banished to Siberia.

The young "Katichka" Deikhman received her schooling at home; among her tutors were the revolutionary thinkers Fedor Nikolaevich L'vov and Mikhail Larionovich Mikhailov, as well as Gorbachevsky. In 1862 the sixteen-year-old Dubrovina's life changed abruptly: Oskar Deikhman was arrested after a political denunciation, an event that does not enter into Dubrovina's exalted descriptions of him and his future career path in *Na Petrovskom zavode.* Deikhman's name was cleared four years later, perhaps as a result of his wife's concerted efforts to convince the authorities in St. Petersburg of her husband's innocence. During this period Ekaterina married the engineer Nikolai Nikolaevich Dubrovin, who had become manager of the Petrovsk factory when Oskar Deikhman had moved to Nerchinsk. Dubrovin was a practical, smart, and honest man and a hard worker, his wife later wrote, but he had "three weaknesses: wine, women, and hunting." The marriage did not last: Dubrovina left her husband several years after the wedding. The couple had one daughter, born after the marriage had already dissolved.

Dubrovina moved to St. Petersburg, where she graduated from the St. Petersburg Higher Women's Courses. Acquainted from her youth with proponents of social change, Dubrovina hosted a "revolutionary salon" during this period and came under suspicion by the government authorities, whereupon she was arrested and exiled briefly. She went on to work at various professions, including midwifery, before settling upon writing as her intended path. The work Dubrovina considered the start of her literary career, the novel *Sfinks* (The Sphinx, 1877), was devoted to the unsatisfactory lot of a middle-class woman. The novel met with poor reviews: Dubrovina's choice of theme and her style were criticized sharply. Dubrovina, however, was far from discouraged, and she continued for the next decades to support herself through her writing, publishing her works under a variety of pseudonyms as well as her own married name.

As Mary Zirin notes, several of Dubrovina's early works are devoted to the wealthy upper classes of St. Petersburg; plot dominates characterization. One such work is *Peterburgskaia l'vitsa. Povest' iz velikosvetskoi zhizni* (The Lioness of St. Petersburg: A Story from the Haut Monde, 1878). At the beginning of the novel a chatty narrator invites the reader into a sumptuous drawing room filled with the idle rich, identified by their titles or fortunes. Chief among these French-speaking Russian aristocrats is the heroine, Valentina Aleksandrovna Saltykova, alone in the capital city while her parents are in Italy. "Pride, vanity, and ambition were developed in her to the highest degree," the narrator states, and then continues rather unfelicitously, "she had no heart, and if she did have one, then she did not have much of one."

The plot revolves around Saltykova's various conquests, who include the sympathetic but rather spineless Sergei Nikolaevich Dobriansky. In a particularly unpleasant act of manipulation, Saltykova convinces Dobriansky to give up a medallion with a picture of his longtime companion, Mar'ia Sergeevna Gorskaia, a hardworking, honest young woman. Thoroughly smitten with Saltykova, Dobriansky capitulates and ends up leaving Gorskaia. Others who fall prey to the "lioness" include the Italian Luigi and the Russian Dmitrii Andreevich Gavrilovsky. The latter, initially resistant to Saltykova's charms, ends up proposing to her, only to have her laugh at him "with a smile of victory." Upon this rejection Gavrilovsky flees to join the army and court danger. Saltykova receives a comeuppance of sorts when one attractive young man, Viktor Petrovich Antonov, rebukes her for her treatment of Gavrilovsky and ends up marrying Gorskaia. A jealous (but somehow unchastened) Saltykova heads off to join her parents in Italy, deigning to permit Dobriansky to follow her hopelessly and desperately. The language of the story is simple, and the plot is predictable. Antonov and the virtuous Gorskaia, one assumes, will live happily ever after, while Saltykova will continue to torture Dobriansky and anyone else she can. Dubrovina's later novella *Sovremennaia Tsirtseia* (A Modern Circe, 1889) features a similarly heartless female leading character who also torments an infatuated group of men.

In 1884 Dubrovina's collection *Ocherki i rasskazy* (Sketches and Stories) was published. As Zirin comments, the stories "became increasingly sophisticated as Dubrovina learned her craft." "Spartanka" (The Spartan Woman), with the epigraph "Noblesse oblige," features as its title character the wealthy, aristocratic military widow Mar'ia Nikolaevna Glovbich, who has lived in Paris and enjoys attending balls. The plot is set in motion when Mar'ia Nikolaevna asks her daughter Nellie why she is constantly reading: "That's not necessary for you, Nellie; you are a rich girl." Much to her horror, Mar'ia Nikolaevna learns that the sensitive Nellie is reading the radical critic Nikolai Aleksandrovich Dobroliubov's work, given to her by a teacher at the local gymnasium. Horrified that her daughter would speak with this teacher, who is "the son of a peasant," Mar'ia Nikolaevna calls her daughter crazy. She advises Nellie to follow the example of her brother Paul, a self-serving snob. Nellie ends up marrying the teacher, and her mother responds by attending a post-Christmas party in deep mourning. She is called a "Spartan" when she tells those surrounding her that her newly married

daughter is now dead to her. When at the end of the story Mar'ia Nikolaevna by chance sees her daughter some time later actually lying dead in her coffin, she proceeds heartlessly to attend an Italian opera. "The death of her recalcitrant daughter," the narrator comments sarcastically, "left a shameful stain on the glorious name of her husband."

In the short, powerful "Mat'" (Mother), the poverty-stricken, lower-class Gerasim Pronin is fleeing from the authorities with his wife, Matrena Mitrevna, and their child. Terrified when he hears people coming after them, Gerasim tries to quiet the crying child and in the process smothers him, much to his wife's horror. While Matrena has not asserted herself earlier in the story, she now gives her husband up to those who are searching for him. "You are looking for Gerasim Pronin?" she asks. "Here he is, in the tree. He has killed a child. Seize him!" In contrast to her portrayal of the heartless Mar'ia Nikolaevna in "Spartanka," in "Mat'" and in various other works Dubrovina writes of the strength and transformative power of maternal love, particularly outside of aristocratic circles. In "Mat'" the outraged Matrena finds surprising strength through bereavement, while in other works motherhood and caretaking give women purpose and a mission.

The story "Greshnitsa" (The Sinner) also features the extraordinary effects of passion and personal commitments. Nil Popov, the son of a village priest, has run away from the seminary and become associated with a bad crowd; he has begun to steal for a living. Nil meets Vera Semiakina, referred to ironically by a sympathetic narrator as a "fallen woman," and the two fall deeply in love. When Nil dies, Vera's hair turns gray in one day. She becomes renowned as a saintly nurse who looks after the poor and tends Nil's grave. As Zirin writes, the stories "share a civic pathos: the rich are uniformly portrayed as oblivious to the sufferings of the less fortunate who cross their paths."

In the 1880s and 1890s Dubrovina turned to historical novels, which, as G. A. Krylova notes, tend to deal more with characters' love affairs than with the historical time frame they address. *Rukhnuvshii velikan* (The Collapsed Giant, 1889), for instance, features the adventures of the beautiful, seventeen-year-old Jadwiga Bokshanskaia, "the only daughter of the marshal of the reigning king, who had died many years earlier in the most secret and most tragic way." The reader then learns that "the romantic story of Viacheslav Bokshansky and the particular kindness of the king to his widow, Jadwiga's mother, as well as the striking beauty of the girl herself made her most interesting in the eyes of the youth of the court." While the narrator claims that the story is about Poland's destruction at the hands of power-hungry leaders, in fact this novel is about people rather than history. The writing is emotional and melodramatic, heightened by illustrations of the heroine and her surroundings. One example of style suffices in this regard: "Jadwiga went pale and convulsively embraced Dmitrii. 'Farewell, farewell! Dying, we will think about each other, and that will make death easier. Do not fear . . . believe me: no one kissed me before you, and after you no one will kiss me either, at least not alive!'" A sensationalist page-turner replete with fanciful events, the novel lacks the skill Dubrovina had demonstrated in shorter forms such as her stories. The novel *Zasluzhennaia kara* (A Deserved Punishment, 1891) features a somewhat similar plotline, as an attractive duo fight the evils of General Aleksei Andreevich Arakcheev, Czar Alexander I's brutal henchman.

By contrast, *Na Petrovskom zavode,* which appeared in 1898, is effective in its relative brevity, strength of characterization of major figures, and descriptive passages. While the work is subtitled "Vospominaniia E. O. Dubrovinoi" (The Reminiscences of E. O. Dubrovina), in fact Dubrovina's own story is not central to the text. The main character of *Na Petrovskom zavode* is the Decembrist Gorbachevsky, who is portrayed in fictionalized and romanticized form, and the plot revolves around his supposed love for Oskar Deikhman's aristocratic sister Liza as well as his relationship with a "woman of the people," the Old Believer Irina Dorozhina. Dubrovina, who figures in the work only as a small girl with long curls, supplied a note to the text in which she claimed that her knowledge of the events described was rooted in her own experiences as an eight-year-old and in her parents' later recollections of that time. The work begins in 1854 and spans nearly a decade.

The reader is treated initially to an evocative description of Dubrovina's native Baikal region and of the milieu in which she grew up: the setting is the Petrovsk factory on a cloudless, warm, humid evening in late May. The narrator soon introduces readers to Dubrovina's parents, identified at this point not by their relationship to the author but simply as the factory director Oskar Deikhman and his wife, who are joined by two close friends. The group is then met by "the engineer Dubrovin," who is carrying the eight-year-old "Katichka" in his arms and laughing at her refusal to go to sleep without her mother's presence. Thus, readers meet the author and, it seems, her future husband.

At this point, except for later digressions into the future career path of Oskar Deikhman and the eventual marriage of Liza, the focus of the narration shifts permanently to the fifty-five-year-old Gorbachevsky, already mentioned by the Deikhmans in the initial scene. The work is a paean to Dubrovina's former teacher, who in Dubrovina's telling is more a sensitive,

aging, ailing man than the singleminded revolutionary other sources portray. Dubrovina also praises the humble Irina, who is so devoted to Gorbachevsky that she weeps for him when she learns of his unsuccessful love for Liza. Gorbachevsky, who through his powerful connections had received permission to return to St. Petersburg earlier, has opted to remain in Siberia; Dubrovina posits his love for Liza Deikhman as a reason. When Liza, his former pupil who loves him as a father figure, begins to show interest in the young man who eventually becomes her husband, Gorbachevsky in pain resists visiting the Deikhmans as had been his habit. Meanwhile, Irina, who has lived with Gorbachevsky for years despite censure from her fellow Old Believers, attempts to understand the cause of her friend's distress. The story ends with Gorbachevsky's death and the letter Irina writes to Oskar Deikhman; having learned earlier of Gorbachevsky's long-standing love for Liza, Irina in her grief writes that there is no point in Liza's crying at his death, given the pain she had caused him while he lived.

Amid these tales of unhappy love, Dubrovina manages to develop these two major characters fairly successfully. Irina provides Dubrovina with a vehicle for lauding the industriousness, caring, and self-sacrifice of non-upper-class women. Yet, Irina is not simply a stereotype. She is a woman with strong emotions, fears, and commitments. Gorbachevsky, meanwhile, is presented as honorable, unwilling to declare himself to Liza because of his prior commitment to Irina. In addition, through these characters' reflections on and reactions to the political changes that occur during this period, Dubrovina is able to inject historical content into her work. Through Irina's eyes readers learn of the death of Czar Nicholas I and then see her worried about Gorbachevsky's emotions and hesitating to tell him about the death of the man who had sentenced him to years in Siberia. Dubrovina portrays Gorbachevsky's shocked and intriguingly respectful response to the demise of the czar; one senses that he has considered the czar a worthy opponent. He prophesies about the new czar, Alexander II: "We may expect great and decisive deeds from our new czar, Alexander II. He is young, smart, and educated in the European fashion. It seems to me that he will bring to fruition all the strivings and tasks of his grandfather, the blessed Alexander." When the new czar does in fact embark upon a program of reforms, Dubrovina's Gorbachevsky, now dying, hails these steps, particularly the abolition of serfdom, with joy. And when the new factory manager Dubrovin condescendingly suggests that the ailing "idealist" is entering a second childhood, the narrator hotly responds that Gorbachevsky was in fact doing nothing of the kind; rather, he had never left his childhood, marked as it had been by "an unwavering faith in people and in the victory of good over evil."

For Dubrovina, writing with the hindsight provided by several more decades that had included events such as the assassination of the "Czar Liberator," who had turned conservative later in his reign, her character Gorbachevsky's idealism must have seemed bittersweet. By this time Dubrovina herself was ailing, and she began to spend increasing amounts of time in Tiflis, where her daughter lived; Dubrovina moved there in 1907. As her health faded, a situation perhaps exacerbated by the opium she claimed to have consumed in great quantities, so too did her renown as an author. Dubrovina had never been lauded by the critics, who considered her writing generally poor, but a mass audience had eagerly perused her often hastily written stories and novels, which appeared for the most part in "light" journals of the day and in separately published editions. Dubrovina's collected works were published at least in part from 1910 to 1911, but by this time, much to Dubrovina's distress, her works no longer met with great popularity. When she died on 10 January 1913 she was largely a forgotten writer; at the end of the twentieth century, there is still no full bibliography of her writings, and there is a dearth of scholarly materials relating to her. Modern reference works have begun to resurrect Dubrovina and her canon, however. Such a task is worthwhile, since her short stories are often well written and effective, and her novels, while not always successful from a literary point of view, are interesting as examples of popular literature of her day. Dubrovina's focus on women's lives and her commitment to the welfare of nonaristocratic women are particularly noteworthy, as is Dubrovina's own experience as a professional woman writer in late-nineteenth-century Russia.

References:

G. A. Krylova, "Dubrovina Ekaterina Oskarovna," *Russkie pisateli 1800–1917, Biograficheskii slovar'* (Moscow: Bol'shaia sovetskaia entsiklopediia, 1992): 190–191;

S. M. Stepniak-Kravchinsky, *Podpol'naia Rossiia* (St. Petersburg, 1907), pp. 177–190;

Mary Zirin, "Dubrovina, Ekaterina Oskarovna," *Dictionary of Russian Women Writers,* edited by Marina Ledkovsky, C. L. Rosenthal, and Zirin (Westport, Conn.: Greenwood Press, 1994): 161–163.

Papers:

Ekaterina Oskarovna Dubrovina's papers are found in St. Petersburg at the Institute of Russian Literature (Pushkin House), and in Moscow at the State Archive of the Russian Federation (GARF, formerly TsGAOR). See also P. V. Bykov's manuscript *Slovar' russkikh zhenshchin-pisatel'nits* in the Bykov fond (fond 118, d. 70) at the Russian National Library in St. Petersburg.

Aleksandr Ivanovich Ertel'

(7 July 1855 – 7 February 1908)

Steven R. Griffin
McGill University

WORKS: *Zapiski stepniaka,* in *Vestnik Evropy,* nos. 1–3, 6, 9, 11 (1880); nos. 2, 5, 7, 9, 12 (1881); nos. 5, 9 (1882); (St. Petersburg, 1883);

Volkhonskaia baryshnia. Povest', in *Vestnik Evropy,* nos. 6–8 (1883);

Miniatiury, in *Otechestvennye zapiski,* no. 4 (1884);

Babii bunt. Dramaticheskaia kartina v 5 deistviiakh, in *Delo,* no. 1 (1884);

Mineral'nye vody. Povest', in *Russkaia mysl',* nos. 2–6 (1886);

Dve pary. Povest', in *Russkaia mysl',* nos. 8, 9 (1887); (Moscow, 1894);

Gardeniny, ikh dvornia, priverzhentsy i vragi, in *Russkaia mysl',* nos. 4–10 (1889); (Moscow, 1890);

Smena, in *Russkaia mysl',* nos. 1–3, 5–7 (1891); (Moscow, 1894);

Kar'era Strukova, in *Severnyi vestnik,* no. 12 (1895); nos. 1–3, 5, 6 (1896);

V sumerkakh. Povest', in *Russkaia mysl',* no. 2 (1898);

Sobranie sochinenii, 7 volumes (Moscow: Moskovskoe Knigoizdatel'stvo, 1909).

Editions and Collections: *Sobranie sochinenii,* 2 volumes, introduced by N. L. Brodsky (Moscow: Knigoizdatel'stvo pisatelei v Moskve, 1918);

Smena, with an introduction by Ivan Alekseevich Bunin (New York: Chekhov Press, 1954);

Zapiski stepniaka, edited by G. V. Ermakova-Bitner, with an introduction by Ia. S. Bilinkis (Moscow: Goslitizdat, 1958);

Volkhonskaia baryshnia - Smena - Kar'era Strukova, edited by Ermakova-Bitner, with an afterword by G. A. Terent'ev (Moscow-Leningrad: Goslitizdat, 1959);

Gardeniny, ikh dvornia, priverzhentsy i vragi (Moscow: Khudozhestvennaia literatura, 1980).

SELECTED PERIODICAL PUBLICATIONS:
"Pereselentsy," *Russkoe obozrenie,* nos. 3, 4 (1878): 26–30;

"Pis'mo iz Usmanskogo uezda," *Slovo,* no. 2 (1879): 16–26;

"Piatikhiny deti. Iz chuzhikh vospominanii," *Vestnik Evropy,* no. 3 (1884);

Aleksandr Ivanovich Ertel'

"Chervonets. Rasskaz," in *Krasnyi tsvetok* (St. Petersburg, 1889);

"Dukhovidtsy," *Russkaia mysl',* no. 12 (1893).

Aleksandr Ivanovich Ertel' remains best known for his epic novel *Gardeniny, ikh dvornia, priverzhentsy i vragi* (The Gardenins, their Servants, Retainers, and Enemies, 1889), although not long after his death in 1908 he was largely forgotten. Ivan Alekseevich Bunin remarked in 1929, "Who has forgotten his friends and contemporaries: Garshin, Uspensky, Korolenko, and Chekhov? In fact, he was no lesser a writer than they (with the exception of Chekhov, of course), and in some respects he was even greater." Ertel's particular contribution to Russian letters lies in his talent as "ethnographer" of the philosophical-religious renaissance that began in the 1880s and 1890s in Russia. Ertel', however, sought through his art not only to convey something of the felt quality and diversity of that cultural revival but also to allow his works to form a dialogue with questions that were both practical and speculative regarding Russia: given a period of dramatic change, what course of action was required? And what sort of future could be hoped for?

In many ways Ertel's body of works reflects his own spiritual and intellectual development. For this reason, his letters—later appreciated for their depth and insight by such writers as Semen Liudvigovich Frank, Mikhail Osipovich Gershenzon, and Petr Berngardovich Struve (all contributors to the 1909 essay collection *Vekhi* [Landmarks])—are invaluable. Ertel' was initially attracted to the populist movement, although his basic philosophy until he was about thirty years old was pessimistic. A turn toward a more hopeful worldview came as he sought direction from Leo Tolstoy: instead of ceaseless, cyclical building and destroying, he found in Tolstoy's teachings the confidence that the "Kingdom of Heaven" was not to be found in some distant future but here and now through efforts to live in harmony with all people. As one brought up among the common people, however, Ertel' did not share Tolstoy's idealized view of the peasant and so could not sustain for long the hope in the transformation of society through basic peasant communities. Against Tolstoy's anarchism, Ertel' sought confidence in progress through institutions and *malye dela* (small endeavors). From the early 1890s onward, progress seemed to him not so inevitable, particularly as his own somewhat frustrated endeavors gave way to what he saw as more fundamental ones—the inculcation of good habits at the "grassroots" level of society and conscientious management of the estates under his care.

Aleksandr Ivanovich Ertel' was born on 7 July 1855 in the village of Ksizovo (near Voronezh). His father, Ivan Aleksandrovich Ertel', was an estate manager and the son of Ludwig Ertel', who as a young soldier in Napoleon Bonaparte's army had been captured and brought to Russia. Ertel's mother was Avdot'ia Petrovna Panova, the illegitimate daughter of a Zadonsk landowner by the name of Beer. From the time he was twelve years old until he was eighteen, Ertel' worked on an estate forty versts or so from home, despite his mother's wish that he enroll in the Voronezh gymnasium. Largely self-taught, as a youth Ertel' read stories from the Bible, world history, and hagiographic works. In his teens he added the works of Ivan Sergeevich Turgenev, Tolstoy's *Voina i mir* (War and Peace, 1863–1869), and other historical novels. In 1875 Ertel'

married Mariia Ivanovna Fedotova, and two years later their daughter Ol'ga was born.

The populist Pavel Vladimirovich Zasodimsky remembered Ertel' at this time as a thoughtful, talented, energetic, and resourceful young man who was close to the peasants. That Ertel' was drawn to the people and their concerns is evident in his first literary work, "Noch' na pokose" (A Night of Haymaking, 1875). In 1879 Ertel' moved to St. Petersburg, where he managed a library opened by Zasodimsky. The latter saw to the publication of Ertel's essays "Pereselentsy" (Emigrants, 1878) and "Pis'mo iz Usmanskogo uezda" (A Letter from the Uezd of Usman', 1879), devoted to peasant matters. In St. Petersburg, Ertel' began the sketches that later came to be part of his *Zapiski stepniaka* (Notes of a Steppe-dweller, 1880–1882), although in 1880, after a severe pulmonary hemorrhage, he decided to return home to his mother's farm on the Griaznusha River. Back home, his health improved, and he met his future common-law wife, Mariia V. Ogarkova, a merchant's daughter from Usman'.

As he later explained in an autobiographical letter of 13 July 1888 to Tolstoy's disciple Vladimir Grigor'evich Chertkov, Ertel' looked back on his years as a novice writer as a period filled "with vague and bitter pessimistic thoughts, tearful pity toward people, and despair in his soul from the conviction that there is nothing to be done." Representative of this period are the *Zapiski stepniaka,* narrated by a certain Baturin, who devotes sketches to the sad lot of the peasants and to the changes in a social landscape whereby passive, long-suffering peasants are challenged by the new "bloodsucking" but efficient types, while well-bred and conservative members of the gentry are replaced by populist-leaning and far more practical, but less refined, individuals. These reflections lead the narrator ultimately, as he writes in his final sketch, to "eagerly await death and the mysterious prospect of turning into nothing." In "Ofitsersha" (The Officer's Wife), Ertel's favorite sketch, Baturin tells how "the officer's wife" came to commit suicide after she realized that her efforts were useless: as the peasants learned to read, they were not helping to bring about the salvation of Russia but were using their learning for evil purposes.

As more than one critic has noted, Ertel's debt to Turgenev in *Zapiski stepniaka* is clear. Reflecting the hunting trips in Turgenev's *Zapiski okhotnika* (Notes of a Hunter, 1852), a trip undertaken here and there by Baturin serves as a pretext for a sketch that might include a description of nature, a study of character types, or a meditation on social change. That the descriptions of nature, in particular, tend to be repetitious and superfluous is suggested by E. Nekrasova, an early critic who faulted Ertel' for descriptive passages that existed for their own sake. By contrast, Soviet critics tended to praise Ertel's descriptive talent, particularly as it portrayed the development of capitalism in prerevolutionary Russia.

In the spring of 1884 Ertel' was arrested for his association with St. Petersburg revolutionaries. While worried in prison about his daughter Ol'ga, who had contracted scarlet fever just before he was arrested (she died while Ertel' was in prison, although he learned of her death only later), and beset by the return of tubercular symptoms, Ertel' experienced a decisive religious conversion while in the Peter and Paul Fortress. Faced with the possibility of his own death there in prison, he later told Chertkov that he had longed to be reconciled with all people and to forgive everyone. His sense of rebirth was enhanced by his release after four months on medical grounds (although he was exiled for four years to Tver') as well as the beginning of his common-law marriage with Ogarkova. In 1884–1885 Ertel' sought treatment in Kislovodsk (Caucasus), and in 1886 their daughter Natal'ia (later Natalie Duddington) was born.

In a letter of 1 March 1885, Ertel' asked for permission to visit Tolstoy to discuss how the principles in Tolstoy's *V chem moia vera* (What I Believe, 1884) were to be put into practice. One of Tolstoy's suggestions was to try to write for the people. Ertel' followed the advice and wrote two stories that reflect his new confidence that the purpose of humanity was to live in brotherhood. The first of these stories, "Spetsialist" (The Specialist, 1885), is the structurally simple story of a police officer's capture of an important criminal and subsequent promotion. The intent of the story is plainly didactic: the officer's wife is interested only in material wealth, and he himself, in prestige, and he will use whatever brutal means he needs to achieve that end. The second story, "Zhadnyi muzhik" (The Greedy Peasant, 1886), likewise simple in structure, is the story of a prodigal son, in which a younger brother forsakes his village in search of the good life, loses everything he has acquired, and is then welcomed home and forgiven. Both stories are inspired by Tolstoy's later teachings that property and money are the source of all evil, that authenticity is to be found in a healthy simple and rural life, away from the excesses and corruption of the city, and that the institutions of Church and State protect the interests of the oppressor. Not only do Ertel's stories uphold these ideas, but in their simplicity of structure and allusions to biblical stories, as in "Zhadnyi muzhik," they stand as models of what Tolstoy later upheld as "universal" art in *Chto takoe iskusstvo?* (What is Art?, 1898).

Collaboration with Tolstoy was brief, however, since Ertel' was suspicious of any doctrine that estab-

lished an agenda on the peasant question without an intimate knowledge of peasant concerns. In any case, as he had written to Matvei Nikolaevich Chistiakov on 5 October 1881, he was more interested in the intelligentsia and its relationship with the people than the people as such. In 1886 Ertel' wrote *Mineral'nye vody* (Mineral Waters), the story of how a young member of the intelligentsia comes to realize, on a trip to a spa, that he is unfit to take part in social concerns. The story is structured to isolate the hero and to distinguish him from all the other characters. As he encounters pessimists, populists, moralizers, and sybarites, the young man is disillusioned by them all, for he finds their lives dreary and full of futile pursuits.

If in *Mineral'nye vody* Ertel' turned his attention to the predicament of the individual in the group, in *Dve pary* (Two Couples, 1887) he challenged Tolstoy's call to the simple life in the interests of the individual. Set in Samara, *Dve pary* tells of the efforts of a populist-minded landowning couple to arrange the life and happiness of a peasant couple. Historical circumstances, including cultural barriers and different native environments, make the couple's attempts to become one with the people not only impossible but also comical. Stylistically, the story represents a middle way between the descriptive, Turgenevan *Zapiski stepniaka* and the simpler and more unadorned stories for the people. In *Dve pary* Ertel's descriptive passages are brief and are better incorporated into the narrative than those in *Zapiski stepniaka*. The work similarly avoids the two poles of blunt didacticism and description for its own sake; the influence of Tolstoy's great novels is evident, while the didactic impulse is transformed into a need to polemicize against him. The result is a story that includes a teaching on the simple life in which Ertel' clearly questions the universality of the call.

In the summer of 1888, while on the farm at Griaznusha (since he was permitted to spend the summers away from Tver'), Ertel' began to work on his magnum opus: *Gardeniny, ikh dvornia, priverzhentsy i vragi.* The novel began to be published the following summer (it came out in book form in 1890), when his internal exile had ended and he was back on the farm. At that time Ertel' and Ogarkova's second daughter, Elena, was born.

A panoramic novel of society in south central Russia in the 1870s, *Gardeniny, ikh dvornia, priverzhentsy i vragi* depicts, as Ertel' explained to Viktor Aleksandrovich Gol'tsev in a letter of 15 October 1889, "that period in public consciousness when ideas are reborn, beliefs are modified, new forms of community powerfully accelerate one's critical stance towards life, when an almost opposite new world-view burgeons." Most of the action takes place on the Gardenin family's ancestral lands, where the confrontation between the old social order and the new is made apparent at various levels: distinctions between social classes are increasingly breaking down, sons no longer follow in their fathers' footsteps, and new forms of belief compete with traditional religion.

Within this context Ertel' traces the spiritual development of his hero, Nikolai Rakhmanny, who with the help of mentors makes the transition from the orthodoxy of his youth through positivism to a philosophy of "small endeavors." The intellectual aspect of his development is intimately linked to the moral one as he, through a series of romantic relationships, learns the value of forgiveness and a life devoted to the well-being of others. Just when the hero finds meaning in a philosophy of small deeds, however, he is confronted, like Baturin in *Zapiski stepniaka,* with a view of change as ceaseless and cyclical, and it undercuts his confidence in lasting progress.

Reception of *Gardeniny, ikh dvornia, priverzhentsy i vragi* has been mixed. On the negative side, some early critics perceived in the novel the lack of an adequate central idea, while others found it overly episodic, so that one could get lost in the parts and miss the whole. Indeed, Ertel' seems to have agreed with such a charge, for in a letter of 15 October 1889 he wrote to Gol'tsev that he had produced "material for a novel, and not a novel." On the positive side, in a preface that he wrote for the novel, Tolstoy praised Ertel's knowledge of folk life and popular language, while Gol'tsev and A. Salikovsky applauded Ertel's impressive acquaintance with various currents in religious thought and rich panorama of life, respectively. True to form, Soviet critics generally regarded the author of *Gardeniny, ikh dvornia, priverzhentsy i vragi* as an artist whose work accurately depicts the collapse of the old social order and the advent of capitalism in Russia.

In late 1890, after a summer of treatment in the Crimea, Ertel' rented a farm at Empelevo (now Trudovoe, near Voronezh) and set to work on his second novel, *Smena* (The Change, 1891). Set in St. Petersburg and on the estate of the Mansurov family in the late 1880s, *Smena* includes a "case study" in philosophical pessimism, whereby the hero, like his counterpart in *Mineral'nye vody,* finds himself gradually isolated from society. Since the individualism of the high society of St. Petersburg, an offer to join a commune, and his aunt's evangelical circle all fail to interest him, Mansurov turns hopefully to a group of people engaged in "the struggle" (efforts for the common good), and decides to return to his family estate. But as a "superfluous man" of sorts, he is unable to engage in that struggle. In any case he has to go abroad for medical treatment, and when he returns he finds himself depressed, contemplating suicide. His life ends in a brothel, where he is killed by a stray bullet.

That *Smena* does not leave philosophical pessimism unchecked is evident in the prominence given to Mansurov's alter ego Alesha, who as a member of the peasant intelligentsia and leader of a new Christian sect represented for Ertel' a greater hope of progress than the *raznochinets.* As he explained in a letter of 9 June 1891 to Petr Fedorovich Nikolaev, "my sympathies are more with the Aleshas than the *raznochinets* . . . because the Aleshas are *more free* than Bazarov [the nihilist of Turgenev's *Ottsy i deti* (Fathers and Sons, 1862)] and his heirs. That strange and complicated way in which Aleshas seek the truth . . . can lead one into a swamp, but it has its merits: here everything is put to the test, experienced." Unlike Mansurov, Alesha manages to find a way through initial depression into a life of learning and service. Summing up his credo in response to another sectarian who insists on the sole authority of the Bible, Alesha argues that Truth is to be found "in pure reason, . . . in the Scriptures, in Socrates the pagan, in books and songs . . . and even in you and me," and that holiness is found in devotion to works of charity.

Reception of *Smena* has been, like that of *Gardeniny, ikh dvornia, priverzhentsy i vragi,* mixed. The most favorable remark was offered by Gleb Ivanovich Uspensky: "He writes so well. It's charming! [Ertel'] has freed himself from Tolstoyan asceticism and given freedom to his great talent. The entire first part is magnificent." But Soviet critics chastised Ertel' for his failure to communicate any hope in the creative strength of the people and for settling for a "small deeds" philosophy, while Nikolai Konstantinovich Mikhailovsky accused Ertel' of "somewhat scornfully and skeptically observing the hubbub of his own creations" so that in the end "what exactly constitutes 'change' in Ertel's novel, . . . [and] in which direction it is headed, whether it leads to good or ill" was unclear. Given Ertel's desire to chronicle change and diversity without pronouncing a final word on the direction change was taking, however, Mikhailovsky's criticism can be understood positively, for it underscores Ertel's ability to tell the story of a society and one of its "superfluous men" during an ideologically chaotic time without rendering his hero entirely superfluous or the struggle that he was unfit to join a useless venture.

From 1891 to 1894 Ertel' occupied himself mainly with famine relief and the founding of a school. But the considerable poverty that he witnessed, the lack of support from the zemstvo in his school project, and the burdensome debts he incurred caused him to question his confidence in small endeavors. While he continued to insist that art should be "saturated with the flesh and blood of reality," as he explained in a letter of 15

January 1893 to Pavel Aleksandrovich Bakunin, he now emphasized that creativity was impoverished if it were not "ignited by the flames of religion or a deep philosophical worldview." With less confidence in any laws of history that guaranteed progress, Ertel' turned in his later works toward more subjective concerns.

In 1893 Ertel' wrote "Dukhovidtsy" (Clairvoyants), a story that raises existential questions of death, hope, and ultimate meaning. Set in a provincial Russian town and narrated by a local resident who has sought to engage himself in "the struggle" and grown weary of it, "Dukhovidtsy" includes another "case study" in philosophical pessimism. The work can be considered Ertel's most psychologically probing piece thus far, for in the story the two principal characters speak at great length about personal concerns. At the heart of the story there is profound despair: society appears to be concerned only with petty affairs, and evil seems to thwart progress and charity, although a somewhat perplexed narrator's hope suggests a response. Moreover, the "decadent" themes of suicide, the extraordinary, and the search for a reality beyond this world all reflect the symbolist trend that was taking root at the time.

On the whole, Soviet critics either ignored the story or found little of value in it. G. A. Kostin wrote that "Dukhovidtsy," along with those works written after it, "no longer had any significant content," while Viacheslav Veniaminovich Nikiforov considered it inferior to Ertel's earlier works because its heroes "even communicate with the world beyond." But in a letter of 25 January 1894, Anton Pavlovich Chekhov recommended "Dukhovidtsy" to Aleksei Sergeevich Suvorin, saying that the story included "poetry and something terrifying in the style of an old fairy-tale. It's one of the best recent items in Moscow."

Ertel's first trip abroad in 1894 to London and Paris gave him part of his setting for his last completed work, *Kar'era Strukova* (Strukov's Career, 1895). Set in the mid 1880s, *Kar'era Strukova* is the story of Natal'ia and Aleksei Strukov's frustrated efforts to bring about social change in their provincial Russian town. After meeting in London, Aleksei and Natasha decide to settle down in a town on the Volga, but soon the ordinariness of life frustrates his efforts as justice of the peace, while her efforts to reform a local school meet with opposition. Bored with life and love, Strukov commits suicide, while Natasha leaves Russia for the sake of her father's health and her sons' education.

The critic I. Dzhonson described the story as "a shining example of the full maturity of Ertel's talent" and a "masterpiece of our literature for its excellent artistic merit, for the brightness and strength of the psychological analysis, for its vivid character portraits, and for the depth of the social, family, and individual issues raised in it." Indeed, *Kar'era Strukova* includes one of Ertel's most individualized characters, Perelygin (Natasha's father), while Natasha herself is one of Ertel's most dynamic characters, for she combines the traits that Ertel' had sought to develop in his earlier heroines: she is close to the people by nature, spiritually motivated, practical, and independent.

From 1896 until his death Ertel' devoted his efforts almost entirely to the oversight of estates owned by Elizaveta Ivanovna Chertkova and Aleksandra Ivanovna Pashkova, with occasional trips abroad. In 1898, with increased responsibilities but with a sense of fulfillment in his work as estate manager, Ertel' left unfinished his last work, *V sumerkakh* (At Twilight, published in part in 1898). By 1904 Ertel' realized that his health was seriously worsening, and in 1906 he moved to Moscow, where he continued his administrative work. He died of a heart attack two years later on 7 February 1908. He was buried at the Novodevichy Cemetery, across from Chekhov's grave.

Letters:
Pis'ma, edited, with an introduction by M. O. Gershenzon (Moscow: I. D. Sytin, 1909).

References:
I. Dzhonson, "Zabytyi pisatel'," *Kievskie Vesti* (23 June 1906);

S. L. Frank, "Pis'ma A. I. Ertelia," in *Filosofiia i zhizn'* (St. Petersburg, 1910), pp. 328–337;

Sebastian Garrett, "A. I. Ertel': Letters to his Daughter," M.A. thesis, University of Birmingham, U.K., 1982;

Steven Griffin, *Alexander Ertel and the Destiny of Russia* (Birmingham, U.K.: Birmingham Slavonic Monographs, 1998);

G. A. Kostin, *A. I. Ertel'. Zhizn' i tvorchestvo* (Voronezh: Knizhnoe izdatel'stvo, 1955);

Viacheslav Veniaminovich Nikiforov, "Tvorchestvo A.I. Ertelia: k peresmotru istoricheskogo-literaturnogo znacheniia," Kandidatskaia thesis, Moscow State University, 1983;

N. S. Parsons, "Alexander Ertel' as a Christian Humanist," *Slavic and East European Review,* 46 (1968): 176–191;

A. P. Spasibenko, *A. I. Ertel': pisatel'-vos'midesiatnik* (Alma-Ata: Nauka, 1966);

Pavel Vladimirovich Zasodimsky, *Iz vospominanii* (Moscow, 1908), pp. 438–450.

Papers:
Aleksandr Ivanovich Ertel's materials are located in the Manuscripts Division of the Russian State Library in Moscow and the Nikitin Museum in Voronezh, Russia.

Ivan Aleksandrovich Goncharov

(6 June 1812 – 15 September 1891)

Galya Diment
University of Washington, Seattle

WORKS: *Obyknovennaia istoriia,* in *Sovremennik,* nos. 3–4 (1847); (St. Petersburg: Biblioteka russkikh romanov, povestei, zapisok i puteshestvii, 1848); translated by Constance Garnett as *A Common Story* (London: Heinemann, 1894; New York: Collier, 1894);

Russkie v Iaponii v nachale 1853 i v kontse 1854 godov (iz putevykh zametok) (St. Petersburg: V tipografii Imperatorskoi Akademii nauk, 1855);

Fregat "Pallada." Ocherki puteshestviia, two volumes (St. Petersburg: I. I. Glazunov, 1858); selections first published as "Putevye zamekti" in *Otechestvennye zapiski, Sovremennik,* and *Russkii vestnik* (1855–1857); translated by N. W. Wilson as *The Voyage of the Frigate Pallada* (London: Folio Society, 1965);

Oblomov, in *Otechestvennye zapiski,* nos. 1–4 (1859); 2 volumes (St. Petersburg: D. E. Kozhanchikov, 1859); translated by C. J. Hogarth as *Oblomov* (New York: Macmillan / London: Allen & Unwin, 1915);

Obryv, in *Vestnik Evropy,* nos. 1–5 (1869); 2 volumes (St. Petersburg, 1870); abridged and translated by M. Bryant as *The Precipice* (London: Hodder & Stoughton, 1915; New York: Knopf, 1915);

Chetyre ocherka (St. Petersburg: Izdanie knizhnoi torgovli Glazunova, 1881)—comprises "Literaturnyi vecher," "Mil'ion terzanii," "Zametki o lichnosti Belinskogo," and "Luchshe pozdno, chem nikogda";

Polnoe sobranie sochinenii, 8 volumes (St. Petersburg: I. I. Glazunov, 1884–1887);

Slugi starogo veka. Iz domashnego arkhiva, edited by N. Forbes (Oxford: Tip. Klarendon, 1918);

Neobyknovennaia istoriia. Neizdannaia rukopis' I. A. Goncharova (Petrograd: Brokgauz-Efron, 1924);

Literaturno-kriticheskie stat'i i pis'ma, edited by A. P. Rybasov (Leningrad: Khudozhestvennaia literatura, 1938);

Nimfodora Ivanovna: Povest'. Izbrannye pis'ma, edited by O. A. Marfinaia-Demikhovskaia and E. K. Demikhovskaia (Pskov: Izd-vo POIUU, 1992).

Ivan Aleksandrovich Goncharov, 1847

Editions and Collections: *Polnoe sobranie sochinenii,* 9 volumes (St. Petersburg: I. I. Glazunov, 1896);

Polnoe sobranie sochinenii, 12 volumes (St. Petersburg: A. F. Marks, 1899);

Polnoe sobranie sochinenii, 4 volumes, incomplete (Petrograd: Literaturno-izdatel'skii otdel Komissariata narodnogo prosveshcheniia, 1918);

Sobranie sochinenii, 8 volumes (Moscow: Pravda, 1952);

Sobranie sochinenii, 8 volumes (Moscow: Goslitizdat, 1952–1955);

Sobranie sochinenii, 6 volumes (Moscow: Goslitizdat, 1959–1960);

Fregat "Pallada." Literaturnye pamiatniki (Leningrad: Nauka, 1986);

Ocherki, stat'i, pis'ma, edited by T. V. Gromova (Moscow: Izd-vo "Pravda," 1986);

Na rodine, edited by V. A. Nedzvetisky (Moscow: Sov. Rossiia, 1987);

Oblomov. Literaturnye pamiatniki (Leningrad: Nauka, 1987);

Polnoe sobranie sochinenii i pisem v dvadtsati tomakh (St. Petersburg: Nauka, 1997–).

Editions in English: *Oblomov,* translated by Natalie A. Duddington (London: Allen & Unwin, 1929; New York: Macmillan, 1929);

Oblomov, translated by David Magarshack (Harmondsworth, U.K.: Penguin, 1954);

The Same Old Story, translated by Ivy Litvinova (Moscow: Foreign Languages Publishing House, 1957);

Oblomov, translated by Ann Dunnigan (New York: Signet, 1963);

The Frigate Pallada, translated by Klaus Goetze (New York: St. Martin's Press, 1987);

An Ordinary Story, translated by Marjorie L. Hoover (Ann Arbor, Mich.: Ardis, 1994);

The Precipice, translated by Laury Magnus and Boris Jakim (Ann Arbor, Mich.: Ardis, 1994).

OTHER: "Son Oblomova. Epizod iz romana," in *Literaturnyi sbornik, s illiustratsiiami* (St. Petersburg: Redaktsiia *Sovremennika,* 1849).

SELECTED PERIODICAL PUBLICATION: "Ivan Savich Podzhabrin," *Sovremennik,* no. 1 (1848).

Although Ivan Aleksandrovich Goncharov wrote several books that were widely read and discussed during his lifetime, he is now best remembered for one novel, *Oblomov* (1859), an indisputable classic of Russian literature that in its artistic stature and cultural significance may be compared to such other masterpieces as Nikolai Vasil'evich Gogol's *Pokhozhdeniia Chichikova, ili Mertvye dushi* (The Adventures of Chichikov, or Dead Souls, 1842), Leo Tolstoy's *Anna Karenina* (1875–1877), and Fyodor Dostoevsky's *Brat'ia Karamazovy* (The Brothers Karamazov, 1879–1880).

Goncharov is often referred to as one of the major Russian realists of the nineteenth century; yet, this formulation, while largely legitimate, often overlooks the rich ambiguity of his works, the psychological complexity of his characters, and the surprising sophistication of some of his literary techniques, which appear to anticipate twentieth-century modernism. Among his modernist admirers were Samuel Beckett, who sometimes signed his letters "Oblomov," and James Joyce, who is said to have recommended only two Russian authors for his grandson to read: Goncharov and Tol-

stoy. Goncharov was also surprisingly and unconventionally frank and even graphic in depicting both male and female sexuality. But above all, Goncharov was a great master at presenting, often in a matter-of-fact and sadly ironic way, conflicting impulses and unresolvable tensions.

Ivan Aleksandrovich Goncharov was born on 6 June 1812 into a well-to-do merchant family in Simbirsk, a medium-sized Volga town that was also the birthplace of one of Goncharov's literary idols and early influences, Nikolai Mikhailovich Karamzin. Simbirsk was provincial and slow-paced; Goncharov, though fond of the place, often described it in somnolent terms. "The whole appearance of my home town," he wrote in 1887, "was a perfect picture of sleepiness and stagnation. . . . One wanted to fall asleep as well while looking at all this immobility, at the sleepy windows with their curtains and blinds drawn, at the sleepy faces one saw inside the houses or on the streets. 'We have nothing to do!,' they seemed to be saying while yawning and lazily looking at you. 'We are in no hurry.'"

Goncharov's father, Aleksandr Ivanovich Goncharov, traded in grain and owned a candle factory. He was sufficiently well known and liked among the merchant population to be elected mayor of Simbirsk several times. He was fifty years old and a childless widower when he married the writer's mother, Avdot'ia Matveevna (neé Shakhtorina), the nineteen-year-old daughter of a merchant. In rapid succession she bore him six children, four of whom survived. Ivan was the Goncharovs' second living child and second son. He was followed by two sisters, Aleksandra and Anna.

Situated in the rural outskirts of Simbirsk, the Goncharovs' estate was so big that, according to Goncharov, it looked like a whole village. His childhood was far from happy, however, for in 1819, when the boy was just seven, his father died. Avdot'ia Matveevna, now in her early thirties, was left with four small children. While Goncharov in later years could hardly remember his father, the strong childhood attachment to his mother lasted for the rest of his life and may explain both the prevalence of fatherless protagonists in his novels and the strength and complexity—unusual for that time—of his female characters. "Our mother was truly bright," Goncharov wrote to his brother, Nikolai, in 1862. "She was undoubtedly smarter than all the women I have known." She was also, apparently, both loving and protective, and a strict disciplinarian.

Goncharov's powerful emotional bond with his mother may also explain why he could be so masterful in depicting a character like Oblomov, whom some critics, such as Natalie Baratoff, see as "a classical example

The building in St. Petersburg where Goncharov wrote his first novel, Obyknovennaia istoriia *(A Common Story),*
first published in Sovremennik *(The Contemporary) in 1847 (photograph by Judith E. Kalb)*

of a man suffering from a severe mother complex." In 1851, the year his mother passed away, Goncharov told his sister Aleksandra: "I feel privileged and I praise God that I had such a mother. There is nothing and no one about whom my thoughts are so radiant and my memories so sacred as about her." In the same letter Goncharov also reminded his sister that she, not he, was their mother's favorite, but he assured her that he did not resent it in the least. In his fiction, however, he chose to make his male protagonists Aleksandr Aduev and Il'ia Oblomov the only children, thus allowing their fictional mothers to dote obsessively on them alone.

Avdot'ia Matveevna came from a less established and less educated merchant family than her husband, making the prospect of single-handedly raising and educating her children difficult. An old friend of the family, the Goncharovs' tenant and the godfather of all four Goncharov children, Nikolai Tregubov, assumed the role of surrogate father and guardian. He was a retired naval officer, rich, well educated, of noble birth, and a bachelor. He was also a Freemason who had settled in Simbirsk upon his retirement, probably because the town had one of the oldest and best-established (albeit outlawed) Masonic lodges in the country. In a rather unusual social arrangement for the time—and one simi-

lar to both Goncharov's own untraditional relationship with a widow and her children toward the end of his life, and some of the unconventional choices his male and female protagonists made—Tregubov moved in with Avdot'ia Matveevna and her children. He occupied half of the house, and, according to Goncharov, the "serfs, cooks, and grooms merged . . . and were placed under my mother's supervision" while Tregubov assumed "all intellectual concerns."

Goncharov seems to have been fond of his kind and easygoing godfather and grateful to him for the help and support he gave the family. Tregubov was, according to Goncharov, "everything that is well expressed by the English word 'gentleman'; . . . he was an unalloyed original of honesty, honor, and nobility." He was also, according to his godson, an Oblomov-like figure who spent most of his days indoors, wearing a dressing gown, reclining after each rich meal, and spoiling the Goncharov children with candy and caresses. But as much as Goncharov may have appreciated Tregubov's gentleness, he was never particularly impressed with how the retired navy officer dealt with his responsibility for their "intellectual concerns." First, the boys studied under the tutelage of a townswoman, who, Goncharov complained later, was "mean and used to hit students on their fingers with a belt if their handwriting was not neat." In 1820 Goncharov was placed in a more satisfactory boarding school, situated on the other side of Volga. An avid reader, he had read all the books in his household by the time he was nine years old, "one after the other, at random, without anyone close by to share impressions or opinions about what I had read."

When Goncharov was ten, his mother and Tregubov sent him to study in Moscow with his older brother at the School of Commerce, a natural place of education for a merchant's son but one Goncharov hated. He spent eight years there, four of them in the same grade simply because he was one of the youngest students. To his brother he confessed later that he could not even bring himself to remember those years, filled as they were with the stupidity, cruelty, and hard-drinking habits of their teachers, as well as with excruciatingly boring class sessions and outdated textbooks. Goncharov concluded that the school was a total waste of their time and their mother's money.

In June of 1830 Goncharov returned to Simbirsk without having graduated from the School of Commerce. A year later, he finally persuaded his mother and Tregubov to let him enroll in the department of philology at Moscow University. While at the university, he studied under some of the most influential minds in the country and also met several important literary figures: Mikhail Iur'evich Lermontov was a fellow student for a short while, and in 1832 Aleksandr Sergeevich Pushkin, whom Goncharov revered above all other writers and poets, visited one of his classes. Upon graduating in 1835, Goncharov moved to St. Petersburg and began working as a translator in the department of foreign trade of the Ministry of Finances.

Goncharov started writing poetry and short stories while a Moscow University student, and he continued to do so in his spare time in St. Petersburg. The only story from that period that was published during Goncharov's life was "Ivan Savich Podzhabrin," written in 1842 and brought out in one of the leading St. Petersburg literary magazines, *Sovremennik* (The Contemporary), six years later, after the success of his first novel. This early work already displays some of Goncharov's major artistic strengths—mostly his dry wit and the natural quality of his dialogues. Both these attributes showed themselves even more dramatically in his subsequent novels. In 1843 Goncharov began working on his first novel, *Obyknovennaia istoriia* (translated as *A Common Story*, 1894), which was published in *Sovremennik* in 1847 and made its author famous.

Obyknovennaia istoriia, which Goncharov intended as a story typical of his entire generation, is at the same time one of the most personal and autobiographical novels of nineteenth-century Russian literature. As a

bildungsroman, *Obyknovennaia istoriia* appears to have followed in the fashionable footsteps of Johann Wolfgang von Goethe's "Wilhelm Meister" novels. The protagonist is a naive and romantic provincial youth whose artistic ambitions and innocent illusions about life are cruelly crushed when he comes to an impersonal and arrogant capital. But most of all, the circumstances of Aleksandr Aduev's early life and his entry into St. Petersburg resemble those of his creator.

Aleksandr Aduev was born in the vicinity of a sleepy provincial town. "How pleasant everything looks there!" Aleksandr exclaims to himself when he first contrasts his native land with the imperial coldness of the huge Russian capital; "the quiet, the stillness, the monotony! In the streets, in the faces of people, the same stillness." Aleksandr's doting mother, his nurse, and his servants all have obvious real-life prototypes in Avdot'ia Matveevna and the Goncharovs' serfs. Goncharov also makes Aleksandr suffer from the same chaotic and largely inadequate early education about which he so bitterly complained to his friends. Aleksandr further shares with the author three years at Moscow University, with his favorite professors. After returning home, Aleksandr longs for and finally reaches St. Petersburg, arriving in the capital full of dreams about a meteoric and meaningful career and speedy success for his verses. Instead, he has to settle for a minor and uninspiring bureaucratic position as a translator in the department of foreign trade.

When he arrives in St. Petersburg, Aleksandr is confronted not only by the indifference of the imperial capital but also by the sarcastic and unsparing pragmatism of his uncle, Petr Aduev, who refuses to coddle his young nephew. Petr is a successful bureaucrat and a part-owner of a china factory. Whereas his nephew is governed solely by his heart, Petr relies on his mind alone. He pitilessly ridicules Aleksandr's provincial upbringing (even though it matches his own), his naive idealism, youthful passions, and literary ambitions.

Goncharov was not the only author at the time to explore the dichotomy between heart and mind. As scholar Irina Paperno has pointed out, by the 1840s, when Goncharov was writing his novel, this opposition had evolved in Russia "into a cultural cliché separated from its original literary and metaphysical contexts." For Vissarion Grigor'evich Belinsky, the most influential Russian critic at the time, and for many of his followers, the choice between the heart and the mind often amounted to the choice between what they called "vulgar idealism" and "reality." The two notions also became stand-ins for the confrontation between the departing sentimentalism and Romanticism, and the burgeoning and much-welcomed realism.

ОБЫКНОВЕННАЯ ИСТОРІЯ

РОМАНЪ

ВЪ ДВУХЪ ЧАСТЯХЪ

Ивана Гончарова

ЧАСТЬ I

САНКТПЕТЕРБУРГЪ
—
1848

Title page for Obyknovennaia istoriia *(A Common Story), which one reviewer praised for its "objective, sculptured depiction of reality"*

This dichotomy was equally symbolic for Goncharov, except, unlike his peers, he did not have clear-cut answers. On the one hand, he was nostalgic for the idealism of his youth and remained loyal to the literary idol of his childhood, the sentimentalist Karamzin, even at a time when it was more than fashionable to attack him. On the other hand, he saw the shortcomings and impractical nature of many Romantic, introspective tendencies in a country that desperately needed pragmatism and the active participation of all of its best and brightest citizens in rebuilding and reorganizing if it were to catch up with the rest of Europe, as Goncharov hoped it would. What Goncharov said about Zakhar, Oblomov's manservant, could have been as easily applied to the author: "He belonged to two epochs, and both left an imprint on him." The writer also preserved this duality and ambivalence in his novel, which neither attains a neat resolution between the two conflicting impulses nor allows one to triumph convincingly over the other.

While the uncle's view of life appears to win at the end, it does so at a terrible cost. The nephew's loss of youthful illusions also brings a loss of joy, including genuine feelings of love. And even Petr's belief in the superiority of his practical ways becomes somewhat shaky at the end. Just as his nephew gets ready to emulate the successful life and career of his uncle, Petr, whose lack of emotions seems slowly to be suffocating his young wife, resigns his high government post and declares that he does "not want to go on living by the head alone."

There is one other character in the novel, however, in whom the balance between reason and emotion seems to have been attained much more successfully than in either Aleksandr or Petr Aduev—and, as in all subsequent novels Goncharov wrote, this most reasonable and balanced person happens to be a woman. Lizaveta Aleksandrovna, whom Petr marries after Aleksandr arrives in St. Petersburg, is, despite being almost as young as Aleksandr, the most mature character in the novel. She thinks and she also feels. She sees the shortcomings of Aleksandr's ardent idealism, but she is also painfully aware of the weaknesses in her husband's overly-practical approach to life. For a while, she serves as a bridge between the two characters, softening the blows for Aleksandr by listening with sympathy to his woes and disappointments, and gently prodding her husband to treat his nephew with more love and understanding.

Yet, Lizaveta's powers are rather limited. Because she is a woman, she is obviously not viewed by either Aleksandr or Petr as a plausible role model: Aleksandr inevitably ends up emulating his uncle rather than his aunt. She is also too unsettled and dissatisfied to serve as a pillar of strength. Even though she has married a man she loved and respected, there is little in their childless marriage that can sustain either her intellectual or emotional needs. Unlike Aleksandr or Petr, as a woman she cannot look for fulfillment outside of her marriage, either in a successful career or in gratifying public activity. Goncharov was seriously concerned with the position of women in his contemporary society and the lack of proper outlets for their talents and energy outside of marriage. At the end of the novel, all indications, including a family doctor's diagnosis, point to a serious nervous disorder that is slowly killing Lizaveta Aleksandrovna, so that Petr's decision to offer a personal sacrifice and stop living "by head alone" may actually come too late to save his wife.

Given that *Obyknovennaia istoriia* was Goncharov's first novel, the complex nature of its probing questions and debates is impressive, as is the natural quality and wit of the exchanges. Equally gratifying is Goncharov's use of the fashionable genre of a bildungsroman to create a novel with no progress, but with a vicious circle, where one character may simply be repeating another character's mistakes and no meaningful development or "education" is truly possible. Yet, the writer's relative immaturity is also apparent. As good as Goncharov's dialogues tend to be, in *Obyknovennaia istoriia* he relies on them too heavily in order to move the plot along. As a result, the exchanges occupy a disproportionately large portion of the novel, making it read at times more like a play. Other weaknesses include the excessively stark nature of the contrast between the uncle and the nephew and the repetitiveness of the examples of their differences.

When the book came out, the weaknesses were largely overlooked, however, and the general critical reaction was enthusiastic. Aleksei Dmitrievich Galakhov, a reviewer for the highly influential *Otechestvennye zapiski* (Notes of the Fatherland), praised it highly: "the character of the novel sharply distinguishes itself by its objective, sculptured depiction of reality which is so rare nowadays given the prevalent desire of writers always to sound their own voices." Goncharov often worried about finding his own, unmistakable voice, but one anonymous critic for *Vedomosti S.-Peterburgskoi gorodskoi politsii* (St. Petersburg City Policy Documents, 8 March 1847) specifically stated: "The talent of Mr. Goncharov is a talent which is original: he goes his own way, imitating no one, not even Gogol—and that is no small deed nowadays." Belinsky, who was quite impressed with Goncharov's first effort, summarized the reaction to *Obyknovennaia istoriia* in St. Petersburg: "Goncharov's novel has created an incredible sensation . . . an unprecedented success! All opinions have been in its favor. . . . His talent is, indeed, remarkable." Leo Tolstoy noted in his diary that he was reading the novel and then recommended it to a friend: "Please read this delightful novel. It teaches you how to live. You see different views expressed here on life, on love. You may not agree with a single one of them but, as a result, your own views become clearer and more intelligent."

As far as Goncharov was concerned, the success of his first novel was both deeply gratifying and quite unexpected. "I was always extremely distrustful of myself," he reminisced in 1875 about his work on *Obyknovennaia istoriia;* "I constantly tortured myself with questions like 'Am I writing total nonsense? . . . is what I write any good? . . . what if it's all rubbish?'" Belinsky's praise flattered him enormously, even if, at times, Goncharov may have found it impossible to agree with the critic's remarks about the novel, such as Belinsky's statement that a better end would have had Aleksandr turn not into his uncle but into "a mystic, a fanatic, a sectarian, better yet . . . a Slavophile." Yet, at least in print, Goncharov never challenged that assertion.

As a writer, Goncharov was riding high. In 1848 he published "Ivan Savich Podzhabrin," which Dostoevsky reviewed positively. A year later, *Sovremennik* published Goncharov's story "Son Oblomova" (Oblomov's Dream), which became chapter 9 of part 1 of the novel. "Son Oblomova" is a masterful performance by Goncharov. The dream takes the protagonist back to his childhood and Oblomovka, its simple pleasures and peaceful sloth and stagnation. At times sounding judgmental, at others nostalgic, Goncharov mixes comedy and pathos, idyll and unvarnished reality, and he does so without any apparent compulsion to resolve the contradictory responses the world of Oblomovka and its inhabitants produce in him or in his readers.

One of the more interesting aspects of "Son Oblomova" is its complex treatment of maternal love. Cherished and worshiped by his mother and her female serf surrogates, who watch the child's every step to make sure he is never exposed to any real or imagined danger, Iliusha Oblomov feels both privileged and trapped. Far from being selfless, maternal love, though genuine and warm, is shown to be at times quite selfish, when affectionate mothering becomes suffocating. Oblomov's mother literally tries to keep him "under wraps"—as when Iliusha manages to get away and throw snowballs with serf boys only to be grabbed by several female hands, wrapped in sheepskins, blankets, and fur coats, and triumphantly carried home. The narrator is highly critical, suggesting that the only good thing the parents could have done in this situation would be to allow the excited and rosy-cheeked Iliusha to continue playing in the fresh, frosty air. Instead, he is not only tightly wrapped in many layers, he is put to bed for three days to recover from the "unfortunate" incident.

While the overly protective mother's efforts to control her child at all times may have been sincerely designed to benefit him, the only true beneficiary appears be the mother, whose peace of mind is never allowed to be disturbed by what is unforeseen or unpredictable. Yet, the blind, all-forgiving quality of maternal love is also all too real and attractive, and so is the peace and tranquility of Oblomovka, even if they are often achieved at the price of mind-numbing boredom. As Vladimir Korolenko wrote in "I. A. Goncharov i 'molodoe pokolenie'" (I. A. Goncharov and the "New Generation"), reprinted in *I. A. Goncharov v russkoi kritike* (I. A. Goncharov in Russian Criticism, 1958), "Son Oblomova" makes it obvious that "Goncharov, of course, mentally rejected 'Oblomovism,' but deep inside he loved it with profound love beyond his control."

The work on *Oblomov* continued for several years after the publication of "Son Oblomova" but was interrupted by several personal losses. Belinsky, whom

ОБЛОМОВЪ

РОМАНЪ

ВЪ ЧЕТЫРЕХЪ ЧАСТЯХЪ

Ивана Гончарова

———

Томъ I

———

Изданіе Д. Е. Кожанчикова

С.-ПЕТЕРБУРГЪ
1859

Title page for Goncharov's best-known novel, Oblomov, *whose title character was considered an accurate representation of a Russian character type (The Kilgour Collection of Russian Literature, Houghton Library, Harvard University)*

Goncharov considered his literary godfather, died in May of 1848. The death of his real godfather, Tregubov, followed a year later. Torn by guilt that he had not seen Tregubov one last time before he died, having not visited his family for almost fifteen years, Goncharov went back to Simbirsk in July of 1849 and spent three months there. He found his family much changed and almost unrecognizable—all except his mother, who, he wrote to a friend, "has aged much less than I expected." While his letters to St. Petersburg friends often contain sarcastic observations about his siblings and former neighbors, they are uniformly respectful and loving when he describes Avdot'ia Matveevna. Within two years, she too was dead, and Goncharov took the loss with difficulty.

Goncharov's grief and his desire to do something so dramatic that it would partially alleviate his pain can explain his unexpected decision (that truly stunned many of his friends, since he was known as both a rather apathetic individual and a creature of comfort) to join the around-the-world voyage of the sailing vessel *Pallas,* which was sponsored by the Russian government. The invitation to become a secretary to the admiral of the frigate *Pallas* was first extended to Goncharov's friend Apollon Nikolaevich Maikov. When Maikov declined it, Goncharov seized the opportunity and offered himself instead. To his friends he explained his decision as, among other things, a tribute to Tregubov, who by his stories had first awakened the boy's curiosity in ships and sea travel. The frigate left from a port near St. Petersburg on 7 October 1852, and for the next two years Goncharov, often seasick and exhausted, sailed around Europe, Asia, and Africa.

The trip was a combination of excruciating tedium and moments of true excitement. Sometimes the ship would be stuck for weeks in the middle of nowhere because there were no winds strong enough to move it along. Cooped up in close quarters with little to do, the crew, including Goncharov, would get restless and testy. In London, he witnessed the funeral procession for former prime minister and Battle of Waterloo hero Arthur Wellesley, first Duke of Wellington. Around the Cape of Good Hope, the ship was tossed around by a severe storm that badly damaged it. When the frigate arrived in Japan, its crew received a message from the St. Petersburg Ministry of Foreign Affairs that they were authorized to negotiate a trade agreement on behalf of the Russian crown. While the ship continued north from Japan on its way back to St. Petersburg, Goncharov chose to end his voyage in the Russian Far East, near the port of Petropavlovsk. He landed there in August of 1854 and then spent another six months slowly making his way through Siberia. In Irkutsk, he visited the families of the exiled Decembrists remaining there, including the Volkonskys, the Trubetskoys, and the Murav'evs. It was a rather daring act for an otherwise cautious man, since the Decembrists were yet to be fully pardoned by the czar, whom Goncharov, as a government official, directly served. He arrived in St. Petersburg in February of 1855. During his travels Goncharov kept detailed journals and copies of his many letters to friends. He used these materials later for publications—first travel essays and then a two-volume book, *Fregat "Pallada"* (1858; translated as *The Voyage of the Frigate Pallada,* 1965).

Even at sea, Goncharov found an apt metaphor for his favorite dichotomy between "idealistic" and "practical": sailing ships versus steamers. As a boy, under the influence of his godfather's nostalgic stories about the sea, he may have learned to romanticize sailing ships, but now he found himself longing for the more modern and comfortable steam variety:

A sailing ship resembles an aged coquette—painted and powdered, with ten petticoats, strapped into a corset in order to impress her lover, succeeding sometimes for a minute. But as soon as youth and health appear, all her endeavors scatter like dust. . . . Some people feel that there is less poetry in a steamer, that it is less tidy, less beautiful. . . . "A steamship can't go like that!" they tell me.—"Yes, but the steamer goes all the time!"

He goes on to record that "at the Admiralty of Portsmouth, they were sawing a completely new sailboat in half, in order to insert the steam machinery."

Another previously idealized concept that suffered much deflation and reevaluation was England. Judging by his early correspondence and the fact that he made Petr Aduev's "English ways" appear attractive in *Obyknovennaia istoriia*, Goncharov had been an Anglophile before he embarked on his journey. But in *Fregat "Pallada"* Goncharov includes—only half in jest—an unflattering description of the country:

England is a savage country, peopled by barbarians, who speak in guttural sounds and live on half-raw meat washed down with spirits; in fall and winter they wander through fields and woods, in summer they crowd together in heaps; they are morose, taciturn, uncommunicative. On Sundays they don't do anything, don't talk, don't smile, put on airs; in the morning they sit in their churches, in the evening they sit at home, all alone, drinking separately; on weekdays they get together, make long speeches and drink in company.

He does, however, go on to acknowledge the importance and "instructiveness" of London museums and monuments, the "Abundance, luxury, taste and display" of stores, and finally, the beauty of English women, who are said to possess "an astonishing color of face" and "are distinguished by their stature, external calm, pride, dignity when they stand, firmness when they walk."

Goncharov's qualified admiration for the English quickly fades again when he encounters them as a colonial power in Africa and Asia. He was not against colonial expansions, and as the Siberian part of his travelogue shows, he welcomed the Russian conquest and colonization of the native peoples of Siberia. He was also not a particular champion of non-European or non-Christian cultures, finding them uncomfortably alien and thus hard to decipher. Yet, Goncharov was troubled by what he perceived to be the cold, cruel, and uncaring treatment of the natives by the English, who to him appeared to be interested only in exploiting the resources and people, giving no consideration to the more noble tasks of enlightening and civilizing the "savages." One could obviously argue as to whether the purposes of the Russians in resource-rich Siberia were

any different or the treatment of the natives any more humane, but that was not Goncharov's argument. He considered the conquest of Siberia to be a true accomplishment by brave Russian pioneers and settlers who, in his view, were both enriching the empire and assuring a better future for the natives.

The reception of *Fregat "Pallada,"* first as essays and then as a book, was quite favorable and helped to cement Goncharov's reputation as a leading writer of his time. Goncharov was not actively working on *Oblomov* during his long journey, but he kept the novel alive in his thoughts. References to *Oblomov* appear often in his letters home, as when he wrote from London to his friend Mikhail Aleksandrovich Iazykov on 3 November 1852: "I haven't given up hope of writing someday a chapter called 'Oblomov's Travel.' There I'll try to describe what it's like for a Russian to reach into his suitcase by himself (and know where things are), to have to look after his own luggage, and to be driven to despair ten times an hour, yearning for Mother Russia, for Philip [Goncharov's manservant], and so forth." When he returned to St. Petersburg, Goncharov attempted to pick up work on *Oblomov* where he had left it three years earlier, but then came further changes in both his personal and professional life, and thus further delays.

Little is known of Goncharov's serious attachments to women prior to 1855. Like Aleksandr Aduev, he probably went through his share of youthful and more mature affairs, but since, like Petr Aduev, he was also careful to destroy potentially embarrassing correspondence, one can only speculate as to who these women might have been. When, upon returning from his voyage, he found himself deeply in love with Elizaveta Tolstaia, that relationship, unlike the earlier ones, soon became widely known and generously documented. Tolstaia was in her mid twenties at the time and strikingly beautiful as well as intelligent, according to many who knew her. In the summer of 1855 she often stayed at the summer residence of their mutual friends, the Maikovs, and Goncharov's visits to them became more frequent than before. Goncharov could never bring himself to throw off the mask of irony and detachment and confess his love fully and unequivocally, but he gave her plenty of hints that his feeling was genuine and all-consuming. "Joking is my element," he wrote to her later that year; "You think I joke because I am gay; but I joked at times when terror and turmoil were in my heart." Terror and turmoil were occasioned by the thought of losing Tolstaia, which he eventually did.

It became clear early on in their relationship that he had a rival for Tolstaia's affections in her first cousin, Aleksandr Musin-Pushkin, and that he, more than Goncharov, could feel assured of reciprocity. Tolstaia was no doubt flattered by the attention and courtship coming from a famous writer and, for a while, she was also happy to engage him in deep philosophical and intellectual discussions. By December of 1855, however, she rather abruptly stopped answering his letters, eliciting desperate pleas from Goncharov, who could no longer maintain the ironic distance he so much prided himself in: "Take away from me this right to speak with you and I shall lack a great deal; the very thread of life will vanish; the very living nerve that connects me with people and society will be paralyzed." Tolstaia got engaged to Musin-Pushkin in the summer of 1856. Marriages between first cousins were frowned upon and needed special permission from the Holy Synod. The couple needed Goncharov, who by then held a fairly high governmental position, to help them get this dispensation. He was successful, and Tolstaia and Musin-Pushkin were married early in 1857. Their union, however, ended six years later when Musin-Pushkin died at the age of thirty-two, leaving his widow with two young sons. For Goncharov, this brief but intense courtship undoubtedly had its impact on the fictional relationship of Oblomov and Ol'ga.

As Goncharov was writing desperate letters to Tolstaia in December of 1855, another dramatic change was taking place in his life: he was seeking a position as a government censor. He had long been dissatisfied with his bureaucratic work in the department of foreign trade, and, wanting to do something more directly connected with literature, he had asked one of his friends, Aleksandr Vasil'evich Nikitenko, who was a censor, to help him obtain a similar position. Nikitenko succeeded, assuring his superiors that Goncharov, because of his intelligence and tact, would make "an honest and good censor." On 23 December Goncharov sent a letter to Tolstaia announcing to her that, beginning in 1856, he would be a senior censor, earning an impressive salary.

His choice to seek and accept this position was startling to many. There was, needless to say, no love lost between Russian writers and the government censors, especially since the censorship under Nicholas I was particularly severe. But Nicholas had just died that year, and a more liberal rule was expected from his son, Alexander II. As a child, Alexander had been tutored by the famous poet Vasilii Andreevich Zhukovsky, and legend had it that Zhukovsky had instilled in the new emperor a love for literature and tolerance for its practitioners. The existence of a new and quite possibly more friendly regime obviously made Goncharov's decision easier, as did perhaps his still-alive hope of winning Tolstaia's heart and hand, for which a new position and impressive salary could be beneficial. (In a letter he informed her of the exact amount of his new annual salary—three thousand rubles. To put this figure into some perspective, Goncharov's salary when he started his government career twenty years earlier was roughly five hundred rubles a year.)

Another factor in his decision to accept the job as a censor was that, unlike several other writers at the time and despite the success of his works, Goncharov still could not afford to live by writing alone. After his mother died, his inheritance consisted mainly of the Simbirsk estate, which she had willed equally to him and his older brother. Since his brother lived in Simbirsk and had a large family, while Goncharov was far away and a bachelor, the writer, in a gesture that he may have come to regret later, chose to relinquish his half of the inheritance. Most important, perhaps, Goncharov, a staunch believer in Western democracies, felt that unless honest and decent people like himself chose to exert influence and accept positions of power in the government, the situation in Russia would never change for the better. But if he expected gratitude from his fellow writers for this "noblesse oblige," he was sorely disappointed. Upon hearing about Goncharov's new position, Aleksandr Vasil'evich Druzhinin, a critic who was usually sympathetic to Goncharov, recorded in his diary: "Such a leading Russian writer should not have accepted a position like that. . . . First of all, it takes too much of his precious time; secondly, public opinion does not like it, and thirdly . . . a writer ought not to be a censor."

By all accounts, Goncharov, who by 1857 had censored about ten thousand manuscript pages, proved to be a reasonable and often sympathetic censor. Yet, his personal reputation among many of his peers appears to have been severely damaged, even though his literary reputation continued to be strong. Typical of such dichotomy is a remark from Dostoevsky in a letter to archaeologist and statesman Aleksandr Egorovich Vrangel in November of 1856. Having attributed to Goncharov "a soul of a bureaucrat" and the "eyes of a boiled fish," he nevertheless added: "God, as if for laughs, endowed him with a brilliant talent." Anton Pavlovich Chekhov, likewise, in a 4 May 1889 letter to publisher Aleksei Sergeevich Suvorin, modified his high praise for Goncharov's talent with this caveat: "though I don't like him as a person." This antagonism toward him as a person, which Goncharov must have felt or known about, can probably help explain, at least to some extent, an odd public dispute that erupted two years after he accepted the position of censor: Goncharov accused Ivan Sergeevich Turgenev of plagiarism.

Their relationship was rather rocky from the start. Fellow writer Avdot'ia Iakovlevna Panaeva recalled in her memoirs that Turgenev was quite envious of the success of Goncharov's first novel and "declared that he had studied Goncharov from all angles and came to a conclusion that he is essentially a bureaucrat, that his interests in life were limited and petty, that his nature knew no spiritual leaps, that he is perfectly content with his small world and is not interested in larger societal issues." Turgenev also allegedly predicted that Goncharov would never write another novel.

How much of the rumor about Turgenev's reaction to his early success ever reached Goncharov is unclear, but on the surface at least, their relationship throughout most of the 1850s appeared friendly and even cordial. Below the surface, however, Goncharov probably resented Turgenev, who was independently wealthy and never had to bother with government positions but was quick to show his contempt for those who had to serve. Yet, for several years after the publication of *Obyknovennaia istoriia*, Goncharov had little reason to vent his irritation, for Turgenev appeared not to be a serious literary rival, limiting himself to minor genres of lyrical stories and essays. Then, in quick succession, Turgenev published two novels, *Rudin* (1856) and *Dvorianskoe gnezdo* (A Nest of Gentry, 1859). When Goncharov made his sensational accusation Turgenev was also in the middle of publishing initial chapters from his next novel, *Nakanune* (On the Eve), which appeared in 1860.

Apparently it was Goncharov's turn to feel envious. He was painfully aware that, as far as his literary reputation went, he had lost time, and perhaps momentum, when he kept postponing work on *Oblomov* and on his next novel, *Obryv* (The Precipice), which did not appear until ten years later but which became a bone of contention in the dispute. Combined with the traumatic relationship with Tolstaia, and the obvious distaste shown by many of his peers and friends for his new job as a censor, the success of Turgenev's *Dvorianskoe gnezdo* appears to have been the last straw that finally unsettled Goncharov. The whole incident happened at the time when *Oblomov* was just coming out, and its success far exceeded that of any of Turgenev's novels to date.

In a letter to Turgenev on 28 March 1859 Goncharov accused him of stealing scenes, themes, and situations from his own unfinished novel, *Obryv,* the completed parts of which Goncharov had read to his acquaintances, including Turgenev. He also criticized Turgenev's novels, and in particular *Dvorianskoe gnezdo*, as superficial and not worthy of Turgenev's talent. Instead, Goncharov suggested, Turgenev should have stayed focused on a lesser genre, such as *Zapiski okhotnika* (Notes of a Hunter, 1852), a collection of sketches of rural life that Goncharov said he had always greatly

ОБРЫВЪ

РОМАНЪ

ВЪ ПЯТИ ЧАСТЯХЪ

ИВАНА ГОНЧАРОВА

ТОМЪ ПЕРВЫЙ

САНКТПЕТЕРБУРГЪ

ПЕЧАТАНО ВЪ ТИПОГРАФІИ МОРСКАГО МИНИСТЕРСТВА,
въ Главномъ Адмиралтействѣ
1870

Title page for Obryv *(The Precipice), Goncharov's last novel*

admired. In short, whether by accusations or flattery, Goncharov was trying hard to talk Turgenev out of being a novelist and thus a competitor.

If Goncharov's personal reputation was already badly hurt by his new government position, this incident appears to have ruined it forever. Turgenev emerged as a hero from it all. Publicly, at least, he behaved nobly and benevolently, first downplaying Goncharov's accusations, then agreeing to have a council of their literary peers—among them Nikitenko, who was one of Goncharov's closest friends—to compare their works and pass judgment. The verdict was in Turgenev's favor. He was cleared of any suspicion of plagiarism, and even Nikitenko had to admit in his diary that Goncharov behaved shamefully: "my friend Ivan Aleksandrovich played a very unenviable role in this event; he showed himself to be some sort of petulant, extremely superficial and coarse human being, while Turgenev . . . conducted himself with great dignity, tact, refinement and that particular grace which is the property of decent people of highly educated society." Turgenev and Goncharov publicly renewed their friendship in 1864, at the funeral of Druzhinin, but their reconciliation was neither genuine nor deep.

If 1859 was the year when Goncharov's personal reputation suffered a perhaps lethal blow, it was also the year that *Oblomov,* which won him immortality as a writer, was published. In the summer of 1857 Goncharov had gone to take the waters in Marienbad; alone there, he finally found himself in the full swing of creating *Oblomov* again. Excited and relieved, he wrote to his friend Ivan Ivanovich Lkhovsky on 2 August 1857: "I arrived here on June 21st . . . and within three days was so bored I wanted to leave. . . . Then around July 25th or 26th I inadvertently opened *Oblomov* and caught fire: by the 31st this hand had written 47 pages! *I have finished the first part, written all of the second, and made quite a dent in the third.* . . . I wrote as though taking dictation. Really, a lot of it simply appeared, unconsciously; someone invisible sat next to me and told me what to write." By the end of August the novel was complete. When *Oblomov* came out, Tolstoy again found himself among Goncharov's most ardent admirers; he wrote to Druzhinin on 16 April 1859: "*Oblomov* is a truly great work, the likes of which one has not seen for a long, long time. . . . I am in rapture over *Oblomov* and keep rereading it." Since the publication of the novel, multitudes of readers and critics have come to share Tolstoy's "rapture" over it. This achievement is remarkable for a book in which the protagonist spends most of his time in bed and little, if any, action ever takes place.

Whatever structure and plot exist in the novel are also quite simple. *Oblomov* consists of four parts and spans roughly fifteen years, occasionally flashing back to the hero's childhood (as with "Oblomov's Dream") and ending several years after Oblomov's death. The main part of the book is much shorter, though: it occupies the spring, summer, and autumn of one year in the life of Il'ia Oblomov. Spring is the season of slumber and reluctant awakening upon his best friend Andrei Stolz's return from abroad. Summer is the season of romance with Ol'ga. Autumn is a return to slumber, which leads to eventual death. Milton Ehre was the first critic to notice that these cycles in *Oblomov* anticipate Northrop Frye's theory of literary myths and archetypes as expressed in Frye's *Anatomy of Criticism* (1957): "The Mythos of Spring: Comedy"; "The Mythos of Summer: Romance"; and "The Mythos of Autumn: Tragedy."

The highlight of the novel, and its only dynamic part, is the protagonist's brief but intense relationship with an intelligent and independent young woman who is still naive enough to think that she may change Oblomov's ways and personality, shaped as they were by many years of parental smothering, early disillusion-

ment in St. Petersburg, and subsequent life of virtual stagnation. As was the case with *Obyknovennaia istoriia, Oblomov* is a perfect antithesis to the bildungsroman and an even more obvious parody of one. Despite the heroic measures undertaken by Stolz and Ol'ga, Oblomov is simply incapable of developing or progressing in the manner expected of him, not only as a human being but also as a literary hero.

Other similarities to the first novel are evident. Ol'ga continues the trend of intelligent and restless women that in *Obyknovennaia istoriia* was started by Lizaveta. An orphan who is being raised by her wealthy and childless aunt, Ol'ga craves intellectual knowledge almost as much as she craves love. Lamenting that women are not taught sciences, she often bombards Oblomov with questions that he has no expertise to answer, at which point she becomes angry at him for having squandered an opportunity to learn that she herself was never given. Their relationship involves a switch of traditional gender roles: she is full of energy and a born leader, whereas Oblomov lacks both initiative and strength. He regards her as being smarter than himself, while she thinks of herself as Pygmalion and Oblomov as her Galatea. Even Ol'ga's eventual marriage to Stolz—who, unlike Oblomov, can answer most of her questions and is prepared to lead rather than be led—fails to fill a significant void in her life.

Another easily recognizable feature in the novel is the presence of well-defined contrasts, although they are no longer quite as stark as they were in *Obyknovennaia istoriia.* Like Aleksandr Aduev, Oblomov embodies mostly "heart" and idealism. Like Petr Aduev, Andrei Stolz primarily stands for "mind" and practicality. Goncharov, however, mutes the distinction here, for unlike Petr, Stolz from the beginning refuses to live "by head alone." Born of a German father and a Russian mother, he combines German pragmatism and energy with Russian generosity and, to a certain extent, spirituality.

Goncharov also tends to treat these dichotomies in *Oblomov* in a more artistic and creative fashion than he had in the earlier novel. Most interesting in this respect is the symbolism of Oblomov's dressing gown, introduced at the beginning of the novel: "He wore . . . a real oriental dressing gown, with no hint whatsoever of Europe." Oblomov temporarily and reluctantly sheds the gown upon Stolz's arrival in favor of a European-looking suit but soon reclaims it as he settles back into his dormant existence under the loving care and supervision of his landlady, Agaf'ia Matveevna, a dull-witted but attractive and hardworking middle-class widow whom he eventually marries. Oblomov's oriental dressing gown indicates the origins of his apathy and passivity. As Russia spans Asia and Europe, the Russians, according to Goncharov, consist of two contradictory natures, Eastern and Western. Despite Stolz's and Ol'ga's many attempts to activate the "Western," industrious, and "socially useful" half in Oblomov, the "Eastern," indolent, easygoing, and dreamy half rules his existence.

In general, while *Oblomov* may strike similar themes and use some of the same literary techniques, it is indisputably a more mature and subtle artistic creation than *Obyknovennaia istoriia*. There are many more characters than in Goncharov's first novel, and the still-frequent colloquial exchanges coexist with long narrative passages that characterize the inhabitants more directly. The arrangement of these passages, which in the case of main characters constitute whole chapters, is rather traditional for nineteenth-century Russian literature and is quite similar to what Turgenev did in his novels. First a character emerges onto the scene and actively participates in it for a while. Then the narrator draws back from the immediate events in the novel in order to introduce the character at more length and depth, including the character's past. Having done that, he picks up the action—or, in the case of Oblomov, mostly inaction—approximately where he had left it.

The narrator of *Oblomov* appears, at first glance, to be a similarly traditional third-person omniscient narrator. In the beginning of the novel he is largely invisible, simply letting his characters do the talking. As the novel progresses, however, he becomes more omnipresent and develops a definite personality. He both describes and judges, freely calling Oblomov's false friends "parasites" or criticizing Oblomov's family for having been overly protective when Il'ia was a child. The seemingly omniscient and judgmental quality of the narrator has led many critics to suggest that he does not differ much from narrators found in many other nineteenth-century Russian and European novels. Yet, such an assessment does not do full justice to the complexity and subtlety of Goncharov's narrative techniques. The narrator's strongly developed moralizing tendencies and his very omniscience are, in a rather startling fashion, constantly undermined by equally strong expressions of ambivalence that reveal someone who may wish he knew all the answers but is honest enough to admit that he does not.

One of the issues the novel raises without necessarily providing any concrete solutions is that of serfdom. In a bit of wishful thinking, Soviet critics used to describe *Oblomov* as a novel "which reflected the anti-serfdom longings of Russian society," as the title page of a 1982 edition exclaimed. Serfdom was, of course, a hotly debated issue in Russian society throughout the 1840s and 1850s, when *Oblomov* was being created. As an institution, serfdom was becoming so unpopular that even Nicholas I, not known otherwise for his liberal tendencies, declared in 1842 that there was "no doubt that serfdom, as it exists at present in our land, is an evil, palpable and obvious to all." He did go on to say, however, that because peasants were not prepared for freedom and would perish without their masters' supervision, "to touch it now would be a still more disastrous evil."

The building in St. Petersburg where Goncharov spent his last thirty years living in a ground-floor apartment (photograph by Judith E. Kalb)

Unlike Gogol's *Mertvye dushi*, *Oblomov* rarely addresses this problem directly. The only serf depicted in detail is Oblomov's manservant Zakhar, who, it turns out, has feelings about serfdom that are similar to those of his master. He too misses Oblomovka and all that it stands for. The narrator explains Zakhar's devotion to the old, traditional ways of life by likening him to a domestic animal: "Zakhar loved Oblomovka as a cat loves its attic, a horse—its stable, a dog—its kennel, in which it was born and grew up." And like a dog, Zakhar also apparently takes for granted that his master is a "superior" creature.

While it is possible that, like many of his contemporaries, Goncharov was uneasy with the institution of serfdom, the novel can hardly be read as a work that unequivocally condemns it. In fact, the narrator appears to take for granted that serfdom exists, and when he blames Oblomov, he blames him not for being a serfowner but for being a bad one. Even though Oblomov daydreams about improvements in his village and discusses them with Stolz, he is both too reluctant to change much in the Oblomovka of his forefathers and too lazy to go there himself to ameliorate his peasants' living and working conditions. He also does not believe that serfs should be educated, suggesting, "Literacy is harmful to a peasant: educate him and he may even refuse to plough." The sentiment echoes the then-famous statement by influential Russian folklorist and lexicologist Vladimir Ivanovich Dal', who wrote in 1856 (while Goncharov was still in the middle of writing his novel): "Literacy by itself is not going to educate a peasant; if anything, it will only confuse him, not enlighten him. A pen is easier than a plough." Stolz's views are more progressive than either Oblomov's or Dal's. As a strong champion of capitalism, he suggests, for example, that peasants should be materially interested in working hard for their masters and that they actually need education precisely so that they can "plough better." Yet, even Stolz does not maintain that the institution of serfdom should be totally eliminated.

But if Goncharov is cautious and even somewhat conservative when it comes to political issues of the day, he is surprisingly bold on some social topics, including female sexuality. There is a strong hint in the novel that the void in Ol'ga's life and her general dissatisfaction may have an added sexual component. At the peak of her relationship with Oblomov, during one of their walks in the dark garden, she even experiences a bewildering sensation that shocks and frightens her and that is referred to as "the lunacy of love." Goncharov's lengthy and graphic description of Ol'ga's strange emotions, which are obviously of a sexual nature, has made some critics identify the scene as a depiction of a female sexual awakening, or even orgasm, unprecedented in Russian literature. Some of Goncharov's contemporaries maintained that the writer based Ol'ga not only on Elizaveta Tolstaia but also, and in large part, on his close friend Ekaterina Maikova, Vladimir Maikov's wife. Maikova—who, in the opinion of many, was an unusually capable, intelligent, and restless woman (as well as, like Ol'ga, a good singer)—also served as a prototype for Vera in Goncharov's next novel, Obryv. Several years after the publication of Oblomov Maikova left her husband, had a child with another man, enrolled in the university classes for women that were just starting to appear in Moscow and St. Petersburg, and became rapidly involved in several radical causes, including women's suffrage. In 1869, the same year

that Obryv finally appeared in Vestnik Evropy (The Herald of Europe), she and her common-law husband joined one of the first Russian communes, in the northern Caucasus.

Among the responses to the publication of Oblomov, the most detailed and celebrated analysis belonged to Nikolai Aleksandrovich Dobroliubov, who in the late 1850s appeared to have assumed Belinsky's mantle as the most influential liberal critic of his generation. In 1879, long after Dobroliubov's death from tuberculosis in 1861, Goncharov credited the critic with having made him better understand his own novel. Called "Chto takoe oblomovshchina?" (What Is Oblomovism?), Dobroliubov's 1859 article treated Oblomov and Oblomovism (or "Oblomovitis") as true manifestations of the Russian national character, with its childlike gentleness and naiveté but also laziness and lack of practicality. He noted that all of Russia is one big Oblomovka, and that Oblomovism is not at all only a feature of the past, as some other critics had suggested. Having thus extolled the novel as a significant social and cultural document of its time, Dobroliubov went on to praise Goncharov's artistic skills: "He reflects every phenomenon of life like a magic mirror; at any given moment, and in obedience to his will, they halt, congeal, and are molded into rigid immobile forms. He can, it seems, halt life itself, fix its most elusive moments forever, and place it before us, so that we may eternally gaze upon it for our instruction and enjoyment."

Goncharov was understandably happy with this article and many other, similarly enthusiastic responses to his novel. The only negative reviews came from the conservative, nationalistic press, upset that the only genuinely positive male character in the novel, Stolz, was half-German. After a short trip abroad with the Maikovs, who were still together at the time, Goncharov tried to settle into finishing Obryv, the original plan for which had been started in the late 1840s and was quite daring. As he wrote in a letter to a friend, the heroine was to fall in love with a liberal artist and "should follow him and abandon her nest, and with her maid should travel through all of Siberia. . . . She would have followed him and partaken in his fate, would have been full of perfectly passionate devotion to him, and, if they had no children, would have sought to make herself useful to others all the while, of course, sharing his views." Maikova had been an early and enthusiastic admirer of this version of Obryv and had helped Goncharov both in planning it and in copying the chapters.

As he was trying to complete his novel, Goncharov began to have serious doubts about its original design. Following the 1862 publication of Turgenev's Ottsy i deti (Fathers and Sons) and then, a year later, the appearance of Nikolai Gavrilovich Chernyshevsky's *Chto delat'?* (What Is to be Done?), it was becoming increasingly clear that the liberalism of the 1840s, to which Goncharov was sympathetic, was quite dead, and the nihilism or radicalism of the 1860s was rapidly gaining ground. While some of his friends, notably Maikova, appeared to have welcomed this new social development, Goncharov, who always preached moderation, responded to it with distrust and even open hostility. He did not like Chernyshevsky's novel, finding it poorly written and politically and ideologically extreme. When, in 1866, despite Goncharov's incessant pleadings and supposedly under the influence of *Chto delat'?,* Maikova left her husband and ran away with a poor, radical-minded student, Goncharov's mind became firmly set against the original plot of *Obryv.*

Obryv held a special place for Goncharov. Knowing that it was, probably, the last novel he would ever write, he tried to put in it all the years of his experience and all the wisdom that he thought he might have gained. "This novel was my life," Goncharov wrote several years after its publication; "I put in it a part of myself, people close to me, my native region, the Volga, my home, in short, all my personal life." He put in it Maikova's personal life as well, for in this novel another intelligent and energetic young woman is dissatisfied with her role in society and is determined to pursue her own, less traditional, path to happiness and satisfaction. Like Maikova, Vera becomes involved with a representative of the "new men," or "nihilists," as they were called at the time. Unlike Maikova, however, Vera, having been seduced by Mark Volokhov, a man who espouses "free love," stays with her family and will probably marry Tushin, a local man who is liberal (in the 1840s sense) yet not "radical." Tushin is a progressive landowner who cares about peasants' needs and can continue to respect Vera despite her "fall," yet he still believes in many traditional values that are anathema to Volokhov.

Because of its long history and different initial designs, *Obryv* often reads like two different novels combined into one. When the reader first meets Vera—who, like Ol'ga, is an orphan and is being raised by her great-aunt—she strikes one as fiercely independent, unusually intelligent, and well read, having consumed every book in the large library of the estate. When Boris Raisky, her cousin, in whose Volga ancestral home they all are living, comes from St. Petersburg to stay with his great-aunt and attempts to court Vera, she displays the kind of unbending pride, strength of character, and sarcastic wit that are rarely expected from either a woman or a poor relative. Raisky, a painter and, in his own right, somewhat of a free spirit (he is, in fact, the original "liberal artist" whom Vera was supposed to follow

Goncharov in 1886

to Siberia), often feels no match to either Vera's intellect or her erudition. In these ways Vera is still as she was intended to be in the early plans for the novel.

But the new man Vera falls in love with, Volokhov, is from the beginning portrayed as a rootless and heartless exile who knows how to destroy but not how to create. After he seduces Vera in the ravine (the *obryv* of the title) on the eve of being sent even further away, she is still determined to follow him; but by then, frustrated with the new ideology and embittered by what he considered Maikova's ill-advised choice, Goncharov was in no mood to let Vera do so. Instead, her great-aunt, Tat'iana Markovna, or Babushka (grandmother), as she is often endearingly called, takes over. After revealing to Vera that she, too, once had an illicit physical relationship with a man she loved, Babushka (with the help of Tushin) attempts to keep Vera away from Volokhov and in the community of "decent," "moral" people. The Vera of the second part of the novel, after the encounter in the ravine, can hardly be recognized as the same independent and strong spirit depicted in the beginning. Deeply repentant and humbled, she now spends much of her time in prayer and is

*Goncharov's grave in the Volkov Cemetery, St. Petersburg
(photograph by Judith E. Kalb)*

ready to become as submissive and obedient as her younger sister Marfenka. Two promiscuous women in the community, the wives of a local teacher and a servant, complete the picture of the danger that moral decay poses to women.

This message was not lost on Maikova. Excited about the appearance of the book, because she thought it was going to develop in accordance with the original design, Maikova felt deeply betrayed once she read the final version of *Obryv*. In the spring of 1869, soon after the publication of the novel, she wrote Goncharov an angry letter and subsequently broke all communications with him. Maikova was not the only one who greeted the novel with hostility. Given that even artistically Goncharov's rather humorless and at times shapeless novel was much inferior to his earlier works, it was an easy target for severe criticism, especially in the Russian liberal press, which hated what they called the "reactionary" underpinnings of the novel. The conservative press liked the novel better than any of his previ-

ous creations; but Goncharov, who still considered himself largely a liberal of the 1840s mold, was uneasy about their praise. He also still could not forgive the same critics who were now lauding *Obryv* their harsh treatment of the German Stolz.

Goncharov's main problem in *Obryv* seems to be that the wounds inflicted by Maikova's action were still too fresh, and his response to her choice still too personal for him to be able to build the necessary artistic distance that he needed in order to create another successful novel. Yet, Goncharov cherished and championed ironic detachment more than most of his peers. He had formulated his notion of detachment back at the time he was writing *Obyknovennaia istoriia:* "a writer only writes to the purpose when not carried away by self-absorption and prejudice. He must cast a calm, radiant glance at life and humanity, otherwise he will express nothing but his own *ego,* which nobody cares a rap about." In the late 1860s, however, his celebrated ironic mask failed him: *Obryv,* with all its promise and ambition, sadly lacks both the authorial calmness and the literary radiance of *Obyknovennaia istoriia* and *Oblomov.*

Early in 1868, a year before *Obryv* appeared, Goncharov retired from his post as a government censor. He spent the next twenty years writing essays and memoirs but not attempting to create another novel. The hostile response to his last published book probably accounted for that. In his essays, he often strove to explain his works to the new generations of readers and to defend *Obryv.* He never completed his memoirs, which by the time of his death still covered only his childhood, youth, and student years. Even while writing them, he continued to guard his privacy fiercely, attacking the excessively "confessional" autobiographies that were becoming popular in the last quarter of the century and even apologizing for his own rather meager reminiscences. Several years before his death Goncharov went a step further and launched a "privacy" campaign, urging his publishers never to print his personal letters and, in fact, to destroy them when all parties involved were no longer alive. He cited the example of England: "In England, if I am not mistaken, there is a law which forbids to mention in print any details of personal, family life of a private citizen without his consent. All this is done even if that life does not contain anything unworthy of publicizing. An Englishman's domestic life, his *home,* are sanctuaries protected from the curiosity of the public. It would have served us well too, especially since we like so much to borrow things from abroad, to borrow this good rule from them!"

In the late 1870s, upon the death of his German manservant Karl Treigut, Goncharov assumed the responsibility for Treigut's widow and young children. In uniting households with an orphaned family of a much-lower social rank, he followed the examples of his real-life godfather and his most famous fictional character. Unlike Oblomov, however, he never married the widow. And unlike Tregubov, Goncharov appears to have been quite concerned and serious about the quality of education the Treigut children were to receive, paying generously for the best schools for them. He formed warm attachments with all three children but was particularly fond of the oldest girl, Sania (Aleksandra) Treigut, who was first sent to a good gymnasium and then a teachers' college. In September of 1891, several months after Sania Treigut's marriage, which he had welcomed, Goncharov died among his adopted family, willing to them all his accumulated assets. He was seventy-nine.

Goncharov's posthumous destiny proved to be almost as unsettled as his life. He was first buried in the cemetery of the Aleksander Nevsky Monastery, in accordance with his wishes. Sixty years later, when the cemetery closed, Goncharov's coffin was moved to the Volkov Cemetery, where many other writers of his generation had been interred. He was ultimately reburied next to Turgenev.

In the years immediately following his death, Goncharov was almost forgotten in Russia. The revolution of 1917, brought about by Mark Volokhov's ideological heirs, ultimately restored him to fame. Together with Mikhail Evgrafovich Saltykov-Shchedrin's famous character Iudushka Golovlev, Goncharov's Oblomov found a permanent home—and thus Soviet immortality—in Communist leader Vladimir Lenin's revolutionary lexicon. "Russia has made three revolutions," the leader of the new Soviet state declared in 1922, "and still the Oblomovs have remained, because Oblomov was not only a landowner, but also a peasant; and not only a peasant, but also an intellectual; and not only an intellectual, but also a worker and a Communist. . . . the old Oblomov has remained, and he must be washed, cleaned, pulled about, and flogged for a long time before any kind of sense will emerge." In 1918, as Soviet Russia was still in the middle of hunger, deprivation, and civil war, admirers even attempted to publish Goncharov's complete works for a new generation of readers but had to abandon the project after the first four volumes.

Many years and leaders later, Goncharov's literary reputation both in Russia and abroad is still far from decided. While few doubt the greatness of his most celebrated novel, Goncharov is not usually included in the pantheon of true Russian literary giants such as Gogol, Tolstoy, and Dostoevsky. In critics' estimation of his talent as a novelist, Goncharov is, in fact, often closest to his neighbor in the Volkov Cemetery

whom he had tried so fiercely to discourage from writing novels.

Letters:

K. Voensky, ed., *I. A. Goncharov v neizdannykh pis'makh k grafu P. A. Valuevu, 1877–1882* (St. Petersburg, 1906);

B. M. Engel'gart, ed., *I. A. Goncharov i I. S. Turgenev: Po neizdannym materialam Pushkinskogo Doma* (St. Petersburg: Academia, 1923);

A. P. Rybasov, ed., *I. A. Goncharov. Literaturno-kriticheskie stat'i i pis'ma* (Leningrad: Khudozhestvennaia literatura, 1938);

E. K. Demikhovskaia and O. A. Demikhovskaia, eds., *Neizdannaia perepiska K. R: Stikhotvoreniia, drama* (Pskov: Izdatel'stvo POIPK, 1993);

Demikhovskaia and Demikhovskaia, eds., *I. A. Goncharov v krugu sovremennikov. Neizdannaia perepiska* (Pskov: Izdatel'stvo POIPK, 1997).

Bibliographies:

Anatolii Dmitrievich Alekseev, *Bibliografiia I. A. Goncharova* (Leningrad: Nauka, 1968);

Garth M. Terry, *Ivan Goncharov: A Bibliography* (Nottingham, U.K.: Astra Press, 1986).

Biographies:

André Mazon, *Un maître du roman russe: Ivan Gontcharov* (Paris: H. Champion, 1914);

E. A. Liatsky, *Goncharov: Zhizn', lichnost', tvorchestvo* (Stockholm: Severnye ogni, 1920);

Liatsky, *Roman i zhizn': razvitie tvorcheskoi lichnosti Goncharova* (Prague: Plamia, 1925);

A. G. Tseitlin, *I. A. Goncharov* (Moscow: AN SSSR, 1950);

A. P. Rybasov, *I. A. Goncharov* (Moscow: Molodaia gvardiia, 1957);

Anatolii Dmitrievich Alekseev, *Letopis' zhizni i tvorchestva I. A. Goncharova* (Moscow: AN SSSR, 1960);

Iurii Loshchits, *Goncharov* (Moscow: Molodaia gvardiia, 1977).

References:

Iulii Aikhenval'd, *Siluety russkikh pisatelei* (Moscow: Nauchnoe slovo, 1906);

Anatolii Dmitrievich Alekseev, ed., *I. A. Goncharov v portretakh, illiustratsiiakh, dokumentakh* (Leningrad: Gos. uchebno-pedagog. izd-vo, 1960);

Natalie Baratoff, *Oblomov. A Jungian Approach: A Literary Image of the Mother Complex* (New York: Peter Lang, 1990);

Jean Blot, *Ivan Gontcharov: Ou le Réalisme Impossible* (Paris: L'Age D'Homme, 1986);

O. M. Chemena, *Sozdanie dvukh romanov. Goncharov i shestidesiatnitsa E. P. Maikova* (Moscow: Nauka, 1966);

Galya Diment, ed., *Goncharov's "Oblomov": A Critical Companion* (Evanston, Ill.: Northwestern University Press, 1998);

Diment, "The Two Faces of Ivan Goncharov: Autobiography and Duality in Obyknovennaja Istorija," *Slavic and East European Journal,* 3 (Fall 1988): 353–372;

Milton Ehre, *Oblomov and His Creator: The Life and Art of Ivan Goncharov* (Princeton: Princeton University Press, 1973);

V. E. Evgen'ev-Maksimov, *I. A. Goncharov: Zhizn', lichnost', tvorchestvo* (Moscow: Gosizdat, 1925);

E. Krasnoshchekova, *Ivan Aleksandrovich Goncharov. Mir tvorchestva* (St. Petersburg: "Pushkinskii fond," 1997);

Krasnoshchekova, *"Oblomov" I. A. Goncharova* (Moscow: Khudozhestvennaia literatura, 1970);

François de Labriolle, "Oblomov n'est-il qu'un paresseux?" *Cahiers du monde russe et sovietique,* 10 (1969): 38–51;

Janko Lavrin, *Goncharov,* Studies in Modern European Literature and Thought (New Haven: Yale University Press, 1954);

Ulrich M. Lohff, *Die Bildlichkeit in den Romanen Ivan Aleksandrovic Goncarovs* (Munich: Otto Sagner, 1977);

Yvette Louria and Morton I. Seiden, "Ivan Goncharov's *Oblomov:* The Anti-Faust as Christian Hero," *Canadian Slavic Studies,* 1 (Spring 1969): 39–68;

Alexandra Lyngstad and Sverre Lyngstad, *Ivan Goncharov* (New York: Twayne, 1971);

Clarence A. Manning, "Ivan Aleksandrovich Goncharov," *South Atlantic Quarterly,* 26 (1927): 63–75;

Milton A. Mays, "Oblomov as Anti-Faust," *Western Humanities Review,* 2 (Spring 1967): 141–152;

D. Merezhkovsky, *Vechnye sputniki: Dostoevsky, Goncharov, Maikov* (St. Petersburg: Izdanie M. V. Pirozhkova, 1908);

Sergio Molinari, *Razionalità ed Emozione: Osservazioni sullo stile di Ivan Goncarov* (Padova, Italy: Marsilio Editori, 1970);

M. V. Otradin, ed., *Roman I. A. Goncharova "Oblomov" v russkoi kritike* (Leningrad: Izdatel'stvo Leningradskogo universiteta, 1991);

Irina Paperno, *Chernyshevsky and the Age of Realism: A Study in the Semiotics of Behavior* (Stanford, Cal.: Stanford University Press, 1988);

Richard Peace, *Oblomov: A Critical Examination of Goncharov's Novel* (Birmingham, U.K.: University of Birmingham, 1991);

N. K. Piksanov, ed., *Goncharov v vospominaniiakh sovremennikov* (Leningrad: Khudozhestvennaia literatura, 1969);

Renato Poggioli, *The Phoenix and the Spider* (Cambridge, Mass.: Harvard University Press, 1957);

V. I. Pokrovsky, ed., *Ivan Goncharov: ego zhizn' i sochineniia* (Moscow: Magazin V. Spiridonova i A. Mikhailova, 1912);

M. Ia. Poliakov and S. A. Trubnikov, eds., *I. A. Goncharov v russkoi kritike* (Moscow: Khudozhestvennaia literatura, 1958);

V. S. Pritchett, *The Living Novel* (New York: Reynal & Hitchcock, 1957);

Mechtild Russell, *Untersuchungen zur Theorie und Praxis der Typisierung bei I. A. Goncarov* (Munich: Otto Sagner, 1978);

Vsevolod Setchkarev, *Ivan Goncharov: His Life and His Works* (Wurzburg, Germany: Jal, 1974);

Leon Stilman, "Oblomovka Revisited," *American Slavic and East European Review,* 7 (1948): 45–77;

Peter Thiergen, ed., *I. A. Goncarov: Beiträge zu Werk und Wirkung* (Köln, Germany: Böhlau Verlag, 1989);

Thiergen, *Ivan A. Goncarov. Leben, Werk und Wirkung. Beiträge der I. Internationalen Goncarov-Konferenz Bamberg, 8.–10. Oktober 1991* (Köln, Germany: Böhlau Verlag, 1994).

Papers:

Ivan Aleksandrovich Goncharov's papers are located in the I. A. Goncharov Museum in his birthplace, Ul'ianovsk (Simbirsk).

Dmitrii Vasil'evich Grigorovich

(19 March 1822 – 22 December 1899)

Maria Rubins
Rice University

WORKS: *Peterburgskie sharmanshchiki,* in *Fiziologiia Peter-*
burga, volume 1, edited by Nikolai Alekseevich
Nekrasov (St. Petersburg, 1845); (St. Petersburg,
1872);

Koshka i myshka, in *Sovremennik,* no. 12 (1845); (St. Petersburg: N. G. Martynov, 1882);

Lotereinyi bal. Povest', in *Fiziologiia Peterburga,* volume 2,
edited by Nekrasov (St. Petersburg, 1845); (St.
Petersburg: N. G. Martynov, 1883);

Derevnia. Povest', in *Otechestvennye zapiski* (1846); (St.
Petersburg: N. G. Martynov, 1882);

Anton Goremyka. Povest', in *Sovremennik,* no. 11 (1847); (St.
Petersburg: N. G. Martynov, 1882);

Bobyl', in *Sovremennik,* no. 3 (1848); (St. Petersburg: N. G.
Martynov, 1882);

Kapel'meister Syslikov, in *Sovremennik,* no. 12 (1848); (St.
Petersburg, 1872);

Pokhozhdeniia Nakatova ili nedolgoe bogatstvo, in *Sovremennik,*
nos. 7, 8 (1849); (St. Petersburg: N. G. Martynov,
1883);

Chetyre vremeni goda, in *Sovremennik,* no. 12 (1849); (St.
Petersburg, 1872);

Neudavshaiasia zhizn', in *Otechestvennye zapiski,* 9 (1850); (St.
Petersburg: N. G. Martynov, 1857);

Svetlo-Khristovo Voskresenie, in *Sovremennik,* no. 1 (1851);
(St. Petersburg, 1879);

Mat' i doch', in *Sovremennik,* no. 11 (1851); (St. Petersburg: N. G. Martynov, 1882);

Proselochnye dorogi. Roman bez intrigi, in *Otechestvennye*
zapiski, nos. 1–7 (1852); (St. Petersburg:
Tipografiia Skariatina, 1872);

Smedovskaia dolina, in *Sovremennik,* nos. 31–32 (1852); (St.
Petersburg, 1857);

Rybaki, in *Sovremennik,* nos. 3, 5, 6, 9 (1853); (St. Peters-
burg: Korolev, 1853); translated by Angelo S.
Rappoport as *The Fishermen* (London: Stanley
Paul, 1916; New York: R. M. McBride, 1917);

Pakhar'. Povest', in *Sovremennik,* no. 3 (1853); (St. Petersburg: N. G. Martynov, 1882);

Svistul'kin, in *Biblioteka dlia chteniia,* no. 1 (1855); (St.
Petersburg: N. G. Martynov, 1882);

Dmitrii Vasil'evich Grigorovich

Zimnii vecher, in *Moskvitianin,* nos. 1, 2 (1855); (St. Petersburg: Sushchinsky, 1883);

Shkola gosteprиimstva, in *Biblioteka dlia chteniia,* no. 9
(1855); (St. Petersburg: N. G. Martynov, 1882);

Pereselentsy. Roman iz narodnogo byta, in *Otechestvennye zapiski,*
nos. 11, 12 (1855); nos. 4–8 (1856); (St. Peters-
burg: Korolev, 1889);

Prokhozhii. Sviatochnyi rasskaz, in *Sbornik dlia legkogo chteniia*, 1 (1856); (St. Petersburg, 1872);

Skuchnye liudi. Fiziologicheskii ocherk, in *Sovremennik*, no. 11 (1857); (St. Petersburg, 1872);

V ozhidanii paroma. Rasskaz, in *Sovremennik*, 8 (1857); (St. Petersburg: N. G. Martynov, 1883);

Stolichnye rodstvenniki, in *Biblioteka dlia chteniia*, nos. 1, 2 (1857); (St. Petersburg: N. G. Martynov, 1883);

Ocherki sovremennykh nravov. Iumoristicheskii rasskaz, in *Sovremennik*, 3 (1857); (St. Petersburg: N. G. Martynov, 1882);

Korabl' Retvizan. God v Evrope i na Evropeiskikh moriakh. Puteshestviia, vpechatleniia i vospominaniia, in *Morskoi sbornik* (1859–1862); *Sovremennik*, no. 3 (1860); *Vremia* (1860, 1863); (St. Petersburg: Tipografiia Skariatina, 1873);

Pakhatnik i barkhatnik, in *Sovremennik*, 11 (1860); (St. Petersburg: N. G. Martynov, 1884);

Pochtennye liudi, obremenennye mnogochislennym semeistvom, in *Russkii vestnik*, 7 (1862); (St. Petersburg, 1872);

Dva generala, in *Russkii vestnik*, nos. 1, 2 (1864); (St. Petersburg, 1864);

Progulka po Ermitazhu (St. Petersburg, 1865);

Guttaperchevyi mal'chik, in *Niva*, nos. 1–3 (1883); *Guttaperchevyi mal'chik. Kar'erist* (St. Petersburg: A. S. Suvorin, 1885);

Stolichnyi vozdukh. Eskiz peterburgskikh nravov, v odnom deistvii (St. Petersburg: N. G. Martynov, 1884);

Akrobaty blagotvoritel'nosti, in *Russkaia mysl'*, nos. 1, 2 (1885); (St. Petersburg: A. S. Suvorin, 1885);

Ne po khoroshu mil,–po milu khorosh, in *Russkii vestnik*, 1 (1889); (St. Petersburg, 1889);

Literaturnye vospominaniia, in *Russkaia mysl'*, no. 12 (1892); nos. 1, 2 (1893); edited by V. L. Komarovich (Leningrad: Academia, 1928);

Polnoe sobranie sochinenii, 12 volumes (St. Petersburg: A. F. Marks, 1896);

Bednyi mal'chik (St. Petersburg: A. S. Suvorin, 1899).

Editions and Collections: *Rasskazy i povesti* (Leningrad: Leningradskoe gazetno-zhurnal'noe i knizhnoe izdatel'stvo, 1952);

Izbrannye sochineniia (Moscow: Khudozhestvennaia literatura, 1954);

Pereselentsy. Roman iz narodnogo byta (Moscow: Khudozhestvennaia literatura, 1957);

Literaturnye vospominaniia (Moscow: Khudozhestvennaia literatura, 1961);

Derevnia. Anton-Goremyka (Moscow: Khudozhestvennaia literatura, 1964);

Rybaki. Povesti (Moscow: Khudozhestvennaia literatura, 1966);

Izbrannoe (Moscow: Khudozhestvennaia literatura, 1976);

Izbrannoe (Leningrad, 1981);

Povesti i ocherki (Moscow: Khudozhestvennaia literatura, 1983);

Izbrannoe (Moscow: Khudozhestvennaia literatura, 1984);

Sochineniia, 3 volumes (Moscow: Khudozhestvennaia literatura, 1988);

Povesti i rasskazy. Vospominaniia sovremennikov, edited by A. A. Makarov (Moscow: Pravda, 1990).

Editions in English: *The Cruel City*, translated by Ernest de Lancey Pierson (New York: Cassell, 1891);

"New Year's Eve," in *Tales from the Russian* (London: Railway & General Automatic Library, 1892);

Russian Sketches, Chiefly of Peasant Life, translated by Beatrix L. Tollemache (London: Smith, Elder, 1913);

Third Russian Book: Extracts from Aksakov, Grigorovich, Herzen, Saltykov, edited by Nevill Forbes (Oxford: Clarendon Press, 1917);

Anton; The Peasant: Two Stories of Serfdom, translated by Michael Pursglove with Nina Allan (Reading, Pa.: Whiteknights Press, 1991).

OTHER: *Pesni i poslovitsy russkogo naroda*, edited by Grigorovich (St. Petersburg: D. V. Grigorovich, 1860);

Literaturnyi sbornik proizvedenii studentov Imperatorskogo Sankt-Peterburgskogo universiteta, edited by Grigorovich, A. M. Maikov, and Ia. P. Panaev (St. Petersburg, 1896).

SELECTED PERIODICAL PUBLICATIONS: "Son Karelina," *Russkaia mysl'*, 1 (1887); "Rozhdestvenskaia noch'," *Russkii vestnik*, 1 (1890); "Gorod i derevnia," *Sbornik Nivy*, 1 (1892).

Dmitrii Vasil'evich Grigorovich was by all accounts a minor prose writer, a dilettante who turned to literature, as he did to the visual arts, not in response to a calling but rather in search of a noble outlet for his ideas and creativity. His position in Russian literary history nevertheless is firmly established for several reasons. Grigorovich was well-known in the contemporary intellectual and creative milieu, and he met scores of famous writers and poets, including Fyodor Dostoevsky, Afanasii Afanas'evich Fet, Ivan Sergeevich Turgenev, Ivan Aleksandrovich Goncharov, Nikolai Alekseevich Nekrasov, Mikhail Evgrafovich Saltykov (pseudonym, Shchedrin), Alexandre Dumas, Leo Tolstoy, and Taras Shevchenko. Some of these literary giants even owed their successful debuts in Russian letters to Grigorovich. For instance, Grigorovich was the first audience for Dostoevsky's inaugural novel, *Bednye liudi* (Poor Folk, 1846), which, without further ado, he hand-delivered to Nekrasov, a prominent poet and the co-owner and chief editor of the influential journal *Sovremennik* (The Contemporary), to arrange for its immediate publication. Much later, Grigorovich championed the young Anton Pavlovich Chekhov, encouraging him to expand his work beyond the short humorous sketches that the novice writer was then publishing under a pseudonym. As far as his own writing is concerned, Grigorovich is best known for several tales for children and adults. His contribution to the Russian novelistic tradition is limited to several long, poorly structured, and tendentious novels in the style of the natural school, and, more importantly, the introduction of the genre of the "peasant novel." During the Soviet era, Grigorovich was fortunate enough to escape oblivion through the eulogy by the Communist literary establishment of his "democratic" views, satirical portrayal of landowners, and sympathy for the underdog.

Grigorovich was born on 19 March 1822. The circumstances of his birth and initial upbringing were quite extraordinary for a man who became a writer in the Russian language. His father, Vasilii Grigorovich, of Ukrainian descent, was a retired army major of modest means who served as a steward on an estate near Simbirsk. In 1825 Vasilii Grigorovich bought his own small estate, Dulebino, in Tula province, but he enjoyed the landowner's lifestyle there for only a few years, as he died when his son was eight years old. Grigorovich's mother, Sidonie (née Varmont), was brought to Russia by her French parents in 1803. After the death of her husband, she became entirely immersed in running her household, delegating Dmitrii's education to her own mother. French, therefore, was the first language Grigorovich began to speak and read at home, while he only occasionally conversed in Russian with serfs of the estate. Unlike the average Russian child, who would have been exposed early on to all kinds of children's books, first by listening and memorizing his favorite fairy tales and then by learning to read them on his own, Grigorovich first laid his hands on a Russian text when he was already eight years old.

In 1832 Grigorovich was enrolled in Jenich's pension in Moscow, then in a gymnasium, and later in the private Monigetti pension, where his teachers were all foreigners and where French was the language of instruction. Since his affinity for the visual arts was already quite strong, Grigorovich also attended the Stroganov School of Drawing. In 1836 Sidonie Grigorovich brought her son to St. Petersburg, the Russian capital, where he began his training at the Kostomarov pension, which prepared boys for entrance exams to the School of Military Engineering, at the time one of the most prestigious institutions in the country. Grigorovich studied at the School of Military Engineering between 1837 and 1840, and was subsequently discharged for failing a math exam and for not saluting the Grand Duke, who was the patron of the school. While the career of a military engineer was no longer an option for Grigorovich, he had received a solid education in the humanities, which, surprisingly, occupied an essential part of the curriculum. During those years, Grigorovich acquired a taste for Russian literature, not without the influence of his fellow student, Dostoevsky.

Upon leaving the School of Military Engineering, Grigorovich studied drawing at the Academy of Fine Arts while also pursuing his passion for theater. His theatrical career was no more successful than his stint as an artist, with only rare appearances on stage as an amateur actor, some stage designing, and an affair with an actress that might have ended in marriage had his mother not threatened to cut off his allowance. Finally, Grigorovich landed an administrative job at the Directorate of the Imperial Theaters. In his spare time, he translated plays from French and wrote original stories.

The first of Grigorovich's stories to appear in print, "Teatral'naia kareta" (The Theater Coach), published in the *Literaturnaia gazeta* (Literary Gazette, 1844), was inspired by the day-to-day life of the theater. Its main character is the prompter Ivan Ivanovich—a humble, inarticulate, and fearful man who was the target of everyone's constant mockery and derision. Ivan Ivanovich's literary ancestor is, doubtless, Akakii Akakievich from Nikolai Vasil'evich Gogol's "Shinel'" (The Greatcoat, 1842). Making his debut in literature with Gogol's theme of the lowly character, Grigorovich repeatedly resorted to Gogolian style and subject matter throughout his literary career.

Around that time, Grigorovich met Nekrasov, who was preparing a compendium of physiological sketches, *Fiziologiia Peterburga* (The Physiology of Petersburg), inspired by a similar French volume. The term "physiology" was made popular by Honoré de Balzac, and the physiological sketch was adopted from West European literature and became a signature genre of the Russian natural school. Its popularity in the 1840s was linked to the considerable rise of journalism, the decline of poetry after the passing of Aleksandr Sergeevich Pushkin's Golden Age, and the search for an adequate form in prose that intensified while the novel was still in its gestation period. Along with Nekrasov, critic Vissarion Grigor'evich Belinsky, the chief advocate of the natural school, promoted the physiological sketch as the best way to portray the lower classes and their social milieu. As a rule, physiological sketches focused on the underbelly of life in a big, modern city, depicting types of urban dwellers, rather than individualized characters, providing detailed sociological commentary and aiming at a photographic representation of reality. Upon Nekrasov's request, Grigorovich contributed *Peterburgskie sharmanshchiki* (The Petersburg Organ-Grinders, 1845) to *Fiziologiia Peterburga,* and this sketch won Belinsky's approval. In the sketch, Grigorovich presents a classification of organ-grinders and, using a fair amount of professional jargon, relates their typical experience without providing any individualistic traits. The overuse of sentimental exclamations and direct addresses to the reader, intended to produce an emotional response, anticipates characteristic elements of Grigorovich's mature writing style.

After a reasonably successful start as a writer, Grigorovich experienced some failures that prompted him to leave the capital for Dulebino, where he spent time observing country life and recording the peasants' idiosyncratic speech. As a result, he wrote the novella *Derevnia* (The Village), published in *Otechestvennye zapiski* (Notes of the Fatherland, 1846), embracing the peasant theme in a style reminiscent of "Dorfgeschichten," or village tales. The plot, focusing on Akulina, a village orphan married against her will to a cruel man who eventually beats her to death, is modeled on a real story told by a sick peasant woman once cured by Grigorovich's mother, who worked as a sort of traditional healer. In a sentimental mode, Grigorovich presents Akulina as a silent sufferer, eschewing any psychological profile for his heroine. While also exposing the cruelty and crudeness of the peasants, Grigorovich is seemingly eager to blame the landowner for the tragic situation; Akulina and Grigory are married on one of the landowner's rare visits to the estate in order to entertain his wife with the exotic folk wedding ritual. The absentee landlord, ignorant of his peasants' real needs and inadvertently responsible for many tragedies, remained a leitmotiv in Grigorovich's works about peasant life.

Irony and sentimentality, related respectively to the landowners and Akulina, are complemented in *Derevnia* with many dialectical words and pretty, but somewhat forced, scenes of nature. In his 1846 survey of Russian literature, Belinsky pointed out Grigorovich's lack of talent for the genre of the tale, compensated to some extent by his gift for physiological writing. While generally enthusiastic about the young author's subject matter, Belinsky referred to the image of Akulina as colorless and nondescript. A caricature that appeared soon after the publication of *Derevnia* ridiculed Grigorovich's urge to depict situations from which he was so dramatically removed by birth, education, and experience: Grigorovich, fashionably dressed, searches for new literary material in a pile of manure near a peasant's hut, while a peasant woman pours a bucket of slop on him from the window above. The caption reads: "Unsuccessful search for Akulinas in the village."

A year later, Grigorovich published another novella in *Sovremennik* titled *Anton Goremyka* (Anton the Wretched), which was received quite warmly by the critics. The novella, compared by some to Harriett Beecher Stowe's *Uncle Tom's Cabin* (1851–1852), focuses on a kind, generous, and hardworking peasant, Anton, who is reduced to complete poverty by the steward of the estate. While Grigorovich mounts his criticism against the landlords, whose absence from their estates gives limitless power over the peasants to covetous and tyrannical stewards, he also exposes the worst traits in the peasants themselves. Forced by the steward to sell his only horse in order to pay his quitrent, Anton sets out for a town fair. There he is swindled by his new acquaintances, who steal his horse and rob him of his last piece of warm clothing, while the witnesses to the crime remain indifferent and unsympathetic. The innocent Anton ends up arrested in the company of highwaymen and sent to Siberia. In an 1847 survey of Russian literature, Belinsky stated that *Anton Goremyka* is not a mere "novella" but a "novel" and called its protagonist a virtually tragic figure. This work displays Grigorovich's stock stylistic features, heavy on sentimentality and local color. While Anton is idealized, his antagonists are presented as one-dimensional villains; the author expresses his sympathy for the main character through frequent exclamations; lyrical descriptions of nature alternate with snatches of local speech.

After writing several more novellas, including *Bobyl'* (The Landless Peasant, 1848) and *Chetyre vremeni goda* (The Four Seasons, 1848), Grigorovich decided to turn to the novel, a genre that was still a work in progress in Russian literature. *Proselochnye dorogi* (By-Ways, 1852), which appeared in seven issues of *Otechestvennye zapiski,* is an episodic novel in two parts. Its plot centers mainly on a provincial landowner, Aristarkh Fedorovich Balakhnov, who tries and fails to purchase land coveted by his enemies and to win local elections. Parallels with Gogol's *Mertvye dushi* (Dead Souls, 1842) are hard to miss, both in the resemblance between the protagonist and Gogol's main character, Chichikov, and in the use of objects to expose the characters' psychology or moral side, as well as satirical tendencies.

With many subplots, Grigorovich's novel is overpopulated, although peasants are conspicuously missing from the vast panorama of provincial characters. Perhaps because of its structural and stylistic infelicities, the critical reception of the novel was rather chilly.

Grigorovich returned to the peasant theme in epic form in his second novel, *Rybaki* (The Fishermen, 1853), published in *Sovremennik*. Together with just a few other writers, including Aleksei Antipovich Potekhin and Nikolai Nikolaevich Zlatovratsky, Grigorovich can be credited with introducing the subgenre of the "peasant novel" into nineteenth-century Russian prose. *Rybaki* is a pastoral idyll, in which the virtues of traditional village life are set off against the morally destructive and rootless lifestyle of the factory. At the center of the novel are the fisherman Gleb Savinov and his sons. Gleb is an authoritative figure who personifies patriarchal values. Two of his sons leave the village to seek their fortunes at fish factories, while the youngest son, Vania, continues his father's occupation until he is recruited into the army. Grigorovich shows how Gleb's harmonious and stable world is destroyed by the impact of his antagonist, Zakhar, a factory worker from a nearby town, whom Gleb temporarily employs. Zakhar has almost no redeeming qualities: he is superficial, selfish, immoral, manipulative, and faithless. He seduces Gleb's adopted son, Grishka, with stories of factory life, inducing him to abandon his wife and steal Gleb's money. Grishka leaves with Zakhar, leads a life of debauchery, and eventually commits suicide. Grigorovich provides only a brief description of the factory, as a crowded, unsanitary place. Turning to the factory town, the narrator seeks to demonstrate how material well-being, bordering on opulence, leads to the loss of moral values, destroys family life, and causes disintegration of the fishermen's community. This ideological streak anticipates Tolstoy's vehement attacks on modern technology, symbolized by the sinister image of the train, which, according to the writer, violates the traditional countryside. Grigorovich's second novel turned out to be too long and repetitive and evoked mixed reactions. The "civic" critic Nikolai Aleksandrovich Dobroliubov, one of the ideological icons of Soviet literary historians, for example, found it tedious and hard to accept.

Grigorovich's third novel, *Pereselentsy* (The Settlers; published in *Otechestvennye zapiski,* 1855–1856), enjoyed moderate success. It traces the trials and tribulations of a poor peasant family. The head of the family, a weak-willed and sickly peasant nicknamed Lapsha (Noodle), so-called because he is remarkably tall and thin, has fathered six children but is incapable of supporting his large household.

РЫБАКИ.

РОМАНЪ ВЪ ТРЕХЪ ЧАСТЯХЪ

ДМИТРІЯ ГРИГОРОВИЧА.

—

ЧАСТЬ ПЕРВАЯ.

SS

САНКТПЕТЕРБУРГЪ.

ВЪ ТИПОГРАФІИ КОРОЛЕВА И КОМП.

—

1853.

Title page for Rybaki *(The Fishermen), one of the prototypes for the Russian "peasant novel"*

His wife, Katerina, is reminiscent of Nekrasov's idealized female types, such as Daria from *Komu na Rusi zhit' khorosho?* (Who Is Happy in Russia?, 1865–1877). Katerina is honest, straightforward, hospitable, and hardworking—a true repository of folkloric peasant values. She has an intuitive moral sense, caring assiduously for her mentally ill sister-in-law, and she acts with dignity before her neighbors and landowners. A loving and caring mother, Katerina is often shown in a natural setting, and the narrator indicates repeatedly that her strength and energy come from her intimate communion with nature and the earth.

When writing about the landowners, the Belitsyns, whose extended residence on the estate was caused by their precarious financial situation and inability to maintain a fashionable lifestyle in St. Petersburg, Grigorovich adopts his usual condescendingly ironic tone. He particularly enjoys mocking Mr. Belitsyn's unrealistic and superfluous projects to improve and embellish his estate—attempts that reveal his incompetence in practical matters. Although the Belitsyns' concern for Lapsha's family is genuine, what they propose does not yield the desired result. Lapsha's family is resettled miles away to watch over one of Belitsyn's distant meadows. The peasants initially welcome this change as a way to escape the hostility directed at them by other villagers, as well as the threats of Lapsha's brother Filip, a fugitive criminal. However, the separation from their native soil proves too hard on Katerina; Filip catches up with them anyway; the meadow does not yield the expected income; and Lapsha barely survives the move, dying shortly thereafter. The end of this long and diffuse novel is not completely pessimistic, however, as Katerina is reunited with her son Petia, kidnapped long before by beggars, and Katerina's older daughter, Masha, marries Ivan, her longtime admirer and protector. *Pereselentsy* displays the same flaws as the rest of Grigorovich's writing—the absence of a firm structure; exalted but uninspired descriptions of natural beauty; one-dimensional characters, either idealized or vilified; the overuse of folksy vocabulary, proverbs, and regional words; an agglomeration of improbable coincidences at the end; and constant recourse to characters' identifying features (such as Lapsha's raised eyebrows or Ivan's broad smile).

Throughout the 1850s Grigorovich continued to write short stories and plays. In 1855, while visiting Turgenev's estate, Spasskoe, Grigorovich staged a satirical sketch, *Shkola gostepriimstva* (The School of Hospitality), which shares some plot elements with Gogol's "Koliaska" (The Carriage, 1836). The protagonist, Avenir Lutovitsyn, invites his St. Petersburg acquaintances to his remote country estate, which he has not visited for years. When he arrives, he finds the place in such a state of disrepair that he tries to escape before his guests arrive. Most of the guests have telling names, indicating a range of repulsive character traits. One character, Chernushkin, has been seen by many as a parody of Nikolai Gavrilovich Chernyshevsky, the radical critic and writer of questionable talent whose fiction was inspired by utopian socialist ideals. In *Shkola gostepriimstva,* Chernushkin writes venomous literary criticism, devoid of even a grain of wit; he is spiteful and tactless, and reeks of overcooked rum. The intended parody was clear to Grigorovich's contemporaries, who were aware of Chernyshevsky's hostile attitude toward Grigorovich's writing. Soviet scholars, however, were at pains to gloss over this animosity between the two

writers, whose ideological positions were so eagerly embraced by the Communist literary establishment. During the Soviet period, Chernyshevsky, who, like Dostoevsky before him, had been subjected to mock execution and then sent to seven years of forced labor in the silver mines of Siberia, was turned into a martyr and a revolutionary icon. For these reasons, Grigorovich scholars, such as V. P. Meshcheriakov, made unconvincing attempts to reconcile the two writers posthumously, writing off the association between the character of Chernushkin and Chernyshevsky as erroneous.

In the 1853 tale *Pakhar'* (The Ploughman), Grigorovich presents another idealized peasant character, Ivan Anisimovich. The narrator takes a Rousseauistic stance, effectively building a contrast between city and country. At the beginning of the tale, he is leaving Moscow, setting out for his country estate, where he spent his childhood years. During his journey he meditates in a sentimental manner on the "bustling and petty" city life, which produces "intellectual and emotional fatigue" and "a sense of dissatisfaction and even regret." Life in the countryside, on the other hand, is simpler, and the soul is more peaceful there in its "meditative dormancy." Grigorovich's excessive lyrical landscape descriptions are complemented with frequent exclamatory addresses to the reader, urging him to know and love the real Russian people as well as their land, songs, and speech. The narrator's heartfelt praise for the Russian land and its inhabitants eventually finds more concrete expression in Ivan and his family. Ivan is dying, an event that gives the narrator an opportunity to review his entire life, creating the flawless portrait of an honest, hardworking man of high moral convictions. Ivan was a plowman, and his exemplary personality is explained through his tight, organic connection to the land. After the description of the funeral, the narrator concludes the tale with a long, pompous soliloquy, almost too dull to read, in which the old man is again eulogized as a model for "all of us meek people."

Whereas Grigorovich's writing might create the impression that he was a grim person, preoccupied with the miserable lot of the poor and a feeling of guilt for his own privileged condition, in reality he was, by all accounts, a larger-than-life, epicurean character. Grigorovich loved all the pleasures that life in the affluent capital had to offer. He appreciated quiet country living as well; however, not all of the time he spent in Dulebino was taken up by a focused observation of the peasants' hardships or diligent recording of the idiosyncratic charm of their speech. Grigorovich had a reputation as a philanderer and had at least one illegitimate child with his village paramour. He was a brilliant storyteller and was always welcome in social circles as a witty interlocutor, even if he tended to talk more than listen. In 1858, when Alexandre Dumas, *père,* was visiting St. Petersburg, Grigorovich escorted the celebrity on sightseeing tours, showing the famous Frenchman around art galleries Grigorovich knew intimately and introducing his guest to a wide range of artists and intellectuals. While in Russia, Dumas began working with Grigorovich on the translation of a minor Russian writer into French and was quite impressed by his partner's command of that language.

In 1858 Grigorovich received an invitation from the Russian Naval Ministry to join the naval vessel *Retvizan* on a five-month-long voyage to Europe. The Naval Ministry had already extended a similar invitation to several other Russian writers, including Ivan Aleksandrovich Goncharov, who sailed to Asia and recorded his impressions in the travelogue *Fregat Pallada* (Frigate Pallas, 1855–1857). Inspired by the example of Goncharov, whom he knew personally, and by the sheer excitement of the prospective voyage, Grigorovich accepted the offer. On the *Retvizan* he visited several ports in Northern and Southern Europe and Palestine, where it stayed anchored for long periods of time, allowing the writer to travel further inland.

As a result of this voyage, Grigorovich wrote the travelogue *Korabl' Retvizan* (The Ship Retvizan, serialized between 1859 and 1863, and published in book form in 1873). The opening pages of the travelogue reflect the narrator's anxiety, caused by constant delays in departure and the general inefficiency and slow pace in preparing the vessel for its mission. The rest presents a lively and informative account of life in France and Spain, covering everything from Parisian night life and entertainment, to the French publishing industry, to the seductive beauty of coquettish Spanish women. Following in the footsteps of Goncharov, Grigorovich attempted to penetrate the character and mores of the nations he described. However, he lacked Goncharov's comparative perspective and only occasionally brought up parallels or contrasts with his native Russia. Grigorovich's second model, mentioned in the text of the travelogue, is Théophile Gautier's *Voyage en Espagne* (Journey to Spain, 1845). Although in the Spanish chapters Grigorovich states his intention not to duplicate what has already been so masterfully portrayed by the French writer, he doubtless adopts Gautier's ecphrastic mode, engaging in lengthy descriptions of art galleries, palaces, and cathedrals. The artwork displayed in the Caridad Church of Seville, featuring

canvases by Bartolomé Estéban Murillo, is rendered in great detail and with the flair of a professional art historian, reminiscent of Gautier's style. (Grigorovich and Gautier shared a deep interest in the visual arts and their verbal representation, as both first tried their hand at painting before turning to literature and later excelled as art critics.) *Korabl' Retvizan* remained unfinished, as Grigorovich never wrote about his visits to Greece and Palestine. Nevertheless, this travelogue is arguably one of his best pieces—an intelligent and perceptive account of contemporary Europe, enthusiastic and open to different cultures and unmarred by any ideological bias, in contrast to so many of Grigorovich's other works.

The middle of the 1860s marked the beginning of a long period of silence for Grigorovich the writer, as he published virtually no fiction. His last novel, *Dva generala* (Two Generals, 1864), appeared in *Russkii vestnik* (Russian Herald) just before this dramatic break in his literary career. Like some other works by Grigorovich, including *Korabl' Retvizan,* this novel remained unfinished, as its projected second part never materialized. The first part focuses on the household of landowner Liuliukov, who is unexpectedly visited by two generals. Grigorovich exploits his gift as a satirist to the utmost in this work, sparing neither Liuliukov's family nor his guests. The older general is a particularly ludicrous character: while serving as university vice chancellor, he insisted that books be checked out from the library and read in alphabetical order. Reading books as one pleases was apparently a clear sign of impermissible freethinking, which the general strove to eradicate in students. Although in fact amusing, this anecdotal episode was recycled by Grigorovich more than once in his other texts. In line with the antinihilist feeling of the time espoused by Dostoevsky and, to a lesser degree, by Turgenev, Grigorovich uses Murzhakhanov, the teacher, and Ol'ga Ivanovna, the governess, to parody nihilism. Overall, the novel was not a success, contributing no doubt to the writer's frustration with his own lack of literary talent.

As years earlier Grigorovich had turned to creative writing after failing in painting, so now he went back to the arts after abandoning literature, but this time in a different capacity. Despite the paucity of his literary accomplishments, Grigorovich had a reputation as a solid writer and, more importantly, all the contacts necessary to obtain a lucrative and intellectually rewarding bureaucratic position in the field of the fine arts. He started a new career as secretary of the *Obshchestvo pooshchreniia khudozhestv* (Society for the Encouragement of the Arts) and eventually set up a new museum under the auspices of the society. In

ПЕРЕСЕЛЕНЦЫ.

РОМАНЪ

ВЪ ПЯТИ ЧАСТЯХЪ

Д. В. ГРИГОРОВИЧА.

САНКТПЕТЕРБУРГЪ.

ВЪ ТИПОГРАФІИ КОРОЛЕВА И КОМ.

1857.

Title page for Pereselentsy *(The Settlers), about the decline of a peasant family sent away from their native village*

1879 Grigorovich toured Europe on behalf of the society, visiting schools of drawing in Vienna, Munich, and Paris, with the purpose of observing innovative methods of instruction and recommending them to Russian art administrators. Along with his purely administrative functions, Grigorovich wrote extensive art criticism, advocating realism in art as much as he did in literature. His in-depth knowledge of the Hermitage collection allowed him to produce a guide to its paintings, published under the title *Progulka po Ermitazhu* (A Stroll through the Hermitage, 1865).

Grigorovich's activities in the literary arena during those years were primarily bureaucratic. He played a major role in organizing Dostoevsky's funeral in 1881. In 1883 he was appointed chairman of the *Litfond* (Society for Aid to Indigent Authors) committee in charge of funeral arrangements for Turgenev, who had died in France.

Shortly before he turned sixty, Grigorovich decided to marry a pleasant Viennese woman in a beautiful ceremony at St. Isaac's Cathedral, the fanciest and most important Orthodox church of the Russian capital. In the years that followed, the couple spent a great deal of time on her estate of Weidlingau, in the vicinity of Vienna.

Whether the change can be attributed to his newfound family happiness or some other source of inspiration, Grigorovich suddenly returned to literature, and in 1883 he published a story, *Guttaperchevyi mal'chik* (The Rubber Boy [so-named because the acrobat protagonist was so pliable he seemed elastic, or made of rubber]), which became an immediate success and remains his best-known work—a classic piece of children's fiction. The story relates the short, tragic life of orphan acrobat Petia, exploited and physically abused by his trainer Becker, who makes his little ward perform complex and exhausting exercises for many hours in a row. Throughout the story Petia does not utter a single word and is consistently portrayed as the helpless, passive victim of his cruel environment. Becker's main method of coaching an acrobat is severe beating, and even the sad clown Edwards, Petia's only protector, cannot shield him from the routine violence. The story, reminiscent of Charles Dickens's sketches, is aimed at arousing pity and compassion in a sympathetic reader. To reinforce this emotion, Grigorovich introduces a stark contrast between Petia's miserable existence and the comfortable and happy childhood of Count Listomirov's three children, who come to the circus to see the performance of the *Guttaperchevyi mal'chik* (Petia's stage name). That performance turns out to be the last for the young acrobat, who dies in the arena as a result of an accident. The children's aunt and governess accompany them home, worrying all along about the trauma the children have just experienced, and their concern highlights the general indifference to the death of the child. The critics extended a warm welcome to this story, pointing out only a few burdensome passages as a minor disadvantage. Turgenev, already on his deathbed, wrote Grigorovich a letter on 1 February 1883, in which he praised the characters' authenticity, while deploring the slow pace of the story, caused by excessively detailed descriptions.

All of Grigorovich's original works subsequent to *Guttaperchevyi mal'chik* fell significantly short of the mark, confirming that the success of the story was an isolated incident. The story *Akrobaty blagotvoritel'nosti* (Acrobats of Charity, 1885), which focused on several characters involved in a charity organization, was so marred by stylistic clichés, heavy-handed imitation of Gogolian imagery, and plot flaws that it arguably deserved Saltykov's pejorative comment: "Kakaia merzost'!" (What a loathsome thing!) Eventually, Grigorovich reworked this story into a play, which lasted six performances in St. Petersburg and was later staged by Konstantin Stanislavsky at the Society for Art and Literature in Moscow. In another story, *Ne po khoroshu mil,–po milu khorosh* (Handsome Is as Handsome Does, 1889), Grigorovich resurrects one of his favorite themes–poor, abused children.

After his return to literature at the end of his life, Grigorovich also wrote the play *Zamshevye liudi* (People of Chamois, 1891) and a couple of physiological sketches, "Kar'erist" (The Careerist, 1883) and "Son Karelina" (Karelin's Dream, 1887), all equally mediocre. "Son Karelina," however, made a positive impression on Chekhov, who wrote Grigorovich a long letter interpreting and praising the sketch. Several stories followed in the early 1890s, including the moralizing tale "Rozhdestvenskaia noch'" (Christmas Night, 1890), portraying a beggar woman, the wife of an alcoholic and a mother of five, and "Gorod i derevnia" (Town and Country, 1892), a tale in the genre of a "season story." In both, Grigorovich is faithful to his penchant for contrast, between rich and poor in the former and between the four seasons in the latter.

Apart from his original writing, Grigorovich continued to translate French fiction. His translation of Prosper Mérimée's *Le Vase etrusque* (1883) was so good it was acknowledged as a standard and was repeatedly reprinted in the twentieth century.

Despite an obvious decline in his literary talent, Grigorovich's fame persisted, and in the last decade of his life he received honors for many works written much earlier. Thus, in 1890 he was awarded the Pogosky gold medal for *Prokhozhii* (The Tramp, 1856), which had been recommended by the Ministry of Education for use in primary schools and public libraries. Grigorovich's collected works in ten volumes came out the same year. Always ready to recycle an old work, Grigorovich created a stage version of *Anton Goremyka,* in collaboration with V. A. Krylov, which ran for several performances at the end of 1893 and was subsequently published in 1894. Recognition of the writer's efforts by the Russian literary establishment culminated in pompous celebrations, replete with dinners and laudatory speeches, on the occasion of the fiftieth anniversary of the beginning of his literary activity in 1893.

Grigorovich had always been proactive in identifying and recommending young promising writers, as the story with Dostoevsky demonstrates. In 1885 he was just as perceptive when he discerned the great Russian writer and playwright Chekhov in Antosha

Chekhonte, the author of humorous mini-sketches. Grigorovich was initially attracted by Chekhov's story "Okhotnik" (The Huntsman), printed in the *Peterburgskaia gazeta* (St. Peterburg Gazette). As he had done many years before with Dostoevsky's *Bednye liudi* (Poor Folk, 1846), he took the story to a publisher who could be influential in promoting the young writer's career. This time the publishing magnate, journalist, and playwright Aleksei Suvorin fell in love with Chekhov's style and soon befriended the novice writer. Grigorovich apparently met Chekhov in Suvorin's house in late 1885, marking the beginning of a friendship that left a prolific correspondence. In 1896, when Grigorovich was already in poor health, Chekhov diagnosed his friend's illness as cancer and predicted that the writer did not have long to live.

Grigorovich's final literary endeavor was his *Literaturnye vospominaniia* (Literary Memoirs, published in *Russkaia mysl'* [Russian Thought], 1892–1893). Because Grigorovich for most of the nineteenth century had witnessed the development of the verbal and visual arts in his country and in Western Europe and was an intimate in so many literary drawing rooms, the memoirs could have become a valuable source of information on major cultural figures. However, Grigorovich's *Literaturnye vospominaniia* cannot be qualified as a reliable document because of its confused chronology and extremely careful, diplomatic tone, which raises suspicions that at times the truth may have been sacrificed to avoid hurt feelings. The memoirs end with the author's withdrawal from literature in 1864 and are primarily interesting as an anecdotal record of the cultural milieu of the time. The sequel to *Literaturnye vospominaniia,* titled *Skuchnyi gorod* (Tedious City), appeared in 1897 and offers a survey of St. Petersburg life from the 1840s to the 1890s.

By the end of his life Grigorovich suffered from a range of illnesses, including heart disease, angina, and dropsy. He spent winters in St. Petersburg and summers on his wife's estate in Austria, from which he managed to travel to Italy and the south of France just a few months before his death. He died in St. Petersburg on 22 December 1899 and was buried next to Turgenev in the Volkovo cemetery.

Grigorovich is clearly a minor author, who perhaps had more "lows" than "highs" in his writing career. In *Speak, Memory,* (1966) Vladimir Nabokov tags him and some other nineteenth-century Russian literary figures as "stupefying bores (comparable to American 'regional writers')." Many contemporaries, including Dostoevsky, were no admirers of Grigorovich's body of works either. Still, he exemplifies essential characteristics of the nineteenth-century literary environment that gave rise to the unprecedented achievements of the Russian novel. His works demonstrate that the bulk of Russian prose never pursued purely aesthetic goals; on the contrary, it was frequently used to express a plethora of ideological, social, philosophical, and religious concerns. The greatest Russian novelists of the time, Dostoevsky and Tolstoy (mutually antagonistic as they may have been), display the same penchant for tendentiousness and moralizing as Grigorovich. But, unlike his greater contemporaries, Grigorovich lacked the spark of genius that could have lifted his writing above didacticism and sentimentality.

References:

Joachim T. Baer, "The 'Physiological Sketch' in Russian Literature," in *Mnemozina: Studia litteraria russica in honorem Vsevolod Setchkarev,* edited by Baer and Norman W. Ingham (Munich: Wilhelm Fink, 1974), pp. 1–12;

N. I. Borodina, "Izobrazhenie zhenshchiny-krest'ianki v povesti Grigorovicha 'Derevnia,'" in *Problemy russkoi literatury. Sbornik trudov,* edited by in A. I. Reviakin (Moscow: Gosudarstvennyi Pedagogicheskii institut, 1973), pp. 72–85;

Rose L. Glickman, "Industrialization and the Factory Worker in Russian Literature," in *Canadian Slavic Studies,* 4, no. 4 (Winter 1970): 629–652;

V. V. Kallash, "Dmitrii Vasil'evich Grigorovich," in his *Ocherki po istorii noveishei russkoi literatury* (Moscow: V. V. Dumnov, 1911), pp. 166–177;

V. Kaminsky, "D. V. Grigorovich," in Grigorovich, *Rybaki. Roman. Povesti* (Moscow-Leningrad: Khudozhestvennaia literatura, 1966), pp. 3–24;

L. M. Lotman, "Roman iz narodnoi zhizni. Etnograficheskii roman," in *Istoriia russkogo romana,* edited by B. P. Gorodetskii and N. I. Prutskov, 2 volumes (Moscow-Leningrad: Nauka, 1964), II: 390–415;

V. P. Meshcheriakov, *D. V. Grigorovich–pisatel' i iskusstvoved* (Leningrad: Nauka, 1985);

M. V. Otradin, "Peterburgskie povesti D. V. Grigorovicha (Problema geroia)," in *Nauchnye doklady vysshei shkoly. Filologicheskie nauki,* 2 (1977): 21–31;

Michael Pursglove, *D. V. Grigorovich: The Man Who Discovered Chekhov* (Aldershot, U.K.: Avebury, 1987);

I. Z. Serman, "Problemy krest'ianskogo romana v russkoi kritike serediny XIX veka," in *Problemy realizma russkoi literatury XIX veka,* by Serman B. I. Bursova (Moscow-Leningrad: AN SSSR, 1961), pp. 162–182;

Evgenii Solov'ev (Andreevich), "D. V. Grigorovich," in his *Ocherki po istorii russkoi literatury XIX veka,* third edition, revised (St. Petersburg: N. P. Karbasnikov, 1907), pp. 137–140;

A. I. Zhuravleva and V. N. Nekrasov, "Grigorovich v russkoi literature," in Grigorovich, *Sochineniia v trekh tomakh,* 3 volumes (Moscow: Khudozhestvennaia literatura, 1988), I: 5–34.

Nadezhda Dmitrievna Khvoshchinskaia
(V. Krestovsky)
(20 May 1824 – 8 June 1889)

Karen Rosneck
University of Wisconsin-Madison

WORKS: *Anna Mikhailovna,* in *Otechestvennye zapiski,* no. 6 (1850);

Iskushenie. Povest', in *Otechestvennye zapiski,* no. 11 (1852); (L'vov: Tip. Stavropigiiskogo instituta, 1890);

Derevenskii sluchai. Povest' v stikhakh in *Panteon* (1853); (St. Petersburg, 1853);

Kto zhe ostalsia dovolen? in *Otechestvennye zapiski,* nos. 4–5 (1853);

Ispytanie, in *Otechestvennye zapiski,* nos. 3–5 (1854); (St. Petersburg, 1883);

Frazy, in *Otechestvennye zapiski,* 8 (1855);

Poslednee deistvie komedii, in *Otechestvennye zapiski,* nos. 1–3 (1856);

Svobodnoe vremia, in *Otechestvennye zapiski,* nos. 11–12 (1856);

Bariton, in *Otechestvennye zapiski,* 10–12 (1857); (St. Petersburg: A. S. Suvorin, 1879); revised edition (St. Petersburg, 1880);

Bratets, in *Otechestvennye zapiski,* no. 10 (1858);

V ozhidanii luchshego, in *Russkii vestnik,* nos. 7–9 (1860); (Moscow, 1861);

Vstrecha, in *Otechestvennye zapiski,* nos. 4–5 (1860); (St. Petersburg, 1880);

Pansionerka, in *Otechestvennye zapiski,* no. 3 (1861); translated, with an introduction, by Karen Rosneck as *The Boarding-School Girl* (Evanston, Ill.: Northwestern University Press, 2000);

Nedavnee, in *Otechestvennye zapiski,* nos. 1–4 (1865); (St. Petersburg: Tip. M. A. Khana, 1880);

Pervaia bor'ba, in *Otechestvennye zapiski,* nos. 8–9 (1869); (St. Petersburg: A. S. Suvorin, 1879);

Bol'shaia medveditsa, in *Vestnik Evropy,* nos. 3–4, 7–9 (1870); 4–6, 11 (1871); (St. Petersburg, 1872);

Al'bom. Gruppy i portrety, in *Vestnik Evropy,* nos. 12 (1874); 2, 9 (1875); 3 (1877); (St. Petersburg: A. S. Suvorin, 1879);

Zdorovye, in *Otechestvennye zapiski,* no. 9 (1883);

Provintsiia v starye gody, 3 volumes (St. Petersburg, 1884);

Nadezhda Dmitrievna Khvoshchinskaia (V. Krestovsky)

Obiazannosti, in *Severnyi vestnik,* nos. 1 (1885); 1, 4, 8, 12 (1886); (St. Petersburg: Izd. Suvorina, 1888).

Editions and Collections: *Romany i povesti,* 8 volumes (St. Petersburg, 1859–1866);

Ocherki i otryvki, 2 volumes (St. Petersburg, 1880–1882);

Povesti, 4 volumes (St. Petersburg: Knizhnyi magazin Novogo vremeni, 1880–1884);

Na pamiat' 1850–1884 (St. Petersburg: A. S. Suvorin, 1885);

Sobranie sochinenii, 5 volumes (St. Petersburg: A. S. Suvorin, 1892);

Polnoe sobranie sochinenii V. Krestovskogo, edited by A. A. Kaspari, 6 volumes (St. Petersburg, 1912–1914);

Povesti i rasskazy (Moscow: Khudozhestvennaia literatura, 1963);

Povesti i rasskazy, edited by M. S. Goriachkina (Moscow: Moskovskii rabochii, 1984).

Editions in English: "On the Way," *Russian Women's Shorter Fiction: An Anthology, 1835–1860,* translated, with an introduction, by Joe Andrew (Oxford: Clarendon Press, 1996), pp. 301–318;

"After the Flood," translated by Karla Solomon, in *Russian Women Writers,* volume 1, edited by Christine Tomei (New York: Garland, 1999), pp. 268–283.

SELECTED PERIODICAL PUBLICATIONS:

"V doroge," *Sankt-Peterburgskie vedomosti,* nos. 209–210 (1854);

"Provintsial'nye pis'ma o nashei literature," *Otechestvennye zapiski* (1861–1863)–comprises eight critical articles;

"Za stenoi," in *Otechestvennye zapiski,* no. 10 (1862);

"Domashnee delo," in *Otechestvennye zapiski,* no. 1 (1864);

"Staryi portret, novyi original," in *Biblioteka dlia chteniia,* no. 2 (1864);

"Ridneva," in *Vestnik Evropy,* no. 12 (1874);

"Veriagin," in *Vestnik Evropy,* nos. 2, 9 (1875);

"Schastlivye liudi," in *Otechestvennye zapiski,* no. 4 (1877);

"Literaturnye besedy," *Russkie vedomosti* (1877–1879)–comprises three critical articles;

"Posle potopa," in *Otechestvennye zapiski,* no. 2 (1881).

Nadezhda Dmitrievna Khvoshchinskaia was one of the most popular and respected Russian writers of the nineteenth century. From 1842 to 1889 she established a substantial reputation as a prose writer, although her literary output also included poetry, drama, translations, and critical articles. Her fictional emphasis on psychological analysis and narrative subjectivity aligns her prose with that of writers such as Ivan Sergeevich Turgenev and Fyodor Dostoevsky, while her thematic examination of individual freedom, social responsibility, love, work, and generational conflict suggests influential predecessors among the works of Aleksandr Sergeevich Pushkin, Ivan Aleksandrovich Goncharov, and Aleksandr Nikolaevich Ostrovsky. Like other Russian nineteenth-century writers, her exploration of family conflicts created a vital, small-scale workshop for examining larger social issues, while avoiding the watchful eye of the censor.

Nadezhda Dmitrievna Khvoshchinskaia was born 20 May 1824 to impoverished gentry in the Pronskii district of Riazan' province. Her mother, Iuliia Vikent'evna Drobyshevskaia-Rubets, of Polish extraction, married Khvoshchinskaia's father at age sixteen. Of Nadezhda's siblings, two sisters, Sof'ia and Praskov'ia, also became writers. Another younger sister died at age eleven; her brother chose an early military career.

Born on the same day but four years apart, Nadezhda and Sof'ia developed a close relationship in early childhood. The two complemented each other in personality; Sof'ia's calm, restrained, and measured intelligence offered a balance to her sister's hot-tempered, more passionate nature. The sisters' intellectual affinity formed the basis for a productive literary partnership that engendered common, though distinctly treated, themes, images, and motifs throughout their works. As a child, Nadezhda edited a literary journal that included submissions from her siblings and was called *Zvezdochka* (The Little Star); it was produced weekly at the home of her aunt and submitted to her father for review. Both Nadezhda and Sof'ia painted in watercolors, and Sof'ia also painted in oils.

Nadezhda apparently enjoyed a happy childhood, despite health problems that persistently plagued her early years, including a bout of rickets that left her with a permanent, deforming curvature of the spine and some facial irregularity. Although she briefly attended a private boarding school between the ages of eleven and twelve, she was largely educated at home by private tutors. While Sof'ia attended the Ekaterinskii Institut in Moscow, Nadezhda attempted to write her first novel with N. E. fon Vinkler, a young girlfriend. Nadezhda taught herself Italian while visiting relatives in Moscow; her mother had taught her French as a child. Endowed with an unusually good memory, she could recite whole pages of poetry or even prose after reading something only twice. As a young girl, she read works by William Shakespeare (in French), Friedrich Schiller, Dante, John Milton, and Nikolai Vasil'evich Gogol. The works of Victor Hugo, Mikhail Iur'evich Lermontov, and George Gordon, Lord Byron remained among her lifelong favorites.

The family's economic situation significantly worsened when accusations of embezzlement cost Nadezhda's father his civil service position. A subsequent legal battle depleted the family's finances still further, forcing him to sell his property and move to a single-story wooden house in the city of Riazan'. Built in the first third of the nineteenth century, the original house still stands at number 10 Kaliaev (formerly Seminarskaia) Street. Although Nadezhda's father maintained his innocence over the next fifteen years, he did not successfully obtain another stable position until 1845.

While largely remembered for her work as a prose writer, Khvoshchinskaia initially began her publishing efforts as a poet. Her first published poem, "Materi" (To My Mother), an encomium to her mother as a source of poetic inspiration, appeared in the journal *Syn otechestva* (Son of the Fatherland) in 1842 when she was eighteen years old. The editor, Konstantin Petrovich Masal'sky, also accepted a novella written by Khvoshchinskaia, but the suspension of the journal prevented its publication. While her poetry continued to appear in journals throughout her lifetime and in anthologies after her death, her desire to publish her poetry in a single collection remained unrealized. More than a hundred poems written during her lifetime have remained unpublished.

Khvoshchinskaia's poetic talent greatly influenced her prose style. While she wrote a large amount of lyric poetry, many other poems address social issues central to her prose work. Her 1856 poem "Slovo" (A Word), which criticizes the egotism and superficiality of life among the privileged classes, has been called an epigraph for her literary work in general. Another poem considers the 1848 revolution in France, a recurrent motif throughout her prose. The anonymous critic of an article published in 1853 for the progressive journal *Otechestvennye zapiski* (Notes of the Fatherland) argued that the poetic sensibility of Khvoshchinskaia's narrative style "comprises the main strength and charm of her talent."

Nikolai Alekseevich Nekrasov, writer and editor for *Sovremennik* (The Contemporary) and Vladimir Zotov, editor of *Literaturnaia gazeta* (The Literary Gazette) after 1847, encouraged Khvoshchinskaia's early experiments with prose in the 1850s. In his review of her novella in verse, *Derevenskii sluchai* (A Country Incident, 1853), Nekrasov argued that Khvoshchinskaia "had set out on a false road," stressing that "she possesses all that is necessary to write prose successfully."

Although she subsequently established a successful career as a prose writer, Khvoshchinskaia's fiction rarely attracted critical acclaim. In an article published in 1880, Petr Nikitich Tkachev argued that critics remained reserved toward Khvoshchinskaia's works because her cultivation of narrative subjectivity defied contemporary aesthetic standards. He contended that her fictional narrators particularly undermined readers' expectations of objectivity by persistently interjecting opinion and judgment into the narrative. More recently, Jehanne Gheith has advanced a similar opinion, arguing that Khvoshchinskaia's works "do not fit the usual categories of society tale, romantic fiction, philosophical novel, physiological sketch, or even realist fiction." As a result, her work "invites, or rather, demands reconceptualizing the history of Russian letters." In a 1994 essay, Arja Rosenholm asserted that Khvoshchinskaia's works suffered poor critical reception because "her fiction and her views on politics did not fit conventional categories."

Khvoshchinskaia published a great deal of prose as well as poetry during the first period of her career, from 1842 to 1860. Her fictional output during this time included her first novella, *Anna Mikhailovna* (1850); the story "V doroge" (1854), translated in 1996 as "On the Way"; the novel *Ispytanie* (The Test, 1854); the trilogy *Provintsiia v starye gody* (The Provinces in Bygone Years, 1850–1856); *Frazy* (Phrases, 1855); *Bariton* (The Baritone, 1857); and the novella *Bratets* (Dear Brother, 1858). More than a dozen stories and novels as well as poetry appeared in journals such as *Otechestvennye zapiski, Literaturnaia gazeta,* and *Illiustratsiia* (Illustration), also edited by Zotov. As an indication of her growing literary reputation, a first edition of her collected prose works began appearing in 1859. However, this attempt to market her fictional works beyond their initial publication in journals proved only modestly successful: just eight hundred copies were sold in three years.

While Khvoshchinskaia published poetry under her own name, she assumed the masculine pseudonym V. Krestovsky to publish her prose fiction. She stubbornly clung to her choice of pseudonym even when the work of another writer with the same name (Vsevolod Krestovsky) appeared in print. Instead of changing her pen name, she simply added the designation "pseudonym" to reduce confusion. Later in her career she adopted additional masculine pseudonyms or initials, such as V. Porechnikov, Nikolai Kuratov, N. Vozdvizhensky, and V. K. to publish her critical essays. Although mention of her feminine identity occurred frequently in early reviews, the critic Vasilii Ivanovich Semevsky noted in 1890 that even in the late 1850s some readers still mistakenly believed that Krestovsky was a man.

Although an immature work, somewhat overburdened with plot twists and secondary characters, Khvoshchinskaia's first novella, *Anna Mikhailovna,* exhibits a surprising number of her later themes and motifs. The novella also powerfully reveals her fully developed talent for witty dialogue. In his 1885 review of this early period of her career, critic Konstantin Konstantinovich Arsen'ev ranked *Anna Mikhailovna* as one of Khvoshchinskaia's most important works.

While visiting an aunt in St. Petersburg with her father, seventeen-year-old Anna Mikhailovna meets Petr Nikolaevich Okol'sky, a twenty-six-year-old civil servant with literary pretensions and a modest salary. Despite the young people's mutual attraction, Anna's father, a widower, selfishly neglects to contract a match for his daughter, since he will lose her attention and housekeeping skills in the home if she marries.

When her father dies later the same year, Anna moves in with her uncle, his wife, and their three daughters.

A few years later, Okol'sky arrives in the city of N. to take possession of an inheritance of land but also establishes a "strange" flirtatious relationship with Anna. He even boldly kisses her hand at Mrs. L.'s home, generating gossip that Anna behaves "freely" with young men. To protect her own daughters from scandal, Anna's aunt responds by pressuring her niece to move out. Anna rejects Okol'sky altogether after he arrives at her rooming house to declare his love but announce his marriage to Anastasie Khlopova in the same breath. In the last paragraph of the novella, the narrator reports that Anna has married and moved to inherited property in the countryside.

A reference in *Anna Mikhailovna* to Samuel Richardson's *Clarissa* (1747–1748) suggests a major literary progenitor of Khvoshchinskaia's novella. Not the first Russian reworking of Richardson's novel, *Anna Mikhailovna* in fact succeeds many works with similar literary origins, such as Pushkin's *Evgenii Onegin* (Eugene Onegin, 1825–1832) and Vladimir Fedorovich Odoevsky's "Kniazhna Zizi" (Princess Zizi, 1839). Both *Anna Mikhailovna* and *Clarissa* depict heroines driven from their families' homes because of socially unsanctioned behavior. Father figures also fail to protect both girls, and both retreat to rooming houses to escape a rake's pursuit.

Khvoshchinskaia continued to explore the lives of provincial women in her first three novels. *Svobodnoe vremia* (Free Time, 1856), published as the first novel of the separately issued trilogy *Provintsiia v starye gody,* depicts the lonely existence of an orphan named Klavdiia Iakovlevna, who lives as little more than a servant in the house of her uncle, Vasilii Ivanovich Kavataev. When her cousin Sergei Pavlovich comes to stay after his university graduation, she discovers passion and also the courage to defy her uncle's authority. The title of the novel suggests both Klavdiia's brief flirtation with freedom in rebelling against her uncle's authority and also Sergei's largely carefree existence before leaving the city of N. for a military career.

In *Kto zhe ostalsia dovolen?* (Who Was Left Satisfied? 1853), the widowed Katerina Mikhailovna Voronskaia strives to contract an advantageous marriage for her unattractive son, Aleksandr. The daughter of a wealthy friend of the family, Nina Aleksandrovna Litvina, arrives for a visit just in time to fulfill Katerina's matrimonial designs. Although Nina lacks the courage to tell her father of her love for Aleksandr's friend Nikolai Beliagin, she successfully avoids an undesired marriage to Aleksandr when

thirty-year-old Nadine Grashkova snares him and his mother's money for herself.

The remaining novel in the trilogy, *Poslednee deistvie komedii* (The Last Act of the Comedy, 1856), reveals a greater sophistication in narrative technique and characterization than Khvoshchinskaia's earlier prose works had. A well-developed third-person narrator depicts characters and events with caustic and comic irony. Khvoshchinskaia's masterful rendering of fresh and pithy dialogue vibrantly animates a pantheon of eccentric characters. Arsen'ev asserted that during the first period of her career, Khvoshchinskaia's talent achieved its "greatest strength" in this novel. He declared that "the hand of the master is seen at every step."

In *Poslednee deistvie komedii,* Andrei Valer'ianovich Orshevsky disrupts family peace and harmony when gambling debts impel him to sell some of his wife's property. To bolster the family's financial stability further, he convinces his son to marry the wealthy widow Artemina. However, Aleksandr's marriage to Artemina will prohibit a union between his sister, Mar'ia, and Grigorii Nestoev, Artemina's brother, according to contemporary law. Andrei's poor fiscal judgment also dooms his daughter's hope for future happiness. The love story of Mar'ia and Grigorii rapidly disintegrates into a hackneyed romantic tragedy: Nestoev dies in a duel, and Nina succumbs to grief six days later. Andrei's wife more successfully responds to her husband's irresponsible mismanagement of family finances. She leaves him to move to her property in Berezovka, repurchased by her friend, the widowed Pelageia Mikhailovna.

In her 1998 essay "Gender," Barbara Heldt notes the frequent presence in Russian novels by writers such as Turgenev and Dostoevsky of a male protagonist's struggle to reclaim a patrimony. Heldt contrasts this common theme among male writers with the more restrictive domestic spaces depicted in most Russian women's fiction. While Khvoshchinskaia's works largely examine domestic conflicts, interestingly, much of her fiction also focuses on her heroines' struggles to obtain or retain an inheritance.

At the end of Khvoshchinskaia's first novella, for example, Anna Mikhailovna at last acquires a home of her own when she inherits property. Andrei's wife, Elena, reclaims her property in *Poslednee deistvie komedii,* rectifying the damages accrued by her husband's incompetent mismanagement of family finances. In *Nedavnee* (Recent Times, 1865), the elderly Agafena Petrovna retains her inherited estate through the fiscal support of her daughter's lover, Colonel Skvoreshchensky. Lisa in "Ridneva" (1874), on the other hand, discovers that her future estate has been sold two weeks before the death of her benefactress.

At the end of 1852, Khvoshchinskaia accompanied her father to St. Petersburg to visit relatives. While there she continued to build her relationship with Andrei Aleksandrovich Kraevsky, editor of *Otechestvennye zapiski,* the journal that later published most of her literary works. During this time, she also met other members of the literary world of St. Petersburg, such as poet Nikolai Fedorovich Shcherbina, who later became a close friend.

Khvoshchinskaia's literary income became necessary for family survival when her father's death in 1856 left the family in an extremely precarious economic condition. She also began to assume responsibility for directing family decisions, living almost exclusively in Riazan' until the fall of 1881. There, she wrote the majority of her literary works in a separate room provided for her use, at the little desk that her father had given her. She and her sister Sof'ia left Riazan' only infrequently to visit St. Petersburg for periods of several months, usually staying at the Znamenskaia Hotel on Vasilevskii Island.

Khvoshchinskaia's works in the 1850s display many of the themes, motifs, and images important to her later fiction. In addition to the struggle to retain a patrimony, the problem of serfdom, the aesthetics of women's writing, the nature of crime and punishment, the dynamics of personal and social responsibility, suicide, "free love," and women's education all received treatment in her fiction. Her works also reveal an array of motifs beginning in the 1850s that suggest intriguing connections to the works of other Russian writers. Her repeated references to dolls, musicians, mirrors, paintings, photographs, America, gossip, doubles and doubling, the act of observation, needlework, and plays by Shakespeare and Ostrovsky form a colorful tapestry of imaginative detail.

Khvoshchinskaia's early story "V doroge" offers an interesting example of her use of double discourse, a frequent stylistic feature of her later works as well. The first-person narrator, a man returning to his hometown on business, recalls his childhood friendship with a girl named Naden'ka. He also recalls his early fascination with the language of business spoken by the townsmen, but in addition he remembers their humiliating references to women. When he and Naden'ka were caught reading in secret as children, he did not defend her or their reading but instead suddenly became ill. After his recovery, the two drifted apart. Unable to confront his childhood betrayal of Naden'ka now as an adult, he flees N. once again when Naden'ka's mother-in-law appears to solicit his

assistance in supporting her deceased daughter-in-law's five-year-old son.

In a 1993 critical study of "V doroge," Arja Rosenholm explores Khvoshchinskaia's use of dual gendered categories such as men/speaking, women/silent throughout the story. Khvoshchinskaia's adoption of a masculine pseudonym and first-person narrator in works such as "V doroge" as well as the later "Za stenoi" (Behind the Wall, 1862) and *Pervaia bor'ba* (First Battle, 1869), provides additional layers of doubling and also further highlights issues of gender in these texts. The narrator's attempts to communicate undifferentiated past happiness through memory reveal dualistic schisms in his consciousness, stemming from the conflicts of his childhood.

Bratets, one of Khvoshchinskaia's most successful early novellas, depicts the outcome of one spoiled son's extended tenure as head of the family. In what is perceived as a threat to family stability, nineteen-year-old Katia, Sergei's youngest sister, seeks happiness and independence by marrying. While Sergei plays a central role in thwarting Katia's marriage plans, other members of the family expose thier own ambiguous intentions by ultimately encouraging the conditions for his destructive visit. In particular, the eldest daughter Praskov'ia's offer of five thousand rubles of her own as a dowry for Katia prompts their mother to send a letter to Sergei, notifying him, as head of the family since his father's death, of the decisions and events coalescing behind his back and without his approval. Viewed by Praskov'ia during childhood as a pretty doll for her own amusement, Katia remains little more than a plaything in the current power struggle between her older brother and sister.

As her career developed, Khvoshchinskaia began to attract a sizable readership for her works, especially among women. Acquainted with her for more than twenty years, novelist Petr Dmitrievich Boborykin attested to the popularity of her works during his youth in an article for *Novosti* (News). Abram Il'ich Reitblat has noted in a study published in 1991 that circulation records from Moscow libraries in 1860 confirm the sizeable readership of Khvoshchinskaia's fiction. Her works were also among those most frequently chosen by schoolteachers for classroom reading during this period.

Despite Khvoshchinskaia's growing success among readers, critics remained reserved during the 1850s, usually criticizing the narrow domestic focus of her plots and themes. In an article in 1856 Nekrasov faulted her prose also for a tendency toward "rezoner-stvo" (intellectualization). He asserted that "if there were less 'literariness' and more life in Krestovsky's novellas, they would arguably be among the best works of the new literature."

Arsen'ev characterized the period beginning in 1860 as the turning point of Khvoshchinskaia's career, asserting that her fiction reached full maturity at this time. Works published in the 1860s included *Vstrecha* (An Encounter, 1860), *V ozhidanii luchshego* (In Hope of Something Better, 1860), *Pansionerka* (1861, translated as *The Boarding-School Girl,* 2000), "Za stenoi"(Behind the Wall, 1862), "Domashnee delo" (A Domestic Matter, 1864), "Staryi portret, novyi original" (An Old Portrait, a New Original, 1864), *Nedavnee* (Recent Times, 1865), and *Pervaia bor'ba* (First Battle, 1869). Her high earnings (100 rubles per signature) for the novel *V ozhidanii luchshego,* published in *Russkii vestnik* (The Russian Herald), distinguished her as the twelfth-highest-paid author in Russia, just behind Nikolai Semenovich Leskov. Her average yearly income had doubled since the 1850s as well.

Khvoshchinskaia also expanded her range of themes during this time. Her creation of more positive character types in the 1860s reflected the more progressive, reformist mood following the emancipation of the serfs and the end of the Crimean War. Her experimentation with double discourse in the early 1850s evolved into a cultivation of multiple, contradictory narrative perspectives that undermined the authority of her omniscient narrators, typical of novels such as *Vstrecha.*

One of the most successful prose works of her career, *V ozhidanii luchshego* (republished in a second separate edition in 1880), also attracted a rare measure of critical acclaim. Focusing on the moral decay of the Russian aristocracy, the novel candidly treated the themes of serfdom, class conflict, and adultery on the eve of the emancipation of the serfs. In 1861 critic Vasilii Petrovich Popov asserted, "The major value of the novel consists of its masterfully depicted characters. This splendid collection of moral monsters is true to the last fiber."

In *V ozhidanii luchshego,* twenty-two-year-old Katerina maintains a love affair with Prince Ivan Desiatov, while still married to Nikolai Aleksinsky. When Ivan shows signs of boredom, Katerina gladly embraces an opportunity to visit her country estate without her husband, knowing that Ivan will be visiting his grandmother in the same district. During this summer sojourn in the country, Princess Desiatova's other grandson, Vasia (age fourteen), vies for his grandmother's favor and inheritance of the Bubnov estate, formerly handed down to daughters in the family.

Khvoshchinskaia's *V ozhidanii luchshego*–like two other contemporary prose masterpieces, Gustave Flaubert's *Madame Bovary* (1856) and Leo Tolstoy's *Anna* *Karenina* (1875–1877)–explores the theme of adultery over a broad social backdrop. However, unlike the heroines of these novels, who meet untimely and even gruesome deaths after their misdeeds, Katerina suffers neither remorse nor any kind of punishment except a superficial display of disapproval from female acquaintances, who snub her for an evening. Even the suicide of her long-suffering husband Nikolai at the end of the novel fails to revive her conscience and only briefly dampens her social life.

In his 1979 *Adultery in the Novel,* Tony Tanner argues that fictional adulterers in nineteenth-century literature provided authors with a means to explore the effects of transgression against social law in general. However, Katerina's adulterous relationship with Ivan fails to produce even the slightest disturbance in the social order. Her country estate manager, Nikolai Mikhailovich Neriatsky, a vociferous critic of upper-class privilege, represents the real danger to social stability. In leaving the family's employment to build an iron factory, he steps outside the social hierarchy based on land ownership, threatening the social order far more than Katerina's illicit relationship with Ivan.

In Khvoshchinskaia's novel *Vstrecha,* writer Vladimir Tarneev takes a four-month vacation at his childhood home in the countryside. Through Varvara Neliubina, the mother of his deceased friend Sergei, he meets Mar'ia Petrovna Panteleva, her three daughters, and the thirty-year-old Aleksandra Grigor'evna Akhtarovskaia. Aleksandra had scandalously left her husband four years earlier and now lives on property inherited from her father. Mar'ia Panteleva's daughter Liudmila, a poet, falls in love with Tarneev, but he likes neither her nor her poetry. Instead, he finds the eccentric fate of Aleksandra more interesting. Also fascinated by Aleksandra, Liudmila contends that this woman's life story would make a good subject for a novel by Tarneev, Aleksandra, or herself. Five years later, Liudmila has issued a collection of her poetry, while Tarneev has stopped writing altogether.

Women as writers appear as characters throughout much of Khvoshchinskaia's fiction. Not always cast as the heroines of her prose works, women writers nevertheless maintain a vibrant and colorful presence within the social landscape. In *Vstrecha,* Liudmila invites Tarneev into her study where she tirelessly subjects him to recitations of her own poetry. Dodo, an "old doll" at thirty, writes poetry and surrounds herself with philosophical companions in the novel *V ozhidanii luchshego.* In *Nedavnee,* Colonel Skvoreshchensky finds himself attracted to Nadezhda Sergeevna because he had heard that she wrote poetry before her marriage. Appearing in the works of earlier Russian writers, such as Elena Gan's

Naprasnyi dar (A Futile Gift, 1842), women writers in Khvoshchinskaia's fiction often provide a vehicle for exploring the social context, form, or content of women's writing in Russia.

Khvoshchinskaia's *Vstrecha* also continued to explore new aesthetic directions. The subjective observations of Khvoshchinskaia's narrator and characters form multiple, contradictory viewpoints that undermine readers' expectations of a single source of narrative objectivity. Although Liudmila suggests that she, Aleksandra, or Tarneev ought to write the story of Aleksandra's life, in fact Khvoshchinskaia remains the author of Aleksandra's story, offering an additional layer of narrative ambiguity to this presentation of contrasting and contradictory viewpoints of Aleksandra's life story.

Published for the first time in 1861 in *Otechestvennye zapiski,* Khvoshchinskaia's extremely popular novella *Pansionerka* (translated into Serbian in 1883, Finnish in 1990, and English in 2000) enjoyed immediate success with readers. Khvoshchinskaia's depiction of the educational experiences of her fifteen-year-old heroine Lelen'ka, a student at a local private boarding school, especially appealed to female readers. Khvoshchinskaia's portrait of the events sparking her young heroine's decision to adopt an independent working life in St. Petersburg in 1860 offered a fresh and lively examination of the challenges presented by emerging new roles for women.

Lelen'ka enjoys her studies at a local private boarding school until conversations with her neighbor Veretitsyn, a young man exiled to the city of N. because of the content of his poetry, incite her to rebel against injustices at home and at school. In suggesting that the great men depicted in her textbooks may have possessed failings or even behaved badly, Veretitsyn encourages Lelen'ka to evaluate knowledge subjectively, not simply to memorize. However, Lelen'ka behaves even more radically, failing her exams in rebellion against the superficiality of her studies. Seeking a refuge from family despotism with an aunt in St. Petersburg after her parents attempt to arrange a marriage for her, Lelen'ka works as a translator at the end of the novella while she studies to become an artist.

An exploration of the theme of women's education, *Pansionerka* also offers a fresh recasting of the familiar male mentor figure depicted in many earlier Russian works. However, unlike the male mentors of novels such as Goncharov's *Oblomov* (1859) and Aleksandr Vasil'evich Druzhinin's *Polin'ka Saks* (1847), Veretitsyn articulates radical approaches to learning that challenge his pupil's worldview. In criticizing the representations of truth provided by Lelen'ka's textbooks and encouraging her to think for herself, he incites his young pupil to rebel against authority at school and at home.

Khvoshchinskaia's tale "Za stenoi" attracted considerable attention from censors, who believed that it advocated the abolition of marriage. It was only published through the persistent and devoted efforts of editor Andrei Kraevsky. The story, however, received unusual praise from Stepan Semenovich Dudyshkin, critic for *Otechestvennye zapiski,* who referred to it in a letter as "masterful." In his opinion, "such a thing could have been written by Turgenev, it's so timely."

Through the thin wall behind his bed, the first-person masculine narrator of "Za stenoi" regularly eavesdrops on conversations conducted by his neighbor, an unemployed violinist. The overly inquisitive narrator had earlier leased part of his apartment to the musician. A widow who had been romantically involved with the violinist several years earlier arrives to declare her love but rejects the musician's proposition that she become his mistress. The story ends abruptly when the woman leaves town, followed shortly afterward by the musician, perhaps in pursuit of his former lover.

References to music and musicians appear in many of Khvoshchinskaia's works. *Bariton,* sometimes compared to Nikolai Gerasimovich Pomialovsky's *Ocherki bursa* (Seminary Sketches, 1860), examines one young man's struggle to realize a career in singing. In "Veriagin" (1875), Adrian suggests to Masha, a lively girl now largely cowed and silent, that she ought to study at a conservatory since her voice had formerly promised much. The pursuit of a singing career in both these works also represents a related search for individual identity and self-expression. In contrast, the musician and the woman in "Za stenoi" orchestrate their voices as a tool to manipulate an eavesdropping neighbor.

A chaotic and often destructive force in Khvoshchinskaia's works, gossip fuels much of the action in *Nedavnee.* Agafena Petrovna Tamanova lives with her thirty-five-year-old daughter, Nadezhda Sergeevna, and Nadezhda's artist-husband, Grigorii Nikolaevich Borovitsky, at Agafena's estate. Renamed by Agafena for Nadezhda, who will receive the estate as part of her dowry, Nadezhdinskoe remains known to almost everyone by its former name, Loskutovshchina. When Grigorii accepts a job in town and begins a flirtation with twenty-two-year-old Nastas'ia Denevskaia, family stability quickly disintegrates. Nadezhda discovers Grigorii's drawing of Nastas'ia in his study and initiates a romance of her own with Colonel Skvoreshchensky. As the marriage breaks up, Agafena's estate

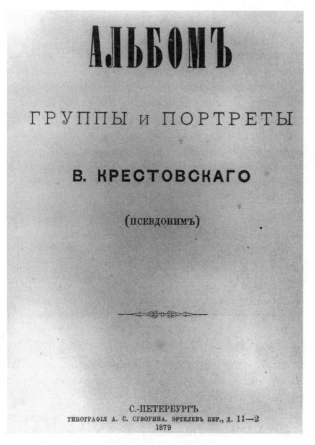

Title page for Al'bom. Gruppy i portrety *(Album. Groups and Portraits), Khvoshchinskaia's most successful collection of short stories (The Lilly Library, Indiana University)*

receives a much needed financial boost from the colonel.

Gossip ruins reputations, wrecks marriages, and wreaks havoc in Khvoshchinskaia's *Nedavnee* to a greater degree perhaps than in any other of the author's works. In that novel Nastas'ia expresses concern that gossip generated by a letter from Grigorii that almost no one has actually read will ruin her good name. However, formal written language fails to offer any contrasting structure of order and stability. At his job Nastas'ia's father blithely but authoritatively signs documents that may be meaningless or even harmful in content without reading or analyzing them. A recurrent motif in Khvoshchinskaia's works, gossip wields destructive power in *Anna Mikhailovna* and *Obiazannosti* (Responsibilities, 1885–1886) as well.

During the 1860s, at the suggestion of Dudyshkin, Khvoshchinskaia began writing critical articles for *Otechestvennye zapiski*. Her first essay appeared in 1861 as part of a series of "Provintsial'nye pis'ma o nashei literature" (Provincial Letters about Our Literature). She reviewed works by several women writers, includ-

ing Kokhanovskaia (Nadezhda Sokhanskaia) and Iuliia Zhadovskaia, in an article devoted to contemporary works, and she opposed art for art's sake in another article. Rejecting the idealization of family relationships, Khvoshchinskaia devoted one essay entirely to the position of women.

Khvoshchinskaia numbered Turgenev among her St. Petersburg friends and acquaintances during the early 1860s. A difficult relationship from the beginning, this friendship did not last. Khvoshchinskaia never wholeheartedly liked Turgenev personally and later combined that with a dislike for him as a writer. However, her inability to maintain an amicable relationship with Turgenev hardly proved unique. Among others, he quarreled with Goncharov in 1859, Tolstoy in 1861, and Dostoevsky in the 1870s.

During this time, Khvoshchinskaia also suffered her greatest personal loss. On 5 August 1865, her sister Sof'ia died from a perforated stomach ulcer. She had just begun to establish her own successful literary career after publishing her first novella in 1857. A talented artist as well, her portrait of painter Aleksandr Ivanov appeared in the Academy of Art exhibition in 1859. Before his death in 1858, Ivanov had invited her to accompany him to Rome as an art student. She was buried in Riazan' at the Spasskii Monastery near the southern side of the altar of the Bogoiavlenskaia Church. Khvoshchinskaia not only became ill herself afterward, but even attempted to poison herself.

A young doctor and acquaintance, Ivan Ivanovich Zaionchkovsky, visited the family with the sisters' other friends during the last days of Sof'ia's illness. He had studied at the Riazan' gymnasium; in 1857 he had entered the School of Medicine at Moscow University. Remembered as honest, gentle, handsome, and delicate, he finished his course of study in 1863, only to be arrested for distributing political literature and sent to prison for eleven months. Thirteen years his senior, Khvoshchinskaia married Zaionchkovsky on 25 September 1865. The couple lived in St. Petersburg until 1866 when he received a position as a district doctor in Riazan'.

A man of high ideals if somewhat ambiguous personal ambition, Zaionchkovsky impulsively quit this job when a man died at the entrance of the hospital because there was no room for him. Illness and frailty acquired during his prison stay finally forced him to travel abroad at a doctor's advice, where he attended lectures at universities in Zurich and Heidelberg. Khvoshchinskaia continued to send money to her husband and even asked editor Mikhail Matveevich Stasiulevich to forward a copy of her newly published *Bol'shaia medveditsa* (Ursa Major, 1870–1871) to him. Referred to by Khvoshchinskaia in a letter to a female friend in 1870 as "an adult child," he never succeeded in getting established in any occupation. His translations of works by Johann Wolfgang von Goethe and the physician Max von Pettenkofer were never published. He died abroad in 1872 of tuberculosis.

Despite tragedy and tumult in her personal life, Khvoshchinskaia persevered in advancing her career. In 1869 *Pervaia bor'ba* garnered praise from both readers and critics. In an article published in 1889, poet Nikolai Konstantinovich Mikhailovsky characterized the novella as "one of the most successful in all of Russian literature."

Republished in a second edition in 1891, Khvoshchinskaia's popular antinihilist novel *Pervaia bor'ba* explores the theme of "free love" through the reminiscences of the first-person narrator, Sergei Nikolaevich. Sergei's father had abandoned his five-year-old son to wealthy relatives in Moscow after his wife's death; when he retrieves the boy eight years later, thirteen-year-old Sergei has become a shallow dandy. The subsequent life of father and son in the provinces becomes a battle. Trying to help Sergei adapt to a life of lesser means, his father secures a job for him as a tutor to the adopted orphan of the aged Smutov sisters. Sergei soon seduces the Smutov's niece, Mar'ia Vasil'evna, and when his father dies, asks her to move to Moscow with him. Mar'ia now faces her own "first battle," pitting her love for Sergei against the prospects of remaining at home with a tarnished reputation. Deciding to accompany Sergei to Moscow, Mar'ia lives with him unmarried for three years before entering a convent.

Contradictory if not completely hypocritical, Sergei supports individual freedom while simultaneously manifesting many of the character defects displayed by the tyrants he claims to abhor. Like Raskol'nikov in Dostoevsky's *Prestuplenie i nakazanie* (Crime and Punishment, 1866), he merely redefines his inadequacies and destructive behavior as characteristic by-products of a superior nature. In contrast with Turgenev's novel of generational struggle, *Ottsy i deti* (Fathers and Sons, 1862), the father in *Pervaia bor'ba* is far less backward and destructive than his son.

Several new works boosted Khvoshchinskaia's career to some prominence in the 1870s. Arsen'ev has argued that Khvoshchinskaia's talent reached its "culminating point" in the novel *Bol'shaia medveditsa*. The group of stories published under the title *Al'bom. Gruppy i portrety* (Album. Groups and Portraits, 1874–1877) also proved successful. In addition to original works such as "Schastlivye liudi" (Happy People, 1877), Khvoshchinskaia published an increasing number of translations in the 1870s. She also began a new series of critical essays or "Literaturnye besedy" (Literary Conversations) for *Russkie vedomosti* (Russian News).

The enormous success of *Bol'shaia medveditsa* (republished in 1872, 1875, and 1883) firmly established Khvoshchinskaia's literary reputation while earning her the third-highest honorarium for a literary work in Russia, just behind Tolstoy and Turgenev. The novel was translated into French in the *Journal de St.-Pétersbourg* in 1870–1872 by Emil-Alix Durand, a professor of French at the St. Petersburg law school and one of the principal translators of Turgenev's works. A major turning point in other ways, *Bol'shaia medveditsa* was Khvoshchinskaia's last novel set in the past.

In *Bol'shaia medveditsa* Katerina, the twenty-two-year-old daughter of Nikolai Stepanovich Bagriansky, a local advocate for the peasantry and official for the Chamber of State Property, falls in love with a married man in 1854. A "strange" girl, she assists her father with business matters, travels unescorted, and reads voraciously. At a ball, Katerina meets Andrei Vasil'evich Verkhovskoy, a young man who has arrived in N. to buy the Spasskoe estate at his wife's request and with her money. At the heart of the novel, an unsolved, alleged theft implicates the foremost political figure of the town, provincial governor Volkarev.

Both Katerina and Andrei struggle against powerful bonds of parental authority and affection to achieve greater personal independence. Katerina's father begs his daughter never to leave him, unlike his son Viktor, who left home early for a military career. In remaining unmarried and refusing Andrei's proposal that she become his mistress, Katerina perhaps unconsciously fulfills her promise to her father. Bagriansky also repays his daughter for her loyalty, bestowing his pension on her after he retires to a monastery. Andrei retains the same idealized love for Katerina that he had had for his mother while continuing to seek greater wealth by marrying a rich, much younger woman after his wife's death.

Observation and surveillance of others, popular activities among Khvoshchinskaia's protagonists, figure prominently in *Bol'shaia medveditsa*. Often observing others or even spying, Verkhovskoy watches Katerina unseen at a distance as she stands outside her new country home under the starlit sky at the end of the novel, just as he had watched her unseen across a ballroom when he first met her. Observance and surveillance also figure centrally in many of Khvoshchinskaia's other works. Varen'ka closely watches her father and his activities without his knowledge in *Obiazannosti*, rifling through his desk and finally learning to her surprise that he writes poetry. In "U Fotografa" (At the Photographer's, 1874), the opening story of *Al'bom. Gruppy i portrety,* a photograph of Talia reduces her to an object of the observations of others.

In her 1995 essay "Love, Attachment, and the 'Objects of Our Regard,'" Jane Costlow examines the important role of the narrator as observer in Turgenev's "Svidanie" (The Meeting, 1850). The power and authority enjoyed by the narrator as a member of the gentry becomes evident when he steps from behind a tree where he had been spying on the peasant woman Akulina. Khvoshchinskaia's fictional exploration of the activity of observation recalls a similar use of the motif. In "U Fotografa" Talia remains a skilled observer of people and events even as her photograph transforms her into a passive object of observation for others.

Khvoshchinskaia's literary success attracted attention outside of Russia as well in the 1870s and 1880s. In an article for *Harper's New Monthly Magazine* in June 1878, the author reported, "Some of the most fruitful and artistic studies of Russian life are found in novels published by women known under the names of Crestovski [Krestovsky], Vovcek [Vovchok], Kokhanovskaia." An article published 7 July 1888 in the *The Athenaeum* by Russian émigré writer and anarchist Petr Kropotkin mentioned Khvoshchinskaia's latest novel, *Obiazannosti:* "A new novel from the pen of that sympathetic lady who signs herself Krestovski (not to be confounded with V. Krestovski) is always welcome."

Khvoshchinskaia also enjoyed many new and ongoing friendships in the 1870s. Goncharov sent her a personal letter in 1872, thanking her for sending a copy of the newly published *Bol'shaia medveditsa.* She continued to enjoy a longstanding friendship with Ol'ga Alekseevna Novikova, a relative and unofficial lobbyist to England, and became even closer to her childhood friend Aleksandra (Markelova) Karrik after the death in 1878 of the latter's husband, Scottish-born photographer William Carrick. Although Khvoshchinskaia had met the writer Mikhail Evgrafovich Saltykov (pseudonym Shchedrin) when he was vice governor in Riazan' from 1858 to 1860, the two did not become close friends until his second term as vice governor from 1867 to 1868. He visited her home in Riazan' in January 1868 to invite her to participate in *Otechestvennye zapiski* on behalf of the new editor of the journal, Nikolai Nekrasov. Saltykov's death in the spring of 1889 particularly distressed her.

As an indication of Khvoshchinskaia's growing literary reputation, Pavel Tret'iakov commissioned the artist Ivan Kramskoy to paint her portrait in 1876 for his collection. Tret'iakov commissioned portraits of other well-known authors during this time, including Goncharov (1865), Tolstoy (1873), Nekrasov (1877), and Dostoevsky (1882). The painting of Khvoshchinskaia that Kramskoy began in Riazan' that February is still owned by the Tret'iakov Gallery in Moscow.

Of all the stories in Khvoshchinskaia's popular *Al'bom* (republished in a second edition in 1889), "Ridneva" enjoyed special success and even international recognition. In "Ridneva," a young woman embarks on an acting career to support herself and her daughter after the death of her husband. Facing endless financial difficulties, Liza Ridneva works long hours only to suffer the tragedy of her daughter's illness and death. Hoping for respite from her struggle to survive, Ridneva returns home to claim an inheritance after the death of the elderly Anna Ivanovna Ridneva and learns that her new property had been sold "lawfully" two weeks before Anna's death. At the end of the story, Ridneva seems deprived of all means of survival when the fatalist and epicurean rake Nikolai Dmitrievich Meniaev suddenly appears at her door. The story was translated into Italian in 1876 by Russian-born Sof'ia de Gubernatis Besobratseff, wife of the Florentine professor Angelo de Gubernatis, and into French by a major translator of Dostoevsky's and Aleksei Feofilaktovich Pisemsky's works, Victor Derély. (Derély translated another story from *Al'bom,* "Veriagin," into French in 1888.)

Besides her original works, Khvoshchinskaia published an increasing number of translations in the 1870s and 1880s. Z. M. Potapova has observed that Khvoshchinskaia almost singlehandedly popularized the newest Italian prose writers and dramatists. From 1879 to 1888 she translated more than twenty works by Giovanni Verga, Anton Barrili, Pietro Cossa, Edmundo de Amicis, Vincenzo Monti, Salvatore Farina, Marchesa Colombi (Maria Antonietta Torriani Torelli-Viollier), and Neera (the pen name of Anna Zucarri). In the mid 1870s she also made her first trip to Italy, to visit the family of Sofia de Gubernatis.

Translations had been an important focus of Khvoshchinskaia's early career as well, reflecting themes that appear throughout her prose fiction. Works exploring women's lives and addressing liberal themes frequently number among her translations, including Federico della Valle's *Medea;* Casimir Delavigne's *Marino Faliero,* a tragedy championing liberalism amidst the corruption of Venice; and Verga's *Nedda,* a sympathetic depiction of Sicilian poverty. Khvoshchinskaia also translated works by women writers such as George Sand (*Gabriel* and *Horace*) and the Marchesa Colombi and Neera.

Although poorly paid, translating provided an increasing share of Khvoshchinskaia's income in the

1880s. The closing of *Otechestvennye zapiski* in 1884, the journal that had published most of her original works, particularly hurt her earnings and morale. Increasing health problems and bouts of depression contributed to reductions in her productivity as well. Still, many works stand out during this period. Like much of her best fiction, *Zdorovye* (The Healthy Ones, 1883) features unusually clever, humorous dialogue and lively characterizations. This novella also presents one of Khvoshchinskaia's most loving and amusing depictions of a mother and daughter. Besides "Posle potopa" (After the Flood, 1881) Khvoshchinskaia published her only full-length novel of this period, *Obiazannosti,* in *Severnyi vestnik* (The Northern Herald) in 1885–1886.

Khvoshchinskaia's themes became darker and more pessimistic in the late 1870s and 1880s. Her fiction during this period typically depicts lonely, isolated idealists, struggling to maintain a sense of hope and direction in a world increasingly dominated by greed and self-interest. A new kind of soulless manipulator populates works such as "Veriagin," *Zdorovye,* and *Obiazannosti.* While similar characters had appeared earlier, such as Sergei in *Pervaia bor'ba* and Volkarev in *Bol'shaia medveditsa,* Khvoshchinskaia's later villains descend to new depths of degradation in a society that offers little hope for love or redemption.

After the fall of 1881, Khvoshchinskaia lived in St. Petersburg with V. A. Moskaleva, a widowed friend from Riazan'. Moskaleva had relocated to St. Petersburg when her husband had accepted a job there in 1876. In 1880–1881 Khvoshchinskaia lived on the fourth floor of an apartment on Novaia Street (now Pushkinskaia). However, St. Petersburg failed to revive her spirits. From the mid 1880s she experienced severe episodes of depression as well as increasing health problems, including recurrent pulmonary inflammations, eventually leading to emphysema. Besides her own afflictions, her mother's blindness and debility depressed her. Many of Khvoshchinskaia's personal letters also persistently express a loss of confidence in her talent.

Khvoshchinskaia's health and spirits declined, however, at the same time that some of the most laudatory reviews of her work appeared in print. In an article written for *Russkoe bogatstvo* (Russian Wealth) in 1880, the critic Mikhail Protopopov added her name to his list of the most talented literary writers in Russia—Turgenev, Tolstoy, Goncharov, Ostrovsky, and Pisemsky. The previous year Boborykin contended in the journal *Slovo* (The Word) that among women writers in Western Europe, only George Eliot could match Khvoshchinskaia's talent.

On 18 February 1880, the young people of Riazan' organized a personal tribute to Khvoshchinskaia's career. In the evening, three hundred to four hundred students gathered on the street outside her home. Surrounding her as she stood on her porch, individual speakers thanked her for her sympathy toward the younger generation and spoke about the meaning of her works in their lives. While Khvoshchinskaia remembered this event as the most valued honor of her career, she also accepted the praise with ambivalence. In a letter reflecting her frequent low spirits during this period, she complained that "this is not like the tributes to Turgenev of last year, but a band of poor children falling all over their widow-mother."

In 1883 the literary world organized a formal gathering in recognition of her career. Attended mostly by women, the event featured an opening statement by the author and playwright Nadezhda Merder. An address with hundreds of signatures from members of the cultural world was presented to her along with a commemorative watch. Offering an assessment of her work that praised her truthful depictions of women's lives, author and critic Mar'ia Tsebrikova characterized Khvoshchinskaia as a role model for other women striving to participate in the public sphere.

Shortly after this event, some women among the cultural elite of Moscow organized a concert to raise money to relieve Khvoshchinskaia's acute poverty. Tsebrikova later presented her with a photo album and seven hundred rubles sent by the organizers of the event. Firmly believing that the concert had been arranged solely out of pity, Khvoshchinskaia never wholeheartedly accepted this expression of gratitude and appreciation.

After her mother's death 26 May 1884 in Riazan', Khvoshchinskaia moved to St. Petersburg in the fall. In these last years of her life, she lived on Maksimilianovskii Pereulok (now Pereulok Pirogova) and Admiralteiskaia Embankment, choosing apartments on the fourth or fifth floors near the Neva for fresh air to facilitate her breathing. Her modest lifestyle incorporated a strict work routine that included rising early to begin writing her fiction in her characteristic, tiny, compressed handwriting style. After work, she enjoyed needlework as a lifelong pastime.

Always protective of her privacy, Khvoshchinskaia not only staunchly refused requests for interviews from biographers during her lifetime, but also disliked attempts to publish her portrait in newspapers and journals. Author and biographer Pavel Vasil'evich Bykov contacted her in 1875 and 1880 to obtain permission to write her biography. After some vacillation, Khvoshchinskaia finally rejected his request, asserting in a letter that "Pseudonyms don't have biographies. What is a pseudonym? No one. So what can be said about one?"

Khvoshchinskaia also returned to writing and publishing critical essays in the 1870s and 1880s. In one of her "Literaturnye besedy" she offered suggestions to prospective writers, such as maintaining chronological charts to record the dates of characters' births and marriages. In another article she developed ideas about writing memoirs, probably in response to encouragement from her editors to write her own life story. As in previous critical essays, she reviewed the works of a variety of authors, including Tolstoy, Vsevolod Mikhailovich Garshin, and Dostoevsky.

In Khvoshchinskaia's novella *Zdorovye,* written in the early 1880s, an indecisive first-person masculine narrator returns to N. when a man named Chernevsky, appearing on behalf of an old friend, Vasilii Petrovich Zaozerov, invites him for a visit. In N. the narrator meets a woman he had once loved: the widow Natal'ia Alekseevna Polivalova, née Dvortsova, who lives in N. with her stepdaughter, Kleopatra. Now forty years old, Natal'ia is a woman "of the most dangerous age." The narrator's renewed attraction to Natal'ia contrasts with his aversion for Zaozerov, who has made an easy transformation from an idealistic mentor of his slightly younger associates of the 1860s to a successful, greedy manipulator of the 1880s. Unlike the narrator of "V doroge," the narrator of this novella finds that he cannot so easily flee his past when events take an unpleasant turn. Instead, he remains waylaid in N. subsequent to a possible lengthy investigation of his travel documents.

In a 1994 article, Mary F. Zirin noted Khvoshchinskaia's frequent incorporation of the motif of needlework in much of her fiction. A traditional mode of creativity for women, needlework in Khvoshchinskaia's works figuratively explores aesthetic problems, while scenes and images incorporated into her characters' embroidery designs contribute to the development of themes and characterization. In *Zdorovye* Natal'ia coyly informs the narrator that she is sewing something for her daughter that she might just keep for herself. The motif also appears in many of Khvoshchinskaia's other works. Twenty-six-year-old Anastasie Khlopova in *Anna Mikhailovna* occupies herself with writing but also displays her talented needlework on the wall, "under glass in gold frames." Needlework also appears as a motif in works such as *Vstrecha, V ozhidanii luchshego,* and *Pansionerka* as well.

In one of Khvoshchinskaia's better stories of the 1880s, "Posle potopa," Nikolai and his brother, just released from a two-year prison term thanks to their uncle's intervention, return home to a family celebration. Apparently suffering from a severe case of survivor's guilt, Nikolai broods over memories of his sister's childhood death and the fate of his less fortunate comrades still in prison. As Nikolai, alone in his room with a revolver, considers suicide while the others celebrate, his mother appears suddenly to stop him. Besides suicide, the story explores a series of thematic pairs—including recollection and forgetfulness, presence and loss, and crime and punishment.

In Khvoshchinskaia's only novel written in the 1880s, *Obiazannosti,* Varen'ka visits her father, Pavel Vasil'evich Kirinov, after leaving her husband. An idealist ready to help every peasant, Pavel seems to turn a deaf ear when Varen'ka tells him that she needs money for her daughter's education. To raise money, Varen'ka sells her property before leaving, depriving her father of a home and income. Although her father finally privately offers money to Varen'ka's servant for those "in need," the reader never learns if Varen'ka will receive the money. A calculating survivor himself, Pavel soon after his daughter's departure marries a young woman with property in order to recoup his losses. All of the characters use the term "responsibility" ambiguously to express genuine feelings of devotion but also to manipulate others for their own self-interest.

Never purely victims, many of Khvoshchinskaia's heroines, including Varen'ka in *Obiazannosti,* are also skillful sexual predators. Varen'ka "catches" a husband by luring an indecisive suitor to a hotel room and plying him with kisses. She then reveals their presence alone together in the hotel to others, manipulating the damaging effects of gossip to force a marriage proposal from him. Andrei's future wife Lidiia in *Bol'shaia medveditsa* advances her own marriage designs by cornering her hapless future husband on a bench and attacking him with kisses. An indecisive, though ambiguously calculating, man without clear career plans and few connections, Andrei soon readily agrees to an advantageous match.

Although funds from her published literary works helped support her and other family members throughout her career, Khvoshchinskaia spent her last days in acute poverty. She died at a summerhouse in Staryi Petergof outside St. Petersburg on 8 June 1889. Nearly destitute, she was buried at the expense of the *Literaturnyi fond* (Literary Fund). In the mid 1890s funds were raised to erect over her grave a white marble monument, depicting an anchor and cross tied to a broken oak entwined with ivy.

Letters:

M. M. Stasiulevich i ego sovremenniki v ikh perepiske, edited by M. K. Lemke (St. Petersburg, 1913), V: 92–130;

"N. D. Zaionchkovskaia," *Literaturnoe nasledstvo,* 51/52 (Moscow: Izd. AN SSSR, 1949), pp. 287–290.

Bibliographies:

S. I. Ponomarev, "Nashi pisatel'nitsy," *Bibliograficheskii slovar' russkikh pisatel'nits* (1889–1891; republished, Leipzig, 1974), pp. 61–71;

D. D. Iazykov, "N. D. Zaionchkovskaia," in *Obzor zhizni i trudov pokoinykh russkikh pisatelei* (St. Petersburg, 1905), IX: 25–30;

K. D. Muratova, *Istoriia russkoi literatury XIX veka: bibliograficheskii ukazatel'* (Leningrad: AN SSSR, 1962), pp. 381–383.

Biographies:

V. I. Semevsky, "N. D. Khvoshchinskaia, biograficheskii ocherk," *Russkaia mysl',* nos. 10–12 (1890);

A. Vinitskaia, "Vospominaniia o N. D. Khvoshchinskoi," *Istoricheskii vestnik,* no. 1 (1890): 146–155;

M. Tsebrikova, "Ocherk zhizni N.D. Khvoshchinskoi-Zaionchkovskoi (V. Krestovskogo-psevdonima)," *Mir Bozhii,* 12 (1897): 1–40;

A. Karrik, "Iz vospominanii o N. D. Khvoshchinskoi-Zaionchkovskoi (V. Krestovsky-psevdonim)," *Zhenskoe delo,* nos. 9–11 (1899);

Russkii biograficheskii slovar' (St. Petersburg, 1901).

References:

K. K. Arsen'ev, "V. Krestovskii (psevdonim)," *Kriticheskie etiudy po russkoi literature,* volume 1 (St. Petersburg: Tip. Stasiulevicha, 1888), pp. 255–350;

A. F. Belousov, "Obraz seminarista v russkoi kul'ture i ego literaturnaia istoriia (ot komicheskikh intermedii XIII veka-do romana Nadezhdy Khvoshchinskoi 'Bariton), in *Traditsiia v fol'klore i literature* (St. Petersburg: Akademicheskaia gimnaziia SPbGU, 2000), pp. 159–176;

Anna Chechneva, "Gore tselogo mira volnuet mne dushu . . . ," *Literaturnaia Riazan'* (1990): 274–279;

Carol Apollonio Flath, "Seminary heroes in Mid-Nineteenth Century Russian Fiction," *Canadian American Slavic Studies,* 24, no. 3 (Fall 1990): 279–294;

Jehanne Gheith, "Nadezhda Dmitrievna Khvoshchinskaia," *Reference Guide to Russian Literature,* edited by Neil Cornwell (Chicago: Fitzroy Dearborn, 1998), pp. 447–449;

Gheith, *(Not) Writing like a Russian Girl: Evgeniia Tur and V. Krestovskii pseudonym* (Evanston, Ill.: Northwestern University Press, forthcoming 2001);

O. Krenzholek, "Problemy literaturnoi pozitsii N. D. Khvoshchinskoi, 1840–1860-kh godov," dissertation, Moscow State University, 1986;

P. Kropotkin, *Ideals and Realities in Russian Literature* (London: Duckworth, 1905), pp. 179–182;

Materialy svoda pamiatnikov istorii i kul'tury RSFSR: Riazanskaia oblast', sost. A. S. Davydova (Moscow: Nauchno-issledovatel'skii institut kul'tury Ministerstva kul'tury RSFSR, 1980), pp. 84–88;

A. P. Mogiliansky, "N. D. i S. D. Khvoshchinskie," *Istoriia russkoi literatury,* volume 9, part 2 (Moscow: AN SSSR, 1956), pp. 228–237;

Kevin Platt, *History in a Grotesque Key: Russian Literature and the Idea of Revolution* (Stanford, Cal.: Stanford University Press, 1997);

Aleksandr Potapov, "'Za pyl'iu proshlogo . . . ,'" *Neizrechennyi svet* (Riazan': Novoe vremia, 1996), pp. 51–62;

Z. M. Potapova, *Russko-ital'ianskie literaturnye sviazi* (Moscow: Nauka, 1973);

Arja Rosenholm, "Auf den Spuren des Vergessens: zur Rezeptionsgeschichte der russischen Schriftstellerin N. D. Chvoščinskaja," *Studia Slavica Finlandensis,* 4 (1989): 63–91;

Rosenholm, *Gendering Awakening: Femininity and the Russian Woman Question of the 1860s* (Helsinki: Aleksanteri-instituutti, 1999);

Rosenholm, "Nadezhda Dmitrievna Khvoshchinskaia," *Dictionary of Russian Women Writers,* edited by Marina Ledkovsky, Charlotte Rosenthal, and Mary F. Zirin (Westport, Conn.: Greenwood Press, 1994), pp. 286–288;

Rosenholm, "N. D. Hvoshchinskaya—1800-luvum venäläinen naiskirjailija yhteisyyden ja yksinäisyyden ristipaineissa," *Slavica Tamperensia,* 1 (1992): 45–92;

Rosenholm, "Rasskazchitsa-pisatel'nitsa v protivorechiiakh ili vzgliad Kassandry," *Russkie pisatel'nitsy i literaturnyi protsess v kontse XVIII-pervoi treti XX vv.,* compiled by M. Fainshtein (Wilhelmhorst: F. K. Göpfert, 1995), pp. 91–114;

Rosenholm, "Eine Reise ins Innere: Die russische Schriftstellerin Nadežda Chvoščinskaja und die weibliche Kreativität," in *Russland aus der Feder seiner Frauen,* edited by F. Göpfert (Munich: Sagner, 1992), pp. 175–194;

Rosenholm, "'Svoe' i 'chuzhoe' v kontseptsii 'obrazovannaia zhenshchina' i *Pansionerka* N. D. Khvoshchinskoi," *"Svoe" i "chuzhoe" v literature i kul'ture* (Tartu, Estonia: Tartu Ülikooli Kirjastus, 1995), pp. 143–166;

Rosenholm, "The 'Woman Question' of the 1860s and the 'Learned Woman,'" *Gender and Russian Literature: New Perspectives,* edited and translated by Rosalyn Marsh (Cambridge: Cambridge University Press, 1996), pp. 112–128;

Rosenholm, "Writing the Self: Creativity and the Female Author: Nadezhda Dmitrievna Khvoshchinskaya (1824–1889)," *Gender Restructuring in Russian Studies* (Tampere, Finland: University of Tampere, 1993), pp. 194–208;

N. V. Shelgunov, "Zhenskoe bezdushie (Po povodu sochinenii V. Krestovskogo-psevdonima)," *Delo,* no. 9 (1870): 1–34;

A. Skabichevsky, "Volny russkogo progressa," in his *Sochineniia* (St. Petersburg, 1903), pp. 817–850;

P. N. Tkachev, "Gnilye korni," *Izbrannye sochineniia na sotsial'no-politicheskie temy v chetyrekh tomakh,* volume 4 (Moscow: Izd. Vsesoiuznogo obshchestva Politkatorzhan i ssyl'no-poselentsev, 1933), pp. 350–412;

Aleksandr Ivanovich Tyminsky, "Poetika prozy N. D. Khvoshchinskoi," dissertation, Moscow Pedagogical University, 1997;

Mary F. Zirin, "Nadezhda Khvoshchinskaia," *Encyclopedia of Continental Women Writers,* edited by Katharina M. Wilson (New York: Garland, 1991), pp. 632–633;

Zirin, "Women's Prose in the Age of Realism," *Women Writers in Russian Literature* (Westport, Conn.: Praeger, 1994), pp. 77–94.

Papers:

Many of Nadezhda Dmitrievna Khvoshchinskaia's letters and other papers are held by the Russian State Archive of Literature and Art (RGALI, formerly TsGALI) f 541, 52 items from 1836 to 1891. The Russian State Library in Moscow also has papers, as do the Russian National Library and the Institute of Russian Literature (IRLI, Pushkinskii dom Pushkin House) in St. Petersburg. Other major depositories of materials related to her life and career are held by the Riazan' Historical-Architectural Museum, the State Archive in Riazan', and the Esenin Local History Museum (497 items) in Konstantinovo.

Viktor Petrovich Kliushnikov

(10 March 1841 – 7 November 1892)

Alexander V. Matyushkin
Karelian State Pedagogical University

(Translated by Sergei Orlov)

WORKS: *Marevo,* in *Russkii vestnik,* nos. 1–3 (1864);
2 volumes (Moscow: Katkov, 1865);

Bol'shie korabli, in *Literaturnaia biblioteka,* nos. 5–12,
17–19 (1867); (St. Petersburg, 1874);

Tsygane, in *Zaria,* nos. 2–4, 6, 7, 10, 12 (1869); (St.
Petersburg, 1871);

Ne marevo, in *Zaria,* nos. 2, 4 (1871);

*Pri Petre. Istoricheskaia povest' vremen preobrazovaniia
Rossii,* by Kliushnikov and Vasilii Ivanovich
Kel'siev (St. Petersburg: A. F. Marks, 1872);

Sem'ia vol'nodumtsev. Roman Ekaterininskogo vremeni, by
Kliushnikov and Petr Nikolaevich Petrov, in
Niva, nos. 1–19 (1872); (St. Petersburg: A. F.
Marks, 1872).

SELECTED PERIODICAL PUBLICATIONS:

FICTION

"Nemaia," *Russkii vestnik,* no. 11 (1864): 291–321;

"Drugaia zhizn'," in *Detskoe chtenie,* nos. 2–9 (1865);

"Baryshnia i barynia (Zapiski doktora)," *Niva,* nos.
4–14 (1874);

"Gosudar'-otrok," *Detskii otdykh,* nos. 1–3, 5, 9, 10, 12
(1881);

"Krepysh," *Russkii vestnik,* no. 1 (1885): 243–310;

"Pliaska mertvyh (Na temu Danse macabre Sen
Sansa)," *Russkoe obozrenie,* no. 12 (1891): 622–
646.

NONFICTION

"M. N. Katkov," *Niva,* no. 31 (1887): 775;

"Sovremennye belletristy. M. V. Krestovskaia," *Moskovskie vedomosti,* no. 154 (1889): 3–4;

"Listok vospominanii k iubileinomu venku," *Niva,*
no. 47 (1890): 1186–1189.

OTHER: *Entsiklopedicheskii vsenauchnyi slovar',* 3 volumes, edited by Kliushnikov (St. Petersburg:
Kh. K. Nebe, 1878–1882).

Viktor Petrovich Kliushnikov

The name of Viktor Petrovich Kliushnikov (also
spelled Kliuchnikov) is often mentioned in histories and
handbooks of Russian literature, but there has been virtually no scholarship devoted solely to him and his
writing. Kliushnikov has been considered a minor literary figure, forgotten by the broader reading public and
interesting to scholars mainly as a representative of the
so-called antinihilist literature that became common in
the 1860s in response to the new radical movement. In

fact, while nihilist characters are found in nearly all of Kliushnikov's works, this theme was not his leading preoccupation throughout his career. Kliushnikov did, however, make his name as an antinihilist writer after the publication of his first novel, *Marevo* (The Mirage, 1864), in which he caricatured the radical revolutionaries and also wrote tendentiously about the Polish uprising of 1863. In spite of many shortcomings in the novel, the publication of *Marevo* was a significant event in Russian literary and social life in the 1860s. It attracted a great deal of negative attention from the radical critics, who took Kliushnikov to task harshly; at the same time, however, it found enormous success with the reading public and brought the writer a brief period of fame.

Kliushnikov continued to write after *Marevo,* producing the novels *Bol'shie korabli* (The Big Ships, 1867) and *Tsygane* (The Gypsies, 1869). Kliushnikov's stories "Krepysh" (The Robust Fellow, 1885), "Pliaska mertvyh (Na temu Danse macabre Sen Sansa)" (Dance of the Dead [On the Theme of Saint-Saëns' 'Danse Macabre'], 1891), and "Baryshnia i barynia (Zapiski doktora)" (The Gentleman's Daughter and the Gentleman's Wife [Notes of a Doctor], 1874), as well as his essays and reviews, are also noteworthy. Kliushnikov worked actively as a translator, supplying Russian translations of the novels of Charles Dickens and Wilkie Collins to the journal *Russkii vestnik* (The Russian Herald), and he devoted nearly half of his life to editorial work at the weekly *Niva* (The Grainfield), which he joined at its inception in 1870.

Viktor Petrovich Kliushnikov was born on 10 March 1841 in the village of Aleksianovka in the Smolensk region to Petr Petrovich Kliushnikov and his wife, Vera Fedorovna (née Ushakova). Kliushnikov's father was a nobleman by birth and a doctor by profession; Kliushnikov was born on his estate but spent his childhood in Moscow. The future writer was educated initially at home, then enrolled first in a private boarding school and later a gymnasium, where he mastered French, German, and English. At the gymnasium under the tutelage of the poet Vasilii Ivanovich Krasov, who was something of a literary authority at the time, Kliushnikov came to love literature. Kliushnikov left the gymnasium with a gold medal for excellent work in 1857 and then followed in his father's footsteps, choosing to study natural sciences at Moscow University; he graduated in 1861.

Immediately after his graduation, Kliushnikov went to stay at the estate of his uncle Ivan Petrovich Kliushnikov, who had been a well-known poet in the 1840s but by this point was leading an uneventful life on his own. The elder Kliushnikov, along with Krasov, had belonged to Nikolai Vladimirovich Stankevich's literary and philosophical circle in the 1830s; other members included Vissarion Grigor'evich Belinsky, Konstantin Sergeevich Aksakov, Mikhail Aleksandrovich Bakunin, Vasilii Petrovich Botkin, and Mikhail Nikiforovich Katkov. All these men remained prominent in Russian literary life: Belinsky as the leading critic of his day, Aksakov as an important Slavophile, Bakunin as a revolutionary, Botkin as writer and critic, and Katkov as editor of *Moskovskie vedomosti* (Moscow News) and founder of *Russkii vestnik*. The time the younger Kliushnikov spent with his uncle influenced his first novel, which featured nature and the life of landowners; particularly important as well was the political unrest associated with the Polish uprising, which was agitating the region at the time.

Like many young people, Kliushnikov did not settle upon a career quickly or easily. He did not turn at this point exclusively to literature, but instead left his uncle's home and returned to Moscow, where he worked for a brief time as an assistant to the secretary of the Eighth Department of the Russian Senate. He shared his early literary attempts only with his fellow participants in artistic salons; he also took part in amateur theatricals, writing plays and participating in their staging. After leaving his work at the Senate, Kliushnikov went on to teach in public and private educational institutions.

Kliushnikov began *Marevo* with the approval of his uncle and published it in 1864 in *Russkii vestnik,* headed by his uncle's former associate Katkov. The work brought Kliushnikov tremendous fame. He chose his themes effectively and succeeded in appealing to readers both emotionally and intellectually. Russian nihilism and the Polish uprising were the foremost issues of the day, and the author's straightforward point of view and opinionated stance met contemporary readers' expectations of politicized literature. An anonymous reviewer in *Syn otechestva* (Son of the Fatherland) attested to the striking impression the work had made initially: "When the beginning of Mr. Kliushnikov's novel was published in *Russkii vestnik,* the majority of the reading public at once distinguished the novel as an extraordinary phenomenon. Mr. Kliushnikov was proclaimed a new, rising star in Russian literature."

Opinions of the novel and its author quickly soured, however; by the time the novel had been published in full, reviews were predominantly harsh. While radical journalists might have been expected to respond negatively to the work, conservative critics also pointed out the artistic shortcomings of the novel. The same anonymous reviewer who had earlier praised the work now implied that Kliushnikov was no more than a mouthpiece for the conservative Katkov's ideas, expressed both in *Moskovskie vedomosti* and in *Russkii vestnik:* "We are observing a well-known point of view.

Devoted to it, the author is not concerned with the artistic quality of his work, but rather presents character after character, speech after speech, in order to make his opinions known about one subject or another. These speeches seem to have been taken entirely from *Moskovskie vedomosti*. The author says nothing new to the public; he's simply repeating what has already been said." The reviewer Evgenii Nikolaevich Edel'son of the journal *Biblioteka dlia chteniia* (Library for Reading) was the only one to support the author.

At the time the novel was published, Kliushnikov was only twenty-three years old. It was clear from the comparisons, allusions, and jokes in the text, understandable only to a narrow circle of readers, that the author had little knowledge of life and was used to writing for a small circle of close acquaintances. The conversations and jests popular in Kliushnikov's circles were not suitable in the context of a novel, and readers were confused by them. The radical critic Dmitrii Ivanovich Pisarev wrote a fascinating analysis of the novel that underlined this particular characteristic. Pisarev wrote his article while imprisoned in the Peter and Paul Fortress in St. Petersburg, and because of these circumstances he was forced to conceal his treatment of Kliushnikov's subject matter in a discussion of the aesthetics of the novel. Pisarev characterized Kliushnikov's style as "wild" because of his constant jumps from one topic to another with no apparent reason or connection. One might think that as a Realist who demanded a strong correspondence between art and reality, Pisarev may have wished for a specifically psychological motivation for these shifts. It is difficult in Kliushnikov's work to find any sort of connection or reason for his changes in topic. The novel seems to be composed of various pieces–phrases or comparisons, conversations, scenes, or even chapters–that do not necessarily fit well together. Taken on its own, each piece appears to be pleasing, but in context can be bewildering. It is difficult to find and follow the thread of the narration, as characters rapidly replace one another.

The novel, however, was convincing to unsophisticated readers, and it seems that Kliushnikov created *Marevo* to conform to the standards of mass literature of his day. Life in its everyday manifestations is expressed precisely as it was commonly accepted to think about it and portray it, and all the characters act just as they would have been expected to act, observing or disregarding the laws of etiquette. A description of the heroine entering a theater is typical in this regard: "Her tall, slender figure, in a black dress with its white teardrops, her severe, thoughtful face, framed by thick locks with no headdress, attracted the attention of the entire pit." Precisely what has attracted the attention of the pit is

not clear: Kliushnikov has not provided sufficient motivation for the response he has asserted. The author does not, however, expect such a question from the reader; he expects the reader to trust him and accept his words. Kliushnikov creates the illusion of complexity in certain scenes in which he develops a simple thought quite intricately. But usually the author openly expresses his attitude toward what he is depicting, and his heroes speak in such a way that their political stance and the author's are clearly understandable from their first phrases. The views the characters have manifested find further expression in their deeds as the plot develops. Kliushnikov also plays on the mass reader's love of easy solutions for complex questions: social conflicts are explained in the novel as a result of forces hostile to the Russian people.

The title of the novel is symbolic. Since the word *marevo* means mirage, in this context Kliushnikov uses it to suggest the falsity of nihilism. This evil is represented in the novel by Vladislav Bronsky, a Polish count. Kliushnikov shared the Russian nationalistic sentiments common at the time of the Polish uprising, and this inclination is clear in his choice of villain. In Kliushnikov's opinion, Poland was the source of nihilism, a disease he felt was aimed at destroying Russia through rebellion. Thus, Kliushnikov has the Polish Bronsky spread the seeds of revolutionary discord among peasants and philistines. At the same time, by perfidiously warning the governor about the planned uprising, Bronsky worms himself into the governor's confidence and gains the right to enter the governor's office at any time. With the help of the young nihilist Kolia, Bronsky stage-manages a riot at the estate of Kolia's uncle Konon Terent'evich, and then insists on the forceful repression of the insurrection; at the same time he prevents the hero, Vladimir Rusanov, from entering into negotiations with the peasants.

In Bronsky's next episode the rebels are armed new arrivals from Poland, secretly brought to Russia because Bronsky's own peasants are not sufficiently reliable: they do not share Bronsky's anti-Russian sentiments, and they are more dissatisfied with their oppression by the landowner than by the policies of the authorities. Bronsky, meanwhile, even as he calls on the peasants to rebel, scorns them and refers to them as "swine." His goal is to create problems between peasants and landowners and then to provoke a severe reaction to the disturbances from the authorities. Then, taking advantage of the ensuing disorder, he plans to conquer the area and become king of Poland. As he tells a young woman whom he has seduced, "My destiny is to shake loose, tear away, drag off anything that collides with me. . . . After that there is only one salvation: to follow me so long as I'm alive." Because of his

The novelist's uncle Ivan Petrovich Kliushnikov, a poet whose country estate inspired his nephew's first novel, Marevo *(The Mirage, 1864)*

lack of scruples, Bronsky seems to survive well. But his child is stillborn, symbolizing the absence of prospects in Bronsky's convictions. It is possible that the character of Bronsky influenced Fyodor Dostoevsky in his depiction of Nikolai Stavrogin and Petr Verkhovensky in *Besy* (The Devils, 1871–1872).

Despite all the support he had received from his uncle and his former associates, Kliushnikov did not spare the liberals of the 1840s from censure in his novel, since he considered their earlier discussions and beliefs to have been another source of misfortune for Russia. He demonstrated this view in the fate of his heroine, Inna Gorobets, a pure and honest young woman who is influenced in her youth by her father, a "man of the forties" whose irresponsible free thinking corrupts her moral principles. Kliushnikov specifically implicated his uncle's circle in this misfortune by inserting into the story letters to the heroine's father from such figures (identified by their initials) as Stankevich, Belinsky, and Krasov, as well as the writers Nikolai Vasil'evich Gogol and Aleksandr Ivanovich Herzen. Kliushnikov was suspected by many of having used original letters in his work, a practice Ivan Sergeevich Turgenev characterized as "impudent."

Immediately classified as an antinihilist novel, *Marevo* joined several other works in this category, the

most famous of which is Turgenev's *Ottsy i deti* (Fathers and Sons, 1862). Other works comparable in their subject matter include Aleksei Feofilaktovich Pisemsky's *Vzbalamuchennoe more* (Troubled Seas, 1863) and Nikolai Semenovich Leskov's *Nekuda* (Nowhere, 1865). Kliushnikov's characters are perhaps more successfully drawn than Pisemsky's. One of his most interesting characters is the hero, the somewhat autobiographical Rusanov. Unlike Bronsky, Rusanov is guided in his actions not by passions and strong emotions but by reason and common sense. A young man of Kliushnikov's age, he has just graduated from the university and has come to stay with his uncle for the summer. In spite of his youth, he regards all new social ideas quite cautiously; he highly values following the examples of his elders; and he condemns individualistic actions. As he writes to his confidante Mal'vina Frantseva Shteinfel'ts, "I will move with the crowd. You can't even imagine how good it is to be one of them."

Kliushnikov portrays Rusanov as a "new man" who represents a practical alternative to the radicals and revolutionaries as well as to the dreamers of the 1840s. Rusanov is close to the peasantry and does not fear negotiating with them when they rise up in revolt. At work he struggles with negligent subordinates and fulfills his duties with remarkable diligence, putting all his documents in order (an important trait, according to Kliushnikov, in a statesman of the "new" type). In spite of his desire to fit in, Rusanov is misunderstood and unappreciated by those around him, and he ends up being forced to resign from his work. Critics felt that Kliushnikov had failed in his attempt to create an ideal hero. While such a hero, working through state channels for moderation and conservatism, would have been acceptable during the period of Czar Nicholas I, by the early 1860s, when the novel was written, state reforms had already been undertaken; so in a sense Kliushnikov was behind the times in his portrayal. Mikhail Evgrafovich Saltykov (N. Shchedrin) called Rusanov a "Don Quixote of conservatism," but one without the slightest shade of irony.

As critics suspected, Katkov probably had a substantial influence on the novel, particularly in the second half, which includes tirades directed at such figures as Herzen and the radical critic Nikolai Gavrilovich Chernyshevsky. In any case, Katkov was certainly pleased with his new author. He published *Marevo* as a book and offered Kliushnikov the chance to become a permanent contributor to *Russkii vestnik*. Kliushnikov's work appeared frequently in *Russkii vestnik* in the 1860s, including his translations of Dickens's *Our Mutual Friend* (1864–1865) and Collins's *The Moonstone* (1868). While he continued producing original literary works as well, he steered clear of political themes and, perhaps for that reason, was gradually forgotten by the public. During this period Kliushnikov attempted to write for children: the result was "Drugaia zhizn'" (Another Life), published in *Detskoe chtenie* (Children's Readings) in 1865. The story of children whose family has just moved to the provinces is told in a lively style and filled with information about agriculture, economics, and rules of conduct, indicating Kliushnikov's apparent didactic intent.

In 1867 Kliushnikov became a member of the *Obshchestvo liubitelei rossiiskoi slovesnosti* (Society of Lovers of Russian Literature), and that same year he published his next novel, *Bol'shie korabli*, in *Literaturnaia biblioteka* (The Literary Library); this work, like *Marevo*, was intended for adults. The novel depicts the love affairs of two young noblemen: the St. Petersburg dandy Aleksandr Astrein and the wealthy factory owner Boris Mezensky. Astrein discovers the meaning of life through love, while Mezensky, a positive example of a contemporary man, is filled with life from the beginning of the story. The novel did not broach the burning issues of the day, and it did not attract much attention from the public. While Kliushnikov did include some of his favorite themes, such as nihilism and the future path of Russia, he did it so weakly and sloppily that the afterword, in which the author's ideas were laid out, seems to have been tacked on to the rest of the novel. The author explained the title with an allegory about big ships after a storm; he most likely had in mind life in Russia following the storm of the "Great Reforms." Kliushnikov took his epigraph to the novel from Aleksandr Sergeevich Pushkin's *Evgenii Onegin* (Eugene Onegin, 1833). In so doing the author wanted to convey to the reader the idea that his novel, like Pushkin's, was written "na staryi lad" (in the old manner), with "predan'ia russkogo semeistva" (Russian family traditions). It might be argued, however, that Kliushnikov understood Pushkin's "traditions" rather peculiarly.

Perhaps Kliushnikov had in mind Pushkin's attempt in *Evgenii Onegin* to find positive traits in all his characters. After *Marevo* Kliushnikov never again portrayed his main characters in a negative light, and instead tried to convince the reader that all the characters were basically good people, simply possessed of shortcomings. Unlike Pushkin, however, Kliushnikov was not successful in his portrayals. The critic Viktor Petrovich Burenin commented astutely that Kliushnikov's main characters in this work were "loafers" who had misbehaved and deserved some sort of light penalty as a result. Burenin characterized *Bol'shie korabli* as a "quasi-artistic work." On the surface, the novel resembles mid-nineteenth-century masterpieces of Russian literature. It combines all the significant themes and problems addressed by the best writers of the time, such

as the superfluous man, the formation of a character's personality, and the role of women in society. But these themes in Kliushnikov's novel are merely stereotyped borrowings from other texts, accomplished in so trite a manner that Burenin compared Kliushnikov's artistic methods to paintings on a snuffbox. Only some individual scenes, such as a description of a student dormitory in the early chapters, are written skillfully and elegantly.

At the end of 1868 Kliushnikov moved to St. Petersburg. Vasilii Vladimirovich Kashpirev, who became editor of *Zaria* (Dawn), had invited Kliushnikov to work on this journal, and Kliushnikov published his next novel, *Tsygane*, in *Zaria* in 1869. The novel focuses on the weak-willed Lev Sergeevich Zarnitsyn and the women around him. Zarnitsyn is motivated purely by his sexual instincts, or, as the author puts it euphemistically, by passion. Kliushnikov links Zarnitsyn's lack of will to the negative ideas that had surrounded and corrupted him during his youth, when he was influenced by nihilist criminals. Zarnitsyn is deeply unhappy and demonically dangerous. He attracts women to him with his magnetism and then makes them as miserable as he is. On the other hand, Zarnitsyn rescues a child from a burning vessel without any hesitation. Kliushnikov appears to sympathize more with Zarnitsyn than with the women he torments. The women themselves are to blame for their own unhappiness; they deserve punishment either because of an unclean past or because of a tendency toward lewdness demonstrated in their submission to carnal desires. Their itinerant lifestyle is symbolically reflected in the title of the novel. Kliushnikov's goal was to produce a moralistic and didactic work in which heroes find salvation through a rational approach to life and through observing common stereotypes.

In his unfinished novella *Ne marevo* (Not a Mirage, 1871), Kliushnikov attempted to depict a new type of positive, conservatively inclined hero. The main character of this work is born into the lower classes but marries a noblewoman. Through his portrayal of the relationship between the spouses, Kliushnikov apparently sought to demonstrate the vices of the gentry, unused to work. Kliushnikov himself, while born a nobleman, nonetheless was forced for much of his life to earn his own living, and he respected work in any form.

In 1870 the publisher Adol'f Fedorovich Marks organized a new journal, the popular *Niva*, and Kliushnikov became the editor. *Niva* was meant for family reading. It included reproductions of famous paintings and photographs, fiction, biographies of leading cultural figures, popular sketches, and articles devoted to local mores, archaeology, the natural sciences, geography, the history of Russia, sports, and notes on new books. This light journal was noteworthy for its attractive design and low price. The principal goal of the editor was independence from "kruzhkovshchina" (literary clannishness) and political stances, and the journal proved remarkably successful, quickly becoming the most popular Russian weekly. No doubt Kliushnikov as editor deserved much of the credit for its success. His contemporaries recalled him as a model editor: benevolent and courteous in his interactions, yet demanding and principled in work-related questions.

In 1876 Kliushnikov began to publish his own journal, *Krugozor* (Horizon), which was based on the same principles as *Niva*. He managed to attract the work of talented writers and critics such as Leskov, Apollon Nikolaevich Maikov, Nikolai Nikolaevich Strakhov, Vsevolod Vladimirovich Krestovsky, and Vasilii Grigor'evich Avseenko. He even included an encyclopedia he had prepared as a free-of-charge appendix to the journal. Nonetheless, the journal was not successful, despite its having a lower price than others of its kind, and *Krugozor* shut down in 1878. Kliushnikov's encyclopedia was also unsuccessful, perhaps because it was poorly put together: Kliushnikov had borrowed the entries from other sources, and his definitions at times lacked accuracy or completeness.

In 1877 Kliushnikov also worked for a brief time as the editor of the newspaper *Sobesednik* (The Interlocutor). Kliushnikov's assignment was supposed to be purely formal: the newspaper was actually to be edited by Iurii Mikhailovich Bogushevich, who was a government employee and as such could not sign off on the newspaper. But Kliushnikov involved himself in the affairs of the paper and took exception to one particular article. When the newspaper was temporarily closed, Kliushnikov took the opportunity to resign from it. He returned to Moscow in 1880 and wrote for *Moskovskie vedomosti* and then *Russkii vestnik*. After Katkov's death in 1887, Kliushnikov moved back to St. Petersburg and edited *Niva* for the rest of his life.

For years Kliushnikov had been neglecting his own writing in order to seek out new talents and edit the work of others. He wrote two historical works for commercial purposes in the early 1870s: *Pri Petre. Istoricheskaia povest' vremen preobrazovaniia Rossii* (Under Peter: A Historical Tale from the Period of Russia's Transformation, 1872), with Vasilii Ivanovich Kel'siev, and *Sem'ia vol'nodumtsev. Roman Ekaterininskogo vremeni* (The Family of Freethinkers: A Novel from the Time of Catherine the Great, 1872), with Petr Nikolaevich Petrov. These works were devoid of artistic merit. The authors interpreted well-known historical works rather roughly, and the plots were artificial. Kliushnikov's story "Gosudar'-otrok" (The Adolescent Sovereign,

1881), intended for children and devoted to the fourteenth-century Russian prince Dmitrii Donskoy, was written in the same way.

Kliushnikov's story "Baryshnia i barynia," on the other hand, has not yet been evaluated as it deserves. In this story Kliushnikov managed at last to find his own themes and manner of expression. The story is devoted to two typical figures in Russian nineteenth-century society: the young lady of the title, and the wife that she eventually becomes. The narrator, Doctor N, develops a theory about the two types. The "Gentleman's Daughter" develops from approximately age thirteen and has a "silly" mother and several older sisters. She represents "the extraordinary combination of an innocent girl and the soul of an experienced woman." Such is Lizaveta Nikolaevna (Betsy), the heroine of the story, who knows life only from novels, thinks in bookish terms, and at the same time manages to behave quite naturally. Her tragedy, according to Doctor N, is that sooner or later she must become a "Gentleman's Wife." This change happens with her obligatory marriage of convenience, which entails her continued search for love and amusement outside the family. Unlike in his previous works, Kliushnikov managed in this story to broaden his picture of the gentry life he knew so well, presenting for the reader's amusement sketches of customs common to the gentry.

Despite a desire to write "a big novel about contemporary life," toward the end of his life Kliushnikov wrote short stories such as "Krepysh" and "Pliaska mertvyh." "Krepysh" joins "Baryshnia i barynia" as one of the best examples of Kliushnikov's work. The limitations of a smaller artistic format kept Kliushnikov from his usual chaotic mode of presentation. The story is based on an intrigue through which the author portrays the development of a Russian businessman who is forced to use cunning and deceit in an effort to conceal his intentions and even his achievements. Kliushnikov shows the dubious value of such success and demonstrates its effects on the protagonist's soul, as the businessman is left motivated solely by the desire to earn more money.

In an 1889 article dedicated to the works of Mariia Vsevolodovna Krestovskaia, Kliushnikov laid out his own artistic credo. A real artistic work, according to Kliushnikov, will be characterized by simplicity, cheerfulness, lyricism, a lack of pretensions, and the portrayal of the inner life of its characters. On the other hand, tendentiousness, artificiality, and a multitude of discourses should not find their way into artistic texts. Kliushnikov's position in this article demonstrates an attempt on his part to combine the aesthetic ideas of the beginning of the century with new artistic approaches. Kliushnikov's conservatism is evident, however, in his analysis of Krestovskaia's language. He praises Krestovskaia for the absence in her works of what he calls "nemetsko-chukhonskie" (German-Finnish) words, which he thought defaced the Russian language, and he gives examples of such "tortures." The words and phrases he mentions nevertheless became common in Russian literary language of the twentieth century.

As a writer, Kliushnikov was a victim of his times. In some ways his talent increased over the course of his career, but his contemporaries—and in particular the reigning critics of the time—valued political content over artistic form. Thus Kliushnikov's best works simply went unnoticed by critics and the reading public. *Marevo* answered the demands of the day through its political focus and therefore met with success. But critics who objected to Kliushnikov's political stance in the novel criticized his shallowness. Thus Kliushnikov began to avoid expressing his opinions clearly, taking refuge instead in hints and allusions. Remembering how freely his *Marevo* had been interpreted, however, he tried to construct his next works in such a way that a reader would not be able to come to an interpretation that the author had not intended. His works then lost their depth, and readers who disagreed with the author's point of view lost interest, seeing in the work only a collection of incongruities. The matter was made worse by Kliushnikov's simplistic approach to the problems and themes his works were intended to discuss—an approach rejected eventually even by the mass reader. Without the public's support for his writing, the shy and modest Kliushnikov feared creating another literary scandal such as his first novel, and he found refuge in journalism. By the end of his life, Kliushnikov's name had been forgotten. His editing had not made him famous, and his new works never achieved the popular success of *Marevo*. Even that novel lost its contemporaneity and perceived relevance as time went by and the political terrain shifted. Kliushnikov died on 7 November 1892. He is buried in the Danilevsky Cemetery in Moscow.

Biographies:

Petr Vasil'evich Bykov, "V. P. Kliushnikov," *Vsemirnaia Illiustratsiia,* no. 1244 (1892): 405–406;

O. E. Maiorova, "Kliushnikov, Viktor Petrovich," in *Russkie pisateli. Biobibliograficheskii slovar';* volume 1 (Moscow: Prosveshchenie, 1990), pp. 347–348;

V. A. Viktorovich, "Kliushnikov, Viktor Petrovich," in *Russkie pisateli 1800–1917: Biograficheskii slovar';* volume 2 (Moscow: Bol'shaia Rossiiskaia Entsiklopediia, 1992), pp. 562–564.

References:

Viktor P. Burenin (as Z.), "Novye knigi. 'Bol'shie korabli.' Roman v trekh chastiakh Viktora Kliushnikova. SPb, 1874," *Sanktpeterburgskie vedomosti,* no. 169 (1874): 1–2;

S. S. Konkin, "Zhurnal 'Russkoe slovo' i antinigilisticheskaia literatura 60-kh godov," *Uchenye zapiski MGPI im. V. I. Lenina,* 160 (1961): 233–258;

"Marevo. Roman G. Kliushnikova," *Syn otechestva,* no. 166 (1864): 1301–1304;

Charles A. Moser, *Antinihilism in the Russian Novel of the 1860s* (The Hague: Mouton, 1964);

Dmitrii I. Pisarev, "Serditoe bessilie," in *Sochineniia,* volume 3 (Moscow: Khudozhestvennaia literatura, 1956), pp. 218–250;

Mikhail Evgrafovich Saltykov (N. Shchedrin), "Tsygane. Roman v 3 ch. Soch. V. P. Kliushnikova. SPb., 1871," in his *Sobranie sochinenii,* volume 9 (Moscow: Khudozhestvennaia literatura, 1970), pp. 426–429;

Iu. Sorokin, "Antinigilisticheskii roman," in *Istoriia russkogo romana,* edited by B. P. Gorodetsky & N. I. Prutskov, volume 2 (Moscow & Leningrad: Nauka, 1964), pp. 103–107.

Papers:

Viktor Petrovich Kliushnikov's papers can be found in St. Petersburg at the Institute of Russian Literature (IRLI [Pushkin House]) and in the Russian State Historical Archive (RGIA, formerly TsGIA).

Aleksandra Petrovna Kobiakova

(1823 – October 1892)

Judith Vowles

WORKS: *Posledniaia kazn'*, in *Sovremennik*, nos. 3–4 (1858);

Semeistvo Podoshvinykh, in *Russkoe slovo*, nos. 1–3 (1860);

Zhenshchina v kupecheskom bytu, in *Russkoe slovo*, nos. 10–12 (1863).

PERIODICAL PUBLICATIONS: "Avtobiografiia," *Russkoe slovo*, no. 7 (1860);

"Prikazchik," *Russkoe slovo*, no. 12 (1860); no. 1 (1861);

"Neozhidannoe bogatstvo," *Russkoe slovo*, nos. 5–6 (1861);

"Drug-priiatel'," *Russkoe slovo*, nos. 11–12 (1861);

"V derevne. Ocherk," *Zaria*, no. 12 (1869);

"Chto drugu nal'esh', to sam vyp'esh'," *Zaria*, no. 2 (1870);

"Svekrov'," *Zaria*, nos. 3–5 (1870);

"Kazennaia kvartira," *Zaria*, nos. 5 and 7 (1870);

"Prianniki," *Zaria*, no. 7 (1871).

One of the few women writers to emerge from the nineteenth-century Russian merchant class, Aleksandra Petrovna Kobiakova documented the dreary life of the provincial merchantry in novels and tales published in the radical press in the early 1860s. Although she was less well known and less prolific than many of her peers, Kobiakova's origins, her subject matter, and the harshly realistic tenor of her prose make her an unusual figure among the Russian women writers whose numbers grew so rapidly during the realist period.

The little that is known about Kobiakova's life comes primarily from the brief "Avtobiografiia" (Autobiography) she published in *Russkoe slovo* (Russian Word) in 1860. She was born in the town of Kostroma in 1823 into the oppressively traditional and patriarchal world of a provincial merchant family. She spent almost forty years in this "kingdom of darkness," as the radical critic Nikolai Aleksandrovich Dobroliubov and the dramatist Aleksandr Nikolaevich Ostrovsky termed the claustrophobic milieu. Her life in Kostroma provided her with abundant material for her fiction. She became

well acquainted with the characteristics of that realm: slow acceptance of change, suspicion of Western ways, superstitious piety and brutality, and ignorance and hostility to education. Although Kobiakova shared her brothers' rudimentary lessons with the local deacon and learned to write as well as read, she was largely self-taught, reading what books she could find. She wrote her first story at the age of twelve. At the age of fifteen, strong-willed and persistent, she endured months of scandal, gossip, and violent family quarrels to escape the arranged marriage that was a merchant daughter's customary lot. For almost five years she enjoyed an unusual degree of freedom. She became engaged to an educated young man from a minor landholding family but broke the engagement when he became tyrannical and scorned her independent mind and literary aspirations.

When Kobiakova was twenty, her father's bankruptcy and death left her and her mother in poverty. For the next ten years Kobiakova earned a meager living by sewing. She wrote her first novel, *Posledniaia kazn'* (The Final Punishment), during this time, but her hopes of selling it came to nothing. Her recollections of her first foray into the publishing world and her meetings with local seminary students and schoolmasters, as well as the writer Aleksei Feofilaktovich Pisemsky, whom she asked for help, reveal a characteristic tenacity but can only hint at the obstacles in her way and her isolation from any kind of literary or even literate community.

In the early 1850s Kobiakova married S. E. Studzinsky, a poor but educated noncommissioned officer from a gentry family. She returned with him to St. Petersburg, where they led a difficult life. He held a minor post in the Senate Survey Department, and she was unable to sell her embroidery. They endured cold and hunger before they were saved from utter destitution by an unnamed benefactor. They evidently had at least one living child, a boy, during this time. Her autobiography merely mentions the burden of caring for children in these years. In 1858 their financial situation improved; Kobiakova finally sold the novel she had written ten years earlier to *Sovremennik* (The Contemporary), one of the leading progressive "thick" journals that championed women's emancipation, not only by printing many essays devoted to the "woman question" but also by publishing women writers.

Although Kobiakova presents *Posledniaia kazn'* as a true story told by her grandmother, who had heard it from her mother-in-law, the novel bears the hallmarks of the historical novels and romances of Mikhail Nikolaevich Zagoskin, Ivan Ivanovich Lazhechnikov, and other Russian followers of Sir Walter Scott popular in the 1830s and 1840s. Set in early-eighteenth-century Kostroma, *Posledniaia kazn'* tells the tale of an ill-starred romance between a young blacksmith and a merchant's daughter. The leisurely, slender plot and overidealized characters (for which Pisemsky had faulted the novel ten years earlier) are given substance by Kobiakova's knowledge of the history, customs, and folk traditions of old Kostroma. Her vivid use of local color and historical material reveals a gift for observation and an eye for telling detail; the dialogue reflects an ear attuned to the speech patterns and cadences of the common people with their colloquialisms, dialect words, and sayings. She transferred these qualities from the historical novel to her realist narratives of contemporary Russian life.

Posledniaia kazn' received little critical notice; but as Kobiakova wrote in her autobiography, the sale of her first novel let her "put down the needle and take up the pen." It also brought her to the attention of the St. Petersburg literary world, in particular the circle associated with the journal *Russkoe slovo*. In the tumultuous period following the Crimean War and the accession of Alexander II in 1855, *Russkoe slovo* pressed for social and political reform in every area of Russian life. Originally intended to provide a middle ground between Westernizers and Slavophiles, the journal grew increasingly radical under the guidance of its editor, Grigorii Evlampievich Blagosvetlov, and its literary critic, Dmitrii Ivanovich Pisarev. Little is known about Kobiakova's place and acquaintances in this circle of "revolutionary democrats." She did, however, publish all her work from the early 1860s—two novels, a novella, two tales, and the autobiography—in *Russkoe slovo*. Kobiakova's bleak representations of Russian society and everyday life or *byt* satisfied Blagosvetlov's commitment to critical realism and the utilitarian demand that literature document the realities of Russian life as a prelude to social reform. She supplied much of the fiction that appeared in the journal between 1860 and 1863—fiction that became, like the journal, increasingly radical.

At the age of almost forty, Kobiakova became one of the rare women writers to make a literary career in St. Petersburg at that time. While her husband's government post made this position practicable, it may be that her background and experiences also allowed her to negotiate the hurly-burly of the St. Petersburg publishing world more readily than other women writers, who, as the literary historian Mary F. Zirin has noted, came primarily from gentry families and either handled their literary affairs by correspondence or found conservative Moscow a more congenial home until the 1880s. Certainly Kobiakova's willingness to publish under her own (unmarried) name was relatively uncommon. Women generally used a pseudonym, often masculine, or anonymity both to shield themselves from the harsh criticism women authors often encountered and also to find a serious audience. Kobiakova found her audience by eschewing privacy and capitalizing on her name and origins, going so far as to publish her autobiography—a practice uncommon among women writers until later in the century. Her lack of formal education and her background were even advantageous. The editor's unusual and enthusiastic introduction to her second novel *Semeistvo Podoshvinykh* (The Podoshvin Family) when it appeared in *Russkoe slovo* in January 1860 welcomed Kobiakova not as a *belletristka,* an educated woman dabbling in literary pursuits, but as a *samouchka,* a self-taught writer whose literary credentials and mastery of her subject came from her life and experiences.

Kobiakova's appearance on the literary scene was well timed. Interest in the world of the Russian merchantry, stirred by Ostrovsky's plays, intensified with the publication of his play *Groza* (The Storm) in 1860. The drama and its remarkable heroine, Katerina, prompted widespread debate in the journals, including Dobroliubov's famous evaluation of the play. His two essays "Temnoe tsarstvo" (The Kingdom of Darkness, 1859) and "Luch sveta v temnom tsarstve" (A Ray of Light in the Kingdom of Darkness, 1860), both published in *Sovremennik,* interpreted the merchant world as a microcosm of a corrupt Russian society and read Katerina's suicide as a last noble gesture of protest against despotism. Kobiakova published *Semeistvo Podoshvinykh* shortly after the first of Dobroliubov's essays and became one of the first and few prose fiction writers to explore the "kingdom of darkness." Although others emerged (among them Aleksandr S. Ushakov, Semen Akimovich Makashin, and Nikolai Aleksandrovich Leiken), the editor of *Russkoe slovo* realized that Kobiakova's gender was an additional advantage. His introduction presented her novel as an artless cry from the heart of a woman whose painful experiences make her unable to keep silent. He implicitly evoked Katerina's image, drawing a parallel between her impassioned yearning for change and Kobiakova's narrative.

In her autobiography Kobiakova declared that she wrote *Semeistvo Podoshvinykh* to serve the estate from which she came by revealing the consequences of "a despotic and senseless upbringing." She wanted to expose the ways in which the family, the very foundation of society and the origin of the most basic social ties, shapes character. In this goal her novel is akin not only to Ostrovsky's dramas but also to such family portraits as Sergei Timofeevich Aksakov's *Semeinaia khronika* (Family Chronicle, 1856), Avdot'ia Iakovlevna Panaeva's *Semeistvo Tal'nikovykh* (The Tal'nikov Family, 1848), and Mikhail Evgrafovich Saltykov's (N. Shchedrin) later novel *Gospoda Golovlevy* (The Golovlevs, 1880). Kobiakova's novel depicts the tyrannical grain merchant Dmitrii Andreevich Podoshvin's patriarchal household in the small Volga town of Prival'sk. Kobiakova traces the complicated web of psychological and emotional ties that bind one person to another in the family of this *samodur*, as Ostrovsky called such ignorant, brutal domestic tyrants. She creates a memorable gallery of men and women whose better natures have been distorted and deformed by Podoshvin's despotic rule. They are more fully realized and complex than those of *Posledniaia kazn';* capable of both good and bad, they cause harm but also arouse pity. Podoshvin is tyrannical but righteous, deploring his son Andriusha's evil ways and chastising him for his own good. Andriusha, once a sweet child, has been transformed by bloody beatings into a drunken wastrel and thief. Kobiakova's female characters are particularly well drawn: Podoshvin's middle-aged, unmarried daughter Feodos'ia Dmitrevna, spiteful and embittered, who knows life and happiness have passed her by; the rude, brazen servant girl Pelageia Osipovna, who sees her own chance for happiness slip away in a pathetic romance; Podoshvin's wife, Mar'ia Borisovna, a kindly woman who knows all her son's vices and nevertheless condemns a naive young woman to be his wife in the vain hope that she will reform him; and her son's bride, Lizaveta Alekseevna Zaponkova, a young penniless girl of gentle manners and some education, whose high minded and somewhat vain naiveté lead her to marry the drunken Andriusha, believing that her love (and reading books together) can civilize and reform her barbarous husband.

Kobiakova represents the suffocating atmosphere of Podoshvin's household in vivid, realistic detail as she traces the course of this calamitous marriage to its end, when Andriusha descends into crime and meets a drunken death. Within the framework of this simple plot, she stages many memorable and dramatic (occasionally melodramatic) scenes, with lively dialogues that capture her characters' idiosyncrasies.

The novel presents its case for the reforms needed at the very heart of society, for the most part without resorting to overt didacticism. The narrator (Kobiakova uses an omniscient third-person female narrator in all her fiction) rarely intrudes. However, Kobiakova gives *Semeistvo Podoshvinykh* a sentimental and improbably optimistic ending: the old tyrant is transformed by the realization that ultimately he is responsible for his son's death. A brief coda to the story, a device Kobiakova used regularly in her fiction, describes the fates of her characters in later years: the father has changed and has learned to treat his dead son's child kindly and lovingly. This unlikely reformation earned the censor's approval of Kobiakova's moderation compared to Ostrovsky's bleak and unregenerate opinions. None of Kobiakova's subsequent fiction ended so optimistically.

Kobiakova's autobiography followed *Semeistvo Podoshvinykh* and attested to her origins and experiences that gave her the right to document merchant life. Yet, her writing is far less naive than the editor asserted. Allusions to the liberal and radical thinkers of her day, including Dobroliubov, reflect her familiarity with the discussions about the "woman question" in the "thick" journals. The sense of political and social obligation to serve society that she expresses reflects the aspirations and ethics of her new milieu. Such autobiographical testaments were not uncommon among the *raznochintsy* (nongentry intellectuals)–Makashin's *Avtobiografiia* (Autobiography) appeared in *Russkaia rech'* (Russian Speech) the following year, for example–but few members of the merchant class, men or women, wrote memoirs. Kobiakova's declaration stands in contrast to the more traditional merchant political stance that the historian Thomas C. Owen has described as "silence, apathy and inaction on public questions."

Although Kobiakova was known primarily for her novels of the provincial merchantry, her next three narratives reached beyond the confines of the merchant household to document the lives of other segments of the Russian population. Her next published piece, "Prikazchik," (The Assistant, 1860–1861), tells the tale of Petr Ivanych Otrubev, a prosperous grain merchant, who is swindled out of a barge-load of grain. The novella begins in a merchant household, and Kobiakova depicts with realistic detail and psychological acuity the self-satisfied and wealthy merchant's pride in his home, with its luxurious Western furnishings, and the wistful and lonely idleness of his wife, Natal'ia Ivanovna, in this splendid cage. The plot, which describes how Otrubev's cousin and assistant Petr Vasil'ich Otrubev and his rascally son defraud their employer and then cheat one another, provides a frame for *ocherki* (sketches) of characters tangential to the story but of great interest in themselves. Kobiakova depicts the religious folk, the wanderers and holy fools who go from house to house. She gives a lively rendition of the conversations of this motley group, some of whom are genuinely devout, while others, such as "Sister" Mamel'fa, make a living by wheedling alms from charitable ladies and monasteries, exploiting superstition and piety alike. Kobiakova also describes the world of the *meshchanstvo* (petty townsfolk) and common laborers. Especially memorable are the scenes of the hard life and rough company of the *burlaki,* or barge haulers; she captures their life of hardship, letting them speak for themselves in richly idiomatic exchanges as they ply their trade along the Volga. However tangential to the plot of "Prikazchik," these *ocherki* reflect Kobiakova's transition to a harsher and more radical representation of Russian life.

In a review of Kobiakova's work that appeared in the newspaper *Russkaia rech'* after "Prikazchik" in 1861, the critic Mikhail Fedorovich De-Pule gave one of the few assessments of her writing. Recently ousted from *Russkoe slovo* by Blagosvetlov for being insufficiently radical in his regard for aesthetic value, De-Pule did much to define the way in which Kobiakova's work is read. The essay, titled "Literatura i obshchestvennyi byt" (Literature and Social Life), applauded the *narodnyi* or "ethnographic" element of Kobiakova's fiction for satisfying the contemporary need for documentary literature in Russia. Disregarding the new subject matter in "Prikazchik," he compared her to Ostrovsky as a writer depicting merchant life, but he insisted that any comparison of their literary skill or their aesthetic value was a "wild and ludicrous idea." In his view Kobiakova's representation of Russian reality was merely a copy, not a literary creation, and Kobiakova herself a mere scribe, not a writer.

De-Pule's distinction reflects a key difference between literary critics who continued to debate the opposing claims of utility and aesthetic value in art. *Russkoe slovo,* guided by Blagosvetlov and the radical critic Pisarev, came down firmly on the side of the former, as did Kobiakova in her next two tales, "Drug-priiatel'" (The Friendly Friend, 1861) and "Neozhidannoe bogatstvo" (The Windfall, 1861). In "Drug-priiatel'" and "Neozhidannoe bogatstvo" Kobiakova again goes beyond the world of the merchantry in unsavory accounts of moral corruption, greed, and venality set amid the squalor of rural and small-town poverty. In "Drug-priiatel'" the steward of an estate plunders his employer's possessions and exploits his own family, until he is found out and hangs himself. The landowner's sordid life is encapsulated in an ugly scene in which he and his friend try to rape the steward's ward. "Neozhidannoe bogatstvo" depicts the miserable life of

the lower clergy and the petty intrigues of money-grubbing small landowners. A poor, elderly deacon who succumbs to the temptation to steal is the focus as events unravel. Kobiakova sympathizes with this "little man" without sentimentalizing him. In both stories Kobiakova uses telling detail rather than an accumulation of facts to convey the wretched lives and *byt* of the rural poor, occasionally inserting brief, lyrical descriptions of the Russian countryside to highlight the man-made nature of the misery she depicts. Typically dialogue functions as a means of characterization. The two stories place her within the tradition of the "natural school" and their followers among the men of the 1860s and such "ethnographic" writers as Vasilii Alekseevich Sleptsov, Aleksandr Ivanovich Levitov, and Fedor Mikhailovich Reshetnikov, whose novel about the barge haulers, *Podlipovtsy* (The Inhabitants of Podlipnaia), appeared in 1864.

In May 1862 the government suspended *Russkoe slovo* for eight months, citing its "harmful tendency." When it reopened Kobiakova returned to the subject of the provincial merchantry in her last and most tendentious novel, *Zhenshchina v kupecheskom bytu* (Woman in Everyday Merchant Life, 1863). Of all her narratives it most directly engages Ostrovsky's dramas. Kobiakova stages the harrowing story of Aniuta Aleksandrovna Lapina's grim marriage to the merchant Matvei Matveich Zhilin as an inverted morality play in which evil triumphs over good, vice over virtue. When Aniuta leaves her loving home for a house dominated by her violently bad-tempered, suspicious husband and presided over by her mother-in-law, the piously sadistic Mar'ia Mikhailovna, and her ill-natured, cruel sister-in-law, the widow Lizaveta Matveevna, she steps into the traditional world of the merchantry as it was perceived by its harshest critics. *Zhenshchina v kupecheskom bytu* catalogues all the vices of this "kingdom of darkness": fanatical belief in tradition; boorish ignorance and hostility toward books and education, especially in women; sexual jealousy and misogyny; physical brutality; social isolation; virulent religiosity; miserliness; and dishonesty. Kobiakova gives substance to these abstractions in the little details and events of Aniuta's daily life as she vainly attempts to escape a situation that becomes desperate when Zhilin begins to beat her in repeated scenes of physical violence that are no less horrifying for being sparely described.

Throughout, the novel alludes to Ostrovsky's plays, *Groza* in particular. As the story unfolds, the parallels between Aniuta's and Katerina's fates grow stronger. Aniuta glimpses a chance for love and happiness when she becomes acquainted with Ivan Sergeevich Kremnitsky, an educated officer from the gentry, stationed in the town with his regiment. The sad predictability of Aniuta's fledgling "romance" has a curiously Chekhovian pathos in the lively atmosphere and cheerful bustle the regiment brings to the sleepy provincial town. Kobiakova's heroine suffers from the same feelings of fear and guilt, but she is less articulate than Ostrovsky's Katerina, as well as more timid. Even as Kobiakova underscores the subtext of her novel with a climactic and dramatic scene in which Aniuta runs wildly through a terrible rainstorm to Kremnitsky's lodgings only to find that his regiment has left town permanently, she emphasizes the differences in the two heroines' ends. Katerina takes her own life, a much-debated conclusion that Dobroliubov's "Luch sveta v temnom tsarstve" interpreted as a final act of heroism and a protest against despotism; Aniuta, however, suffers a drearier, long-drawn-out fate. To find a few moments of oblivion she takes to drink, secretly selling off her few personal possessions to supply herself at first with Madeira, and later with the cheapest rum. Kobiakova figures Aniuta's fate in her disfigurement: the lovely young woman becomes an ugly, bloated slattern, perishing "as so many thousands of women perish in this bottomless maelstrom we call the marriages and family life of the Zhilins of our society." The novel closes with a quotation from an old love note from Kremnitsky trying to persuade Aniuta to meet him: "Isn't death better than this slow, dreary torment?" Questioning Dobroliubov's interpretation, Kobiakova reaches the same conclusion that Pisarev did somewhat later in his better-known challenge to Dobroliubov, the essay "Motivy russkoi dramy" (Motives in a Russian Drama, 1864): Aniuta's fate is neither dramatic nor poetic, but rather the realistic fate of a victim of despotism.

At stake in these interpretations is the political question: What is to be done? Kobiakova's answer to this question, and the distance between the optimistic conclusion of *Semeistvo Podoshvinykh* and the bleak verdict of *Zhenshchina v kupecheskom bytu,* reflect the extent to which her work had changed and become more radical over time. Unlike Podoshvin, Zhilin learns nothing; and unlike the Podoshvins—whose humanity Kobiakova reveals by showing glimpses of what might have been, thus making them pitiable, even tragic—the Zhilins are purely evil. They are unchanging and unchangeable; no reform is possible, only a more revolutionary extirpation.

Zhenshchina v kupecheskom bytu was Kobiakova's final contribution to *Russkoe slovo.* When her husband resigned from government service in 1862, Kobiakova returned to Kostroma and bought a small landholding. After debts forced the sale of the property in 1867, she moved into town, where her son was enrolled in the gymnasium. Early in 1868 she received financial assis-

tance from the Literary Fund, a charity set up to aid struggling writers and scholars, and returned to St. Petersburg. She published a handful of slight stories in the short-lived Slavophile journal *Zaria* (Dawn, 1869–1872), as did several other writers formerly associated with *Russkoe slovo.* Once again she drew on her experiences in Kostroma. "V derevne. Ocherk" (In the Country. A Sketch, 1869) details the petty struggles of small landowners. "Kazennaia kvartira" (The Government Apartment, 1870) follows a minor government official and his family as they slide into poverty. "Chto drugu nal'esh', to sam vyp'esh'" (You'll Get Yours, 1870) and "Svekrov'" (Mother-in-Law, 1870) sketch characters from provincial life. "Prianniki" (Spice Cookies, 1871), an uncharacteristically amusing story about a lost basket of sweetmeats, was the last of her works to appear in print. Nothing is known about the last twenty years of Kobiakova's life.

By the time of her death in St. Petersburg in October 1892 Kobiakova appears to have been largely forgotten. In her essay "Russkie zhenshchiny-pisatel'nitsy" (Russian Women Writers, 1876), the feminist critic and social activist Mar'ia Konstantinovna Tsebrikova mentions Kobiakova as a woman who struggled free from the merchant class, but aside from such occasional references to her origins, Kobiakova escaped notice. Her slight body of work was never collected or reprinted and has since remained generally unknown. Unlike other nongentry women writers of her time, such as the proletarian writer Anna Aleksandrovna Kirpishchikova, who wrote similar "ethnographic" accounts of peasants and workers in the Urals, Kobiakova was never republished in the Soviet period. Apparently her work did not reflect the nascent revolutionary struggles of factory workers and the peasantry. This indifference to her writing persists in the late twentieth century. She has yet to find a place in studies of realist writers of the 1860s or in the histories of Russian women's writing that takes full account of her literary achievements.

References:

Edith W. Clowes, "Merchants on Stage and in Life: Theatricality and Public Consciousness," in *Merchant Moscow: Images of Russia's Vanished Bourgeoisie,* edited by James L. West and Iurii A. Petrov (Princeton: Princeton University Press, 1998), pp. 147–159;

Toby W. Clyman and Judith Vowles, eds., *Russia Through Women's Eyes. Autobiographies from Tsarist Russia* (New Haven & London: Yale University Press, 1996), pp. 60–74;

Ol'ga Demidova, "Kobiakova," translated by Andrea Lanoux, in *Dictionary of Russian Women Writers,* edited by Marina Ledkovsky, Charlotte

Rosenthal, and Mary Zirin (Westport, Conn.: Greenwood Press, 1994), pp. 301–302;

Demidova, "Russian Women Writers of the Nineteenth Century," in *Gender and Russian Literature. New Perspectives,* edited by Rosalind Marsh (Cambridge: Cambridge University Press, 1996), pp. 92–111;

Mikhail Fedorovich De-Pule, "Literatura i obshchestvennyi byt," *Russkaia rech',* no. 61 (July 1861): 129–133;

Muriel Joffe and Adele Lindenmeyr, "Daughters, Wives, and Partners: Women in the Moscow Merchant Elite," in *Merchant Moscow: Images of Russia's Vanished Bourgeoisie,* edited by West and Petrov (Princeton: Princeton University Press, 1998), pp. 99–108;

V. Kastorsky, *Pisateli-kostromichi XVIII-XIX vv.* (Kostroma: Kostromskoe knizhnoe izdatel'stvo, 1958);

Catriona Kelly, *A History of Russian Women's Writing 1820–1992* (Oxford: Clarendon Press, 1994);

Kelly, "Teacups and Coffins: the Culture of Russian Merchant Women, 1850–1917," in *Women in Russia and Ukraine,* edited and translated by Marsh (Cambridge: Cambridge University Press, 1996), pp. 55–77;

Hugh McLean, "Realism," in *A Handbook of Russian Literature,* edited by Victor Terras (New Haven & London: Yale University Press, 1985), pp. 363–367;

Derek Offord, "Literature and Ideas in Russia after the Crimean War: the 'Plebeian' Writers," in *Ideology in Russian Literature,* edited by Richard Freeborn and Jane Grayson (New York: St. Martin's Press, 1990), pp. 47–78;

Thomas C. Owen, *Capitalism and Politics in Russia: A Social History of the Moscow Merchants, 1855–1905* (Cambridge: Cambridge University Press, 1981);

Proza pisatelei-demokratov shestidesiatykh godov XIX veka (Moscow: Gosudarstvennoe izdatel'stvo 'Vysshaia shkola', 1962);

Richard Stites, *The Women's Liberation Movement in Russia: Feminism, Nihilism, and Bolshevism* (Princeton: Princeton University Press, 1985);

T. V. Timofeeva, "Kobiakova," in *Russkie pisateli 1800–1917. Biograficheskii slovar',* volume 2 (Moscow: Nauchnoe izdatel'stvo "Bol'shaia rossiiskaia entsiklopediia" Fianit, 1992), p. 574;

G. A. Tishkin, *Zhenskii vopros v Rossii 50-60-e gody XIX v.* (Leningrad: Izdatel'stvo Leningradskogo universiteta, 1984);

Mar'ia Konstantinovna Tsebrikova, "Russkie zhenshchiny-pisatel'nitsy," *Nedelia,* nos. 21–22 (1876): 698–700;

L. E. Varustin, *Zhurnal "Russkoe slovo," 1859–1866* (Leningrad: Izdatel'stvo Leningradskogo universiteta, 1966);

Vechnye vskhody. Sbornik ocherkov o pisateliakh Kostromskogo kraia (Iaroslavl': Verkhne-Volzhskoe knizhnoe izdatel'stvo, 1986);

Mary F. Zirin, "Women's Prose Fiction in the Age of Realism," in *Women Writers in Russian Literature,* edited by Toby W. Clyman and Diana Greene (Westport, Conn.: Greenwood Press, 1994), pp. 77–94.

Papers:

Aleksandra Petrovna Kobiakova's papers are located at the Russian State Historical Archive (RGIA, formerly TsGIA), in St. Petersburg, f. 1349, op. 5, d. 3583, under her husband's name (S. E. Studzinsky).

Vsevolod Vladimirovich Krestovsky

(10 March 1839 – 18 January 1895)

Grazyna Lipska Kabat
University of Toronto

WORKS: *Besenok. Povest'*, in *Svetoch,* no. 1 (1861); (St. Petersburg, 1861);

Ne pervyi i ne poslednii. Neokonchennye zapiski studenta, in *Russkii mir* (19 April – 10 June 1861);

Stikhi, 2 volumes (St. Petersburg: A. Ozerov, 1862);

Sochineniia, 2 volumes (St. Petersburg: F. Stellovsky, 1862);

Peterburgskie trushchoby. Kniga o sytykh i golodnykh, in *Otechestvennye zapiski,* nos. 10–11 (1864); nos. 1–6, 9–12 (1865); nos. 1–12 (1866); 4 volumes (St. Petersburg: M. O. Vol'f, 1867);

Fotograficheskie kartochki peterburgskoi zhizni. Ocherki (St. Petersburg, 1865);

Peterburgskie tipy. Ocherki (St. Petersburg, 1865);

Peterburgskie zolotopromyshlenniki (St. Petersburg, 1865);

Sochineniia, 2 volumes (St. Petersburg: F. Stellovsky, 1866–1867);

Povesti, ocherki i rasskazy (St. Petersburg: Tip. Iu. And. Bokgama, 1868);

Krovavyi puf, first part published as *Panurgovo stado,* in *Russkii vestnik,* nos. 1–4, 6–7, 10–12 (1869); unauthorized edition, 3 volumes (Leipzig: V. Gergard, 1870); second part published as *Dve sily,* in *Russkii vestnik,* nos. 2–4, 6, 9–12 (1874); republished together as *Krovavyi puf. Khronika o novom smutnom vremeni gosudarstva Rossiiskogo,* 4 volumes (St. Petersburg: Tip. M. O. Ettingera, 1875);

Malen'kie rasskazy, ocherki, kartinki i legkie nabroski (St. Petersburg: Izd. A. Bazunova, 1870);

Na zapade i na vostoke. Ocherki (St. Petersburg: Izd. A. Bazunova, 1872);

Vne zakona. Fel'etonnyi roman, in *Russkii mir* (1872–1873); (St. Petersburg, 1873);

Istoriia 14-ogo ulanskogo Iamburgskogo polka (St. Petersburg, 1873);

Na trave. Iz ocherkov kavaleriiskoi zhizni. Rasskazy, in *Niva,* nos. 1–3, 26–31 (1874); (St. Petersburg: Izd. Komarova, 1889);

Iz pokhodnykh ocherkov (St. Petersburg, 1874);

Vsevolod Vladimirovich Krestovsky

Dedy. Istoricheskaia povest' iz vremen imperatora Pavla I, in *Russkii mir* (6 June – 31 December 1875); (St. Petersburg: "Obshchestvennaia pol'za," 1876);

Istoriia Leib-gvardii ulanskogo ego Velichestva polka (St. Petersburg, 1876);

Dvadtsat' mesiatsev v deistvuiushchei armii, 1877–1878, 2 volumes (St. Petersburg: Tipografiia Ministerstva vnutrennikh del, 1879);

V gostiakh u emira Bukharskogo. Putevoi dnevnik, in *Russkii vestnik,* nos. 2–3, 5–8 (1884); (St. Petersburg, 1887);

V dal'nikh vodakh i stranakh, in *Russkii vestnik,* nos. 1–2, 4, 6–7, 9, 11–12 (1885); nos. 1–3, 5–8, 10–11 (1886); nos. 3–7, 11 (1887); (Moscow: Vek, 1997);

Zhid idet, first part published as *T'ma egipetskaia. Roman,* in *Russkii vestnik,* nos. 1–5, 7, 10, 12 (1888); (St. Petersburg: "Obshchestvennaia pol'za," 1889); second part published as *Tamara Bendavid. Roman (Prodolzhenie romana "T'ma egipetskaia"),* in *Russkii vestnik,* nos. 2, 4, 6, 10, 12 (1889); nos. 1–7 (1890); (St. Petersburg: "Obshchestvennaia pol'za," 1890); third part published as *Torzhestvo Vaala. Roman (Prodolzhenie romanov "T'ma egipetskaia" i "Tamara Bendavid"),* in *Russkii vestnik,* nos. 5, 7–11 (1891); nos. 1–3, 5 (1892);

Ocherki kavaleriiskoi zhizni (St. Petersburg, 1892).

Editions and Collections: *Sobranie sochinenii,* 8 volumes, edited by Iulii Luk'ianovich Elets (St. Petersburg: "Obshchestvennaia pol'za," 1899–1900);

Peterburgskie trushchoby, 3 volumes, edited by I. N. Kubikov (Moscow-Leningrad: "Academia," 1935–1937);

Peterburgskie trushchoby, 2 volumes, edited by T. Ornatskaia, with an introduction by M. Otradin (St. Petersburg: Khudozhestvennaia literatura, 1993);

T'ma egipetskaia, Tamara Bendavid, Torzhestvo Vaala, Dedy (Moscow: Kameia, 1993);

Peterburgskie tainy. Roman (Moscow: Eksmo, 1994);

Vne zakona (Moscow: Sovremennik, 1995);

Krovavyi puf, 2 volumes (Moscow: Sovremennyi pisatel', 1995);

Peterburgskie trushchoby, 4 volumes (Moscow: Terra, 1996);

Ocherki kavaleriiskoi zhizhni (Moscow: Voennoe Izd-vo, 1998);

Peterburgskie trushchoby, 2 volumes (Moscow: Eksmo, 1998).

Edition in English: *Knights of Industry* (New York, 1909).

OTHER: Poetry in *Pesni russkikh poetov,* edited by Ivan N. Rozanov (Leningrad: Sovetskii pisatel', 1957);

Poetry in *Poety 1860-kh godov,* edited by Isaak Grigor'evich Iampol'sky (Leningrad: Sovetskii pisatel', 1968);

"Pesni i romansy" and *Dedy,* in *Russkaia istoricheskaia povest',* volume 2, edited by Iurii Antonovich Beliaev (Moscow: Khudozhestvennaia literatura, 1988).

SELECTED PERIODICAL PUBLICATIONS:

"Liubov' dvorovykh," *Biblioteka dlia chteniia,* no. 8 (1859);

"Pogibshee, no miloe sozdanie," *Vremia,* no. 1 (1861);

"Sfinks," *Russkoe slovo,* no. 12 (1861);

"Pchel'nik," *Russkoe slovo,* no. 3 (1862).

Vsevolod Vladimirovich Krestovsky was a remarkably well-known and popular writer in his own time, a fact that makes more interesting not only his subsequent obscurity but also the resurgence of his works in late-twentieth-century Russia. Because Krestovsky was an acute observer and because he wrote much like a reporter, his works provide an interesting record of his epoch and also serve as an important reflection of the populist fervor that ran through the Russia of his day and that has been appearing once again in modern Russia as a product of similarly unsettled times. Although Krestovsky is generally considered a writer of historical fiction, unlike most writers in this genre Krestovsky did not write about earlier historical periods. Instead, he wrote about the period in which he lived and about those events that were taking place even as he was describing them in his notebooks. His major works of fiction, revolving around the great conflicts of his times, were created within the very milieu they seek to describe and understand.

Except for commentary inspired by the publication of his works and a few biographical notes, little information or primary material concerning Krestovsky's life has survived. Almost all known biographical material was summarized by his friend and biographer Iulii Luk'ianovich Elets and presented as an introduction to the publication of Krestovsky's complete set of works in 1899. Vsevolod Vladimirovich Krestovsky was born in the village of Malaia Berezianka in the province of Tarashchany near Kiev on 10 March 1839. Krestovsky's family, although only minor nobility, nevertheless imposed upon him the sense of his upper-class background, which no doubt partially accounts for the attitudes he adopted throughout his later years.

From 1850 to 1857 Krestovsky was a student in the First Petersburg Gymnasium. Apparently he showed little interest in his studies until a Russian language teacher noticed his talent as a writer. He had written a story, "Vecher posle grozy" (Evening After the Storm), based on the memories of his years spent in the Ukrainian countryside. The teacher, Vasilii Ivanovich Vodovozov, predicted a brilliant literary future for Krestovsky and continued to encourage him throughout his life.

Already acquainted with some of the leading liberal and radical writers of the day, Krestovsky was more interested in the possibility of a literary career than in political events. In 1857, at eighteen years of age, he enrolled in the historical-philological department of St. Petersburg University. In 1858 his mentor Vodovozov introduced him to the famous poet Lev Aleksandrovich Mei, through whom Krestovsky met many of the most influential writers and critics of the

КРОВАВЫЙ ПУФЪ

ХРОНИКА

О НОВОМЪ СМУТНОМЪ ВРЕМЕНИ

ГОСУДАРСТВА РОССІЙСКАГО

СОЧИНЕНІЕ

Всеволода Крестовскаго

ТОМЪ I.

С.-ПЕТЕРБУРГЪ

Типографія м. о. эттингера. (Казанск. ул., д. № 14—37).

1875.

Title page for Krovavyi puf *(The Bloody Bluff), parts of which
are set during the 1861 student demonstrations in St. Petersburg
and the 1863 uprising in Poland (The Kilgour Collection of
Russian Literature, Houghton Library,
Harvard University)*

day, such as the well-known critic and editor Vladimir Rafailovich Zotov, the writer Mikhail Andreevich Zaguliaev, and the poets Nikolai Ivanovich Krol', Konstantin Konstantinovich Sluchevsky, Fedor Nikolaevich Berg, and Apollon Aleksandrovich Grigor'ev. At the same time Krestovsky was also frequenting the leftist radical literary circle of Dmitrii Ivanovich Pisarev and becoming well acquainted with the satirist Vasilii Stepanovich Kurochkin, future editor of the left-wing journal *Iskra* (The Spark), along with other revolutionary democrats such as Nikolai Gavrilovich Chernyshevsky, Ivan Ivanovich Panaev, Nikolai Alekseevich Nekrasov, and Grigorii Evlampievich Blagosvetlov. The conflicting influences of these often antagonistic literary circles—one conservative, the other radical—had a profound impact on Krestovsky's work.

Krestovsky left the university two years after entering it, most likely to pursue a literary career. His

first published work, a translation of Horace's "Ode to Chloris," had appeared in *Obshchezanimatel'nyi vestnik* (The Herald of General Divertissement) in 1857; it was followed in a later issue of the same journal by a rhymed tale, "Ofitsersha" (Wife of an Officer), together with his first piece of prose, "Perepiska dvukh uezdnykh barishen'" (Correspondence of Two Provincial Ladies), as well as a satirical essay called "Splosh' da riadom" (Very Often), which appeared in *Iskra* in 1859. Krestovsky's early works, generally following lyrical and romantic patterns, also included "Liubov' dvorovykh" (Peasant Love, 1859) in *Biblioteka dlia chteniia* (Library for Reading); "Pchel'nik" (Beekeeper, 1862) and "Sfinks" (Sphinx, 1861), in *Russkoe slovo* (The Russian Word); "Pogibshee, no miloe sozdanie" (Lost but Nice Creature, 1861), in *Vremia* (Time); and the novel *Ne pervyi i ne poslednii* (Not the First, Not the Last, 1861), in *Russkii mir* (Russian World). By 1861 and 1862 the novella *Besenok* (Little Devil) had appeared in the journal *Svetoch* (Light of Knowledge) as well as a long poem, "Kalinka perekhozhaia" (Passing Viburnum), and a cycle of poems under the title of "Khandra" (Melancholy).

Favorite themes, such as the fate of a virtuous woman abandoned by a man of weak character, and Krestovsky's basic technique of subsuming the story line to elaborate descriptive passages, were already evident. Aleksandr Petrovich Miliukov reviewed Krestovsky's early prose, comparing the style with that of Nikolai Vasil'evich Gogol's *Pokhozhdeniia Chichikova, ili Mertvye dushi* (The Adventures of Chichikov, or Dead Souls, 1842) and at the same time acknowledging Krestovsky's literary talent. Yet, critics of Krestovsky's early work, while recognizing his skill as an observer and as a writer, generally did not approve of his simplistic characters.

In 1862 a two-volume collection of Krestovsky's poetry was published. Many of the poems ("Vladimirka," for example) showed a decided democratic tendency or an interest in popular social issues. This collection, which also included "Ispanskie motivy" (Spanish Motifs), made Krestovsky quite famous in literary circles, even though some critics ridiculed it or were scandalized by the sexual tone of some of the poetry. The general public, however, was far from shocked: many read and memorized these poems. Krestovsky continued writing poetry throughout the late 1850s and into the early 1860s, as well as publishing his many translations of German poetry. His most popular work was a group of romances or poetry set to music, which eventually acquired the status of folk songs and are still popular even at the end of the twentieth century—for example, the gypsy romances "Pod dushistoiu vetv'iu sireni" (Under the Fragrant Branch of Lilac) and "Dai mne ruchku, kazhdyi pal'chik" (Give Me Your Hand, Every Finger); the folk song "Van'ka-kliuchnik" (Vanka the Key Keeper); and the fairy tale "Kolobok, kolobok" (Little Round Loaf of Bread).

Of all Krestovsky's acquaintances during this period, perhaps the most interesting, certainly from a literary point of view, was Fyodor Dostoevsky. During these university years Krestovsky met Dostoevsky at one of the Thursday literary meetings held at Miliukov's house. Krestovsky's poetry at this time was considered quite liberal and showed a marked sympathy toward the poor and needy. Thus, his poem "Zhnitsa" (Harvest Hand, 1859), which was published in *Russkoe slovo* and, in the same year, the short story "Liubov' dvorovykh," made him temporarily attractive to Dostoevsky's camp of *pochvenniki* (those who sought a return to Russian roots combined with a knowledge of Western culture). Dostoevsky, in fact, in a 3 May 1860 letter to his actress friend Aleksandra Ivanovna Shubert, precisely describes his feelings toward the younger writer: "Videl Krestovskogo. Ia ego ochen' liubliu" (I saw Krestovsky. I love him very much).

Dostoevsky was apparently fond of Krestovsky's early poetry, especially "Vesennie nochi" (Spring Nights) and "Solimskaia Getera." (Solim's Hetairai), both published in 1860. His influence on Krestovsky during the early 1860s seems evident, especially in the use of themes such as the necessity of "teaching the people" and bringing them closer to the intelligentsia. These ideas are also found in Krestovsky's review for the first issue of *Russkoe slovo* in 1861 of a book of folk tales collected by Ivan Aleksandrovich Khudiakov. Krestovsky, although briefly fascinated by Dostoevsky's use of double psychology, could not or would not introduce a similar device into his own works.

Peterburgskie trushchoby (The Slums of Petersburg), Krestovsky's first major novel, was originally published as a serial between 1864 and 1866 in the journal *Otechestvennye zapiski* (Notes of the Fatherland). From the beginning the book caused quite a stir. For some it was a remarkable socialist document, while for others it offended good taste. Those who saw the book as a proper attack on a society badly in need of reform linked Krestovsky to the young radical movement, whereas others thought the book little more than a typical boulevard novel replete with fantastic or even shocking adventures. While much of the narrative revolves around a rather typical counterpoint between callous nobility and unfortunate innocents, there is also an apparently realistic portrait of many aspects of St. Petersburg society. Krestovsky's St. Petersburg is ruled by depravity, which succeeds in undermining the social fabric of the city by forcing the poor to be criminals in order to survive while the nobility indulge their corrupt natures, wasting their patrimonies without remorse.

The novel, subtitled *Kniga o sytykh i golodnykh* (A Book About the Well-Fed and the Hungry), focuses on the depredations of the Shadursky family: the prince; his wife, the princess; and their son, Vladimir. According to the prologue, twenty years before the action of the story, the prince had seduced princess Anna Tchetchevinskaia. The prince learned about Anna's child, Masha, at the same time that he discovered his wife in the arms of their servant, Mordenko. The result of that union was also a child, Ivan Veresov. The plot focuses primarily on the struggles of Masha and Ivan, both of whom are cruelly cast out into the sordid St. Petersburg underworld so that the Shadursky family can maintain appearances, and on the story of another woman, Beroeva, who is raped by Vladimir Shadursky and must eventually flee St. Petersburg in order to survive. For the most part the noble characters end badly, while the evil characters go unpunished. Vladimir even manages to marry well, rescuing his family's name and fortune, and to live quite happily.

What made the novel successful were Krestovsky's often brilliant sketches of the darker side of St. Petersburg through which Masha and Ivan are forced to travel. Their adventures lead them in a downward spiral through an increasingly infernal universe, passing through the world of low bars and taverns, prisons, hospitals, the vicious Court of Malinik ruled by criminals, and the infamous Viazemskaia Lavra, a once-luxurious complex of buildings taken over by the most miserable inhabitants of the city. Finally, moving from the world of physical deterioration to one of spiritual disintegration, the author guides readers through the world of bordellos, where Masha has finally been forced to work and where she dies of tuberculosis, and the world of the cardsharpers, where nothing is what it seems and where appearance and depravity have their final triumph.

Krestovsky's stated purpose in writing the novel was to uncover the hidden plague of misery that lay beneath the false appearance of a depraved nobility. His vision of depravity in this work is rather sophisticated, as he insists that crimes committed from surfeit are far more depraved than those committed from poverty. The impetus behind the action of the novel is Prince Shadursky's demand that the family's noble appearance cannot be compromised and that no crime is too base to maintain that appearance. That paradox is at the root of the plague that infests St. Petersburg and makes depravity the actual ruler of the city. Thus, the essence of Krestovsky's social doctrine is the recognition that what passes for vice or depravity among the poor is really deprivation. While the poor are deprived

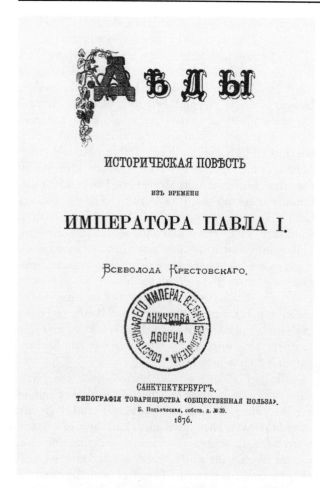

Title page for Dedy *(Grandfathers), set during 1796–1801,
the reign of Czar Paul I (The Kilgour Collection of Russian
Literature, Houghton Library, Harvard University)*

of the luxury of human feeling, the rich have allowed the very luxury of their lives to stifle emotion and reduce feeling to simple instinct.

Krestovsky's most caustic passages, however, are reserved for the social reformers whose commitment to reform derives only from a posturing that is itself a false appearance, one that so corrupts society that it no longer distinguishes between good and evil or reality and appearance. Thus, Beroeva and Masha are continually labeled as liars, while their attackers and detractors are always thought to be persons of noble spirit. This social blindness does not uncover the "plague" and therefore encourages its spread throughout Russia.

Although the book was extremely popular when it was released, critical opinion on *Peterburgskie trushchoby* was split, in some cases simply along what might be described as "party lines." Because Krestovsky, by the time the book was published, had apparently deserted the radical cause and moved to the conservative camp, radical critics saw the work as an oversimplification, a

series of "photographic sketches" that captured only surface reality and concentrated on what was sordid in order to shock the reader rather than enlighten him. There was also a claim, supported even by some modern critics, that Krestovsky had plagiarized this work either from an unfinished work of Nikolai Gerasimovich Pomialovsky or from Eugène Sue's *Les Mystères de Paris* (The Mysteries of Paris, 1842–1843).

The most serious critical attacks came from those in Dostoevsky's circle, such as Dmitrii Vasil'evich Averkiev, who believed that Krestovsky ultimately did not control his material. In fact, the book has always received mixed reviews. Evgenii Solov'ev, in a 1907 study, perhaps best summarized the conflicting strains of Krestovsky criticism at the time by pointing out that the novel was extremely popular; that it may have drawn on another writer's work; that it includes an often terrifying picture of the St. Petersburg slums; that it resembles some earlier French works; and that the plot offers no real solutions or possibility of redemption. The most trenchant criticism of Krestovsky came from Arsenii Ivanovich Vvedensky, who pointed to the failure of the work ultimately to achieve any depth or understanding in the manner of Dostoevsky. If Averkiev and Vvedensky believed that Krestovsky failed, Vasilii Grigor'evich Avseenko, however, offered an entirely different opinion, praising the general conception of the book and the author's commitment to revealing the manner in which vice pervades all levels of society. For Avseenko the accurate and often sordid picture of life in the slums finally gives rise to a telling satire that mirrors the shortcomings of Russian society.

What finally emerges from the critical controversy, however, is that the greatest merit in Krestovsky's first novel lay in the description of what he saw and not in his ability to transform or analyze that reality. This characteristic became even more of an issue in his later works and probably explains why, at the end of his career, he actually preferred writing minor histories or descriptions of the various places he was assigned to work.

At the time of his marriage to the young actress Varvara Dimitrievna Grineva and throughout 1861 and 1862 Krestovsky worked as a critic, developing *pochvennik* ideas while simultaneously continuing to follow in Pisarev's footsteps. But in 1863 Krestovsky turned decisively away from nihilist theory and began to attack his former colleagues among the radicals. Perhaps reflecting the upsurge in nationalism that followed the Polish Uprising of 1863, he also published anti-Polish poems and mocked the enthusiasm with which Chernyshevsky's book *Chto delat'?* (What Is to Be Done? 1863) was generally received in literary circles. For many Russians, and especially for Krestovsky, the

Polish Uprising discredited the radical program while lending credence to the conspiracy theories that became popular in the literature of the period and in Krestovsky's most important work, *Krovavyi puf* (The Bloody Bluff, 1869, 1874).

Even more important than the break with Pisarev and the other radicals was Krestovsky's break with Dostoevsky. It is hard now to tell exactly why and when this relationship cooled. V. A. Viktorovich speculates that it could have been a matter of money: Krestovsky's first major work, *Petersburgskie trushchoby,* had originally been intended for Dostoevsky's journal *Epokha* (Epoch). Because the journal could not afford the fee Krestovsky wanted, he gave it instead to Andrei Aleksandrovich Kraevsky's journal, *Otechestvennye zapiski.* An apparent repercussion of Krestovsky's decision to publish with Kraevsky were two devastating reviews that followed: Grigor'ev's "O borzoopisanii radi pechatnogo lista" (About Writing for the Sake of Writing) in *Iakor'* (Anchor), and Averkiev's "Vsiakomu po plechu" (Anyone Can Do It) in *Epokha.* Both of these well-known critics were extremely close to Dostoevsky, and both reviews maintained that Krestovsky sold his talent for money. Dostoevsky himself also became quite critical of Krestovsky's literary work, especially of the first part of *Krovavyi puf,* pointing to descriptions that captured only the surface of each situation while avoiding any profound treatment of ideas or problems.

Krestovsky's travels to Warsaw during 1865 and 1866, along with later trips to the Volga region, provided much of the background material for *Krovavyi puf.* Unlike *Peterburgskie trushchoby,* this new work bitterly attacked the radical critics with whom Krestovsky had maintained close relationships earlier. *Krovavyi puf* searches out a new "plague" and a new hidden enemy, uncovering a plot that threatens not just the health of one Russian city but the security of all of Russia and its people. In this case the infection, spread by the secret societies that are trying to undermine all of Russian society, is even more resistant than the one spread by the poverty of *Peterburgskie trushchoby.* The evil characters in this novel are not simply criminals, driven to crime by circumstances that they cannot control; they are a willful and self-conscious organization of Poles and nihilist radicals who are planning to engage in sabotage against the Russian state.

Krestovsky's newly expressed hatred of the radical camp reflected his turn to the political right. The events of 1861, such as peasant uprisings and student unrest, had provoked strong opinions within intellectual circles. No doubt Krestovsky's initial flirtation with the radicals derived more from the intense atmosphere of university life in the late 1850s than from any deep-

seated political convictions. Elets also suggests that Krestovsky's shift to the Right was a response to the unfavorable criticism his early work had received from the radicals. But whatever personal motives may have driven Krestovsky at this time, his break with the radicals also simply reflected divisions that were taking place throughout Russian society.

Krovavyi puf is divided into two books: *Panurgovo stado* (Panurge's Herd), published in *Russkii vestnik* (The Russian Herald) in 1869, and *Dve sily* (Two Forces), published in the same journal in 1874. On an historical level the novel revolves around four major events: the massacre at Snezhki (Bezdna, the greatest peasant uprising to follow the 1861 emancipation of the serfs), the closing of the university in St. Petersburg after student demonstrations in 1861, the St. Petersburg fires of 1862, and the Polish Uprising of 1863. For the most part the story traces the adventures of Khvalyntsev, a young Russian who finds himself caught up, more as a bystander than a participant, in these momentous events. Throughout the novel, good and innocent characters are regularly betrayed or misled by evil ones. Thus, the young student Shishkin, the innocent Anna, and the Polish noblemen Bejgusz and Khvalyntsev (both of whom have fallen in love with perfect Russian women, Susanna and Tat'iana) are all deceived by characters such as the nihilist agitator Svitka, the "new man" Poloiarov, the Catholic priest Kuncewicz, and the Polish Countess Marzecka.

Dve sily moves the action from Russia to Poland and concentrates on the struggle between several opposing forces: Catholic and Orthodox churches, Pole and Russian, and corrupt nobility and innocent peasant. Krestovsky's Polish peasants, in fact, hate their Polish masters and love the Russian czar. The hero, Khvalyntsev, becomes the guest of a complete hypocrite, the Polish landowner Pan Kotyrlo. At the end of the novel most of the conspirators are thriving, thanks to the forgiving nature of the Russians, except for Svitka, who is to be hanged. Bejgusz dies of tuberculosis without contacting his wife, Susanna, while Khvalyntsev ends up being nursed back to health by Tat'iana.

Despite the obvious element of propaganda, Krestovsky's novel is an often rich picture of the events that were then taking place in Russia. At the same time, however, Krestovsky adopted an attitude that placed history in the service of politics. Even the representation of the radicals, "new men," and communes, at times reminiscent of Dostoevsky's scathing portrait in *Besy* (The Devils, 1871–1872) is colored by the need to link that movement with the central theme of the Polish conspiracy and its secret infestation at every level of Russian society. Krestovsky portrays Russia as being

Krestovsky's grave in the Volkov Cemetery, St. Petersburg
(photograph by Judith E. Kalb)

ies, some earlier critics such as Elets rejected the idea that Krestovsky's reactionary ideas flawed the novel. Avseenko, also defending the novel, claimed that this work was much more mature than *Peterburgskie trushchoby,* especially given the clever device of using a simple hero like Khvalyntsev, whom he describes as wholesome and a carefully wrought and finished character. Nevertheless, most critical discussions of this work focus on Krestovsky's attack on the nihilists. The distortion of the nihilist movement and Krestovsky's attempt to link it to the "Polish intrigue" seemed not only far-fetched but intentionally misleading. More serious, however, is the criticism of scholar Zbigniew Baranski, who posited that Krestovsky not only oversimplified the Polish revolutionary movement but also failed to break new ground as an artist. The complaint is ultimately that Krestovsky avoided complex situations and ideas rather than confronting a more problematic truth. One might argue that whether one admires Krestovsky's satirical presentation of these events or believes that it was only crass propaganda, the problem with this novel is that the author's political viewpoint increasingly overwhelms the characters and sweeps them away within a universe that is too closed and predictable. This tendency became even more problematic in Krestovsky's final novel.

A major turning point in Krestovsky's life occurred in June 1868 when he entered the 14th Cavalry of the Iamburg Regiment in Grodno as a noncommissioned officer, following in the footsteps of both his father and grandfather. At this time he was writing for the journal *Zaria* (Dawn) and publishing in *Russkii mir* (Russian World), *Niva* (The Grainfield), *Krugozor* (Horizon), and *Vsemirnaia illiustratsiia* (World Illustrated). He also published a series of essays idealizing life in the army, *Ocherki kavaleriiskoi zhizni* (Essays about the Life in Cavalry), some of which appeared in book form in 1892. These essays led to Krestovsky's major "military" work, *Istoriia 14-ogo ulanskogo Iamburgskogo polka* (History of the 14th Regiment of Iamburg Cavalry, 1873) and the subsequent request of Czar Alexander II that he write *Istoriia Leib-gvardii ulanskogo ego Velichestva polka* (History of His Majesty's Life-Guard Regiment of the Lancers, 1876). While Krestovsky was working on his military histories, he was collecting material that he used in his only truly historical novel, *Dedy* (Grandfathers, 1875), about the times of Paul I—a work that tried to convince his contemporaries that the dark side of Paul's rule had been greatly exaggerated and that he did not deserve his bad reputation.

During the period from 1877 to 1888 Krestovsky became the first journalist officially assigned by the government to serve as a war correspondent, and he worked in that capacity throughout the Russian-Turk-

under active attack by its enemies and easily victimized because of its native generosity and liberal tendencies. From Krestovsky's point of view the Polish conspiracy was easy to recognize because of the omnipresence of Polish influences in contemporary Russian society. Like the articles of the conservative journalist Mikhail Nikiforovich Katkov, Krestovsky's novel was intended as a clarion call awakening Russians to the threat posed by Polish nationalism and the Catholic Church.

The novel seems to lack a strong central voice, because its main character, Khvalyntsev, is easily duped and quite weak. This weakness, however, was Krestovsky's intention. Khvalyntsev is dominated by events and becomes a vehicle for reflecting the effects of those events rather than rising above them and focusing the reader's attention on his own actions. Thus, Khvalyntsev's weakness is a device that allows for the easy play of historical forces that might have been more effective if the author's vision of history had been less prejudiced.

Although Soviet critics were generally appalled by Krestovsky's treatment of radicals and revolutionar-

ish War of 1877–1878. His articles appeared in the newspaper *Pravitel'stvennyi vestnik* (Government Herald), and his *ocherki* (sketches) in *Russkii vestnik,* the journal in which he later published *Dvadtsat' mesiatsev v deistvuiushchei armii 1877–1878* (Twenty Months in the Front Line Army, 1877–1878, 1879). For that work the czar rewarded him with a valuable ring. In his official position, from 1880 to 1881 Krestovsky also served as secretary to the chief of the Pacific Ocean Squadron, while continuing to work as a correspondent and to write for *Pravitel'stvennyi vestnik* and the journal *Morskoi sbornik* (Maritime Collection). He also published a series of works drawing on his travels, such as the sketches *V dal'nikh vodakh i stranakh* (In Far Countries and Waters, 1885–1887) and descriptive pieces such as *V gostiakh u emira Bukharskogo* (Visit to the Emir of Bukhara, 1884) and *Putevoi dnevnik* (Travel Journal, 1884). During this period Krestovsky often wrote commentaries on foreign policy, always expressing a nationalistic and anti-German point of view. The best known of these works were "Nasha budushchaia voina" (Our Future War), "Po povodu odnogo ostrova" (Regarding a Certain Island), and "Gadaniia o budushchem" (Speculation about the Future). Later he produced a series of articles known as "Pod vladichestvom zemstva" (Under the Power of the Zemstvo), and "Promyshlennye i torgovye tsentry Rossii" (Industrial and Business Centers of Russia).

Krestovsky's personal life also changed dramatically in these years. On 25 October 1885 he married the widow Evdokia Stepanovna Lagoda, with whom he had five children. Unlike his first marriage, which had ended in divorce in 1875, this one was extremely happy. In 1887 Krestovsky returned to the frontier and wrote "Vdol' avstriiskoi granitsy" (Along the Austrian Border), and he continued traveling throughout Russia. By 1888 he was made a colonel and, at the same time, released his final major work.

Zhid idet (The Jew is Coming, 1888–1892), published in *Russkii vestnik,* was strongly influenced by the pan-Slavic sentiment surrounding the Russian-Turkish War. The novel opposed Jew and Christian just as Krestovsky's earlier work had opposed Pole and Russian. In both works the success of the former is in large part based on the naiveté and good nature of the latter. The stated, anti-Semitic purpose of the book is to make society aware of yet another threat, one even more insidious than that of depravity or nihilism. The novel was divided into three books: *T'ma egipetskaia* (Egyptian Darkness, 1888), *Tamara Bendavid* (1889–1890), and the unfinished third volume, *Torzhestvo Vaala* (The Victory of Baal, 1891–1892). While on the surface each volume follows the adventures of Tamara Bendavid, there is a parallel plot charting the machinations of the Kagal, a

Jewish secret society described by Krestovsky as intent on gaining control of Europe through control of the world's wealth.

Tamara's adventures, beginning with her father's death and a struggle within Jewish society over position and money, make her easy prey for the scheming Russian Count Karzhol, already the lover of Ol'ga Ukhova, who is pregnant with his child. Tamara's love for the count and the emphasis on love in the New Testament convince her that she must convert to Christianity. A cruel pogrom forces Tamara to leave the convent she has recently entered and to go to St. Petersburg. The story then follows Tamara to the battle of Plevna, where she works as a nurse and meets the noble Captain Alturin. Instead of accepting their mutual love, Tamara insists on remaining faithful to the ignoble Count Karzhol. Finally, after meeting with Ol'ga, Tamara recognizes Karzhol's treachery and leaves to become a teacher in the new zemstvos. There, however, even in remote villages, she finds only pettiness and scheming. At the end, reunited with her friend Lubuskha after a terrible illness, she attempts to reconcile herself with her grandfather.

Krestovsky was always fascinated by his subject, no matter how much he disliked it, but he presents Jewish practices and customs as repugnant and alien. Furthermore, by having Jewish characters offer up perverse readings of the Old Testament as evidence of their eventual "world domination," Krestovsky makes them an easy target for satire. Despite these gross distortions, however, *Tamara* is Krestovsky's most complex and interesting character, a young woman whose heart and soul become a battlefield not only between the forces of love and devotion but also between the demands of family, religion, and culture. Tamara's passivity as a character links her to many of Krestovsky's earlier creations. Her simplicity makes her unable to distinguish between different passions, such as the love she has for Karzhol and the love she discovers in the New Testament. This tendency to level his characters and make them almost caricatures affects much of the thematic treatment as well. All the problems in Russian society, according to Krestovsky's novel, can be traced to the Jews, just as in earlier works they could be traced to the Poles or to a depraved nobility. Although Krestovsky claims to reveal what he takes to be a grand Jewish conspiracy, he cannot ignore the corruption he sees at every level of Russian society, even within the Christian church. His criticism of Christianity was too strong in fact for Katkov, who declined to publish the work.

The novel received little critical attention and was generally viewed as a failure that marked the end of Krestovsky's career as a writer. An anonymous reviewer in *Russkii vestnik* (1898) took a different position, praising Krestovsky for his portrayal of Jewish life in Russia. Vvedensky also praised the novel, actually endorsing Krestovsky's "tendentiousness" as one of many valid approaches to the subject matter of the novel. What he really points to, however, is the tension between the author's dislike of the Jews and his fascination with his subject. This perspective marks what can be called Krestovsky's "lesser vision," or his failure to pursue the complexities his own researches uncovered.

After this last major novel Krestovsky continued writing articles on various nonliterary subjects, such as fortifying the Russian frontiers. Doubtless because of these articles, in 1892 he was appointed editor of the official government newspaper *Varshavskii dnevnik* (Warsaw Daily). The first issue of the paper to appear with his name as editor was published on 7 October 1892, a date especially chosen by Krestovsky because it marked the thirty-fifth anniversary of his literary work. The job in Warsaw proved demanding, especially given the usual problems with censorship. Not surprisingly, Krestovsky suffered from a continuing nervous condition that may have led to his final illness. Only one story remains from this period, "Kak my s Solomonom Solomonovichem ekhali iz Chushki-Makhaly v Gornyi Studen'" (How Salomon Salomonovich and I Traveled from Chushki-Makhaly to Gornyi Studen'). He did not even finish the third and last part of *Zhid idet*.

Toward the end of his life Krestovsky became quite religious. With his liver, kidneys, and heart all failing at the same time, he realized that he was dying and talked freely about his impending death with his friends. According to Krestovsky's friend A. Sidorov, Krestovsky died at 11:45 P.M. on 18 January 1895 at the age of fifty-five. The eyewitness accounts reveal that only a few close friends came either to the service or the funeral in Warsaw. His remains were moved to St. Petersburg and buried at the Aleksandr Nevsky monastery. The funeral in St. Petersburg was much better attended, both by friends and colleagues. Later his body was moved to the Volkov Cemetery at Literatorskie mostki.

The final word on Krestovsky's life belongs to Sidorov, who, in his article following Krestovsky's death, referred to him as a man "made out of steel," or a man who was stronger than he may have seemed. Like many of the intelligentsia of his day, he flirted with the current ideas and parties of the 1860s and then chose a career and point of view which, no matter how distasteful it may seem to modern readers, seems consistent with his past and his character.

Biographies:
"Sovremennye russkie pisateli," *Ogonek,* 18 (1880): 346–349;

M. I. Semevsky, *Znakomye. Al'bom M. I. Semevskogo* (St. Petersburg, 1888), pp. 326–327;

A. Sidorov, "Poslednie dni zhizni i deiatel'nosti Vs. Vl. Krestovskogo," *Russkoe obozrenie,* 2 (1895): 888–891;

Ia. Posadsky, "Iz mestnykh literaturnykh vospominanii. Priezd v Kazan' Vsevoloda Krestovskogo," *Volzhskii vestnik,* (1898): 392–417;

I. K. Markuze, "Vospominaniia o V. V. Krestovskom," *Istoricheskii vestnik,* 3 (1900): 979–1003;

V. Iakimov, "V. V. Krestovsky v Nakhichevani," *Istoricheskii vestnik,* 3 (1902): 951–955.

References:
Irina Ashcroft, "*Petersburgskie trushchoby:* A Russian Version of *Les Mystères de Paris,*" *Rèvue de Littérature Comparée,* 53 (1979): 163–174;

Dmitrii Vasil'evich Averkiev, "Vsiakomu po plechu," *Epokha,* 2 (1865): 12–30;

Vasilii Grigor'evich Avseenko, "Novye sochineniia Vsevoloda Krestovskogo," *Russkii vestnik,* 3 (1875): 315–342;

Iu. Barabash, "Sii raznorodnye o nem suzhdeniia," *Voprosy literatury,* 3 (1985): 102–107;

Zbigniew Baranski, "Powstanie styczniowe v literaturze rosyjskiej," in *Dziedzictwo literackie powstania styczniowego,* edited by J. Z. Jakubowski (Warsaw: Panstwowy Instytut Wydawniczy, 1964), pp. 515–548;

A. I. Batiuto, "Antinigilisticheskii roman 60–70-kh godov," in *Istoriia russkoi literatury v 4-kh tomakh,* edited by N. I. Prutskov, volume 3 (Leningrad: Nauka, 1982), pp. 279–300;

Batiuto, "Turgenev i nekotorye pisateli antinigilisticheskogo napravleniia," in *Turgenev i ego sovremenniki,* edited by M. P. Alekseev (Leningrad: Nauka, 1977), pp. 49–69;

Batiuto, *Tvorchestvo I. S. Turgeneva i kritiko-esteticheskaia mysl' ego vremeni* (Leningrad: Nauka, 1990);

Vasilii Grigor'evich Bazanov, *Iz literaturnoi polemiki 60-kh godov* (Petrozavodsk: Gosizdat, 1941);

Fedor N. Berg, "V. V. Krestovsky," *Russkii vestnik,* 2 (1895): 355–359;

G. A. Bialy, *Istoriia russkoi literatury* (Moscow-Leningrad: AN SSSR, 1956);

"Delo Krestovskogo," *Otchestvennye zapiski,* 4 (1876): 275–280;

A. Dolinin, *Dostoevsky i drugie* (Leningrad: Khudozhestvennaia literatura, 1963);

Dolinin, *Poslednie romany Dostoevskogo* (Moscow-Leningrad, 1963);

Savelii Dudakov, *Istoriia odnogo mifa* (Moscow: Nauka, 1993);

N. Frisov, "V redaktsii zhurnala Russkoe slovo," *Istoricheskii vestnik,* 5 (1914): 494–499;

E. G. Gaintseva, "Antinigilisticheskaia belletristika *Russkogo vestnika* 1870-kh godov," in *Problemy poetiki russkoi literatury XIX veka* (Moscow: Moskovskii Pedinstitut, 1983);

Gaintseva, "Avseenko i Russkii vestnik 1870-kh godov," *Russkaia literatura,* 2 (1989): 70–84;

Apollon Aleksandrovich Grigor'ev [Grebeshkov], "O borzoopisanii radi pechatnogo lista," *Iakor',* no. 1 (1864);

Isaak Grigor'evich Iampol'sky, ed., *Poety "Iskry,"* 2 volumes (Leningrad: Sovetskii pisatel', 1987);

Andrei Leskov, *Zhizn' Nikolaia Leskova* (Moscow: Khudozhestvennaia literatura, 1984);

Aleksandr Petrovich Miliukov, "Mertvye dushi bol'shogo sveta," *Svetoch,* 2 (1861): 23–44;

Vladimir Osipovich Mikhnevich, *Nashi znakomye* (St. Petersburg: Tip. E. Goppe, 1884);

Charles A. Moser, *Antinihilism in the Russian Novel of the 1860's* (The Hague: Mouton, 1964);

"Na vse otozvalsia, ni do chego ne dogovorilsia," *Russkoe slovo,* 3 (1863): 45–53;

"Novosti literatury. Vs. Vl. Krestovsky. *Ocherki kavaleriiskoi zhizni* i *T'ma egipetskaia,*" *Russkii vestnik,* 3 (1898): 386–389;

Jan Orlowski, *Z dziejow antypolskich obsesji w literaturze rosyjskiej* (Warsaw: Wydawnictwa Szkolne i Pedagogiczne, 1992);

Longin Fedorovich Panteleev, *Vospominaniia* (Moscow: Khudozhestvennaia Literatura, 1958);

Mikhail Evgrafovich Saltykov (N. Shchedrin), "Stikhi V. Krestovskogo," *Sovremennik,* 1–2 (1863): 129–136;

N. V. Shelgunov, L. P. Shelgunova, and M. L. Mikhailov, *Vospominaniia,* edited by E. Vilenska, E. Ol'khovsky, and L. Roitberg, 2 volumes (Moscow: Khudozhestvennaia literatura, 1967);

A. Skabichevsky, *Istoriia noveishei russkoi literatury 1848–1908* (St. Petersburg, 1909);

Skabichevsky, *Literaturnye vospominaniia* (Moscow-Leningrad, 1928);

I. Skachkov, "Introduction," in *Peterburgskie trushchoby,* by Krestovsky (Moscow: Pravda, 1990);

N. N. Skatov, ed., *Istoriia russkoi literatury XIX v (vtoraia polovina)* (Moscow: Prosveshchenie, 1991);

Evgenii Solov'ev, *Ocherki iz istorii russkoi literatury XIX veka* (St. Petersburg: Kartasnikov, 1907);

N. Solov'ev, "Dva romanista," *Vsemirnyi trud,* 12 (1867): 35–66;

Iu. S. Sorokin, "Antinigilisticheskii roman," in *Istoriia russkogo romana,* 2 volumes (Moscow-Leningrad: Nauka, 1964), pp. 97–120;

Sorokin, "K istoriko-literaturnoi kharakteristike antinigilisticheskogo romana (Dilogiia Vs. Krestovskogo 'Krovavyi Puf')," *Doklady i soobshcheniia,* 3 (1947): 79–87;

Nikolai Nikolaevich Strakhov, "Vospominaniia o F. M. Dostoevskom" (St. Petersburg, 1883);

N. D. Tamarchenko, "Krestovsky," in *Russkie pisateli,* edited by P. A. Nikolaev, volume 1 (Moscow: Prosveshchenie, 1990), pp. 370–372;

A. A. Tseitlin, "Siuzhetika antinigilisticheskogo romana," *Literatura i marksizm,* 2 (1929): 57–74;

L. E. Varustin, *Zhurnal "Russkoe slovo" 1859–1866* (Leningrad, 1966);

V. A. Viktorovich, "Dostoevsky i Vs. Krestovsky," *Materialy i issledovaniia,* 9 (1991): 92–116;

Viktorovich, "Krestovsky," in *Russkie pisateli,* edited by P. A. Nikolaev, volume 3 (Moscow: Bol'shaia Rossiiskaia Entsiklopediia, 1994), pp. 146–149;

Viktorovich, "Vsevolod Krestovsky: legendy i fakty," *Russkaia literatura,* 2 (1990): 44–56;

E. N. Vodovozova, *Na zare zhizni* (Moscow: Khudozhestvennaia literatura, 1964);

"Vs. Vl. Krestovsky 'T'ma Egipetskaia,' 'Tamara Bendavid.' Rom. Peterburg 1889 i 1890 gg," *Russkii vestnik,* 10 (1890): 240–243;

Arsenii Ivanovich Vvedensky, "Sovremennye literaturnye deiateli. Vsevolod Vladimirovich Krestovsky," *Istoricheskii vestnik,* 12 (1890): 734–754;

V. A. Zaitsev, "Rasskazy V. Krestovskogo: Peterburgskie tipy; Peterburgskie zolotopromyshlenniki; Fotograficheskie kartochki," *Russkoe slovo,* 7 (1865): 68–70;

I. Zamotin, "Publitsisticheskaia belletristika 60–70 godov," in *Sorokovye i shestidesiatye gody* (Warsaw, 1911);

Zamotin, "Tendentsioznaia belletristika 60-kh–70-kh godov," in *Istoriia russkoi literatury XIX veka,* edited by D. N. Ovsianniko-Kulikovsky, volume 4 (Moscow, 1910), pp. 129–160.

Papers:

Vsevolod Vladimirovich Krestovsky's papers can be found in the Institute of Russian Literature (IRLI, Pushkin House) in St. Petersburg, fond 129; the Russian State Historical Archive (RGIA, formerly TsGIA) in St. Petersburg, fonds 1343 and 776; the Russian State Archive of Military History (RGVIA, formerly TsGVIA) in Moscow, fond 400; and the State Archive of the Russian Federation (GARF, formerly TsGAOR) in Moscow, fonds 95 and 109.

Ivan Afanas'evich Kushchevsky

(? 1847 – 12 August 1876)

Judith E. Kalb
University of South Carolina

WORKS: *Nikolai Negorev, ili Blagopoluchnyi rossiianin,* in
Otechestvennye zapiski, nos. 1–4 (1871); (St. Petersburg: A. F. Bazunov, 1872); translated, annotated,
and with an introduction by D. P. and B. Costello
as *Nikolai Negorev, or the Successful Russian. A Novel by
Ivan Kushchevsky* (London: Calder & Boyars, 1967;
New York: St. Martin's Press, 1972);

Malen'kie rasskazy, ocherki, kartinki i legkie nabroski (St.
Petersburg: A. F. Bazunov, 1875);

Neizdannye rasskazy (St. Petersburg: Kn. mag. "Novoe
Vremia," 1881).

Editions: *Nikolai Negorev, ili Blagopoluchnyi rossiianin,* afterword by M. Goriachkina (Moscow: Khu-
dozhestvennaia literatura, 1958);

Nikolai Negorev. Roman i malen'kie rasskazy, compiled,
annotated, and with an introduction, by N.
Iakushin (Moscow: Sovetskaia Rossiia, 1984);

*Nikolai Negorev, ili Blagopoluchnyi rossiianin. Roman, rasskazy,
fel'etony,* compiled, with an afterword, by V. F. Uli-
andro (Irkutsk, 1988).

OTHER: "V Peterburg! (na medovuiu reku Nevu!),"
in *Peterburg v russkom ocherke XIX veka,* edited by
M. V. Otradin (Leningrad: Izd. Leningradskogo
universiteta, 1984), pp. 308–316.

SELECTED PERIODICAL PUBLICATION:
"Ne stol' otdalennye mesta Sibiri (Nabroski iz vospominanii ssyl'nogo)," as Khaidakov, *Otechestvennye zapiski,*
no. 7 (1875).

Ivan Afanas'evich Kushchevsky

In an 1895 article, an impassioned critic called for
the literary resurrection of Ivan Afanas'evich Kushchevsky–critic, journalist, and author of one highly
regarded novel, *Nikolai Negorev, ili Blagopoluchnyi rossiianin*
(Nikolai Negorev, or the Successful Russian, 1871). The
novel, which has been characterized by the well-known
Russian literary historian D. S. Mirsky as an "unsur-
passed picture of the change that transformed the Russia of Nicholas I into the almost anarchic Russia of the
sixties," was in fact republished in 1917, and again during the Soviet period, and it was published in English
translation in 1967. Yet, the renown the author and his
work might have encountered never materialized.
Instead, Kushchevsky found a home as a minor figure
in Soviet literary encyclopedias, mentioned briefly as a

writer of radical or revolutionary prose, and he was virtually ignored in most Western criticism.

Biographical details about Kushchevsky's life are scarce: his birth date is unknown, and his place of birth was disputed for some time. It seems, however, that Ivan Afanas'evich Kushchevsky was born in Achinsk, in Siberia, in 1847. His father was a titular councillor of no great means. Kushchevsky's father died when Ivan was a small boy, and the family settled in Barnaul, where Ivan received his elementary education. He went on to study at the Tomsk gymnasium, upon which to a large extent he based his description of the gymnasium attended by Nikolai Negorev, the main character of his eponymous novel. According to the Siberian regionalist, activist, ethnographer, and historian Nikolai Mikhailovich Iadrintsev in an 1876 obituary for the writer that appeared in the newspaper *Sibir'* (Siberia), the Tomsk gymnasium was a fertile ground for writers. In the 1860s students often joined together for literary evenings and contests; the gymnasium students even produced their own newspaper. Iadrintsev writes that Kushchevsky was already noteworthy at this stage of his life for his literary talent. Kushchevsky entered the gymnasium during the Crimean War, another fact that made its way into his novel.

After leaving the gymnasium in 1864 at an uncle's behest, Kushchevsky returned briefly to Barnaul. Later that year, at age seventeen, he set out for St. Petersburg. Like many other young men coming to St. Petersburg from the provinces, he hoped to make his fortune in the capital city. In his autobiographical sketch "V Peterburg! (na medovuiu reku Nevu!)" (To Petersburg! To the Honeyed River Neva!, 1875), Kushchevsky recalled his initial, excited impressions of the city: "We've arrived. Everything is strange, everything is new, everything is striking," and further, "And it was all wonderful to me. . . ." Sadly, Kushchevsky's dreams of an exalted life in the big city were not fulfilled. While he had planned to attend the university, he did not have enough money to do so, though he was able at some point to audit several courses. Instead, he settled into a variety of menial jobs; those listed in "V Peterburg! (na medovuiu reku Nevu!)," which at the very least provides examples of the type of employment in which Kushchevsky was engaged, include factory labor, fruit vending, and work on the St. Petersburg wharves.

The critic A. G. Gornfel'd notes that while there are few details on this part of Kushchevsky's life, one can assume that it was miserable: Kushchevsky was poverty-stricken, hungry, and exhausted. This difficult time is reflected in his early works—short stories and sketches—which appeared in *Deiatel'nost'* (Activity), *Narodnyi golos* (The People's Voice), *Iskra* (The Spark), and

Peterburgskii listok (The Petersburg Page) beginning in early 1866. Kushchevsky was influenced in these works by the radical critics Nikolai Gavrilovich Chernyshevsky and Nikolai Aleksandrovich Dobroliubov. Kushchevsky wrote of the difficulties of life in the slums of St. Petersburg and of the harsh fate of the poor in a city indifferent to them. He ran into difficulties with the censors as he attempted to publish his manuscripts: his first story, "Pogibshii chelovek" (The Ruined Man), written in 1865, was not published until 1869, under a different title, "Utonuvshie" (The Drowned Ones). In 1867 Kushchevsky wrote a biography of Aleksandr Nikolaevich Radishchev, whose *Puteshestvie iz Peterburga v Moskvu* (Journey from St. Petersburg to Moscow, 1790) had earned its author Siberian exile for its radical treatment of Catherine II's Russia. Kushchevsky's life was further complicated, and his political convictions most likely strengthened, when he himself was arrested for two weeks in April of 1866. N. Iakushin notes that the arrest was one of many that occurred in the wake of the student Dmitrii Karakozov's 1866 attempt on the life of Czar Alexander II. An official noted Kushchevsky's "suspicious" clothing and long hair, and the young man was taken away for questioning. He was released when no proof emerged to demonstrate a connection to the attempted assassination of the czar.

According to a tale that appears in Kushchevsky's sketch "V Peterburg! (na medovuiu reku Nevu!)" and has been taken as autobiographical in several treatments of him, at one point during this period the young man dropped a heavy package into the river, landed in the water himself, caught cold, and ended up in the hospital. The story may be apocryphal, and its timing is disputed: some critics date the fever-inducing dousing to an earlier phase in Kushchevsky's St. Petersburg existence and assert that a journalist Kushchevsky met during his hospital stay then introduced him to the literary ways of the capital, while others place it in 1870, the year of the composition of *Nikolai Negorev, ili Blagopoluchnyi rossiianin*. Regardless, Kushchevsky experienced a hospital stay in 1870, which provided him the respite necessary to produce his one complete novel. Moved by his poverty to request public assistance at this point, Kushchevsky wrote in a letter that he was selling his meager hospital food in order to purchase candles to light his nocturnal writing spells.

Kushchevsky wrote *Nikolai Negorev, ili Blagopoluchnyi rossiianin* from July to November 1870. The novel met with the praise of Nikolai Alekseevich Nekrasov, who welcomed the opportunity to publish it in the first four issues of *Otechestvennye zapiski* (Notes of the Fatherland) in 1871; the novel was published as a separate volume in 1872. Nekrasov also supplied financial and emotional assistance to the young writer.

"V Peterburg! (na medovuiu reku Nevu!)" tells of the main character's excitement when "N.N.," the editor of a leading journal, sends him a letter congratulating him on a fine piece of work. "He himself, that genius whose own works I knew by heart, whom I had idolized, . . . he himself with his own hand was writing to me, to pitiful, poor, and insignificant me!" The "genius" then proceeds to show up in his younger colleague's hospital room, where the latter bursts into "unwilling" tears and receives from his hero two hundred rubles in payment for his work. Nekrasov was not alone in his positive assessment of the novel, which was lauded in various reviews. Kushchevsky was called a potential Russian Charles Dickens for his bildungsroman featuring Nikolai Negorev, whom the reader first sees as a child, then as a schoolboy, then as a university student, and finally as a self-satisfied and reactionary government bureaucrat.

While *Nikolai Negorev, ili Blagopoluchnyi rossiianin* has generally been viewed from a sociopolitical point of view, focusing less on the artistic merit of the work than on its message, recent criticism has ranged further. Robert Szulkin's 1986 article on the novel rejects the previous utilitarian approach to examine instead Kushchevsky's artistic achievement in creating a main character who is, Szulkin writes, "a complex and modern 'type,'" one comparable to Fyodor Dostoevsky's "Underground Man." Both points of view provide insight into the novel. *Nikolai Negorev, ili Blagopoluchnyi rossiianin* provides a fascinating window into the world of the 1850s and 1860s: the reader encounters the major political, social, and cultural events and trends of the day—including, among others, the Crimean War; the death of Czar Nicholas I in 1855; the educational reforms under Czar Alexander II; the liberation of the serfs; the works of Chernyshevsky, Dobroliubov, and Ivan Sergeevich Turgenev; the growing interest in science; and the "woman question." Through the saga of Nikolai Negorev—who renounces his liberal convictions for a comfortable, safe, and "successful" life—Kushchevsky demonstrates his belief that the "liberals" of the 1860s were possessed merely of shallow convictions that turned easily and conveniently into bourgeois complacency when expedient. Meanwhile, Kushchevsky's characterizations are at times remarkable; Mirsky describes them as worthy of comparison with those of Leo Tolstoy in his *Voina i mir* (War and Peace, 1863–1869). Beyond the title character, other noteworthy figures include Nikolai's brother Andrei, an openhearted and committed revolutionary; his sister Liza, eager to devote herself passionately to "the people's" cause but ending instead as a poverty-stricken but proud housewife; his fiancée, Sof'ia Lokhova, a "new woman" who falls in love with Nikolai despite her radical convic-

tions; and, most of all, his friend Sergei Overin, a revolutionary modeled in part on Chernyshevsky's hero Rakhmetov in *Chto delat'?* (What Is to Be Done?, 1863). In addition, the novel's light and enjoyably humorous tone, surprising perhaps given Kushchevsky's sad life experiences at the time of the composition of the work, is striking and bears witness to the good humor the author himself is said to have demonstrated on various occasions.

In a sense the political content of the novel is encompassed in the complex relationship between Nikolai and his brother Andrei, one year older: while Nikolai chooses his safe path, Andrei ends up in exile in Switzerland after joining a revolutionary cell and evading government capture. The differences between the two brothers are brought out from the beginning of the novel. Told in the first person, the work commences with the twelve-year-old, motherless, and awkward Nikolai's describing his joyous, physically imposing elder brother's antics and his own relationship to them. Many of the adult Nikolai's qualities, from careful reserve and self-control to defensiveness and self-analysis, are evident in Nikolai's early words: "Reading Plutarch and finding that almost all great men abstained from games at my age, I suppressed my envy and imagined rather that I had been born a great man, and that instead of having physical prowess I was superior to my brother in the intellectual sphere." Nikolai is at times horrified by his sunny-tempered, open-minded brother, particularly when Andrei demonstrates his attachment to "the people" by inviting into his home and heart such strays as the "dirty," "brown" boy he meets in their village (the disgusted and panic-stricken Nikolai is convinced that Andrei will catch a disease from the child). Nikolai admits that he does not love his brother as he should. He appears as well to have little use or respect for his father, an eternally laughing and rather endearing man who cares not a whit for his obvious financial difficulties: he has sold most of his assets, including the majority of the serfs attached to his former estate of Negorevka, a name that appropriately suggests happiness and lack of care.

Kushchevsky has set the stage well. Nikolai and Andrei then go off to school in the company of the orphaned Semen Novitsky, who is attending seminary to become a priest. (In a typically humorous touch, Kushchevsky, perhaps influenced by Nikolai Gerasimovich Pomialovsky's *Ocherki bursy* [Seminary Sketches], titles his second chapter "The Seminarist, Essential to All Contemporary Stories, Appears.") True to form, Andrei, who has been sent to a military school, befriends not only the impecunious seminarist but also Nikolai's classmates at his gymnasium. Nikolai, on the other hand, stands apart as he observes the religious mania of his new, eccentric friend Overin, the drunken and incompetent schoolmasters who scarcely attempt to teach but occupy themselves rather in beating their charges, and the tortured relationships between the lordly seniors and their minions in less advanced classes. Nikolai also notes with envy the cultured ways of the aristocratic, French-speaking Shramm family, including their scion, Nikolai's classmate Volodia, and, aware of the social benefits therein, he applies himself to learning French. With the exception of Overin, turned eventually from religious ascetic to military zealot, the students and teachers all virtually ignore the Crimean War; after a description of newspaper coverage of the war and popular rumors about it, Nikolai, narrating, concludes, "In general few people were interested in the war, and I heard about it from my father only in passing. Such was the time when I entered the gymnasium."

With the death of the czar in 1855, the situation at school gradually changes: as Nikolai notes, "It was a transitional period." Beatings are outlawed, and the incompetent teachers are replaced by knowledgeable and committed pedagogues, one of whom suggests that the students create their own literary journal. The "liberal" Volodia meanwhile has introduced his schoolmates to journals that included the works of Chernyshevsky, Dobroliubov, Vissarion Grigor'evich Belinsky, Turgenev, and Aleksei Feofilaktovich Pisemsky. Discussions rage among the boys over literature, censorship, superfluous men, and double meanings. Encouraged by Andrei, Overin now becomes a voracious reader. Ever sensitive to the trends of the day, Nikolai, too, "acquires liberal convictions," convictions that he eventually and painlessly sloughs off. Andrei and Overin recognize the "safe" nature of Nikolai's beliefs, as opposed to their own more serious commitments. While a personal break does not occur at this point, an intellectual one does, when Overin and Andrei write their own journal in response to the one Nikolai has produced with Volodia and other classmates. Mocking the moderates mercilessly and hilariously, Andrei writes a story in which his little brother seeks to murder him, and Volodia is referred to as an idiot, even as Overin produces a counterculture diatribe lauding lawbreaking but virtuously needy bribe takers and condemning Nikolai and his ilk: "You, Nikolenka Negorev, will not take bribes, because you don't dare to: you're afraid of what people will say about you. Your children could be dying, and you still wouldn't accept bribes because others think it's a vice."

Once the young men have moved on to attend university, the split between Nikolai and his companions deepens. Andrei has become a radical, while Nikolai has recognized that "the best way to become

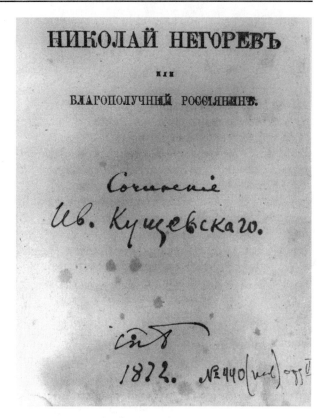

Half-title in a copy of Nikolai Negorev, ili Blagopoluchnyi rossiianin (Nikolai Negorev, or The Successful Russian, 1872), the novel that inspired one reviewer to predict Kushchevsky would be the Russian Charles Dickens (The Lilly Library, Indiana University)

noticed and to set oneself apart from the crowd of liberals is to preach (at that time it was necessary to preach something) conservative ideas" and, thus, has "turned into a conservative." While Nikolai's turn to conservatism appears unprincipled, it suits his cautious nature. Andrei, disgusted at the onerous terms under which the serfs are being liberated, informs Nikolai of his revolutionary involvement, but Nikolai refuses to listen, admitting to Andrei that he is frightened and to himself that he has realized "that it is much more advantageous to be a loyal citizen."

Upon the death of his father, Nikolai becomes the head of the Negorev household, despite his being the younger brother. Such a role gives him the opportunity to dominate his sister Liza, an earnest liberal who is infatuated with Overin, and to preach conservatism to her, albeit ineffectively. Liza is friendly with two sisters, Ol'ga and Annin'ka, with whom she sets up a school for poor children. The women also seek to further their own education at the university, and Ol'ga, when she grows tired of the school where she is teaching, in a reference to Chernyshevsky's novel *Chto delat'?* dreams of starting a dressmaking cooperative. Nikolai is attractive to both Ol'ga and Annin'ka, and he becomes romantically involved with the latter, occasioning some remarkably straightforward descriptions of the physical effects of sexual passion. In a further example of his lack of commitment, however, Nikolai leaves Annin'ka to become engaged to Sof'ia Vasil'evna Lokhova, who, much to Nikolai's relief, lacks Annin'ka's sexual nature, though she is quite radical politically. Kushchevsky vouchsafes to Sof'ia Vasil'evna a tirade about the plight of women in a male-dominated society that sees women as toys rather than people: "How degrading it is to be a thing, a body, something pleasant to others, something they desire to acquire!"

By the end of the novel, Overin has been condemned to exile in Siberia after a period of revolutionary activity working with peasants in the countryside; Volodia has met the same fate, while Andrei has escaped to Europe. Nikolai, too, makes an escape of sorts: when Sofi'a Vasil'evna dies after being arrested, Nikolai moves to St. Petersburg, where he advantageously marries the pregnant daughter of a powerful man and in so doing advances his career substantially. When his sister and her husband come to visit him, Nikolai keeps them waiting to satisfy his own ego, and then finds difficulty in summoning up any warm feelings even for the sister for whom he had once cared: he has, as he puts it, "frozen all the flowers of his heart." The final chapter of the novel lacks the light and humorous tone of the previous chapters, as Nikolai loses his link to other human beings and therefore his own humanity.

Characterizing *Nikolai Negorev, ili Blagopoluchnyi rossiianin* as an undervalued work, Maksim Gorky wrote that Kushchevsky's novel portrayed "the transformation of a hero into a lackey." In fact, though, one might suggest that the message of the book is not entirely clear. On the one hand, the "loyal" and "successful" Nikolai is portrayed quite negatively: while in prison, Overin tells the visiting Nikolai, "In order to avoid being left without a pastry, you're ready to condemn millions to death!" Meanwhile, the heroic revolutionaries of the book—openhearted, self-sacrificing, and idealistic—appeal to the reader's sympathies. The reader must regret Nikolai's triumph and the exile of Andrei and Overin; Gornfel'd notes that more than twenty years after the novel's publication, people could still recall the impression made on them by Overin. And yet the strength of Kushchevsky's characterization of Nikolai and his assigning of the narration to this rather objectionable character inject some doubt into this scenario. As Szulkin writes, Nikolai is "not easily graspable"; he responds to nature and to beauty and at least at the beginning of the book is sen-

sitive and at times emotional. In contrast to Szulkin's more conflicted view of Nikolai, Victor Terras argues in his *History of Russian Literature* (1991) that Kushchevsky's "artistic tact caused him to present Negorev as a normal human being, with the result that the very message of the novel became ambiguous: maybe Negorev was right and the revolutionary idealists wrong." Meanwhile Overin, for all his admirable qualities, is seen even by his fellow revolutionary Andrei as a Don Quixote type—a dreamer, humorous at times, unable to function productively in the "real world." I. P. Viduetskaia writes that Kushchevsky's sympathies lay with the Overins of Russia, but he doubted their ability to make meaningful changes in the world. The Nikolai Negorevs were certainly not the answer, however: the final picture in the novel of a friendless and coldhearted Nikolai clashes with the last chapter's title: "Ia sozdaiu svoe blagopoluchie" (I Arrive at Success).

Kushchevsky grew increasingly disenchanted with Russian life in the years following the publication of his novel. He attempted another novel, fragments of which were published in the newspaper *Novosti* (The News) in 1873. He never completed it, however, and, convinced that it was not worth keeping, burned the manuscript. Kushchevsky soon found himself in the same position he had occupied before his literary success: he was writing stories and sketches for various publications and struggling to earn a living wage. In 1875 he published his *Malen'kie rasskazy, ocherki, kartinki i legkie nabroski* (Short Stories, Sketches, Pictures, and Drafts), which received mixed reviews. The story "Dva nigilista" (Two Nihilists) recalls both Turgenev's *Ottsy i deti* (Fathers and Sons, 1862) and *Nikolai Negorev, ili Blagopoluchnyi rossiianin* in its portrayal of two family members, in this case a father and a son, who represent very different political trends. General Anton L'vovich Konoplianikov is open, loving, and filled with concern for those less fortunate than he; like Overin, he is compared to Don Quixote. His son Anton Antonovich, however, is similar to Nikolai Negorev in his coldness, lack of sympathy for the poor people he encounters through his work, and interest only in himself. In "Liberal'nyi barin" (The Liberal Gentleman), Kushchevsky mocks what he saw as the hypocrisy of the moderate liberals: his main character, Arkadii Il'ich, is lazy, ineffectual, and quick to blame others—including poverty-stricken employees—for his own mistakes. "Zimnii vecher v bol'nitse" (A Winter Evening at the Hospital) juxtaposes the stories told by men gathered in a hospital ward on a blustery evening to the conditions they encounter in the hospital. Both "Liberal'nyi barin" and "Zimnii vecher v bol'nitse" were published in an 1881 posthumous collection of Kushchevsky's stories.

Kushchevsky also wrote criticism during this period, evaluating various new literary works in reviews that appeared in *Novosti,* and he published a series of feuilletons about contemporary Russia. He may also have written, under a pseudonym, the ethnographic sketches "Ne stol' otdalennye mesta Sibiri (Nabroski iz vospominanii ssyl'nogo") (The Not So Distant Places of Siberia. [Sketches from the Recollections of an Exile], 1875), though his authorship has been disputed. Kushchevsky's feuilletons were clever at times, revealing touches of his humor, but overall they do not compare to his novel. Kushchevsky was spiraling downward, spending time in taverns drinking and losing his will to create and live productively. When he ended up once again in the hospital at the end of his life, he set about writing an autobiography in an attempt to explain himself and the paths he had chosen. "I want to say only that a writer-proletarian, working for the sake of a piece of bread, is a product of a transitional period. The Maecenases [patrons] are no more, but a reading public does not yet exist. It is considered a gift of God to have ten thousand subscribers to a daily newspaper. In spite of the high price of our newspapers, the publisher can scarcely make ends meet and is barely in a position to pay a writer 5 kopecks a line." Kushchevsky added, "I was not the only one like this."

Kushchevsky died of emphysema in the hospital on 12 August 1876 at age twenty-nine. His posthumous volume *Neizdannye rasskazy* (Unpublished Stories) was published in St. Petersburg in 1881. Evaluating this volume negatively, a critic noted, "If only, after his *Nikolai Negorev,* Kushchevsky had progressed as much as he in fact regressed, we would be able to talk of him now without exaggeration as a great writer. But it did not turn out that way." Kushchevsky himself tried to explain this fact in the brief pages of his attempted autobiography, attributing his difficulties to the economic hardships he had almost constantly faced. Echoing his words, Iadrintsev wrote in Kushchevsky's obituary that the native Siberian had been unable to find a lasting place in the Petersburg metropolis. In fact, Kushchevsky's novel deserves to find a place at last in the Russian literary canon so that new generations can learn from his depiction of a given moment in Russian history, admire his skillfully drawn characters, and enjoy the lightness of his literary touch and his delightful sense of humor.

Biographies:

Nikolai Mikhailovich Iadrintsev, "I. A. Kushchevsky," *Sibir',* no. 40 (3 October 1876): 7–8; on-line at <http://arw.dcn-asu.ru/~sokol/altai/literature/jadrin/cusc.html>;

S. N. Iuzhakov, ed., "Kushchevsky, Iv. Afanas'ev.," in *Bol'shaia entsiklopediia* (St. Petersburg, 1903), II: 718–719;

I. P. Viduetskaia, "Kushchevsky, Ivan Afanas'evich," in *Russkie pisateli. Biobibliograficheskii slovar'* (Moscow: Prosveshchenie, 1990), I: 391–393;

M. T. Pinaev, "Kushchevsky, Ivan Afanas'evich." *Russkie pisateli 1800–1917. Biograficheskii slovar'* (Moscow: Bol'shaia rossiiskaia entsiklopediia, 1994), III: 252–253.

References:

M. Goriachkina, "Posleslovie," in I. A. Kushchevsky, *Nikolai Negorev ili Blagopoluchnyi rossiianin* (Moscow: Khudozhestvennaia literatura, 1958), pp. 321–342;

V. Gorlenko, "Pisatel'-proletarii," *Moskovskoe obozrenie,* no. 41 (1877): 263–270; no. 42, (1877): 307–311;

A. G. Gornfel'd, "I. A. Kushchevsky," in I. A. Kushchevsky, *Nikolai Negorev, ili Blagopoluchnyi rossiianin* (Moscow: Zadruga, 1917), pp. 1–56– previously published as "Zabytyi pisatel'," in *Russkoe bogatstvo,* 12 (1895): 143–180;

N. Iakushin, "Pisatel'-proletarii," in I. A. Kushchevsky, *Nikolai Negorev. Roman i malen'kie rasskazy* (Moscow: Sovetskaia Rossiia, 1984), pp. 3–22;

Istoriia russkoi literatury (Moscow: Nauka, 1964), III: 507–509;

D. S. Mirsky, *A History of Russian Literature. From Its Beginnings to 1900,* edited by Francis J. Whitfield (New York: Vintage, 1958), pp. 300–301;

Robert Szulkin, "Nikolai Negorev: A Voice from the Void." *Studies in Russian Literature in Honor of Vsevolod Setchkarev,* edited by Julian W. Connolly and Sonia I. Ketchian (Columbus, Ohio: Slavica, 1986), pp. 243–254.

Papers:

Ivan Afanas'evich Kushchevsky's papers can be found at the Russian National Library and at the Institute of Russian Literature (Pushkin House) in St. Petersburg.

Nikolai Semenovich Leskov
(M. Stebnitsky)
(4 February 1831 – 21 February 1895)

Gabriella Safran
Stanford University

WORKS: *O raskol'nikakh goroda Rigi* (St. Petersburg, 1863);

Rasskazy M. Stebnitskogo (N. S. Leskova) (St. Petersburg, 1863);

Tri rasskaza M. Stebnitskogo (St. Petersburg, 1863);

Nekuda, in *Biblioteka dlia chteniia,* nos. 1–5, 7–8, 10–12 (1864); (St. Petersburg, 1865);

Oboidennye, in *Otechestvennye zapiski,* nos. 9–12 (1865); (St. Petersburg: A. A. Kraevsky, 1866);

Ostrovitiane, in *Otechestvennye zapiski,* nos. 11–12 (1866); (St. Petersburg: A. A. Kraevsky, 1867);

Rastochitel', in *Literaturnaia biblioteka,* 7 (1867); (St. Petersburg, 1868);

Povesti, ocherki i rasskazy M. Stebnitskogo (St. Petersburg, 1867);

Zagadochnyi chelovek. Epizod iz istorii komicheskogo vremeni na Rusi s pis'mom avtora k Ivanu Sergeevichu Turgenevu, in *Birzhevye vedomosti,* nos. 51, 54, 56, 58, 60, 64, 66, 68, 76, 78 (1870); (St. Petersburg: Bezobrazova, 1871);

Na nozhakh, in *Russkii vestnik,* nos. 10–12 (1870); nos. 1–8, 10 (1871); (Moscow, 1871);

Smekh i gore. Raznokharakternoe pot-pourri iz pestrykh vospominanii poliniavshego cheloveka, in *Sovremennaia letopis',* nos. 1–3, 8–16 (1871); (Moscow: V Univ. tip., 1871);

Soboriane. Stargorodskaia khronika v 5-ti ch., in *Russkii vestnik,* nos. 4–5, 7 (1872); (Moscow: V Univ. tip., 1872; St. Petersburg, 1878); translated by Isabel Florence Hapgood as *The Cathedral Folk* (New York: Knopf, 1924; London: John Lane, 1924);

Sbornik melkikh belletristicheskikh proizvedenii N. S. Leskova-Stebnitskogo (St. Petersburg, 1873);

"Zapechatlennyi angel," in *Russkii vestnik,* no. 1 (1873); republished in *Zapechatlennyi angel. Rozhdestvenskii rasskaz; Monasheskie ostrova na Ladozhskom ozere. Putevye zametki vestnik,* no. 1 (1873); (St. Petersburg: Izd. Bazunova, 1874);

Nikolai Semenovich Leskov, 1892

Ocharovannyi strannik, in *Russkii mir* (1873); (St. Petersburg: Tip. Doma prizreniia maloletnykh bednykh, 1874); translated by A. G. Paschkoff, edited, with an introduction, by Maksim Gorky, as *The Enchanted Wanderer* (New York: McBride, 1924; London: Jarrolds, 1926);

Zakhudalyi rod. Semeinaia khronika kniazei Protozanovykh. Iz zapisok kniazhny V. D. P., in *Russkii vestnik,* nos. 7–8, 10 (1874); (St. Petersburg: A. Bazunov, 1875);

Pavlin. Rasskaz; Detskie gody. Iz vospominanii Merkula Prao-tseva, in *Niva*, nos. 17–24 (1874); (St. Petersburg: Izd. Bazunova, 1876);

Na kraiu sveta (Iz vospominanii arkhiereia), in *Grazhdanin*, no. 52 (1875); nos. 1–4, 6 (1876); (St. Petersburg, 1876);

Velikosvetskii raskol. Grenvil' Val'digrev lord Redstok, ego zhizn', uchenie i propoved', in *Pravoslavnoe obozrenie*, nos. 9–10 (1876); no. 2 (1877); republished as *Velikosvetskii raskol (Lord Redstok, ego uchenie i propoved')*. *Ocherk sovremennogo religioznogo dvizheniia v peterburgskom obshchestve* (Moscow, 1877; St. Petersburg: V. Tushnova, 1877); translated by James Y. Muckle as *Schism in High Society: Lord Radstock and His Followers* (Nottingham, U.K.: Bramcote, 1995);

Vladychnyi sud. Byl' (Iz nedavnikh vospominanii. Pendant k rasskazu "Na kraiu sveta"), in *Strannik*, nos. 1–2 (1877); (St. Petersburg, 1877);

Nekreshchennyi pop. Neveroiatnoe sobytie (Legendarnyi sluchai), in *Grazhdanin*, nos. 23–29 (1877); (St. Petersburg: M. I. Popova, 1878);

Melochi varkhiereiskoi zhizni (Kartinki s natury), in *Novosti i birzhevaia gazeta*, nos. 236, 239, 240, 244, 248, 253, 259, 265, 272, 278, 285, 292, 298 (1878); (St. Petersburg: I. L. Tuzov, 1879); revised and enlarged (St. Petersburg, 1880);

Russkie bogonostsy. Religiozno-bytovye kartiny (St. Petersburg: A. S. Suvorin, 1880)—comprises *Na kraiu sveta* and *Vladychnyi sud;*

O prepodavanii Zakona Bozhiia v narodnykh shkolakh (St. Petersburg: A. S. Suvorin, 1880);

Tri pravednika i odin Sheramur (St. Petersburg: A. S. Suvorin, 1880);

Khristos v gostiakh u muzhika. Rasskaz, in *Igrushechka*, no. 1 (1881); Posrednik edition (Moscow: Sytin, 1885);

Russkaia rozn'. Ocherki i rasskazy (St. Petersburg, 1881);

Levsha, first published as *Skaz o tul'skom kosom Levshe i o stal'noi blokhe (Tsekhovaia legenda)*, in *Rus'*, nos. 49–51 (1881); republished as *Skaz o tul'skom Levshe i o stal'noi blokhe (Tsekhovaia legenda)* (St. Petersburg: A. S. Suvorin, 1882);

Evrei v Rossii (St. Petersburg, 1884)—published anonymously in an edition of fifty copies for the government's Pahlen Commission; translated by Harold Klassel Schefski as *The Jews in Russia: Some Notes on the Jewish Question* (Princeton: Kingston Press, 1986);

Sviatochnye rasskazy (St. Petersburg: M. O. Vol'f, 1886);

Skazanie o Fedore khristianine i o druge ego Abrame zhidovine, in *Russkaia mysl'*, no. 12 (1886); (Moscow, 1887);

Rasskazy kstati (St. Petersburg: M. O. Vol'f, 1887);

Povesti i rasskazy N. S. Leskova (St. Petersburg: A. S. Suvorin, 1887);

Starye gody v sele Plodomasove. Tri ocherka (St. Petersburg: A. S. Suvorin, 1888);

Inzhenery-bessrebrenniki. Iz istorii o trekh pravednikakh (St. Petersburg: A. S. Suvorin, 1888);

Sovestnyi Danila i prekrasnaia Aza. Dve legendy po starinnomu prologu (Moscow, 1889)—*Sovestnyi Danila* first published as "Dve legendy po starinnomu Prologu. I. Sovestnyi Danila," in *Novoe vremia* (3 February 1888); *Prekrasnaia Aza* first published as "Zhenskie tipy po Prologu. Prekrasnaia Aza," in *Novoe vremia* (5 April 1888) and republished as *Prekrasnaia Aza. Legenda po starinnomu prologu* (Moscow: I. D. Sytin, 1890);

Sobranie sochinenii, 10 volumes (St. Petersburg: A. S. Suvorin, 1889–1890); volumes 11–12 (St. Petersburg: A. F. Marks, 1893, 1896);

Lev startsa Gerasima. Vostochnaia legenda (Moscow: I. D. Sytin, 1890);

Figura. Rasskaz (Moscow: I. D. Sytin, 1890);

Povest' o bogougodnom drovokole (Moscow, 1890);

Gora. Roman iz egipetskoi zhizni, in *Zhivopisnoe obozrenie*, nos. 1–12 (1890); (St. Petersburg: Tip. S. Dobrodeva, 1890);

Nevinnyi Prudentsii. Skazanie (Moscow, 1892);

Pustopliasy. Sviatochnyi rasskaz, in *Severnyi vestnik*, no. 1 (1893); (Moscow, 1893);

Durachok (Moscow, 1894);

Zaiachii remiz. Nabliudeniia, opyty i prikliucheniia Onopriia Pereguda iz Peregudov (Moscow: "Krug," 1922).

Editions and Collections: *Polnoe sobranie sochinenii*, 36 volumes (St. Petersburg: A. F. Marks, 1902–1903);

Evrei v Rossii; neskol'ko zamechanii po evreiskomu voprosu, edited by Iu. Gessen (Petrograd: Gosudarstvennoe izdatel'stvo, 1919);

Sobranie sochinenii, 11 volumes, edited by V. G. Bazanov, B. Ia. Bukhshtab, A. I. Gruzdev, S. A. Reiser, and B. M. Eikhenbaum (Moscow: Gos. izd. khud. lit., 1956–1958);

N.S. Leskov o literature i iskusstve, edited by I. V. Stoliarova and A. A. Shelaeva (Leningrad: Izd-vo Leningradskogo universiteta, 1984);

Chestnoe slovo, edited by L. Anninskii (Moscow: Sov. Rossiia, 1988);

Na nozhakh (Moscow: Russkaia kniga, 1994);

Polnoe sobranie sochinenii, 30 volumes planned, edited by K. P. Bogaevskaia, I. P. Viduetskaia, A. A. Gorelov, N. I. Liban, M. L. Remneva, Stoliarova, and V. A. Tunimanov (Moscow: Terra, 1996–);

Neizdannyi Leskov, edited by Bogaevskaia, O. E. Maiorova, and L. M. Rozenblium, *Literaturnoe nasledstvo*, volume 101 (Moscow: Nasledie, 1997).

Editions in English: *The Sentry and Other Stories,* translated by A. E. Chamot (London: John Lane, 1922; New York: Knopf, 1923);

The Musk-Ox and Other Tales, translated by R. Norman (London: Routledge, 1944);

The Enchanted Pilgrim, and Other Stories, translated by David Magarshack (London & New York: Hutchinson, 1946);

The Amazon, and Other Stories, translated by Magarshack (London: Allen & Unwin, 1949);

Selected Tales, translated by Magarshack (New York: Farrar, Straus & Cudahy, 1961);

Lefty, Being the Tale of Cross-Eyed Lefty of Tula and the Steel Flea, translated by George Hanna (Moscow: Progress Publishers, 1965);

Satirical Stories of Nikolai Leskov, translated and edited by William B. Edgerton (New York: Pegasus, 1969);

The Sealed Angel and Other Stories, translated and edited by K. A. Lantz (Knoxville: University of Tennessee Press, 1984);

Five Tales, translated, with an introduction, by Michael Shotton (London: Angel Books, 1984);

Vale of Tears; and, On Quakeresses, translated by James Y. Muckle (Nottingham, U.K.: Bramcote, 1991);

On the Edge of the World, translated by Michael Prokurat (Crestwood, N.Y.: St. Vladimir's Seminary Press, 1992).

OTHER: "Produkt prirody," in *Put'-doroga. Nauchno-literaturnyi sbornik v pol'zu Obshchestva dlia vspomoshchestvovaniia nuzhdaiushchimsia pereselentsam* (St. Petersburg: K. M. Sibiriakov, 1893).

Author of a few tendentious novels and a vast number of newspaper articles, reviews, government reports, and letters, Nikolai Semenovich Leskov is more admired and discussed a century after his death than he was in his own time. He developed a signature style in his stories and novellas, creating memorable characters, often from the lower classes, the clerical estate, or minority ethnicities or religions. Each character speaks in a carefully crafted, distinctive language rather than in standard literary Russian. For most of Leskov's intellectual contemporaries, his complex prose was a distraction from the progressive ideology that, they thought, motivated worthwhile literature. For the Formalist critics of the early twentieth century, however, his prose style exemplified *skaz,* the device an author uses to convince a reader that the voice reproduced on the page is genuine. In the 1890s a few critics began to recognize Leskov's achievements, but an ill-deserved reputation as a religious and political conservative condemned him in the eyes of his liberal contemporaries, as well as Soviet critics and censors. His works

were seldom read during the first decades of Soviet rule. The first modern scholarly edition of some of his works appeared in the 1950s, and an informative biography written by his son, Andrei Leskov, was published in 1954. With the advent of glasnost, or "openness," in the 1980s, Leskov reemerged as a popular and controversial writer. A host of new editions appeared, culminating in the first complete edition of his works, which began to appear in 1996 and includes articles and letters as well as fiction. At the same time, a lively debate has begun over Leskov's significance for Russian intellectual and literary history. Some contemporary scholars assert that he and his best-known characters are voices from the Russian people, representatives of a genuine national spirit and carriers of a deep folk religiosity. Others see him as primarily an innovative artist whose nuanced and multivoiced portrayals of the peoples of the Russian Empire reveal the complexity of his views of nation and culture.

Although critics since Maksim Gorky have enthusiastically repeated Leskov's assertion that he "knew the [Russian] people since childhood," his class origins were remarkably diverse. Nikolai Semenovich Leskov was born on 4 February 1831, when his family lived in the small city of Orel, south of Moscow. Although he was legally a member of the gentry, his paternal grandfather was a priest. His father had trained for the priesthood, but then refused ordination and became a civil servant instead. His maternal grandmother was a merchant's daughter who married into a family of impoverished gentry of peasant origin. This mixture of ancestors made Leskov a *raznochinets* (a person of various estates) and a member of the new class of landless intellectuals that began to fill the professions in the Russian cities from the 1840s. (Critics such as Vissarion Gigor'evich Belinsky and Nikolai Gavrilovich Chernyshevsky and writers such as Gleb Ivanovich Uspensky and Anton Pavlovich Chekhov were also *raznochintsy.*)

When Leskov was a child, his father lost his job, and the family moved to a small farm near Orel. Along with the children of some wealthy relatives, he was educated by tutors until age eight. At ten he began to study in a gymnasium in Orel, where he remained for five years. Not having distinguished himself as a scholar, he dropped out and entered the civil service as a clerk in Orel. For three years, he copied documents, read voraciously, and enjoyed the company of a few provincial intellectuals. In 1849 he went to Kiev to visit a relative, managed to transfer to a post in the civil service there, and stayed for seven years. He worked in an army recruitment office, a fascinating and problematic place. Leskov's awareness of the injustice of the system by which boys were selected for twenty-five-year terms of military service, and his exposure to the personal and family crises that the selection process engendered, fed into much of his later work. In fiction and nonfiction, he explored the morally ambiguous position of the person compelled to carry out orders that he knows to be wrong, and he experimented with what Hugh McLean calls "camouflaged" criticism of unjust state practices, producing descriptions that the authorities might see as innocent but that a knowing reader would recognize as damning.

Throughout his twenties, Leskov continued his project of self-education. He read widely, mostly in Russian and occasionally in French. Unlike most of the Russian intellectuals of his time, he was interested in the cultures and literatures of other Slavic peoples: he became fluent in Polish and Ukrainian during his Kiev years, and later he studied Czech. In April 1853 he married Olga Vasil'evna Smirnova, with whom he had two children, Dmitrii (born 1854), who died in 1856 or 1857, and Vera (born 1856). Leskov's choice of wife proved unwise, and by 1862 the marriage had ended after a long period of separation.

In 1857 Leskov left Kiev, moved his family to Penza and spent the next three years in the employ of Alexander Scott, an uncle by marriage. A Russified Englishman and the son of a British Nonconformist, Scott was a businessman and estate manager. Leskov worked for him as a commercial agent, traveling widely and amassing the impressions and stories that later filled his prose. His letters to his uncle revealed an unexpected literary talent. For the rest of his life, as he worked to market his writings, Leskov traded energetically on his image as an expert in matters far beyond the ken of most urbanites. In formal terms Leskov's narrators often take the viewpoint from which Leskov observed his surroundings while working for Scott or in the Kiev recruitment office: a sympathetic fly on the wall, a semi-educated, somewhat privileged person whom fate has allowed to witness the dramatic lives of the lower classes.

After he returned to Kiev in 1860, already almost thirty years old, Leskov began to write for publication with an anonymous notice in the 18 June 1860 issue of the *Ukazatel' ekonomicheskii* (The Economic Index), protesting that the price of a newly permitted Russian translation of the Gospels had been unjustifiably marked up. Until 1860 Russians had had no access to any part of the Bible in their native language. Educated churchmen read it in Greek; the intelligentsia, if they cared to, could read it in French; and the illiterate heard sections of it read during religious services in Church Slavonic. In speaking out for the newly granted right to read the Bible in Russian, Leskov touched on topics that continued to fascinate him long after his literary debut: education and literacy, the vagaries of book pub-

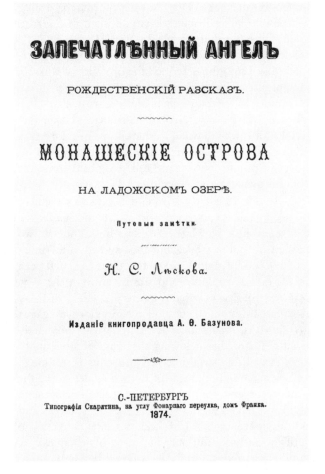

Title page for the first book publication of Leskov's Zapechatlennyi angel *(The Sealed Angel) and* Monasheskie ostrova na Ladozhskom ozere *(Monks' Islands on Lake Ladoga)*

lishing and sales, the relation between Church and State, and the role of Bible-reading in Eastern Orthodoxy. Even while he created some of the most sympathetic portraits of the Orthodox clergy in Russian literature and celebrated such national religious institutions as icon-painting and pilgrimages to monasteries, Leskov just as frequently criticized—more and more overtly over time—the emphasis the Church placed on ritual over an individual's unique encounter with faith. His insistence in 1860 on the importance of an individual's reading of the Bible was only the first manifestation of what critics such as James Y. Muckle have seen as his Protestant tendencies.

Moving to St. Petersburg in 1861, Leskov associated with radical writers, enjoyed the support of a liberal patron, experimented with various political stances, and wrote journalism and opinion pieces. His first attempts at fiction date to this time as well: in "Pogasshee delo" (A Case that was Dropped; first published in *Vek* [The Age], 25 March 1862), "Razboinik" (The Robber; first published in *Severnaia pchela* [The Northern Bee], 23 April 1862), and "V tarantase" (In a Coach; first published in *Severnaia pchela,* 4 May 1862), he described the brutality of Russian peasant life. The dark tones of these stories bring them close to the naturalism of writers such as Gleb Ivanovich Uspensky, Nikolai Vasil'evich Uspensky, and Fedor Mikhailovich Reshetnikov, but Leskov's focus on the sins and sufferings of the clergy and on the charms and horrors of folk religiosity emerges from his own experiences and beliefs.

An absurd event put an end to Leskov's popularity within the literary circles in which the naturalists were published. In May 1862 fires broke out at two markets in St. Petersburg and then spread to an entire neighborhood. Rumors spread that these fires had been set by radical students, and unrest grew in the city. Leskov wrote an editorial for *Severnaia pchela* (30 May 1862) arguing that, if the police had evidence against any students, they should formally charge those individuals, rather than allowing the mass of students to suffer from the suspicions of the crowd. Although Leskov apparently thought of himself as defending the students (at least the majority of innocent ones), many people perceived him as attacking radical students and radicals in general. All of Leskov's later attempts to clarify what he meant only increased his enemies' ire, and the controversy gradually aroused immense hostility in him.

Travel offered Leskov a refuge from politics. His peregrinations had an explicitly literary goal. For three months of 1862 he journeyed through Eastern Europe, sending back "diary entries" to *Severnaia pchela* on what he saw in Grodno, Lvov, and other equally uncommon destinations for the Russian traveler (who tended to pass through the western provinces of the Russian Empire as quickly as possible in order to reach Paris or a German resort). In these travel articles Leskov revealed the curiosity of an ethnographer, equally interested by the holiday customs of the Jews of Pinsk, the business practices of Vilna hoteliers, and recent Czech literature. After a few months spent café hopping with the Slavic intellectuals of Paris, he returned to St. Petersburg but soon found a government commission to take him back to the western provinces. In Riga and Pskov, he investigated the underground schools established by Old Believers (schismatics who refused to accept Russian church reforms introduced in the seventeenth century). Published in 1863, his report of their activities reveals a belief in religious tolerance and a fascination with the schismatics' archaic culture and language. He later published articles based on the report in newspapers and magazines.

During his travels, Leskov produced the first of the long stories on which his reputation as a fiction writer is based. In "Ovtsebyk" (The Musk-Ox; first published in *Otechestvennye zapiski* [Notes of the Fatherland], April 1863), an idealistic priest's son, absurd but somehow saintly, wanders through Russia, working thanklessly to improve the peasants' life. In "Zhitie odnoi baby" (Life of a Peasant Martyress; *Biblioteka dlia chteniia* [Library for Reading], July and August 1863), a peasant woman's life is ruined by the grasping men in her family. Both protagonists may be seen as early examples of the concern that distinguished Leskov from the naturalistic writers: his impulse, explicitly articulated later, to depict good people rather than focusing on the evil nourished by the peasants' poverty and exploitation.

Having returned to St. Petersburg in 1863, Leskov began to write in the only form that could legitimatize him—in his own eyes as well as those of his public—as a serious writer. His first novel, *Nekuda* (No Way Out), published serially in the January–December 1864 issues of *Biblioteka dlia chteniia,* a middlebrow "thick journal," was a cruel roman à clef that mocked the liberal patroness who had abandoned him and the radical youth who had despised him ever since his editorial about the St. Petersburg fires. In *Nekuda* a few high-minded young people imagine that by leaving their families and living in communes, they will help bring about a better future for Russia. They are surrounded by quarrelsome whiners, cynics, and untrustworthy Poles. (Like other Russian intellectuals, Leskov became less sympathetic toward the Poles after the 1863 Polish uprising against Russian rule.) The immediate target was a commune organized by Vasilii Alekseevich Sleptsov, whom Leskov had met and disliked; the more distant one was Nikolai Gavrilovich Chernyshevsky's radical classic, *Chto delat'?* (What Is To Be Done?), published in 1863. One of the most influential works of the Russian nineteenth century, *Chto delat'?* depicts a cohort of "new people" who escape their suffocating family lives, reimagine sexual morality, educate themselves, and live communally. Usually called "nihilists," the characters Chernyshevsky described inspired not only a host of real-life imitators but also an array of critical responses in the form of "anti-nihilist novels" such as *Nekuda.*

The radicals responded to Leskov's antinihilism with their most powerful ammunition. In the March 1865 issue of *Russkoe slovo* (Russian Word) the brilliant young critic Dmitrii Ivanovich Pisarev excoriated Leskov as a treacherous spy and questioned whether any self-respecting, right-thinking editor would ever be willing to publish his work again. For the next twenty years the liberal press in the capitals heeded Pisarev, and Leskov found his stories welcome only in the most conservative or obscure periodicals. These circumstances, as well as Leskov's anger, motivated him to attack the nihilists in more works: *Oboidennye* (The Bypassed; first published in *Otechestvennye zapiski,* 15 September – 15 December 1865), which argued for an alternative, less ideological way of re-imagining family life; *Zagadochnyi chelovek* (An Enigmatic Man; first published in *Birzhevye vedomosti* [Stock-Exchange News], 1870), Leskov's "biography" of his idealistic friend Arthur Benni; and the eight-hundred-page novel *Na nozhakh* (At Daggers Drawn; first published in *Russkii vestnik* [Russian Herald], 1870–1871), depicting a generation of entirely cynical "radicals" who have lost their idealism and seek only to exploit each other and the rest of society. Leskov's artistic failure in this work was probably sharpened by Fyodor Dostoevsky's far more successful realization of the same idea soon after with his portrayals of Stavrogin and Verkhovensky in *Besy* (The Devils; 1871–1872). In spite of several attempts, Leskov never finished another novel.

Leskov was not entirely sidetracked from writing short fiction by his polemics or the attempt to write a novel. In Dostoevsky's short-lived journal *Epokha* (Epoch), Leskov published "Ledi Makbet mtsenkogo uezda" (Lady Macbeth of Mtsenk) in 1865. Katerina L'vovna Izmailova is a slim, strong young woman from a poor family who has made an advantageous match with Zinovii Borisovich, a merchant and an older man. Childless and bored, she flirts with his worker Sergei during one of Zinovii's business trips. Sergei climbs through her window that night, and they begin a passionate affair. After her father-in-law discovers them and beats Sergei, Katerina dispatches her father-in-law with poison, and when Zinovii returns from his travels, the lovers kill him too and bury the corpse in the basement. Finally pregnant, Katerina establishes Sergei in her bedroom and relishes her physical relationship with him. Her confidence that her child will inherit Zinovii's estate is shaken, however, when a distant relative—a young boy—appears. A crowd peering through the window sees her suffocate the child. On their way to Siberia to serve their sentences for murder, Sergei rejects Katerina for another female convict, a prostitute. Driven almost mad by anger and desire, Katerina drowns herself and her rival. One of Leskov's most popular stories, "Ledi Makbet mtsenkogo uezda" was made into an opera (1930–1932) by Dmitrii Shostakovich.

Citing the relatively standard language, the compellingly developed plot, and the strongly sexual heroine, critics see the story as atypical for Leskov. Its title, though, may provide a way to situate it meaningfully within his writings. Like Ivan Sergeevich Turgenev's

Title page for Leskov's religious tale Na kraiu sveta *(On the Edge of the World), with the book stamp of the czar's personal library at Anichkov Palace (The Kilgour Collection of Russian Literature, Houghton Library, Harvard University)*

"Gamlet Shchigrovskogo uezda" (A Hamlet of the Shchigry District, 1849), Leskov's story asks the reader to recognize the Russian provincial as a worthy literary subject, a complex human being whose life could be as dramatic as a tragedy by William Shakespeare. At the same time Leskov questions that Western model, whose insufficiency is clear from the beginning to anyone familiar with the real Lady Macbeth (unlike her, Katerina wants the man, not the power). As Katerina and the convoy of prisoners proceed farther and farther east, the departure from the Shakespearean prototype becomes ever more obvious. In this tension between title and topic, the text addresses one of Leskov's perennial concerns: the gap separating Russia from the West and the absurdity of any superficial attempt to bridge it. Finally, the story illustrates a little-known side of Leskov's art: his abiding fascination with the connections between strength of will and physical violence. Although Leskov is well known for satirizing the state and lauding the virtuous individual, he also describes characters, such as Katerina, whose forceful personalities distinguish them from their colorless neighbors and seem to attract the narrator, even as their bloodthirstiness appalls him.

The sympathetic depiction of Katerina's predicament before Sergei comes along indicates that in spite of his scorn for the radicals, Leskov shared their interest in the "Woman Question." He seems to have agreed with most of the Russian intelligentsia of his time that if women were not allowed to earn a living "honestly," they might turn to prostitution. Unlike the more-cynical French writers and intellectuals of their time, nineteenth-century Russians tended to see prostitutes primarily as victims of madams, pimps, and clients, and they told stories about the evil circumstances—such as poverty, ignorance, and greedy parents—that combined to lead innocent young girls into the brothel, as with Sonia in Dostoevsky's *Prestuplenie i nakazanie* (Crime and Punishment, 1866). Leskov touched on the theme of prostitution in "Voitel'nitsa" (The Battle-Axe; first published in *Otechestvennye zapiski,* 1 April 1866), where Domna Platonovna, a procuress who has come from the Orel region to St. Petersburg, convinces Lekanida, a young Polish woman who has left her husband, to become the mistress of a wealthy general. The relationship between the two women repeats the familiar narrative about the prostitute and her exploiter: Lekanida is weak, romantic, unrealistic, and unaware of the consequences of her actions, while Domna Platonovna is calculating and strong, with little patience for Lekanida's romantic illusions.

As usual, Leskov's story differs from the polemical prototype in its language. Domna Platonovna, who tells the story, speaks in a combination of earthy provincial expressions and poorly remembered, hilariously distorted bourgeois euphemisms (for unmentionable topics such as a bath or pregnancy). Her better-educated listener, a fellow countryman from Orel, notices her malapropisms but admires her plump beauty and brisk efficiency. Literary scholar Dmitrii S. Likhachev has suggested that in such tales Leskov employed the narrator as a diversion. That is, by agreeing with the narrator, the reader might arrive at a "false ethical evaluation." If one recognizes the absurdity of Domna Platonovna's self-satisfied narration of her triumphs and the frame narrator's spineless refusal to challenge her, however, one might reject the "false" evaluation and decide that both narrators are morally suspect in the persecution of the hapless Lekanida. In this story and many later ones, Leskov's structure and language were calculated to provoke exactly this sort of readerly rebellion, and many reviews attest that he succeeded. Nonetheless, in "Voitel'nitsa" the procuress emerges as a far more attractive figure than her victim. In supplying men with women and vice versa, Domna Platonovna does not have only profit in mind; instead, as the narrator observes, she is an "artist, absorbed in her creations," and a far more original figure than the stereotypically drawn Lekanida. Inès Müller de Morogues has pointed out a connection between Leskov and his heroine: for both the compulsion to create proves more powerful than the reinforcement of conventional morality.

In 1867 Leskov wrote his only play, *Rastochitel'* (The Spendthrift; first published in *Literaturnaia biblioteka* [Literary Library], 1 and 15 July 1867), about a noble young man defrauded of his inheritance by an evil guardian. This denunciation of cruelty in the provincial merchant class recalls the works of Aleksandr Nikolaevich Ostrovsky, the reigning master of the Russian stage. When this rather weak work was attacked in the press, Leskov did his best to defend it, even going so far as to publish an anonymous article explaining the plausibility of the plot.

The episode reveals the fluidity of Leskov's attitudes toward truth, fiction, and the printed word. Using various pseudonyms (M. Stebnitsky until the early 1870s), he published assorted articles and regular newspaper columns as well as stories in his effort to support himself and his family (which by the mid 1860s included a common-law wife, Katerina Bubnova, her four children, and their mutual child, Andrei). He also occupied a small government post, and when the opportunity arose he wrote on commission for the government or private individuals. Typically for his era, he did not place an enormous emphasis on originality. He had a habit of reusing material from one article in another while often revising his own views on a given topic, though he did not always admit it. He also copied passages from the works of others (especially when his readers were unlikely to know the source), making whatever changes he thought might contribute to the appeal of the text. He crossed the barriers between fiction and nonfiction in both directions, not only inserting fictional embellishments and unverified, "borrowed" material in his articles, but also presenting his fictional texts as fact. In titles and subtitles he insisted that his stories were really "scenes from nature" or "a real occurrence," that they emerged directly "from my recent reminiscences" or "from my observations." Many stories begin with an explanation of the circumstances under which the narrator (usually fairly explicitly identified with the author) heard the stories and how he knew that his interlocutors were telling the truth.

This entanglement of fact with fiction speaks to both Leskov's historical context and his distinctive artistry. On the one hand, he used a typical realist device when he insisted that his fiction is not fictional; unlike the "artificial" creations of Romantic and other earlier writers, it is an unedited slice of life, full of the rough, ugly substance of reality. Leskov's *skaz* reinforces this impression. In a letter translated by McLean, Leskov claimed that his art was really only a kind of careful stenography: "This colloquial, vulgar, florid language in which many pages of my works are written was not invented by me, but overheard from the peasant, the semi-intellectual, the fine talkers, the holy fools, and the pious souls. People reproach me for this 'mannered' language. . . . But don't we have plenty of 'mannered' people?" On the other hand, his elaborate legitimation of his narrative voice in this comment and throughout his writings might distinguish him from other realists. Just as later generations of writers and critics understood his *skaz* as a complex artistic creation, so too his use of pseudonyms, his challenges to generic boundaries, and his elaborate structures built on the contrasting styles of overlapping narrators, give his work an unusual multivoicedness.

One of Leskov's most successful and least generically conventional texts, a "chronicle," appeared in 1872 in Mikhail Nikiforovich Katkov's *Russkii vestnik* (The Russian Herald) under the title *Soboriane* (Cathedral Folk). Katkov, a conservative, anti-Polish nationalist and a good judge of literature, provided an outlet for Leskov's most important work of the early 1870s. Leskov had planned a lengthy series of stories, relating several centuries of the history of Stargorod (Old Town), featuring the Russian Orthodox priests, aristocrats, Old Believers, and unrecognized saints of the town. Fragments of that larger project survive as freestanding works—including "Kotin doilets i Platonida" (Kotin the He-Cow and Platonida), first published in *Povesti, ocherki i rasskazy M. Stebnitskogo* (Tales, Sketches and Stories of M. Stebnitsky, 1867), whose hero believed he was a girl until adolescence, then matured into an asexual creature who adopts helpless orphans, and "Starye gody v sele Plodomasovo" (Old Times in the Village of Plodomasovo; first published in *Syn otechestva* [Son of the Fatherland], 1869), about eighteenth-century aristocrats intoxicated by the absolute power that they wield over their families and serfs. Other sections of the project that were ultimately folded into *Soboriane* include "Chaiushchie dvizheniie vody" (Waiting for the Moving of the Waters; first published in *Otechestvennye zapiski*, 15 March – 15 April 1867), which draws its title from John 5:3–4, and "Bozhedomy" (Dwellers in the House of God; first published in *Literaturnaia biblioteka*, January – February 1868).

Eventually published as a three-hundred-page book, *Soboriane* tells the story of the priest of Stargorod, Father Savelii Tuberozov, and his two subordinates, the diminutive Father Zakhariia Benefaktov and the strong but childlike Dean Akhilla Desnitsyn. Although Leskov seems to have turned his back on the St. Petersburg radicals in this work, provincial Stargorod has a nihilist as well: the schoolteacher Varnava Prepotensky, who offends Akhilla by planning to use a human skeleton in his anatomy lessons. The bulk of the book is cast as Tuberozov's diary, which depicts his unending struggle with forces of darkness. At the beginning he recounts his battle against the Old Belief. He resists the immoral and ineffective tactics that his superiors in the church want him to use to stamp out the heresy, and also opposes the government, which abets the worst offenders within the church. Tuberozov next takes on more modern enemies: the atheist and former revolutionary Termosesov, who schemes to destroy Tuberozov's relations with his superiors, and the entire unbelieving upper class, which supports Orthodoxy as a means to keep the peasants in check but cannot imagine it as a faith that an educated person can take seriously.

Part of the power of this work lay in its relevance to the situation of the Russian church. In 1858 Father Ivan Belliustin had written *Opisanie sel'skogo dukhovenstva* (A Description of the Village Clergy), a harsh exposé of the economic and moral degradation of the provincial clergy, for which he blamed the church hierarchy. Shocked by his revelations, Russians debated reforming the ecclesiastical schools and the church economy over the next decade. Leskov was far from the only respected writer to address ecclesiastical topics: both Tolstoy and Dostoevsky touched on the division between the educated classes and those charged with instructing them in religion, and both addressed the broader problem of reconciling science and faith. Yet, Leskov's work stands out in its sympathetic portrait of a clergyman. Rather than focusing on the religious peregrinations of the educated, he examined the other side, a priest who is relatively low in the hierarchy. In so doing, he combined two seemingly irreconcilable perspectives. Conservatives delighted in his portrayal of an Orthodox priest as a proud, intelligent, ethically unimpeachable figure. By implication it presented the Orthodox Church as a source of genuine morality, a religion that an educated adult need not be embarrassed to espouse. Liberals, however, could read the book as a cynical indictment of a Russian church in which a brave man with strong faith is ultimately destroyed by his inflexible, self-interested superiors.

Soboriane was not the only work of the early 1870s to showcase Leskov's convincing images of Russian life. In the two-hundred-page *Smekh i gore* (Laughter and

Grief; first published in *Sovremennaia letopis'* [Contemporary Chronicle], 1871), he told a series of tales united only by the narrator's thesis that Russian life is full of unpleasant surprises—such as betrayals by friends and family, incursions by the secret police, highway extortion, and street violence. Humor lightens the gloomy picture of Russian life, making Leskov's satire age better than that of Mikhail Evgrafovich Saltykov (N. Shchedrin), the best-known satirist of the age. The form of Leskov's book recalls the realist "zapiski" (notes) that trade on the impression of immediacy. The best-known examples were produced by Turgenev in *Zapiski okhotnika* (A Hunter's Notes, 1852) and Dostoevsky in *Zapiski iz mertvogo doma* (Notes from the House of the Dead, 1861). Walter Benjamin has suggested that Leskov's technique in *Smekh i gore* is appealingly archaic, like stories related by one worker to another during work. The setting makes possible an endless collection of tales with no necessary internal causal relation among them. Unlike a bildungsroman, a novel of education, stories such as Leskov's do not insist on a hero whose positive development may teach the reader something as well. Indeed, the Russia that Leskov depicts is hopelessly stagnant, incapable, like the hero, of any evolution. Benjamin's vision of the writer's atavism, however, denies the degree to which Leskov's form is rooted in late-nineteenth-century urban life, especially in the newspaper columns that he produced regularly. This forum encouraged precisely the stringing together of incidents and the combination of humor and pessimism that characterize *Smekh i gore*.

During the first half of the 1870s Leskov produced two of his best-known and most frequently anthologized works, which—with the 1881 story *Levsha* (The Lefthander)—gave him the reputation of being a defender of the Russian people and their cultural heritage. In the summer of 1872 he visited the islands in Lake Ladoga, north of St. Petersburg, a region well known for its wooden architecture, its preservation of a tradition of oral folk poems called *byliny,* and monasteries such as the one on the island of Solovki (which functioned under the Soviets as a prison for political offenders). The trip inspired *Ocharovannyi strannik* (The Enchanted Wanderer; first published in *Russkii mir* [Russian World], 1873). As a youth, Ivan Severianovich Fliagin, a tall and powerful man born into serfdom, thoughtlessly kills a monk. The monk's ghost tells him in a dream that he will endure many trials and then become a monk himself. After inadvertently killing another man, a Tatar, in a gruesome "whipping duel," Fliagin flees east and finds himself living among the Tatars. Although they give him wives with whom he has children, he misses Christian Russia and returns home. There he works for a buyer of horses for the army and fights his urge to drink until it overpowers him. In the grip of vodka, he squanders state money on a gypsy woman. Betrayed by another, she convinces Fliagin to kill her because she cannot bring herself to commit suicide. Full of remorse, he volunteers to serve in the army in the Caucasus, where he deliberately risks his life over and over before finally entering the monastery at Solovki.

The hero of *Ocharovannyi strannik* is often seen as representing Russia or the Russians. Indeed, Leskov had originally titled the work "Russkii Telemak" (A Russian Telemachus) or "Chernozemnyi Telemak" (A Black-Soil Telemachus). The evocation of Telemachus, the son of Odysseus, indicates that Leskov believed he had written a national epic that might rival Homer's. By identifying his hero with the son of a Greek hero, Leskov suggested, in the ideological vocabulary of his time, that his epic told the story of a younger nation, one whose time had not yet come. Leskov eventually settled on a title that decreases this comparative focus. He called his hero a *strannik,* a word that means wanderer, but that has a religious overtone. Fliagin is "enchanted" by the fate that compels him to wander until he becomes a monk, but the term also signals that the text might be read as a Russian fairy tale. Leskov heightened this impression by comparing Fliagin to Il'ia Muromets, the powerful Russian fighter who stars in many of the *byliny*. In doing so, as A. A. Gorelov has noted, he displayed a fashionable familiarity with Russian folklore. Members of the St. Petersburg intelligentsia were all reading the first significant collections of folk tales, songs, and sayings, which were just being published in the early 1870s. The similarities between Leskov's story and the *byliny* go beyond the title and the hero. Like an oral folk genre, the story is composed of a string of incidents, seemingly infinitely expandable, featuring a single hero. The primitive, almost cartoon-like presentations of human lives and deaths also recall the world of the folktale. (The characters fall in love with or kill each other abruptly and with seemingly little thought.) By stylizing the folk legend in evocative language, entirely unlike the realist depictions of peasant life of his era, Leskov produced what his contemporaries read as a paean to the Russians' physical strength, endurance, and loyalty to their fatherland and Church, in spite of the alcoholism, brutality, and fatalism that cripple them.

Leskov's other major work of 1873, "Zapechatlennyi angel" (The Sealed Angel; first published in the January 1873 issue of *Russkii vestnik*), also focuses on Russian national identity. A group of travelers at an inn on a snowy night listens to a tale about a community of Old Believer stonemasons, who are building a bridge for an English firm in Kiev. All goes well until scandal erupts. Policemen confiscate the community's collection of ancient icons, including their guardian, an angel icon, and seal them with red sealing wax. The narrator, Mark, travels to find an Old Believer icon painter, who makes an exact copy of the stolen angel icon. In a dramatic finale, the stonemasons' leader crosses the Dnieper on the icy chains of the uncompleted bridge during the Christmas service in order to substitute the new icon for the stolen one. By a "miracle" (revealed later to have natural causes), the seal on the substitute icon disappears, convincing the Old Believers to renounce their heresy and convert to the state religion.

In the stonemasons' explanation of the importance of their icons to their English employer, Leskov displayed extensive knowledge of the schools, techniques, history, and philosophy of icon painting. He had learned some of it from a St. Petersburg icon painter, Nikita Savostianovich Rachaiskov. Leskov's visits to Rachaiskov's studio are recorded in Andrei Leskov's biography of his father. He knew that, as John of Damascus had argued, icons not only substitute for biblical text by teaching Scripture to the illiterate, but can be more persuasive than the written word by representing an embodied form of the holy to humans. Mark explains this theology in his colorful language:

> Not everyone is given to understand Scripture, and the minds of the uncomprehending are darkened even in prayer: one man hears proclaimed "mercies rich and abundant" and bows down all athirst, thinking at once that they are talking of money. But when he sees before him the whole picture of heavenly glory, then he contemplates life's higher prospect and understands how he can achieve this goal, because it's all clear and comprehensible here. (translation from Kenneth Lantz)

In centering his story around the icon, Leskov created a virtual icon of an inspirational, inclusive Russianness, which brings together the former Old Believers and their former tormenters in admiration of an authentic national art form. Although he later blamed his patriotic, conciliatory ending on the conservatism of Katkov, the editor of *Russkii vestnik,* Leskov motivated it throughout the text, and the overtly Romantic nationalism of "Zapechatlennyi angel" undoubtedly reflected the artist's mood at the time. By reclaiming the icon, a symbol of ancient Russian folk culture, as the heritage of all modern Russians (not just Old Believers), Leskov modeled the creation of a new nation out of its cultural heritage by means of high art. His success in this task may account for the popularity of the story. For example, the Empress Maria Aleksandrovna requested a private reading by the author, and Anton Pavlovich Chekhov complained about trying to write in his family's crowded apartment while his father read

Leskov in 1889 (engraving by V. V. Mate after a portrait by I. E. Repin)

"Zapechatlennyi angel" out loud to his mother in another room.

The popularity of "Zapechatlennyi angel" did not usher in an easier life for its author. His second marriage was in trouble, and he had broken with Katkov over the editor's emendations to his mediocre, unfinished *Zakhudalyi rod* (A Decrepit Clan), which Katkov had begun to publish in *Russkii vestnik* (July, August, and October 1874). *Zakhudalyi rod* centers on the efforts of a virtuous widow-landowner princess to find a teacher who can educate her two sons to be moral individuals.

Leskov took his second trip to Paris in 1875. On his return he published several strong works that betray an increasing cynicism about Orthodoxy. In the 28 December 1875 – 8 February 1876 issues of Prince Vladimir Petrovich Meshchersky's ultra-right-wing *Grazhdanin* (The Citizen), he published *Na kraiu sveta* (On the Edge of the World). It begins with what sounds like a nod to the nationalism that made "Zapechatlennyi angel" so popular: a wise bishop concludes on the basis of the icon that the faith of the Russians is superior to that of other Christians, precisely because of its simplicity. The comparison motivates a story from the churchman's younger days, when he served in Siberia.

Orthodox churchmen in the Far East were expected to work to convert the natives, but Father Kiriak, an older priest who had been in Siberia for many years and knew the natives' language, mysteriously refused to participate in a campaign to baptize as many of them as possible as quickly as possible. As he and the narrator embarked on a journey into the wilderness, Kiriak chose a baptized native as his guide and driver, assigning the narrator to a pagan one. When a snowstorm developed, the pagan saved the narrator by huddling with him under the snow and then skiing away for provisions. Meanwhile, the "Christian" driver abandoned Kiriak, who soon died. At the end of the story the reader learns that a host of pagans eventually converted to Christianity, represented for them by Kiriak and his faith. Among the many admirers of this story was Konstantin Pobedonostsev, a powerful right-wing ideologue and official, who gave a copy to his pupil, the future Alexander III. Presumably, he did not read the story as indicating that because religious ritual is meaningless without true faith, which can never be bought or required under duress, the legal enforcement of Orthodoxy is entirely pernicious.

Two years later, Leskov concealed the same moral in two more stories, *Nekreshchennyi pop* (The Unbaptized Priest; first published in *Grazhdanin,* 13–31 October 1877) and *Vladychnyi sud* (Episcopal Justice; first published in *Strannik* [Wanderer], January–February 1877). *Vladychnyi sud,* set in the army-recruitment bureau in Kiev where Leskov had worked during the reign of Nicholas I, addresses one of the most vexed problems of the era, the "Jewish Question." The hero, a Jewish bookbinder, tries frantically to rescue his only son from recruitment into the army. In the notorious practice called "cantonism," boys from populations that the czar wished to reform (such as Jews, Old Believers, and criminals) could be taken into the army as young as twelve years old. Kept apart from their families, they began their official twenty-five-year term of service after they reached eighteen. In Leskov's story the bookbinder hires an adult Jew to take the place of his child, but the substitute recruit then tries to avoid military service by converting to Russian Orthodoxy. (By law only a Jew could substitute for another Jew in the army.) After much pleading, the archbishop of Kiev declares the substitute recruit "unworthy" of conversion, thus forcing him to enter the army. The bookbinder's son is released, after which he dies. At the end of the story the narrator meets the bookbinder again and finds out that he has converted to Orthodoxy. Leskov explicitly connected *Vladychnyi sud* to *Na kraiu sveta* in its first lines, where he explains that, like the earlier story, *Vladychnyi sud* exemplifies the heroism of an archbishop; at the same time *Vladychnyi sud* also implicitly criticizes a church in which the heavy hand of the state has made rituals such as baptism meaningless.

To criticize the behavior of Russian Church toward Russians, Leskov had chosen to describe its dealings with first Siberian natives and then Jews. The exotic subjects undoubtedly distracted the censors, who may have found it less disturbing for a writer to describe Jews and pagans as participating in Christian ritual without demonstrating real faith than if he had shown Russian Orthodox peasants behaving the same way. At the same time, by picturing the Russian Empire as home to so many ethnicities and religions, Leskov took the position of a cosmopolitan liberal who can understand and enter into dialogue with every kind of person. Even his language, as Boris M. Eikhenbaum has noted, indicates the complexity of his notion of Russianness. In regard to one of the most controversial and reputedly least assimilable or "Russifiable" minorities, the Jews, this consciously assumed broadminded stance allowed Leskov to depict the Jewish bookbinder, at the end of the story, as a better Christian than many "born" Christians. As an intellectual, Leskov seemed to feel obliged to make a statement on the "Jewish Question" in his work. He produced a few stories—such as "Rakushanskii melamed" (The Melamed of Osterreich; first published in *Russkii vestnik,* March 1878) and "Zhidovskaia kuverkollegiia" (Yid Somersault; first published in *Gazeta A. Gattsuka* [A. Gattsuk's Gazette], 1882)—that invoke Russian stereotypes about Jews. He also wrote a lengthy series of ethnographic articles about Jewish rituals (1880–1884), which led him to accept a commission from the Jewish magnate Baron Horace O. de Günzburg to write *Evrei v Rossii* (The Jews in Russia, 1884), a surprisingly entertaining book-length defense of Jews for the Pahlen Commission, headed by Count Konstantin Ivanovich Pahlen and formed to discuss the laws concerning the Russian Empire's Jewish population. Leskov concluded his published remarks on the topic with a sermon for religious tolerance included in a rather dull later work, *Skazanie o Fedore khristianine i o druge ego Abrame zhidovine* (The Tale of Fedor the Christian and his Friend Abram the Jew; first published in *Russkaia mysl'* [Russian Thought], December 1886). Leskov's changing depictions of Jews and Judaism parallel his fictional and nonfictional treatments of other religious and ethnic minorities in the Russian Empire: Poles, Germans, Ukrainians, and Old Believers. In each case he frequently repeated folk stereotypes (such as snobbish Poles and punctilious Germans), but just as often he mocked Russians and their prejudices.

Among the religious minorities that interested Leskov was a Russian Protestant movement called Radstockism (or Pashkovism). In an 1876 report, *Veli-*

Leskov's study in St. Petersburg during the 1890s

kosvetskii raskol (A High-Society Schism; first published in *Pravoslavnoe obozrenie* [Orthodox Review], September and October 1876, and February 1877), about the phenomenon of an Englishman nobleman–Granville Augustus Waldegrave, third Baron Radstock–preaching in Russia, Leskov alternately praised and attacked the Radstockites and their Orthodox foes. He returned to the theme of clerics in *Melochi v arkhiereiskoi zhizni* (Little Things in a Bishop's Life; first published in *Novosti i birzhevaia gazeta* [News and Stock-Exchange Gazette], 14 September – 20 November 1878), which reveals bishops as human, often self-interested and petty, and frequently suffering from constipation. This popular work finally improved Leskov's reputation among the radicals, and, not coincidentally, got him into trouble with the authorities. Published in a liberal year, it was withdrawn from libraries in 1884, and in 1889 it also provoked the seizure and incineration of volume 6 of his collected works, an event on which Leskov blamed the onset of his heart problems.

The enormous energy that Leskov put into depicting Jews and Christians, Poles and Germans, had far less impact on his reputation than a single story, *Levsha* (The Lefthander), first published as *Skaz o tul'skom kosom Levshe i o stal'noi blokhe (Tsekhovaia legenda)* (The Tale of the Crosseyed Lefthander from Tula and the Steel Flea [A Workshop Legend]) in *Rus'* (17–31

October 1881). The tale begins when a Don Cossack, Platov, accompanies Czar Alexander I on a voyage to England. The Englishmen show the emperor and his entourage around the country, inviting them into factories as well as palaces. While Alexander admires, Platov scoffs at what he sees as an attempt to make Russian workmen look bad by comparison. He is especially disgruntled when the Englishmen give the czar a miniature steel flea, too small to see with the naked eye, that dances when wound up with a key. Under the next czar, Nicholas I, Platov finds the opportunity for revenge on the Englishmen. He brings the steel flea to the workmen of Tula and commands them to best it. They supply it with miniature shoes. When the Englishmen see it, they invite the Lefthander, one of the Tula workmen, to visit them. Although they offer to keep him in England, he insists on returning to Russia. He and an English soldier engage in a drinking contest on the way back, and when they arrive in St. Petersburg, English doctors quickly cure the English sailor from his hangover, but the poor Lefthander dies of exposure, never having been able to tell the czar what he discovered in England: that the Russians would do well to imitate the English and stop cleaning their muskets with brick dust. This information, the narrator notes, might have helped the Russians win the Crimean War (1853–1856).

For more than a century, some Russian critics have praised *Levsha* as an example of the superiority of untutored Russian native genius over anyone with a Western education, while other critics have pointed out the subtext that praises the way workers are treated in the West and unmasks Platov as an autocratic bully. Even the Lefthander's craftsmanship is ultimately inferior: once the flea is shod, it can no longer dance. (Never having had the opportunity to learn the basic laws of physics, the Tula masters could not account for the effect the weight of the miniature shoes had on the tiny motor that made the flea's legs move.) *Levsha* epitomizes what Leskov called his "ricochet" technique: a story appears to be aimed at one target, and then suddenly turns around and decimates another.

The narrative of the inventive Lefthander has generated another story, centering on Leskov's attempt to receive credit for his inventiveness: *Levsha* includes far more and far funnier malapropisms than Domna Platonovna's speech in "Voitel'nitsa." The descriptions of the English factory reveal the limitations of the narrator's knowledge and vocabulary. In William Edgerton's inventive attempt to translate the stunning collection of puns, the story includes "nautical whether-meters, gamble-hair coats for the infantry, and waterproof rein coats for the cavalry." In the first edition of this story, as in so many others, Leskov included a foreword accounting for this language by describing the "real teller" of the tale: in this case, an elderly canary-keeping "Tula gunsmith," still in good health and living in Sestroretsk near St. Petersburg. Charmed by the wordplay, reviewers took the author at his word and gave him kudos not for his brilliant linguistic inventiveness, but merely for so accurately recording another's speech. Wanting full acknowledgment for his hard work, Leskov was forced to recant his introduction and eventually wrote letters to the newspapers and inserted comments in his later stories revealing his "fraud," insisting that he had invented the gunsmith and his language out of whole cloth. In spite of his efforts he was never able to eradicate the myth that he had simply recast a preexisting "armory legend." Boris Bukhshtab has described how scholars vied to discover Leskov's "original" and account for the writer's ingenious "adaptation" of it.

None of Leskov's subsequent works achieved the later renown of *Levsha*. The story, and the attendant popular confusion between the author and the talented Russians he described, may have reinforced his confidence in himself as a master of the miniature, an acknowledged expert in shorter prose forms. In his last decade and a half, he created several collections of stories in small genres that he defined or popularized: Christmas stories, tales of righteous people, and revisions of Russian Orthodox legends. In 1886, perhaps

trading on the popularity of "Zapechatlennyi angel," he published *Sviatochnye rasskazy* (Stories of the Christmas Season). According to Leskov's definition of the genre, such works are all set during the Christmas season and feature the supernatural, a moral, and a happy ending. Among Leskov's Christmas stories is "Prividenie v inzhenernom zamke" (Apparition in the Engineers' Castle, first published in *Novosti i birzhevaia gazeta*, 5–6 November 1882), set in the eighteenth-century St. Petersburg palace where Paul I had met a grisly death in 1801 at the hands of a group of conspirators that included his own son. Now the children who attend the engineering school located in the building delight in frightening each other with ghostly pranks. Set to keep vigil at the corpse of the school's hated director, they are primed for terror when a spectral gray figure appears. As in "Zapechatlennyi angel," Leskov takes care to insert a prosaic explanation, which does nothing to invalidate the magical transformation of the children's character. An even more dramatic human metamorphosis drives another "Christmas story." In "Zver'" (Wild Beast; first published in *Gazeta A. Gattsuka*, 25 December 1883), an effective story with a sentimental ending, an evil landowner turns into a virtuous patron of the poor after he witnesses the touching love between his serf Ferapont and a pet bear and then hears a priest explain a Christmas song to some children.

The possibility of human reform intrigued Leskov more and more in the 1880s. He included *Levsha* and *Ocharovannyi strannik* in a collection called "pravedniki" (righteous people), which was published in 1889 as the second volume of his collected works. In reaction to the tendency of Realist writers such as his friend Aleksei Feofilaktovich Pisemsky to illustrate the worst aspects of life and the worst kinds of people, Leskov explained, he had deliberately set about creating pictures of positive humans, who might by their example inspire others to reform. He had already imagined such a mechanism in *Na kraiu sveta*, where the memory of the virtuous Father Kiriak convinces the pagans to convert, and *Vladychnyi sud*, where the archbishop's merciful ruling inspired the bookbinder to become a Christian. In the late 1870s and 1880s Leskov set about creating more such stories, each featuring a person who behaves morally while flouting convention and resisting temptation. For example, in "Odnodum" (Singlethought; first published in *Ezhenedel'noe novoe vremia* [Weekly New Times], 20 and 27 September 1879), a Bible-reading provincial stuns his superiors and society by insisting on living only on his salary as a policeman and resolutely turning down all opportunities to take bribes. In "Chelovek na chasakh" (The Sentry; first published in *Russkaia mysl'*, April 1887), the *praved-*

nik (righteous man) suffers more for his virtue. Standing guard at the Winter Palace in St. Petersburg, the soldier Postnikov realizes that a man is drowning in the Neva only a few steps away. Although he knows that if he leaves his post for any reason, he will be punished by being forced to run the gauntlet (effectively a death penalty), he nevertheless runs to the river and rescues the man. When his superior finds out, he "arranges" matters and saves Postnikov from punishment for his "crime" (another man gets a medal for the brave rescue, and Postnikov gets a mere two hundred lashes).

Postnikov is one of many Leskovian heroes who is whipped. Leskov said that seeing a woman flogged publicly inspired him to write "Ledi Makbet mtsenkogo uezda," and he offered memorable punishment scenes in "Tupeinyi khudozhnik" (The Toupee Artist; first published in *Khudozhestvennyi zhurnal* [Art Journal], February 1883), about a serf who works as a theatrical hairdresser for one of the troupes of serf actors maintained by the wealthiest landowners, and tries heroically but unsuccessfully to save his sweetheart, an actress, from the evil master's clutches. Rather than arguing, like many liberal intellectuals, only for the elimination of corporal punishment, Leskov depicted physical violence as intrinsic to Russian life, its legal system, and relations between classes and even within families. An especially bitter meditation on the impossibility of eradicating flogging appears in the 1893 "Produkt prirody" (A Product of Nature), based on Leskov's experiences working for his uncle Alexander Scott, transporting peasants against their will from one part of Russia to another. The narrator's misguided kindheartedness influences him to permit a group of men to leave the barge on which they are traveling for a bathhouse. When they take advantage of their temporary freedom to run away, a single police scribe captures them, flogs them all, and returns them, aided considerably by the serfs' willingness to hold each other down for the whipping. The incident recalls Leskov's cynical statement that on the next day after the triumph of the ideas that Chernyshevsky expressed in *Chto delat'?*, the Russian people would immediately choose "the fiercest policeman" to maintain order. The combination of a critical presentation of Russian life and cynicism about any "quick fix" solutions gave Leskov's later stories some of their power, though it made it impossible for him to publish some of them.

Given Leskov's increasing hostility to the state and his ongoing opposition to Orthodox ritual, it is not surprising that he found common cause with the best-known radical Christian literary philosopher in Russia, Leo Tolstoy. In his later years Tolstoy articulated his hostility to Church and State in his retellings of stories from the Prolog, a Byzantine collection of sermons, histories, and tales about saints. Leskov, who met Tolstoy

in 1887, declared him a "wise man" and sought his advice. Although Tolstoy did not entirely reciprocate Leskov's respect, he published several of Leskov's stories at his publishing house, Posrednik (Intermediary), which was dedicated to supplying the peasants with morally useful reading material. Although Tolstoy and his followers worried that the ornate quality of Leskov's language might confuse the uneducated reader, they liked his story *Khristos v gostiakh u muzhika* (Christ Visits a Muzhik; first published in *Igrushechka* [Toy], January 1881), about a falsely accused man who confronts and forgives the man who has had him sent to Siberia. They were even more charmed by the sketch "Pod Rozhdestvo obideli" (Offended Before Christmas; first published in the *Peterburgskaia gazeta* [The Petersburg Gazette], 25 December 1890), in which a merchant, rather than punishing a child whom he finds casing his home for a gang of thieves attempting to rob him, instead adopts the boy, thereby teaching him not to judge his fellow man. During Leskov's Tolstoyan years, he followed the master's example with several stories based on themes from the Prolog. Leskov's versions of the genre of the *zhitie* (saint's life) include *Prekrasnaia Aza* (Beautiful Aza; first published in *Novoe vremia* [New Times], 5 April 1888), about a pagan woman who gives her fortune away to save a would-be suicide, is forced into prostitution, and is eventually baptized by angels; and *Gora* (The Mountain; first published in *Zhivopisnoe obozrenie* [Picturesque Review], 1890), in which a free-thinking goldsmith, who heroically resists the temptation of a beautiful woman, has the faith required physically to move mountains. Leskov set these works in Roman times and devoted tremendous attention to the exotic, luxurious surroundings. He defended his new Tolstoyan faith in "Polunoshchniki" (Night Owls; first published in *Vestnik Evropy* [The Herald of Europe], November–December 1891), about a conflict between Tolstoyans and the nationalistic, purportedly miracle-working priest John of Kronstadt, narrated by a woman reminiscent of Domna Platonovna.

In the last years of his life, already suffering from heart trouble, Leskov produced a few final bitter stories, depicting Russia as—in the title of "Zagon" (Cattlepen; first published in *Knizhki nedeli* [Booklets of the Week], November 1893)—a dark, dismal prison, maintained by the innocent benightedness of the poor and the willful ignorance of the upper classes. In "Zimnii den'" (A Winter's Day; first published in *Russkaia mysl'*, September 1894), a few Tolstoyans can do little to lighten the bleak atmosphere of a house full of self-serving voluptuaries. In his last years Leskov wrote two works that he could not publish during his lifetime: "Administrativnaia gratsiia" (Adminstrative Grace), about the authorities' manipulations of liberal society, which make it turn against its own best members, and "Zaiachii remiz" (The Rabbit Warren), a linguistic tour de force, combining Russian, Ukrainian, and Church Slavonic in the story of a petty official's paranoid hunt for radicals in a sleepy Ukrainian town, and his subsequent mental breakdown. Profoundly dissatisfied with the country he had so brilliantly depicted, Leskov died on 21 February 1895.

Bibliographies:

P. V. Bykov, *Bibliografiia sochinenii Nikolaia Leskova s nachala ego literaturnoi deiatel'nosti–1860 god po 1887 god (vkliuchitel'no)* (St. Petersburg, 1889);

Bykov, "Bibliografiia sochinenii N. S. Leskova za tridtsat' let (1860–1889)," in *Sobranie sochinenii N. S. Leskova* (St. Petersburg: A. S. Suvorin, 1890), X: i–xxv;

Inès Müller de Morogues, *L'oeuvre journalistique et littéraire de N. S. Leskov: Bibliographie* (New York: Peter Lang, 1984);

V. N. Sazhin, *N. S. Leskov: rukopisnoe nasledie: katalog* (Leningrad: Gos. publichnaia biblioteka im. M. E. Saltykova-Shchedrina, 1991).

Biographies:

Rostislav Ivanovich Sementkovsky, *N. S. Leskov. Kritiko-biograficheskii ocherk* (St. Petersburg, A. F. Marks, 1902);

A. I. Faresov, *Protiv techenii. N. S. Leskov. Ego zhizn', sochineniia, polemika i vospominaniia o nem* (St. Petersburg: M. Merkushev, 1904);

Andrei Leskov, *Zhizn' Nikolaia Leskova po ego lichnym, semeinym i nesemeinym zapisiam i pamiatiam* (Moscow: Gos. izd. khud. lit., 1954);

Leonid Petrovich Grossman, *Nikolai Semenovich Leskov* (Moscow: Znanie, 1956);

B. M. Drugov, *N. S. Leskov: Ocherk tvorchestva* (Moscow: Gos. izd. khud. lit., 1957);

Hugh McLean, *Nikolai Leskov: The Man and His Art* (Cambridge, Mass. & London: Harvard University Press, 1977);

Vladimir Semenov, *Nikolai Leskov–Vremia i knigi* (Moscow: Liubiteliam ros. slovesnosti, 1981).

References:

L. Anninsky, *Leskovskoe ozherelie* (Moscow: Kniga, 1982);

V. G. Bazanov, *Iz literaturnoi polemiki 60-kh godov* (Petrozavodsk: Gos. izd-vo Karelo-Finskoi SSR, 1941);

Walter Benjamin, "The Storyteller: Reflections on the Works of Nikolai Leskov," in *Illuminations: Essays and Reflections,* edited by Hannah Arendt, translated by Harry Zohn (New York: Schocken, 1969);

Viktor Bogdanov, ed., *V mire Leskova: sbornik statei* (Moscow: Sovetskii pisatel', 1983);

Boris Bukhshtab, "Ob istochnikakh 'Levshi' N. S. Leskova," *Russkaia literatura,* no. 1 (1964);

Danilo Cavaion, *N. S. Leskov: saggio critico* (Florence, Italy: G. C. Sansoni, 1974);

Cavaion and P. Cazzola, eds., *Leskoviana* (Bologna: Editrice CLUEB, 1982);

B. S. Dykhanova, *V zerkalakh ustnogo slova (Narodnoe samosoznanie i ego stilevoe voploshchenie v poetike N. S. Leskova)* (Voronezh: Izdatel'stvo voronezhskogo universiteta, 1994);

Boris M. Eikhenbaum, "N. L. Leskov (K 50-letiiu so dnia smerti)," in *O proze. Sbornik statei* (Leningrad: Khud. lit. 1969);

A. A. Gorelov, *N. S. Leskov i narodnaia kul'tura* (Leningrad: Nauka, 1988);

Maksim Gorky, "N. S. Leskov," in *Sobranie sochinenii v tridtsati tomakh* (Moscow: Gos. izd. khud. lit., 1953);

K. A. Lantz, *Nikolay Leskov* (Boston: Twayne, 1979);

Dmitrii S. Likhachev, *Literatura–real'nost'–literatura* (Leningrad: Sovetskii pisatel', 1984);

James Y. Muckle, *Nikolai Leskov and the "Spirit of Protestantism"* (Birmingham, U.K.: Department of Russian Language and Literature, University of Birmingham, 1978);

Inès Müller de Morogues, *"Le problème féminin" et les portraits de femmes dans l'oeuvre de Nikolaj Leskov* (New York: Peter Lang, 1991);

Gabriella Safran, *Rewriting the Jew: Assimilation Narratives in the Russian Empire* (Stanford, Cal.: Stanford University Press, 2000);

Irina Vladimirovna Stoliarova, *V poiskakh ideala: Tvorchestvo N. S. Leskova* (Leningrad: Izd-vo LGU, 1978);

Irma Pavlovna Viduetskaia, *Nikolai Semenovich Leskov* (Moscow: Znanie, 1979);

A. L. Volynsky, *N. S. Leskov* (St. Petersburg: Epokha, 1923);

Irmhild Christina Weinberg, "The Organic Worldview of Nikolaj Leskov," dissertation, Columbia University, 1996.

Papers:

Archives of Nikolai Semenovich Leskov's papers are located at the Institute of Russian Literature (IRLI, Pushkin House), the Russian State Historical Archive (RGIA, formerly TsGIA), and the Russian National Library (RNB), all in St. Petersburg; the Russian State Archive of Literature and Art (RGALI, formerly TsGALI) and the Russian State Library (RGB) in Moscow; and the Orel State Museum of I. S. Turgenev (OGMT) in Orel.

Dmitrii Narkisovich Mamin
(D. Sibiriak; also known as Mamin-Sibiriak)
(25 October 1852 – 2 November 1912)

Liubov' Minochkina
Cheliabinsk State University

(Translated by J. Alexander Ogden)

WORKS: *V vodovorote strastei,* as E. Tomsky (St. Petersburg, 1876);

Privalovskie milliony. Roman v 5-i chastiakh, in *Delo* (January–October 1883); (Moscow: D. Efimov & M. Kliukin, 1897); translated by V. Shneerson as *The Privalov Fortune* (Moscow: Foreign Language Publishing House, 1958);

Gornoe gnezdo. Roman, in *Otechestvennye zapiski,* nos. 1–4 (1884); (Moscow: I. A. Ponomarev, 1890);

Zhilka, in *Vestnik Evropy,* nos. 1–4 (1884); republished as *Dikoe schast'e. Roman* (St. Petersburg: Redaktsiia zhurnala *Zvezda,* 1896);

Na ulitse. Roman, in *Russkaia mysl',* nos. 3–8 (1886);

Zolotopromyshlenniki. Bytovaia khronika v 4-kh deistviiakh, in *Nabliudatel',* no. 10 (1887);

Imeninnik. Roman, in *Nabliudatel',* nos. 1–4 (1888);

Ural'skie rasskazy, 2 volumes (Moscow: I. A. Ponomarev, 1888, 1889);

Tri kontsa. Ural'skaia letopis', in *Russkaia mysl',* nos. 5–9 (1890); (St. Petersburg: O. Popova, 1895);

Zoloto. Roman, in *Severnyi vestnik,* nos. 1–6 (1892); (St. Petersburg, 1895);

Vesennie grozy. Roman v 3-kh chastiakh, in *Mir Bozhii,* nos. 1–10 (1893); (Moscow: D. Efimov, 1895);

Bez nazvaniia. Roman, in *Mir Bozhii,* nos. 1–10 (1894);

Cherty iz zhizni Pepko, in *Russkoe bogatstvo,* nos. 1–10 (1894); (Moscow: I. D. Sytin, 1896);

Detskie teni. Rasskazy (Moscow: Posrednik, 1894);

Sibirskie rasskazy (Moscow: V. V. Chicherin, 1895);

Khleb. Roman, in *Russkaia mysl',* nos. 1–8 (1895); (Moscow: Redaktsiia zhurnala *Russkaia mysl',* 1896);

Po novomu puti. Roman, in *Mir Bozhii,* nos. 1–9 (1896);

Brat'ia Gordeevy. Okhoniny brovi (Moscow: Biblioteka Russkoi mysli, 1896);

Dmitrii Narkisovich Mamin (D. Sibiriak)

Alenushkiny skazki (Moscow: I. N. Kushnerev, 1897); translated by Irim Zheleznova as *Tales for Alyonushka* (Moscow: Progress, 1978);

Sviatochnye rasskazy (St. Petersburg, 1898);

V doroge. Ocherki i rasskazy (Moscow: D. Efimov & M. Kliukin, 1898);

175

Legendy (St. Petersburg, 1898);

V glushi. Povesti i rasskazy (Moscow: D. Efimov & M. Kliukin, 1898);

Noktiurny (St. Petersburg, 1899);

Osennie list'ia. Ocherki i rasskazy (Moscow, 1899);

Rannie vskhody. Roman (St. Petersburg, 1899);

Padaiushchie zvezdy. Roman, in *Russkoe bogatstvo,* 1–8 (1899); (Moscow: M. V. Kliukin, 1900);

Obshchii liubimets publiki. Roman (St. Petersburg: "Izdatel'," 1899);

Malinovye gory (St. Petersburg, 1899);

Po Uralu. Rasskazy i ocherki (Moscow, 1900).

Collections: *Sobranie sochinenii,* 5 volumes (St. Petersburg, 1912–1913);

Polnoe sobranie sochinenii, 12 volumes (Petrograd: A. F. Marks, 1915–1917);

Sobranie sochinenii, 4 volumes (Moscow-Leningrad, 1927–1928);

Sobranie sochinenii, 12 volumes (Sverdlovsk, 1948–1951);

Sobranie sochinenii, 8 volumes (Moscow: Khudozhestvennaia literatura, 1953–1955);

Sobranie sochinenii, 6 volumes (Moscow, 1980–1981);

Izbrannye proizvedeniia, 2 volumes (Moscow, 1988).

Dmitrii Narkisovich Mamin, who wrote under the pseudonym D. Sibiriak, was the most significant writer from the region of the Ural mountains that separate European Russia from Siberia and a leading figure in late nineteenth-century Russian literature. His works were popular with both the general reading public and other writers. Author of fifteen novels and hundreds of stories, sketches, and tales, he was also an interesting journalist, finding his own themes and a distinctive voice. Accounts by many contemporaries attest to Mamin's important place in Russian literary life and the generally high regard in which contemporaries held his talent. In 1887 Vladimir Galaktionovich Korolenko wrote of Mamin's "striking store of artistic strength," his "clarity of mind," and his ability to characterize people "faithfully and forcefully." Nikolai Semenovich Leskov, attracted by the "freshness and immediacy of the writer's talent," was "ecstatic" over the novel *Zoloto* (Gold, 1892), and he gave the novel *Khleb* (Bread, 1895) a similarly high evaluation. Anton Pavlovich Chekhov announced that "positively wonderful things" could be found in Mamin's works and that in several stories Mamin had portrayed the common people just as well as Leo Tolstoy in *Khoziain i rabotnik* (Master and Man, 1895). Chekhov noted the integral and organic qualities of Mamin's heroes and their immediacy and freshness, saying, "His language is real." Maksim Gorky wrote, "Everywhere his talent is strong and bright."

Professional critics, however, did not immediately appreciate the innovations in Mamin's works, persistently characterizing him as a *"mestnyi bytopisatel'"* (chronicler of everyday regional life)–hence, his supposed lack of attention to intellectual truth-seekers (the traditional heroes of the Russian literary classics) and hence, too, his supposed distance from those classics. More recent researchers of Mamin's novelistic output have shown that in fact his naturalistic tendencies took literature in new directions; he made substantive innovations in the portrayal of the great masses of humanity and the psychology of social populations. Thus, he introduced fundamental changes to the Russian social-psychological novel, contributing significantly to Russian literature in the last decades of the nineteenth century; the little-studied naturalism of his works of the 1880s and 1890s is also interesting in its relationship to Emile Zola's naturalism. Mamin categorized himself as a writer of regional literature and explained much in his work by his blood ties to his native Urals. Others also noticed the strength of this connection; in the words of one contemporary, Mamin "was all, entirely, from the Urals, in his temperament, in his manner, in his perceptions, in his thinking . . . a thick-set, strong, and bold person, as if hewn from wood." Mamin's works, then, raise theoretical and practical questions about the relationship between *oblastnichestvo* (writing focused on local color) and innovation.

Dmitrii Narkisovich Mamin was born on 25 October 1852 into the family of a priest. His father, Narkis Matveevich Mamin, was a deeply honest, fair, and humane person, a democratic thinker in the spirit of his time. He held to strict principles of self-restraint, and he taught his son: "You are well-fed and clothed, and you are warm–everything else is just caprice." This modest man, who had a strong impact on his son's development, had a particular interest in education. Young Dmitrii's mother, Anna Semenovna, a deacon's daughter, also valued books. In her own notebooks she pondered whether her children would be "honest people, industrious, abstemious, and helpful to others." Mamin, noting the role of his family in his literary beginnings, thought that "in ways every one of us is the living outcome of our ancestors." Such views explain Mamin's interest, expressed in his novels, in biological heredity and, given his own background, in the history of the Russian clergy.

Mamin grew up in the Visimo-Shaitansky factory settlement, located in one of the most beautiful parts of the Urals. The "dear green mountains" surrounding the village, the fast-flowing rivers Shaitanka and Visim, and the particular customs of the Urals and their astonishing inhabitants all served as sources for the writer's works. The life of the Mamin family was inseparably tied to the life of the factory and his father's parishioners. From childhood Mamin learned about the lives and problems of the workers, and he absorbed the rich, figurative language of the folk. At first Mamin followed in his father's footsteps: he graduated from the Ekaterinburg ecclesiastical school and entered the Perm' seminary. Soon, however, he became exasperated with what he considered to be a dead, scholastic education, cut off from the interests of life. After four years at the seminary, Mamin, who had been studying on his own quite assiduously for some time, set off in August of 1872 for St. Petersburg and entered the Medico-Surgical Academy, one of the best educational institutions of the time. In outlook Mamin sympathized with the Populists, but at this point he had no time for "going to the people" to learn and to teach, as so many students were doing at the time. Rather, he immersed himself in writing, initially as a newspaper reporter. One of his early assignments was to report on the meetings of the scholarly societies in the capital.

At this time Mamin also began to write absorbing page-turners: stories about runaways, brigands, abusive bailiffs, and the inhabitants of secluded Old Believer hermitages. These works included the stories "Startsy" (The Elders, 1875), "Starik" (The Old Man, 1876), "V gorakh" (In the Mountains, 1876), "Krasnaia shapka" (The Red Hood, 1876), and others. All were based on real facts of life in factory towns, familiar to Mamin since his youth. Even in these first stories, which were published in the weekly journal *Syn otechestva* (Son of the Fatherland), Mamin showed himself to be an expert on folklore. In these stories, however, the devices of popular literature prevailed, as they did in his first novel, *V vodovorote strastei* (In the Whirlpool of Passions, 1876).

In 1877, as the result of a lingering pulmonary illness, Mamin broke off his studies and returned to the Urals. Another reason for the move was a change in his spiritual points of reference: he lost his faith in the exceptional importance of thought and advanced social ideas, and in their place he now desired a return to his native roots—to real life in the reinvigorating Russian countryside. The now adult Mamin came to grasp the "particular life of the Urals" anew, undertaking lengthy trips to Isim, Nizhnii Tagil, Ekaterinburg, and other places, and at one point traveling all the way to the steppes of Bashkiria to undergo a koumiss cure.

On 24 January 1878 Mamin's father died unexpectedly of pneumonia. Care for the family's welfare fell on Mamin's shoulders, and he worked to the point of exhaustion on his journalistic endeavors and on giving private lessons. Living in Ekaterinburg, he entered into a common-law marriage with Mariia Iakimovna Alekseeva, the former wife of the manager of the Verkhnesaldinskii factory. Alekseeva was one of the most educated women in the Urals, and she also introduced Mamin into the life of the local factory elite.

Mamin's second spate of literary attempts turned out to be unusually successful, bringing swift results in the publishing world. From January to October 1883 the journal *Delo* (The Cause) published his first significant work, the novel *Privalovskie milliony* (Privalov's Millions), and that same year in *Otechestvennye zapiski* (Notes of the Fatherland) Mikhail Evgrafovich Saltykov-Shchedrin published a group of Mamin's sketches, "Zolotukha" (Scrofula), informing his co-editor Grigorii Zakharovich Eliseev that these were "wonderful sketches about gold-mining in the style of Bret Harte." In these sketches, as in the cycles "S Urala" (From the Urals), "Ot Zaural'ia do Volgi" (From Beyond the Urals to the Volga), and "Ot Urala do Moskvy" (From the Urals to Moscow), written in the early 1880s, Mamin introduces lively and colorful material documenting daily life in the Urals. A filial love for his native land and a heightened sense of homeland are evident in his articles and sketches of the period. Mamin wrote to his brother Vladimir, "Homeland is our second mother, and all the more so a homeland like the Urals. Remember 'brother Antei' and his fellow heroes who, falling onto the damp earth, redoubled their might tenfold. This idea has great merit. The time of the cosmopolitans has passed; what's necessary is simply to be a person who doesn't forget his family, loves his homeland, and works for his fatherland." Mamin further emphasized his allegiance to his native Urals region by beginning to use the pseudonym "D. Sibiriak" (D. Siberian) in the early 1880s; he kept this pseudonym for the rest of his career.

The outline of the novel *Privalovskie milliony* changed several times. In an early variant, the work was to be a trilogy, "Kamennyi poias" (The Stone Belt); it was to feature the successive development of different types of Ural mill owners. Mamin planned to start with the first, hearty industrialists who had come from the working masses to lay the basis for the development of the Urals; these men had worked their way up through willpower, energy, and exceptional intelligence. Mamin then planned to move on to their degenerate heirs. He later rejected the idea of this epic trilogy, but the idea of the degeneration of the Ural industrialists remained central to the novel that eventually became *Privalovskie milliony*. Mamin based the life of Pavel Guliaev in the novel on facts from the biographies of the Ekaterinburg gold-hunters Anika Riazanov and Lev Rastorguev; unlike Guliaev, his son-in-law Aleksandr Privalov forgets his responsibilities after the death of his father-in-law and sinks into monstrous luxury, prodigality, and a life of scandals. Mamin explained such degradation as a consequence of the specific mining conditions in the Urals.

Д. Маминъ-Сибирякъ.

СИБИРСКIЕ РАЗСКАЗЫ.

СОДЕРЖАНIЕ:

1. Сибирскіе орлы. — 2. Главный баринъ. — 3. Звѣрство. — 4. На перевалѣ. — 5. Не у дѣлъ. — 6. Подснѣжникъ. — 7. Кладъ. — 8. Морокъ. — 9. Пріисковый мальчикъ. — 10. Крестникъ. — 11. Удивленный человѣкъ. — 12. Мизгирь.

Типографія В. В. Чичерина.
прот. Марьиной сл., за Калера-Коллеж. вал., соб. д., 2 от. Моск. уѣзда
1895.

Title page for Sibirskie rasskazy *(Siberian Stories), in which Mamin collected some of his short fiction about life in the Ural Mountains*

Government circles protected the mine owners, investing them with privileges and a monopolistic freedom from competition. Thus, they facilitated the development of parasitism among the owners, as they benefited from the unremunerated labor of the workers.

The theme of bad heredity continues in the fate of Aleksandr's son Sergei Privalov, who finds himself the center of attention of the inhabitants of Uzel, who have noticed what kind of people the descendants of the Privalov-Guliaev stock are. But the hero's social and genetic inheritance is not one-sided. He exhibits honesty, generosity, a popular instinct for good, and a moral sense developed by a university education.

Sergei is preoccupied with a high-minded idea—to return his debt to the workers, whose labor created the mills, and to the Bashkirs, whose land had been taken for the plants through deceitful means. The trustees Liakhovsky and Polovodtsov turn out to be stronger than Privalov, using all means at their disposal, including their inherited vices of destructive passion and sen-

suality, to fight for the millions at stake. Polovodtsov wagers the honor of his wife, Antonida Polovodtsova, and of his favorite girl, Zosia Liakhovskaia. In this company Sergei Privalov sinks lower and lower. But Mamin has his own way of viewing and conforming to the laws of genetics. I. A. Dergachev, one of the most significant scholars of Mamin's works, notes that "In the theme of 'inheritance' the writer goes beyond the bounds of biological conceptions. More important for him is the 'compressed experience of generations,' finding expression in the entire conduct of a person—the social experience." Inherited features are closely linked to the development on a national scale of the mining and metallurgical operations in the Urals. Privalov himself perceives this "system of parasitism" that has existed for one hundred and fifty years.

Another scholar, G. K. Shchennikov, suggests that the novel is not only about the degeneration of the exploiters but also about the quick degradation of people who represent deeply rooted Russian character traits. Mamin raised an acute problem still relevant today—the question of whether the good qualities of a nation can be perverted in a relatively short historical period under the influence of unnatural systems of economic management. Mamin's answer is clear not only in Sergei Privalov's fate but also in the general picture of widespread exploitation, adventurism, venality, and moral decay that the novel presents. As Dergachev notes, the personality of Mamin's hero is revealed "as a result of diverse forces that act on it, from physical nature and inherited characteristics to the most general social processes in the lives of the people. The individual is presented neither in the capacity of a self-conceited 'shaper of history' nor in the capacity of a tragically pitiful unit, crushed by hostile circumstances."

In this novel Mamin also acquainted his readers with a broad spectrum of provincial society in the Urals—colorful industrialists of the old generation such as Bakharev, who is caught up in his activities and feels himself responsible for the development of what he had begun; the successful gold-hunter Danila Shelekhov; the lawyer and virtuoso swindler Nikolai Verevkin; and the "lionesses" of local society. To these latter, Mamin juxtaposes the Bakharev household, with the stable Old-Believer life of its women and its democratically oriented young people. Nadezhda, the daughter of the "founder" Bakharev, is endowed with a moral sense as pure as that of the women in the novels of Ivan Sergeevich Turgenev. Dreaming of doing practical good deeds, she "goes to the people" and, breaking relations with her family, becomes a schoolteacher.

Mamin's next novel, *Gornoe gnezdo* (A Mountain Nest, 1884) has a sharply satiric style quite different from that of Mamin's other works. Meditating on the twenty years of the development of Russia since the reforms of the early 1860s, the writer showed that, since the overthrow of serfdom, the statutes regulating the relations between workers and their factories had limited the rights of workers and created a system of total domination by the administration. The "mountain nest" of the title refers to these owners, overseers, and bureaucrats—the "gentry," as the locals call them. To them are juxtaposed the common people—the factory artisans, whose interests Mamin sees as the interests of the nation as a whole. The common people await the arrival of their master, the mill owner Laptev, who lives abroad. The plot unfolds along the lines of Nikolai Alekseevich Nekrasov's "Zabytaia derevnia" (A Forgotten Village, 1855), lines from which Mamin takes for an epigraph: "Here comes the master, / The master will settle things between us."

The end of the novel makes clear that this hope has been a utopian one. Laptev is a degenerate type, absolutely indifferent to his business affairs, the factories, and the workers. His interests are food, women, and entertainment. He has no strength of will, and he is ruled by his retinue, who compete for a leading position in the factory management. This competition is shown as a series of absurd, masquerade-like episodes. Meanwhile, no one pays any heed to the interests of the workers.

In his portrayals of the common people, Mamin does not hide ingrained habits, such as their blind faith in the master, but at the same time he shows the workers to be strong and skillful masters of their iron-working trade. Dergachev has noted that the common people's point of view, appearing in laughter and in comic evaluations of other characters, ironically illuminates the squabbles of those higher up. Thus, for example, the artisans acidly give their opinion of the Scottish kilt worn by Laptev: "It's well-known that laws aren't written for the masters" (playing on the folk saying "laws aren't written for fools").

In the mid 1880s Mamin, still living in Ekaterinburg, was elected to the city council; during this period he also traveled regularly around the Urals, gathering material for his stories. All of his earnings came from literary work; as he wrote to his mother in a letter dated 30 November 1885, "Turgenev reworked all his articles nine times, and I barely have time to write a rough draft; if I rework something twice I am horrified at the luxury."

Discussing his *Ural'skie rasskazy* (Ural Stories), published in a two-volume edition in 1888 and 1889, Mamin wrote, "This is the best that I have." The stories focus on nature and on the varied types of prospectors, artisans, free hunters, vagabonds (or *letnye* [fliers], as they are called in the Urals), tramps, actors, and priests.

Evident again is Mamin's love for his native land, about which he liked to repeat words heard in his childhood: "The Urals, the Urals! A stone body, a fiery heart!" With the publication of these stories Mamin established himself definitively, finding recognition among critics and readers. Contemporaries were struck by his astonishing knowledge of the life, labors, and mores of the socially varied population of the Urals. They also noted Mamin's ability to link the personality of workers and the character of their work and to incorporate details from daily life into a folkloric expression of the common people's worldview, psychology, emotions, and aesthetic conceptions.

Such features give a reader of *Ural'skie rasskazy* a sense of the epic foundation of life. Mamin uses folkloric elements to include the working man in a national and folk whole. Readers were attracted by Mamin's ability to sculpt personalities plastically, in relief, drawing them in dramatic and tragic collisions. The writer himself said, "You can't avoid strong character types here; take your brush and paint. . . . If life in the capitals takes away people's individuality and bleaches away all color, then as far as character types are concerned the Urals are an unquenchable source of something miraculous and incredible that is created all around." Thus, in his story "Boitsy" (Fighters) Mamin portrays the colorful rafter and barge-hauler Savka. At first he is presented as an unprepossessing drunkard, a "hopeless case," but during a timber-rafting session along the river Chusovaia he is transfigured, revealing willpower, character, practicality, energy, artistry in his work, talent, and inspiration. Other such original figures from the common people include gold-searchers ("Zolotukha"), vagabonds escaped from hard labor, tramps ("Bashka"), and hunters ("Na shikhane" [On the Summit] and "Groza" [The Storm]).

Scholars have more than once noted a connection between *Ural'skie rasskazy* and Turgenev's *Zapiski okhotnika* (A Hunter's Sketches, 1847–1851), finding similarities in the ways the stories are unified through the image of the narrator, in the means and style of narration, and in the authors' descriptions of scenery. The difference between the two works lies in Mamin's fundamentally democratic nature. In social status he is closer to the common people than Turgenev; this fact explains the absence of idealization of the people and of a search for "holy people" in the folk, such as wanderers to holy places or folk philosophers. Reality itself is most important for the storyteller—the life experience of his heroes gathered through their work and through the practice of everyday life.

Over the years Mamin became increasingly drawn to novels dedicated to broad social processes as reflected in the fate, not of an exceptional individual, but of a whole multifaceted environment. The process of history, and in particular a socially significant occurrence at a particular moment of crisis, lies at the basis of Mamin's Urals cycle of novels, *Tri kontsa. Ural'skaia letopis'* (Three Ends: A Urals Chronicle, 1890), *Zoloto,* and *Khleb.* In *Tri kontsa,* this historical process is seen in the transition from serfdom to capitalism; in *Zoloto* it is seen in the transition to a "privately owned gold industry," enabling the development of individual interests in private property; and in *Khleb* it is in the organization of the All-Russian grain market in the region beyond the Urals and the accompanying new phenomena characteristic of capitalism—the organization of a market, a bank, and competition.

Focusing his attention on the chronology of historical events, Mamin chooses the moment that is decisive in determining the direction of life into the future, and he times his opening of the novel to coincide with it. In *Tri kontsa* this moment is the formal announcement of "freedom," the consequences of which are then traced. In *Zoloto* it is the news of the replacement of State mines with "free rents," bringing with it the formation of artels of "equals" and the development of interests in private property and the pursuit of the "filthy kopek." In *Khleb* it is the quick invasion of capital together with the appearance of the merchant Kolobov, followed by shrewd businessmen of the new breed. The opening is given meaning in the speeches of Kolobov to his old friend, the merchant Lukovnikov. Kolobov says that he has come not only to look for a bride for his son Galaktion, but also to "get married" himself by the river Kliuchevaia: "I'm throwing aside the factories and bringing my whole family to the Kliuchevaia. . . . Ah, what a wonderful place! . . . Later I'll put up a little windmill." Returning from his meeting with Lukovnikov along Bread Street, Kolobov thinks about "how everything here will be different in a few years." A similar situation—a family's move to a new place and its subsequent disintegration—is portrayed in Gorky's novel *Delo Artamonovykh* (The Artamonov Affair, 1925).

The novel *Tri kontsa* chronicles the events of ten post-reform years. As always in Mamin's writing, the origins of the reform are not clear; instead, emphasis is placed on the destructive forces at work. In the course of the novel the complete annihilation and impoverishment of the workers takes place. The author traces this phenomenon in the fates of his heroes and in emotional pictures of the migration of entire settlements (the *kontsy,* or "ends," of the title)—Samosadka, Pen'kovka, and Kerzhatsky konets. Mamin portrays representatives of various social groups, from the member of the intelligentsia who has lived abroad (Mukhin) to the member of a religious sect (Konon) and serf brigands. As in a psychological

novel, the heroes' fates (in this case the fates of Mukhin and his daughter) are important throughout *Tri kontsa,* but their fates do not exhaust the complex movement of the social and economic world portrayed in the novel. Significantly, Mamin portrays a change in types of factory managers: the manager Luka Nazarych, a peasant and "petty old tyrant" who under serfdom squeezed "the whole mining region in an iron vice," is replaced by Golikovsky, a "shrewd mine operator of the new type" and a member of the middle-class intelligentsia.

The main focus of the writer's attention in *Tri kontsa,* however, is on the working masses and their fate. They, too, are not homogeneous in the degree of their involvement in the various historical processes at work. The movement of time also brings different social types of women—from the cook Domnushka to Annushka, the mischievous wife of a soldier, and from various types of factory women and Old Believers to the *intelligentka* Niurochka Mukhina. The "environment" of secondary characters that constitutes the "background" for the action in the novels of Turgenev and Tolstoy comes to the fore in Mamin's novels, and secondary figures attain significance as "typical" elements of the complex mechanism of reality.

In *Tri kontsa,* Mamin presents three ethnic groups: settlers from the Tula Province ("great Russians"), settlers from the Chernigov Province ("khokhly," slang for Ukrainians), and the native Ural population—the *kerzhaki* (the name given to the Old Believer schismatics living in the Urals). In the novel, Mamin explores the obliteration of territorial isolation, ethnographic boundaries, and religious differences. This process is revealed mostly through the history of interactions among several families from different *kontsy.* "Our *kontsy* are all mixed up," concludes the character Tais'ia, telling of the new ties between villages. In writing about the dissolution of ethnographic boundaries, Mamin was depicting a process he believed was taking place in his own homeland. After the czar's manifesto emancipating the serfs is read, a mass migration begins, the result of an "age-old yearning for one's own land," but at the same time people become more *self*-conscious, not wanting to submit to the head of a clan or large family. The naturalistic tendencies evident here and elsewhere in the novels of Mamin are related to particular features of Fedor Mikhailovich Reshetnikov's "folk realism" and to the sociological realism of Saltykov-Shchedrin.

In the novel *Zoloto,* Mamin gives a similar faction-by-faction analysis of the mine population—from the manager and member of the intelligentsia Karachunsky to the "mine girl" Oksa. The prospectors themselves are varied, reflecting whole epochs of Urals mining operations—Mina Kleimeny, an old hard-laborer;

Rodion Potapych Zykov, an experienced mine foreman who went through training back in the days of serfdom; the "small proprietor" Kishkin, who has grown rich under the newly developing middle-class social order; and those who in the post-reform period use illegal methods to buy up "State gold" for a higher price than is paid by the company, such as the gold-buyers Iastrebov and Petr Vasil'ich, son of the old woman Luker'ia. The social composition of the women is also diverse—from those "enslaved to housework" to those working in the mines. As in *Tri kontsa,* the reader also encounters a tavern keeper, a priest, and Old Believers.

Zoloto, using the story of the large family of the mine foreman Rodion Potapych Zykov, traces the decline of patriarchal moral concepts and of stable family ties and customs under the influence of the seductive power of gold. As the result of freedom, workers who have been attached to State industries all their lives receive the right to mine gold themselves at the Kedrov dacha, and all are seized by the excitement of quick profits. Even the righteous old woman Luker'ia becomes greedy—bossing her granddaughters, whom she sees as potential matches for the rich mine folk. The reckoning that takes place among associates is a bloody one. Mamin shows, however, that the soul cannot become reconciled to such a perversion of nature: he depicts the suicide and derangement of people in the final part of the novel. The worker Matiushka, murderer of three others, takes his own life. The old mine foreman Rodion Zykov, seeing the decline in morals as a result of the free mining of gold, fills the mineshaft with water where a vein rich in gold had been found and laughs "with an already insane laugh." The theme of gold fever reaches a breaking point for the nation as a whole. Tracing the succession of types of merchants in several generations of the middle-class Kolobov family, Mamin depicts the old man Kolobov as a pioneer, representing "capitalism in its early years," while his son Galaktion is a businessman of the new type, creating a fortune out of nothing.

In *Khleb,* monopolistic capital invades the grain-growing region beyond the Urals. The characters in the foreground include grain traders, vintners, and banking tycoons. Mamin shows how the local patriarchal merchant class (Malygin, Lukovnikov, and others) sinks into ruin, supplanted by shrewd businessmen of the new type (Stabrovsky, Shtoff, and Echkin). Mamin also portrays a progression of the intelligentsia in the novel, from the *kulak* lawyer Myshnikov to the new intelligentsia, represented by the teacher Kharchenko and Usten'ka Lukovnikov.

The plot of *Khleb* investigates the whole banking mechanism in detail, showing all sides of its functioning. Beginning their industrial activity, the shrewd new businessmen first clamor for the opening of a bank. Mamin shows that the emergence of the bank is a direct consequence of the growth of industry and the middle class in the region. In the grain business in particular huge sums are moved about, and desperate competition runs rampant. "Zapol'e funds are moved around wholesale in the grain exchange, and it has become impossible for the average merchant to exist without credit." The writer reveals the all-encompassing influence of the bank on the lives of the most varied social groups and individuals, showing how the activity of the Trans-Ural Commercial Bank affects the economic life of all the citizens of Zapol'e: a whole range of new enterprises open, and the utter ruin of small-scale millers, such as Kolobov, begins. The bank only helps those firms whose affairs are going successfully, such as Prokhorov. "Its force is huge, inexhaustible," the clerk Zamaraev says of the bank to the miller Ermilych; "It takes everyone into its clutches, sure as death."

Competition leads to the fabulous enrichment of some at the expense of others, and Mamin shows how the local government itself is transformed into an arm of the Trans-Ural Commercial Bank. "Money gave power," writes Mamin in the novel, "and of this [the people of] Zapol'e became more and more convinced—specifically money in an organized form, like some kind of army. Earlier there had been simply 'fat cats' whose influence did not cross the boundaries of a tight circle of their close associates and buyers, while now capital, passing through the furnace of the bank, has formed itself into some kind of elemental force, crushing everything in its path."

Mamin's plot investigates the effects of money on people's fates; he was one of the first in Russian literature to document these sociological changes of the post-reform period. A. Nalimov, writing about the novel *Khleb,* states that "often his picturesque documents are valuable precisely from a sociological perspective." Mamin's fellow writer Pavel Vladimirovich Zasodimsky wrote admiringly about this feature of the novels of his time: " . . . the contemporary novel in many of its representations outpaced political economy and sociology, feeding them a mass of laws that had not yet entered into the bounds of science." He continues, "Shchedrin and Uspensky, Mamin-Sibiriak and Karonin did more to clarify the essence of the economic structure of society than did the [theories of] political economy predominating at that time."

Mamin's three novels about society in the Urals attracted widespread critical attention and often provoked a comparison to the works of Emile Zola. Mamin's "Zolaism" cannot be reduced to the use of the motif of biological inheritance as found in *Privalovskie milliony.* Mamin, like Zola, concentrates attention on "a certain social community" and "not on one central hero." Following Zola's dictates, Mamin for years collected and studied the materials and documents on which he based his novels, striving for an almost scientific precision in the description of workers, the processes of production, and the machinations of the stock markets. Like Zola, Mamin investigated the relationships between people and "social-economic organisms." His analysis of the social forces at work in his trilogy of Urals novels can be compared to Zola's Rougon-Macquart cycle, which includes such novels as *Le ventre de Paris* (The Belly of Paris, 1874), *Germinal* (1885), and *L'Argent* (Money, 1891).

On the basis of his social novels Mamin can also be compared to Petr Dmitrievich Boborykin, who in fact often consciously followed the ideas of Zola. Boborykin and Mamin reflect different forms of processes taking place in Russian reality in the 1870s–1890s. Boborykin knew St. Petersburg and Moscow, the centers and citadels of the nation's capitalism, and he observed the rise of the Russian middle class, formed on the European model. Mamin was utterly rooted in the Urals, where the processes of capitalist development took place under conditions of the preservation of many forms of pre-Emancipation economics and their consequent social relations. The writers not only observed different processes, but they also saw and understood them differently, resorting to dissimilar artistic forms. While Mamin, like Zola, investigates the mechanisms of the action of the market and bank, as well as the capitalization of social relations, in Boborykin's novels the socio-economic process remains beyond the bounds of the work, and the hero or heroes only talk about it. Thus, in Boborykin's novel *Kitai-gorod* (1883, named for the merchant section of Moscow), which deals with the birth of the Russian cultured middle class in the 1870s, the heroes only make proclamations about the place and role of the merchant class, which already occupies a dominant place in Russian life. Mamin, on the contrary, uses concrete scenes, situations, and images to show the omnipotence of capital, creating situations that force the reader to draw conclusions; he directs the reader's attention toward the complexity and, at the same time, the logic of social development.

Some critics have noted the epic tone of Mamin's novels: private life in his novels is connected with epic folk memory, as expressed in the folkloric elements of the novel. Folk sayings, which often give a commonsense evaluation of socio-economic events, take what is depicted beyond the bounds of the immediate, contemporary world into the world of folk epic. Epic roots also determine the distinctness of Mamin's vivid and colorful heroes, even though the author concentrates his attention on the environment and not on personalities themselves.

Even as Mamin's Urals novels were attracting a wide reading audience, events in his personal life created a scandal in Ekaterinburg society. In 1890 a traveling actress, Mariia Moritsovna Abramova, attracted his attention while she was on tour in Ekaterinburg, and Mamin fell deeply in love with her, divorcing his wife and marrying Abramova in January of 1891. The couple soon moved to St. Petersburg, where Mamin began to work for several of the leading periodicals.

Cherty iz zhizni Pepko (Features from the Life of Pepko), one of Mamin's most interesting and original novels, was serialized in *Russkoe bogatstvo* (Russian Wealth) in 1894. The work was accorded wide recognition by Mamin's contemporaries. This novel was largely autobiographical, but its focus was not on the individual and the individual experience (as in, for example, Leo Tolstoy's trilogy *Detstvo* [Childhood, 1852], *Otrochestvo* [Boyhood, 1854], and *Iunost'* [Youth, 1857]), but rather on general laws of people's youth in a given circle. The narrator of the novel, Vasilii Ivanovich Popov, lays out the story of his youth and that of his friend Agafon Pavlovich, also surnamed Popov, who has the nickname Pepko.

Mamin also devoted considerable energy to writing stories and tales for children. The stories were tremendously popular, and during his lifetime Mamin became one of the most famous and best-loved children's writers of Russia. He began to write for his daughter Alenushka, born to Abramova in March of 1892. One day after giving birth, Abramova died, leaving Mamin inconsolable. Only his concern for Alenushka and the need to look after her saved him. Thus, his famous *Alenushkiny skazki* (Tales for Alenushka, 1897) came into being.

Mamin's children's stories draw on a tradition of Russian literary fairy tales leading back to Pushkin and appropriating many of the features of folktales. In *Alenushkiny skazki* (as, for example, "Lesnaia skazka" [A Forest Tale] and "Svetliachki" [Fireflies]), there are none of the usual traditional fantastic elements, fanciful and far-fetched images, characters, and objects associated with fairy tales. Events are transported instead into the sphere of everyday reality: real forests, bogs, streams, henhouses, and cottages of the Urals. The fairy-tale heroes are normal animals, birds, insects, and fish, but Mamin gives them human features. The stories exhibit a lovingly poetic relationship with nature.

Mamin does use traditional fairy-tale images of animals, such as the cowardly and boastful hare, the clumsy bear, and the stupid wolf, but their characteristics are fleshed out psychologically and, unlike in the folkloric fairy tale, they take on real, concrete details of daily life. Another idiosyncrasy of the writer's fairy-tale images is a skillful combination of traditional features with natural physiological attributes—a supple, precise description of the conduct, movement, and habits of beasts, birds, and fish. Furthermore, the human features of the beasts and birds of the *Alenushkiny skazki* are specifically those of children. In "Skazka pro khrabrogo Zaitsa-dlinnye ushi-kosye glaza-korotkii khvost" (The Tale of the Brave Hare Long-Ears-Slant-Eyes-Short-Tail), for example, the conduct of the cowardly Hare and the childlike intonations of his speech sound much like a child boasting without restraint: "'I'm not afraid of anybody!,' he cried to the entire forest. 'I'm not at all scared, and that's that. . . . I'm not afraid of the wolf, or the fox, or the bear—not of anyone!'"

In a letter dated 11 February 1893 Mamin wrote, "I now write first and foremost about children, and my Alenushka serves as a living model." Often, speaking animals, birds, and insects conduct themselves like children. Childlike in this way are the carefree, happy, and naively egotistical Koziavochka (Buglet), introducing herself to the world, and the boastful Komar Komarovich (Mosquito Mosquitovich). Direct, childlike relations link Vorobei Vorob'evich (Sparrow Sparrovich) and Ersh Ershovich (Spikey Spikeson), who steal each other's loot and conduct naive arguments about whether it is better to live in the river or on the roof.

Another cycle for children, collected in *Detskie teni* (Children's Shadows, 1894), presents stories about gold-seekers, raftsmen, and old hunters who live as wardens at fishing camps or in remote forest hamlets. These include "Zimov'e na Studenoi" (Winter Quarters on the Studenaia), "Emelia-okhotnik" (Emelia the Hunter), "Priemysh" (The Foster-Child), "Seraia Sheika" (Grey-Neck), "Vol'nyi chelovek Iashka" (Iashka the Freeman), and "Bogach i Eremka" (The Rich Man and Eremka). The people Mamin presents have not had easy lives. Living in nature, they are left alone with the woods and river for months at a time. They preserve a noble humanity, goodness, wisdom, and poetic quality, and they strongly feel the harmony of nature and the fatal consequences of breaking natural laws. Such heroes and such intimately simple stories about them had not previously existed in Russian children's literature.

Among Mamin's children's stories are also works with a sharply social content, such as the story "Pod zemlei" (Under the Earth), in which the prospector Rukobitov along with his young son Mikhalko sets off on Christmas Eve for a dangerous, illegal gold-mining expedition. In the thick of work a mine foreman scares them off, and Mikhalko spends the whole night at the base of the mineshaft until Grandmother Denisikha gets him out. She goes in despair directly to the engi-

Mamin's grave in Volkov Cemetery, St. Petersburg (photograph by Judith E. Kalb)

neer in the master's house, where children decked in their holiday finery are playing around the Christmas tree. The children in these stories live the hard life of their fathers and therefore grow up early. Mamin depicts this life with both sadness and humor. One Urals newspaper aptly noted that Mamin was "close to the soul of the people and the soul of children."

At the turn of the century Mamin grew close to the major writers of the new generation—Chekhov, Alexsandr Ivanovich Kuprin, Gorky, and Ivan Alekseevich Bunin—all of whom valued his works highly. During his final years the writer was seriously ill. On 26 October 1912 the anniversary of his forty years of literary activity was celebrated, but Mamin could barely recognize the well-wishers who came to congratulate him, and a week later, on 2 November, he died. In a letter sent for the jubilee and signed by many émigrés, Gorky wrote, "When a writer deeply feels his blood tie to the people this gives him beauty and strength. All your life you have felt that creative link and have shown it wonderfully in your books, having opened up a whole region of Russian life that before you was unknown to us. Your native land has something to thank you for, our friend and teacher."

References:

E. A. Bogoliubov, *Tvorchestvo D. N. Mamina-Sibiriaka. Vyp. 1* (Perm', 1944);

I. A. Dergachev, "D. N. Mamin-Sibiriak i narodnichestvo 90-kh godov," *Russkaia literatura 1870–1890-kh godov,* Sb. 2 (Sverdlovsk: Ural. un-t, 1969);

Dergachev, "D. N. Mamin-Sibiriak v istorii russkogo romana," *Russkaia literatura 1870–1890-kh godov,* Sb. 6 (Sverdlovsk: Ural. un-t, 1974);

Dergachev, "Gleb Uspensky i Mamin-Sibiriak," *Russkaia literatura 1870–1890-kh godov,* Sb. 8 (Sverdlovsk: Ural. un-t, 1978);

Dergachev, *Mamin-Sibiriak. Lichnost'. Tvorchestvo,* second edition (Sverdlovsk, 1981);

Dergachev, "Peizazh D. N. Mamina-Sibiriaka: shkola, struktura, funktsiia," *D. N. Mamin-Sibiriak–khudozhnik. Sbornik nauchnykh trudov* (Sverdlovsk: Ural. un-t, 1989);

Dergachev, "Zhanr legendy v tvorchestve D. N. Mamina-Sibiriaka i puti razvitiia russkoi literatury," *Russkaia literatura 1870–1890-kh godov,* Sb. 5 (Sverdlovsk: Ural. un-t, 1979);

M. Kitainik, *D. N. Mamin-Sibiriak i narodnoe tvorchestvo* (Sverdlovsk: Sverdlovskoe Kn. Izd-vo, 1955);

N. Kremianskaia, *D. N. Mamin-Sibiriak kak detskii pisatel'* (Sverdlovsk: Oblgiz, 1952);

A. I. Lazarev, "Fol'klorizm kak khudozhestvennyi printsip D. N. Mamina-Sibiriaka," *D. N. Mamin-Sibiriak–khudozhnik. Sbornik nauchnykh trudov* (Sverdlovsk: Ural. un-t, 1989);

L. I. Minochkina, "Geroi sotsial'nykh romanov D. N. Mamina-Sibiriaka 'Tri kontsa,' 'Zoloto,' 'Khleb,'" *Russkaia literatura 1870–1890-kh godov* (Sverdlovsk: Ural. un-t, 1983);

Minochkina, "Mamin-Sibiriak i Boborykin: K voprosu o tipologii realizma," *Russkaia literatura 1870–1890-kh godov* (Sverdlovsk: Ural. un-t, 1981);

Minochkina, "Psikhologizm i sotsial'naia etika v romanakh D. N. Mamina-Sibiriaka 'Tri kontsa,' 'Zoloto,' 'Khleb,'" *Russkaia literatura 1870–1890-kh godov* (Sverdlovsk: Ural. un-t, 1984);

Minochkina, *Sotsial'nyi roman D. N. Mamina-Sibiriaka ("Tri kontsa," "Zoloto," "Khleb") v istorii russkogo romana 90-x godov XIX veka: Uch. posob. po spetskursu* (Cheliabinsk, 1988);

Minochkina, "Stilisticheskoe vyrazhenie epicheskogo nachala v sotsial'nykh romanakh D. N. Mamina-Sibiriaka," *Russkaia literatura 1870–1890-kh godov* (Sverdlovsk: Ural. un-t, 1979);

Minochkina, "Tipologiia form povestvovaniia v romanakh D. N. Mamina-Sibiriaka 90-kh godov," *Problemy tipologii literaturnogo protsessa* (Perm': Permskii gos. un-t, 1985);

G. K. Shchennikov, "D. N. Mamin-Sibiriak," *Literatura Urala. Ocherki i portrety: Kniga dlia uchitelia* (Ekaterinburg: Izd-vo Ural'skogo un-ta, 1998);

Shchennikov, "Modifikatsiia izvestnykh literaturnykh tipov v 'Ural'skikh rasskazakh' D. N. Mamina-Sibiriaka," *D. N. Mamin-Sibiriak–khudozhnik. Sbornik nauchnykh trudov* (Sverdlovsk: Ural. un-t, 1989);

Shchennikov, "Naturalizm sotsial'nogo romana D. N. Mamina-Sibiriaka," *Vestnik Cheliabinskogo gosudarstvennogo universiteta,* series 2, no. 1 (Filologiia, 1996);

V. I. Udalov, "Printsipy dramaturgii D. N. Mamina-Sibiriaka," *Russkaia literatura 1870–1890-kh godov,* Sb. 6 (Sverdlovsk: Ural. un-t, 1974);

B. Udintsev, *Fol'klor v zapisnykh knizhkakh D. N. Mamina-Sibiriaka* (Sverdlovsk: Sred.-Ural. kn. izd-vo, 1966).

Papers:

Dmitrii Narkisovich Mamin's papers can be found in the Russian State Archive of Literature and Art (RGALI, formerly TsGALI), the Russian State Library (RGB, formerly the Lenin Library), and the Sverdlovsk Literary Museum.

Anastasiia Iakovlevna Marchenko
(T. Ch., A. Temrizov)
(1830 – 1880)

Mary F. Zirin

WORKS: *Putevye zametki*, as T. Ch. (Odessa: K. I. Totti, 1847; expanded edition, 2 volumes, 1849);

Ternistyi put'. Roman, as T. Ch., in *Otechestvennye zapiski*, no. 10 (1849): 133–192;

Dina. Roman, as T. Ch., in *Otechestvennye zapiski*, no. 2 (1853): 1–76; no. 3 (1853): 215–256; no. 4 (1853): 1–120;

Umnaia zhenshchina. Povest', as T. Ch., in *Biblioteka dlia chteniia*, no. 10 (1853): 71–132; no. 11 (1853): 1–98;

Vokrug da okolo. Povest', in *Otechestvennye zapiski*, 6 (1855): 357–416; no. 7 (1855): 5–70;

Gory. Povest', in *Otechestvennye zapiski*, no. 5 (1856): 61–162;

Na pokhode. Sovremennaia povest', in *Russkii vestnik*, no. 17 (1857): 77–128; no. 18 (1857): 344–394;

Myl'nye puzyri. Roman, 3 volumes (St. Petersburg: Izd. A. Smirdina, 1858);

Salamandra. Povest', in *Otechestvennye zapiski*, no. 9 (1859): 1–98;

Moi geroi i geroini, as M-r-o (Moscow: [Tip.] Razvlechenie, 1861);

Razluchniki. Roman, as A. Temrizov (St. Petersburg: Tip. D-ra M. Khana, 1869).

SELECTED PERIODICAL PUBLICATIONS:
"Pozdno. Povest'," in *Sovremennik*, no. 4 (1848): 77–130;
"Teni proshlogo. Povest'," in *Otechestvennye zapiski*, no. 5 (1850): 1–64;
"Serdtse s peregorodkami. Rasskaz," in *Biblioteka dlia chteniia*, no. 1 (1853): 81–104.

In 1847 Anastasiia Iakovlevna Marchenko's *Putevye zametki* (Travel Notes) heralded a generation of Russian women authors—among the most prominent were Nadezhda Dmitrievna Khvoshchinskaia (V. Krestovsky), Avdot'ia Iakovlevna Panaeva, and Evgeniia Tur—who were to transform fiction writing into a viable profession for their sex. The ecstatic reception that critics gave the book—two *povesti* (novellas or long stories)

Anastasiia Iakovlevna Marchenko (T. Ch., A. Temrizov)

signed T. Ch. and clearly the work of a woman—must have encouraged other aspiring writers and especially those who, like Marchenko, lived in the provinces.

Marchenko's career in Russian literature has been obscured by her leading what she called in *Razluchniki* (Homewreckers—literally, separators, 1869) a "dualistic life" as private woman and public writer. While she was serious about her craft, she veered between anonymity (adopting the initials T. Ch. for early works) and an evident desire for recognition for

185

fiction published under her own name (A. Marchenko) between 1855 and 1859. *Razluchniki,* her last novel, appeared under a male pen name, A. Temrizov. She used other initials (A. M., M., and T. Z.) for minor pieces. Marchenko has also been identified as the author of six stories published as *Moi geroi i geroini* (My Heroes and Heroines) under the pseudonym M-r-o by the weekly illustrated magazine *Razvlechenie* (Entertainment) in 1861, as well as the story "Zagadochnyi gost'" (The Mysterious Guest) and many sketches and verses that appeared under the same pen name in that magazine in the 1870s. Her 1853 "Serdtse s peregorodkami" (A Heart with Partitions), a light tale about a topic she took seriously (men's penchant for dispersing love frivolously), and humorous passages in her more serious fiction demonstrate that she was a capable author of the formulaic pieces in which *Razvlechenie* specialized. Those late works, however, belong to an evolving school of popular writings for lower middle-class urban readers and are not discussed in this essay.

In a biographical sketch published in 1889, Ekaterina Nekrasova describes Marchenko as a talented "representative . . . of a George-Sandian tendency" in Russian literature, but Marchenko portrays situations and settings from her own life with a specificity that rises above foreign models. Her protagonists are Russianized Ukrainian gentry, most of whom live on country estates or in small towns and rely on visits to the cosmopolitan Black Sea port of Odessa for cultural diversion and medical treatment. The women travel to St. Petersburg only to settle lawsuits over land, and the men, to advance their careers. Brought up to speak fluent French and perhaps English or German as well as Russian, they are at ease in Western Europe. Marchenko alternates between concentration on a single plot and a polyphonic interweaving of plots involving a number of characters. Nikolai Vasil'evich Gogol obviously influenced her frequent interpolations of bits of local color and, in *Myl'nye puzyri* (Soap Bubbles, 1858), the introduction of the "diary of a madman." There are elements of sentimentalism (the use of journals and letters in which her heroines explore their emotions, sometimes in inflated Sandian rhetoric), and much of her fiction continues the tradition of the "society tale," with its ironic plots centered on upper-class mating rituals (salons, balls, the theater, masquerades, and outings). The corrosive power of gossip is a major element in her version of the genre. Marchenko is gifted at pointed portrayals of eccentric noblewomen, doting mothers, scheming female rivals, and other ladies of varying ages. Fathers are usually insignificant or absent. The corrupting force of hereditary wealth is a theme throughout her writings: gender games underline the ways in which smug aristocrats exploit poorer gentry.

All of Marchenko's fiction toys with contemporary concepts of gender. Young women are meticulously drawn, often in contrasting pairs of "feminine" (flighty, self-absorbed, cushioned by wealth, and immune to close attachments) and "strong" (independent, attentive to others, relatively poor, and passionate). Unlike the heroines of Ivan Sergeevich Turgenev, who wait within a family setting for men to liberate them, Marchenko's women earn at least a modest living and seek to move as equals in society. A repeated plot line is their struggle to reach "rational independence" and yet find love in circles that offer only weak, spoiled, but charming men (for whom Marchenko's keyword is "vanity"). These heroes, particularly those in her early tales, have "feminine" traits and are as underdescribed as Russian heroines are in contemporary fiction by men. There is a maternal element along with the passion in her heroines' choices: the heroines are usually older than their immature love-objects.

The few details known of Anastasiia Iakovlevna Marchenko's life come from Nekrasova's somewhat unreliable sketch, which closely follows Marchenko's portrayal of the early years of the heroine of *Razluchniki.* Marchenko's father was Ukrainian, her mother Polish, and she grew up on the paternal estate near Chigirin in Kiev province. She and her siblings were educated at home by a capable governess, with other teachers brought in to impart the artistic skills prized in gentry circles. Her works are sprinkled with epigraphs, citations, and references from a wide variety of Western writers—including Dante, Edward Bulwer-Lytton (both quoted in French), Mikhail Iur'evich Lermontov, Aleksandr Sergeevich Pushkin, Etienne Pivert de Sénancour (his *Obermann*), Johann Wolfgang von Goethe (his *Faust*), Friedrich von Schiller, Rodolphe Töpffer, André Chenier, Jean Paul Richter, Benjamin Franklin, William Shakespeare, and George Gordon, Lord Byron. Music, opera in particular, plays a key role in her fiction, and most of her heroines are talented musicians.

At the age of twelve Marchenko suffered a crisis in health, diagnosed as an aneurysm, and the previously self-willed, active girl began to write seriously during this period. Like many gentry, her father was profligate, and the family's idyllic country existence ended abruptly when he was paralyzed by a stroke brought on by futile struggles against debt. The Marchenkos moved to Odessa, and to help support them, at sixteen Anastasiia began giving music lessons in a private school—an experience she ascribed with some acerbity to the heroine of *Myl'nye puzyri.* When Marchenko's health again failed, she brought out notebooks of stories she had written and chose two that had passed her self-imposed test of letting a year elapse before deciding whether or not they were worth preserving. She was fortunate to find an honest bookseller, Karl Totti, to publish them. A major reason for the ecstatic reviews *Putevye zametki* received from important critics in Moscow and St. Petersburg was the novelty of its publication in Odessa: the book was hailed as a harbinger of a developing provincial literature. Vissarion Grigor'evich Belinsky called it "the only remarkable piece . . . to come out this year. . . . Much heartfelt warmth, much feeling; life not always comprehended or comprehended in a feminine way. . . ." The reviewer for *Finskii vestnik* (Finnish Herald), while also lavishing praise, noted that Marchenko did not "striv[e] for a resolution of contemporary problems, she only resolves problems close to the feminine heart."

In Marchenko's foreword to *Putevye zametki,* she explains the travel of the title as a journey through the "eternal kaleidoscope" of humanity. The first story, "Tri variatsii na staruiu temu" (Three Variations on an Old Theme), is remarkable for its economy. The reader learns nothing about the narrator that does not relate to her loving fascination with a "boy" five years younger, and she describes him only at three distinct epochs—at fifteen (nicknamed Lelia), at twenty (a Frenchified Aleksis), and at thirty as a prematurely pompous government official (Aleksei Petrovich). Marchenko claimed to have written the second tale, "Guvernantka," at fourteen, and her choice of governess as heroine, perhaps the first in Russian literature, is a tribute to her own teacher. The work is dedicated to Vladimir Aleksandrovich Sollogub, an author noted for society tales, and, like "Tri variatsii . . .", offers a clever adolescent's slant on the genre. Franz Peter Schubert's "Wanderer" fantasy becomes a leitmotiv for Elena Linkevich's fate—maintaining her independence while serving in other people's homes. The rich man Elena loves has no intention of marrying a woman without property, and she is too proud to ask the poor man who loves her to share her modest life. At the end, from a window in the private boarding school where she has found a niche that suits her, she sees a cavalcade of her aristocratic friends on horseback, still engaged in the old mating rituals.

The 1849 second edition of *Putevye zametki,* also published in Odessa, added three more tales. "Tantseval'nyi uchitel'" (Dance Master) reflects the Russian "natural school" of the 1840s, with its emphasis on the "insulted and injured." It is also one of Marchenko's few attempts at narration from a male viewpoint. The tale is framed in Gogolian humor: two satirically treated families of Ukrainian gentry import an alcoholic dance master for their children, and the comedy of his inept lessons gives way to a tragic outcome. A widower, he is devoted to his nine-year-old son, who falls mortally ill and, as the neighbors' governess, Elena (presumably the heroine of "Guvernantka"), watches with

him at the boy's bedside, the dance master tells her the story of his decline from a promising future as a wealthy man's godson-ward into poverty and alcoholism. The other two tales, "Chetvert' zhizni chelovecheskoi" (One-Fourth the Human Lifespan) and "Pozdno!" (Too Late!), are more experimental and complex, intermingling the lives of a number of figures and delineating the shifting attractions among them. "Chetvert' zhizni chelovecheskoi" starts with a Gogolian-tinged description of the life of a Ukrainian town (with a brief reprise near the end) and then shifts into a society tale with an admixture of epistolary novel and Sandian pathos. "Pozdno!" depicts an elaborate mating chain among five characters, in which poor but proud Aleksandrina is odd woman out.

Ternistyi put' (The Thorny Path, 1849), subtitled a novel despite its brevity, traces the contrasting fates of two provincial gentry girls, both spoiled by doting widowed mothers. The resolution is typical of Marchenko's use of contrasting types: Ninochka, a rich girl, ends up trapped in a disastrous marriage and permanent infantilism; the impoverished Mimishka grows into self-sufficient womanhood. The work is marred by an unpleasant tinge of anti-Semitism, as "yids" prey on the financial ineptitude of Mimishka's mother. "Teni proshlogo" (Shades of the Past) is Marchenko's attempt at portraying a devalued romantic hero, whom Nekrasova calls "Onegin in caricature." All of these tales, written before Marchenko turned twenty, are distinguished by terse exposition and lively command of language.

Marchenko finds ingenious ways to use setting as an organizing principle in four works published between 1853 and 1856. The omniscient narrator of her novel *Dina* (1853) describes the work as having "no heroes, and no heroines; these are all people who submit to the influence of circumstances and appearance . . . all this is a chain of ordinary stories." Several of its interlocking plots, however, owe more to opera than to everyday life, and thematic references to opera (Gaetano Donizetti's *Lucia di Lammermoor* and Wolfgang Amadeus Mozart's *Don Giovanni* in particular) reinforce those melodramatic elements. The novel is centered on an affectionately described rundown cottage in a provincial town and traces the lives of four children born there. Their newly widowed mother, Klavdiia Nikolaevna, is forced to give up three of them to friends to raise—Pavel and Varia, both adolescents, to a rich and eccentric countess from Moscow; and her younger daughter, Nadia, to a principled governess with no fixed abode. Klavdiia Nikolaevna is to concentrate on raising Misha, the youngest child, and retaining the cottage. As they separate, the family members agree that some day they will be reunited to meet there once a week.

Varia, brought out into high society, chooses to marry a corrupt rich man rather than an honorable poor one and is later seduced by a conscienceless rake; her marriage and reputation ruined, she returns to her mother's house. Pavel realizes his childhood dream of becoming a doctor, and the countess sets him up in practice in his hometown. A long chapter describing a day Pavel spends visiting patients is Marchenko's one attempt at portraying men's work. His lasting grief is to lose the battle to save several patients he has come to love. Nadia and Misha are devoted to art. Nadia becomes an internationally famous opera singer, the eponymous Dina (Marchenko does not reveal the secret of the name–or even mention it–until halfway into the novel), and then gives up her career to be with her mother and tutor the sons of her disgraced sister Varia. Misha becomes a sculptor, and the months Nadia-Dina spends with him in Germany give Marchenko a chance for another spate of local color, as the family's neighbors in a quiet backstreet of Leipzig observe the exotic Russians in their midst. Misha fades away, heartbroken, when a statue he has submitted to an exhibit in Florence is accidentally smashed. Back home Dina settles down to educate her nephews to become artists–and "honest and steadfastly good people." This concatenation of unlikely events, with even more melodramatic aspects than an outline can suggest, is redeemed by Marchenko's gift for effective individual scenes and observed detail.

The narrator of *Umnaia zhenshchina* (A Clever Woman, 1853) declares an intention of telling a "happy, quiet, soothing tale–a tale with a happy ending" and "a hero and heroine . . . who possess no heroic qualities at all." This time the description is apt. The third major protagonist is Odessa itself, lovingly described in all its moods and seasons. The clever woman of the title and an "old bachelor" are country neighbors, both bruised by earlier attempts to find love and somewhat hostile to each other. They meet by chance in Odessa, where both have come for their health. After months of verbal sparring driven by fears of further disillusionment, they at last come to terms with their pasts and decide to marry. A happy life as Gogolian old-world landowners lies ahead.

Vokrug da okolo (A Near Miss, 1855) has an even simpler linear plot and, like "Umnaia zhenshchina," is set in Odessa. The narrator defines its theme as the "Gordian knots" of modern psychology. Rita Torsina strikes up a flirtatious acquaintance and clandestine correspondence with the most extreme example of a feminized man in Marchenko's work–an idle, aesthetically inclined "porcelain doll" named Valentin. When he

breaks up with her because he wants something more ethereal in romance than her frank common sense can provide, she turns to a family friend, a ship's officer who has been her confidant since childhood, and asks: was that love? He reassures her that it was only a near miss, and that real love is yet to come.

Gory (Hills, 1856) is set in aristocratic circles in St. Petersburg. It is one of Marchenko's most economical and effective tales. Ol'ga, a young provincial landowner spending the winter in the capital to settle a lawsuit, suffers a near-fatal infatuation with a handsome but shallow man-about-town, Boris. Marchenko uses two extended tropes for the affair: artificial sledding hills that offer proper St. Petersburgers a site for discreet flirtation, where Ol'ga meets Boris and becomes addicted to swooping downhill kneeling behind him; and a near-fatal influenza brought on by exposure to both Boris and the elements. Ultimately, she recovers her health and her emotional equilibrium, wins her lawsuit, and quits St. Petersburg in relief.

In the mid 1850s Marchenko published a few lyrics in *Otechestvennye zapiski* (Notes of the Fatherland) and *Panteon* (Pantheon) and patriotic verse on the occasion of the Crimean War in *Russkii invalid* (Russian Veteran). Her "contemporary novella" *Na pokhode* (On Campaign, 1857) is set amid the influx of troops into Ukraine on their way to the front. Three young women fall in love with officers: Mashen'ka and Buteev, both adolescents, are prototypical idealistic lovers; the social butterfly, Kitti, becomes the object of a cruel game played by two heartless rakes; and Vera, in her mid-twenties and disillusioned with the possibility of finding love, is attracted to Lavrenetsky, who looks much less attractive in civilian clothes (yellow gloves!) than in uniform. As Vera tartly remarks, " like Franklin, I paid too much for the whistle." None of the romances outlasts the war, but Marchenko's heroines are resilient enough to chalk up their failed romances to experience. The tale is engaging, despite its confusion of narrative techniques: it begins with letters from the three women to a first-person narrator, a friend who interacts with them in succeeding scenes, offering advice they rarely take; this personal viewpoint gradually gives way to semiomniscient narration.

All that is known about Marchenko's adult life is that, probably in the mid 1850s, she married an officer in the Russian army. She lived for a time in St. Petersburg and spent the rest of her life in Kherson. Most of her later heroes are military men, depicted on leave or at leisure.

Marchenko's last three major works–*Myl'nye puzyri, Salamandra* (1859), and *Razluchniki*–are dedicated to the fate of a single heroine, Iuliia. Marchenko's foreword defines the "soap bubbles" of *Myl'nye puzyri* as the self-deluding illusions by which people make their lives palatable, but which inevitably burst, leaving only a "murky drop" of water behind. At least 25 passages of the novel's 140,000 words apply the trope to twists of the plot, which centers on "a woman, endowed with a strong soul, [who], like an alchemist, cannot resist . . . searching for . . . the philosopher's stone—an emotion equal in force to her capacity to feel." Orphaned, Iuliia is forced by debt to sell her modest Ukrainian farm and take a post teaching music in Odessa. Her marriage for love to a wealthy country neighbor her own age, Aleksandr Ulimov, seems like a fairy tale, until her husband begins developing signs of insanity. The first third of the novel deals mainly with the couple's trip abroad for Iuliia's health, as she buckles under the strain of Aleksandr's growing peculiarities. The section ends with his death in a luxurious asylum in Paris.

The two remaining volumes of *Myl'nye puzyri* treat Iuliia Ulimova's further brushes with love. Left a modestly independent widow, she moves to Odessa. Each of the two younger men for whom she develops a passion turns out only to reflect the aspects of her own principled character that he assumes in her company. Both are even more easily influenced by less scrupulous people—in one case, an older woman, and in the other, a Mephistophelian fellow officer—who succeed in alienating them from Iuliia. Unable to transmute these base metals into her gold, she is relieved to be called home to her native province to care for her elderly father-in-law.

Marchenko relieves this narrow concentration on a single protagonist by introducing subsidiary characters, viewpoints, and settings. The novel begins with a largely irrelevant but colorful section on the history and contemporary culture of the neighborhood in which the Ulimovs grew up, a touch of exoticism prompted perhaps by nostalgia for her childhood home, but surely also by the appeal to Russian readers of quaint Ukrainian mores. Marchenko's characters enliven the pages of the novel and relieve the pessimistic tone and its overlong delineations of Iuliia's shifting emotions. These characters include wise French counselors who see Iuliia through her ordeal in Paris, the inmates of Aleksandr's asylum and their delusions of grandeur, a Russian disciple of Friedrich Wilhelm Joseph von Schelling whose philosophical bent is merely excuse for idleness, the hypocritically moralistic baroness to whom one of Iuliia's admirers is devoted, a woman bareback rider in the St. Petersburg circus who is Iuliia's other suitor's lover, and an officer who plays tunes on his horn to set his hounds baying in concert.

Marchenko's thesis that principled, proud women tend to fall in love with men who become better people in their company, while remaining susceptible to baser influences as well, is developed further in "Salamandra" and *Razluchniki*. They are also the first works in which she treats contemporary sexual mores openly. In "Salamandra" the ward of a wealthy woman falls in love with her benefactor's nephew, Grisha, and, pressed hard by the ardent youngster, agrees to live with him but will not marry him without his mother's consent. As a result, despite the fact that she earns her own living and maintains a modest household, she falls into the category of *camelia* (kept woman), rejected by the aristocratic society that Grisha continues to frequent. Salamandra is the nickname given the heroine—because she speaks of love with such fiery passion—by a circle of men who have come to respect her. At the end, the couple marry, but only after Grisha has matured enough to realize that his happiness lies with Salamandra and the unpretentious life they can share as equals.

Perhaps because Marchenko reflects her own past in describing that of her heroine, Nekrasova dismisses *Razluchniki,* published under an undecipherable male pen name and featuring a male narrator, as a spiteful depiction of the author's in-laws. It is, rather, novel-as-tract, peppered with key words and phrases in enlarged italics to make sure the reader grasps its didactic criticism of contemporary society. The plot is simple. After nearly a decade of marriage, Dem'ianov is seduced away from Nadezhda Ivanovna and their three children by a scheming girl, who is urged on by her half brother and his wife, Dem'ianov's sister. Marchenko makes her target explicit: Nadezhda Ivanovna "had up to that point thought that the new people were the nihilists, the heroes of . . . [Nikolai Gavrilovich Chernyshevsky's] 'Chto delat'?'" but now she is faced with opposition from even newer people who "become angry only if the hero of the romance returns to the bosom of his real family, to the path of duty, honor, and morality." Marchenko's novel raises a problem largely ignored by the radicals of the 1860s. What is to become of the children of these so-called liberated people? Women are raised to be responsible mothers, but "where are those prepared to be *fathers?* Where are those whose goal is the material well-being, moral upbringing, and intellectual education of children . . .? They exist!—but rarely, and the majority of men play the role of male animal (*samets*) rather than father." Nadezhda Ivanovna comes in for her share of blame; her sin, she finally recognizes, is idolatry. Married for love to a young man who has been indulged since childhood without countervailing moral or intellectual influence, she has betrayed her principles by settling for "being useful" to him—restoring the estate he had plundered for his pleasures and creating an elegant setting in which he can entertain his cronies. Her blind naiveté has left her helpless to counteract the homewreckers who use Dem'ianov's weakness to their financial and social advantage. For the first time in Marchenko's works, biblical citations displace references to secular literature, as Nadezhda Ivanovna turns for consolation to what remains—her children and her religion.

Marchenko died of unknown causes in Kherson in October or November 1880. She had never, throughout her career, again received the kind of fulsome, albeit condescending, praise that greeted *Putevye zametki*. Her protofeminist attempts throughout her fiction to dispute the restrictive concept of masculinity/femininity promulgated by her male peers went either unrecognized or ignored by contemporary critics. Over the next decades liberal men (among them, Aleksander Vasil'evich Druzhinin, Ivan Sergeevich Turgenev, and Chernyshevsky) treated women's presumed physical, intellectual, and

cultural inferiority as a problem for Russian society overall, while depictions of interactions between the sexes by Marchenko and other women writers were relegated to the category of "women's literature."

References:

Ekaterina S. Nekrasova, "Anastasiia Iakovlevna Marchenko ('T. Ch.' ili 'A. Temrizov'), 1830–1880," *Kievskaia starina,* 11 (1889): 392–422;

P. A. Nikolaev, ed., *Russkie pisateli 1800–1917. Biograficheskii slovar'* (Moscow: Bol'shaia rossiiskaia entsiklopediia, 1994), III: 536–537;

Irina Savkina, *Provintsialki russkoi literatury. (Zhenskaia proza 30–40-kh godov XIX veka). FrauenLiteraturGeschichte: Texte und Materialen zur russischen Frauenliteratur* (Wilhelmshorst: Verlag F. K. Göpfert, 1998), VIII: 58, 59, 126–129.

Papers:

The Russian National Library, St. Petersburg, holds correspondence between Anastasiia Iakovlevna Marchenko and the editors of *Otechestvennye zapiski* and *Sovremennik*.

Boleslav Mikhailovich Markevich

(1822 – 6 November 1884)

Denis Akhapkin
St. Petersburg University

(Translated by Judith E. Kalb)

WORKS: *Tipy proshlogo,* in *Russkii vestnik,* 8–12 (1867); (Moscow, 1867);

Kn. Grigorii Shcherbatov o gr. Uvarove, in *Sovremennaia letopis'* (1, 8, 15 February 1870); (Moscow, 1870);

Zabytyi vopros, in *Russkii vestnik,* 1–4 (1872); translated by the Princesses Ouroussoff as *The Neglected Question,* 2 volumes (London: H. S. King, 1875);

Marina iz Alogo Roga, in *Russkii vestnik,* 1–3 (1873); (Moscow: V Univ. tip., 1873);

Chetvert' veka nazad, in *Russkii vestnik,* 4, 6–8, 10–12 (1878); 2 volumes (Moscow: Tip. M. N. Lavrova, 1879);

Kniazhna Tata, in *Russkii vestnik,* no. 7 (1879);

Lesnik, in *Niva,* nos. 41–45 (1880);

Perelom, in *Russkii vestnik,* nos. 2, 3, 5, 6, 9, 10 (1880); nos. 1, 3, 6–8, 11, 12 (1881); 2 volumes (St. Petersburg: Izd. Novogo vremeni, 1882);

Povesti i rasskazy (St. Petersburg: Tip. Obshchestvennaia pol'za, 1883);

Bezdna, in *Russkii vestnik,* nos. 1–4, 7–9, 11 (1883); nos. 5–11 (1884); (Moscow, 1883–1884);

Chad zhizni. Drama v piati deistviiakh. Zaimstvovana iz romana Perelom (St. Petersburg: Tip. Obshchestvennaia pol'za, 1884).

Editions and Collections: *Na povorote* (St. Petersburg: Izd. M. O. Vol'fa, 1874)—comprises *Marina iz Alogo Roga* and *Zabytyi vopros;*

Polnoe sobranie sochinenii, 11 volumes (St. Petersburg: Tip. A. M. Kotomina, 1885);

Polnoe sobranie sochinenii, 11 volumes (Moscow: V. M. Sablin, 1912).

SELECTED PERIODICAL PUBLICATION:
"Dve maski. Sviatochnyi rasskaz," *Russkii vestnik,* no. 12 (1874).

Boleslav Markevich is one of those writers who has suffered at the hands of the critics, both during his

Boleslav Mikhailovich Markevich

lifetime and posthumously. This situation is easily explained: possessed of definite talent but also of views considered reactionary, Markevich was a tempting target for critics of almost all persuasions and schools. He has entered the history of Russian literature as the object of his contemporaries' biting epigrams, the stooge of the editor and publisher Mikhail Nikiforovich Katkov, and a harsh critic of Ivan Sergeevich Turgenev, on the one hand, and on the other hand as Czar

Alexander III's favorite writer and an author whose novels enjoyed enormous popularity with the reading public. At the same time, Markevich's works reveal important aspects of the literary and social conditions in the second half of the nineteenth century, and as such they are worthy of interest. In addition to his novels, Markevich contributed many journalistic pieces to popular periodicals; often these appeared anonymously or under a pseudonym.

As the literary scholar Konstantin Fedorovich Golovin noted in 1897, "In spite of the embittered critiques that his novels inspired, which tried to lower him to the level of a simple pamphleteer, it is impossible to deny Markevich's literary significance. Even those characters whom he drew in a thoroughly partisan manner are almost always striking and bold." Golovin concluded that this ability to portray his characters effectively and concretely to his readers was precisely what rendered Markevich worthy of a prominent and lasting place in Russian belles lettres.

Boleslav Mikhailovich Markevich was born in 1822 to a noble family of Polish extraction, and he spent the first part of his life in Kiev. Little is known about his early years. He was educated at home until approximately fourteen years of age. One of his earliest literary memories, recounted in his memoir *Iz prozhitykh dnei* (From Bygone Days, first published in his collected works in 1885), deals with the writer at age eight: "My generation was essentially 'raised on Pushkin.' I was in my ninth year when the last song of *Onegin* fell into my hands. . . . I remember to this day how impressed I was by the musical charm of the first lines I read." Several years later a similar sensation struck Markevich when he read *Vechera na khutore bliz Dikan'ki* (Evenings on a Farm near Dikanka, 1831–1832) by Nikolai Vasil'evich Gogol. At that moment Markevich understood that in order to produce an impression on the reader, it was not essential to have "rhymes and measured lines."

Markevich's education at home was managed by his tutor V. G. Iushkov, whom Markevich later portrayed under the same name in his well-known trilogy of novels *Chetvert' veka nazad* (A Quarter Century Ago, 1878), *Perelom* (The Break, 1880–1881), and the unfinished *Bezdna* (The Abyss, 1883–1884). Before enrolling in the Rishel'evskii lycée in Odessa, Markevich spent two years on his father's estate in Volynskii province, where he was taught by a French tutor. Markevich later portrayed this tutor in the novel *Zabytyi vopros* (1872; translated as *The Neglected Question,* 1875). In his memoirs he recalled,

> We studied literally all day long, from nine o'clock in the morning until three (that is, until dinner), and then from six to nine . . . and this was without a break,

year-round, in winter just as in summer. . . . In two years with him I went through an entire course in French grammar and literature, from Alain Chartier and Charles d'Orleans, poets of the fourteenth and fifteenth centuries, to Victor Hugo and the Romantics inclusively, and I became an expert in all the subtleties of French versification.

In 1836 the family moved to Odessa, where Markevich entered fifth grade at the lycée. Because of the training he had received at home, his studies came easily to him, and in 1838 he became a student in the juridical section of the lycée; as he later recalled, "I entered into the juridical section for lack of anything better to do, given that I was drawn exclusively to philology, and not to the study of the law." Markevich devoted most of his attention to studying Roman and Russian literature. He graduated in 1841, one of six graduates awarded a certificate of excellence.

While still a student, Markevich had been writing verse and literary articles that were published in the newspaper *Odesskii vestnik* (Odessa Herald), and he continued this activity after he moved to St. Petersburg, where in 1842 he began to work in the Ministry of State Property. Markevich was making quite a career for himself in the capital city: he turned up in the best aristocratic circles, impressing high society with his quick wit and dramatic talents. His life during this period is captured in part in the 1889 *Vospominaniia* (Memoirs) of fellow writer Avdot'ia Iakovlevna Panaeva (which are, of course, not free of the later common evaluation of Markevich as a reactionary and stooge):

> He was strikingly handsome and he knew it. He didn't give literature a thought at this time; all his energies were focused on entering the highest social circles. In addition to his handsome exterior, Markevich had a worldly polish. One elderly lady of the court, Potemkina, who played an important role in the aristocracy, took him under her wing, and Markevich became a ballroom dancer, receiving invitations to balls in the highest society.

Markevich was also a skilled reciter and had great stage talent, as is evident from the 1867 correspondence relating to the Aleksandrinskii Theater production of *Smert' Ioanna Groznogo* (Death of Ivan the Terrible), a tragedy by Aleksei Konstantinovich Tolstoy, with whom Markevich was friendly over many years. Markevich had agreed to advise the actor A. A. Nil'sky, who was playing Boris Godunov; the correspondence touched on various aspects of speech, intonation, and conduct on stage.

In 1848 Markevich moved to Moscow, where until 1853 he worked in various bureaucratic capacities under General Governor Arsenii Andreevich Zakrevsky, whom he also depicted, though under a different name, in his trilogy. From the beginning of Markevich's writing career his works shared a trait that earned them popularity among the reading public of the day: he filled his works with characters who had prototypes among either the author's acquaintances or leading figures of state. This prototypical basis gives lasting historical value to Markevich's works.

Markevich returned to St. Petersburg in 1854 and continued his bureaucratic work as head clerk in the State Chancellery; starting in 1863 he worked at the Ministry of Internal Affairs. His career moved along successfully, and in 1866 he assumed a post at the Ministry of Education.

In the 1860s Markevich was an active contributor to *Moskovskie vedomosti* (Moscow News) and *Russkii vestnik* (Russian Herald), edited by Katkov. Given the latter's reactionary and antireform positions, this association gained Markevich no popularity among liberal critics and writers. Markevich's first novel, *Tipy proshlogo* (Types of the Past), appeared in *Russkii vestnik* in 1867 and was published in book form the same year. The subject matter is rather artificial: critics noted that it had been taken more from the works of George Sand than from Russian reality. At the center of the tale is the fate of a radical from the peasantry, who has been raised by a gentleman and poisoned morally by the European culture that has been forcibly cultivated in him.

Markevich's next novel, *Zabytyi vopros,* appeared in *Russkii vestnik* in 1872. It is devoted to a polemic with the views of radical writers on the question of "female emancipation." Markevich constructs this viewpoint somewhat artificially, taking the idea of emancipation to its extreme in order to end the novel by criticizing it:

> Among the innumerable new *questions* that have been raised by the *new times,* the right of a woman to dispose of herself as she will, according to the demands of her own heart, occupies a significant role, and it has found for itself a number of quick-witted and heated, if not always talented, defenders. But carried away by their generous desire to help a "living soul" out from under the yoke of a "narrow morality" and a "conventional obligation," the champions of woman's freedom carelessly forget about another living soul, another being worthy of defense—they forget about the child of this woman when they permit her to exchange one object of affection freely for another, pitilessly trampling on everything that she finds to be a "foolish obstacle."

One of the central problems posed by Markevich in *Zabytyi vopros* is that of education. This question is also at the heart of his next novel, which is probably the best known of all his works: *Marina iz*

Alogo Roga (Marina from Alyi Rog), published in *Russkii vestnik* in 1873. In terms of its subject matter the novel is similar to Turgenev's *Dvorianskoe gnezdo* (A Nest of the Gentry, 1859), and critics both at the time and later took Markevich to task for this resemblance. However, the portraits of some of Markevich's characters, particularly secondary ones, are undoubtedly successful. Aleksei Konstantinovich Tolstoy esteemed the novel highly; his native Krasnyi Rog probably supplied a name for the setting. This work, which was subjected to the vehement criticism of the Populist critic Nikolai Konstantinovich Mikhailovsky in *Otechestvennye zapiski* (Notes of the Fatherland) immediately upon its appearance, defends the worth of the classical education system and the advantage of a focus on the humanities rather than practical areas such as the natural sciences or business. The positive heroes of the novel discuss almost exclusively linguistic themes, presenting Sanskrit and ancient Hebrew derivations, while those characters who are not particularly positive speak about Darwinism and lucidly explain the way financial intrigues work. The discussions about Darwinism infuriated Marxist-leaning critics. Mikhailovsky exhibited such a reaction to the heroine, who unsuccessfully tries to combine diametrically opposed political and philosophical positions (it must be noted that Markevich in no way demonstrates any sort of solidarity with her thinking):

> A little sociological theory comes into her head: weren't the elegant counts and princes around her just those higher, better sorts, picked out from the common herd by the same process according to which the monkey had earlier separated itself out, and then that same common herd? Not only is this theory in its own way no worse than others, but in fact it is precisely the very theory that is made up and given approbation by many scientific and non-scientific realists, both European and native Russian. They anticipated poor Marina from Alyi Rog's theory; they have robbed Mr. Markevich's orphan.

Markevich's denunciation of financial intrigues in *Marina iz Alogo Roga* was followed by his attacks against the immorality and lack of principles found in "nihilists and *raznochintsy*" (people from mixed classes), in a series of articles published in the newspaper *Moskovskie vedomosti,* under the title "S beregov Nevy" (From the Banks of the Neva, 1879). However, in 1875 a huge scandal broke out in which Markevich was implicated in large-scale bribery. He was charged with accepting five thousand rubles for his help (using his official position) in the transfer of *Moskovskie vedomosti* to the hands of the Ministry of Education, which in practical terms meant the transfer of the lease from Valentin Fedorovich Korsh to the banker Fedor Petrovich Baimakov, with all the financial profits and losses that this shift entailed. Despite Markevich's claims of innocence, he was dismissed from the Ministry within twenty-four hours and deprived of the court title of "chamberlain" that he had received earlier. He had to leave the capital city quickly, and he did not return until 1877, by which point the incident had been minimized with Katkov's help: Markevich was said to have filled out financial forms incorrectly upon receiving an advance for subsequent publications.

From the late 1870s to the early 1880s Markevich worked on his trilogy. Purely artistic concerns are secondary in these volumes, unlike his previous novels, and the main characteristics of these works are the haste in which they were written (often on commission for *Russkii vestnik*) and the depiction of political trends. The novels inspired many sharp responses from critics and researchers in the nineteenth century and continued to do so in the twentieth. An excerpt from the Soviet critic Anatolii Ivanovich Batiuto's article in *Istoriia russkoi literatury* (The History of Russian Literature, 1982) serves as a typical example of this approach to Markevich's work:

> The spiteful haste with which the anti-nihilists worked, their tendentious subjectivity, the close link between their convictions and reactionary ideology, and, finally, the minimal talent of the majority of these authors—all this led to a situation in which the anti-nihilist novel assumed a place on the farthest periphery of the literary reflection of socio-political life of that epoch; it functioned as an ignominious monument to obscurantism and brutish hatred towards everything forward-thinking and honest.

The first novel, *Chetvert' veka nazad,* was published in *Russkii vestnik* in 1878. In it Markevich set forth the idea that liberalism, even the most moderate, played into the hands of the revolutionary movement. Despite the simplistic and schematic structure of the novel (composition never was Markevich's strong suit), it includes several successful moments, among which many critics noted the description of the staging of the tragedy *Hamlet* at the estate of the protagonists, the Princes Shastunov.

During the interval between the publication of this novel and its successor, Markevich landed in the center of another scandal, this time linked to Turgenev. After the publication in November 1879 of Turgenev's introduction to the emigré writer Ivan Iakovlevich Pavlovsky's autobiographical story "En cellule. Impressions d'un nihiliste" (From the Cell: Impressions of a Nihilist) in *Le Temps,* Markevich

responded with an article from the series "S beregov Nevy" in *Moskovskie vedomosti* (9 December 1879). In it he accused Turgenev (with whom he had once maintained friendly relations) of "the urge towards crass popularization" and of "turning somersaults before the nihilists." Many contemporaries assessed the article as a reaction to the fact that Turgenev in his *Nov'* (Virgin Soil, 1877) had caricatured Markevich under the name of Ladislas. Markevich's article appeared to be an undisguised political denunciation, and as such it called forth an entire series of sharp responses from contemporaries. One of the best known of these responses was an epigram by Dmitrii Minaev in which Minaev punned on the very idea of denunciation.

The novel *Perelom* was published in *Russkii vestnik* in 1880 and 1881. Some time later Markevich adapted *Perelom* for the stage, under the title *Chad zhizni* (The Haze of Life, 1884). The novel was devoted to the time just before the emancipation of the serfs in 1861, and the editorship at *Russkii vestnik* almost immediately asked Markevich for a continuation of the story. In a letter to historian and commentator Petr Karlovich Shchebal'sky, Markevich wrote about his resulting novel in progress, *Bezdna:* "*Russkii vestnik* is demanding it from me. And the editors even thought of the title: *Over the Abyss,* that is, the unravelling of our society, the final years of the last reign, an epic, and the first of March [the assassination of Czar Alexander II] to finish with. It's a task that I can't even imagine how to deal with!" Most of Markevich's contemporaries took the novel as filled with mean-spirited insinuations; however, shortly after the writer's death Golovin remarked upon the paradox, not immediately noticed, of this work and of the late work of the writer as a whole: "Now and then he very accurately brings to light the internal disintegration of the governmental organization, often becoming, consciously or not, an ally of sedition."

Golovin also assessed the issue of the complex mutual relations between Markevich and the literary process of his time quite accurately. Raised on the literary traditions of Russia in the 1840s, Markevich was closer to them than to the movements of his own day. Markevich proved unable to resolve this contradiction. His work on *Bezdna* was left unfinished; those parts of the novel that had been written were published in *Russkii vestnik* in 1883 and 1884. Markevich died on 6 November 1884. The following year, relying on his discussions with Markevich, the writer Vsevolod Vladimirovich Krestovsky wrote an afterword in which he laid out the rest of the novel as the author had planned it. Markevich is buried in the Aleksandr Nevsky Cemetery in St. Petersburg.

Letters:

Pis'ma B. M. Markevicha k gr. A. K. Tolstomu, P. K. Shchebal'skomu i dr. (St. Petersburg: Tip. Obshchestvennaia pol'za, 1888);

Aleksei Konstantinovich Tolstoy, *Sobranie sochinenii,* volume 4 (Moscow, 1969).

Bibliography:

Semen Afanas'evich Vengerov, *Istochniki slovaria russkikh pisatelei,* volume 4 (Petrograd, 1917).

References:

Anatolii Ivanovich Batiuto, "Antinigilisticheskii roman 60-70-kh godov," in *Istoriia russkoi literatury,* edited by N. I. Prutskov, volume 3 (Leningrad: Nauka, 1982);

Konstantin Fedorovich Golovin (Orlovsky), *Russkii roman i russkoe obshchestvo* (St. Petersburg: Tip. A. A. Porokhovshchikova, 1897);

Vsevolod Vladimirovich Krestovsky, "Posleslovie k romanu Markevicha 'Bezdna,'" *Russkii vestnik,* no. 2 (1885): 849–853;

Nikolai Konstantinovich Mikhailovsky, "Chetvert' veka nazad. Pravdivaia istoriia. Sochinenie B. M. Markevicha," in his *Polnoe sobranie sochinenii,* volume 10 (St. Petersburg, 1913);

Mikhailovsky, "Iz literaturnykh i zhurnal'nykh zametok 1873 g. ('Prekrasnaia Marina iz Alogo Roga i g. Markevich o darvinizme')," in his *Polnoe sobranie sochinenii,* volume 1 (St. Petersburg, 1911), pp. 922–931;

Mikhailovsky, "'Zabytyi vopros' g. B. Markevicha," in his *Polnoe sobranie sochinenii,* volume 10 (St. Petersburg, 1913), pp. 579–581;

I. Mikhnevich, *Istoricheskii obzor sorokaletiia Rishel'evskogo litseia s 1817 po 1857 gody* (Odessa: V Tip. L. Nitche, 1857);

Orest Fedorovich Miller, *Russkie pisateli posle Gogolia,* part 2 (St. Petersburg, 1886);

Charles A. Moser, *Antinihilism in the Russian Novel of the 1860s* (The Hague: Mouton, 1964);

Avdot'ia Iakovlevna Panaeva (Golovacheva), *Vospominaniia* (Moscow: Pravda, 1986);

P. K. Shchebal'sky, "Roman iz epokhi osvobozhdeniia krest'ian ['Perelom']," *Russkii vestnik,* no. 3 (1882);

I. T. Trofimov, "Roman I. S. Turgeneva 'Nov' i obshchestvenno-literaturnaia bor'ba 70-kh godov," *Tvorchestvo I. S. Turgeneva. Sbornik statei,* edited by S. M. Petrov and Trofimov (Moscow: Gos. Uchebno-pedagog. izd-vo, 1959);

A. G. Tseitlin, "Siuzhetika antinigilisticheskogo romana," *Literatura i marksizm,* no. 2 (1929);

I. I. Zamotin, "Tendentsioznaia belletristika 70-kh godov. Markevich," in *Istoriia russkoi literatury XIX veka,* edited by D. N. Ovsianiko-Kulikovsky, volume 4 (Moscow, 1910).

Papers:

Boleslav Mikhailovich Markevich's papers are found in St. Petersburg at the Russian State Historical Archive (RGIA, formerly TsGIA).

Pavel Ivanovich Mel'nikov
(Andrei Pechersky)
(25 October 1818 – 1 February 1883)

Veronica Shapovalov
San Diego State University

WORKS: *Dorozhnye zapiski na puti iz Tambovskoi gubernii v Sibir'*, in *Otechestvennye zapiski*, nos. 11–12 (1839); nos. 3–4, 8–10, 12 (1840); nos. 3–4, 9–10 (1841); nos. 2–3 (1842);

Nizhegorodskaia iarmarka v 1843, 1844 i 1845 godakh (Nizhnii Novgorod, 1846);

Krasil'nikovy, in *Moskvitianin*, no. 8 (1852);

Otchet o sovremennom sostoianii raskola v Nizhegorodskoi gubernii (1853);

Starye gody, in *Russkii vestnik*, no. 7 (1857);

Medvezhii ugol, in *Russkii vestnik*, no. 8 (1857); (Moscow: Gos. izd-vo khudozhestvennoi literatury, 1917);

Nepremennyi, in *Russkii vestnik*, no. 12 (1857);

Babushkiny rosskazni, in *Sovremennik*, nos. 8, 10 (1858);

Ukazatel' dostoprimechatel'nostei Nizhnego Novgoroda (Moscow, 1858);

Imeninnyi pirog, in *Russkii vestnik*, no. 2 (1858); (Moscow: Gos. izd-vo khudozhestvennoi literatury, 1955);

Zauzol'tsy [unfinished], in *Russkii dnevnik*, nos. 119, 125, 131, 133, 137 (1859);

Grisha. Rasskaz iz raskol'nichego byta, in *Sovremennik*, no. 3 (1861); (St. Petersburg: Obshchestvennaia pol'za, 1861);

Pis'ma o raskole, in *Severnaia pchela* (1862); (St. Petersburg: V tip. N. Grecha, 1862);

O russkoi pravde i pol'skoi krivde (Moscow, 1863);

Istoricheskie ocherki popovshchiny, in *Russkii vestnik*, no. 5 (1864); nos. 5, 9 (1866); no. 2 (1867); (Moscow: V Univ. tip. (Katkov), 1864);

Opisanie prazdnenstva, byvshego v S.-Peterburge 6–9 aprelia 1865 goda po sluchaiu stoletnego iubileia Lomonosova (St. Petersburg, 1865);

Kniazhna Tarakanova i printsessa Vladimirskaia (Moscow, 1868);

Za Volgoi, in *Russkii vestnik*, nos. 6–7, 10, 12 (1868);

V lesakh, in *Russki vestnik*, nos. 1, 3, 5, 8 (1871); nos. 1, 3, 6, 8 (1872); nos. 2, 5, 8, 9, 12 (1873); nos. 4, 5, 8,

Pavel Ivanovich Mel'nikov (Andrei Pechersky)

12 (1874); no. 4 (1875); 4 volumes (Moscow: V Univ. Tip. (Katkov), 1875);

Na gorakh, in *Russkii vestnik*, nos. 5, 10 (1875); nos. 8, 10 (1876); nos. 5–7, 9–10 (1877); nos. 1, 5, 8, 11 (1878); nos. 9, 12 (1879); nos. 3, 5, 8 (1880); nos. 2–3 (1881); 4 volumes (Moscow-St. Petersburg: M. O. Vol'f, 1881);

Rasskazy Andreia Pecherskogo (P. I. Mel'nikova) (Moscow: Universitetskaia tip., 1876).

Editions and Collections: *Polnoe sobranie sochinenii,* 14 volumes (Moscow-St. Petersburg: M. O. Vol'f, 1897–1898);

Polnoe sobranie sochinenii, 7 volumes (St. Petersburg: A. Marks, 1909);

Krasil'nikovy. Dedushka Polikarp (Moscow: Rodnaia Rech', 1917);

V lesakh, 2 volumes (Moscow-Leningrad: Academia, 1936–1937);

V lesakh, 2 volumes, edited by I. S. Ezhov (Moscow: Goslitizdat, 1955);

Na gorakh. Prodolzhenie rasskazov "V lesakh," 2 volumes, edited by K. N. Polonskaia (Moscow: Goslitizdat, 1956);

Medvezhii ugol i drugie rasskazy (Moscow: Gos. izd-vo khudozhestvennoi literatury, 1960);

Sobranie sochinenii, 6 volumes (Moscow: Pravda, 1963);

Sobranie sochinenii, 8 volumes (Moscow: Pravda, 1976);

V lesakh (Moscow, 1977);

Ocherki mordvy (Saransk: Mordovskoe knizhnoe izdatel'stvo, 1981);

Obzhivaia merzlomu (Moscow: Sovetskaia Rossiia, 1984);

Povesti i rasskazy (Moscow: Sovremennik, 1985);

Starye gody. Rasskazy i ocherki (Moscow: Moskovskii rabochii, 1986);

Babushkiny rosskazni: Povesti i rasskazy (Moscow: Pravda, 1989).

OTHER: "Zapiska o russkom raskole," in *Sbornik pravitel'stvennykh rasporiazhenii o raskole* (London: Izdanie V. I. Kel'sieva, 1866);

Otchet o sovremennom sostoianii raskola v Nizhegorodskoi gubernii na 1853 g., in *Sbornik Nizhegorodskoi uchenoi arkhivnoi komissii, v pamiat' P. I. Mel'nikova (Andreia Pecherskogo),* volume 9, part 2 (Nizhnii Novgorod, 1910).

SELECTED PERIODICAL PUBLICATIONS:
"Poiarkov," *Russkii vestnik,* no. 2 (1857);

"Dedushka Polikarp. Rasskaz," *Russkii vestnik,* no. 5 (1857);

"Razbor dramy Ostrovskogo *Groza,*" *Severnaia pchela,* no. 42 (1860);

"U Makar'ia," *Severnaia pchela,* no. 144 (1860);

"Blagodetel'nitsa," *Sovremennik,* no. 8 (1863): 267–348;

"Staroobriadcheskie arkhierei," *Russkii vestnik,* nos. 4–6 (1863);

"Tainye sekty," *Russkii vestnik,* no. 5 (1868);

"Belye golubi," *Russkii vestnik,* nos. 3, 5 (1869);

"Materialy dlia istorii khlystovskoi i skopcheskoi eresei," *Chteniia v Imperatorskom Obshchestve Istorii i Drevnostei Rossiiskikh pri Moskovskom Universitete,* nos. 1–4 (1871); no. 1 (1873);

"Raskol'nichii Apokalipsis," *Chteniia v Imperatorskom Obshchestve Istorii i Drevnostei Rossiiskikh pri Moskovskom Universitete,* no. 2 (1873);

"Spasenie zhizni imperatora Nikolaia Pavlovicha," *Russkii arkhiv,* no. 2 (1879): 140–141;

"Vospominanie o grafe S. S. Lanskom," *Russkii arkhiv,* no. 2 (1879): 251–254.

Pavel Ivanovich Mel'nikov, who wrote fiction under the pseudonym Andrei Pechersky, is one of the most-controversial writers of Russian literature. While highly praised by many writers and critics, such as Mikhail Evgrafovich Saltykov (N. Shchedrin), who considered Mel'nikov "the explorer of Russian nationality," he was scorned by others—among them Leo Tolstoy, who accused Mel'nikov of a "false attitude towards the Russian people." The diversity of opinion can be attributed largely to Mel'nikov's work at the Ministry of Internal Affairs, where between 1850 and 1866 he served as an official on special assignments connected with the matters of the Schism (a split in the Russian Orthodox Church that originated in the seventeenth-century rejection by the Old Believers of new church reforms). As a government official, Mel'nikov participated in the conversion of Old Believers to Russian Orthodoxy and in the closing of Old Believer cloisters in Nizhnii Novgorod province. In the 1850s through the 1860s, when Mel'nikov's literary reputation was being formed, the democratic concept that a writer should cater to the needs of society was in vogue. Mel'nikov's views and suggestions on the Schism, outlined in his *Otchet o sovremennom sostoianii raskola v Nizhegorodskoi gubernii* (Report on the State of the Schism in Nizhnii Novgorod, 1853), which was intended for the Ministry of Internal Affairs, were looked upon by his critics as his literary credo. Since the characters of his epic-length novels *V lesakh* (In the Woods, 1871–1875) and *Na gorakh* (On the Hills, 1875–1881) are Old Believers, the ideas in his *Otchet o sovremennom sostoianii raskola v Nizhegorodskoi gubernii* often became the measure of the literary merits of both novels.

Opponents and admirers of Mel'nikov's literary works agreed on one point: he gave a precise description of the everyday life, religious ceremonies, customs, and traditions of the Old Believers of the Transvolga region. As early as 1875 the famous Russian historian Dmitrii Ivanovich Ilovaisky, praising *V lesakh,* noted that "the novel may be called an artistic ethnography." Since then, in both Russian prerevolutionary and Soviet literary criticism, Mel'nikov's novels have been associated with the ethnographic novel. In *Istoriia russkoi literatury* (History of Russian Literature, 1956) and *Istoriia russkogo romana* (History of the Russian Novel, 1964), the Soviet critic Larisa M. Lotman gives brief analyses of *V lesakh* and *Na gorakh,* stressing their connection with Russian folklore. Likewise, the majority of published articles on Mel'nikov's literary works deal exclusively with the various aspects of folklore in his works. His works are steeped in Russian mythology and Russian folk and biblical symbolism; however, his novels go far beyond the frame of the ethnographic novel. He turned to the crucial theme of Russian literature—the search for a supreme truth. In his works Mel'nikov shows man as prey to mysterious forces within and without that can lead to his destruction, both moral and physical. Mel'nikov uses middle-class characters to show that tragedy often arises out of social and class experience. His novels form a link between the Russian literary traditions of the nineteenth century and the works of the Russian Symbolists at the turn of the twentieth century.

Pavel Ivanovich Mel'nikov was born on 25 October 1818 to a noble family whose roots date back to the times of the sixteenth-century czar Ivan the Terrible. Pavel's father, Ivan Ivanovich Mel'nikov, participated in the Napoleonic wars and after his retirement from the military settled in Nizhnii Novgorod, where he married Anna Pavlovna Sergeeva, the daughter of Pavel Pavlovich Sergeev, a Nizhnii Novgorod landowner. Anna Pavlovna was a voracious reader; her father had collected a large library, and she loved Russian literature and history. Along with a French tutor, Anna Pavlovna was her son's teacher. By the time Pavel was ten years old, he could recite Aleksandr Sergeevich Pushkin's *Poltava* (1829) and long excerpts from *Evgenii Onegin* (1825) along with Pierre-Jean de Béranger's songs in French. He copied the works of Pushkin, Anton Antonovich Del'vig, Evgenii Abramovich Baratynsky, and Vasilii Andreevich Zhukovsky into special thick copybooks.

After graduating from the Nizhnii Novgorod gymnasium in 1834, Mel'nikov entered Kazan University, where he studied history and literature. He graduated from the university in 1837 and took a position teaching history in the Perm gymnasium. While living in Perm, he traveled around the region visiting local factories and salt mines and collecting ethnographic and historical data about the region. As a result of this extensive research he wrote *Dorozhnye zapiski na puti iz Tambovskoi gubernii v Sibir'* (Travel Notes on the Way from Tambov Province to Siberia)—nine essays about the history and economics of the region. These essays were published in *Otechestvennye zapiski* (Notes of the Fatherland) between 1839 and 1842.

In 1839 Mel'nikov was transferred to the Nizhnii Novgorod gymnasium. The routine of gymnasium teaching bored him; however, he had several talented students with whom he stayed friendly for the rest of his life. One such student was Konstantin Nikolaevich Bestuzhev-Riumin, who later became a prominent historian and journalist. In Nizhnii Novgorod, Mel'nikov became close to Dmitrii Nikolaevich Tolstoy, the director of one of the largest fairs in Russia—the Nizhnii Novgorod Fair. On Tolstoy's advice, Mel'nikov started his research on the Old Believers, who had many cloisters in the Transvolga region. Through Tolstoy he became acquainted with Old Believer antique book collectors and dealers. Although at that time he could not afford to buy old books and manuscripts, he did not miss an opportunity to read them. His interest in old Russian texts was encouraged by Andrei Aleksandrovich Kraevsky, the editor of *Otechestvennye zapiski,* and later by historian and journalist Mikhail Petrovich Pogodin. Mel'nikov met Pogodin in 1841 during Pogodin's visit to Nizhnii Novgorod. Together they searched for rare items at book and antique dealers at the Nizhnii Novgorod Fair. In his letters to Pogodin, Mel'nikov discussed various finds in detail. He arranged for Pogodin to buy a letter written by Archbishop Iakov, several letters about Old Believers written by Peter the Great, and a letter by the statesman Artemii Volynsky. Gradually, Mel'nikov started acquiring such items himself. In later years his book and manuscript collection included more than three thousand volumes. Mel'nikov also made a *starinshchik* (an old book dealer) one of the main characters in *Na gorakh.*

In Nizhnii Novgorod, Mel'nikov began his serious studies of Russian history. He was especially interested in the history of the Transvolga region. Mel'nikov was the first historian to work extensively in the local archives. In 1841 Minister of Education Sergei Semenovich Uvarov appointed Mel'nikov a corresponding member of the Commission on the Study of Old Texts and assigned him to sort out the archives of the provincial revenue department and the monasteries in Nizhnii Novgorod province.

Mel'nikov regularly published his historical, archaeological, and ethnographic essays in *Otechestvennye zapiski, Nizhegorodskie gubernskie vedomosti* (Nizhnii Novgorod Province News), *Moskvitianin* (The Muscovite), and *Literaturnaia gazeta* (Literary Gazette). His first story, "El'pifidor Perfil'erich," written in the style and manner of Nikolai Vasil'evich Gogol, was published in 1840 in *Literaturnaia gazeta.* Mel'nikov did not like the story and later wrote to his brother, "I'll never forgive myself for publishing such a disgusting piece. If I only could, I would have gathered all the copies . . . and thrown them into the stove. I am still a bad judge of character, and I solemnly promise not to write poetry or prose until I know life better."

In 1841 Mel'nikov married Lidiia Nikolaevna Belokopytova, the daughter of a poor landowner

Mel'nikov's house in Liakhovo (from Sbornik v pamiat' Mel'nikova, *1910)*

from Arzamas. Many years later, Mel'nikov portrayed her grandfather, the governor of Arzamas, as Sergei Mikhailovich Churilin, one of the protagonists of the story "Babushkiny rosskazni" (Grandmother's Tall Tales, 1858). Lidiia Nikolaevna had tuberculosis, and all of their seven children died in infancy; Lidiia Nikolaevna died in 1848. Recalling these years, Mel'nikov wrote in his diary, "My wife was sick and unable to go out. Expenses increased, but my income did not. I did not go out and studied a lot at home." In 1845 the governor of Nizhnii Novgorod, Mikhail Urusov, invited Mel'nikov to become the editor of the unofficial part of the newspaper *Nizhegorodskie gubernskie vedomosti*. Under Mel'nikov's editorship the newspaper became a serious literary publication devoted to ethnography, history, literature, and theater. Writers Vladimir Aleksandrovich Sollogub and Mikhail Vasil'evich Avdeev were among the contributors.

In 1847 Mel'nikov became an official on special assignment in Urusov's office. The majority of Mel'nikov's assignments were connected with the Schism. At the request of the government, he assembled a detailed description of the Old Believer cloisters in the region. Mel'nikov wrote in his diary about his work, "I have studied all kinds of heresies—from *popovshchina* (Old Believers who followed priests) to *skoptsy* (castrates). I am well acquainted with the teachings of sectarians of all persuasions—from *khlysts* (flagellants) to *skoptsy,* with all their rituals. . . . I even wrote down their songs." Mel'nikov's knowledge of Old Believer teachings and rituals made him indispensable in the conversion of Old Believers to Russian Orthodoxy. On his assignments Mel'nikov had to travel extensively around the region. He became a legendary figure among Old Believers: he was a government official who did not take bribes and was able to find and confiscate icons, books, and even bells (various policies

Mel'nikov undertook in regard to the Old Believers were seen as intolerant). There were folk tales about Pavel Ivanovich striking a deal with the devil and gaining the ability to see through walls. In a folk song he was referred to as a king of Babylon–"Nebuchadnezzar Pavel Ivanovich sails in a boat with thirty-two oars and gives orders like a general." During a cholera epidemic in the fall of 1847, Mel'nikov spent six weeks among boat haulers inspecting the ships arriving at the Nizhnii Novgorod Fair. He worked undercover so that no one would find out the real purpose of the inspection and spread panic at the fair.

While working for the governor, Mel'nikov continued his journalistic and historical work. In 1847 he gave free public lectures on Russian history and on the history of Nizhnii Novgorod–an unheard-of occurrence in a town without a university, as one contemporary later observed. In 1849 Mel'nikov renewed his acquaintance with ethnographer Vladimir Ivanovich Dal' (they had first met in St. Petersburg in 1845). Soon the acquaintance deepened into a friendship as they spent long hours working together on old Russian manuscripts. Mel'nikov recalled, "I visited Dal' almost every day, and we spent whole evenings looking at acts of the Commission on the Study of Old Texts, manuscripts, and saints' lives, searching for archaic words and explaining them by their remnants, which were preserved throughout various isolated corners of Russia." Mel'nikov was one of the few who helped Dal' with his renowned work, *Tolkovyi slovar' zhivogo velikorusskogo iazyka* (Reasoned Dictionary of the Living Great-Russian Language, 1863–1866). The research material, as well as his conversations with Dal', influenced Mel'nikov immensely. Dal' encouraged Mel'nikov to write the long story *Krasil'nikovy* (The Krasil'nikovs, published in *Moskvitianin* in 1852) and even suggested a pen name for him–Andrei Pechersky, from Pecherka, the part of Nizhnii Novgorod where he lived. Mel'nikov always considered Dal' his literary mentor.

Among Mel'nikov's friends was Aleksandr Dmitrievich Ulybyshev, a writer and music critic who was also a contributor to St. Petersburg periodicals. In 1850 Ulybyshev wrote a drama, *Raskol'niki* (The Schismatics), which was performed in his home in the 1850s and published in *Russkii arkhiv* (Russian Archive) in 1886. Ulybyshev touched upon several problems that Mel'nikov, as a specialist on matters of the Schism, considered important. Also in 1850 Mel'nikov was assigned to the Ministry of Internal Affairs with special commissions concerning the Schism and Old Believer cloisters in Nizhnii Novgorod province. Mel'nikov lived in Nizhnii Novgorod, where he continued his historical and ethnographical research, publishing some of his essays in *Otechestvennye zapiski* and *Moskvitianin*.

In October 1853 Mel'nikov married Elena Andreevna Rubinskaia, the great-granddaughter of the local magnate K. M. Von-Rebinder. Mel'nikov's best men were Sollogub and Sergei Timofeevich Aksakov, and the priest conducting the wedding service was Aleksandr Ivanovich Dobroliubov, father of the critic Nikolai Aleksandrovich Dobroliubov. Mel'nikov and his wife had six children: Andrei (who also became an historian and ethnographer), Nikolai, Aleksei, Mariia, Elena, and Sofiia.

Mel'nikov's assignments at the Ministry of Internal Affairs required him to travel extensively in the Transvolga region. In 1853 he worked on his *Otchet o sovremennom sostoianii raskola v Nizhegorodskoi gubernii*. By that time he had become Russia's leading specialist on matters of the Schism. His report included sociological, statistical, and geographical data on the Old Believers, detailed descriptions of their cloisters, and an evaluation of their beliefs and morals. One of the issues–the malfeasance and corruption among small parish clergy–preoccupied Mel'nikov as a government official, and later he turned to it in his novels *V lesakh* and *Na gorakh*. In the late 1850s the "clerical question" was widely discussed, not only among intellectuals but also in the Holy Synod and in the government. The issue was brought to the attention of Alexander II, and the discussion eventually resulted in Church reforms.

In his spare time Mel'nikov continued his literary work. He wrote two stories about life and morals of the eighteenth century–*Starye gody* (Bygone Years), published in *Russkii vestnik* (The Russian Herald) in 1857, and *Babushkiny rosskazni,* published in *Sovremennik* (The Contemporary) in 1858. In both stories Mel'nikov presented the eighteenth century as a period of abuse of power and lack of justice, which ultimately corrupted not only wealthy landowners but their serfs as well. The main character of *Starye gody,* Prince Zaborovsky, has a passion for wild debauchery; he is sadistically cruel and vengeful and likes theatrical performances on a grand scale, as they assure him of his power. Evil and injustice permeate not only the provinces but also the court. In *Babushkiny rosskazni* Mel'nikov portrays Catherine II forgiving one of her subjects at the request of a bright and educated young woman, Nasten'ka Borovkova. However, Catherine does not hesitate to arrange Nasten'ka's marriage to a boorish, uneducated military man whom she appoints the governor of a remote, small, provincial town in Siberia. *Starye gody* was so popular that a bookdealer named Sveshnikov cut out the pages from *Russkii vestnik,* made booklets, and sold them for one silver ruble apiece. Mel'nikov protested the sale of these booklets: "I did not give any rights to anyone for such a sale and I respectfully ask bookdealers and buyers to consider these booklets to be sold without the consent and even the previous knowledge of the author."

In 1857 Mel'nikov published "Dedushka Polikarp" (Grandfather Polikarp), "Poiarkov," *Nepremennyi* (Indispensable), and *Medvezhii ugol* (Godforsaken Hole) in *Russkii vestnik*. He masterfully depicted life in the remote corners of the Russian provinces. Many of his characters, as well as the details of everyday life, came from his travels in the Transvolga districts. According to Mel'nikov, in his stories he "brought out into the open all the abuse of power that had been committed in darkness."

The theme of searching for an ultimate truth appears for the first time in Mel'nikov's story *Grisha* (published in *Sovremennik* in 1861). In this story Mel'nikov portrays a young Old Believer, Grisha, who appears ready to commit his life to religious deeds but instead commits a crime. The story is saturated with folk songs, legends, and images. Mel'nikov's stories brought him immediate recognition as one of the leading writers of the time. His works were praised by Nikolai Gavrilovich Chernyshevsky, Nikolai Alekseevich Nekrasov, and Saltykov. However, government officials were pleased neither with his stories nor with the fact that a representative of the Ministry of the Internal Affairs happened to be a writer (despite the pseudonym, his identity was well known). After the publication of *Medvezhii ugol* in *Russkii vestnik*, a complaint was submitted to Alexander II. According to Mel'nikov's biographer, Pavel S. Usov, Alexander dismissed the complaint with the words, "Really, Mel'nikov knows better the state of affairs in your department." Nevertheless, the censors did not allow the publication of a separate collection of Mel'nikov's short stories. The collection was published only in 1876. The Minister of Internal Affairs, Sergei Lanskoy, asked Mel'nikov in a personal conversation to stop writing for journals.

Mel'nikov, however, did not abandon his literary work: in 1859, using his connections at the Ministry of Internal Affairs, he obtained permission to publish a daily newspaper, *Russkii dnevnik* (Russian Daily). The newspaper published local news, and it had sections on arts and sciences as well as on literature and bibliography. Mel'nikov, who was the main editor, also took charge of the literature section. Aleksandr Ivanovich Artem'ev was Mel'nikov's partner and first assistant in the production of *Russkii dnevnik*. There Mel'nikov published his story "Na stantsii" (At the Station) and the unfinished novel *Zauzol'tsy* (1859), which became the first draft for the novel *V lesakh*. But Mel'nikov's position in government service again interfered with his literary and journalistic career. His prominent post at the Ministry of Internal Affairs was

well known to the reading public, which therefore considered the newspaper an official publication of the Ministry. Lanskoy received many complaints about the material published in *Russkii dnevnik*, and he offered Mel'nikov a choice—retire or close the newspaper. Civil service was Mel'nikov's only source of income, so he closed *Russkii dnevnik* in July 1859.

Mel'nikov continued his journalistic work in *Severnaia pchela* (The Northern Bee), the newspaper edited by Usov. In *Severnaia pchela* Mel'nikov published his review of Aleksandr Nikolaevich Ostrovsky's play *Groza* (The Storm, 1860), the stories "U Makar'ia" (At Makar'evskaia Fair, 1860) and "V Chudove" (In Chudovo, 1862), the essay "Predanie o sud'be Tarakanovoi" (Legend about Tarakanova's Fate, 1860), and *Pis'ma o raskole* (Letters on the Schism, 1862). Mel'nikov was hesitant to publish *Pis'ma o raskole* in the newspaper not only because of his official position in government service but also because of his previous encounters with censorship. *Pis'ma o raskole* was published without the name of the author. In this work Mel'nikov entered into polemics with liberals, who considered Old Believers to be one of the main forces in opposition to the government, and with ultraconservatives, who labeled Old Believers the enemies of the Orthodox faith. Fanaticism was the main aspect of the Schism that alienated Mel'nikov; he felt that fanaticism leads to inhumanity, cruelty, and ultimately the rejection of Christian dogma. Explaining his position, Mel'nikov wrote, "Old Believers did not and still do not represent any danger to the state and social well being. The two-hundred-year-old persecution of Old Believers as well as the restrictions on their rights were excessive and even harmful. Old Believers deserve to enjoy all civil rights."

Mel'nikov's extensive travels and his contacts with Old Believers and sectarians of various creeds provided him with vast material about the Schism and sects. In the 1860s Mel'nikov published essays on the Schism and sectarianism—"Staroobriadcheskie arkhierei" (Old Believer Archbishops, 1863), *Istoricheskie ocherki popovshchiny* (Historical Essays on Popovshchina, 1864–1867), "Tainye sekty" (Secret Sects, 1868), and "Belye golubi" (White Doves, 1869).

The summer of 1862 in St. Petersburg was marked by fires. The house in Troitskii Lane where Mel'nikov lived with his family was spared by fire, but many of his personal papers, manuscripts and books from his collection, and an old family icon (dating back to the time of Ivan the Terrible and given to one of Mel'nikov's forefathers) were stolen during the evacuation of the house. Popular rumor accused the Poles of arson. Personal loss was an important reason for Mel'nikov's accepting the assignment from the Minister of Internal Affairs to write a booklet for popular read-

Mel'nikov in the 1870s (engraving after a portrait by Ivan Kramskoy)

ing, *O russkoi pravde i pol'skoi krivde* (On Russian Truth and the Polish Lie, 1863). The booklet was purely nationalistic and aimed against the Polish uprising, which called for independence from Russian rule. The liberal and democratic reading public immediately labeled Mel'nikov reactionary and ultraconservative.

In the 1860s Mel'nikov worked with archival materials and was particularly interested in Russian history of the eighteenth century. He turned to one of the most tragic and mysterious incidents in Russian history: the life story of a woman known as Elizaveta Alekseevna Tarakanova, who claimed to be the illegitimate daughter of Empress Elizaveta and Count Aleksei Razumovsky. In an 1860 essay for *Severnaia pchela* Mel'nikov made an attempt to trace the fate of Avgusta Tarakanova, the empress's real daughter, only briefly mentioning the impostor. In 1866 he returned to the theme again, this time focusing on the impersonator, who was imprisoned in the Peter and Paul Fortress at the behest of Catherine II and died there. At the time of publication, Mel'nikov's study *Kniazhna Tarakanova i printsessa Vladimirskaia* (Princess Tarakanova and the Princess of Vladimir, 1868) was viewed as an attempt not only to

interpret a sensational event of the eighteenth century but also to answer the questions remaining about the true identity of the mysterious woman who called herself the daughter of the Russian empress. The public and the critics were disappointed in Mel'nikov's work: there were no sensational discoveries of new documents, and none of the mysteries surrounding Elizaveta's daughter was solved. For Mel'nikov, however, the sensational aspect of the intrigue was not important. He was exploring the tragedy of a strong individual caught in a complex network of human relationships that were beyond her control.

In *Kniazhna Tarakanova i printsessa Vladimirskaia* Mel'nikov presents the biography of an impostor, based on historical documents. In this biography he uses elements characteristic of fictional prose: adventure, mystery, seduction, and betrayal. The genre of literary biography in mid-nineteenth-century Russian and European literature tended to focus on the lives of prominent people—writers, philosophers, and political leaders. Thus, Mel'nikov was an exception in producing a literary biography of an adventuress.

Mel'nikov approached his subject with careful scholarship, and extensive footnotes highlight his effort to render the narration as close to recorded facts as possible. Furthermore, historical references define the stance the author adopts toward the action: he distances himself from the events, and as he deals with historical facts, he tries to be objective.

In *Kniazhna Tarakanova i printsessa Vladimirskaia* Mel'nikov continues the theme of pretense—emphasized by the discrepancy between reality and name—that already existed at the time in Russian literature. He portrays a whole gallery of "impostors" at all levels of society: Count Aleksei Razumovsky, whose name was changed from Rozum and who had never been in any military campaign, though he held the rank of a general field marshal; Count Aleksei Orlov, who handed out titles like a member of the royalty; the Cossack rebel leader Pugachev; and several other rebels who called themselves Czar Peter III. The choice of characters is meaningful: in Mel'nikov's work impostors are in power, and thus they are responsible for the appearance and existence of impostors of a lower rank. He directly links the impersonator of Elizaveta's daughter to Catherine II: neither has a legal right to the Russian throne, and both are part of a conspiracy that may lead either to the throne or to their imprisonment and death. Mel'nikov questions Catherine's right to the throne, and by doing so, transfers the conflict between Catherine and Tarakanova from the level of monarch and subject to that of two equal human beings. Mel'nikov notes that the truth about the conspiracy surrounding the impostor is of no interest to

Catherine. None of the Polish conspirators involved was even questioned, although there was enough evidence to prove their participation.

Mel'nikov portrays Tarakanova as a courageous and daring woman. She is an adventuress whose courage is recognized even by her enemies. During the ordeal of her imprisonment, Tarakanova behaves with dignity and even arrogance toward her captors. Whether she has been sincere in her testimony remains a mystery; but she is adamant about her story, and nothing can make her change it. Of all the people arrested in connection with her case, she is the most noble and tragic. She is the one who has been betrayed by everybody and who must pay with her life, not only for her own ambitions but also for the ambitions of other people who readily forgot the "princess" as soon as it was convenient.

The unusual structure of *Kniazhna Tarakanova i printsessa Vladimirskaia* contributed to its cold reception. Tarakanova is a real historical character, but her true identity remains unknown. Thus, as a protagonist, she exists on the borderline between documented history and fiction. She remains the center of the narration throughout, and in describing episodes from her life Mel'nikov uses various compositional devices and techniques that enable him to evoke a full spectrum of emotions. Describing her childhood and early adventures, Mel'nikov uses the elements of an adventure novel: mystery, intrigue, meetings in an old empty house, and sea voyages during a storm. From the moment Count Orlov decides to capture the impostor, the narration suddenly changes: all the adventure elements are gone, and from this point tragedy dominates the narration. In the final chapters Mel'nikov's heroine acquires the status of a tragic hero: she is physically broken but continues to progress morally.

In 1866 Mel'nikov retired from the Ministry of Internal Affairs and settled with his family in Moscow. For a short time he edited the literary section of *Russkie vedomosti* (Russian News), but after a conflict with its editor, Mikhail Nikiforovich Katkov, he stopped working for this publication. In 1868 Mel'nikov and his family moved into a small apartment in Dal's house. Although as the leading expert on the Schism and the Transvolga region he occasionally fulfilled assignments for the Ministry of Internal Affairs, Mel'nikov had to rely on his literary work as the main source of income. In Moscow he began working on his epic-length novels *V lesakh* and *Na gorakh*.

V lesakh originated in 1861, when Mel'nikov was assigned to accompany the Grand Prince Nikolai on his trip down the Volga. Mel'nikov was Nikolai's guide at the Nizhnii Novgorod Fair; he acquainted the prince with folk legends, tales, and details of the everyday life of the Old Believers. Nikolai made Mel'nikov promise to write down his stories of "how people live in the woods, in the Transvolga region." Mel'nikov made two attempts to fulfill his promise: he returned to the material in *Zauzol'tsy* and he wrote a story, "Za Volgoi" (On the Left Bank of the Volga), published in *Russkii vestnik* in 1868.

The action of *V lesakh* takes place between 1846 and 1853. At the center is the family of an Old Believer Transvolga merchant, Patap Maksimych Chapurin, and the love affairs of his two daughters, Nastia and Parasha. Chapurin is not only a successful and respected businessman but also a warden of a Schismatic chapel in Gorodets. Besides the chapel, Chapurin supports the Komarov cloister, and he has petitioned the governor many times on the Old Believers' behalf. His favorite daughter, Nastia, falls in love with Aleksei, Chapurin's servant. Aleksei is a skillful craftsman, and for his excellent work and quick wits Chapurin has made him a manager of the house and workshops. Nastia and Aleksei plan to marry even if they have to elope. Chapurin, who has different plans for his daughter, has already chosen Nastia's future husband; but she threatens to take the veil in the Old Believer cloister instead. Soon Nastia realizes that she has been mistaken in Aleksei—he is driven in life only by money and wealth. She falls ill, and on her deathbed she tells her parents that she is pregnant but that she forgives Aleksei the wrong he did her. She has sacrificed everything for her love.

An elopement, however, does take place in the Chapurin family: Parasha marries Vasilii Borisych, an Old Believer envoy from Moscow who turns out to be a womanizer. Chapurin suffers humiliation at the hands of Aleksei, unhappiness at the deaths of Nastia and then Parasha, bitter disappointment in Vasilii Borisych, and finally the long torment of the illness and death of his wife. Yet, all the misfortunes that befall Chapurin do not break his spirit; in spite of all his sufferings, he remains the same monolithic character. He is vain, yet generous; short tempered, yet just; fearsome in anger, yet kind. No matter how contradictory these qualities are, there are no shades of gray in his character. Chapurin does not break his ties with the village where he lived for many years; in his dress and manner, he adheres to the customs of his forefathers. In the business world, Chapurin has the reputation of an honest and respectable man. For Mel'nikov, Chapurin is the ideal Russian merchant: honest, kind, reasonable, and just.

V lesakh, dedicated to Alexander III, was published between 1871 and 1874 in *Russkii vestnik* and as a separate edition in 1875. It was a great success, and Mel'nikov became one of the most popular writers of the day. The well-known arts patron Pavel Tret'iakov commissioned the famous artist Ivan Kramskoy to paint Mel'nikov's portrait. In 1874 Mel'nikov celebrated the thirty-fifth anniversary of his literary career. In Moscow his circle of friends included Aleksei Feofilaktovich Pisemsky, who at that time was working on his novel *Masony* (The Masons, 1880); Apollon Nikolaevich Maikov; historians Dmitrii Ilovaisky and Bestuzhev-Riumin; and a well-known book collector, Aleksei Khludov. By that time Mel'nikov had become a member of various historical, archaeological, and ethnographical societies. For a long time he attended the meetings of the *Obshchestvo liubitelei rossiiskoi slovesnosti* (Society of Lovers of Russian Literature). To work on *Na gorakh*, Mel'nikov would escape to Liakhovo, his small estate in the vicinity of Nizhnii Novgorod. *Na gorakh* is Mel'nikov's last work.

Na gorakh is to a great extent the continuation of *V lesakh*. The main theme is the search for an absolute truth. In these novels not only individuals but also entire religious groups are involved in this search: pilgrims from various monasteries look for lands where the old faith is preserved untouched, and in frequent debates, Old Believer cloisters try to decide what exactly is the ultimate religion. In *Na gorakh*, for the first time in Russian literature, the search for truth is undertaken by a young woman. Her religious quest is also distinctive in nineteenth-century Russian literature because Mel'nikov brings his heroine into contact with the sect of the *khlysts*.

Dunia Smolokurova, the heroine of *Na gorakh*, is a highly unusual character in Russian literature. Dunia is the only daughter of a rich Old Believer fish merchant, Marko Danilych Smolokurov. The Smolokurovs belong to the nouveau riche class, and the family wealth is based on stolen money. Dunia's mother dies before the girl is two years old, and Dunia is brought up by her father and Dar'ia Sergeevna, a close friend of Dunia's mother. For Marko Danilych, Dunia becomes a living reminder of his late wife and his short happiness with her. His business brings millions, but money for its own sake is of no importance to Smolokurov: he thinks only of Dunia's benefit and wealth. Cruel and rude with everybody else, he is kind and loving with her. Dunia's upbringing is significantly different from that of the majority of her contemporaries: in his fanatical love for his daughter, Marko Danilych never limits her freedom. Dunia receives her education in the Komarov cloister, and her teachers are the most knowledgeable nuns. In the cloister she lives in a separate house built by her father for her and Dar'ia Sergeevna. Smolokurov likes to read and has collected a big library; he encourages his daughter to read as well. Dunia's world is devoid of any trace of romance or romantic love, however: Smolokurov acquires books only on history and geography, considering novels and drama to be impious and idly entertaining.

Dunia's quest for the true religion is not connected with family happiness or money: "Not to bridegrooms but to knowledge of good and truth did her soul strive." Dunia's search for the true religion brings her to the sect of the *khlysts*. She breaks with her family and fully embraces her new faith. Dunia participates in the *khlysts'* meetings, prays fervently, and experiences hypnotic trances during which she "prophesies." A growing awareness of the discrepancies between the sectarians' teachings and their actions, however, and her dissatisfaction with the answers of sect members to her questions lead Dunia to recognize her mistakes and leave the sect.

Dunia's spiritual quest is closely tied with her social quest. Her return home coincides with her father's illness and death. Her social position changes as she becomes a rich, independent woman. She begins to resemble her father, an imperious and short-tempered man, though, unlike her father, Dunia is just and honest. Dunia's moral strength is so powerful that even her godfather, Chapurin—a man intolerant to any obstruction of his own will—must yield to it. Dunia marries for love, as she had decided long before that she would. However, she is well aware of her spiritual and moral superiority over her husband, merchant Petr Stepanych Samokhvalov. This superiority is noticed by others: "God gave her good sense and good character and if she manages to keep her husband at her command they will have order in their household and everything."

The family theme dominates both of the novels. For all Mel'nikov's characters, family history and roots are of the utmost importance. Each character's family history is a separate plot; all of these threads comprise the mainstream of life. For Mel'nikov's characters, the family is the beginning and the end: they reveal themselves in their relationships, and their attitude toward the family indicates the nature of their personalities. Thus, Chapurin's foreman Aleksei Lokhmaty's first step toward moral degradation is his contempt for his family. The notion of family is present even in the cloister: not only does Mother Manefa retain close ties with her brother, Patap Maksimych, but she also raises in the cloister her illegitimate daughter, Flenushka, who succeeds her in the position of mother superior. Although the world tempts Flenushka, family ties are stronger than all temptations: she takes holy vows and stays with her mother.

A prominent theme of Russian literature—the theme of fathers and sons, the conflict between the old and young generations—is closely connected with the family theme and acquires new dimensions in

Mel'nikov's novels. There are no discussions or arguments between fathers and sons about the new ways of life. A new generation of educated Russian merchants tries to preserve its ties with Russian national traditions. However, the first and foremost link in the chain of keeping up with tradition–family ties–has in a sense already been severed. This conflict is not initiated by the new generation, but instead is brought by strangers from the outside: in each case a son is taken from his family and sent to Moscow to study commerce by the will of someone who has more power than his father–a governor or mine owner. Mel'nikov does not even mention these men's names, as the names themselves are not important: these people act as the hand of Fate. The new ways come with the progress of time; they are inevitable and unavoidable. The old generation gives way to the new seemingly without resistance: older characters do not condemn and disinherit their sons. The only thing the sons do not get is their fathers' blessing, which is extremely important in the Russian traditional system of values. All the characters are well aware of it, and all of them realize a moral loss that no money can compensate.

V lesakh and *Na gorakh* are deeply rooted in Old Russian literature, such as saints' lives, pilgrimages, and stories from the Apocrypha and the Prolog. They are saturated with myth, legend, and folk beliefs. They include a detailed and precise ethnographic description of everyday life of the Old Believer communities. Yet, these novels touch upon themes and social issues that were widely discussed in intellectual circles of the time. The connection between Old Russian literature and social issues is not artificial: Mel'nikov depicts a society in which the traditions of Old Russian literature are definitely kept alive. Thus, *V lesakh* and *Na gorakh* constitute a distinctive link between Old Russian literature and Russian literature of the mid nineteenth century.

Tragedy permeates the lives of Mel'nikov's characters. The destruction of the Old Believer cloisters in the nineteenth century is only one of the many changes that take place across the country. Significantly, the characters of *V lesakh* and *Na gorakh* constantly travel down the Volga River, maintaining close business and religious contacts with Moscow and St. Petersburg. Although Mel'nikov acknowledges the necessity of industrial progress, he also portrays the losses that civilization brings to the lives of his characters. The changing world is hostile or, at best, indifferent to Mel'nikov's characters. Happiness is achieved not by changing or reforming the world, but by comprehending and accepting it in all its complexity.

In *V lesakh* and *Na gorakh* vivid, mystical images and symbols and a rich, detailed vision of everyday life are intermingled. Many images of the novel appear

Mel'nikov's grave at the Krestovozdvizhenskii monastery

to be introduced as circumstantial detail, but they reappear in subsequent chapters as keys to the meaning of the narration. This saturation with mythical images as well as an exquisite accuracy in describing the details of Old Believers' everyday life made Mel'nikov's novels the main "reference books" on the Schism for the Russian Symbolists. The characters in these novels also inspired a series of paintings by the famous Russian artist Mikhail Vasil'evich Nesterov: *Khristova nevesta* (Christ's Bride, 1887); *Za privorotym zel'em* (The Love Potion, 1887); *Velikii postrig* (Taking the Veil, 1897); *Na gorakh* (On the Hills, 1896); and *Na Volge* (On the Volga, 1905).

Mel'nikov was afflicted by gout and gradually lost his ability to move and to write. He dictated the last chapters of *Na gorakh* to his wife and lived to see the publication and the success of his novel. When Alexander III learned about Mel'nikov's illness, he sent the writer two thousand rubles for a trip to the Crimea. However, doctors were convinced that Mel'nikov would not survive the trip. He died on 1 February 1883 in Nizhnii Novgorod. Peasants from Mel'nikov's estate, Liakhovo, came on foot to Nizhnii Novgorod to attend the funeral and carried his coffin from the church to Krestovozdvizhenskii monastery, where Mel'nikov was buried. Mel'nikov occupies a distinctive place in Russian literature: his novels are inseparable from the mainstream of Russian literature of the nineteenth century both thematically and in form. At the same time, his works serve as a connection between Old Russian literature and modernism.

Letters:

"Pis'ma P. S. Usovu," *Novoe vremia*, 25–28 (1883);

"Pis'ma E. A. Mel'nikovoi," *Istoricheskii vestnik*, 1 (1884): 47–54; 11 (1884): 359–360; 12 (1884): 564–566, 586–588;

"Pis'mo A. P. Shirinskomu-Shikhmatovu," *Istoricheskii vestnik*, 10 (1884): 32–35;

"Pis'ma k A. P. Valuevu," *Istoricheskii vestnik*, 12 (1884): 539–542, 547–561;

"Pis'mo N. I. Subbotinu," *Istoricheskii vestnik*, 12 (1884): 566–567;

"Pis'ma k D. N. Tolstomu," *Trudy Riazanskoi gubernskoi arkhivnoi komissii za 1887 god* (Riazan', 1888), pp. 2–10;

"Pis'mo K. I. Tikhonravovu," *Materialy dlia biografii K. N. Tikhonravova* (Vladimir, 1909), pp. 216–219;

"Pis'mo F. M. Dostoevskomu," *Iz arkhiva Dostoevskogo* (Moscow-Petrograd, 1924), pp. 38–40;

"Pis'mo A. A. Kraevskomu," *Literaturnoe nasledstvo*, 56 (1950), pp. 162–164.

Biographies:

Pavel S. Usov, "P. I. Mel'nikov (Andrei Pechersky). Ego zhizn' i literaturnaia deiatel'nost'," in P. I. Mel'nikov (Andrei Pechersky), *Polnoe sobranie sochinenii*, volume 1 (St. Petersburg: M. O. Vol'f, 1897), pp. 3–316;

L. A. Anninsky, *Tri eretika: povesti o A. F. Pisemskom, P. I. Mel'nikove-Pecherskom, N. S. Leskove* (Moscow: Kniga, 1988).

References:

A. [V. G. Avseenko], "Eshche raz o narodnosti i kul'turnykh tipakh," *Russkii vestnik*, 3 (1876): 77–85;

A., "Khudozhestvennoe izuchenie raskola," *Russkii vestnik*, 1 (1874): 352–378;

N. Ia. Agafonov, "Kazanskaia geroinia *V lesakh* Andreia Pecherskogo," *Istoricheskii vestnik*, 1 (1902): 210–228;

E. A. Antsupova, "K probleme kharakterov v romanakh P. I. Mel'nikova (A. Pecherskogo) *V lesakh* i *Na gorakh*," in *Problemy russkoi literatury: Sbornik trudov*, edited by Aleksandr Ivanovich

Reviakin (Moscow: Moskovskii gos. pedagog. in-t im. V. I. Lenina, 1973), pp. 123–139;

V. F. Botsianovsky, "Ostrovsky i Mel'nikov Pechersky," in *Sbornik statei k sorokaletiiu uchenoi deiatel'nosti akademika A. S. Orlova*, edited by V. N. Peretts (Leningrad: izd-vo Akademii nauk SSSR, 1934), pp. 64–74;

N. Cheremnykh, "Lichnaia biblioteka P. I. Mel'nikov-Pecherskogo," *Volzhskii al'manakh*, 8 (1952): 375–377;

K. V. Chistov, "P. I. Mel'nikov-Pechersky i I. A. Fedosova," *Slavianskii fol'klor* (Moscow: Nauka, 1972), pp. 313–327;

Thomas H. Hoisington, "Dark Romance in the Provincial Setting: Mel'nikov-Pecherskij's *The Krasil'nikovs*," *Slavic and East European Journal*, 22 (1978): 15–25;

Hoisington, "Mel'nikov-Pechersky: Romancer of Provincial and Old Believer Life," *Slavic Review*, 33 (1974): 679–694;

Hoisington, "Romance—a Congenial Form: Mel'nikov-Pecherskii's *Grandma's Yarns* and *Olden Times*," *Russian Review*, 36 (1977): 463–476;

L. K. Il'insky, "P. I. Mel'nikov (Andrei Pechersky)," *Russkii filologicheskii vestnik*, 67 (1912): 1–48;

Dmitrii Ivanovich Ilovaisky, "P. I. Mel'nikov i ego 35-letniaia literaturnaia deiatel'nost'," *Russkii arkhiv*, 1 (1875): 77–85;

A. A. Izmailov, "Bytopisatel' vzyskuiushchikh grada," *Ezhemesiachnoe nauchno-populiarnoe prilozhenie k "Nive,"* 1 (1908): 454–482;

V. A. Kaminsky, "P. I. Mel'nikov (Andrei Pechersky)," *Russkii filologicheskii vestnik*, 2 (1908): 374–380;

"Kniazhna Tarakanova i printsessa Vladimirskaia," *Otechestvennye zapiski*, 3, no. 6 (1868): 203–209;

"Kniazhna Tarakanova i printsessa Vladimirskaia," *Sovremennoe obozrenie*, 2, no. 4 (1868): 30–38;

I. M. Kolesnitskaia, "P. I. Mel'nikov-Pechersky," *Literaturnoe nasledstvo*, volume 79 (Moscow: Izdatel'stvo Akademii nauk SSSR, 1978), pp. 581–591;

K. E. Korepova, "Fol'klor narodov Povo'zh'ia v istoriko-etnograficheskikh rabotakh P. I. Mel'nikov-Pecherskogo," *Fol'klor narodov RSFSR* (Ufa, 1976), pp. 161–167;

S. F. Librovich, "Originaly Mel'nikov-Pecherskogo," *Na knizhnom postu: Vospominaniia, zapiski, dokumenty* (Petrograd-Moskva: M. O. Vol'f, 1916), pp. 145–148;

Larisa M. Lotman, "P. I. Mel'nikov-Pechersky," *Istoriia russkoi literatury*, volume 9 (Moscow-Leningrad: Izdatel'stvo Akademii nauk SSSR, 1956), pp. 198–227;

Lotman, "Roman iz narodnoi zhizni. Etnograficheskii roman," *Istoriia russkogo romana,* volume 2 (Moscow-Leningrad: Izdatel'stvo Akademii nauk SSSR, 1964), pp. 405–415;

D. A. Markov, "Osobennosti leksiki romana Mel'nikov-Pecherskogo *V lesakh,*" *Uchenye zapiski Moskovskogo oblastnogo pedagogicheskogo instituta imeni Krupskoi,* 7 (1961): 3–39;

N. M. Meleshkov, "K biografii P. I. Mel'nikova-Pecherskogo," *Uchenye zapiski gor'kovskogo gosudarstvennogo pedagogicheskogo instituta,* 129 (Gorky, 1972), pp. 127–134;

P. O. Pilashevsky, "K voprosu o kompozitsii i stile romana P. I. Mel'nikova *V lesakh,*" *Izvestiia Nizhegorodskogo gosudarstvennogo universiteta,* volume 2 (Nizhnii Novgorod, 1928), pp. 330–347;

Sbornik Nizhegorodskoi uchenoi arkhivnoi komissii, volume 9, part 1 (Nizhnii Novgorod, 1910);

Veronica Shapovalov, "From *White Doves* to *Silver Dove:* Andrei Belyi and Mel'nikov-Pecherskii," *Slavic and East European Studies Journal,* 4 (1994): 591–602;

Shapovalov, "Khlystovskaia bogoroditsa: k istorii razvitiia literaturnogo tipa," *Studia Slavica Hungarica,* 40 (1995): 153–164;

Shapovalov, "P. I. Mel'nikov-Pecherskii in the History of the Russian Novel," dissertation, University of Illinois, Urbana, 1988;

S. V. Sheshunova, "Mel'nikov," in *Russkie pisateli, 1800–1917: Biograficheskii slovar',* volume 3, edited by P. A. Nikolaev (Moscow: Bol'shaia Rossiiskaia Entsiklopediia, 1994), pp. 578–582;

V. F. Sokolova, "Eshche raz o fol'klornykh istochnikakh romana P. I. Mel'nikova-Pecherskogo *V lesakh,*" in *Poetika i stilistika russkoi literatury* (Leningrad: Nauka, 1971), pp. 180–186;

Sokolova, "K voprosu o tvorcheskoi istorii romanov P. I. Mel'nikova-Pecherskogo *V lesakh* i *Na gorakh,*" *Russkaia literatura,* 3 (1970): 107–118;

Sokolova, "Ostrovsky i Mel'nikov-Pechersky," in *Russkaia literatura 1870–1890 godov,* Trudy ural'skogo gosudarstvennogo universiteta imeni Gor'kogo, 8 (Sverdlovsk, 1975), pp. 65–73;

Sokolova, *P. I. Mel'nikov-Pechersky: Ocherk zhizni i tvorchestva* (Gorky, 1981);

Z. I. Vlasova, "Fol'klor o Groznom u P. I. Mel'nikova i N. K. Miroliubova," *Russkii fol'klor,* volume 20 (Leningrad, 1981), pp. 107–157;

Vlasova, "P. I. Mel'nikov-Pechersky," in *Russkaia literatura i fol'klor: Vtoraia polovina 19 veka,* edited by A. A. Gorelov (Leningrad: Nauka, 1982), pp. 94–130;

V. A. Volodina, "Istoricheskii ocherk P. I. Mel'nikova *Kniazhna Tarakanova i printsessa Vladimirskaia,*" in *Pisatel' i literaturnyi protsess: Sbornik nauchnykh statei,* Tadzhikskii gosudarstvennyi universitet, 6 (Dushanbe, 1979), pp. 89–106;

Volodina, "Nachalo literaturnogo puti P. I. Mel'nikova-Pecherskogo," in *Pisatel' i literaturnyi protsess: Sbornik nauchnykh statei,* Tadzhikskii gosudarstvennyi universitet, 5 (Dushanbe, 1974), pp. 193–215;

A. P. Zmorovich, "O iazyke i stile proizvedenii P. I. Mel'nikova," *Russkii filologicheskii vestnik,* 1–2 (1916): 172–191.

Papers:

Pavel Ivanovich Mel'nikov's papers are located in Moscow at the Russian State Archive of Literature and Art and in St. Petersburg at the Institute of Russian Literature (Pushkin House) and the Russian National Library.

Mikhail Larionovich Mikhailov

(3 or 4 January 1829 – 2 or 3 August 1865)

Clark Troy
Harriman Institute, Columbia University

WORKS: *Adam Adamych*, in *Moskvitianin*, nos. 18–20 (1851); (St. Petersburg: V. I. Gubinsky, 1890);

Mar'ia Ivanovna, in *Otechestvennye zapiski*, nos. 6–8 (1853);

Sviatki. Ocherki i rasskazy, in *Otechestvennye zapiski*, no. 3 (1853); (St. Petersburg: Korolev, 1854);

Pereletnye ptitsy, in *Otechestvennye zapiski*, nos. 9–12 (1854); (St. Petersburg, 1889);

Strizhovye nory, in *Otechestvennye zapiski* (1855);

V provintsii, 2 volumes in 1 (St. Petersburg: Riumin, 1859)—comprises volume 1: *Adam Adamych*, "On. Dnevnik uezdnoi baryshni," "Kruzhevnitsa," "Poet," "Skromnaia dolia," "Synok i mamen'ka," "Kumushki," and "Skripach"; volume 2: *Pereleynye ptitsy* and "Izgoev";

Blagodeteli, in *Russkoe slovo*, nos. 6–8 (1859); (St. Petersburg: V. I. Gubinsky, 1891);

Tetushka, in *Russkoe slovo*, no. 1 (1860);

Russkie skazki dlia detei (St. Petersburg: Osviannikov, 1864);

Sibirskie ocherki, in *Delo*, nos. 7–9 (1867);

Za predelami istorii. Kartiny zhizni za million let, in *Delo*, nos. 3–4 (1869); (Moscow: Sytin, 1898);

Zhenshchiny, ikh vospitanie i znachenie v sem'e i v obshchestve. Zhenshchiny v universitete. Dzhon Stiuart Mill' ob emansipatsii zhenshchiny. Uvazhenie k zhenshchinam. Vospominaniia o Mikhailove N. V. i L. P. Shelgunovykh (St. Petersburg: Kartavov, 1903);

Zapiski (1861–1862), edited by A. A. Shilov (Petrograd: Byloe, 1922);

Vospominaniia, by Mikhailov, N. V. Shelgunov, and L. P. Shelgunova, edited by E. Vilenska, E. Ol'khovsky, and L. Roitberg, 2 volumes (Moscow: Khudozhestvennaia literatura, 1967).

Editions and Collections: *Stikhotvoreniia* (Berlin: Georg Stilke, 1862);

Sobranie stikhotvoreniia (St. Petersburg: M. M. Stasiulevich, 1890);

Sochineniia M. Mikhailova (St. Petersburg: V. I. Gubinsky, 1890);

Polnoe sobranie sochinenii M. L. Mikhailova, edited by P. V. Bykov, 4 volumes (St. Petersburg: Marks, 1913);

Mikhail Larionovich Mikhailov, 1861

Polnoe sobranie stikhotvorenii, edited by N. S. Ashukin (Moscow-Leningrad: Academia, 1934);

Sochineniia v dvukh tomakh, volume 1, edited by P. S. Fateev (Chita, 1950);

Sobranie sochinenii v piati tomakh, volume 1, edited by Militsa Vasil'evna Nechkina (Chkalov, 1951);

M. L. Mikhailov. Sobranie stikhotvorenii, edited by Iu. D. Levin (Leningrad: Sovetskii pisatel', 1953);

Sochineniia v trekh tomakh, edited by B. P. Koz'min, 3 volumes (Moscow: Goslitizdat, 1958);

Adam Adamych i drugie: Izbrannye proizvedeniia, edited by G. G. Elizavetina (Moscow: Pravda, 1991).

TRANSLATIONS: Heinrich Heine, *Pesni Geine v perevode M. L. Mikhailova* (St. Petersburg: Iakov Trei, 1858);

Nemetskoe izvestie o russkikh pisateliakh. 1768. (Moscow: Grachev, 1862).

SELECTED PERIODICAL PUBLICATIONS:
"Nash dom," *Biblioteka dlia chteniia* (1855);
"Parizhskie pis'ma I–VI," *Sovremennik,* nos. 9–12 (1858); no. 2 (1859): "Sovremennoe obozrenie" section;
"Londonskie zametki I–IV," *Sovremennik,* nos. 6–9 (1859): "Sovremennoe obozrenie" section;
"Ural'skie zametki (Iz putevykh zametok 1856–1857)," *Morskoi sbornik,* no. 9 (1859): unofficial section, 1–29;
"Zametka o Lermontove," *Sovremennik,* no. 2 (1861).

P. V. Bykov, writing a biographical sketch of Mikhail Larionovich Mikhailov for a 1913 edition of Mikhailov's collected works, opined that it would be hard to find another writer who had been so quickly forgotten. Mikhailov's rapid descent into oblivion was aided by an official ban on the mention of his name in print following his 1862 deportation to a Siberian labor camp, where he died in 1865. While Mikhailov's reputation as a martyr flourished among late-nineteenth-century populists, the prohibition against mentioning him in print insured that even the better-than-average reader remained more or less ignorant of him right up until the revolution. Another salient fact in Mikhailov's life story was passed over in silence for even longer: his open love affair with Liudmila Shelgunova, the wife of Mikhailov's good friend, the progressive man of letters Nikolai Vasil'evich Shelgunov. This liaison was glossed over until 1929, when it was one of the focal points of T. A. Bogdanovich's book on radical marital arrangements in the 1860s; then it vanished again from Soviet biographies of Mikhailov, owing to Soviet prudishness, only to be reacknowledged in the 1960s. More than most, Mikhailov's legacy has suffered from censorship of both the official and consensual varieties.

All repressive measures aside, Mikhailov was never entirely forgotten, and he has been claimed in the twentieth century by several constituencies for a variety of reasons. Mikhailov was an active man of letters, writing prose fiction, verse, criticism, and journalism. While two of his novels, *Adam Adamych* (1851) and *Pereletnye ptitsy* (Migrating Birds, 1854) were well known in their day, later generations—including Aleksandr Aleksandrovich Blok, Nikolai Andreevich Rimsky-Korsakov, and Petr Il'ich Tchaikovsky—esteemed him highly for his translations of the works of Heinrich Heine and other poets. The Bolsheviks and Soviets, following in the populist tradition, at times regarded Mikhailov as a great revolutionary predecessor. Postwar Western scholars, led by the historian Richard Stites, have focused on Mikhailov's crucial role in the formulation and discussion of the "woman question" in the early 1860s.

Mikhail Larionovich Mikhailov was born on 3 or 4 January 1829 in Orenburg, and he and his sister and three brothers grew up in the Ural town of Iletskaia Zashchita, about sixty-five kilometers south of Orenburg. As was the case with so many of his colleagues in progressive St. Petersburg literary circles of the 1850s and 1860s, Mikhailov's family originated well outside the salons of the capitals. Mikhailov's grandfather, a serf on the Aksakov estate in Orenburg province, cleverly earned the gratitude of his owner and thereby his freedom. Mikhailov's father solidified the family's ascent by marrying a Russified Kyrgyz princess and working his way through the ranks of the bureaucracy to attain the title of court counselor by the time he retired.

Mikhailov and his siblings obtained a good home education. Despite being nearly blind because of a congenital defect in his eyelids (ameliorated by surgery performed by the ethnographer Vladimir Ivanovich Dal'), Mikhailov soon distinguished himself in the study of languages. In 1841 Mikhailov's mother died, followed only four years later by his father. Relatives arranged for the Mikhailov brothers to be moved to Ufa so that they could study at the gymnasium there. In 1846 the brothers were to be enrolled in the College of Mines in St. Petersburg, but Mikhailov was not admitted owing to his poor eyesight. None too distressed at his failure to gain access to a practical education, Mikhailov attended St. Petersburg University as an auditor. At the university Mikhailov quickly befriended Nikolai Gavrilovich Chernyshevsky, who proved an invaluable contact in later years as editor of *Sovremennik* (The Contemporary) and leader of Russia's new generation.

Even prior to his arrival in the capital in 1846, Mikhailov had successfully submitted two poems for publication in Nestor Vasil'evich Kukol'nik's journal *Illiustratsiia* (The Illustration), inaugurating a career of intensive contribution to and collaboration with the chief Russian journals that continued until his incarceration in 1861. From 1846 to 1848 Mikhailov published a host of original and translated verse in such periodicals as *Illiustratsiia* and *Literaturnaia gazeta* (Literary Gazette). Between 1845 and 1848 Mikhailov's poems developed from an imitative, epigonic Romanticism to a verse that reflected the lessons of Vissarion

Grigor'evich Belinsky and the "natural school" and was oriented around more concrete social questions.

In 1848 the monetary demands of living in St. Petersburg, combined with the need to help support a younger sister who remained in Ufa, drove Mikhailov to leave the capital and accept an administrative post in the Salt-Farming Administration of Nizhnii Novgorod. Over the course of four years in the civil service Mikhailov rose in rank considerably. Although he worked full-time, Mikhailov was nonetheless able to maintain a frenzied level of intellectual and literary activity while in Nizhnii Novgorod. He frequented the theater, studied English and read assiduously from English literature, and contributed poems, translations, sketches, and reviews regularly to St. Petersburg and Nizhnii Novgorod periodicals. He also wrote many of his most accomplished prose works, including the novella *Adam Adamych* and the novel *Pereletnye ptitsy*. In 1851 *Adam Adamych* was published in Mikhail Petrovich Pogodin's journal *Moskvitianin* (Muscovite), and it was so successful that Mikhailov decided to leave his administrative post and return to St. Petersburg to devote himself entirely to a literary life.

Adam Adamych was praised in its day for its depiction of the everyday life of the provinces, to which Mikhailov was so faithful that Pogodin almost rejected the book for publication on the grounds that it was "too dirty" (though commercial concerns held sway in the end). The novella opens with a sentimental scene of its title character, a provincial German tutor, before quickly descending in tone to the "low" material to which Pogodin (and Dal' before him) had objected. The novella is not long on plot, and in many ways Adam Adamych serves primarily as a Shklovskian "device" facilitating the display of a gallery of typical provincial characters and their foibles. Notable among these are the head steward, Tat'iana Vasil'evna—who carries on affairs with both her master, Maksim Petrovich Zhelnobobov, and his eldest son—and the debauched and lazy tutor Zakurdaev. Tension between Adam Adamych's carnal lust for the local miller's comely wife and his wish to better himself socially through a liaison with a widowed pseudointellectual salon hostess drives what little narrative there is. In the end, Adam Adamych dies, seemingly of humiliation, after being—in the course of one day—caught by the miller in bed with his wife and then laughed off the stage while reading a poem at one of the widow's cultural evenings. For all his weaknesses, Adam Adamych is the only vaguely sympathetic character in the novella, but he is a mock sentimental victim of a provincial society exceeding that found in Nikolai Vasil'evich Gogol's fictions in its nastiness.

Adam Adamych did not pass unnoticed by the critics of the early 1850s. While the reviewer for *Sovremennik* called it a "remarkable" work by an "indubitable talent," Apollon Aleksandrovich Grigor'ev wrote in *Moskvitianin* that Mikhailov copied too indiscriminately from reality. Another critic in the same journal, however, likened Mikhailov's talents to those of the painter Pavel Andreevich Fedotov, saying that the two shared an ability to find humor in the negative sides of humanity, before going on to fault Mikhailov for overemphasizing "society's shortcomings and vices." In any case, the critical response to his first novel led Mikhailov to tell Pogodin that he would thereafter write in a more moderate tone.

Upon his return to St. Petersburg in 1852, Mikhailov began to publish vigorously in several of the leading journals in the capital, including *Sovremennik* and *Otechestvennye zapiski* (Notes of the Fatherland). Mikhailov became an entirely professional man of letters, managing to feed, entertain, and clothe himself entirely on what he earned from his literary activity. Meeting his expenses was no mean feat, for Mikhailov earned the reputation of a bon vivant extraordinaire in the St. Petersburg literary circles of the 1850s, which were themselves quite given over to festivity. Moreover, because of the medical problem with his eyelids, Mikhailov's eyes drooped constantly; seemingly to make up for his somewhat bizarre and slightly off-putting visage, Mikhailov invested substantial effort and resources in his clothing and haberdashery. Most probably on account of a similar wish to make up for perceived superficial shortcomings, the young writer also devoted himself assiduously to cultivating the favor of women.

All his efforts notwithstanding, Mikhailov apparently had no lasting liaisons with members of the opposite sex until the winter of 1855–1856, when he made the acquaintance of Liudmila Shelgunova, the wife of Nikolai Shelgunov. The two men became friends, with Shelgunov assenting to his wife's affair with Mikhailov as a show of support for women's freedom to determine their own destinies. In time, Shelgunova bore Mikhailov's child, who was named Mikhail Nikolaevich Shelgunov and who was educated by Nikolai Shelgunov following Mikhailov's death. Mikhailov and the Shelgunovs lived together and traveled through Western Europe, and the men in time worked together to distribute revolutionary literature. When Mikhailov was arrested in 1861, he maintained that he alone was guilty of acts in which he had collaborated with Shelgunov and others, and when Mikhailov was deported to Siberia, the Shelgunovs followed him into exile until they themselves were arrested.

The first two chapters of Mikhailov's second novel, *Pereletnye ptitsy,* were published in June 1854 in the journal *Otechestvennye zapiski.* Where *Adam Adamych* had almost fallen prey to the censorious impulses of its publisher, *Pereletnye ptitsy* encountered considerable resistance on the part of the official censor, who objected, once again, to the "low" and "dirty" nature of Mikhailov's scenes, characters, and language. Only after the novelist agreed to several changes did the censor approve the remaining chapters for publication. In a subsequent version of the novel, published in an 1859 collection, Mikhailov restored many of the excisions made by the censor and more starkly underscored the distinctions between his positive and negative characters. This later edition served as the basis for all Soviet reprints.

Conceived and written during Mikhailov's theater-intensive stay in Nizhnii Novgorod, *Pereletnye ptitsy* claims the inarguable distinction of being the first Russian novel written about the provincial theater. Despite its clearly delineated subject matter, however, the novel lacks narrative unity and focus. Mikhailov's practically omniscient first-person narrator begins by focusing on one theatrical troupe, only to have his attention decisively usurped by another troupe two-thirds of the way through the novel. Similarly, the reader is presented with a succession of major characters, introduced at regular intervals right up until the last quarter of the novel, as well as detailed presentations of the backstage intrigues of both theatrical companies and of the foibles and anxieties of their many constituent members. Although the talented but debauched actor Mirvolsky occupies center stage of the novel more than any other character, he proves to be a negative character for whom positive counterweights do not appear until much later in the novel. In the end, Mirvolsky's tale turns out to be nothing more than a dominant anecdote that dissolves in the multiple plot threads with which it is entwined.

At some level, however, the structural problems of the novel indicate that, despite the many plot twists Mikhailov threw into it, narrative was not his primary concern. If the roaming heroes of Gogol, Faddei Venediktovich Bulgarin, and Mikhail Iur'evich Lermontov had allowed their authors to describe a wide variety of social and geographical settings, Mikhailov's multiple "migrating birds" afforded him even greater range. Mikhailov's narrator lingers over inns, pubs, wayside huts, streets, ferries, apartments, flophouses, boulevards, markets, and theaters across far-flung Russian territories from St. Petersburg to the village of Bor near Turukhtansk. Mikhailov populates his multifarious locales with a similarly wide assortment of humanity, from petty and vain actresses and noble peasant moth-

Nikolai Vasil'evich Shelgunov and his wife, Liudmila,
Mikhailov's close friends and collaborators

ers to wily innkeepers and pool-shark actors. Each time a major character enters the novel, the reader is presented with a lengthy and detailed version of the character's life up until that moment in the narrative. One would say that these "backstories" hinder the development of the story, were it not apparent that the narrative itself quite purposefully ushers them into being.

Mikhailov completed and published two other novels: *Mar'ia Ivanovna,* which appeared in *Otechestvennye zapiski* in 1853, and *Blagodeteli* (The Benefactors), which came out in *Russkoe slovo* (The Russian Word) in 1859. Neither of these novels attracted much attention at all, the latter not even meriting inclusion in P. V. Bykov's 1913 "complete" edition of Mikhailov's works, despite being listed in the bibliography of that edition. *Mar'ia Ivanovna* depicts the stultification of a provincial woman's life and has attracted scholarly attention almost exclusively for the portrait it provides of a *raznochinets* (mixed class) tutor who, like Borsky in *Pere-*

letnye ptitsy, strives heroically to rise above the constraints of his milieu.

Mikhailov also published several works of short fiction between 1852 and 1860. Mikhailov's stories take place almost exclusively in the provinces, and many of them depict the passive and vulnerable character of the provincial woman's life. In the 1852 "On. (Iz dnevnika uezdnoi baryshni)" (Him. [The Diary of a Provincial Noblewoman]), a young woman carries on a clandestine affair with an unnamed dandy, only to find herself betrothed to an unattractive older man and her lover relatively indifferent. "Kruzhevnitsa" (The Lacemaker), also published in 1852 in *Sovremennik,* describes how an urbane nobleman dazzles and befuddles a small-town girl and then leaves her behind. Other stories, such as "Nash dom" (Our House, 1855), a rare St. Petersburg story, and *Strizhovye nory* (Martins' Lairs, 1855), set among retired officers and Cossacks in the Urals, come closer to the physiological tradition, focusing less on individual psychology and more on manners and everyday life. In all of his fiction Mikhailov displays a keen ear for dialect and a penchant for the less attractive sides of life, from physical detail to social and psychological situation. Like Aleksei Feofilaktovich Pisemsky, Mikhailov shone particularly in the attention he paid to the inner world of secondary characters.

In the latter half of the 1850s, a pair of trips influenced Mikhailov's development considerably. In 1856 the writer traveled to his native Urals on a commission from the Naval Ministry, part of the same program that produced such notable works as Ivan Aleksandrovich Goncharov's *Fregat "Pallada"* (The Frigate *Pallas,* 1858). Over the course of a year and a half, Mikhailov discharged his mission of assembling ethnographic data and stories by and about the fishermen and boatmen of the region. He also planned two large works based on his travels and studies, though little of what he wrote was cleared by the censor. More important, the writer, long an admirer of Belinsky and an associate of Chernyshevsky and Nikolai Alekseevich Nekrasov, and thus clearly associated with the so-called Gogolian school of socially conscious literature, witnessed firsthand the privations of Russian provincial serfs and colonial minorities. The trip to the Urals marks Mikhailov's definitive political radicalization.

Mikhailov published a book of his translations of Heine in 1858, just two years after the German poet's death. This collection was one of the high points in Mikhailov's career, eliciting favorable reviews in most of the leading Russian journals. Mikhailov had been translating Heine since the beginning of his literary career and had always avowed a particular affinity for him. This work forms the main part of his legacy as a translator, along with his version of Friedrich Schiller's

Kabale und Liebe (Cabal and Love, 1784), which attained canonical status in the Soviet period. Mikhailov was a productive translator. Out of some five hundred published poems, roughly four-fifths were translations from German, English, French, Slavic, and even Asian poets. As his views moved increasingly to the Left, Mikhailov selected politically pointed poems for translation as a way of eluding the censor. More theoretically inclined than most of his contemporaries, Mikhailov attended as much as possible to the maintenance of the rhythmic texture of his originals and called in his reviews for similar formal fidelity.

Also in 1858 Mikhailov embarked on the second of his formative journeys, setting off for Paris to join the Shelgunovs. In Paris, Mikhailov studied utopian socialism and held long discussions with the feminists who managed and frequented the hotel where he and the Shelgunovs stayed, including Eugénie d'Héricourt, one of the first woman doctors in Europe. Early in 1859 the writer traveled to London to meet Aleksandr Ivanovich Herzen and Nikolai Platonovich Ogarev, publishers of the progressive journal *Kolokol* (The Bell). During his time abroad, Mikhailov dispatched two series of politically charged articles to *Sovremennik: Parizhskie pis'ma* (Parisian Letters) and *Londonskie zametki* (London Notes). In these articles Mikhailov began his career as a partisan publicist, inveighing against the repressive bourgeois-catholic atmosphere of Napoleon III's France and the unspeakable poverty that undergirded the industrial preeminence of England.

While in France, Mikhailov also completed a set of articles that later distinguished him as a social journalist-activist, if not quite as an original thinker. Mikhailov's series of articles on the "woman question" appeared at irregular intervals in *Sovremennik* between 1860 and 1861. In these articles Mikhailov adopts a rational and pragmatic stance in favor of women's rights. Polemicizing with recent and surprisingly reactionary books by Jules Michelet and P. J. Proudhon, Mikhailov begins by stating that woman's subjugation originally derives from her relative physical frailty, a fact no longer relevant in modern society. Mikhailov's subsequent main points are that women's education must be brought in line with that of men; that women must be provided with career options outside the home; and that marriage must be based on choice, not on force and property exchange. In the final analysis, Mikhailov advanced the outrageously radical position that women are people and should be treated as such. To seal this point, he translated and published an article by John Stuart Mill and Harriet Taylor advocating the enfranchisement of women, an idea doubly outlandish in the context of Russia at that time, but one nonetheless in line with Mikhailov's thinking.

Late in 1859 Mikhailov returned to St. Petersburg and once again settled into a schedule of frenetic literary activity. He translated poems, reviewed works of foreign literature, contributed many articles to the encyclopedia project of the future populist leader Petr Lavrovich Lavrov, and for all practical purposes edited the journal *Russkoe slovo*. But Mikhailov's most significant publication was the revolutionary pamphlet "K molodomu pokoleniiu" (To the Young Generation), written with Shelgunov. The extent of Mikhailov's authorship remains unclear, but he contributed greatly to the success of the project. In the summer of 1861 Mikhailov traveled to London, had this proclamation printed on Herzen's press, and then smuggled six hundred copies of it into Russia on his person and under a false bottom in his suitcase. With the help of the Shelgunovs and Aleksandr Serno-Solov'evich (who fathered Shelgunova's second child), Mikhailov distributed his pamphlets in early September and was arrested on the fourteenth of that month. He spent the rest of his life in government custody, the first victim of Czar Alexander II's political repressions. Immediately after his arrest, progressive St. Petersburg activists gathered in editorial offices to try to effect his release, signing petitions and delivering them to the Third Section, but to no avail. In London, Herzen and Ogarev soon printed a special appendix to *Kolokol*, "Mikhailov i studentskoe delo" (Mikhailov and the Student Affair).

Throughout his incarceration and interrogation, Mikhailov protected his friends and cohorts, insisting that he had worked alone. In December 1861 he was sentenced to six years of hard labor in the mines, and in March 1862 he arrived at the Kazakovsky gold mines in the Zabaikal'e region. Mikhailov chronicled his trip from St. Petersburg to Siberia in a memoir titled *Zapiski (1861–1862)* (Notes [1861–1862]), which was published only in the twentieth century. Mikhailov's brother Petr worked as an engineer at Kazakovo, and he arranged for Mikhailov to be spared hard labor and to live with him; the Shelgunovs joined them in the spring of 1862. The Shelgunovs were arrested and dispersed by the beginning of 1863, and Mikhailov was transferred to an actual prison camp. Mikhailov died in August 1865 of inflammation of the kidneys.

In many ways, the arrest and exile of Mikhailov marked the beginning of the end of the 1860s in Russia, even though these events took place early in the decade. Mikhailov was the first significant figure to be arrested, but by the end of the summer of 1862, Chernyshevsky was in jail; Nikolai Aleksandrovich Dobroliubov was dead; *Kolokol* was in decline; and both *Sovremennik* and *Russkoe slovo* had been shut down temporarily. But Mikhailov's importance as a revolutionary martyr should not obscure his literary significance. Mikhailov's translations of Heine and Schiller survived into the twen-

tieth century, even as reprints of his novels and shorter prose fiction continue to take readers into distant and unfamiliar corners of Russia's past.

Biography:
P. S. Fateev, *Mikhail Mikhailov–Revoliutsioner, pisatel', publitsist* (Moscow: Mysl', 1969).

References:
N. Belozersky, "Ot Peterburga do Nerchinska (Novye materialy dlia biografii poeta M. L. Mikhailova)," *Russkaia mysl'*, no. 12 (1902);

V. V. Bogatov, *M. I. Mikhailov–myslitel' i revoliutsioner* (Moscow, 1959);

T. A. Bogdanovich, *Liubov' liudei shestidesiatykh godov* (Leningrad: Academia, 1929), pp. 35–50, 264–420;

B. P. Koz'min, "N. G. Chernyshevsky i M. L. Mikhailov," *Voprosy istorii*, no. 7 (1946): 3–25;

M. L. Lemke, *Politicheskie protsessy M. L. Mikhailova, D. I. Pisareva, i N. G. Chernyshevskogo (po neizdannym dokumentam)* (St. Petersburg: O. N. Popov, 1907);

Iu. D. Levin, "M. L. Michajlovs Beziehungen zu Deutschland und zu deutschen Zeitgenossen," *Zeitschrift fur Slawistik*, no. 7 (1963): 487–514;

Levin, "Poslednii roman M. L. Mikhailova: K 100-letiiu so dnia smerti pisatelia," *Izvestiia Akademii nauk SSSR: Seriia literatury i iazyka*, 24, no. 4 (1965): 287–298;

N. Meshchersky, "Mikhail Larionovich Mikhailov i ego literaturnaia komandirovka v Orenburgskii krai," *Stepnye ogni*, no. 4 (1941): 152–181;

V. Miiakovsky, "M. L. Mikhailov," *Golos minuvshego*, no. 9 (1915);

Irina Paperno, *Chernyshevsky and the Age of Realism: A Study in the Semiotics of Behavior* (Stanford, Cal.: Stanford University Press, 1988), pp. 147–150;

Richard Stites, *The Women's Liberation Movement in Russia* (Princeton, N.J.: Princeton University Press, 1978), pp. 38–47;

A. F. Zakharkin, "Novye materialy o poete-revoliutsionere M. L. Mikhailove," *Izvestiia Akademiia nauk SSSR*, 12, no. 5 (1953): 417–438.

Papers:
Mikhail Larionovich Mikhailov's papers can be found in the Russian State Archive of Literature and Art (RGALI, formerly TsGALI) in Moscow, fond 1111, and in the Institute of Russian Literature (IRLI, Pushkin House) in St. Petersburg, fond 547. Further information on Mikhailov's papers can be found in L. P. Klochkova, "Rukopisi Mikhailova," in *Biulleteni Rukopisnogo otdela Pushkinskogo doma*, volume 5 (Moscow-Leningrad: Akademiia nauk SSSR, 1955).

Daniil Lukich Mordovtsev

(7 December 1830 – 10 June 1905)

Dan I. Ungurianu
Vassar College

WORKS: *Malorusskii literaturnyi sbornik* (Saratov, 1859);

Samozvantsy i ponizovaia vol'nitsa, 2 volumes (St. Petersburg & Moscow: Izd. M. O. Vol'fa, 1867);

Russkie gosudarstvennye deiateli proshlogo veka i Pugachev (1868);

Novye russkie liudi, in *Vsemirnyi trud,* 5–8 (1868); (St. Petersburg, 1870);

Znameniia vremeni, in *Vsemirnyi trud,* 1–7 (1869); (St. Petersburg, 1870);

Gaidamachina. Istoricheskaia monografiia, 2 volumes (St. Petersburg: K. N. Plotnikov, 1870);

Politicheskie dvizheniia russkogo naroda. Istoricheskaia monografiia, 2 volumes (St. Petersburg: S. V. Zvonarev, 1871);

Nakanune voli. Arkhivnye siluety, in *Delo* (1872);

Poslednie gody raskol'nich'ikh skitov na Irgize (1872);

Dvizheniia v raskole (1874);

Russkie istoricheskie zhenshchiny. Populiarnye rasskazy iz russkoi istorii. Zhenshchiny dopetrovskoi Rusi (St. Petersburg: K. N. Plotnikov, 1874);

Russkie zhenshchiny novogo vremeni (St. Petersburg: A. Cherkesov, 1874);

Idealisty i realisty, in *Novoe vremia* (1876); (St. Petersburg: A. S. Suvorin, 1878);

Desiatiletie russkogo zemstva (St. Petersburg: A. A. Kraevsky, 1877);

Nashi okrainy (St. Petersburg, 1877);

Lzhedmitrii (St. Petersburg: Tip. Ministerstva putei soobshcheniia [A. Benke], 1879);

Nanosnaia beda (St. Petersburg: A. S. Suvorin, 1879);

Dvenadtsatyi god, in *Nedelia,* nos. 2–3, 9–12 (1879); (St. Petersburg, 1879);

Tsar' i getman, in *Ezhened. "Novoe vremia" za 1879 g.,* 1–3 (1879); (Moscow, 1880);

Solovetskoe sidenie (Moscow, 1880);

Velikii raskol, in *Russkaia mysl',* nos. 1–8 (1880); (St. Petersburg: Tip. Ministerstva putei soobshcheniia, 1881);

Mamaevo poboishche (St. Petersburg, 1881);

Poezdka k piramidam (St. Petersburg, 1881);

Daniil Lukich Mordovtsev

Poezdka v Ierusalim, in *Istoricheskii vestnik,* 10–11 (1881); (St. Petersburg, 1881);

Gospodin velikii Novgorod (Moscow, 1882);

Sagaidachnyi (St. Petersburg, 1882);

Na Ararat (St. Petersburg, 1884);

Arkhimandrit-getman (Moscow, 1884);

Iz prekrasnogo daleka (St. Petersburg: Tip. N. A. Lebedeva, 1884);

Po Italii, in *Nabliudatel',* 1–8 (1884); (St. Petersburg, 1884);

Po Ispanii, in *Vestnik Evropy*, 1–3 (1884); (St. Petersburg, 1884);

Istoricheskie povesti (St. Petersburg, 1885);

Opovidannia (St. Petersburg, 1885);

Tsar' Petr i pravitel'nitsa Sof'ia (1885);

Pokhorony, in *Nabliudatel'*, 1–8 (1885); (St. Petersburg, 1886);

Avantiuristy, in *Istoricheskii vestnik*, 10–12 (1885); (St. Petersburg, 1886);

Iz zhizni. Povesti i rasskazy (St. Petersburg, 1885);

Nash Odissei, in *Nedelia*, 3–6 (1886); (St. Petersburg, 1886);

Novye liudi (St. Petersburg: Tip. N. A. Lebedeva, 1886);

Aforizmy (St. Petersburg: Tip. V. S. Balasheva, 1886);

Kum Ivan, in *Istoricheskii vestnik*, 1 (1887); (St. Petersburg: A. S. Suvorin, 1887);

Beglyi korol', in *Nedelia*, 10–12 (1887); (St. Petersburg: Tip. N. A. Lebedeva, 1888);

Tri byli (St. Petersburg, 1888)–includes "Kum Ivan," "On idet," and "Sila very";

Iz proshlogo (St. Petersburg, 1888);

Pozdniaia liubov', in *Nabliudatel'*, 5–12 (1888); (St. Petersburg, 1889);

Teni minuvshego (St. Petersburg: V. A. Nemetti, 1888);

Professor Ratmirov, in *Knizhki "Nedeli,"* 1–2 (1889); (St. Petersburg, 1889);

Istoricheskie propilei, 2 volumes (St. Petersburg: Tip. N. A. Lebedeva, 1889);

Zamurovannaia tsaritsa, in *Severnyi vestnik*, 5–7 (1890); (St. Petersburg: Tip. V. I. Shteina, 1891);

Za ch'i grekhi? in *Istoricheskii vestnik*, 1–9 (1890); (St. Petersburg, 1891);

Zhertvy vulkana (St. Petersburg, 1891);

Tsar' bez tsarstva (St. Petersburg, 1891);

Za vsemirnoe vladychestvo (1891);

Mezhdu Stsilloi i Kharibdoi (St. Petersburg, 1892);

Bez titula. Byli i rasskazy (St. Petersburg, 1894)–includes *Kavkazskii geroi;*

Zhelezom i krov'iu, in *Nabliudatel'*, 3–8 (1894); (St. Petersburg, 1896);

Svetu bol'she, in *Nabliudatel'*, 1–3 (1895); (St. Petersburg: Tip. gaz. "Novosti," 1896);

Boginia Izida-svakha (St. Petersburg, 1895);

Govor kamnei (St. Petersburg: A. Benke, 1895);

Mest' zhretsov (1895);

Prometeevo potomstvo, in *Nabliudatel'*, nos. 2–7 (1896); (St. Petersburg: A. E. Landau, 1897);

Irod (St. Petersburg, 1897);

Poslednie dni Ierusalima (St. Petersburg, 1898);

Derzhavnyi plotnik (St. Petersburg, 1899).

Editions and Collections: *Sobranie sochinenii*, 50 volumes (St. Petersburg: Izd. N. F. Mertsa, 1901–1902);

Polnoe sobranie istoricheskikh romanov, povestei i rasskazov, 33 volumes (St. Petersburg: Izd-vo P. P. Soikina, 1914);

Polnoe sobranie sochinenii, 12 volumes (Petrograd, 1915);

Sobranie sochinenii, 14 volumes (Moscow: Terra, 1996).

SELECTED PERIODICAL PUBLICATIONS:
"K slovu ob istoricheskom romane i ego kritike. (Pis'mo v redaktsiiu)," in *Istoricheskii vestnik*, 6 (1881): 642–651;

"Timosh i Fanatik" (St. Petersburg, 1891).

A prolific writer of a prolific age, Daniil Lukich Mordovtsev was extremely productive as a journalist, historian, and novelist. His journalism is relevant within the context of the era of the Great Reforms. His historical research reflects the turn of Russian historiography to the study of grassroots movements. His first novels are of interest as a part of the argument about the "new men" begun by Ivan Sergeevich Turgenev and Nikolai Gavrilovich Chernyshevsky. But his foremost contribution is in the area of the historical novel. Although Mordovtsev did not create a single masterpiece of lasting importance, his many novels on subjects from the Russian and Ukrainian past earned him a place in the rich tradition of Russian historical fiction. In addition to Russian, Mordovtsev wrote in his native Ukrainian, and, although his output there is rather modest, he is warmly remembered in Ukrainian culture. Mordovtsev did not belong to any single literary or political group, but all of his work is permeated with "democratic" sympathies that can be viewed as a version of moderate populism.

Daniil Lukich Mordovtsev was born on 7 December 1830 in the village of Danilovka in the Territory of the Don Cossack Army (now in the Volgograd Oblast) into the family of an estate steward. His father, who died before Daniil was a year old, was a descendant of Zaporozhian Cossacks; his mother was the daughter of the local priest. Mordovtsev received his initial schooling at home, reading Church Slavonic books under the guidance of his kinsman, a sacristan. At the age of nine he was sent with his two elder brothers to the district school in the town of Ust'-Medveditskaia on the Don River. Among the biggest challenges facing the boy, who had grown up in a Ukrainian-speaking environment, was mastering the Russian language. In 1844, following his brother's lead, Mordovtsev moved to the city of Saratov and entered the second grade of the local gymnasium. There he was among the best students and showed impressive linguistic aptitude (in addition to Ukrainian, Russian, and Slavonic, Mordovtsev knew Latin, Greek, Hebrew, French, German, Tatar, and Kalmyk). At the gymnasium Mordovtsev also became friends with several talented young men, including Chernyshevsky's relative Aleksandr Nikolaevich Pypin, who later became a prominent historian, ethnographer, and philologist.

In 1850 Mordovtsev applied to Kazan University, intending to enroll in the Department of Physics and Mathematics; however, the members of the examination board were so impressed by his proficiency in classical languages that they steered him to the Department of Philology. A year later he transferred to St. Petersburg University, where he majored in Russian history and philology. (Among his professors was the patriarch of the Slavic linguistics Izmail Ivanovich Sreznevsky.) Upon graduating with a gold medal in 1854, Mordovtsev, much to the surprise of his friends, married an acquaintance from Saratov, Anna Nikanorovna Paskhalova (née Zaletaeva). A well-educated woman and a literary figure in her own right, she was seven years older than Mordovtsev and had four children from her previous marriage. In 1855 the couple moved back to Saratov, where they found themselves in the atmosphere of the liberal "spring" that preceded the Great Reforms.

In Saratov, Mordovtsev began his career in the civil service and joined the Ministry of the Interior, where he served from 1856 to 1873, attaining the rank of *kollezhskii sovetnik* (the civilian equivalent of colonel). At this time he also met the exiled historian and Ukrainophile Nikolai Ivanovich Kostomarov, who was serving as the secretary of the Provincial Statistical Committee. Largely under Kostomarov's influence, Mordovtsev embarked upon his literary career in 1859–1861, publishing a narrative poem and several short stories in Ukrainian. Initially, he acted as Kostomarov's assistant and also co-edited *Saratovskie gubernskie vedomosti* (The Saratov Province Gazette). Using his access to local archives, Mordovtsev wrote many articles pertaining to history and to the current state of affairs in the province, which appeared in both local and central newspapers. He also paid tribute to the prevailing critical mood, publishing a number of biting social exposés. As his relations with the Saratov authorities deteriorated, Mordovtsev moved to St. Petersburg in 1864, but life in the capital proved to be too taxing, and in 1867 he returned to Saratov.

During the 1860s, Mordovtsev undertook extensive historical research and published several monographs on various popular movements and uprisings in the seventeenth and eighteenth centuries. The most important of these works were *Samozvantsy i ponizovaia vol'nitsa* (Impostors and Outlaws of the Lower Volga, 1867), *Russkie gosudarstvennye deiateli proshlogo veka i Pugachev* (Russian Statesmen of the Last Century and Pugachev, 1868), *Gaidamachina* (The Gaidamak Movement, 1870), and *Politicheskie dvizheniia russkogo naroda* (Political Movements of the Russian People, 1871). His shorter historical works were later collected in the two-volume edition *Istoricheskie propilei* (Historical Propylaea, 1889). The grassroots focus of these studies was in tune with the populist concerns of the time and won praise from many reviewers in leading periodicals and from professional historians. (Aside from Mordovtsev's friends Kostomarov and Pypin, the latter included the oldest Russian historian, Mikhail Nikolaevich Pogodin.) At one point there was even a serious discussion of offering Mordovtsev a professorship in Russian history at St. Petersburg University, but Mordovtsev showed little interest in pursuing the matter. Mordovtsev's books were also avidly read by young radicals, who dreamed of igniting new popular revolts. For the same reason, his writings met with disapproval from conservatives and put the censors on guard. The most controversial of Mordovtsev's monographs, *Nakanune voli. Arkhivnye siluety* (On the Eve of Freedom. Archival Silhouettes, 1872), dealt with the recent past of Russia and described the dire plight of the serfs in Saratov province on the eve of the Emancipation of 1861. The serialized publication of the book was interrupted by the censor in 1872 (a separate edition of 1889 was likewise banned, with printed copies destroyed), and after the ensuing scandal Mordovtsev had to resign his commission in the Ministry of the Interior.

In the late 1860s Mordovtsev also published his first novels—*Novye russkie liudi* (The New Russian Men, 1868) and *Znameniia vremeni* (Signs of the Time, 1869)—which dealt with the topical issues of the "New Man" and the position of young intellectuals as compared with the *narod* (common people). Although somewhat vague and contradictory, these novels lean toward a moderate version of populism, as their characters renounce revolutionary agitation and concede that, instead of trying to guide the people, intellectuals should learn from them. The novels inspired mixed responses—especially negative was a review in *Otechestvennye zapiski* (Notes of the Fatherland) by Mikhail Evgrafovich Saltykov; overall, however, the novels met with considerable interest on the part of the "democratic" reading public. Subsequent commentators noted certain "prophetic" elements in these works that in a sense predicted the failure of the so-called "going to the people" movement of the mid 1870s.

In 1873 Mordovtsev moved to St. Petersburg for the third time and reentered the civil service, now in the statistical department of the Ministry of Communications; he served until 1886, when he retired with the rank of *deistvitel'nyi statskii sovetnik* (civilian major general). In the early 1870s he was quite active as a journalist, addressing among other matters the state of the Russian provincial press and summarizing the first decade of the *zemstvos,* the local self-governing bodies that had been introduced during the Great Reforms. (This work appeared in *Otechestvennye zapiski* in 1875–1876 and in a separate edition in 1877.) All the drawbacks of the *zemstvo* system notwithstanding, Mordovtsev painted it as a beneficial institution, one that provided a constructive venue for the energy of the masses that had formerly found an outlet in mutiny and rebellion.

Mordovtsev also continued his historical studies and wrote two monographs on the fashionable subject of Old Believers—*Poslednie gody raskol'nich'ikh skitov na Irgize* (The Last Years of the Schismatics' Hermitages on the Irgiz, 1872) and *Dvizheniia v raskole* (Currents in the Schism, 1874). He also published two collections dealing with the increasingly topical "woman question"—*Russkie istoricheskie zhenshchiny. Populiarnye rasskazy iz russkoi istorii. Zhenshchiny dopetrovskoi Rusi* (Russian Historic Women. Popular Stories from Russian History. Women of the pre-Petrine Russia, 1874) and *Russkie zhenshchiny novogo vremeni* (Russian Women of the New Time, 1874). These popularized historical sketches served as a stepping-stone to the next phase of Mordovtsev's literary career.

In the mid 1870s Mordovtsev turned to the genre of the historical novel, which had been proliferating rapidly on Russia's literary scene. According to his subsequent explanations, his goal was to reach out to broader audiences. This goal was fulfilled as Mordovtsev became one of the most widely read historical novelists of his day. (His main competitors were Count Evgenii Andreevich Salias de Turnemir, Grigorii Petrovich Danilevsky, and Vsevolod Sergeevich Solov'ev.) Mordovtsev was also among the most prolific authors of Russia, writing more than thirty historical novels and tales, many of which went through several editions.

Mordovtsev considered historical novels a branch of popular historiography, as did other contemporary writers; their mission was to use an entertaining form for educational purposes. Not by chance, many of his works first appeared in *Istoricheskii vestnik* (Historical Herald), a journal that published historical fiction along with research papers and primary sources. This tendency was much in tune with the general outlook of the positiv-

ist historiography common at the time. However, Mordovtsev did not curb his flights of fancy in these novels. He concocted far-fetched connections between historical figures and made rather improbable pronouncements on the part of his characters (as one unsympathetic reviewer noted, "Mr. Mordovtsev has a bad habit of putting the rubbish that occurs to him into the mouths of people who could never have imagined anything of the kind"). And yet, such license occured only in the "gray" areas of history; Mordovtsev did not allow himself any deliberate distortions of established facts. Mordovtsev believed that filling in the blanks in primary sources was a prerogative of the novelist, who adds psychological analysis to the historian's tools.

Mordovtsev's views were compatible with those of his era, when literature was perceived as a means of quasi-scientific description and explanation of reality. What distinguishes Mordovtsev from many other historical novelists is his open tendentiousness—one, though, that is grounded in a populist concept of art and, as far as the historical novel is concerned, finds a precedent in Leo Tolstoy's *Voina i mir* (War and Peace, 1863–1869) and in the historical fiction of Mordovtsev's mentor Kostomarov. As Mordovtsev declared in his manifesto "K slovu ob istoricheskom romane i ego kritikakh" (Apropos of the Historical Novel and Its Critics, 1881): "The historical novel cannot help but serve the tasks of the present."

Especially biased are Mordovtsev's early historical works, beginning with his first historical novel, *Idealisty i realisty* (Idealists and Realists, 1876). Spanning the period from 1711 to 1722, *Idealisty i realisty* portrays a grim picture of the reforms of Peter the Great. In his criticism of Peter, Mordovtsev does not in fact proceed from a Slavophile premise, as he admits that Peter was perhaps correct in moving Russia in a westward direction. However, Mordovtsev laments the cruelty of the reforms, emphasizing that the suffering inflicted upon the common people was needless and excessive. This view reflects Mordovtsev's core historical belief, according to which history can be seen as a field of contestation between the "centripetal" and "centrifugal" forces, the former being embodied in the state, the latter, in the people. Not denying the role of the centripetal forces in historical progress, Mordovtsev sympathizes with the centrifugal ones, since the state embodies the principle of coercion, while the potential for free historical development lies within the people. In the novel, these forces are dubbed "realism" and "idealism." The "realists" may prevail, but moral truth remains on the side of the "idealists." Mordovtsev concludes,

Focused around Peter I, the realism of the early eighteenth century was confronted with an equally powerful idealism . . . it dwelt in the adepts of the old, in the [Old Believer] Schism; it hid in the forests and deserts and it faced death–fearlessly, heroically–at the stake, at the executioner's block, through impalement or self-conflagration. . . .

The "idealists" in the novel are represented by Peter's conservative son, Czarevich Aleksei, by many clergymen and common people, and by the main character of the novel, Captain Vasilii Levin, who is based on an actual historical figure. Crushed by a personal drama (the love of his life becomes a nun in order to avoid a marriage arranged by Peter) and appalled by what he sees around him, Levin turns into Peter's staunch opponent. Like many Russians of his time, Levin comes to believe that Peter is the Antichrist. Levin retires from the military, takes monastic vows, and, eventually, meets a martyr's death after publicly denouncing Peter and preaching the end of the world. In contrast to the selfless and sincere "idealists," Peter's supporters are a corrupt, predatory, and self-seeking breed. (They also turn out to be among the spiritual ancestors of the modern Russian bourgeois.) While the "reformers" rape and pillage the country, their leader acts in the novel as a veritable sadistic monster. Such a negative treatment of Peter provoked a storm of refutations from various quarters, but Mordovtsev did not budge and in later editions even published the piece under the title *Ten' Iroda* (The Shadow of Herod), implying that Peter was a Russian incarnation of the biblical villain. Mordovtsev changed his position only toward the end of his life, presenting an apologetic view of Peter in the novel *Derzhavnyi plotnik* (The Royal Carpenter, 1899). However, his early anti-Petrine stance set an important precedent in Russian literature; the novel is also noteworthy as an obvious source for *Antikhrist (Petr i Aleksei)* (The Antichrist [Peter and Alexis], 1904), the closing piece in the historical trilogy by Dmitrii Sergeevich Merezhkovsky.

During subsequent years, Mordovtsev published many novels covering a wide range of subjects from Russian and Ukrainian history: the first Russian victory over the Tartars in *Mamaevo poboishche* (The Massacre of Mamai, 1881); the fall of Novgorod in *Gospodin velikii Novgorod* (Lord Novgorod the Great, 1882); the Time of Troubles in *Lzhedimitrii* (The False Dmitrii, 1879); Ukrainian Cossacks in the early seventeenth century in *Sagaidachnyi* (Sahaidachny, 1882); the rise and fall of Patriarch Nikon and the Schism in *Velikii raskol* (The Great Schism, 1880) and *Solovetskoe sidenie* (The Siege of Solovki, 1880); the clash between young Peter I and

his half sister in *Tsar' Petr i pravitel'nitsa Sofia* (Czar Peter and Regent Sofia, 1885); the challenges to the recently formed Russo-Ukrainian union during the war with Sweden in *Tsar' i getman* (The Czar and the Hetman, 1879); the Moscow plague of 1771 in *Nanosnaia beda* (Calamity Brought from Afar, 1879); Napoleon's invasion in *Dvenadtsatyi god* (The Year 1812, 1879), and others.

Although Mordovtsev's views of particular figures and events sometimes vacillated, his approach to the past in these works is based upon the same set of principles as in his first novel and in his previous historical studies. The writer is sympathetic to popular movements and "centrifugal forces" in general; this latter tendency goes hand in hand with the ardent Ukrainian nationalism Mordovtsev had manifested already in *Idealisty i realisty*. There, Mordovtsev has Peter voice the following praise for Ukraine and warning to Russia:

The Little-Russian [i.e., Ukrainian] nation is both very clever and very shrewd. Like a hard-working bee, it provides the Russian state with the best intellectual honey and the best wax for the candle of Russian enlightenment, but it has a sting as well. As long as Russians love and respect it, it will be a beast of burden and a source of light for the Russian realm; but if they encroach upon its freedom and its language, dragon's teeth will grow out of it, and the Russian realm will not profit.

A corollary to this belief is Mordovtsev's pronounced anti-Moscow stance. In *Gospodin velikii Novgorod*, he unconditionally sides with the Novgorodians, who fight a losing battle against the "Muscovite pest," and presents an unattractive portrait of Ivan III. In *Lzhedimitrii*, Mordovtsev even goes against his usual "democratic" leanings–portraying the people of Moscow as a dark, blind, and cruel force that mindlessly destroys Dmitrii, that "great Sphinx of history."

In the early 1880s, Mordovtsev began extensive foreign travels, which inspired several vividly written travelogues: *Poezdka k piramidam* (A Trip to the Pyramids, 1881), *Poezdka v Ierusalim* (A Trip to Jerusalem, 1881), *Iz prekrasnogo daleka* (From the Beautiful Afar, 1884), *Na Ararat* (To Mount Ararat, 1884), *Po Ispanii* (Through Spain, 1884), *Po Italii* (Through Italy, 1884). In 1886, after a series of personal crises (the death of his wife and suicide of a stepson), Mordovtsev retired from the civil service, moving in with the family of his brother in Rostov-on-Don. His continued travels provided him with the impetus for quite a few historical novels set in the ancient world. Emulating the success of the German professor-novelist Georg Ebers, Mordovtsev published several Egyptian novels: *Zamurovannaia tsaritsa* (The Immured Queen, 1890), *Mest' zhretsov* (The Revenge of the Priests, 1895), and *Boginia Izida-svakha* (The Goddess Isis as a Match-Maker, 1895). Refreshing his background in the classical languages, Mordovtsev also wrote two Roman novels—*Za vsemirnoe vladychestvo* (For World Domination, 1891) and *Zhertvy vulkana* (Volcano Victims, 1891)—and two novels of ancient Israel—*Irod* (Herod, 1897) and *Poslednie dni Ierusalima* (The Fall of Jerusalem, 1898). According to the unanimous verdict of critics, these novels are among the weakest of Mordovstev's works, but they are not devoid of interest, as they signaled a shift away from the domination of domestic Russian subjects in Russian historical fiction. At the same time Mordovtsev wrote several pieces dealing with the Russian conquest of the Caucasus: *Tsar' bez tsarstva* (A King without a Kingdom, 1891), *Zhelezom i krov'iu* (With Iron and Blood, 1894), and *Kavkazskii geroi* (The Caucasian Hero, 1894). *Kavkazskii geroi* is devoted to the Dagestani warlord, Hadji Murad, the title hero of Tolstoy's late masterpiece *Khadzhi Murat* (1904). A considerable portion of *Zhelezom i krov'iu* describes the ill-fated mission to Teheran led by Aleksandr Sergeevich Griboedov, whose demise was later described in one of the finest of Soviet historical novels, *Smert' Vazir-Mukhtara* (The Death of Vazir-Mukhtar, 1928), by Iurii Nikolaevich Tynianov. However, there is no evidence that either Tolstoy or Tynianov was familiar with these particular pieces, which, like the rest of Mordovtsev's *senilia*, are among his least successful works.

The most valuable part of Mordovtsev's novelistic legacy consists of the novels dealing with Russian and Ukrainian history that Mordovtsev wrote during the decade between the mid 1870s and the mid 1880s. In them Mordovtscv drew upon his unquestionable historical erudition and his intimate familiarity with a wide range of primary sources. He also made rather effective attempts at linguistic stylization in the speech of his characters. Recent commentators have pointed to the structural particularities of Mordovtsev's novels—the multiplicity of characters and the interlacing of many plotlines, a technique that creates a stereoscopic panorama of history. However, this tendency is a common one in realistic epics and can hardly be seen as Mordovtsev's innovation. Moreover, this alleged architectonic complexity in Mordovtsev's work does not seem to be an entirely intentional device, but rather a consequence of improvisation, bordering on looseness and lack of structure. A more plausible achievement on Mordovtsev's part lies in his rendering of the formulaic

and "archetypal" nature of the medieval mind; this achievement is, however, undermined by instances of blatant modernization and incursions of the authorial voice, with its naive commentary and clumsy lyricism. Indeed, even Mordovtsev's best works are marred by verbosity and a certain sloppiness resulting from the haste in which he wrote. Yet, all possible criticism aside, Mordovtsev stands out as one of the most prominent historical novelists of his day and as a notable figure in the tradition of Russian historical fiction in general.

Mordovtsev died in the spa resort of Kislovodsk on 10 June 1905 and was buried in Rostov-on-Don. Shortly before his death there was a celebration marking fifty years of his literary career. Respectful speakers noted his continuing popularity and extraordinary productivity (according to one estimate, his complete works would have made up 129 volumes of printed text). Mordovtsev remained a widely read author in the decade preceding the Revolution. After 1917, however, he was virtually forgotten, although two or three of his works were published by émigré presses. In the Soviet Union, Mordovtsev's Ukrainian oeuvre was more durable, while only the quasi-populist *Znameniia vremeni* appeared in Russian. Overall, by the mid 1980s, like many other once-popular writers of historical fiction, Mordovtsev's works had disappeared from the reading scene. They made a comeback, though, during perestroika and the post-Soviet era, when, as a result of a renewed obsession with history, the pre-Revolutionary historical novel found a niche in the omnivorous book market of the new Russia.

Biographies:

P. V. Bykov, "D. L. Mordovtsev. Kritiko-biograficheskii ocherk," in Daniil Lukich Mordovtsev, *Polnoe sobranie istoricheskikh romanov, povestei i rasskazov,* volume 1 (St. Petersburg: Izd-vo P. P. Soikina, 1914), pp. ii–xxxviii;

V. S. Momot, *Daniil Lukich Mordovtsev: Ocherk zhizni i tvorchestva* (Rostov-na-Donu, 1978).

References:

F. I. Bulgakov, "V zashchitu istorii v istoricheskom romane (Pis'mo v redaktsiiu)," in *Istoricheskii vestnik,* 6 (1881): 835–837;

N. G. Il'inskaia, "Mordovtsev, Daniil Lukich," in *Russkie pisateli, 1800–1917, biograficheskii slovar',* volume 4 (Moscow: Bol'shaia rossiiskaia entsiklopediia, 1999), pp. 126–130;

Susan Layton, "Imagining the Caucasian Hero: Tolstoj vs. Mordovcev," in *Slavic and East European Journal,* 30, no. 1 (1986): 1–15;

Nikolai Konstantinovich Mikhailovsky, "Roman-icheskaia istoriia. *Idealisty i realisty.* Istoricheskii roman D. L. Mordovtseva," in his *Sochineniia,* volume 6 (St. Petersburg: Izdanie zhurnala *Russkoe Bogatstvo,* 1896–1897), pp. 251–278;

V. S. Momot, "D. L. Mordovtsev v russkoi kritike," in *Filologicheskie nauki,* 124, no. 4 (1981): 23–27;

S. I. Panov and A. M. Ranchin, "D. L. Mordovtsev i ego istoricheskaia proza," in Daniil Lukich Mordovtsev, *Za ch'i grekhi? Velikii raskol* (Moscow: Pravda, 1990), pp. 5–30;

Mikhail Evgrafovich Saltykov, "*Novye russkie liudi.* Roman D. Mordovtseva," in his *Polnoe sobranie sochinenii,* 20 volumes (Moscow: GIKhL, 1933–1939), VIII: 395–400;

Aleksandr Mikhailovich Skabichevsky, *Istoriia noveishei russkoi literatury. 1848–1892 gg.,* third revised edition (St. Petersburg: Izdanie F. Pavlenkova, 1897);

N. Sokolov, "Petr Velikii i Val'ter-Skotty-mogil'shchiki," in *Russkaia starina,* 2 (1894): 191–209; 3 (1894): 164–192;

N. Subbotin, "Istorik-belletrist," in *Russkii vestnik,* no. 5 (1881): 149–216.

Papers:

Major holdings of Daniil Lukich Mordovtsev's papers can be found in the Russian National Library, fond 494, in St. Petersburg; the Russian State Archives of Literature and Art (RGALI, formerly TsGALI), fond 320, in Moscow; the State Archive of the Odessa oblast, fond 146; and the Academy of Sciences of the Ukraine in Chernigov, fond 24.

Innokentii Vasil'evich Omulevsky
(Innokentii Vasil'evich Fedorov)
(26 November 1836 [or 21 October 1837] – 26 December 1883)

Alexander V. Matyushkin
Karelian State Pedagogical University

(Translated by Anton Shabaev, Natalia Savina, and Sarah Young)

WORKS: *Mitskevich v perevode Omulevskogo* (St. Petersburg, 1857);

Shag za shagom, in *Delo,* nos. 1–4, 6, 12 (1870); republished as *Svetlov, ego vzgliady, kharakter i deiatel'nost'* (St. Petersburg: Tip. A. Morigerovskogo, 1870–1871); republished as *Shag za shagom. (Svetlov, ego vzgliady, kharakter i deiatel'nost')* (Moscow & Petrograd: GIZ, 1923); republished as *Shag za shagom* (Irkutsk, 1950);

Popytka—ne shutka, partial publication (halted by censors) in *Delo,* no. 1 (1873): 199–239;

Pesni zhizni. Stikhotvoreniia (St. Petersburg: Biblioteka A. Ivanova, 1883);

Derevenskie pesni (St. Petersburg: Biblioteka A. Ivanova, 1884);

Zemnoi rai i taina kar'ery. Iumoristicheskie stikhotvoreniia (St. Petersburg: Biblioteka A. Ivanova, 1884);

Prouchili (Moscow, 1926);

Proza i publitsistika, compiled by N. V. Minaeva and Valentin Dmitrievich Oskotsky (Moscow: Sovetskaia Rossiia, 1986)—includes "Uchenye razgovory," *Sof'ia Bessonova,* and *Novyi gubernator.*

Editions and Collections: *Polnoe sobranie sochinenii,* 2 volumes, edited by Petr Vasil'evich Bykov (St. Petersburg: A. F. Marks, 1906);

Sobranie sochinenii, volume 2, edited by Mark Konstantinovich Azadovsky and Ieremiia Iakovlevich Aizenshtok (Irkutsk: Vostochnosibirskoe kraevoe izd-vo, 1936);

Izbrannye stikhotvoreniia, edited by S. Krasnoshtanova (Khabarovsk: Khabarovskoe khizhnoe izd-vo, 1961);

Shag za shagom: Romany, rasskazy, compiled by N. V. Minaeva and Valentin Dmitrievich Oskotsky (Irkutsk: Vostochno-Sibirskoe knizhnoe izda-

Innokentii Vasil'evich Omulevsky (Innokentii Vasil'evich Fedorov)

tel'stvo, 1983)—includes the most complete publication (based on Omulevsky's rough draft) of *Popytka—ne shutka.*

OTHER: "Neopublikovannye stikhotvoreniia," edited by I. G. Vasil'ev, in *Uchenye zapiski Leningradskogo gosudarstvennogo pedagogicheskogo instituta imeni A. I. Gertsena,* volume 170 (Leningrad, 1958), pp. 213–319;

"Stikhi," in *Poety-demokraty 1870–1880 gg.* (Moscow-Leningrad: Sovetskii pisatel', 1962), pp. 95–132.

TRANSLATION: Kazimir Zalevsky, *Marko Foskarini* (St. Petersburg: Redaktsiia zhurnala *Zhivopisnoe Obozrenie*, 1877).

The name of Innokentii Vasil'evich Omulevsky means little to most Russian readers today. He is remembered, perhaps, only in Siberia, for his poetry. Omulevsky considered poetry to be his main concern: from that genre he earned his living and found consolation during the difficult periods of his life. Nevertheless, in the history of Russian literature Omulevsky figures as the author of a novel about the "new people" of the 1860s and 1870s, *Shag za shagom* (Step by Step, 1870). The novel caused a sensation at the time and was popular among several generations of educated readers. Until the Soviet period many young people, discontented with the existing social and political system, were inspired by its ideas and program for living. Vladimir Galaktionovich Korolenko, in his study of the generation of the 1870s titled *Istoriia moego sovremennika* (1922; translated as *The History of My Contemporary,* 1972), recalled how much people enjoyed reading Omulevsky's novel alongside Daniil Lukich Mordovtsev's *Znameniia vremeni* (Signs of the Times, 1869) and Nikolai Gavrilovich Chernyshevsky's *Chto delat'?* (What Is To Be Done? 1863). In the Soviet period the novel re-created for younger readers the heroic image of fighters for the "public good," ready to sacrifice their lives for the sake of future revolutions. While *Shag za shagom* cannot be called artistically outstanding, Omulevsky honestly and sincerely portrays his ideal way of life. The novel remains interesting as an historical source describing the mood of the youth of the 1860s and 1870s, and as the sum of the writer's moral search.

Omulevsky's real name was Innokentii Vasil'evich Fedorov. His exact date of birth has not been decisively determined: the service record (personal file) of Vasilii Nikolaevich Fedorov, the writer's father, indicates the year as 1837, but biographers of the writer traditionally prefer 1836. Omulevsky's birthplace, however, is well known to all his readers. The *napolovinu avtobiograficheskii* (half-autobiographical) novel *Shag za shagom* lovingly depicts the settlement of Petropavlovsk-Kamchatsky, Russia's main port in the Far East, located on the Kamchatka peninsula, where the writer spent the first six years of his life. The main character of the novel, Aleksandr Vasil'evich Svetlov, spends his childhood and reaches moral maturity in "Petropavlovsky Port."

Omulevsky's father, like the fictional Svetlov's, was in government service. Having dropped out of the local school, Vasilii Fedorov had begun employment as a copyist in the Yakutsk circuit court in 1819; by 1858 he had risen to the position of collegiate counselor, thus making his way through half of the Table of Ranks as the result of honest and assiduous work. He was awarded a distinguished service medal for twenty-five years of irreproachable service. The writer's mother became the prototype of Svetlov's mother; both came from merchant families that were fairly well-to-do by Irkutsk standards. The first name of Omulevsky's mother was Pavla; according to some sources her maiden name was Podikova, while others give it as Vasil'eva.

In 1842 Vasilii Fedorov was transferred to Irkutsk, where he occupied high positions in the town and provincial police system. He bought a house on Bol'shaia Street and rented it out. The rent formed his third and most significant source of income, after his salary and pension from service in Kamchatka. In 1846 young Innokentii entered the classical gymnasium, but he did not gain his true education there. He became friendly with exiled Poles and Decembrists (the latter, frequently portrayed as the first Russian revolutionaries, had been exiled to the Irkutsk region after their attempted uprising in 1825). There were many such exiles in the town, and the young man's personality took shape in an atmosphere in which the main priorities were, as he later recalled, "respect for the individual, moral purity and proper behavior." Omulevsky started reading widely, and he enthusiastically studied Polish. In the gymnasium he was concerned only with literature. His first attempts at poetry—humorous poems and epigrams—were often taken away by the school principal, who would then come to Omulevsky's home to complain to his parents. After six years of education Omulevsky gave up the gymnasium, dropping out without getting his certificate; he refused to take an examination on scripture and theology.

Under pressure from his father, Omulevsky started a career in state service, but he was not enthusiastic about it and devoted all his free time to reading and translating the famous Polish poet Adam Mickiewicz. The young man longed to go to St. Petersburg and in 1856 entered the law faculty of St. Petersburg University at his own expense. Academics, however, did not much interest the future writer. His father was sending more than enough money, and Omulevsky, little concerned with the future, was abusing his freedom. He was living in the center of the political life of the country, and he quickly grasped the significant role that literature then played in Russian society. In 1857 he published his first book, *Mitskevich v perevode Omulevskogo* (Mickiewicz in Omulevsky's Translation). He wrote in his introduction: "I am starting out on my public way, and, as a mere mortal entering a vast field, I hold onto the hand of the immortal." Thus, Omulevsky entered the literary arena for the first time as a poet. As he explained later, his pen name was formed from the word *omul'*, the name of his favorite Siberian fish. Omulevsky's initial aspirations for fame and glory, however, did not work out. The collection did not attract much attention. Only Nikolai Aleksandrovich Dobroliubov, in one of the anonymous reviews in *Sovremennik* (The Contemporary), mentioned the translator Omulevsky and cited two of his poems, remarking that the author, "although he writes in prose, certainly wants his prose to be taken for poetry." The poems were indeed simple versifications of sonnets by Mickiewicz, written without regular meter and abounding in long-outdated romantic clichés.

A year later Omulevsky gave up the university and found employment in state service as a special missions functionary to the governor of Vitebsk. However, high society and literature took first place for him. He wrote his first significant poem, a Tatar legend titled "Tri promakha" (Three Failures, 1861), which was later published in the journal *Vek* (The Century). Omulevsky was little interested in a career in the civil service, and he soon retired. He started wandering around Russia and ended up in St. Petersburg again.

Omulevsky at this point decided to become a professional writer and dreamed of establishing his own satirical newspaper. This decision was mainly influenced by a group of fellow Siberians at St. Petersburg University, where the young poet found his first readers and enthusiastically participated in social activities. The *zemliaki* (compatriots), as they called themselves, organized parties that combined wine, conversation, and politics. Readings and plans for restructuring Siberia were discussed. With the beginning of significant reform in the country heralded by the emancipation of the serfs in February of 1861, independent social activity became considerably more dangerous for the *zemliaki*. For participating in demonstrations and student gatherings stimulated by the closure of the university in the fall of 1861, some of the members of the Siberian circle were arrested.

At the same time, Omulevsky was leading a tempestuous, bohemian life. He was gifted with a handsome appearance, wit, and spontaneity, and, as his friends recalled later, he easily became popular with women. Rumors about his behavior reached his father, who stopped sending money to his son and insisted that he come home. *Shag za shagom* hardly mentions the St. Petersburg life of the central character, but impressions of life upon his return to Irkutsk—public activity, meetings with friends and parents—are portrayed in detail. While living in Irkutsk, Omulevsky published his first original prose works: the stories "Sibiriachka" (The

Siberian Woman) and "Mednye obrazki" (Copper Icons), which appeared in N. S. Shchukin's collection *Sibirskie rasskazy* (Siberian Tales, 1862) and also in the newspaper *Amur* (The Amur, named for a river in Siberia).

Provincial life, however, did not appeal to Omulevsky, and three years later he came back to St. Petersburg. His works began appearing frequently in St. Petersburg publications, including *Sovremennik, Russkoe slovo* (The Russian Word), *Zhenskii vestnik* (The Herald of Women), *Delo* (The Cause), *Luch* (The Ray), *Iskra* (The Spark), *Budil'nik* (The Alarm Clock), and *Peterburgskii listok* (The Petersburg Newssheet). His works of this period were mostly denunciatory and parodic poems. Many of them revealed the influence of Nikolai Alekseevich Nekrasov's poetry, an influence that lasted for Omulevsky's entire creative career. The main themes of the poems were the denunciation of bureaucrats, as in "Priznanie" (Confession); the problem of "fathers and children," interpreted by Omulevsky as an opposition between different views of life, as in "Zabudem te frazy, kakimi nas s detstva . . ." (Forget the phrases that since childhood . . .); the "woman question," closely related to family issues, as in "Zadushevnaia beseda" (Soul-to-Soul Conversation), "Svetskoi devitse" (To a Society Maiden), and "Nashei podruge zhizni" (To Our Girlfriend, Life); and the questions of love for the motherland and the fight for liberty, as in "Svoboda" (Freedom) and "Vse na svete tryn-trava" (There is no power that is able to frighten us). The poet tried to unmask the existing order and conservative traditions, as well as to create the image of a protagonist fighting for the new society. His poem "Delo" was especially popular among the *raznochintsy* ("mixed-class" intellectuals). It begins:

Svetaet, tovarishch! . .
Rabotat' davai!
Raboty usilennoi
Trebuet krai . . .

(The day is breaking, comrade! . .
Let's work!
The land demands
Hard work . . .)

All these issues were also reflected in the novel *Shag za shagom,* which was published in *Delo* in 1870 and appeared as a separate edition in 1871 under the title *Svetlov, ego vzgliady, kharakter i deiatel'nost'* (Svetlov, His Views, Personality, and Activity). The journal version of the novel was significantly censored. The censor initially refused to permit the third part, because its first chapter described a workers' strike at a state factory that ended with the lashing and banishing of the director, who had embezzled public funds. Finally, the editor managed to convince the Committee on the Press to grant permission to publish the third part without its first chapters. Omulevsky then had the chance to publish his novel as a separate edition without preliminary censorship; however, he used this opportunity to restore all the pieces earlier withdrawn by the censors, violating the regulations in force. The authorities were angry. They did not dare destroy the novel or apply sanctions to its author at the time, but the consequences became clear when attempts were made to publish reprint editions. Twice, in 1874 and 1896, entire print runs of the novel (2,200 and 3,200 copies respectively) were completely destroyed despite frantic resistance by the publishers. In 1906, in the aftermath of the first Russian revolution, the censored version appeared in the *Polnoe sobranie sochinenii Omulevskogo* (Complete Collected Works of Omulevsky) edited by Petr Vasil'evich Bykov. The novel began to be reprinted regularly only in the 1950s.

Shag za shagom enjoyed tremendous success among readers, and the first edition sold out quickly, mainly because it was immediately placed on the list of books forbidden in libraries and reading rooms. This ban added an aura of mystery to the novel and its author, more than compensating for any artistic defects. The print run was insufficient, and many people tried to rewrite the novel by hand in order to have a personal copy. The number of handwritten copies made can be guessed from the fact that even in the middle of the twentieth century they could still be found in Siberian bookstores.

Among critics *Shag za shagom* aroused varying responses, but the talent of the author was acknowledged both by the critic of the radical *Otechestvennye zapiski* (Notes of the Fatherland), Mikhail Evgrafovich Saltykov (N. Shchedrin), and the critic of the conservative *Vestnik Evropy* (Herald of Europe), Konstantin Konstantinovich Arsen'ev. Saltykov wrote: "Not making any comparisons, we can say conscientiously that Mr. Omulevsky in the artistic sense stands far ahead of more experienced fiction writers, who go hand in hand with him in the same honest direction of literature, but at the same time do not show any hope of freeing us from unsubstantiated assertions." In his review Saltykov brought together two novels written with the same aim: Fyodor Dostoevsky's *The Idiot* (1868) and Omulevsky's *Shag za shagom*. As the critic noted, both works were attempts to portray the writer's ideal: a positively beautiful person, a person of the future. But while Dostoevsky's character is presented in a way that is intentionally close to life, Omulevsky's character is clearly an ideal. His last name, deriving from the word *svet* (light), has a symbolic meaning: Svetlov is a person who brings light. All his deeds are positive, and nothing

dims his image. Korolenko compared him with a well-cleaned copper basin. Omulevsky consistently avoids expressing psychological details in his narrative; he presents Svetlov as if from a bird's-eye view. This tradition originated in Chernyshevsky's *Chto delat'?* and was motivated by the goals of revolutionary propaganda. A new personality had to be portrayed as moving confidently and consistently toward those goals.

Omulevsky's views are presented neither in the ideas conveyed in discussions between the characters, nor in the narrative comments, but in the action itself. In order to be more persuasive, the writer shows his character in normal, everyday situations. As he writes in the final chapter:

> We have deliberately presented you, the reader, with the figure of Svetlov in his everyday life, in all its insignificance, and, at the risk of boring you with details, we have placed our character in numerous unremarkable situations: thus you will be able to judge him much more accurately. At important moments in their life sometimes even the most mediocre people are suddenly seized by life's hot influx and rise, so to speak, to the occasion; but an author has the right to show you only those outstanding personalities who at every minute stand up confidently on the grounds of their own beliefs.

Omulevsky places his story in opposition to fairy tales, but the life of his main character develops as smoothly and freely as the plot of a fairy tale. It could not be otherwise: at that time people like Svetlov barely existed in Russia, and the writer was compelled to imagine his character and present him in a way that would make him an attractive example for readers.

Aleksandr Vasil'evich Svetlov possesses a strong will, and he consistently, "step by step," reaches his goals, never losing self-confidence. He successfully completes his university studies, quickly finds profitable work as a tutor, and always has a decent income. When he decides to establish a school for the people, he overcomes all obstacles, and his enthusiasm is contagious. Under his influence El'nikov, a friend of Svetlov's, starts treating poor people for free. Even after ending up in jail for participating in a workers' strike, Svetlov cheers up those who come to visit him.

The image of Svetlov was meant to contradict the image of "nihilists" that was popular at that time. Starting with Bazarov, the hero of Ivan Sergeevich Turgenev's *Ottsy i deti* (Fathers and Sons, 1862), nihilists had been depicted as long-haired, carelessly dressed, untidy, bad-mannered people. Svetlov, on the contrary, is courtly and dressed with style. His natural ability to communicate is noticed by various characters, including a representative of the local authorities, his cousin

Aniuta, and the workers at El'tsin factory. Unlike Bazarov, Svetlov has concrete creative goals. He is successful in love, unembarrassed by romantic desires, and fond of classical literature. Margarita Dmitrievna Zinov'eva has suggested that Svetlov was based on the *novye liudi* (new people) or *realisty* (realists) featured in articles by Dmitrii Ivanovich Pisarev, including Pisarev's interpretation of Bazarov. The critic Arsen'ev suggested that Omulevsky was also influenced in this portrayal by *In Reih' und Glied* (In Rank and File, 1867) by the German writer Friedrich Spielhagen, a work that was enormously popular at the time. In Arsen'ev's opinion, the very title *Shag za shagom* exemplifies the essential idea of *In Reih' und Glied*.

The goals portrayed by Omulevsky take on particular interest when viewed in historical perspective. Svetlov fights for civil rights and thinks that children deserve these same rights. While teaching children he ignores traditional pedagogical techniques based on memorization and instead substitutes conversations on subjects that are important for children, providing them in leisurely fashion with the most diversified information on all spheres of life, including both general school subjects and social knowledge heretofore ignored in Russian schools. Svetlov also has respect for all living beings. He explains to his younger brother Vladimirko that "even a bedbug should not be killed"; rather, "it is necessary to act in such a way that they don't breed in the room–keep the rooms clean."

In Omulevsky's opinion, Chernyshevsky-style striving for personal freedom and that of others has only one limit: not to do what causes harm to others. This absence of traditional restraining factors is further emphasized in Omulevsky's unusual treatment of sexual relationships. Svetlov in principle refuses to have a family and leads an almost ascetic life, as a true revolutionary should. Although women want him to be liberated sexually, they realize that any intimate relationship they might have with him would not last long.

Such opinions were much too daring for many audiences in nineteenth-century Russia. The censor Matveev wrote in his official report: "Through Svetlov the author propagandizes for the emancipation of the personality from all ties of public order and undermines the obedience of wife to husband, children to parents, etc." Omulevsky's positive characters are similarly emancipated with respect to religion. They pray with the workers at school at the beginning of their classes, but they do not believe in God and think it necessary to demonstrate this fact every time they get a chance. Thus, El'nikov asks to have Auguste Comte's *Cours de philosophie positive* (Course of Positive Philosophy, 1830–1842) read to him before he dies.

The principle of "step-by-step" development is also relevant to Omulevsky's construction of his main character. He shows that even in childhood Svetlov has a feeling of social equality and love for living beings. The legacy of the Decembrists, which guides and legitimates the activity of "the new people," also plays a great role in the novel. The novel in general shows connections between generations at various levels. Svetlov encapsulates the best features of the older generation while rejecting its defects.

In creating the main characters of the novel, Omulevsky allowed himself to be governed by his ideological views, and therefore, despite all the charm of these characters, there is much that is artificial in them. Negative characters receive a similarly biased portrayal. But some background characters are free of ideology, and from an artistic point of view their portrayals are the most successful. One such character is Svetlov's uncle, Aleksei Petrovich Sosnin, who, with a gun in his hand, demands a return of affections from the woman he loves ("she has become a woman of fire, her arms cannot be pulled from my neck even by ropes"). Sosnin also keeps money on the floor in a corner of his room ("where would you find a better place for this trash?"). Another is Svetlov's brother Vladimirko, who interrupts Svetlov's lessons with unexpected, childishly naive questions.

In Omulevsky's novel *Popytka–ne shutka* (An Attempt is No Joke, 1873) the writer finds an organic artistic form for his romantic ideas. In this work social romanticism gains a mystic tone that eliminates all the psychological tensions typical of *Shag za shagom*. The censors, however, still did not approve. Like *Shag za shagom*, this novel was returned to the editor of *Delo*. The epigraph, "posviashchaetsia russkoi zhenshchine" (dedicated to a Russian woman) was quite daring, and after publication of only the first three chapters in *Delo*, the novel was banned. These chapters were more romantically extravagant than politically dangerous, but they were still significantly censored. The censors considered them to be undermining to the foundations of society. At the same time (and the prohibited novel probably played a role in this event) Omulevsky was called to account for an "oskorblenie Velichestva" (insult to the Royal Family) he had made while drunk. He was imprisoned in Petropavlovsk fortress and then, by orders of the court, in the Litovsky castle. *Popytka–ne shutka* was not published in full until 1983.

Omulevsky spent the time in prison working on the novel *Novyi gubernator* (The New Governor, published for the first time in 1986), but he wrote only the first part and then stopped for unknown reasons. This time the positive character and center of the narrative is a figure of authority–the governor of the town of

Zemel'sk. However, Omulevsky did not mean to flatter the authorities. The honest governor makes all the unattractive realities of Russian bureaucracy even more obvious. He is an exception among officials and from the beginning is confronted with the reluctance of his colleagues, who are unwilling to agree with his principles.

After a short sentence Omulevsky was set free, but his life continued to be troubled. In 1874 he suffered from a serious ocular disease that nearly resulted in blindness. In despair he started drinking heavily. His contemporaries recalled that he would sell his last clothes to buy a drink, and when drunk he would insult even close friends. With disease there also came poverty, from which even restored eyesight and zealous work did not save him. Original poems and translations of the Polish poet Vladislav Syrokomla (Ludvig Kondratovich), to whom Omulevsky felt spiritually close, were not as popular with readers as his novels had been, while his prose was suppressed by censors. On 21 March 1877 Omulevsky wrote to his friend Aleksandr Konstantinovich Sheller: "my situation is terrible, hopeless. . . . It almost concerns my very life. . . . If it weren't for self-respect, I think I'd put an end to it." His parents could not help either. In 1868 their profitable rent-earning house burned down, and the family had to take shelter in a tiny house on the outskirts of town, living on Vasilii Fedorov's pension from his service in Kamchatka.

The situation was aggravated by Omulevsky's extreme scrupulousness. Bykov recalled that when he was living in the most terrible poverty, Omulevsky would not offer his work to publications whose ideas and positions he did not share, "preferring to submit a poem to some insipid edition like a fashion magazine with a literature section." Sheller, known for his kindness to fellow writers, managed to relieve Omulevsky's situation by finding a job for him at *Zhivopisnoe obozrenie* (Picturesque Review), where Omulevsky stayed until the end of his life. There he published his own poetic works as well as a column in verse and prose, titled "Mimoletnye nabroski" (Fleeting Sketches), written under the pseudonym "Veselyi poet" (the Merry Poet). For the supplement to *Zhivopisnoe obozrenie* Omulevsky translated from Polish Kazimir Zalevsky's drama *Marko Foskarini* in 1877.

In the late 1870s Omulevsky married E. I. Ivanova, sister of the owner of a reading library in St. Petersburg. Vasilii Fedorov died in 1879, and Omulevsky hurried to Irkutsk to share with his brother their father's remaining small inheritance–a house on the outskirts of town. However, when he arrived, the town was on fire. Along with nearly all the wooden buildings of Irkutsk, Fedorov's small house was ruined. Omu-

levsky's mother survived, but she and her son did not get along and lived apart. Omulevsky rented a tiny room, where he and his pregnant wife listened to the constant quarrels of the owners behind the thin wooden wall of the apartment. The family had practically no source of income. Omulevsky started drinking again and this time contracted delirium tremens, ending up at the local hospital. Immediately after his recovery he sold the land on which his parents' house had stood and used the money to return to St. Petersburg in the summer of 1880, intending to start working and publishing actively again.

Following the suggestion of his wife's brother, A. A. Ivanov, Omulevsky collected his best original and translated poems in one book, and in 1883 it was published under the title *Pesni zhizni* (Songs of Life). Omulevsky's poems are not distinguished by refined artistic form; they are rather publicistic, too general, and seldom concretized through individualism. They have little poetic originality, but nonetheless win over the reader with their spontaneity, sincerity, and intimacy. These are indeed songs, hymns to the living. Though many of the poems are full of unconcealed bitterness, even during his most difficult years the poet remained optimistic, and his writings always expressed hope in a brighter future that would make suffering through all the hardships of the present worthwhile.

First and foremost Omulevsky addressed young people, advising the younger generation to search for new, authentic ideals, to work hard for them, and to sacrifice themselves if necessary. His poetry became a passionate sermon, the goal, as he saw it, of poetry. In Omulevsky's opinion the poet is a special person, able to understand and feel much that is inaccessible to ordinary people. Thus, the main task of a poet is to help people see the true meaning of life, which is inseparably connected to ideals of truth and good, moral purification, liberty, and labor. Omulevsky's talent as a poet is particularly obvious in the sections called "Sibirskie motivy" (Siberian Motifs) and "Derevenskie pesni" (Village Songs). The twentieth-century writer Kornei Ivanovich Chukovsky thought that Omulevsky had understood and conveyed the psychology of the Russian people better than Nekrasov.

Critics, however, were more or less indifferent to the collection, and the public was also uninterested in the book. Meanwhile, zealous work and a predilection for wine quickly exhausted the writer's health. He was taken ill with consumption. There was no money for treatment or even basic household needs. During his last three months the writer did not even have enough clothing to leave the house. On 26 December 1883 Omulevsky died of a heart attack. Those who came for a last good-bye were shocked by his poverty–there was neither decent clothing to put on the deceased nor a table on which to lay him out. Money for the funeral and the support of his wife and three small children was collected by the writer's admirers, friends, and colleagues. Omulevsky's fate was not unusual; many Russian writers in this period of transition after the reforms ended up in similarly dire straits.

Besides his novels and poems, Omulevsky's most successful works are his stories "Sibiriachka," "Ostrozhnyi khudozhnik" (The Jail Artist, 1882), "Bez krova, khleba i krasok" (Without Shelter, Bread, and Paints, 1883), "Sutki na stantsii" (A Day at the Station, 1904), and "Uchenye razgovory" (Educated Talks, 1986). All of them were "captured from nature," but, unlike naturalistic prose, they are full of lyricism and the author's sympathy for his main characters.

Omulevsky certainly belongs to the ranks of distinguished Russian writers of the nineteenth century. From the beginning, however, his artistic talent was under heavy pressure from ideology. Readers demanded ideas and trends from the literature of the 1860s, while the organic qualities of Omulevsky's work were lyricism and spontaneity. Adjusting his writings to the requirements of the time diminished their artistic merits. As a result, Omulevsky's most colorful images are background characters or characters in short stories. The other hindrance to Omulevsky's career and artistic development came from his problems with censorship. Until the end of his life Omulevsky was distressed about the fate of several of his literary efforts that had never made it into print. Collected after his death, these manuscripts confirm their author's positive assessment and his place in Russian literature.

Biographies:

Petr Vasil'evich Bykov, "I. V. Fedorov (Omulevsky). (Biograficheskii ocherk)," introduction to *Polnoe sobranie sochinenii Omulevskogo (I. V. Fedorova),* edited by Bykov, volume 1 (St. Petersburg: A. F. Marks, 1906), pp. 3–26;

Ivan G. Vasil'ev, "Materialy k biografii I. V. Fedorova-Omulevskogo," *Uchenye zapiski LGPI im. A. I. Gertsena,* 198 (1959): 301–305.

References:

Eduard A. Abel'tin, *Pesnia–svoboda moia: Ocherk zhizni i tvorchestva I. V. Fedorova-Omulevskogo* (Krasnoiarsk: Izdatel'stvo Krasnoiarskogo universiteta, 1987);

Abel'tin, "Roman I. V. Fedorova-Omulevskogo 'Shag za shagom' (voprosy metoda i stilia)," in *Voprosy russkoi literatury, Uchenye zapiski MGPI im. V. I. Lenina,* 389 (1970): 296–316;

Vasilii G. Bazanov, *Iz literaturnoi polemiki 60-kh godov* (Petrozavodsk: GIZ KFSSR, 1941);

Kornei Ivanovich Chukovsky, "Asketicheskii talant (Omulevsky i ego tvorchestvo)," *Ezhemesiachnoe literaturnoe i nauchno-populiarnoe prilozhenie k "Nive",* no. 9 (1906): 123–134;

N. F. Chuzhak, "'Sibirskie motivy' u I. V. Fedorova-Omulevskogo v otnoshenii formy i soderzhaniia," *Sibirskii arhiv,* no. 2 (1913): 61–77;

Vladimir Galaktionovich Korolenko, *The History of My Contemporary,* translated and abridged by Neil Parsons (London: Oxford University Press, 1972);

E. V. Petukhov, *Fedorov-Omulevsky (Ocherk ego zhizni i literaturnoi deiatel'nosti)* (Tomsk, 1900);

A. L. Rubanovich, "'Sibirskie motivy' I. V. Fedorova-Omulevskogo," *Trudy Irkutskogo gosudarstvennogo universiteta im. A. A. Zhdanova,* 16, Seriia istoriko-filologicheskaia, 3 (1956): 64–84;

Ivan G. Vasil'ev, "Osnovnye motivy liriki Omulevskogo," *Uchenye zapiski LGPI im. A. I. Gertsena,* 210 (1959): 67–79;

Vasil'ev, "Roman I. V. Fedorova-Omulevskogo 'Shag za shagom,'" *Uchenye zapiski LGPI im. A. I. Gertsena,* 245 (1963): 89–100;

Margarita Dmitrievna Zinov'eva, "Bazarovskii tip v tvorchestve I. V. Omulevskogo (Fedorova) (Stat'ia 1)," in *Voprosy russkoi i sovetskoi literatury Sibiri (Materialy k "Istorii russkoi literatury Sibiri"),* edited by V. G. Odinokov (Novosibirsk: Nauka, 1971), pp. 164–183;

Zinov'eva, "Stilevye osobennosti romana I. V. Omulevskogo 'Shag za shagom,'" in *Ocherki literatury i kritiki Sibiri (XVII-XX vv.),* edited by Iurii Sergeevich Postnov (Novosibirsk: Nauka, 1976), pp. 150–164;

Zinov'eva, "Tipologicheskie cherty revoliutsionno-prosvetitel'skogo realizma v romane I. V. Omulevskogo 'Shag za shagom' (K kharakteristike metoda)," in *Problemy literatury Sibiri XVII–XX vv. (Materialy k "Istorii russkoi literatury Sibiri"),* edited by Postnov (Novosibirsk: Nauka, 1974), pp. 78–89;

Zinov'eva and A. L. Rubanovich, "I. V. Fedorov-Omulevsky (1836–1883)," in *Ocherki russkoi literatury Sibiri,* edited by Odinokov, volume 1 (Novosibirsk: Nauka, 1982), pp. 403–416.

Papers:

Innokentii Vasil'evich Omulevsky's papers are located in the Russian State Archive of Literature and Art (RGALI, formerly TsGALI, in Moscow), fond 371, and in the Russian State Historical Archive (RGIA, formerly TsGIA, in St. Petersburg), fond 776.

Avdot'ia Iakovlevna Panaeva
(N. Stanitsky)
(31 July 1820 - 30 March 1893)

Susan Conner Olson

WORKS: "Semeistvo Tal'nikovykh. Zapiski, naiden-nye v bumagakh pokoinitsy," in *Illiustrirovannyi al'manakh Sovremennika* (1848); republished as *Semeistvo Tal'nikovykh. Povest'* (Leningrad: Academia, 1928);

Bezobraznyi muzh. Povest' v pis'makh, in *Sovremennik,* no. 4 (1848);

Tri strany sveta, by Panaeva (as N. Stanitsky) and Nikolai Alekseevich Nekrasov, in *Sovremennik,* nos. 10–12 (1848); nos. 1–5 (1849); (St. Petersburg, 1849);

Paseka. Povest', in *Sovremennik* (1849);

Mertvoe ozero, by Panaeva (as N. Stanitsky) and Nekrasov, in *Sovremennik,* nos. 1–10 (1851); (St. Petersburg: V Tip. Eduarda Pratsa, 1852);

Melochi zhizni, in *Sovremennik,* nos. 1–4 (1854); (St. Petersburg, 1854);

Vozdushnye zamki. Povest', in *Sovremennik,* no. 3 (1855);

Stepnaia baryshnia, in *Sovremennik,* no. 8 (1855);

Domashnyi ad, in *Sovremennik,* no. 9 (1857);

Russkie v Italii. Povest', in *Sovremennik,* no. 2 (1858);

Roman v peterburgskom polusvete, in *Sovremennik,* nos. 3–4 (1860); (St. Petersburg: V Tip. K Vul'fa, 1863);

Zhenskaia dolia, in *Sovremennik,* nos. 3–5 (1862); (St. Petersburg, 1864);

Fantazerka, in *Sovremennik,* no. 9 (1864);

Istoriia odnogo talanta, in *Niva,* nos. 24–34 (1888);

"Vospominaniia," in *Istoricheskii vestnik,* nos. 1–11 (1889); republished as *Russkie pisateli i artisty. 1824–1870* (St. Petersburg: V. I. Gubinsky, 1890); republished as *Vospominaniia. 1824–1870* (Leningrad: "Academiia," 1927);

Zheleznodorozhyi mir (St. Petersburg, 1890).

Edition in English: "The Young Lady of the Steppes," in *Russian Women's Shorter Fiction: An Anthology 1835–1860,* translated by Joe Andrew (Oxford: Clarendon Press, 1996).

SELECTED PERIODICAL PUBLICATIONS: "Neostorozhnoe slovo," *Sovremennik,* no. 3 (1848);

Avdot'ia Iakovlevna Panaeva (from Russkie pisateli, 1800–1917: Biograficheskii slovar', *volume 4 [1999])*

"Zhena chasovogo mastera," *Sovremennik,* no. 2 (1849);

"Neobdumannyi shag. Rasskaz," *Sovremennik,* no. 1 (1850);

"Kapriznaia zhenshchina," *Sovremennik,* no. 12 (1850);

"Zheleznaia doroga mezhdu Peterburgom i Moskvoiu. Fiziologicheskii ocherk," *Sovremennik,* no. 11 (1855);

"Dvorniazhka," *Niva,* nos. 49–51 (1889);

"Petukh," *Ezhemesiachnye literaturnye prilozheniia k zhurnalu "Niva,"* no. 11 (1891);

"Siroty," *Ezhemesiachnye literaturnye prilozheniia k zhurnalu
 "Niva,"* no. 3 (1893).

Avdot'ia Iakovlevna Panaeva's significance as a
writer of fiction has long been eclipsed by her literary
and artistic memoirs, written toward the end of her life
in the late 1880s and detailing the lives of the writers
associated with the leading liberal "thick" journal of the
mid nineteenth century, *Sovremennik* (The Contemporary). Panaeva played an integral part in the establishment and ongoing support of this journal, which served
as a medium for the naturalistic and democratic writings of such authors as Nikolai Alekseevich Nekrasov,
Ivan Sergeevich Turgenev, Dmitrii Vasil'evich Grigorovich, Nikolai Gavrilovich Chernyshevsky, and
Nikolai Aleksandrovich Dobroliubov. In addition to
feeding, supporting, and sometimes housing the contributors, Panaeva edited manuscripts and wrote her
own short stories and novels that were published in the
journal under the male pseudonym "N. Stanitsky." All
of her works, which follow a naturalistic style typical of
the period, revolve around the problems of social
hypocrisy and the exploitation of women—themes that
were close to Panaeva's own unhappy experiences.

Panaeva was born Avdot'ia Iakovlevna Brian-
skaia on 31 July 1820 to theatrical parents, Anna
Matveevna Stepanova and Iakov Grigor'evich Briansky. She and her siblings did not experience an idyllic
family life. Friends have attested that much of her
early life can be judged by her first work of fiction,
"Semeistvo Tal'nikovykh" (The Tal'nikov Family,
1848), which offers a harsh and gruesome picture of a
prison-like childhood under uncaring parents. She
received a somewhat meager education at the St.
Petersburg Theatre School, but she managed to cultivate an interest in literature by escaping from stage
rehearsals to read books under the desk in her father's
off-limits library.

When she was sixteen she met the rising writer
Ivan Ivanovich Panaev, who was working with her
father to stage one of his translations of a William
Shakespeare play as a benefit performance. After a two-
and-a-half-year courtship, Panaev still could not convince his mother to consent to his marrying the daughter of a lowly artisan, so the couple eloped in 1839.

This dramatic escape from her repressive home
gave Panaeva her first taste of the kind of freedom that
became so important to her fictional heroines. V. A.
Panaev recalled in his 1893 "Vospominaniia" (Memoirs) that Panaeva was like "a bird freed from her
cage," literally running and frolicking in the gardens at
Panaev's country estate, where she and her husband
honeymooned briefly before he took her to St. Petersburg. There he paraded her before the literary and

social elite, who were impressed with the unusual, dark-
complexioned beauty; she was admired by almost all of
the artists of her day, including Fyodor Dostoevsky,
who fell in love with her briefly and may have modeled
some of his female characters after her.

While still on their honeymoon, the Panaevs
met the already well-known literary critic Vissarion
Grigor'evich Belinsky. They formed an immediate,
close, and lasting friendship that influenced the literary careers of both husband and wife. Panaeva wrote
Belinsky carefree letters describing her excitement at
the new literary sphere in which she found herself and
apologizing for her poor writing skills, which she suddenly realized had never been developed. Belinsky
encouraged Panaeva to write and helped instill in her
a sense of pride in her natural sincerity and naiveté,
which she found to be quite at odds with her new
social surroundings.

Her carefree happiness did not last long. She soon
discovered that her husband was far more interested in
his wardrobe, gambling, and other women than in her.
Panaev's humiliating open love affairs and carousing
lifestyle ultimately pushed Panaeva closer to her husband's good friend and business associate, Nekrasov,
who pursued her for six years and even jumped into
the river Volga to prove his devotion before she suc-
cumbed to his advances.

In the meantime, however, Panaeva cultivated
her role as the official hostess for her husband's literary
circle of friends, who were first associated with the journal *Otechestvennye zapiski* (Notes of the Fatherland) and
later *Sovremennik,* which Panaeva helped convince her
husband and Nekrasov to purchase in 1846. At first
Panaeva took no part in the literary gatherings besides
pouring tea and feeding the attendees, a feat by no
means immaterial and one that appropriated all of her
time and resources. She gradually became more active
at the meetings, and she spoke out vehemently in
defense of writers from the provinces or lower social
classes, such as Dostoevsky, Chernyshevsky, and
Dobroliubov. This behavior earned her the eternal
annoyance of writers from the more conservative upper
classes, such as Turgenev and Count Vladimir Aleksandrovich Sollogub. The two camps were already at
odds with one another over the future direction of
Sovremennik. A final break occurred in 1858 with the
departure of the conservatives. Panaeva was clearly on
the side of the liberal seminarists who subsequently
turned the journal into the leading forum for revolutionary democratic writings, earning her the later
respect of Soviet scholars.

No doubt influenced by these literary gatherings
and encouraged by both Belinsky and Nekrasov,
Panaeva took on more responsibilities for the journal,

such as reading and correcting manuscripts and eventually writing her own fiction. Her first work, *Semeistvo Tal'nikovykh,* followed the early intention of *Sovremennik* to depict the ugly realities of everyday life, a literary trend promoted by Belinsky and known as Naturalism. In *Semeistvo Tal'nikovykh* Panaeva took this trend to the extreme and into the sacred ground of the family hearth, shocking even her friends with graphic scenes and an antisentimental narrative tone. This pseudo-autobiographical work depicts the squalor of a presumably respectable middle-class home in which the children suffer from an embarrassing poverty of dress and a disgraceful lack of parental attention. Their father beats them during drunken rages or ignores their existence altogether, while their mother doles out verbal abuse and keeps them locked up so that she will not have to be reminded of their money-draining presence. Meanwhile, the harsh governess takes out her bitter frustration on the children by forcing them to kneel for hours at a time. Their grandmother "entertains" them with horrifying fairy tales of robbers and cruelty, and the children try to find their own amusement by playing with the bugs that infest their prison-like quarters.

The story caused the entire publication in which it was printed to be banned by the censors for "undermining parental authority." The publication, *Illiustrirovannyi al'manakh* (An Illustrated Almanac, 1848), had been designed as a special supplement of *Sovremennik.* However, copies of the banned almanac were pilfered from storage and circulated unofficially, instantly making Panaeva's pseudonym "N. Stanitsky" famous. Most critics and readers seemed to recognize the author's identity, and some even referred to the story as "The Briansky Family" after Panaeva's maiden name.

Although the story garnered her critical respect, especially among the Naturalist camp, Panaeva soon found that many of her friends shunned her in public and spread rumors that Nekrasov and Panaev were the real authors behind her work. Further fueling social censure, in 1848 Panaeva and Nekrasov moved in together, apparently with the consent of her husband, who continued to live in the same house. She became known in the most unflattering terms as "one of those emancipated types," having taken George Sand's emancipation of the heart beyond acceptable boundaries.

The social abuse to which she was subjected is indicated by almost all of her fictional works that followed, in which heroines grapple with the no-win situation of either following their hearts and being ostracized, or suppressing their integrity in order to conform to societal rules. In some of her first stories, such as *Bezobraznyi muzh* (An Ugly Husband, 1848) and "Zhena chasovogo mastera" (The Watchmaker's Wife, 1849), the naive and energetic young heroines fall prey

to embittered mothers, greedy husbands, or their own unrealistic fantasies, and end up prostituting their minds as well as their bodies for societal acceptance. Panaeva laments that neither familial upbringing nor traditional education equips girls with a practical understanding of real life, and so they become the unknowing victims of their own naiveté, easily exploited by others. Because of their neglected or impractical education, girls are not able to recognize the shallow hypocrisy that lurks behind the seemingly glamorous allure of high society, or the importance of financial security, or even the nature of sexual attraction. Sex assumes an important role in Panaeva's works. Young girls are never told that there is such a thing as passion, and so they either mistake it for love, or they do not discover passion at all until after they are married off to passionless or abusive men. "Neostorozhnoe slovo" (A Careless Word, 1848) and *Paseka* (The Apiary, 1849) are good examples of stories that depict heroines discovering sexual attraction too late, and because they must repress it, they become just as cold and heartless as their surrounding society.

With the exception of *Semeistvo Tal'nikovykh,* which is told from the point of view of the female protagonist, Panaeva's stories are usually narrated by the male persona Stanitsky, a self-proclaimed traveling litterateur whose chief function in the stories is to provide ironic social commentary. Her stories are filled with melodramatic scenarios, chit-chat, and intrigues, frequently at the expense of plot and character development but providing ample material for the narrator's sarcastic denunciations of high-society hypocrisy and the exploitation of women. Panaeva, like many of the writers associated with *Sovremennik,* was less concerned with literary artistry than with the message of her works. She once told Belinsky that she just did not have the patience to write "smoothly or prettily," a weakness complicated by the fact that many of her works were written hurriedly for the express purpose of providing Nekrasov and Panaev with material for their publication.

The years between 1848 and 1854 were the height of the censorship terror in Russia, and journal editors had to scramble for material. In 1848 six stories slated for publication in *Sovremennik* were rejected by the censor in one month alone. According to Panaeva's memoirs, Nekrasov proposed to Panaeva and Grigorovich the undertaking of a jointly authored novel in order to fill up the empty space. The three worked together to come up with ideas for a novel in the popular French tradition of Eugène Sue and Victor Hugo. Panaeva wrote a melodramatic birth scene in which the new mother decides to give up her infant son in order to save him from her abusive husband. This chapter

The writer Ivan Ivanovich Panaev, whom Panaeva married in 1839

served as the prologue for *Tri strany sveta* (Three Corners of the World), which was published in 1848 and 1849. Because the novel was not finished when the first chapters were published, Nekrasov and Panaeva had to sign a guarantee for the censors that "good would prevail and evil would be punished" in the novel. Even so, they had great difficulties getting the pages past the censors, and they would often have to rewrite entire chapters just days before publication. Perhaps this hasty revision of the work is one reason for its highly disjointed plotline and poorly developed characters, which critics were vocal in pointing out. Despite its artistic flaws, however, the novel was extremely successful among readers, a fact attested to by its separate publication in 1849 and republication in 1852, 1872, and three more times in the twentieth century.

The novel features two highly dramatic story lines, one following the travels of the hero, Kaiutin, to eastern Russia and Russian America, and one depicting the romantic intrigues surrounding the heroine, Polin'ka, who stays behind in the city. Kaiutin's travels are a series of anecdotal sketches, with an abundance of local flavor, regional dialects, and colloquial proverbs following Nekrasov's prosaic and poetic writing style. Some of the sketches are humorous, such as the description of the hero's eccentric uncle, while others are purely adventurous. Kaiutin travels to the harsh and monotonous Russian countryside, learns to harvest, takes barges down a tumultuous river, and then heads off to Siberia, where he masters the hunt and has many near-death experiences. Meanwhile, Polin'ka is left in St. Petersburg, where she fights off the unwanted attentions of an evil, hunchbacked moneylender who doggedly pursues her and eventually kidnaps her. She manages to escape and takes a position as a maidservant in the household that happens to belong to the first woman who cruelly rejected the advances of the hunchback when he was younger. Kaiutin eventually returns for Polin'ka in the end, and as they start their life together they realize that life is a mixture of happiness and sadness, of adventure and boredom–a "happy ending" rather lukewarm at best.

Critics traditionally have assumed that Nekrasov was behind the Kaiutin story line, and some insist that the entire novel was written by Nekrasov. Although it has been published in Nekrasov's collected works without credits to any other authors, the novel appeared in *Sovremennik* under the names of both Nekrasov and N. Stanitsky. Panaeva asserts in her memoirs that she and others, such as her husband and Aleksandr Vasil'evich Druzhinin, took part in the writing of the novel, but she also notes that because so many of their colleagues were appalled by the idea of a novel written by multiple authors, she offered to remove her name from the credits. Critics called the practice of multiple authorship "preposterous buffoonery" and derided the journal for a sequel to be titled "Ten Corners of the World" with just that many authors behind it.

Panaeva's themes, style, and characterizations are obvious throughout the entire Polin'ka story line and even in some of the more melodramatic sketches mixed in with Kaiutin's travels, such as the tragic tale of an artist, later published as a short story, "Portretist" (The Portrait Painter, 1856), under Panaeva's pen name. Polin'ka is a typical Panaeva heroine: she is young, energetic, and so beautiful that all of the men desire her, causing her all sorts of troubles. She is also one of Panaeva's few strong heroines who manages to escape exploitation by her innate down-to-earth understanding of society, money, and sex. Polin'ka is never deceived into desiring social acceptance, preferring hard work and independence to petty societal intrigues. She helps fund Kaiutin's travels because she recognizes the importance of financial security to making their relationship work. Finally, Polin'ka realizes the difference between the passionate love she feels for Kaiutin and the friendly love she feels toward her golden-hearted neighbor Karl Ivanych, who looks after her devotedly while Kaiutin is away. This particular type of strong female character can only be found in one other work by Panaeva, the short story *Stepnaia baryshnia* (Young Lady of the Steppes, 1855), which features a country outcast who knows her mind and heart well enough to refuse the misplaced charity of an eligible bachelor from the upper class.

Panaeva developed the ironic juxtaposition of passion and friendship hinted at in *Tri strany sveta* with full force in her later works. Having discovered from her marriage to Panaev that love cannot survive without passion, Panaeva discovered with Nekrasov the difficulties in keeping passion alive in the face of everyday realities. Just one year into their affair, petty domestic squabbles over financial matters and even issues so mundane as what to have for dinner turned their house into a battlefield. Nekrasov took out his frustration by turning to drink, women, and gambling, frequently bringing prostitutes home with him and creating loud, drunken scenes with Panaeva, which shamed and embarrassed even his friends. Their hellish rows and passionate reconciliations lasted for the entire fifteen years of their tumultuous affair and found their way into the fictional works of both writers. Nekrasov, in his famed "Panaeva cycle" of poems, lamented the petty arguments and "despotic tears" that killed the poetry of his love affair, while Panaeva in her short stories and novels tried to determine ways to make a relationship work. As one of her heroines mused, "There is much more to making a marriage work than just love: the first passion fades and then you have to make the love continue somehow."

Nekrasov and Panaeva's disillusionment with their love affair can be seen in their next novel written together, just after their first parting and reconciliation. *Mertvoe ozero* (The Dead Lake, 1851), published in *Sovremennik* in fifteen parts and later published separately twice, features a disheartening ending in which almost all of the characters are either destroyed or consigned to a life of domestic suffering. Plagued by a mind-numbing array of unrelated plots and subplots, jumpy dialogue, and characters who disappear for several chapters and then reappear with a complete turnaround in personality, the novel has almost no inner structure. While this disorganization may be a sign of multiple authors behind the project, censorship no doubt had a great impact on the writing of this novel as well. Nekrasov begged his friends not to judge these works too harshly because the authors could only do so much with what was allowed. The grotesque menagerie of characters earned the novel notoriety among conservative critics as the "masterpiece of the Natural School," while liberal critics praised it as Russia's first realistic depiction of provincial theater life.

Only about a third of this rambling novel clearly reflects the stylistic and thematic inclinations of Panaeva. These chapters feature Panaeva's typical heroines, who are repressed and taken advantage of by bitter old women or unscrupulous men. Eventually these girls are destroyed, like the half-gypsy girl Liuba, or they become bitter and old themselves, like the actress Liubskaia and the mistreated ward Zina. The only one to end up happily is the country-bred Nast'ia, who is rescued from her sufferings by a loving father and noble fiancé; they all decide to move back to the country, where they will live off the land in complete disregard for monetary riches.

Of the three "main" plotlines in the novel, by far the most entertaining one deals with the inner workings of theater life. This milieu is depicted as a hyperbolic extension of everything bad in society, comprised almost exclusively of gossip, intrigue, envy, and egos. The actors and actresses connive and backstab their way to the top, only to be replaced by younger, more energetic connivers and backstabbers. This depiction coincides with Panaeva's later description of the St. Petersburg theater in her memoirs. The plotline is not necessarily Panaeva's alone, however, as many critics have concluded, based solely on biographical evidence. There are many stylistic marks in this subplot indicating that the novel may represent a more integrated joint writing effort on the parts of Nekrasov, Panaeva, and perhaps others. The vivid portrait of the three sisters who dress like men, smoke, drink, never wash their greasy hair, and brush their teeth with tobacco (which must have driven the anti-Naturalistic critics to despair) reads more like a scene out of Nekrasov or Panaev's writings. In addition, the proverb-littered colloquial speech, the attention to scenic and other details such as male grooming habits, and the extremely bitter ending that goes to great lengths to punish the heroines are a far cry from Panaeva's other works. However, the love plot featuring a golden-hearted man rejected because of a lack of passion, as well as the unpleasant female tête-à-têtes, are quite familiar to the reader of Panaeva's fiction.

Her two novels with Nekrasov helped Panaeva polish her writing skills and establish her reputation as a writer of the Natural School. Both novels feature detailed descriptions of the grungy aspects of daily life, and the intimacy of episodes such as the childbirth scene in *Tri strany sveta* prompted one conservative critic to plead, "Spare us, Messieurs Naturalists!" Panaeva's successive works, written apart from Nekrasov, show far less interest in naturalistic details as she began to focus on the issues surrounding "the woman question."

In Russia, public debate over women's lack of freedom began in the 1840s with the ideal of the "emancipation of the heart" inspired by the works of George Sand. Works in the 1850s and 1860s shifted the focus of the woman question to the status of educational and social opportunities, and the crowning achievement in the defense of the liberation of women is considered to be Chernyshevsky's 1863 novel, *Chto delat'?* (What Is to be Done?). His heroine, Vera Pavlovna, set the example of the new emancipated woman, who had broken out of the narrow family role and earned her own living, thanks largely in part to the two rational men who love her.

Panaeva's works show far less optimism in the promises of women's emancipation, reflecting her own experiences as an "emancipated" woman. Her next novel, *Melochi zhizni* (The Details of Life, 1854), shows how far society is from its purported agenda of liberation and freedom. In this novel women are powerless to construct a life of happiness for themselves because they are completely at the mercy of their husbands, mothers, or benefactors.

The novel is composed of another double plotline, following the fates of two different young girls who fall into similarly unhappy marriages. Elena Andreevna is young, beautiful, energetic, intelligent, and possesses a childlike naiveté. Blinded by poetic fantasies of love, she marries the rather foppish Boris Fedorich, whose interests—spending money, hobnobbing with high society, and clipping his fingernails—Elena does not share. Elena ends up staying at home, making jam and reading books with her more intellectual neighbor, with whom she has much more in common, but who again lacks the physical draw. Elena's unhappiness eventually hardens her and gives her what others refer to as a masculine coldness. In contrast to Elena, Natal'ia Grigor'evna is almost crushed by her unhappy match, and she is constantly in tears. Natal'ia is pawned off on an old bachelor feeling the need for a wife of some sort; he cages her up in a stark and depressing fifth-floor apartment and refuses to let her see anyone or read any books for fear that she will get dangerous ideas. The only human companionship she has is listening to her passionate neighbors fight and make up on the other side of her bedroom wall.

There is no payoff at the end of this novel: everyone ends up poorly. Elena continues her spouseless existence without any hope left in her at all, and Natal'ia is whisked away to an even more-remote prison, where she continues to live in solitary monotony for the rest of her life. The only ones who make out well in the end, writes the narrator, are people who live solely for themselves and bring pain to others around them, such as the heartless husbands.

The story offers intriguing parallels to Panaeva's life. Like Elena, Panaeva had beauty, pride, and strong individualism that alienated her from other women, who managed to ostracize her from the rest of society via rumors, gossip, and intrigue. Panaeva, like her heroine, refused to be crushed by her position as a social outcast, and she prided herself on what she called her "masculine" independence of opinion and thought that gave her strength to endure public humiliations and lonely nights, first with her husband, then with her lover. The contrasting story of Natal'ia Grigor'evna is most likely a fictionalized depiction of Panaeva's friendship with Elizaveta Bogdanovna Granovskaia, to whom the novel is dedicated. Granovskaia and Panaeva became close friends in 1852 as social outcasts. Granovskaia's quiet shyness earned her public ridicule, but this trait is reflected sympathetically in the character of Natal'ia Grigor'evna, whose subjugation to a cruel husband was a variation on Granovskaia's tearful subservience to a tyrannical father.

Although *Melochi zhizni* garnered considerable attention for its focus on the subjugation of women to their husbands, critics denounced the novel for the usual reasons Panaeva's work was attacked: poor character development and overly melodramatic scenes. The novel is not without successful moments, however, such as the character of the candy-gobbling, platitude-mouthing Irina Andreevna, who heads the "orphanage" for poor girls, and the depiction of the dull monotony of Natal'ia Grigor'evna's apartment prison. More importantly, *Melochi zhizni* succinctly articulates the theme that is central to almost all of Panaeva's works: that women must be educated in matters of real life in order to be able to come to terms with the mundaneness inherent in life and love. As Elena explains to her neighbor, "When you marry, be mindful of the things that seem the least important. Believe me, they are the most potent poison to any kind of happiness." In Panaeva's worldview, the key to life is in the details, not in great events or tragedies. Women must learn that life is not always glamorous, and love is not always passionate. They must realize the cold fact that "It takes a lot of money to support the poetry of love."

The idea of financial security, always a prominent theme in Panaeva's works, took on new significance for her beginning in 1853, when she became involved in a messy civil proceeding after being accused of embezzling funds from a friend's estate. This new scandal dragged on until 1860, when Nekrasov paid the fines for her. This act earned Panaeva the resentment of many of Nekrasov's friends and almost all Nekrasov scholars even through the twentieth century. Her experiences with broken friendships only added to her disillusionment and found voice in her next works.

If, in Panaeva's earlier works, there was some compensatory sense of friendship or camaraderie between similarly persecuted heroines, her later fiction shows how even friendship can bring on more suffering and humiliation. These later works develop a good girl versus bad girl duality, in which two female opposites forge a friendship in the face of their mutual sufferings from egotistical men and social exile, only to be betrayed by each other's backstabbing, selfish behavior. *Domashnii ad* (A Domestic

Hell, 1857), features an older female mentor who alienates and destroys her younger, more naive friend looking to her for advice. Neither of these women is portrayed in the most sympathetic light; Panaeva's heroines take on more ambiguity with her later works. The typical heroine is still lively, beautiful, and independent of thought, but neither her pride nor her naiveté is portrayed unsympathetically as the ultimate cause of her downfall. An extreme example is the short story *Vozdushnye zamki* (Castles in the Air, 1855) in which both the naive young girl and the despotic older woman in whom she places her trust are portrayed as unattractive, shallow creatures addicted to cigarettes and tacky fashions. This story, which ends with a gang rape, is one of Panaeva's harshest attacks on upper-middle-class society and the provincial misses who are willing to sacrifice everything to be a part of it.

Haunted by betrayed friendships, her continual fights with Nekrasov, his endless cycle of affairs and abandonment, and their inability to conceive children who would live past infancy, Panaeva began questioning her ability to continue her role as an emancipated woman at the center of a prominent and demanding literary salon. In 1856 she wrote to her brother-in-law: "am I really capable of being satisfied with just the contentment of female egoism? That is, of surrounding myself with a crowd of young men, listening to their compliments and declarations, flirting. Sometimes I think I am capable, but then it's all so repulsive and cheap that I become vile to myself." However, Panaeva felt that she, like other women, really had no choice in controlling her fate once she had submitted to the wishes of society, which stripped her of even the most fundamental human rights. In a 28 January 1857 letter to I. A. Panaev she wrote sarcastically, "Isn't that awful? I consider myself, a woman, to be a person! Forgive me."

Panaeva's next novel, *Roman v peterburgskom polusvete* (Romance in the St. Petersburg Demimonde, 1860), expounds the theme of female powerlessness and subversively equates women's position to that of serfs. In this novel, both women and serfs are punished if they try to educate themselves, live independently, or refuse to conform to the socially condoned standards of hypocrisy and greed. Their only choice is to live and die in suffering and ignorance. Such an overt condemnation of upper-class tyranny over serfs and women could only have been published during the brief thaw in Russia's strict censorship rules between 1856 and 1862, when several works questioning the propriety of serfdom appeared. While these controversial writings dealt with issues surrounding the 1861 Emancipation Act that freed the serfs, Panaeva's novel is distinctive in equating the debates over serfdom and the woman question.

The novel revolves around Aniuta, a young, spirited provincial miss, who is sold off by her impoverished drunkard father to a heartless aunt who forces her into a life of slavery, first to the uncaring, hypocritical society that inhabits the St. Petersburg demimonde, and later to a reactionary, abusive husband. Although Aniuta tries to escape with the help of her idealistic childhood friend from the lower classes, she is ultimately caught.

The novel makes clear that Aniuta's story is not unique—it is a repetition of what happens to every girl who thinks and feels with liveliness and a sense of self. Although Aniuta vows she will be stronger, she is ultimately powerless in the face of society and family. Even the representative of the working-class democrats, Karsanov, is incapable of helping. Karsanov is a different kind of "superfluous man." He is the educated, deep-thinking, deep-feeling kind of individual from the middle class who can do nothing to improve the situation of women or serfs, because he has no power to influence society. The only figures with power in society are those with money, who have learned how to exploit others in order to accumulate more wealth.

The exploitation of the serfs is symbolized by the story of Aniuta's nanny. Having been forced to abandon her beloved husband and infant when she was ordered by the landowners to become Aniuta's wet-nurse, she throws all of her love and devotion onto the child. When Aniuta is sent off to St. Petersburg, however, the nanny is forbidden to accompany her. Her masters even set the dogs on her when she tries to follow Aniuta. By the end of the novel, she is unceremoniously kicked out of the house, and she wanders the estate grounds in a state of madness and starvation.

The novel gave rise to harsh criticism—not just among the conservative critics, who took political exception to the portrayal of the condition of serfs, but also among the more sympathetic liberal critics, who called her novel "tendentious" and rebuked her for resorting to lurid scenes and one-sided characterization to make her point. Indeed, her descriptions of the evil deeds committed by Aniuta's family and the St. Petersburg demimonde society are almost beyond imagination. An example is Gavril Antonovich, a tyrannical secretary who whips the serfs, hangs the dog, exiles the maids to the pig sties, destroys the flowers in the garden, and forbids Aniuta to read or step out of her room. On the whole, critics found her complaints against high society and the victimization

Nikolai Alekseevich Nekrasov, Panaeva's lover and her collaborator on two novels

of women so tiresome and fiercely cynical in this novel that they felt the reader was left "cold."

Several of Panaeva's characters escape from this one-sided type of characterization, however. Following Panaeva's emerging sense of ambivalence toward her heroines, Aniuta is rather ambiguously portrayed as a standoffish girl who has grown up selfish and overly proud. Aniuta's illegitimate half sister, Duniasha, is an even more interesting character. Duniasha faces a different kind of exploitation because of her illegitimacy: her parents have paid gypsies to educate her in the arts of drinking and seduction so that she can "entertain" their male dinner guests. Because she has been treated cruelly since birth, she has a cruel streak in her that is only broken in the end by patient compassion and kind words from Karsanov. She tells him: "I always thought how nice life might be if only somebody would speak to me as you have done. Nobody has ever said a kind word to me, ever. But I am still not so evil . . . here I am now, ready to walk through fire for you."

That a scorned woman might be looking for a kind word echoes what Panaeva wrote in letters to friends and later expressed in her memoirs. She explains her aura of aloofness toward others by the fact that "Nobody was ever tender with me, therefore I was never very receptive to tenderness." While her childhood experiences may have left her scarred, her adulthood experiences proved no less difficult. Although she endured fifteen years of Nekrasov's chronic irritability and affairs with other women (including one that left him painfully ill with syphilis), she gained no benefit. When Panaev suddenly in 1862, Nekrasov did not offer to marry Panaeva. Instead, he demanded that she play hostess to the mistresses he brought into their house. One year later, Nekrasov literally kicked Panaeva out and moved in with a French actress who was then living in St. Petersburg. Panaeva found herself abandoned and completely shunned by society.

Not surprisingly, her next novel was an impassioned outcry against men. *Zhenskaia dolia* (A Woman's Lot, 1862), published in *Sovremennik,* reflects her state of absolute disillusionment with husbands, lovers, fathers, and society in general. In contrast to her previous works, in which mothers or female mentor figures or even the heroines themselves were also somehow to blame for the degraded state of women in society, this novel argues that men are the base cause of all female suffering. Her heroine summarizes the theme of the novel succinctly: "Until men themselves become more moral, there can be no 'emancipation' for women."

The plot, which is similar to previous stories by Panaeva, features a lively, naive young girl who falls in love with an unscrupulous and carousing young fop. There is no one to help prevent the heroine from making a big mistake by marrying the abusive young man, because her mother has already suffered tremendously from the tyranny of her husband and fears opening her daughter's eyes to what she calls the depravity of men. The heroine's father is an even more unscrupulous villain who would like nothing more than to see his own daughter suffer, and society does not care one way or the other what happens to her.

In the novel Panaeva goes to great lengths to show the extent of man's moral corruption, even hinting at such tabooed topics as domestic violence and forced abortion. The narrator is quick to point out that while wives endure their husbands' blows and mistresses abort their lovers' illegitimate children, society turns a blind eye and encourages women to continue to trust that these same men will educate and "liberate" them. The narrator scoffs at this misplaced trust, warning women, "don't expect anything from the emancipation of women! This idea is being preached just as fruitlessly as is kindness toward fellow man, which has been bandied about for so long. And do you really not see that a woman, having fallen under the spell of emancipation and having given herself up to a man without any kind of civil bond, that she won't also perish in a state of degraded slavery and even more shame?"

As might be expected, the novel met with an extremely harsh critical reception. While some critics rebuked her characters for "stupidity," others decried the novel as a denouncement of the ideals of women's emancipation. The leading nihilist critic Dmitrii Ivanovich Pisarev went even further in his criticism, calling the novel a "wooden-headed tragedy" filled with "putrid trash and noxious crap." Revealing much about the contemporary male point of view toward women, Pisarev rebuked "Stanitsky" for being too ignorant to realize that men are, by the fact of their superior mental development, already superior morally to women, and that it is up to women to stop being the simpleminded victims, luring men into seducing them because they do not know enough to hide their charms.

Zhenskaia dolia was Panaeva's last novel. In 1864 she married Apollon Filippovich Golovachev, a minor critic who had been hired to work as a journalist and secretary for *Sovremennik* the previous year. With Golovachev, when she was well into her mid forties, she finally bore a healthy child, Evdokia Apollonovna, who later became a writer under her married name of Nagrodskaia. Panaeva devoted herself to her new role of mother. However, in 1877 her husband died, leaving her and her daughter penniless; so Panaeva turned again to writing.

Knowing well the popular appetite for gossip and petty details, Panaeva chose as her subject matter her reminiscences of the famous people she knew best, including prominent actors as well as the *Sovremennik* circle of writers. Published in 1889 in *Istoricheskii vestnik* (Historical Herald) simply as "Vospominaniia" (Memoirs) under her married name of Golovacheva, her memoirs were subsequently published in 1890 (as *Russkie pisateli i artisty. 1824–1870* [Russian Writers and Artists: 1824–1870]) and republished in 1927, 1933, 1948, 1956, and 1972. These sensationalistic memoirs can be considered Panaeva's most successful work. On the whole, contemporary critics received them warmly. As one of the few women in Russian letters to be granted access to the male-dominated club of literary movers and shakers, Panaeva offered amusing and revealing insights into this sphere. Twentieth-century social historians have claimed that her memoirs are "the most valuable source for the study of the history of Russian literature."

Because they have been read almost exclusively as a sociological work documenting a past era, her memoirs are most often rebuked for what made them so successful in their day: their gossipy nature. Panaeva's memoirs paint vivid portraits not of great giants of literature, but of everyday men and women simply trying to make a living. In a stream-of-consciousness, anecdotal style, complete with reconstructed dialogue and detailed descriptions of mannerisms and dress, Panaeva depicts Nekrasov at his writing desk in his dressing gown, Chernyshevsky and Dobroliubov eating kasha at the dinner table, Turgenev waxing on about the poetic inspiration of society ladies, Belinsky testing her naïveté with racy jokes, and Victor Hugo gobbling homemade Russian cooking as though it were a gourmet feast. This kind of detail later caused critics to accuse her of "impoverishing and simplifying the souls" of the great artists of the nineteenth century. The critic Kornei Chukovsky lamented, "It is as if she were listening to a symphony by the greatest maestros, but heard only the chirping of crickets."

By focusing on the factual nature of these memoirs, critics for the most part have missed the richness of Panaeva's text, which is marked by lively narration and nuanced self-representation. Although on the surface she is always a background figure, a narrator of others' lives, Panaeva inadvertently creates a self-portrait that is not only entertaining but also revealing. Panaeva uses dialogue and mannerisms to highlight personality traits that stand for larger social issues upon which she can safely offer her own opinion. Dramatist Aleksandr Aleksandrovich Shakhovskoi, for example, becomes representative of the demeaning mores of the theater, which Panaeva mocks by humorously recounting his habitual manner of harassment: "Use your own voice! You're squawking! You, my dear little idiot, have no ear! Where is your sense of rhyme? You need to take a visit to the nursery, not to the stage." Similarly, her admiration for Belinsky's proletarianism, Panaev's humanitarianism, and Nekrasov's uneducated simplicity comes across in their dialogue and mannerisms. Turgenev in particular provides Panaeva with an amusing means for polemicizing about such topics as the Russian artistic tradition versus the European, the aristocracy versus the working class, high society superficiality, and women's rights.

After her memoirs were published and until her death in 1893, Panaeva continued to support her family by writing. She wrote several short stories for the rather second-rate journals *Niva* (The Grainfield) and *Sbornik Nivy* (Collection from *Niva*), a step that was not easy for her to take. She wrote in 1889, "If not for the fear that my little grandchildren might die of hunger, I would not for anything in the world show my face in any editorial office, so difficult it is to endure their unceremonious attitude towards me, a forgotten author of a past literary era."

On 30 March 1893, at the age of seventy-two, Panaeva died from complications of pneumonia. With the exception of her memoirs, her works have remained mostly forgotten until late in the twentieth century. While her works might seem dated in terms of artistry and melodrama, her themes and ideas are still topical: love, passion, social hypocrisy, childhood repression, domestic violence, and sexual abuse. In her work Panaeva strove to show the importance of giving women the freedom and the education to live life, not to put them on display in social circles or cage them up in prison-like rooms. Living, in Panaeva's view, is physical and active, from the most mundane household chores to the most passionate lovemaking. Life is most often dirty, and, like love, it requires hard work. In Panaeva's world, those with the cleanest fingernails are the most unfortunate failures in life.

Letters:

Russkie propilei, edited by M. O. Gershenzon, volume 4 (Moscow: Sabashnikovy, 1917), pp. 83–86, 95–98, 117;

N. A. Nekrasov, in *Literaturnoe nasledstvo,* volume 49/50 (Moscow: Akademiia Nauk SSSR, 1946), pp. 549–550;

V. G. Belinsky i ego korrespondenty, edited by N. L. Brodsky (Moscow, 1948), pp. 217–223;

N. A. Nekrasov, in *Literaturnoe nasledstvo,* volume 53/54 (Moscow: Akademiia Nauk SSSR, 1950), pp. 117–119;

Voprosy literatury, 11 (1979): 239–246.

Bibliography:

Dmitrii Dmitrievich Iazykov, *Obzor zhizni i trudov pokoinykh russkikh pisatelei umershikh v 1893 godu* (Petrograd: A.S. Suvorin, 1916), pp. 71–73.

Biographies:

V. A. Panaev, "Vospominaniia," *Russkaia starina,* 8 (1893);

Maksim Alekseevich Antonovich, "Vospominaniia," *Shestidesiatye gody* (Moscow-Leningrad: Academia, 1933), pp. 33–248;

Dmitrii Vasil'evich Grigorovich, *Literaturnye vospominaniia* (Moscow: Khudozhestvennaia literatura, 1987), pp. 147–272.

References:

Kornei Chukovsky, "Panaeva i Nekrasov," in *Semeistvo Tal'nikovykh. Povest'*, by Panaeva (Leningrad: Academia, 1928);

Chukovsky, *Zhena poeta* (Petrograd: Epokha, 1922);

Vladislav Evgen'evich Evgen'ev-Maksimov, Introduction to *Tri strany sveta*, by Panaeva (Moscow: Respublika, 1994);

Evgen'ev-Maksimov, *Sovremennik v 40-50 gg.* (Leningrad: Izd. pisatelia, 1934);

Richard Gregg, "A Brackish Hippocrene: Nekrasov, Panaeva, and the 'Prose in Love,'" *Slavic Review* (December 1975): 735–751;

Kseniia Sergeevna Kurova, *Literaturnoaia deiatel'nost' A. Ia. Panaevoi* (Alma-Ata, 1951);

Kurova, "Tvorchestvo A. Ia. Panaevoi v 60-e gody," *Uchenye zapiski Kazakhskogo universiteta*, 14 (1952): 39–58;

Marina Ledkovsky, "Avdotya Panaeva: Her Salon and Her Life," *Russian Literature Triquarterly*, 9 (1974): 423–432;

V. N. Sorokin, "Roman Tri strany sveta (k voprosu o tvorcheskom sodruzhestve N. A. Nekrasova i A. Ia Panaevoi)," *Uchen. zap. Vinnitskogo ped. in-ta im. N. Ostrovskogo*, 21 (1963);

M. Tsebrikova, "Russkie zhenshchiny-pisatel'nitsy," *Nedelia*, 21/22 (1876): 703–705;

Mary Zirin, "Butterflies with Broken Wings? Early Autobiographical Depictions of Girlhood in Russia," in *Gender Restructuring in Russian Studies*, edited by Marianne Liljeström, Elia Mäntysaari, and Arja Rosenholm (Tampere: University of Tampere, 1993), pp. 267–272.

Papers:

Avdot'ia Iakovlevna Panaeva's papers can be found in the Russian State Archives of Literature and Art (RGALI, formerly TsGaLI) in Moscow, fond 382, and in the Institute of Russian Literature (IRLI [Pushkin House]) in St. Petersburg, fond 155.

Aleksei Feofilaktovich Pisemsky

(11 March 1821 – 21 January 1881)

Alexandra Sosnowski
McGill University

WORKS: *Tiufiak,* in *Moskvitianin,* nos. 19–21 (1850); (Moscow, 1850); translated by Ivy Litvinova as *The Simpleton* (Moscow: Foreign Language Publishing House, 1959);

Sergei Petrovich Khozarov i Mari Stupitsyna. Brak po strasti, in *Moskvitianin,* nos. 4–7 (1851); (St. Petersburg: Stellovsky, 1861);

Komik, in *Moskvitianin,* no. 21 (1851); (St. Petersburg, 1861);

Bogatyi zhenikh, in *Sovremennik,* nos. 10–12 (1851); nos. 1–5 (1852); (Moscow, 1855);

Ipokhondrik, in *Moskvitianin,* no. 1 (1852); (St. Petersburg, 1861);

M-r Batmanov, in *Moskvitianin,* nos. 17–18 (1852); (St. Petersburg: Stellovsky, 1861);

Pitershchik, in *Mosvitianin,* no. 23 (1852); (St. Petersburg: Stellovsky, 1861);

Razdel, in *Sovremennik,* no. 1 (1853); (St. Petersburg, 1861);

Leshii. Rasskaz ispravnika, in *Sovremennik,* no. 11 (1853); (St. Petersburg: Stellovsky, 1861);

Povesti i rasskazy, 3 volumes (Moscow: Stepanova, 1853);

Fanfaron. Odin iz nashikh snobsov, in *Sovremennik,* no. 8 (1854); (St. Petersburg, 1861);

Veteran i novobranets. Dramaticheskii sluchai iz 1854 goda, in *Otechestvennye zapiski* (1854); (St. Petersburg, 1861);

Plotnich'ia artel'. Derevenskie zapiski, in *Otechestvennye zapiski,* no. 9 (1855); (St. Petersburg: Stellovsky, 1861);

Ocherki iz krest'ianskogo byta (St. Petersburg: Tip. A. Dmitrieva, 1856);

Staraia barynia, in *Biblioteka dlia chteniia,* no. 2 (1857); (St. Petersburg: Stellovsky, 1861);

Boiarshchina, in *Biblioteka dlia chteniia,* nos. 1–2 (1858); (St. Petersburg, 1861);

Tysiacha dush, in *Otechestvennye zapiski,* nos. 1–6 (1858); 2 volumes (St. Petersburg: Tip. I. I. Glazunova, 1858); translated by Litvinova as *One Thousand Souls* (Moscow: Foreign Language Publishing House, 1958; New York: Grove, 1959);

Gor'kaia sud'bina, in *Biblioteka dlia chteniia,* no. 11 (1859); (St. Petersburg: Tip. I. I. Glazunova, 1860); trans-

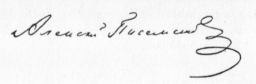

lated by A. Kagan and G. R. Noyes as "A Bitter Fate," in *Masterpieces of the Russian Drama,* edited by Noyes, volume 1 (New York & London: Appleton, 1933), pp. 407–456;

Starcheskii grekh. Sovershenno romanticheskoe prikliuchenie, in *Biblioteka dlia chteniia,* no. 1 (1861): 1–90; (St. Petersburg: Stellovsky, 1861);

Sochineniia, 4 volumes (St. Petersburg: Stellovsky, 1861–1867);

Bat'ka, in *Russkoe slovo,* no. 1 (1862); (St. Petersburg, 1866);

Vzbalamuchennoe more, in *Russkii vestnik,* nos. 3–8 (1863); 3 volumes (Moscow: Univ. tip., 1863);

Russkie lguny, in *Otechestvennye zapiski,* no. 1 (1865): 88–116; no. 2 (1865): 483–496; no. 4 (1865): 501–524; (Moscow: Goslitizdat, 1955);

Samoupravtsy, in *Vsemirnyi trud,* no. 2 (1867); (St. Petersburg, 1867);

Poruchik Gladkov, in *Vsemirnyi trud,* no. 3 (1867); (St. Petersburg, 1872);

Byvye sokoly, in *Vsemirnyi trud,* no. 9 (1868); (St. Petersburg, 1918);

Liudi sorokovykh godov, in *Zaria,* nos. 1–9 (1869); (St. Petersburg, 1869);

V vodovorote, in *Beseda,* nos. 1–6 (1871); 3 volumes (Moscow: Izd. brat'ev Salaevykh, 1872);

Vaal, in *Russkii vestnik,* no. 4 (1873); (Moscow, 1873);

Podkopy (Khishchniki), in *Grazhdanin,* nos. 7–10 (1873); (St. Petersburg, 1873);

Komedii, dramy i tragedii, 2 volumes (Moscow: Univ. tip., 1874);

Prosveshchennoe vremia, Russkii vestnik, no. 1 (1875): 68–139;

Finansovyi genii, in *Gazeta A. Gattsuka* (1876); (Moscow, 1876);

Meshchane, in *Pchela,* nos. 18–49 (1877); (St. Petersburg: M. O. Mikeshin, 1878);

Masony, in *Ogonek,* nos. 1–52 (1880); 2 volumes (St. Petersburg: Izd. G. Goppe, 1880–1881).

Editions and Collections: *Sochineniia. Posmertnoe polnoe izdanie,* 20 volumes (St. Petersburg: M. O. Vol'f, 1883–1886; second edition, 24 volumes, 1895–1896);

Polnoe sobranie sochinenii, 8 volumes, with a biographical sketch by V. V. Zelinsky (St. Petersburg: A. F. Marks, 1910–1911);

Sobranie sochinenii, 9 volumes (Moskow: Izd. Pravda, 1959).

Edition in English: *Nina; The Comic Actor; An Old Man's Sin,* translated by Maya Jenkins (Ann Arbor, Mich.: Ardis, 1988).

SELECTED PERIODICAL PUBLICATIONS:

"Nina: Epizod iz dnevnika moego priiatelia," *Syn otechestva,* no. 7 (1848): 3–30;

"Vinovata li ona?" *Sovremennik,* no. 2 (1855): 217–304.

In Russian literary circles Aleksei Feofilaktovich Pisemsky has generally been regarded as a second-rate writer. Yet, for a brief time at the onset of his career the immense popularity of his works ranked him with the leading writers of his time. Pisemsky was compared favorably with such masters of Russian letters as Fyodor Dostoevsky, Leo Tolstoy, Ivan Sergeevich Turgenev, and Nikolai Semenovich Leskov. Writing to Turgenev in 1863, Dostoevsky described Pisemsky as "a colossal literary name." While not a writer of Tolstoy's or Dostoevsky's caliber, Pisemsky's insightful renderings of Russian provincial life have earned him a place among the masters of nineteenth-century Russian literature.

The son of Feofilakt Gavrilovich Pisemsky and Avdot'ia Alekseevna Shipova, Aleksei Pisemsky was born on 11 March 1821 (some sources say 10 March 1820), just northeast of Moscow, on the family estate at Ramen'e in the Chukhloma district of Kostroma Province. His father, a lieutenant colonel in the military, was a strict disciplinarian. His mother was loving but weak and high-strung. The only surviving child of nine siblings, young Aleksei was doted on and enjoyed a happy childhood. His early schooling was entrusted to local tutors. Then, in 1835, when he reached the age of fourteen, Aleksei was enrolled in Kostroma gymnasium, where he acquired a taste for adventure stories, developed a passion for literature, and discovered theater. On the encouragement of his literature teacher, A. F. Okatov, Aleksei's performance in school amateur productions soon led to playwriting. Pisemsky's gifts for theater served him well, winning him popularity among his fellow students and later garnering public acclaim for him as an eloquent reader.

In 1840, after completing secondary school at the Kostroma gymnasium, Pisemsky entered Moscow University, from which he graduated in 1844. He was enrolled in mathematical studies but devoted much time to literary subjects, regularly attending lectures on literature. Lacking a strong command of any foreign language, he became acquainted with foreign literature by way of Russian translations. At the end of his university studies, Pisemsky graduated not only with standing in mathematics, but also well versed in Western and Russian literary classics. After university, family duties recalled him to Kostroma: his father's death a year earlier, his mother's serious illness, and various domestic difficulties left him no alternative but to return to the family estate. There he secured a civil-service post as special agent attached to the military governor of Kostroma Province. During this period Pisemsky's closest literary contact was the poet Pavel Aleksandrovich Katenin, who served as a mentor to the fledgling writer.

In 1848 Pisemsky married the eighteen-year-old Ekaterina Pavlovna Svin'ina. She had excellent literary connections and was also able to help Pisemsky by copying his writing. The couple had four sons and a daughter; only two sons and their daughter survived to maturity. Pisemsky also fathered an illegitimate daughter by an anonymous seamstress. Given Pisemsky's many weaknesses, which included alcoholism, Ekaterina Pavlovna was a fortunate choice, for she kept him on course through many difficult times. Yet, he seems not to have appreciated her fine qualities; in his novel *Vzbalamuchennoe more* (Troubled Seas; first published in *Russkii vestnik* [The Russian Herald], 1863), Pisemsky rather meanly disclosed his opinion of Ekaterina's shortcomings in the frigid character of Evpraksiia.

The year of his marriage also marked Pisemsky's official literary debut. In 1848, through the influence of his former university professor, Stepan Petrovich Shevyrev, Pisemsky's short love story "Nina" appeared in the Moscow literary journal *Syn otechestva* (Son of the Fatherland). During this first decade of his writing career a variety of topics drew his interest. Ultimately, however, he focused on family relationships, particularly on the challenges of love and marriage. This theme dominates twelve of the sixteen pieces he published before his first full-length novel, *Tysiacha dush* (One Thousand Souls) was serialized in *Otechestvennye zapiski* (Notes of the Fatherland) in 1858. His interest in the role of women in the context of family and marriage had been inspired by the writings of French novelist George Sand (Lucile-Aurore Dupin). Like Sand, Pisemsky explored freedom of sentiment and women's right to love. But Pisemsky's views on these matters diverged markedly from Sand's. Pisemsky modified Sand's notion of free love for women to mean a woman's right to choose a husband.

Of the works published during the first decade of his writing career, two short stories, *Tiufiak* (The Simpleton; first published in *Moskvitianin* [The Muscovite], 1850) and *Ocherki iz krest'ianskogo byta* (Sketches of Peasant Life, 1856), were universally acclaimed. Both stories explore love, individual choice, and marital relationships. In *Tiufiak* Pisemsky demonstrates how naiveté can lead to tragic consequences in life and in marriage. The central characters—Pavel Beshmetov and his intended, Iuliia—are far apart emotionally, spiritually, and morally. They are destined never to breach the gulf that separates them, for their union is being arranged without Iuliia's consent. For both characters, their trusting illusions about life, their personal shortcomings, and the inexorable pressures of social convention destine them to bleak and unhappy lives. *Ocherki iz krest'ianskogo byta,* on the other hand, depicts in penetrating detail the myriad nuances of Russian peasant culture. Pisemsky traces the ways in which city values corrupt rural virtues, spawning tragedy in the lives of his peasant heroes. Yet, even as he describes the subtleties of daily peasant life, Pisemsky refrains from pressing his own biases on the reader. Pisemsky's *Ocherki iz krest'ianskogo byta* is artistically neutral. He offers no clear-cut solutions to the dilemmas that beset his characters. This highly detailed, yet neutral, style drew praise and attention to Pisemsky's early works. In Pisemsky's characters, readers recognized types common in Russian society. His candid images of peasant life drew high praise from his literary

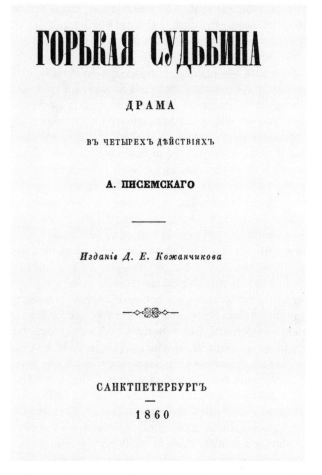

Title page for an edition of Pisemsky's play Gor'kaia sud'bina *(A Bitter Fate), first published in* Biblioteka dlia chteniia *(Library for Reading) in 1859*

contemporaries, both radicals and conservatives. Each faction claimed Pisemsky as an advocate of its cause.

Pisemsky's talents as a playwright and orator came together at the end of the 1850s, as his writing advanced to a new level of sophistication. Two works display this synthesis of his strengths: the novel *Tysiacha dush* (1858) and the play *Gor'kaia sud'bina* (A Bitter Fate; first published in *Biblioteka dlia chteniia* [Library for Reading], 1859). These two works placed him among the important writers of the epoch.

Kalinovich, the hero of *Tysiacha dush,* is a type familiar from Pisemsky's earlier works. Driven by aspirations for material wealth, Kalinovich determines to make a name for himself by achieving something noteworthy. In this quest he is none too scrupulous about the means he uses to achieve his goals. Kalinovich is not an honorable man, but, as Pisemsky reveals, he is a man of his time and place. Through his depiction of this character, Pisemsky probes the mores of provincial society and the values of his contemporaries. The picture that emerges is one of a corrupt Russian society in which good seems to be achieved only by evil means. This view of the dark side of Russia allowed Pisemsky to elevate a scoundrel to the status of hero and to justify his character's nefarious deeds. Kalinovich's wrongdoing enriches him materially and socially; yet, his success exacts a high price. For example, Kalinovich's betrayal of his true love, Nastia Godneva, does lead to wealth, but he is left with a cheerless marriage to the unattractive Polina. Who, Pisemsky seems to ask, is beyond reproach in such a corrupt setting? Who among Kalinovich's contemporaries is virtuous enough to pass judgment on the actions of this venal hero?

Pisemsky's *Gor'kaia sud'bina* also portrays the social milieu darkly. Structurally and psychologically, the brilliant play is one of Pisemsky's most interesting and complex early works. The action involves a love triangle made up of Lizaveta, her serf-husband Ananii, and her lover, a landowner. Despite appearances to the contrary, however, the tension does not emanate from a master-peasant conflict. The sources of the tension are far deeper and more personal. Although the play does not focus on questions of women's emancipation, it does revolve around the question of a woman's right to choose love. This dilemma leads to the tragic ruin of the proud and upright Ananii, who is ravaged by moral torment when he learns of his wife's love for the master. Wracked by the opposing strains of pride and of love, Ananii is driven to murder a guiltless child. In 1860 this powerful drama shared the prestigious Uvarov prize for drama with Aleksandr Nikolaevich Ostrovsky's *Groza* (The Storm, 1859). In Pisemsky's thought, the key to enduring and happy relationships between men and women is love—hence the failure of Kalinovich's marriage to the wealthy Polina in *Tysiacha dush,* and the tragic disintegration of the serf Ananii in *Gor'kaia sud'bina.*

During the 1850s Pisemsky grew increasingly dissatisfied with provincial life. He longed for the stimulation of Russian cultural centers. Through works such as *Tiufiak, Tysiacha dush,* and *Gor'kaia sud'bina* he had gained a following among the radicals, who claimed him as an ally. When Pisemsky finally abandoned provincial life in 1854, he did not choose Moscow, capital of the conservative Slavophiles, but St. Petersburg, the center of the Westernizers, or radicals. This choice was surprising. Although Pisemsky generally steered clear of politics, he was at heart committed to the existing monarchical system and opposed to revolutionary transformations. His conservative leanings became more visible in 1856, when he agreed to join Grand Duke Konstantin Nikolaevich's expedition to Astrakhan'. This venture sent established writers to lesser known parts of the empire to write informational materials for the public and the government. In 1857 he further revealed his political leanings when he became co-editor with Aleksandr Vasil'evich Druzhinin

of the conservative *Biblioteka dlia chteniia.* By 1860, having overcome his fondness for alcohol, Pisemsky had taken over from Druzhinin as chief editor of *Biblioteka dlia chteniia.*

During the 1860s Pisemsky's well-known antinihilist feuilletons exposed his conservatism. Though the feuilletons were satirical, directed primarily at the Russian bureaucracy and its milieu, they attacked many concerns dear to the radicals. Even his comments on the "woman question," in the feuilletons attributed to "Salatushka" and "Nikita Bezrylov" (published in *Biblioteka dlia chteniia,* 1861–1862), demonstrate that despite his admiration for George Sand, Pisemsky was not in favor of all the demands promoted by the supporters of women's struggle for equal rights. The radicals' bitter reactions to Pisemsky's feuilletons (which according to him had been misinterpreted)—including a challenge to a duel—provoked violent controversy in St. Petersburg, causing Pisemsky to withdraw from literary activity for some time, thus fueling his hostility toward the radical camp.

Pisemsky's true ideological orientation was soon confirmed yet again. In 1863 he left St. Petersburg for Moscow on an invitation from Mikhail Nikiforovich Katkov, editor of *Russkii vestnik* (The Russian Herald), to join Katkov's journal as director of the literary section. The journal, known for its conservatism in political affairs, was openly critical of the radicals. Pisemsky's conflict with the radicals peaked in 1863, after the publication of his antinihilist work *Vzbalamuchennoe more* in *Russkii vestnik.* Setting him firmly within the conservative camp, the work prompted many debates, critical articles, and polemics. The novel is highly representative of the 1860s, a decade in which politics were eagerly discussed, but its severely antiradical bias contrasts significantly with Pisemsky's previous objective style, and, thus, the work was disappointing to many readers.

Vzbalamuchennoe more is an attempt to describe the major social and intellectual movements of Russian society. It criticizes the radicals' political convictions and impugns their social and moral principles. In it Pisemsky also returned to the notion of female emancipation, which had gained considerable attention in the 1860s as a core issue endorsed by radicals and nihilists. Given Pisemsky's bitter feelings toward the radicals, it is not surprising that *Vzbalamuchennoe more* casts a critical light on their notion of erotic freedom, which he equates with sexual promiscuity. In contrast to the nihilist's stereotypical emancipated woman—plain, eccentric, and living a blameless life of self-abnegation—Pisemsky's heroine, Sofi Leneva, is sensual, beautiful, and a courtesan. Yet, in *Vzbalamuchennoe more* Pisemsky's critical barbs are directed more at the radicals and nihilists than at the concept of female emancipation. He denounces the radical and nihilist position on feminism because in his view, by the 1860s, the radicals and nihilists had debased the true meaning of emancipation to faddism and sexual promiscuity. Both in *Vzbalamuchennoe more* and in his next novel, *Liudi sorokovykh godov* (Men of the 1840s; first published in *Zaria* [Dawn], 1869), Pisemsky characterized nihilist women as shallow, undiscerning characters who adopt nihilism only because it is the latest trend.

With the exception of the short-story collection *Russkie lguny* (Russian Liars; first published in *Otechestvennye zapiski*, 1865), most of Pisemsky's written output during this decade consisted of novels and plays, largely concerned with social problems, sexual passion, and Russian society, both past and present. Pisemsky's most interesting play of this period is the disquieting *Byvye sokoly* (Worldly Wise Falcons; first published in *Vsemirnyi trud* (World Labor, 1868), about an incestuous relationship between a father and daughter that ends in childbirth and the murder of the father by a serf whom he had mistreated. Because of this daring subject matter, Pisemsky had little expectation that it would be published and even less that it might be staged. In fact, however, a slightly modified version of *Byvye sokoly* was performed in Russian theaters to considerable acclaim. Yet, this success contributed little to Pisemsky's financial well-being.

In 1866, after twelve years of trying to support his family from his income as a professional writer, Pisemsky returned to the civil service, becoming councillor at the Moscow Provincial Directory. While the position offered little in the way of intellectual stimulation, it provided the security of a fixed income.

By the time *Liudi sorokovykh godov* was published in 1869, Pisemsky had faded from the literary map. Not only was he forced to publish his work in obscure journals, but he was also virtually ignored by the critics. An historical novel and a memoir, *Liudi sorokovykh godov* includes many autobiographical revelations set against the panorama of complex social currents that coursed through Russia in the 1840s. The adventures of the character Pavel Vikhrov, a figure who resembles Pisemsky, include events from the author's childhood and his civil service work in Moscow, as well as revealing four love affairs, of which Vikhrov's relationship with Mari Eismond was the most enduring. This long novel went almost entirely unnoticed.

In 1871 Pisemsky attempted to reestablish himself in the literary fold. With the novel *V vodovorote* (In the Whirlpool; first published in *Beseda* [Talk], 1871) he ingratiated himself with Russian radicals by amending his depiction of their social movements. The central figure of the novel, Elena Zhiglinskaia, is a radical and a woman; and the enduring challenge of female emancipation is a primary theme of the work. With this novel, Pisemsky advanced beyond the idea of sentimental freedom that was characteristic of his earlier prose works. For the first

Caricature of Pisemsky in the 1860s by A. I. Lebedev (from Russkie pisateli, 1800–1917: Biograficheskii slovar', *volume 4 [1999])*

time he looked at female emancipation as a complex systemic issue rather than a matter of domestic arrangements. Elena is not confined to acting out the roles of daughter, wife, and mother in a home environment. Rather, Pisemsky places her beyond the domestic orbit, showing her involved in the social, economic, and political spheres.

Pisemsky's Elena is a new radical woman, one who not only sets rational goals but pursues them with single-minded determination. No other Pisemsky heroine is gifted with such intellect, passion, grace, and integrity of character. *V vodovorote*, in fact, relies on the classic motif of a heroine's disillusionment with a hero who fails to live up to her standards. But in this work even Pisemsky's hero breaks with the usual role assigned the male lead in Russian novels of this genre. Rather than making him the dominant character in the work, Pisemsky instead assigned this role to Elena. Pisemsky's fundamental conservatism, however, seems to surface in Elena's fate. Despite his remarkable empathy for the trials of his male and female heroes, Pisemsky may still have had deep reservations about female emancipation and been cynical

ВЗБАЛАМУЧЕННОЕ
МОРЕ.

—

РОМАНЪ ВЪ ШЕСТИ ЧАСТЯХЪ.

А. Ѳ. Писемскаго.

—

ТОМЪ I.

ЧАСТЬ ПЕРВАЯ И ВТОРАЯ..

МОСКВА.
ВЪ УНИВЕРСИТЕТСКОЙ ТИПОГРАФІИ
(Катковъ и Кⁿ).
1863.

Title page for the first volume of Pisemsky's antinihilist novel
Vzbalamuchennoe more *(Troubled Seas), with the*
book stamp of the palace library at Tsarskoe Selo
(The Kilgour Collection of Russian
Literature, Houghton Library,
Harvard University)

Genius; first published in *Gazeta A. Gattsuka* [A. Gattsuk's Gazette], 1876), *Khishchniki* (The Plunderers, 1873; also titled *Podkopy* [Mines]), and *Prosveshchennoe vremia* (The Enlightened Time; first published in *Russkii vestnik,* 1875)—examine the same problem.

Pisemsky was an observer of his times. He beheld a world in which aristocratic origins, influential connections, or substantial independent means had long been obligatory criteria for securing a decent place in society. Throughout most of the nineteenth century, only a tiny minority had been privy to these advantages. The arrival of capitalism in Russia at the end of this century did not eradicate inequality. On the contrary, under capitalism material wealth became the exclusive criterion for access to prestige, power, and influence. For Pisemsky, then, capitalism, with its infinite capacity to seduce people into the bondage of material wealth, stood for superficiality, which he had criticized throughout his literary career. Thus, in the final stretch of his writing career, the impact of capitalism on Russia, with its capacity to upset and undermine traditional ways, values, and mores, became the focal subject of Pisemsky's plays and novels, though matters of love and improved status for women within the family circle remained significant themes. In his final novels and in several dramas, Pisemsky endorsed women's traditional and central role in family life, confining his views on emancipation of women to the domestic realm of love, marriage, and the family. Pisemsky's narrow definition of emancipation is clear in the characters of the leading females in his two final novels. Domna Osipovna in *Meshchane* and Susanna Ryzhova in *Masony* are models of virtue and of convention.

In these late novels Pisemsky seems to have been searching for the positive and the ideal in the Russian social landscape, both past and present. *Meshchane* focuses on the uneven contest between expanding capitalism, which Pisemsky depicts as sinister, and the waning aristocracy, which he portrays as noble (betraying perhaps, his own deep-seated yearning for membership in that exclusive fold). *Masony* harkens back to the long-vanished romantic period of the 1830s, when the tightly knit fraternal order of Masons held sway. Although the relative weight of historical and Masonic detail in this novel is not great, Pisemsky does present the Masons and their rituals in a positive light. Here again, the positive emphasis on convention, community, and cohesion seems to demonstrate Pisemsky's fundamental conservatism.

The decade of the 1870s was especially difficult for Pisemsky on a personal level. Deteriorating health forced him to seek release from his civil-service post, and in 1872, at the relatively young age of fifty-one, he was officially permitted to retire. Not long after his retirement, Pisemsky's two surviving sons suffered tragic fates, dispiriting Pisemsky profoundly. The younger son, Nikolai, a

about the likelihood of constructive change in Russian society and politics.

By the 1870s Pisemsky had given up trying to court the public, which in any case had proven recalcitrant. His works of this period—particularly his two final novels, *Meshchane* (The Bourgeois; first published in *Pchela* [The Bee], 1877) and *Masony* (The Masons; first published in *Ogonek* [The Flame], 1880)—steer clear of political issues. Instead, they dwell on the emergent capitalism in Russia and its effect on people's lives. His heroes are portrayed as vulnerable pawns of overwhelming external forces. Like his contemporary Dostoevsky, Pisemsky was more interested in exploring the moral disintegration wrought by burgeoning capitalism than in contemplating its social implications. In the play *Vaal* (Baal, 1873), for example, money emerges as a transcendent motivation, usurping traditional values and virtues. Several of Pisemsky's plays from this period—such as *Finansovyi genii* (The Financial

mathematician, had always been a joy to his parents. But in 1874 without warning Nikolai committed suicide while preparing to enter the Communications Institute in St. Petersburg. His older brother, Pavel, had also been successful in the academic world, and in 1876, at the age of twenty-six, on his return from Berlin, where the Pisemskys had visited him after burying Nikolai, he joined the law faculty at Moscow University. It soon became apparent, however, that he was mentally unbalanced. Relinquishing his position, Pavel suffered mental illness for the rest of his life.

No doubt, concern over Pavel's illness contributed to Pisemsky's depression. After the publication of *Masony* in 1880, his health worsened. In early 1881 a series of gala evenings were held in honor of Aleksandr Sergeevich Pushkin. Turgenev, Dostoevsky, and Pisemsky read from the poet's works with Pisemsky, the grand orator, delivering several splendid readings. This event was Pisemsky's final moment in the limelight; he died shortly thereafter, on 21 January. Pisemsky's funeral was modest, attended only by close relatives and a handful of friends. He was buried at the Novodevichy monastery in Moscow. One week later Russia observed the funeral of Dostoevsky with far greater pomp and ceremony. The contrast could not have been more poignant, as the literary critic A. I. Kirpichnikov so aptly observed twelve years after these events: "The death of Dostoevsky was a misfortune which all Russia grieved; the death of Pisemsky . . . was hardly noticed. Dostoevsky is exalted and placed alongside Turgenev and L. Tolstoy; Pisemsky is abandoned, humiliated and almost forgotten."

Pisemsky's writings demonstrate his conviction that the primary responsibility of literature is the accurate portrayal of social life and culture. He opposed any schematization in literary portrayal and strove to create plausible, realistic heroes. Rather than painting his characters as unblemished saints or thorough villains, Pisemsky imbued them with virtues and flaws. More often than not, his hero is a man or woman of complex personality, full of inner contradictions. Pisemsky saw individuals as infinitely complicated beings who in various life circumstances could and would act in unpredictable ways. Pisemsky never provided readers with detailed accounts of his heroes' life stories. In this sense his approach to literary portrait and character presentation is especially close to that of Turgenev. Like him, Pisemsky always introduces characters fully formed and at some crossroads in their adult life.

Pisemsky used mimicry, gesture, and dialogue to avoid the problem of stasis and to inject his characters with vitality. In the main, his characters reveal themselves directly, through dialogue. This technique, which he used widely, is strongly reminiscent of the methods employed in theatrical drama and exhibits Pisemsky's thespian roots. In Pisemsky's fiction dialogue represents approximately 70 percent of the text. Pisemsky's plot arrangements are also typical of the theater. His plots usually advance through a series of dramatic scenes that function in much the same way as they do in plays, building suspense to the final denouement. In fact, with only minor modification, many of his prose works could be adapted for the stage.

It was not until the end of his writing career, most notably in the novel *V vodovorote,* that Pisemsky reached the pinnacle of his skill as a storyteller and an artist. In this work most of his typical literary devices are masterfully executed. Characters are richly dimensioned, with complex relationships; plot and structure are elegantly suspenseful. *V vodovorote* continues to draw the attention of many scholars today, some of whom consider Elena to be the most captivating female character in Russian literature.

Letters:

Pis'ma, edited by M. K. Kleman and A. P. Mogiliansky (Moscow: Izd-vo Akademii nauk SSSR, 1936);

K. I. Tiun'kin, "Pisemsky i Turgenev v ikh perepiske," *Literaturnoe nasledstvo,* 73 (Moscow, 1964): 129–137;

"Pis'ma A. F. Pisemskogo 1855–1879," edited by I. I. Anisimov and others, in *Literaturnoe nasledstvo,* 73 (Moscow, 1964): 138–194.

Biographies:

S. A. Vengerov, *A. F. Pisemsky* (St. Petersburg: M. O. Vol'f, 1884);

A. M. Skabichevsky, *A. F. Pisemsky, ego zhizn' i literaturnaia deiatel'nost'. Biograficheskii ocherk* (St. Petersburg: Obshchestvennaia pol'za, 1894);

I. I. Ivanov, *A. F. Pisemsky* (St. Petersburg: Tip. I. N. Skorokhodova, 1898);

Claude Backvis, "Un témoin négligé d'une grande époque: le romancier Pisemskij," *Revue des études slaves,* 32 (1955): 42–55;

P. V. Annenkov, "Khudozhnik i prostoi chelovek. Iz vospominanii ob A.F. Pisemskom," in his *Literaturnye vospominaniia* (Moscow, 1960), pp. 489–526;

A. F. Koni, "A. F. Pisemsky," in his *Vospominaniia o pisateliakh* (Leningrad: Lenizdat, 1965), pp. 89–96.

References:

A. I. Beletsky, "V masterskoi khudozhnika slova," *Izbrannye trudy po teorii literatury* (Moscow: Proveshchenie, 1964), pp. 51–233;

P. N. Berkov and M. K. Kleman, "Literaturnyi put' Pisemskogo," in *Izbrannye proizvedeniia,* by Pisemsky (Moscow & Leningrad: Khudozhestvennaia literatura, 1932), pp. 3–22;

M. P. Eremin, *A. F. Pisemsky* (Moscow: Znanie, 1956);

Eremin, "Vydaiushchiisia realist," in *Sobranie sochinenii*, volume 1 (Moscow: Izd. Pravda, 1959), pp. 3–52;

F. Evnin, *A. F. Pisemsky. K 125-letiiu so dnia rozhdeniia* (Moscow: Izd. Pravda, 1945);

M. M. Gin, "A. F. Pisemsky i ego roman *Tysiacha dush*," in *Tysiacha dush* (Petrozavodsk: Gosudarstvennoe izdatel'stvo Karelo-Finskoi SSR, 1955), pp. 475–493;

N. N. Gruzinskaia, "Khudozhestvennoe svoeobrazie romana A. F. Pisemskogo *V vodovorote*," *Uchenye zapiski Tomskogo gosudarstvennogo universiteta imeni V. V. Kuibysheva*, 62 (1966): 261–274;

Gruzinskaia, "Sredstva raskrytiia kharaktera glavnogo geroia v romane A. F. Pisemskogo *Meshchane*," *Uchenye zapiski Tomskogo gosudarstvennogo universiteta imeni V. V. Kuibysheva*, 54 (1965): 29–38;

Maya Jenkins, "Pisemsky's *Bitter Fate:* The First Outstanding Drama of Russian Peasant Life," *Canadian Slavonic Papers*, 3 (1958): 76–88;

Jenkins, "A Study of A. F. Pisemsky and His Fate in Russian Literature," dissertation, University of London, 1976;

I. V. Kartasheva, "Ideino-khudozhestvennoe svoeobrazie romana A. F. Pisemskogo *Tysiacha dush*," dissertation, Kazan', 1963;

A. I. Kirpichnikov, "Dostoevsky i Pisemsky (Opyt sravnitel'noi kharakteristiki)," in his *Ocherki po istorii novoi russkoi literatury* (St. Petersburg: L. F. Panteleev, 1896), pp. 258–340;

V. Ia. Lakshin, "Spor o Pisemskom dramaturge," *Teatr*, 4 (1959): 94–97;

Jules Lemaitre, "Pisemsky," *Impressions de théâtre*, 5 (1891): 69–81;

L. M. Lotman, "Pisemsky–romanist," in *Istoriia russkogo romana*, edited by A. S. Bushmin, and others, volume 2 (Moscow & Leningrad: AN SSSR, 1964), pp. 121–148;

Charles A. Moser, *Pisemsky: A Provincial Realist* (Cambridge, Mass.: Harvard University Press, 1969);

V. A. Mysliakov, "Saltykov-Shchedrin o Pisemskom," *Russkaia literatura*, 4 (1971): 90–98;

A. Nalimov, "Zabyt li Pisemsky?" *Obrazovanie*, 7–8 (1901): 125–139;

Michael Manning Lane Pearson, "A Comparative Study of the Art of A. F. Pisemskij: *Tysjača duš* and the Novels of the Last Period," dissertation, University of California, Los Angeles, 1974;

Sergei Plekhanov, *Pisemsky* (Moscow: Molodaia gvardiia, 1986);

P. G. Pustovoit, *A. F. Pisemsky v istorii russkogo romana* (Moscow: Izdatel'stvo Moskovskogo universiteta, 1969);

Pustovoit, "K istorii romana A.F. Pisemskogo *Tysiacha dush*," *Vestnik moskovskogo universiteta*, 6 (1966): 80–90;

Pustovoit, "Portretnoe masterstvo Pisemskogo-romanista," *Filologicheskie nauki*, 4 (1966): 43–54;

Pustovoit, "Sposoby motirovki v romanakh Pisemskogo 50–60 godov," *Filologicheskie nauki*, 2 (1967): 3–13;

A. A. Roshal', "Iz nabliudenii nad tvorcheskoi istoriei romana A. F. Pisemskogo *Masony*," *Russkaia literatura*, 1 (1963): 180–84;

Roshal', *Pisemsky i revoliutsionnaia demokratiia* (Baku: Azerbaidzhanskoe gos. izdatel'stvo, 1971);

Roshal', "Tvorchestvo Pisemskogo v 40–50 gody (Pisemsky v *Moskvitianine*)," dissertation, Leningrad State University, 1948;

Julian Schmidt, "Turgenev und Pisemsky," *Bilder aus dem geistigen Leben unserer Zeit*, 4 (1875): 250–267;

N. Skatov, "Ob odnom epizode romana A. F. Pisemskogo *Liudi sorokovykh godov*," *Russkaia literatura*, 3 (1964): 201–203;

Jolanta Sklad, "Poglady estetyczno-literackie Pisemskiego," *Slavia Orientalis*, 4 (1978): 493–507;

Sklad, "Proza powiesciowa Aleksego Pisiemskiego," dissertation, University of Warsaw, 1979;

Jolanta Skrunda, "Powiesc Aleksego Pisiemskiego *Wir*," *Slavia Orientalis*, 1 (1986): 47–64;

Skrunda, "*Tysiac dusz* Aleksego Pisiemskiego czyli miraze pracy u podstaw," *Slavia Orientalis*, 2 (1986): 231–257;

R. E. Steussy, "Pisemskij's Talent as a Novelist," dissertation, Harvard University, 1959;

M. K. Tsebrikova, "Gumannyi zashchitnik zhenskikh prav (Po povodu romana g. Pisemskogo *Liudi sorokovykh godov*," *Otechestvennye zapiski*, 2 (1870): 209–228;

Tsebrikova, "Roman Pisemskogo o geroe vremeni," in *Tysiacha dush*, by Pisemsky (Moscow: Khudozh. litra, 1965), pp. 3–21;

Jenny Woodhouse, "A. F. Pisemsky: The Making of a Russian Novelist," *Forum for Modern Language Studies*, 20 (1984): 49–69;

Woodhouse, "A Realist in a Changing Reality: A. F. Pisemsky and *Vzbalamuchennoe more*," *Slavonic and East European Review*, 4 (1986): 489–505.

Papers:

Major holdings of Aleksei Feofilaktovich Pisemsky's papers are in Moscow at the Russian State Library (formerly the Lenin Library), fond 407, and the Russian State Archive for Literature and Art (RGALI, formerly TsGALI), fond 375; and in St. Petersburg at the Russian National Library, fond 584, and the Institute for Russian Literature (IRLI, Pushkin House), fond 232.

Nikolai Gerasimovich Pomialovsky

(11 April 1835 – 5 October 1863)

Carol Apollonio Flath
Duke University

WORKS: *Meshchanskoe schast'e,* in *Sovremennik,* no. 2 (1861);

Molotov, in *Sovremennik,* no. 10 (1861);

Ocherki bursy, in *Vremia,* nos. 5, 9 (1862); *Sovremennik,* nos. 4, 7 (1863); (St. Petersburg: Tip. K. V. Trubnikova, 1871); translated by Alfred R. Kuhn as *Seminary Sketches* (Ithaca, N.Y.: Cornell University Press, 1973).

Editions and Collections: *Povesti, rasskazy i ocherki,* 2 volumes, compiled by N. A. Blagoveshchensky (St. Petersburg, 1865);

Polnoe sobranie sochinenii, 2 volumes, compiled by Blagoveshchensky (St. Petersburg: S. V. Zvonarev, 1868);

Polnoe sobranie sochinenii, 2 volumes (St. Petersburg: Prosveshchenie, 1913);

Ocherki bursy (Moscow: Molodaia gvardiia, 1928);

Meshchanskoe schast'e (Moscow: Zhurnal'no-gazetnoe ob"edinenie, 1932);

Polnoe sobranie sochinenii, 2 volumes, edited by I. G. Iampol'sky (Moscow & Leningrad: Academia, 1935);

Sochineniia, edited by N. P. Dmitriev (Moscow: Goslitizdat, 1935);

Sochineniia (Moscow: Pravda, 1949);

Sochineniia, edited by Iampol'sky (Moscow & Leningrad: Goslitizdat, 1951);

Ocherki bursy (Saratov, 1955);

Ocherki bursy (Moscow: Gosudarstvennoe izdatel'stvo detskoi literatury, 1957);

Meshchanskoe schast'e, Molotov (Moscow: Gosudarstvennoe izdatel'stvo detskoi literatury, 1957);

Ocherki bursy (Kiev, 1958);

Sochineniia (Moscow & Leningrad: Khudozhestvennaia literatura, 1965);

Povesti (Moscow, 1973);

Sochineniia, edited by Iampol'sky (Leningrad: Khudozhestvennaia literatura, 1980);

Izbrannoe (Minsk: Nauka i Tekhnika, 1980).

SELECTED PERIODICAL PUBLICATIONS:

"Vukol," *Zhurnal dlia vospitaniia,* no. 1 (1859);

Nikolai Gerasimovich Pomialovsky

"Zimnii vecher v burse," *Vremia,* no. 5 (1862);

"Bursatskie tipy," *Vremia,* no. 9 (1862);

"Zhenikhi bursy," *Sovremennik,* no. 4 (1863);

"Beguny i spasennye bursy," *Sovremennik,* no. 7 (1863);

"Andrei Fedorych Chebanov," *Sovremennik,* no. 10 (1863): 551–560;

"Porechane," *Russkoe slovo,* no. 10 (1863): 1–36;

"Perekhodnoe vremia bursy," *Sovremennik,* no. 11 (1863);

"Brat i sestra," *Sovremennik,* no. 3 (1864): 150–154; no. 5 (1864): 101–154;

"Makhilov," *Sovremennik,* no. 5 (1864): 155–168;

"Danilushka," *Zhenskii vestnik*, no. 3 (1867): 89–105.

Nikolai Gerasimovich Pomialovsky was known as a creature of his time, rather than a master of it. Yet, a reading of his works proves this valuation to be an unfair assessment of a serious, talented, and original writer. Pomialovsky's publishing career lasted a meager four years (1859–1863), a period during which the greatest Russian novelists–Fyodor Dostoevsky, Leo Tolstoy, and Ivan Sergeevich Turgenev–as well as the radical critics Nikolai Gavrilovich Chernyshevsky, Nikolai Aleksandrovich Dobroliubov, and Dmitrii Ivanovich Pisarev were making their marks on history. Like many other young graduates of Russian Orthodox seminaries during the early liberalism of Alexander II's regime, Pomialovsky turned his back on a career in the church to engage in civic and literary activism. His hospitalizations for alcohol-related illness and his early death at the age of twenty-eight were sadly typical of these *shestidesiatniki* (people of the 1860s). Pomialovsky left to posterity a small but significant body of writing, most notably the horrifying *Ocherki bursy* (Seminary Sketches, 1862–1863), a naturalistic, autobiographically based depiction of life in a Russian religious school that is unequaled in its genre in Russian literary history. Pomialovsky's work influenced other novelists, notably Chernyshevsky, Dostoevsky, and Turgenev.

Nikolai Gerasimovich Pomialovsky was born on 11 April 1835, the third son of eight children of Gerasim Pomialovsky and his wife, Ekaterina Alekseeva. Gerasim served as the deacon of the cemetery church of Mary Magdalene in Malaia Okhta, a small settlement of peasants and tradespeople outside St. Petersburg. Pomialovsky spent his early childhood roaming the still-unspoiled countryside around his village, where he developed a taste for fishing. The countryside later served the adult Pomialovsky as a refuge and stood in implicit contrast to many aspects of the harsh urban world he portrayed in his sketches of school life. Although Pomialovsky was too much of a realist to present an idyllic view of nature as a cure for the problems of urban life, his writing manifests a deep affection and longing for the countryside. Ultimately his fate proved that a faith in nature was insufficient to withstand two forces that were present from his earliest childhood: vodka and "the cemetery" (depression). Western assumptions of high moral virtue among members of the clergy are often irrelevant in the Russian context, at least during Pomialovsky's lifetime. With some notable exceptions, lower-level church officials lived in poverty and had a largely justified reputation for drunkenness and corruption. Pomialovsky reported that he was first drunk at the age of seven. His father officiated at many funerals,

which may have been on the writer's mind when he created the character Cherevanin's *kladbishchenstvo* ("cemetery" nihilism) in *Molotov* (1861).

As Pomialovsky suggested in his semiautobiographical sketch "Danilushka" (written in 1858 or 1859 but not published until 1867), in the countryside the child learns without textbooks; he lives in harmony with the adult world and nature; and he enjoys a complete and wholesome freedom. Pomialovsky's lifelong devotion to questions of education, in his civic activities and in his writing, drew on such a vision of childhood. The corruption of innocence begins when the child is removed from the lap of nature and is sent away to attend school in the city, a moment that is dreaded by the child and his family as *chto-to nedobroe* (something evil). In 1843, at the age of eight, after being taught the basics of reading and writing by his father, Pomialovsky left for church school at the famous Aleksandr Nevsky monastery in St. Petersburg, within whose walls he spent half his life.

Pomialovsky's experiences at school are the single most important influence on his mature writing, much of which can be seen as an attempt to overcome and counteract the deficiencies of his education. The grief of the weeping mother at her child's departure, described in the conclusion to "Danilushka," is amply justified by the fate that awaits the child at school.

Pomialovsky's happy, curious, and intelligent young protagonist is replaced by a new autobiographical figure, the naive Karas' (Carp), whose grim initiation into school is meticulously described in the fourth sketch in *Ocherki bursy*, "Beguny i spasennye bursy" (Seminary Escapees and Survivors, 1863). The Nevsky seminary combined lower schools and the seminary proper, with all out-of-town students living in the dormitory, or *bursa* (in contemporary usage the term referred metonymically to the whole school, including the seminary proper). Pomialovsky and his contemporaries reported a stultifying curriculum, with teaching methods ranging from mind-numbing memorization and recitation to a wide variety of forms of physical abuse, from hair pulling and pinching to brutal whipping. With some pride, Pomialovsky reported having endured four hundred floggings during his time at school.

The many kinds of students Pomialovsky described in his sketches represent a variety of responses to the cruel pedagogical system. Some students, such as the vicious Tavlia, remained on a primitive animal level, communicating with others primarily through beatings and games involving the infliction of physical pain. Others, such as the pathetic Semenov, disliked for his weakness and privileged family background, became informers and suffered cruel punishments at the hands of their fellow students. Former fellow students reported that Pomialovsky was a "survivor" like his character Goroblagodatsky—strong, defiant, and universally respected and feared by his classmates. Such students refused to let the educational system crush their spirits and independence of mind. During his years in the seminary, Pomialovsky seems to have undergone an evolution from the naive, deeply religious, and spirited Karas' to the inveterate, cynical rebel Goroblagodatsky.

Pomialovsky's literary activity began in the seminary, where he developed a passion for reading works of literature, including those of Russian writers slipped quietly into the otherwise dry curriculum by intrepid younger teachers whose zeal for their subject distinguished them from their colleagues. The majority of the teachers, however, were at best apathetic and at worst violent and sadistic. Inspired by his reading and a growing awareness of new, activist intellectual trends taking shape in Russian public life, Pomialovsky joined with his schoolmates to establish a school journal, *Seminarskii listok* (Seminary Leaflet), of which he became the editor and chief contributor. His writings for the journal include earnest exercises in philosophy, such as a semiblasphemous essay on whether or not animals have souls. In the journal he also published his first work of fiction, the fragment "Makhilov," about a grown seminary student who secretly has a wife and baby in town. ("Makhilov" was published posthumously in *Sovremennik* [The Contemporary] in 1864). This story bears traces of the *bogatyr'* seminarist type—the swaggering, larger-than-life hero bequeathed to Russian literature by earlier writers such as Nikolai Vasil'evich Gogol and Vasilii Trofimovich Narezhny. The students' excitement about their journal and their plans to expand it beyond the walls of the seminary aroused the suspicions of the administration, which expelled eight student journalists. The journal withered away after its seventh issue, and Pomialovsky, as was to be his pattern after each disappointment, took solace in vodka.

The system of education offered Pomialovsky a negative example against which he built the short life remaining to him after his graduation in 1857, thirty-seventh in a class of fifty. As with many other seminary students of his generation, far from molding Pomialovsky into a docile servant of Russian Orthodoxy, the church school embittered him and fueled him with a powerful desire to offer the younger generation something better. After graduation, Pomialovsky earned a meager living through mostly church-related odd jobs. He put his pedagogical ideas into practice by tutoring his younger brother for several months. At the same time he embarked on an intense self-education program to compensate for the defects of his schooling. He read

Title page for Pomialovsky's influential Ocherki bursy *(Seminary Sketches), first published in* Vremia *(Time) and* Sovremennik *(The Contemporary) in 1862 and 1863*

and studied the classics of Russian literature, as well as the latest issues of journals, particularly the articles of Chernyshevsky and Dobroliubov in *Sovremennik*. Pomialovsky also explored philosophy and wrote articles on education, which have not survived. His first adult publication was a "psychological sketch" titled "Vukol," which, to his surprise, appeared in 1859 in *Zhurnal dlia vospitaniia* (Journal for Education). Like much of his fictional writing about children, "Vukol" aims to show the effects of a coarse environment and corporal punishment on the psychology of an innocent child. The artistic and analytical elements are balanced in the story and attempt to communicate Pomialovsky's central pedagogical concerns; the story breaks off, like "Danilushka," with the child's enrollment in school.

On advice from his friends Pomialovsky began attending lectures at St. Petersburg University, where a liberalized admissions policy had sparked an enormous influx of new students from the unprivileged classes. The changes in the Russian educational system during this period reflected the overall upheaval in Russian society following the death of Nicholas I. Pomialovsky's interest in education led him to participate in the Sunday-school movement, which tried to bring literacy to the lower classes. He was one of the most enthusiastic organizers and effective teachers in a large Sunday school in St. Petersburg that served some eight hundred students.

Pomialovsky's first significant literary work was the novella *Meshchanskoe schast'e* (Bourgeois [or Middle Class] Happiness), published in Nikolai Alekseevich Nekrasov's *Sovremennik* in 1861. The protagonist is Egor Ivanych Molotov, whose quest for "happiness" serves as the central plotline in both this novella and its sequel, *Molotov,* which was published later that same year. Molotov represents a new kind of hero in Russian literature, the *raznochinets* (a nongentry intellectual), who rises from poverty to take his place among the increasing numbers of white-collar workers in mid-nineteenth century Russia. In a sweeping approach that characterizes all his major (mostly unfinished) literary projects, Pomialovsky led his hero through several different occupations and social environments. Orphaned as a child, Molotov is taken in and given a solid education by an aging professor, who dies as Molotov begins his university studies. Molotov later serves as a kind of clerk and tutor in a family of landed nobility, the Obrosimovs, until an overheard conversation reveals to him their condescending attitude toward him because of his lower-class origins. A letter conveniently arrives from his friend Andrei Negodiashchev offering him a government job, and the novella ends with Molotov's tactful departure from the estate of the "negodiai, aristokratishki, bary-kulaki" (good-for-nothing aristocratic kulak-scoundrels).

Molotov's harsh judgment of his benefactors remains unspoken; his disillusionment does not lead to an open confrontation, and his departure from the Obrosimov family is ostensibly harmonious. As in the sequel, the plot of *Meshchanskoe schast'e* features a sense of measure and accommodation to social realities: an individual may not be able to change the world, but he might find a place for himself in it. Still, the promise of "happiness" offered in Pomialovsky's title is not delivered to the protagonist in this first novella. Negodiashchev's unabashed careerism and manipulation of his official position do not portend a comfortable future in the civil service for a man of conscience. Furthermore, the promise of romance remains unfulfilled. Before his departure, Molotov rejects the advances of Lenochka, a naive, forward country girl clearly derived from Turgenev's works, particularly "Asia" (1858). Representative of the times is a discussion on women's emancipation, in which Obrosimov's daughter, the sophisticated young widow Liza, educates Lenochka about the topic, distilling

it down to a woman's right to choose her own husband. Molotov's sympathy, like that of the reader, is with the spontaneous, honest Lenochka rather than the well-educated but unkind Liza, but this feeling does not prevent him from abandoning her to embark on his new career. Liza's condescending nickname for Lenochka, "kiseinaia devushka" (the girl in muslin), provided the critic Pisarev with a title for his laudatory 1865 review of Pomialovsky's two novellas.

At times Molotov's musings hover at the boundary between fiction and social theory. It would appear that a young, talented, and well-educated man, without family encumbrances and empowered by the breakdown of class boundaries, would enjoy a great deal of freedom to determine his own fate and contribute to society. But Molotov discovers that his freedom is illusory and reaches the conclusion that labor is the same as slavery:

> One needs to have patronage and money, to be subservient, to seek favors, and to inform on others; these and other such qualities are necessary to gain the right to do honest labor. But here the employer practically always lords it over his employee . . . ; in all spheres of Russian labor that bring in income, the subordinate is a beggar who receives sustenance from his boss, who acts as a benefactor.

This situation leads to a philosophy of defeatism: "I do nothing: thus I am free; I hire others to work for me: thus I am independent. I work hard—this means I am a slave; I hire out my labor—this means I am eating others' bread." The energetic and independent Molotov sheds these dangerous thoughts in good time, but a similarly defeatist philosophy is propounded with conviction by his friend, the artist Cherevanin, in the sequel. The relevance of these ideas in the volatile political environment of the early 1860s was not lost on Pomialovsky's readers.

Pomialovsky began *Molotov* with a family chronicle of the upwardly mobile Dorogov family, whose energetic matriarch builds, through years of hard work and thrift, a comfortable "bourgeois" existence for her descendants. The novella hinges on the classic plot of a girl's resistance to a lucrative arranged marriage. At the crucial moment Nadia Dorogova, unwilling to marry the elderly "general" Podtiazhkin, conveniently finds herself in love with Molotov, who has long been like a member of her family. The originality of Pomialovsky's treatment of this theme lies first in his emphasis on the engagement as the culminating moment in the Dorogov's overall family history and second in his underemphasis of the romantic element and conflict in favor of the triumph of "reason." Nadia's parents have put her under house arrest in an attempt to force her to accept Podtiazhkin's suit, and Molotov is banned from the house. Tension builds. Realizing, like a good man of the 1860s, that he must take action ("nado deistvovat'"), Molotov goes straight to his rival's house. There, rather than provoking a duel, he informs Podtiazhkin directly that Nadia does not love him, that in fact she is his own, Molotov's fiancée, and that it is immoral to force girls to marry men they do not love. This declaration is enough to dissuade the general, who is "not inclined to marry a girl who is capable of falling in love" and who has had his eyes on an alternate in any case. Thus, reason coincides with everyone's self-interest, and marriage coincides with love.

In many ways Pomialovsky's novella anticipates the better-known *Chto delat'?* (What Is to Be Done?, 1863), which Chernyshevsky wrote during his imprisonment in the Peter and Paul Fortress in 1862–1863. Indeed, Pomialovsky's two novellas and *Ocherki bursy* were among the works Chernyshevsky read in the fortress. The reader of *Chto delat'?* recognizes the influence of Pomialovsky's description of Nadia's house and family, elements of her characterization, as well as that of Molotov (particularly his self-control, appetite, practicality, and rationality), the theme of the "new man" (Pomialovsky's *homo novus*), the discussions of women's emancipation (including mentions of "blue stockings"), and above all, the happy ending in which reason triumphs over passion, with love surviving as well. The obstacles facing an energetic man in his attempt to take "action" in society are a central theme of both writers and reflect heated discussions of this politically loaded issue in literature and public life in the early 1860s. Particularly in *Meshchanskoe schast'e,* Pomialovsky's style, characterizations, and plot construction are indebted to Turgenev's early works, while the independence, practicality, and rationality of Pomialovsky's hero, as well as the theme of "nihilism" in both *Meshchanskoe schast'e* and *Molotov,* anticipate Turgenev's *Ottsy i deti* (Fathers and Sons, 1862). A reading of these two works confirms the contemporary critical judgment of Pomialovsky's importance in the development of Russian literature in the 1860s. Soviet criticism lauds Pomialovsky as a pioneer in portraying the struggles of a "plebeian" *raznochinets* to take his place in public life, and sees him as an important contributor to the development of the positive hero. The modern reader may notice a particular poignancy in the independence of Pomialovsky's hero, whose freedom from the encumbrances of family and social class tends to isolate him from others; his "aloneness" is a recurring theme. Molotov's acquaintance, the degenerate artist Cherevanin, bears the full burden of this isolation. Cherevanin's nihilistic philosophy, labeled *kladbishchenstvo,* seems to derive as much from his failures at love as

from an informed philosophy of life; but his outlook is immediately relevant to the social radicals in Pomialovsky's readership. If the practical Molotov represents an accommodation to the limited opportunities of life, Cherevanin reflects the darker side of Pomialovsky's outlook during the last years of his life.

The two novellas established Pomialovsky's place in the circle of literati connected with *Sovremennik*. His talent was recognized by the most prominent writers and critics of the time, and he participated in their literary readings and gatherings. His social activism grew, accompanied by an increasingly radical outlook that corresponded to the spirit of the times. He continued his work in the Sunday school and supported the St. Petersburg University students during the unrest of the fall of 1861. In discussions with fellow members of the chess club in 1862 Pomialovsky proposed that they work together to produce a novel that would provide a contemporary "physiology" of St. Petersburg, with the various authors each describing a particular segment of society. Nothing came of the project, but the novel Pomialovsky was writing at the time of his death, "Brat i sestra" (Brother and Sister, 1864), was similarly ambitious in scope.

Pomialovsky is best known and remembered for the sketches of seminary life that he published in 1862–1863 in Dostoevsky's journal *Vremia* (Time) and in *Sovremennik*. If Pomialovsky's two novellas are derivative of his reading and reflect the literary trends of his time, *Ocherki bursy* is a completely original phenomenon in Russian literature, the product of the author's bitter personal experience, passion, sense of mission, and considerable literary talent. The sketches derive their form from the physiological sketch, which was a central genre of the Russian Natural School of the 1840s, but Pomialovsky's efforts far surpass their predecessors in artistic quality. Each of the sketches consists of scenes of particular aspects of seminary life loosely structured around a plot involving one or two vividly portrayed protagonists. The structure of the sketches reverses the hierarchies of mainstream fiction: the "crowd" and the setting that normally serve as background to a central plot are foregrounded, with the protagonist's "story" threading quietly, but memorably, through the chaos. "Zimnii vecher v burse" (A Winter Evening in the Seminary) tells the story of the seminarists' revenge on the "townie" and informer Semenov. "Bursatskie tipy" (Seminary Types) features a description of the boys' trip to the bathhouse, and the rampages in town that accompany it; a theme of the demonic runs through the sketch, particularly in the story of Aksiutka and "Satan-Ipse," who collaborate in a thieving expedition. Brutal beatings follow. The third sketch, "Zhenikhi bursy" (Seminary Suitors), exposes

ing," which are immediately followed by scene after scene of brutal games centering on the mutual infliction of physical pain.

The originality, quality, and relevance of the sketches were immediately recognized by contemporary critics. Particularly memorable is Dmitrii Pisarev's extended 1866 essay "Pogibshie i pogibaiushchie" (The Dead and the Dying). Pisarev developed an exhaustive comparison of Pomialovsky's work with Dostoevsky's *Zapiski iz mertvogo doma* (Notes from the House of the Dead, 1861–1862), whose serial publication overlapped that of *Ocherki bursy* and which clearly influenced Pomialovsky's work. Pisarev reduced these two brilliant literary works to sources of factual evidence in a sociological study and concluded that conditions in the *bursa* were infinitely worse than those in Dostoevsky's labor camp. His study is a covert criticism of the Russian educational system and of Russian society in its entirety.

Critics also recognized the originality of Pomialovsky's harsh vision of childhood, which challenged the idyllic, "golden, happy childhood" tradition established by such aristocratic writers as Tolstoy (in *Detstvo, Otrochestvo, Iunost'* [Childhood, Boyhood and Youth, 1852–1857]) and Sergei Timofeevich Aksakov (in *Detskie gody bagrova-vnuka* [Childhood Years of Bagrov's Grandson, 1856]). In addition to the considerable critical attention it inspired, *Ocherki bursy* sparked a wave of memoirs by "survivors" of a seminary education, which were published in a wide variety of journals in the 1860s.

With each new work Pomialovsky gained in skill and self-confidence. In his unfinished novel "Brat i sestra" he planned to provide a sweeping picture of urban life in St. Petersburg, following the decline of his protagonist from the highest level of society to its lower depths. In this sense Pomialovsky can be seen as working at fulfilling his proposal for a "physiology" of St. Petersburg, but with himself as the sole author. He also began a story, "Porechane" (River Folk, 1863). At the same time, according to his friends and acquaintances, Pomialovsky was going on extended binges, during which he would disappear into the most disreputable areas of the city. Pomialovsky hoped to redeem some value from these moral lapses by using his experiences as raw material in his writing. At some point, he fell in love and courted the daughter of an official in the civil service, but he was refused her hand because of his lower-class background and lack of career promise. Fame led to disillusionment with his new acquaintances in the literary world. True to the commonly held stereotypes of "seminarists," he allowed himself to

Pomialovsky's grave, in Volkov Cemetery, St. Petersburg
(photograph by Judith E. Kalb)

the inhumanity of the matchmaking process by which a seminary student is married off to a needy, and newly fatherless, priest's daughter. The fourth sketch, "Beguny i spasennye bursy" (Seminary Escapees and Survivors), follows the autobiographical protagonist's early experiences in the seminary.

All the sketches, including the unfinished fifth sketch (and, presumably, the planned fifteen or so that were to follow it), share a common theme: the horrors of a religious education system that corrupts its students and turns innocent young boys into cruel, cynical atheists. Throughout the sketches, the reader is aware of Pomialovsky's implicit criticism of the abuses and repressions of Russian society as a whole, although such links are never expressed openly. Pomialovsky's style features a highly original combination of schoolboy slang and Russian Orthodox language that is doubly jarring for the naturalism of the events and characters depicted. Irony borders on bitter cynicism, as in the opening words of the first sketch, "Class is over. Children are play-be disruptive, crude, and deliberately provocative at public gatherings.

Pomialovsky's growing reputation and skill as an artist was thus paralleled by a downward spiral in his personal life. Periods of abstention from drink were inevitably followed by long binges. His loyal friend and biographer N. A. Blagoveshchensky reported an emotional conversation in which the author blamed the seminary for his drinking problem: "The accursed seminary drained my willpower and taught me to drink. Later, the conditions of life itself were miserable, and ultimately I just got used to it. . . . But I still want to live; I have a lot of work to do, I still have strength, but nothing will come of it unless I can stop [drinking]. . . ." Pomialovsky's last recovery from alcohol-related illness was short and was followed almost immediately by a sore on his leg that he neglected until it turned gangrenous. This infection was the cause of his death on 5 October 1863.

Nikolai Gerasimovich Pomialovsky's life and fate were typical of many of the *raznochintsy* of the mid-nineteenth century. Like other peers who left behind a career in the lower clergy, he struggled to overcome overwhelming burdens that faced him from his earliest youth: poverty, drunkenness, and an abusive, inadequate education. His writings represent the best these "new men" had to offer: talent, energy, conscience, and a passionate desire to work for positive social change. The radical currents of the early years of Alexander I's reign offered an unprecedented opportunity for Pomialovsky and others like him to contribute fully to public life. His works, particularly his masterpiece *Ocherki bursy,* are still well worth reading.

Letters:

Pis'ma, in volume 2 of *Polnoe sobranie sochinenii,* edited by I. Iampol'sky (Moscow & Leningrad: Academia, 1935), pp. 267–279;

"Pis'ma: N. A. Nekrasovu (1863)," commentary by V. E. Evgen'ev-Maksimov, *Literaturnoe nasledstvo* (1949): 51–52.

Biographies:

N. A. Blagoveshchensky, "Nikolai Gerasimovich Pomialovsky," *Sovremennik,* 101, no. 3 (1864): 115–154; republished in *Polnoe sobranie sochinenii,* edited by I. Iampol'sky, volume 1 (Moscow & Leningrad: Academia, 1935), pp. xv–xlvi;

V. S. Val'be, *Pomialovsky* (Moscow: Zhurnal'no-gazetnoe ob"edinenie: *Zhizn' zamechatel'nykh liudei,* 1936);

I. G. Iampol'sky, *Pomialovsky. Lichnost' i tvorchestvo* (Moscow & Leningrad: Sovetskii pisatel', 1968).

References:

S. T. Akhumian, "Bursatskaia leksika 'Ocherkov bursy' N. G. Pomialovskogo," *Nauchnye trudy Erevanskogo universiteta,* 57, no. 4, part 2 (1956): 149–174;

Akhumian, "Mesto N. G. Pomialovskogo v istorii russkoi literatury i russkogo literaturnogo iazyka," *Uchenye zapiski Erevanskogo russkogo pedagogicheskogo instituta,* 7 (1956): 317–353;

E. P. Andreeva, "N. G. Pomialovsky v bor'be za boevoe demokraticheskoe iskusstvo," *Uchenye zapiski Magnitogorskogo pedagogicheskogo instituta,* 2 (1949): 254–320;

P. V. Annenkov, "Russkaia belletristika v 1863 godu. G-n Pomialovsky," *Peterburgskie vedomosti,* 5 (6 ianv., 1863): 1–2; republished in his *Vospominaniia i kriticheskie ocherki,* volume 2 (St. Petersburg, 1879), pp. 244–257;

V. P. Bartsevich, "Preemstvennost' i polemika (O povestiakh Pomialovskogo i romane Chernyshevskogo *Chto delat'?*)," *Voprosy slavianskoi filogoii* (Saratov, 1963): 101–117;

Bartsevich, "Realizm pravdy bez vsiakikh prikras ('Ocherki bursy' Pomialovskogo)," in *N. G. Chernyshevsky, Stat'i, issledovaniia, materialy* (Saratov, 1962), pp. 126–150;

P. Bibikov, "Po povodu odnoi sovremennoi povesti. (Nravstvenno-kriticheskii etiud). ["Molotov"]," *Vremia,* 1, otdel 1 (1862): 31–57;

V. A. Desnitsky, "N. G. Pomialovsky. Ocherk zhizni i tvorchestva," *Literaturnaia ucheba,* 4 (1935): 13–39;

Desnitsky, "Tvorchestvo Pomialovskogo," in his *Izbrannye stat'i po russkoi literature XVIII–XIX vekov* (Moscow & Leningrad, 1958);

Carol Apollonio Flath, "N. G. Pomialovskij's *Seminary Sketches:* Context and Genre," dissertation, University of North Carolina, 1987;

I. A. Goncharov, "[Tsenzorskii otzyv ob ocherke 'Beguny i spasennye bursy'], 23 iulia 1863 g.," *Severnye zapiski,* 9 (1916): 139–140; republished in *Polnoe sobranie sochinenii,* volume 2 (Moscow & Leningrad: Academia, 1935), pp. 318–319;

Maksim Gorky, *Istoriia russkoi literatury* (Moscow, 1939), pp. 241–245;

I. G. Iampol'sky, *N. G. Pomialovsky. Kritiko-biograficheskii ocherk* (Moscow: Goslitizdat, 1941);

Iampol'sky, "Ocherki bursy N. G. Pomialovskogo," *Literaturnaia ucheba,* 12 (1938);

Iampol'sky, "Pomialovsky," in *Istoriia russkoi literatury,* volume 8, part 1 (Moscow & Leningrad: Akademii nauk SSSR, 1956), pp. 536–561;

Incognito [E. Zarin], "Mezhdu starym i novym. (Povesti, rasskazy i ocherki N.G. Pomialovskogo, tt. I, II)," *Otechestvennye zapiski,* 159, no. 4 (1865): 525–542; 160, no. 5 (1865): 133–154;

T. V. Kevlishvili, "Osobennosti leksiki i frazeologii 'Ocherkov bursy' N. G. Pomialovskogo," *Trudy Tbilisskogo pedagogicheskogo instituta,* 11 (1957): 197–212;

V. Kostrica, *Literarni Odkaz N.G. Pomjalovskeho* (Olomous, 1983);

N. Kotliarevsky, "Ocherki iz istorii obshchestvennogo nastroeniia v shestidesiatykh godakh. Dva literaturnykh portreta, v kotorykh molodezh' 1855–1861 godov sebia ne uznala. (Molotov i Bazarov)," *Vestnik Evropy,* 11 (1914): 171–202;

V. L-v, "Shkol'nye gody N. G. Pomialovskogo," *Istoricheskii vestnik,* 7 (1896): 158–170;

L. M. Lotman, *Realizm russkoi literatury 60-kh godov deviatnadtsatogo veka* (Leningrad: Nauka, 1974);

"Nikolai Gerasimovich Pomialovsky (Nekrolog)," *Biblioteka dlia chteniia,* 9 (1863): 158–160;

M. M. Orlov, *Iazyk N. G. Pomialovskogo* (Rostov na Donu, 1958);

Orlov, "Publitsisticheskaia leksika i frazeologiia v iazyke N. G. Pomialovskogo," *Uchenye zapiski Balashovskogo pedagogicheskogo instituta,* 2 (1957): 336–374;

Orlov, "Slavianizmy v proizvedeniiakh N. G. Pomialovskogo," *Uchenye zapiski Rostovskogo n/D. universiteta,* 52 (1957): 119–150;

V. P. Ostrogorsky, *N. G. Pomialovsky. Etiudy o russkikh pisateliakh* (Petersburg, 1889);

D. I. Pisarev, "Mysliashchii proletariat," *Russkoe slovo,* 1, otdel 2 (1865): 1–42; republished as "Roman kiseinoi devushki," in his *Sochineniia,* volume 3 (Moscow: Goslitizdat, 1956), pp. 185–217;

Pisarev (N. Ragodin), "Pogibshie i pogibaiushchie," in *Luch. Ucheno-literaturnyi sbornik,* volume 1 (Petersburg, 1866), pp. 32–96; republished in his *Sochineniia,* volume 4 (Moscow: Goslitizdat, 1956), pp. 86–139;

A. I. Plotnikova, "O nekotorykh osobennostiakh ideinogo soderzhaniia romana-dilogii N. G. Pomialovskogo 'Meshchanskoe schast'e' i 'Molotov'," *Sbornik nauchnykh statei Barnaul'skogo pedagogicheskogo instituta,* 2 (1957): 151–216;

Plotnikova, "Ob osobennostiakh khudozhestvennoi formy romana-dilogii N. G. Pomialovskogo 'Meshchanskoe schast'e' i 'Molotov'," *Sbornik nauchnykh statei Barnaulskogo pedagogicheskogo instituta,* 3 (1958): 198–264;

E. A. Podshivalova, "K voprosy o tipologii formal'no-soderzhatel'nogo edinstva russkogo realisticheskogo romana 40–60-kh godov XIX veka: A. I. Gertsen, N. G. Pomialovsky, N. G. Chernyshevsky," in *Problemy sovremennoi filologii: Dialektika formy i soderzhaniia v iazyke i literature* (Perm: Permskii gosudarstvennyi universitet, 1982), pp. 139–140;

"Pomialovsky, ego tipy i ocherki," *Biblioteka dlia chteniia,* 4 (1863);

R. D. Ponomareva, *Zhanrovye iskaniia russkoi literatury 60-kh godov XIX veka i tvorchestvo N. G. Pomialovskogo* (Iakutsk: Iakutskii gosudarstvennyi universitet, 1988);

[A. N. Pypin], "Sochineniia Pomialovskogo," *Sovremennik,* 105, no. 12, otdel 2 (1865): 61–84;

P. N. Sakulina, "N. G. Pomialovsky," in *Istoriia russkoi literatury XIX v.,* volume 3, edited by D. N. Ovsianiko-Kulikovsky (Moscow: Mir, 1909), pp. 332–342;

V. N. Sazhin, *Knigi gor'koi pravdy: N. G. Pomialovsky, "Ocherki bursy," F. M. Reshetnikov, "Podlipovtsy," V. A. Sleptsov, "Trudnoe vremia," Sud'by knig* (Moscow: Kniga, 1989);

S. E. Shatalov, "O ritme povestvovaniia N. G. Pomialovskogo," *Trudy Uzbekskogo universiteta,* novaia seriia, 72 (1957): 165–178;

S. V. Shuvalov, "Tvorchestvo Pomialovskogo (K istorii raznochinskogo stilia 60-kh godov)," *Russkii iazyk v sovetskoi shkole,* 5 (1931): 48–68;

V. Sovsun, "Sotsiologicheskie osnovy tvorchestva Pomialovskogo," in *Literaturovedenie. Sbornik statei,* edited by V. F. Pereverzev (Moscow, 1928), pp. 231–272;

I. Voronov, "Pomialovsky (Pedagogicheskie mysli i detskie tipy)," *Vestnik vospitaniia,* 5 (1914): 160–187;

N. P. Zhdanovsky, "O khudozhestvennom svoeobrazii povestei N. G. Pomialovskogo," *Voprosy literatury,* 8 (1958): 181–199;

Zhdanovsky, *Realizm Pomialovskogo (Voprosy stilia)* (Moscow: Izdatel'stvo Akademii nauk SSSR, 1960).

Papers:

Many of Nikolai Gerasimovich Pomialovsky's papers have been lost. Most of the manuscript for the sketch "Beguny i spasennye bursy" is preserved in the archive of A. N. Pypin at the Institute of Russian Literature of the Academy of Sciences in St. Petersburg (Pushkin House), and four pages of it are in the Russian State Library in Moscow. Some letters are in the manuscript divisions of the Institute of Russian Literature, and the Russian State Library, as well as the Saltykov-Shchedrin Library in St. Petersburg and the Fyodor Dostoevsky archive in the State Archive of the Era of Serfdom (*Gosudarstvennyi Arkhiv Feodal'no-krepostnicheskoi epokhi:* GAFKE). Some documents are preserved with the papers of N. A. Blagoveshchensky in the manuscript division of the Institute of Russian Literature.

Aleksei Antipovich Potekhin

(1 July 1829 - 16 October 1908)

Sonia I. Ketchian

Davis Center for Russian Studies, Harvard University

WORKS: *Tit Sofronov Kozonok*, in *Moskvitianin* (1850s);

Krest'ianka, in *Moskvitianin* (1853); (Moscow: Tip. L. Stepanovoi, 1854);

Shuba ovech'ia—dusha chelovech'ia, published as *Brat i sestra*, in *Moskvitianin* (1854);

Sud liuskoi—ne Bozhii (1854);

Chuzhoe dobro v prok neidet, in *Otechestvennye zapiski*, 103 (1855);

Krushinsky. Roman, in *Biblioteka dlia chteniia*, nos. 1–6, 9–10 (1856); (St. Petersburg, 1857);

Mishura. Komediia, in *Russkii vestnik*, 13 (1858); (Moscow, 1858);

Burmistr. Povest', in *Biblioteka dlia chteniia*, no. 2 (1859);

Reka Kerzhenets. Povest', in *Sovremennik*, no. 2 (1859);

Noveishii orakul. Komediia, in *Sovremennik*, no. 3 (1859);

Vakantnoe mesto. Komediia, in *Otechestvennye zapiski*, no. 11 (1859); (St. Petersburg, 1870);

Bednye dvoriane. Roman, in *Biblioteka dlia chteniia*, nos. 2–6 (1861); (St. Petersburg, 1863);

Zhenskaia ispoved'. Povest', in *Russkoe slovo*, 4 (1862);

Otrezannyi lomot'. Komediia, in *Sovremennik*, no. 10 (1865); (St. Petersburg, 1865);

Vinovataia. Komediia, in *Sovremennoe obozrenie*, no. 1 (1868);

Rytsari nashego vremeni. Komediia, in *Otechestvennye zapiski*, no. 2 (1869);

Sochineniia, 7 volumes (St. Petersburg: K. N. Plotnikov, 1873–1874);

Khai-devka. Neokonchennyi etiud, in *Skladchina. Literaturnyi sbornik* (St. Petersburg: Tip. A. M. Kotomina, 1874); republished as *Khai-devka. Povest'*, in *Vestnik Evropy*, no. 3 (1875);

Khvoraia. Povest', in *Vestnik Evropy*, nos. 2–3 (1876); (Moscow: Posrednik, 1887);

Okolo deneg. Roman iz sel'skoi i fabrichnoi zhizni, in *Vestnik Evropy*, nos. 10–12 (1876); (St. Petersburg, 1877);

Na miru. Povest', in *Vestnik Evropy*, nos. 4–5 (1877); (St. Petersburg, 1879);

Vygodnoe predpriiatie. Komediia, in *Vestnik Evropy*, no. 1 (1878); (St. Petersburg, 1878);

Molodye pobegi. Povest', in *Vestnik Evropy*, nos. 10–12 (1878); no. 3 (1879);

Aleksei Antipovich Potekhin

Ivan-da-Mar'ia. Povest', in *Niva* (1880);

Posle osvobozhdeniia. Rasskazy iz krest'ianskogo byta, 3 volumes (St. Petersburg: A. S. Suvorin, 1891);

Sochineniia, 12 volumes (St. Petersburg: Prosveshchenie, 1903–1905).

Editions and Collections: *Izbrannye proizvedeniia* (Ivanovo: Gos. izdatel'stvo Ivanovskoi oblasti, 1938);

Izbrannye proizvedeniia (Ivanovo: Ivanovskoe knizhnoe izdatel'stvo, 1960).

SELECTED PERIODICAL PUBLICATIONS:
"Zabavy i udovol'stviia v gorodke. Ocherki," *Sovremennik,* no. 7 (1852);

"Otryvok iz romana," *Moskvitianin,* no. 8 (1852);

"Barynia. Sel'skaia idilliia," *Biblioteka dlia chteniia,* no. 10 (1859);

"Zakulisnye tainy," *Sovremennik,* no. 3 (1861);

"Vecherinka u bednoi rodstvennitsy," *Sovremennik,* no. 9 (1863);

"Dva okhotnika. Rasskaz," *Biblioteka dlia chteniia,* no. 8 (1864);

"Derevenskie miroedy. Ocherk," *Vestnik Evropy,* nos. 4–5 (1880);

"Iz teatral'nykh vospominanii," *Russkaia mysl',* no. 2 (1894); *Teatr i iskusstvo,* 40–41 (1901).

Well known for his innovative plays, which total one-fourth of his works, Aleksei Antipovich Potekhin also wrote essays, sketches, stories, novellas, and novels. Championing peasant equality at the time of serfdom, he was an authority on the life, culture, mores, and language of the Russian peasant, as well as an ardent environmentalist and sensitive advocate for improving women's plight. Potekhin's writings were appreciated by Leo Tolstoy, who in an 18 February 1887 letter to Potekhin wrote, "I believe that in dramatic and theatrical matters after Ostrovsky there is no expert better than you, also that in matters of the people's life no expert can equal you, that I am aware of myself." While serfdom was still an institution, Potekhin wrote the first full-length Russian peasant play, *Sud liudskoi–ne Bozhii* (Human Judgment Is Not That of God, 1854), and the first Russian novel with a serf girl as its heroine, *Krest'ianka* (The Peasant Girl, 1853)–influencing Tolstoy, Aleksei Feofilaktovich Pisemsky, and Aleksandr Nikolaevich Ostrovsky. Despite his renown among his contemporaries, Potekhin's works have not been translated into English.

Aleksei Antipovich Potekhin was born on 1 July 1829 in the town of Kineshma in the province of Kostroma to Antip Makarovich Potekhin and Anfisa Alekseevna (née Iudina). Of ancient impoverished lineage, he was the second son in a harmonious and pious family of nine sons and two daughters. Antip Makarovich was a treasurer in the Kineshma District Court, and the well-educated Anfisa Alekseevna tutored their children. Learning and music were important in their lives. Later Potekhin explored some aspects of their family life through the eyes of his distanced autobiographical hero Boria in "Shest'desiat let nazad: Iz neokonchennogo romana" (Sixty Years Ago: From an Unfinished Novel; *Pushkinskii sbornik,* 1899). This subtle psychological depiction of bickering children, nannies, parents, and servants seems to diverge greatly from the idyllic childhood Potekhin remembered in letters.

After graduating from the Kostroma gymnasium, Potekhin entered the Demidov Lycée in Iaroslavl' to study under the well-known professor K. D. Ushinsky, whose influence remained with Potekhin. He graduated in 1849 with the first gold medal in the history of the school for his essay "Opeka i popechitel'stvo" (Trusteeship and Guardianship). In it he explored the possible brutality of guardianship, whether of parents or of legally appointed caretakers. Some of these notions were developed in Potekhin's plays, notably in *Vygodnoe predpriiatie* (A Lucrative Enterprise, 1878).

Potekhin's love for the theater began in childhood. In high school he staged and acted in plays and drew the decorations. In subsequent years his acting in amateur productions and his stage decorations won praise. Potekhin's acting talent made him a superb reciter. He was called on later in life to participate in many commemorative evenings, including those honoring Aleksandr Sergeevich Pushkin and Nikolai Vasil'evich Gogol. Marriage to his neighbor Mariia Petrovna Kondrat'eva soon after graduation and family responsibilities cut short Potekhin's dream of professional acting. In his only existing diaries, which date from this period, he wrote of courting and winning Mariia Petrovna, who was engaged to another and whose father opposed Potekhin's suit. She chose the shy, tall, bearded Potekhin, who supplied her with books by George Sand and other French writers. As far as can be determined, the couple had seven children: Varvara, Angelina, Leonid, Raisa, Valerii, Pavel, and Nikolai.

To support his family, Potekhin served as "chinovnik osobykh poruchenii pri gubernatore" (a special aide to the governor) with the rank of collegiate secretary, first in Iaroslavl' and next for two years in Kostroma. He met Pisemsky, who was also serving on the administrative board of the province. In 1851 Potekhin's first review appeared in *Moskovskie vedomosti* (Moscow News). "Benefis aktera moskovskogo teatra Shumskogo" (The Benefit Performance of the Moscow Theater Actor Shumsky) resulted in a raise for Shumsky. At the invitation of Mikhail Katkov, editor of *Moskovskie vedomosti,* to submit original writing, Potekhin wrote the ethnographical essays "Put' po Volge v 1851 godu" (Along the Volga Waterway in 1851) and "Uezdnyi gorodok Kineshma" (The District Town of Kineshma, 1852). Ethnographical observation remained a distinctive part of his prose works. Drawing on his observations as a governor's aide, Potekhin published in *Sovremennik* (The Contemporary) the Gogolesque sketch "Zabavy i udovol'stviia v gorodke" (Entertainment and Pleasures in the City, 1852) and his first work of fiction, "Otryvok iz romana" (Excerpt from a Novel) in *Moskvitianin* (The Muscovite, 1852). Potekhin wrote with his heart, his conscience, and strong democratic and feminist proclivities. His ideas reflect in a Russian context those of progressive French and American writers. While peasants pitted against the upper classes and privileged persons often emerge as positive characters, most of his peasant characters are far from positive. Rather, the victors are more often than not the negative, darker forces in life.

During frequent trips to Moscow, Potekhin became friendly with Ostrovsky's circle, and in 1852 he also became involved with the so-called young editorial staff of the journal *Moskvitianin,* whose Slavophile leanings he espoused. Potekhin recalled the time in his undated and unpublished "Vospominaniia o znakomstve s I. F. Gorbunovym v 1852–1853 godakh" (Recollections of My Acquaintance with I. F. Gorbunov in the Years 1852–1853). Unable to devote himself wholly to literature, Potekhin sought to relocate to Moscow, one of the principal centers of Russian culture, but he was unsuccessful in securing a position as an inspector of the Second Moscow High School or in the Naval Ministry. Nonetheless, he resigned his post in the province while continuing his search for suitable employment in Moscow. Letters to the editor of *Moskvitianin,* Mikhail Petrovich Pogodin, were no help, for Pogodin made payments to his contributors most reluctantly. Consequently, on 30 March 1855, Potekhin was obliged to enter military service as "lieutenant and adjunct of detachment no. 148" without being able to purchase the required horse. His military experience was brief, and Potekhin returned to his close contacts with the peasants he so admired. Because of his choice of subject matter, some people of his social class felt Potekhin was wasting his talent.

Potekhin's writings span forty years, falling into three periods. During the first, 1851–1855, he employed peasant themes in a variety of genres and forms: ethnographic sketches, three peasant plays, two novels, a short story, and two novellas. In his prose of this period, primal realism is peppered with sentimental thoughts and addresses to the reader. In the second period, 1856–1867, the gentry is predominant in the six character plays, the two vaudevilles, the story "Barynia" (The Mistress, 1859), and the novel *Bednye dvoriane* (Poor Noblemen, 1861). Potekhin also continued to write ethnographic sketches focusing on peasants. During the third period, 1868–1881, Potekhin produced his last original character play, *Vygodnoe predpriiatie,* and the essay-like works "Krest'ianskie deti" (Peasant Children) and "Derevenskie miroedy" (Village

Usurers, 1880), which display residual traits of the ethnographical sketches. The prose fiction of this period focuses exclusively on peasants and includes *Khvoraia* (The Sickly Woman, 1876), "Porchenaia" (The Spoiled One, 1881), and *Ivan-da-Mar'ia* (Ivan and Maria, 1880). With *Okolo deneg* (Around Money, 1876), as well *Na miru* (In the Village Community, 1877) and its remarkable sequel *Molodye pobegi* (Young Shoots, 1878–1879) Potekhin became a pioneer in the depiction of the initial stages of the peasants' proletarization, which he deemed as deplorable as alcoholism.

Potekhin's first play, the peasant drama *Sud liudskoi–ne Bozhii,* has the distinction of having been sanctioned by Prince Konstantin Romanov. This play was the longest Russian dramatic work portraying the peasantry yet written. Its publication in 1854 antedated by one year the publication of Ostrovsky's first peasant drama, *Ne tak zhivi kak khochetsia* (Live Not As You Want, 1855). Like each of Potekhin's ten full-length plays, his first dramatic effort consists of four acts. The prevailing leitmotif of all Potekhin's peasant works is articulated in *Sud liudskoi–ne Bozhii* through the retort to the rather comical landowner Skripunov by the peasant hero Ivan, who attributes to peasants the same subtlety of emotion as the upper class: "a po tebe–kakoe-de u muzhika serdtse, kakoe-de u nego chuvstvie" (according to you–what kind of heart can a muzhik have, what kind of feeling can he have). Employing local color, folklore, superstition, and customs, this play has an original, suspenseful plot. Paternal damnation of the intimacy between Matrena and the carefree orphan Ivan sets the plot in motion. Only through forgiveness and humility can the once-proud Old-Believer father Nikolai Spiridonych atone for his mistakes. The scene of public atonement finds repeated resonance in Pisemsky, Leo Tolstoy, and Fyodor Dostoevsky. Matrena's ultimate decision to spend her life serving her father frees Ivan to enlist in the army (his surrogate family), but, as in Potekhin's later novel *Krushinsky* (1856), the overbearing despotic parent is thus punished because his daughter will not marry and bear children. The ambience of the play is colored by Matrena's temporary insanity and by a consideration of the role of fate. The play is also remarkable for its well-drawn characters, notably Ivan, the neighbor Akulina, and the old soldier Egor. As in all Potekhin's plays, tension is maintained throughout. Unlike his next two peasant plays, this first play rests on peasantry's past.

Potekhin's first novel, *Krest'ianka,* is the fast-paced, dialogue-propelled story of a serf girl who steps across class lines to freedom before the official emancipation of the Russian peasants in 1861. In two parts of twelve chapters each–with additional folk flavor from the sayings and proverbs used for the chapter titles–the novel traces the transformation and failed love of virtuous Annushka, the daughter of well-to-do serf parents. Formerly a typical peasant serf, Annushka maintains ties with her natural family, while successfully turning herself into a genteel young lady, the adopted daughter of a German estate manager, Avgust Knabe.

The eleven-year-old Annushka's wistful gazing outside the estate fence leads to her being befriended by Anchen Knabe. Subsequently, she advances from a nominal servant to Anchen's equal. After the German girl's early demise, Annushka takes Anchen's place, and with the permission of Annushka's peasant parents Anchen's father formally adopts their daughter. Throughout this action Annushka assumes a seemingly passive role, as Anchen and her kindly sentimental mother, Amaliia Fedorovna, arrange everything, even buying the Russian girl's freedom. Yet, Anna, as she is now called, has willed everything and has been able to convey her wishes tacitly. Once her peasant origin is revealed to her love interest, the neighboring landowner Dmitrii Gubov, he cannot bring himself to marry her, and she successfully resists his attempts to make her his mistress. Scenes filled with details of customs and local color, such as serf men and women reaping rye on Gubov's estate under his watchful eye, anticipate Tolstoy's Levin working with the peasants in the fields in *Anna Karenina* (1875).

In part 2, when Anna returns to her peasant home following the death of her adoptive mother, her family finds her re-assimilation trying. The cultural chasm between them and Anna is wider than she will admit. Anna's inability to readjust to peasant life results in Avgust Knabe's finding her a position as a governess, creating another unusual twist–a peasant teaching the nobility. For Potekhin, a peasant was the equal of a nobleman in emotions and learning ability and could excel with the proper education. In his works, social inequality in marriage can be surmounted by a woman if she has chosen a nobleman who is truly wealthy and strong, but it fails if the man is her social inferior.

Potekhin's sequel to *Krest'ianka* is a play, *Shuba ovech'ia–dusha chelovech'ia* (The Coat Is Sheepskin–the Soul, Human, 1853), the only such switch in genre known in Russian literature. Because the stringent theatrical censor rejected the original title, *Brat i sestra* (Brother and Sister)–under which the play appeared in *Moskvitianin* in 1854–the title given the play in both editions of Potekhin's works is *Shuba ovech'ia–dusha chelovech'ia,* which comes from the epigraph to part 1 of *Krest'ianka.* The same words are also spoken by Anna's father, Ivan Prokhorov, who deplores her education and gentrification. A twelve-year ban on stage performance undercut the sensational impact of the play during serfdom. Potekhin's plays always reached the stage

belatedly, and other playwrights borrowed his innovative conceits from the published texts. The female characters in *Shuba ovech'ia–dusha chelovech'ia* served as prototypes for Ostrovsky's *Les* (The Forest, 1871).

The events of the three-year lapse between the end of the novel and the time period of the play are filled in meagerly. Of the characters in the novel only Anna Ivanovna and her now-freed brother Zosima, to whom the title refers, appear in the play. Whereas Aleksandr Ivanovich Herzen's *Soroka-vorovka* (The Thieving Magpie, 1846) questions the gifted serf actress's fate with "Zachem razbudili tebia?" (Why Did They Awaken You?), Potekhin resolves the question by freeing his heroine in the novel and finding her an appreciative counterpart in the play, the wealthy landowner Aleksei Dmitrich Radugin–through the seemingly naive intervention of her adoring brother Zosima. His freedom from serfdom, attained through an advance on Anna's salary, has brought confidence to Zosima, who plans to become a merchant. As in the novel, Potekhin broaches the themes of servants' resenting Anna Ivanovna, rivalry among servants (so crucial later in *Krushinsky*), "samodur" (interpersonal tyranny), and corrupt civil servants, a theme that reached its apogee in the play *Mishura* (Tinsel, 1858). In *Krest'ianka* Anna Ivanovna's father, Ivan Prokhorov, questions whether one can remain a good pure Russian despite the influences of foreign language, religion, and culture. In the novel and play alike, Potekhin reinforces the notion that, when foreign influences do not dominate, they can enrich one's life, as they do for Anna Ivanovna, who retains her genuine Russian soul.

The staging in 1856 of Potekhin's third, and last, peasant play, *Chuzhoe dobro v prok neidet* (No Good Comes of Another's Belongings, 1855), brought him and the actor Aleksandr Evstaf'evich Martynov fame and recognition. This peasant play is the only one of his works about which Potekhin commented extensively, focusing on its staging and Martynov's personal stage interpretation. The plot, which is the simplest of the three plays, has a linear structure with a singleness of movement. It concerns the successful peasant innkeeper Stepan Fedorov, whose older, married, money-loving son, Mikhailo, finds a wallet full of money after the visit of two merchants. Stepan appropriates the money. Extravagant Mikhailo goes downhill, carousing and nearly murdering his father. The second son, submissive and "naive" Aleksei, and his mother, Maremiana, subtly prod the family into returning the wallet. The focus of the play is not on crime but rather on human psychology and values, notably on the insidious corrupting influence of ill-begotten money. As in Tolstoy's *Fal'shivyi kupon* (The Falsified Check, 1911), where an uncompassionate father's false accusations prompt fifteen-year-old Mitia Smokovnikov into forging a check that induces criminality in all subsequent possessors, in Potekhin's play Stepan's lack of faith in his son compounds Mikhailo's resentment and protest.

Although Potekhin's longest novel, *Krushinsky,* was published in 1856, it better fits his second period because of its lack of peasant protagonists and its narrative structured through dialogue. It resembles a society tale with its driving society gossip and love angle. Yet, it also recalls *Krest'ianka* and *Shuba ovech'ia* because the eponymous hero, a sexton's son risen to the status of a brilliant military doctor, falls in love with a wealthy young noblewoman. Fashioned in three parts, the novel traces this budding love, its acknowledgment, gossip and intrigues, and a tragic finale in which Krushinsky dies, leaving Nadia Korkina to spinsterhood, after her family's near financial ruin at the hands of a titled, fraudulent, non-Russian suitor.

Potekhin's "slice of life" scenes admirably depict the fluctuation, repetition, and tedium of ordinary social interaction. He excels in showing the process by which proud and audacious Krushinsky becomes caught up in social banality. Extensive dialogue and brilliant social banter are interfaced with short passages of explanatory prose, all of which subtly convey psychology and underlying motivation. Symbolism—such as the connection of Krushinsky, whom Nadia's maid calls "krasnoe solnyshko" (shining sun), to a ray of sunlight entering Nadia's bedroom—adds another dimension to the novel. As an epilogue, the unexpected marriage of Krushinsky's sister to his faithful older friend Captain Dobrago lends an optimistic closure to an otherwise disheartening novel.

Like most of Potekhin's plays, *Mishura* was banned for years. These bans undermined the effectiveness of his plays and probably discouraged him from writing more dramatic works. *Mishura* treats the appearance in Russian society of a new sort of university-educated official, who claimed to be honest while holding out for higher stakes than the petty bribes and favors corrupt officials had taken in the past. Potekhin's protagonist, Pustozerov, is one of these new bureaucrats, while Anisim Fedorovich represents the old order. Of impoverished aristocratic lineage, Pustozerov takes advantage of Anisim Fedorovich's beautiful pension-educated daughter Dasha, who is dazzled by the young man's rhetoric and, expecting love to conquer all obstacles, attempts to prove her love for Pustozerov physically. Yet, once the prosperous industrialist Zolotarev obtains a desirable position for Pustozerov in St. Petersburg—as recompense for Pustozerov's agreeing not to prosecute

Zolotarev's friend—Dasha's lover abandons her for a future wealthy bride. The love interest notwithstanding, the emphasis of the drama remains on the antihero Pustozerov's official dealings and his driving ambition. The effective open ending leaves Dasha's fate unresolved. The masterfully painted characters and several elements, including mention of an incognito visit by the governor, recall Gogol's *Revizor* (The Inspector General, 1836). Once again, Potekhin's technique involves stringing scene on scene and applying heavy coloration. Pustozerov resembles the "new" characters in Anton Pavlovich Chekhov's play *Ivanov* (1889), in which gradual disclosure displaces development.

In 1856 Potekhin, Pisemsky, and Sergei Vasil'evich Maksimov were invited to participate in a literary-ethnographic expedition on the Volga River, organized by the Grand Duke Konstantin Nikolaevich. Potekhin later recommended that Ostrovsky participate as well. Assigned the section from the mouth of the Oka River to the city of Saratov, Potekhin published several essays on his observations: "Lov krasnoi ryby v Saratovskoi gubernii" (Catching Red Fish in the Saratov Province, 1857), considered his best; *Reka Kerzhenets* (The River Kerzhenets, 1859), which is vaguely evocative of Jack London's tales of Alaska and avoids the sentimental addresses to the reader; "S Vetlugi" (From the Vetluga, 1861); and "Na nochlege" (Staying Overnight). The grand duke commended Potekhin's work.

After the expedition Potekhin was once more in need of employment. From the late 1850s until 1864 he served as an agent for the management of the estates of A. M. Golitsyna and her daughter E. L. Ignat'eva in the villages of Gor'ky and Karabikha in the province of Iaroslavl' in the late 1850s to 1864. He was possibly working for the two women in a higher capacity as late as 1873, judging by business reports sent to him that year. From 1869 to 1874, Potekhin was a landowner in the Mogilev Province, where—beginning in September 1869—he spent a year as editor of the unofficial part of the local newspaper, *Mogilevskie gubernskie vedomosti* (Mogilev Province News).

Potemkin's 1865 play, *Otrezannyi lomot'* (Alienated Son) was banned for fifteen years following its fifteenth performance. Potekhin's protagonist, the disinherited son Nikolai Khaziperov, has relinquished ties with the ruling class into which he was born and with his wealthy family, not only with his despotic father but also with his cowering mother and sister, who, as in Dostoevsky's *Khoziaika* (The Landlady, 1847) crave a stronger person's despotic yoke. Returning after five years in the hope that tensions have lessened, Nikolai realizes that the two women are complete strangers to him in ideology and feelings, as they accept his father's increased tyranny. After his sister, Natasha, offers to reject her impecunious democratic suitor, Demkin, if her father will send away his mistress, Nikolai leaves forever. The conflict is one of generations, of fathers and sons, and the theme carries over into the peasant life depicted in the play as well. The play—whose title derives from the elder Bazarov's utterance in Ivan Sergeevich Turgenev's *Ottsy i deti* (Fathers and Sons, 1862) following his son Evgenii's first departure—strongly recalls Turgenev's novel. Much more goal-oriented than Turgenev's Bazarov, Nikolai survives alone as a nihilist.

In concentration and expressive spareness, especially in his middle period, Potekhin's prose evokes that of Pushkin. Nature and landscape descriptions are restricted mainly to Potekhin's sketches. In its spareness Potekhin's prose fiction, almost devoid of landscape and nature descriptions, recalls the prose of Dostoevsky. Lively, expertly modulated dialogue remains the salient mode of characterization and conveyance of remarkable nuances as he perpetuates realistic traditions.

Potekhin anticipated Tolstoy in preaching "all-forgiving love and a life dedicated to the benefit of others." Just as the vicious circle of evil is ended in Tolstoy's *Fal'shivyi kupon* only when Mitia Smokovnikov dedicates his life to others, so too in *Chuzhoe dobro v prok neidet* evil is overcome by all-forgiving love. The notion of all-forgiving love is taken to the extreme in Potekhin's first published novella, *Tit Sofronov Kozonok* (which appeared in the 1850s), in which the affluent peasant Onufrii Kuzmich forgives the man who killed his only grandson, to the extent that he takes the wife of the murderer, Kozonok, into his home. Potekhin's novellas *Na miru* and the superbly constructed *Khvoraia,* with its undercurrent of apathy and "turning the other cheek," won praise from Tolstoy.

Selfless kindness in the peasant novella *Na miru* and its sequel—the novel *Molodye pobegi*—causes the undoing of its practitioners. With the establishment of nascent capitalism, the only victors are the *kuptsy* (merchants), as Potekhin calls them, and those willing to work for them servilely in any capacity. The naive, intelligent, and talented Fedia and his sister Anna fall victim to Kirill, the spoiled and destructive only son of the self-made wealthy peasant elder Fedot Semenych. In *Na miru* responsible and hard-working Anna seems the ideal wife for the carousing and gambling Kirill, but she fails to change him. Instead, he steadily accelerates his deplorable activities until two peasants discover him selling the harness he has stolen from his father-in-law. In retaliation Kirill sets fire to their houses. The flames engulf half the village, and he is apprehended and imprisoned. The fast-paced narrative relies on dialogue authentically duplicating peasant parlance. Each character has his own distinctive way of speaking; the best are the fair peasant elder and the inquisitive and multitalented youth Fedia, who learned physics and mechanics through reading.

In *Molodye pobegi,* as in *Okolo deneg,* amorphous revolutionary stirrings begin among peasants who have become the new proletariat. *Molodye pobegi* is a darkly realistic novel with superb structure, characterization, and plot development. No longer adhering to a linear structure, Potekhin opens the novel as young, literate Fedia (now called Fedor) is convincing his father, Gerasim Dmitrich, to let him work in a factory rather than till the land and marry the girl chosen for him. Setting off for town, Fedor thinks back at length about when he was eighteen and living with Fedot Semenych's family to work for them while Kirill served his prison sentence. He recalls his friendship with the village teacher, Vasilii Iakimych (who was also a character in *Na miru*), and his meeting the strikingly beautiful Parania, a peasant who, like her mother, Dar'ia Tikhonovna, looks like an aristocrat. Parania's parentage is uncertain. Dar'ia served in the home of a member of the gentry, and the novel merely hints at the way in which she entertains her raucous male visitors. Dar'ia artfully wheedles money from Fedor, whose intention to marry the largely indifferent Parania is as quixotic as his dreams of becoming wealthy by working at a factory and inventing machines.

Fedor convinces Dar'ia that she and Parania should move with him to the factory town, where Fedot Semenych has arranged for an acquaintance, the wealthy factory owner Kuz'ma Ivanych Koshatnikov, to give Fedor a job. Just as they antagonized Kirill in *Na Miru,* Fedor's autodidactic knowledge and aspirations irritate the anti-intellectual Kuz'ma, who places the young man in a lowly job. Fedor becomes involved in an unauthorized school for the workers that has been established at the factory by Kuz'ma's progressive-minded son Aleksandr, who is under the bullying intellectual spell of the radical impetuous governess Alena Nikolaevna. The embittered former convict Kirill, who has come to stalk Parania and take revenge on Fedor, informs on the group and his nemesis Fedor in return for a supervisory position at the factory. Unspecified retaliation comes swiftly and without elaboration; Fedor and Alena are apparently sent to Siberian prison camps, and Fedot Semenych laments, "Ekh, zadarom propala zolotaia golovushka" (Hey, a golden boy was ruined for nothing!). At their first meeting Kuz'ma had cast a salacious eye on Parania and entrusted the rest to his subservient manager. Dar'ia accepts the position of Kuz'ma's housekeeper with Parania as the sexual prize.

The rise of the merchant class to a new industrialist class that is replacing the gentry is depicted in the ruthless characterizations of Kuz'ma and his underlings. Industrialists chopping down old-growth forests and desecrating the beauty of the Russian manor house, which was probably built by the famous architect Rastrelli, announce the unwelcome advent of capitalism. The idea that industrialists should build their factories in cities rather than despoil the pristine beauty of the country or harm the peasants is repeated throughout the narration.

As early as 1870, Potekhin was concerned about the impoverishment of the theater—despite excellent indigenous Russian plays by Ostrovsky, Pisemsky, and Turgenev, as well as his own works, and a tradition of brilliant actors such as Pavel Stepanovich Mochalov, Mikhail Semenovich Shchepkin, Aleksandr Evstaf'evich Martynov, and Sadovsky. Considering Potekhin's characters their best roles, talented actors such as Modest Ivanovich Pisarev, E. Martynov, Maria Nikolaevna Ermolova, Mariia Gavrilovna Savina, Vera Fedorovna Komissarzhevskaia, and A. M. Chitau chose his plays for their benefit performances. With the help of Ostrovsky and others, Potekhin drew up and implemented theatrical reforms. In 1881 a committee that included Potekhin and Ostrovsky reviewed the situation in the Imperial Theaters. In April of 1882 Potekhin was named manager of the dramatic troupes in St. Petersburg and Moscow with Ivan Aleksandrovich Vsevolozhsky as director. Potekhin poured all his energy and talents into making his position a success. As a result, he wrote no more original works. His only writings during the period were unpublished stage adaptations of earlier works. Ostrovsky and Dmitrii Vasil'evich Averkiev opposed the unification of the Moscow and Petersburg troupes. Ostrovsky coveted Potekhin's position; and on Potekhin's retirement as manager of the Moscow branch in 1886, Ostrovsky and Apollon Nikolaevich Maikov were appointed to the position.

Potekhin introduced many improvements in the theater. Some of his ideas were too innovative for the time and were abandoned—notably, inviting the press to dress rehearsals, as in Western Europe, because the famous actors left the play before opening night if the press reacted critically to such previews. He was criticized for allegedly promoting the staging of his own plays and those of his brother Nikolai. Actually, theater records show that Potekhin's plays were staged less frequently during his years as manager than in earlier years. The records further demonstrate that before Potekhin became manager his plays drew full houses, while other plays made less money at the box office. Yet, the weekly paper *Sufler* (The Prompter) hounded Potekhin and his actress daughter Raisa.

One of Potekhin's accomplishments as manager was his role in obtaining permission to stage Tolstoy's *Vlast' t'my* (The Power of Darkness, 1887), and he put much effort and expertise into assuring ethnographic authenticity for depicting Tula Province in the production. In sending his drama to the actress M. G. Savina in 1886, Tolstoy signaled his faith in Potekhin, writing: "I agree to everything that the theatrical censorship finds necessary to change in order to soften it, if those changes are approved by A. A. Potekhin, whom I trust absolutely."

After leaving his position in the Imperial Theater, Potekhin participated in establishing the Obshchestvo vspomoshchestvovaniia stsenicheskim deiateliam (Society for Aid to Stage Workers), later renamed Russkoe teatral'noe obshchestvo (Russian Theatrical Society), and served as its president for ten years. He also organized the first conference of stage workers. A special fund in honor of Potekhin was established to assist needy actors and their families.

In 1900 Potekhin, Tolstoy, Chekhov, Vladimir Galaktionovich Korolenko, and Vladimir Sergeevich Solov'ev were awarded the degree of Honorary Academician in Artistic Literature. The fiftieth anniversary of Potekhin's literary debut was commemorated in 1901 with fanfare and much praise. By then Potekhin was a sick man with a nervous disorder, possibly Parkinson's disease, that impeded concentration and writing. The struggles of life had transformed the optimistic lover of humankind into a rather pessimistic, critical old man. Trips to the Caucasus in 1905 and 1907 brought little improvement to his health, and he died on 16 October 1908. During the Soviet era, Potekhin faded into unwarranted obscurity. His remarkable, pioneering legacy in literature, drama, and the theater remains to be reevaluated, and his writings await translation into English.

Letters:

"Neizdannye pis'ma sovremennikov k L. N. Tolstomu," *Voprosy literatury,* no. 11 (1960): 76–80;

P. M. Tamaev and others, "Iz perepiski A. A. Potekhina i M. P. Pogodina (1850-e gg.)," *Fol'klor i literatura Ivanovskogo kraia,* 1 (1994): 109–119.

Biographies:

B. B. Glinsky, "A. Potekhin (Materialy dlia biografii)," *Istoricheskii vestnik,* 12 (1908): 987–1004;

I. Vinogradov, "Melochi dlia biografii A. F. Pisemskogo i A. A. Potekhina," *Izvestiia Otdeleniia russkogo iazyka i slovesnosti,* 13, no. 3 (1908): 322–327.

References:

Petr Dmitrievich Boborykin, "A. Potekhin," *Izvestiia Otdeleniia russkogo iazyka i slovesnosti,* 7, book 1 (1902): 17–38;

Nikolai Aleksandrovich Dobroliubov, "Mishura. Komediia v 4-kh destviiakh A. Potekhina," *Sovremennik,* no. 8 (1858): 209–231;

Andrew Donskov, "The Changing Image of the Peasant in Nineteenth Century Russian Drama," *Suomalainen Tiedeakatemia. Toimituksia,* Series B, volume 177 (1972);

Sergei Vasil'evich Kastorsky, "Pisatel'-dramaturg A. A. Potekhin," in *Iz istorii russkikh literaturnykh otnoshenii XVIII–XX vekov,* edited by Kastorsky (Moscow & Leningrad: AN SSSR, 1959), pp. 177–198;

Sonia I. Ketchian, "The Plays of Aleksej Potexin," dissertation, Harvard University, 1974;

Pavel Viacheslavovich Kupriianovsky, ed., *Stat'i o russkoi i zarubezhnoi literature* (Ivanovo, 1966), pp. 67–93;

Nikolai Semenovich Leskov, "Russkii dramaticheskii teatr v Peterburge," *Otechestvennye zapiski,* no. 3 (1867): "Sovremennaia khronika" section, 40–47;

Lidiia Mikhailovna Lotman, *A. N. Ostrovsky i russkaia dramaturgiia ego vremeni* (Moscow & Leningrad: Akademiia nauk SSSR, 1961), pp. 148–159;

Lotman, "Dramaturgiia shestidesiatykh godov. (Obshchii obzor)," in *Istoriia russkoi literatury,* volume 8, part 2 (Moscow & Leningrad: AN SSSR, 1956), pp. 357–362;

P. Morozov, "Pisatel'-narodnik A. A. Potekhin," *Mir Bozhii,* 11 (1901): 236–251;

Aleksandr Nikitenko, "Otrezannyi lomot'. Komediia v 4-kh deistviiakh A. Potekhina," in his *Tri literaturno-kriticheskie ocherka* (St. Petersburg, 1866), pp. 17–37;

Mikhail Evgrafovich Saltykov (N. Shchedrin), "Nashi bezobrazniki. Stseny N. A. Potekhina," *Sovremennik,* no. 1 (1864);

Aleksandr Mikhailovich Skabichevsky, *Sochineniia,* third edition, volume 1 (St. Petersburg, 1903), pp. 787–818;

Anna Ivanovna Zhuravleva, ed., *Russkaia drama epokhi A. N. Ostrovskogo* (Moscow: Moskovskii universitet, 1984), pp. 7–38.

Fedor Mikhailovich Reshetnikov

(5 September 1841 – 9 March 1871)

Denis Akhapkin
St. Petersburg University

(Translated by Judith E. Kalb)

WORKS: *Podlipovtsy. Etnograficheskii ocherk (iz zhizni burlakov),* in *Sovremennik,* nos. 3–5 (1864); (St. Petersburg: Izd. S. V. Zvonareva, 1867);

Stavlennik, in *Sovremennik,* nos. 6–8 (1864);

Gornorabochie, partial publication in *Sovremennik,* nos. 1–2 (1866);

Glumovy, in *Delo,* no. 2 (1866); nos. 3, 4, 7, 9 (1867); (St. Petersburg: Izd. Knigoprodavtsa I. L. Tuzova, 1880);

Gde luchshe? in *Otechestvennye zapiski,* nos. 6–10 (1868); (St. Petersburg: Izd. S. V. Zvonareva, 1869);

Sochineniia: Ocherki, rasskazy i stseny, two volumes (St. Petersburg, 1869);

Svoi khleb, in *Otechestvennye zapiski,* nos. 3–8 (1870); (St. Petersburg: Izd. K. N. Plotnikova, 1871);

Znakomye portrety (St. Petersburg: Izd. V. V. Obolenskogo, 1878);

V omute, in *Russkoe bogatstvo,* nos. 5–6 (1887); (St. Petersburg: V. V. Komarov, 1887).

Editions and Collections: *Sochineniia,* two volumes, introduction by Gleb Ivanovich Uspensky (Moscow: Izd. K. T. Soldatenkova, 1874);

Sochineniia, two volumes (St. Petersburg: Izd. F. Pavlenkova, 1890);

Polnoe sobranie sochinenii v dvukh tomakh, edited by A. M. Skabichevsky (St. Petersburg: P. V. Lukovnikov, 1904);

Iz literaturnogo naslediia F. M. Reshetnikova, edited by I. I. Veksler (Leningrad-Moscow: Akademiia Nauk SSSR, Institut russkoi literatury, 1932);

Izbrannye sochineniia, edited by I. S. Panov and P. F. Riumin (Sverdlovsk, 1933);

Polnoe sobranie sochinenii v shesti tomakh, edited by Veksler (Sverdlovsk: Sverdlovskoe obl. izd-vo, 1936–1948);

Izbrannye proizvedeniia, two volumes (Moscow: Goslitizdat, 1956).

Fedor Mikhailovich Reshetnikov during the 1860s

SELECTED PERIODICAL PUBLICATIONS:
"Maksia," *Sovremennik,* no. 10 (1864): 379–423;

"Vospominaniia detstva," *Russkoe slovo,* nos. 10–11 (1864);

"Mezhdu liud'mi (Iz vospominanii proshlogo)," *Russkoe slovo,* nos. 1–3 (1865);

"Pokhozhdeniia bednogo provintsiala v stolitse," *Sovremennik,* nos. 11–12 (1865);

"Nikola Znamensky," *Otechestvennye zapiski,* no. 21 (1867): 1–30;

"Stseny iz dramy 'Raskol'nik,'" excerpts edited by Gleb Ivanovich Uspensky, *Nevskii al'manakh,* 2 (1917): 85–107.

Among the writers long classified as "Realists," Fedor Mikhailovich Reshetnikov occupies a special place, even though only one of his books, *Podlipovtsy* (The Inhabitants of Podlipnaia, 1864), achieved renown. This privileged position is linked primarily to the fact that in any discussion of realism and naturalism in nineteenth-century Russian literature Reshetnikov is acknowledged as exhibiting the highest degree of correspondence between literature and reality, text and biography. Some critics saw this characteristic as the main deficiency in Reshetnikov's prose, noting the writer's striking inability to manage his material, to transform life experiences into a literary text, and to separate out the unnecessary and add in what was lacking. Others saw in this tendency the most worthwhile element of his work: for example, Mikhail Evgrafovich Saltykov (N. Shchedrin) wrote of Reshetnikov, "He feels the truth, he writes the truth, and from this truth (*pravda*) the tragic deeper truth (*istina*) of Russian life flows forth to such an extent that it becomes understandable even without any particular effort on the writer's part." This "tragic truth," like Reshetnikov's prose, becomes even more understandable when one takes into account the writer's biography.

Fedor Mikhailovich Reshetnikov was born on 5 September 1841 in Ekaterinburg into the family of a traveling postman. Reshetnikov's father, Mikhail Vasil'evich Reshetnikov, was a drunkard who left the family shortly after his son's birth; Reshetnikov's mother took her ten-month-old son with her to relatives in Perm in search of refuge. Soon after their arrival in Perm, terrified by the sight of an enormous fire that by a miracle had avoided the home where they were staying, his mother fell into a fever and shortly thereafter died in the hospital. Thus, the boy remembered neither his father nor his mother, though it is possible that dim recollections of his mother were incorporated into Reshetnikov's female characters.

After his mother's death Reshetnikov was left in the care of his uncle Vasilii Vasil'evich Reshetnikov, who was working at the time as a senior sorter at the Perm post office, where he received a small salary that was hardly sufficient for his own family, let alone another mouth to feed. Reshetnikov's uncle had particular opinions about the boy's education and future path. Convinced that the highest aspiration available to one of his circle and social position was a position as a post-office employee, which permitted one to avoid dying of hunger and, albeit barely, to make ends meet, Reshetnikov's uncle began to prepare his nephew for just such a career.

Literacy was an essential element of this plan, but neither the uncle nor those around him saw any need for the child to learn any more than was necessary to read addresses on envelopes and to sort them in accordance with these addresses. Initially the uncle tried to teach the child himself, but the latter, by nature playful and restless, was often distracted and unable to focus, which in turn led to the only educational method the uncle knew of: flogging. At times the child was beaten so severely that blood came to his throat. Such punishment was common to the circles to which Reshetnikov belonged.

In 1850 Reshetnikov's uncle sent him off to be educated at a seminary. Reshetnikov's works depict that life as a senseless and harsh one that extinguished the best instincts and was most difficult for the kind and weak. Yet, initially, after his uncle's home, the boy actually liked the seminary. Later, unable to stand the systematic beatings, he ran from the place, having stolen a fisherman's boat. This attempted flight proved unsuccessful: Reshetnikov was caught and beaten to such an extent that he had to spend three months in the hospital. After recovering he did manage to run away, and he spent some time traveling through the Perm region. He lived with workers in a factory, and he wandered around with beggars who forced him to drink vodka, sing, and dance for handouts. Through these situations he encountered the harsh and half-wild Perm reality that, when portrayed in his novels and stories, stunned an entire generation of Russian readers.

Returning to his uncle's home, the boy turned inward, spoke with no one, and responded to beatings with displays of temper. For instance, in revenge for one typically unfair beating, he shoved a dead cat into the household kneading trough along with some dough. When this escapade was discovered, Reshetnikov was nearly beaten to death. Also during this period Reshetnikov's acquaintance with the written word began in earnest—at first with books taken furtively from the trunk that stood unwanted in the cellar, and then with newspapers at the post office where his uncle had sent him to work in 1851 and where he ran errands for various bureaucrats.

Information about this period of Reshetnikov's life comes primarily from his autobiographical novella, *Mezhdu liud'mi* (Among People, published first in segments in 1864 and 1865), and also from a series of letters in which he told acquaintances about his childhood. The writer noted at one point that studying at the local school where his uncle sent him had been basically useless: "For three years I was in the first grade and understood nothing. The teachers were not concerned with our mental development, but instead taught us to cram and never explained anything. Besides which, the teachers considered it a pleasure to beat us. I didn't run away, because I was already used to beatings."

In order to improve his teachers' attitude toward him, Reshetnikov began to bring them newspapers from the post office; at first he tried to return these to their proper place but then for all intents and purposes stole them. When this theft was discovered, the matter went to trial. Because of the defendant's youth and his penitence, the sentence was limited to a three-month exile in the Solikamskii Monastery. This exile proved to be beneficial: customs in the monastery were much milder than at his uncle's home, and Reshetnikov left the place having acquired a deep sense of religious devotion, even though he admitted that life there had not been distinguished by piety: "Within a week I learned of the impiety of the monks, how they drank wine, swore, ate meat, and gallivanted."

Much of Reshetnikov's reading in 1857 and 1858, after he had left the monastery, centered on books with spiritual content; moreover, he began his own writing, and one of the genres he attempted was that of the homily. Reshetnikov's development was helped further by his uncle's transfer to Ekaterinburg. Left for the first time in years to his own devices, Reshetnikov began to study diligently and to write extensively. His notes are filled with descriptions of happenings in village life, portraits of acquaintances, and lyrical sketches. Few of Reshetnikov's early works have survived, and some of them exist only in the Populist writer Gleb Ivanovich Uspensky's retellings in his biographical introduction to Reshetnikov's 1874 collected works. Almost all of these early works draw on Reshetnikov's own life.

In 1859, after completing his studies at the local school, Reshetnikov moved to his uncle's home in Ekaterinburg and began to work at the main court (*uezdnyi sud*). Serving in one of the least prestigious capacities of the court, as an aide to the head of the unskilled laborers' department (the branch of the court that dealt with the complaints of simple workers), and receiving a meager salary of only three rubles per month, Reshetnikov nonetheless took pride in his work and in his affiliation with the court. At this time he wrote the three-part narrative poem "Prigovor" (The Verdict). He then turned to drama: his next work was "Panich," a three-act play in verse. These works have not survived, but Uspensky, who had read them, set forth their contents in his own work.

From the start of his belletristic activity, Reshetnikov also engaged in journalistic pursuits. His work in court frequently gave him the opportunity to associate with simple workers from the mint and other businesses. Influenced by these contacts, Reshetnikov began to write articles that exposed the inhuman conditions faced by workers. These articles have not survived, and the titles of only two of them are known: "Chernoe ozero" (The Black Sea) and "Delovye liudi" (Businessmen) (circa 1860–1861). The articles were not published but nevertheless played a significant role in the writer's life. When in the middle of 1861 Reshetnikov moved to Perm to seek out a life independent of his uncle's guardianship, he had difficulty finding work because of rumors about his authorship of such articles.

At last Reshetnikov found steady employment in Perm as a clerk at the provincial revenue department, where he worked from 1861 to 1863. This period proved to be quite important to Reshetnikov's development as a writer. Plans for many of the works he published later in life, as well as the rough drafts inspired by these plans, arose at this time. And his first published work appeared: the article "Biblioteka dlia chteniia chinovnikov Permskoi Kazennoi palaty" (The Library of the Perm Revenue Department Workers) was published in the newspaper *Permskie gubernskie vedomosti* (Perm Province News). During these years Reshetnikov also produced the story "Skripach" (The Fiddler, 1861), published in a 1932 collection of his works, and the play *Raskol'nik* (The Dissenter, 1862), excerpts of which were published in 1917. Both works are devoted to a description of the difficult lives of simple workers and their families, a central theme in all of Reshetnikov's works. Yet, unlike his later writing, these works treat the theme in a somewhat melodramatic manner characterized by romantic exaggerations in the description of backbreaking work, material deprivation, and corporal punishment. "Skripach" also demonstrates Reshetnikov's close links to oral folk poetry and folk lyric songs—connections that he developed in many later works.

Also at this time Reshetnikov first became interested in the coexistence of Russian Orthodox and pagan observances in the Perm province; he discussed aspects of this phenomenon in his article "Sviatki v Permi" (Christmastide in Perm), also published in *Permskie gubernskie vedomosti*. He later reworked this theme in the story "Nikola Znamensky" (1864–1865), published in *Otechestvennye zapiski* (Notes of the Fatherland) in 1867.

After a time provincial life began to pall for the young author, who wished to benefit others through his writings. He began to seek a way to move to St. Petersburg and seized the first available opportunity, taking advantage of a chance acquaintanceship with a St. Petersburg government inspector visiting Perm. Reshetnikov had copied papers for him and earned his approval; the inspector now helped Reshetnikov find a position as a clerk in St. Petersburg, where he moved in the autumn of 1863.

Despite the advice of his highly placed acquaintance that he abandon literature, Reshetnikov felt strongly that

of the clothing and food of the peasants and barge-haulers) only strengthens this supposition.

The reading public quickly seized upon Reshetnikov's novella, which has remained the best-known of his works (Podlipnaia, the name of the village described in the work, has become almost as much of a literary commonplace as Oblomovka, the setting of Ivan Aleksandrovich Goncharov's 1859 novel, *Oblomov*). While the lives of peasants and barge-haulers had been described frequently in previous works, the concentration of endless misery and cruelty that marks the story, along with the surprising feeling of authenticity in the descriptions of Reshetnikov's main characters, Pila and Sysoiko, combined to make Reshetnikov seem almost the first discoverer of this theme. In the comments he supplied to the separate edition of the work that appeared in 1868, Reshetnikov wrote:

> The inhabitants of the cities spread along navigable rivers often come across ship workers, but few know of the everyday life of the barge-haulers, who spend almost their entire lives floating wooden barges down the Chusovaia, Kama, and Volga rivers. Therefore the author of the sketch *Podlipovtsy* with all truthfulness and clarity and without embellishment has presented to the reader the life of these poor, *beaten down and wild to the eye* [the italicized words were excised by the censor] people of Northeastern European Russia. In the first section we see pictures of the regions where Pila and Sysoiko live, their mores and customs, their simplicity, and their family life, having taken shape in their distinctive form, and, finally, the sole possibility of escaping from such a destructive life, the desire to become a barge-hauler and the striving for that. In the second part we see pictures of barge-hauling life in all its stark reality.

Immediately after the initial publication of *Podlipovtsy*, this depiction of life "in all its stark reality" resulted in polemics from the critics. Dmitrii Vasil'evich Averkiev asserted himself as an opponent of the story in an article in Fyodor Dostoevsky's journal *Epokha* (Epoch). Averkiev claimed that Reshetnikov's work was marked by unnecessary sentimentality, that it slandered "the people," who were portrayed as savages, and furthermore that the author demonstrated a lack of knowledge of peasant life and falsified its language. Dmitrii Ivanovich Pisarev countered this argument in the journal *Russkoe slovo* (The Russian Word), writing, "As for Mr. Reshetnikov, one can criticize him for a certain dryness in his manner of exposition, but certainly not for a lack of knowledge of that life. Anyone who has read even one of his stories must be convinced that Mr. Reshetnikov describes only those phenomena that he himself has seen very closely, studied carefully, or even experienced himself."

Pisarev's words came closer to the truth. As for Reshetnikov's supposed falsification of language, Averkiev's words become more understandable when one takes

*Reshetnikov's grave in the Volkov Cemetery, St. Petersburg
(photograph by Judith E. Kalb)*

his calling lay precisely there and not in bureaucratic work. On the other hand, until nearly the end of his life he saw himself as a retired clerk, and he sought at first to become a chronicler of the everyday life of bureaucratic circles. But he was most successful in descriptions of what he had known since childhood, drawing on his knowledge of the life of the Perm peasants and the barge-haulers' artel.

Reshetnikov's novella *Podlipovtsy* appeared in the third and fourth issues of Nikolai Alekseevich Nekrasov's journal *Sovremennik* (The Contemporary) in 1864, with the subtitle *Etnograficheskii ocherk* (An Ethnographic Sketch). According to those who knew Reshetnikov, he had already written a rough draft of the manuscript when he moved to St. Petersburg. Because no copy of this original draft has survived, it is impossible to judge the extent to which the author reworked his material, but it seems likely that the revisions were not extensive. Everything in the tale would have been known to Reshetnikov in Perm, and the factual basis of the text (which includes precise references to the layout of the village of Podlipnaia, the price of bread, and particulars of flour supplies for the peasants, as well as detailed descriptions

into account the fact that Reshetnikov was one of the first Russian writers to depict quite precisely the peculiarities of dialectical speech, and not only lexical peculiarities but also phonetic and syntactical ones. For one unfamiliar with dialectical speech, this tendency looked almost like a deliberate attempt to destroy the Russian language.

One of the central motifs of the story is that of the peregrinations of enormous masses of people. Following the reforms of 1861, peasants were permitted to move in search of better work. This theme links the story with Reshetnikov's later works.

After the appearance of *Podlipovtsy,* Reshetnikov wrote a great deal. Among the works published between 1864 and 1865 were *Stavlennik* (The Protégé), a novella about seminary life published in *Sovremennik* in 1864; the short story "Maksia" (Maksia), published in *Sovremennik* in 1864; and the autobiographical novella *Mezhdu liud'mi.* This last work was intended for *Sovremennik* but was rejected by the editors because of its "weak" composition. *Mezhdu liud'mi* was published instead in segments in *Russkoe slovo:* "Vospominaniia detstva" (Recollections of Childhood) and "Mezhdu liud'mi (Iz vospominanii proshlogo)" (Among the People [Recollections of the Past]) appeared in 1864 and 1865. *Russkoe slovo* rejected the third part, "Pokhozhdeniia bednogo provintsiala v stolitse" (Adventures of a Poor Provincial in the Capital), which appeared in *Sovremennik* in 1865. *Mezhdu liud'mi* was published in full for the first time in Reshetnikov's two-volume collected works that came out in 1869.

In January of 1865 Reshetnikov married Serafima Semenovna Kargopolova, who had graduated from the obstetrics institute in St. Petersburg. She later became the prototype for one of the characters in Reshetnikov's final novel, *Svoi khleb* (One's Own Bread, 1870). The same year Reshetnikov wrote the novel *Gornorabochie* (The Miners), the first part of which was published in *Sovremennik* at the beginning of 1866. After *Sovremennik* was closed later that spring by the government, however, the rest of the novel remained unpublished.

In order to compose *Gornorabochie* and later novels, Reshetnikov undertook a trip to the Urals, where, intent on becoming better acquainted with the lives of the workers there, he lived with them and even worked in a local factory. He wrote to his acquaintance Nikolai Aleksandrovich Blagoveshchensky about the experience: "I was at four factories in the Perm province; I worked in Motovilikha at a foundry, and I almost got bruised by a winch. I could work only at night, in peasant clothing. I told them I was a seminarian, ready to join the recruits."

The extraordinarily difficult working conditions and lives of the workers of the Urals (familiar to Reshetnikov since his youth) were portrayed through the experiences of several of Reshetnikov's characters in *Gornorabochie:* the laborer Gavrila Tokmentsov, who returns from work

every day utterly exhausted and beaten down; his elder son, Pavel, who is flogged to death; his wife, who is beaten savagely for her attempt to defend her son; and his daughter, who is raped by the policeman Artamonov. Portraying this horrific world of violence and cruelty, Reshetnikov does not propose any means of escaping the situation or improving it. In fact, at approximately this time he wrote in his diary (published in his 1936–1948 collected works): "Now I understand very well that those who fight for freedom are either wealthy people or those who enjoy the respect of those who oppress humanity. People don't have true freedom. They will always be subjugated to others, and will be dependent on the rich. A poor person with paltry knowledge can't even think about freedom. Take me, the retired clerk, as an example."

Reshetnikov's next novel, *Glumovy* (The Glumovs), published in the journal *Delo* (The Cause) in 1866 and 1867, similarly provides no escape from the hardships it portrays. The novel describes the doomed members of the Glumov family, nearly driven to the grave by the harsh living conditions they face. In this novel, however, there is a new tendency: the author pays particular attention to the central female character of the novel, Praskov'ia Ignat'evna. Through his portrayal of her fate, Reshetnikov demonstrates the difficult circumstances faced by Russian women of the working class. She loses her father early, endures the insanity of her mother, and experiences an unhappy marriage, a stillborn child, constant need, and hard labor at the factory and in the employ of others. All this hardship is followed by illness and an early death. Reshetnikov writes, "The fate of the simple Russian working woman is to labor hard. Her entire life, until old age, so long as she is not replaced by a good helper, consists of work."

The next year, in 1868, Reshetnikov's new novel *Gde luchshe?* (Where Better?), considered by many critics his best, appeared in the journal *Otechestvennye zapiski.* The title of the novel clearly calls to mind Nekrasov's poem *Komu na Rusi zhit' khorosho?* (Who Lives Happily in Russia?, written between 1863 and 1878), the "Prologue" of which had already appeared in print in *Sovremennik.* Reshetnikov's novel continued the theme, familiar from his earlier work, of the migration of people in search of a better fate. This time Reshetnikov's heroes are workers in salt mines and gold mines, railroad construction workers, and St. Petersburg laborers. One of the central characters of the novel, as in the previous one, is a working woman, Pelageia Prokhorovna Mokronosova. Saltykov described this character as "representative of lovely Russian womanhood." Pelageia has the best human characteristics: humanity, love toward those close to her, industry, energy and commitment to achieving her goals, honesty, and responsiveness. Yet, these qualities are ultimately insufficient: her fate turns out to be an unhappy one, as after long trials, difficult physical labor, and insulting relationships, she ends up dying young. A similar fate awaits other characters in the novel as they attempt to respond to the title question, which nonetheless remains unanswered.

Lidiia Mikhailovna Lotman has compared this novel with Leo Tolstoy's *Voina i mir* (War and Peace, 1863–1869): "Despite the difference in the two writers' artistic talents, one can note basic traits they have in common. They have both created large epic novels, in which people's lives are portrayed through a historical prism. The central image in Reshetnikov's *Gde luchshe?* and in Tolstoy's *Voina i mir* is the movement of huge masses of people through space, giving the impression of an explosion in the historical activity of humankind."

Reshetnikov's last novel, *Svoi khleb,* published in *Otechestvennye zapiski* in 1870, was dedicated in full to the situation of Russian women. In many ways the novel echoes Nikolai Gavrilovich Chernyshevsky's novel *Chto delat'?* (What Is to Be Done?, 1863). In *Svoi khleb* Reshetnikov also turned to a portrayal of the bureaucratic milieu, a subject that came less easily to him, as various critics have suggested. However, the author's desire to present a new type of Russian woman as his heroine did not go unnoticed by the critics. M. K. Tsebrikova wrote in 1872, "Reshetnikov is hardly the first and certainly will not be the last of our writers to think up this type of heroine, who has been taught–not by a book and not by someone else's words, but by life itself–to break all ties to a life of idleness and plunge instead into a life of labor and deprivations, in order to secure her independence."

One can speak about just such a "life of labor and deprivation" in relation to Reshetnikov himself. Despite his artistic productivity, Reshetnikov found it difficult by the end of his life to feed himself and his family. He also tended to give what little he had to those who needed it more. The difficult conditions of his life, added to hereditary alcoholism that had begun manifesting itself in the writer's youth, affected his health, and Reshetnikov died of emphysema on 9 March 1871 at age twenty-nine. He never finished his next novel, "Chuzhoi khleb" (Another's Bread), which had been intended as a continuation of *Svoi khleb.*

Bibliography:

I. I. Veksler, "Izbrannaia bibliografiia F. M. Reshetnikova," in *Polnoe sobranie sochinenii,* volume 6 (1936), pp. 403–421.

References:

Dmitrii Vasil'evich Averkiev, "Po povodu samopriznanii dvukh peterburzhtsev," *Epokha,* book 11 (1864): 3–5;

A. G. Bednov, *Tvorchestvo Fedora Mikhailovicha Reshetnikova* (Arkhangelsk, 1956);

E. A. Bogoliubov, "Novoe o Reshetnikove," *Prikam'e,* no. 2 (1941);

K. Filippova, *Mezhdu liud'mi: Povest' o pisatele F. M. Reshetnikove* (Sverdlovsk, 1952);

A. L. Kavurov, "Razvitie zhanra ocherka v tvorchestve F. M. Reshetnikova," in *Problemy razvitiia zhanrov v russkoi literature XVII–XIX vv.,* edited by N. N. Bulgakov and others (Dnepropetrovsk: Dnepropetrovskii gos. universitet, 1985);

Lidiia Mikhailovna Lotman, *Realizm russkoi literatury 60-kh godov XIX v.* (Leningrad: Nauka, 1974);

Lotman, "Reshetnikov," in *Istoriia russkoi literatury v 10 t.,* edited by M. P. Alekseev and N. F. Bel'chikov, volume 8, chapter 1 (Moscow-Leningrad, 1956), pp. 597–616;

I. A. Manuilova, *Krest'ianstvo v proizvedeniiakh F. M. Reshetnikova (peterburgskogo perioda)* (Chardzhou: Uchenye zapiski Chardzhouskogo ped. instituta, 1959);

Manuilova, *Osobennosti stilia F. M. Reshetnikova* (Chardzhou, 1961);

Dmitrii Ivanovich Pisarev, "Progulka po sadam rossiiskoi slovesnosti," *Russkoe slovo,* 3 (1865);

Mikhail Evgrafovich Saltykov (N. Shchedrin), "Naprasnye opaseniia," *Otechestvennye zapiski,* 10 (1868);

V. N. Sazhin, *Knigi gor'koi pravdy: N. G. Pomialovsky "Ocherki bursy," F. M. Reshetnikov "Podlipovtsy," V. V. Sleptsov "Trudnoe vremia"* (Moscow: Kniga, 1989);

L. S. Sheptaev, "Tvorchestvo F. M. Reshetnikova," in *Proza pisatelei-demokratov shestidesiatykh godov XIX veka,* edited by I. G. Vasil'ev, Z. A. Vorob'eva, and others (Moscow: Vysshaia shkola, 1962);

A. M. Skabichevsky, "Zhivaia struia," *Otechestvennye zapiski,* 4 (1868): 166–170;

M. P. Tseboeva, "Literaturnaia bor'ba vokrug tvorchestva F.M. Reshetnikova v 60-e–70-e gody XIX v.," *Uchenye zapiski Kishinevskogo gosudarstvennogo universiteta: Filologiia,* volume 22 (Kishinev, 1956), pp. 35–46;

M. K. Tsebrikova, "Letopis' temnogo liuda: (Romany, povesti i rasskazy F. Reshetnikova)," in her *Russkie obshchestvennye voprosy: Sbornik "Nedeli"* (St. Petersburg: P. A. Gaideburov & E. I. Konradi, 1872), pp. 75–152.

Papers:

Fedor Mikhailovich Reshetnikov's archive is found in the Russian National Library in St. Petersburg and at the Institute of Russian Literature (Pushkin House) in St. Petersburg.

Mikhail Evgrafovich Saltykov
(N. Shchedrin; also known as Saltykov-Shchedrin)
(15 January 1826 – 28 April 1889)

Susan E. Kay

WORKS: *Gubernskie ocherki. Iz zapisok otstavnogo sovetnika N. Shchedrina. Sobral i izdal M. E. Saltykov,* in *Russkii vestnik,* nos. 4–6 (1856); nos. 1, 6–8 (1857); (Moscow: M. Katkov, 1857);

Satiry v proze, in *Sovremennik* (1860–1862); (St. Petersburg: K. Vul'f, 1863);

Nevinnye rasskazy, in *Russkii vestnik* (1857); *Biblioteka dlia chteniia* (1858); *Atenei* (1858); *Moskovskii vestnik* (1859); *Sovremennik* (1859–1863); (St. Petersburg: O. I. Bakst, 1863);

Pompadury i pompadurshi. Izdal M. E. Saltykov (Shchedrin), in *Sovremennik* (1863–1864); *Otechestvennye zapiski* (1868–1871, 1873); (St. Petersburg: V. V. Prats, 1873); translated by David Magarshack as *The Pompadours: A Satire on the Art of Government* (Ann Arbor, Mich.: Ardis, 1985);

Priznaki vremeni, in *Sovremennik* (1866); *Otechestvennye zapiski,* nos. 8, 11 (1868); no. 1 (1869); *Pis'ma o provintsii,* in *Otechestvennye zapiski,* nos. 2, 4–5, 9–10 (1868); nos. 3, 8, 11 (1869); nos. 3, 4, 9 (1870); republished together as *Priznaki vremeni i Pis'ma o provintsii* (St. Petersburg: V. V. Prats, 1869);

Istoriia odnogo goroda, in *Otechestvennye zapiski,* no. 1 (1869); nos. 1–4, 9 (1870); (St. Petersburg: A. A. Kraevsky, 1870); translated by I. P. Foote as *The History of a Town* (Oxford: Meeuws, 1980);

Gospoda tashkenttsy. Kartina nravov. Izdal M. E. Saltykov (Shchedrin), in *Otechestvennye zapiski,* nos. 10–11 (1869); nos. 9, 11 (1871); nos. 1, 9 (1872); (St. Petersburg: V. V. Prats, 1873);

Sbornik. Rasskazy, ocherki, skazki, in *Sovremennik* and *Otechestvennye zapiski* (1869–1879); (St. Petersburg: A. A. Kraevsky, 1881);

Dnevnik provintsiala v Peterburge, in *Otechestvennye zapiski,* nos. 1–6, 8, 10–12 (1872); (St. Petersburg: V. V. Prats, 1873);

Blagonamerennye rechi, in *Otechestvennye zapiski* (1872–1876); 2 volumes (St. Petersburg: A. A. Kraevsky, 1876);

Mikhail Evgrafovich Saltykov (N. Shchedrin)

Nedokonchennye besedy, in *Otechestvennye zapiski,* no. 11 (1873); no. 11 (1874); nos. 1–9 (1875); and (1882–1884); (St. Petersburg: M. M. Stasiulevich, 1884);

V srede umerennosti i akkuratnosti, in *Otechestvennye zapiski,* nos. 9–11 (1874); 9–11 (1876); nos. 8–11 (1877); (St. Petersburg: V. I. Likhachev & A. S. Suvorin, 1878);

Sovremennaia idilliia, in *Otechestvennye zapiski,* nos. 2–4 (1877); nos. 3–4 (1878); nos. 9–10, 12 (1882); nos.

269

1, 5 (1883); (St. Petersburg: Izd. N. P. Karbasnikova, 1883);

Skazki i rasskazy (St. Petersburg: V. V. Obolensky, 1878);

Ubezhishche Monrepo, in *Otechestvennye zapiski,* no. 8 (1878); nos. 2, 8, 9, 11 (1879); (St. Petersburg: A. S. Suvorin, 1880);

Kruglyi god, in *Otechestvennye zapiski,* nos. 2–3, 8–12 (1879); (St. Petersburg: A. S. Suvorin, 1880);

Gospoda Golovlevy (St. Petersburg: A. S. Suvorin, 1880); translated by Athelstan Ridgway as *The Gollovlev Family* (London: Jarrold, 1916); translated by Avrahm Yarmolinsky as *A Family of Noblemen* (New York: Boni & Liveright, 1917);

Za rubezhom, in *Otechestvennye zapiski,* nos. 9–10 (1880); nos. 1, 2, 5–6 (1881); (St. Petersburg: A. A. Kraevsky, 1881);

Chuzhuiu bedu rukami razvedu, first published as "Chuzhoi tolk," in *Otechestvennye zapiski,* no. 12 (1880); unexpurgated version published as *Chuzhuiu bedu rukami razvedu* (Geneva: M. Elpidin, 1880);

Pis'ma k teten'ke, in *Otechestvennye zapiski,* nos. 7–8, 11–12 (1881); nos. 1–5 (1882); (St. Petersburg: A. A. Kraevsky, 1882);

Poshekhonskie rasskazy, in *Otechestvennye zapiski,* nos. 8–12 (1883); (St. Petersburg: M. M. Stasiulevich, 1885);

Pestrye pis'ma, in *Vestnik Evropy,* nos. 11–12 (1884); nos. 1, 4, 6 (1885); nos. 9–10 (1886); (St. Petersburg: M. M. Stasiulevich, 1886);

23 skazki (St. Petersburg: M. M. Stasiulevich, 1886);

Melochi zhizni, in *Vestnik Evropy,* nos. 11–12 (1886); nos. 1–4 (1887); (St. Petersburg: M. M. Stasiulevich, 1887);

Poshekhonskaia starina (St. Petersburg: M. M. Stasiulevich, 1890);

Novye skazki dlia izriadnogo vozrasta (Geneva: M. Elpidin, 1893).

Collections: *Sochineniia,* 9 volumes (St. Petersburg: M. M. Stasiulevich, 1889–1890);

Polnoe sobranie sochinenii, 12 volumes, fifth edition (St. Petersburg: A. F. Marks, 1905–1906);

Sobranie sochinenii, 6 volumes, edited by K. Khalabaev and Boris Eikhenbaum, with a biographical sketch and commentary by Ivanov-Razumnik (Moscow-Leningrad: GIZ, 1926–1928);

Polnoe sobranie sochinenii, 20 volumes (Moscow-Leningrad: GIKhL, 1933–1941);

Sobranie sochinenii, 20 volumes in 24 (Moscow: Khudozhestvennaia literatura, 1965–1976);

Selected Satirical Writings, edited, with an introduction and notes in English, by I. P. Foote (Oxford: Clarendon Press, 1977).

Editions in English: "Konyaga," "A Visit to a Russian Prison," and "The Governor," in *The Village Priest*

and Other Stories from the Russian of Militsina and Saltikov, translated by Beatrix L. Tollemache, with an introduction by C. Hagberg Wright (London: Unwin, 1918);

Fables, translated by Vera Volkhovsky (London: Chatto & Windus, 1931);

How a Muzhik Fed Two Officials, translated by Volkhovsky (London: Chatto & Windus, n.d.);

Tales from M. Saltykov-Shchedrin, translated by D. Rottenberg, edited by J. Gibbons (Moscow: Foreign Language Publishing House, 1956);

The History of a Town; or, The Chronicle of Foolov, translated and edited by Susan Brownsberger (Ann Arbor, Mich.: Ardis, 1982);

The Golovlevs, translated by I. P. Foote (Oxford & New York: Oxford University Press, 1986).

SELECTED PERIODICAL PUBLICATIONS:
"Dlia detei III. Godovshchina," *Otechestvennye zapiski,* nos. 2–3 (1869);

"Dlia detei V. Dobraia dusha," *Otechestvennye zapiski,* nos. 2–3 (1869);

"Dlia detei VI. Isporchennye deti," *Otechestvennye zapiski,* no. 9 (1869): 273–310;

"V bol'nitse dlia umalishennykh," *Otechestvennye zapiski,* nos. 2, 4 (1873);

"Son v letniuiu noch'," *Otechestvennye zapiski,* no. 8 (1875);

Kul'turnye liudi, parts 1–4, *Otechestvennye zapiski,* no. 1 (1876): 119–158;

"Deti Moskvy," *Otechestvennye zapiski,* no. 1 (1877);

"Bol'noe mesto," *Otechestvennye zapiski,* no. 1 (1879).

In May 1881 Ivan Sergeevich Turgenev professed the opinion to Sergei Nikolaevich Krivenko that the mantle of responsibility for Russian literature had fallen to the writer Mikhail Evgrafovich Saltykov. The following year Turgenev wrote to Saltykov: "You are Saltykov-Shchedrin, a writer who is destined to leave a great mark on our literature." Turgenev was not alone in his admiration for Saltykov, whom contemporaries often compared favorably with Leo Tolstoy and Fyodor Dostoevsky. His reputation and readership, however, have not stood the test of time well. He was revered and often quoted in Soviet times—Lenin was a particular devotee—but this attention resulted more because of his trenchant criticism of life under the czars than because of his literary talent. Of the twenty volumes of Saltykov's writing, only *Gospoda Golovlevy* (The Golovlev Family, 1880), *Istoriia odnogo goroda* (The History of a Town, 1870), and the *skazki* (fairy tales) retain any real popularity among Russian readers, and only these works and a few other shorter ones are available in translation for non-Russian-speaking readers.

In a review written in English for *The Academy* about *Istoriia odnogo goroda* in March 1871, Turgenev described Saltykov as "the Russian [Jonathan] Swift." Saltykov was not particularly impressed with the comparison, and his dismissive response was, "I reread Swift recently . . . he is difficult to read without commentaries, so did not make a particularly strong impression on me." Saltykov is no less difficult than Swift to understand without the assistance of a commentary. In 1882 Saltykov conceded that contemporary readers read his work "guessing at its sense and target" and that their children and grandchildren "would not be able to take a step without commentaries." First and foremost, Saltykov was a chronicler and fierce critic of his own time. He used the weapon of satire to attack what he described as the *zloba dnia* (the evil of the day). In Saltykov's view, many of these evils were occasioned by the way in which society was controlled. Overt dissent against the czarist autocracy in nineteenth-century Russia was not permitted, however, and the exigencies of censorship meant that this criticism had to be oblique. From these conditions resulted Saltykov's particular brand of "coded satire," as it was described in *The Times Literary Supplement* of August 1966, in one of the few articles written about Saltykov in English. To appreciate the full meaning of a Saltykov work requires not only a knowledge of the period but also an understanding of his code. Thus, many readers are deterred. This difficulty results in great loss in two respects. Perhaps better than any of his contemporaries, Saltykov illumines the mores and attitudes of his time. This quality gives his works particular significance as historical documents. Of at least equal importance is the sophistication of Saltykov's satirical literary style; Turgenev said of Saltykov, "as a satirist he has no equal."

Saltykov's best-known work, *Gospoda Golovlevy,* is generally accepted as a novel. However, Saltykov was not a novelist in the same sense as Turgenev, Tolstoy, or Dostoevsky. Saltykov's novels either developed almost by accident, as does *Gospoda Golovlevy,* or were his own idiosyncratic version of the novel form, which he defended thus: "I consider my *Sovremennaia idilliia, Golovlevy, Dnevnik provintsiala,* and others as true novels; although they are apparently made up of separate stories, whole periods of our life emerge." In setting forward his blueprint for a new Russian novel, Saltykov saw himself as following in the tradition of Nikolai Vasil'evich Gogol, "who long since predicted that the novel must step outside the family." Refuting the description of *Sovremennaia idilliia* (Contemporary Idyll, 1883) as a *sbornik* (collection) rather than a novel, Saltykov compared it to Gogol's *Mertvye dushi* (Dead Souls, 1842), Charles Dickens's *Pickwick Papers* (1837), and Miguel de Cervantes's *Don Quixote* (1605, 1615). In

truth, many of Saltykov's works hover on the boundary between *sbornik* and picaresque novel. The most usual form taken by his works has been defined best by the Russian Saltykov scholar A. S. Bushmin, who called it the *problemnyi tsikl* (problem cycle), a form that blends journalism and creative prose. Saltykov wrote as a journalist before he became a creative writer; the metamorphosis was gradual and never complete. He saw the potential of creative literature for putting across his radical beliefs: "of particular importance is the influence of that branch of literature which is called belles-lettres, because that branch is the most comprehensible to the majority." Creative literature had greater appeal than straightforward polemic; disguising the message was also easier in creative literature, and thus the writer could evade the censor's ban. The "problem cycle" is a series of essays on related topics; their relationship is often indicated in the title. The subjects Saltykov chose were material for articles, but his method and strongly creative style raise these series to literature. The cycles were published one episode at a time in a periodical, generally over a period of at least two years, and Saltykov was often engaged on several cycles simultaneously. He then revised the episodes, and they were published together in book form. Each of his works combines the elements of creative literature and tendentious journalism in differing proportions. They also differ in the extent to which the finished cycle has a continuous narrative thread and may thus be considered a novel. The evidence indicates that Saltykov's works grew spontaneously as he wrote them. There is nothing resembling a plan preserved among Saltykov's manuscripts. Occasionally there is a penciled note in the margin—an idea to be incorporated in the episode in progress, but nothing more premeditated.

Mikhail Evgrafovich Saltykov was born on 15 January 1826 in the village of Spas-Ugol in the Tver' province. At the age of ten he entered the Moscow Institute for the Nobility and two years later transferred to the lycée at Tsarskoe selo, where he became a member of the circle surrounding a much older pupil, the socialist Mikhail Vasil'evich Petrashevsky. At the lycée Saltykov also began to write verse, the first published example of which was "Lira" (Lyre) in *Biblioteka dlia chteniia* (Library for Reading, 1841), and reviews for the journals *Otechestvennye zapiski* (Notes of the Fatherland) and *Sovremennik* (The Contemporary). After leaving the lycée, Saltykov joined the civil service in St. Petersburg, where he maintained his association with Petrashevsky and also continued writing, although after the lycée he no longer wrote any poetry. In response to the publication of his story "Zaputannoe delo" (Muddled Business, first published in *Otechestvennye zapiski,* 1848; revised and published in *Nevinnye rasskazy* [Innocent

Saltykov pouring forth his characters on a cover for a special 1880
supplement to Strekoza *(Dragonfly)*

Tales, 1863]), Saltykov was exiled from the capital to
serve in the provincial town of Viatka, where he lived
for almost eight years. His father died in 1851 during
the period when Saltykov was in Viatka. Saltykov's
father, Evgraf Vasil'evich Saltykov, was from an old,
noble, but impoverished family. He was a weak character, and when he married, he left the running of the
family affairs to his wife, Ol'ga Mikhailovna. She was
the daughter of a merchant and, after her marriage,
devoted herself to the enlargement of the Saltykov
estate. By the mid 1850s she had increased the family
fortunes to the ownership of three thousand serfs. In
1872 the death of Sergei Saltykov, one of Saltykov's
four brothers, plunged the family into a lawsuit over the
question of inheritance. Saltykov had not received any
income from the family estates for ten years and, seemingly, was also going to be deprived of his share of the
inheritance. He was also in debt to his mother, who had
lent him the money to buy a small estate of his own,
which brought no income. Although his mother's role
in the attempt to defraud him was obvious, Saltykov
laid the blame at the door of his eldest brother, Dmitrii.
His mother and his brother Dmitrii provided Saltykov
with the inspiration for his most powerful characters—
Iudushka Golovlev and Arina Petrovna Golovleva.

    During his exile in Viatka, Saltykov stopped writ-
ing. However, on his return to St. Petersburg in 1856 he
renewed his literary activity with *Gubernskie ocherki* (Pro-

vincial Sketches, 1857), a work based on his experiences in Viatka and the first he published under his pen
name of N. Shchedrin. In June 1856 he married Elizaveta Apollonovna Boltina in Moscow. For ten of the
next twelve years Saltykov divided his time between
writing and his duties as a provincial civil servant. For
financial reasons he continued this latter work, except
for the short period 1862–1864. His intention had been
to found his own journal, *Russkaia pravda* (Russian
Truth), and in March 1862 he had left the civil service
with that aim. However, the censor refused permission,
and Saltykov accepted the invitation of the editor
Nikolai Alekseevich Nekrasov to join the editorial staff
of the radical journal *Sovremennik,* which had reopened
in December 1862 after being closed for eight months.
He only stayed with *Sovremennik* for two years, during
which time he wrote principally articles, rather than creative literary work. In 1864 he returned to service in
the provinces in Tula, Penza, and Riazan'. He retired
from the civil service in June 1868 to concentrate on his
literary career.

    In January 1868, after protracted negotiations
with the owner, Andrei Aleksandrovich Kraevsky,
Nekrasov took over control of the journal *Otechestvennye
zapiski.* From that time began the journal's renaissance
as the leading radical voice in Russia. After the authorities had closed *Sovremennik* two years previously, Nekrasov was not allowed to publish *Otechestvennye zapiski* in
his own name, and Kraevsky remained as nominal editor, though his only involvement in the journal was
financial. Furthermore, Nekrasov was officially forbidden to employ two of his former collaborators from
Sovremennik, Iulii Galaktionovich Zhukovsky and Maksim Alekseevich Antonovich. But he was joined by two
other writers who had worked on the journal with
him—Grigorii Zakharovich Eliseev and Saltykov.
Saltykov began to contribute to *Otechestvennye zapiski* as
soon as Nekrasov took over, and later that year he was
appointed editor of the creative literature section. After
Nekrasov's death in 1877, Saltykov took overall editorial responsibility and continued his close association
with the journal until its final closure by the authorities
in 1884. The years 1868 to 1884 were the most productive period of Saltykov's literary career. The journal
gave him an almost constant vehicle for his work.

    During his first years with *Otechestvennye zapiski,*
1868–1870, Saltykov both started and completed *Pis'ma
o provintsii* (Letters about the Provinces, 1869), *Istoriia
odnogo goroda,* and his cycle of children's stories, *Dlia
detei* (For Children, first published in *Otechestvennye
zapiski,* 1869); he continued work on two cycles begun
in *Sovremennik—Pompadury i pompadurshi* (Pompadours and
their Consorts, 1863–1873) and *Priznaki vremeni* (Signs
of the Times, 1866–1869)—and wrote the first episode

of *Gospoda tashkenttsy* (The Gentlemen from Tashkent, 1869–1873). *Pis'ma o provintsii* and *Priznaki vremeni* are both examples of his "problem cycle" form. In *Pis'ma o provintsii,* Saltykov used a quasi-epistolary form to discuss events in provincial life in what was, for him, a fairly intimate, gentle tone. *Priznaki vremeni* is a much more sharply satirical anthology of essays on contemporary phenomena, with a suitably flexible title that allowed Saltykov to include any subject that caught his attention. The collection *Dlia detei* comprised, according to Saltykov's preface, the first contributions to a children's reader, which consisted of prose stories by himself and verse by Nekrasov. The claim that this work was intended as children's literature was somewhat disingenuous, described as a "malicious joke" in one contemporary review. Whether or not Saltykov ever had a sincere intention to produce a children's anthology, the project did not progress beyond six stories. These six included three of only six *skazki* Saltykov ever published in *Otechestvennye zapiski,* since the majority were written after its closure: "Povest' o tom, kak odin muzhik dvukh generalov prokormil" (The Story of How One Peasant Fed Two Generals), "Propala sovest'" (Loss of Conscience), and "Dikii pomeshchik" (The Wild Landowner). One further work, "Igrushechnogo dela liudishki" (Little People of the Toy Business), written in 1880, though later included in Saltykov's collection of *skazki,* is not a true example of the genre but the first and only sketch in a series he planned on *liudi-kukly* (doll-people). Saltykov's *skazki* have retained the popularity that his more topical works soon lost. Their message is much simpler. Even when first written, they were aimed, if not at children, certainly at a less sophisticated audience than the rest of his work. In a letter of condolence to Saltykov's widow, Tiflis workmen, writing of Saltykov's influence, made special reference to the *skazki,* "which we love and understand better than his other stories." In his *skazki* Saltykov observes the established conventions of that genre, using the set phrases, proverbs, and archaic vocabulary associated with folk literature. "Propala sovest'," in which conscience appears in tangible form, is reminiscent of the seventeenth-century poem *Povest' o Gore i Zlochastii* (The Tale of Woe and Misfortune). In "Dikii pomeshchik" the landowner despises his serfs. But when deprived of them, he becomes wild; hair grows all over his body; and he takes to living in the forest. "Povest' o tom, kak odin muzhik dvukh generalov prokormil" represents a microcosm of Russian society. Two generals and a peasant find themselves stranded on an uninhabited island, but their behavior is still totally governed by their class relationship. Both *skazki* point to the same moral. The dependency of the upper classes on the lower in no way inhibits them from feeling superior.

In the preface to *Istoriia odnogo goroda* Saltykov, posing as editor rather than author, describes the work as a *letopis'* (chronicle). But, insofar as the work follows the chronicle form, the intention is to parody it rather than to simulate it, and Saltykov abandons the pretense when it becomes irksome. As Saltykov himself wrote, in particular reference to *Istoriia odnogo goroda:* "I have never restricted myself with form, and use it only to the extent which I find necessary." In fact, in its structure, *Istoriia odnogo goroda* has many affinities with satires such as Swift's *Gulliver's Travels* (1726) or Gogol's *Mertvye dushi.* In those works the heroes' travels and various encounters give rise to the different episodes. In *Istoriia odnogo goroda* the encounters between the inhabitants of the town of Glupov (from *glupyi,* stupid) and their successive governors initiate the action. The work exists on three levels of meaning: the narrative chronicle of the town of Glupov, a satirical account of Russian history, and a satire on contemporary political structure and the relationship between the governing and the governed.

Many contemporary critics took the historical framework of the work at face value, found an historical prototype for each character, and labeled it "historical satire." Saltykov dismissed this interpretation: "Paramosha is by no means only Magnitsky, but also Count D. A. Tolstoy, and even not Count D. A. Tolstoy but all the people of a certain party in general." He added that *Istoriia* was "not historical but completely ordinary satire . . . aimed at those characteristic features of Russian life which make it not completely comfortable." If history was not Saltykov's target, it most certainly was his inspiration. The similarity between events in Glupov and actual Russian history of the chronicled period (1731–1825) becomes ever more evident as the work progresses. There are close similarities between Count Aleksei Andreevich Arakcheev and Ugrium-Burcheev, whose lunatic plans for Glupov are an exaggerated version of Arakcheev's military colonies; between the czar's adviser Mikhail Mikhailovich Speransky and the reformer Benevolensky; between Czar Paul and Negodaev; and between Czar Alexander I and Grustilov.

Saltykov's characters were, in the view of contemporary critics, caricatures of the originals, a technique that he sometimes used to excess. Konstantin Konstantinovich Arsen'ev wrote of *Istoriia* in *Vestnik Evropy* (European Herald): "Colors are laid on too thickly, irony becomes cartoon, events and characters depicted in the form of caricatures sometimes become almost unrecognizable." However, none of Saltykov's caricatures are without some foundation in reality. In one of the most fantastic, the governor's head is replaced with a musical instrument capable of playing only two refrains: *razoriu* (I'll destroy) and *ne poterpliu* (I won't put up with it). The idea that a czarist official entertained only those two thoughts when dealing with his subordinates is not so incredible. Other town governors are no less bizarre. They include Pryshch, whose head is eaten when discovered to be made from pâté; Klementii, the former Italian cook who was noted for his flying activities and who would have flown away had he not caught his coattails on the town spire; and the immensely tall Baklan, "direct descendent of Ivan the Great (the well-known bell-tower in Moscow), who died during a storm which snapped him in half."

This grotesque procession of characters and their bizarre antics is indeed entertaining, but those of Saltykov's contemporaries who continued in the 1870s to refer to Saltykov's "innocent humor," echoing a description first applied by Dmitrii Ivanovich Pisarev in *Russkoe slovo* (The Russian Word) in 1864, missed the point. In other works Saltykov sought to discredit czarist authority by polemic. In *Istoriia odnogo goroda* he employs humor, ridicule, and the grotesque to the same end. The office of town governor, and, by extension, czarist officialdom as a whole, is discredited by the semihuman misfits who aspire to it in Glupov. Their whole "chronicle" is recounted without any overt criticism by an apparently naive chronicler, who employs the style of hagiography and epic folktale, as well as the chronicle, to recount their exploits, but to read between the lines is not difficult.

In *Istoriia odnogo goroda* Saltykov displays literary skill that goes beyond a talent for humor and fantasy. One of the most outstanding passages in the book is the fire scene in "Solomennyi gorod" (Town of Straw). This description not only captures the color, smell, and texture of the fire in evocative and realistic detail, but it also conveys the mood of panic among the townsfolk and the aftermath of despair. The humorous tone is also abandoned in the denouement of *Istoriia odnogo goroda* for one of sinister menace. As a result of the lunatic Arakcheevian regime of Ugrium-Burcheev, the usually submissive Glupovians "suddenly grew ashamed." Resentment against him grows, and finally his order for the appointment of spies drives the Glupovians to what? To revolt? The reader can only conjecture, for here the manuscript, so the reader is told, breaks off. Only one fragment remains, concerning the arrival of "it" a week later. The two main theories advanced by scholars on the identity of "it" are reaction and, conversely, revolution. The more plausible is the former, given the fear displayed by the Glupovians as "it" arrives and the governor's calm pronouncement, "it is coming," which seems to fit with his prophesy: "One comes after me more terrible than I." If a parallel is drawn between Glupovian history and Russian history, the sudden resistance of the townsfolk represents the Decembrist revolt in 1825, and the appearance of "it" represents the accession of the conservative Nicholas I.

The enduring popularity of *Istoriia odnogo goroda* almost certainly has resulted from its being a nearly continuous humorous satirical narrative, without the theoretical discussions and digressions that characterize the majority of Saltykov's works. *Pis'ma o provintsii* and *Priznaki vremeni* have not enjoyed such continuing success. However, they were important landmarks in the development of the quintessentially Saltykovian style and, as such, are more typical of the canon of his works. In particular, they played an important role in the development of what Saltykov called his Aesopian, or slave's, language. This language was a coded manner of expression that the censor was prepared to pass, while more overt criticism would have been rejected. It obscured the message and limited the circle of Saltykov's readership. The writer himself recognized this limitation, admitting that the mass of people could derive no benefit from his writing: "The street cannot read between the lines, and for them the slave's language did not and cannot have any educative significance." The slave's language was a kind of shorthand in which a particular psychology or situation was implied by one metaphorical key word that only the regular reader would recognize. Examples of such Saltykovisms that appear in *Pis'ma o provintsii* and *Priznaki vremeni* include *pirog* (pie) or *kusok* (bite)—spoils of office; *stolp* (pillar)—pillar of reactionary society; and *kraeugol'nye kamni* (cornerstones)—family, state, property, and patriotism abused as an excuse for parental despotism, tyranny of officialdom, greed, and exploitation of war. These sociopolitical phenomena identified by Saltykov took on increasing importance in his later works.

Saltykov's work in the intervening years between his two acknowledged masterpieces—*Istoriia odnogo goroda,* completed in 1870, and *Gospoda Golovlevy,* begun in 1875—were in a mold similar to *Pis'ma o provintsii* and *Priznaki vremeni* and brought the writer no lasting fame. These years were, however, a period of intensive and significant literary activity, curtailed only by incapacitating ill health in the early months of 1874. This illness resulted in Saltykov's first journey abroad, which he took on his doctor's advice the following year. Saltykov's strength gave out under the strains, both physical and mental, that he endured in the first years of this decade. In his personal life the births of a son in 1872 and a daughter in the following year were burdens as well as occasions of great joy for the writer. He confided in a letter to a friend, not long after the birth of his son: "I am already approaching the age of fifty and the sentiment of an old man makes me glad at this birth—but the thought that I *must* live to sixty-six to see this young man on his feet simply overwhelms me." Since

1863 Saltykov had been supporting himself and his wife, and now children, by his own earnings. These earnings, especially since he had retired from the civil service and devoted himself completely to writing, were far from considerable, and he was even, on occasion, reduced to borrowing money. Few people were aware of Saltykov's poor circumstances. He was, after all, from a family with both breeding (on his father's side) and wealth (on his mother's). On the birth of his children it became imperative for Saltykov to retrieve the inheritance of which he had been defrauded, and he devoted much energy to this end with little success.

If Saltykov found his personal life troublesome, he certainly could not turn outside it for solace. His children at least were a bright spot in his private life, but in society at large he saw a picture of unrelieved gloom. From Saltykov's point of view, the beginning of the new decade was a period of the profoundest disillusionment. Just when the political and social reforms of the 1860s should have been developing into maturity, they were fading and withering. Dealt several blows by the reactionary mood of a government seeking to emasculate its own progressive measures, Saltykov felt that the reforms had been further betrayed by his own class. Members of the liberal intelligentsia who had campaigned for the emancipation of the serfs, which occurred in 1861, and had so keenly supported the *zemstva* (land councils) were now dissociating themselves from both. Saltykov found this new mood of Russian society both repugnant and dangerous, and he devoted his literary talent to exposing it—lampooning it with satirical wit and demolishing it with argument. One technique he used was to "borrow" characters from the earlier works of other writers and develop them in accordance with the spirit of the times. For example, in their Saltykovian regeneration Turgenev's Rudin and Lavretsky completely abandon their liberal ideals. Some of Saltykov's most vehement attacks of the period were leveled against the weakness of writers who had abandoned their principles. Cowardly liberal publicists are labeled the *penkosnimateli* (skimmers of froth). Their golden rule of writing is "without letting pass a single question of contemporary importance to discuss everything in such a way that nothing can come of it." In the works of these years he also sought to expose the rule of terror that unchallenged repressive measures were bringing about.

In 1873 Saltykov finally finished *Pompadury i pompadurshi*, a cycle begun ten years earlier in *Sovremennik* under the title *Gubernatorskie rasskazy* (Provincial Tales). The pompadours in question are town governors; the *pompadurshi* are their mistresses. Early chapters of the work resemble *Istoriia odnogo goroda* in both subject and technique. In fact, *Istoriia odnogo goroda* grew out of the

first chapters of *Pompadury i pompadurshi* and developed at its expense. Episodes conceived by Saltykov for *Pompadury i pompadurshi* were eventually incorporated in *Istoriia odnogo goroda* and others transplanted to *Istoriia odnogo goroda* after first being published in *Pompadury i pompadurshi*. Later chapters of *Pompadury i pompadurshi* are less humorous and more polemical. "On" (He) and "Pompadury bor'by ili prokazy budushchego" (Battling Pompadours or Future Mischief) deal with the betrayal by the liberals of their ideals. In "Zizhditel'" (The Founder) Saltykov writes of the emasculation of literature resulting from the replacement of preliminary censorship by punitive censorship. Intended as a liberalization of the press when first introduced in 1865, the harsh and arbitrary way in which punitive censorship was implemented in the 1870s meant that Saltykov was frequently torn between his desire as a writer to express his deeply held views and his duty as editor to safeguard *Otechestvennye zapiski* from closure by the censor. Described by Saltykov as *rasskazy* (tales), there is a narrative connection among some of the earlier episodes of *Pompadury i pompadurshi*, but to describe the work as a *gubernatorskii roman* (provincial novel), as Bushmin does, is to deny its episodic, anthology-like character.

Gospoda tashkenttsy, published in *Otechestvennye zapiski* between October 1869 and September 1872, is a series of sketches that culminates in four major character studies. Saltykov's Tashkentians, named in honor of those Russians who had captured Tashkent in 1865 in the name of civilization, are individuals who are prepared to act as the government agents of oppression. When the work was published as a separate edition in 1873, Saltykov subtitled it *Kartina nravov* (A Tableau of Manners) and described it thus in the preface: "It was my intention to write, if not a novel in the proper sense of the word, then at least a complete tableau of manners." In the work itself, Saltykov's rejection of the novel form is more categorical: "I do not intend to write a novel, although the campaign of any one of the Tashkentians could offer much that is confused, complicated and even striking." He does, however, allocate himself the role of "collector of material" for the new Russian novel. The four "parallels" or character studies, subtitled "Tashkenttsy prigotovitel'nogo klassa" (Tashkentians of the Preparatory Class), which are the greater and more striking part of *Gospoda tashkenttsy*, are more than just a "collection of material." Each parallel seems on the point of developing into a fully fledged novel when the author abandons it. Each is a forerunner of *Gospoda Golovlevy*, an embryonic family chronicle in which not only is the central figure drawn with great insight and depth, but also his family and friends, his surroundings and home, and all the influences that

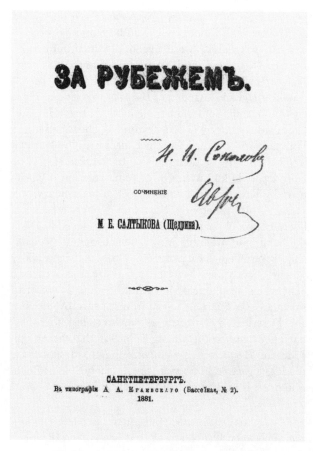

Title page for Za rubezhom *(Abroad), Saltykov's humorous novel about Russian tourists in Western Europe, inscribed by the author to N. I. Sokolov (The Kilgour Collection of Russian Literature, Houghton Library, Harvard University)*

formed his character. A promised sequel to "Tashkenttsy prigotovitel'nogo klassa," to be titled "Tashkenttsy v deistvii" (Tashkentians in action) was never written.

Dnevnik provintsiala v Peterburge (The Diary of a Provincial in St. Petersburg, 1873) relates the encounters and often fantastic adventures of a liberal landowner who, following the emancipation of the serfs, has difficulty finding a role for himself in the countryside. He first devotes his energies to the zemstvo, but, finding its powers limited and its members reactionary, he becomes disillusioned and abandons the provinces for St. Petersburg. Longin Fedorovich Panteleev, a frequent visitor to Saltykov's home during his last years, recalled in his memoirs that Saltykov described *Dnevnik provintsiala v Peterburge* as a novel, alongside his much greater works—*Gospoda Golovlevy* and *Sovremennaia idilliia*. It certainly has the most continuous narrative thread of any work Saltykov had thus far written and even has some cliff-hanger chapter endings. Although he admitted to finding them restrictive, Saltykov even faithfully

observes the limits imposed by the diary form. For once he manages to resist his habit of slipping out of the assumed character of the narrator to preach his own viewpoint to the reader. This restraint benefits the literary integrity of the work, but it caused some confusion over its message. He complained of one critic: "It seems that in reading *Dnevnik* he did not understand the main point: that *Dnevnik* is narrated by a third party whose opinions are an expression of the opinion of the crowd, and in no way mine."

At the end of *Dnevnik provintsiala v Peterburge* Saltykov promises the reader a sequel to the provincial narrator's adventures. In this sequel, *V bol'nitse dlia umalishennykh* (In the Hospital for the Insane, published in *Otechestvennye zapiski,* 1873), which only got as far as an unfinished third chapter, the provincial narrator is committed to a mental home by a police officer. *V bol'nitse dlia umalishennykh* includes some of Saltykov's most forceful condemnations of the dangers and threats of life in a politically repressive atmosphere. Some contemporaries felt he exaggerated the situation. Dostoevsky remarked, "The theme of Shchedrin's satire is that there is a police officer hiding somewhere, listening to his conversations and reporting on him; and, because of this, Mr. Shchedrin finds life unbearable."

Writing in 1869 in *Gospoda tashkenttsy,* Saltykov had dismissed novels devoted to the family circle (*proizvedenie semeistvennosti*) as outmoded. Paradoxically, he himself is best remembered as the author of *Gospoda Golovlevy,* a family chronicle that is certainly a novel, if an imperfectly constructed one, which he wrote between October 1875 and May 1880. The paradox is not quite as great as it might seem. Saltykov did not begin writing *Gospoda Golovlevy* with the intention of producing a novel, family or otherwise. *Gospoda Golovlevy* began as part of another work, and its first four episodes were published in *Otechestvennye zapiski* as part of the "problem cycle" *Blagonamerennye rechi* (Loyal Speeches, 1872–1876). However, by the time Saltykov was engaged on the fifth episode he was aware that the saga of the Golovlevs was developing beyond his original intention. He wrote to Nekrasov: "I regret having included these stories in *Blagonamerennye rechi,* it would have been better to print them under a separate heading 'Episodes from the life of a family.'"

These comments came after a shaky start. Saltykov was initially so dissatisfied with *Gospoda Golovlevy* he did not even want to publish the second episode. However, his contemporaries were of a contrary opinion. On reading the first episode, Turgenev wrote in a letter to Saltykov in October 1875: "It is so good that the thought occurs—why does not Saltykov, instead of writing fragments, write a full-scale novel." Turgenev's words appear prescient. However, there is no evidence that Saltykov was persuaded to Turgenev's point of view. On the contrary, Saltykov's correspondence reveals that each successive episode of *Gospoda Golovlevy* was intended to be the last, until the work finally came to an end with the episode "Raschet" (The Reckoning), titled "Reshenie" (Conclusion) in the original journal version.

Blagonamerennye rechi (1876), the cycle out of which *Gospoda Golovlevy* evolved, is devoted to the abuse of three of the four "cornerstones," as Saltykov calls them, of Russian society: *semeistvennost'* (family), *sobstvennost'* (property), and *gosudarstvennost'* (state). The first episodes of *Gospoda Golovlevy* are among several that explore the abuse of the family. As with all the episodes in *Blagonamerennye rechi,* those that finally were included in *Gospoda Golovlevy*–"Semeinyi sud" (Family Tribunal), "Po rodstvennomu" (Like Good Relatives), "Semeinye itogi" (Family Scores), and "Plemiannushka" (Little Niece)–are complete narratives in themselves and can be understood independently of one another. "Semeinyi sud" deals with the return to his mother's estate of the disgraced son, Stepan Golovlev, and his sentence to a solitary life of poverty in one of the outbuildings; it concludes with Stepan's death. "Po rodstvennomu" concerns events in the Golovlev family ten years later, relating the death of another son, Pavel.

The early sections of *Gospoda Golovlevy* are disjointed compared with other nineteenth-century novels. Events are not presented chronologically. For example, the events of the fifth episode, "Nedozvolennye semeinye radosti" (Illicit Family Pleasures), are contemporaneous with the end of episode 3 and the beginning of episode 4. The family matriarch, Arina Petrovna Golovleva, dies at the beginning of episode 4 and has to be resurrected by the author to take part in the events of episode 5. Contemporary critics, accustomed to the much more consistent form and narrative construction of the late-nineteenth-century Russian novel, felt that such liberties were a weakness of *Gospoda Golovlevy.* According to a February 1890 review in the journal *Nedelia* (The Week), "It is a work without a story, without a plot, without proper construction . . . the most complete of all Saltykov's works suffers from deficiencies of completeness and of form." Episodes of Saltykov's earlier work, *Gospoda tashkenttsy,* were embryonic novels, the potential of which Saltykov deliberately curtailed. The subject of *Gospoda Golovlevy* seems to have taken hold of Saltykov and developed into a novel almost in spite of his declared intentions. Perhaps the strong autobiographical content of the work caused this occurrence. The senior Golovlev generation, Vladimir Mikhailych and his wife, Arina Petrovna, greatly resemble Saltykov's parents. The father, prematurely in his dotage, lives the life of a recluse. The mother is a strong matriarch who has devoted herself to increasing the family estates. Her affectionless and autocratic treatment of her children mirrors Saltykov's childhood experiences. The principal character of the work is the arch-hypocrite Iudushka Golovlev, who devotes his life to ensuring that he becomes the sole inheritor of all the family fortune, even when his aim results in degradation and penury for other family members. Saltykov referred to his brother Dmitrii as "my evil demon" and confided in a letter: "I portrayed him as Iudushka."

Iudushka Golovlev stands out among Saltykov's creations as the most powerful of his psychological portraits. By this period Saltykov had largely moved away from the satirical caricatures of *Istoriia odnogo goroda* and *Pompadury i pompadurshi* to much deeper characterization. Iudushka's prototype can be seen in the pious hypocrite Sofron Khmylov in *Gospoda tashkenttsy*. But if Iudushka was the culmination of a trend that had been developing in Saltykov's writing, the portrait also acquired added force from the writer's personal involvement with his subject. The character of Iudushka does not immediately take center stage in *Gospoda Golovlevy*. The first episode is dominated by Arina Petrovna. However, it does reveal something of his fawning obedience as a child, behavior that induced his mother to show favoritism to him but also "gave rise in her heart to a vague feeling of alarm at something mysterious and evil." The reader also learns how he was given the nickname Iudushka, little Judas, by his brother Stepan. His real name was Porfirii.

At the time of the first episode Iudushka is a civil servant in St. Petersburg, a career that has turned him into a pettifogging windbag. In this first episode, Iudushka takes his first steps toward the acquisition of the entire Golovlev fortune by persuading his mother not to give the prodigal Stepan the small property she had intended, but instead to leave him destitute. Stepan predicts of his brother: "He knows how to worm his way into a person's soul. What's more he'll settle her, the old witch; he'll suck the estate and the capital out of her." And so it proves in the second episode. Iudushka persuades Arina Petrovna to divide up the estate to his advantage and eventually drives her out of her home. Although Iudushka is now dominant within the Golovlev family, he does not dominate the second episode. The main focus is still on family relationships and the family as a context for oppression rather than on the single character of Iudushka.

"Semeinye itogi" was originally intended to be the last episode devoted to the Golovlevs. In this episode, however, the psychological portrait of Iudushka begins to take over from the theme of family life as the focal point of the work. Saltykov became so involved with this new aspect of the work that he continued it for a further four episodes in which Iudushka's character is not only revealed in greater depth but also is seen to develop. In particular, Saltykov explores the character of Iudushka as representative of a peculiarly Russian type of hypocrisy, fostered by his petty activity as a civil servant and his unbridled authority and life of indolence as a landowner: "If he was a hypocrite, then he was a hypocrite of a peculiarly Russian type, that is simply a man without any moral code, not knowing any truth except that set out in ABC books. He was ignorant to a degree, litigious, a liar, a windbag and, to crown all, was afraid of the devil." By the penultimate episode, "Vymorochnyi" (Forfeited Property), Iudushka has caused the death of or alienated all those close to him. He becomes a recluse, passing his time brooding on the wrongs done to him by others and mentally revenging himself on them. In the final episode, "Raschet," Iudushka is introduced to the attractions of alcohol by his niece Annin'ka. During their drunken orgies she taunts Iudushka with the calamities and misfortunes of which he has been the cause: "With merciless importunity she unearthed the Golovlev archive, and in particular she liked to taunt Iudushka by proving that the star role in all these acts of mutilation was shared by him and his grandmother."

Gradually this constant nagging has an effect on Iudushka, and his conscience begins to stir within him. Saltykov tells the reader: "Amazingly it seemed that he was not completely without conscience, but that it was just exhausted, forgotten, as it were." To escape from the torments of his past Iudushka toys with the idea of suicide. He sets out in the middle of the night to seek forgiveness at his mother's grave. Next morning he is found dead by the roadside. By his powerful description of Iudushka's mental anguish at the end, Saltykov elevates him to a tragic figure.

Is the awakening of Iudushka's conscience credible? Is it consistent with his character as developed throughout the work? Ivan Aleksandrovich Goncharov, for one, thought not. In a letter to Saltykov written before *Gospoda Golovlevy* was finished, he wrote, that Iudushka "will never hang himself, as you will see yourself when you get to the end. He may develop however you wish, . . . but reform—no, no and again no!" There is no record of a reply from Saltykov to this letter. Iudushka's death brings the work to a dramatic denouement, but Saltykov had never shown himself to be governed by such structural concerns before, particularly if they conflicted with the inherent truth of his message. Perhaps in Iudushka's repentance and death Saltykov was playing out a fantasy of a similar fate for his brother Dmitrii.

The characterization of Iudushka and the interaction of the Golovlev family members are the qualities that make *Gospoda Golovlevy* a powerful work. But they are not its only strength as a piece of prose fiction. The family chronicle is set against the vividly depicted background of the Russian countryside. Before *Gospoda Golovlevy,* Saltykov's works had been set either in St. Petersburg or in provincial towns such as those to which he had been posted as a civil servant. The disputed inheritance took Saltykov many times to Spas-Ugol and the other Saltykov properties in the years prior to writing *Gospoda Golovlevy.* He made good use of this experience in his re-creation of the atmosphere of the Russian country estate, the minutiae of activity, and the influence of the passing seasons, which seem to echo the mood of the narrative. Contemporaries praised the literary artistry of *Gospoda Golovlevy.* A review published in *Molva* (Rumor) in 1876 comments: "We think that the artist in him will soon overcome the satirist." Turgenev wrote to Saltykov to praise his descriptive powers, singling out for particular praise a description of Arina Petrovna dissolving into bitter tears.

Saltykov set out his purpose in writing *Blagonamerennye rechi* thus: "I have dealt with the family, with property, with the state and have given to understand that these are no longer true coin, that it has come to pass that those principles in whose name freedom is restricted are no longer principles, even to those people who make use of them." *Blagonamerennye rechi* is a diffuse collection of essays, stories, and sketches that all appeared under that heading in *Otechestvennye zapiski* from 1872 to 1876. It is a perfect example of a Saltykov "problem cycle" because it is the problem or theme that connects the works. "Loyal speeches" express conservative views, the "disloyal" are those of progressive leanings. The episodes can be crudely divided according to whether they deal with family, state, or property. However, the division is not rigid; some episodes shed light on more than one of the "cornerstones."

The first two separate editions of *Blagonamerennye rechi* each appeared in two volumes, introduced by the episodes "V doroge" (On the Road) and "Opiat' v doroge" (Back on the Road) respectively. As their titles suggest, these episodes take the form of a travelogue probably inspired by Saltykov's journeys to and from Spas-Ugol as he was struggling over the family inheritance. Narrated by a landowner who is trying to sell Chemezovo, his dilapidated country estate, they relate his encounters and conversations while en route there on one of his periodic visits and are full of descriptions of landmarks and views. The landowner whose fortunes are in decline, the *vetkhii chelovek* (decrepit man), is one of the main types that people *Blagonamerennye rechi.* General Utrobin in "Otets i syn" (Father and Son) is one such character. His fortunes decline after the eman-

Saltykov's study in his house on Liteinyi Prospekt, St. Petersburg (watercolor by Vargina, 1880s; State Literary Museum)

cipation, but they are dealt a final blow by the son on whom he dotes, who forges his father's signature on an IOU. The other major type is the *novyi chelovek* (new man) or *chumazyi* (dirty-faced), the peasant turned wealthy merchant and property owner. The new man Derunov is the central figure in two narrative episodes of *Blagonamerennye rechi:* "Stolp" (Pillar) and "Prevrashchenie" (Transformation). The first charts his rise. The second, written four years later, finds him installed in the Hotel Europe in St. Petersburg with his daughter-in-law, living a life of idleness and revelry and thus most likely destined for the same ultimate decline as the "decrepit man."

"Kuzina Mashen'ka" (Cousin Mashen'ka) and "Nepochtitel'nyi Koronat" (Disrespectful Koronat) also form a character sketch in two episodes. Narrated by the owner of Chemezovo, they describe his cousin's ruthless repression of her children. Her son Koronat is a rare type in the Saltykov cast of characters, a new man in the style of Turgenev's "nihilist" Bazarov. Koronat wants to become a doctor in order to help people, but Mashen'ka has made him train as a lawyer because the material rewards are greater. Saltykov had claimed in *Dnevnik provintsiala v Peterburge* that he rarely depicted such characters because he found virtue difficult to portray. He had even criticized Turgenev for presenting Bazarov too negatively, describing his portrayal as "a slander on the aspirations of the younger generation."

Koronat, however, is not an attractive character, and Saltykov's own approval of the Bazarovian type seems less than wholehearted.

Despite Saltykov's strong radical credentials as editor of *Otechestvennye zapiski,* his commitment to fashionable radical views was not always evident. The episode of *Blagonamerennye rechi* titled "Po chasti zhenskogo voprosa" (On the Subject of Female Emancipation) takes the form of a dialogue between two friends on women's rights—one pro, the other con. Both attract Saltykov's irony in equal measure, so that, as contemporary critics remarked, to tell where his sympathies lay was impossible.

The third "cornerstone," the state, is dealt with in an episode titled "V druzheskom krugu" (In a Circle of Friends), which uses the same discussion format as "Po chasti zhenskogo voprosa." It is also the subject of "Tiazhelyi god" (A Difficult Year), which, in its style and subject, resembles *Istoriia odnogo goroda* and *Pompadury i pompadurshi.* The chief representative of the new breed of *chinovniki* (civil servants), who oppress in the name of the state, is Kolotov. He is depicted in the episode "Okhraniteli" (The Protectors—a title that bears uncanny similarity to the name of the *okhranniki,* the czarist secret police who emerged in the next decade). Kolotov describes his own ilk as "the militant bureaucratic army, all young people, all born conservatives." The principal achievement of *Blagonamerennye rechi* was the creation of characters such as Kolotov, Derunov, and General Utrobin (the *chinovnik,* the "new man," and the "decrepit" man), who were at the same time individual characters and the embodiment of a social trend. This achievement was recognized by Arsen'ev in an article for *Vestnik Evropy* in 1883:

> Mr. Saltykov succeeded in catching a type in the process of its development, fixing on its characteristics at the very moment of their birth. . . . To achieve such success means to be at one and the same time both thinker and artist—thinker in order to observe and correlate a whole sequence of analogous phenomena, artist in order to concentrate and embody them in one living figure.

The character types that dominate Saltykov's other works of the second half of the 1870s are the *kul'turnyi chelovek* (cultured man) and the "Molchalins." They both appear in the work *V srede umerennosti i akkuratnosti* (Amidst Moderation and Conscientiousness, 1874–1877). It is a work of hybrid form. Although it is not a novel with a continuous narrative thread, there are recurrent characters who appear in narrative episodes. These episodes are interspersed with passages of reflection, internal monologue by the narrator, and dialogue with his cynical alter ego Glumov. The work is constructed in two halves. The first is titled *Gospoda Molchaliny* (The Molchalins); the second, *Otgoloski* (Echoes). For the most part the first section deals with the character of the Molchalins and the second with the "cultured man." Saltykov's Molchalin has developed from the arrogant toady created by Aleksandr Sergeevich Griboedov in his 1823–1824 play *Gore ot uma* (Woe from Wit). Molchalin is a faceless bureaucrat who is indispensable to his superiors. His main characteristics are moderation and conscientiousness. The "cultured man" is the upper-class member of the intelligentsia who finds himself no longer with a contribution to make to society in the politically repressive atmosphere of the 1870s. He lives like an émigré in his own country with, as the narrator of *V srede umerennosti i akkuratnosti* declares, "nothing apart from a place to live and the zealous surveillance of the police. We have neither honest nor dishonest work, nothing to stir us to activity."

V srede umerennosti i akkuratnosti describes the "cultured man" dissipating his time in the capital. *Ubezhishche Monrepo* (My Sanctuary Monrepos, 1878–1879) relates the life of the cultured man on his country estate. *Ubezhishche Monrepo* is a fictional memoir. It relates a continuous chain of events from the moment the narrator settles on his newly acquired small country estate until his departure. The abortive populist movement, when young, idealistic members of the intelligentsia went to

the countryside to preach revolution, culminated in the trials of 1874–1877 and also resulted in greater vigilance in the surveillance of the activities of the intelligentsia in the countryside. The narrator of *Ubezhishche Monrepo,* retired cornet Progorelov, is the victim of a cat-and-mouse game by the local policeman Gratsianov, who tries to trick him into an expression of radical views. Saltykov wrote thus in defense of this portrayal to the censor Vasilii Vasil'evich Grigor'ev: "The thought behind my story is that since our administration brought into the foreground questions of so-called internal politics, for even quite moderate liberals, if they are not justices of the peace or members of the land councils, life in the provinces, and in particular in the villages, has become almost unthinkable."

Although he satirized Progorelov's weakness, Saltykov shows some sympathy for him. He does not do so with all his portraits of "cultured men." Saltykov's intention was to create in *Kul'turnye liudi* (Cultured People, published in *Otechestvennye zapiski,* 1876) a work modeled in its form on *Pickwick Papers.* The subject matter was to be a satire on the antics of the Russian cultured classes during their travels abroad, based on Saltykov's observations during his travels to Europe in 1875–1876. The work was left incomplete, however, before the main characters even reached foreign soil. Saltykov blamed ill health, which, he said, made it impossible to write in the humorous vein that *Kul'turnye liudi* required: "There is so little humor in me at the moment that I must give up *Kul'turnye liudi* for a time." In fact, he never returned to it. However, he did create the character of Prokop, or more correctly re-create him, as he had already played the role of narrator's friend in *Dnevnik provintsiala v Peterburge.* Prokop is caricatured as a buffoon, lacking in any conscience or psychological depth; clearly Saltykov had no sympathy with his particular breed of "cultured man."

Sbornik. Rasskazy, ocherki, skazki (Collection: Stories, Sketches, Tales, 1881) is, as the title implies, an anthology of separate works. There were originally six of them, though in some separate editions Saltykov also included his early *skazki.* The works range from "Deti Moskvy" (Moscow's Children), a straightforward essay on the degeneracy of Moscow youth, to Saltykov's finest short story, "Bol'noe mesto" (Painful Spot). The main character of "Bol'noe mesto" is Razumov, a bureaucrat in the Molchalin mold. Dismissed by a superior who was irritated by Bazumou's reputation for indispensability, Razumov finds comfort only in the memory of past duties fulfilled and news of his adored son. This comfort is shattered, however, when his son admits that he is ashamed of his father's past career; the shame ultimately leads to Razumov's suicide. His gradual realization that his whole life has been misspent, wasted on a mistaken concept of duty, is told with agonizing pathos.

Razumov's love for his son shows him to be a much more sympathetic character than his calculating and emotionless attitude toward his public duties indicate. The same is also true of Molchalin. Molchalin's son is one of those brought to trial after "going to the people." Saltykov described Molchalin's anguished attempts to secure his son's release in an episode of *V srede umerennosti i akkuratnosti* titled "Chuzhuiu bedu rukami razvedu" (I Throw up My Hands at the Misfortunes of Others), written in 1877. However, rejected by the censor, it did not appear in print until 1880, in a more innocuous form, as "Chuzhoi tolk" (The Opinions of Others) in *Otechestvennye zapiski.* When he sent the manuscript of "Chuzhuiu bedu rukami razvedu" to the critic Pavel Vasil'evich Annenkov, Saltykov denied that it was an explicit criticism of Turgenev's portrayal of the *narodniki* (populists) in *Nov'* (Virgin Soil, 1877). Saltykov did, however, concede that he was "absolutely opposed to that position which Turgenev has chosen for himself." In fact, Saltykov achieves little better than Turgenev when he attempts to portray the young radical generation. Razumov and Molchalin's son are rather aloof, shadowy figures; their parents are the characters who evoke sympathy. Saltykov's other attempt at such a character was not much more successful. The schoolteacher Kramol'nikov in the *Sbornik* sketch "Son v letniuiu noch'" (Dream on a Summer Night) is notable as the mouthpiece for an impassioned speech on the sufferings of the peasantry but remains a two-dimensional creation. Saltykov, like Turgenev, was on the wrong side of the generation gap when it came to understanding young radicals. As he admitted to Annenkov in 1879, "with the passage of time I more and more feel myself to be a man of the forties."

Saltykov's ambivalence toward the liberal generation of the 1840s is apparent in the works he wrote for *Otechestvennye zapiski* in the final years before its closure by the censor in April 1884. Saltykov berates the liberal, now referred to as *srednii chelovek* (the average man), for his betrayal of liberal ideals, motivated by *shkurnyi instinkt* (the instinct to save his own skin). Saltykov is not totally without sympathy, however. The persecution of the liberal intelligentsia increased after the assassination of Alexander II on 1 March 1881. *Pis'ma k teten'ke* (Letters to Auntie, 1882) was started not long afterward. The auntie of the title, to whom the fifteen letters are addressed, is the liberal intelligentsia. Saltykov encourages them not to give up their ideals: "I ask you, dear auntie: do not weaken." The tone is one of reassurance and encouragement, such as an affectionate nephew might well adopt toward his aunt. In Saltykov's words, the work is "a sequence of letters

exclusively concerning contemporary life," and with the exception of a few narrative and descriptive interludes, the form is that of an essay. Government policies during Count Nikolai Pavlovich Ignat'ev's period as minister of the interior are examined in some detail. The controversial nature of its subject matter increased the popularity of the work at the time but also attracted criticism from the censor. Soon after Ignat'ev's appointment Saltykov learned from his predecessor as minister of the interior, Count Mikhail Tarielovich Loris-Melikov, that Ignat'ev had formed a secret organization called the *sviashchennaia druzhina* (sacred host) to root out radical opinion. Saltykov described the *druzhina* in the third letter, calling it *chastnaia initsiativa spaseniia* (private salvation initiative), but the letter was banned by the censor. This rejection resulted in a clamor for manuscript copies.

In the final letter Saltykov maintains his tone of encouragement to the liberals, telling them that much depends on them and their attitudes and that they are still a force in contemporary Russia. In another quite different work of almost exactly the same period he turned the full force of his satire on the *srednii chelovek,* who abandoned his ideals. *Sovremennaia idilliia* is another of Saltykov's "accidental novels." The first episode was written hurriedly, in two evenings, to fill a gap caused by the censor's ban on the final chapter of *V srede umerennosti i akkuratnosti* in February 1877. This work is closely related to the previous work, opening with an episode that involves all three of its main characters: Molchalin, the narrator of *V srede umerennosti i akkuratnosti,* and his alter ego, Glumov. Molchalin comes to tell the narrator that he must *pogodit'* (wait a bit). By this instruction he means eschew all political activity. The first episode has no chapter number, ends with the apparently successful achievement of the hero's aim to "wait a bit," and has a certain self-sufficiency that indicates that Saltykov did not initially intend to pursue the work further. Subsequent chapters, by contrast with this rounded ending, finish on notes of anticipation or at points at which the fortunes of the heroes are suffering a reversal, indicating the important role that Saltykov now assigned to the narrative thread.

In *Sovremennaia idilliia* Saltykov takes his heroes on a journey, both physical and spiritual. The physical journey is a nightmare flight through Russia during which fantastic adventures befall them. The spiritual journey is from *blagonamerennost' vyzhidaiushchaia* (uncommitted loyalty) to *blagonamerennost' voinstvuiushchaia* (militant loyalty), passive acceptance of reaction to active support. In a letter to the literary scholar and historian Aleksandr Nikolaevich Pypin, a regular contributor to *Vestnik Evropy,* Saltykov refuted the suggestion made in that journal that *Sovremennaia idilliia* was an anthology,

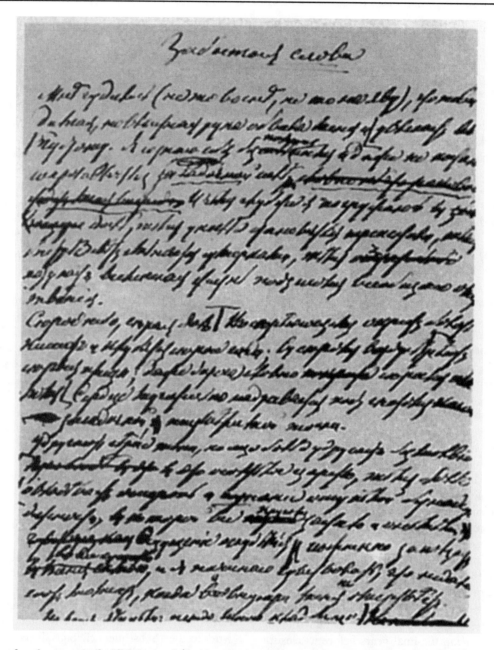

Page from the manuscript for "Zabytye slova" (Forgotten Words, 1889), one of the works Saltykov was writing at the time of his death (Institute of Russian Literature, Academy of Sciences [Pushkin House], St. Petersburg)

comparing it with *Pickwick Papers, Mertvye dushi,* and *Don Quixote. Sovremennaia idilliia* does indeed resemble these works, all of which are satirical mock epics. Together with *Dnevnik provintsiala v Peterburge, Sovremennaia idilliia* comes closest to the novel of the contemporary man for which Saltykov set forward the blueprint in *Gospoda tashkenttsy,* the novel that takes place "on the street, in a public place–anywhere, only not at home; and, moreover, ends in the most unusual, unforeseen manner." The episodic nature of these picaresque works gives scope to include a variety of digressions and inserted scenes, some of them utterly fantastic. Typical in *Sovremennaia idilliia* is

the story of Rededia's exploits, an allegorical account of General Mikhail Grigor'evich Cherniaev's career. In these later works Saltykov increasingly lampoons scarcely disguised contemporary figures. Another digression from the exploits of the heroes is the trial of the gudgeon, in court for fomenting rebellion after being left behind when the other fish depart for a new breeding ground. Despite its translation into animal terms, this attack on the judicial process and on political repression of the innocent resulted in the seizure of the copy of *Otechestvennye zapiski* in which it was published, later commuted to a second warning.

Sovremennaia idilliia ends abruptly with the appearance of "Shame" in a dream to the heroes. Within the text of *Sovremennaia idilliia* itself, stepping outside the persona of the narrator for once, Saltykov expresses his surprise to find the work coming to such a premature end: "I myself had not reckoned that the word 'end' would be written so soon, and proposed to take my heroes through all the ordeals which form the natural conditions of a career in self-preservation." Although he defended the ending in the letter to Pypin as no less natural than a denouement involving marriage or retirement to a monastery, to his co-editor Eliseev he confesses that he "somehow screwed up *Sovremennaia idilliia*." He then goes on to say, "I will give up my literary activity here."

Following a second warning from the censor in January 1883, Saltykov had been afraid to publish his work in *Otechestvennye zapiski* lest the publication result in the closure of the journal. The only new literary work he published during the next seven months was the closing chapter of *Sovremennaia idilliia*. When he took up writing again, it was with a spoof first chapter of *Poshekhonskie rasskazy* (Tales of Poshekhon'e, 1885) devoted to ribald fairy stories. As it developed further, *Poshekhonskie rasskazy* showed itself as a work somewhat in the mold of *Istoriia odnogo goroda,* but less successful than that earlier work. As the microcosm of Russia, Glupov is replaced by Poshekhon'e, a setting taken from Russian folklore, where it was a byword for ignorance and disorder. Events are traced in its history from the prereform era through to the postreform reaction. After a timorous first two chapters, Saltykov resolved, "I am gradually transferring *Poshekhonskie rasskazy* on to more serious ground—we shall see what comes of that: perhaps a third warning." In the ensuing chapters there are some powerful scenes exposing political repression and resultant cowardice among the liberals, presented in the form of conversations, speeches, and narrative incident. However, because the work developed apparently without any overall plan, the result is rather fragmented.

With *Za rubezhom* (Abroad, 1881), started in 1880 during his second visit to Europe, Saltykov finally produced his chronicle of the behavior of Russians abroad that he had promised with *Kul'turnye liudi*. In addition, the work deals with the political situation in Europe and draws comparisons between Russia and western Europe. The Russian tourists are treated with ironic humor, memorably the pair who can find nothing better to do in Paris than sit in the Russian restaurant, compiling "statistics" on the use made of a nearby urinal. Saltykov was disappointed by France, a country whose revolutionary ideals had inspired his youth. He now found it to be "a republic without republicans, with a bloated bourgeoisie at the head." The most memorable of the comparisons he draws between Russia and Europe takes the form of a dream. In this dream an encounter takes place between two boys, a German "boy in trousers" and a Russian "boy without trousers." Despite the evident greater poverty of the Russian boy, symbolized by his lack of trousers, his position is superior, for whereas the German has sold his soul to the devil, the Russian has given his away "and can take it back again." The story of the two boys is one of three such short fantastic playlets that are interwoven into the journal/travelogue form of *Za rubezhom*. The others are "Graf i reporter" (The Count and the Reporter) and "Torzhestvuiushchaia svin'ia ili razgovor svin'i s pravdoi" (The Triumphant Pig or a Conversation between a Pig and Truth), in which the pig devours truth.

Kruglyi god (Year Round, 1880) also makes use of the journal form. Starting with the first chapter, "Pervoe ianvaria" (First of January), published in the January 1879 edition of *Otechestvennye zapiski*, Saltykov apparently intended to chronicle events taking place each month. Saltykov was unable to keep to this schedule, and the April chapter appeared five months late. The plan was further thwarted by the censor, who banned publication of "Pervoe iiunia" (First of June) and the final chapter. Though ostensibly a chronicle of current events, actual events are only hinted at in *Kruglyi god*. Saltykov defined the theme of the work as *gosudarstvennost'* (state). It traces the activities and development of the new generation of conservative statesmen through the journal of an indulgent elderly uncle who chronicles his nephews' deeds and records his conversations with them. Chief among these nephews is Fedin'ka, whose success is based on abuse of his fatherland; he treats it as a pie from which he seizes the largest slice possible. As Saltykov says, "the fatherland-pie—that is the ideal beyond which these immature but impudent minds do not go."

The last work that Saltykov published in *Otechestvennye zapiski* was an episode of *Mezhdu delom* (By the Way), in April 1884. This diffuse collection, subtitled *Zametki, ocherki, rasskazy i. t. d.* (Notes, Sketches, Stories, etc.) was later published in a separate edition under the title *Nedokonchennye besedy* (Unfinished Conversations, 1884). This title referred to the interruption in Saltykov's conversations with his reader caused by the closure of *Otechestvennye zapiski*. The final episode, written for the May edition, was overtaken by the closure of the journal and only appeared in the first separate edition. On seeing this separate edition Saltykov commented, "The book has turned out to be rather motley, for it comprises articles published at different times over a period of eight years."

After all Saltykov's apprehensions, when *Otechestvennye zapiski* was finally closed by the authorities, the stated reason had nothing to do with his writing but was caused by the "close link with a revolutionary organization of collaborators on the journal." The official notice cited that three of its contributors had been arrested: Krivenko, a member of the editorial board; the critic Mikhail Alekseevich Protopopov; and the writer Aleksandr Ivanovich Ertel'. Saltykov was devastated by the closure of *Otechestvennye zapiski:* "In my old age and sickness I have become a misanthropist and have even become unaccustomed to loving. I loved only one thing, that semi-abstract creature, which is called the reader. And now they have separated me from him." The closure of *Otechestvennye zapiski* meant that there was no remaining radical journal in Russia as a medium for Saltykov's work. Despite his gloomy prediction, the closing did not result in the cessation of his literary activities. Instead, he turned to the liberal journals with which he previously had been at ideological loggerheads. The first work he published after the closure of *Otechestvennye zapiski* was the first letter of *Pestrye pis'ma* (Motley Letters, 1884–1886; book publication, 1886), in the November 1884 edition of the liberal journal *Vestnik Evropy*. It had first been accepted by the Moscow newspaper *Moskovskie vedomosti* (Moscow Gazette) but was not published because of the sensitive atmosphere created by student disturbances in Moscow at the beginning of October. Saltykov was convinced that his article would also be removed from *Vestnik Evropy*. This fear was not realized, although censor Vladimir Maksimovich Vedrov remarked that with its publication *Vestnik Evropy* had departed from its usual tradition and adopted "reprehensible views." Saltykov published nine *Pestrye pis'ma* in *Vestnik Evropy* over the following two years. The first letter expressed his dismay at the lack of loyalty of the readers of *Otechestvennye zapiski,* who had raised little protest at its closure, and in general the articles were an attack on the "motley" people whose political allegiances changed according to the predominant political climate.

At the same time he was writing *Pestrye pis'ma,* Saltykov was also engaged on the writing of *skazki,* to which he had returned in 1882. Three works—"Premudryi peskar'" (The Wise Gudgeon), "Samootverzhennyi zaiats" (The Selfless Hare), and "Bednyi volk" (The Poor Wolf)—had been intended for the February edition of *Otechestvennye zapiski.* But the journal had just received its second warning in January, so instead Saltykov published them abroad in the émigré journal *Obshchee delo* (General Business). They were reprinted in the January 1884 edition of *Otechestvennye zapiski.* Four more *skazki* destined for the February edition were removed by the censor, so a third cycle intended for March was retrieved from the printers. Fifteen of Saltykov's *skazki* were published in *Moskovskie vedomosti* between December 1884 and December 1886. Not all

of Saltykov's *skazki* were published in his lifetime. A collection of twenty-three appeared in two editions (1878, 1886), and he was working on a third edition at the time of his death. However, all thirty-two appeared for the first time only in the collected works of 1906. In his *skazki* Saltykov gave a fantastic, allegorical treatment, often transported into the animal kingdom, to the same themes as he dealt with in his other works. For example, several *skazki* are devoted to the cowardice of the liberals, such as the wise gudgeon "who lived for more than a hundred years and trembled all the time." In turning down Saltykov's request to produce a cheap edition of his *skazki,* censor Nikolai Egorovich Lebedev remarked, "What Saltykov calls *skazki* do not fit that name. His *skazki* are the same satire, biting, tendentious and directed against our social and political system."

Melochi zhizni (Trivia of Life, 1887) is a series of satirical sketches published in 1886 and 1887, some in *Russkie vedomosti,* others in *Vestnik Evropy.* They consist of a brilliantly drawn spectrum of character portraits from almost all circles of Russian society—including peasants, landowners, civil servants, and newspaper editors—all of whom serve to prove Saltykov's thesis that Russians of that time preferred not to be plagued by ideas but rather to focus on the trivia that made their lives more comfortable.

The last work that Saltykov wrote before his death was the semi-autobiographical chronicle *Poshekhonskaia starina* (Old Times in Poshekhon'e, 1890), published between October 1887 and March 1889 in *Vestnik Evropy.* It has received little recognition. Through its depiction of scenes, both rural and urban (in Moscow), everyday activities, and family events and relationships, it evokes Russian life in a noble family of average status before the liberation of the serfs. It is not the idealized "nobleman's nest" portrayed by Turgenev but a much harsher picture, in which peasants are subject to the vagaries and cruelties of serfdom and even noblemen's children live in circumstances of relative squalor and almost total emotional deprivation. Through it Saltykov seems to be searching for the roots of his own character. As usual, Saltykov warns his reader not to confuse the narrator with himself; but the autobiographical signals are present. The narrator's mother, Anna Pavlovna Trapeznaia, is of merchant stock and enriches the family by her acquisitions of property and serfs; the father is educated and from the nobility but elderly and ineffectual. Saltykov's approach had mellowed somewhat since he had depicted his family in *Gospoda Golovlevy: Poshekhonskaia starina* is without the dark, tragic, violent atmosphere of the earlier work.

Poshekhonskaia starina relates only the childhood of the narrator, and in the final episode the narrator hints at a sequel. However, Saltykov died the month after this episode was published, on 28 April 1889. He was buried next to Turgenev in the Volkov Cemetery. The final words written to his son were: "Above all love your native literature and the calling of writer prefer to all others." Saltykov's own life had been one of single-minded commitment to the calling of writer. Vladimir Galaktionovich Korolenko wrote of him: "He was a writer to a greater extent than all other writers. Apart from their writing everyone has a personal life and we more or less know about it. Of Saltykov's life in recent years we know only that he wrote."

Bibliographies:

L. M. Dobrovol'sky, *Bibliografiia literatury o M. E. Saltykove-Shchedrine,* 1848–1917 (Moscow-Leningrad: Akademiia Nauk SSSR, 1961);

V. N Baskakov, *Bibliografiia literatury o M. E. Saltykove-Shchedrine, 1918–1965* (Moscow-Leningrad: Nauka, 1966);

Saltykov-Shchedrin, 1826–1976: stat'i, materialy, bibliografiia, edited by A. S. Bushmin (Leningrad: Nauka, 1976).

Biographies:

S. N. Krivenko, *M. E. Saltykov, ego zhizn' i literaturnaia deiatel'nost'. Biograficheskii ocherk* (St. Petersburg: Obshchestvennaia pol'za, 1891);

K. M. Saltykov, *Intimnyi Shchedrin* (Moscow-Petrograd: GIZ, 1923);

S. A. Makashin, *Saltykov-Shchedrin. Biografiia,* volume 1, second edition (Moscow: Goslitizdat, 1951);

Ia. E. El'sberg, *Saltykov-Shchedrin. Zhizn' i tvorchestvo* (Moscow: Goslitizdat, 1953);

V. Ia. Kirpotin, *Mikhail Evgrafovich Saltykov-Shchedrin, Zhizn' i tvorchestvo* (Moscow: Sovetskii pisatel', 1955);

M. E. Saltykov-Shchedrin v vospominaniiakh sovremennikov, edited by S. A. Makashin (Moscow: Khudozhestvennaia literatura, 1957);

E. I. Pokusaev and V. V. Prozorov, *M. E. Saltykov-Shchedrin. Biografiia* (Leningrad: Prosveshchenie, 1969);

Makashin, *Saltykov-Shchedrin na rubezhe 1850–1860 godov: Biografiia* (Moscow: Khudozhestvennaia literatura, 1972);

A. P'ianov, ed., *M. E. Saltykov-Shchedrin i Tver'* (Moscow: Moskovskii rabochii, 1976);

A. M. Turkov, *Saltykov-Shchedrin* (Moscow: Sovetskaia Rossiia, 1981);

Makashin, *Saltykov-Shchedrin: Seredina puti, 1860-e–1870-e gody: Biografiia* (Moscow: Khudozhestvennaia literatura, 1984);

E. D. Petriaev, *M. E. Saltykov-Shchedrin v Viatke* (Kirov: Volgo-Viatskoe knizhnoe izdatel'stvo, 1988);

Makashin, *Saltykov-Shchedrin: poslednie gody, 1876–1889: Biografiia* (Moscow: Khudozhestvennaia literatura, 1989);

K. I. Tiun'kin, *Saltykov-Shchedrin, Zhizn' zamechatel'nykh liudei,* series 3, no. 694 (Moscow: Molodaia gvardiia, 1989);

E. N. Stroganova, ed., *M. E. Saltykov-Shchedrin: tverskie stranitsy zhizni* (Tver': Tverskoi gos. universitet, 1996).

References:

K. K. Arsen'ev, *Saltykov-Shchedrin* (St. Petersburg: Obshchestvennaia pol'za, 1906);

A. P. Auer, *Poetika simvolicheskikh i muzykal'nykh obrazov M. E. Saltykova-Shchedrina* (Saratov: Saratovskii universitet, 1988);

Auer, *Saltykov-Shchedrin i poetika russkoi literatury vtoroi poloviny XIX veka* (Kolomna: Kolomenskii pedagogicheskii institut, 1993);

V. D. Babkin, *Narod i vlast': Opyt sistemnogo issledovaniia vozzrenii M. E. Saltykova* (Kiev: Manuskript, 1996);

S. Borshchevsky, *Shchedrin i Dostoevsky: Istoriia ikh ideinoi bor'by* (Moscow: Goslitizdat, 1956);

A. S. Bushmin, *Evolutsiia satiry Saltykova-Shchedrina* (Leningrad: Nauka, 1984);

Bushmin, *Khudozhestvennyi mir Saltykova-Shchedrina* (Leningrad: Nauka, 1987);

Bushmin, *M. E. Saltykov-Shchedrin* (Leningrad: Prosveshchenie, 1970);

Bushmin, *Saltykov-Shchedrin: Iskusstvo satiry* (Moscow: Sovremennik, 1976);

Bushmin, *Satira Saltykova-Shchedrina* (Moscow-Leningrad: Akademiia Nauk SSSR, 1959);

Bushmin, *Skazki Saltykova-Shchedrina* (Moscow-Leningrad: Goslitizdat, 1960);

E. Draitser, *The Comic Art of Saltykov-Shchedrin* (Ann Arbor: University of Michigan Press, 1987);

Draitser, *Techniques of Satire: The Case of Saltykov-Ščedrin* (Berlin & New York: Mouton de Gruyter, 1994);

A. I. Efimov, *Iazyk satiry Saltykova-Shchedrina* (Moscow: Moskovskii universitet, 1953);

Ia. E. El'sberg, *Stil' Shchedrina* (Moscow: GIKhL, 1940);

V. E. Evgen'ev-Maksimov, *V tiskakh reaktsii. K stoletiiu rozhdeniia M. M. Saltykova-Shchedrina* (Moscow-Leningrad: GIZ, 1926);

I. P. Foote, "M. E. Saltykov-Shchedrin: *The Golovlyov Family,*" *Forum for Modern Language Studies,* 4, no. 1 (1968): 53–63;

Foote, "Reaction or Revolution: The Ending of Saltykov's *History of a Town,*" *Oxford Slavonic Papers,* new series, 1 (1968): 105–125;

M. S. Goriachkina, ed., *M. E. Saltykov-Shchedrin v russkoi kritike* (Moscow: Goslitizdat, 1976);

Goriachkina, *Satira Saltykova-Shchedrina* (Moscow: Prosveshchenie, 1965);

K. N. Grigor'ian, *Roman M. E. Saltykova-Shchedrina "Gospoda Golovlevy"* (Moscow-Leningrad: Akademiia Nauk SSSR, 1962);

N. V. Iakovlev, *Poshekhonskaia starina M. E. Saltykova-Shchedrina* (Moscow: Sovetskii pisatel', 1958);

I. T. Ishchenko, *Parodii Saltykova-Shchedrina* (Minsk: BGU, 1973);

V. Ia. Kirpotin, *Filosofskie i esteticheskie vzglyady Saltykova-Shchedrina* (Moscow: Goslitizdat, 1957);

Kirpotin, *M. E. Saltykov-Shchedrin. Literaturno-kriticheskii ocherk* (Moscow: Sovetskii pisatel', 1939);

II. G. Kupferschmidt, *Saltykow-Stschedrin, philosophisches Wollen und schriftstellerische Tat* (Halle: Niemeyer, 1958);

A. Lavretsky, *Shchedrin—literaturnyi kritik* (Moscow: GIKhL, 1935);

Literaturnoe nasledstvo, volumes 11–12, 13–14 (Moscow, 1933);

N. K. Mikhailovsky, *Kriticheskie opyty II. Shchedrin* (Moscow: Iakovlev, 1890);

V. A. Mysliakov, *Saltykov-Shchedrin i narodnicheskaia demokratiia* (Leningrad: Nauka, 1984);

D. P. Nikolaev, *Satira Shchedrina i realisticheskii grotesk* (Moscow: Khudozhestvennaia literatura, 1977);

Nikolaev, *Smekh Shchedrina: Ocherki satiricheskoi poetiki* (Moscow: Sovetskii pisatel', 1988);

M. S. Ol'minsky, *Shchedrinskii slovar'* (Moscow: GIKhL, 1937);

Ol'minsky, *Stat'i o Saltykove-Shchedrine* (Moscow: Goslitizdat, 1959);

N. N. Pokrovsky, ed., *M. E. Saltykov kak satirik, khudozhnik i publitsist: Iz kriticheskoi literatury o Saltykove* (Moscow: Sklad v knizhnom magazine V. S. Spiridonova i A. M. Mikhailova, 1906);

E. I. Pokusaev, *Revolutsionnaia satira Saltykova-Shchedrina* (Moscow: Goslitizdat, 1963);

Z. T. Prokopenko, *M. E. Saltykov-Shchedrin i I. A. Goncharov v literaturnom protsesse XIX veka* (Voronezh: Voronezhskii universitet, 1989);

V. V. Prozorov, *O khudozhestvennom myshlenii pisatelia-satirika; nabliudeniia nad tvorcheskim protsessom M. E. Saltykova-Shchedrina* (Saratov: Saratovskii universitet, 1965);

P. Reifman, *M. E. Saltykov-Shchedrin: Tvorcheskii put'* (Tartu: Tartuskii gos. universitet, 1973);

R. Risaliti, *Saltykov-Ščedrin* (Pisa: Libreria goliardica, 1968);

V. N. Baskakov and V. V. Prozorov, eds., *Saltykov-Shchedrin i russkaia literatura* (Leningrad: Nauka, 1991);

Nikolaev, ed., *M. E. Saltykov-Shchedrin i russkaia satira XVIII–XX vekov,* edited by D. P. Nikolaev (Moscow: Nasledie, 1998);

R. D. Kuznetsova, ed., *M. E. Saltykov-Shchedrin: Problemy mirovozzrenia, tvorchestva, iazyka: Materialy konferentsii* (Tver': Tverskoi gos. universitet, 1991);

Foote, ed., *Saltykov-Shchedrin's The Golovlyovs: A Critical Companion* (Evanston, Ill.: Northwestern University Press, 1997);

Kuznetsova and E. N. Stroganova, eds., *M. E. Saltykov-Shchedrin v zerkale issledovatel'skikh pristrastii: materialy nauchnoi konferentsii* (Tver': Tverskoi gos. universitet, 1996);

K. Sanine, *Saltykov-Chtchedrine, sa vie et ses oevres* (Paris: Institut d'études slaves de l'Université de Paris, 1955);

N. Strelsky, *Saltykov and the Russian Squire* (New York: Columbia University Press, 1940);

I. T. Trofimov, *Revoliutsionnaia satira Saltykova-Shchedrina i russkaia literatura* (Moscow: Prosveshchenie, 1967);

D. I. Zaslavsky, *Saltykov-Shchedrin; kritiko-biograficheskii ocherk* (Moscow: Khudozhestvennaia literatura, 1939).

Papers:

The Institute of Russian Literature, St. Petersburg, has a considerable archive of Mikhail Evgrafovich Saltykov's manuscripts and correspondence. For a detailed list of this archive and other smaller holdings see *Literaturnoe nasledstvo,* volume 13–14, pp. 591–624.

Aleksandra Stanislavovna Shabel'skaia

(1845 – 1921)

Martha Kuchar
Roanoke College

WORKS: *Gore pobezhdennym,* in *Delo,* nos. 1, 3, 5 (1881); (St. Petersburg, 1881);

Magistr i Frosia, in *Russkaia mysl',* nos. 8–9 (1883);

Nabroski karandashem (St. Petersburg: M. M. Stasiulevich, 1884);

Pid Ivana Kupala (Kiev, 1887);

Tri techeniia, in *Severnyi vestnik,* nos. 1–5 (1888);

Druz'ia, in *Russkoe bogatstvo,* nos. 2–12 (1894).

OTHER: "Motia," in *Pamiati Belinskogo,* edited by Grigorii Aleksandrovsky (Moscow: Tovarishchestvo tipografii A. F. Mamontora, 1899), pp. 313–320;

"Po uzen'koi dorozhke," in *Pushkinskii sbornik (v pamiat' stoletiia dnia rozhdeniia poeta),* edited by V. V. Mate (St. Petersburg: A. S. Suvorin, 1899), pp. 474–483.

SELECTED PERIODICAL PUBLICATIONS:

"Miron i Annushka," *Otechestvennye zapiski,* no. 12 (1881);

"Paraska," *Otechestvennye zapiski,* no. 5 (1882);

"Nakanune Ivana Kupala," *Otechestvennye zapiski,* no. 9 (1882);

"'Hola pani,'" *Russkaia mysl',* no. 12 (1883);

"Ne vyderzhal," *Severnyi vestnik,* 10 (1887): 155–193;

"Pozhar," *Severnyi vestnik,* 11 (1887): 59–85;

"Talant," *Russkoe bogatstvo,* 12 (1887): 121–158;

"Legenda," *Russkoe bogatstvo,* 1 (1896): 92–128;

"Tkachi," *Novoe slovo,* 12 (1896): 1–49.

Aleksandra Stanislavovna Shabel'skaia was a prolific writer who left behind an impressive body of prose fiction. Her narratives, mostly set in Ukrainian provinces where she spent most of her life, vividly describe life during the second half of the nineteenth century.

As with many other women writers of her era, little is known about Shabel'skaia's life. The questions begin with her name. While some historians once assumed that Shabel'skaia was her surname, most now believe that it is a pseudonym. Some scholars—such as F. A. Brokgauz, I. A. Efron, and Stepan Ivanovich Ponomarev—have thought that her married name was "Montvid" and that her maiden name was unknown. This belief seems to be grounded in the assertion of Mikhail Evgrafovich Saltykov (N. Shchedrin) in an 1882 letter to Ivan Sergeevich Turgenev that Shabel'skaia was "'Monvid-Monvizh' by her husband and 'Tolochinova' by her lover." But in 1995 Ippolit Vasil'evich Zborovets' postulated on the basis of archival records that Montvid was Shabel'skaia's maiden name and that her married name was Tolochinova (or "Tolochynov" in Ukrainian). This theory finds some support in works by earlier scholars such as Aleksandr L'vovich Flekser-Volynsky, Ivan Filippovich Masanov, and Oleksei Ivanovych Dei. Shabel'skaia used other pseudonyms as well: Born (probably a surname), Vrag (Enemy), and Shabel'sky (the masculine version of Shabel'skaia).

Despite such uncertainty, it is possible to construct at least a partial biography. Aleksandra Stanislavovna Montvid was born in 1845 in the province of Khar'kov in eastern Ukraine. According to Zborovets', her home was the village of Maiachok in the Izium district. Her roots are generally agreed to have been Lithuanian and aristocratic, but by her generation the family had been classed as petty (not high) gentry. Little more is known about her early life, though according to Zborovets', much information can be found in unpublished manuscript reminiscences–titled "Detstvo" (Childhood), "Otrochestvo" (Adolescence), and "Iunost'" (Youth)–purported to exist in the Shabel'skaia archives in Kiev (Kyiv in Ukrainian).

In the days before women won admittance to universities or were enrolled in secondary schools, Montvid attended the Khar'kov Institute for Daughters of the Nobility, one of only a handful of such schools for nineteenth-century women. After graduation in 1858, she worked for a time as an *akusherka* (midwife), a craft she subsequently described in some of her fiction, such as *Magistr i Frosia* (The Master of Arts and Frosia, 1883). Perhaps she met the man who may have been her husband, Mykola Tolochinov, whom the *Encyclopedia of Ukraine* (English edition, 1993) describes as a medical scholar and obstetrician-gynecologist of wide repute, while she was learning or practicing midwifery.

Shabel'skaia's earliest known publications date to the early 1880s. Her place of residence in those years has not been firmly fixed. In 1882 Saltykov told Turgenev that Shabel'skaia was then living in Kiev, and Zborovets' says Shabel'skaia lived mostly in Khar'kov from 1885 until 1908. If she were married to or living with Tolochinov, Shabel'skaia may have been in those cities with him. He is said to have lectured in Kiev until 1885 and in Khar'kov after that. Since Shabel'skaia's first novel, published in 1881, is set in a fictional version of Khar'kov, she may have spent time in that city earlier than 1885. It is possible that she and Tolochinov had two residences, since Tolochinov seems to have had professional ties to both cities.

The gaps in Shabel'skaia's biography offer a challenge to scholars, who have also tried unsuccessfully to compile a complete bibliography of her writings. Most of her published narratives and plays were serialized in Russian journals during the 1880s and 1890s and have not been republished in the twentieth century. Lists of her writings, mostly dating from the turn of the twentieth century, include works that have not been located. Perhaps some were circulated in manuscript or as single printed volumes. Yet, even Shabel'skaia's available works represent a prodigious output: some two thousand pages of narrative written over two decades. A complete recovery of her writings could double this number.

Shabel'skaia's works include novels, short stories, and plays. She made her literary debut with *Gore pobezhdennym* (Woe to the Vanquished). First serialized in *Delo* (The Cause), a journal known for its radical political leanings, in 1881, the novel was published as a separate volume later that year. *Gore pobezhdennym* features a large cast of characters, mostly drawn from government, academe, and commerce; debates about political and social issues constitute much of the interest of the novel. The plot involves local elections and the intrigues that go along with them in the city of Khorzai, a thinly disguised version of Khar'kov. At the heart of the novel, as in many of Shabel'skaia's works, is a story about family ties–in this case, those binding the Bilibins and Lebedas to others in their community–and about the betrayal of those ties.

After *Gore pobezhdennym,* Shabel'skaia wrote the slender novel *Magistr i Frosia.* First published in 1883 in the journal *Russkaia mysl'* (Russian Thought), it was republished a year later, when Shabel'skaia included it in a collection of her fiction titled *Nabroski karandashem* (Pencil Sketches, 1884). *Magistr i Frosia* documents the relationship between Petr Ivanovich Sokolov and Evfrosiia Vasil'evna Akimova (Frosia), a Russian couple who have traveled from St. Petersburg to Vienna to advance Petr Ivanovich's career. After an unsuccessful attempt to defend a doctoral dissertation in Russia, Petr (the master of arts) has gone to Austria to complete a projected study of "the foundations of government." In the process he has turned bitter and resentful toward the Russian academy, calling it a "despicable corporation," and he has acquired conservative views. Those views, however, do not prevent him from "keeping" Frosia, despite the fact that he is already married.

The illicit affair turns sour in the Austrian capital. By the time the novel opens, Petr Ivanovich has already tired of Frosia. He installs her in separate quarters and, although he rarely visits her, he expects her to stay indoors and be happy. When she escapes and finds herself surrounded by admirers, he becomes obsessed with the idea of controlling her completely: "He had a burning desire to possess her," to "tyrannize over her." Although slavishly devoted to Petr Ivanovich at first, Frosia comes to recognize his intellectual and moral weakness and steels herself to break free: "If I can shake this yoke, I will never again submit to anyone." By this time, however, she is pregnant. Petr Ivanovich heartlessly agitates for an end to the pregnancy, but Frosia will not abort the fetus and gives birth to their daughter. Petr Ivanovich's callousness almost causes the infant's death, and Frosia returns with the child to the protection of her brother's home in St. Petersburg. The novel illustrates the harm that comes from the actions of men who have not progressed, who have become like the "fathers" of an era long past rather than the "sons" and leaders of a new, reformist Russia. Shabel'skaia refers explicitly to Turgenev's novel *Ottsy i deti* (Fathers and Sons, 1862).

In 1888 Shabel'skaia published *Tri techeniia* (Three Currents). The writer Vladimir Galaktionovich Korolenko, who was Shabel'skaia's editor for this novel, called it a *romanishche,* a word best translated as "a novel and a half" or simply as "a hefty tome." The title refers to the three women who dominate the interests of the central character, Konstantin Mikhailovich Mal'vinsky (Kostia): Varvara Petrovna Mal'vinskaia, the forty-five-year-old long-suffering mother of Kostia and of seven other children who perished in infancy; Mar'ia Semenovna Lebedeva, a relatively unattractive twenty-one-year-old wealthy heiress, who has a taste for expensive, flashy clothes and manages her affairs—and her men—with an iron fist (hence, her nickname "kulak-baba" [the iron-fisted woman]); and Lidia Fedorovna Litvinova, roughly eighteen years of age, an orphan and Kostia's cousin, a "wild child" who feels perennially uncomfortable in the "egotistical" environment of the aristocracy and longs to return to her parental estate and her beloved gardens.

The plot focuses on the return of Kostia after a five-year banishment from the home of his now-deceased father. At twenty-five he is a changed man, bearing, in word and deed, the signs of illness, of sated love, and of a kind of Byronic weariness. Having converted to a hybrid form of Buddhist austerity and Christian evangelism, he preaches the new religion to anyone in his birthplace who will listen. He exhorts his listeners to shed material things, let go of worldly vanities, and obey the word of the Bible. Over the course of the narrative, Kostia's "apostolic aspirations" sound increasingly tinny—and suspiciously inauthentic—both to his interlocutors and to the reader. On the other hand, his exhortations captivate Mar'ia and Lidia, who soon fall in love with him.

As Shabel'skaia unfolds the story of their relationships, she makes a familiar tale interesting by manipulating the point of view. For the most part, the novel is narrated from a third-person, omniscient point of view, but the story slips into a limited point of view at inter-

vals. These multiple viewpoints allow the reader to see an action or idea from several different perspectives. With these shifts and the fast-paced action of incident and crisis, the novel occasionally rises to the pitch of a soap opera, but the reader never loses interest and involvement in the story.

In 1894 the journal *Russkoe bogatstvo* (Russian Riches) published Shabel'skaia's last novel, *Druz'ia* (Friends). As her contemporaries noted, Shabel'skaia filled her novels with references to current events. For example, Flekser-Volynsky observed that her subjects were those discussed in the daily press, while Il'ia Nikolaevich Ignatov noted that in novels such as *Druz'ia* Shabel'skaia set the action in towns and cities familiar to her and to her readers and alluded to actual people. He also charged that Shabel'skaia had populated the book with pointedly defined moral agents: the good and the bad, the demonic and the angelic. From the international scene to scandals in local governments, she wrote knowledgeably about Eastern and Western Europe, citing specific ideological skirmishes, parliamentary debates, and political negotiations.

Shabel'skaia's *povesti* (tales) began to appear in 1881, the same year as her first novel. Over the years, she published many of them in *Otechestvennye zapiski* (Notes of the Fatherland), *Russkaia mysl', Severnyi vestnik* (The Northern Herald), and *Russkoe bogatstvo*. After reading the story "Paraska" (the title is the heroine's name) in the May 1882 issue of *Otechestvennye zapiski,* Turgenev heralded her arrival on the literary scene. Writing to Saltykov, who was then editor of *Otechestvennye zapiski,* he said: "I congratulate you for discovering this strong and fresh talent; please send her my regards." Saltykov did not share Turgenev's enthusiasm, though he based his dislike on personal rather than aesthetic grounds.

Some of Shabel'skaia's earliest stories were collected in *Nabroski karandashem,* and after 1884 each of the stories she published intermittently over the next two decades appeared under the rubric *Nabroski karandashem.* Clearly she intended the reader to make connections among her stories and to regard them as an interrelated whole. Some of her shorter fiction was also published in separate volumes.

The turn-of-the-century literary historian Aleksandr Mikhailovich Skabichevsky preferred Shabel'skaia's stories to her novels, perhaps because for the most part they avoid Shabel'skaia's tendency to fill her novels with generous detail and to recapitulate. Her stories are spare, finely chiseled works that move with energy and grace. Like her novels, though, they can be surprising amalgams of humor and wrenching seriousness. While her novels feature the upper classes, in her shorter fiction Shabel'skaia lavished great care on her treatment of the underclasses, notably the peasants and house servants of the mid to late nineteenth century. More often than not, Shabel'skaia's peasants are Ukrainian, or in the derogatory language of the day, *khokhly:* "The *khokhly* who lived at the borders of the gentry lands didn't bother to learn their difficult names; they simply called the lieutenant 'the fellow with the nose hairs' and the colonel 'the fellow who mutters to himself,'" Shabel'skaia wrote in "Miron i Annushka" (Miron and Annushka, 1881). Ukrainian or Russian, as peasants they exist "at the borders" of the established order. The poor, orphaned, and mistreated heroine, Annushka, has outgrown her clothes and, with no money to replace them, wears tatters that reveal her shoulders and breast: "She had nothing with which to cover herself." Her nakedness is a metaphor for a poor girl's vulnerability.

The theme of stripping away a person's humanity recurs in the 1883 story "'Hola pani'" (a Ukrainian phrase meaning "naked lady"). By a curious reversal, however, it is a woman of the gentry, Varvara Iakovlevna Konti, née Ishinskaia, who finds her circumstances stripped down. She loses everything–her land, her home, her heirlooms–because of her late husband's profligacy and the ruthless cunning of Amel'ian Burlachko, proprietor, like his father before him, of the tavern Naked Lady. In many ways the story presages Anton Pavlovich Chekhov's 1903 play *Vishnevyi sad* (The Cherry Orchard). Children of the working class, Burlachko in "'Hola pani'" and Lopakhin in *Vishnevyi sad* are self-made men who manage to displace members of the landed gentry from their ancestral homes. In Shabel'skaia as in Chekhov, the sound of the felling of an ancient tree, symbolic of the passage from the old to the new, ends the work. Change does not come easily, Shabel'skaia seems to say; someone always pays. In "'Hola pani'" Varvara Iakovlevna's daughter Lelichka, who was born the day serfdom officially ceased to exist, has returned home from boarding school to find that "home" is now the Naked Lady. She has been stripped of her identity.

Like Turgenev in his *Zapiski okhotnika* (A Hunter's Notes, 1852), Shabel'skaia characterized the common folk as colorful and even predictable but, at the same time, as people with complex inner lives. They can be kind and cruel, sympathetic and unattractive, pitiful victims and wretched exploiters. There is a tension in most of her stories that makes their resolutions difficult to predict. Skabichevsky particularly valued these tensions, as well as Shabel'skaia's ability to breathe life into relations between the lower and upper classes.

While the rare individual, such as Amel'ian Burlachko, can rise from poverty, most of the underclass in Shabel'skaia's stories cannot. An intransigent political, social, and economic order has rendered them immobile. In many cases the rich find out that money is not everything, but to a poor person money can mean the difference between life and death. The sick child of a rich parent receives house calls from a physician who earns five hundred rubles per visit, but the sick child of a poor peasant, who earns half that amount in a year, relies on charity to receive any treatment at all. Shabel'skaia's fiction suggests that, despite the abolition of serfdom, circumstances had not changed much for the Russian peasantry of the late 1800s. Two to three decades after serfdom ended, she depicted problems that still persisted, in some instances even worse than before, because abolition had succeeded in setting adrift the "liberated" serfs, tearing them from the security of ownership. Before 1861, they had been slaves to their masters, but they had known their place. Twenty or thirty years later much was expected, but little could be accomplished with the peasants' meager resources: they had no land, no money, no meaningful education, and little motivation to get ahead.

In addition to portraying the general malaise of her time, Shabel'skaia also focused on a particular kind of social disorder, the ill treatment of women. Most of her heroines are approximately eighteen years old, an age at which they are, in most ways, naive and full of desire. Soon, however, they learn about human cruelty, unkind fate, and the urgent need for self-reliance. In "Nagornoe" (Hilltop), first published in the collection *Nabroski karandashem,* the master rapes his servant girl, who develops "a loathing toward men. . . . All their faces transformed into the beastly face" of her transgressor. The rape results in a pregnancy, for which she, not her master, is blamed. Shunned by her fiancé and her family, she gives birth to a stillborn child and dies in the process, delirious and alone.

In Shabel'skaia's fiction women in all walks of life are victims of their men, while the men, with rare exceptions, are remarkably selfish, egotistical, or pathologically cruel. "He dehumanized her, humiliated her, deprived her of friendships," says the narrator of "'Hola pani.'" Across class lines, men exploit women, using them for pleasure and then discarding them. Women constitute an underclass that does not deserve its punishment. Shabel'skaia's heroines are flesh and blood women, not the sometime pale sisters of earlier Russian fiction. During the first half of the nineteenth century, when a female character said she could not endure her situation, generally she meant "I will die," and usually she did. In Shabel'skaia's work, when Frosia says in *Magistr i Frosia:* "I cannot endure this!" she means "I won't stand for it," and she does not. Shabel'skaia's women expect respect, access to education, and the opportunity to succeed. Their determination makes their defeat all the more disturbing.

Shabel'skaia's story "Pozhar" (Fire, 1887) includes another of her major themes: the idea that privilege begets violence. In this story Valerian Andreevich Zaretsky, a landowner who has essentially dissipated his wealth, looks for a way to raise money and settles on the idea of burning alive his herd of eighty insured horses. His cruelty to the animals matches his vindictiveness toward humans, especially his coachman Nikola, whom he makes the scapegoat for the fire. Like many other aristocrats, Zaretsky is vain, exploitative, and dishonest. Even worse, as Shabel'skaia makes clear, he misbehaves with impunity. The law will not touch him because the law is on the side of might.

A story such as "Pozhar" suggests Shabel'skaia's links to European naturalism: she does not avoid naturalistic details and sensational events. With scenes describing the slitting of chickens' throats for a great repast and pack dogs tearing apart the carcasses of horses, Shabel'skaia spares the reader little. Such details do not appear gratuitous; instead, they follow Shabel'skaia's general desire to overturn taboo and to stretch the boundaries of narrative subject and style. The sexual innuendoes common in her work shocked such critics as Korolenko.

Furthermore, Shabel'skaia's stories show her skillful use of the techniques of drama. She arranged scene and action with a dramatist's eye for suspense and the compelling event. The reader notices her deft handling of dialogue, particularly in her later fiction. She was also successful as a playwright: one of the stories in *Nabroski karandashem* became the basis for her Ukrainian-language play, *Pid Ivana Kupala* (Ivan Kupala Eve). Published in Kiev in 1887, the four-act play retells the story "Nakanune Ivana Kupala" (On the Eve of Ivan Kupala Day), which Shabel'skaia had written in Russian and published in *Otechestvennye zapiski* in 1882 before collecting it in *Nabroski karandashem* in 1884. The celebrated Ukrainian poet, dramatist, and stage director Mikhailo Petrovich Starytsky brought Shabel'skaia's *Pid Ivana Kupala* to the stage, winning considerable acclaim. Shabel'skaia may have written a half-dozen other plays (comedies), though their location has not been determined. Zborovets' suggests that the renowned Russian playwright Aleksandr Nikolaevich Ostrovsky assisted Shabel'skaia in the writing of dramatic literature.

Shabel'skaia's *Nabroski karandashem* appeared intermittently throughout the 1890s. Two of her last known stories appeared in 1899 in memorial volumes dedicated to the great Russian poet Aleksandr Sergeevich Pushkin and to the influential Russian literary commentator Vissarion Grigor'evich Belinsky. The "pencil sketch" included in the Pushkin volume allows the reader to measure Shabel'skaia's aesthetic matu-

rity. "Po uzen'koi dorozhke" (Along the Narrow Path, 1899) calls to mind two of Tolstoy's stories: *Smert' Ivana Il'icha* (The Death of Ivan Ilyich, 1886) and *Khoziain i rabotnik* (Master and Man, 1895). In her story Shabel'skaia created tension by putting in uncomfortably close proximity two characters whose prior relations have made them mortal enemies. The story is told essentially as a set of interior monologues, alternating between the two characters: a judge who, like Tolstoy's Ivan Ilyich, is dying from a tumor that has emerged after a fall, and a peasant farmer who has been deprived of home and hearth and who has been exploited by more-powerful people for their own purposes. Shabel'skaia experimented successfully with stream of consciousness, employing a kind of austere, wordless exchange between the two main characters, a silent meeting of the minds conveyed through interior monologue within the fabric of the narrative. The two characters communicate through a nervous laugh, a grunt, or a heavy sigh. In the process their humanity emerges, and bonds of forgiveness and love develop between them. Thus, like Tolstoy, Shabel'skaia created resolution in the unexpected sympathy that develops between the pair. There is a difference, however. While Tolstoy situated the change of heart in the member of the gentry, Shabel'skaia placed the change in the peasant—"Let living things live; let them go free and breathe"— thus seeking to demonstrate the intelligence and complexity of the common man.

Little is known of Shabel'skaia's life and work after 1899. Bibliographies list no original publications after that time; she may have stopped writing. Tolochinov died in 1908, and, according to Zborovets', Shabel'skaia moved to Kiev a year later. She resided in Kiev until her death in 1921, at the age of seventy-six. According to one source, Shabel'skaia's complete works were published during the second half of the 1890s, but no copies have been located.

Bibliographies:

Stepan Ivanovich Ponomarev, *Nashi pisatel'nitsy. Bibliograficheskii slovar' russkikh pisatel'nits'* (St. Petersburg: Akademiia nauk, 1891), p. 73;

Il'ia Nikolaevich Ignatov, *Gallereia russkikh pisatelei* (Moscow: S. Skirmunt, 1901);

F. A. Brokgauz and I. A. Efron, eds., *Entsiklopedicheskii slovar'*, volume 39 (St. Petersburg, 1908), p. 84;

S. A. Vengerov, ed., *Istochniki slovaria russkikh pisatelei*, volume 4 (Petrograd, 1917), p. 405;

I. V. 'Vladislavlev'-Gulbinsky, *Russkie pisateli: Opyt bibliograficheskogo posobiia po russkoi literature XIX–XX st.*, fourth edition (Moscow: Gosudarstvennoe izdatel'stvo, 1924);

Ivan Filippovich Masanov, *Slovar' pseudonimov russkikh pisatelei, uchenykh i obshchestvennykh deiatelei* (Moscow: Vses. Khnizhnaia palata, 1956–1960), volume 3, p. 249; volume 4, p. 323;

Oleksei Ivanovych Dei, *Slovnyk ukrains'kykh pseudonimiv ta kryptonimiv (XVI–XX st.)* (Kiev: Naukova dumka, 1969), p. 396;

"Bio-bibliograficheskii ukazatel' noveishei russkoi belletristiki (1861–1911)," *Entsiklopedicheskii slovar' T-va "Br. A. i. I. Granat i Ko."* (Moscow: Vasanta, 1996), p. 732.

Biographies:

Mary Zirin, "Shabel'skaia, Aleksandra Stanislavovna," *Dictionary of Russian Women Writers*, edited by Marina Ledkovsky, Charlotte Rosenthal, and Zirin (Westport, Conn.: Greenwood Press, 1994), pp. 565–566;

Ippolit Vasil'evich Zborovets', "Shabel's'ka, Oleksandra Stanislavivna," in *Literaturna Kharkivshchyna: Dovidnyk,* edited by M. F. Het'manets' (Khar'kov: Maidan, 1995), pp. 344–345.

References:

Aleksandr L'vovich Flekser-Volynsky, *Kniga velikogo gneva: Kriticheskie stat'i, zametki, polemika,* second edition (St. Petersburg: Trud, 1904), p. 198;

V. G. Korolenko, *Sobranie sochinenii,* volume 10 (Moscow: Gosudarstvennoe izdatel'stvo, 1956), pp. 64–65, 79–82;

"Montvid," in *Bol'shaia entsiklopediia,* volume 13 (St. Petersburg: Prosveshchenie, 1903), p. 367;

I. Z. Pidkova and R. M. Shust, eds., *Dovidnyk z istorii Ukrainy,* volume 3 (Kiev: Geneza, 1999), pp. 517–519;

Mikhail Evgrafovich Saltykov, *Sobranie sochinenii,* volume 9, book 2 (Moscow: Khudozhestvennaia literatura, 1977), pp. 117–119;

N. A. Siroshtan, ed., *Istoriia mist i sil Ukrains'koi RSR: Khar'kovskaia oblast'* (Kiev: Radians'ka entsyklopediia, 1967);

Aleksandr Mikhailovich Skabichevsky, *Istoriia noveishei russkoi literatury 1848–1903 gg.,* fifth edition (St. Petersburg: Obshchestvennaia pol'za, 1903), pp. 402–403;

Danylo H. Struk, ed., "Kharkiv" and "Tolochynov, Mykola," in *Encyclopedia of Ukraine* (Toronto: University of Toronto Press, 1993), volume 2, pp. 441–449; volume 5, p. 234;

Ivan Sergeevich Turgenev, *Polnoe sobranie sochinenii i pisem,* volume 13, book 1 (Moscow-Leningrad: AN SSSR, 1968), pp. 266, 542;

O. E. Zasenko, ed., "M. P. Starytsky," *Istoriia ukrains'koi literatury,* volume 4, book 2 (Kiev: Naukova dumka, 1969), pp. 327–333.

Papers:

Archival material, including some of Aleksandra Stanislavovna Shabel'skaia's manuscripts, can be found in the National Archives at Kiev and in the Filial TsGIA at Khar'kov.

Aleksandr Konstantinovich Sheller
(A. Mikhailov)
(30 July 1838 – 21 November 1900)

Olga Shitareva
Moscow State University

and

J. Alexander Ogden
University of South Carolina

WORKS: *Gnilye bolota. Istoriia bez geroia*, in *Sovremennik*, nos. 2–3 (1864); (St. Petersburg, 1867);

Zhizn' Shupova, ego rodnykh i znakomykh. Avtobiografiia, in *Sovremennik*, nos. 2–3, 6–8 (1865); (St. Petersburg, 1866);

V chadu glubokikh soobrazhenii. Roman v trekh knigakh, in *Zhenskii vestnik*, nos. 1, 4 (1866); nos. 5, 6, 9 (1867);

Zasorennye dorogi, in *Delo*, no. 1 (1866); republished in *Zasorennye dorogi. Roman.–S kvartiry na kvartiru. Rasskaz* (St. Petersburg: V. E. Genkel', 1868);

Gospoda Obnoskovy. Roman, in *Delo*, nos. 3–7 (1868); (St. Petersburg, 1870);

Ocherki prirody i byta Belomorskogo kraia Rossii. Okhota v lesakh Arkhangel'skoi gubernii (St. Petersburg: Tip. Retgera i Shneidera, 1868);

Pod gnetom okruzhaiushchego. Povest', in *Delo*, nos. 11–12 (1868);

Proletariat vo Frantsii, 1789–1857. Istoricheskie ocherki (St. Petersburg, 1869);

V razbrod. Iz istorii nashei sem'i. Roman, in *Delo*, nos. 8–12 (1869); (St. Petersburg, 1870);

Assotsiatsii. Ocherk prakticheskogo primeneniia printsipa kooperatsii v Germanii, v Anglii i vo Frantsii (St. Petersburg: Tip. A. M. Kotomina, 1871);

Les rubiat–shchepki letiat. Roman v dvukh chastiakh, in *Delo*, nos. 1–12 (1871); (St. Petersburg, 1872);

Sochineniia, 6 volumes (St. Petersburg: A. I. Bortnevsky, 1873–1875);

Ekonomicheskie palliativy (St. Petersburg: A. I. Bortnevsky, 1874);

Osnovy obrazovaniia v Evrope i v Amerike (St. Petersburg: D. E. Kozhanchikov, 1874);

Aleksandr Konstantinovich Sheller

Khleba i zrelishch. Roman, in *Delo*, nos. 1–7 (1875); (St. Petersburg, 1876);

Grachevy iz Grachovki. Ocherki i vospominaniia, in *Delo*, nos. 4–5 (1875); (St. Petersburg, 1875);

Starye gnezda. Roman, in *Delo,* nos. 10–12 (1875); (St. Petersburg, 1875);

Nasha pervaia liubov'. Iz vospominanii (St. Petersburg, 1876);

Pogibaiushchie v detstve sily. Ocherki obshchestvennoi zhizni (St. Petersburg, 1877);

Bespechal'noe zhit'e. Roman, in *Delo,* nos. 1–5 (1878); (St. Petersburg, 1879);

Nashi deti. Ocherki (St. Petersburg: R. Golike, 1880);

Chuzhie grekhi. Roman (St. Petersburg: Imp. Akademii nauk, 1880);

Gol'. Roman, in *Russkaia mysl',* nos. 1–4, 6–12 (1882); 2 volumes (St. Petersburg, 1883);

Nad obryvom. Roman.–Pis'ma cheloveka soshedshego s uma (St. Petersburg, 1884);

Muzh i zhena.–Nasedka.–Nashi blizhnie (St. Petersburg, 1884);

Nasha pervaia liubov'.–Lytkiny.–Prokliatyi dar (St. Petersburg, 1884);

I molotom i zolotom. Roman, in *Zhivopisnoe obozrenie,* nos. 1–12 (1884); (St. Petersburg: V. I. Gubinsky, 1885);

Razrublennyi uzel. Roman (St. Petersburg, 1886);

Prorok. Roman (St. Petersburg, 1886);

V omute (St. Petersburg, 1886);

Milye bezdel'niki (St. Petersburg, 1886);

Bezdomniki. Roman, 2 volumes (St. Petersburg: V. I. Gubinsky, 1886–1887);

Padenie. Roman (St. Petersburg: S. E. Dobrodeev, 1887);

Na raznykh beregakh. Roman (St. Petersburg, 1887);

Alchushchie. Roman (St. Petersburg, 1887);

Blaga zhizni. Roman (St. Petersburg: S. E. Dobrodeev, 1888);

Ne nam sudit'. Povest'.–Belaia noch'.–Chto bylo ee schast'em.–Diadia Kolia.–Na puti k izvestnosti (St. Petersburg, 1889);

Otshchepenets. Roman (St. Petersburg: V. I. Gubinsky, 1889);

Iz-za vlasti. Istoricheskii roman-khronika, supplement to *Zhivopisnoe obozrenie* (St. Petersburg, 1889);

Pobediteli. Roman, in *Severnyi vestnik,* nos. 1–4 (1889); (St. Petersburg, 1889);

Revoliutsionnyi anabaptizm. Istoricheskie ocherki (St. Petersburg: S. E. Dobrodeev, 1889);

Deti ulitsy. (Razorennye berlogi). Roman, supplement to *Zhivopisnoe obozrenie* (St. Petersburg, 1890);

Dvorets i monastyr'. Istoricheskii roman-khronika iz vremen velikogo kniazia Vasiliia Ivanovicha i tsaria Ioanna Groznogo, supplement to *Zhivopisnoe obozrenie* (St. Petersburg, 1890);

Rtishchev. Roman, in *Severnyi vestnik,* nos. 10–12 (1890); (St. Petersburg, 1891);

Tina. Roman, in *Severnyi vestnik,* nos. 10–12 (1890); (St. Petersburg, 1890);

Zagublennaia zhizn'. Roman, supplement to *Zhivopisnoe obozrenie* (St. Petersburg, 1891);

Iz triasiny na dorogu. Roman, in *Nabliudatel',* nos. 1–4 (1892);

Esfir'. Istoricheskaia povest' iz drevne-persidskoi zhizni.–Paskhal'naia noch'.–Povrezhdennyi.–Soblazn–Veshnie grozy–Puchina–Otchet (St. Petersburg: V. I. Gubinsky, 1892);

Trudnye gody. Povest', in *Mir Bozhii,* nos. 9–11 (1892);

Obida, in *Severnyi vestnik,* nos. 11–12 (1892);

Pozolochennyi pozor (skol'zkii put'); i, Zagublennaia zhizn'. Roman i povest' (St. Petersburg: V. I. Gubinsky, 1893);

Savonarola, ego zhizn' i obshchestvennaia deiatel'nost' (St. Petersburg, 1893);

Sovest' zazrila, in *Nabliudatel',* nos. 1–3 (1893);

Polnoe sobranie sochinenii, 15 volumes (St. Petersburg: A. F. Marks, 1894–1895);

Iz rasskazov. "Kontsy i nachala," in *Nabliudatel',* nos. 1–5 (1895);

Grekhi ottsov. Roman, in *Nabliudatel',* nos. 1–4 (1896); republished as *Grekhi proshlogo* (St. Petersburg, 1897);

Les dremuchii. Povest', in *Zhivopisnoe obozrenie,* no. 1 (1897);

Smena pokolenii. Roman, in *Nabliudatel',* nos. 1–4 (1897);

Shkola zhizni. Roman.–Glukhaia rozn'. Povest'.–Posle nas. Povest' (St. Petersburg, 1900);

Nikolai I, ego lichnost', pravlenie, dekabristy (London, 1906).

Editions and Collections: *Polnoe sobranie sochinenii,* 16 volumes, edited by A. M. Skabichevsky (St. Petersburg: A. F. Marks, 1904);

Les rubiat, shchepki letiat: Roman, edited by G. G. Elizavetina (Moscow: Khudozhestvennaia literatura, 1984);

Dvorets i monastyr'. Istoricheskii roman-khronika vremen velikogo kniazia Vasiliia Ivanovicha i tsaria Ioanna Groznogo (Moscow: Sovetskii pisatel'-Olimp, 1991);

Chuzhie grekhi (Moscow: Zenit, 1994).

The career of the popular and prolific novelist, journalist, editor, and translator Aleksandr Konstantinovich Sheller was intrinsically linked to the hopes and disappointments of the 1860s. Seeing himself as the chronicler of the lives of the "new people" of the time, the "men of the sixties," Sheller (writing under the pseudonym A. Mikhailov) focused his attention in his more than one hundred novels and stories on the strivings of this generation for self-improvement and self-transformation. Avidly read by the young people of the 1860s and 1870s, Sheller's works regularly received positive reviews from the critics only early in his career; they soon started criticizing his heavy-handed moralizing, artificiality, and lack of originality. But Sheller's popularity with the reading public endured. Addressing the question of why "over three decades the best, most advanced, thinking people have kept engrossing themselves in

Sheller's novels and still consider him among the most appealing and useful writers," the critic Aleksandr Mikhailovich Skabichevsky answered, "The reason could not be clearer or simpler: they love Sheller, and so assiduously read him because he concerns himself in his novels directly with portrayals of the mental and moral development of his contemporaries, over three decades, in different layers of society. I am convinced that in all of Russia you could not find one thinking person who has not experienced something like what is experienced by the heroes of Sheller's novels."

Aleksandr Konstantinovich Sheller was born on 30 July 1838 in St. Petersburg, from birth a member of the *raznochintsy* (people of mixed class) who were to play such an important role in the intellectual life of the 1860s. His father, Konstantin Sheller, an ethnic Estonian of peasant background, had graduated from a theatrical school and for some time performed in an orchestra, after which he served at the Imperial Court. Konstantin Sheller was characterized by a sense of inborn dignity and courage much admired by his son: the writer endowed many heroes of his novels with his father's character traits. The writer's mother was of aristocratic origin, a member of an impoverished noble family who nonetheless shared her husband's views concerning the importance of hard work. She then became the archetype for many of Sheller's fictional Russian women–pure, self-sacrificial, and loving. In his novel *Gnilye bolota* (The Putrid Bogs, 1864) Sheller wrote admiringly of a Russian woman inspired by his mother's image.

From childhood Sheller learned about the difficulties of the life of common people–specifically the lower stratum of city dwellers. He observed drunken men, downtrodden women, and homeless children. At the same time, his family life was characterized by a special moral and spiritual climate, which formed the foundation of his personality and influenced all his later life. In addition to his parents, he was influenced by his maternal grandmother, a lady with certain aristocratic claims, who dreamed that her grandson would become a member of high society. Her plans for him resulted in a certain discord, as Sheller tried to respond to the various problems connected with his family's social status.

Sheller studied privately and later gained the right to audit courses at St. Petersburg University, though he failed to graduate because of the temporary closure of the university in 1861. After leaving the university he traveled abroad while working as a private secretary to Count Apraksin. As a student, Sheller had begun writing for the journal *Vesel'chak* (The Jolly Fellow), publishing feuilletons under an anagram of his name, A. Relesh. Sheller also wrote poetry, and the publication of his poetry in the journal *Sovremennik* (The Contemporary) in 1863 marked the true beginning of his long creative career. Skabichevsky recounts that the poems were submitted without Sheller's knowledge by a childhood friend, Andrei Mikhailov. When published, they were attributed to the submitter and appeared under the name "A. Mikhailov." Sheller kept this name as a pseudonym throughout his publishing career.

In his poetry Sheller expressed ideas common among Russian nineteenth-century democratic poets, glorifying his "hero of proud patience and powerful labor" in poems such as "Dolia bedniaka" (A Poor Man's Lot), "Slabyi, bol'noi . . . " (Weak, sick . . .), and "Smert' bedniaka" (Death of a Poor Man), in which he recounts the hard life of those at the depths of the city. His lyrical hero is a representative of the Russian lower classes, who sees poetry as one of the ways to serve high and noble ideas.

Sheller is also known to have completed many poetic translations. He is responsible for translating the poetry of Adelbert von Chamisso, Ferdinand Freiligrat, Barry Cornwall, Edgar Allan Poe, and others. Attracted by the folk motifs in Sandor Petefi's poetry, Sheller was the first to introduce the latter to Russian readers. He considered Petefi's poetry to be similar to that of the Russian poet Aleksei Vasil'evich Kol'tsov and to that of Robert Burns.

Sheller's novel *Gnilye bolota,* published when the author was only twenty-five, gained him his first significant literary success. The novel appeared in *Sovremennik* in 1864, and it piqued Russian readers' interest in spite of the critics' rather reserved but generally favorable reactions. The novel is subtitled *Istoriia bez geroia* (A Story without a Hero), but in fact it chronicles the youth of Aleksandr Rudy. In an "Author's Preface" Sheller alerts his readers not to expect a typical novel, ending in a death or a marriage, saying that his book has neither "astonishing scenes, nor love, nor crime, nor a hero." Sheller's first-person narrator tells the story of his childhood and school years, and the novel analyzes in detail everything with which the child comes into contact–all the factors and circumstances influencing the maturation of his character, soul, and heart. The writer's aim was to describe the process of his protagonist's character formation–in so doing, portraying the character of a man who could make possible a better future for Russia.

As he demonstrates in *Gnilye bolota,* Sheller did not believe that political and violent social upheavals could change Russian life for the better. Although he shared many of the ideas of the radicals and populists—Sheller was an admirer of the critic Vissarion Grigor'evich Belinsky and also paid tribute to Nikolai Gavrilovich Chernyshevsky and Nikolai Aleksandrovich Dobroliubov, considering them all to be enlighteners who influenced Russian readers in a necessary and noble direction and fought in their publications for human rights—he also differed in important ways from them. He insisted on a nonviolent solution to Russia's problems, one based on principles of high moral consciousness and responsibility for every action. Correspondingly, he filled his novels with philosophical discourses on important moral and social issues of the day, such as the social position of women and the upbringing of the younger generation. In so doing, he hoped to inspire his readers, too, to consider their place in society.

Sheller's second novel, *Zhizn' Shupova, ego rodnykh i znakomykh. Avtobiografiia* (The Life of Shupov, His Relations and Friends. An Autobiography) was serialized in *Sovremennik* in 1865. Narrated, like *Gnilye bolota,* in the first person, *Zhizn' Shupova, ego rodnykh i znakomykh* presents the moral lessons of Pavel Konstantinovich Shupov's early years, from childhood to his university years. Born into a noble family, Shupov is cast out by his father after his mother's death, and he grows up in the poor family of his godfather, Leliushin, forming a close bond with the young Kol'ka Leliushin. The boys are separated when Shupov goes off to a private school but are reunited for their university studies. In his depiction of children's impressionability and of the indignities and stupidity of school life, Sheller drew extensively on his own experience, and *Zhizn' Shupova, ego rodnykh i znakomykh,* like *Gnilye bolota,* has often been seen as entirely autobiographical and has been used therefore as a major source on Sheller's own life. Sheller leaves his characters not at the end of their lives, but at their beginning: playing with readers' desire to know what happens next, Shupov says near the end,

> you can make of me and my friends whatever you want, because we ourselves stand here questioning as we enter the doors of the future; we know only that we ourselves have opened these doors, that no "grandmother" got our foot in for us and no aunt four times removed used her connections to dispatch various lackeys to clear the road for us, help us up the stairs, and fling open the doors for us. What we have done, we have done ourselves! Directing my gaze into the future, I only hope that all of us will be happy and can do at least a little for our own children, so that those children will not have the bitter right to be our opponents . . . [and] will not suffer the terrible moments I suffered when meeting my own father again: may all members of

the family learn to respect and love one another, and thus also learn to respect others not tied to them by blood.

Sheller's first two novels established the pattern for his fiction as a whole. He focused his attention on the characters' upbringing and education, assigning the utmost importance to such aspects as mental stability, consistency, independence, hard work, optimism, and the formation of a firm, far-seeing consciousness. Sheller constantly emphasized that hard work and the continual acquisition of knowledge enhance the quality of human life. Intellectual development prevents people from being lost in the impersonal crowds engaged in aimless struggles.

Because of his interest in character formation, Sheller frequently concentrates on the childhood years of his characters and on the problems of children's lives in nineteenth-century society. These problems were as important to him as they were to Leo Tolstoy, Fyodor Dostoevsky, and Charles Dickens. (Dickens's novels were in fact influential in Sheller's writing; in translation they had been his parents' favorite reading, and Skabichevsky notes that in addition to a Dickensian proclivity for external detail, "in Sheller's novels you will find characters, dramatic situations, and scenes that remind you of Dickens.") In his books Sheller often depicts his characters' childhoods as unhappy, full of humiliations and offenses, thus attracting attention to the emotions and feelings of the children and demanding respect for their tears and sufferings. He writes, "You should know that they never leave such imprints in any grown-up as they do in a child's character, drying him up, making him hard-hearted, gradually destroying his faith in any good. . . ." Sheller depicts as unhappy not only the children of the poor but also those from the well-to-do families; the child's happiness or unhappiness simply depends on how much love he or she receives. Thus, the protagonist of *Zhizn' Shupova, ego rodnykh i znakomykh* is unhappy because his mother had died when he was still a child, and his father does not love him.

Sheller's interest in childhood development was not confined to literature. Like many in his generation, Sheller devoted considerable energies to education reform and the study of new pedagogical methods. Immediately after leaving the university, he founded a school for poor children, who paid only thirty to sixty kopeks a month to attend. Sheller's school also provided Saturday lectures for adults. The school survived until 1863, when it was closed by the government in part of a larger reactionary move against such institutions. Sheller also discussed problems of upbringing and education in detail in journalistic articles and essays such as "Pervonachal'noe obrazovanie vo Frantsii" (Elementary Education in France, in *Delo* [The Cause], 1871), "Pervonachal'noe obrazovanie v Prussii, Shveitsarii i Soedinennykh Shtatakh" (Primary Education in Prussia, Switzerland, and the United States, 1873), and "Osnovy narodnogo obrazovaniia v Rossii" (Fundamentals of Popular Education in Russia, 1874).

Educators, in Sheller's view, needed to take a scientific approach to the education of the younger generation: education should be strict, consistent, truthful, accurate, enlightening, and useful. The writer appears to have assumed a firm and negative attitude toward the predominance in young people of fantastic imaginings, emotions, and overexcitement. Instead, their personalities should be shaped by a realistic attitude toward life, genuine humanism, and nobility of character. In *Zhizn' Shupova, ego rodnykh i znakomykh,* for example, a teacher describes his ungifted pupils and their problems in the following way: "Never-ending dormancy, sleep, and an inactive, lazy society have put an end to their mental development; they show a desire to rest and a complacency, especially in those cases when they have managed to establish their superiority over others. This is the first sign of imminent human failure. One must never calm down and rest; it is always necessary to think, to be on the alert, to meditate and to act."

Even as he was establishing himself as a novelist and social activist, Sheller was equally busy working as a contributor and editor for many progressive journals. The editor Grigorii Evlampievich Blagosvetlov invited him to edit the foreign section of *Russkoe slovo* (Russian Word), and when that publication was closed, Sheller moved to Blagosvetlov's new venture, *Delo*. He also worked for *Zhenskii vestnik* (Women's Herald), *Nedelia* (Week), and, later in his career, edited the weekly journal *Zhivopisnoe obozrenie* (Picturesque Review) and the newspaper *Syn otechestva* (Son of the Fatherland).

Gnilye bolota and *Zhizn' Shupova, ego rodnykh i znakomykh* set the stage for Sheller's subsequent novels. The satirist Mikhail Evgrafovich Saltykov, reviewing Sheller's next novel, *Zasorennye dorogi* (Littered Roads, 1866), wrote, "Mr. Mikhailov has written quite a lot, but everything newly written turns out to be a repetition of *Gnilye bolota*—and, unfortunately, a rather weak repetition." Of *Zasorennye dorogi,* Saltykov writes, "There is no doubt that the layer of life that is placed before our eyes here is clogged up quite adequately with litter; but in order to have the

right to be indignant about this litter it is necessary at the very least to be able to call it by name." Saltykov finds Sheller's complaints about contemporary life to be insufficiently clear and his characters to lack firm convictions: "the most elementary principles of *belles lettres* demand that a narrator at the very least explain the inner motives that govern his heroes. In Mr. Mikhailov's writings the characters knock around from corner to corner without any motives at all—even without any outward reason: they are simply puppets on strings." Saltykov's observations about the repetitiveness of Sheller's works were repeated in various forms by many other critics.

Skabichevsky, who also considered the vision of life put forward in *Gnilye bolota* emblematic of all of Sheller's work, defined this view of life as follows: "life is presented as a ceaseless struggle between two opposing elements: on the one hand, an environment of good-for-nothing idleness, of triumphant people idly chatting; on the other, an environment of honest toil, originally for one's daily bread, and, in the higher spheres of mental development, with the goal of spreading around oneself light, knowledge, truth, and good." The tension between these two elements is found within Sheller's heroes themselves; typically, Skabichevsky points out, the battle often makes up the whole content of the novel, but in the end, good prevails, and the heroes set out on a progressive path into the rest of their lives. In focusing on this inner development, though, Sheller carefully avoids chance or external distractions, a choice that contributes to the artificiality of his novels. Skabichevsky writes,

> Sheller specializes to such a degree on strict depictions of only the mental and moral development of his contemporary generation that he carefully avoids any accidental catastrophes whatsoever that, while they might move readers and make them appalled and indignant at the imperfections of our life, would not be relevant to the matter at hand. . . . The goal of his narration is in no way to suggest to us how unstable our human happiness is in this world, but, on the contrary, to suggest what a stable and rational happiness people can create by way of mental and moral development.

In his novel *Gospoda Obnoskovy* (The Obnoskov Family, 1868), Sheller once again presents a clash between petty and senseless established tradition and the suffering, forward-looking people of the new era. The Obnoskovs represent the old system of reliance on privilege, connections, and inherited wealth. But when the kindly family elder is dying, he decides not to will his inheritance to his undeserving relations but rather to distribute the better part of it to the people about whom he actually cares. Much of the novel depicts the squabbles, subterfuges, and senseless machinations that ensue. The new generation is represented by Grunia, daughter of a professor, who has married into the hapless Obnoskov family but then escapes, fleeing abroad. Sheller leaves his readers with hope for the "new people" and an epitaph for the Obnoskovs.

Throughout his career Sheller continued his journalistic work, and many of the themes of his fiction and his journalism were closely connected. In addition to his studies of elementary education, Sheller had an abiding interest in a range of other social and historical topics. His nonfiction writings include "Ocherki iz istorii rabochego sosloviia vo Frantsii" (Sketches from the History of the Working Class in France, *Nedelia* [The Week], 1868), "Zhilishcha rabochikh" (Workers' Lodgings, *Delo,* 1870), "Proizvoditel'nye assotsiatsii" (Productive Associations, *Delo,* 1870), and "Politicheskie prava i ekonomicheskaia neuriaditsa" (Political Rights and Economic Disorder, *Delo,* 1872). Later in his career Sheller's publicistic works included studies of revolutionary Anabaptism and of Girolamo Savonarola and Tommaso Campanella.

Sheller's biographers note that he demonstrated both warmth and dignity in his treatment of others. Following the ideals of many Russian nineteenth-century intellectuals, Sheller attempted to help the needy, and he was particularly known for assisting young writers. Indeed, he was extravagant in this respect, and while his tireless literary endeavors earned him respectable amounts of money, whatever he had he gave away to those who needed it more. In his reminiscences of Sheller, his contemporary Ryshkov recalls that, in his generosity, Sheller often put those in need on a stipend, and they would come to him in droves to collect a regular payment.

Sheller's readiness to help and to look for the good in human nature was reflected in his writing, too. Unlike the strident tone of many of the 1860s radical critics, many of whose ideas he was propagating, Sheller's works convey rather a sense of compassion and a measured willingness to consider all sides of any debate or action. Of this quality, Skabichevsky writes,

Is it necessary to add that at the basis of all of [Sheller's] analyses and discussions there lie humanitarian ideas of unity in a spirit of love, brotherhood and forgiveness? You will not find one line in Sheller's novels that would embitter readers or in

any way cast a shadow over them, arousing spite or hatred. Filled with a purely Christian meekness and humility, A. K. Sheller, on the contrary, is ceaselessly guided by the humanitarian principle that to understand all is to forgive all, and the most extreme degree of his condemnation goes no further than a sad lament that "they know not what they do."

Sheller's next novel, *Les rubiat—shchepki letiat* (When Trees are Felled, Chips Will Fly) was serialized in *Delo* during the course of 1871 and appeared as a separate publication the following year. The novel centers on three heroes: Aleksandr Prokhorov and Ekaterina and Anton Prilezhaev. After their father's death Ekaterina and Anton become impoverished but realize that they have to fight for themselves and for their right to be happy. Depending on their circumstances, their notion of happiness gradually changes. Eventually, they realize that happiness is the ability to earn a living, to study, and to fight against injustice. Sheller once again describes the life of the 1860s, including in his text animated discussions of the Crimean War, peasant reform, and social discontent. Sheller portrays Ekaterina and Aleksandr, who participate actively in such discussions, as unusual personalities, differing from those around them because of their strong convictions and dignity—traits of character that enable them to fight, to occupy a worthy place in their society, and to be independent and free.

Sheller's cycle of novels *Muratovy* (The Muratovs) occupied him for nearly a decade from the mid 1870s to the mid 1880s. Included in the series were the novels *Starye gnezda* (Old Houses of Gentlefolk, 1875), *Khleba i zrelishch* (Provide Them with Bread and Circuses, 1875), *Bespechal'noe zhit'e* (Life Without Sorrow, 1878), *I molotom i zolotom* (By Hammer and Gold, 1884), *Sovest' zazrila* (Conscience, 1893), and "Vne zhizni" (Beyond Life). The latter novel was left unfinished. In the series as a whole the author's aim was to chronicle the life of a family of the Russian gentry during the second part of the nineteenth century. Saltykov criticized Sheller for laying special emphasis on the personal responsibility of every character for his deeds, arguing that literature should be aimed at exposing negative aspects inherent in the foundations of contemporary Russian society as a whole.

Devoted to his parents, Sheller had dedicated *Gnilye bolota* to them, underlining his personal belief in connections between generations even as he built upon a literary tradition (marked most notably by Ivan Sergeevich Turgenev's Bazarov in *Ottsy i deti* [Fathers and Sons], 1862) that emphasized a break between the old and the new. Sheller's mother died in 1877 and his father in 1888; in caring for his ill father and at the end of his life, otherwise alone, Sheller came to depend increasingly on the selfless devotion of his cousin Tat'iana Nikolaevna Fedorova, who looked after him and took care of many of his business affairs. Sheller's own health began failing the same year his father died, but he continued both his editing work (now for *Zhivopisnoe obozrenie* and *Syn otechestva*) and his own writing, publishing several novels in the late 1880s and 1890s.

Taken as a whole, Sheller's novels present a diverse panorama of Russian life of the late nineteenth century, glossed with philosophical interpretation and serious observations in the spirit of the 1860s. It can be argued that in forming a rounded picture of an historical period, the works of a writer considered to be minor can be an important supplement to the works of a Tolstoy or Dostoevsky. Sheller's best novels record a difficult social transition in Russian history—the decline and fall of old values and the slow emergence of a new way of life and of new people, governed by rationalism and influenced by a modern upbringing and education. Contrary to Chernyshevsky's heroes, who wanted to destroy the old world, Sheller and his heroes were not iconoclasts. Sheller's outlook was positive, and he professed reforms, not revolutions. He always worked for the enlightenment of Russian society, something best accomplished by reaching young people and those who taught them. In a private letter written toward the end of his career, Sheller wrote,

> Looking back after more than thirty years on the path I have taken I see that I always strove to say what I considered to be necessary and useful in our society. I tried to show parents and teachers how they, in not wanting or knowing how to fulfill their sacred obligations, ruin their children and turn them into enemies. . . .

Aleksandr Konstantinovich Sheller died on 21 November 1900 and was buried at the Mitrofan'evsky Cemetery in a grave between his mother and father. Summing up his career and his significance for Russian literature, Skabichevsky writes, "not only in his industriousness, but in his entire character and in all his habits Sheller embodied in his life that same new ideal that he advocated in his works." The topical and tendentious nature of many of his novels, however, caused them to be largely ignored after his death. Several have been reprinted in the 1980s and 1990s, and significant new scholarship on Sheller has begun to appear.

Letters:

To A. L. Volynsky [A. L. Flekser], 10 January 1895; in A. L. Volynsky, *Russkie kritiki* (St. Petersburg, 1896), p. 480;

To N. A. Nekrasov, 1 December 1864; in *Vestnik Evropy*, 4 (1915): 142.

Bibliographies:

N. N. Bakhtin and P. Dilaktorsky, "Materialy dlia *Slovaria russkikh pisatelei*: A. K. Sheller," *Literaturnyi vestnik,* no. 8 (1901): 295–300;

"Materialy dlia slovaria russkikh pisatelei: A. K. Sheller," extracted by B. M. Gorodetsky from the bibliographic archive of S. A. Vengerov, *Literaturnyi vestnik,* no. 2 (1901): 149–163.

References:

G. A. Bialy, "Proza shestidesiatykh godov," *Istoriia russkoi literatury,* no. 8, part 1 (Moscow: AN SSSR, 1956), pp. 292–295;

A. I. Faresov, *Aleksandr Konstantinovich Sheller. Biografiia i moi o nem vospominaniia* (St. Petersburg, 1901);

Faresov, "Belletrist-vospitatel'," *Knizhki "Nedeli,"* no. 11 (1898): 118–125;

Faresov, "'Lishnii chelovek' na Zapade i nash 'delovoi,'" *Zhivopisnoe obozrenie,* nos. 22, 25, 26, 30 (1884);

Faresov, "Sovremennye literaturnye deiateli. A. K. Sheller," *Istoricheskii vestnik,* no. 2 (1896): 558–577;

Faresov, "Tragizm A. K. Shellera," *Istoricheskii vestnik,* no. 4 (1901): 163–197;

Faust Shchigrovskogo uezda [S. A. Vengerov], "Iznanka stolichnoi zhizni (Khleba i zrelishch. Roman A. Mikhailova)," *Novoe vremia,* 163 (12 August 1876): 1–2;

K. Golovin, *Russkii roman i russkoe obshchestvo* (St. Petersburg, 1897);

Maral Muradovna Kadzharova, "K biografii A. K. Shellera-Mikhailova (o nachale literaturnoi deiatel'nosti)," *Russkaia literatura,* no. 3 (1992): 141;

Kadzharova, "Romany A. K. Shellera-Mikhailova 1860-kh godov," dissertation, St. Petersburg State University, 1995;

N. Z. Kokovina, "A. K. Sheller-Mikhailov v chitatel'skoi situatsii 1860-kh godov," *Literaturnoe proizvedenie i chitatel'skoe vospriiatie* (Kalinin, 1982);

Kokovina, "A. K. Sheller-Mikhailov v demokraticheskikh izdaniiakh 60-70-kh godov XIX v," *Filologicheskie nauki,* no. 4 (1983): 80–84;

Kokovina, "O chitatel'skoi orientatsii tvorchestva A. K. Shellera-Mikhailova," *Khudozhestvennoe vospriatie: problema teorii i istorii* (Kalinin, 1988);

P. Krasnov, "Chutkii pisatel'," *Trud,* no. 9 (1894): 688–695;

O. F. Miller, *A. K. Sheller* (St. Petersburg, 1889);

A. Nalimov, "Pedagogicheskie idei Shellera-Mikhailova," *Russkaia shkola,* no. 10 (1910): 118–124;

L. E. Obolensky, "A. K. Sheller (Mikhailov)," *Russkoe bogatstvo,* no. 10 (1888): section 2, 177–183;

S. S. Okreits, "My ne soglasny, a mezhdu tem–my ne pravy . . . (A. K. Mikhailov v druzheskikh rukakh g. Postonogo)," *Biblioteka deshevaia i obshchedostupnaia,* no. 7 (1873): 73–88;

Okreits, "Pechal'nyi povorot," *Biblioteka deshevaia i obshchedostupnaia,* no. 3 (1873): 3–29;

Mikhail Evgrafovich Saltykov, "*Bespechal'noe zhit'e.* A. Mikhailov. Roman," *Otechestvennye zapiski,* no. 8 (1878): section "Novye knigi," 234–237;

Saltykov, "*V razbrod:* Roman v dvukh chastiakh A. Mikhailova," *Otechestvennye zapiski,* no. 2 (1870): section "Novye knigi," 265–270;

Saltykov, "*Zasorennye dorogi* i 'S kvartiry na kvartiru': Roman i rasskaz soch. A. Mikhailova," *Otechestvennye zapiski,* no. 9 (1868): section "Novye knigi," 46–52;

Aleksandr Mikhailovich Skabichevsky, "A. K. Sheller." *Russkaia mysl',* no. 1 (1895): section 2, 100–121; no. 2 (1895): section 2, 72–104;

Skabichevsky, "Belletristy-publitsisty," *Istoriia noveishei russkoi literatury* (St. Petersburg, 1897);

Skabichevsky, "Sentimental'noe prekrasnodushie v mundire realizma," *Otechestvennye zapiski,* no. 9 (1873): section 2, 1–34;

P. N. Tkachev, "Tendentsioznyi roman," *Izbrannye sochineniia na sotsial'no-politicheskie temy,* volume 2 (Moscow, 1932), pp. 360–435.

Aleksei Konstantinovich Tolstoy

(24 August 1817 – 28 September 1875)

Susan McReynolds
Northwestern University

WORKS: *Upyr'*, as Krasnorogsky (St. Petersburg, 1841);

Kniaz' Serebriany. Povest' vremen Ioanna Groznogo, in *Russkii vestnik*, nos. 8–10 (1862); (St. Petersburg: D. E. Kozhanchikov, 1863); first translated by Princess M. Galitzine as *Prince Serebrenni*, 2 volumes (London: Chapman & Hall, 1874);

Smert' Ioanna Groznogo, in *Otechestvennye zapiski*, no. 1 (1866): 1–116; (St. Petersburg: Tip. Morskogo ministerstva, 1866); translated by I. Henry Harrison as *The Death of Ivan the Terrible* (London: F. B. Kitto, 1869);

Stikhotvoreniia (St. Petersburg: Tip. Morskogo ministerstva, 1867);

Tsar' Fedor Ioannovich, in *Vestnik Evropy*, no. 5 (1868); (St. Petersburg: Tip. F. Sushchinskogo, 1868); translated by Jenny Covan as *Tsar Fyodor Ivanovitch* (New York: Brentanos, 1922);

Tsar' Boris, in *Vestnik Evropy*, no. 3 (1870); (St. Petersburg: Tip. F. Sushchinskogo, 1870);

Sadko, in *Russkii vestnik*, no. 1 (1873); (St. Petersburg: Tip. A. Benke, 1905);

Son statskogo sovetnika Popova (Berlin: B. Behr's Buchhandlung, 1878); republished as "Son Popova," as Koz'ma Prutkov, in *Russkaia starina*, no. 12 (1882): 701–712.

Editions and Collections: *Polnoe sobranie stikhotvorenii*, 2 volumes (St. Petersburg: Tip. M. Stasiulevicha, 1876);

Polnoe sobranie sochinenii, edited by D. N. Tsertelev, 4 volumes (St. Petersburg, 1882–1883);

Polnoe sobranie sochinenii, edited by P. V. Bykov, 4 volumes (St. Petersburg: A. F. Marks, 1907);

Polnoe sobranie stikhotvorenii, edited by Isaak Grigor'evich Iampol'sky (Moscow: Sovetskii pisatel', 1937);

Dramaticheskaia trilogiia, edited by Iampol'sky (Leningrad: Sovetskii pisatel', 1939);

Sobranie sochinenii, edited by Iampol'sky, 4 volumes (Moscow: Khudozhestvennaia literatura, 1963–1964);

Sobranie sochinenii A. K. Tolstogo, 4 volumes (Moscow: Biblioteka Ogonek, 1969, 1980);

Aleksei Konstantinovich Tolstoy in the 1860s

O literature i iskusstve (Moscow: "Sovremennik", 1986);

Protiv techeniia, edited by Viacheslav Trofimovich Kabanov (Moscow: Knizhnaia palata, 1997);

Izbrannye sochineniia, 2 volumes (Moscow: Literatura, 1998).

Editions in English: *Prince Serebryani: An Historical Novel of the Times of Ivan the Terrible and of the Conquest of Siberia*, translated by Jeremiah Curtin (New York: Dodd, Mead, 1892);

Czar Fyodor Ioannovitch, translated by Alfred Hayes, with a preface and appendix by C. Nabokoff (London: Kegan Paul, Trench, Trübner, 1924);

The Death of Ivan the Terrible, translated by Hayes, with a preface by Nabokoff (London: Kegan Paul, Trench, Trübner, 1926);

A Prince of Outlaws (Prince Serebryany), translated by Clarence Manning (New York & London: Knopf, 1927);

The Death of Ivan the Terrible, translated by George Rapall Noyes, in *Masterpieces of the Russian Drama* (New York: Appleton, 1933);

Vampires; Stories of the Supernatural, translated by Fedor Nikanov, edited by Linda Kuehl (New York: Hawthorn Books, 1969).

PLAY PRODUCTIONS: *Smert' Ioanna Groznogo,* St. Petersburg, Aleksandrinskii Theatre, 12 January 1867;

Posadnik (Castellan). St. Petersburg, Aleksandrinskii Theatre, 1877;

Tsar' Boris, Moscow, Pushkin Theatre, 1881;

Tsar' Fedor Ioannovich, St. Petersburg, Suvorin's Theatre of the Literary-Artistic Circle, 1898.

SELECTED PERIODICAL PUBLICATIONS:
"Greshnitsa. Poema," *Russkaia beseda,* no. 9 (1858): 83–88;

"Vasilii Shibanov. Ballada," *Russkii vestnik,* no. 17 (1858);

"Ioann Damaskin. Poema," *Russkaia beseda,* no. 13 (1859): 5–30;

"Don-Zhuan," *Russkii vestnik,* no. 4 (1862);

"Bog i baiadera. (Magadeva i baiadera)," *Russkii vestnik,* no. 9 (1867);

"Bylina," *Vestnik Evropy,* no. 2 (1868);

"Pesnia o Garal'de i Iaroslavne," *Vestnik Evropy,* no. 4 (1869);

"Pesnia o trekh poboishchakh," *Vestnik Evropy,* no. 5 (1869);

"Pesnia o pokhode Vladimira na Korsun," *Vestnik Evropy,* no. 9 (1869);

"Pesnia o potoke-boratyre," *Russkii vestnik,* no. 7 (1871);

"Il'ia Muromets. Bylina," *Russkii vestnik,* no. 9 (1871);

"Ballada s tendentsiei ('Poroi veseloi maia')," *Russkii vestnik,* no. 10 (1871);

"Portret. Povest' v stikhakh," *Vestnik Evropy,* no. 1 (1874);

"Drakon. Rasskaz v stikhakh, XII veka, s ital'ianskogo," *Vestnik Evropy,* no. 10 (1875);

"La Famille du Vourdulak," French original translated as "Sem'ia Vurdalaka. Iz vospominanii neizvestnogo," *Russkii vestnik,* no. 1 (1884).

Aleksei Konstantinovich Tolstoy transcends the labels used to categorize the people and works of art emblematic of his age. Neither a Slavophile nor a Westernizer, radical nor conservative, Tolstoy cultivated lyric and dramatic verse in an epoch famous for its ideologically charged prose. Tolstoy is remembered for his lyric and satirical poetry, the historical novel *Kniaz' Serebriany* (Prince Serebriany, 1862), and his trilogy of historical dramas in verse based on the reigns of the medieval rulers Ivan the Terrible, his son Fedor, and Boris Godunov. Tolstoy's reputation as a novelist has been overshadowed by his accomplishments as one of the outstanding poets and dramatists of the later nineteenth century, but *Kniaz' Serebriany,* like his drama and verse, is an artistically and politically complex and sophisticated text. It includes insights into some of the tragic dilemmas of Russian history that remain relevant and compelling today.

During his own lifetime, appreciation of Tolstoy's multifaceted literary achievements was hampered by the battle lines that divided educated Russian society into antagonistic camps of radicals and conservatives, both of which courted but failed to win his allegiance. Then, under Soviet rule, Tolstoy's impressive output of generically and ideologically complex works was forced into the inappropriate Procrustean bed of what Isaak Grigor'evich Iampol'sky, prominent Soviet editor and scholar of Tolstoy's works, calls the "shkola chistoi poezii" (school of pure art). Now the engaging humanism that informs Tolstoy's life and art can be approached with the appreciation it merits. Tolstoy defended artistic and civic freedom from the dictates of both the regime and its opponents, dedication acknowledged in Ivan Sergeevich Turgenev's remark on Tolstoy's death that "Tolstoy's humane nature shines through and breathes in everything he wrote."

Tolstoy's mother, Anna Alekseevna Perovskaia, was a descendent of the last Ukrainian hetman, Kirill Grigor'evich Razumovsky. The Razumovskys rose to social prominence, political influence, and wealth under Empress Catherine II. Tolstoy's grandfather, Count Aleksei Kirillovich Razumovsky, served as a senator under Catherine II and as a minister of public education under Alexander I. With Mariia Mikhailovna Sobolevskaia, Count Razumovsky had several illegitimate children, including Tolstoy's mother, who was born in 1799. An Imperial decree in the early nineteenth century granted the children of this union legitimacy, noble status, and the name Perovsky. Like her siblings, Anna Alekseevna led a life of privileged interaction with the Imperial court. At seventeen, she married Count Konstantin Petrovich Tolstoy. Born in 1780, Count Tolstoy was decorated for bravery in military service against France and Sweden before pursuing an undistinguished career of state service in the Senate and at the State Bank in St. Petersburg.

The marriage that took place between Anna Alekseevna and Count Tolstoy in St. Petersburg in

November 1816 was in many ways a mismatch. Besides the almost twenty-year age difference dividing them, the bride and groom came from vastly different backgrounds—the Tolstoys were old, impoverished nobility, while the Perovskys had new wealth and status that entitled them to enjoy the privileges of highest St. Petersburg society. Anna Alekseevna separated from her husband immediately after the birth of their son on 24 August 1817, taking the child to her family's Ukrainian estates, where her brother, Aleksei Alekseevich Perovsky, assumed the role of father to the child; Count Tolstoy essentially disappeared from his son's life. Aleksei Tolstoy's earliest childhood was divided between the Perovsky family estates Krasnyi Rog, built by the famous architect Rastrelli, and Pogorel'tsy. An atmosphere of luxurious refinement reigned in both homes and formed a gracious counterpart to the beauty of the Ukrainian countryside that made a strong impression on Tolstoy, a precocious child sensitive to his surroundings.

Tolstoy's idyllic early childhood in the Ukrainian countryside ended in 1826, when Anna Alekseevna joined her brother in St. Petersburg, where Perovsky was serving on an Imperial committee on education. Life in the capital furthered Tolstoy's literary development. Known by the nom de plume Antonii Pogorel'sky, Tolstoy's uncle belonged to the intellectual and artistic elite of St. Petersburg; Pogorel'sky's short stories, written during the late 1820s, were extremely successful and highly esteemed by his contemporaries. Aleksandr Sergeevich Pushkin especially valued one of Pogorel'sky's Romantic tales, and Petr Andreevich Viazemsky called Perovsky "our genuine, our only novelist" in a letter to A. I. Turgenev from February 1833. Perovsky shared his adolescent nephew's poetic experiments with his literary friends, and in 1835 Perovsky was able to tell his nephew that the verses had met with Vasilii Andreevich Zhukovsky's approval. Well acquainted with Pushkin, Nikolai Mikhailovich Karamzin, Viazemsky, and Zhukovsky, a former member of the literary group Arzamas and connected to the Pleiad, Perovsky exerted a strong influence on Tolstoy, an influence most clearly reflected in Tolstoy's early fondness for Romantic and fantastic themes.

The beauty of the Ukrainian countryside, exposure to artistic success and the literary circles of St. Petersburg through his uncle, and the family's first trip to Europe in the late 1820s and early 1830s were the most important formative influences on Tolstoy's development as a writer. A sense of love for and affinity with the West, first evoked in the ten-year-old Tolstoy's marveling at the treasures of Italian museums, cities, and artists' studios visited with his mother and uncle, inured him as an adult to the nationalism of both Slavophiles

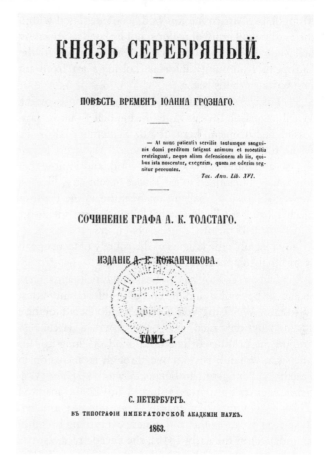

Title page for Tolstoy's historical novel Kniaz' Serebriany (Prince Serebriany), *first published in* Russkii vestnik (The Russian Herald) *in 1862 (The Kilgour Collection of Russian Literature, Houghton Library, Harvard University)*

and radicals. This first of many European visits instilled in Tolstoy the enduring conviction that he, and Russia, were part of Europe. "Khomiakov's Slavophilism troubles me when he places us above the West on the basis of our Orthodoxy," he wrote to his friend, literary advisor, and unofficial agent, Boleslav Mikhailovich Markevich in January 1870.

Thus, despite the aristocratic repugnance for the modernizing, bureaucratic autocracy of St. Petersburg that Tolstoy shared with the Slavophiles, he was never the Slavophile some contemporaries and the Soviet regime held him to be. The sense of belonging to Europe awakened during this first trip abroad and his refusal to idealize the Orthodox faith and humility as the true nature of the Russian people led him to reject the Slavophile version of Russian history. Konstantin Sergeevich Aksakov dreamed of resurrecting a *staraia Rus'* (ancient Russia) that had never existed, Tolstoy wrote in a letter to the historian and editor Mikhail Matveevich Stasiulevich in 1869, because the real, pre-

Mongol, pre-Muscovite *Rus'* had been integrated within the European family of nations, not isolated as Aksakov believed. The conviction that Russia belonged to the European community informs Tolstoy's art from his first writings to his last.

Tolstoy's description of his first glimpse of the Wartburg castle reveals his enduring belief that he possessed a European heritage. In September 1867 he wrote to his wife, Sof'ia Andreevna: "My heart began to beat and jump in the knightly world, and I know that previously I belonged to it." Prince Serebriany, like the heroes of Tolstoy's ballads, or *byliny,* bears the features of chivalrous medieval knights. Young, pure, idealistic, and dedicated to lofty causes, characters such as Serebriany resemble the knights of the courtly old European world that so appealed to Tolstoy.

Two of Tolstoy's most beautiful lyric poems, written at the beginning and end of his life, openly attest to Johann Wolfgang von Goethe's influence. Goethe's poem "Mignon's Lied" (Mignon's Song), a lyrical reverie on the beauties of Italy and *Sehnsucht* (longing) for one's native land, best known through its inclusion in Goethe's bildungsroman *Wilhelm Meister's Lehrjahre* (Wilhelm Meister's Apprenticeship, 1795–1796), inspired Tolstoy to write "Ty znaesh' krai, gde vse obil'em dyshit" (You know the land, where everything breathes abundance) in the early 1840s, the decade of Tolstoy's own lyric apprenticeship. Published in *Sovremennik* (The Contemporary) in 1854, Tolstoy's poem preserves the rhythm and reverie of Goethe's hymn to the land "where the lemons bloom," while extending the original poem in an historical direction and adding references to events of Ukrainian and Russian history to the homage of the poem to the beauty of Ukraine.

Near the end of his life, Tolstoy found inspiration in Goethe again. "Mailied" (May Song), Goethe's poem of youthful exuberance in love and spring, dating from his early *Sturm und Drang* (Storm and Stress) period, is the clear subtext of "To bylo ranneiu vesnoi" (It was in early spring), written in May 1871 and published in *Vestnik Evropy* (The Herald of Europe) that same year. Tolstoy modestly called his poem a "small pastoral, taken from Goethe" on sending it to Markevich soon after its completion. Much more than a translation, this poem, like "Ty znaesh' krai," is a lovely example of Tolstoy's rare ability to blend cultures and epochs into a voice unmistakably his own and of his capacity for appropriating and "russifying" the products of European culture in a way that carries a common tradition further, while blatantly rejecting the potential aesthetic and ideological sterility of all forms of national chauvinism. Set to music by Petr Il'ich Tchaikovsky and Nikolai Andreevich Rimsky-Korsakov, "To bylo ranneiu vesnoi" exemplifies Tolstoy's gift for raising art above national and temporal boundaries and inspiring others across generic divides, while still maintaining a distinctively individual and Russian voice.

The indelible impressions Europe left on Tolstoy as a young boy were soon joined to others when the family returned to Russia. Most notable was the exposure to Russian history he gained through his work at the Moscow Archives of the Ministry of Foreign Affairs. At the Moscow Archives, where Tolstoy began work as a sixteen-year-old in 1834 after being educated at home, his tasks included selecting and describing ancient documents. While gaining firsthand exposure to Russian history through this work at the Moscow Archives, Tolstoy also received tutoring in history and philosophy from professors at Moscow University.

Though the idealistic group of thinkers known as the *Liubomudry* (Society of Lovers of Wisdom) was physically gone from the Moscow Archives by the time Tolstoy arrived, and though the trend in Russian thought and letters was by this time—the mid 1830s—already leaning toward realism and Hegelianism, Tolstoy seems to have absorbed the legacy of German Romantic idealism that still lingered in the Moscow Archives and lived on in aristocratic pockets of Russian life. The intellectual atmosphere of the Moscow Archives, Moscow University, and aristocratic salons of the 1820s and early 1830s contributed to the imitative dimension of Tolstoy's life and art. Romantic idealist themes such as the sacred calling of the artist, the separation of real and ideal realms, and the artist's privileged access to the ideal are the topics of many of Tolstoy's works and are especially prevalent in the first ballads and lyric poems written in the late 1830s and early 1840s; however, they never dominated Tolstoy's art or worldview.

In 1835 Tolstoy received his university diploma and the right to government service as an official of the first rank. He took a leave of absence from the Moscow Archives one year later to accompany his mother and physically ailing uncle abroad. Perovsky died in his nephew's arms in Warsaw, leaving Tolstoy his entire fortune. After a brief period in St. Petersburg, Tolstoy returned to Europe as part of a Russian mission to the German Diet in Frankfurt-am-Main in 1837, where he visited Zhukovsky and met Nikolai Vasil'evich Gogol. In 1838 Tolstoy accompanied Zhukovsky and the future Alexander II to Italy, where Tolstoy spent part of the year living on Lake Como and spent the winter of 1838–1839 in Livorno with his mother.

Like his first trip abroad, this time spent in Europe stimulated Tolstoy's imagination. Experiences in Italy inspired him to compose three short, fantastic tales in the Gothic style at which his uncle had been so adept. Written in French, Tolstoy's "La Famille du Vourdulak" (The Vourdulak Family) was translated and published by Markevich in *Russkii vestnik* (The Russian Herald) in 1884. "Le rendez-vous dans trois cents ans" (The Reunion in Three Hundred Years) was first published in Paris in 1912, and a Russian translation appeared in *Russkie vedomosti* (Russian News) in 1913. *Upyr'* (Vampire), the only one of the three stories originally written in Russian, became Tolstoy's first publication, in May 1841.

Tolstoy's literary debut was epigonic in every way. Formally and thematically, *Upyr'* belonged to a past epoch of Russian literature; interest in such fantastic tales had long since peaked and waned. While Russian letters were becoming an increasingly professional field of mass commercial publishing, Tolstoy's literary life still revolved around the aristocratic salons of the capitals. Tolstoy read *Upyr'* before Zhukovsky and Vladimir Fedorovich Odoevsky at Vladimir Aleksandrovich Sollugub's salon in April 1841, one month before the story appeared in a limited edition under the pseudonym Krasnorogsky, a name derived from his maternal estate of Krasnyi Rog. *Upyr'* was the subject of sarcastic reviews in the press. But the story evoked a cautiously positive response from the critic Vissarion Girgor'evich Belinsky, who praised the new author's obvious literary talent in an 1841 review in *Otechestvennye zapiski* (Notes of the Fatherland), while criticizing his youthful excesses in the outdated fantastic style.

Although Tolstoy's first three attempts at prose ran counter to contemporary Russian literary trends, his beginnings as a prose writer illustrate the complexity that characterizes his career, for his next attempts at prose, two realistic nature sketches and a Gogolian tale of adventure on the road, published in the early 1840s, were on the cutting edge of Russian literary and social trends. "Dva dnia v kirgizskoi stepi" (Two Days in the Kirgiz Steppe) and "Volchii priemysh" (The Wolf's Foster Child), published in 1842 and 1843, respectively, attracted little public attention, probably because they were printed in the *Zhurnal konnozavodstva i okhoty* (Journal of Horse Breeding and Hunting), a specialized magazine with limited circulation. First-person narratives of rural experience told in simple yet elegant prose, these stories are early examples of the lyrical realism that Russian artists such as Ivan Turgenev and Sergei Timofeevich Aksakov later developed to such great heights. "Artemii Semionovich Bervenkovsky," first published in *Vchera i segodnia* (Yesterday and Today), a literary compendium compiled by Count Vladimir Aleksandrovich Sollogub in 1845, is a travel anecdote suggestive of Gogol's *Mertvye dushi* (Dead Souls, 1842, 1855). Finding himself stranded on the road, the narrator turns to the nearest landowner, Bervenkovsky, for help. One of Tolstoy's humorous pieces, the story satirizes the traditional Russian landowning class, laughing

at its wasteful expenditure of energy on such useless and eccentric pursuits as Bervenkovsky's attempt to construct a *perpetuum mobile*.

The contrast between the talented but derivative gentleman author of the first three tales and the formally innovative, socially insightful writer of the next three stories illustrates the most consistent and compelling quality of Tolstoy's art—its relentless drive to internal self-criticism and even self-parody. An internal dialectic fuels Tolstoy's art: every positive thesis is countered by its antithesis. Each tenet of Romantic idealism that receives serious expression is accompanied by its equally serious or parodic opposite. Belief in an ideal realm of pure forms and eternal beauty, defense of the artist's special access to that realm and his need for creative freedom, love for Western Europe, nostalgia for a perceived waning of Russia's nobility—all are presented by Tolstoy as serious theses, but none is allowed to stand unchallenged. To each of these theses, Tolstoy poses an equally sincere antithesis or a parodic inversion through satire.

A dialogue between withdrawal from the real world for the service of art and ideals, on the one hand, and a commitment to social engagement and civic responsibility, on the other, is carried on among different texts or within individual works. Early in his career Tolstoy tended to create monological lyrics and ballads: different poems speak in different voices, reflecting on one another and at times parodying one another. Later, as Tolstoy's art became more sophisticated, he produced internally dialectical or dialogical works, such as *Kniaz' Serebriany* and the trilogy, each of which carries many voices and views within itself.

Returning to Russia from Frankfurt and Italy in the early 1840s, Tolstoy plunged into an active social life in St. Petersburg. While his official career at Court proceeded under the watchful and ambitious eyes of his mother—from 1842 to 1846 he received a series of promotions that advanced him from the rank of "Titular Councilor" to "Councilor of the Court"—Tolstoy was also developing as a poet. Although he published little—only one poem appeared in the 1840s—Tolstoy cultivated his poetic repertoire over the course of the decade, perfecting his talents in the lyric, experimenting with the appropriation of folk forms, and exploring the artistic and critical potential of humor and political satire. Tolstoy's writings over the 1840s and 1850s display an impressive diversity in genre and voice, ranging from the drama, aphorisms, and satirical poems of Koz'ma Prutkov to Tolstoy's lyric and satirical verse and ballads.

Tolstoy's early poems are distinguished by the Romantic idealist themes inspired by the atmosphere at the Moscow Archives and Moscow University, but

СМЕРТЬ ІОАННА ГРОЗНАГО,

ТРАГЕДІЯ

ВЪ ПЯТИ ДѢЙСТВІЯХЪ.

Графа А. К. ТОЛСТАГО.

САНКТПЕТЕРБУРГЪ.
ПЕЧАТАНО ВЪ ТИПОГРАФІИ МОРСКАГО МИНИСТЕРСТВА,
въ Главномъ Адмиралтействѣ.
1866.

Title page for Tolstoy's Smert' Ioanna Groznogo *(The Death of Ivan
the Terrible), the first in a trilogy of historical plays depicting the
rise and fall of Boris Godunov*

they also strike notes of social criticism and point
ahead to future formal developments in Russian
poetry. Often elegiac and reminiscent of a Zhuk-
ovskian melancholy, and frequently nostalgic for lost
ways of life, these early lyrics constitute the most conservative body of Tolstoy's texts, both formally and
thematically. His first known poem, "Prosti" (Farewell),
probably written in the late 1830s when he broke off a
romance with a woman of whom his mother disapproved, offers the poet's beloved consolation in the
belief of reunion in the other, better world to come
after this one. "Prosti" points ahead to Tolstoy's later
Romantic idealist appropriation of "Don-Zhuan" (Don
Juan), published in 1862, the same year as *Kniaz' Serebriany.* In both "Prosti" and "Don-Zhuan," earthly love
is either thwarted or ultimately dissatisfying; it functions as a premonition of a higher, spiritual realm
where the true, spiritual nature of love will be revealed.
Dedicated to Wolfgang Amadeus Mozart and E.T.A.
Hoffmann—whom Tolstoy (in a letter to Markevich
from March 1860) called the first to see Don Juan as a
"seeker of an ideal, and not just a simple playboy"—

Tolstoy's "Don-Zhuan" shows the influence of Pushkin's *Kamennyi gost'* (The Stone Guest, 1830).

Tolstoy wrote twelve poems in the 1840s; some
express a Romantic idealist view of the superiority of
art to life and exude an aristocratic nostalgia that many
of his contemporaries and Soviet critics identified as evidence of Tolstoy's improper class consciousness. "Shu-
mit na dvore nepogoda" (A Storm Sounds in the Yard)
and "Pustoi dom" (The Empty House), both written in
the 1840s and published in 1856–in *Otechestvennye zapiski*
and *Russkii vestnik,* respectively–reflect on the theme of
forgotten aristocratic dignity, lost in the modern state.

"Kolokol'chiki moi" (My Bluebells) and "Oi
stogi, stogi" (Haystacks, Haystacks), written in the
1840s and published in *Sovremennik* in 1854, were
immediate sensations and remained two of Tolstoy's
most popular works; in a letter to Sof'ia Andreevna
from October 1856, Tolstoy called "Kolokol'chiki
moi" one of his "most successful things." The poem
exemplifies Tolstoy's complexity: the lifelong opponent of nationalism, Slavophilism, and the Muscovite
state, who became an outspoken critic of the regime's
russification policies in Poland after the uprising of
1863, Tolstoy nevertheless wrote two folk-style poems
that express the hope that Moscow, the "svetlyi grad"
(bright city) of "My Bluebells" and the "orel" (eagle)
of "Haystacks, Haystacks," will unite the Slavic peoples. The different Slavic tribes are the "haystacks"
who appeal to "Nash otets dalekii . . . Groznyi, svet-
lookii!" (Our far-away father . . . mighty, bright-eyed!).

Tolstoy's life and work defy simple classification
as conservative or progressive; the dialectical quality
of his views is apparent in the differences between the
original, prepublication version of "Kolokol'chiki moi"
and the Pan-Slavist poem that was eventually published. In place of the calling of Russia to unite the
Slavic lands, the first version of "Kolokol'chiki moi"
emphasizes longing for the pre-Muscovite past, for
Novgorod, and for a Russia led by aristocratic, powerful noblemen, the boyars: "Novgoroda l' vam zhal'? /
Dikoi li svobody?" (Do you miss Novgorod? / Wild
freedom?) the first poem asks the flowers. "Vy zvenite
o bylom, / Vremeni dalekom, / Obo vsem, chto otts-
velo, / Chego net uzh bole, / O boiarakh na Rusi, / O
kazatskoi vole!" (You ring about the past, / Long ago
times, / About everything that has faded, / that is no
more, / About the boyars in Rus', / About Cossack
freedom!).

The 1850s marked the high point of Tolstoy's
poetic production; in 1856 alone Tolstoy published
more than twenty-four poems and ballads in diverse
journals. The decade was also the time of Tolstoy's
close collaboration with and then his parting from
widely disparate circles of Russian intellectual life. His

collaboration with Nikolai Alekseevich Nekrasov and the liberal circles around *Sovremennik* lasted from 1854 until 1857, when Tolstoy broke ties with them. A period of collaboration with *Russkaia beseda* (Russian Talk) and close interaction with Slavophiles Aleksei Stepanovich Khomiakov, Konstantin Sergeevich Aksakov, and Ivan Sergeevich Aksakov followed. But Tolstoy's relations with the Slavophiles, like those with the Natural School around Nekrasov, were short-lived; no movement or journal could house him. Later, in the 1860s, Tolstoy published in both Mikhail Nikiforovich Katkov's reactionary *Russkii vestnik* and the liberal journal *Vestnik Evropy,* since he regarded no political philosophy as having exclusive claim to himself or to the truth.

Tolstoy's ballads, or *byliny* (he made no distinction between the terms), from the 1840s and 1850s reveal his growing interest in the reign of Ivan the Terrible (1533–1584) and the events leading to the *Smutnoe vremia* (Time of Troubles) in the early seventeenth century. Tolstoy drew on Karamzin's *Istoriia gosudarstva Rossiiskogo* (History of the Russian State, 1818–1829) and other historical sources for the topics of ballads such as *Vasilii Shibanov* and *Kniaz' Mikhailo Repnin* (Prince Mikhailo Repnin), written in the 1840s and published in 1858 and 1867, respectively. In the tale of *Kniaz' Mikhailo Repnin,* inspired by Prince Andrei Mikhailovich Kurbsky's sixteenth-century *Istoriia Ioanna Groznogo* (History of Ivan the Terrible), Tolstoy describes how the boyar Repnin weeps at the sight of the drunken czar dancing with his *skomorokhi* (traveling minstrels) and reproaches the czar for degrading his rank and surrounding himself with the *oprichnina* (a militarized government branch created by and under the direct control of the czar). Ivan can bear no criticism and stabs Repnin in a fit of rage when the boyar refuses to join the revelry; Ivan then descends into a fit of grief and self-recrimination. The emotional volatility from murderous rage to exaggerated self-abnegation and back to rage again are a constant feature of all of Tolstoy's representations of Ivan. Ivan's humiliation of Repnin in this ballad predicts his humiliation of the boyar Morozov, whom he dresses as a jester at a feast in *Kniaz' Serebriany.*

Karamzin's *Istoriia* provided the source for the ballad *Vasilii Shibanov,* in which Ivan impales Kurbsky's faithful messenger in the foot; despite torture, Shibanov remains faithful to Kurbsky. *Staritskii voevoda* (The Governor of Staritsk), written in 1858 and published that year in *Russkii vestnik,* adumbrates the paranoia and cruelty that dominate Ivan's character in *Kniaz' Serebriany* and *Smert' Ioanna Groznogo* (The Death of Ivan the Terrible, 1866). Rumors of treason reach Ivan's ears, and he performs a sadistic parody of a coronation, dressing the old man under suspicion in regal robes and placing him on the throne before stabbing him in the heart. Ballads

of the 1840s and 1850s, such as *Staritskii voevoda,* based on events of the sixteenth century, anticipate the development of Ivan's character in the novel and drama, and reveal Tolstoy's growing interest in history.

In 1858 Tolstoy published more than thirty poems. The year marked a turning point in his career. In the late 1850s Tolstoy began the transition from lyric to narrative and narrative-in-verse that culminated in *Kniaz' Serebriany* and the historical trilogy. The narratives-in-verse "Greshnitsa" (The Sinner, written in 1857) and "Ioann Damaskin" (John of Damascus, written in 1859) were both published in Aksakov's *Russkaia beseda* in 1858 and 1859.

During these years a series of official appointments bound Tolstoy increasingly to the intimate circle of the Imperial family, ties that Tolstoy always experienced as personally oppressive and as irreconcilable with his art. In fact, much of his life was spent rattling the golden chains that bound him to the Court, since he and the future Alexander II had both been eight years old when Tolstoy was presented to the heir apparent as one of a select circle of playmates. Tolstoy was appointed Master of Ceremonies at Court in 1851, and Alexander II named Tolstoy an aide-de-camp the day of his coronation in 1856. When Tolstoy finally liberated himself from his official duties in 1861, he insisted on the incompatibility of art with any and all forms of worldly "service." In his letter to the emperor, Tolstoy writes, "Service, *whatever it might be,* is deeply opposed to my nature. . . . I thought . . . that I could conquer the nature of the artist in me, but experience has shown, that I fought futilely with it. *Service and art are incompatible.*"

But Tolstoy served his ideals well. His own life exemplified a successful combination of loyalty to civic ideals and adherence to a strict code of personal honor, a combination sought for but never satisfactorily achieved by his sixteenth-century characters, such as Serebriany and Boris Godunov. The spirit of personal independence and civic responsibility motivating Tolstoy's desire to leave government service and devote himself to art also led him to intervene in public affairs. He interceded on behalf of figures as disparate as Ivan Aksakov (in 1862), Ivan Turgenev (in 1863), and Nikolai Gavrilovich Chernyshevsky (in 1864) with Alexander II. Tolstoy's personal intervention with the emperor helped mitigate Turgenev's punishment for his words on the death of Gogol, but Tolstoy's courageous defense of Chernyshevsky, a man whose views on art and society were antithetical to Tolstoy's own, unfortunately had no effect with Alexander. Friendship and collaboration across class and ideological lines were typical of Tolstoy, who by the end of his life maintained close ties with only a few authors, including Afanasii Afanas'evich Fet, Ivan Aleksandrovich Goncharov, and Markevich.

Tolstoy's novel *Kniaz' Serebriany* was already conceived in his imagination in the 1840s; there is some evidence that he began work on it then, possibly as a drama rather than a novel. By 1850, when he was stationed in Kaluga, his work on the novel had progressed far enough to allow him to read parts of it to Gogol and A. O. Smironova-Rosset, the wife of the provinicial governor and friend of Pushkin and Gogol. Then the great lyrical decade of the 1850s intervened; Tolstoy's correspondence attests to an abiding commitment to *Kniaz' Serebriany,* but he put active work on the novel aside. Besides his bursts of lyric creativity, state service occupied Tolstoy's attention during the 1850s. Tolstoy wanted to perform active military service in the Crimean War, but he contracted typhus and spent 1855–1856 recuperating in Odessa.

In 1850 Tolstoy had met Sof'ia Andreevna Miller (née Bakhmeteva) at a ball. Unhappily married to a man who would not grant her a divorce, Sof'ia Andreevna became Tolstoy's de facto wife until they were finally able to marry on 3 April 1863, a marriage expedited not only by her divorce but also by the death of Tolstoy's possessive mother. Sof'ia Andreevna joined Tolstoy in Odessa despite gossip, and Alexander II requested daily telegrams reporting Tolstoy's condition. One felicitous result of the otherwise ill-fated journey to the Crimea was the composition of the *Krymskie ocherki* (Crimean Sketches), a collection of fourteen poems that were published in 1856 and 1867.

After his release from state service in 1861, Tolstoy retired to his estates at Pustyn'ka (near St. Petersburg) and Krasnyi Rog (in Chernigovsky province). His relations with the emperor cooled, but his friendship with the empress, Mariia Aleksandrovna, grew closer. She became Tolstoy's literary confidante, with whom he shared works in progress. In 1860 Tolstoy wrote to Markevich that he had completed the second part of a novel begun in the 1840s and that he had written a "dramaticheskaia poema" (a dramatic poem), "Don-Zhuan." Tolstoy continued to work on *Kniaz' Serebriany* throughout 1861 at Krasnyi Rog, and the novel, dedicated to Empress Mariia Aleksandrovna, was published in *Russkii vestnik* in 1862.

Kniaz' Serebriany portrays fictional and historical events from the latter period of the reign of Ivan the Terrible. The novel shows the struggle between Ivan, who is trying to break the independent strength of the boyars with his *oprichnina,* and the aristocratic spirit of independence and dignity embodied in fictional boyars, such as Prince Serebriany and Druzhina Andreevich Morozov. The melancholy theme that the era of aristocratic glory lies in the past—expressed in the poems and ballads of the 1840s and 1850s—is developed with much more sophistication in *Kniaz' Serebriany* and then the dramatic trilogy, in which it appears in dialectical form. In these later texts, the thesis of the value and importance of the old nobility is countered by the antithetical insight that its qualities have become not merely useless but actually harmful to Russia.

Thus Ivan, whom the novel portrays as a fascinating psychological anomaly, is not the object of Tolstoy's severest recrimination; nor are Ivan's *oprichniks,* who are shown to be unfortunate perversions of human nature. The boyars, whose admirable values paradoxically result in their complicity with Ivan, elicit Tolstoy's deepest indignation. The moral code that distinguishes Serebriany and Morozov from "new men," such as Boris Godunov, who advances to great power and prestige over the course of the novel and trilogy, also renders them unwilling to challenge the moral outrages perpetrated by Ivan and the *oprichniks,* because such resistance sometimes requires compromises in dignity or honesty. In the foreword to *Kniaz' Serebriany,* the author writes "that while reading the sources the book more than once fell from his hands and he threw down the pen in disgust, not so much from the thought that Ivan IV could exist, but that a society could exist which would look on him without disgust."

The figure of Boris Godunov represents a tragic synthesis of a positive ethic of state service—upheld as a worthy goal—and a negative excess of personal ambition: Boris is willing to resort to any means in the service of desirable goals. The amoral, politically cunning means by which Godunov attempts to realize his positive goals for Russia meet with success in *Kniaz' Serebriany* and *Smert' Ioanna Groznogo,* in which Godunov rises to great power and brings about the abolition of the wicked *oprichnina.* But his willingness to walk a crooked path—"ia ne priamoiu, a okol'noiu dorogoi idu" (I walk a devious road, not a straight one), he tells Serebriany—finally dooms him to self-destruction in the final play and condemns Russia to the sufferings of the Time of Troubles.

The conflict between the simple chivalry of characters such as Serebriany—whose values of honesty, loyalty, and individual dignity the novel shows to be obsolete—and the skillful political calculation of Godunov, who is willing to use deceitful and demeaning techniques in the pursuit of honorable ends, produces the tragic paradox of Russia's modernization in the novel and trilogy. The boyarstvo's adherence to a strict code of personal morality is upheld as the basis of all true service, but it also hampers progress by rendering boyars such as Serebriany incapable of combating Ivan's despotism and his *oprichnina.* Tolstoy, who embodied the best qualities its apologists and he himself ascribed to the old boyarstvo–independence, disdain for careerism or personal advantage, and an unwavering sense of honor and duty–critically questioned the role his class had played in the tragedies of Russian history that enthralled him.

Before the action of the novel begins, the reader is told in the opening pages, Ivan had sent Prince Serebriany to negotiate peace with Lithuania, but "Serebriany was not born for negotiations." Serebriany will not resort to deceit, even to pursue an advantageous peace for Russia: "Rejecting the subtlety of diplomatic procedure, he wanted to conduct the affair honestly, and, to the extreme annoyance of his secretaries, he allowed them no intrigues." Serebriany greets Ivan's decision to cease negotiations and resume the war joyfully, and he shows his merits on the battlefield to be superior to those at the negotiating table.

Returning to Russia after years of fighting in Lithuania, Serebriany finds his homeland changed almost beyond recognition: Ivan rules capriciously and despotically, and the *oprichnina,* whom Serebriany encounters with disbelief for the first time in the opening pages of the novel, terrorizes boyars and peasants. Because Serebriany refuses to compromise his honesty or dignity, he undergoes a series of misadventures. A brave soldier, Serebriany eagerly defends the innocent from *oprichniks* with physical violence, but he is unwilling to protect himself or anyone else if doing so requires guile. His first meeting with *oprichniks,* whom he finds plundering a defenseless village, ends with his violent attack on the czar's men; only the appearance of a gang of bandits, who try to explain to him who the *oprichniks* are, prevents him from killing them. His friend Morozov, whom Serebriany visits after the attack, tries to detain him because he knows that Ivan will condemn Serebriany to death for the attack on the *oprichniks* if he appears before the czar; but Serebriany insists that his life is in the hands of God. Asserting that "it is not right to try to extend it [life] by cunning longer than God wills," Serebriany appears before the czar at the risk of his life.

Serebriany escapes execution only with the help of the bandits. When they break into his prison cell to rescue Serebriany from execution, moreover, he refuses to leave, insisting that he gave his word to accept the czar's judgment. The bandits forcibly rescue him; having fallen into their hands, he acquiesces to their demand that he be their new ataman and leads them to victory against the Tartars. When Ivan seeks to reward Serebriany by making him an *oprichnik,* Serebriany requests permission to go to the Siberian frontier instead; he leaves Russia for Siberia, where he seeks and finds a soldier's death in battle.

Unable to adapt to Ivan's autocratic state, Serebriany finds himself pushed to the margins of Russian society–literally in his self-imposed exile to Siberia and figuratively in his alliance with the bandits, outcasts who, despite their ignoble pursuit of theft, embody positive values of loyalty and honesty among themselves. The other major characters suffer equally tragic endings. Elena, the woman Serebriany had loved before going to Lithuania, has married his old friend Morozov. Believing Serebriany to have fallen in battle, Elena, subject to the unwelcome attentions of an *oprichnik,* seeks protection through her marriage. By marrying Elena, however, Morozov arouses the wrath of Ivan, who had supported his *oprichnik's* suit for her hand.

Like Serebriany, Morozov embodies noble honesty and fealty to the czar and refuses to resort to deception or debase himself. Angry that Morozov has married Elena despite his support of the *oprichnik's* suit for her hand, Ivan orders Morozov to sit at the czar's table beneath Boris Godunov, who possesses no noble rank. Morozov refuses, and Ivan punishes Morozov's disobedience with banishment from his sight. Morozov expresses no resentment but instead mourns his exile from Ivan's good graces: "It grieved the boyar not to see the sovereign's eyes, but he did not bring shame upon his family, he did not sit beneath Godunov!" When Serebriany meets Morozov again after his long absence in Lithuania, the prince asks Morozov why he is in disgrace; "because I preserve old custom, maintain boyar honor, and don't bow to new people!" Morozov exclaims. Morozov prides himself on his unwavering dedication to speak his mind before the czar, even at the risk of his own life. After being subjected to repeated humiliations by Ivan, including (in addition to being commanded to sit beneath Boris Godunov at the czar's table) being dressed as Ivan's jester and witnessing the sacking and burning of his home by *oprichniks,* Morozov is finally executed, beheaded in public ceremony. Elena retreats to a nunnery. The novel ends shortly before Ivan's death, with the conquest of Siberia by Cossack bands.

Kniaz' Serebriany is an indictment of the autocratic despotism Tolstoy found embodied in Ivan the Terrible. All natural feeling and decency have left Ivan, who delights in bloodshed and suffering. When in a good mood, the narrator observes, Ivan "dozed or drove to the prison to torture some poor person. This horrible sight seemed to amuse him: he returned with a look of heartfelt satisfaction; he joked, conversed more cheerfully than usual." Charismatic and eloquent, with his smile Ivan charms even those who suffer from his cruelty. Endowed with an "uncommon gift for words," he can mesmerize even good people: "It happened that good people, hearing the tsar, were convinced of the

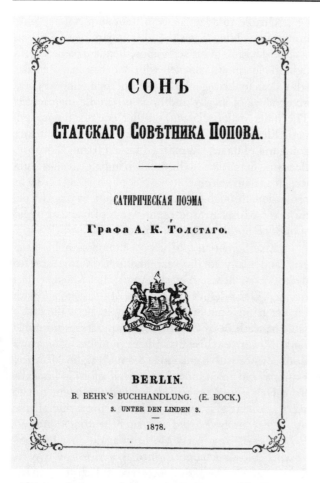

СОНЪ

Статскаго Совѣтника Попова.

САТИРИЧЕСКАЯ ПОЭМА

Графа А. К. Толстаго.

BERLIN.
B. BEHR'S BUCHHANDLUNG. (E. BOCK.)
3. UNTER DEN LINDEN 3.

1878.

Title page for Son statskogo sovetnika Popova *(The Dream of State Councillor Popov), Tolstoy's satirical poem on the civil service and police*

necessity of his horrible measures, and, while he spoke, believed in the fairness of his executions." When his notorious adviser and henchman Grigory Luk'ianovich Skuratov-Bel'sky, nicknamed Maliuta, insinuates that the czarevitch is guilty of plotting against his father, Ivan's unnatural wrath drives him to order the murder of his own son, who is abducted at his command but is rescued by the same bandits who had saved Serebriany from execution.

Tolstoy portrays the *oprichnina* as a scourge on all honest people, pillaging Russia with savage brutality and specifically intent on the liquidation of the boyars as a class. Maksim Skuratov accuses his father, Maliuta, of murdering innocent boyars: "Not because of their guilt, but out of evil you cut boyars heads off!" He exhorts his father to admit that he seeks the boyars' extermination, not the just punishment of treason; admit, Maksim taunts Maliuta, "that you indiscriminately want to destroy the boyars by the roots!"

Maliuta relishes the opportunity to humiliate Serebriany, imprisoned and facing interrogation.

Maliuta says that he and his ilk are just little people before the great princes from ancient families, who have never soiled their hands with blood and torture; he adds that it is said their blood is even different from his. Threatening the prince with a knife, Maliuta whispers, "Allow, father-prince . . . allow me, before the interrogation, just for fun, to see your boyar blood!" and he would have tortured Serebriany if not for the intervention of Boris Godunov.

But despite Ivan's creation of the *oprichnina* and his violation of the trust and responsibility placed in him as czar, no one, not even his victims, questions his right to rule. The psychological mechanisms by which Ivan deflects guilt from himself are shown to be the same sources of the passivity and fatalism that prevent the best of Russian society, boyars such as Serebriany and Morozov, from opposing him. All of his subjects, from the boyars to the bandits and *oprichniki,* uphold Ivan's sanctity as their God-given ruler. Just as Ivan believes himself to be God's emissary on earth, his subjects, too, explain all his actions as divinely ordained and preclude any criticism of him as not just treasonous but even heretical. Although he is visited by fantastic visions of his victims and the terrors of hell, Ivan ascribes these fleeting visions and the temporary mood of contrition and mercifulness that accompanies them to the work of the devil, trying to lead him astray from his divinely appointed task of cleansing Russia of treason.

Like Ivan, Serebriany and Morozov explain the czar's actions in religious terms, as punishment sent to them and Russia for their sins. They justify and exonerate Ivan, the vessel of the divine will, as a victim of evil, deceitful friends. The czar, they say, is enthroned by God "chtoby karat' i milovat'" (to punish and pardon). Upholding the principle of divine right, they insist that the czar must decide whom to punish and whom to forgive; if Ivan errs in judgment, "not the Czar is to blame for that, but his informers!" "We have angered God," Morozov tells Serebriany; "he has darkened the Czar's bright eyes!" Serebriany concurs with Morozov's interpretation of Ivan's behavior, affirming "it is God punishing us!"

Although Ivan abuses his power, the boyars cannot imagine being without a ruler. Telling Serebriany how Ivan attempted to abdicate the throne and how the boyars pleaded with him to remain in power, Morozov says, "we could not be without a Czar," and he describes how a great wail arose from Moscow on Ivan's departure: "Who will rule over us now!" Morozov concludes, "Let his holy will be done," and the boyars' discussion of Ivan ends with their toast to the czar and the wish that God open his eyes.

The fool Vasia recognizes Serebriany and Morozov as his brothers. "You are my brother!" Vasia exclaims on meeting Serebriany on a Moscow street, "you are just as blessed as I. And your mind is no greater than mine . . . I see your whole heart. You are pure there, pure, there is naked truth there; you and I are both fools!" Serebriany, just arrived in Moscow after his absence in Lithuania, is looking for his old friend Morozov and asks Vasia where the boyar lives. On hearing Morozov's name, Vasia exclaims that Morozov is one of them. When Serebriany later tells Morozov of his encounter with Vasia, Morozov remarks that Ivan fears Vasia and expresses the belief that such honesty and purity offer the solutions to the problems of Russia: "if there were more such holy people, then there would be no *oprichnina!*"

But the novel repudiates Morozov's self-serving interpretation of history, revealing that the blessed foolishness of Vasia and the boyars, while admirable, is incapable of resisting the evil of autocracy. During this dark period of Russian history, the best servant of the national good is paradoxically Boris Godunov, who combines a self-interested quest for power with a realism that allows him to achieve more concrete good than Serebriany or Morozov. Unlike the boyars, who abstain from cunning no matter what the consequences of such abstention for themselves or Russia, Boris Godunov is willing to use any means to attain his goals. He saves the city of Riazan' from being gambled away to the Tartars by Ivan, who has had too much to drink and makes a boastful bet; he saves Serebriany's life; he tries to explain to the prince that unconditional honesty is not always the best way to achieve good, but Serebriany does not comprehend him. Observing that Ivan trusts Godunov, Serebriany, who persists in believing that Ivan is simply unaware of the *oprichnina's* evil deeds, insists that Godunov should inform the czar of the truth. Boris replies that it is easy to tell the truth but that such honesty is often purposeless and even counterproductive.

While the novel does represent a generic shift from poetry to prose, it incorporates many stylistic features that had become trademarks of Tolstoy's lyrics. As in his poetry, Tolstoy's language in his novel moves up and down the stylistic register, from lofty Biblical passages—often used by Ivan in (often mock) contrition or when he is blasphemously appropriating the voice of God to mete out punishment or grant forgiveness—to the language of bandits and peasants. The novel includes several songs closely modeled on existing folk songs. In his quest for historical verisimilitude, Tolstoy relied on the works of Karamzin and contemporary ethnographers, from whom he borrowed material details of everyday life for his portrait of sixteenth-century Muscovite life and mores. The novel also includes frequent intrusions by Tolstoy, who engages in lyrical rev-

erie and descriptions of nature reminiscent of his early poems and nature sketches.

Tolstoy's conception of the artist's relationship to history had progressed since the composition of his historical ballads. In the foreword to *Kniaz' Serebriany,* Tolstoy defended artistic freedom, asserting that he had taken artistic liberties with the historical facts as a way to arrive at a greater effect, as he did with his "inexact" or "careless" poetry. Admitting that he had changed some dates and details, Tolstoy wrote that his goal was not merely the accurate description of events, but the "izobrazhenie obshchego kharaktera tseloi epokhi" (representation of the general character of the whole epoch). Some scenes closely adhere to their representation in Karamzin's *Istoriia,* such as Serebriany's combat with a bear in the Sloboda, the attack and burning of Morozov's house by *oprichniki,* and the descriptions of public executions.

The fantastic, which had figured prominently in Tolstoy's early lyric poetry and ballads, plays a new role in the novel: rather than requesting the reader's suspension of disbelief, Tolstoy uses the fantastic to historicize the world and characters of the novel. Ivan is not the only character to experience the supernatural. Besides the czar's nocturnal visions of his murdered victims, the novel portrays a miller who lives in the forest and practices sorcery and whom many characters seek out for magic charms and divinations of the future.

Kniaz' Serebriany was largely dismissed by critics as an anachronism. The historical novel had been popular with Russian readers in the 1830s, and the review of *Kniaz' Serebriany* that appeared in *Russkoe slovo* (The Russian Word) in 1863 was typical of the criticism: the reviewer asked how the author could "sympathize with what turned to dust long ago" if he is acquainted with the questions and tasks confronting the present age. But the public greeted the novel with enthusiasm and made it a popular success. It went through three print runs during Tolstoy's lifetime and was translated into French, German, English, Polish, and Italian. Turgenev recommended *Kniaz' Serebriany* to a French publisher for translation, noting that it was "in the spirit of Walter Scott . . . entertaining, well-constructed and well written." Critics, though, have noted that Tolstoy's novel bears some resemblance to Mikhail Nikolaevich Zagoskin's 1829 novel *Iurii Miloslavsky.*

The clash of the boyartsvo's aristocratic code of honesty and individual dignity with despotism and political cunning, a clash Tolstoy found embodied in the tragic events and figures of the sixteenth century, continued to preoccupy him after the completion of *Kniaz' Serebriany.* Tolstoy's dramatic trilogy covers the years 1584–1605, from the last days of Ivan's reign up to the death of Boris Godunov. Like *Kniaz' Serebriany,* the trilogy explores the origins of despotism in the psychology of characters such as Ivan, and it investigates the reasons why individuals and an entire society passively endure tyranny. For the trilogy, as for the novel, Tolstoy relied primarily on Karamzin. Tolstoy began work on *Smert' Ioanna Groznogo* as soon as *Kniaz' Serebriany* was published, while he was living in Dresden during the winter of 1862–1863.

One of the clearest expressions of the conflict between aristocratic values and political necessity is offered by Boris Godunov in *Smert' Ioanna Groznogo*. In the plays, as in *Kniaz' Serebriany,* Tolstoy's portrait of Godunov balances appreciation of Godunov's indisputable services to Russia with moral censure of the means by which he serves his country; this censure ends when Boris's unethical means cause his downfall in the final play, *Tsar' Boris* (Czar Boris). Godunov's inner speech is concealed from the reader in *Kniaz' Serebriany,* but his first monologue in *Smert' Ioanna Groznogo* reveals the psychological sources of Boris's actions, consistent through each of Tolstoy's texts. Reflecting on the difference between a "novyi chelovek" (new man) such as himself and the boyars, Godunov compares his fate to that of the boyar Zakhar'in:

Kak by rad ia, otets moi, bez uklona
Vsegda vpered idti priamym putem!
No mozhno li mne? Ty znaesh' gosudaria,
Ty znaesh' protivnikov moikh
. . . .
Chto delat' mne? Ia dolzhen ne usypno
Za kozniami vragov moikh sledit'
I khitrosti protivostavit' khitrost'
Il' otkazat'sia dolzhen navsegda
Sluzhit' zemle

How happy I would be, old man, without bowing
To walk always forward along a straight path!
But is it possible for me? You know the sovereign,
You know my opponents
. . . .
What can I do? I must tirelessly
Follow the intrigues of my enemies
And counter cunning with cunning
Or give up forever
Service to my country.

For Tolstoy himself, there was no higher moral imperative than to "idti priamym putem" (walk along a straight path) always and in all things, but he unsparingly exposed the disastrous consequences of such rigidity. He also traced the inevitable destructiveness of moral compromise, the alternative to the boyars' ethical absolutism embodied in the rise and fall of Godunov and the advent of the Time of Troubles. In the world of *Kniaz' Serebriany* and the plays,

ethical absolutism and flexibility both result in tragedy. A sense of resignation envelops Tolstoy's account of the decline of noble values.

As in *Kniaz' Serebriany,* the boyars of *Smert' Ioanna Groznogo* are politically ineffectual, divided among themselves by petty disputes over rank and incapable of conceiving any alternative to passive endurance of Ivan's despotism. Ivan, sunk in remorse over his murder of his eldest son, asks the boyars to nominate a new czar to replace him. Instead of seizing the opportunity, they cannot agree on which of them should take precedence and prefer to remain subject to Ivan, who was made czar by God rather than by election, for "his anger and mercy are both from God." One boyar insists that they should replace Ivan, because the czar's madness poses a greater threat to Russia than external enemies such as the Tartars, but his warning goes unheeded; Ivan has devastated the country, the majority avers, "but without a Czar it would be even worse."

As in *Kniaz' Serebriany,* Ivan vacillates between holding himself to a moral standard of behavior and believing himself to be above such standards, as God's anointed representative. His feelings of remorse and guilt over killing his son dissipate instantly when he hears of Russian military victories, and he relapses into megalomania. Godunov's character also develops consistently from his portrait in the novel. While the boyars are rendered helpless by their antiquated ideas about rank and cannot agree on a course of action, Boris skillfully manipulates them to endorse his proposal. Because he understands Ivan's character, Boris proposes that they beseech the czar to remain on the throne. While he is motivated by the desire to preserve his own power, which at this point still depends on the favor he enjoys with Ivan, Boris's actions nevertheless preserve the boyars from almost certain execution–by the time they appear before him, Ivan has undergone a change of heart and no longer wishes to abdicate. Had they elected a replacement for him, Ivan surely would have killed them.

Tolstoy finished a complete version of *Smert' Ioanna Groznogo* at the end of 1863, but it did not appear until he entrusted it to Goncharov, who struggled with official obstacles to its publication before he finally succeeded in printing it in *Otechestvennye zapiski* in 1866. After this initial print run, Tolstoy added some of the most significant lines of the play, including those spoken at the conclusion by the boyar Zakhar'in at the sight of Ivan's corpse: "Forgive us all! There is the punishment of autocracy! / There is the result of our collapse!" Empress Mariia Aleksandrovna helped raise money for the staging of the play, and with her support prominent scholars and artists were enlisted in its production. The play premiered before Alexander II in St. Petersburg in

January 1867 at the Mariinskii Theater. While the press was critical, the play enjoyed the support of the emperor and empress, who attended performances twice.

Tolstoy began composing *Tsar' Fedor Ioannovich* in 1864 and worked on the play through 1867, while supervising the production of *Smert' Ioanna Groznogo* and publishing the only volume of his collected poetry printed during his lifetime. The play was published in *Vestnik Evropy* in 1868, but it was never performed while Tolstoy was alive. Unlike Tolstoy's representations of historical characters in *Kniaz' Serebriany* and the other plays, the portrait of Fedor is entirely Tolstoy's poetic creation, an original departure from the treatment of Fedor in historical sources such as Karamzin. Tolstoy's Fedor is related to Dostoevsky's Prince Myshkin: like Myshkin, Fedor is an utterly meek, benevolent man, incapable of anger or egoism, whose goodness has mixed effects on the world around him. Boris Godunov, the advocate of modernizing reform, and Prince Ivan Petrovich Shuisky, leader of the boyars, are locked in a deadly struggle for power, but Fedor, who cannot grasp the political dimension of events, is unaware of the reasons for their antagonism and attempts to reconcile them. His good intentions go tragically wrong, however, and Fedor becomes the unwitting cause of a series of murders. Shiusky's murder at the end of the play paves the way for Godunov, who has been running the country as Fedor's brother-in-law and closest adviser, to consolidate his power. Fedor was Tolstoy's favorite character, and *Tsar' Fedor Ioannovich* his favorite play.

In Tolstoy's representations, both Ivan and Boris—who seeks to make positive, enlightened reforms in Russia—are obsessed with exculpating their personal, moral guilt as irrelevant in light of their public achievements. Tolstoy began *Tsar' Boris,* the final play of the trilogy, in 1868; completed in the fall of 1869, it was published in *Vestnik Evropy* in 1870. Although it passed censorship, the play was not accepted by Imperial theaters and was not performed until 1881. *Tsar' Boris* begins with Boris's triumphant coronation after the death of his brother-in-law Fedor. Boris begins as an enlightened reformer, dedicated to the progress and reintegration of Russia within Europe. Although he is ultimately punished with dishonor and death for his attempt to bring about good ends by immoral means—he has ascended the throne because he has removed Fedor's half brother Dmitrii from the succession by murder—Boris is a complex, ambiguous character. His mistaken belief that he can buy the throne and the future of Russia with his soul takes him in a circle, back to the violence and brutality typical of Ivan, instead of forward. Like Ivan, Boris thinks that Russia needs him and that his goals justify his means.

The similarities between Ivan and Boris deepen as Boris finds himself increasingly enmeshed in the despotic abuses from which he had hoped to lead Russia away, shown to be the inevitable consequence of his sin. But Boris also expresses some of Tolstoy's most cherished hopes, as he attempts to reestablish the ties of Russia to the West after the isolation of the Tartar occupation and Muscovy. Boris dies an ignoble death, his crime perceived even by his own son, but the play also creates sympathy for him as one whose good intentions and accomplishments are forgotten. Fedor was morally pristine but brought about tragedy; Godunov is punished for trying to separate personal morality from public actions, but he has been the creator of much good.

Tolstoy's novel and trilogy are some of the most insightful interrogations of despotism in Russian literature, investigating its sources in the psychology of figures such as Ivan and pursuing its bases of support in individual human souls and group psychology. As a member of the highest nobility, Tolstoy knew firsthand the continuing injustices and humiliations perpetrated by the autocrat against the class descended from the sixteenth-century boyars, whom he accused of formally fulfilling the letter of their honor code rather than its spirit. Unlike his noble characters, Tolstoy rejected a fatalistic acceptance of autocracy and oppression as God's will. Had his ancestors understood the true meaning of honor, the tragic outcomes of the novel and plays suggest, the course of Russian history might have been different. To Tolstoy, who believed that pre-Muscovite Russia had been a European country rather than an Asiatic despotism, the tyrannical rule of Ivan the Terrible might have remained an isolated anomaly rather than establishing a precedent for subsequent Russian rulers.

While researching the historical background of *Tsar' Boris,* Tolstoy became interested in what he called the Norman period of Russian history. After completing the first act of *Tsar' Boris,* he put it aside in order to write a series of ballads that emphasized the integration of Kiev into and prominence in Western Europe. "Pesnia o Garal'de i Iaroslavne" (Song about Harald and Iaroslavna, 1869) recounts the courtship and marriage of the eleventh-century Kievan princess and the Norwegian king. "Pesnia o pokhode Vladimira na Korsun" (Song of the March of Vladimir to Korsun, 1869) describes the conversion of the Eastern Slavs to Christianity. "Pesnia o trekh poboishchakh" (Song of Three Battles, 1869) compresses historical dates to portray three decisive battles of European history—the battles of York and Hastings, and the battle between the Slavs and the Polovtsians on the Dniepr—as taking place on a single day; Tolstoy wrote to Stasiulevich that he hoped to underscore the communality of Kiev with Europe.

All three ballads were written and published in *Vestnik Evropy* in 1869, after which Tolstoy returned to the composition of *Tsar' Boris,* writing to Stasiulevich, "Normandy distracted me."

Tolstoy's health and finances declined in the late 1860s, and he went abroad each year after 1863 to seek relief from headaches and asthma. Pressed by his financial difficulties and poor health, Tolstoy worked tirelessly, devoting himself primarily to the composition of satirical verse critical of the conservatism of the establishment and the extremism of the radicals, both of which Tolstoy held to be misguided. He was elected to the literary section of the Russian Academy in 1873. Tolstoy died at Krasnyi Rog on 28 September 1875 after spending the winter of 1873–1874 in Italy at the invitation of the empress and spending several months in Karlsbad. He is buried in the village church at Krasnyi Rog.

Letters:

Polnoe sobranie sochinenii, volume 4 (St. Petersburg: A. F. Marks, 1907);

Sobranie sochinenii, volume 4 (Moscow: Khudozhestvennia literatura, 1964).

Bibliography:

G. I. Stafeev, *A. K. Tolstoy, Bibliograficheskii ukazatel'* (Briansk: Priokskoe knizhnoe izdatel'stvo, 1969).

Biographies:

A. Nikitin, "Graf A. K. Tolstoy v literature 60-kh godov," in *Russkii vestnik,* no. 2 (1894): 303–320;

A. A. Kondrat'ev, "K biografii A. K. Tolstogo," in *Novyi put',* no. 1 (1904): 181–208;

A. Levenstim, "Graf A. K. Tolstoy. Ego zhizn' i proizvedeniia," *Vestnik Evropy,* no. 10 (1906): 487–520;

V. Pokrovsky, ed., *Aleksei Konstantinovich Tolstoy. Ego zhizn' i sochineniia,* second edition, expanded (Moscow: Sklad v Knizhnom magazine V. Spiridonova i A. Mikhailova, 1908);

Kondrat'ev, ed., *Graf A. K. Tolstoy. Materialy dlia istorii zhizni i tvorchestva* (St. Petersburg, 1912);

A. Lirondelle, *Le poète Alexis Tolstoi. L'homme et l'oeuvre* (Paris: Hachette, 1912);

G. I. Stafeev, *Serdtse polno vdokhnoven'ia. Zhizn' i tvorchestvo A. K. Tolstogo* (Tula: Priokskoe knizhnoe izdatel'stvo, 1973);

Dmitrii Zhukov, *Aleksei Konstantinovich Tolstoy* (Moscow: Molodaia gvardiia, 1982).

References:

Margaret Dalton, *A. K. Tolstoy* (New York: Twayne, 1972);

Nikolai Fedorovich Denisiuk, comp., *Kriticheskaia literatura o proizvedeniiakh gr. A. K. Tolstogo* (Moscow: A. S. Panafidina, 1907);

Edward Seymour Lee, "A. K. Tolstoy: Life and Lyric Poetry," dissertation, University of Pittsburgh, 1985;

A. P. Obolensky, "A. K. Tolstoy and the West," in *Transactions of the Association of Russian-American Scholars in the United States,* no. 10 (1976): 69–76;

F. E. Paktovsky, *Graf A. K. Tolstoy i ego poeticheskoe tvorchestvo* (Kazan': Imperatorskii universitet, 1900);

A. V. Rianovsky and L. Prednewa, "A. K. Tolstoy: A Remembrance and Appreciation," in *Transactions of the Association of Russian-American Scholars in the United States,* no. 10 (1976): 47–67.

Leo Tolstoy

(28 August 1828 – 7 November 1910)

Edward Wasiolek
University of Chicago

WORKS: *Detstvo i Otrochestvo. Sochinenie grafa L. N. Tolstogo* (St. Petersburg: E. Prats, 1856)—*Detstvo* first published as *Istoriia moego detstva* in *Sovremennik,* no. 9 (1852), section 1: 5–104; *Otrochestvo* first published in *Sovremennik,* no. 10 (1854): 81–146;

Voennye rasskazy (St. Petersburg, 1856)—comprises "Sevastopol' v dekabre mesiatse," first published in *Sovremennik,* no. 6 (1855): 333–348; "Sevastopol' v mae," first published as "Noch' vesnoiu 1855 goda v Sevastopole" in *Sovremennik,* no. 9 (1855), section 1: 5–30; and "Sevastopol' v avguste 1855 goda," first published in *Sovremennik,* no. 1 (1856), section 1: 71–122; translated by Isabel Florence Hapgood as *Sevastopol* (New York: Crowell, 1888);

Dva gusara. Povest', in *Sovremennik,* no. 5 (1856), section 1: 5–63;

Iunost', in *Sovremennik,* no. 1 (1857), section 1: 13–163; republished in *Detstvo, Otrochestvo, Iunost'* (Moscow, 1885);

Semeinoe schast'e, in *Russkii vestnik,* nos. 7–8 (April 1859): 435–473; (Moscow, 1886); translated by Nathan Haskell Dole as *Family Happiness: A Romance* (New York: Crowell, 1888);

Kazaki, in *Russkii vestnik,* no. 1 (January 1863): 5–154; (Moscow, 1886); translated by E. Schuyler as *The Cossacks: A Tale of the Caucasus in 1852* (New York: Scribners, 1878);

Polikushka, in *Russkii vestnik,* no. 2 (February 1863): 587–644; (Moscow, 1887); translated as *Polikouchka* (New York: Lovell, 1888);

Sochineniia, 2 volumes (St. Petersburg: F. Stellovsky, 1864);

Voina i mir, first two parts published as *Tysiacha vosem'sot piatyi god,* in *Russkii vestnik* (1865–1866); (Moscow: Katkov, 1866); expanded and republished as *Voina i mir. Sochinenie grafa L. N. Tolstogo,* 6 volumes (Moscow, 1868–1869); translated as *War and Peace,* 3 volumes (London: Vizetelly, 1886);

Azbuka, 4 volumes (St. Petersburg: Zamyslovsky, 1872);

Novaia azbuka (Moscow: Tip. A. Tarletskogo i M. Terikhova, 1875);

Leo Tolstoy

Anna Karenina, in *Russkii vestnik* (1875–1877); 3 volumes (Moscow, 1878); translated by Dole (New York: Crowell, 1886);

Ispoved' (Geneva: M. Elpidin, 1884);

V chem moia vera (Moscow: Kushnerev, 1884); translated as "What I Believe" in *Christ's Christianity* (London: Kegan Paul, 1885);

Tak chto zhe nam delat'? [What Then Must We Do?], censored edition published as *Kakova moia zhizn'?*

(Geneva: M. Elpidin, 1886); restored and republished as *Tak chto zhe nam delat'?* (Moscow: "Trud i volia," 1906); first translated by Hapgood as *What to Do? Thoughts Evoked by the Census of Moscow* (New York: Crowell, 1887);

Smert' Ivana Il'icha, in *Sochineniia grafa L. N. Tolstogo. Chast' dvenadtsataia* (Moscow, 1886); translated by Dole as *The Death of Ivan Ilyitch* in *Ivan Ilyitch and Other Stories* (London: Scott, 1887);

Vlast' t'my [The Power of Darkness] (Moscow: Izdanie Posrednika, Tip. I. D. Sytina, 1887); first translated as *The Domination of Darkness: A Drama in Five Acts* (Chicago: Sergel, 1890);

Kratkoe izlozhenie Evangeliia (Geneva: M. Elpidin, 1890);

Kreitserova sonata (Geneva: M. K. Elpidin, 1890); translated as *The Kreutzer Sonata* (Chicago: Sergel, 1890);

Issledovanie dogmaticheskogo bogosloviia (Geneva: M. Elpidin, 1891);

O zhizni (Geneva: M. Elpidin, 1891);

Soedinenie i perevod chetyrekh evangelii, 3 volumes (Geneva: M. Elpidin, 1892–1894);

Skazki i byli (St. Petersburg: Izdanie M. B. Kliukina, 1893);

Tsarstvo Bozhie vnutri vas (Berlin: Izdanie Avgusta Deibnera, 1893–1894); translated by Constance Garnett as *The Kingdom of God is Within You* (New York: Cassell, 1894);

Khoziain i rabotnik, in *Severnyi vestnik*, no. 3 (1895), section 1: 137–175; (Moscow: Izdanie Posrednika, 1895); translated by Ardern George Hulme-Beaman, with an introduction by William Dean Howells, as *Master and Man* (New York: Appleton, 1895);

Poslednie proizvedeniia grafa L. N. Tolstogo, zapreshchennye v Rossii (London: Tip. Fonda Vol'noi russkoi pressy, 1895);

Chto takoe iskusstvo? in *Voprosy filosofii i psikhologii*, no. 5 (1897): 979–1027; no. 1 (1898): 5–137; (Moscow: Izdanie Posrednika, 1898); translated by Aylmer Maude as *What is Art?* (New York: Crowell, 1899);

Voskresenie, in *Niva* (1899); (Purleigh, Malden, Essex, U.K.: Izdanie Vladimira Chertkova, 1899); translated by Louise Maude as *Resurrection*, 3 volumes (New York: Dodd, Mead, 1899);

Polnoe sobranie sochinenii, zapreshchennykh russkoi tsenzuroi, L. N. Tolstogo = Oeuvres complètes interdites en Russie de Leon Tolstoy, 2 volumes, edited by Vladimir Grigor'evich Chertkov (Christchurch, Hants, U.K.: Izd-vo "Svobodnogo slova," 1901–1903);

Zakon nasiliia i zakon liubvi (Christchurch, Hants, U.K.: Svobodnoe Slovo, 1909);

Zhivoi trup, in *Russkoe slovo*, 23 (1911); edited by Chertkov (Moscow: Izdanie A. L. Tolstoi, 1912); trans-

lated by Anna Evarts as *The Living Corpse: A Drama in Six Acts and Twelve Tableaux* (Philadelphia: Brown, 1912);

D'iavol (Moscow: Izd. gr. A. L. Tolstoi, 1911); translated by Aylmer Maude as *The Devil* (London: Allen & Unwin, 1926);

Posmertnye khudozhestvennye proizvedeniia L'va Nikolaevicha Tolstogo, 3 volumes, edited by Chertkov (Moscow: Izdanie Aleksandry L'vovny Tolstoi, 1911–1912);

Khadzhi-Murat (St. Petersburg: R. Golike i A. Vil'borg, 1912); translated by Aylmer Maude as *Hadji Murad* (New York: Dodd, Mead, 1912);

Neizdannye rasskazy i p'esy, edited by S. P. Mel'gunov, T. I. Polner, and A. M. Khir'iakov (Paris: Izdanie T-va "N. P. Karbasnikov," 1926);

Russkie knigi dlia chteniia, 4 volumes (Moscow-Leningrad: Detgiz, 1946).

Editions and Collections: *Sochineniia grafa L. N. Tolstogo*, 20 volumes, 12th edition (Moscow: I. N. Kushnerev, 1911);

Polnoe sobranie sochinenii, 24 volumes, edited by P. I. Biriukov (Moscow: I. D. Sytin, 1912–1913);

Polnoe sobranie sochinenii, 90 volumes, edited by Vladimir Grigor'evich Chertkov (Moscow: Goslitizdat, 1928–1958);

Sobranie sochinenii, 14 volumes, edited by S. P. Bychkov (Moscow: Goslitizdat, 1951–1953);

Sobranie sochinenii v dvadtsati tomakh, edited by N. N. Akopova and others (Moscow, 1960–1965);

Pedagogicheskie sochineniia (Moscow: Pedagogika, 1989);

Polnoe sobranie sochinenii v sta tomakh, volume 1, edited by L. D. Gromova-Opul'skaia and others (Moscow: Nauka, 2000).

Editions in English: *Childhood. Boyhood. Youth*, translated by Isabel Florence Hapgood (New York: Crowell, 1886);

My Confession (New York: Crowell, 1887);

Count Tolstoi's Gospel Stories, translated by Nathan Haskell Dole (New York: Crowell, 1890);

The Complete Works of Lyof N. Tolstoi, 24 volumes in 12, translated by Hapgood, edited by Dole (New York: Thomas Y. Crowell, 1898–1911);

Anna Karenin, 2 volumes, translated by Constance Garnett (London: Heinemann, 1901);

What Is Religion, edited by Vladimir Grigor'evich Chertkov and A. S. Fifield (New York, 1902);

Selected Works, translated by Aylmer Maude (London: Oxford University Press, 1903);

War and Peace, translated by Garnett (London: Heinemann, 1904; revised, London: Heinemann, 1914);

The Power of Darkness, translated by Louise and Aylmer Maude (New York: Funk & Wagnalls, 1904);

Plays, translated by Louise and Aylmer Maude (New York: Funk & Wagnalls, 1904);

Works of Count Lev N. Tolstoy, 12 volumes, translated and edited by Leo Wiener (New York: Willey Book Co., 1904);

Twenty-three Tales, translated by Louise and Aylmer Maude (London & New York: Oxford University Press, 1906);

The Novels and Other Works of L. N. Tolstoi, 24 volumes, edited by Dole (New York: Scribners, 1907);

The Diaries of Leo Tolstoy, 1842–1852, translated by C. J. Hogarth and A. Sirnis (London, 1917);

The Journal of Leo Tolstoy, translated by Rose Strunksy (New York: Knopf, 1917);

The Dramatic Works of Lyof N. Tolstoi, translated by Dole (New York: Crowell, 1923);

The Private Diary of Leo Tolstoy, 1853–1857, edited by Aylmer Maude, translated by Louise and Aylmer Maude (Garden City, N.Y.: Doubleday, Page, 1927);

The Cossacks (New York: Grossett & Dunlap, 1928);

The Works of Leo Tolstoy, Tolstoy centenary edition, 21 volumes, translated by Aylmer and Louise Maude and J. D. Duff (Oxford & London: Oxford University Press, For the Tolstoy Society, 1928–1937);

Anna Karenina, 2 volumes, translated by Louise and Aylmer Maude, revised (London: Oxford University Press, 1939);

Anna Karenin, translated by Rosemary Edmonds (Baltimore: Penguin, 1954);

War and Peace, 2 volumes, translated by Edmonds (Baltimore: Penguin, 1957);

The Death of Ivan Ilytch and Other Stories, edited by David Magarshack (New York: New American Library, 1960);

The Kreutzer Sonata, The Death of Ivan Ilytch and Other Tales, translated by Aylmer Maude (London: Oxford University Press, 1960);

Last Diaries, translated by Lydia Weston-Kesich and edited by Leon Stillman (New York, 1960);

Anna Karenina, translated by Magarshack (New York: New American Library, 1961);

Fables and Fairytales, translated by Ann Dunnigan (New York: New American Library, 1962);

Hadji Murat: A Tale of the Caucasus, translated by W. G. Carey (London: Heinemann, 1962; New York: McGraw-Hill, 1965);

War and Peace, translated by Aylmer Maude, edited by George Gibian (New York: Norton, 1966);

The Great Short Works of Leo Tolstoy, translated by Louise and Aylmer Maude (New York: Harper & Row, 1967);

The Portable Tolstoy, selected, with a critical introduction, biographical summary, and bibliography, by John Bayley (New York: Viking, 1978);

Tolstoy's Diaries, 2 volumes, edited and translated by R. F. Christian (New York: Scribners, 1985; London: Athlone Press, 1985);

Tolstoy's Short Fiction, edited and with revised translations by Michael R. Katz, Norton Critical Edition (New York: Norton, 1991);

Tolstoy: Plays, translated by Marvin Kantor with Tanya Tuklinsky (Evanston, Ill.: Northwestern University Press, 1994–1998);

Anna Karenina, edited by George Gibian, Norton Critical Edition, second edition (New York: Norton, 1995);

War and Peace, edited by Gibian, Norton Critical Edition, second edition (New York: Norton, 1996);

Divine and Human, and Other Stories, edited and translated by Gordon Spence (Evanston, Ill.: Northwestern University Press, 2000);

Tolstoy as Teacher: Leo Tolstoy's Writings on Education, edited by Robert Blaisdell (New York: Teachers & Writers Collaborative, 2000).

PLAY PRODUCTIONS: *Vlast' t'my,* Moscow, Skomorov Teatr, 1895;

Zhivoi trup, Khudozhestvennyi Teatr, October 1900.

OTHER: *Plody prosveshcheniia. Komediia v 4-kh deistviiakh,* in *V pamiat' S. A. Iur'eva* (Moscow, 1890);

Krug chteniia, 2 volumes, edited by Tolstoy (Moscow: Kushnerev, 1906); translated by L. Lewery as *The Cycle of Reading: Thoughts of the World's Greatest Authors on Truth, on Life and the Ways Thereof,* edited by Lewery (New York: International Library, 1911);

Na kazhdyi den', edited by Tolstoy (Moscow: Tip. Vil'de, 1909).

Leo Tolstoy is one of the most important novelists in Western literature. The breadth of his vision and the range of his accomplishments are immense. His 1928–1958 collected works comprise 90 volumes, and a projected new edition will reach at least 134 volumes. Tolstoy was a novelist, educator, farmer, critic, and aesthetician. He was not only the writer of *Voina i mir* (War and Peace, 1865–1869), *Anna Karenina* (1875–1877), and dozens of short works, but also, in the last twenty years of his life, a sage who commanded the attention of people all over the world. The editor of *Novoe vremia* (New Times) said at the turn of the twentieth century that Russia had two czars, one in St. Petersburg and one in Iasnaia Poliana (Bright Glade, Tolstoy's estate). Although he did not come to the attention of

Tolstoy in 1855

the department of Turkish-Arabic studies and then transferred to law. Tolstoy's university professors noted his linguistic gifts; by the end of his life Tolstoy had studied more than a dozen languages and was proficient in many of them, including English, German, and French.

Tolstoy's life at the university was the one led by many young men of his class: the pursuit of pleasure in cards, wine, and women. Yet, even in these early years Tolstoy's pleasure-seeking came into conflict with a ferocious morality. Beginning in 1847 Tolstoy kept a diary (which occupies thirteen volumes in the 1928–1958 collected edition of his works), and his struggles against a life of idleness are recorded there. Tolstoy left the university in 1847 without receiving a degree and shortly thereafter moved back to Iasnaia Poliana, which he had received as an inheritance from his father. He settled down to manage the estate and to improve the lot of his peasants. The next few years were a period of experimentation, as Tolstoy sampled aristocratic life in Moscow in 1848, studied law in St. Petersburg in 1849, and also, at the end of 1850, began his writing career, with an unpreserved story about gypsies and then "Istoriia vcherashnego dnia" (History of Yesterday), which is lost as well. He also began work on *Detstvo* (Childhood, 1852) at this time.

In May 1851, in circumstances similar to those of his character Dmitrii Olenin in *Kazaki* (The Cossacks, 1863), Tolstoy left for the Caucasus, where his brother Nikolai was serving in the Russian army. Tolstoy volunteered for action with Russian troops fighting the Chechens. He described his experiences in stories such as "Nabeg" (The Raid, 1853) and "Rubka lesa" (The Wood Felling, 1855), both published in the journal *Sovremennik* (The Contemporary). In 1852 Tolstoy published *Detstvo*, the first part of a trilogy, in *Sovremennik;* he published the second part, *Otrochestvo* (Boyhood), in 1854. The third part, *Iunost'* (Youth), was published in 1857. Tolstoy became a commissioned officer in 1854 and went on to serve on the Danube and then in the Crimea, participating in the siege of Sevastopol during the Crimean War, for which he was decorated for bravery. He recorded his impressions of the siege in three sketches for *Sovremennik:* "Sevastopol' v dekabre mesiatse" (Sevastopol in December, 1855), "Sevastopol' v mae" (Sevastopol in May, 1855), and "Sevastopol' v avguste 1855 goda" (Sevastopol in August 1855, 1856). The stories are on-the-spot descriptions of the siege and as such are historical fact, but they are also fiction in the sense that Tolstoy used his artistic skill to render them dramatic and interesting. Tolstoy came to St. Petersburg in 1855 and developed friendships with various prominent literary figures, including Ivan Sergeevich Turgenev, Ivan Aleksandrovich Goncharov, Aleksandr

the West until the 1870s by way of Ivan Sergeevich Turgenev's introduction, by the turn of the century Tolstoy commanded the respect and even adoration of Western literary circles. His writing style was one of simplicity, clarity, and force.

Count Lev Nikolaevich Tolstoy was born on 28 August 1828 on the estate Iasnaia Poliana, in the province of Tula, approximately 140 miles from Moscow. He was one of five children of Count Nikolai Il'ich Tolstoy and his wife, Mariia Nikolaevna Tolstaia, née Princess Volkonskaia. Tolstoy's family belonged to the oldest Russian nobility: Tolstoy was related on his mother's side to the aristocratic Trubetskoy, Golitsyn, and Odoevsky families. On his father's side Tolstoy was descended from one of the first Russians to receive the title of *graf* (count): Tolstoy's ancestor Petr Andreevich Tolstoy had won the title in service to Peter I. The writer's father had fought in the war of 1812. Tolstoy lost his mother in 1830, when he was nearly two, and his father in 1837, when he was nine; he and his siblings moved to Kazan', where they were brought up by their father's distant relative "Auntie" T. A. Ergol'skaia, to whom Tolstoy was devoted. In 1844 he entered the University of Kazan', where he enrolled in

Nikolaevich Ostrovsky, and Nikolai Gavrilovich Chernyshevsky. He retired from the military in 1856, noting in his diary that a military career was not the right choice for him. Growing tired of literary life in the capital, in 1857 Tolstoy toured France, Italy, Germany, and Switzerland. By the end of the decade he had moved back to Iasnaia Poliana.

Tolstoy's creative life can be divided into several periods: the early period, beginning with the publication of *Detstvo* in 1852 and lasting until 1863, when he began work on *Voina i mir;* the mature or great period from 1863 to 1878, when he wrote and published *Voina i mir* and *Anna Karenina;* and finally the years from 1878, when Tolstoy experienced a religious conversion and reexamination of his beliefs and strove to construct a new worldview, until his death in 1910. In this last period he wrote a series of novellas, including *Smert' Ivana Il'icha* (The Death of Ivan Il'ich, 1886), *Kreitserova sonata* (The Kreutzer Sonata, 1890), *D'iavol* (The Devil, written in 1889–1890 and published posthumously in 1911), *Khoziain i rabotnik* (Master and Man, 1895), *Otets Sergii* (Father Sergius, 1898), and *Khadzhi-Murat* (Hadji-Murad, 1912), as well as the full-length novel *Voskresenie* (Resurrection, 1899). Also in this last period he wrote several theological and socioeconomic works, as well as a major work on aesthetics, *Chto takoe iskusstvo?* (What Is Art?, 1897–1898).

In his early period Tolstoy experimented with many different forms (diary, sketch, short story, short novel), but his emphasis was already on realism for didactic ends. Tolstoy believed that art was not an end in itself, but that it existed to serve social and moral purposes. In this respect he was squarely in the tradition of Russian writing in the nineteenth century. Goncharov, Turgenev, and Nikolai Vasil'evich Gogol, to name just a few, saw art as a means to perceive more finely and creatively where Russian society was at present and where it should go. Art threw a light over circumstantial reality, and by way of that light, the artist was able to guide society.

Tolstoy's narrative mode tends toward exposition rather than drama and dialogue. His goal is to explain and teach rather than to affect emotions by extreme situations and rhetorical effects. *Detstvo* comprises a series of the impressions of adult life experienced by an eleven-year-old narrator. The child tries to make sense of the world about him, and his consciousness and its growth are the focuses of the work. Chernyshevsky noted early and accurately in a review of *Detstvo* in 1856 that Tolstoy was trying to give the reader "chistotu nravstvennogo chuvstva" (the purity of moral feeling). The purity that Chernyshevsky refers to is a state of being unsullied by social forces. Tolstoy believed that people are born with a "pure" consciousness that is pro-

gressively molded and distorted by society and civilization. Sophistication, intellect, and even culture itself are seen as obstacles to truth and reality. In that sense the growth of the child's consciousness is also a record of his progressive corruption by society.

For example, the young narrator of *Detstvo,* Nikolai Irten'ev, is asked at one point to prepare a gift for his grandmother's name day. He decides to write a poem for her, and in writing it, he finds that the rhyme scheme forces him to say what he does not want to say: specifically, that he loves his grandmother as much as his mother. He finishes the poem with reluctance and a sense of betrayal and expects to be punished at the presentation for his false feelings. Instead, he is praised by the adults. Poetry—and by extension, art—distorts his feelings and manipulates him to lie. The adults around him receive a lie as truth because they have already lost their sense of pure and true feeling. This incident is the first expression of Tolstoy's antipathy to the formal aspect of art, and it anticipates his work later in life.

Tolstoy's moral world is anchored in clarity and directness. Right and wrong, "good" people and "bad" people, are concretely delineated. The firmness of Tolstoy's moral universe does not deprive it of complexity, however, as the later novels *Voina i mir* and *Anna Karenina* particularly reveal. This complexity is shown by the difficulties his characters encounter in finding happiness and "the truth," although these entities do exist. In most cases, Tolstoy's characters are diverted from their quest and cannot find their way. Tolstoy assumes that there is an objective world; that is, that reality does not depend on one's feelings, as the Romantics had believed, or on one's particular point of view. While dreams, fantasies, reconstructions, and various other distortions may be diverting, reality will remain. Tolstoy felt that one had to bring oneself into alignment with objective reality in order to live a fulfilled and authentic life. Tolstoy's objective reality is not, however, a social one: social reality, and even civilization, are themselves distortions, as seen to a degree in *Detstvo.* This distinction would seem to imply that in order to touch objective reality, one must become "desocialized" and even "decivilized." Indeed, many of the high points in Tolstoy's creative world take place in natural or elemental settings and in states of consciousness divested of habitual, distorting modes of thinking, feeling, and perceiving. Some of this philosophy is evident in the opening pages of the novel *Semeinoe schast'e* (Family Happiness, 1859), also part of Tolstoy's early period.

The novel begins with the thoughts and feelings of the seventeen-year-old Masha (Mariia Aleksandrovna). Masha's mother has recently died, and the house is given over to mourning and gestures of respect for her death. Winter frost has dimmed the windows,

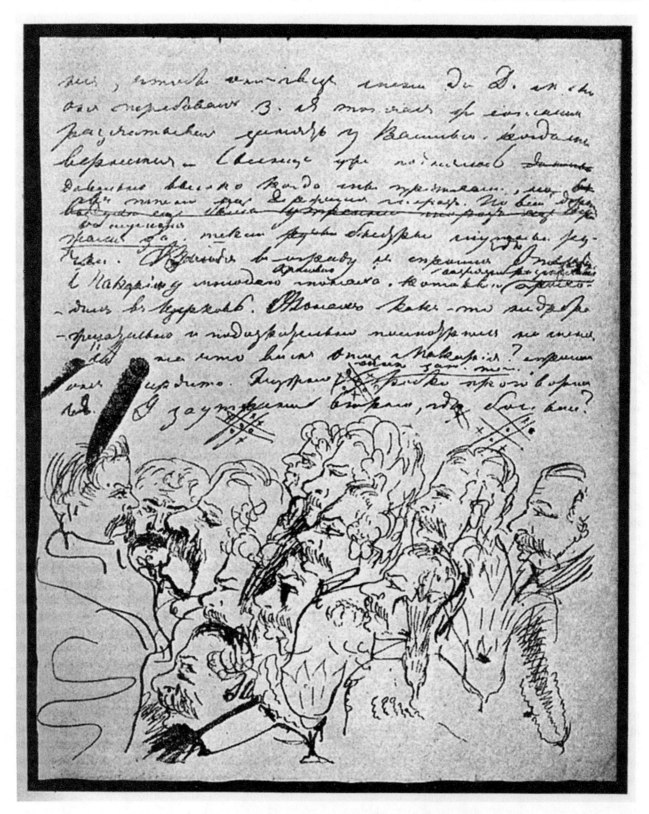

Page from the manuscript for Iunost' *(Youth), first published in* Sovremennik *(The Contemporary)*
in 1857 (from Ernest J. Simmons, Leo Tolstoy, *1946)*

and snowdrifts have almost covered the manor house. Just as winter has "buried" the house, grief has "buried" the thoughts and feelings of the people inside. The business of living has been suspended by the convention of grief. The inhabitants live in a ritualistic repetition of gestures and feelings that are commanded by society. A kind of conventional reality is superimposed on "real reality" and in fact controls and even obliterates it. The pantomime is interrupted only when a neighbor, Sergei Mikhailovich, visits the family. Sergei refuses to be immobilized by grief. He insists that Masha play her music, read, and develop her life. The opening pages of *Semeinoe schast'e* are a remarkable example of how a social form can impoverish life. Such emotions as grief, sorrow, and respect for the dead are not ordinarily seen as impoverishing impulses, but Tolstoy suggests in these opening scenes that they can function as such.

The rest of the novel is an examination of how conventions affect marriage. Masha is a young girl when she marries the thirty-four-year-old Sergei, and her expectations of marriage are unrealistic. She expects the feelings of courtship to continue, and when they do not, she looks for them elsewhere. She finds them, or thinks she finds them, in the artificial life of the city, where she takes flattery and flirtation for true feelings. Masha almost destroys her marriage when she is seduced by city life and her delight in the superficialities of high society into neglecting her husband and child. The final scenes of the novel, however, take place in the country, as husband and wife sit on a veranda reminiscing about the course of their marriage. Sergei tells his young and distraught wife that "v kazhdoi pore est' svoia liubov'" (Each time of life has its own kind of love). What he means is that one must accept the necessary changes that the realities of age, motherhood, and time bring, and that one must not cling to the past. The heady romance of first love has its time, as do motherhood and mature love. Regret for a lost emotion or images of a different kind of love result not only in unreal emotions but in a distance from the reality of one's present love.

The 1850s, the decade when Tolstoy was establishing himself as a writer, were a time of intense political debate about the future of Russia and especially about the subject of freeing the serfs. Russia's defeat in the Crimean War provoked political protests and additional debate. Critics such as Chernyshevsky, Nikolai Aleksandrovich Dobroliubov, and Dmitrii Ivanovich Pisarev urged radical reform. They railed against the gradualism of the previous generation's politics and urged immediate and even violent action. There was a class difference between these critics and the previous generation, who were for the most part noblemen with a stake in gradual reform. The new generation, repre-

sented by Chernyshevsky, Dobroliubov, and Pisarev, was made up of a new class of reformers called *raznochintsy* (people of varied classes). They were not landowners; they were mostly university trained, and some came from theological and civil-servant backgrounds. They demanded a literature of radical social reform, socially and politically relevant. Some of the older generation attempted to meet their demands, notably Turgenev. He responded by writing a series of novels on contemporary themes, such as *Rudin* (1856), *Dvorianskoe gnezdo* (A Nest of Gentry, 1859), *Nakanune* (On the Eve, 1860), and *Ottsy i deti* (Fathers and Sons, 1862).

Tolstoy, however, appeared indifferent to the political realities of the day. While almost everyone was debating the liberation of the serfs and political reform, Tolstoy was writing of how the consciousness of a child is formed, what makes marriage work, and how best to die. Such themes, no matter how universal, seemed to be almost an affront to contemporary discussions of Russia's needs. Critics had greeted Tolstoy's *Detstvo*, and to some extent his Sevastopol sketches, with warm and even lavish praise: Nikolai Alekseevich Nekrasov esteemed *Detstvo* highly, and an early review in *Sovremennik* claimed that the novel was "from beginning to end truly wonderful." By 1856, however, when Tolstoy published "Metel'" (The Snow Storm) and "Dva gusara" (The Two Hussars) in *Sovremennik*, "Utro pomeshchika" (A Landlord's Morning) in *Otechestvennye zapiski* (Notes of the Fatherland), and *Otrochestvo*, praise for his writings was beginning to cool. Much of this lack of interest had to do with the perception that his works lacked contemporary social and political content. *Semeinoe schast'e*, for instance, met with meager reaction; *Sovremennik* made no reference to it, and the few critics who did review it praised the execution of the story but found the theme old and irrelevant to contemporary issues. Tolstoy's one seeming nod to political reality was perhaps his novel *Polikushka* (1863), the story of a peasant with feelings and a conscience superior to those of his masters. But there is nothing overtly political in the story, and it was published after the liberation of the peasants.

Many critics thus did not fully appreciate Tolstoy's short novel *Kazaki*, which is the masterpiece of Tolstoy's pre–*Voina i mir* period; Turgenev, however, considered it to be superior to the later novel, and Pavel Vasil'evich Annenkov, in an 1863 article, named it one of Russia's best recent novels. Tolstoy had begun *Kazaki* in 1852 while he was serving in the Caucasus, but he did not complete it until 1862; the novel was published in *Russkii vestnik* (The Russian Herald) in 1863. The novel describes the life of Dmitrii Olenin, a spoiled officer who abandons Moscow for the Caucasus, where he expects to be purified and renewed. His mind is filled with romantic banalities about beautiful women, dangerous escapades, and heroic deeds. Yet, the reality of Caucasian village life, which Tolstoy describes with vivid precision, is anything but romantic. The villages are filled with mud, smoke, girls driving cattle, and men bringing in firewood. The story follows the familiar Tolstoyan course of "deromanticization." Tolstoy had little patience with romanticism, either in literature or in life. Romanticism as he understood it was an idealization of life, and as such a departure from the objective reality he so prized. Olenin is gradually shorn of his romantic anticipations and compelled to see the reality of Cossack life. Yet, he never fully abandons the imaginary life he brings with him.

While hunting one day Olenin discovers a stag's lair, and the following day he decides to lie in it. He experiences a causeless joy and a love of everything, feeling himself so much a part of nature that he invites the mosquitoes to devour him. The Muscovite Olenin, the privileged nobleman, the romantic quester for renewal, and indeed all of the Olenins of the past fall away, and a new Olenin, at one with elemental nature, appears, at least for a short while. This state is spoiled when Olenin begins to think about what he has experienced there. He reverts to his normal mode of thinking and interpreting and comes to the conclusion that what he has learned from the experience in the stag's lair is to sacrifice himself for others. But in fact there was nothing in the experience about self-sacrifice; this idea is a false conceptual re-creation.

Much about *Kazaki* is a proving ground for *Voina i mir*. The clarity of Tolstoy's ethnographic descriptions of Cossack life, the attention to minute sensuous details, the vividness of the battle scenes, and the brilliance of many of the characterizations all preview what Tolstoy accomplished on a much larger scale in the later novel.

In addition to producing a considerable literary corpus during this early period, Tolstoy was deeply involved in the late 1850s and early 1860s in educational theory and practice. In 1860 and 1861 he returned to Europe, traveling to France, Germany, Italy, and England to visit schools and survey educational practices. Tolstoy put his views on education into practice by setting up a school in the manor house on his estate and assisting in the opening of more than twenty additional schools in surrounding villages. While Tolstoy's educational theories struck many as bizarre, there was much in them that anticipated some of the theories in twentieth-century American education. Tolstoy urged complete liberty for the students, with no rote learning or compulsion. The desire to learn, he felt, should come from students and not from the outside. Even the content of what they were to learn was to come from indi-

vidual needs, rather than from general prescriptions. As one might expect, chaos reigned in the classroom, but according to Tolstoy the students eventually settled down and were eager to learn and to explore the world around them and inside of them. Tolstoy himself taught classes; in 1862 and 1863 he also edited a pedagogical journal called *Iasnaia Poliana,* which was reviewed positively by Ivan Sergeevich Aksakov and by Chernyshevsky, and he wrote many articles on education. After the freeing of the serfs, Tolstoy's school and journal were closed.

In 1862 Tolstoy married Sof'ia Andreevna Bers, the daughter of a Moscow doctor. He was thirty-four; she was eighteen. When Tolstoy gave her his diaries to read before their marriage, the innocent Sof'ia Andreevna was shocked to learn of his previous sexual relationships, including one with a peasant woman that had resulted in the birth of an illegitimate child. This discovery later made its way into *Anna Karenina,* in which the innocent Kitty Shcherbatskaia learns before her marriage to Konstantin Levin about her fiancé's past dalliances. The Tolstoys' marriage lasted forty-eight years, and Tolstoy was initially delighted with married life: he wrote in a diary entry of 5 January 1863, "Domestic happiness has swallowed me completely." While the union grew stormy over the years, Sof'ia Andreevna was a faithful companion, copying *Voina i mir* by hand several times, bearing thirteen children, and handling household duties as Tolstoy devoted himself to managing the Iasnaia Poliana estate.

In 1863, the year following his marriage, he began the first jottings of what became *Voina i mir*. For a time Tolstoy had considered writing an epic about the Decembrists, the noblemen involved in the palace revolution of 1825. His work on this novel led him to the conclusion that the revolt of 1825 had its roots in the political agitation of the early 1820s, which are pictured in nascent form in the first epilogue of *Voina i mir*. This conclusion led Tolstoy to the Napoleonic invasion of 1812, which decisively put Russia into contact with European life and liberalization. In turn the Napoleonic invasion led Tolstoy to work on the seeds of the invasion in the events of 1805, the year in which *Voina i mir* begins. Tolstoy published thirty-eight chapters of the work-in-progress under the title *Tysiacha vosem'sot piatyi god* (The Year 1805) in *Russkii vestnik* in 1865 and 1866; these chapters correspond roughly to the first twenty-five chapters of the final text.

Voina i mir was published between 1868 and 1869 in six volumes. It was favorably received, and still-living veterans of the war of 1812 commented extensively on Tolstoy's description of the military events. By and large, these veterans found Tolstoy's depiction of the battle scenes in the novel to be accurate. Critics meanwhile were fascinated by the form of the novel and attempted fruitlessly to define it by genre. Nikolai Nikolaevich Strakhov called the novel an "epopeia v sovremennykh formakh iskusstva" (epic in contemporary forms of art) and then described it as a "family chronicle." The writer Maksim Gorky later compared the novel to Homer's *Iliad*. Most contemporary critics found Tolstoy's philosophical, theorizing chapters, especially in the second epilogue, intrusive and a blemish on the novel. Such criticism led Tolstoy in 1873 to put out an edition with these sections excised, along with his extensive use of French in characters' conversations. But in 1886 and subsequent editions Tolstoy restored the chapters on the theory of history, and all further editions included them. (In modern Russian editions the French is preserved in footnotes, but in Anglo-American editions the French has largely been translated into English.)

Voina i mir came late to the attention of readers in the West; it was not widely discussed by English critics until the first decade of the twentieth century, when such writers as E. M. Forster and Virginia Woolf praised it. In the United States the novel was well received by such critics as William Dean Howells and Lafcadio Hearn. Almost alone Henry James denigrated it, calling the novel a "loose baggy monster" and dismissing it on formal grounds. His disciple Percy Lubbock faulted the novel for having no center. Indeed, *Voina i mir,* with its multiple lines of action and centers of consciousness, is definitely at odds with the James-Lubbock concept of a good novel as narrated from the point of view of a single consciousness. Yet, Tolstoy worked hard on the novel and was acutely conscious of matters of composition and structure. The novel has a center, but one that is more complex, mysterious, and difficult to reach than in the James-Lubbock restricted conception of "center" and "form."

Voina i mir alternates between domestic scenes and military scenes. The domestic part of the novel follows the fates of three families: the Bolkonskys, the Rostovs, and the Kuragins. The Kuragins are the "bad" family; the Rostovs, the "good" family; and the Bolkonskys, a complex mixture of "good" and "bad." Vasilii Kuragin, the father, is an aristocrat with considerable influence at court, adept at the intrigues of high society, and intent always on furthering his own ends and those of his three children. His daughter, Hélène, is stunningly beautiful, vapid, sensuous, and self-interested. His son Anatole is also handsome, pleasure-seeking, and unconcerned when his actions harm others. The third Kuragin child, Hippolyte, is mentally handicapped, and his senseless utterances on social occasions are taken often by high society as having some special import. Families, for Tolstoy, have a common behavioral essence, modi-

Sof'ia Andreevna Bers in 1860, two years before her marriage to Tolstoy

fied by the circumstances of age and situation. The Kuragins are all corrupt, but in different ways. Hélène and Anatole, both young and handsome, are corrupted by a predatory sensuality, and their father by a predatory political sense. All of them seek to advance themselves at the expense of others. They live in St. Petersburg, the home of the court and the most sophisticated people, and therefore, for Tolstoy, the most corrupt Russian city.

The Bolkonskys live in the country. They are rigid, high-minded, truthful, principled and severe in the judgment of others and of themselves. The father, Nikolai Bolkonsky, is a former military officer and favorite of the court who has exiled himself to his estate voluntarily because of his disgust at court intrigues. He leads a life of impeccable and rigid regularity and busies himself with turning out snuffboxes on a lathe and solving problems in geometry. These activities counter what he considers to be the two most serious vices that afflict humanity: sloth and ignorance. Nikolai has two children: Andrei and Mar'ia. Prince Andrei resembles his father in his sense of honor and the rigidity of his character, but his ideals have not yet been transformed into the cynicism of his father, at least not in the beginning of the novel. Like his father, Andrei is contemptuous of high society and intent on seeking military fame. He is the most complex character in the novel, and his search for truth is both long and riveting. Princess Mar'ia is not traditionally attractive; she is self-effacing, loving, and deeply religious. She is terrified of her father, and the relationship between them is one of bitterness and denial. She exhibits a vein of the Bolkonsky character in the severity of her self-denial and later in her upholding of the Bolkonsky honor.

The Rostovs are open, joyous, generous, and in love with life. Natasha, who is the heroine of the novel, is everyone's darling because of her spontaneity and openness to life. Her brother Nikolai is impetuous and good of heart. The elder Rostov is generous to a fault, but a thoughtless and incompetent manager of the Rostov estates. None of the Rostovs are reflective or intellectual. They meet life without passing it through the nets of self-reflection and analysis, as do the Bolkonskys. The Rostovs live in Moscow, the provincial capital, and are thus partly removed from the corruption of St. Petersburg.

There is one other important character who is not a member of these three families: Pierre Bezukhov, the illegitimate son of Prince Bezukhov. Early in the novel Pierre is legitimized by his dying father and inherits his wealth. Pierre is impetuous, genuine, and easily duped. His fate is intertwined with the fates of the three families. He is first the prey of the Kuragins and is manipulated into a marriage with Princess Hélène. He is also a close friend of Andrei, and their various interactions define important points in the novel. Both Pierre and Andrei search for the "truth," that is, for the plenitude of life. Pierre in the end marries Natasha Rostova.

The military and domestic events touch and interpenetrate at various points during the novel, and there is an overall analogy between the two spheres of life. Apart from his careful and accurate description of the various battles, Tolstoy also provides a realistic view of what happens on the battlefield. The Romantic view of war was still the vogue in Western literature when he wrote *Voina i mir*. Stendhal had shown a different view of war in his description of the battle of Waterloo in his novel *La Chartreuse de Parme* (The Charterhouse of Parma, 1839), a work that was part of Tolstoy's library. Tolstoy was, however, the first to mount a long and sustained attack on the Romantic view of war. He influenced other such attacks, notably Stephen Crane's *The Red Badge of Courage* (1895) and Ernest Hemingway's *A Farewell to Arms* (1929). Nikolai Rostov, for example, goes off to war carrying with him all the romantic conventions of military warfare. He sees himself as charging gloriously at the enemy and wrenching victory from defeat, without thought of gore or injury. But in his engagements he finds war to be confusion and himself capable of cowardice. Despite these experiences, Nikolai quickly rethinks the events so that they fit his preconceptions, rather than reality. Andrei, on the other hand, is more realistic and honest. He starts out with romantic preconceptions, but when he encounters the confusion and gore, and the lies of others, he insists on seeing war as it actually is.

On the eve of the battle of Austerlitz a military briefing takes place in the presence of German, Polish, and Russian commanders. Weierothe, the German general, outlines the dispositions of the troops for battle the next day in great detail and explains how the fighting is expected to go. The Russian general Mikhail Illarionovich Kutuzov, on the contrary, sleeps through the briefing, snoring audibly. Kutuzov clearly has a low opinion of military briefings, and when the meeting is done he tells Andrei that the battle will be decided on the field rather than the blackboard. The next day bears out Kutuzov's words, because, despite the refined strategy, nothing works out as it was planned. Napoleon Bonaparte's troops are not where they are supposed to be, and the confusion is such that the allied positions are quickly muddled. The French come upon the Russians unexpectedly, and the battle of the three leaders quickly turns into a rout of the allies and a complete victory for the French. Andrei, in the face of the fleeing Russians, picks up the regimental flag and briefly rallies the troops, but he is seriously wounded and left for dead on the battlefield. The victorious Napoleon comes upon him, and Andrei, semi-delirious, listens to his vainglorious words. Andrei is lying on his back and gazing at the sky, and the voice of Napoleon sounds like the buzzing of a fly in contrast to the infinity he sees in the sky and his soul. This experience is one of the high points of *Voina i mir*.

The generals at the Battle of Austerlitz, with the exception of Kutuzov, believe that they can understand and direct the lives of thousands of soldiers. Austerlitz shows, however, that generals and their strategies do not guide the course of the battle. Instead, that course is determined by those who are closest to the actual events—that is, by the interaction of thousands of ordinary soldiers. The farther up one is in the chain of command, the farther one is from the course of events, and the less one understands or directs what is happening on the battlefield. The view of the battle directed by strategy and the commands of its generals is an illusion. Tolstoy reserves his harshest criticism for Napoleon and his pretensions of military genius. Tolstoy's military hero is Kutuzov, the Russian commander in chief, who permits events to unfold by themselves.

Tolstoy's view of battlefield events as guided by an incomprehensible but necessary force is in keeping with his view of history, a central theme of the novel. History, too, and even personal history, is guided by a force beyond the prediction or understanding of individuals. The force that governs the lives of individual characters is the same as that which governs historical and military events. To the extent that one moves with this current, one is in touch with real life; to the extent that one attempts to guide, manipulate, and command life, one is stricken with sterility and unreality. Much of the interest in the novel is in understanding how various characters interact with the current of life. One can flow with it, resist it, or step outside of it. If one flows with the current, one experiences harmony and happiness. Outside the current there is only illusion and unhappiness. The axis of Tolstoy's moral world turns not on good and evil, but on the plenitude or emptiness of life.

One can conceive of this world by positing a center, in which life beats full, and a series of concentric circles that measure how far one is from the plenitude of life. One can then place the various characters on one of these circles or even in the center. There is no movement for characters such as the Kuragins, who remain on the outermost circle, where they spin lifelessly. Natasha, Pierre, Nikolai, Mar'ia, and especially Andrei move among the inner circles. A few of the characters touch the center, but none, not even Natasha, remains in the center for long. No one tries harder to find the truth than Andrei, and he often draws close to that magic center. Yet a repelling force keeps him from touching that core: his intellect, his habit of placing things at a distance by conceptualizing, and his inability to accept without question himself and his life in the immediate moment. He is only in touch with a more authentic self at moments when his guard is down, such as on the battlefield at Austerlitz. Andrei is never able fully to permit himself to be other than his conception of himself, however. Even on his deathbed, as he slips in and out of life, Andrei has something too conscious in his perceptions. The repelling force, then, is some form of command or desire for command over life— one's own and those of others.

Pierre, on the other hand, less intelligent than Andrei and less realistic in his thoughts and aims, does touch the magic core. Imprisoned by the French during the occupation of Moscow, he loses his faith in the goodness of man and indeed in all meaning of life when he hears the French executing their prisoners. Because he lets go of his beliefs and expectations, he is ready to permit a different and better reality to awaken in himself. In order to arrive at the "truth," Pierre must divest himself of his social clothing, not only literally but also figuratively, internally. Pierre learns the truth from the peasant sage Platon (Plato) Karataev. Platon accepts unquestionably that he is not in control of life, that he is a servant of God, and that the future is not in his hands. He lives so completely in the present moment that he does not know how a sentence will end when he begins it. He is captive neither of memory nor of past affections.

Isaiah Berlin had something of this schema in mind when in his seminal essay *The Hedgehog and the Fox* (1953) he wrote, "What is it that Pierre has learnt, of which Princess Marie's marriage is an acceptance, that Prince Andrey all his life pursued with agony? Like Augustine, Tolstoy can only say what it is not." But Tolstoy does in fact say what "it" is, not as a formula, a conclusion, or a schema but through his characters and what they experience. Perhaps the best example of this phenomenon is the scene in which Natasha attends a ball. If there is a center where life beats full, it is in this scene, generally acknowledged as one of the high points of *Voina i mir*. Natasha is a young girl of sixteen and not particularly intelligent. There is little consistency in her actions, and her emotions are fluid and almost fickle. She changes suitors with regularity. It is hard to see why Tolstoy would have chosen her as someone to embody his conception of truth or the plenitude of life; yet, at the ball she is unimpressed, indeed not even conscious of the importance of the various nobles, of rank and influence. Rather, she is living her own life with intensity, so much so that Tolstoy describes her as "blinded" by the lights and glitter about her and "deafened" by the sound of the crowd. The condition of touching the center is that one lives one's own life and feelings fully, intensely, and without reservation, rather than living with socially approved feelings or distancing one's feelings by judgment and reflection.

This point can be clarified by comparing Natasha with Mar'ia. The latter is a "good" woman: she is self-sacrificing, devoted to her father, and devoutly religious. Yet, there is no joy in her life. She is somber and heavy in thought and action. Her chief trait is self-sacrifice, whereas Natasha's chief trait is a kind of absorption in herself and in the moment. Mar'ia lives for the other world; Natasha lives for this world. Mar'ia lives for others; Natasha lives for herself, in the sense of experiencing concretely and immediately her own feelings, rather than feelings imposed upon her. The contrast between Natasha and Mar'ia touches on Tolstoy's conception of morality. Mar'ia's conventional morality does not give her happiness. It traps her into feelings and actions that are at odds with her actual feelings. Mar'ia's repetitive and inflexible self-sacrifice is reminiscent of the desiccating conventional grief that darkened Masha's house in the beginning of *Semeinoe schast'e*. Tol-

Tolstoy in 1868

stoy places himself on the side of genuine feelings and speaks out against those that are socially or religiously imposed. He writes at one point in *Voina i mir* that people are good when they are happy, and not happy because they are good.

The Battle of Borodino is fought, and neither side can claim a decisive victory. Nevertheless, the Russians retreat and give up Moscow in order to save their army. French troops enter Moscow and find a deserted city, except for a few thousand stragglers. Andrei, who recovered after Austerlitz, has been mortally wounded in this new battle, and he hovers between life and death in one of the wagons in the courtyard where the Rostovs are staying. Pierre is captured by the French and thrown into prison, where he comes to his illumination about life and his place in it. History and its mysterious, incomprehensible current have swept all of these characters, and the Russian nation, to the brink of extinction. Yet, history will also take them to ends that they had not foreseen.

Tolstoy attempts to characterize and define the "logic" of history in his second epilogue to the novel. The epilogue has been widely criticized as an inappropriate and barren theoretical argument. Berlin was one

of the few critics to take these chapters seriously. He was convinced, as have been many critics, that Tolstoy was a strict determinist, and that Tolstoy's view of history leaves no room for individual liberty. Berlin sees the basic dilemma of the novel as a conflict between freedom and necessity. According to Berlin, Tolstoy created characters whose vitality and choices presupposed free choice, and yet he insisted in his theoretical chapters that man is not free. Berlin writes that Tolstoy is

above all obsessed by his thesis—the contrast between the universal and all-important but delusive experience of free will, the feeling of responsibility, the values of private life generally, on the one hand; and on the other, the reality of inexorable historical determinism, not, indeed experienced directly, but known to be true on irrefutable theoretical grounds. This corresponds in its turn to a tormenting inner conflict, one of many, in Tolstoy himself, between the two systems of value, the public and the private. On the one hand, if those feelings and immediate experiences, upon which the ordinary values of private individuals and historians alike ultimately rest, are nothing but a vast illusion, this must, in the name of the truth, be ruthlessly demonstrated, and the values and the explanations which derive from the illusion exposed and discredited.

The contradiction that Berlin sets up is true only if one accepts the idea that Tolstoy believed in strict necessity, a proposition that would make individual choice illusory. Tolstoy denigrates the "great man" theory of history and is at pains to argue that history is moved by forces other than the commands of leaders. Napoleon was bound to be defeated, and his commands were empty gestures before the great forces of history that moved him and his armies. But then it becomes unclear what Tolstoy means when he speaks of man as nowhere freer than on the battlefield, and when he makes repeated statements in his rough drafts that fatalism is nonsense. The answer to this dilemma may lie in Tolstoy's peculiar yet important definition of freedom. Tolstoy does not have in mind, clearly, a view of freedom as the freedom to move events. Man is not free to initiate events. He cannot step out of history. Every action is necessarily the consequence of the events that come before the action and necessarily condition it. By "free," then, Tolstoy must mean a freedom that does not exclude necessity, a "free necessity," or a free will that coincides with necessity.

Tolstoy finishes the dramatic portions of the novel in the second epilogue with a summary of the fates of the principal characters, nine years after the war of 1812. The epilogue in its expository form has struck most readers as rapid, dry, and lacking in dramatic interest. Pierre is married to Natasha; Mar'ia is married to Nikolai. Many readers have been shocked by the transformations: Natasha has become a somewhat stout and doting mother, uninterested in politics or anything other than her domestic affairs. Nikolai, the volatile and capricious hussar, has become a dour but successful manager of his estates. Pierre has become involved in liberal politics and even in conspiratorial circles. The transformations of Pierre and Nikolai are not so drastic: throughout the novel Pierre has sought the betterment of society and its people, and Nikolai is still a hot-headed, impassioned defender of the czar and the status quo. The portrait of Natasha, however, has been hard for many readers to accept. The spellbinding girl of the ball is now a housewife whose interests seem to be limited to husband and children. Tolstoy may be intentionally disappointing the reader's romantic expectations. On the other hand, Tolstoy always considered mother-hood the sacred mission of women, so from this point of view Natasha has not degenerated but has continued in the natural course of things.

Voina i mir enjoyed a huge success in Russia–the patriotic subject matter was both popular with and familiar to readers–and the years of its writing and early reception were the happiest of Tolstoy's life. Both Tolstoys were in good health; there was a constant stream of visitors to the estate; and Tolstoy enjoyed the family life he had wanted. Still, Tolstoy began to feel considerable restlessness as the years progressed. It was understandably difficult to go from *Voina i mir* to another major work. He worked on a novel about Peter I, but after a time gave that up. He learned Greek and had a fleeting passion for astronomy. In 1873 he summered in Samara and became involved in famine-relief efforts there. He took up his educational work once again and in 1875 wrote primers for schools: *Novaia azbuka* (New Primer) and *Russkie knigi dlia chteniia* (Russian Readers). He attempted to get the government to adopt his educational theories; eventually many Russian schools used his teaching materials. The family was also touched by death during this restless period: in 1873 the Tolstoys' little boy Petr died; in 1874 Tolstoy's favorite aunt passed away; and a year later the Tolstoys lost two more children, Nikolai and Varvara. The somber tones of *Anna Karenina* may in part be attributed to these personal losses.

Tolstoy began *Anna Karenina* in 1873, and the novel was serialized from 1875 to 1877 in *Russkii vestnik*. The beginnings are perhaps biographical, since Tolstoy was present at the inquest of a neighboring noble-woman who had committed suicide over an unrequited love. The early drafts present, more or less, the portrait of a conventional "bad" woman: audacious, gossiped about, and provocative. Tolstoy only slowly came to see Anna with more sympathy. The novel has a tension, at times almost unbearable, between a woman's immoral

act and the considerable sympathy and even love she provokes. Until *Anna Karenina,* there had been no such loves or tragedies in Tolstoy's work. He had, of course, depicted love and physical passion in previous works: there are seductions, romantic flights, and even irrational actions following on the impulses of passion. But physical passion and the temporary derangements of orderly life that it entails are treated in the works up to *Anna Karenina* as "errors" that can be corrected by experience, proper conditions, and the counsel of others. Anna is different and troubling. Something beyond Anna's control, and perhaps beyond even Tolstoy's understanding, turns her from a beautiful, intelligent, and wise creature into a tormenting and tormented being, wracked by jealousy and determined to visit hurt upon those around her.

Matthew Arnold, who first read the novel in a French translation, wrote one of the first reviews in English of *Anna Karenina* in 1888. Arnold seizes upon the disturbing view of a woman of good character and background who is dragged irretrievably along a path of self-destruction. He writes, "In our high society with its pleasure and dissipation, laxer notions may to some extent prevail; but in general an English mind will be startled by Anna's suffering herself to be so overwhelmed and irretrievably carried away by her passion, by her almost at once regarding it, apparently, as something which it was hopeless to fight against."

Tolstoy juxtaposes the destructive love between Anna and her lover, Vronsky, with the healthy love between another couple, Kitty and Levin: familiar, comforting, blessed by progeny and common devotion, and grounded in family and community. The question of what makes one love "bad" and the other "good" is difficult to answer. Anna and Vronsky are powerfully and fatefully attracted to each other. Kitty and Levin's love, on the other hand, seems to be untainted by physical passion, as Levin has an idealized love for Kitty. Levin and Kitty are bound by their family and by a growing respect for one another, but they lead largely separate lives, with each little interested in what occupies the other. Levin is consumed by the responsibilities of his estates and especially by his search for the meaning of life, a subject in which Kitty is uninterested. Levin reads the works of German philosopher Arthur Schopenhauer, and Kitty worries about whether she has enough clean sheets for her guests. A certain distance from each other seems to be one of the reasons that the marriage flourishes. Anna and Vronsky's love, on the other hand, is characterized on Anna's part by her demands for Vronsky's presence and for his emotional involvement, and, near the end, by a frenetic fear that he will leave her. The reader is fascinated by Anna and Vronsky's love and especially by her fate. Anna

Anton Pavlovich Chekhov, Maksim Gorky, and Tolstoy

husband are his big ears, his weight, his supercilious manner, and other physical detractions. At home Anna attempts to busy herself with her child, Serezha, but uncharacteristically loses her temper with a seamstress about the alteration of some dresses. Clearly, her perceptual and emotional landscape has changed, whatever her intentions and actions. What had been comforting and familiar to her before is now irritating and unsatisfying. Something overrides not only her past tranquility and habits but also, and more ominously, her present intentions. She becomes helpless before the attraction, and before reason and will; the force that has taken possession of Anna will release her only in death.

Vronsky's actual seduction of Anna—or more accurately, the immediate aftermath of the seduction—is described in a painful scene of little more than a page. Vronsky tries to support Anna as she is about to slip to the floor. He is helpless before the enormity of her shame and suffering. The seduction is likened to murder; and when Vronsky renews his kisses he is compared to a killer hacking at a dead body. Anna is bathed in self-humiliation and despair. The scene prefigures everything that is in store for them. Anna's agony will not lessen, and the love will only deepen in hurt for her and for him. The scene also shows that Vronsky does not know how to support Anna, as he will not throughout the novel. He has seen the love affair only in conventional terms, as the normal pursuit by an attractive bachelor of a beautiful married woman. His habits have been engaged, but not his deepest feelings. His capacity for feeling is limited; hers is infinite.

Anna's need for love, even physical love, is frantically possessive. She had married Karenin, a considerably older man and one authoritative in manner, under circumstances that suggest a forced marriage. Vronsky, meanwhile, is an honorable but weak person. He is baffled by Anna and her love and is drawn unwillingly into the whirlpool of her destructive emotions. It may be that in falling in love with Vronsky, Anna repeats with variation the humiliation of marrying Karenin. Vronsky seems, however, to be the antithesis of the heavy-footed, sententious, bureaucratic Karenin. He is, after all, a dashing guardsman, handsome and charming. Yet, psychic repetitions take place under a screen of superficial differences. Vronsky, too, is interested in politics, although he must set aside his ambitions under the emotional onslaughts of Anna's demands and societal condemnation of their affair, which moves beyond the realm of the socially sanctioned. Karenin is a relentless social creature: every aspect of his life, including his religion, is a strict observance of what society requires. Vronsky is no different. He does set aside his proper life to attend to Anna's needs. But the differences that fester between them have to do with Vronsky's desire to make

hurts her husband, gives pain and confusion to her son, destroys her family life, and visits pain and suffering on her lover. Yet, she sweeps the reader into her emotional orbit, and the reader becomes privy to the pain and humiliation that she suffers.

As the novel begins, Anna is on her way to smooth over the minor domestic tragedy of her brother Stiva Oblonsky's betrayal of his wife, Dolly, sister to Kitty, in an affair with the family's governess. (Stiva is an incorrigible bon vivant; unlike Anna, however, Stiva does not meet with disaster as a result of his infidelity.) On her way to see Dolly and to intercede for her brother, Anna meets Vronsky at a railway station in Moscow, and the attraction between the two is immediate and intense. Anna fights it by trying to take up the routine of her former life, but without success. Tolstoy records her futile efforts to combat her attraction, symbolized by a powerful snowstorm when Anna returns on the train to St. Petersburg after meeting Vronsky. Anna's husband, Aleksei Karenin, meets her at the railway station, and the first things she notices about her

their love lawful through legal marriage, a situation that at times threatens Anna's ability to keep her son.

The joint crisis of husband and lover comes at Anna's near death in childbirth (the child is Vronsky's). Karenin experiences a religious illumination under the strain of the situation and forgives Anna for her transgression. He is ready to grant her everything at this point, even her son and her lover. Anna is overwhelmed by his generosity, and they are briefly reconciled. But the inner force that has driven Anna to the near destruction of husband and lover, and of herself, reasserts itself and drives Anna away from her husband. Anna and Vronsky are reconciled and go abroad so that they can live openly together. She does not take her son with her, as Karenin had offered, and she explains her decision as not wanting to take advantage of his generosity.

During the first months of bliss abroad, Anna barely thinks of her son. And on her last day alive, when for a few minutes her madness ceases and she is able to see her situation clearly, she admits to herself that having both her child and Vronsky would not have made any difference. She needs her son when she feels that Vronsky's love for her is diminishing, which suggests that what drives her to misery is the inability of Vronsky to love her as she wishes. Vronsky gives her everything he is capable of giving her: he forsakes his career, the approbation of his family, and the bachelor life he loves. One might argue that he behaves decently and honorably to her. He is a conventional man and gives her an honorable and conventional love. But Anna wants and needs something else. She has had a conventional love with her husband, a love that later she compares to death. Vronsky has aroused a deep and mysterious need in her that he is not then able to fill. The result is Anna's suicide.

Anna's last day on earth depicts most heartrendingly her pain and a sense of helplessness before the forces that are driving her to destruction. Anna and Vronsky have come to St. Petersburg from their country estate to wait for Karenin's answer to Anna's request for a divorce. When it becomes clear that Karenin will not grant the divorce, Anna is anxious to leave for the country. Vronsky wants to delay the departure for a few days because of business affairs, and Anna becomes insistent. It appears that nothing Vronsky can do will calm or satisfy her demands: she rejects every gesture of conciliation from him and then at the same time frantically desires his presence. In several remarkable scenes Tolstoy describes Anna's sense of panicked loneliness. She cannot recognize herself in a mirror; bread and cheese on a table fill her with disgust; she does not know where to go and to whom to turn. When Vronsky goes off to see his mother about a business matter,

she sends a telegram for him to return, and when she receives an answer that he cannot, she rushes to intercept him at a railway station. She fails to do so and finds herself alone on the station platform, feeling abandoned and desperate. She is in a place where all the passengers except her have goals; all are meeting or saying goodbye to loved ones. In a state of desperate confusion, Anna goes to the end of the railway platform, which shakes as a freight train approaches, and measures the distance between wheels to throw herself under an oncoming train. She is held back on her first try by a red handbag she is carrying, but her second attempt is successful.

The various reasons offered for Anna's suicide are many, and none is fully convincing. She kills herself because she had a loveless marriage; because she lived in a society that would not permit the kind of love she had for Vronsky; because she flouted conventional opinion and then could not bear rejection by society; because she could not have both lover and son; because she received God's vengeance for an immoral relationship (the epigraph, "Vengeance is mine; I will repay," has been noted in support of this last reading). There are strong reasons to see sex as the demonic power that destroys her, especially in view of Tolstoy's increasingly negative attitude toward sex. Anna's abrupt change of character coincides with her sexual affair with Vronsky, and the destructive consequences follow upon the inception of the affair. Tolstoy believed that the individual had an inner sanctity that ought not to be violated by others. Sex for him was a massive aggression and violation of this sanctity. But Anna wants more than sex, more than the kind of love Karenin and Vronsky can offer her; and she wants more, apparently, than what maternal love can bring her. There is no question that she loves her son; the painful scene in which she appears for his birthday despite the interdiction of her husband is evidence of her—and her son's—love and loss. Still, Vronsky's love or what she seeks in Vronsky's love is greater than her love for Serezha. The most common, and in a sense the most persuasive, explanation for her suffering and tragedy has been the argument that she suffers because she cannot have both lover and son. And yet Karenin, after the near-death reconciliation, offers her both.

Thus, the novel seems to undermine every explanation that is put forth. Yet, the reader remains drawn by the fate of a woman who on rational grounds does not deserve such interest. There must be something in her and her fate with which the reader identifies powerfully, something that inspires sympathy, compassion, even love. It may be simply the recognition that something like her fate can be the reader's as well, that there are forces in the universe and within people that are

Tolstoy reading a work to his disciple Vladimir Grigor'evich Chertkov, who edited many of Tolstoy's posthumously published works

incomprehensible and uncontrollable, forces that can override one's goodwill, reason, and intentions.

In the last chapter of *Anna Karenina* Tolstoy attempts to reassert the life of Levin against the tragedy of Anna. Levin has tortured himself with the meaning of life and sought the truth by reading through the works of many philosophers. They are of no help to him, and he comes to the point of considering suicide. He is saved by the words of a peasant who says that while one man may live for his own needs, another lives for his soul and does not forget God. These words hit Levin with a blinding light, and he interprets the peasant's words to mean that one is not to live for reason or desire. The years of self-torture lift from his soul, and a saving truth is revealed to him. Levin's illumination seems imposed and arbitrary, however. If so, this falsity is an indication of how Tolstoy was driven to deliver himself and his readers from the awful truth of Anna's tragic life. If dramatic intensity is some gauge of the vitality and truth of a character, then Anna, not Levin, carries the truth.

The novel ends with an argument about Russian volunteers going off to help the Serbs in their revolt against Turkish Ottoman rule. In a dialogue with his half brother, Koznyshev, Levin questions the sincerity of the volunteers and the role of the press in whipping up a war fever. Koznyshev insists that a spontaneous feeling is motivating the volunteers to action against the

atrocities committed by the Turks against their "Slavic brothers." Levin says that he does not feel such a motivation. Levin's remarks enraged Fyodor Dostoevsky, who wrote two long articles on *Anna Karenina*. In the second of these articles Dostoevsky objected to Levin's views about the war, insisting with vehemence that the Russians must help their Slavic brethren. Tolstoy's editor Mikhail Nikiforovich Katkov was also profoundly disturbed by Tolstoy's stand against the Russian aid to the Serbs and refused to publish this last chapter in *Russkii vestnik,* substituting instead a summary. Tolstoy later published the novel with the last chapter intact. Dostoevsky did, however, admire the novel enormously as a whole; his opinion differed from that of Turgenev, who found the second part of the novel "trivial and boring."

After, and perhaps during, the publication of *Anna Karenina* between 1875 and 1877, Tolstoy experienced a profound spiritual change, one similar in ways to that undergone by the semiautobiographical Levin. Tolstoy left an account of this change in a work titled *Ispoved'* (My Confession, 1884), a record of his loss of meaning in his life and work. Tolstoy was healthy and famous; he had vast wealth and a loving wife and children; and yet he experienced a profound emptiness and meaninglessness in the core of his being. He tells the reader that it was as if wherever he turned, despite his riches, he ended up at a precipice. He had noticed, however, that while the peasants on his estate were poorly clad, lived in shabby and leaking huts, and had no prospect of bettering their futures, they were nonetheless happy. He came to the conclusion that they knew what the meaning of life was and he did not. So Tolstoy became a peasant, in the sense of living as they lived, or at least attempting to do so. He dressed as the peasants did, ate the same food, and worshiped with them. The prospect of the great Count Tolstoy, author of *Voina i mir* and *Anna Karenina,* genuflecting in a country church at the side of peasants, was striking indeed. Yet, while Tolstoy worshiped he could not keep his mind from working, and soon he was questioning the priest's words and actions. This questioning process led Tolstoy to try to understand what the Russian Orthodox religion consisted of, and this study led him in turn to examine the biblical texts in their original Hebrew and Greek. Tolstoy already knew Greek, and he rapidly learned Hebrew. The conclusion he came to was that the contemporary practice of Russian Orthodoxy was base, crude magic, and that Orthodoxy was a monstrous distortion of "true" Christianity. Such a view, especially when Tolstoy began to make it public, did not endear him to Church authorities or to the czar, and eventually, after the publication of his final novel, *Voskresenie,* Tolstoy was excommunicated from the Orthodox Church in 1901 as a heretic.

When Tolstoy immersed himself in theological studies, he stopped writing fiction, much to the distress of his reading public. He turned instead to a reevaluation of every aspect of contemporary life, publishing his views in nonfictional tracts on art, education, economic and social relations, and family life. In the early 1890s he wrote such theological works as *Issledovanie dogmaticheskogo bogosloviia* (A Criticism of Dogmatic Theology, 1891) and *Soedinenie i perevod chetyrekh evangelii* (Union and Translations of the Four Gospels, 1892–1894), in which he reinterpreted the New Testament and excised from it all mention of miracles. In Tolstoy's new "Anarchical Christianity," Christ emerges as a wise teacher and not as a transcendent and divine God. Similar views were expressed in smaller volumes such as *V chem moia vera* (What I Believe, 1884). And in *Tak chto zhe nam delat'?* (What Then Must We Do?, 1886) Tolstoy took up the problem of poverty. In his *Tsarstvo Bozhie vnutri vas* (The Kingdom of God Is Within You, 1893–1894) he preached nonviolent anarchism.

Tolstoy's bold views on religion, sex, education, government, and art brought him increasingly to the attention of various segments of the Russian public, and visitors came to him for advice. At first these visitors were a trickle, then a stream, and by the mid 1890s, a torrent. Writers, students, the old and the young, the rich and the poor all came to see Tolstoy and to seek his counsel. There was hardly a Russian writer of the time who did not visit him, including Gorky, Anton Pavlovich Chekhov, and Ivan Alekseevich Bunin. Increasingly Tolstoy came to the attention of the larger world as well: such figures as George Bernard Shaw and Mahatma Gandhi (then a journalist in the Union of South Africa) corresponded with him, as did Woodrow Wilson briefly, before he became president. By the mid and late 1890s Tolstoy had become a kind of prophet, the carrier of a modern and "purified" Christianity.

Communes in keeping with Tolstoy's principles were organized in England, on the Continent, and in the United States. Tolstoy believed that no one should live off the work of another, and he counseled that people should grow their own food, make their own clothing, and in general consume as little as possible. He himself attempted to make his own shoes, an activity that resulted in bad shoes and neglect of his estates, which could have fed many. He was against private property, paying taxes, and serving in the army. He believed that government had no right to interfere in the lives of individuals. He believed the less education, the better. His views on sexual relationships went through several stages: he first counseled monogamy, but then reasoned that if sex was wrong outside of marriage, it was also wrong inside marriage. When it was pointed out to him that in a few generations the human race would disappear, he said that one must never compromise with principle. He also condemned all Western art, with few exceptions, as useless and even corrupt.

Perhaps none of Tolstoy's views provoked more disagreement than those on art. In his *Chto takoe iskusstvo?,* on which he worked for more than a decade, he rejected almost all the art of the Western world, his own earlier works included. He insisted that what society considered to be art was an elitist activity, cultivated to protect the interests of a leisure class. He was against schools of art, since nothing ought to be taught. He reserved his deepest criticism for William Shakespeare's works, which he considered to be not only poor but actually corrupting. *Chto takoe iskusstvo?* is a masterfully written treatise, though its conclusions are debatable. One should note, however, that while Tolstoy was condemning what is conventionally called "art," he was at the same time championing another kind of art. "Real" art for him was as necessary and universal as air or food, and therefore should be available for all people. Conventional art was not only class-bound but based on imitation—that is, on willed and artificial emotions. Tolstoy's definition of true art is based on the communication of emotion, sincerely felt and received. True art serves the end of uniting people, whereas conventional art divides people. Perhaps Tolstoy's most controversial proposition was that a work is not true art if it cannot

Tolstoy with his youngest daughter, Aleksandra

ther the best nor worst of students. He marries, not because of love or passion, but because his fiancée is from the right class and fits in with his social set. He makes his way through bureaucracy by way of the proper deference and obedience, furnishes his apartment with the right objects, entertains the right people, and serves the right things. He becomes a judge, with children and a comfortable lifestyle.

Then a seemingly trivial accident occurs: one day, while showing a draperer how to hang a curtain, Ivan Il'ich falls off a ladder and hurts his side. The injury does not seem serious, but the pain returns and with time begins to interfere with Ivan's "pleasant and proper" life. The doctors cannot diagnose it; Ivan Il'ich cannot understand it; and family and friends progressively ignore it. After a time Ivan Il'ich comes to hate those about him, especially his wife, as the pain progressively seeps into every part of his life and isolates him from everyone, except for one sympathetic peasant lad. Uncorrupted by societal influence, this youth is the only character who seems to feel genuine compassion for the judge. Ivan Il'ich moves from ignoring the pain, to protesting against the injustice of his suffering, and then finally to accepting his inevitable death. In the last hours of his life, he finds pity and forgiveness for his wife and family and accepts his fate. With this acceptance, Ivan Il'ich enters a place of light, and then realizes that the pain and death are gone. The ending is Christian in its symbolism and has been criticized as arbitrary.

The pain, which is never named, is called "it" throughout the novel. In Russian, Tolstoy assigns this "it" a feminine gender, thus linking "it" to such grammatically feminine Russian nouns as *smert'* (death), *bol'* (pain), and *zhizn'* (life). Life leads to death, but the acceptance of death is also a form of life. Tolstoy seems to argue that a life that attempts to seek pleasure only becomes a living death. Ivan Il'ich's society has attempted to eliminate pain or its derivatives from life. Compassion, however, is shared pain, and a society without shared pain and a corresponding consciousness of death is a society that has eliminated much of what makes people truly human.

Khoziain i rabotnik is another work that is spare in detail, actors, and plot. In this work Tolstoy has reduced existence to its most elemental features: life and death, rich and poor, material and spiritual, powerful and humble. He also uses the most basic archetype on which to structure his tale: the journey from life to death. A rich peasant (kulak) sets off with his worker Nikita in the face of a snowstorm to buy a patch of woods for profit. The difference between the rich man and the poor man is marked without subtlety: Brekhunov, the rich man, has two coats; the poor man

be understood by everyone. The test of genuineness in art is that it excludes no one. This point meant, for some at least, that the most ignorant peasant was a judge of artistic worth. This argument seemed outrageous to many, yet Tolstoy puts forth his case with great cogency and considerable persuasion.

After not publishing any fiction for nearly a decade, Tolstoy in his last period created a series of works in keeping with his newly formulated artistic principles. Such short novels as *Smert' Ivana Il'icha*, *Khoziain i rabotnik*, *Khadzhi-Murat*, and *Otets Sergii* are among his best works. Tolstoy's works of this period are consciously pedagogical, moral, and didactic, with universal themes. He eschews technical and stylistic mannerisms, pruning his works of descriptive detail and pursuing a simple and direct writing style. Perhaps the greatest of these postconversion works is *Smert' Ivana Il'icha*. Ivan Il'ich is Everyman in his aspirations, pleasures, marriage, and aims in life. He wants to live a proper and pleasurable life, and all his capacities are directed to the attainment of these ends. The words "priiatno i prilichno" (pleasantly and properly) are expressed with incantatory repetition, almost like the heartbeat of his life. He does everything to please the powers that be. He goes to law school, where he is nei-

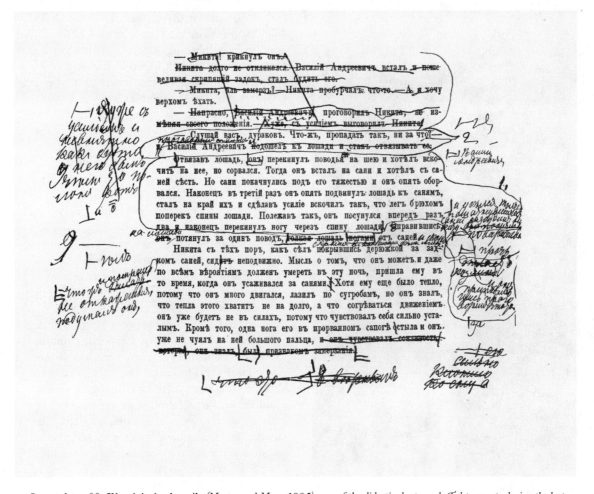

Corrected proof for Khoziain i rabotnik *(Master and Man, 1895), one of the didactic short novels Tolstoy wrote during the last period in his career (from Nathan Haskell Dole,* The Life of Count Lyof N. Tolstoi, *1911)*

Nikita has only a shred of a coat. Brekhunov is florid from drink and good food; Nikita is skinny and pale. Brekhunov has been stealing from his worker by withholding his wages and forcing him to buy his goods at elevated prices from Brekhunov. The bulk of the story has to do with the difficulty and ultimate impossibility of finding "the way." Repeatedly, Brekhunov forces his way despite the severity of the storm and the counsel of others. The two men finally get lost and stuck in the snow, and the scene of the figures buried in the stark whiteness of the snow and the prospect of death has a terrifying existential character. The snow throughout is linked to death and annihilation. Snow literally obliterates all the markings of civilization: roads, signposts, fields. Faced with freezing and death, the rich peasant lies on his servant in an attempt to keep warm. In the morning the two men are found: Brekhunov is dead, and Nikita is alive. The ending, didactic in nature, has often been read as an example of Christian sacrifice of one human being for another. But it can be argued that

though the story describes the giving of one life for another, this act is not necessarily Christian, or even an act of love. When Brekhunov lies on Nikita, he is not thinking of God or Christianity or sacrificial love. Rather, he is thinking of keeping himself warm and saving his own life, and there is no other way of doing it but by way of his fellow man. If there is a parable in the tale, it is that people are alone in the universe and have only one another.

Of all Tolstoy's postconversion novels, *Kreitserova sonata* is perhaps the most notorious because of its view of sexual relations. The novel is narrated by the half-mad Pozdnyshev, who tells his life story to several of his fellow passengers on a train: a lawyer, a woman of the higher classes, and a peasant. Pozdnyshev tells how he lived a corrupted life, one in accordance with the conventions of the time. These conventions train women to accept a life focused on satisfying men's sexual appetites: women are marketed like cattle to the highest bidder, and they themselves strive by way of

Tolstoy and his wife, six weeks before his death in 1910

dress, gestures, and makeup to render themselves as attractive as possible and to command the highest price. When the listening lawyer and woman insist that love is a union of minds and souls, Pozdnyshev snorts with disgust. He has killed his wife because, enraged by jealousy and by his own appetites, he suspected her in an unsubstantiated affair with a musician. Tolstoy suggests that the proper relation between human beings is respect for each other's person, and if it were not for a corrupt society, human beings would not indulge in "unnatural" (that is, sexual) acts. The novel was not published in Russia until 1891, and only then by way of a personal plea from Tolstoy's wife to the czar; but it was widely circulated in manuscript and lithograph form and fascinated and enraged many. High government officials urged the czar to punish Tolstoy, and the work was banned in the United States by postal authorities.

Also during this later period, in 1884, Tolstoy and his disciple Vladimir Grigor'evich Chertkov founded a nonprofit publishing house called "Posrednik" (The Intermediary), meant to aid in the publication and distribution of inexpensive works for the peasantry. (Chertkov, who had met Tolstoy in 1883 and shared many of the writer's views, became close to Tolstoy during this time despite Sof'ia Andreevna's fervent dislike of him.) In 1886 Tolstoy wrote the play *Vlast' t'my* (The Power of Darkness, 1887), a peasant drama produced successfully by Konstantin Sergeevich Stanislavsky in the 1890s. During the 1890s Tolstoy also helped with famine-relief efforts in various regions, organizing free meals for starving peasants.

Tolstoy's last major novel was *Voskresenie,* written over a period of ten years and serialized in *Niva* (The Grainfield) in 1899. The novel was written to help the Dukhobors, a religious sect persecuted by the government for its beliefs; its members wished to immigrate to Canada. The Dukhobors were against owning private property and in favor of Christian communal living, and as such their beliefs were similar to those of Tolstoy. He and his followers had been helping the Dukhobors for several years but finally saw that the only solution was emigration. Canada was willing to accept them, but money was needed to defray the cost of travel and resettlement. Tolstoy agreed to write *Voskresenie* and to use the royalties for this purpose. While Tolstoy had refused payment for works published after 1881, in this case he entered into a contract with a publisher.

The idea for the novel came from friend and jurist Anatolii Fedorovich Koni, who recounted the true story of a young man who seduced an orphan girl of sixteen and then abandoned her to a life of prostitution and misery. The girl was later arrested and tried for stealing, and one of the jurors was her seducer. The conscience of the seducer was touched, and in an effort at personal redemption he married the girl. In *Voskresenie* Tolstoy reworked this story into a tale of great complexity and social import, raging against the many injustices that he saw in Russian society. While some of the artistic integrity of the novel is compromised by Tolstoy's invectives against social abuses, Tolstoy is at his best in his depiction of the various stages of love between the young woman, Maslova, and her seducer, Nekhliudov. Redemption, Nekhliudov quickly learns, is more difficult and complicated than seeking official justice. When he offers to marry Maslova, Nekhliudov believes that he has redeemed his wrong. To his surprise and to the surprise of most readers, Maslova refuses his offer. She does so because she knows that as the wife of Nekhliudov she would be returning to the place she had been: not only to the memory of the painful seduction, but also to the prison of dependency on Nekhliudov's generosity. Maslova recognizes at some level that only she can redeem herself.

Voskresenie was acclaimed in Russia, on the Continent, and in the United States. The young poet Aleksandr Blok described the novel as a "testament from the departing generation to the new one," and the French novelist Romain Rolland, who was influenced by Tolstoy, wrote that *Voskresenie* was "one of the most beautiful poems about human suffering." Meanwhile, other readers were shocked by Tolstoy's unorthodox portrayal of the Russian Church in the novel. Sof'ia Andreevna, for one, found his description of the Orthodox liturgy distressingly cynical. Konstantin Pobedonostsev, Procurator of the Holy Synod, was appalled by the content and popularity of the book. On 24 February 1901 Tolstoy, who had, in the church's thinking, used his literary talent to attack the Russian Orthodox faith, was excommunicated. Tolstoy, however, was pleased with *Voskresenie,* feeling that he had succeeded in his desire to produce literature meant for "the people" in keeping with his beliefs.

At the turn of the century Tolstoy was in frail health but still productive. He spent a portion of 1901 in the Crimea to recover from various illnesses and while there spent time with Chekhov and Gorky. Tolstoy's play *Zhivoi trup* (The Living Corpse) had been staged in 1900 and the story "Posle bala" (After the Ball) appeared in 1903. Tolstoy was basking in worldwide fame. He put together several collections of philosophical and moral texts, including *Krug chteniia* (Cycle of Reading, 1906) and *Na kazhdyi den'* (For Every Day, 1909), and visitors continued to pour into Iasnaia Poliana. Meanwhile, Russia entered into a stormy political period, losing the Russo-Japanese War (Tolstoy, who despite himself had felt patriotic feelings during the war, wrote that a Christian nation such as Russia should not be engaging in war, which explained the Russian defeat) and plunging into the chaos of the 1905 revolution.

The unrest on the political front was mirrored inside the Tolstoy household during the last decades of Tolstoy's life. *Kreitserova sonata* and its biographical resonances had long pointed to the strains that were afflicting the Tolstoys' marriage. Their daughter Masha, who had been devoted to her father's teachings, died in 1906. Trying to live according to the well-known principles that he preached, Tolstoy sought to give away his property, especially his exclusive and profitable rights to the works he was publishing in Russia and abroad. Sof'ia Andreevna, trying to raise the large brood of Tolstoy children and to maintain the estate, objected vehemently to this plan. The two finally arrived at a compromise in which Sof'ia Andreevna would retain the rights to the preconversion works, while Tolstoy would give away the rights to the postconversion works. Tolstoy's decision led to a scramble among publishers to profit from his works and to the publication of sloppy editions. Sof'ia Andreevna felt increasingly neglected and ignored by her busy husband. Preaching love and brotherhood to the world, Tolstoy experienced bitterness and discord at home.

This discord reached its lowest point in the last year of Tolstoy's life. Sof'ia Andreevna became increasingly jealous and erratic in her actions. She threatened suicide repeatedly to provoke Tolstoy's attention, and the strain of her quarrels with her husband began to affect her mental health. On 28 October 1910 Tolstoy lay in bed in his study and heard his wife rifling through his papers. The eighty-two-year-old Tolstoy arose and decided that he had to leave Iasnaia Poliana and its noxious atmosphere. He awoke D. P. Makovitsky, his wife's personal physician, and his youngest daughter, Aleksandra, and told them that he wanted to leave. He was taken to a train station, where he boarded a third-class car. Two days later he was taken off the train because he had become too ill to travel further, and he was lodged in the station house of a small railway junction at Astapovo. The world soon knew his whereabouts, and the small town was besieged with reporters and even moviemakers. Upon learning where he was, Sof'ia Andreevna rushed to his side, but his supporters did not permit her to see him until his final day, when he was already in a coma. He died on 7 November 1910.

Despite Tolstoy's excommunication and his attacks on the government, the czar decreed a day of mourning upon Tolstoy's death, and newspapers were bordered in black in his memory. Tolstoy's body was brought back to Iasnaia Poliana and was buried on the side of a ravine, where he and his brothers as children had played a game of searching for a green stick that supposedly had on it the secret of human happiness.

Letters:

Pis'ma L. N. Tolstogo k dukhobortsam (Berlin: Izd. G. Shteinitsa, 1902);

Pis'ma L. N. Tolstogo, 2 volumes, edited by P. A. Sergeenko (Moscow: K-vo "Kniga," 1910–1911);

Novyi sbornik pisem L. N. Tolstogo, selected by P. A. Sergeenko (Moscow: A. A. Levenson, 1912);

Pis'ma grafa L. N. Tolstogo k zhene, 1862–1910, edited by A. E. Gruzinsky (Moscow: A. A. Levenson, 1913; second edition, revised, 1915);

Perepiska L. N. Tolstogo s N. N. Strakhovym, 1870–1894 (St. Petersburg: Izd. Obshchestva Tolstovskogo muzeia, 1914);

Lev Tolstoi i russkie tsari, 1862–1905, edited by Vladimir Grigor'evich Chertkov (Moscow: "Svoboda" i "Edinenie," 1918);

Tolstoi's Love Letters, With a Study on the Autobiographical Elements in Tolstoi's Work by Paul Biryukov, translated by S. S. Koteliansky and Virginia Woolf (Richmond, U.K.: L. & V. Woolf, 1923);

Pis'ma Tolstogo i k Tolstomu: Iubileinyi sbornik, edited by A. E. Gruzinsky (Moscow: Gos. izd-vo, 1928);

The Letters of L. Tolstoy and his Cousin Countess Alexandra Tolstoy, 1857–1903, translated by Leo Islavin (New York: Dutton, 1928);

L. N. Tolstoi i N. N. Ge: Perepiska (Moscow: Academia, 1930);

Korrespondenty L. N. Tolstogo, compiled by F. V. Buslaev, edited by N. N. Gusev (Moscow: Gos. sotsial'no-ekonomicheskoe izd-vo, 1940);

Leo Tolstoy, Correspondence, 2 volumes, edited and translated by R. F. Christian (New York: Scribners, 1978);

Lev Tolstoi, perepiski s russkimi pisatel'iami, 2 volumes, edited by S. Rozanova (Moscow: Khudozhestvennaia literatura, 1978);

Mahatma Gandhi and Leo Tolstoy: Letters, edited by B. Srinivasa Murthy (Long Beach, Cal.: Long Beach Publications, 1987);

Perepiska L. N. Tolstogo s sestroi i brat'iami, edited by N. A. Kalinina, V. V. Lozbiakova, and T. G. Nikiforova (Moscow: Khudozhestvennaia literatura, 1990);

L. N. Tolstoi i P. V. Verigin: Perepiska, edited by A. A. Donskov (St. Petersburg: Bulanin, 1995);

Leo Tolstoy–Peter Verigin: Correspondence, edited by Donskov, translated by John Woodsworth (New York: Legas, 1995);

L. N. Tolstoi i M. P. Novikov: Perepiska, edited by Donskov (Munich: Verlag Otto Sagner, 1996);

L. N. Tolstoi i T. M. Bondarev: Perepiska, edited by Donskov (Munich: Verlag Otto Sagner, 1996);

L. D. Gromova-Opul'skaia and Z. N. Ivanova, comps., *Novye materialy L. N. Tolstogo i o Tolstom: iz arkhiva N. N. Guseva = New Tolstoy Materials From the N. N. Gusev Archive* (Munich: Verlag Otto Sagner, 1997);

L. N. Tolstoi i F. A. Zheltov: Perepiska, compiled by Liudmila Gladkova, edited by Donskov (Ottawa: Slavic Research Group at the University of Ottawa, 1999);

L. N. Tolstoi i S. A. Tolstaia: Perepiska s N. N. Strakhovym (Ottawa: Slavic Research Group at the University of Ottawa / Moscow: State L. N. Tolstoy Museum, 2000).

Bibliographies:

Iu. Bitovt, *Graf L. Tolstoi v literature i iskusstve: Podrobnyi bibliograficheskii ukazatel' russkoi i inostrannoi literatury o gr. L. N. Tolstom* (Moscow: Tip. T-va I. D. Sytina, 1903);

B. S. Bodnarsky, *Bibliografiia proizvedenii L. N. Tolstogo: Opyt sistematicheskogo ukazatelia* (Moscow, 1910);

A. L. Bem, *Tolstovskaia bibliografiia za 1913: Obzor russkikh knig i povremennykh izdanii* (St. Petersburg: Izd. Tolstovskogo muzeia, 1915);

Bem and V. I. Sreznevsky, *Bibliograficheskii ukazatel' tvorenii L. N. Tolstogo* (Leningrad: Izd-vo Akademii nauk SSSR, 1926);

V. S. Spiridonov, *L. N. Tolstoi: Bio-bibliografiia* (Moscow: Academia, 1933);

F. V. Buslaev and I. K. Luppol, *Rukopisi L. N. Tolstogo: Katalog* (Moscow: Gos. biblioteka SSSR im. V. I. Lenina, 1937);

Ernest J. Simmons, "Recent Publications on Lev Nikolaevich Tolstoi," *Slavonic and East European Review,* 20 (1941): 338–346;

E. N. Zhilina and B. Ia. Bukhshtab, *Lev Tolstoi, 1828–1910: Ukazatel' osnovnoi literatury* (Leningrad: Gosfinizdat, 1941);

Zhilina and Morachevsky, *Lev Nikolaevich Tolstoi: Ukazatel' literatury,* second edition (Leningrad: Izd. Gos. publichnoi biblioteki im. M. E. Saltykova-Shchedrina, 1954);

V. A. Zhdanov, E. E. Zaidenschnur, and E. S. Serebrovskaia, *Opisanie rukopisei khudozhestvennykh proizvedenii L. N. Tolstogo* (Moscow: Izd-vo Akademii nauk SSSR, 1955);

Zhilina and Morachevsky, *Lev Nikolaevich Tolstoi, 1828–1910: Bibliograficheskii ukazatel' i metodicheskie materialy v pomoshch' bibliotekariu* (Leningrad: Gos. publichnoi biblioteki im. M. E. Saltykova-Shchedrina, 1960);

N. G. Sheliapin and others, eds., *Bibliografiia literatury o L. N. Tolstom, 1917–1958* (Moscow: Izd-vo Vses. knizhnoi palaty, 1960);

T. L. Motyleva, *Khudozhestvennye proizvedeniia L. N. Tolstogo v perevodakh na inostrannye iazyki* (Moscow: Izd-vo Vses. knizhnoi palaty, 1961);

Motyleva, ed., *Tolstoi i zarubezhnyi mir* (Moscow: Nauka, 1965);

R. B. Zaborova, *Rukopisnye materialy otnosiashchiesia k L. N. Tolstomu: katalog* (Leningrad: Gos. publichnaia biblioteka im. M. E. Saltykova-Shchedrina, 1966);

Motyleva, ed., *Voina i mir za rubezhom* (Moscow: Sovremennyi pisatel', 1978);

Garth M. Terry, "Tolstoi Studies in Great Britain: A Bibliographical Survey," in *New Essays on Tolstoi,* edited by M. V. Jones (Cambridge: Cambridge University Press, 1978), pp. 223–250;

David R. Egan and Malina A. Egan, *Leo Tolstoy, An Annotated Bibliography of English Language Sources* (Metuchen, N.J.: Scarecrow Press, 1979);

Patrick J. Wreath and April I. Wreath, "Leo Tolstoi: A Bibliography of Criticism in English, From the Late Nineteenth Century Through 1979," *Canadian-American Slavic Studies,* 14 (1980): 466–512;

Munir Sendich, "Tolstoj's *War and Peace* in English: A Bibliography of Criticism (1879–1985)," *Russian Language Journal,* 41 (1987): 219–279;

Sheliapin and others, *Bibliograficheskii ukazatel' literatury o L. N. Tolstom, 1974–1978* (Moscow: Izd-vo Knizhnaia palata, 1990);

I. Borisova, *Neizvestnyi Tolstoi v arkhivakh Rossii i SShA: Rukopisi, pis'ma, vospominaniia, nabliudeniia, versii: So 108 fotografiiami* (Moscow: AO Tekhna-2, 1994);

Sheliapin and others, *Bibliograficheskii ukazatel' literatury o L. N. Tolstom 1979–1984* (Moscow: Nasledie, 1999).

Biographies:

P. A. Sergeenko, *Kak zhivet i rabotaet gr. L. N. Tolstoi* (Moscow: I. N. Kushnerev, 1898); translated by Isabel Florence Hapgood as *How Count Tolstoy Lives and Works* (New York: Crowell, 1899);

Dmitrii Sergeevich Merezhkovsky, *L. Tolstoi i Dostoevskii: zhizn' i tvorchestvo,* fourth edition (St. Petersburg: Obshchestvennaia pol'za, 1909); translated as *Tolstoi as Man and Artist, with an Essay on Dostoievski* (Westminster: Archibald Constable, 1902);

Aylmer Maude, *The Life of Tolstoy,* 2 volumes (New York: Dodd, Mead, 1910);

A. V. Zaikin, *Apostol mira i liubvi: Lev Nikolaevich Tolstoi: Ego zhizn' i trudy* (St. Petersburg: Smysl' zhizni, 1911);

Pavel I. Biriukov, *Lev Nikolaevich Tolstoi,* 4 volumes (Moscow: Gos. izd-vo, 1911–1923); republished as *Biografiia L. N. Tolstogo,* 2 volumes (Moscow: Algoritm, 2000);

N. N. Gusev, *Dva goda s L. N.Tolstym* (Moscow: "Posrednik," 1912);

V. I. Sreznevsky and A. L. Bem, eds., *Tolstoi: Pamiatniki tvorchestva i zhizni,* 4 volumes (Petrograd: Ogni / Moscow: Zadruga, 1914–1923);

Maksim Gorky, *Reminiscences of Leo Nikolaevich Tolstoy,* translated by S. S. Koteliansky and Leonard Woolf (New York: Huebsch, 1920);

Percy Lubbock, *The Craft of Fiction* (London: Cape, 1921);

Vladimir Grigor'evich Chertkov, *The Last Days of Tolstoy,* translated by Nathalie A. Duddington (London: Heinemann, 1922);

Boris M. Eikhenbaum, *Lev Tolstoi,* 2 volumes [volume 1, *50-e gody;* volume 2, *60-e gody*] (Leningrad: Priboi, 1928–1931); volume 2 translated by Duffield White as *Tolstoi in the Sixties* (Ann Arbor, Mich.: Ardis, 1982);

Il'ia L'vovich Tolstoi, *Moi vospominaniia,* second revised edition (Moscow: Mir, 1933); translated by Ann Dunnigan as *Tolstoy, My Father: Reminiscences* (Chicago: Cowles Book Co., 1971);

Tatiana A. Kuzminskaia, *Tolstoy as I Knew Him* (New York: Macmillan, 1948);

Alexandra Tolstoy, *Tolstoy: A Life of My Father,* translated by Elizabeth Reynolds Hapgood (New York: Harper, 1953);

N. N. Gusev and V. S. Mishin, eds. and comps., *L. N. Tolstoi v vospominaniiakh sovremennikov,* 2 volumes (Moscow: Gos. izd-vo khudozh. literatury, 1955; second revised edition, 1960);

Eikhenbaum, *Lev Tolstoi: Semidesiatye gody* (Leningrad: Sovetskii pisatel', 1960); translated by Albert Kaspin as *Tolstoi in the Seventies* (Ann Arbor, Mich.: Ardis, 1982);

N. K. Gudzii, *Lev Tolstoi: Kritiko-biograficheskii ocherk,* third edition, revised (Moscow: Gos. izd-vo khudozh. lit-ry, 1960);

V. B. Shklovsky, *Lev Tolstoi* (Moscow: Molodaia gvardiia, 1963; English edition, Moscow: Raduga, 1988);

Henri Troyat, *Tolstoi* (Paris: Hachette, 1963); translated by Nancy Amphoux as *Tolstoy* (Garden City, N.Y.: Doubleday, 1967);

Valentin Bulgakov, *The Last Year of Tolstoy,* translated by Ann Dunnigan (New York: Dial, 1971);

B. S. Meilakh, *Ukhod i smert' L'va Tolstogo,* second edition (Moscow: Khudozhestvennaia literatura, 1979);

L. D. Gromova-Opul'skaia, *Lev Nikolaevich Tolstoi: Materialy k biografii s 1886–po 1892 g.* (Moscow: Nauka, 1979);

V. Ia. Linkov and A. A. Saakiants, *Lev Tolstoi: Zhizn' i tvorchestvo* (Moscow: Russkii iazyk, 1979);

K. N. Lomunov, *Zhizn' L'va Tolstogo* (Moscow: Khudozhestvennaia literatura, 1981);

Martin Green, *Tolstoy and Ghandi* (New York: Basic Books, 1983);

Nikolai Ardens, *Zhivoi Tolstoi: Zhizn' L'va Nikolaevicha Tolstogo v vospominaniiakh i perepiske* (St. Petersburg: Lenizdat, 1995).

References:

Matthew Arnold, "Count Leo Tolstoi," in his *Essays in Criticism: Second Series* (London & New York: Macmillan, 1888);

John Bayley, *Tolstoy and the Novel* (London: Chatto & Windus, 1966);

Isaiah Berlin, *The Hedgehog and the Fox* (New York: Simon & Schuster, 1953);

S. P. Bychkov, *Lev Nikolaevich Tolstoi v russkoi kritike* (Moscow: Gos. izd-vo khudozh. lit-ry, 1952);

Nikolai Gavrilovich Chernyshevsky, "Detstvo i otrochestvo, Voennye rasskazy grafa Tolstogo," *Sovremennik*, 12 (December 1856): 53–64;

R. F. Christian, *Tolstoy, A Critical Introduction* (Cambridge: Cambridge University Press, 1969);

Fyodor Dostoevsky, *Dnevnik pisatelia za 1877 goda* (Paris, n.d.), pp. 268–270, 275–311;

Ann Edwards, *Sonya, the Life of Countess Tolstoy* (New York: Simon & Schuster, 1980);

Vladimir Ermilov, *Tolstoi-romanist: "Voina i mir," "Anna Karenina," "Voskresenie"* (Moscow: Khudozhestvennaia literatura, 1965);

Kathryn B. Feuer, *Tolstoy and the Genesis of* War and Peace (Ithaca, N.Y.: Cornell University Press, 1996);

Richard F. Gustafson, *Leo Tolstoy, Resident and Stranger: A Study in Fiction and Theology* (Princeton: Princeton University Press, 1986);

William Dean Howells, "Lyof Tolstoy," in *The Library of the World's Best Literature, Ancient and Modern,* edited by Charles Dudley Warner, volume 45 (New York: The International Society, 1897), pp. 14985–14994;

A. V. Knowles, ed., *Tolstoy: The Critical Heritage* (London: Routledge & Kegan Paul, 1978);

Janko Lavrin, *Tolstoy: An Approach* (New York: Macmillan, 1946);

K. Leont'ev, *O romanakh gr. L. N. Tolstogo, Analiz, stil' i veianie* (Moscow: Tip. Sabina, 1911);

György Lukács, *Studies in European Realism,* translated by Edith Bone (London: Hillway, 1950);

Amy Mandelker, *Framing* Anna Karenina: *Tolstoy, the Woman Question, and the Victorian Novel* (Columbus: Ohio State University Press, 1993);

Gary Saul Morson, *Hidden in Plain View* (Stanford, Cal.: Stanford University Press, 1987);

Donna Tussing Orwin, *Tolstoy's Art and Thought, 1847–1880* (Princeton: Princeton University Press, 1993);

Dmitrii Ivanovich Pisarev, "'Tri smerti,' rasskaz gr. L. N. Tolstogo," *Rassvet,* 12 (December 1859): 63–74;

Natasha Sankovitch, *Creating and Recovering Experience: Repetition in Tolstoy* (Stanford, Cal.: Stanford University Press, 1998);

Ernest J. Simmons, *An Introduction to Tolstoy's Writings* (Chicago: University of Chicago Press, 1968);

George Steiner, *Tolstoy or Dostoevsky* (New York: Knopf, 1959);

Edward Wasiolek, *Tolstoy's Major Fiction* (Chicago: University of Chicago Press, 1978);

A. N. Wilson, *Tolstoy* (New York: Norton, 1988);

Virginia Woolf, "The Russian Point of View," in her *The Common Reader* (New York: Harcourt, Brace, 1925);

Vasilii Apollonovich Zelinsky, comp., *Russkaia kriticheskaia literatura o proizvedeniiakh L. N. Tolstogo,* 8 volumes (Moscow: Tipo-lit. V. Rikhter, 1897–1903).

Papers:

The Tolstoy Museum and Archive (Gosudarstvennyi muzei L. N. Tolstogo. Otdel rukopisei) is probably the most complete and most centralized of any archive of a Russian author. Founded in 1912, it came under the jurisdiction of the People's Commissariat for Education in 1917, then the Academy of Sciences of the USSR (1939–1953), and since 1953 has been independently administered by the Ministry of Culture. It is the depository for almost all of Leo Tolstoy's manuscripts, personal papers, and other materials, dating from the beginning of the nineteenth century. In addition to material on all of the Tolstoy family, the archive contains material relating to Tolstoy's friends, colleagues, and acquaintances. For a brief but thorough history of the museum and all its divisions, as well as a list of published and unpublished guides and finding aids to the Museum and Archive, see "Gosudarstvennyi muzei L. N. Tolstogo," in *Archives of Russia: A Directory and Bibliographic Guide to Holdings in Moscow and St. Petersburg,* English-language edition, edited by Patricia Kennedy Grimsted, volume 2 (Armonk, N.Y.: M. E. Sharpe, 2000), pp. 917–920.

Evgeniia Tur
(Elizaveta Sailhas de Tournemir)
(12 August 1815 – 15 March 1892)

Christine D. Tomei
Slavic Seminar, Columbia University

WORKS: *Oshibka,* in *Sovremennik,* 10 (November–December 1849): 137–284;

Dolg, in *Sovremennik,* 11 (1850): 5–60;

Plemiannitsa, in *Sovremennik,* nos. 1, 4 (1850); (Moscow, 1851);

Dve sestry, in *Otechestvennye zapiski,* 75 (1851);

Antonina and *Pervoe aprelia,* in *Al'manakh "Kometa"* (Moscow, 1851);

Chuzhaia dusha–potemki. Pogovorka, in *Otechestvennye zapiski,* 81 (1852): 1–30;

Tri pory zhizni, in *Biblioteka dlia chteniia,* 117 (1853); (Moscow: V. Got'e, 1854);

Zakoldovannyi krug, in *Otechestvennye zapiski,* 92 (1854): 139–240;

Starushka, in *Russkii vestnik,* no. 1 (1856): 32–113; 229–365;

Na rubezhe, in *Russkii vestnik,* no. 11 (1857): 803–884; no. 12 (1857): 37–104, 331–368;

Parizhskie pis'ma, in *Russkii vestnik,* no. 7 (1858);

Povesti i rasskazy, 4 volumes (Moscow: Kontragentstvo po torgovle proizvedeniiami pechati na stants. zh.d., 1859);

Povesti i rasskazy, 3 volumes (Moscow: Katkov, 1859);

Tsvetochnitsa, in *Otechestvennye zapiski,* no. 10 (1859);

Zhemchuzhnoe ozherel'e. Skazka (Moscow, 1870);

Khrustal'noe serdtse (Moscow, 1873);

Zvezdochka (Moscow, 1873);

Semeistvo Shalonskikh. Iz semeinoi khroniki (St. Petersburg: Tip. M. M. Stasiulevicha, 1880);

Mucheniki Kolizeia. Istoricheskii rasskaz dlia detei (Kaluga, 1884);

Ocherk zhizni i deianii Innokentiia, mitropolita Moskovskogo (Moscow, 1884);

Tri rasskaza dlia detei (St. Petersburg, 1884);

Zhitie prepodobnogo ottsa nashego Ksenofonta, suprugi ego Marii i dvukh synovei ego, Ionna i Arkadiia (St. Petersburg, 1884);

Cherez krai (Moscow, 1885);

Evgeniia Tur (Elizaveta Vasil'evna Sailhas de Tournemir; from I. N. Ignatov, Gallereiia russkikh pisatelei, *1901)*

Deti korolia Liudovika XVI (Moscow, 1885);

Zhizn' sviatogo Makariia Egipetskogo (Moscow: V Univ. tip. M. Katkova, 1885);

Kniazhna Dubrovina (Moscow, 1886);

Bor'ba ispantsev s mavrami i zavoevanie Grenady (St. Petersburg: Tip. M. M. Stasiulevicha, 1887);

Sergei Bor-Ramenskii (Moscow, 1888);

Sviashchennaia istoriia Vetkhogo Zaveta (Moscow: Univ. tip., 1888).

Edition in English: *Antonina,* translated by Michael R. Katz (Evanston, Ill.: Northwestern University Press, 1996).

TRANSLATIONS: *Katakomby* (Moscow, 1866); *Poslednie dni Pompeii,* in *Detskii otdykh,* nos. 1–4 (1882).

SELECTED PERIODICAL PUBLICATIONS:
"Krymskie pis'ma," *Sankt-Peterburgskie vedomosti,* nos. 254, 257 (1852); nos. 203, 209, 214, 234, 241, 255, 261, 266 (1853);
"Zhizn' Zhorzh-Sanda," *Russkii vestnik* (May 1856): 79–93; (June 1856): 693–715; (August 1856): 667–708;
"Vospominaniia," *Poliarnaia zvezda* (1881).

For the literary world of the late 1840s and early 1850s, Elizaveta Sailhas de Tournemir, writing under the pen name Evgeniia Tur, was one of the most important figures in Russia. Her novels, replete with social themes made famous by George Sand, met with overwhelmingly positive reviews, and she rose swiftly to a prominence unusual among women writers. In the 1860s she changed venues, working primarily as a literary critic but also founding and running an important literary journal, *Russkaia rech'* (Russian Speech). After a move abroad and the closing of her journal, she continued to write criticism, and eventually she turned to children's literature. In each of these areas her contribution was considerable, although only in the last years of the twentieth century has her work been seriously evaluated. As a woman, she was regarded by literary historians as inferior to her male contemporaries, and her reputation fell into decline for decades.

A member of the prominent Sukhovo-Kobylin family, Evgeniia Tur was born Elizaveta Vasil'evna Sukhovo-Kobylina on 12 August 1815 in Moscow. Literature was a part of family life, as her mother, Mariia Ivanovna (née Shepeleva), hosted literary salons in the house while Tur was growing up. In addition to Tur's own literary successes, her brother Aleksandr Vasil'evich Sukhovo-Kobylin became a well-known playwright. Education was an important part of Tur's life as well, and it became one of the dominant themes in her literature and her primary purpose for writing in her later years. Tur learned foreign languages, especially French, as a young girl. Later, her tutors included some of the most famous figures in Moscow, including the poet Semen Egorovich Raich (pseudonym Amfiteatrov) and the historian Mikhail Petrovich Pogodin, both of whom may have had lasting influences on her work. Nikolai Ivanovich Nadezhdin, a professor who was also a jour-

nalist, editor, and critic residing in Moscow before a Siberian exile, was a longtime tutor. He had more than a superficial influence on Tur—he was, at one time, her intended husband as well. When Tur's parents rejected Nadezhdin as a suitor for their daughter in 1835, the two planned an elopement, which for various reasons did not come to pass. However, Nadezhdin's most lasting influence on Tur may have been his belief that literature should become a synthesis of Romanticism and Classicism, as the types of experimentation with genre that she later developed in her socially realistic novels demonstrate.

Tur's private life took an unpleasant turn after the missed elopement with Nadezhdin. Not only were her dreams of independence quashed—a young, unmarried woman was restricted from almost all public activities unless chaperoned—but her parents then proceeded to take her abroad and, in 1837, to marry her to a poorly heeled Frenchman of aristocratic background but weak character. André Sailhas de Tournemir, a titled count, returned with Tur to Russia, where he promptly wasted her dowry of 80,000 rubles. Shortly afterward he was banished from Russia and returned to France—not for theft, since Tur's right to the dowry he had squandered was not supported by law, but for dueling. Tur's decision to remain in Russia, living principally upon the largesse of a sister and her own earnings, may have had a practical basis, since there were three children—Masha, Ol'ga, and Evgenii—to feed. Evgenii Andreevich Sailhas later became an historical novelist.

Issues concerning women occupy a great deal of Tur's fiction. Like Fyodor Dostoevsky, Tur searched for a compelling, active role for a female protagonist who is often sexually or socially subservient and is also kept from independent activity by restrictive laws. Like Sand, Tur changed the narrative focus to a woman's view. Exceptional women had yet to make frequent appearances in Russian literature, however, and Tur was careful to keep her women characters ordinary, thus providing a more realistic field for playing out the changing hierarchy of values affecting women's lives during the years she was writing.

The main character in Tur's first novel, *Oshibka* (The Mistake, 1849), is Ol'ga, a woman of twenty-eight who embodies many traits uncharacteristic of women in the fiction that had been written by men. For example, she is not described as attractive, being neither pretty nor plain, but her features are "overall harmonious, even and peaceful." For this ordinariness, the narrator begs the reader "ne serdites', chitatel'" (don't be angry). Ol'ga represents a move toward the prosaic atypical of Russian literature of the time: female characters were either romanticized or taken to task for a lack of romantic qualities. Tur's male protagonist, Slavin, is associated with *slava* (glory) by name, but is described in a manner distinctly inglorious. He is weak-willed and superficial, commanding position and wealth but lacking any truly redeeming character traits. In Slavin, Tur made an unusual move for her day, both in the contradictory naming and in his gender role: Slavin is not only not dominating, but banal.

The novel incorporates lengthy epistles that set the plot in motion. Slavin's mother, in a reply to her son's request for her blessing on his marriage to Ol'ga, encapsulates the central conflict of the novel: the proposed marriage of a well-to-do, society-oriented man to a woman of lower status. She tells him that Ol'ga "will never know how to fill her position in society, support your name and connections with dignity, make your drawing room one of the significant gathering places of the town, or be able to shine in society by virtue of her wit, her beauty or charm." Ol'ga's poor background, which has left her so ignorant that she cannot even put on her underclothes properly ("ne obladaet dazhe tain-ogo odevat'sia s isskustvom"), is certain to prove insurmountable in a role in higher society.

The major issues in the novel are not so much personal as institutional and social; the "villain" is the laws restricting women and their functions in society. Also at work is a complex social code in which value is assigned according to clothing and livery, rather than in consideration of one's character.

The proposed marriage between Ol'ga and Slavin is shown quite realistically as two completely different things to the two principals. His treatment of the obstacles (he has been attracted to someone else; she harbors grave doubts) is different from hers. Moreover, Slavin is portrayed as a slave to convention, and the institutional obstacles separating them (which appear most clearly when they are in public) lead to a breaking point in their relationship. Slavin tells Ol'ga, "You have no conception at all about duty, and you completely despise social opinion. A woman in particular should respect general opinion, bow to it and never deviate from the rules everyone finds pleasant." He thus inadvertently reproaches her for not being like his mother, who has "never deviated a single step from the rules and customs everyone found pleasant." He sees the wisdom of his mother's letter, and Ol'ga finds herself out of her element in society.

The conclusion of the novel is quite original. Ol'ga does not commit suicide, her usefulness as a woman rebuked. There are no hysterics, conflagrations, or murders. Instead, Ol'ga goes to her mother, telling her that her love will save Ol'ga and that the withholding of this maternal affection would destroy her. She decides to live with her mother, loving her; and her mother, suddenly remembering that Ol'ga is her child and not barter for some future welfare, makes a peace that promises to be permanent and mutually satisfactory. Slavin, meanwhile, takes off with a young princess who knows little but promises to keep him in society, where he feels the greatest contentment. The "mistake" of the title does not occur, and a happy ending ensues for all. Instead of punishing the foolish or rejecting innovation, the ending accommodates people's limitations and failings; and social convention, while providing an insuperable obstacle for women, does not preclude some alternative fulfillment of individuals' needs. These are some of the major themes and circumstances that are worked out in different ways throughout Tur's canon.

It is possible that Tur did not see the problems in this work as "women's" or "men's," but as reflective of a general plight in society, which she left indeterminate. To some extent, this generality might have contributed to the eventual fading of her literary reputation. Without a direct reproach or a defined problem, her writing seemed to lack a specific goal, a feature increasingly seen as crucial in Russian letters. Yet, Tur's works do represent the general scheme of purely romantic convention in an unconventional way. Her greatest deviation is that the narrative proceeds not as the exploit of a man, but as the evolution of a social problem that often involves a woman and her place in society. Scholar Jehanne Gheith has argued that Tur "writes new roles for old heroines," for while her female characters may resemble those of earlier male writers such as Aleksandr Sergeevich Pushkin or Mikhail Iur'evich Lermontov, Tur makes them leading characters in her writing and gives them new roles to play.

Oshibka met with a positive critical reception. In 1850 Aleksandr Nikolaevich Ostrovsky gave special praise in *Moskvitianin* (The Muscovite) to Tur's characterizations. Tur's next novel, *Plemiannitsa* (The Niece, 1851), is also well written and may have been one of the best novels published that year. Among Tur's works *Plemiannitsa* stands out for clarity of plot and execution, possibly because of some autobiographical elements. It carries forward many of the themes set out in *Oshibka*. Mar'ia, who is later Masha, the title heroine, loses both her parents before her sixth birthday. Her father, Aleksandr Bel'sky, was a spendthrift, while her mother was empty-headed. The mother, while pregnant, finds out by accident that her husband's holdings are being auctioned off, and the shock of this news brings about a premature stillbirth and her own death. Bel'sky, who had been as "dobr kak mat'" (tender as a mother) to his wife and to Mar'ia, is sent reeling back to his sister's and, after a time, he goes to the Caucasus, where he is quickly killed. Young Mar'ia is then left with her unmarried aunt, Varvara Petrovna Bel'skaia.

The theme of the ward's plight crops up persistently in Tur's work and appears full force in *Plemiannitsa*.

ПОВѢСТИ

и

РАЗСКАЗЫ

ЕВГЕНІИ ТУРЪ.

IV.

СТАРУШКА.

МОСКВА.

Контрагентство по торговлѣ произведеніями
печати на станц. ж. д.

Title page for Starushka *(The Old Woman), volume 4 of Tur's*
Povesti i rasskazy *(Tales and Stories, 1859); this story
of a failed marriage first appeared in* Russkii vestnik
(The Russian Herald) in 1856.

While Pushkin had in ways glossed over dependence, despondency, abuse, and neglect in the life of a ward in his "Pikovaia dama" (Queen of Spades, 1834), Tur expends considerable effort relating from their point of view the problems underage progeny or wards faced as victims of a brutally unfair system. Her descriptions of their mistreatment, told in the first person, might be considered the most compellingly realistic psychological portraits in this period of Russian literature.

Mar'ia is soon pictured as a young woman of almost eighteen (she somehow ages eleven years in the same time as her aunt gains twenty-three) who finds herself with three men attached to her: her former tutor, a distant relative who is also a rich prince, and the prince's friend. She thrives in this environment, and her rude aunt, intent on planning a successful match, tones down the mistreatment she has visited upon her niece. However, at a critical moment, the aunt again asserts herself, attempting to force the prince to commit to a marriage and in the process embarrassing him enormously.

While Tur narrates this episode in the third person, she relates the inconsequential status of the ward quite eloquently. Mar'ia stands above the shameful conduct of her aunt, but is nonetheless condemned by Varvara Petrovna. Mar'ia exclaims, "I am going to my room as I am ordered. You can do whatever you want here, but it goes against all manner of fairness. Auntie can allow someone into her house or not, as she wishes, but to interfere with the affairs of my heart, to offend my pride by proposing me to a well-to-do and important man, goes against my will!"

In *Oshibka* Ol'ga is reproached for not being like Slavin's mother; in *Plemiannitsa* Mar'ia is reproached because in ways she wants to be similar to the parental figure involved, in this case her aunt. The two most important words in Mar'ia's declaration concern *volia* (will or freedom) and *gordost'* (pride). They echo the description given of the aunt at an age approximate to Mar'ia's at the beginning of the novel: "Varvara Petrovna was known throughout the entire province as the most *proud* and unapproachable [eligible] bride." Clearly Varvara Petrovna recognizes pride in a young woman, because she has so embodied it herself. She answers Mar'ia's accusation: "She defends her pride. . . . Listen to her . . . and why bring up pride when she has never had it. I'll prove my right in deed, ingrate!" Mar'ia's will or freedom has been denied through an assertion of her aunt's rights, a huge issue that of course had affected Tur herself, since she had been disposed of in marriage against her will.

Though Mar'ia ends up happily with her former tutor, at this point she marries the prince and suffers the burden of an unequal marriage, which eventually overcomes her entirely because of a rival with whom she cannot compete. This situation mirrors the outcome of an inset story, *Antonina* (1851), which was published separately from *Plemiannitsa* and comprises volume three of that four-volume work. The heroine of *Antonina,* though loved by a prince, loses him because of her position in life. However, the themes in *Antonina* of abused children and of women prohibited in their freedom of choice and movement by patriarchal laws rival Dostoevsky's in the inset story of the Grand Inquisitor in *Brat'ia Karamazovy* (The Brothers Karamazov, 1879–1880). Antonina tells her story in the first person, as the victim, and the cruelty and despotism with which she is treated are related quite realistically, without superfluous flourishes or sentimental reaction. As such, this story constitutes a highly unusual phenomenon in nineteenth-century Russian literature.

Plemiannitsa met with considerably favorable reviews and secured Tur's place in the esteem of the readership of the time. The novel was read at court and well received. Negative criticism was sparse, consisting of a few words disparaging women in general. In an 1852 review in *Sovremennik* (The Contemporary) typical of this phenomenon, Ivan Sergeevich Turgenev praised the work but also denigrated women's writing—criticism that was distressing to Tur, who expected to be treated as an equal on the basis of her talent and her accomplishments. Citing *Antonina* in particular, Turgenev also noted that part of Tur's work would remain in Russian literature, and he was certainly correct in at least one sense: Tur's writings provided him and many other male writers with valuable source material for their own work. Indeed, Leo Tolstoy at one point casually admitted in a letter that he planned on reworking a Tur story for his own. In fact, it was not unusual at this time to borrow the writings of others, and it seems quite likely that there was unself-conscious use of her work in various authors' writings during this decade and the next.

Tur continued developing her previously established themes in subsequent work: the novella *Dve sestry* (Two Sisters, 1851), a continuation of *Antonina;* the plays *Pervoe aprelia* (First of April, 1851) and *Chuzhaia dusha–potemki* (A Foreign Soul–Darkness, 1852); and an attempt at an epistolary novel, *Zakoldovannyi krug* (The Enchanted Circle, 1854). At this point Tur was experimenting in form rather than content. As a play, *Chuzhaia dusha–potemki* lists a cast of characters and is presented in lines; however, the subtitle of the work is *Pogovorka* (Folk Saying), and the list of characters does not include Pensky, one of the leading personages and the conscience of the play. Pensky arrives and finds out about the impending marriage of twenty-five-year-old Polina to Nevzorov, a man of forty years. However, there is an interesting reversal between the sexes in this work, as Pensky is the one who mourns Polina's intended "barbarous union" and the potential loss of her youthful dreams and ardor.

Zakoldovannyi krug presents a collection of letters that do not form a correspondence but instead constitute a virtual chorus of missives addressing the activities of an individual to whom the letters themselves are not directed. Thus there are excerpts from the diary of Dunia, and then letters from Aniuta to Sasha. From the point of view purely of innovation, *Zakoldovannyi krug* may be Tur's most ambitious effort, striving as it does to produce multiple impressions of what would otherwise be assumed a single reality. Her presentation yields diverse subjective standpoints of various characters without ever reaching a complete consensus; the idea of "one right way" does not underlie every action or decision. Thus, Tur moves away from the idealized focus of much of the literature by men of her day and anticipates twentieth-century literary experiments in the diverse ways a single moment may be apprehended by different individuals.

Tur's next novel, *Tri pory zhizni* (Three Ages of Life, 1853), was quite ambitious in another sense. The novel takes its characters from birth through final maturity and, as before, engages in describing the mores and laws of the times, especially as they affect women. The story concerns a family of three siblings: an older sister, a younger sister, and a brother, who are quite close. The younger sister dies prematurely, and the brother, Oginsky, leaves his home in grief. Years later, he reappears to try to save his surviving sister and her family from financial ruin and seems to fall in love with Lina, the daughter of his former nurse and companion. She alone seems to understand him and draw him out of his usual misery. However, at the critical moment, he cannot maintain his faith in her, and she rushes off, never to be seen again. Like many of her predecessors in Tur's prose, she sends back a hefty missive describing her feelings, but their tie is forever broken. So is Oginsky, who moves to town, never marries, and foolishly squanders his fortune on anyone who asks for money.

In terms of the evolution of Tur's literary heroines, Lina is a reversal, for although she is described as "over-proud" like her predecessors, she declares that serving someone in love is preferable to remaining unattached: "I assure you . . . that knowing that I am everything for another, that I am his soul, his goal, his blessing—that is truly happiness; that really means living with a purpose. To be born for someone else means finding and understanding one's own significance." Indeed, Lina suffers from extreme dedication: "Lina was one of those women who know no boundaries to devotion, and who, having taking something upon themselves, carry the idea of duty to the extreme, secretly delighting in the sacrifice." In another reversal, the forty-year-old Oginsky reproaches twenty-five-year-old Lina: "These are the subtleties of a carping conscience . . . and I am amazed that you, an elevated and independent nature, subjugate yourself to vacuous popular opinion." Thus all the relations between the sexes Tur had established in her previous works are contradicted in *Tri pory zhizni*.

Tri pory zhizni did not meet with a positive reception; Nikolai Gavrilovich Chernyshevsky was one of several disappointed critics. Tur continued to experiment, however, mostly with forms, though much of her later fiction, such as the 1856 *Starushka* (The Old Woman), also failed to find critical success. In *Starushka* Tur took on the persona of a male narrator and then turned to the framed inset piece of the written memoir of a woman, in whose voice the remainder of the story is told. Perhaps most compelling is the depiction of the failure of a marriage and the muting of the woman's voice over time. Stepanida, who is described as extremely intelligent, describes in detail how her marriage was transformed from a relationship of mutual respect to a haunted silence of complete restraint, in deference to the exaggerated position of her husband. She laments, "in Leon's hard hands I became a machine which at the slightest signal was supposed to fulfill his commands." The narrative of the doomed woman is haunting in its realism and quite compelling artistically.

Although Tur's later fiction was not as popular as her earlier works had been, she was nonetheless selected for the honor of becoming a member of *Obshchestvo liubitelei rossiiskoi slovesnosti* (The Society of Lovers of Russian Literature) in 1859. Tur had long maintained a salon frequented by many of the leading writers of the day. From approximately the mid 1850s to the mid 1860s she began to devote more attention to criticism, which earned praise from her contemporaries. Her list of articles is long, with the first an 1856 biographical sketch of George Sand that appeared in *Russkii vestnik* (The Russian Herald), edited by Mikhail Nikiforovich Katkov. Further articles published in *Russkii vestnik* included review articles on the work of Jules Michelet and on Elizabeth Gaskell's biography of Charlotte Brontë.

In 1860 Tur argued with Katkov over a literary disagreement and broke with his journal. Against the odds, Tur went on to found her own journal, *Russkaia rech'*, the following year. *Russkaia rech'* was one of the first journals edited and published by a woman in Russia, although many women had previously played active roles in publication. The journal helped to provide a literary start for many well-known writers, such as Nikolai Semenovich Leskov and Vasilii Alekseevich Sleptsov. *Russkaia rech'* had a relatively short run, ending production in early 1862, mainly because Tur could not attract sufficient support for it.

Matters were also complicated by the fact that Tur was no longer living in Russia when the journal closed; she had left for France the previous November for what seem to have been political reasons. Tur's son had been active in student uprisings in 1861, and Tur apparently had supported the students; this support led to her being put under observation by the police. She lived in France for ten years, continuing to hold her salon and to produce critical works; for instance, Tur published a series called *Parizhskoe obozrenie* (The Parisian Review) regularly in *Golos* (The Voice). Tur became more conservative politically later in life.

In her last period, from the mid 1860s until her death, Tur turned to children's literature, where she found an authentic voice of her own. The lengthy embellishment of her earlier prose gave way to a shorter, more direct establishment of manners. She also wrote and translated historical works. Her works of this period include *Katakomby* (Catacombs, 1866), a translation of Cardinal Wiseman's *Fabiola*, about a woman who con-

verts to Christianity; *Semeistvo Shalonskikh* (The Shalonsky Family, 1880), about the Napoleonic invasion as recalled by a girl; and a translation (from Edward Bulwer-Lytton) called *Poslednie dni Pompei* (The Last Days of Pompeii, 1882). In 1881 Tur also began writing her memoirs, which were published in part in *Poliarnaia zvezda* (Polar Star) that year. Her works for children were extremely popular, and she continued to work on them until shortly before her death in 1892 in Warsaw at the home of her son-in-law.

While Tur's initial success in belles lettres did not last, she nevertheless made an important contribution to Russian literature. In an age that was formalizing relations between groups and the sexes, Tur wrote in a far from fashionable manner. Not only could a father be as "nice as a mother," but a man in love could be "childish" and truly love a woman. In an age that became famous for its psychological novels, Tur's style embodied a logic whereby a man could be held responsible for his actions and a woman did not necessarily feel sorry for him. Thus Tur's psychology reflected a nonmale reality. Tur's realism was evidently too real for her time, but to modern readers it presents new potential as a rich source of cultural understanding.

Bibliography:

Bibliograficheskii slovar' russkikh pisatel'nits, edited by N. N. Golitsyn (St. Petersburg, 1889).

References:

Jane Costlow, "Speaking the Sorrow of Women: Turgenev's 'Neschastnaia' and Evgeniia Tur's 'Antonina,'" *Slavic Review,* 2 (1991): 328–335;

Jehanne M. Gheith, "Evgeniia Tur," in *Dictionary of Russian Women Writers,* edited by M. Ledkovsky, C. Rosenthal, and M. Zirin (Westport, Conn.: Greenwood Press, 1994), pp. 667–672;

Gheith, "Evgeniia Tur," in *Russian Women Writers,* edited by C. D. Tomei, volume 1 (New York: Garland, 1999), pp. 349–369;

Gheith, "In Her Own Voice: Evgeniia Tur, Author, Critic, Journalist," dissertation, Stanford University, 1992;

Jennifer Lonergan, "Evgeniia Tur 1815–1892. Prose Writer and Translator," in *Reference Guide to Russian Literature,* edited by Neil Cornwell (London: Fitzroy Dearborn, 1998), pp. 840–841;

O. V. Nikolaeva, "Tur, Evgeniia," in *Russkie pisateli,* edited by P. A. Nikolaev, volume 2 (Moscow: Prosveshchenie, 1990), pp. 311–313;

Wanda Laszczak, *Zaryszycia i tworczosci Eugenii Tur* (Opole: Wyzsza Szkola Pedagogiczna, 1987).

Ivan Sergeevich Turgenev

(28 October 1818 – 22 August 1883)

Nicholas G. Žekulin
University of Calgary

WORKS: *Parasha. Rasskaz v stikhakh* (St. Petersburg, 1843);

Neostorozhnost', in *Otechestvennye zapiski*, no. 10 (1843); translated by M. S. Mandell as *Carelessness*, in *The Plays of Ivan S. Turgenev* (New York: Macmillan / London: Heinemann, 1924);

Razgovor. Poema (St. Petersburg, 1845);

Bezdenezh'e, in *Otechestvennye zapiski*, no. 10 (1846); translated by Mandell as *Broke*, in *The Plays of Ivan S. Turgenev* (New York: Macmillan / London: Heinemann, 1924);

Gde tonko, tam i rvetsia, in *Sovremennik*, no. 11 (1848); translated by Margaret Gough as *One May Spin a Thread Too Finely; A Comedy in One Act*, in *Fortnightly Review*, 85, new series 91 (April 1909);

Kholostiak. Komediia v 3-kh deistviiakh, in *Otechestvennye zapiski*, no. 9 (1849); (St. Petersburg, 1860); translated by Mandell as *The Bachelor*, in *The Plays of Ivan S. Turgenev* (New York: Macmillan / London: Heinemann, 1924);

Dnevnik lishnego cheloveka, in *Otechestvennye zapiski*, no. 4 (1850); translated by Henry Gersoni as *The Diary of a Superfluous Man*, in *Mumu, and The Diary of a Superfluous Man* (New York & London: Funk & Wagnalls, 1884);

Provintsialka, in *Otechestvennye zapiski*, no. 1 (1851); (St. Petersburg, 1860); translated by Mandell as *The Country Woman*, in *The Plays of Ivan S. Turgenev* (New York: Macmillan / London: Heinemann, 1924);

Zapiski okhotnika [A Hunter's Notes], 2 volumes (Moscow: v Universitetskoi tipografii, 1852); third revised, expanded edition (St. Petersburg: Stasiulevich, 1880); first translated by James D. Meiklejohn [from the French translation by Ernest Charrière] as *Russian Life in the Interior; or, The Experiences of a Sportsman* (Edinburgh: Black, 1855);

Mesiats v derevne. Komediia v 5 deistviiakh, in *Sovremennik*, no. 1 (1855); translated by Mandell as *A Month in*

Ivan Sergeevich Turgenev, 1879

the Country, in *The Plays of Ivan S. Turgenev* (New York: Macmillan / London: Heinemann, 1924);

Zavtrak u predvoditelia, in *Sovremennik*, no. 8 (1856); translated by Mandell as *An Amicable Settlement*, in *The Plays of Ivan S. Turgenev* (New York: Macmillan / London: Heinemann, 1924);

Rudin, in *Sovremennik*, nos. 1–2 (1856); first translated [from the French and German translations] as *Dimitri Roudine*, in *Every Saturday*, 3 (January–April 1873); (New York: Holt & Williams, 1873);

Povesti i rasskazy I. S. Turgeneva, 3 volumes (St. Petersburg: Prats, 1856);

Nakhlebnik [The Dependent], published as *Chuzhoi khleb,* in *Sovremennik,* no. 3 (1857); translated by Mandell as *The Family Charge,* in *The Plays of Ivan S. Turgenev* (New York: Macmillan / London: Heinemann, 1924);

Dvorianskoe gnezdo [A Nest of the Gentry], in *Sovremennik,* no. 1 (1859); (Moscow: Glazunov, 1859); first translated by W. R. S. Ralston as *Liza* (London: Chapman & Hall, 1869);

Nakanune, in *Russkii vestnik,* no. 1 (1860); translated by C. E. Turner as *On the Eve: A Tale* (London: Hodder & Stoughton, 1871);

Sochineniia I. S. Turgeneva. Ispravlennye i dopolnennye, 4 volumes (Moscow: Osnovsky, 1860);

Ottsy i deti, in *Russkii vestnik,* no. 2 (1862); (Moscow: Soldatenkov, 1862); translated by Eugene Schuyler as *Fathers and Sons* (New York: Leypoldt & Holt, 1867);

Sochineniia (1844–1864), 5 volumes (Karlsruhe: Br. Salaevy, 1865);

Dym, in *Russkii vestnik,* no. 3 (1867); (Moscow: Br. Salaevy, 1868); translated by Rowland Crawley [from the 1868 French translation] as *Smoke; or, Life at Baden* (London: Richard Bentley, 1868);

Sochineniia (1844–1868), 7 volumes (Moscow: Br. Salaevy, 1868–1869; supplementary volume 8, 1871);

Veshnie vody [Spring Torrents], in *Vestnik Evropy,* no. 1 (1872); first translated by Sophie Michell Butts as *Spring Floods,* in *Eclectic Magazine,* 18–19 (October 1873 – March 1874) and together with *A Lear of the Steppe* (New York: Holt, 1874);

Sochineniia, 8 volumes (Moscow: Br. Salaevy, 1874–1875);

Nov', in *Vestnik Evropy,* nos. 1–2 (1877); 2 volumes (Leipzig: Gerhard, 1877; Moscow: Salaev, 1878); first translated by T. S. Perry [from the French and German translations] as *Virgin Soil* (New York: Holt, 1877); another translation by Ashton Dilke [from the Russian] (London: Macmillan, 1878);

Sochineniia (1844–1868–1874–1880), 10 volumes (Moscow: Nasl. Br. Salaevykh, 1880);

Stikhotvoreniia v proze, in *Vestnik Evropy,* no. 12 (1882); translated as *Poems in Prose* (Boston: Cupples-Upham, 1883) and by M. C. Rayner [from the German translation?] as *Senilia. Prose Poems by Ivan Turgeneief,* in *Macmillan's Magazine,* 49 (November–December 1883);

Polnoe sobranie sochinenii. Posmertnoe izdanie, 10 volumes (St. Petersburg: Glazunov, 1883–1884).

Editions and Collections: *Stikhotvoreniia* (St. Petersburg, 1885);

Sochineniia, 12 volumes (Moscow-Leningrad: GIZ, 1928–1934);

Polnoe sobranie sochinenii i pisem, 28 volumes (Moscow-Leningrad: AN SSSR, 1960–1968); revised edition, 30 volumes planned (Moscow: Nauka, 1979 –).

Editions in English: *Turgénieff's Works,* 8 volumes (New York: Holt, 1867–1885);

The Novels of Ivan Turgenev, 12 volumes, translated by Constance Garnett (London: Heinemann / New York: Macmillan, 1894–1899);

The Novels and Stories of Ivan Turgenieff, 16 volumes, translated by Isabel Hapgood (New York: Scribners, 1903–1904);

First Love and Other Stories, translated and edited by Richard Freeborn (Oxford & New York: Oxford University Press, 1989);

Sketches from a Hunter's Album, translated by Freeborn (Harmondsworth, U.K.: Penguin, 1990);

A Month in the Country, translated and edited by Freeborn (Oxford & New York: Oxford University Press, 1991);

Fathers and Sons, translated and edited by Freeborn (Oxford & New York: Oxford University Press, 1991);

The Essential Turgenev, edited by Elizabeth Cheresh Allen (Evanston, Ill.: Northwestern University Press, 1994)–includes *Rudin, A Nest of the Gentry, Fathers and Sons,* and *Hamlet and Don Quixote;*

Fathers and Sons, translated and edited by Michael Katz, Norton Critical Edition (New York & London: Norton, 1995);

Rudin and *On the Eve,* translated and edited by David McDuff (Oxford & New York: Oxford University Press, 1999).

SELECTED PERIODICAL PUBLICATIONS:
"Andrei Kolosov," in *Otechestvennye zapiski,* no. 11 (1844);

"Khor' i Kalinych," in *Sovremennik,* no. 1 (1847);

"Zhid," in *Sovremennik,* no. 11 (1847);

"Petushkov," in *Sovremennik,* no. 9 (1848);

"Mumu," in *Sovremennik,* no. 3 (1854);

"Dva priiatelia," in *Sovremennik,* no. 1 (1854);

"Iakov Pasynkov. Iz vospominanii cheloveka v otstavke," in *Otechestvennye zapiski,* no. 4 (1855);

"Perepiska," in *Otechestvennye zapiski,* no. 1 (1856);

"Faust," in *Sovremennik,* no. 10 (1856);

"Asia," in *Sovremennik,* no. 1 (1858);

"Gamlet i Don Kikhot," in *Sovremennik,* no. 1 (1860);

"Pervaia liubov'," in *Biblioteka dlia chteniia,* no. 3 (1860);

"Prizraki," in *Epokha,* no. 1 (1864);

"Sobaka," in *Sankt-Peterburgskie vedomosti,* no. 85 (1866);

"Istoriia leitenanta Ergunova," in *Russkii vestnik*, no. 1 (1868);

"Brigadir," in *Vestnik Evropy*, no. 1 (1868);

"Neschastnaia," in *Russkii vestnik*, no. 1 (1869);

"Strannaia istoriia," in *Russkii vestnik*, no. 1 (1870);

"Stepnoi korol' Lir," in *Vestnik Evropy*, no. 10 (1870);

"Stuk . . . stuk . . . stuk! . . ," in *Vestnik Evropy*, no. 1 (1871);

"Nashi poslali! Epizod iz istorii iiun'skikh dnei 1848 g. v Parizhe," in *Nedelia*, no. 1 (1874);

"Punin i Baburin," in *Vestnik Evropy*, no. 4 (1874);

"Chasy," in *Vestnik Evropy*, no. 1 (1876);

"Rasskaz ottsa Alekseia," in *Vestnik Evropy*, no. 5 (1877);

"Starye portrety. (Otryvki iz vospominanii—svoikh i chuzhikh)," *Poriadok*, nos. 1, 4 (1881);

"Pesn' torzhestvuiushchei liubvi," in *Vestnik Evropy*, no. 11 (1881);

"Otchaiannyi," in *Vestnik Evropy*, no. 1 (1882);

"Klara Milich. (Posle smerti)," in *Vestnik Evropy*, no. 1 (1883).

Henry James—friend, colleague, and student—said of Ivan Sergeevich Turgenev that he was "in a peculiar degree what I may call the novelist's novelist, an artistic influence extraordinarily valuable, and ineradicably established." Turgenev himself was much more modest; in a letter to Sergei Timofeevich Aksakov in 1856, well after the publication of Turgenev's first major triumph, *Zapiski okhotnika* (A Hunter's Notes, 1852) and even after his first novel, *Rudin* (1856), he wrote, "I am one of the writers of the interregnum—the era between [Nikolai Vasil'evich] Gogol and a future chief"; for Turgenev that future chief turned out to be Leo Tolstoy. For all his modesty, however, Turgenev was the first Russian writer to achieve an international reputation; from the late 1860s on, most of his works appeared in French, English, and German almost simultaneously with their Russian publications. There was virtually no major European author with whom he was not personally acquainted, and many younger writers of the later nineteenth century openly acknowledged his influence on their writing. Most of the world saw him as the Russian writer par excellence before coming to see him as a member, with Tolstoy and Fyodor Dostoevsky, of the great Russian triumvirate. Eventually, however, he was eclipsed, in the twentieth century, which sought spicier fare, by his two compatriots.

Within Turgenev's substantial body of works there are six novels. He himself established this canon when he provided an introduction for them in the ten-volume 1880 collected edition of his works (in which the novels occupied volumes three through five):

In deciding in the forthcoming edition to publish all the novels I have written (*Rudin, A Nest of the Gentry, On the Eve, Fathers and Sons, Smoke,* and *Virgin Soil*) in chronological order, I consider it not inappropriate to explain, briefly, why I have done so. I wanted to provide those of my readers who take upon themselves the trouble of reading these six novels in a row the opportunity to ascertain for themselves graphically to what extent those critics who accuse me of having betrayed previously held views, of apostasy etc., are justified. On the contrary, it seems to me that I might more likely be accused of excessive constancy and invariability, so to speak, of path chosen. The author of *Rudin*, written in 1855, and of *Virgin Soil*, written in 1876, is one and the same person. Throughout all this time I tried, to the best of my strength and ability, conscientiously and impartially, to depict and embody in appropriate characters both what Shakespeare calls 'the body and pressure of time' [in English in the original], and the rapidly changing physiognomy of cultured Russians, who were above all the object of my observations.

This apologia serves as a useful yardstick, for while writing his novels, and even after their publication, Turgenev was far from consistent in his use of genre designation, not infrequently referring to the novels as "povesti" (novellas). Turgenev's novels, of a modest length by nineteenth-century standards (let alone by comparison with the popular perception of the elephantine dimensions of "the Russian novel"), are indeed distinguished from his novellas—not by length or by a distinction in protagonists, as much as by their context, a context that attempts to identify a specific and particular phenomenon or stage in the development of Russian society. Thus, the novel *Dym* (Smoke, 1867) and the novella *Veshnie vody* (Spring Torrents, 1872) have a similar story line: both are set, for much of their plots, in Germany, but the novella does not include the context of a critical examination of the diverse post-emancipation Russian groups abroad that is found in the novel. And while *Ottsy i deti* (Fathers and Sons, 1862) remains for most readers Turgenev's crowning achievement, his reputation among his contemporaries was established by *Zapiski okhotnika* (many people believed, on little direct evidence, both in Russia and, especially, abroad, that this work had a major impact on the future Alexander II in his determination to emancipate the Russian serfs). Turgenev's stories and novellas were widely admired for their delicate artistry, and many German writers, such as Theodor Storm and Paul Heyse, derived their understanding of the novelle as a genre from Turgenev's novellas. His plays, in particular *Mesiats v derevne* (A Month in the Country, 1855), are now seen as important precursors for the theater of Anton Pavlovich Chekhov.

Turgenev's parents, Sergei Nikolaevich and Varvara Petrovna (née Lutovinova) Turgenev (from David Magarshack, Turgenev: A Life, *1954)*

Ivan Sergeevich Turgenev was born on 28 October 1818 in the provincial town of Orel, the second son of Varvara Petrovna (née Lutovinova) and Sergei Nikolaevich Turgenev. After an extremely difficult childhood, Varvara Petrovna had inherited substantial estates, of which Spasskoe-Lutovinovo in Orel Province was the crown jewel, making her one of the richest landowners in the district. Not long afterward, in 1816, she had married the somewhat younger Sergei Nikolaevich Turgenev, a notoriously handsome cavalry officer. With Sergei Nikolaevich's retirement from active duty in 1821, the family moved to Spasskoe, thus beginning an association with a place that remained important throughout Turgenev's life.

Turgenev's early life at Spasskoe was interrupted in May 1822 by a family journey through Western Europe that lasted about a year. Then, in February 1824, the Turgenevs moved to Moscow, where in 1827 Ivan began his formal schooling, alternating between local schools (usually when his father was abroad for health reasons) and private tutors, and receiving a broad education that had an emphasis on languages (French, German, Latin, and Greek, as well as Russian). In 1833 Sergei Turgenev petitioned Moscow University for Ivan to sit the requisite exams for entrance to the Philology Faculty, even though he had not yet reached the minimum age of seventeen. Eventually,

thanks to the intervention of the Minister of Education, an exemption was received. That summer, while Ivan was preparing for his entrance exams, the Turgenev family lived in a dacha outside Moscow. Among their neighbors was the Shakhovskoy family. Ivan became attracted to the daughter, Ekaterina, only to discover that among the several rivals for her affections was his father, an episode that later formed the story line of his short story "Pervaia liubov'" (First Love, 1860), by his own admission Turgenev's favorite among his works. Having passed the entrance exams, Ivan began his university studies in the fall of 1833, although only a year later he transferred to St. Petersburg University. In St. Petersburg he lived with his father (until Sergei Nikolaevich's death on 30 October 1834) and his elder brother, Nikolai, a student in a military academy.

Ivan Turgenev's interest in literature was awakened early. In a short autobiographical note written in 1872, he states that his initiation into Russian literature was at the hands of Leontii Iakovlevich Serebriakov, one of his mother's literate serfs at Spasskoe. The work Serebriakov chose for this first exposure was Mikhail Matveevich Kheraskov's epic poem "Rossiiada" (1779). Throughout his childhood and youth Turgenev read widely in the literature of several languages. His mother, who is often depicted as a typically narrow-minded, despotic serf owner of the time (and who served as the prototype of such characters in many of her son's literary works), had an extensive library and was, in fact, widely read, particularly in French literature of the late eighteenth century. His father had some contacts among Russian literary figures, including the poet Vasilii Andreevich Zhukovsky and the historical novelist Mikhail Nikolaevich Zagoskin. By the time of his transfer to St. Petersburg University in 1834 Turgenev was himself writing poetry, including a "slavish imitation of Byron," as he himself subsequently described it, the dramatic poem *Steno* (not published until 1913). In October 1836 Ivan Turgenev's name first appeared in print, under a review of a travelogue to venerated Russian holy places. His first original piece, the lyric poem "Vecher" (Evening; published anonymously), then appeared in the January 1838 issue of the journal *Sovremennik* (The Contemporary). During his time at St. Petersburg University, Turgenev not only read the works of the most prominent contemporary writers but also encountered most of them, however briefly and incidentally. He was one of the students for Gogol's ill-fated and short-lived (1835) experiment at becoming a professor of history. Turgenev briefly saw Aleksandr Sergeevich Pushkin twice within days of his fatal duel in January 1837, and obtained as a keepsake that he treasured all his life, a lock of the dead poet's hair. Nearly two years later, in December 1839, he saw Mikhail Iur'evich Lermontov at a masquerade ball.

Although Turgenev successfully completed the Philological Faculty of St. Petersburg University in 1836, he returned the following year to improve his standing and to obtain the degree of Candidate, which would permit him to continue his studies. Thus, in May 1838, Turgenev embarked on the steamer *Nicholas I* for Germany. The steamer caught fire in sight of its destination, an incident that Turgenev later described in a sketch, "Une incendie en mer" (Fire at Sea; originally in French, dictated to Pauline Viardot from his deathbed and published in 1883), in which he did not attempt to cover up the panic that engulfed him at the prospect of dying at the tender age of nineteen. Turgenev described his attitude of mind at leaving Russia to take up studies in philosophy at Berlin University in the 1869 introduction to his "Literaturnye i zhiteiskie vospominaniia" (Memoirs of Literature and Life):

> I spent about two years (on two separate occasions) in Berlin. . . . I threw myself head first into the 'German Sea,' in which I was supposed to be cleansed and reborn, and when I finally surfaced from its waves, I was a 'Westernist' and remained one forever. . . . I could not breathe the same air, I could not remain in close proximity to that which I hated. I absolutely had to get away from my enemy in order to strike all the more strongly from afar. In my eyes that enemy had a

definite physiognomy, had a specific name: that enemy was serfdom.

While in Berlin, Turgenev became close to fellow Russians Nikolai Vladimirovich Stankevich, who, following his early death in June 1840, became the model for many characters of the noblest spirit in Turgenev's later works (including Pokrovsky in *Rudin* and the title-hero of the story "Iakov Pasynkov"); Timofei Nikolaevich Granovsky, who became an historian; and in 1840 Mikhail Aleksandrovich Bakunin, the future anarchist. Turgenev became a habitué of the salon of the Frolov family, which was frequented by many prominent Germans, including Karl Werder, the student of and successor to Georg Wilhelm Friedrich Hegel as Professor of Philosophy at Berlin University; the explorer Alexander von Humboldt; Karl Varnhagen von Ense, the critic and essayist; and Bettina von Arnim, well known for her memoirs of Johann Wolfgang von Goethe. Goethe became, along with William Shakespeare, one of the authors whose works Turgenev cherished and which he knew by heart almost in their entirety. Throughout his time in Germany, Turgenev continued to write poetry, and his lyric verse appeared from time to time in the Russian periodical press.

In May 1841 Turgenev returned to Russia. Even before visiting his mother at Spasskoe, he made a trip, the first of several, to the estate of the Bakunin family at Premukhino, where he, for a time, became romantically entangled with Bakunin's sister Tat'iana. At Spasskoe, Turgenev was supposed to be studying for his comprehensive exams, which he took at St. Petersburg University in April–May 1842. On 26 April, Turgenev's daughter, Pelageia, was born, the product of an affair with Avdot'ia Ermolaevna Ivanova, one of his mother's seamstresses at Spasskoe. The contrast between an ideal, intellectual, largely platonic love and an erotic relationship that was physical and not infrequently socially unequal was later featured in a variety of guises in Turgenev's works, appearing sometimes in the form of rivals for the hero's affections, sometimes as a dichotomy that the heroine had to try to dispel in the hero's expectations.

After he successfully completed his comprehensive exams, only a dissertation lay between Turgenev and a possible academic career. He never wrote the dissertation. His narrative poem *Parasha* appeared as a small brochure in April 1843 and served as the official start of his literary career, sealed by approval (albeit in an anonymous review) from the fiery leading critic of the "young" generation, Vissarion Grigor'evich Belinsky. In June, Turgenev was appointed to a minor post in the Ministry of Internal Affairs in the office of Vladimir Ivanovich Dal', the famous lexicographer, col-

Turgenev at twenty-one (from David Magarshack, Turgenev: A Life, *1954)*

lector of folk sayings and proverbs, and author of sketches from Russian village life published under the pseudonym of Kazak Lugansky. In October of that same year, St. Petersburg went wild over the appearances at the opera of the French diva Pauline Viardot-Garcia. On his twenty-fifth birthday Turgenev first met Pauline Viardot's husband, Louis Viardot, a political writer and journalist of socialist bent, a prominent Hispanist whose translation of Miguel de Cervantes's *Don Quixote* into French remains in print to this day, an art lover and art historian of some repute and no less avid a hunter than Turgenev himself. On 1 November, a date he celebrated annually to the end of his life, Turgenev was introduced to Pauline as "a young Russian landowner, a capital huntsman and a bad poet." Turgenev was smitten by the accomplished singer, whom many considered to be singularly unattractive, except for her large eyes. She was, however, one of the most intelligent and talented women of her age and mesmerized audiences with the power of her performances as both actress and singer. Turgenev's acquaintance with Pauline Viardot determined much of the future course of his life, for she was never far from his thoughts, and, whenever possible, he was never far from her in person.

Their relationship has been the subject of much speculation among both Turgenev's contemporaries and subsequent generations (and especially, and usually negatively, among his compatriots), particularly on the subject of whether or not it always remained "platonic." Although in early years the relationship had its ups and downs, it eventually settled into a lasting and deep friendship. Interestingly, Turgenev's friendship with Louis Viardot never suffered the occasional vagaries of his relationship with Pauline, remaining close and strong until Louis's death, a scant few months before Turgenev's own.

The "bad" poet continued to write and publish lyric verse in many journals. He also continued to expand his circle of acquaintances among Russian intellectuals from both the St. Petersburg and the Moscow groups; in February 1843 he had become a member of Belinsky's intellectual circle (in which he most likely met the man who later became one of his closest friends and his principal literary adviser, Pavel Vasil'evich Annenkov). A year later, in February 1844, Turgenev met Aleksandr Ivanovich Herzen, who later became the editor of the influential émigré journal *Kolokol* (The Bell), and in April of that year he met some of the founding members of the Slavophile circle, including Iurii Fedorovich Samarin and Konstantin Sergeevich Aksakov. Turgenev's future lay with prose, and the first of his stories, "Andrei Kolosov," appeared in the November 1844 issue of the journal *Otechestvennye zapiski* (Notes of the Fatherland), although still alongside a lyric poem ("K ***" [To ***]) and still under his customary pseudonym of the time, "T. L." (the initials of his paternal and maternal [Lutovinov] surnames). Rounding out Turgenev's diverse activities during this period were a review of a recent translation by Mikhail Petrovich Vronchenko of Goethe's *Faust,* which Turgenev used as a vehicle for elaborating his own views on the title hero, and work on a translation of Gogol's works into French, which he undertook together with Stepan Aleksandrovich Gedeonov (who became the director of both the Hermitage Museum and the Imperial Theaters) and Louis Viardot. This undertaking was the first of a series of joint efforts between Turgenev and Louis Viardot to bring to the attention of the French reading public works by the major Russian authors (Pushkin, Lermontov, and Gogol), as well as, later, Turgenev's own works in translations that avoided the often violent distortions of the originals that were not uncommon in the translation practice of the day.

With the increase in his literary activity, Turgenev requested and received permission to leave his post in the Ministry of Internal Affairs (April 1845), ostensibly for reasons of health. No longer restrained by a government position, he left Russia in early May, not long after the Viardots, and joined them at Courtavenel, their estate in France, south of Paris, which for several years became the base of his literary and personal activities. There, not long after his arrival in France, Turgenev first met one of his early literary idols, George Sand, who had been a mentor to Pauline since the latter's childhood.

In early November 1845 Turgenev returned to Russia in time for Pauline's third consecutive season of engagements in both Russian capitals. He once again became involved in the literary and intellectual life of St. Petersburg, committing himself to assist the major undertaking by the writers Nikolai Alekseevich Nekrasov and Ivan Ivanovich Panaev—the publication of the journal *Sovremennik*. The first issue under the new management was published in January 1847, and Turgenev contributed a cycle of nine lyric poems under the title "Derevnia" (The Country), a review, and, hidden in the back section, "Smes'" (Miscellany), an anonymous sketch, "Khor' i Kalinych" (Khor' and Kalinych), to which the editors had appended a subtitle, "Iz zapisok okhotnika" (From A Hunter's Notes). Thus, inconspicuously and somewhat inauspiciously, began the series that established Turgenev as a major writer, not only in Russia but also around the world.

Zapiski okhotnika occupied much of Turgenev's literary attention for the next several years. Although the extent of the political influence of the sketches has often been exaggerated, they nonetheless were a significant element in the pressure that built up in Russian society for the emancipation of the serfs. Emerging out of the genre of the "physiological sketch," they went beyond the rather unadorned depiction characteristic of that genre with its sociological bent and emphasis on the lower classes. The original twenty-two stories (three were added in the 1870s) presented a wide variety of characters, particularly rich in diversity regarding the peasants (thereby countering the perception of the peasants as an indistinguishable, gray mass), but without excessive eulogizing. Equally importantly, the depiction of the landowners showed that serfdom was, in its different way, no less destructive economically, but especially spiritually, on that class. Using the narrative device of a hunter from the landowning class wandering through the countryside encountering and observing, Turgenev also filled his sketches with superbly rich descriptions of the Russian countryside, another hallmark of his talent.

In mid January 1847 Turgenev left Russia for Berlin. In May, Belinsky arrived there in a futile attempt to counteract the ravages of his tuberculosis. Together he and Turgenev went to the spa town of Salzbrunn, where they were joined by Annenkov. With Annenkov filling his customary role as sounding board, Turgenev

continued working on *Zapiski okhotnika,* while Belinsky took the opportunity of being away from spying eyes in the Russian post office to write his famous "Letter to Gogol," accusing Gogol of having betrayed, in his *Vybrannye mesta iz perepiski s druz'iami* (Selected Passages from a Correspondence with Friends, 1847), what Belinsky saw as Gogol's mission of exposing the social ills of Russia. Despite the apparent flightiness of his personal life (which friends and acquaintances noted and decried), Turgenev continued to work hard at his *Zapiski okhotnika* and other works: "Petr Petrovich Karataev" (not originally designated as part of *Zapiski okhotnika*) appeared in the February 1847 issue of *Sovremennik;* "Ermolai i mel'nichikha" (Ermolai and the Miller's Wife"), "Moi sosed Radilov" (My Neighbor Radilov), "Odnodvorets Ovsianikov" (The Smallholder Ovsianikov), and "L'gov" appeared in the May issue; and "Burmistr" (The Overseer) and "Kontora" (The Office) appeared in October. The sketches "Malinovaia voda" (Malinovaia Spring), "Uezdnyi lekar'" (A Country Doctor), "Biriuk" (A Surly Fellow), "Lebedian'," "Tat'iana Borisovna i ee plemiannik" (Tat'iana Borisovna and her Nephew), and "Smert'" (Death) then all appeared in the February 1848 issue, while the last of the sketches written abroad, "Gamlet Shchigrovskogo uezda" (A Hamlet of the Shchigry District), "Chertopkhanov i Nedopiuskin" (Chertopkhanov and Nedopiuskin), and "Les i step'" (Forest and Steppe) were published a year later, in February 1849. Besides the sketches, the story "Zhid" (The Jew) had been published in the November 1847 issue and the curiously Gogolian story "Petushkov" in the September 1848 issue of *Sovremennik*, while the novella *Dnevnik lishnego cheloveka* (The Diary of a Superfluous Man) appeared in the April 1850 issue of *Otechestvennye zapiski*. A first-person account, on the eve of his death that occurs on 1 April, by a man who considers his entire life to have been a futile waste, this story provided the name to a phenomenon that subsequent critics have sometimes seen as the hallmark of the Russian literary male hero, his superfluousness in life.

While still working on the sketches for *Zapiski okhotnika,* Turgenev began to turn his attention to drama. Two plays, *Neostorozhnost'* (Imprudence) and *Bezdenezh'e* (Penniless), had been published as early as 1843 and 1846 respectively in the journal *Otechestvennye zapiski,* but only in the late 1840s and early 1850s did the theater attract his intense attention. Drama by its nature endured a double censorship at this time, requiring separate permission for publication and for performance. Turgenev's plays suffered from the vagaries of this dual system, although they fared slightly better in his obtaining permission for staging than for printing. The play *Gde tonko, tam i rvetsia* (The Weakest Link

Breaks First) was published in the November 1848 issue of *Sovremennik,* but it was not produced on stage until December 1851. *Nakhlebnik* (The Dependent), dedicated to the outstanding actor of his day, Mikhail Semenovich Shchepkin, was banned by the print censorship in February 1849, a ban that lasted until 1857. Turgenev quickly replaced that play with a second comedy for Shchepkin, *Kholostiak* (The Bachelor), which was published in the September 1849 issue of *Otechestvennye zapiski* and soon after was first performed on the stage of the Aleksandrinskii Theater in St. Petersburg. By contrast, *Zavtrak u predvoditelia* (Breakfast at the House of the Marshal of the Nobility) was delayed by the print censorship that same September 1849 but allowed for the stage in October. *Provintsialka* (A Provincial Lady) was published in the January 1851 issue of *Otechestvennye zapiski* and shortly after was performed in Moscow. Interestingly, the most ambitious of Turgenev's plays, originally titled "Student" (The Student) and eventually renamed *Mesiats v derevne,* was not designated for a particular actor. It occupied Turgenev intensively for approximately one year until he sent off a draft to the editors of *Sovremennik* in April 1850. It was quickly banned by the censorship and did not appear until January 1855, when Turgenev revised the play and adopted its final title. Despite the fact that most of Turgenev's plays were sought out by and even written expressly for and at the request of prominent actors of the day, Turgenev himself denigrated his talent as a dramatist. When he finally permitted the inclusion of his plays as a separate volume (volume seven) in the 1868–1869 edition of his collected works, he prefaced their publication with the comment: "Since I do not acknowledge any dramatic talent in myself, I would not have submitted just to the request of the publishers wanting to publish as complete an edition of my works as possible, if I did not think that my plays, though unsatisfactory on stage, might be of some interest when read." No one was as astonished as the author when *Mesiats v derevne* was revived to tremendous popular acclaim in 1879. Nonetheless, the attention to dramatic writing at this stage in his career played an important part in the development of Turgenev's talents as a writer. While the sketches in *Zapiski okhotnika* were from the first noted for their descriptions, dramatic writing helped hone Turgenev's skills in the use of dialogue, an element that became especially important in his novels.

Turgenev's extended stay abroad lasted until June 1850. Although he used his time, spent primarily in Paris and Courtavenel, to good effect (emerging as one of the major contributors to *Sovremennik* as its editors tried to establish it with the Russian reading public), significant reasons for his continued absence from Russia were tense relations with his mother and her refusal to fund him (including the funds for him to return home). His extended stays at Courtavenel–often in the absence of Louis and Pauline Viardot, as she was now at the height of her career and enjoying particular success in Britain–were a form of keeping living expenses low. Among his Russian friends was the Herzen family and, although they later parted ways both publicly and privately, at this time Turgenev and Aleksandr Herzen provided each other with intense intellectual stimulation in exploring a wide variety of political and social issues of the day. Turgenev was on a short visit to Brussels when he learned of the start of the 1848 Revolution in Paris, and he hurried back to observe events, in which quite a few of his Paris friends and acquaintances were actively involved to varying degrees. At the height of the uprising, in May and June, Turgenev observed the fighting on the barricades in the streets of Paris. His impressions of those events are reflected in his 1874 story-reminiscence "Nashi poslali!" (Our People Sent Me!), and on those barricades the title hero of his first novel, *Rudin,* modeled on Mikhail Bakunin, dies in a later addition to the work.

Turgenev arrived in St. Petersburg on 20 June 1850 and quickly went on to Moscow. Among the people he saw there soon after his arrival was his eight-year-old daughter, Pelageia. In a letter that determined her future life, Turgenev wrote to Pauline Viardot about her, asking for advice on what he should do with her. Pauline's response was to offer to bring the girl up in her own family, a decision that Turgenev welcomed, since he thought that this solution would free his daughter from all the legal and social problems in Russia associated with her illegitimacy. Pelageia was dispatched to Paris in late October, but the decision proved the source of difficulties and friction for many years. Nor did the situation with his mother improve. Following a major clash, Turgenev and his brother broke relations with their mother and left for the small estate that they had inherited from their father. In November, Varvara Petrovna fell seriously ill. Turgenev dashed to Moscow from St. Petersburg but arrived just after her funeral. Her diary revealed to him a remarkably complex, if not particularly pleasant, woman, whose death ended her efforts to ensure that neither of her sons inherited anything. In any case, Turgenev found himself a relatively wealthy landowner (although the inheritance did little to put an end to later money problems), but above all, by an earlier arrangement with his brother, the master of his beloved Spasskoe, the spot that continued to draw him to Russia throughout his life and where he most frequently went in order to refine drafts of his major works.

In the summer of 1850, in the country, Turgenev began the final set of sketches of *Zapiski okhotnika,* each devoted to particularly striking individuals from among the peasants. He transformed a singing competition he witnessed into the sketch "Pevtsy" (The Singers); a peasant valet who imitated the cruel nonchalance of his master became the model for the main protagonist of "Svidanie" (The Tryst)—both published in the November 1850 issue of *Sovremennik*. A group of small boys spending the night around a fire while guarding a herd of horses is depicted in "Bezhin lug" (Bezhin Meadow, published in the February 1851 issue of *Sovremennik*), while Turgenev's interest in the semi-hidden life of the members of the religious sects of Russia emerges in the singular character of the dwarf in "Kas'ian s Krasivoi Mechi'" (Kas'ian from Krasivaia Mech', published in the March 1851 issue of *Sovremennik*). Despite the considerable and generally favorable attention that *Zapiski okhotnika* had attracted among both the reading public and the critics, Turgenev for some time had been aware that the sketches needed to be something more than the sum of their parts, and he devoted considerable attention to compiling lists, identifying various stories for the series (some of which were never written or completed), and even pondering the order for a future edition of the collected sketches. This collection appeared, under rather dramatic circumstances, in 1852.

In October 1851 Turgenev met Gogol again, no longer as an anonymous student in Gogol's ill-fated history class but as a young writer whose works Gogol had noted with appreciation. Gogol died not long afterward, on 21 February 1852. For Turgenev, as for so many writers of his generation, Gogol's works (particularly as interpreted by Belinsky) had been the source of inspiration for their socially conscious writing. Under the impact of Gogol's death, which Turgenev considered to be of momentous significance because he saw in Gogol "a continuator of [the work of] Peter the Great," he wrote a short obituary that, in accordance with imperial instructions to minimize the reactions, was banned by the St. Petersburg censors. Turgenev sent his obituary to Moscow, where it appeared, with just his initial, on 13 March in the newspaper *Moskovskie vedomosti* (Moscow News), unleashing a storm upon Turgenev's head. As a result of a denunciation, the incident went to Nicholas I, who ordered Turgenev placed under arrest for a month, followed by exile under police observation on his estate. Turgenev's arrest, which occurred on 16 April, and imprisonment at a local police station, were not particularly harsh. Turgenev could be, and was, visited by many friends, some of whom brought him books, until the practice had to be stopped because of the crowds involved. He himself was able to write; "Mumu," the touching story of a deaf serf and the dog his mistress forces him to drown because it disturbed her rest was written during this

Pauline Viardot, the actress and singer who was close to Turgenev for most of his life (engraving by Lallemand after a portrait by N. Ploszczynski)

time. Furthermore, well-connected friends of Turgenev, especially Aleksei Konstantinovich Tolstoy and Sof'ia Ivanovna Meshcherskaia, made concerted efforts to try to involve the heir to the throne in Turgenev's case. Turgenev finished his imprisonment and on 18 May headed into exile at Spasskoe.

Many have suggested (and Turgenev himself always believed as much) that Turgenev's arrest and exile were not the result of his Gogol obituary but a punishment for *Zapiski okhotnika*. The chronology of their publication as a separate edition of twenty-two sketches in two volumes (the sketch "Dva pomeshchika" [Two Landowners], although written in 1847, was first added in this edition) indicates that the two events moved in separate bureaucratic channels. The censorship passed both volumes of *Zapiski okhotnika* a few days before the publication of Turgenev's Gogol obituary, and the printing continued in Moscow throughout Turgenev's arrest in St. Petersburg. The printed books did go to the Main Censorship Office for review in late May, but Turgenev himself, while in Moscow on his way into exile, discussed with his Moscow friends the advisability of delaying the release. The books eventually went on sale in early August 1852, swiftly bringing down retribution on the head of Vladimir Vladimirovich L'vov, the censor who had passed them; he was officially relieved of his duties (with loss of pension) on 12 August. Sales, however, were not stopped, and the book sold out within six months. There was, however, an effective ban on reviews and analyses in the press.

Nor were the terms of Turgenev's exile severely restrictive, since he was permitted to travel to the provincial capital of Orel and around the province, visiting neighbors and indulging in his passion for hunting. He did not, however, receive permission to leave the province, and so in March 1853 he traveled secretly with a false passport to Moscow to meet with Pauline Viardot, on tour in Russia for the last time. Finally, in November 1853, through the efforts of his friends, Turgenev was reprieved and given permission to return to St. Petersburg.

With the publication of the separate edition of *Zapiski okhotnika,* Turgenev began to consider seriously the future direction of his writing, searching for a "new manner," one that did not involve making a "triple extract" of peasant life for readers to "sniff." In response to encouragement from several quarters, he turned his attention to a novel, "Dva pokoleniia" (Two Generations). He completed the first part in March 1853, but the decidedly mixed verdict of friends who read the work persuaded him to abandon it, and only a short extract, reminiscent of the style of *Zapiski okhotnika,* was ever published (the remainder has been lost), under the title "Sobstvennaia gospodskaia kontora" (The Estate Privy Office, 1859). However, even as Turgenev was turning away from *Zapiski okhotnika,* the sketches were beginning to make their way into Europe. A French translation by a former private tutor in Russia, Ernest Charrière, was being prepared. It appeared in Paris in April 1854, not long after the start of the Crimean War, an event that greatly contributed to the impact of these "Photographs from Russian Life," as a lengthy review of Charrière's translation in the English journal *Frazer's Magazine* dubbed them.

Herzen was the person who had first brought Turgenev's name as a writer before the European public when he praised *Zapiski okhotnika* in his study *Du développement des idées révolutionnaires en Russie* (On the Development of Revolutionary Ideas in Russia), which appeared in Paris in March 1851, with a German translation following in April. Not long afterward, the earliest translations, into German, had been undertaken by

August Viedert, a young man of German origin who had been a member of both Moscow and St. Petersburg intellectual circles and who had met Turgenev during the winter of 1850 and 1851. Viedert's translations of individual sketches had begun to appear in periodicals in both Russia and Germany even before the publication of the collection in 1852. With Theodor Storm acting as intermediary, he arranged for half the stories to appear in what became volume one of *Aus dem Tagebuch eines Jägers* (From the Diary of a Hunter), published in Berlin in October 1854. To Viedert's subsequent lifelong chagrin, the publisher, Heinrich Schindler, turned to someone else, August Boltz, for the second volume, published in April 1855, since Boltz was willing to do the translations for half the price. The Viedert volume, in a translation that Turgenev greeted with thanks for its honesty and elegance, attracted wide attention in the German press and established Turgenev's reputation among the German literati. It also served to provide Turgenev an introduction into American letters when the translation was one of several works discussed in a review article, "Slavery in Russia," published in the *North American Review* (April 1856) by "Mrs. T. Robinson" (Therese von Jakob, a cultural philologist).

Charrière's 1854 French translation, however, established Turgenev's name among the European reading public. Under the fanciful title *Mémoires d'un Seigneur Russe, ou Tableau de la Situation actuelle des Nobles et des Paysans dans les Provinces Russes* (Notes of a Russian Lord, or a Picture of the Current Condition of Nobles and Peasants in the Russian Provinces), it was published in a popular edition by a major publishing house, Hachette, and went through three editions, the last with eleven reprints over nearly fifty years. Like the title, the translation was fanciful, frequently embellishing Turgenev's text with Charrière's own additions, no doubt because Charrière assumed that they corresponded more with the readers' expectations, since his preface was surprisingly perspicacious about both the significance and the artistic merits of Turgenev's original. In that preface, Charrière began the tradition of comparing *Zapiski okhotnika* with Harriet Beecher Stowe's *Uncle Tom's Cabin* (1851–1852), indicating a preference for the Russian work because of the absence in it of excessive sentimentality. Charrière then helped assure the success of his enterprise by sending a copy of his translation to the prominent French writer Prosper Mérimée, who responded by publishing an extensive review in the foremost French journal of the day, the *Revue des Deux Mondes* (1 July 1854), a warm review in which Mérimée did not hesitate to draw on Charrière's preface in assessing the work. From France, the book made its way across the English Channel. Several journals noted it in reviews, often with extracts translated from Charrière's translation, and the whole appeared in Edinburgh in 1855 under the title *Russian Life in the Interior, or The Experiences of a Sportsman* in a translation by James D. Meiklejohn that occasionally treated Charrière's French in as cavalier a fashion as Charrière had treated Turgenev's original. Reactions to the work in both France and Britain were, however, most notable for their chauvinism against this picture of life in the country ruled "by the world's arch-enemy, the Emperor Nicholas." As M. K. Kleman showed, the chauvinistic reactions as much as, if not more than, the translation itself prompted from Turgenev an official letter of protest against Charrière's version.

While Turgenev was establishing a foothold outside of Russia, following his release from exile in November 1853, he was assuming an active role in the literary and intellectual life of the capital, meeting with colleagues to discuss new works and attending the theater and concerts. His social life was by no means confined to littérateurs; not long after his return, he met a distant relative, Ol'ga Aleksandrovna Turgeneva, with whom he established a largely platonic relationship that some of his friends thought might lead to a marriage proposal. No proposal was made, although Ol'ga Aleksandrovna was the inspiration for the much-suffering heroine Tat'iana Shestova of Turgenev's novel *Dym*. Throughout this period Turgenev continued to write and publish. The story "Dva priiatelia" (Two Friends) appeared in the January 1854 issue of *Sovremennik*, "Mumu" in the March issue, and "Iakov Pasynkov" in the April 1855 issue of *Otechestvennye zapiski*. Turgenev also devoted considerable attention to bringing before the public the poetry of Fedor Ivanovich Tiutchev, Evgenii Abramovich Baratynsky, and the translations of the odes of Horace by Afanasii Afanas'evich Fet. Turgenev then spent the summer of 1855 at Spasskoe, much of the time devoted to the writing of *Rudin*, his first published novel.

Returning to St. Petersburg in mid October 1855, Turgenev read his new work to friends and colleagues from the *Sovremennik* circle. Throughout his life Turgenev sought reactions to his works prior to final changes and publication. In his early years these "consultations" were often quite broad (readings of new works by authors to groups of colleagues was a quite common phenomenon); later in life, when he was living abroad, he tended to choose a more select group of like-minded friends, among whom Annenkov eventually became the most important and occasionally the sole arbiter. Although these consultations led to changes, Turgenev seems to have sought the reactions in order to learn where he was being "misread," that is, where reactions to elements in his works were not those that he had anticipated, and the changes effected were

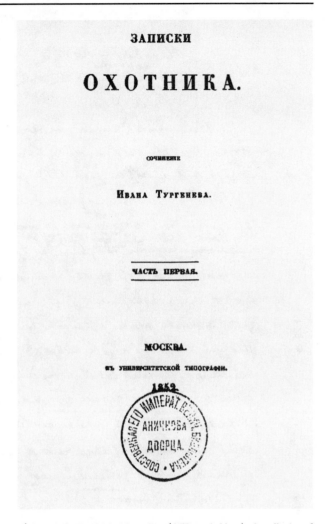

Title page for Zapiski okhotnika *(A Hunter's Notes), the collection of sketches that established Turgenev's literary reputation among his contemporaries (The Kilgour Collection of Russian Literature, Houghton Library, Harvard University)*

designed to avoid such "misreading" rather than to alter his works in any fundamental or substantive way. The reading of *Rudin* provided him with "useful suggestions," which Turgenev took into account before the novel appeared in two parts in the January and February 1856 issues of *Sovremennik*. The novel, the eponymous hero of which had been modeled in some respects on Bakunin, explored the gulf between idealistic ideas and their implementation. The arrival of Dmitrii Rudin at the country estate of Mme. Lasunskaia sets her world ablaze. Rudin's noble-sounding speeches inspire Lasunskaia's daughter, Natasha, into thinking that here is the man who can encourage, instruct, and provide the opportunity for her to transfer her own idealistic yearnings into a meaningful life. As happens all too often with Turgenev's heroines, however, her hopes are disappointed, because the male protagonist proves unable to transfer his own words and sentiments into deeds.

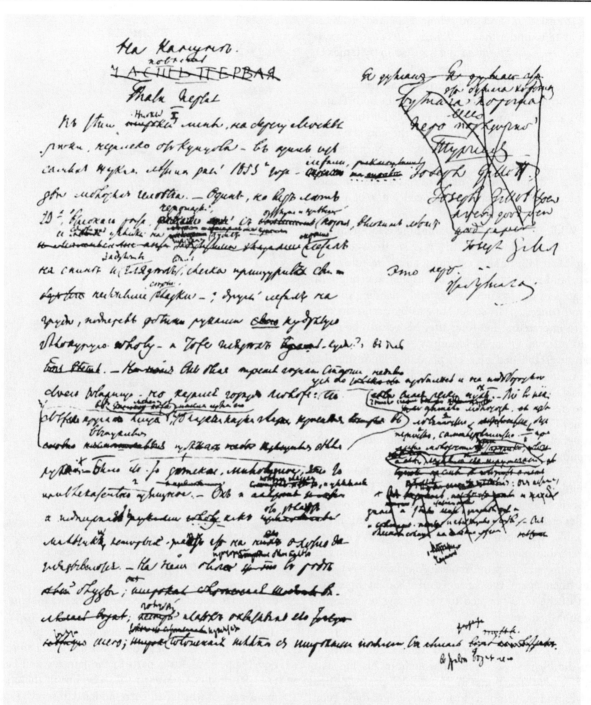

First page of a draft for Turgenev's novel Nakanune *(On the Eve), published in* Russkii vestnik *(The Russian Herald) in 1860*
(from Avrahm Yarmolinsky, Turgenev, The Man, His Art and His Age, *1959)*

Natasha's assignation with Rudin, at which love and aspirations are to become united, finds Rudin unable to commit himself to either. Another of the protagonists in the novel, Lezhnev, defends Rudin, suggesting that his ability to inspire others with his words is a positive characteristic in itself, and Turgenev added an epilogue in 1860 in which Rudin dies fighting on the barricades in Paris in 1848, though those fighting beside him know him only as an anonymous Pole. Nonetheless, the gulf between words and deeds, under the rather broad designation of "the superfluous man," came to be depicted as a fundamental flaw in the Russian male psyche and to occupy considerable attention. Turgenev and other writers of his generation explored the "superfluous man," searching for the causes of the phenomenon in contemporary sociopolitical circumstances as well as in the hero's personal psychology and upbringing.

Rudin was greeted largely positively as a significant milestone in Turgenev's writing career. Attracting less notice than the novel was a story also published in *Otechestvennye zapiski* in the January 1856 issue— "Perepiska" (A Correspondence)—which Turgenev had been working on for nearly a decade and which includes many of the themes that continued to occupy him throughout his literary career. The corpus of Turgenev's published works now made possible a collected edition. Turgenev sold the rights to such an edition (excluding *Zapiski okhotnika*) to Annenkov, who brought out a three-volume edition under the title *Povesti i rasskazy I. S. Turgeneva* (The Novellas and Stories of I. S. Turgenev) in November 1856. This edition provided the opportunity for important retrospective articles by Aleksandr Vasil'evich Druzhinin in *Biblioteka dlia chteniia* (Library for Reading, nos. 2, 3, and 5, 1857) and Stepan Semenovich Dudyshkin (*Otechestvennye zapiski*, nos. 1 and 4, 1857).

Among the major events of late 1855 was the arrival in St. Petersburg of Leo Tolstoy, then a young frontline officer, who until recently had been in besieged Sevastopol'. He arrived in mid November and moved in with Turgenev. Tolstoy's work had attracted attention from the first, with Turgenev among his most enthusiastic admirers. Tolstoy's stories from the siege of Sevastopol' ("Sevastopol' in December" in the June 1855 issue of *Sovremennik* and "Sevastopol' in May" in the September issue) had set the seal on his reputation as a major new talent. The vastly different characters of the two writers probably made inevitable the extremely turbulent nature of their relationship—at times close, more often hostile. Tolstoy had a high opinion of *some* of Turgenev's works; Turgenev, in contrast, always acknowledged Tolstoy's talent, even when their personal relationship was at its worst.

With the conclusion of hostilities in the Crimean War (February 1856) Turgenev could consider once again the possibility of traveling abroad, and on 21 July 1856 he left for Europe and a reunion with Pauline Viardot, her family, and his daughter, whom he barely knew. As he himself admitted later, he had virtually nothing in common with his daughter: "She likes neither music, nor poetry, neither Nature, nor dogs, and I like nothing else," Turgenev once admitted to Countess Lambert. Turgenev's letters of this period are filled with complaints about his health, although the exact nature of his illness is never specified. (Tolstoy, who visited Paris from February until early April and with whom Turgenev undertook trips into the French provinces, was inclined to see it as both physical and psychological, the latter at least a function of his far from straightforward relationship at this time with Pauline Viardot.) In May 1857 Turgenev traveled to England for an extended visit, during which he made the acquaintance of many prominent British figures—including Thomas Carlyle, William Makepeace Thackeray, Thomas Macaulay, Benjamin Disraeli, and Florence Nightingale and her family at their country home near Salisbury. Turgenev spent much of the summer and beyond visiting a variety of spas and doctors in an attempt to rid himself of his mysterious illness. In July he was taking the waters in Sinzig, where he began his story "Asia" (1858), set in that small town on the Rhine. In late September, instead of returning to Russia as had been his intention, he suddenly decided to spend the winter in Rome. While in Rome, Turgenev completed "Asia" and sent it to the *Sovremennik* editors, where it appeared in the January issue for 1858.

Although Nekrasov, the editor-in-chief of *Sovremennik*, was thrilled with "Asia," an intensely beautiful story of indecision and lost opportunities, this work in some ways marks the beginning of a major sea change in Russian intellectual life, the break between the "liberals," Turgenev's "Generation of the 40s," and the next generation, the radicals of the 1860s, whose leaders had gathered around *Sovremennik*. Although only the previous year (as announced in the October 1856 issue of *Sovremennik*, in which Turgenev's story "Faust" had also appeared), a group of authors that included Turgenev, Tolstoy, and the playwright Aleksandr Nikolaevich Ostrovsky had signed an exclusive contract for their work to appear in *Sovremennik*, for a variety of reasons, including long-standing but unfulfilled promises, Turgenev's name continued to appear in a variety of journals until the final break with *Sovremennik* in 1859. In the middle of January 1858, the leading figure among the *Sovremennik* radicals, Nikolai Gavrilovich Chernyshevsky, published an article in the journal *Atenei* (Athenaeum) under the title "Russkii chelovek na

Turgenev at forty-four

state of completion that made possible circulating them among his friends and advisers. Much of the summer and autumn of 1858 were spent hunting and working on his second novel, *Dvorianskoe gnezdo* (A Nest of the Gentry, 1859). With the manuscript complete, he left Spasskoe for St. Petersburg. There, in mid November, Annenkov read the novel to a group of Turgenev's friends and colleagues. Turgenev himself, rendered mute by a severe attack of bronchitis, attended the reading, at which the work was enthusiastically received. No less important for Turgenev was the opinion of Countess Elizaveta Egorovna Lambert, a member of the higher aristocracy, to whom Turgenev had become quite close and whose religious asceticism had been an influence on the character of the heroine of the novel, Liza Kalitina.

In *Dvorianskoe gnezdo* Turgenev directs attention to the chaotic diversity of influences that go into the social and psychological makeup of his protagonists; it is a chaos that those of good will must struggle to overcome. The hero, Fedor Lavretsky, son of a peasant girl and her master's son, is a victim of the eccentric Anglophile views on a Spartan education espoused by his father, himself the product of a peculiar upbringing. Innocent in the ways of the world, Lavretsky marries a vacuous society woman, who leaves him for a young lover in Paris. Lavretsky returns to Russia and visits a distant relative, Mar'ia Dmitrievna Kalitina. The cross section of provincial characters who meet in her house includes Vladimir Panshin, an upwardly mobile bureaucrat and dilettante; Christopher Lemm, an intensely serious elderly German music teacher; and Marfa Timofeevna, the hostess's old aunt, who maintains in her own rooms a ménage in which traditional "old" Russian values predominate. While Mar'ia Dmitrievna is the social center of this society, its main attraction and spiritual oasis is her daughter, Liza. Lavretsky and Liza are drawn together by a common sense of idealism, although neither knows exactly how to channel it. When the rumor of the death of Lavretsky's wife reaches them, the path appears open for them to unite and implement their idealism together. The sudden appearance of Lavretsky's wife brings this dream to a crashing end. Liza sees their love as a punishment for selfishly having sought personal happiness to the detriment of duty. Her response is to enter a monastery, where she can expiate not so much her own "sins" as those of her family, leaving Lavretsky to undertake a modest program of reform on his own estates.

The novel, in which the Westernist and agnostic Turgenev introduced a Slavophile hero and a deeply religious heroine, appeared in the January 1859 issue of *Sovremennik* to acclaim from across the ideological spectrum, an accomplishment that was not repeated in Rus-

rendez-vous" (A Russian Man at a Rendezvous, 1858), which used "Asia" as the pretext for criticizing the liberals precisely for their indecisiveness. This attack was soon followed by another from the other prominent radical in *Sovremennik,* Nikolai Aleksandrovich Dobroliubov. Dobroliubov's review of Annenkov's biography of Nikolai Vladimirovich Stankevich, who had always represented an ideal for the liberals, took the opportunity to challenge the premise of the dichotomy between duty and personal happiness that had been at the heart of Turgenev's "Faust," a story in which the hero-narrator introduces the heroine, whose mother had deliberately shielded her from any contact with the world of emotions, to Goethe's *Faust.* The consequences are dramatic and fatal for the heroine, torn between duty to her mother's strictures and the happiness of love. Although there were those who came to the public defense of the liberals, the split became increasingly acerbic, and the breach was never healed.

In early June 1858 Turgenev returned to Russia, leaving St. Petersburg almost immediately for Spasskoe. In what remained a habit throughout the remainder of his life, even when he began his major literary works abroad, he retreated to Spasskoe to bring them to a

sian intellectual life for decades. Indeed, perhaps the only blot on Turgenev's literary horizon was the accusation of plagiarism made against him by Ivan Aleksandrovich Goncharov, whose slow pace of writing let him believe that those who heard him read extracts from his unfinished works (and indeed some who did not) were stealing his themes and ideas and incorporating them into their own works.

Not content to rest on his accomplishments, Turgenev almost immediately began preliminary work on his next novel, *Nakanune* (On the Eve, 1860). In March 1859 he went to Spasskoe in order to work on *Nakanune,* but he returned to St. Petersburg in late April, leaving almost immediately for Europe. By mid September, he was back in Russia and at Spasskoe in order to work on the new novel. His other task while on his estate was to begin work on a settlement with his peasants in anticipation of the emancipation process that had become the major interest and concern in Russia. He was still at Spasskoe on 8 November, the day of the inaugural meeting of the *Obshchestvo dlia posobiia nuzhdaiushchim literatoram i uchenym* (Society for Aid to Needy Authors and Academics), an organization in which from the beginning he had taken a keen interest. Back in St. Petersburg, Turgenev took his role in the new organization seriously. In January 1860 he read his programmatic essay "Gamlet i Don Kikhot" (Hamlet and Don Quixote) at a fund-raiser for the literary fund; the text was published in the January 1860 issue of *Sovremennik,* the last work by Turgenev to appear in that journal. In "Gamlet i Don Kikhot" Turgenev argued that these literary figures are emblematic of two fundamental and opposite human psychological principles; Hamlet represented the egotistical principle, paralyzed by excessive analysis and, especially, self-analysis; Don Quixote represented the selfless principle, handicapped in turn by the inability to see reality accurately and therefore prone to waste that noble selflessness on inappropriate causes. All humans, suggested Turgenev, fall somewhere on the axis between these two extremes, exhibiting the two principles in some particular combination. Many subsequent commentators routinely identified Turgenev's heroes with the Danish prince and his heroines with the Spanish knight.

Turgenev's new novel, *Nakanune,* appeared at the beginning of February 1860 in a double issue of *Russkii vestnik* (The Russian Herald). This novel was not as well received as its predecessor had been. Even before publication, Countess Lambert in particular had rejected it outright, and only the careful efforts of Annenkov and others prevailed upon the insecure author not to abandon or destroy it.

Once again Turgenev created an idealistic heroine in search of a like-minded hero who could help translate that idealism into practical action, something that the position of young women in contemporary society made impossible for the heroine on her own. In *Nakanune,* the independent-minded heroine, Elena Stakhova, appears to have found a solution to this dilemma by choosing a young Bulgarian student, Dmitrii Insarov, whose own idealism is clearly focused and directed on the grandly noble cause of the liberation of his native country from the Turks. In contrast to his Russian contemporaries, Insarov appears as a model of strength, determination, and, most notably, action. Despite the obstacles, which include Insarov's serious illness, Elena and Insarov marry and leave to take up the liberation struggle, but Insarov dies of tuberculosis in Venice on the eve of their departure for the Balkans. Once again the fates (and the author) seem to punish those who attempt to combine personal happiness with selfless idealism. All traces of Elena disappear following a storm in the Adriatic the night that she leaves with Insarov's body; there are rumors of her death, but there are counter-rumors of a mysterious foreign lady alongside insurrection forces in Herzegovina.

Attacks on the novel from Turgenev's former colleagues at *Sovremennik* came quickly. In the March issue, Chernyshevsky published his review under the title "Kogda zhe pridet nastoiashchii den'?" (When Will the Real Day Come?). True, Elena had found a hero to match her own idealism, and Insarov actually seemed to possess the ability to translate his idealism into action, but Insarov is not Russian and that was what provoked Chernyshevsky's polemical stance. Taking advantage of the changed possibilities under Alexander II, Chernyshevsky became more overtly political in his review, not interested in the character of the main hero as much as in deploring the absence of idealistic action among Russians. At the height of the critical discussions surrounding *Nakanune,* Turgenev's story "Pervaia liubov'" appeared to no less mixed reviews, with some critics actually accusing the author of immorality. Even the preparation of a new edition of his collected works, *Sochineniia I. S. Turgeneva. Ispravlennye i dopolnennye* (Works of I. S. Turgenev: Corrected and with Additional Material, published in Moscow in four volumes, 1860), did not go smoothly, as friends of Turgenev began to accuse the publisher, Nil Andreevich Osnovsky, of being a swindler (not entirely without justification; Osnovsky did print more copies than he was entitled to under the contract). Nor had Turgenev's conflict with his confrere Goncharov gone away. Goncharov's accusation of plagiarism led to an informal arbitration hearing on 29 March 1860, at which the judges—Annenkov, Druzhinin, and Dudyshkin—found Turgenev not guilty, declaring that any apparent similarities between Turgenev's novels and Goncharov's works were a factor of their all having emerged "from one and the same Russian soil." Less than a month later, Turgenev once again left St. Petersburg and proceeded to take the waters at the German spa town of Soden. While there, he read the works of the materialistic philosopher Karl Vogt, part of the preparations that led to his next and most famous novel, *Ottsy i deti*.

Since many of his friends and acquaintances were in Europe that summer, Turgenev tried to organize a grand gathering on the Isle of Wight for August. Not all of those whom Turgenev had been cajoling went to Ventnor, but a small colony of Russians did gather. Two projects eventually emerged from the sojourn on the Isle of Wight. As the forces that led to the emancipation of the serfs continued to gather steam, many Russians turned their attention to education in the realization that without widespread public education, the success of political reform would be severely compromised. Nothing lasting came from the noble call for an *Obshchestvo dlia rasprostraneniia gramotnosti i pervonachal'nogo obrazovaniia* (Society for the Propagation of Literacy and Elementary Education) that the group in Ventnor elaborated. The other project, despite an initial setback, did make a lasting impression on Russian life and culture. Turgenev later recalled that he confided the preliminary idea of his future novel to an unnamed fellow Russian in Ventnor (probably Vasilii Petrovich Botkin) and was shocked to hear that, in the opinion of this friend, Turgenev had already treated what he himself considered to be a profoundly new phenomenon in Russian life in the character of Rudin. As a result of this surprising comment, Turgenev abandoned even thinking about this new work for several weeks, but once he returned to France (where he quickly retreated to the peace of Courtavenel), he began to work on the ideas and characters of *Ottsy i deti*. Consequently, Turgenev was in Paris when he heard the news of the Emancipation of the Serfs on 6 March 1861. Nonetheless, the need to finish *Ottsy i deti,* as much as any political imperative, took him back to Russia and to Spasskoe in May 1861. While at Spasskoe, he visited his neighbor, the poet Afanasii Afanas'evich Fet, and Tolstoy. Turgenev's hopes that his and Tolstoy's past misunderstandings might be overcome were dashed as they had a heated quarrel (the subject of which was the issue of charity and, specifically, Turgenev's approbation of his daughter's performing charitable deeds at the insistence of her English governess, Maria Innis; Tolstoy was opposed to anything that could be construed as "compulsory" in charity). The argument got out of hand, written apologies got lost in transportation, and for a period of time, two of the most prominent writers in Russia appeared to be headed toward fighting a duel. (Turgenev's sense of the absurdity of the situation was quickly transferred

artistically into *Ottsy i deti* with its no less ridiculous duel between Pavel Petrovich Kirsanov and Bazarov.) Despite these dramatic events, both Turgenev's arrangements with his peasants and his work on *Ottsy i deti* went well, and he left Spasskoe for Moscow on 29 August, where he left his manuscript with the editor of *Russkii vestnik,* Mikhail Nikiforovich Katkov, and returned to Paris.

In *Ottsy i deti,* Arkadii Kirsanov, recently graduated from a university, returns to the estate of his father, Nikolai Petrovich Kirsanov, in the company of Evgenii Bazarov, a student of medicine and other natural sciences. There is immediate tension between the generations, as the mildly liberal ideas of Nikolai and his brother Pavel clash with Bazarov's extreme empiricist materialism that denies all abstractions and is proudly called "nihilism" by Bazarov's newest acolyte, Arkadii. While in the local provincial town, the young men encounter a youthful widow, Anna Odintsova, to whom Arkadii is attracted and who, surprisingly, from the first, nonplusses the usually sanguine Bazarov. Instead of going on to visit Bazarov's long-suffering parents, the young men go to stay at Odintsova's estate. While Bazarov denies the existence of emotional attraction, Odintsova avoids it, because it cannot be controlled, and strict order is the only thing that provides meaning in her empty life. Nonetheless, Bazarov and Odintsova are attracted to each other and in the battle between Bazarov's denial and Odintsova's avoidance, Bazarov is forced to change. Ruthlessly honest in everything, he finds himself obliged to admit that he has fallen in love with Odintsova, as a result of which the premises of his philosophy are shown to be false. Bazarov's life thus loses all meaning, and he dies after carelessly cutting himself while performing an autopsy. With him dies his challenge to accepted views and customs, as represented by the Kirsanov family, including Arkadii, who marries Odintsova's younger sister, Katia, and settles with his father to run the estate in anticipation of the forthcoming emancipation. What survives Bazarov is a vague memory of his challenge and the profound love of his aging parents.

Katkov's somewhat fearful reaction to the manuscript of the novel anticipated the rift that the novel provoked in Russian society. As Annenkov wrote to Turgenev, it was difficult to determine whether the author himself considered the principal hero, Bazarov, as "a source of productive strength for the future or the putrid abscess of a barren civilization." As a result, Katkov could see in Bazarov an apotheosis of the worst aspects of the young radicals, while those radicals saw the same Bazarov as a cruel distortion of an entire generation. Turgenev himself acknowledged as much in a letter to Fet, in which he declared that he himself did not know if he loved or hated his hero. Later, in his apologia for the novel, "Po povodu «Ottsov i detei»" (On the Subject of *Ottsy i deti*), he suggested that he was in fundamental agreement with Bazarov's worldview in everything but his views on art. While this bald statement might seem to underplay the crucial importance of art in Turgenev's own worldview, it does underscore Turgenev's interest in philosophical ideas in the novel. The novel appeared in the February 1862 issue of *Russkii vestnik,* Turgenev having prevailed upon Katkov not to break it up. Initial reactions were generally favorable; Annenkov noted that among the younger generation in particular there were many enthusiastic supporters. They realized, he observed, that they were the subject matter of the novel, while the older generation simply did not understand it. But, warned Annenkov prophetically, the "*Sovremennik* clique" had not yet had its say. That came in an acerbic article (under a title that played on the famous novel by Lermontov), "Asmodei nashego vremeni" (An Asmodeus of Our Time) by Maksim Alekseevich Antonovich, that set out "the party line," that the character Bazarov was a vicious attack upon the young radicals. Although the even more radical Dmitrii Ivanovich Pisarev welcomed Bazarov as an accurate portrait of a "nihilist" in his article named after that hero, which appeared in *Russkoe slovo* in 1862, Antonovich's view prevailed (arguably for more than a century). Most people continued to read what is fundamentally a philosophical novel, in political terms, as a conflict between two generations, rather than as a conflict between two ways of looking at life, with Bazarov representing a rationalistic, materialistic view taken to its extreme. Such a view denies the element of irrationality that was all too evident for Turgenev, and an irrational element, Bazarov's falling in love with Anna Odintsova, is what ultimately undermines Bazarov's worldview and leads, seemingly inescapably, to his premature death. Annenkov's original assessment had concluded with the warning: "It will make a lot of noise—expect that," and, after the publication of the novel, he added, "It is good to be a novel writer, but to throw into the public arena something resembling a moral gauge, against which everyone measures himself, cursing the reading shown by the gauge, and equally angry when that reading is low and when it is high, that means rising above the level of a novel into the sphere of a public homily." Not all readers were prepared to measure themselves; they preferred to measure Turgenev and find him wanting. His reputation among a whole generation of young Russians remained tarnished, while at the same time he all too often found himself lumped in with a reactionary camp for which he had little sympathy. The word *nihilist* that he had introduced in the novel (although not invented) began to be

Title page for Ottsy i deti *(Fathers and Sons), Turgenev's best-known novel, which depicts the generational conflicts of his time*

identified with young radicals (not only in Russia, but eventually abroad as well), so much so that he noted bitterly (once again in "Po povodu «Ottsov i detei»") that when he was in St. Petersburg in 1862 at the height of a period of civil unrest that brought with it widespread arson, he was accosted by an acquaintance on Nevskii Prospect who upbraided him: "Look what *your* nihilists are doing! They're burning Petersburg!" Even before the publication of *Ottsy i deti,* Turgenev started writing a pessimistic essay-story concerned with the transitory nature of all human affairs and with the place of art in human civilization, under the title "Dovol'no" (Enough). Why, wonders the anonymous artist-narrator, subject oneself to the laughter of the "cold crowd" or "the judgment of the idiot"? "The rest is silence . . . " concludes the story (in English), quoting Hamlet's final words before his death.

Pauline Viardot officially retired from her operatic career in the summer of 1863, and for a variety of reasons, including their political opposition to the régime of Napoleon III in France, she and Louis

Self-caricature drawn by Turgenev in Paris, circa 1878–1879 (from Avrahm Yarmolinsky, Turgenev, The Man, His Art and His Age, 1959)

decided to take up residence in the popular and cosmopolitan spa town of Baden-Baden, the gateway to the German Black Forest, where they had often spent the summer months between engagements and where Pauline quickly established an international reputation as a singing teacher. Turgenev, therefore, had also begun to gravitate toward Baden-Baden, although he did not officially move there until after his daughter's marriage on 25 February (new style) 1865 to Gaston Bruère, the manager of a glass factory in Rougemont, south of Paris. From Baden, Turgenev eventually set out, in early January 1864 after many delays ascribed to ill-health, to St. Petersburg to face a Senate Commission of Enquiry into his contacts "with the London Émigrés," that is, with Herzen and his collaborator, Nikolai Platonovich Ogarev. The irony of this summons was not lost on Turgenev, since Herzen had begun to attack Turgenev publicly in a series of eight articles under the title "Kontsy i nachala" (Endings and Beginnings, *Kolokol*, 1862–1863). Turgenev's appearance before the committee proved a formality, but Herzen chose to seal the rift between them with a published comment about a "gray-haired Mary Magdalene of the male gender, who had lost all her teeth and hair as a result of her repentance." Nor, in the aftermath of the controversy surrounding *Ottsy i deti,* was Turgenev eager to return actively to writing. His few works of this period, "Prizraki" (Apparitions, 1864), published in Dosto-

evsky's journal *Epokha* (Epoch), and "Sobaka" (The Dog, completed in April 1864, but not published until March 1866, in *Sankt-Peterburgskie vedomosti*), included mysterious, even supernatural, elements that ran counter to the literary tenor of the time. Not until late 1865 did he begin what became his fifth, and most ideological, novel, *Dym*.

Turgenev's first attacks of what was to become his constant companion, gout, delayed his departure for Russia with the manuscript of *Dym*. He eventually arrived in St. Petersburg in late February 1867, where on 26 February he read the story "Istoriia leitenanta Ergunova" (The Story of Lieutenant Ergunov, 1868) and the first chapters of *Dym* to a group that included Botkin and Annenkov. He also gave public readings from the novel for charity, all of which were met with approbation. The critical response to the novel following its appearance in the March 1867 issue of *Russkii vestnik* was much less favorable. If readers had not been certain whom Turgenev was attacking in *Ottsy i deti*, his attacks in *Dym* seemed to be directed at everyone and everything.

For many readers and critics, the familiar Turgenev love triangle is somewhat obscured in *Dym* by the ideological wranglings that surround it. The novel is set primarily in Baden-Baden, where Grigorii Litvinov finds himself on his way home to Russia following four years of studies in Europe to learn the basic principles to make the estate he inherited from his father a viable economic concern following the emancipation of the serfs. He is in Baden to meet his fiancée, Tat'iana Shestova, another of Turgenev's idealistic young women, and her aunt. His apparently straightforward future is shattered by the intrusion of Irina Ratmirova, a grande dame (modeled in part on Alexander II's mistress) with whom Litvinov had been in love as a student before she broke with him to embark on her social "career." Bored with her life, Irina feels her old attraction for Litvinov, but she is unwilling to give up her social position for him, while Litvinov, in the end, retains just enough self-esteem not to accept a position as her lover. Having broken his engagement, Litvinov leaves Baden alone, when Irina decides at the last minute not to join him, and returns to Russia, where he begins to apply the principles he has learned to the management of his estate and is eventually rewarded with the possibility of reestablishing relations with Tat'iana.

Irina, through her husband, provides the link with one of the groups that Turgenev targets in *Dym* for his bitter criticism and thus emerges as the unifying center of the novel. General Ratmirov belongs to a group of high society "Generals," resident in Baden, whose apparent disdain for Russia includes a pernicious chauvinism. Opposing them is a mixed group of radicals, who represent a new Slavophile socialism that is at least in part derived from the ideas of Herzen and his circle. Thus, for Turgenev, the similarities between them, rather than the surface opposition, lie at the heart of his criticism. Both groups deal in abstracts; both are far removed from any practical realities; and both ignore what for Turgenev remains the necessary element for the future of Russia–hard work in the context of the lessons of Western "civilization" in the broadest sense. That viewpoint is presented by one of Turgenev's most problematic protagonists, Sozont Potugin, whose unsuccessful personal life stands in sharp contrast with the forcefulness of his Westernist views. Nor is Potugin a minor character in the novel; as early as in his drafts and subsequently in letters, Turgenev actually identifies him as "the main character of the entire story." What thus emerges is a novel about the dangers of empty arrogance, whether that of the Generals or of the radicals, against which is set the inner strength of modest aims and humility, coupled with hard work, represented by Litvinov. Not surprisingly, Turgenev himself faced a barrage of negative criticism for his novel, together with accusations that his absence from Russia undermined his ability to understand and write about it, and he seriously considered giving up writing.

With the marriage of his daughter, Turgenev had begun the process of "letting down roots" in Baden-Baden. He built an impressive villa on what were then the outskirts of Baden, next door to the Viardots' chalet. Admittedly, financial difficulties caused by the incompetence of his aging uncle Nikolai Turgenev, who was acting as his estate manager in Russia, meant that Turgenev had to "sell" the villa to Louis Viardot before he finally moved in in April 1868. Even before Turgenev moved in, his villa had been the venue for a series of operettas composed by Pauline Viardot to librettos by Turgenev and performed by her family and pupils before audiences that often included royalty (Augusta, Queen of Prussia was a particularly enthusiastic supporter) and the political and artistic élite of Europe that gathered in Baden. These events contributed to the view that Turgenev, by nature of a melancholy and pessimistic disposition, considered the Baden years perhaps the happiest time of his life. He lived in peace and harmony next to the family whom he deeply loved (the Viardots' second daughter, Claudie, was his favorite among the Viardot children, and his affection for her almost rivaled that for her mother). The idyll, however, did not last; it was destroyed by the Franco-Prussian War of 1870–1871. Although the Viardots at first welcomed the defeat of Napoleon III, the occupation of France eventually forced them to move to London, where Turgenev followed them, before they

returned to their house in Paris in October 1871. They offered Turgenev the top floor of that house as a residence, and Turgenev, having disposed of his estate in Baden, established residence there. Three years later, Turgenev and the Viardots bought a property above the Seine in Bougival, a short distance downriver from Paris, where, in 1875, Turgenev built for himself the chalet in which he later died.

Despite Turgenev's sense that he had been abandoned by Russian readers, interest in his works, as manifested in regular and updated editions of his collected works, suggests that there was a steady demand for them. In 1865 the Moscow publisher F. Salaev had issued a five-volume collected edition, *Sochineniia (1844–1864)* (Works [1844–1864]). Printed in Karlsruhe, this collection constituted a third cumulative edition. The same publisher also published the fourth edition in seven volumes, under a similar title, *Sochineniia (1844–1868)* in 1868–1869, to which a supplementary eighth volume was added in 1871. Nor did Turgenev actually give up writing, as he had threatened, in the aftermath of the reception of *Dym* in Russia. He found a literary home, more congenial than the *Russkii vestnik* of the increasingly reactionary Katkov, in the journal *Vestnik Evropy* (The Herald of Europe), edited by the liberal historian Mikhail Matveevich Stasiulevich, and from 1868 virtually all his remaining literary works appeared there. Over a period of about a decade he produced a relatively small body of novellas and stories that explored interesting, occasionally esoteric or even paranormal, aspects of Russian life, often historical and always centered on a distinctive individual. After the accusations of being a traitor who despised and rejected Russia, he created a gallery of striking, if singular, Russian portraits in "Istoriia leitenanta Ergunova" (1868), "Brigadir" (The Brigadier, 1868), "Neschastnaia" (An Unfortunate Woman, 1869), "Strannaia istoriia" (A Strange Story, 1870), "Stepnoi korol' Lir" (A King Lear of the Steppes, 1870), and "Stuk . . . stuk . . . stuk! . . " (Knock . . . Knock . . . Knock! . ., 1871). A similar interest in the extraordinary inspires the story of Luker'ia, a saintly paralyzed peasant; her story, "Zhivye moshchi" (The Living Relics, 1874), was one of three added to *Zapiski okhotnika*. If some of his friends were consternated by this assault, albeit by the author himself, on what was seen as a "classic," its impact on his old idol George Sand was a letter of praise: "*All* of us have to come and learn from you." The exception to this trend was the somewhat nostalgic replay of the theme of *Dym*, shorn of its ideological polemic, in *Veshnie vody* in 1872, but that novella was followed by a return to the unusual and esoteric in "Punin i Baburin" (Punin and Baburin, 1874), "Chasy" (The Watch, 1876), and "Rasskaz ottsa Alekseia" (Father Alexis's Tale, 1877). All of these new

Turgenev in September 1879 (portrait by Pauline Viardot; from Avrahm Yarmolinsky, Turgenev, The Man, His Art and His Age, *1959)*

works were added to the successive editions of Turgenev's collected works issued by Salaev. The sixth edition in eight volumes with just the title *Sochineniia* appeared in 1874 and, after the death of the founder of the firm, his successors published the seventh edition, in ten volumes, under the cumulative title *Sochineniia (1844–1868–1874–1880).*

While the period following the publication of *Dym* marked the lowest ebb of Turgenev's reputation in Russia, it simultaneously marked the confirmation of his reputation—and influence—abroad as a major literary figure. He was well established among French writers, particularly close to George Sand and Gustave Flaubert. A German publisher, Erich Behre, had begun a collected edition of Turgenev's works, beginning with *Ottsy i deti* in 1869, that eventually encompassed twelve volumes before it was completed in 1884. Turgenev was attracting the attention of the young American writers associated with the *North American Review,* especially Henry James and William Dean Howells. An American, Eugene Schuyler, had made one of the first English translations from the original Russian, rather than from a French translation, with his *Fathers and Sons,* which became the first volume of an eight-volume *Turgénieff's Works,* published by Holt (1867–1885). In England William Ralston of the British Library served as translator (his classic translation of *Dvorianskoe gnezdo* under the title *Liza* was in print until recently) and tire-

less promoter, although at least some in Britain, such as George Eliot, always read Turgenev's works in French.

During the 1870s Turgenev's visits to Russia had become only occasional, but he maintained his extensive reading of the Russian press and contacts with a wide variety of Russians. As a result, as early as 1872, he began to think about a phenomenon, still in its infancy, the *narodnik* movement, which expressed the selfless desire of young Russians to "repay" the debt they felt they owed to the emancipated serfs (for all the privileges that the privileged youths and their ancestors had received as a result of the institution of serfdom). This phenomenon fascinated Turgenev and persuaded him once more to turn to the novel in order to describe it to his still largely unsuspecting countrymen. He complained about a lack of information, and the gestation time was unusually long for him, but in 1876 he finally found himself able to work seriously on his last novel, *Nov'* (Virgin Soil). He spent the summer of 1876 at Spasskoe, completing the novel, and following Annenkov's enthusiastic approval, *Nov'* finally appeared in the first two issues of *Vestnik Evropy* for 1877.

In *Nov'* Turgenev's hero, Aleksei Nezhdanov, is hired by Boris Sipiagin, a government official with a reputation as a political "up-and-comer" and proud of what he describes as his "liberal" views, as a tutor for his young son for the summer. Nezhdanov, described by Turgenev as a "romantic of realism," is associated with the new generation of radicals, who see their task as partly education, partly revolutionary agitation among the peasant masses. They are diverse in age and in social origin, ranging from noblemen to provincial merchants, but united in a rather naive idealism. At the Sipiagins, Nezhdanov quickly finds a sympathetic soul mate in an idealistic young woman, Marianna Sinetskaia, the niece of Valentina Sipiagina. Marianna's antipathy is directed at her uncle and aunt, whose veneer of liberalism hides a deep-seated reactionary selfishness. Eventually Nezhdanov and Marianna "elope" to the factory run by a practical manager, Vasilii Solomin, determined to begin their work among the people together. Unfortunately, Nezhdanov's efforts at "going to the people" prove farcical (he is unable to handle the vodka that he is made to drink), thereby exacerbating the contradictory impulses that are a part of Nezhdanov's character. He loses whatever convictions he had in his cause and thereby sees himself as betraying Marianna, as a result of which he sees no option for himself but to commit suicide. This personal tragedy permits Marianna to join forces with Solomin, a man whose vision of the future is radically different. A practical man "in the American mold," Solomin rejects the naive goals of the radicals in favor of practical improvements that he believes can be achieved only through a long series of small steps.

Turgenev's house in Bougival, 1881

Preliminary reaction to *Nov'* was largely negative, but the accusations that Turgenev was woefully out of touch with Russian reality quickly dissipated when the first of the mass *narodnik* trials, the so-called "Trial of 50," was held in February–March 1877. The trial seemed to confirm Turgenev's assessment of the naive, and at times inept, idealism of many in the *narodnik* movement, to the point that some commentators even suggested that Turgenev had been privy to secret materials in advance of the trial. However, while Turgenev's reputation as a keen observer, even an anticipator, of the "body and pressure of time," was finally confirmed by this novel, it has never achieved a general appreciation, and perhaps the presence in this novel of a rare, positive figure in the low-key, practical Solomin has prevented most critics from seeing this last novel as the equal in artistic terms of Turgenev's earlier efforts in the genre. The character of Solomin does seem in some respects like wishful thinking on Turgenev's part. He can, however, be seen rather as the precursor of that class of engineers and other practical intellectuals who played an important part in the economic and intellectual blossoming of Russia at the turn of the century and who, in the opinion of some later writers such as Aleksandr Isaevich Solzhenitsyn, might well have been the saving of Russia, but for the disaster of the First World War and their systematic extermination by the young Soviet regime that followed it.

The fortunes of *Nov'* were in some ways a forerunner of a change in Turgenev's own personal fortune among his Russian readers. The confirmation of the change came in 1879, when he was lionized and feted everywhere he went during a visit to Russia, most especially and gratifyingly by students. The "young" generation of the 1860s that had rejected and vilified him had itself been replaced by a still younger generation that appreciated and venerated him as a writer. That this reception was not an anomaly was shown the following year, when he traveled again to Russia, this time to take part in the great national celebration of Pushkin, culminating with the dedication of Aleksandr Opekushin's famous Pushkin monument in Moscow. The celebrations surrounding this event included his selection to the status of an honorary member (that is, an honorary degree recipient) of Moscow University as well as dinners and speeches organized by the *Obshchestvo liubitelei rossiiskoi slovesnosti* (Society of Lovers of Russian Letters), of which he had been a member since 1859. Of all the speeches delivered over two days, Dostoevsky's is the one that has passed into legend, a legend that suggests that this speech annihilated that of his perceived rival. Certainly Dostoevsky's chauvinistic exaltation of Pushkin as a universal genius marks the beginning of the virtual deification of Pushkin in Russian culture, and beside it Turgenev's more cautious praise inevitably pales, even if it is the more perspicacious in its assessment of the writer whom Turgenev always considered the greatest in Russia.

Turgenev's renewed popularity in Russia echoed the consolidation of his eminence in Europe. In 1878 he was the vice president of the International Literary Congress held in Paris to coincide with the International Exhibition. Turgenev found his chores frustrating (the president, Victor Hugo, took his duties honorifically), but the congress was devoted to the crucial issues of authorial rights and copyright. A year later, Turgenev was honored with a Doctorate of Civil Laws from Oxford University, somewhat to his astonishment, since he had written a poem, "Kroket v Vindzore" (Croquet at Windsor, 1876, not published in Russia until 1881), with less than flattering comments about Queen Victoria, in response to the Turkish actions in Bulgaria that had culminated in the Balkan Crisis and the Russo-Turkish War of 1877–1878. He assumed a more prominently public role in émigré circles in Paris. He was a leading light in the establishment of–and a fund-raiser for–a Russian reading room for impoverished students, later named in his honor Bibliothèque russe Tourguenoff (1875) and an *Obshchestvo vzaimnogo vspomozheniia i blagotvoritel'nosti russkikh khudozhnikov v Parizhe* (Society for Assistance to Russian Artists, 1877). Turgenev had always been keenly interested in art, and although he was more favorably disposed to the Russian school of art than to the Russian school of music, his personal collection of paintings was devoted primarily to non-Russian artists–Flemish masters and French painters of the Barbizon school in particular. The economic downturn as a result of the Balkan Crisis forced him to sell his personal collection in April 1878. He had extensive contacts among all classes of Russians in Paris, from visiting dignitaries to radical émigrés, the latter bringing down on him the secret attention of the French police authorities and, posthumously, a variety of accusations of support for Russian terrorists.

Whether the cause was the success of *Nov'* or the change in his Russian fortunes, the remaining few years of Turgenev's life brought a remarkable late flowering of his talent. These late works are often filled with a rich autumnal glow that some critics see as a foreshadowing of the fin de siècle. To a certain extent inspired by the *Trois Contes* (Three Tales, 1877) of his friend Flaubert, two of which he translated into Russian and published in 1877, Turgenev also turned to an historical and exotic subject in his story "Pesn' torzhestvuiushchei liubvi" (A Song of Love Triumphant, 1881), set in sixteenth-century Ferrara and exploring the power of suppressed love, aided and abetted by potions and tricks from the mysterious Orient. Turgenev also began what looked like a new series of character sketches to match at the end of his career *Zapiski okhotnika* at the begin-

ning. Only two stories, however, from *"Otryvki iz vospominanii–svoikh i chuzhikh"* (Extracts from Memoirs–My Own and Those of Others) were completed and published: "Starye portrety" (Old Portraits, 1881) and "Otchaiannyi" (The Desperado, 1882). Stasiulevich, his editor at *Vestnik Evropy*, persuaded Turgenev to select fifty of the reflective miniatures that collectively became known as *Stikhotvoreniia v proze* (Poems in Prose, 1882; a further thirty-one were posthumously published by André Mazon in 1930). Turgenev had been writing them since about 1877, and among the gems published during his lifetime was his paean to his native language "Russkii iazyk" (The Russian Language). "Porog" (The Threshold), his no less famous "ode" to an anonymous young Russian woman willing to do anything, including crime and self-sacrifice, for her idealistic cause, and considered for that a saint by some and a fool by others, was eventually excluded at Turgenev's insistence from publication. Circulating clandestinely, this last incarnation of Turgenev's idealistic heroine soon became something of a rallying cry among young radicals, whose judgment, unlike the author's, was unequivocal. Turgenev's final work, the story "Klara Milich" (1883), carries the subtitle "Posle smerti" (After Death). It also returns to a theme that had always underlain Turgenev's world, the power of love–in this case, a love so powerful that it "conquers" death itself. The eponymous heroine, unable to satisfy her love in life, commits suicide and only then succeeds in capturing the affections of the hero, Iakov Aratov, who quickly follows her to the grave in order to be united there with his beloved.

This spate of literary activity, after his regular declaration in the aftermath of reactions to *Nov'* that he was abandoning writing forever, belied the seriousness of Turgenev's health. Although often considered something of a hypochondriac, Turgenev, despite his extremely large physical frame, had always had rather delicate health. The first signs of the back pain that proved to be a symptom of his spinal cancer manifested themselves as early as July 1876, but for a long time Turgenev's doctors tended to concentrate on possible heart damage from his years of suffering from gout. In 1881 he made his last visit to Russia, spending much of the summer at Spasskoe, where he was visited by Tolstoy, repaying the visits that Turgenev had made to his estate, Iasnaia Poliana, in 1879. From the beginning of 1882, Turgenev's health deteriorated rapidly, and he spent much of the remaining twenty months of his life in often excruciating pain that, in the end, even morphine could only mask for short periods of time. This situation was not helped by the breakdown of the marriage of his daughter, who fled from her husband in February 1882 with their two children and had to go into hiding in Switzerland. Turgenev's ill health and the need to consider providing for his daughter and grandchildren persuaded him to try to sell his works in perpetuity, but the efforts of his reluctant agents, including Annenkov and Stasiulevich, were unsuccessful. In the end, he did sign a contract with the publisher Glazunov for a seventh collected edition of his works and even read the proofs of some of the volumes, but the edition appeared in December 1883 as a "posthumous" edition.

Despite the efforts of a multitude of doctors, none of whom really knew what Turgenev was suffering from, and brief and occasional respite from pain, the inevitable end became increasingly apparent. On 14 January (new style) 1883 he was operated on for the removal of a hypogastric protrusion, but this condition was merely a distraction from the main event. Bulletins about Turgenev's health appeared regularly in the European newspapers, and many Russians were vociferous in their condemnation of what they claimed was his "forced" detention away from Russia and neglect by the Viardot family. Unbiased reports speak of the extraordinary care he received at the hands of his longtime friends, despite the serious illness of Louis Viardot, who himself died on 5 May (new style) 1883. The two friends saw each other briefly when Turgenev was carefully transported to Bougival on 28 April. Worried about the state of his health, Pauline Viardot had telegraphed Annenkov, urging him to come and see Turgenev before it was too late; Annenkov came from Baden-Baden at the end of April for what was their last meeting. Turgenev himself, no longer able to write, dictated his final stories to Pauline Viardot: the account, in French, of the fire aboard the *Nicholas I* from his first trip to Berlin University in 1838 and "Une fin" (The End), a character sketch of Talagaev, a landowner whose behavior and attitudes had remained fundamentally unchanged despite the emancipation of the peasants, in a macaronic mixture of languages. In his chalet at Bougival, surrounded by the family he loved, Ivan Turgenev died on 3 September (22 August) 1883.

Formalities took a considerable time, but following a service in the Russian Orthodox Church on 6 September, on 1 October Turgenev's mortal remains began the long journey back to Russia. There was an impressive send-off from the Gare du Nord, attended by approximately four hundred people, among whom journalists noted Emile Zola and Alphonse Daudet, both of whom considered themselves influenced by Turgenev. The body was escorted to Russia by Stasiulevich and, representing the Viardot family, his favorite, Claudie, and her husband, Georges Chamerot. On 27 September (9 October) a huge crowd (including students from several institutions—classes had been canceled) lined the streets of St. Petersburg, carefully watched by wary police, to mark their respect and

Turgenev's grave in the Volkov Cemetery, St. Petersburg

salute the massive procession consisting of nearly 180 delegations (but no representatives of the government) that accompanied the bier to Turgenev's final resting place in the Volkov Cemetery.

Letters:

Nouvelle correspondance inédite, 2 volumes, edited by Alexandre Zviguilsky (Paris: Librairie des Cinq Continents, 1971–1973);

Lettres inédites à Pauline Viardot et à sa famille, edited by Henri Granjard and Zviguilsky (Lausanne: Editions L'Age d'Homme, 1972);

Letters, 2 volumes, translated, edited, and with an introduction by David Lowe (Ann Arbor, Mich.: Ardis, 1983);

Turgenev's Letters, selected, translated, edited, and with a preface by A. V. Knowles (London: Athlone Press, 1983);

Perepiska I. S. Turgeneva, 2 volumes (Moscow: Khudozhestvennaia literatura, 1986).

Bibliographies:

Rissa Yachnin and David H. Stam, *Turgenev in English. A Checklist of Works by and about Him* (New York: New York Public Library, 1962);

Bibliografiia literatury o I. S. Turgeneve 1918–1967 (Leningrad: Nauka, 1970);

N. N. Mostovskaia, "Bibliografiia literatury o I. S. Turgeneve. 1968–1974," in *Turgenev i ego sovremenniki* (Leningrad: Nauka, 1972), pp. 237–273;

Mostovskaia, "Bibliografiia literatury o I. S. Turgeneve. 1975–1979," in *Turgenev. Voprosy biografii i tvorchestva* (Leningrad: Nauka, 1982), pp. 224–252;

Katherina Filips-Juswigg and JoAnne Murphy, "Bibliography of Publications in English on I. S. Turgenev for 1965–80," Association of Russian-American Scholars in the USA, *Transactions,* 16 (1983): 347–353;

Allan J. Urbanic and Barbara T. Urbanic, comps., "Ivan Turgenev: Bibliography of Criticism in English, 1960–83," *Canadian-American Slavic Studies,* 17, no. 1 (1983): 118–143;

Nicholas G. Žekulin, *Turgenev. A Bibliography of Books 1843–1982 By and About Ivan Turgenev* (Calgary: University of Calgary Press, 1985);

Mostovskaia, "Bibliografiia literatury ob I. S. Turgeneve. 1980–1986," in *Turgenev. Voprosy biografii i tvorchestva* (Leningrad: Nauka, 1990), pp. 255–283;

Patrick Waddington, "A Bibliography of Writings by and about Turgenev, Published in Great Britain up to 1900," in his *Ivan Turgenev and Britain* (London & Providence, R.I.: Berg Publishers, 1995), pp. 213–240;

Waddington, "Select Chronological Bibliography of Writings on Turgenev, Published in Great Britain from 1901 to the Present," in his *Ivan Turgenev and Britain* (London & Providence, R.I.: Berg Publishers, 1995), pp. 241–252;

Žekulin, *Ivan Turgenev. An International Bibliography, 1983– .* (Ongoing electronic bibliography at <http://www.acs.ucalgary.ca/~zekulin/tbibl/index.html>).

Biographies:

Avrahm Yarmolinsky, *Turgenev, The Man, His Art and His Age* (New York: Century, 1926 / London: Hodder & Stoughton, 1927; revised edition, New York: Orion Press, 1959 / London: Deutsch & Toronto: Burns & MacEachern, 1960 / New York: Colliers, 1961);

M. K. Kleman, *Letopis' zhizni i tvorchestva I. S. Turgeneva* (Moscow-Leningrad: Academia, 1934);

David Magarshack, *Turgenev: A Life* (London: Faber & Faber, 1954; New York: Grove, 1954);

I. S. Turgenev v vospominaniiakh sovremennikov, 2 volumes (Moscow: Sovremennik, 1969; revised edition, Moscow: Khudozhestvennaia literatura, 1983);

V. S. Pritchett, *The Gentle Barbarian: The Life and Work of Turgenev* (London: Chatto & Windus / New York: Random House, 1977; New York: Random House, 1978);

Leonard Schapiro, *Turgenev. His Life and Times* (Oxford & Toronto: Oxford University Press / New York: Random House, 1978);

N. S. Nikitina, *Letopis' zhizni i tvorchestva I. S. Turgeneva (1818–1858)* (St. Petersburg: Nauka, 1995);

N. N. Mostovskaia, *Letopis' zhizni i tvorchestva I. S. Turgeneva (1867–1870)* (St. Petersburg: Nauka, 1997);

Mostovskaia, *Letopis' zhizni i tvorchestva I. S. Turgeneva (1871–1875)* (St. Petersburg: Nauka, 1998);

Patrick Waddington, *Turgenev's Mortal Illness from its Origins to the Autopsy* (Pinehaven, New Zealand: Whirinaki Press, 1999).

References:

M. P. Alekseev, "Turgenev–propagandist russkoi literatury na Zapade," in his *Izbrannye trudy,* volume 4 [t. IV] ("Russkaia kul'tura i ee mirovoe znachenie"), edited by V. N. Baskakov and N. S. Nikitina (Leningrad: Nauka, 1989), pp. 268–307;

Alekseev, ed., *I. S. Turgenev. Voprosy biografii i tvorchestva* (Leningrad: Nauka, 1982);

Alekseev, ed., *Turgenev i ego sovremenniki* (Leningrad: Nauka, 1977);

Alekseev, ed., *"Zapiski okhotnika" I. S. Turgeneva (1852–1952). Sbornik statei i materialov* (Orel: Orlovskaia pravda, 1955);

Elizabeth Cheresh Allen, *Beyond Realism: Turgenev's Poetics of Secular Salvation* (Stanford: Stanford University Press, 1992);

Joe Andrew, "The Lady Vanishes: A Feminist Reading of Turgenev's *Asya,*" *Irish Slavonic Studies,* no. 8 (1987): 87–96;

A. I. Batiuto, "Turgenev i Belinsky (K voprosu ob ideino-esteticheskikh sviaziakh)," *Russkaia literatura,* no. 2 (1984): 50–73;

Batiuto, *Turgenev–romanist* (Leningrad: Nauka, 1972);

Batiuto, *Tvorchestvo I. S. Turgeneva i kritiko-esteticheskaia mysl' ego vremeni* (Leningrad: Nauka, 1990);

Batiuto, "Vokrug epopei (I. S. Turgenev i L. N. Tolstoy v 1860–1870-e gody)," *Russkaia literatura,* no. 4 (1989): 28–52;

Isaiah Berlin, *Fathers and Children (Romanes Lecture 1970)* (Oxford: Clarendon Press, 1972);

G. A. Bialy, *Turgenev i russkii realizm* (Moscow-Leningrad: Sovetskii pisatel', 1962);

K. I. Bonetsky, ed., *Turgenev v russkoi kritike. Sbornik statei* (Moscow: Goslitizdat, 1953);

Peter Brang, "Turgenev and the -isms," *Russian Literature*, 16, no. 4 (1984): 305–322;

N. L. Brodsky, *Turgenev i russkie sektanty* (Moscow: Nikitinskie subbotniki, 1922);

Kenneth N. Brostrom, "The Heritage of Romantic Depictions of Nature in Turgenev," in P. Debreczeny, ed., *American Contributions to the IXth International Congress of Slavists* (Columbus, Ohio: Slavica, 1983), II: 81–95;

Brostrom, "The Journey as Solitary Confinement in *Fathers and Children*," *Canadian-American Slavic Studies*, 17, no. 1 (1983): 13–38;

N. F. Budanova, *Dostoevsky i Turgenev: Tvorcheskii dialog* (Leningrad: Nauka, 1987);

Budanova, *Roman I. S. Turgeneva Nov' i revoliutsionnoe narodnichestvo 1870-kh godov* (Leningrad: Nauka, 1983);

V. P. Burenin, *Literaturnaia deiatel'nost' I. S. Turgeneva. Kriticheskii etiud* (St. Petersburg: Suvorin, 1884);

Jane T. Costlow, "'Oh-là-là' and 'No-no-no': Odintsova as Woman Alone in *Fathers and Children*," in Sona Stephan Hoisington, ed., *A Plot of Her Own: The Female Protagonist in Russian Literature* (Evanston, Ill.: Northwestern University Press, 1995), pp. 21–32;

Costlow, *World Within Worlds: The Novels of Ivan Turgenev* (Princeton, N.J.: Princeton University Press, 1990);

R. Iu. Danilevsky, "'Nigilizm' (K istorii slova posle Turgeneva)," in N. N. Mostovskaia and N. S. Nikitina, eds., *I. S. Turgenev. Voprosy biografii i tvorchestva* (Leningrad: Nauka, 1990), pp. 150–156;

April FitzLyon, "I. S. Turgenev and the 'Woman' Question," *New Zealand Slavonic Journal* (1983): 161–173;

FitzLyon, "An Unpublished Novel by Turgenev?" Association of Russian-American Scholars in the USA, *Transactions*, 16 (1983): 213–224;

Richard Freeborn, "Bazarov as a Portrayal of a Doomed Revolutionary," *New Zealand Slavonic Journal* (1983): 71–83;

Freeborn, "Turgenev and Revolution," *Slavonic and East European Review*, 61, no. 4 (1983): 518–527;

Freeborn, *Turgenev: The Novelist's Novelist. A Study* (London: Oxford University Press, 1960);

M. O. Gershenzon, *Mechta i mysl' I. S. Turgeneva* (Moscow: Knigoizd-vo pisatelei v Moskve, 1919; reprinted as *Brown University Slavic Reprint*, 8, in Providence, R.I.: Brown University Press, 1970);

Royal Alfred Gettmann, *Turgenev in England and America* (Urbana: University of Illinois Press, 1941; reprinted, Westport, Conn.: Greenwood Press, 1974);

Henri Granjard, *Ivan Tourguénev, la comtesse Lambert et "Nid de Seigneurs"* (Paris: Institut d'Etudes Slaves, 1960);

L. D. Gromova (Opul'skaia), "Turgenev i Lev Tolstoy (Istoriia druzhby i polemiki)," in P. G. Pustovoit, *I. S. Turgenev i sovremennost'. Mezhdunarodnaia nauchnaia konferentsiia, posviashchennaia 175–letiiu so dnia rozhdeniia I. S. Turgeneva* (Moscow: Filologicheskii fakul'tet Moskovskogo gos. universiteta, 1997), pp. 11–19;

Joan Delaney Grossman, "Transformations of Time in Turgenev's Poetic," *Stanford Slavic Studies*, 4, no. 1 (1991): 382–400;

Boris Groys, "Tourguéniev et l'historique du nihilisme européen," *Cahiers Tourguéniev-Viardot-Malibran*, no. 7 (1983): 65–72;

Alekseï Guédroïtz, "Pushkinskie rechi Turgeneva i Dostoevskogo," Association of Russian-American Scholars in the USA, *Transactions*, 17 (1984): 253–260;

N. M. Gut'iar, *Ivan Sergeevich Turgenev* (Iur'ev: Tip. K. Mattisena, 1907);

Edmund Heier, "Duty and Inclination in Turgenev's 'Faust'," in John Whiton and Harry Loewen, eds., *Crisis and Commitment: Studies in German and Russian Literature in Honour of J. W. Dyck* (Waterloo, Ont.: University of Waterloo Press, 1983), pp. 78–86;

Ludmilla Hellgren, *Dialogues in Turgenev's Novels: Speech Introductory Devices* (Stockholm: Almqvist & Wiksell [*Stockholm Studies in Russian Literature*, 12], 1980);

Harry Hershkowitz, *Democratic Ideas in Turgenev's Works* (New York: Columbia University Press, 1932; reprinted, New York: AMS Press, 1973);

Michael Holquist, "Bazarov and Sečenov: The Role of Scientific Metaphor in *Fathers and Sons*," *Russian Literature*, 6, no. 4 (1984): 359–374;

Ulrich Huber-Noodt, *L'Occidentalisme d'Ivan Tourguénev* (Paris: Champion, 1922);

S. Hutchings, "Love of Words/Words of Love: Self-Sacrifice, Self-Identity and the Struggle with Dualism in Turgenev's *Rudin*," *The Slavonic & East European Review*, 76, no. 4 (1998): 614–632;

Eva Kagan-Kans, *"Hamlet and Don Quixote." Turgenev's Ambivalent Vision* (The Hague & Paris: Mouton [*Slavistic Printings and reprintings*, 288], 1975);

Rainer Kessler, *Zur Form und Kritik in I. S. Turgenevs "Zapiski ochotnika." Fünf Aufsätze* (Frankfurt am Main: Peter Lang, 1979);

R.-D. Kluge, "Sektanstvo i problema smerti v 'Zapiskakh okhotnika' I. S. Turgeneva," *Slavica*, 23 (1986): 25–36;

A. V. Knowles, *Ivan Turgenev* (Boston: Twayne, 1988);

W. Koschmal, *Von Realismus zum Symbolismus. Zu Genese und Morphologie der Symbolsprache in den späten Werken I.S. Turgenevs* (Amsterdam: Rodopi [*Studies in Slavic Literature and Poetics,* 5], 1984);

G. B. Kurliandskaia, *Metod i stil' Turgeneva-romanista* (Tula: Priokskoe knizhnoe izd-vo, 1967);

Iu. V. Lebedev, "Prekhodiashchee i vechnoe v khudozhestvennom mirosozertsanii I. S. Turgeneva," in *I. S. Turgenev: mirovozrenie i tvorchestvo, problemy izucheniia. Mezhuzovskii sbornik nauchnykh trudov* (Orel: Min-vo Prosveshcheniia RSFSR; OGPI, 1991), pp. 3–10;

Nicholas Lee, "Exposure to European Culture and Self-Discovery for Russians and Americans in the Fiction of Ivan Turgenev and Henry James," in P. Debreczeny, ed., *American Contributions to the IXth International Congress of Slavists* (Columbus, Ohio: Slavica, 1983), II: 267–283;

V. Ia. Linkov, "Romany Turgeneva i roman epopeia L. Tolstogo *Voina i mir,*" *Izvestiia Akademii nauk SSSR. Seriia literatury i iazyka,* 42, no. 6 (1983): 515–524;

Literaturnoe nasledstvo, 73 (2 parts: "Iz parizhskogo arkhiva I. S. Turgeneva"); 76 ("I. S. Turgenev. Novye materialy i issledovaniia") (Moscow: Nauka, 1964; 1967);

David Lowe, *Turgenev's* Fathers and Sons (Ann Arbor, Mich.: Ardis, 1983);

Lowe, ed., *Critical Essays on Ivan Turgenev* (Boston, Mass.: G. K. Hall, 1988);

Iu. V. Mann, "I. S. Turgenev i vechnye obrazy mirovoi literatury (Stat'ia Turgeneva 'Gamlet i Don-Kikhot')," *Izvestiia Akademii nauk SSSR. Seriia literatury i iazyka,* 43, no. 1 (1984): 22–32;

V. M. Markovich, *Chelovek v romanakh I. S. Turgeneva* (Leningrad: Izd-vo Leningradskogo gos. universiteta, 1975);

Irene Masing-Delic, "The Metaphysics of Liberation: Insarov as Tristan," *Welt der Slaven,* 32 (N.F. XI), no. 1 (1987): 59–77;

Masing-Delic, "Philosophy, Myth and Art in Turgenev's *Notes of a Hunter,*" *Russian Review,* 50, no. 4 (1991): 437–450;

Masing-Delic, "Schopenhauer's Metaphysics of Music and Turgenev's *Dvorjanskoe gnezdo,*" *Welt der Slaven,* 31, no. 1 (1986), (N.F. X, 1): 183–196;

Sigrid McLaughlin, *Schopenhauer in Ruland: Zur literarischen Rezeption bei Turgenev* (Wiesbaden: Harrassowitz, 1984);

John Mersereau, Jr., "Don Quixote-Bazarov-Hamlet," in P. Debreczeny, ed., *American Contributions to the IXth International Congress of Slavists* (Columbus, Ohio: Slavica, 1983), II: 345–355;

N. N. Mostovskaia and N. S. Nikitina, eds., *I. S. Turgenev. Voprosy biografii i tvorchestva* (Leningrad: Nauka, 1990);

A. B. Muratov, *I. S. Turgenev posle "Ottsov i detei" (60-ye gody)* (Leningrad: Leningradskii gos. universitet, 1971);

Muratov, *Povesti i rasskazy I. S. Turgeneva 1867–1871* (Leningrad: Leningradskii gos. universitet, 1980);

Muratov, *Turgenev-novellist (1870–1880-e gg)* (Leningrad: Leningradskii gos. universitet, 1985);

E. Naiman, "Ne grešno li èto želanie?: *Nakanune,* Failure, and the Psychopoetics of Literary Evolution," *Wiener Slawistischer Almanach,* 31 ("Psychopoetik. Beiträge zur Tagung «Psychologie und Literatur»") (Munich: 1991), pp. 101–116;

L. N. Nazarova, *Turgenev i russkaia literatura kontsa XIX–nachala XX vv.* (Leningrad: Nauka, 1979);

Michael Nierle, *Die Naturschilderung und ihre Funktion in Versdichtung und Prosa von I. S. Turgenev. Studien zur Geschichte der russischen Literatur des 19. Jahrhunderts* (Bad Homburg, Berlin & Zurich: Gehlen, 1969);

N. S. Nikitina, "I. S. Turgenev nakanune razryva s *Sovremennikom,*" *Russkaia literatura,* no. 3 (1987): 151–157;

N. Noskov and G. Tumin, comps., *Slovar' literaturnykh tipov,* volume 1: *Turgenev* (St. Petersburg: Vskhody, 1908);

L. N. Os'makova, "'Tainstvennye' povesti i rasskazy I. S. Turgeneva v kontekste estestvenno-nauchnykh otkrytii vtoroi poloviny XIX veka," Nauchnye doklady vysshei shkoly, *Filologicheskie nauki,* 139, no. 1 (1984): 9–13;

Jochen-Ulrich Peters, *Turgenevs "Zapiski ochotnika" innerhalb der očerk-Tradition der 40-er Jahre. Zur Entwicklung des realistischen Erzählens in Russland* (Berlin & Wiesbaden: Harrassowitz, 1972);

Dale E. Peterson, "From Russia with Love: Turgenev's Maidens and Howell's Heroines," *Canadian Slavonic Papers,* 26, no. 1 (1984): 24–34;

P. G. Pustovoit, *I. S. Turgenev–khudozhnik slova* (Moscow: Izd-vo Moskovskogo gos. universiteta, 1987);

Victor Ripp, *Turgenev's Russia. From* Notes of a Hunter *to* Fathers and Sons (Ithaca, N.Y. & London: Cornell University Press, 1980);

Hugo Tauno Salonen, *Die Landschaft bei I. S. Turgenev* (Helsingfors: Kirjapaino-Osakeyhtiö Sana, 1915);

Frank Friedeberg Seeley, *Turgenev: A Reading of His Fiction,* Cambridge Studies in Russian Literature (Cambridge, New York, Port Chester, Melbourne & Sydney: Cambridge University Press, 1991);

I. S. Shatalov, ed., *I. S. Turgenev v sovremennom mire. Sbornik statei* (Moscow: Nauka, 1987);

Shatalov, ed., *Khudozhestvennyi mir I. S. Turgeneva* (Moscow: Nauka, 1979);

I. Sukhikh, comp., *Roman I. S. Turgeneva* Ottsy i deti *v russkoi kritike. Sbornik statei* (Leningrad: Izd-vo Leningradskogo gos. universiteta, 1986);

Peter Thiergen, *Lavreckij als "Potenzierter Bauer": Zu Ideologie und Bildsprache in I. S. Turgenevs Roman* Das Adelnest (Munich: Verlag Otto Sagner, 1989).

Thiergen, "Turgenevs *Dym:* Titel und Thema," in *Bausteine zur Geschichte der Literatur bei den Slaven,* 18 (Köln & Wien: Böhlau Verlag, 1983), pp. 277–311;

Thiergen, "Zum Problem des Nihilismus in I. S. Turgenev's Roman *Väter und Söhne," Die Welt der Slaven,* 38 (N.F. 17), 2 (1993): 343–359; also in *Russkaia Literatura,* no. 1 (1993): 37–47;

A. G. Tseitlin, *Masterstvo Turgeneva-romanista* (Moscow: Sovetskii pisatel', 1958);

Turgenevskii sbornik. Materialy k Polnomu sobraniiu sochinenii i pisem I. S. Turgeneva, 5 volumes (Leningrad: Nauka, 1964–1969);

Glyn Turton, *Turgenev and the Context of English Literature 1850–1900* (London & New York: Routledge, 1992);

Semen Vengerov, *Russkaia literatura v ee sovremennykh predstaviteliakh. Kritiko-biograficheskie etiudy. I. S. Turgenev* (St. Petersburg: Tip. Vil'kina i Ettingera, 1875);

Patrick Waddington, "No Smoke Without Fire: The Genesis of Turgenev's *Dym,*" in Arnold McMillin, ed., *From Pushkin to* Palisandriia: *Essays on the Russian Novel in Honour of Richard Freeborn* (New York: St. Martin's Press, 1990), pp. 112–127;

Waddington, "The Role of Courtavenel in the Life and Work of Turgenev," in J. Douglas Clayton, ed., *Issues in Russian Literature before 1917* (Columbus, Ohio: Slavica Publishers, 1989), pp. 107–132;

Waddington, "Turgenev and Pauline Viardot: An Unofficial Marriage," *Canadian Slavonic Papers,* 26, no. 1 (1984): 42–64;

Edward Wasiolek, "Bazarov and Odintsova," *Canadian-American Slavic Studies,* 17, no. 1 (1983): 39–48;

Wasiolek, Fathers and Sons. *Russia at the Crossroads* (New York: Twayne, 1993);

James B. Woodward, "*Aut Caesar aut nihil:* The 'War of Wills' in Turgenev's *Ottsy i deti,*" *Slavonic and East European Review,* 64, no. 2 (1986): 161–188;

Woodward, "Hamlet, Don Quixote, and the Turgenevian Novel," *Die Welt der Slaven,* 34, no. 1 (1989): 58–69;

Woodward, *Metaphysical Conflict: A Study of the Major Novels of Ivan Turgenev* (Munich: Verlag Otto Sagner, 1990);

Woodward, "The 'Roman Theme' in Turgenev's *Nov',*" in his *Form and Meaning: Essays on Russian Literature* (Columbus, Ohio: Slavica Publishers, 1993), pp. 94–105, 339–341;

Woodward, "Turgenev's 'Constancy' in His Final Novel," in Arnold McMillin, ed., *From Pushkin to* Palisandriia: *Essays on the Russian Novel in Honour of Richard Freeborn* (New York: St. Martin's Press, 1990), pp. 128–148;

Woodward, *Turgenev's* Fathers and Sons (Bristol: Bristol Classical Press, 1996);

Woodward, "Turgenev's 'New Manner' in His Novel *Dym,*" in his *Form and Meaning: Essays on Russian Literature* (Columbus, Ohio: Slavica Publishers, 1993), pp. 75–93, 337–339;

Nicholas G. Žekulin, "P. V. Annenkov i *Ottsy i deti,*" *Russkaia literatura,* no. 1 (1998): 3–15;

V. Zelinsky, comp., *Sobranie kriticheskikh materialov dlia izucheniia proizvedenii I. S. Turgeneva,* 2 volumes (Moscow, 1905–1908);

Zs. Zöldhelyi-Deák, "'Stikhotvoreniia v proze' I. S. Turgeneva. K probleme zhanra," *Russkaia literatura,* no. 2 (1990): 188–194;

Zöldhelyi-Deák, "Turgenev i novye khudozhestvennye iskaniia v kontse XIX–nachale XX veka," *Studia Russica* (Budapest), 6 (1983): 113–123.

Papers:

Ivan Sergeevich Turgenev's papers are widely scattered; the largest collections are in the Bibliothèque Nationale (Paris), the Institute of Russian Literature (Pushkin House) of the Russian Academy of Sciences (St. Petersburg), the Russian National Library (St. Petersburg), and the State Literary Museum (Moscow). Descriptions of these collections (not entirely up-to-date) are to be found in André Mazon, *Manuscrits parisiens d'Ivan Tourguénev. Notices et Extraits* (Paris: Champion, 1930); *Biulletin Gosudarstvennogo Literaturnogo muzeia, No. 1: I. S. Turgenev. Rukopisi, perepiska, dokumenty* (Moscow: Zhurnal'no-gazetnoe ob"edinenie, 1935); Gos. Publichnaia biblioteka, *Trudy Otdela rukopisei: Rukopisi I. S. Turgeneva. Opisanie* (Leningrad: 1953); and *Opisanie rukopisei i izobrazitel'nykh materialov Pushkinskogo doma,* volume 4: I. S. Turgenev (Moscow-Leningrad: Izd-vo Akademii Nauk SSSR, 1958).

Marko Vovchok
(Mariia Aleksandrovna Vilinskaia)
(10 December 1833 – 28 July 1907)

Jane Costlow
Bates College

WORKS: *Narodni opovidannia* (St. Petersburg: P. A. Kulish, 1858 [1857]); volume 2 (St. Petersburg, 1862); published in part in the author's translation from Ukrainian to Russian in *Russkii vestnik,* nos. 13–15 (1858); no. 3 (1859); translated into Russian by Ivan Sergeevich Turgenev as *Ukrainskie narodnye rasskazy* (St. Petersburg: Izd. Kozhanchikova, 1859); translated by N. Pedan-Popil as *Ukrainian Folk Stories,* edited by H. B. Timothy (Saskatoon: Western Producer Prairie Books, 1983);

Rasskazy iz narodnogo russkogo byta (Moscow: Izd. K. Soldatenkova i N. Shchepkina, 1859);

Institutka, translated into Russian by Turgenev in *Otechestvennye zapiski,* 1 (1860); translated by Oles Kovalenko as *After Finishing School* (Kiev: Dnipro, 1983);

Novye povesti i rasskazy (St. Petersburg: Izd. D. Kozhanchikova, 1861);

Povistki (narodni opovidannia) (St. Petersburg: Izd. N. Tiblena, 1861–1862);

Skazki (St. Petersburg, 1864);

Opovidannia (St. Petersburg, 1865);

Sochineniia, 3 volumes (St. Petersburg: I. Papin, 1867);

Zhivaia dusha. Roman, in *Otechestvennye zapiski,* 1–3, 5 (1868); (St. Petersburg, 1868);

Zapiski prichetnika, in *Otechestvennye zapiski,* 9–12 (1869); 10–11 (1870);

Sochineniia, 4 volumes (St. Petersburg: I. Papin, 1870–1874);

Sbornik rasskazov v proze i stikhakh. (St. Petersburg: Tip. A. M. Kotomina, 1871);

Skazki i byl' (St. Petersburg: Tip. A. A. Kraevskogo, 1874);

V glushi. Roman, in *Otechestvennye zapiski,* 7–10, 12 (1875); (St. Petersburg, 1876);

Marusia. Povest' (St. Petersburg: Izd. Spb. Kom. Gram., 1896);

Polnoe sobranie sochinenii, 8 volumes (Saratov: Izd. knizhnogo magazina "Saratovskogo dnevnika," 1896–1898).

Editions and Collections: *Narodnye rasskazy i skazki* (Moscow, 1954);

Rasskazy iz narodnogo russkogo byta. Zhivaia dusha; roman. (Kiev: Khudozhestvennaia literatura, 1954);

Sobranie sochinenii, 3 volumes (Moscow, 1957);

Tvori, 7 volumes (Kiev: Naukova dumka, 1964–1967);

Izbrannoe: Rasskazy, povesty, skazki (Moscow: Khudozhestvennaia literatura, 1976);

Narodni pisni v zapisakh Vovchok (Kiev, 1979);

Tvori, 2 volumes (Kiev: Naukova dumka, 1983);

Narodni opovidannia (Kiev: Drukarnia Petra Bars'koho, 1983);

Fol'klorni zapysy Marka Vovchka ta Opanasa Markovycha (Kiev: Naukova dumka, 1983);

Tiulevaia baba. Rasskazy. Povesti. Skazki (Moscow: Khudozhestvennaia literatura, 1984).

Editions in English: *Melasia and the Bear,* translated by Mary Skrypnyk (Kiev: Veselka, 1980);

Karmelyuk: A Tale, translated by Oles Kovalenko (Kiev: Dnipro, 1981).

SELECTED PERIODICAL PUBLICATIONS:
"Chervonnyi korol'," *Russkii vestnik,* 3 (1860);

"Likhoi chelovek," *Russkii vestnik,* 1 (1861);

"Zhili da byli tri sestry," *Sovremennik,* 9, 11 (1861);

"Glukhoi gorodok," *Russkoe slovo,* 2 (1862);

"Puteshestvie vo vnutr' strany," *Otechestvennye zapiski,* 4 (1871);

"Teploe gnezdyshko. Povest'," *Otechestvennye zapiski,* 6–7 (1873).

Marko Vovchok (born Mariia Aleksandrovna Vilinskaia) was a writer of short stories and novels in Russian and Ukrainian who achieved some prominence in the mid-nineteenth century as the author of peasant tales and satirical accounts of the Russian gentry. Vovchok also worked as an editor at *Otechestvennye zapiski* (Notes of the Fatherland) and elsewhere, and she was active as a translator of at least five languages. Closely bound up in the literary life of her day, she was the addressee of poems by Taras Shevchenko and Nikolai Alekseevich Nekrasov. Briefly championed by mid-nineteenth-century radical critics as an important voice in the chorus of "denunciatory prose," Vovchok was uneven in her achievement as a writer. Her prose and its reception nonetheless suggest some of the intense forces at work in mid-nineteenth-century Russia and the ways in which ideological concerns came to impinge upon literary careers.

Mariia Aleksandrovna Vilinskaia was born on 10 December 1833 into a family of mixed Polish-Ukrainian-Russian lineage and spent much of her early life in the region of Orel, in central European Russia. Her father was an army officer; her mother's family were provincial gentry. After her father's death in 1840 Vilinskaia was educated as a "poor relation" in the homes of two different aunts and briefly in a private school for girls (one of the "closed institutes," the educational merits of which she later satirized in *Institutka* [The Institute Girl, 1860]) in Kharkov. While Orel is associated in the literary his-

tory of this period with a whole host of cultural luminaries–Ivan Sergeevich Turgenev, Nikolai Semenovich Leskov, Dmitrii Ivanovich Pisarev, Afanasii Afanas'evich Fet, and Timofei Nikolaevich Granovsky, among others–the life of a provincial "backwater" is depicted in unrelentingly dismal tones in Vilinskaia's prose. Small provincial towns in her later novels are hothouses of petty vanities, oppressive and stifling to the few souls who rise above concerns with career and successful marriage.

Vilinskaia's own biography, however, departed sharply from the trajectory of such plots in her novels. In the mid 1850s Orel became the settling place for many Ukrainian nationalists, who had been exiled from Ukraine in the wake of the suppression of intellectual circles fighting for national and cultural dignity. Among them was A. Markovich, an ethnographer and champion of Ukrainian culture. Vilinskaia met and fell in love with Markovich; the pair married in 1851 and traveled together to the environs of Kiev, where Markovich continued his work as an ethnographer. In this period Vilinskaia (now Markovich) herself began ethnographic work, which led clearly into her work as the author of short fiction. Settled in a small village, traveling throughout the rural settlements around Kiev, she gathered songs and stories from Ukrainian peasant women. While this work was conceived initially as part of broader efforts to retrieve and celebrate national cultural heritage, the experience led her in the late 1850s to write the first of her "peasant stories," tales in two languages (the first in Ukrainian, the second in Russian) that draw on ethnography and oral traditions but offer sharp denunciations of serfdom and class inequity. At this point she adopted the pen name Marko Vovchok. The Ukrainian-language *Narodni opovidannia* (Tales from Ukrainian Life) was published as a small volume of stories in late 1857–early 1858. The stories appeared in the author's own Russian translation in *Russkii vestnik* during 1858. Turgenev's translation was published in Russian in 1859 as *Ukrainskie narodnye rasskazy.*

Vovchok's tales are marked by the particularities of their narrative form: each story is narrated by a peasant woman, whose diction is sprinkled with the lilting, alliterative qualities of stylized folk speech. These women tell tales of love, loss, separation, and the abuses of unrestrained power: most frequently the "masters" are the means of separating young lovers, but the forces ranged against happiness seem occasionally even more encompassing, as when plotting stepmothers and elders interfere. By and large in these stories, however, the powers of good and evil are clearly demarcated: landowners are willfull and

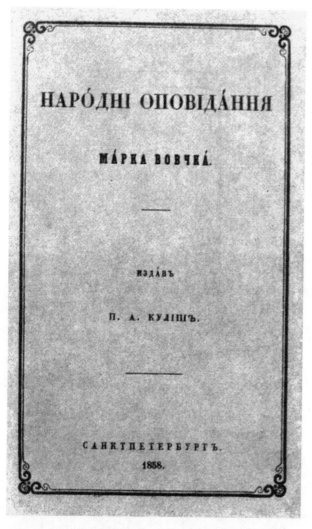

Title page for the first volume of Vovchok's Narodni opovidannia
*(Tales from Ukrainian Life), the work that established
her literary reputation*

a closet, her hair cut off) suggests an almost gothic sensibility. (One of Vovchok's biographers indeed mentions that Anne Radcliffe was one of Vovchok's favorite authors in childhood.) The gentry estates of these stories are monstrous enclosures of human emotion and potential; there is never any way out: the controlling powers are too all-encompassing and too brutal. "Igrushechka" (The Plaything) is perhaps paradigmatic in this regard: the peasant girl stolen from her mother and brought to the manor house as a "plaything" for the master's daughter tells a story of darkness, death, separation, and defeat. The master's daughter is briefly awakened by the serf girl's stories of another way of life, but that awakening is stifled by her parents, and she fades slowly into illness, which is clearly symptomatic of the stifling of spirit. The serf girl, meanwhile, falls in love with a kind peasant, but their love is dashed when the masters are forced to sell the estate to an unscrupulous new owner. Love never ends well in these stories, and promises of a new consciousness are either stifled or snuffed out.

Vovchok's stories made her reputation as a writer and elicited both high praise and significant critical controversy. Published at a moment of intense anticipation and dispute over what was to be the fate of serfdom in Russia, the stories became occasions for disputes that were both aesthetic and political. Radical critics—including such major figures as Aleksandr Ivanovich Herzen and Nikolai Aleksandrovich Dobroliubov—hailed Vovchok as a compelling voice in the battle for human rights. More moderate liberalizing forces also acknowledged the power of the stories, as when Ivan Turgenev—virtually identified with the difficult terrain of "moderate" politics in pre-Emancipation Russia and himself an undisputed master of Russian prose—translated Vovchok's Ukrainian tales into Russian. The storm surrounding the stories was intensified by the appearance of an impassioned essay in *Vremia* (Time) titled "G–n –bov i vopros ob iskusstve" (Mr. –Bov and the Question of Art, 1861) by the young Fyodor Dostoevsky, just recently returned from imprisonment and exile in Siberia. Dostoevsky's essay uses Vovchok's stories as grounds to attack the radical camp in the person of Dobroliubov; for Dostoevsky, the most damning thing about the stories is what he perceived as their estrangement from real Russian peasant life. Vovchok's peasants, Dostoevsky claims, smack of European pastoral and bear no resemblance to the "true" Russian peasantry. Radical critics' championing of the stories turned indeed less on the high aesthetic merits of the stories than on their spirited attempts at denunciation of injustice. Vovchok's nar-

evil, petty monsters of caprice, while the peasantry are noble and downtrodden, capable of firm loyalties and strong emotion. Thus, in "Masha" the quick-witted heroine resists her situation by feigning sickness; her tyrannical mistress calls her a fool, while those in her own village are uncomprehending at her disinclination to work; in "Nadezhda" peasant lovers are separated by the machinations of an evil woman from another village; and in "Sasha" the mistress's son falls in love with a serf girl, professes his willingness to defy conventions and marry, but ultimately capitulates to parental and societal pressures and abandons his pregnant beloved.

In many of these stories the peasant women's powerful but repressed emotions lead to illness and even death; the prevalence of motifs of enclosure and incarceration (the heroine of "Sasha" is locked up in

ratives thus were quickly swept up in the "accursed questions" of mid-century Russian criticism, a stance of denunciation and subordination of aesthetic to political concerns that the narratives themselves make abundantly evident.

While Turgenev's own "peasant tales" may indeed be seen as models of a sort for Vovchok's stories of Ukrainian and Russian peasant life, in terms of style her stories are more markedly influenced by folk traditions in diction and imagery, and their narrative strategies are far simpler than Turgenev's *Zapiski okhotnika* (A Hunter's Notes, 1847–1851). Turgenev's stories are narrated by a gentry hunter whose political and human allegiances are muted and complex, but Vovchok adopts a narrative voice that is much more clearly denunciatory. Like Turgenev a member of the gentry, Vovchok nonetheless takes on in her short narratives the voice of a peasant woman, drawing on stylizations of peasant diction from oral poetry. Her stories were a part of the movement to "humanize" the peasant through narratives that demonstrate that the capacity for humanity lodges more deeply in the heart of the peasantry than in the cold egos of the gentry. Contemporary critics' descriptions ranged from "poetic" to "saccharine" in characterizing the tone of Vovchok's prose. Sentimental and relatively simplistic, the stories nonetheless struck a strong chord in a society deeply engaged in a debate over social structures and human potential.

Vovchok's career as a writer began with this early success as a writer of short narratives grounded in sentimentalized native traditions; her subsequent prose continued in this vein, though much less intensely. Beginning in the spring of 1859 Vovchok began a series of travels that kept her abroad for the next eight years. After visits to Dresden, London, Ostend, Brussels, Heidelberg, and Switzerland in 1859–1860, in the fall of 1860 she settled in Paris, where she lived until 1867, building a circle of both French and Russian acquaintances that included Leo Tolstoy, Evgeniia Tur, and Nikolai Aleksandrovich Dobroliubov (whom she met on a trip to Italy). While abroad, Vovchok continued to write short fiction (stories, novellas), some of which focused on the lives of Russian peasants, but she also attempted to extend her range to longer forms and other topics; her aesthetic and style in these works owes much more to nascent Realism than to the romanticized oral traditions of Ukraine and peasant Russia. In a series of novellas and novels written in the early 1860s, Vovchok focuses on the grotesque vanities of the rural gentry of Russia, sometimes structuring her plot around a "positive" figure (frequently a heroine) whose alienation from this milieu is intense. The

impetus away from "peasant" prose toward satirical accounts of provincial gentry and the narrative "search" for a positive hero or heroine was conditioned at least in part by broader cultural and political forces. Social critics' attention shifted after 1861 away from the peasantry (now nominally liberated from serfdom) toward the educated sectors of Russian society, whose capacity for action and radical reform of their lives was seen as key to broader changes. Radical critics in the late 1850s received Vovchok's work enthusiastically and laid claim to her as a "progressive" writer, a role she was clearly determined to fill.

The themes and strategies of Vovchok's peasant tales are still apparent in *Institutka,* which, like the earlier stories, narrates an insider's view of the petty tyrannies of estate women's lives. The "institutka" is a spoiled young woman who has completed her education at one of the elite closed institutes for women; she returns to the estate to torment the narrator and ultimately to bring down ruin on her dreams of happiness and marriage. "Likhoi chelovek" (A Person with Flair, 1861) explores the "dual suitor" plot from the vantage point of the peasantry when a village girl's affections shift from the stolid but kind Mikailo to the much more dashing Petr. The denouement of the story is once again tragic: the spirited Petr is evidently not made for the settled role of husband, and he becomes a *beglets*—a vagabond or runaway—who on a final return to his native village kills his wife. Confessing to the murder, he says only that life with her was "a burden"; the story ends in rumors that he has ended his own life on the road to Siberia, having worn himself out with sorrow for the woman he killed. The story repeats the motifs of love tormented, challenged, and abandoned but suggests a different chain of responsibility, and torment as much inner as outwardly imposed.

In other stories written in this period Vovchok explores the lives of women on Russian gentry estates, as well as the lives of women who live at the mercy of wealthy relatives, as she herself had as a young woman in Orel. The possibilities for women in these stories are enormously restricted, and even the happy denouements remain conventional. In "Chervonnyi korol'" (King of Hearts, 1860) a young woman's "enclosure" is both spatial and psychic: trapped within the expectations of a conventional woman's life and manipulated by her aunt's matrimonial scheming, the bride-to-be sinks into a kind of madness symbolized by her obsessive laying out of cards, a form of fortune-telling, in which she seeks endlessly for the promised "king of hearts." In this story as elsewhere in Vovchok's stories, superstition and gaming become important motifs in the author's critique of gentry women's elegant entrapment. In "Glukhoi gorodok" (A God-Forsaken Town, 1862) Nastia, the heroine, is brought up by a wealthy aunt and uncle determined to marry her off to a wealthy, older merchant. Nastia finds refuge in an otherwise wholly inhospitable world in the home and garden of an elderly townswoman. When Nastia and the woman's son fall in love and plan to marry, Nastia's relatives lock her up at their country estate and scheme to thwart the couple's plans. Nastia's beloved suitor manages to rescue her, and the couple are married. The motif of enclosure and escape is used again in this narrative, but with a happier denouement than those found elsewhere in Vovchok's prose.

The satirical element, however, comes to dominate Vovchok's prose of the 1860s and 1870s in a series of narratives, both short and long, which depict the foibles and frivolities of provincial Russian society in the period of post-Emancipation reforms. Vovchok's cast of unpromising characters hardly leaves readers optimistic about the possibilities for any deeper transformation of Russian society. The plot of escape, which continues to appear in these narratives, is shown to work desperately against forces deeply entrenched and almost irrationally hostile to emancipation.

Vovchok meanwhile had returned to Russia in February of 1867, and she quickly reimmersed herself in Russian literary life. She worked as editor of the foreign literature section of *Otechestvennye zapiski* (1868–1870) and later edited the journal *Perevody luchshikh inostrannykh pisatelei* (Translations of the Best Foreign Writers, 1871–1872).

While the satirical vein in Vovchok's work is most evident in her novels *Zhivaia dusha* (A Living Soul, 1868), *Zapiski prichetnika* (Clerical Notes, 1869–1870), and *V glushi* (In the Hinterland, 1875), satire—which contemporary critics noted as a move on her part toward Realism—dominates in other shorter work from this period as well. "Puteshestvie vo vnutr' strany" (A Journey into the Heartland, 1871) uses the space of a second-class train car to assemble a group of Russians representative of various social and political persuasions—a conservative apologist for Slavdom; assorted merchants and bureaucratic bootlickers; and an emancipee, who voices, with shrill obviousness, didactic outrage when she expresses dismay at one passenger's purchase of an orange in the presence of an impoverished elderly woman. While the work begins with sprightly and pointed sparring among the travelers, the voice of denunciation that comes to predominate levels the narrative into predictability and shrillness, its own

polemic as desperate and insistent as that of the indignant and embattled emancipee.

The theme of gentry women's lives and of the possibilities of escape from conventional "plots" for women is most explicitly and extensively developed in Vovchok's *Zhivaia dusha*. The novel combines vitriolic satire of the provincial gentry with the plot of a young woman's liberation from that milieu. Masha, the heroine of the novel, lives as a dependent with her aunt in the provincial city of "N–," a city and a household inhabited seemingly exclusively by hypocritical and petty types, whose verbal allegiance to Russia and freedom in no way unsettles the domestic comforts of the existing order, from which they all apparently benefit. Masha is serious, even stern, and ill at ease in this milieu (motifs familiar to contemporary readers from a novel such as Turgenev's *Nakanune* [On the Eve, 1860]); she is determined to leave the nest of hypocrisy and comfort behind and find her own way in the world. Her determination to leave is strengthened by the arrival on the scene of a mysterious male outsider whose speech marks him at once as actively committed to the cause (vaguely stated—perhaps for reasons of censorship—but obviously allied to progressive concerns). Masha's departure from her aunt's home brings down wrath and opprobrium on the heroine; she, however, is undeterred and unmoved by her aunt's hysterical reactions and supports herself in modest accommodations through sewing and tutoring a merchant's children. Throughout the novel she spurns the advances of various eligible bachelors (the novel begins with a rare moment of levity and the sprightly presentation of a "dual suitor" plot); the novel closes with a glimpse of domestic happiness attained with the "mysterious stranger" of the novel, Zagainy, in whom intellectual and political goals have been reconciled. The implications of the ending are that in this marriage Masha has discovered neither enclosure nor ill-gained comfort but an oasis of love that will aid the labors of political change. Thus, the marriage plot, so aggressively refuted in the actions of the novel (and in a series of references to the "fairy tales" with which society entices women into subservience), is redeemed in its ending, with a vision of new revolutionary matrimony.

The differences between this novel and Vovchok's earlier, shorter prose are instructive and striking. *Zhivaia dusha* differs from the stories not only in length—the novel displays a propensity for turgid accounts of petulant provincial lamentations that hardly sustain the reader's interest—but in point of view. Whereas the early stories are all told through the eyes of peasant narrators (many of whom are women), *Zhivaia dusha* adopts the device of an omniscient narrator, although Vovchok's commitment to the narrator's voice seems to waver. In the early chapters of the novel the narrator is witty and sharp, almost playful. The opening chapter, after quickly drawing a portrait of the city of N–, moves into Masha's aunt's drawing room presided over by the young girl Katia and her cat, "Drug" (Friend). The early chapters promise a narrative that will be as lively as Katia, playful and leavened with antics that show up the pomposity of the world around her without being too didactic. The spirit of Katia, however, soon cedes to the spirit of Masha: serious and stern. Vovchok's omniscient narrator quickly adopts what is essentially Masha's point of view, with a correspondingly more judgmental and rigid perspective. The loss of humor–and of a point of view outside that of the one-dimensional, dogmatic heroine–is a loss for the novel as a whole. Indeed, one of the lamentable consequences of Masha's departure from her aunt's house is the abrupt decline of Katia, who clearly suffers deeply at the loss of a young woman "role model" in an otherwise stifling house. The overly stern, judgmental character of Masha suffers for its severing from the liveliness of Katia.

Zapiski prichetnika, published in heavily censored form in 1869–1870, was Vovchok's last major literary work. The novel is justly regarded as an anticlerical novel (its distinctly negative portrait of the clergy occasioning its treatment by the censor), but in narrative form it represents an interesting variation on Vovchok's other satirical, "denunciatory" prose. Written in the first person, the novel presents the world of the provincial Orthodox clergy (priests and their families, deacons, cantors, and the "white" or monastic clergy) as seen through the eyes of a young boy, nine years old as the work begins. The Russia of the novel is as dominated as that of any Vovchok narrative by obtuseness, petty vanities, and insatiable tyrants. In this particular provincial corner, the priest's wife's despotic whims take center stage; her husband's misdemeanors and corrupt behavior are more hidden, though more fundamental, since they bespeak a deeply malignant religious authority. The boy narrator witnesses the wife's shrill outbreaks and his parents' obsequious deferrals to ecclesiastical authority. The complications of the plot, such as they are, are introduced by the arrival of a young deacon of higher moral standards who has the strength of character to stand up to the corrupt priest. The priest's daughter–the object of the boy's childish affections–has managed not to inherit her mother's shrewishness and has clear (to the reader) sympathies for the deacon who stands up to her father.

Vovchok in 1903

When the couple's wanderings in the woods are found out, the father-priest packs them both off to points unknown, actions that quite undo the young narrator. Both objects of affection and moral strength in an otherwise bleak spiritual landscape have been taken from him. After his mother's death (another "blow of fate"), he comes through a series of circumstances to set off for a distant monastery as the charge of a priest who is victim to fits and visions. When the boy arrives, he discovers an unspeakably corrupt monastic institution–but also (to his surprise, if not the discerning reader's) the deacon who had been so abruptly spirited away.

The novel is incomplete and leaves the reader hanging at this moment of reunion (wondering still where the priest's daughter might be). The maneuvers of melodrama, in both plot and character, are evident in this novel: the priest's wife is drawn with cartoonish extremity, and the power of evil personages over the innocent is, despite the deacon's fortitude, incontrovertible. As the boy says at one point, "the good are always lost." The power of darkness in this microcosmic corner of Russia is absolute.

What distinguishes *Zapiski prichetnika* from Vovchok's other longer prose–from *Zhivaia dusha* in particular–is her choice of narrative strategy, the element of the novel that is perhaps most successful. The voice of the narrator (himself an ecclesiastic, of modest position) remembering the events of his boyhood is more nuanced than that of *Zhivaia dusha* and harks back in a formal sense to Vovchok's early stories, which were all told in the first person. The narrator of *Zapiski prichetnika* is both voyeur (watching events in the priest's courtyard through a convenient hole in the fence) and participant; through him, Vovchok grants some of her characters–most notably the boy's father–sympathy and a measure of understanding. The boy's father is well-intentioned but weak, and when he signs a letter of betrayal that seals the renegade deacon's fate, the boy is put in the difficult position of condemning emotionally the actions of a man he nonetheless loves. Such nuance is not generally a feature of Vovchok's prose. While the narrator's stance and some of his rendering of childhood perception demonstrate greater skill than that evidenced in *Zhivaia dusha,* Vovchok's narrative still leans heavily on melodrama and a near-gothic sensibility, and her plots repeat monotonously the plight of the innocent at the hands of the mighty. The imbalance of power and virtue first sketched out in her stories of Russian peasant life are still in place, despite the passing of serfdom. Whether or not the stories record "reality," they come close to inducing a sense of helplessness, reinforcing precisely that inclination to inactivity that they presumably sought to battle; the powers of the world are so deeply entrenched and evil that one can do nothing against them.

While Vovchok had entered Russian letters as something of an outsider, a provincial who took the St. Petersburg literary world by storm, throughout the 1860s and early 1870s her position as an established figure in Russian literary life was firm. Her personal life was marked by a continued disdain for established mores: her reputation weathered a series of unconventional relationships with men, including an affair with her distant relation, the radical critic Dmitrii Ivanovich Pisarev; a rupture with Markovich; and a lengthy involvement with Aleksandr Passek, son of the memoirist Tat'iana Passek. Upon her return from abroad in the late 1860s Vovchok undertook, together with her mother, the management of a translation cooperative, which produced many translations of both popular and serious works–Jules Verne's stories of adventure and travel paying the bills for a translation of Charles Darwin's *On the Origin of the Species* (1859). The most humbling experience of Vovchok's career as a writer occurred in connection with the translation undertakings: one of her translators was accused of having plagiarized an existing translation of a tale by Hans Christian Andersen. Vovchok's disillusionment with Russian literary circles in the wake of this scandal appears to have been profound; from 1878 she published virtually nothing, spurning involvement with the world of radical literary politics that had been the center of her life for almost twenty years. The last thirty years of her life were spent largely outside the world of Russian letters, in various small towns throughout rural European Russia, to which she traveled with her second husband, Mikhail Demianovich Lobach-Zhuchenko. Vovchok died on 28 July 1907.

The trajectory of Marko Vovchok's reputation is deeply interconnected with the literary politics of both the nineteenth and twentieth centuries. Initially heralded as a champion of the enserfed peasantry, Vovchok's affiliation with radical politics continued into the 1860s, when her narrative turn toward Realism accorded with programmatic calls for new, active heroes and heroines. By the late 1860s, when a new generation of still more intransigent critics took center stage, Vovchok's critical star had begun to set: Petr Nikitich Tkachev, among others, ridiculed *Zhivaia dusha,* denouncing its inordinate attention to the inner life of a "lady." Nonetheless, Vovchok fared well in the Soviet era. Her posthumous fate was determined by the tendency of Soviet literary politics to canonize critical Realism and radical critics of the pre-revolutionary period as forerunners of twentieth-century Socialist Realism. In an entirely different vein, Vovchok has a legacy in Ukrainian literary history because of her involvement with Markovich and the ethnographic-cultural work of Ukrainian nationalists of the mid-nineteenth century.

Feminist criticism has yet to examine exhaustively Vovchok's position as a woman writer and her obvious focus on women's lives, both under serfdom and in the claustrophobic world of provincial "reform" Russia. Interest in Vovchok today stems in part from this focus on women's lives and fates. While her own critical consciousness was aimed primarily at forms of class inequity, the attention she gives in both short and longer prose to women's lives suggests her relevance for scholars of women's writing and history. As scholars of American letters have attempted to recover and to some extent redeem the rhetoric of literary sentimentalism as it was used to denounce antebellum society in the United States, so may scholars of the Russian Empire come to a fuller understanding of Vovchok's often "gothic" sensibilities and melodramatic visions of good and evil.

Letters:

Listy do Marka Vovchka, 2 volumes (Kiev: Naukova dumka, 1979);

Listy Marka Vovchka, 2 volumes (Kiev: Naukova dumka, 1984).

Biographies:

E. P. Brandis, *Marko Vovchok* (Moscow: "Mol. Gvardiia," 1968);

B. B. Lobach-Zhuchenko, *Litopis zhittia i tvochosti Marka Vovchka* (Kiev: Dniepro, 1983);

Lobach-Zhuchenko, *O Marko Vovchok* (Kiev: Izdatel'stvo khudozhestvennoi literatury "Dniepro," 1987).

References:

Victor O. Buyniak, "Marko Vovchok and Leo Tolstoi," *Canadian Slavonic Papers,* 14 (1972): 300–314;

Nikolai Dobroliubov, "Cherty dlia kharakteristiki prostogo naroda," *Sovremennik,* 9 (1860);

Fyodor Dostoevsky, "Mr. –Bov and the Question of Art," *Dostoevsky's Occasional Writings,* selected, translated, and with an introduction by David Magarshack (New York: Random House, 1963), pp. 86–137;

Katerina Horbatsch, *Die Russischen und die Ukrainischen Volkserzahlungen von Marko Vovchok* (Frankfurt: Kubon & Sagner, 1978);

V. A. Nedzvetskii, "Dve kriticheskikh stat'i Pisareva o Marko Vovchke," *Voprosy russkoi literatury,* 1, no. 21 (1973): 64–70;

Petr Tkachev, "Podrostaiushchie sily," *Delo,* 9–10 (1868).

Papers:

Marko Vovchok's papers and manuscripts are held primarily in the Institute of Russian Literature and Art (Pushkin House) in St. Petersburg, fond 174. There are also holdings in the Shevchenko Institute and in the Central Academic Library of the Ukrainian Academy of Sciences, both in Kiev. Family archives in Moscow (Lobach-Zhuchenko) and Kiev (Doroshkevich) also include some relevant materials.

Pavel Vladimirovich Zasodimsky
(Vologdin)
(1 or 4 November 1843 – 4 May 1912)

J. Alexander Ogden
University of South Carolina

WORKS: *Greshnitsa; Volchikha; A ei veselo–ona smeetsia* (St. Petersburg: A. Bazunov, 1873)–"Greshnitsa" first published in *Delo,* nos. 1, 3 (1868); "Volchikha" first published in *Delo,* no. 12 (1868); "A ei veselo–ona smeetsia" first published in *Delo,* no. 4 (1870);

Khronika sela Smurina, in *Otechestvennye zapiski,* nos. 8–10, 12 (1874); (St. Petersburg: V Tip. Kraevskogo, 1875);

Povesti iz zhizni bednykh. Temnye sily, Staryi dom, Durak (St. Petersburg, 1876);

Kto vo chto gorazd, in *Slovo,* nos. 1–5 (1878); (St. Petersburg, 1878);

Lesnoe tsarstvo (Zyrianskii krai), in *Slovo,* nos. 9–11 (1878);

Stepnye tainy, in *Russkoe bogatstvo,* 1–2, 5–7 (1880); (St. Petersburg: R. Golike, 1881);

Chto seiali, to i pozhali, as L. Valevskaia, in *Russkoe bogatstvo* (1882);

Stepan Ogon'kov, in *Delo,* nos. 4–5 (1882);

Zadushevnye rasskazy, 2 volumes (St. Petersburg: F. Pavlenkov, 1883–1884);

Po gradam i vesiam (Iz istorii nashego vremeni), in *Nabliudatel',* nos. 1–5 (1885); (St. Petersburg: Tip. A. I. Transhelia, 1885);

Pesnia speta, in *Severnyi vestnik,* nos. 6–8 (1888);

Byval'shchiny i skazki (St. Petersburg: A. F. Devrien, 1888);

Bludnyi syn, in *Mir Bozhii,* nos. 10, 12 (1893);

Legendy. Graf Boregar i Agnesa Tusenel'. Nevedomyi stradalets (St. Petersburg: M. V. Kliukin, 1893);

Grekh. Roman, in *Russkoe bogatstvo,* nos. 1–3 (1893); (St. Petersburg: Tipo-lit. B. M. Vol'fa, 1893);

Iz detskikh let. Vospominaniia i rasskazy (Moscow: M. V. Kliukin, 1894);

Sobranie sochinenii, 2 volumes (St. Petersburg: I. N. Skorokhodov, 1895);

Svet i teni. Rasskazy dlia starshego vozrasta (St. Petersburg, 1895);

Vostochnyi magazin, in *Novoe slovo,* nos. 1–3 (1895);

Pavel Vladimirovich Zasodimsky

V zimnie sumerki. Sbornik byval'shchin, rasskazov i skazok (Moscow, 1901);

Nasledie vekov. Pervobytnye instinkty i ikh vliianie na khod tsivilizatsii (St. Petersburg: Izd. Knizhnogo sklada "Shkol'noe Delo," 1902);

V Krymu. Gorod smerti i vesel'ia, Na mogilakh (Moscow: I. D. Sytin, 1902);

Dedushkiny rasskazy i skazki, third edition (Moscow: I. D. Sytin, 1905);

Vesna idet. Iz derevenskoi zhizni (Moscow: I. D. Sytin, 1905);

Iz vospominanii (Moscow: I. D. Sytin, 1908);

Chudodeistvennaia fleita. Sbornik rasskazov (Moscow: I. D. Sytin, 1908);

Arfa zvuchala. Starinnaia legenda, second edition (Moscow: I. D. Sytin, 1910);

Despotizm. Ego printsipy, primenenie ikh i bor'ba za despotizm (St. Petersburg: M. M. Stasiulevich, 1911).

Editions and Collections: *Khronika sela Smurina,* introduction by V. Gura (Vologda, 1956);

Khronika sela Smurina, afterword by S. Rozanova (Moscow: Khudozhestvennaia literatura, 1959);

Greshnitsa; Temnye sily, with an introduction by Rozanova (Moscow: Khudozhestvennaia literatura, 1959);

Khronika sela Smurina. Roman; Vospominaniia, edited by O. V. Shelepina (Arkhangel'sk: Severo-Zapadnoe knizhnoe izd-vo, 1986).

OTHER: "Iz derevenskoi glushi," in *Put'-doroga. Nauchno-literaturnyi sbornik v pol'zu Obshchestva dlia vspomoshchestvovaniia nuzhdaiushchimsia pereselentsam* (St. Petersburg: K. M. Sibiriakov, 1893);

"Pavel Vladimirovich Zasodimsky" [autobiographical sketch], in *Pervye literaturnye shagi: Avtobiografii sovremennykh russkikh pisatelei,* compiled and edited by F. F. Fidler (Moscow: I. D. Sytin, 1911), pp. 214–215.

SELECTED PERIODICAL PUBLICATIONS:
"Avtobiografiia. (Pis'mo k redaktoru *Golosa*)," *Golos* (Khar'kov), 4 (1908): 50–52;

"Avtobiograficheskaia zametka," *Golos minuvshego,* 5 (1913): 145–149.

A prolific and long-lived writer of *narodnik* (populist) orientation, Pavel Vladimirovich Zasodimsky was actively involved in Russian literary life from the late 1860s until his death in 1912. He contributed to (and at times helped edit) the major "progressive" journals of his time, and he was personally acquainted with many important populist writers—including Nikolai Vasil'evich Shelgunov, Petr Lavrovich Lavrov, Nikolai Konstantinovich Mikhailovsky, Gleb Ivanovich Uspensky, and Nikolai Nikolaevich Zlatovratsky. He also knew Innokentii Vasil'evich Omulevsky (Innokentii Vasil'evich Fedorov), Aleksandr Ivanovich Levitov, Ivan Alekseevich Bunin, and Dmitrii Narkisovich Mamin (D. Sibiriak)—and he corresponded with Leo Tolstoy. Contemporaries found him personable, and he was known for helping beginning writers and others in need. Critics, both contemporary and posthumous, however, have

tended to minimize the literary significance of Zasodimsky's works. In the opinion of one critic, for example, "since he values primarily ideological content, [Zasodimsky] clearly concerns himself very little with the artistic presentation of his tales and novels. Their composition is often quite unsuccessful. . . ." Yet, Zasodimsky's writings—most notably his novel *Khronika sela Smurina* (Chronicle of the Village of Smurino, 1874)—were widely read, and they reflected the author's considerable experience as a witness to the plight of Russia's peasantry and as an observant traveler to Russia's regions (Vologda, Zyriansk, Bashkiria, Novgorod, Pskov, Tambov, and elsewhere). Zasodimsky's work was also important in contributing to the formation of the popular image of the rich peasant kulak, as Cathy A. Frierson discusses in her 1993 book *Peasant Icons: Representations of Rural People in Late Nineteenth-Century Russia.* Later a prominent writer for children, Zasodimsky seems to have established the fundamentally gloomy tone of many of his future literary works in his own childhood: a tale he wrote at the age of nine began, "It was a dark night. The wind howled dolefully, and rain was falling." The heroine of the story becomes an orphan when her father is executed for a terrible crime and her mother consequently goes mad from grief; the child herself ends up dead from cold and hunger at the entrance to a church. This work apparently established the predilection for Bulwer-Lyttonesque "dark and stormy nights" later evident in many of Zasodimsky's mature works.

Zasodimsky was born in the city of Velikii Ustiug in the Vologda province on 1 November 1843. The precise date is disputed; while Zasodimsky himself gave 1 November as his birth date, some sources give 4 November instead. Zasodimsky's father, Vladimir Mikhailovich Zasodimsky, worked in government service until his son was nine; thereafter (already in his fifties) he retired and volunteered as an officer in the popular militia during the Crimean War. The elder Zasodimsky was restrained and rather cold in his relations with his son. The boy turned to his mother, Ekaterina Pavlovna (née Zasetskaia), as his protector and intermediary. He later wrote of her: "I have met in my time kind and beautiful women, but my mother both was and remains for me the very best, the kindest, and the most beautiful of women."

The Zasodimsky family came from the nearby small town of Nikol'sk, and they moved back there when Pavel was four months old. He spent the first nine years of his life in this "remote little hamlet, lost in the woods"; locals were fond of saying "Not even the mail goes further than our Nikol'sk!" Both the landscape and its remoteness had a formative influence on Pavel, shaping themes and descriptions in his work. Recalling the surrounding forests, he wrote in later life: "these evergreens, pines and shaggy spruce trees, constantly before my eyes in the days of my early childhood, were vividly imprinted in my lively child's mind and forever have remained my favorite trees." That imprint reappeared in his nature descriptions in both fiction works and in his long article "Lesnoe tsarstvo" (The Forest Kingdom, 1878). The sense of being on the edge of the world contributed to the young Zasodimsky's fascination with everything from far away, and he eagerly listened to the stories of the wanderers, exiles, and peddlers who were all welcome in their house.

In his memoirs, especially *Iz vospominanii* (From My Reminiscences, 1908), Zasodimsky dwells lovingly on his childhood (he reaches the chapter "My First Steps in the Literary World" nearly two hundred pages into the latter work). "My childhood," he writes, "was light and happy. It had everything: bright sunshine or quiet moonglow, clear skies, flowers, smiles and tender caresses." The boy's main occupation was reading, and his reading was constant and indiscriminate, drawing on whatever was available from peddlers, his father's collection, or servants. He consumed Bible stories, Daniel Defoe's *Robinson Crusoe* (1719), and tales of travel to Africa and Australia; memorized most of Petr Pavlovich Ershov's *Konek-Gorbunok* (The Humpback Horse, 1834), and passages from the works of Aleksandr Sergeevich Pushkin; and later read novels and tales by Mikhail Nikolaevich Zagoskin, Eugène Sue, Vladimir Aleksandrovich Sollogub, Sir Walter Scott, Osip Ivanovich Senkovsky, and many others. By the age of eight he had also learned French and German from one of his maternal aunts.

While his sister, Liza, spent summers with their father at home, the young Zasodimsky traveled with his mother to her country home, Miroliubovo, far from Nikol'sk and located beside the Arkhangel'sk road. Along this road the boy watched wanderers, pilgrims, parties of prisoners, trained bears, and—on one occasion—even a camel. Also with his mother, he frequently visited the various estates of his maternal grandfather, Pavel Mikhailovich Zasetsky, a hereditary nobleman of the province, retired sailor, and important landowner. Zasodimsky recalled Zasetsky's favorite residence, Fominskoe, as one of the best estates near Vologda; it included a huge house surrounded by gardens, greenhouses, orangeries, and avenues of lindens, birches, and evergreens. Zasetsky had served in the navy under Paul I, and he

decorated the rooms of this house with portraits and statuettes of his hero.

In contrast to the wealth of the Zasetskys, the Zasodimsky family's means were meager, but they were able to send their son to the Vologda gymnasium as a boarding student (1856–1863). During these seven years, Zasodimsky watched a slow transformation take place within the enclosed world of his school, mirroring Russia's larger transformation as it moved from the rule of Nicholas I and defeat in the Crimean War to the era of the Great Reforms under Alexander II. Corporal punishment became rarer, and reading habits changed. Instead of sentimental novels and historical romances, Zasodimsky and his classmates now read Nikolai Alekseevich Nekrasov, Ivan Aleksandrovich Goncharov, Mikhail Evgrafovich Saltykov (N. Shchedrin), and Ivan Sergeevich Turgenev–"especially Turgenev"–Zasodimsky recalled in his memoirs: "his Lavretsky, Rudin, Bazarov seized us to the quick and became obsessions." A similar transformation of gymnasium life in these years of reform was vividly portrayed in literature by Zasodimsky's contemporary Ivan Afanas'evich Kushchevsky in his 1871 novel *Nikolai Negorev*.

Unmoved by his father's appeal to take a position in the provincial government, Zasodimsky left for the university in St. Petersburg, where he studied law. After two years Zasodimsky left the university without graduating to take a position as a private tutor to a family in the Saransk district. After a year and a half, he left for Moscow and there began his literary career.

Zasodimsky started his first story, "Greshnitsa" (The Sinner), in January 1867 and finished it after moving to St. Petersburg in February. The story is a depressing and rather derivative tale about a young woman betrayed by her lover who, with no means to raise the child she has borne, becomes a prostitute and then dies—alone, sick, and forgotten. Looking around for a journal in which to publish it, Zasodimsky was unable to turn to the ones familiar from his school days, *Sovremennik* (The Contemporary) and *Russkoe slovo* (The Russian Word), since both had been shut down by the government in the wake of Dmitrii Karakozov's attack on Alexander II in 1866. Zasodimsky instead took the story to *Delo* (The Cause), not at first realizing that Grigorii Evlampievich Blagosvetlov, former editor of *Russkoe slovo,* was its unofficial editor and publisher (although banned from an official capacity after the closure of his previous journal). Zasodimsky was delighted to meet Blagosvetlov and through him to be connected to the radical writers and critics who had grouped around him at *Russkoe slovo,* including Dmitrii Ivanovich Pisarev, Afanasii Prokof'evich Shchapov, Shelgunov, Aleksandr Konstantinovich

Sheller (A. Mikhailov), and Petr Nikitich Tkachev. Looking back later in his life in *Iz vospominanii,* Zasodimsky defended Blagosvetlov against a frequent charge that he cared only for the ideological content of a work and nothing for form. This defense of Blagosvetlov could have been a self-defense as well, since a similar charge often was leveled at Zasodimsky himself over the course of his career. Recalling what he had learned from his first editor, Zasodimsky remembered Blagosvetlov's telling him at their first meeting, "Today's writers are careless; they don't pay attention to form—and that's a big mistake on their part. . . . Form is very important, and a work must be diligently polished. . . . Any work of literature must have an idea, but it doesn't need sermonizing from the author. . . . He must instruct only through artistic images."

Zasodimsky spent 1868–1869 back in Vologda. He continued to contribute to *Delo* and became acquainted with a fellow contributor also living in Vologda, the radical journalist Shelgunov. Through Shelgunov he also had occasion to meet another leading populist, Petr Lavrovich Lavrov. Zasodimsky's next long story, *Temnye sily* (Dark Forces, first published in *Delo,* 1870), was written "under the influence of conversations with Shelgunov and of the drunken, unfortunate, impoverished people around me: carpenters, tailors, shoemakers, and all kinds of working people." The story was dedicated to Shelgunov.

Temnye sily is typical of Zasodimsky's early stories in its detailed focus on the lives of the desperately poor and in its unremittingly depressing tone. It is the story of a carpenter, Nikita Petrov, and his family. Nikita can think of only one bright day in all his fifty years—a day around Easter when, as a small boy, he accompanied his father to ring the church bells of the town. Much more common, though, are Nikita's memories of beatings and of his father's heavy fist raised against him, and now, worn down by a life he hates, he frequently turns to the tavern. But even drunk, he cannot escape the one, interminably sad note ringing in his head, painfully rending his heart and clouding his thought, and at these moments he feels "an irresistible need to smash something—his children, the dishes, the old, three-legged bench, or his wife. . . ." After narrating Nikita's life story in some detail, Zasodimsky gives similar details about Nikita's four children; he offers a detailed enough picture of his characters' miserable life stories to make the reader pity them even when they lash out senselessly or violently at the world around them. The reader has a much harder time, however, taking a personal interest in their lives, since all have been so warped by poverty and hardship that they have few remaining hopes or emotions to which the reader

can relate. On the few occasions when they do exhibit any yearning or desire, they usually suffer even more. Nikita's one vision of true happiness comes in a dream he has after sitting up with a friend, Ivan Mudry ("the wise"), who reads to him from an old, leather-bound book that includes millennial pronouncements from Revelation. Zasodimsky emphasizes that Nikita is not fated to experience happiness in this world.

Returning to St. Petersburg in the fall of 1869, Zasodimsky soon became closely acquainted with the Siberian writer Omulevsky. At a New Year's party at Omulevsky's house, Zasodimsky met his future wife, Aleksandra Nikolaevna Bogdanova, then a seventeen-year-old gymnasium student. Bogdanova was soon receiving supplementary tutoring in history and Russian literature from the impoverished young writer. At first refused as a suitor by Bogdanova's father, Zasodimsky considered turning to the ritual Russian folk practice of abducting his intended, but the father soon reconsidered, and the wedding took place on 30 August 1870. In their nearly forty-two years of married life, Aleksandra Nikolaevna was often a sounding board for her husband's work, and she herself wrote stories and tales that were published in various collections and journals for children.

Over the course of the next two years Zasodimsky's work continued to appear regularly in *Delo*—including "Mnogo li sveta v nashem prosveshchenii" (Is There Much Light in Our Enlightenment? 1870), "A ei veselo—ona smeetsia" (But She's Happy—She's Laughing, 1870), and a half dozen other articles and stories. Poor, out of work, and suffering insomnia in the St. Petersburg summer "white nights," Zasodimsky also began writing children's stories. His first story, "Zagovor sov" (The Owls' Conspiracy) appeared in *Detskoe chtenie* (Children's Readings) and was based on his memories of events and stories from his childhood. Zasodimsky did not set out to write for a children's audience, and he attributed the subsequent success of his stories for children to his never adopting a sugary, pandering tone but instead always writing for them in the same way that he wrote for adults.

In need of money and a change of scene, and increasingly motivated by the new populist idea of "going to the people," Zasodimsky accepted an offer to become a village schoolteacher, teaching for much of 1871 in a one-room schoolhouse near Borovichi in the Novgorod province at a salary of twenty-five rubles a month. The patron of the school was Sof'ia Aleksandrovna Leshern, younger daughter of the nobleman on whose estate it was located. Zasodimsky met her through the populist Feofan Nikandrovich Lermontov; in his memoirs he described her in terms that exemplify the heroine of a novel of the 1870s: "She was all fire, flame; always carried away . . . ready for self-sacrifice, ready to forget herself for the sake of an idea, for the sake of the good of society." (Leshern was later imprisoned and sentenced to death for her involvement in radical circles, a sentence commuted to hard labor.) As a teacher, Zasodimsky got to know peasant families well, and he prided himself on his knowledge of country life, gained over the course of a lifetime. In *Iz vospominanii* he wrote, "For me, knowledge of the *narod* [common people] was a completely natural consequence of the course of my whole life. I never set out to study the *narod,* never looked on the *narod* as an object of analysis, never went to the *narod* with a preconceived program 'to gather data'; but I would be a simpleton not to know the *narod,* having lived for entire years—from early childhood—together with them."

Back in St. Petersburg, the Zasodimsky family lived in a damp, cold apartment while Zasodimsky continued to write, and his wife continued her studies. Poverty led to personal loss: their first son died for lack of proper medical attention. Noting the bitter irony of the situation, Zasodimsky later wrote, "he died, I think, because I didn't have three rubles to call the doctor and buy medicine; yet money appeared for the funeral." That night friends took his wife to stay with them while Zasodimsky, sitting beside his son's body, stayed up finishing a promised article.

The early chapters of Zasodimsky's first and most influential novel, *Khronika sela Smurina,* were written while he was teaching in the Novgorod province, and many scenes and characters were based on his surroundings both there and in his subsequent wanderings around the Tver' province. Having had a falling out with Blagosvetlov, he turned to the prestigious *Otechestvennye zapiski* (Notes of the Fatherland), which had in the 1870s a decidedly populist orientation under the joint editorship of Nekrasov and Saltykov. Serialization began during the height of the "going to the people" movement, in the summer of 1874.

The geography of the fictional village in the novel captures the class conflict within it: the left bank of the river Vozhitsa is densely populated by the poor, while the right bank, called Zakruch'e, has new, tall, two-story houses occupied by kulaks. "Kulak," the first chapter of the novel, simply presents one of the most successful of these peasants, Grigorii Ivanovich Prokudov. Prokudov, it seems, "lived only in order to become rich. . . . Every moment of his existence, every transaction—clearly even the most insignificant one—played its role in the cause of enrichment." This wealth comes at the direct expense of his neighbors: "Prokudov held his fellow villagers in his hand, held them not in spiked gauntlets, but as if in fetters. But he put on these fetters so tenderly and softly that their wearers didn't feel the touch of his hands on them at all; it seemed to everyone that the fetters had been placed on them not by Grigorii Ivanovich, but by someone else—some bad person."

Prokudov is only one of many kulaks who have enslaved the poor, left-bank peasants in a nefarious system in which the latter, mostly smiths and craftsmen, have to buy their iron and other raw materials from the kulaks at inflated prices and then sell back their nails and other finished goods for little or no profit. One poor but resourceful, self-educated, and self-confident peasant, Dmitrii Kriazhev, sees a way out of this impasse. Kriazhev has already made several trips to the nearby town and has brought goods home with him from the stores there, bypassing the kulaks' monopoly. On one visit to town, he hears talk of a peasants' savings bank, run by peasants for their own mutual aid. Inspired, he finds a booklet on the subject, buys it, and spends long hours mulling over possible applications of the idea to Smurino.

Soon Kriazhev, in spite of the opposition of the kulaks, has set up the savings bank as well as an artel' (workers' cooperative) to buy iron and sell nails without the participation of the kulaks. But nothing works out as planned. The kulaks fight back with every available means, trying to turn both the villagers and the authorities against Kriazhev. Even when these techniques fail, the kulaks gain the upper hand in the end. Both the artel' and the bank fail to help the workers; the bank, in fact, becomes a tool of the kulaks. Kriazhev is no more successful in love than he is in his plans for reform. After long resisting the evident interest of Evgeniia (niece and ward of Prokudov), he falls in love with her, and they have a joyful period of love together, even though he makes clear that his first commitment is to the people's cause and he can never marry her. But Evgeniia's relatives are appalled and take all their wrath out on the young woman, who falls ill and dies even as she works in the field, a sickle in her hand. Just as the "dark forces" of oppressive poverty and misfortune had oppressed the characters in Zasodimsky's earlier story, in Smurino, too, the villagers lead lives of inescapable suffering. Near the end of the novel, Zasodimsky pictures this oppression as "the seal of the Antichrist." Kriazhev sees that "'people's lives are cramped and stifling. Who put this seal in place, and how can it be removed?' Kriazhev did not know. Neither books nor people had told him this. . . . And in the future, no matter how much Kriazhev tried to scrutinize it, he did not see anything new."

The original title of the book was "Pechat' Antikhrista" (The Seal of the Antichrist), but Saltykov found this title unclear and potentially alarming; he suggested the final title to Zasodimsky, at the same time insisting that Zasodimsky choose a pseudonym to mask his defection from *Delo*. Thus, *Khronika sela Smurina* appeared under the name "Vologdin," a pseudonym that Zasodimsky kept for much of his subsequent writing. For the journal publication in *Otechestvennye zapiski* the last chapter, which Saltykov considered too dangerous to pass the censors, was drastically cut; Zasodimsky chanced restoring the cut passages for the separate book publication of the novel and was lucky to have it passed without problems.

The novel evoked a mixed and tendentious critical reaction; conservatives saw the novel as a threat, while populists were divided in their interpretations. Many considered the intelligent, motivated, and well-groomed Kriazhev too good to be true. They also saw him as a pale copy of the hero of *In Reih' und Glied* (In Rank and File, 1866) by the German novelist Friedrich von Spielhagen, a charge that had also been leveled against Omulevsky's novel *Shag za shagom* (Step by Step, 1870). The radical critic and revolutionary Tkachev asserted in the third article of his series "Muzhik v salonakh sovremennoi belletristiki" ("The Peasant in the Salons of Contemporary Literature") that *Khronika sela Smurina* was based much more on the love relationships, individualism, and attitudes found among "cultured people" than among the peasant masses. Furthermore, according to Tkachev, Zasodimsky showed no awareness of the changes in peasant life and of the role of the kulak since the reforms of the 1860s: "Just as he reproduces the 'inner, mental world' of the muzhik by modeling it on the inner world of a cultured person, so, too, he reproduces the inner life of the post-Reform countryside by modeling it on the pre-Reform countryside." Zasodimsky's response to such critics was simple. In an unpublished autobiographical sketch he wrote, "Critics unfairly jeered at me, saying that I copied Dmitrii Kriazhev from Spielhagen's Leo, that I invented and fabricated everything, and that a peasant like Kriazhev—interested in social concerns, selfless, and highly developed morally—could never exist in reality. But in fact my Kriazhev is none other than a peasant of the Pskov province, Maksim Burunov. . . ." In spite of its mixed reviews, *Khronika sela Smurina* was extremely popular, and both the individual issues of *Otechestvennye zapiski* in which it appeared and the separate edition of the novel sold out almost immediately.

Over the next several years Zasodimsky moved frequently, spending some time in Vologda, returning to St. Petersburg, and then settling in Usman' in the Tambov province, where his wife, who had trained as a midwife, received a position. While in St. Petersburg, he was for a time a regular contributor of articles to *Birzhevye vedomosti* (Stock Exchange News); subsequently, he wrote several "Letters from the Provinces" and other articles for *Molva* (Rumor). In Usman' Zasodimsky met the aspiring writer Aleksandr Ivanovich Ertel'; the two formed a friendship that lasted throughout their lives. Zasodimsky was never destined to spend long in one place, and looking back on his life in his memoirs, he wrote, "All my life, it seems, I have been unpacking and packing up my suitcase and setting out to move on. I am so used to fate's throwing me from corner to corner, giving me no rest in this world, that it even seems strange to me when I happen to live in one place for six or eight months."

Zasodimsky's observations of life in the Tambov region became the basis for his second novel, *Kto vo chto gorazd* (Each in His Own Way, 1878), a depiction of the plight of poor peasants in Podlesnoe. These peasants have gained nothing from the Emancipation and are oppressed by kulaks, just as the villagers of Smurino were. Once again Zasodimsky portrays an attempted struggle against this oppression, led by the brothers Kuzemkin. But while the Podlesnoe residents are happy to listen, ultimately they are no more interested in changing the existing order than are the poor peasants in Zasodimsky's earlier novel. While Zasodimsky's writing had matured and his novel was praised by critics for its careful, factual portrayal of village life, *Kto vo chto gorazd* did not give rise to passionate critical debates of the sort inspired by *Khronika sela Smurina*.

Kto vo chto gorazd appeared in the first issues of *Slovo* (The Word), started in 1878 out of a combination of the earlier *Molva* and *Znanie* (Knowledge). Other contributors to the new journal included Petr Dmitrievich Boborykin, Aleksei Antipovich Potekhin, and Uspensky. Zasodimsky continued to publish frequently in *Slovo* during the next three years, although as the journal was forced by the authorities to subdue its populist stance and change editors, he also turned elsewhere. He returned, however, to serve as the acting editor for *Slovo* (the censor would not allow him to assume the title permanently). For a brief period in late 1880 and 1881, until the journal was shut down in the wake of the assassination of Alexander II, Zasodimsky worked energetically on *Slovo* and attracted several good contributors.

Meanwhile, his own work had been appearing more and more in *Russkoe bogatstvo* (Russian Wealth).

This St. Petersburg monthly was under new management, and from the very beginning Zasodimsky helped to shape its populist leanings as editor of the "Russian Life" section, in which he was responsible for projecting the collective editorial orientation of the journal. Zasodimsky's work appeared in every issue of *Russkoe bogatstvo* for three years, often several times in the same issue under different pseudonyms ("G. Vladimirov," "Skitalets" [Wanderer], "Staryi vorobei" [Old Hand; literally, Old Sparrow], and others). Starting in 1883, Zasodimsky also contributed many works to the journal *Nabliudatel'* (The Observer) but stopped when it adopted an anti-Semitic orientation.

Zasodimsky continued his association with many revolutionary populists. Although not directly involved in the revolutionary movement or political conspiracy himself, he provided a gathering place for his friends by founding a private library in the late 1870s on the Nevskii Prospect of St. Petersburg. This library soon became a preferred meeting place for populists and revolutionaries. Many of Zasodimsky's friends and acquaintances were imprisoned for the 1877 "Trial of the 193," including Leshern, the patron of his one-time provincial school. Zasodimsky attended parts of this trial and also went with Ertel' to the famous trial of the revolutionary Vera Zasulich in 1878, found innocent for her attempt on the life of St. Petersburg's military governor. In 1879, advised by friends to leave St. Petersburg, Zasodimsky handed over the running of his library to Ertel' and returned with his wife to the Vologda province. On his aunt's small estate of Gorka he found a productive place to work, and he frequently returned to it, well into the 1890s, writing many of his novels and long stories, articles, and works for children there during this period.

One of the novels he worked on in Vologda was *Stepnye tainy* (Secrets of the Steppe), which was serialized in 1880 in the first issues of the renewed *Russkoe bogatstvo*. Based, like *Kto vo chto gorazd*, on Zasodimsky's experiences in the Tambov region, the new novel focused on relations between kulaks and gentleman landowners. Zasodimsky does not hesitate to demonize his main kulak character, Ivan Afanas'evich Rukavitsyn. Rukavitsyn and other similar exploiters, "supple and slippery as an eel, but a million times more noxious than an eel," present a growing threat to Russian society, since they, "under various names and aliases, from various classes and professions, slip in everywhere now . . . [and] put down roots to the detriment of the future welfare of the *narod*. . . ." As always, Zasodimsky showed that the poor peasants and the urban workers suffered the consequences of this exploitation.

Another novel, *Chto seiali, to i pozhali* (They Reaped What They Sowed, published in *Russkoe bogatstvo* under the pseudonym L. Valevskaia, 1882), dealt with the history of the noble Tamanov family. The novel was a failure, and Zasodimsky later omitted it from his *Sobranie sochinenii* (Collected Works, 1895). Nikolai Ivanovich Iakushin, author of a study on Zasodimsky's life and works, comments laconically on this work: "The story of the economic and moral breakdown of a noble family. A theme that was not new for Russian literature. Zasodimsky did not add anything new to it."

In the 1870s and 1880s Zasodimsky also continued his regular contribution to *Detskoe chtenie* and its supplement, *Pedagogicheskii listok* (Pedagogical Newssheet). In the early 1880s, in the wake of the closure of *Slovo* and under the reaction that set in under Alexander III, Zasodimsky gave particular attention to his writing for children, publishing the two-volume collection *Zadushevnye rasskazy* (Heartfelt Stories) in 1883–1884. In the foreword to these volumes, Zasodimsky explained the sad tone of the stories, writing, "In the real world, as in these little tales, there is incomparably more sorrow than joy; and in life, just as in this little book, you see tears much more frequently than a happy, shining smile." Zasodimsky's children's stories were extremely popular, going through several reprint editions with large print runs. As Antonina Petrovna Babushkina, historian of Russian children's literature, writes, "love for humanity, sympathy for the common people, and heartfelt warmth are features of Zasodimsky's writing that truly make him a writer for children."

In 1885 Zasodimsky published a new and successful novel in *Nabliudatel'* titled *Po gradam i vesiam* (Around Cities and Villages). Its hero, the populist Feofan Mikhailovich Veriugin, is based on Feofan Nikandrovich Lermontov, and additional characters are based on other political figures with whom Zasodimsky was acquainted in the early 1870s, as the author states in *Iz vospominanii*. As Iakushin has noted, though, the physical description of the hero and many of his experiences are based on Zasodimsky himself. Veriugin devotes himself to spreading revolutionary ideas among the peasants, but by the end of the novel he increasingly sees urban workers as the revolutionary force of the country. (The work thus particularly pleased Soviet critics.) Unlike most of Zasodimsky's works, *Po gradam i vesiam* has a hopeful ending. Veriugin imagines a brilliant sun rising over the world, "illumining cities and villages with its happy rays, penetrating even the wildest and most remote thickets, and everywhere—across the whole face of the earth—pouring out life and happiness. . . ."

In the late 1880s and early 1890s Zasodimsky was attracted to Tolstoy's teachings and carried on a lively correspondence with Tolstoy himself and with his disciple Vladimir Grigor'evich Chertkov. In Zasodimsky's first letter, from 28 December 1890, he refers to his enclosed story "Pered potukhshim kamel'kom" (Before the Extinguished Hearth, published in 1891) and asks Tolstoy, "Can literary works like my story deflect a person even a little from evil?" Tolstoy, who by this point had rejected much of the Russian and Western literary heritage as worthless, reassured Zasodimsky that "This is that very art which has a right to exist." In 1892 the two authors also discussed famine relief efforts in which both were involved. During this period several of Zasodimsky's works were issued by the Tolstoyan publishing house, Posrednik (The Intermediary).

As a young participant in Russian life of the 1860s and 1870s who lived a long life for his time, Zasodimsky was, in the words of one reviewer marking Zasodimsky's twenty-five years in literary life, "one of the last of the Mohicans" from that era in which writers were thoughtful and inspired by lofty strivings. As a survivor from that earlier era, Zasodimsky was fated to give many speeches at funerals and memorials to his old friends and colleagues. *Iz vospominanii* describes many of these events and includes sections on his former editor Blagosvetlov and on Nekrasov, Vsevolod Garshin, Uspensky, and Shelgunov. As a result of his speech at Shelgunov's funeral in 1891, Zasodimsky was exiled from St. Petersburg for a time and was put under police surveillance for the rest of his life.

Zasodimsky's last novel, *Grekh* (Sin, 1893), was submitted to several journals before being accepted by *Russkoe bogatstvo*. Grigorii Petrov (nicknamed Chaban) is a wealthy peasant whose life is transformed when he unwittingly is responsible for the death of his beloved daughter-in-law. While he previously cared only for hard work and scorned those less fortunate as "good for nothings," Chaban now transforms his life and generously helps anyone in need.

In the early 1890s Zasodimsky worked to put together a collection of his fiction, both short and long, and a selection from his journalistic articles as well. This collection appeared in 1895 as the two-volume *Sobranie sochinenii*. In addition to his novels written over the previous two decades, Zasodimsky had continued to write *povesti* (long tales) in the spirit of his early works such as *Temnye sily;* many of these works appeared in his *Sobranie sochinenii*. Often little differentiates his long stories from his novels other than the frequent subtitles, "a novel" or "a *povest'*." In length, the novels are only marginally longer than the more substantial of the tales. Zasodimsky's novels, stories, and journalistic works are also similar in having for the most part the same subject matter—peasant or village life in the Russian provinces, often seen from a pessimistic point of view. The *Sobranie sochinenii* includes a few exceptions to this usual subject matter, such as stories about the Middle Ages and the ancient world.

During the final seventeen years of his life, Zasodimsky continued writing stories for children and adults, produced various journalistic articles, and concentrated on his memoirs, the largest part of which he revised, added to, and collected as *Iz vospominanii*. Zasodimsky spent much of the last dozen years of his life in Novgorod province, near the village of Opechenskii Posad (and, after 1911, in a small house in the village itself). He died there on 4 May 1912. His wife survived him by eight years, living to receive a pension from the Soviet government.

While Zasodimsky had largely outlived his generation, his dedication to the Russian people was greatly admired, and he was widely mourned in obituaries. "The last populist has died!" began one obituary. "Everyone who knew P. V. Zasodimsky loved him," noted another; "meek, delicate, very humble in his life, he wanted to comfort, help, and give charity to everyone." As a "democratic" writer in the revolutionary tradition, Zasodimsky was given some attention in the Soviet period. Editions of *Khronika sela Smurina* appeared in the 1950s and 1960s, as well as Iakushin's book-length study of his life and works and several shorter analyses. Zasodimsky's legacy to the post-Soviet period seems to be his children's stories (some of which are reprinted and anthologized) and some of his writings on the Russian provincial regions; the web page for the far northern Komi Republic offers his complete "Lesnoe tsarstvo" online, commenting that it is "one of the best works of Russian literature about the land of the Komi."

Letters:

"L. N. Tolstoy i P. V. Zasodimsky," in Leo Tolstoy's *Perepiska s russkimi pisateliami*, edited by S. Rozanova (Moscow: Khudozhestvennaia literatura, 1962), pp. 657–662.

Bibliographies:

P. A. Dilaktorsky, *Vologzhane-pisateli. Materialy dlia slovaria pisatelei, urozhentsev Vologodskoi gubernii* (Vologda, 1900), pp. 30–36; also in *Izvestiia Vologodskogo obshchestva izucheniia Severnogo kraia,* 1 (1914): 73–76;

R. N. Krendel', ed., *Russkie pisateli vtoroi poloviny XIX–nachala XX vv. (Do 1917 goda): Rekomendatel'nyi ukazatel' literatury,* part 3 (Moscow: Ministerstvo kul'tury RSFSR, 1963), pp. 170–177.

Biographies:

Nikolai Ivanovich Iakushin, *Po gradam i vesiam: Ocherki zhizni i tvorchestva Zasodimskogo* (Vologda: Severo-Zapadnoe Izd-vo, 1965);

S. V. Kuznetsova, "Zasodimsky," in *Russkie pisateli: Bio-bibliograficheskii slovar',* edited by P. A. Nikolaev (Moscow: Prosveshchenie, 1990), I: 320–322;

E. A. Shpakovskaia and E. A. Rogalina, "Zasodimsky," in *Russkie pisateli, 1800–1917: Biograficheskii slovar',* edited by Nikolaev (Moscow: Bol'shaia Rossiiskaia Entsiklopediia, 1992), II: 327–330.

References:

V. K. Arkhangel'skaia, "Zasodimsky i fol'klor," in her *Ocherki narodnicheskoi fol'kloristiki* (Saratov, 1976);

Antonina Petrovna Babushkina, *Istoriia russkoi detskoi literatury* (Moscow: Gos. uchebno-pedagogicheskoe Izd-vo, 1948), pp. 426–430;

Cathy A. Frierson, *Peasant Icons: Representations of Rural People in Late Nineteenth-Century Russia* (New York: Oxford University Press, 1993), pp. 156–157;

Viktor Vasil'evich Gura, "Zasodimsky i ego *Khronika sela Smurina,*" in his *Iz rodnikov zhizni* (Vologda: Severo-Zapadnoe Izd-vo, 1964), pp. 162–197;

P. Nikitin [P. N. Tkachev], "Muzhik v salonakh sovremennoi belletristiki," *Delo,* no. 3 (1879), section 2: 1–28; also in Tkachev, *Izbrannye sochineniia,* volume 4 (Moscow: Obshchestvo politkatorzhan, 1932), pp. 233–253;

M. A. Protopopov, "Pisatel'-optimist," *Russkoe bogatstvo,* 9 (1895), II: 101–118;

O. V. Sheliapina, "O prototipakh *Khroniki sela Smurina,*" *Sever,* 5 (1971);

A. M. Skabichevsky, "Zasodimsky," *Novoe slovo,* 4 (1896), section 2: 51–73; 5 (1896), section 2: 123–139;

A. P. Spasibenko, *Pisateli-narodniki* (Moscow: Prosveshchenie, 1968), pp. 229–267;

M. K. Tsebrikova, "Belletrist-narodnik (Sobranie sochinenii P. Zasodimskogo)," *Russkaia mysl',* 2 (1896), II: 58–82.

Papers:

Institutions holding Pavel Vladimirovich Zasodimsky's papers include the Russian State Archive of Literature and Art (RGALI, formerly TsGALI), and the Russian State Library (formerly the Lenin Library), both in Moscow.

Nikolai Nikolaevich Zlatovratsky

(14 December 1845 – 10 December 1911)

William Nickell

University of California, Santa Cruz

WORKS: *Krest'iane-prisiazhnye,* in *Otechestvennye zapiski,* no. 12 (1874), no. 3 (1875); *Bytovye ocherki N. N. Zlatovratskogo. Krest'iane-prisiazhnye. Sredi naroda* (St. Petersburg, 1875);

Satiricheskie rasskazy zolotogo cheloveka, as Malen'kii Shchedrin (St. Petersburg: V. Demakov, 1876);

Zolotye serdtsa. Listki iz zagublennoi povesti, in *Otechestvennye zapiski,* nos. 4–5, 8, 12 (1877); (St. Petersburg: V tip. A. A. Kraevskogo, 1878);

Ustoi. Istoriia odnoi derevni, in *Otechestvennye zapiski* (1878–1883); (Moscow, 1884);

Derevenskie budni, in *Otechestvennye zapiski,* nos. 3–4, 8, 10, 12 (1879); (St. Petersburg: V tip. A. A. Kraevskogo, 1882);

Narodnyi vopros v obshchestve i literature, as N. Oransky, in *Russkoe bogatstvo,* no. 3 (1880): 25–48; no. 5 (1880): 1–16; no. 6 (1880): 1–20;

Sochineniia, 3 volumes (Moscow: I. N. Kushnerev, 1884–1889);

Bezumets, in *Russkie vedomosti* (1886);

Sobranie sochinenii, 2 volumes (Moscow: Russkaia mysl', 1891);

Belyi starichok, in *Russkoe bogatstvo,* no. 3 (1892); (Moscow, 1906);

Novye rasskazy (Moscow, 1895);

Sochineniia, 3 volumes (N.p., 1897);

Derevenskii korol' (Moscow: Posrednik, 1905);

Kak eto bylo. Ocherki i vospominaniia iz epokhi 60-kh godov (Moscow: I. D. Sytin, 1911);

Rasskazy (St. Petersburg: Gosudarstvennoe izdatel'stvo, 1919).

Editions and Collections: *Sobranie sochinenii,* 8 volumes (St. Petersburg: Prosveshchenie, 1912–1913);

Izbrannye proizvedeniia (Moscow: Goslitizdat, 1947);

Ustoi. Istoriia odnoi derevni (Moscow: Goslitizdat, 1951);

Vospominaniia (Moscow: Goslitizdat, 1956);

Nado toropit'sia. Siroty 305 versty (Moscow: Goslitizdat, 1961);

Nikolai Nikolaevich Zlatovratsky

Derevenskie budni, in *Pis'ma iz derevni. Ocherki o krest'ianstve v Rossii vtoroi poloviny XIX veka* (Moscow: Sovremennik, 1987);

Derevenskii korol' Lir. Povesti, rasskazy, ocherki (Moscow: Sovremennik, 1988).

SELECTED PERIODICAL PUBLICATIONS:

"V arteli (Iz zapisok peterburgskogo proletariia)," *Otechestvennye zapiski,* no. 6 (1876);

"Barskaia doch'. Rasskaz doktora," *Russkaia mysl'*, nos. 6, 12 (1883);

"Skitalets," *Otechestvennye zapiski*, no. 9 (1883);

"Moi videniia. Rasskaz odnogo malen'kogo cheloveka," *Russkaia mysl'*, no. 4 (1885);

"Gorod rabochikh," *Russkaia mysl'*, no. 7 (1885);

"Karavaev i ego zhena," *Severnyi vestnik*, no. 2 (1885);

"Ocherki narodnoi zhizni," *Severnyi vestnik*, no. 2 (1886);

"Kak eto bylo. Moi malen'kii dedushka i Fimushka," *Russkaia mysl'*, no. 12 (1890);

"Mechtateli. Rasskaz," *Russkoe bogatstvo*, no. 4 (1893).

Nikolai Nikolaevich Zlatovratsky is remembered as an icon of the populist movement in Russian prose that flowered in the period following the emancipation of the serfs in 1861. He was primarily known as a writer of novels and short fiction, though he also produced works of literary and social criticism. He firmly believed in the social function of literature, and he wrote with a passionate desire to achieve the democratic goals of his day. His literature was largely tendentious and often didactic, aimed imparting the wisdom of native Russian patriarchal traditions and, particularly, of the peasant commune, or *mir*. As Zlatovratsky worked to articulate the superiority of these traditions, he often documented their decay as he described the increasing encroachment of post-emancipation values upon village culture.

Zlatovratsky's works center on the character types that he knew best—the peasants and democratic *raznochintsy*, or members of various middle classes. His familiarity with the peasant idiom enabled him to depict village life with realistic vitality; his belief in the moral superiority of the Russian folk, however, led to criticism that he sugarcoated his characterizations. His oeuvre is often contrasted with that of the more pessimistic Gleb Ivanovich Uspensky, who referred to the idealized peasant as a "chocolate muzhik." (Maksim Gorky later called Zlatovratsky a *sladkoglasnyi obmanshchik* [sweet-talking deceiver].) Zlatoratsky's style was, in a sense, a sort of protosocialist realism, in that his mimesis was colored with this idealism. But whereas the "great time" of socialist realism was a projection of the yet unrealized Soviet ideals and was thus oriented toward the future, for Zlatovratsky it emerged from the past. The bright future was to be found by returning to the fundamentals of native communal life—by throwing off the corrupting influences of the present and embracing the earth and its oldest traditions as a saving force.

Critics of Zlatovratsky's day repeatedly referred to him as a "Romantic" realist. While at times he was faulted for this quality, Zlatovratsky himself defended it; the Russian folk, he argued, were themselves inherently romantic and idealistic by nature. Even his more ethnographic works, such as *Derevenskie budni* (Everyday Life in the Village, 1879), retained this romantic quality. The boundaries

between fact and fancy were always somewhat indistinct for Zlatovratsky. This characteristic is a distinguishing feature in his work: his works of fiction, likewise, have a strong ethnographic element.

Closely identified with the populist period, Zlatovratsky outlived its popularity and spent his last years in relative obscurity. He was so absorbed in the spirit of the 1860s that when it passed, he seemed lost, lingering on as a venerated but peripheral and anachronistic reminder of the past.

The son of Nikolai Petrovich Zlatovratsky and his wife, Mar'ia Iakovlevna (née Chernysheva), Nikolai Nikolaevich Zlatovratsky was born on 14 December 1845 in the town of Vladimir, one of the "Golden Ring" towns north of Moscow. His father was a minor official in the Vladimir bureaucracy, and the large family was of modest means. Though they had been economically secure in Zlatovratsky's childhood, by the time he attended high school the family had fallen on harder times, and Zlatovratsky was required to help his father with his work. The family had been of peasant birth until the generation of his great-grandfather, who had entered the priesthood: the family name was evidently derived from the Church of Nikolo-Zlatovratsky, where he had served. Zlatovratsky's grandfather also entered the priesthood and likewise served in a Vladimir church. Although Zlatovratsky's father attended a seminary, he ultimately abandoned family tradition to pursue a civil career.

The origins of Zlatovratsky's populist sympathies are detailed in his memoirs. As a child, he spent considerable time living with his grandfather in a village near Vladimir, where he learned of the peasants' milieu and witnessed the abuses they suffered. One particular incident that left a vivid impression in his memory was the march of a large crowd of peasants, numbering in the hundreds, being sent off by their master to work in Siberia. More important, however, Zlatovratsky came of age during the period of the emancipation, and as a young boy he was surrounded by people who celebrated and directly participated in the reforms undertaken by Czar Alexander II. Zlatovratsky's father was of democratic leanings and served on a provincial committee dealing with the financial concerns of the peasants; he also organized and worked in the first public library in Vladimir. Zlatovratsky often helped his father in the library and subsequently cited this experience as his initiation into the world of literature. The connection between democratic principles and the literary impulse was reinforced in other ways as well. In 1861 the radical critic Nikolai Aleksandrovich Dobroliubov, who was a schoolmate and close friend of Zlatovratsky's uncle, Aleksandr Petrovich Zlatovratsky, visited the family home. At that time Zlatovratsky's father was taking part in the organization of the first independent newspaper in Vladimir, and Dobroliubov promised to participate. Zlatovratsky, who later used his uncle's unfinished memoirs as the basis for a piece on Dobroliubov, was clearly attracted to the heroic and democratic potential of literature as represented by such men as Dobroliubov. Zlatovratsky used the first wages he collected from giving private lessons to purchase the collected works of the critic Vissarion Grigor'evich Belinsky.

Zlatovratsky was initially schooled at home and subsequently studied at the Vladimir gymnasium. At this time he began his first literary experiments–"secret exercises," as he described them, in writing poetry in the manner of Aleksei Vasil'evich Kol'tsov. Later he was much taken by the work of Nikolai Alekseevich Nekrasov. Zlatovratsky's poetry showed the civic-mindedness of his models, as well as a faith in science. His first prose efforts were in the style of Ivan Sergeevich Turgenev and Nikolai Gerasimovich Pomialovsky, and also included a play modeled on the works of Aleksandr Nikolaevich Ostrovsky. Zlatovratsky also tried his hand as an editor at the gymnasium, producing a student journal, *Nashi dumy i stremleniia* (Our Thoughts and Strivings).

In 1864 Zlatovratsky graduated from the Vladimir gymnasium and passed his exam as surveyor-assessor. His work in this field gave him extensive contact with peasant life in the environs of Vladimir; his memoirs later revealed that many characters in his literary works were based on real-life acquaintances from his work as a surveyor. Though he had excelled on his graduation exam, Zlatovratsky nonetheless was not admitted to Moscow University. The following year, determined to continue his education, he began auditing courses in the historical-philological department of the university. Without financial support, however, he was forced to abandon this plan, and he moved to St. Petersburg, where he hoped to receive a government stipend to study at the St. Petersburg Technical Institute. When once again his plans did not work out, he abandoned his studies because of financial hardship. In 1866 Zlatovratsky began work as a copyeditor for the newspaper *Syn otechestva* (Son of the Fatherland); the same year "Chuprinskii mir," appearing under the pseudonym N. Cherevanin, was published in *Otechestvennye zapiski* (Notes of the Fatherland). Over the next several years, Zlatovratsky's short pieces began to appear in many journals, particularly in the satirical journals *Iskra* (The Spark) and *Budil'nik* (Alarm Clock).

As was typical of moderately successful plebeian writers of his day, pragmatic issues continued to plague Zlatovratsky. In this initial phase of his career as a writer, he supposedly could not afford to buy ink, and he wrote with *sin'ka* (diluted blueing) that he had to request from his landlord. As Zlatovratsky later recalled in his memoirs, in his youth he was continually confronted with doubts as to his calling as a writer, suffering through both inspirational and economic privations that led to pro-

longed periods of creative inactivity. Some of these hardships are described in his story "V arteli (Iz zapisok peterburgskogo proletariia)" (In the Artel [From the Notes of a Petersburg Proletarian], 1876). Finally, he collapsed in the street in St. Petersburg and had to be taken to a nearby hospital. After being discharged, Zlatovratsky decided to return to Vladimir, where he spent some time recuperating before beginning work on what became his first major literary success, the short novel *Krest'iane-prisiazhnye* (Peasant Jurors), first published in *Otechestvennye zapiski* (1874–1875). The story describes the journey of eight peasants to serve on a jury in an arson trial. Leaving their village and traveling by foot to the town where the trial is to be held, they cross significant representational boundaries, entering an alien world in which their traditional ways are in conflict with the educated and comparatively cosmopolitan views of the townspeople. Significantly, the setting allowed Zlatovratsky to thrust the moral and judicial systems of the *mir* into favorable comparison with those of the provincial government.

Zlatovratsky sent the novel to Mikhail Evgrafovich Saltykov and Nekrasov at *Otechestvennye zapiski,* in which it was published; it subsequently appeared in a separate edition in 1875. The following year a second book appeared, a collection of minor pieces derived from Zlatovratsky's work as a surveyor; many of these works had appeared previously in the satirical journals *Iskra* and *Budil'nik*. The collection, *Satiricheskie rasskazy zolotogo cheloveka* (The Satirical Stories of a Man of Gold, 1876), was published under the pseudonym Malen'kii Shchedrin (Little Shchedrin). The pseudonym acknowledged Zlatovratsky's debt to Saltykov (whose pseudonym was Shchedrin). Saltykov's patronage had been vital to establishing Zlatovratsky's literary career. As editor of *Otechestvennye zapiski,* Saltykov had not only encouraged Zlatovratsky and published many of his most important early works, but Saltykov had also supplied Zlatovratsky with much-needed monetary advances. Saltykov also assisted in the separate publication of *Derevenskie budni* in 1882.

Whereas *Krest'iane-prisiazhnye* had described the peasants outside their native milieu, many of Zlatovratsky's stories from this period were centered in the *mir*. Zlatovratsky complained that Russian literature had not yet offered a representation of the Russian peasant in this truly native environment, and he sought to correct this oversight. By the 1870s, however, the *mir* was already decaying, as the longstanding ways of the commune were being affected by changing economic conditions. Zlatovratsky endeavored to reconstruct this crumbling world in his writing, often by pointing out contrasts between the past and the present. Many of his early stories feature a character by the name of Vas'ka Gor'ianov–an ambitious *kulak* (well-to-do peasant) whose behavior highlights the virtues of the traditions he displaces. Zlatovratsky's *Zolotye serdtsa* (Golden Hearts, 1877) is a collection of portraits of young democratic enthusiasts who renounce their worldly concerns and devote their lives to the service of the people. The main hero openly defends his own (and Zlatovratsky's) romanticism, arguing that it is the mark of any nation that is uncivilized—a positive attribute in the context of Zlatovratsky's populism. Uncivilized romanticism might be better, he argued, than the narrow ideals of more pragmatic cultures.

In fall 1876 Zlatovratsky married Stefaniia Avgustinovna Ianovskaia, daughter of a doctor from Vladimir. They subsequently had four children: Nikolai, Aleksandr, Sof'ia, and Stefanina. After his marriage Zlatovratsky began spending his summers in the villages surrounding Vladimir, where he continued to familiarize himself with the contemporary peasant life that he described in his next work, the larger, more programmatic *Ustoi* (Foundations, 1883). Initially written as a drama, the first version was sent to Nikolai Konstantinovich Mikhailovsky in 1876, who declined to publish it. In 1877 Zlatovratsky began transforming the piece into a novel, a process that continued sporadically over the next six years. It was published in piecemeal fashion between 1878 and 1883 in *Otechestvennye zapiski*, after which it was substantially reworked into a more cohesive whole for publication in the first edition of Zlatovratsky's collected works (1884–1889). *Ustoi*, the longest of Zlatovratsky's novels, is generally considered his most important work. Again, Zlatovratsky documented the emerging changes confronting the village and its fundamental institution, the *mir*; while the traditional "old truth" is portrayed as superior, it is clearly being supplanted by the "new truth" of a nascent village capitalism.

The novel is set in the small, provincial, yet somewhat mythical village of Dergach. Anna, the daughter of one of the peasant artel members, rejects the love of a poor villager and marries Peter Volk, a young kulak who has been "educated" in the city, having been an apprentice at a factory. Her family increasingly mixes with that of her new husband and adopts some of its economic interests, including plans for mills and various other enterprises. The young Peter Volk is, in fact, disenchanted with the city: he sincerely cares for the countryside and believes he can improve it by bringing in new ways. He is confident that a growing sense of self-determination among the peasants will lead to a better future for the village: as the peasants become economically enfranchised, they will make better use of the land and the labor force at their disposal. For Zlatovratsky, however, this notion subverts the fundamental connection of the peasant to the land. In his view, all of the troubles in the village come from the influence of the town, without which "the village would continue to live in heavenly peace." A section of the novel, "Son schastlivogo muzhika" (The Dream of a Happy Peasant), can be read as a separate piece. It depicts the pre-reform

village, isolated from external authority, governing itself according to long-standing, patriarchal laws. Like the dreams of Nikolai Gavrilovich Chernyshevsky's Vera Pavlovna in *Chto delat'?* (What Is to Be Done? 1863) or Ivan Aleksandrovich Goncharov's *Oblomov* (Oblomov, 1859), it stands in contrast to the reality depicted in the novel, in which a "new law," the law of capitalism, is compromising the foundations of peasant life to which the title of the novel refers—the *mir* and the village artel.

Ustoi is long and episodic. Many readers have felt that in it the author unintentionally reveals the weaknesses in his patriarchal "foundations": his hero, the truth-seeking Min Afanas'ich, is himself adrift, wandering from his native home in search of truth. Stylistically, the novel is written in a rather affected language, as the Russian countryside is laden with Homeric atmosphere. Saltykov, who was publishing the work in *Otechestvennye zapiski*, objected to this style, arguing that it was unnatural and innapropriate to the subject matter. The contemporary critic V. V. Chuiko suggested that Zlatovratsky was not so much studying folk life as he was fantasizing about it according to his own prescriptive designs. Zlatovratsky defended his style, however, and employed similar folk motifs in other works, including his 1886 *Bezumets* (Madman), which was written as a modern *bylina* (folk tale), with the main character as a model of the heroic populist.

During this time Zlatovratsky also contributed regularly to many important journals, including *Severnii vestnik* (The Northern Herald), *Russkaia mysl'* (Russian Thought), *Slovo* (The Word), *Nedelia* (The Week), and *Russkoe bogatstvo* (Russian Riches). Zlatovratsky was one of the founders of the latter journal, for which he initially served as editor. In 1880 he contributed a long, programmatic piece to the journal under the pseudonym N. Oransky—*Narodnyi vopros v obshchestve i literature* (The Question of the Folk in Society and Literature). *Derevenskie budni*, a cycle of nonfiction studies of peasant society, was an ambitious attempt to describe the intrinsic principles of village life—those constants that resisted the various impulses of historical change.

Zlatovratsky's greatest popularity came during the late 1870s and early 1880s. His subsequent decline can in many ways be connected to the evolution of the political climate during the years that followed. The period of optimism surrounding the emancipation came to a close, and new political agendas formed in response to the repressive regimes of Alexander III and Nicholas II. As the reactionary positions of the autocracy intensified a desire for change on the part of the Russian people, Marxism made increasing inroads, and Zlatovratsky's democratic romanticism (or "folk socialism," as Pavel Nikitich Sakulin called it) fell out of style. The traditional communal structure of the village continued to disintegrate, making a populist utopia increasingly difficult to imagine.

Zlatovratsky's later stories—such as "Skitalets" (The Wanderer, 1883) and "Barskaia doch'" (The Baron's Daughter, 1883)—depict the ensuing ideological crisis in populism and the frustrated efforts of the democratic intelligentsia to merge with the peasants and effect permanent change in society. Zlatovratsky also began to consider more urban themes, perhaps reflecting his experience living in Moscow, where he took a permanent apartment in 1884 in which he continued to reside until the end of his life. His 1885 "Gorod rabochikh" (City of Workers) was a pessimistic account of the tribulations of peasants who had recently relocated in the city to find work in factories. "Mechtateli" (Dreamers, 1893) concerned a rebellious worker protesting against social injustice. At the same time, however, Zlatovratsky continued to explore his favorite motifs: "Derevenskii korol' Lir" (A Provincial King Lear, 1889), for example, considered the conflicts between traditional village life and capitalist ideas arriving from the city.

Though the first edition of Zlatovratsky's collected works, which began appearing in 1884, was included in a list of books prohibited by imperial proclamation from circulation in public libraries (a ban that was not lifted until 1909), his days as an important spokesperson for the opposition were coming to an end. The regime was at this time much more concerned with the novelist and social thinker Leo Tolstoy, who was beginning to attract followers to his own brand of populism. Zlatovratsky was among those who were influenced by Tolstoy's views. The two writers met in the fall of 1883 and maintained frequent contact and correspondence over the next ten years.

Tolstoy's stylistic and ideological influence has been noted in Zlatovratsky's stories of the period—including "Moi videniia. Rasskaz odnogo malen'kogo cheloveka" (My Visions. The Story of an Insignificant Man; *Russkaia mysl'*, 1885), "Kak eto bylo. Moi malen'kii dedushka i Fimushka" (How it Was. My Little Grandfather and Fimushka; *Russkaia mysl'*, 1890), and *Belyi starichok* (The White Old Man, *Russkoe bogatstvo*, 1892). The first of these stories featured a "great man" figure modeled on Tolstoy, to whom the story was dedicated. Though they often disagreed on fundamental principles (and particularly on the issue of nonviolence), the two writers nonetheless found a great deal of common ground, and they undertook several projects together. In 1889, for instance, Tolstoy approached Zlatovratsky with an offer to edit a new journal, *Sotrudnik* (Coworker). In the early 1890s Zlatovratsky's "Iskra Bozhiia" (Spark of God, 1892) and several other stories were published by Posrednik, the Tolstoyan publishing house. Though the two writers did not see each other after Tolstoy ceased wintering in Moscow in the 1890s, their association continued until Tolstoy's death. In 1908 Zlatovratsky published an essay marking Tolstoy's eightieth birthday, and Zlatovratsky's last pub-lished piece during his lifetime is believed to have been his obituary for Tolstoy in *Russkie vedomosti* (Russian News) in November 1910.

In the mid 1880s, Zlatovratsky organized "Shakespearean evenings" in his Moscow home; the gatherings were attended by important writers and critics of the time, including Konstantin Dmitrievich Bal'mont, Dmitrii Narkisovich Mamin (D. Sibiriak), Aleksandr Mikhailovich Skabichevsky, and Konstantin Mikhailovich Staniukovich. As Ivan Belousov recalls, Zlatovratsky's evenings were always on Saturday, as many of those in his circle worked during the week. Refreshments were always modest (one bottle of vodka for the whole crowd), but the discussions were lively. Belousov was among many young, self-educated writers who received Zlatovratsky's help and encouragement. In 1893, with money from an inheritance, Zlatovratsky was able to purchase a country home outside Moscow, where he spent his summers and again hosted a literary salon.

At the turn of the century Zlatovratsky was actively involved in the "Moscow Literary Wednesdays" organized by N. D. Teleshov. He also worked for the journals *Sem'ia i shkola* (Family and School), *Detskoe chtenie* (Children's Readings), and *Vestnik vospitaniia* (Educational Herald). No longer a major figure in the literary establishment, he now engaged in minor literary activities, writing critical reviews and essays as well as bibliographical entries and encyclopedia articles on Russian literature. During the 1905 Revolution, he and his family hosted a detachment of workers in their apartment on Moscow's Malaia Bronnaia Street; Zlatovratsky's daughter served as a nurse in support of the revolutionaries. Though he continued in this way to support the democratic movement as it developed, Zlatovratsky's voice was no longer prominent: his article marking the event, "Tri legendy russkoi revoliutsii" (Three Legends of the Russian Revolution), remained unpublished until after his death. Zlatovratsky's article anticipated the famous revolutionary poem "Dvenadtsat'" (The Twelve, 1918) by the Symbolist poet Aleksandr Aleksandrovich Blok in describing the revolutionaries as bearers of a new cross, harkening the arrival of a kingdom of God on earth.

Zlatovratsky did not escape poverty even in his later years, which were spent in relative isolation in Moscow with the financial support of the philanthropic Literary Fund. He continued to receive respect for his past contributions, however, and enjoyed the celebration of his thirty- and forty-year jubilees in 1897 and 1907. In 1909 Zlatovratsky was named an honorary member of a literary academy. Quietly he pursued more serious undertakings, working on memoirs of his early years and preparing an eight-volume edition of his works, which appeared in 1912–1913, after his death. Zlatovratsky's memoirs, first published in 1908–1910, offer a fascinating look at his early years and the period of reform that had influenced him so strongly. These recollections end with the year 1864; details from his later years can be found in his literary memoirs, as well as in the reminiscences of his daughter, Sofiia. A 1911 collection of Zlatovratsky's memoirs, some of them reworked, was published separately under the title *Kak eto bylo* (How It Was). His literary criticism was not published in any of his collected works and still has not been republished.

Zlatovratsky's last years were also marked by ill health. He suffered from frequent and severe headaches and was extremely emotional. His friends and family tried to spare him upsetting situations, which often caused him to break down and weep. His death was reportedly stimulated by one of these reactions. On 10 December 1911 Zlatovratsky read in the newspapers that the Holy Synod had placed another prohibition on the circulation of his works, which only two years earlier had been freed from a similar prohibition enacted in 1884. Upset by this news, he reportedly took to his bed and died later that day.

Even during his final years when he was no longer a prominent literary figure, Zlatovratsky maintained a strong desire to communicate his ideas to the public. Negotiating with the publisher over the last edition of his collected works, Zlatovratsky was concerned that the price for the eight volumes was to be set at twelve rubles; he feared that the edition would be unaffordable to anyone but a few wealthy literary historians. While this consideration reveals that his populist impulse was still strong, it likely also indicates a certain awareness of the diminished popular interest in his literary legacy. His prefaces to his works repeatedly indicate his disappointment in the quality of his often hurried literary efforts, as well as in the ultimate effect of his labors. At the time of his death he was remembered with respect and a touch of nostalgia by those who mourned the loss not only of a dedicated worker for the cause but also the hopes and dreams of a bygone era. Zlatovratsky's ideals were fondly remembered but were considered largely outdated. Attending Zlatovratsky's funeral, Vladimir Kranikhfel'd noted that those in attendance were largely the writer's gray-haired contemporaries. The event failed to resonate with the younger generation, who were largely unacquainted with his work, as Zlatovratsky himself well knew. His grave, marked with a simple wooden cross, lies with those of several other populists in a corner of the Vagankova Cemetery in Moscow.

References:

I. A. Belousov, *Literaturnaia Moskva. Pisateli iz naroda. Pisateli-narodniki* (Moscow: Glavlit, 1926);

Iurii Bunin, "Pamiati Zlatovratskogo," *Vestnik vospitaniia*, no. 1 (1912): 110–120;

V. V. Bush, "N. N. Zlatovratsky," in *Ocherki literaturnogo narodnichestva* (Leningrad & Moscow: Glavlitizdat, 1931)–includes Zlatovratsky's early poetry;

V. V. Chuiko, "Sentimental'noe narodnichestvo. N. Zlatovratsky," *Nabliudatel'*, no. 11 (1887): 147–162;

M. M. Fillippov, "Narodnik-idealist," *Delo*, no. 6 (1886): 72–101;

N. Gorbanev, "Zlatovratsky v otsenke Plekhanova," *Russkaia literatura*, no. 3 (1963): 145–149;

Vladimir Kranikhfel'd, "N. N. Zlatovratsky," *Sovremennyi mir*, no. 1 (1912): 316–325;

S. B. Mikhailova, "Zlatovratsky i L. Tolstoi," *Russkaia literatura*, no. 4 (1969): 136–147;

A. A. Mokrushin, "Realizm rasskazov i povestei N. N. Zlatovratskogo 70-kh gg.," in *Uch. Zap. Moskovskogo pedagogicheskogo instituta im. N. P. Krupskoi* (1958);

P. Nikitin (P. N. Tkachev), "Muzhik v salonakh sovremennoi belletristiki," *Delo*, no. 8 (1879): 1–31;

M. Protopopov, "Posledovatel'nyi narodnik (Sobranie sochinenii N. Zlatovratskogo)," *Russkaia mysl'*, no. 5 (1891): 114–130;

A. N. Pypin (as A. V–n), "Narodniki i narod. Sobranie sochinenii N. Zlatovratskogo, tt. I i II," *Vestnik Evropy*, no. 2 (1891): 655–695;

P. Sakulin, "Narodnichestvo N. N. Zlatovratskogo," *Golos minuvshego*, no. 1 (1913): 117–133;

K. G. Semenkin, *N. N. Zlatovratsky. Ocherki zhizni i tvorchestva* (Iaroslavl': Verkhne-Volzhskoe kn. izdvo, 1976);

Aleksandr Mikhailovich Skabichevsky, "Novyi chelovek derevni (*Ustoi*)," in *Belletristiki-narodniki* (St. Petersburg, 1888); also in *Istoriia noveishei russkoi literatury*, seventh edition (St. Petersburg, 1909);

A. P. Spasibenko, *Pisateli-narodniki* (Moscow, 1968);

M. Tsebrikova, "Narod v literaturnykh eskizakh. Povesti i rasskazy Zlatovratskogo," *Delo*, no. 8 (1882): 1–34;

A. Vvedensky, "Proizvedeniia Zlatovratskogo," in *Literaturnye kharakteristiki*, second edition (St. Petersburg: M. P. Mel'nikov, 1910), pp. 456–511.

Papers:

Nikolai Nikolaevich Zlatovratsky's papers are located in the Institute of Russian Literature (IRLI), St. Petersburg (f. 111, nos. 2704–2749). No. 2721 is a bibliography, collected by Zlatovratsky. His letters to various recipients can be found at the same archive. Additional letters are located in the Russian State Archive of Literature and Art (RGALI, formerly TsGALI), Moscow (f. 202), the Russian State Historical Archive (RGIA, formerly TsGIA), St. Petersburg, the L. Tolstoy State Museum, Moscow (f. 776, f. 777), and the State Archive in Vladimir.

Books for Further Reading

Allen, Elizabeth Cheresh, and Gary Saul Morson, eds. *Freedom and Responsibility in Russian Literature*. Evanston, Ill.: Northwestern University Press, 1995.

Andrew, Joe. *Russian Writers and Society in the Second Half of the Nineteenth Century*. Atlantic Highlands, N.J.: Humanities Press, 1982.

Andrew. *Writers and Society During the Rise of Russian Realism*. Atlantic Highlands, N.J.: Humanities Press, 1980.

Belknap, Robert, ed. *Russianness: Studies of a Nation's Identity*. Ann Arbor, Mich.: Ardis, 1990.

Berlin, Isaiah. *Russian Thinkers*. London: Hogarth Press, 1978.

Berry, Thomas Edwin. *Plots and Characters in Major Russian Fiction*. 2 volumes. Hamden, Conn.: Archon, 1977.

Boyd, Alexander T. *Aspects of the Russian Novel*. Totowa, N.J.: Rowman & Littlefield, 1972.

Brooks, Jeffrey. *When Russia Learned to Read: Literacy and Popular Culture, 1861–1917*. Princeton: Princeton University Press, 1985.

Bushmin, A. S., and others, eds. *Istoriia russkogo romana*. 2 volumes. Moscow: Akademiia Nauk SSSR, 1962–1964.

Chances, Ellen. *Conformity's Children: An Approach to the Superfluous Man in Russian Literature*. Columbus, Ohio: Slavica, 1978.

Čiževskij, Dmitrij. *History of Nineteenth-Century Russian Literature,* translated by Richard Noel Porter, edited by Serge A. Zenkovsky. Volume 2: *The Realistic Period*. Nashville: Vanderbilt University Press, 1974.

Čiževskij. *Russian Intellectual History,* translated by J. Osborne. Ann Arbor, Mich.: Ardis, 1978.

Clowes, Edith W., Samuel D. Kassow, and James L. West, eds. *Between Tsar and People: Educated Society and the Quest for Public Identity in Late Imperial Russia*. Princeton: Princeton University Press, 1991.

Clyman, T. W., and D. Green, eds. *Women Writers in Russian Literature*. Westport, Conn.: Greenwood Press, 1994.

Cornwall, Neil, ed. *Reference Guide to Russian Literature*. London: Fitzroy Dearborn, 1998.

Debreczeny, Paul, and Jesse Zeldin, eds. and trans. *Literature and National Identity: Nineteenth-Century Russian Critical Essays*. Lincoln: University of Nebraska Press, 1970.

Eklof, Ben, and others, eds. *Russia's Great Reforms, 1855–1881*. Bloomington: Indiana University Press, 1994.

Fanger, Donald. *Dostoevsky and Romantic Realism: A Study of Dostoevsky in Relation to Balzac, Dickens, and Gogol*. Chicago: University of Chicago Press, 1965.

Fennell, John, ed. *Nineteenth-Century Russian Literature: Studies of Ten Writers.* Berkeley: University of California Press, 1973.

Forster, E. M. *Aspects of the Novel.* New York: Harcourt, Brace, 1927.

Frank, Joseph. *Through the Russian Prism. Essays on Literature and Culture.* Princeton: Princeton University Press, 1990.

Freeborn, Richard. *The Rise of the Russian Novel: Studies in the Russian Novel from "Eugene Onegin" to "War and Peace."* Cambridge: Cambridge University Press, 1973.

Freeborn. *The Russian Revolutionary Novel: Turgenev to Pasternak.* Cambridge: Cambridge University Press, 1982.

Garrard, John, ed. *The Russian Novel from Pushkin to Pasternak.* New Haven: Yale University Press, 1983.

Gheith, Jehanne M., and Barbara T. Norton. *An Improper Profession: Women, Gender, and Journalism in Late Imperial Russia.* Durham, N.C.: Duke University Press, 2001.

Gifford, Henry. *The Novel in Russia: From Pushkin to Pasternak.* London: Hutchinson, 1964.

Ginzburg, Lydia. *On Psychological Prose,* translated and edited by Judson Rosengrant. Princeton: Princeton University Press, 1991.

Golovenchenko, F. M., and S. M. Petrov. *Istoriia russkoi literatury XIX veka.* 2 volumes. Moscow: Izd-vo Ministerstva Prosveshcheniia, 1960–1963.

Golovin, K. F. (Orlovsky). *Russkii roman i russkoe obshchestvo.* St. Petersburg: A. A. Porokhovshchikov, 1897; republished, Leipzig, 1974.

Griffiths, Frederick T., and Stanley J. Rabinowitz. *Novel Epics: Gogol, Dostoevsky, and National Narrative.* Evanston, Ill.: Northwestern University Press, 1990.

Grivtsov, Boris. *Teoriia romana.* Moscow: Gosudarstvennaia akademiia khudozhestvennykh nauk, 1927.

Gutsche, George J., and Lauren G. Leighton. *New Perspectives on Nineteenth-Century Russian Prose.* Columbus, Ohio: Slavica, 1982.

Heldt, Barbara. *Terrible Perfection: Women and Russian Literature.* Bloomington & Indianapolis: Indiana University Press, 1987.

Hingley, Ronald. *Russian Writers and Society, 1825–1904,* second revised edition. London: Weidenfeld & Nicolson, 1977.

Hoisington, Sona Stephan, ed. *A Plot of Her Own: The Female Protagonist in Russian Literature.* Evanston, Ill.: Northwestern University Press, 1995.

Istoriia russkoi literatury. 11 volumes. Moscow: Akademiia Nauk SSSR, 1941–1956.

Jackson, Robert L. *The Underground Man in Russian Literature.* The Hague: Mouton, 1958.

Jacobson, Helen Saltz, ed. and trans. *Diary of a Russian Censor: Alexander Nikitenko.* Amherst: University of Massachusetts Press, 1975.

Jones, Malcolm V., and Robin Feuer Miller, eds. *The Cambridge Companion to the Classic Russian Novel.* Cambridge: Cambridge University Press, 1998.

Kelly, Aileen M. *Toward Another Shore: Russian Thinkers Between Necessity and Chance.* New Haven & London: Yale University Press, 1998.

Kelly, Catriona. *A History of Russian Women's Writing 1820–1992.* Oxford: Oxford University Press, 1994.

Kravtsov, N. I., ed. *Istoriia russkoi literatury vtoroi poloviny XIX veka.* Moscow: Prosveshchenie, 1966.

Lavrin, Janko. *An Introduction to the Russian Novel.* New York: Methuen, 1942.

Layton, Susan. *Russian Literature and Empire.* Cambridge: Cambridge University Press, 1994.

Ledkovsky, Marina, Charlotte Rosenthal, and Mary Zirin, eds. *A Dictionary of Russian Women Writers.* Westport, Conn.: Greenwood Press, 1994.

Levitt, Marcus C. *Russian Literary Politics and the Pushkin Celebration of 1880.* Ithaca, N.Y. & London: Cornell University Press, 1989.

Marsh, Rosalyn, ed. and trans. *Gender and Russian Literature: New Perspectives.* Cambridge: Cambridge University Press, 1996.

Martinsen, Deborah A., ed. *Literary Journals in Imperial Russia.* Cambridge & New York: Cambridge University Press, 1998.

Mathewson, Rufus W., Jr. *The Positive Hero in Russian Literature,* second edition. Stanford, Cal.: Stanford University Press, 1975.

Matlaw, Ralph E., ed. *Belinsky, Chernyshevsky, & Dobrolyubov. Selected Criticism.* Bloomington & London: Indiana University Press, 1962.

Mirsky, D. S. *A History of Russian Literature,* edited and abridged by Francis J. Whitfield. New York: Knopf, 1949.

Morson, Gary Saul, ed. *Literature and History: Theoretical Problems and Russian Case Studies.* Stanford, Cal.: Stanford University Press, 1986.

Morson. *Narrative and Freedom: The Shadows of Time.* New Haven: Yale University Press, 1994.

Moser, Charles A. *Aesthetics as Nightmare: Russian Literary Theory, 1855–1870.* Princeton: Princeton University Press, 1989.

Moser. *Antinihilism in the Russian Novel of the 1860s.* The Hague: Mouton, 1964.

Moser, ed. *The Cambridge History of Russian Literature,* revised edition. Cambridge: Cambridge University Press, 1992.

Nabokov, Vladimir. *Lectures on Russian Literature,* edited by Fredson Bowers. London: Weidenfeld & Nicolson, 1982.

Nikolaev, P. A., general editor. *Russkie pisateli, 1800–1917: Biograficheskii slovar'.* 4 volumes to date. Moscow: Bol'shaia rossiiskaia entsiklopediia, 1992 –   .

Ovsianiko-Kulikovsky, D. N., ed. *Istoriia russkoi literatury XIX v.* 5 volumes. Moscow: Mir, 1911.

Paperno, Irina. *Suicide as a Cultural Institution in Dostoevsky's Russia.* Ithaca, N.Y. & London: Cornell University Press, 1997.

Pares, Bernard. *A History of Russia.* New York: Knopf, 1953.

Phelps, Gilbert. *The Russian Novel in English Fiction*. London: Hutchinson, 1956.

Phelps, William Lyon. *Essays on Russian Novelists*. New York: Macmillan, 1911.

Pomper, Philip. *The Russian Revolutionary Intelligentsia,* second edition. Arlington Heights, Ill.: Harlan Davidson, 1991.

Reeve, Franklin. *The Russian Novel*. New York: McGraw-Hill, 1966.

Riasanovsky, Nicholas V. *A History of Russia,* sixth edition. New York & Oxford: Oxford University Press, 2000.

Rowe, W. W. *Patterns in Russian Literature II: Notes on Classics*. Ann Arbor, Mich.: Ardis, 1988.

Seeley, Frank F. *From the Heyday of the Superfluous Man to Chekhov*. Nottingham: Astra Press, 1994.

Shklovsky, E. A., ed. *Entsiklopediia literaturnykh geroev. Russkaia literatura vtoroi poloviny XIX veka*. Moscow: Olimp, 1997.

Shklovsky, Viktor. *Khudozhestvennaia proza. Razmyshleniia i ravgovory*. Moscow: Sovetskii pisatel', 1959.

Simmons, Ernest J. *Introduction to Russian Realism*. Bloomington: Indiana University Press, 1965.

Stavrou, Theofanis G., ed. *Art and Culture in Nineteenth-Century Russia*. Bloomington: Indiana University Press, 1983.

Steiner, George. *Tolstoy or Dostoevsky: An Essay in the Old Criticism*. New Haven: Yale University Press, 1996.

Stites, Richard. *The Women's Liberation Movement in Russia. Feminism, Nihilism, and Bolshevism*. Princeton: Princeton University Press, 1978.

Terras, Victor. *A History of Russian Literature*. New Haven & London: Yale University Press, 1991.

Terras, ed. *Handbook of Russian Literature*. New Haven: Yale University Press, 1985.

Todd, William Mills, III. *Fiction and Society in the Age of Pushkin: Ideology, Institutions and Narrative*. Cambridge, Mass.: Harvard University Press, 1986.

Todd, ed. *Literature and Society in Imperial Russia, 1800–1914*. Stanford, Cal.: Stanford University Press, 1978.

Venturi, Franco. *Roots of Revolution*. Introduction by Isaiah Berlin. New York: Knopf, 1964.

Vogüé, Eugène-Melchior, vicomte de. *The Russian Novel,* translated by Colonel H. A. Sawyer. London: Chapman & Hall, 1913.

Wachtel, Andrew. *The Battle for Childhood: Creation of a Russian Myth*. Stanford, Cal.: Stanford University Press, 1990.

Walicki, Andrzej. *A History of Russian Thought From the Enlightenment to Marxism*. Stanford, Cal.: Stanford University Press, 1979.

Wellek, René. *A History of Modern Criticism: 1750–1950*. Volume 4: *The Later Nineteenth Century*. New Haven: Yale University Press, 1965.

Contributors

Denis Akhapkin . . . . *St. Petersburg University*

Jane Costlow . . . . *Bates College*

Galya Diment . . . . *University of Washington, Seattle*

Andrew M. Drozd . . . . *University of Alabama*

Carol Apollonio Flath . . . . *Duke University*

Steven R. Griffin . . . . *McGill University*

Grazyna Lipska Kabat . . . . *University of Toronto*

Judith E. Kalb . . . . *University of South Carolina*

Susan E. Kay . . . . *Newcastle upon Tyne*

Sonia I. Ketchian . . . . *Davis Center for Russian Studies, Harvard University*

Martha Kuchar . . . . *Roanoke College*

L. K. Mansour . . . . *United States Military Academy*

Alexander V. Matyushkin . . . . *Karelian State Pedagogical University*

John McNair . . . . *University of Queensland*

Susan McReynolds . . . . *Northwestern University*

Liubov' Minochkina . . . . *Cheliabinsk State University*

Harriet Murav . . . . *University of California at Davis*

William Nickell . . . . *University of California, Santa Cruz*

J. Alexander Ogden . . . . *University of South Carolina*

Susan Conner Olson . . . . *Phoenix, Arizona*

Ekaterina Rogatchevskaia . . . . *University of Glasgow*

Karen Rosneck . . . . *University of Wisconsin–Madison*

Maria Rubins . . . . *Rice University*

Gabriella Safran . . . . *Stanford University*

Veronica Shapovalov . . . . *San Diego State University*

Olga Shitareva . . . . *Moscow State University*

Alexandra Sosnowski . . . . *McGill University*

Christine D. Tomei . . . . *Slavic Seminar, Columbia University*

Clark Troy . . . . *Harriman Institute, Columbia University*

Dan I. Ungurianu . . . . *Vassar College*

Judith Vowles . . . . *New York, New York*

Edward Wasiolek . . . . *University of Chicago*

Nicholas G. Žekulin . . . . *University of Calgary*

Mary F. Zirin . . . . *Altadena, California*

Cumulative Index

Dictionary of Literary Biography, Volumes 1-238
Dictionary of Literary Biography Yearbook, 1980-1999
Dictionary of Literary Biography Documentary Series, Volumes 1-19
Concise Dictionary of American Literary Biography, Volumes 1-7
Concise Dictionary of British Literary Biography, Volumes 1-8
Concise Dictionary of World Literary Biography, Volumes 1-4

Cumulative Index

DLB before number: *Dictionary of Literary Biography,* Volumes 1-238
Y before number: *Dictionary of Literary Biography Yearbook,* 1980-1999
DS before number: *Dictionary of Literary Biography Documentary Series,* Volumes 1-19
CDALB before number: *Concise Dictionary of American Literary Biography,* Volumes 1-7
CDBLB before number: *Concise Dictionary of British Literary Biography,* Volumes 1-8
CDWLB before number: *Concise Dictionary of World Literary Biography,* Volumes 1-4

E

M

ISBN 0-7876-4655-5

90000

9 790787 646553